CAUCASUS
Erevan
Mt Ararat
Nakhichevan
CASPIAN SEA
Khoy
Great Zab R.
Tabriz
Urmia
Naghada
Ushnaviyeh
Mahabad
Rowandoz
Arbil (Hawler)
Saguez
Tehran
Sulaimani
Little Zab R.
Kirkuk
Halabja
Sanandaj
Hamadan (Ecbatan)
Khanaqin
IRAN
Kirmanshah
Mandali
Arak
Baghdad
Elam
Tigris R.
Euphrates R.
Shatt Al-Arab
IRAQ
Basra
MOUNTAINS
KUWAIT
PERSIAN GULF
SAUDI ARABIA
0 100 200 300
Kilometres

FIRE, SNOW & HONEY

VOICES FROM KURDISTAN

Essays, life stories, poems, short fiction and fables contributed by people from Kurdistan

EDITED BY GINA LENNOX

with a foreword by Mme Danielle Mitterrand

HALSTEAD PRESS

SYDNEY MMI
Published by Halstead Press
19a Boundary Street,
Rushcutters Bay, New South Wales, 2011

 Typeset by Brevier Design, Kensington, N.S.W. Printed in Melbourne, Victoria, by Brown Prior Anderson.

National Library cataloguing in publication entry:

Fire, snow and honey : voices from Kurdistan.

Bibliography.
Includes index.
ISBN 1 875684 70 0.

1. Kurds – Australia – Literary collections.
I. Lennox, Gina. II. Mitterand, Danielle.

A820.80891597

ACKNOWLEDGEMENT

The publisher is grateful to Alison White, Tracey Ann Rankin, Adam Smith, Ginger Briggs, Skye O'Neill, Kristin Westlake, Kylie Prats, David Cece and Sonia Markovtzev for their work in editing, preparing the text and typesetting.

This project was assisted by The Myer Foundation through the Jesuit Refugee Service, the Commonwealth Government through the Australia Council for the Arts, and the NSW Ministry of the Arts.

THE MYER FOUNDATION

Australia Council for the Arts

1901-2001 Centenary of Federation

Table of Contents

Pronunciation Guide

a'a — pronounced as the long 'a' in bath
aw — pronounced 'ow' as in 'cow'
c — in part III pronounced as 'j'
ç — in part III pronounced 'ch'
e — pronounced 'e' as in egg
jh — pronounced 's' as in vision
kh — pronouced with more emphasis on the'h'
ir — pronounced 'eer' as in peer
oo — pronounced 'oo' as in book
ou — pronounced 'oo' as in spoon
'rr' — pronounced as a heavy, rolling 'r'
q — pronounced 'gkh', with more emphasis on the 'k'

Foreword

by Madame Danielle Mitterrand

The Kurds and I have a long history. We have memories in common which our relationship and joint histories are founded upon.

They have confidence in my initiatives for peace because they know my persistence in convincing people that they have a right to their own place on our earth, in the same way as those who have appropriated it do.

Thus, for more than fifteen years, I have taken every opportunity to alert not only French but also European and international public opinion to the injustice done to the Kurdish people. The United Nations Human Rights Commission, the European Parliament, the US Congress, my Nobel Peace Prize friends, heads of state and governments have all heard me speak about the Kurds.

What can we do for the Kurds, divided between four countries, continually in conflict, so that they can live in peace and justice with their compatriots: Turks, Arabs, Iranians and others?

I think that our role is to have the legitimacy of Kurdish cultural, civic and political claims recognised in the countries in which they live. It is no longer acceptable, under the pretext of not interfering in the internal affairs of sovereign states, to close our eyes to the massive violations of the rights of Kurds, while declaring our duty to help people in danger, *peoples* in danger.

Representatives of civil society and public opinion, we also have a role in denouncing civil wars, massacres, the destruction of villages and massive deportations carried out by sovereign states against their own populations. It is our responsibility as citizens of this planet to demand that our leaders act in such a way as to bring the warring parties around to dialogue and a peaceful solution.

It is regrettable to note that in Turkey, generals continue to lead the *danse macabre* of a deadly armed conflict and refuse to consider a political and peaceful solution to the Kurdish problem. They are forever brandishing the spectre of war against a population which is only seeking recognition of its existence and its legitimate rights. Under the pretext of fighting "terrorism", they maintain a state of seige in the Kurdish region, destroying villages and obliging the population to flee. They lose no opportunity of stifling any democratic demands. The Kurdish democratically elected representatives are rotting in prison. The decision of the European Court of Human Rights which declared their trials unfair, has not changed in any way the fact that these representatives continue to remain in prison, while our European governments, members of the European Council, intervene on their behalf. Also, the Turkish army, in spite of international laws, violates Iraqi borders, while pursuing Kurds who have found refuge in that country. In doing so, it breaks the conventions and international agreements it has signed.

In Iraq, where for more than ten years, part of the Kurdish region has been under the control of the UN, the Kurds are no longer subjected to extermination campaigns led by the Iraqi regime of the 1980s. They have rebuilt their villages, but continue to live in terror and fear of the return of their persecutors. Is it necessary to remind people of the Anfal campaigns, of the chemical and biological gassings carried out against the Kurdish population?

In Iraq, weakened by a decade of economic sanctions, which strike at the most disadvantaged and weakest sectors of the population, the desire to rid the country of Kurds, is the political backdrop of Saddam Hussein's regime. In allowing terror and insecurity to rule, it is encouraging, if not inciting, the people to choose exodus.

In the current context of the globalisation of economies, finance and communication, it is time to install a global justice so that dictators, and all those responsible for crimes against humanity, may be brought before an international criminal court, which would have the means to render justice. Thus, Saddam Hussein, and the like, would suffer a check to their destructive excesses, and the states which support and arm them receive a reminder of their duty to establish peace.

The Kurds of Iran have also suffered political repression since 1979 and the establishment of the Islamic Republic. The Kurdish political parties are outlawed and exiled. Their pacifist leaders have been assassinated in Europe. An acceptable solution to the Kurdish problem in that country, negotiated by Kurdish representatives and Iranian leaders, is possible, on the basis of a real international political and democratic will.

The Kurds in Syria have no cultural rights and cannot fulfil their civic responsibilities if they declare their ethnic origin. Like everywhere in Kurdistan, the Kurdish region in Syria remains underdeveloped. The Kurds in this country demand recognition of their cultural rights and the return of those people expelled from their land during the 1960s.

So what can we do? Close our eyes in the name of economic and financial imperatives to the atrocities committed in the region against a civilian population, living on its own territory, but deprived of its most basic rights? Isn't it time to choose moral firmness in which the advantages are indisputable under any circumstance? Shouldn't we establish the means to achieve a peaceful solution acceptable to everyone?

Shouldn't Europe, which instigated the division of the Kurdish region, take the necessary measures so that in the absence of their own state, the Kurds have the possibility to live in liberty and democracy, with respect for their cultural traditions, in peace with themselves and with the peoples around them?

The Kurdish problem is part of a worldwide movement of solidarity in resistance to commercial forces, which do not hesitate to exploit the possessions they buy with investment dollars, to the detriment of native populations and with the complicity of governments. The weight of market policy and free trade rules allow for every kind of compromise up to the abandonment of the defence of human rights, the basis of democratic European constitutions. Yet the conventional discourse has hardly changed over the years, despite the information and denunciations of NGO humanitarian field workers.

Europe no longer has confidence in itself. It will become mature when it learns to speak with a single voice to declare that its European policy is not subject to imperatives imposed on it by a global imperialism which becomes even more threatening when it feels itself challenged. Consequently, at the signing of trade agreements, Europe contents itself with a democracy clause, alibi for its good conscience, but invokes the right not to interfere before sending the issue back to the warring parties. This attitude has been interpreted by many European citizens as an act of cowardice.

Parliamentarians more in tune with public opinion respond to these injustices, but it is governments that have the final say in deciding the overall policy to follow, and the influence of their most persuasive means to ensure that the peace process is established in countries where the Kurds live, particularly in Turkey.

In 1999, the main Kurdish armed resistance movement in Turkey decided to put an end to the armed struggle, and become a political organisation which will achieve its aims through political and peaceful methods. It is the start of an encouraging evolution which should be taken into consideration. We should help Kurdish political movements to begin a dialogue with the leaders of their countries and to come to a democratic and peaceful solution, even more now that Turkey is an official candidate for entry into the European Union.

Finding a political and peaceful solution to the Kurdish problem now is necessary more than ever. We have a large population, with a very high birth rate, living in an area which has the largest reserves of water in the region. Peace in the whole region will be determined by peace and stability in the territories inhabited by Kurds.

Optimistic and confident about the future, I believe that the Kurdish problem, outstripping its regional framework, has become a European, indeed a global problem. Therefore it would be best dealt with by the international community. Certainly, a recognition of Kurdish cultural rights by the regimes involved, even more in Turkey than in Iraq, Iran and Syria, is far from being achieved, but the Kurds' peaceful struggle continues and peace is their strength.

Almost everywhere in the world, diverse initiatives are increasingly promoting awareness. *Fire, Snow and Honey: Voices from Kurdistan* is an example. With the aim of tackling all aspects of Kurdish life, the ambition of this book is to act as a living witness of the Kurdish people in the millennium, of their past, but also of their present so that the future can take note.

Why Care?

Introduction by Gina Lennox

While I was tearfully undergoing crises of belief—both spiritual and human—due to an avalanche of love and war experiences in this book, many non-Kurds around me were asking, "What have the Kurds got to do with you or me?" Or I was told, "People deserve what they get." Such questions and comments inspired this introduction: "Why is the plight of the Kurdish people relevant to you?"

In a general sense, although our sensitivities may be media-blunted, if we stop caring about our fellow human it reflects on ourselves and the world we create. Ignorance can be bliss. It can also pave the path to hell on earth.

But more importantly, I believe the Kurds, who claim to be the largest nation of people without a homeland, are on a front line of struggle that all of us face in a world that is being rapidly transformed by global forces. In their present form, these forces show little regard for human rights, democratic process or the environment. The Kurdish people's aspirations for cultural integrity, religious freedom, economic sustainability and political self-determination are those of all humanity. Thus the reasons for their present circumstances need to be understood for their own sake and also as invaluable insights into the state of the world: "There but for the grace of God go I." As the world shrinks, we must start thinking about solutions.

The momentum of modernism is forcing us all to face new frontiers of a personal, sociopolitical and ecological nature. It can be argued that those who are making the critical decisions are not the leaders of nation states but a faceless group of international financiers, weapons and chemical manufacturers who are neither democratically elected nor accountable to the people. Throughout history there have always been elites subjugating the people for their own benefit, but never before have they had the technological means to make the world their chessboard. This grand imperialism has become known as globalisation. Many peoples, including the Kurdish, became its victims in a carve-up of Africa and the Middle East after World War One and of Asia after World War Two. More recently, many living in more privileged societies have been made aware of its consequences.

Likewise, it was only in the last decade of the twentieth century that the plight of the Kurdish people became more generally known. After Saddam Hussein, president of Iraq, invaded Kuwait in August 1990 and the Americans and their allies chose to defend Kuwait's oil fields, the Allies feared chemical attack above all. It was then that the media mentioned Saddam Hussein's previously ignored chemical attacks on Kurdish civilians in 1987–88, culminating in the chemical bombing of the town of Halabja, where between 5000 and 12,000 civilians were killed. Have you ever seen the pictures of dead babies wrapped in the arms of mothers lying in the streets?

After the Allies' victory in forcing Iraq's withdrawal from Kuwait, the world media followed the uprising of the Shi'ite Arabs in the south and the Kurds in the north of Iraq in March 1991. Reports continued to cover the two million Kurdish refugees fleeing from Saddam's tanks and helicopters across snow-covered mountains into Iran and Turkey, an estimated 500 people a day dying from cold, hunger and illness. Then silence.

But eight years later, in February 1999, the Kurds hit the world stage once again with reports of Kurdish demonstrations outside Greek embassies around the world. The demonstrations were in response to a Kurdish leader from Turkey, Abdullah Ocalan, having been arrested in Nairobi and taken back to Turkey as a result of a collusion of international forces acting outside the law. The justification of these agencies was that Ocalan was a terrorist. Kurds consider him a leader of a nation. Since 1984 he had directed an armed struggle against the Turkish government's systematic policy of genocide of its 19 million Kurds. It was subsequently reported that he was to be kept in isolation on the prison-island of Imrali. Then silence.

So who are these people? By consensus, rather than any accurate census, they are a nation of between 25 and 40 million Indo-European people, who unlike many ancient peoples, have miraculously survived many thousands of years in a region called Kurdistan. Evidence of culture and burial rituals in the area date back to 35,000 BC. Evidence of the first agriculture, pastoralism and village life has been found in the fertile mountains of Kurdistan, a part of the Fertile Crescent, dating back to 11,000 BC. Seven and a half thousand years ago, their homeland gave birth to the precursors of 'civilisation', defined in terms of the development of a hierarchical society where an elite can accumulate wealth through agriculture, crafts, including metallurgy and trade, thus building public buildings and trans-community power structures. Subsequently many kingdoms and empires were established in the area.

While oppression of the Kurds began in earnest with the invasion of Islamic forces in the seventh century and continued with the invasions of Mongol and Turkic tribes from Asia, it was not until 1639 that Kurdistan was divided between the Ottoman and Safavid Empires. Despite this division, many Kurdish emirates remained largely independent of their overlords. This long-held autonomy was lost completely in 1923, when the League of Nations divided Kurdistan between Turkey, Iraq, Iran and Syria (small parts having already been incorporated into the Soviet Union's republics of Armenia and Georgia). Ever since, Kurdish freedom fighters, writers, politicians and ordinary citizens have been executed or sentenced to long terms in prison for wanting the right to speak and write in their own language and have a say in their own affairs.

Few Jews, Christians, or Muslims realise that their religious and cultural heritage is entwined with the Kurds. Kurdistan is classified as northern Mesopotamia. It was in Kurdistan that the earliest monotheistic religion, known as Ezidism, was practised. (The other ancient monotheistic religion of the Mandaeans, which continues to be practised by Sabeans in the south of Iraq and Iran, may have a common heritage.) Noah's ark is said to have come to rest in Kurdistan. Abraham is believed to have escaped to Kurdistan, where members of his family lived, because his city-state of Ur was under threat of invasion around 2300 BC. In 600 BC Nebuchadnezzar II, thought by some to be Ezidi, conquered Jerusalem. The Jewish leaders were taken to Babylon and were exposed to ancient Sumerian and Akkadian cuneiform tablets outlining legends of Adam, the first offspring of a god and man and a great king saving his family, animals and seeds from a flood by building a boat. It was in Babylon that the exiled Jews began compiling the present-day Torah and some archeologists believe it was in this time that Jews became truly monotheistic. This was the time of the Mede dynasty, the Medes being Ezidi and one of the ancestral people of the Kurds. The empire of Medea extended from Cappadocia to Tehran and, some say, as far as Afghanistan. The half-Mede, half-Persian 'King of Kings' Cyrus the Great, was responsible for releasing the Jews from their captivity in Babylon in 539 BC, although Babylon remained a centre of Judaism for many centuries.

Later, the teachings of the Medean prophet Zoroastra, who can be seen as a reformer of Ezidism, described a struggle between good and evil and states of heaven and hell, concepts which were to have a profound impact on the Christian and Muslim religions. Similarly striking echoes of Ezidi and Zoroastrian rituals are found in all three modern monotheistic religions.

Thus this microcosm of the Fertile Crescent has impacted on history for at least 13,000 years, as it continues to do. The eight-year Iraq-Iran War was a direct outcome of an agreement to stop the Kurdish revolution in Iraq five years earlier and Saddam Hussein's invasion of Kuwait was one outcome of the Iraq-Iran War.

Since the division of Kurdistan in 1923 there have been over 50 Kurdish uprisings. All have been cruelly squashed. The Kurdish homeland has been systematically wiped of its villages, agriculture and people. Between 1960–2000, a minimum of 10,000 Kurdish villages and their agricultural base have been destroyed. At least 500,000 men, women and children have been slaughtered by their own governments. Going back to World War One, this figure easily could exceed one million, not counting the 800,000 Kurds killed during World War One (of whom 500,000 were civilians), the 700,000 Kurds killed by Russians and Armenians and the hundreds of thousands killed in World War Two, when the Kurds fought on the side of the British. As well, about seven million in Turkey and Iraq have been deported from villages into camps and overcrowded towns with no compensation and no work. Up to one million have become political prisoners. These figures are estimates—there are no accurate statistics.

In terms of systematic government policy, as opposed to an irregular outburst of violence or international war, the scale of this genocide is comparable to the worse genocides of the twentieth century: the 40 million killed, frozen or starved by Stalin's programs and purges in the 1930's and 40's; the 35 million Chinese starved and killed by Mao Tse Tung's polices between 1949 and 1970, including the two million killed in the Chinese Cultural Revolution of 1966–69; the one to two million Christian Armenians killed between 1915 and 1922 by the Ottomans and Mistefa Kemal in Turkey; the six million Jews and six million non-Jews killed in Nazi concentration camps between 1939 and 1945; and the 1.5 million Cambodians killed by Pol Pot's bullets, overwork and famine between 1975 and 1977. In fact in the twentieth century, it is estimated that 100 million people have died by their government's own hand, compared to the 40 million who were killed by international war.

The Kurdish genocide has at least three distinguishing features. Most importantly, it is internationally supported by the Western World in terms of military hardware and the training and financing of the governments that carry it out. This applies particularly to

Turkey, its government by far the worst oppressor of Kurds. As well, its sheer time scale exceeds all others, for it continues to the present day. Thirdly, there is no end in sight.

So why does the West, so willing to go to war against Milosevic in the former Yugoslavia, with the UN and other agencies increasingly intervening in internal affairs in the name of human rights, continue to supply its military and financial aid to Turkey and other countries which deny human rights to Kurds?

Historically the Kurds have always been a fiercely independent people living on some of the richest agricultural lands in the Middle East. This land is situated on the path of the old Silk Road and thus has been subject to invasion from all sides. The Kurds' land-locked homeland has been kept an educational and economic backwater, even after the British discovered some of the world's richest oil fields there in the 1890s. Unlike the Jews and other oppressed peoples, because the Kurds form tribal societies separated by mountains, with many religious and political persuasions, dialects and alphabetic scripts, they have been unable to unite and take advantage of the window of opportunity to form a nation state between 1920–1923.

Arguably, the next significant opportunity to declare an independent state is being missed at this present time. After the USA and its Allies declared a no-fly zone in northern Iraq, banning Iraq's airforce north of the 36 Parallel, the Kurdish people elected a regional government, proposing to become part of a democratic confederation of Iraq. While most non-assimilated Kurds dream of an independent Kurdistan, the leaders have resisted putting a referendum to the people, arguing that to establish an independent Kurdistan is unrealistic, justifiably fearing a bloodbath.

Personally, I do not know which is harder to achieve—democracy in Iraq, Turkey, Iran and Syria, or a nation state called Kurdistan, although more people would benefit from the former.

Today the Kurds are estimated to number 19 million in Turkey (28.4% of the population), 6.4 million in Iraq (24 %), nine million in Iran (12.6 %) and 1.6 million in Syria (9.2 %). There are populations in Armenia, Georgia, Russia, Jordan, Lebanon and Palestine, an estimated 200,000 Jewish Kurds living in Israel, and growing diasporas in Europe, the home of about one million Kurds, the USA and Canada, where more than 35,000 Kurds now live, and Australia, the home of some 12,000.

What is most relevant for the future of Kurdistan is that the sources of the rivers that supply water and electricity to Iraq, Iran, Turkey, Syria and other countries lie in the mountains of Kurdistan. Water is the future's elixir and far more essential to life than oil. As oil was in the 20th century, water will be to the 21st, Kurdistan being rich in both. As well, overland access to the oil-rich republics of the former Soviet Union is through Kurdistan. For these and other reasons of sovereignty and the strength of existing alliances, neither the ruling nation states nor their international allies want a united independent Kurdistan, or a series of autonomous, federal states within present borders.

However the changing dynamic between nation states, international organisations such as the United Nations, the International Monetary Fund, the World Bank and the World Trade Organisation, as well as international financial and business monopolies, may have huge impacts on the Kurdish struggle. With the increase in the Kurdish population relative to other peoples in the region and their recent and rapid social evolution in terms of urbanisation and education, the communicative power of new technologies exposing people in both Kurdistan and the diasporas to diverse ideas, the growing empowerment of Kurdish women, the possibility that Turkey will join the European Union and, above all, the looming ecological crunches, who knows what the future will bring? If the Kurds devise some long-range, well thought-out strategies in terms of the role they can play in the Middle East and take advantage of sudden changes, they may realise their dream.

Nevertheless, the obstacles appear overwhelming. With enforced urbanisation the Kurds are losing their primary source of independence: life in sustainable villages. Natural resources such as the forests that feed the river systems have all but been destroyed. No oil refineries, food processing or manufacturing industries are being developed in Kurdistan and they continue to face very strong opposition on all government fronts. In lurching from one crisis to another they remain fractionalised and the need for charismatic leaders who demand absolute loyalty (from family to nation) is perpetuated.

Good leaders continue to be assassinated as was Qazi Muhammad in 1947 and Dr Abdul Rahman Qassemlou in 1989, or exiled as was Mostefa Barzani in 1946 and 1975, or imprisoned as was Leyla Zana in 1994 and Abdullah Ocalan in 1999. To survive other leaders have been forced into dubious alliances, defying the Kurdish saying 'Even if the enemy becomes a bridge, do not cross it'.

Moreover, a militant form of Islam is gaining a political and social foothold in Kurdistan. In one terrible scenario, Kurdistan will become part of a larger dynamic that may be fostered to replace communism: that of a militant form of political Islam being the new enemy of the Judeo-Christian West.

Western readers may dismiss the Kurds' unenviable predicament as being no concern of theirs, but no Western consumer can turn away from the Kurds' plight unless they deny their own culpability. Most of us in Western societies live relatively well from the exploitation of others.

If nothing else, the Kurdish struggle is of relevance for purely selfish reasons. The wheels within wheels turn rapidly in Kurdistan and magnify the forces and patterns at play in the world. These forces are causing more and more people to flee as refugees. You may find one is your neighbour. It is highly likely you will live or work beside a refugee, whose life experiences are so foreign it is as if he or she comes from another planet. Then there are the controversies of what to do with asylum seekers. In Australia we imprison them in detention camps! Do we have any idea of what they have been through already? To listen to or read about the Kurds' history, culture, society and individual experiences enhances one's understanding of people, society and international processes. This helps us reflect on the nature of our own society and our rights and responsibilities in it.

As more people in Western societies question the ecologically unsustainable and inequitable world the present international order is producing, there may come a time when they want to change the way it is operating. They will then have to ask themselves: When should we take a stand? What strategies should we employ? What processes do we want to put in place to minimise harm and maximise the rights of the individual while also enhancing the common good? In a world facing ecological crises, this common good is global. Thus we can all learn from the international nature of the Kurdish struggle.

Mostly this struggle has been violent. The sociopolitical climate is a determining factor. When national and international bodies are based on nationalistic, religious, capitalist, communist or other one-dimensional criteria, the people struggling against these forces also tend to use nationalism, religion or social class to unite. Their means of struggle reflect the means by which the rulers stay in power. In this way, cycles of oppression are perpetuated.

The cost of armed struggle is enormous, as will be shown in this book, yet few oppressed peoples have achieved liberation through peaceful means. Even the famous case of Gandhi's passive resistance in India involved decades of bloodshed between Hindus and Muslims before and after independence. Other exceptions to armed struggle are Tibet's and Burma's, their outcomes yet to be determined. Many indigenous populations' aspirations for self-determination have gained some ground in the last forty years—since 1967 Australia's indigenous people have become citizens of their own country—but this is because the people in power have had a change of consciousness. Obviously this is the preferable way for Kurds too.

The stakes are also high. Many Kurds in this book talk about a wish for democracy and freedom although they have little experience of either. In the West many take our system of democracy for granted. Yet democracy of the people, as opposed to democracy practised within a ruling body, or the development of institutions to make democracy possible, is a fairly recent phenomenon, with the outstanding exception of Greek states in the fifth century BC. Two and a half thousand years ago, all male citizens of Athens over the age of eighteen, irrespective of their economic status, directly elected people into office. Office bearers were paid, which opened positions to the less privileged, and were subject to annual elections.

From the 1760s England allowed male landowners to vote in a constitutional monarchy, but modern democracies only developed in America after the War of Independence in 1775 and the establishment of a constitution in 1798, then in France, on and off during the 1800s. Universal suffrage, where women had the right to vote as well as men, is as recent as 1902 in Australia (excluding the indigenous nations), 1918 in Britain and 1920 in the USA.

The transition from a monarchy or republican dictatorship to democracy is a long, hard road—one that can change direction gradually, by subtle processes, or suddenly by coup, war or revolution. It can be argued that genuine democracy is realised and maintained only in societies where there is tolerance and trust. In dictatorships you simply imprison or kill your enemy. In a genuine democracy there should be no threat of death, imprisonment or economic hardship when an individual or group shows signs of weakness or lawful dissent. There have to be checks and balances to enable economic sustainability and a high standard of education for all, a free decentralised media, an independent and accessible justice system, a military controlled by a democratically elected parliament and public accountability for all private and public institutions. The size of these institutions and the regions they control are also important considerations. Now assess what is happening in our democratic nation states according to the above criteria.

Today so-called democracy exists in relatively few countries. While these societies enjoy a degree of tolerance, social mobility and choice as never before, we are maybe too trusting of the strength of the fragile institutions that support democracy, especially as they are being increasingly undermined by transnational monopolies, international laws, and decisions made by unelected elites.

All Western democracies are based on the rule of the majority. Yet even this principle needs to be rethought in an increasingly pluralistic world due to its failure to represent diverse groups, especially the disadvantaged, at all levels of decision making.

While working on this book, and reflecting on the significance of the development of democracy in the 20th century, I became aware of the strong parallels between the tools of social control—namely, the use of violence, imprisonment and food queues in the Middle East—and the use of TV violence, unemployment and the bureaucratic queues in Western societies. The fear, insecurity, distrust and pessimism produced by these tools of control, coupled with a lack of social services, produce divided, easily manipulated societies.

Another observation was how a society's dynamics can completely change in just 10 to 20 years. This change can be the result of a people's movement such as women's liberation or civil rights, or the Iranian revolution of 1979. Or it can be designed from the top, as in Mistefa Kemal's and Saddam Hussein's fascist regimes and the economic rationalists' neo-liberalism that is determining the New World Order.

These dramatic political, social and economic changes have a huge effect on individual behaviour and thinking. For example, when people say "Greed is fundamental to human nature," one only has to think of all the peoples around the world, including the Kurds, who have lived a village life for aeons and who were and still are more than willing to share what little they have. Many cultures believe in sacrificing their personal well-being for the common good. Yet because capitalism thrives on individualism, we are taught to think and behave as if the need for independence, profit, power and pleasure invariably determine the human condition. I would argue they are more usually the characteristics of leaders.

Freedom is a complicated concept, yet it is a word that has inspired many revolutions and evolutions. What does it really mean, even if defined as freedom from oppression? How a young Kurd might define it may be quite distinct from Buddha's definition. To be free to drive a car on the road, one must follow the road rules. Self-determination or freedom of choice carries with it responsibility. Liberty and equality, individual freedom and the notion of the common good, are values which impact on each other and are often at cross purposes.

What is most frightening is the number of revolutions, including those you will read about, which have had no detailed blueprint for replacing the present situation with something more just. Often there is blind hope that change will be for the better, yet little preparation for it. But as will be shown in this book, it is becoming increasingly vital to think about the issues and to put into place practices, even of a personal or underground nature, to ensure a better future.

This book is made more significant in that it is the first time Kurds from all over Kurdistan have had the opportunity to speak for themselves in English, occasionally using Kurdish words that, in their nation of origin, they may go to prison for using. Their essays, life stories, short fiction and poems represent a time of social revolution and evolution.

Until now, most books about the Kurds have been authored by non-Kurdish, male observers using a single voice of authority. Past books have concentrated on Kurdish history and politics invariably from the male standpoint. Yet it is my view that only by attempting to understand the richness, diversity and vagaries of individual experience, memory and belief can one fully explore the interrelationship of the Kurdish predicament, especially in terms of man and woman, family and nation and its application to our own survival.

My interest in the Kurdish people goes back to 1991, when I heard about their plight in northern Iraq. It developed in 1994 when Michelle James, a woman who lived next to a Kurdish refugee family in Melbourne, asked me to do some research for a documentary. My interviews with Kurds from northern Iraq became a series of three radio documentaries for the ABC. The stories haunted me for four years, so it seemed they deserved a book.

What initially attracted me was these people's sense of humanity in the face of extreme suffering. I was curious to know how they survived mentally and emotionally. Through working on this book I have come to understand the sources of the Kurdish people's strength. Most of all, strong beliefs can make suffering easier to bear than if one is alienated from belief. I decided our beliefs, rather than the availability of food or our life experiences, make us who we are. Also, collective forms of suffering can ease the pain more than if one suffers in isolation. As well, human nature is so plastic it can adapt to the most horrific conditions.

However I soon became aware of the terrible debilitating effects of centuries of oppression. Behind the humanity was sometimes a substrate of depression, anger and distrust. This was understandable, given the extremity of suffering. An intolerance to difference and a readiness to pass judgement, so harsh that few can survive unscathed, were also understandable, given the culture of community, the dictates of Islam and recent history. What underscored all this was a lack of forgiveness, especially of Kurds of other political persuasions. Again, this is understandable. The more violent the suffering, the harder it is to forgive, but without forgiveness, one cannot rise above past experience.

At times I became frustrated by extreme passions that fuelled noble dreams, which were disconnected from a will to act. People talked about unity—again, a hard goal in any society—but when given the opportunity to unite, were hesitant. As one individual said, "I am a sick person because I come from a sick nation. It is sick because it has existed in a state of war and oppression for 1400 years." Yet it is a miracle of humanity that in this book you will read about so many intelligent, compassionate, brave, stoic and refreshing dimensions to the Kurdish psyche. Since the late 1980's a new psychology is developing in Kurdistan, one that is far more willing to embrace democratic processes.

Starting with my contacts from 1994 and with help from Michelle James in Melbourne and Dr Peter Cavanagh in Sydney, I made further connections with the Australian-

Kurdish community. Partial funding came from the Community Cultural Development Program of the Australia Council for the Arts (1998) and later from The Myer Foundation through the Jesuit Refugee Service in Sydney (2000), as well as the NSW Ministry of the Arts (2000).

Over three years, I interviewed people and connected with others who wrote their own essays or short stories either in Kurdish, Arabic or English. The criterion for selection was that all contributors had to be residing in Australia.

It was particularly hard to find Kurdish women willing to go through the process. Many were housebound and felt they did not have sufficient English, or were too shy, claiming they lacked knowledge and experience to make a significant contribution. Those who worked and had a family felt pressured for time. In Middle Eastern societies, very personal matters are not openly discussed and the Kurdish diaspora continue to be influenced and fragmented by Kurdish stereotypes, values and politics. Even Kurdish associations in Australia are often answerable to a party back in Kurdistan.

The other area of difficulty was interviewing people from northern Kurdistan sympathetic with PKK. No-one was willing to speak in detail as an individual or as a spokesperson for PKK. I can think of a number of reasons. The Kurds in Turkey have been denied and oppressed more than any other Kurds. This does little for confidence and self esteem. The nature of PKK is a reaction to the extreme fascism of Kemalism. Many outsiders view the organisation as terrorist, but see other Kurdish political groups as justified in their struggle. Since Ocalan's imprisonment, the Turkish government lets Ocalan rule from his prison cell, no-one knowing whether his often-surprising statements are the result of brainwashing or government censorship. PKK has chosen to keep Ocalan as their leader as a show of loyalty and defiance. In the midst of all the confusion as to the future direction of PKK and fear of retribution by both government and PKK, people were unwilling to commit themselves to print and often those who did so spoke anonymously, unwilling to reveal personal details.

Each interviewing process took between three and 14 hours of tape, four contributors being interviewed through a translator. Interviews were then transcribed and with English being a second language, the same amount of time, or more, was spent checking details with each contributor. Many were reminded of experiences that they preferred to forget. Public domain facts were checked with reference books wherever possible.

Then the editing process began. In the editing, patterns and rhythms of speech were rarely retained, because of the difficulties of reading English as a second language, but Kurdish, Arabic, Turkish and Farsi words were kept as important dimensions of Kurdish culture. Once the interview had become a working draft of oral history, with further points of confusion or details being clarified, the contributors were shown their stories to read, check and change. This is a critical stage in the oral history process. The spoken word is often more ambiguous than the written and in an interview, especially in a person's second, third or fourth language, time sequences, details and emphasis can be inadvertently misrepresented.

When reviewing their story, contributors could choose to change their names and cut or change anything. A number of revealing details had to be cut because of a concern for the safety of family and friends back in Kurdistan or fear of reprisal by governments if they returned to Kurdistan. Only two contributors chose to pull out of the book entirely, even though to speak out and be published is a very courageous act, not only because of the danger but also because much of the material is controversial. That so many decided to use real names and retain the details of villages, dates and opinions is a testimony to their personal bravery, love for their people and country, their wish to inform the world and their heartfelt desire for change.

After a contributor approved a draft of their story, it was further polished and edited for structure, flow and avoidance of repetition. However, it was important to retain differences of observed or remembered fact, myth and opinion, even if contradictory, because the relativity of reality informs our thoughts, choices and actions. In relation to these discrepancies of personal truth, some Kurds involved expressed a concern that this book would too much reflect the capricious views of 'ordinary' people. Yet I believe these are as important as those of the academics, which are also included. In all societies, large numbers of people lack the knowledge or time to explore the depth of issues. Their mentality can be formed by myths and rumours, but these often have great social influence, particularly in societies where there are few academics and which rely on oral tradition.

The book is divided into four sections. These divisions are as artificial as the borders that divide Kurdistan, but for ease of understanding I decided to structure the book in this way because the modern history of southern Kurdistan (northern Iraq) is so different to that of northern Kurdistan (eastern Turkey and north-west Syria) and eastern Kurdistan (north-west Iran).

As for those who chose to write in Kurdish or Arabic and have their work translated, it soon became apparent that translation is an art in itself. Many thanks to Haji Alhajani, Eziz Bawermend, Hussein Tahiri, Isma'il Qaradghi, Benaz, Omar Sheikhmous, Dr Muhammad Kamal, Dr Toma Hamid, Kamran Avin and Gafoor Muhamad from Kurdistan, Sam Zakhary from Egypt, Myra Cheera from Lebanon, and Loretta Jew and Skye O'Neill from Australia for their work in translating. Also, thanks to Dana Kadar for checking facts and supplying additional material for 'A Musical and Poetic Tradition'.

I also extend my gratitude to Eziz Bawermend for supplying list upon list of Kurdish proverbs, which he had translated. These have been used as titles for many contributions. Much appreciation also to Rebwar Tahir for his painting for the front cover, Abdulwahab Talabani for checking all pronunciations and spelling of non-English words and names, and Hussein Khoshnow for his map of Kurdistan and its emirates.

Thanks as well to the transcribers Jane Stevenson, Dawn Webb and Terri Kibbler, who had to deal with broken speech patterns, accents and foreign nouns and also to the Australian Kurdish Community Association, the Australian Kurdish Association, the Kurdish Association of NSW, Komita Kurdistan of Australia, the Kurdish Association of Victoria, the Australian Kurdish Community of Victoria and the Australian Kurdish Association of Queensland, as well as the Liverpool Migrant Resource Centre, all of whom supported various grant applications. For the design of the book, Kylie Prats of Brevier Design deserves all credit.

Most of all, I wish to express my deepest appreciation and respect for the Kurdish people who shared so much of their life experiences, time, patience and generous hospitality. When I made my initial approach, they had no idea about the length and depth of the journey on which they were embarking! I might add—nor did I!

It is hoped that this book will inspire much-needed archeological and other academic research. Most of all it is hoped that it will contribute to a sense of empowerment, for the Kurds to feel no longer 'we have no friends but the mountains'. Healing the psychological trauma of an abused individual is hard enough. Having a whole population suffering from generations of physical and emotional trauma requires an international political and socioeconomic movement to support constructive processes, to allow a time of peace so people can gain a sense of safety and start thinking, rather than reacting in the midst of adrenalin-charged danger. For the Kurdish people to realise their dream of being recognised as a nation and to be able to live in peace with their neighbours in whatever way this can be negotiated, they need friends, both individuals and institutions.

We can choose to be ostriches sticking our heads in the sand and saying, "I'm okay," or "I have too many problems to worry about yours." But if chaos theory is correct, that the movement of a butterfly's wing can cause a cyclone somewhere else, then how much more concerned should we be about the ongoing denial of 40 million people in a major world crossroad?

Existing powers have the ability to control populations and exploit the world's resources as never before. Yet thanks to better education and communication, to the potential power of a collective mind and to united action and the global nature of social and ecological problems that make change imperative—coupled with the laws of synchronicity, chance and those of a metaphysical nature—no major event, process or outcome is ever completely in the control of a few humans, no matter how powerful.

Knowledge is one form of power. Compassion is one form of humanity. My greatest source of hope is humankind's miraculous capacity to transcend suffering with a vision that is qualitatively different from anything it has experienced. Individuals who do this can inspire others to work patiently towards a more peaceful, democratic world.

— 1 —

LIFTING THE VEIL

ABOUT **Dr Hussein Tahiri**

See 'Life's Legacy: Blood Cannot Be Washed With Blood'

The Kurds and their Origins

An essay by Dr Hussein Tahiri

The origin of the Kurds is a controversial issue in Middle Eastern history because the Kurds form the fourth largest nation in the region and their territory has been divided among four nation-states: Turkey, Iran, Iraq and Syria. This division has caused a politicisation of the Kurds' origins. Some ruling states have sometimes tried to deny them recognition as a separate people, claiming they are part of the ruling nation. They have falsified history and recruited academics in order to achieve this.[1] The most glaring example is in Turkey, where the majority of Kurds live. Ever since the suppression of the Kurdish revolt of Dersim in 1938, the Turkish state has claimed that Kurds are 'mountain Turks'.[2] The hypocrisy of their claim is demonstrated when the Turkish state protests to international bodies against Bulgaria denying the identity of Turks in Bulgaria, while it continues to deny the identity of the Kurds in Turkey.

At times, Kurds have been regarded as Arabs, such as in the work of Arab historian Masudi.[3] Other academics have ignorantly regarded the Kurds and their language, literature and history as Persian.[4] Classical authors often refer to the 'Iranic people', including those living in Anatolia, as 'Persian'. This has given some justification for the ruling governments in Iran to relate the Kurds to Persians. However, the term 'Iranic people' includes people known as Kurd, Lur, Azeri, Baluchi and Afghani, as well as some people of Anatolia.[a]

Of one thing we can be sure: the Kurds cannot be Turk, Arab *and* Persian, as no historian claims that Turks are Arab and Persian or any other combination. Trying to relate the Kurds to a ruling nation only shows the depth of political confusion on the part of these states. Therefore, the origin of the Kurds needs to be scientifically studied, taking into account the Kurds' history, early tribal composition, geographical location, language and religion.

Myths must be distinguished from historical facts. There are several legends about the origin of the Kurds. One legend regards the Kurds as the most ancient people of the civilised world. Ancient Sumerian and Akkadian tablets describe a great flood when the King of Shuruppak (Noah in the Torah and the Bible, Nuh in the Qur'an) landed in Kurdistan on Judi Mountain, in the Ararat Range, near the Turkish, Iraqi and Iranian borders. From ancient times, the letter 'g' has been interchangeable with 'j', and likewise the letters 't' and 'd', so 'Judi' is the same as 'Guti'. Noah is said to have built a village called Bikhurdi. Historical evidence suggests that an Indo-European people known as the Guti are one of the ancestors of the Kurds. They are believed to have settled in the region by 2250 BC. Therefore, according to the legend of Noah, the Kurds are descended from the most ancient civilised people of the Fertile Crescent.[5]

Another myth says that King Suleiman (Solomon) wanted to add 400 beautiful girls from the West to his harem. On the way, *jinn* raped them, and the children from this intercourse are said to be the ancestors of the Kurds.[6]

Yet another legend relates the Kurds to the people who survived the cruelty of King Azhdehak, also known as Zohag, Dahak and Zahak. This legend recounts that two snakes grew on Azhdehak's shoulders. Each day, these snakes had to be fed the brains of two young human beings. Taking pity on the people, the king's cooks, Armaiel and Garmaiel, would substitute a sheep's brain for one of the human beings and smuggle the survivor to the mountains. These survivors are said to be the ancestors of the Kurds.[7]

Whether or not this legend is based on history, it has penetrated deeply into Kurdish folklore. Many Kurds regard Newroz, the Kurdish New Year, as a symbol of freedom and a celebration of the victory of the people over the cruelty of Azhdehak. They give a political colour to Newroz, describing the Kurdish revolts of the 20th century as uprisings against the Azhdehaks of this era.

The debate over the identity of the historical Azhdehak has significant implications. In the Kurdish history book called the *Sharafnameh* (1597), Amir Sharaf Khan Bitlisi claims that the tyrant Zahak was the fifth king of the Pishdadian, an Iranian dynasty of ancient times. He established a reign of terror over Iran and Turan after the death of the fourth Pishdadian king, King Jamshid.[8] People continue to argue over whether the Pishdadian were Kurd or Persian. However, Mehrdrad Izady, a Kurdish scholar from Iran now based in the USA, puts forward the theory that Azhdehak was the last Mede king, who was defeated by his half-Persian grandson Cyrus the Great. Given the evidence that Kurds are descended from the Medes, if Izady's theory is correct, there is some contradiction in the Kurds' celebration of the defeat of the last Mede king. Izady suggests that it was only after his defeat that Azhdehak acquired his demonic reputation,[9] because during his reign, the ancient religions known as the 'Cults of the Angels' greatly influenced the newly developing religion of the prophet Zoroastra. For instance, this influence introduced the priestly office of the *magi* into Zoroastrianism. Zoroastrianism became the state religion of the Achaemanids, the empire established by Cyrus the Great, and Izady hypothesises that it was probably as a reaction to this influence that Zoroastrians gave Azhdehak the title of demon. The legend was subsequently incorporated into Zoroastrianism and into Iranian mythology and literature. If this was the case, the Kurds are celebrating a Persian victory over their ancestors and a negation of their original religion and its influence on Zoroastrianism.

There is no verifiable historical basis for any of these legends, so it is best to look elsewhere for evidence of the origin of the Kurds. There are two major theories. One view is that of V. Minorsky, a Russian linguist, who states that the Kurds are of Indo-European origin. Another view, held by N. J. Marr, also a linguist, relates the Kurds to Asian peoples such as the Khaldes, Georgians and Armenians.[10] However, the view of many scholars is that the Kurds are an amalgamation of native peoples and migrating Aryan tribes who settled in the area.[11]

There is archeological evidence that 10,000 years ago pastoralists and agriculturalists inhabited Kurdistan's mountains and plains. A distinct culture known as the Halaf developed from 6300 BC. A Halaf town near the Khabour River in north-east Syria dates from 5050 BC. Other towns have been discovered, varying in size from one to eight hectares. The Halaf culture has been labelled 'trans-egalitarian', or a precursor to the age of civilisation, defined by inherited social stratifications, which featured in the southern Ubaid and Sumer cultures. There is evidence that the Halaf towns had granaries, large adobe houses, cobbled streets and drainage systems. They traded in pottery, had intersettlement communication and could have influenced the Ubaid and Sumer civilisations.

By 4300 BC the Halaf culture was superseded by the Ubaidian culture, either from the south or by an evolution of Halaf culture itself, the Ubaids lasting another millennium or more in the north. The Ubaids hierarchical social structure is more evident in that some of their houses are very large, up to 240 square metres and they also built large public buildings, including temples to the Anunnaki god, Enki.[b/12]

In the south, the Ubaids were replaced by the Sumers during the fourth millennium BC, when recorded history began, and in the north by the Hurrians by 2600 BC. The Hurrians may have been Halafian people who wanted to reassert their dominance over Kurdistan's mountains,[13] or a newly arrived people from the north or east. From the end of the third millennium BC, they were in Urmia and could be related to the Subareans. By 1700 BC, they formed the majority of the population in the Mitanni empire, which spread west as far as Lake Van in modern-day Turkey and south into Syria, until 1350 BC, when the Assyrians became dominant. Although the Hurrians lost their independent identity by the late second millennium BC, their religion, myths, art and culture were to influence the Hittites, Scythians and Medes.[14] They spoke a language close to modern Chechen and Lezgian, which belong to the north-east Caucasian family of languages, Alarodian.[15] Wilhelm Gernot believes that the Hurrians are the pre-Aryan ancestors of the Kurds,[16] whereas N. J. Marr, probably by using the same Hurrian ancestry, relates the Kurds to Asians.

It has been established that waves of Aryan migration into the area began from about 2300 BC. Few scholars are willing to commit themselves to explaining the ambiguous origin of the Aryans; however, scholars like S. G. Talageri indicate that Iranians and other Indo-Europeans originally lived in southern Russia, passing through Central Asia to settle in Iran. He rejects the view that the Aryans' original homeland was in Central Asia, in the Pamir region, or in Russian Turkestan.[17]

The already-mentioned Guti are one of the early Indo-European tribes who settled in Kurdistan and are therefore thought to be one of the forebears of the Kurds. They became a political force for 100 years in the third millennium BC, overthrowing the scholastic Akkadians and conquering the city of Babylonia in 2230 BC, to be defeated by Utu-khegal of Uruk in 2130 BC. They again reasserted their dominance in the second millennium, when they briefly overthrew the Assyrians.[18] Frank Hole, an American scholar, locates the Guti in the mountain valleys of Iranian Kurdistan, north and south-west of Kirmanshah.[19] According to Thomas Bois, the Gutis inhabited the mountains to the east of the Little Zab River, near the Diyala River.[20] Shaykh A. Waheed, from Pakistan, locates the Gutis' land around the Lower Zab, the Tigris, the hills of Sulaimani and the

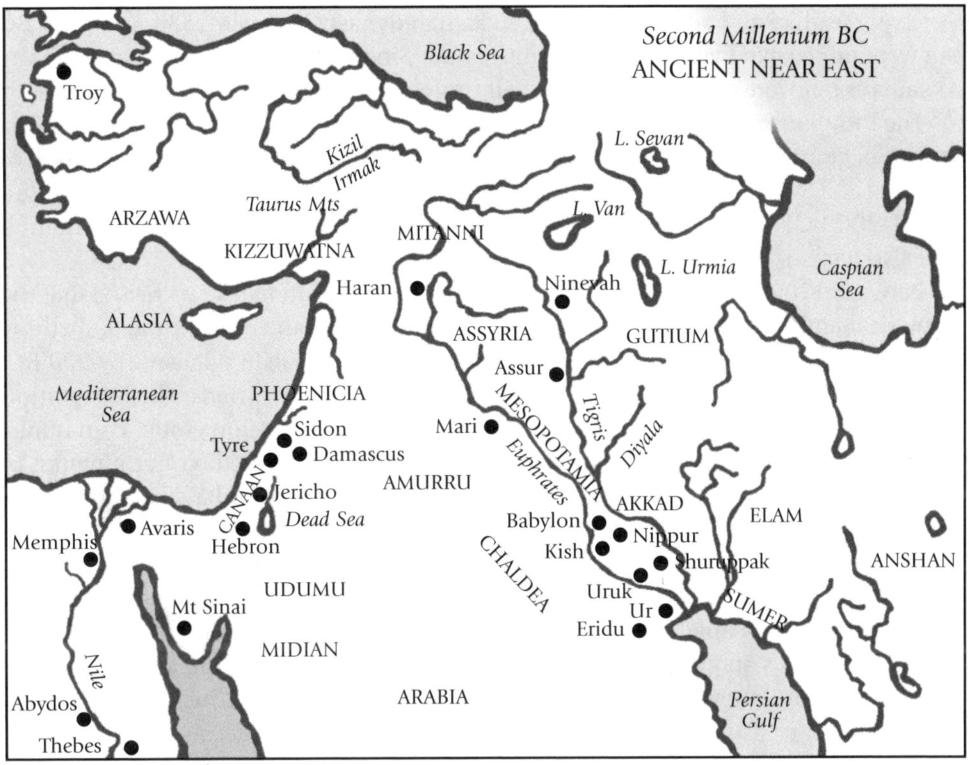

River Diyala, with their capital, Arrepkha, near the town of modern-day Kirkuk.[21] These locations would tend to undermine the theory that relates the Guti to Mount Judi. However, one can conclude that the Guti occupied a portion of Kurdistan for a considerable time and therefore could be ancestors of the Kurds.

Aryan migration was to change the structure of Kurdistan's society forever. Aryans formed the aristocracy of the Mitanni, Kassite and Hittite kingdoms, the common people remaining Hurrian.[22] From old texts, the Kassites appear to have been in the area known as Luristan from the third millennium BC. They borrowed the cuneiform script and laws from the Sumerians, were polytheistic, and worshipped the horse as sacred, horses being vital for war and trade.[23] According to Frank Hole, the Kassites occupied Babylonia from 1800 BC and were dominant for six centuries. They traded and had political marriages with the Egyptian pharaohs, but in the first millennium, they were forced to withdraw to the Zagros Ranges when the Assyrians expanded their empire.[24] However, the Kassites managed to prevent the Assyrians going further east. After being conquered by Alexander the Great in 330 BC, they regained their independence and, according to Thomas Bois, expanded their domination to Elam.[25] So the Kassites are another tribe who could have contributed to the formation of the Kurdish people.[26] One view regards them as the ancestors of the Guran Kurds, who continue to live around Kirmanshah and Elam in Luristan, in modern Iran.[27]

Likewise, the Lullubi people inhabited the Sherizor plain of the Zagros Range. They were very warlike and active during the Akkadian dynasty between 2334 and 2154 BC but were subjugated by the Akkadian king Naram-Sin. Later they helped bring down the Akkadians but were overshadowed by their more powerful neighbours.[28]

The Indo-European tribe of the Hittites had more success. They appeared in Anatolia by the beginning of the second millennium BC and became a dominate power of Anatolia and Syria in the Old Kingdom (late 1600s–1500 BC) and in the New Kingdom (1400–200 BC). During these times, they took over Babylonia, fighting the Mitanni, and also Ramses II of Egypt in the famous battle of Kadesh.[29]

Between 1200 and 900 BC, the flow of Aryan immigration had so increased that the numerical and material superiority of the Aryans absorbed the old cultural and ethnic structures of Kurdistan and the rest of the Iranian and Anatolian plateaus. By 900 BC, the Aryan groups were fully integrated with the pre-existing Hurrians. This integration changed the culture and structure of society from a Paleo-Caucasion group to an Iranic, Indo-European one that survives to the present day.[30] However, the intermingling of native people and various Indo-European tribes did not create a unitary political entity. Kurdistan continued to be ruled by different tribes. Sometimes, a strong tribe would form a kingdom and expand its territory; at other times, each tribe would have its own kingdom, exchanging knowledge and trade with neighbouring kingdoms. This fragmentation of people and cross-pollination of cultures has aroused much debate among academics and caused some confusion as to who are the true ancestors of the Kurds. Yet I have shown that the pre-Mede ancestors could well include the Halafs, Ubaids, Hurrians, Guti, Mitanni, Kassite, Lullubi and Hittite tribes.

By the eighth century BC, two other peoples had settled in Kurdistan. The warlike Scythians are believed to be either an Indo-European people from north of the Black Sea or an Asiatic people.[31] The other was the Medes, an Indo-European people who migrated from east Iran during the mid-ninth century BC. In the *Ganjineh-e-Kurdistan*, or *Treasury of Kurdistan*, a unique 3000-year-old document discovered in Kurdistan, the fine art in the region is described. It is shown that there were clear similarities between the arts of the Medes and Scythians, famous for their gold and electrum animal-decorated ornaments, elaborate royal grave mounds and horsemanship.[32] It is the Medes who are considered the most important forebears of the Kurds.

The ninth-century BC cuneiform clay tablets of the Assyrians[c] record two major groups of Iranians: the Medes and the Persians. At the time of this record, the Medes were more widespread and more powerful than the Persians.[d 33] By the seventh century BC, the Medes had expanded their domination over most of the Middle East. According to the Greek historian Herodotus (484–424 BC), an extensive empire known as Medea was formed in 727 BC.[34] The Medes elected their first king, Deioces, also known as Deiokes or Dayaukku, who built his capital, Ecbatan, near modern-day Hamadan. His son Phraotes, named Kashtariti by the Assyrians, succeeded him. Between 625 and 523 BC, the Scythians pushed south and assumed dominance in the area, before they were defeated in 625 BC by the Mede king Cyaxares. By 612 BC, the Median Empire was so strong that, in alliance with the Babylonians, it destroyed Nineveh and defeated the Assyrians.[35]

The Mede Empire is most likely to have been a confederation of kingdoms, hence the title 'king of kings' given to Cyaxares. Under him, the Medes spread over vast territory. They organised themselves into three main provinces: Greater Mede (Iraq Ajami), Atropatenus Mede (Azerbaijan) and Rhages Mede (a district around present-day Tehran).[36] Izady states that Cyaxares extended Medea west to the banks of the Halys River, the ancient name of the Kizilirmaq River, near Ankara (Medea included the Kingdom of Cappodocia),[37] and east beyond Kurdistan. The king Rshti-vega Azhi Dahak was to be the last Mede king. In 550 BC, he was defeated by his half-Persian grandson Cyrus the Great, who founded the Persian dynasty of the Achaemeniads.[38] Like his Mede forebears, Cyrus was also known as 'king of kings'.

So what happened to the Medes? Although their territory was occupied by Persians from 550 BC, the Medes, with their power structures and military, survived. There is no indication that they were assimilated by Persians or migrated. In 220 BC, the historian Polybius wrote about the Kurti who inhabited Medean territory, including eastern Anatolia, where the Kurds still live.[39] T. Wahby, a Pakistani military officer and scholar, who studied the fourth-century Christian Aramaic records of Arbil,[e] states that historical evidence shows that by the end of the Sassanian era (637 AD), the name 'Mede' continued to exist in different forms, including 'Mad', 'May', 'Mas', 'Maday' and 'Madaya'. The name appeared as 'Mah' in the early Islamic period. All these names denoted areas in Kurdistan. He also discovered close relations between personal names of the Median and Kurdish language. Wahby concludes that the Medes survived the Sassanian Empire and the Kurds of today are their descendants.[40]

Some linguists support this view. Wahby uses Minorsky's work to show that the Kurdish language bears close relationship to the north-west Iranian language group, thus adding to the evidence suggesting that Kurds are descended from the Medes.[41] Many researchers agree.[42] However, as I have shown, other tribes also could have contributed to the ancestry of the Kurds. The question then arises: when did the Kurdish people come to be known as 'Kurd', with a homeland called 'Kurdistan'?

There have been many historical names related to the word 'Kurd', including Qutil, Kurtie, Karduch and Carduk. Despite differences in the way these names are spelled or pronounced, almost all historians locate the people to which they refer in the same region. Izady states that the Qutils, in the late third millennium BC, united many other tribes and succeeded in expanding their rule outside Kurdistan. He mentions one clan of Qutils whom Sumerians called the Subiru or Saubaru. According to Izady, the Saubarus are the present-day Zibaris, a Kurdish tribe who live in northern Iraq, near the border with Turkey, where the Saubarus lived 4000 years ago.[43]

Akkadian tablets dated 1400 BC indicate that a kingdom called Qortie or Kurtie was situated in the north of Mesopotamia and extended to the shores of Lake Van.[44] Sir Henry Rawlinson, a British scholar, deciphered cuneiform inscriptions related to Kur-ti or Kurtie from an ancient Assyrian site. He located Kurtie to the east of Lake Van.[45]

Xenophon (430–352 BC), a student of Socrates who became a Greek historian and army commander, describes the retreat of the Greek army of 'Ten Thousand' (400–401 BC) from the warlike Karduchoi living in the east of Botan, which was to become a Kurdish emirate of the Ottoman Empire. The name Karduchoi has subsequently been found on the left bank of the Tigris River, near Mount Djudi.[46] Pliny, a Roman historian, located Carduci or Cordueni around the Tigris.[47] Thus, the people known as the Karduchs (and variations of this word) had been living in the region for a long time.

Apart from the Kurds, who else could the Karduchs be? Professor Lehmann-Haupt states that the Karduks may not be the ancestor of the Kurds, that they may be the ancestors of the Georgian-Kartuelians.[48] Also, Karduks or Carduks could be related to the Chaldeans and the Khaldes of Urartu.[49] However, the Kurds speak an Indo-European language, while the Khaldes and Georgians do not.[50] Furthermore, the ancient land of the Karduchoi is populated by modern-day Kurds. There is no historical indication, as far as I am aware, that the people called the Karduchoi, or a variation of the word, migrated to a territory outside Kurdistan. Therefore, one can conclude the Karduchs were the Kurds. The different forms of spelling or pronunciation, Karduchoi, Kurtie and so on, can be attributed to the way a word in different languages is spelled or pronounced.[f] This is what Frederick Millingen believes. Focusing on different variations of the word 'Kurd' in different languages, he states that there is no doubt the Kurds of today are the Karduks of 23 centuries ago.[51] Hence, the Karduks were one of the ancestors of the Kurds. However, some scholars challenge this theory.

One challenger is Dr Mackenzie. Using linguistic evidence, he rejects that the Kurds are descendants of the Medes, saying that the Kurdish language belongs to the south-west Iranian language group, not to the north-west, as V. Minorsky claims.[52] W. J. Marr stresses another view. He claims that the Kurds are a native people from Asia Minor, relatives of the Khaldes, Georgians and Armenians. He states that the Kurdish language was formed in the region, but puts emphasis on the social and economic changes as having transformed Kurdish from a language akin to Georgian and Khaldi to a language akin to the Indo-European group.[53]

However, most scholars agree that modern Kurdish is one of the Indo-European group of languages. It is outside the scope of this chapter to explore the linguistic details, but suffice it to say that Kurdish shares a great number of words with English, as in *ster* (star), *dale* (dole), *der* (door), *roobar* (river), *rhubarg* (rhubarb) and so on, as well as with the Indo-European language of Sanskrit, as in *tanoor* (tandoor) and *na'an*.

Meanwhile, the Kurdish language continues to be the target of misinterpretations,[54] the main controversy being how much it is related to the language of the Medes. As already stated, Wahby uses V. Minorsky's work on the north-west Iranian language group and his own research in Arbil to establish the Mede ancestry of the Kurds from a linguistic point of view. Even Marr, who believes that the Kurds are native to the area, does not deny that Kurdish is classifiable as an Indo-European language.

Nevertheless, some 20th-century Turkish scholars have tried to show that Kurdish is an ancient form of Turkish, even though Turkic peoples began arriving in the area as recently as 950 years ago and the word samples one Turkish scholar used were not even Turkish but were derived from Arabic.[g] Also, no-one who masters Kurdish and Turkish can claim that there is any relationship between the languages, in either words or grammar!

Other views maintain that the Kurdish language is a kind of corrupted Persian[55] or has been influenced by 'Middle Persian' and belongs to the Iranian south-west language group.[56] There are ways in which Kurdish and Persian are related. However, the similarities do not indicate that Kurdish is a dialect of Persian, and if one of these languages were a derivation of the other, then the historical evidence—that the Medes ruled an extensive empire before the Persians—would suggest it was more likely that Persian is derived from the language of the Medes. Supporting such a view is the fact that the mother of Cyrus the Great, the founder of the first Persian Empire, was a Mede and no-one can deny that families, particularly mothers, shape the language of their children. Likewise, the Parthians, who were dominant in Iran between 200 BC and 140 AD, accused Ardashir I, founder of the Sassanian Empire, of being born into a Kurdish family.[57]

Minorsky's work supports the argument that the north-west Iranian language groups could not have developed without being affected by the Medes' Indo-European language.[58] He believes that before the Kurds scattered to the mountains, their language was shaped and spoken by the vast majority of people over a large area. Wahby uses Minorsky's arguments and his own study of fourth-century Aramaic records of Arbil to endorse this view.[59]

Whoever influenced who, it can be shown that modern Kurdish is a unitary language, with its own distinguishable characteristics, and includes a number of dialects and subdialects distinguishable by variations of accent and words. This diversity of dialects is natural in such a mountainous area, where pre-20th-century communication was difficult and where, after the Medes, the Kurds failed to form a unified political entity over a large territory, thereby failing to develop a standardised language. Yet the mere survival of closely related Kurdish dialects in such conditions points to a common origin.

Kurdish dialects include Kurmanji, Sorani, Gurani, Hawrami and Dimili (also known as Zaza). The variations between them have led some scholars to separate some dialects from mainstream Kurdish, claiming that there is no relation between them in either words or grammar! Kurdish is generally divided into two main branches: Kurmanji and Pahlawani. Kurmanji is further divided into northern Kurmanji, which includes Bahdinani, and southern Kurmanji, which includes Sorani. Even so, Bahdinani and Sorani are very close. After a week or so of being together, speakers of each dialect can communicate easily. Pahlawani is subdivided into Hawrami, Dimili (or Zaza) and Gurani,[60] and these subdialects can be further subdivided.

It is the Pahlawani dialects that are the most controversial, because of politically based attempts to separate the Dimili and Gurani dialects from the Kurdish language, especially for the Dimili-speaking people of Turkey. The confusion arises because, while these two dialects are closely related, the Gurani are located in eastern Kurdistan (Iran) and the Dimili live in northern Kurdistan (Turkey). The reason for this separation is that Pahlawani was spoken throughout much of Kurdistan before internal migrations of people in the 16th century. From this time, Kurmanji expanded south and north to replace Pahlawani. As a result, Pahlawani became confined to two distinct areas—one in the north and the other in the south.[61] As well, for a long time, Gurani was the poetic language of the Ardalan and Baban ruling families. It was regarded as a very civilised and polished dialect of Kurdish.[62] Dimili did not have the same prestige, but it was spoken by a large number of people until the Turkish government outlawed it.[h]

A glance at history will confirm that Dimili is a Kurdish dialect. Dimilis are believed to be the descendants of the Daylamites. Daylam is a geographical area located in present-day Gilan, in Iran, from where the Daylamites began their expansion in early medieval times. This has led some scholars to think that the Daylamites were originally located outside Kurdistan and were not Kurds. However, pre-Islamic history indicates that the Daylamites lived in Anatolia. The *Bundahishn*, one of the Zoroastrian holy books, and Christian church archives of late classical Arbil locate the Daylamites at the headwaters of the Tigris River. Furthermore, Dimilis are Alevi[i] who still practise some ancient Kurdish beliefs and rituals.[63] Shaykh Waheed states, "The old Cappadocian language is the basic constituent of this [Dimili] language."[64] Cappadocia was a Mede kingdom.[65] Amir Sharaf Khan Bitlisi included both Guranis and Dimilis among the Kurds in the *Sharafnameh*, in 1597.[66] Therefore, regarding Guranis and Dimilis as Kurds is not a new phenomenon. Linguistic evidence also suggests that Dimili and Gurani are Kurdish dialects.

The history of the Kurds in the last 2000 years is well documented. The term 'Kurd' developed to its current shape during the Sassanian era (224–637 AD). Artakhshir-e-Papakan (or Ardashir-e-Babakan), chief of the Fars, established the Sassanian capital at Ctesiphon, near modern Baghdad, and described the 'Madiq' or 'Mede' Shah-e-Kurdan, or 'King of the Kurds', among his opponents. Thus it can be said that the words 'Karduchoi', 'Kurtie' and variations developed into the word 'Kurd' and in the early Islamic period, following the defeat of the Sassanians at the battle of Qadisiya in 637 AD, the word 'Kurd' became widely used.

After the Muslim invasion, Arab historians kept extensive records. Kurdistan was an important land road to Anatolia, Iran and the rest of Asia. Following the first contact between Kurds and Arab Muslims, in 637 AD, when Tikrit and Hulwan were occupied, Sa'ad ibn Abi Waqas subjugated Mosul and its Kurdish population,[67] but the Islamic occupation of Kurdistan did not go smoothly. It was only after bloody fighting that the Kurds were subdued, and afterwards, the Kurds repeatedly revolted. Nevertheless, many Kurds converted to Islam. By this time, the Sassanian and Byzantine Empires were in decline, and in the power vacuum, the Kurds managed to establish a number of kingdoms with their own administrative and military structures.

The first significant Kurdish dynasty was that of the Shaddadis. The Shaddadis ruled between 951 and 1088 AD in the north of Kurdistan, the Caucasus and Armenia.[68] Likewise, between 990 and 1069 AD, the Marwanids ruled Diyarbakir, Jeziri and several towns in Armenia.[69] They are said to have had a good relationship with the neighbouring Byzantine Empire, which extended to Anatolia. A century later, between 1169 and 1250 AD, the Ayyubi dynasty came to power. Its founder was Salahaddin Ayyubi, a Kurd who formed an Islamic empire in Egypt and Syria. He is well known in the West because he fought the Crusaders and defeated Richard the Lionheart in 1187, formalising the victory in 1192.[70] It was the Ayyubiads who were overtaken by the Seljuk Turks in 1250. However, it must be said the Ayyubiad Empire was not a Kurdish but an Islamic empire, so many Arabs regard it as an Arab Muslim empire, even though Salahaddin and some of his ruling administrators and military leaders were Kurdish.

Other Kurdish kingdoms did not reach the heights of the Ayyubi Empire, because they did not use Islam to unite the different peoples and expand their territory over large areas. Nevertheless, Kurdish kingdoms were numerous, and can be distinguished from fiefdoms because they had their own fortress-castles, civil administrations and military aristocracies that governed a number of tribes. Often, they were brought undone by power struggles between tribes, and these betrayals made them vulnerable to outside forces. This was the case for the Hasanwayhid dynasty, formed by the Barzani tribe between 959 and 1015 AD, the last ruler being famous for his concern for social justice. Contemporary with this dynasty, Amir Sharaf Khan Bitlisi, in the *Sharafnameh*, names two other Kurdish kingdoms, Greater Lur and Minor Lur, the Lurs being regarded as Kurds until this time.[71]

While the Ayyubiads were regarded as Arab, other Kurdish dynasties were considered Persian. Abu Muslim Khurasani's dynasty, between 754 and 770 AD, is described as Persian in Iranian schoolbooks because he served Islam and Persia, even though he was of the Rawendi tribe from Azerbaijan.[72] Likewise, between 1752 and 1795, the Zand dynasty in Iran is considered Persian even though its founder, Karim Khan-e-Zand, who became Shah of Persia, was from a Kurdish tribe from Ighar, between Hamadan and Malayir.[73] The Zands were overthrown as a result of an insider's collusion with Persian forces.

Nevertheless, Kurdish dynasties were relatively secure in their independence until 1055, when successive invasions of Turkic tribes from the plains of central Asia began. By 1071, the Turks occupied the towns of Malatya, Kayseri and Konya, forcing the Greek Byzantine Empire to retreat to Asia Minor. An influx of other tribes from Asia followed, including the Seljuk Turks from 1037, the Mongols in the 13th century and the Tartars of Tamerlane in the 1380s.[74]

From the beginning of the 13th century, the Turkic nomads dominated the region. Kurdistan was their pathway for invading the Byzantine Empire, which they defeated in 1453. On their way, they destroyed many cultures and ethnic groups and overthrew many independent Kurdish kingdoms.[75] However, under the Seljuks from 1250 and the Ottomans from 1300, some Kurdish principalities survived, or were revived, as were others under the Safavids in Persia, who ruled between 1499 and 1736.

The Kurds continued to enjoy a large degree of autonomy under the Ottomans and Safavids until the early 16th century, when tensions rose between the two empires. On 23 August 1514, as a result of war, Kurdistan was divided for the first time between the two empires, the division being formalised in 1639. One cause of tension was sectarian antagonism. The Ottomans were Sunni. The Safavids were Shi'ite. Many Kurds were Sunni, so the Ottoman sultan, Selim, wanted to use the Kurds against the Safavids, while also focusing on eastern Europe. In return for their military support, the Kurds were given relief from paying taxes and continued to have freedom in their internal affairs.

The Ottomans formed 16 autonomous Kurdish emirates or principalities, which were basically tribal confederacies, and these continued until the mid-19th century.[76] The Persians also allowed the Kurds under their jurisdiction independence until the mid-19th century, by which time both empires began centralising their governments, subjugating the Kurdish principalities and leaving the Kurds to face an uncertain future. This led to many uprisings, which continue to the present day. Thus the Kurds have survived as a distinct nation.

The final area of scholarship to be considered in support of the ancient origin of the Kurds is religion. Like the Kurdish language, the original religions of the Kurds are the subject of many disputes. Muhammad Abbasi, an Iranian historian, states that the Kurds were probably Zoroastrians before converting to Islam. To substantiate this claim, he mentions the remains of the ancient fire temples in Kurdistan, such as the great temple of Azar Gashnisb at Takht-e-Suleiman (Shiz Ginzik), in Iran. The Sassanian kings used to visit this temple and use its fire to light other fire temples.[77]

The prophet known as Zoroastra, Zaradash or Zartosht (628–551 BC) was born in Kurdistan, to the west of Lake Urmia. On going to the mountains, he had a vision of the great god Ahura Mazda, creator of all that is good, and began to teach. However, many researchers argue it is unlikely that the Kurds were Zoroastrians. One such researcher is Brigadier General Sir Percy Sykes. In 1930, he wrote that while Zoroastra taught the new religion for a decade in Kurdistan, he could not influence the people, so he travelled to north-east Persia and Afghanistan, where he had more success.[78] Zoroastra's religion became the official religion of the Achaemanids, and spread to India, where the Parsees still practise it. Consequently, while there are many Zoroastrians among the Persians, there is no Kurd who is Zoroastrian. However, many Kurds have retained the religion known as Ezidi,[j] often written as 'Yezidi' or 'Yazidi'.

There is much ambiguity surrounding the Ezidi religion. It is not known who founded it. Neither Ezidism nor any other religion has any documentation on its foundation, so it has been subject to many interpretations. This could partly be due to its emphasis on secrecy and hereditary, it having been an oral tradition passed down through Ezidi families until the 12th century.

Some regard it as a derivative religion that borrowed from Islam, Christianity and other faiths.[79] Others, using similarities between 'Yazidi' and 'Yazid', have related it to Yazid ibn Mu'awiyya, an apostle of the prophet Muhammad and caliph after Ali, and conclude that Ezidis are of the Arab race.[80]

Historically, Ezidis have been much hated and persecuted by the Muslims, especially the Shi'ites, who have wrongly accused them of being Satan-worshippers. This is because although Ezidis believe there is only one God, they believe that Ta'us,[k] the Peacock Angel, does not represent evil as does Satan in Christianity and Islam. Instead, they believe Malak Ta'us is one of the archangels and was partly responsible for creating the material world. When Malak Ta'us refused to bow to Adam, God ostracised him but afterwards forgave him, and their respect for him as an angel has been the source of many misunderstandings.

Another view maintains that the Ezidi religion is so old, its very antiquity has made its origin hard to trace.[81] This view is probably the most authentic. Ezidis believe theirs is the first monotheistic religion. Its antiquity is supported by the importance it places on the sun and fire in its worship and rituals, and by its influence on Zoroastrianism. This influence would indicate that the religion must be older than 600 BC.[l]

The controversy over whether Ezidism is an offshoot of Islam has at its source the existence of Ezidis' primary avatar, the Sufi Shaykh Adi. He lived in the 12th century, in Syria, then travelled to Mosul in Iraqi Kurdistan. His burial site and temple are found in Lalish, also in Iraqi Kurdistan. He revitalised the religion and, influenced by Islam, is said to have written the first Ezidi holy books.

Today, the population of Ezidis is estimated to be between 70,000 and 150,000 in the towns of Mosul and Sheikhan (in Iraq), Diyarbakir (in Turkey), Halab (Aleppo, in Syria), Erevan (in Armenia) and around Tiflis (in Georgia). There are also some Ezidis living in Iran. A decade ago, they were twice this number.[82] It is hard to arrive at accurate figures, although the decline is real. Muslim hostility towards them has led some to practise Islam, while others choose not to identify themselves, or to stop practising their religion. Many have scattered, and even their fellow Kurds have massacred some. Nevertheless, most scholars consider the original religion of the Kurds to be the Ezidi religion and view this religion as very ancient, which would also support the ancient origins of the Kurdish people.

Other religions could have coexisted with Ezidism, some surviving to this day, beside or in combination with Islam, but with some practices and beliefs that originate before Islam.[83] Two of these religions are Alevism, which is practised in Turkey and Syria, and Yarsanism[m], also known as Ahl-e-Haqq or Aliolahi. These two religions continue to exist under the name of Shi'ite Islam because both worship Ali, the first Shi'ite Imam and fourth caliph in Islam, as their primary avatar, or 'universal spirit'. For this reason, they are known as 'those who side with Ali'. Yet the Alevi called Qizilbash,[n/84] and many other Alevi, do not observe the five pillars of Islam, and their fundamental theology sharply contradicts the Qur'an's theology, as any independent, non-Semitic religion might. As well, they have secret ceremonies and esoteric doctrines, which can be related to their ancient forebears. These bear close relation to the ancient Aryan cults of angels and fire rituals, and include an annual gathering festival called Jem, also practised by the Ezidis and Yarsanis.[85]

The Yarsanis or Ahl-e-Haqq mainly live in eastern Kurdistan. They have their own cosmology, sharing with the Ezidi the belief in one creator God and a universe that can be divided into two distinct but interrelated worlds: outer and inner, each with its own order and rules. Both religions believe in the incarnation of God in human form, one such incarnation being Ali, and that the human soul is transformed over many animal and human lifetimes until it reaches purification. It has been suggested that the incorporation of Islamic figures into their cosmology was a survival strategy.

There are also Kurds who are Jewish and Christian, Kurds having long been neighbours with the Nestorian, Assyrian and Chaldean Christians. Otherwise, many Kurds are Sunni Muslims, with some Shi'ites now living in the Bakhtaran (Kirmanshah) and Elam provinces of Iran, as well as in Iraq.

To solve the controversies surrounding the origin of the Kurds, I have considered historical, geographical, linguistic and religious evidence. It appears that the history of a developed agrarian culture in Kurdistan dates back over 10,000 years and that the Kurds probably had a multiplicity of ancestors, both native to the area and from the Aryan tribes who began migrating to Kurdistan from 2300 BC. With the Indo-European influx, the social landscape changed completely and by 900 BC the indigenous people had become aryanised. Before this date and afterwards, over a period of several thousand years, various kingdoms, including that of the Medes, influenced each other as they rose and fell from dominance. As a result, the Kurds' multiple ancestors were not confined to the Zagros Mountains but extended south to the upper and middle Euphrates and Tigris Rivers and west to ancient Assyria and Anatolia, north into Armenia and east into Iran.[86]

Through linguistic evidence, it was shown that the Indo-European language of Kurdish can be related to the language of the Medes and that people in the area were known as the Kardochoi, Kurtie, Qutil and so on. Some of these names could have existed before Aryan migration and some were Aryan tribes. The word 'Kurd' came into common usage in Sassanian times.

After the introduction of Islam, Kurdish history is better documented. While forced to convert to Islam from more ancient religions, the main one being Ezidi, and 500 years later facing setbacks from the invading Turkic tribes, Kurdish dynasties continued to rule their own territory under the Ottoman and Safavid Empires until the mid-19th century.

Thus the evidence shows that despite incredible odds, the Kurds have survived as a distinct people in great numbers in an area known as Kurdistan, albeit with close ties to other peoples in the region. This did not prevent their land being divided following World War One, the break-up of the Ottoman Empire and the downfall of the Qajars in Iran. Consequently, the origin of the Kurds has become a political issue. Yet even with all the controversy surrounding their origins, one thing is certain: the relatively recent division of Kurdistan has translated into a struggle for identity and a heightened sense of Kurdish nationalism.

ABOUT Dr Muhammad Kamal

Muhammad Kamal was born on 26 August 1955 in Kirkuk and grew up in Sulaimani, two cities in southern Kurdistan (northern Iraq). In 1977, after completing a Diploma of Education, he became a primary school teacher for three years. At the end of 1979, he left Iraq to seek higher education and study philosophy. Receiving a PhD in philosophy in 1988, he spent 10 years from 1985 lecturing in the philosophies of Kant and Hegel at the University of Karachi. In 1994, he migrated to Australia, and now works as a lecturer in the Institute of Asian Languages and Societies at the University of Melbourne. He is the author of three books: *Hegel's Metalogic* (1989), *Towards Hegel's Anthropology* (1992) and *Heterodoxy in Islam: A Philosophical Study* (1992), and has published articles in English and Kurdish, his main interests being the philosophies of Hegal, Sartre and Heidegger.

Religion and Faith in Kurdistan

An essay by Dr Muhammad Kamal

Kurdish history is usually written in terms of conflict—much of it bloody, due to the Kurds' long struggle for self-determination. Studies of Kurdish society and culture have also tended to focus on this political history rather than on the belief systems and religious philosophies informing this history. Yet much of the structure of Kurdish society is based on religious beliefs and traditions, these having formulated and transformed symbolism into frames of meaning in the life of the people. An objective appreciation of this process is essential to an understanding of the course of Kurdish history.

To explicate Kurdish religious beliefs from the large number of religious clusters and symbols in Kurdistan, I have chosen specific examples on the basis that these groups and symbols have exerted an enduring impact on the cultural life of the Kurds, surviving to the present day. I do not cover all religious groups. Although some groups have different names, many follow the same system of belief, so a separate account of each would be repetitive. I include significant Arabic words, with their English translations, because they are fundamental concepts in Middle Eastern culture.

The history of religion in Kurdistan can be divided into two periods: pre-Islamic and post-Islamic. This division is historical rather than theoretical. The pre-Islamic period should not be mistaken for the period of Al-jahiliyyah, or 'Age of Ignorance', the term applied to pre-Islamic Arab society when the Arabs were said to be idolaters living in ignorance of the religious doctrines and principles of monotheism.[87] In contrast, the beliefs and practices of the Al-jahiliyyah period of Arabia did not dominate the religious and social life of the Kurds. Kurds were not polytheists and, unlike the Arabs, did not practise female infanticide.[88] On these grounds, it can be argued that the conversion of

Kurds to Islam was not based on a perception of cultural inferiority, but was the result of political defeat from 637 AD.

Pre-Islamic Religions

In the pre-Islamic period, the Kurds practised various forms of religion. They were Ezidis, Zoroastrians, Jews and Christians.

Although Zoroastrianism is no longer extant in Kurdistan, many Kurds in southern Kurdistan, Armenia and Georgia are still Ezidis and have striven to retain their faith. Ezidism is a national Kurdish religion, in the sense that it is peculiar to the Kurds. From the beginning, its followers preferred to keep their faith secret. Also, since they did not have an early tradition of writing down their beliefs and rituals, they transmitted these orally from one generation to another, a factor that has hampered researchers and scholars.

The written documents of the Ezidis, which may be called their foundation texts, appeared only in the 12th century. The first text is the *Hymn* and the second is *Kitab e-Jelwa* or *Book of Revelation*, written by Shaykh Adi bin Musafir. The third text is *Mes-haf-e Resh*, written by Shaykh Hasan bin Adi, the great-nephew of Shaykh Adi.

The founder of the Ezidi religion is unknown. There is no reference to such a figure in the tradition of the Ezidis or in the chronicles of the religions of the Middle East. According to the Ezidis, their religion is one of the most ancient systems of monotheistic belief. Shaykh Hasan bin Adi maintains in *Mes-haf-e Resh* that Ezidis existed during the time of the ancient Assyrians and that the Assyrian kings, for example Nesrukh, Kamush and Artimus, were Ezidi, as were Nebuchadnezzar in Babylon (also known as Babel), Ahasuerus in Persia and Aghriqalus in Constantinople.[89] Shaykh Hasan bin Adi's claim is not based on scientific fact, but it is well established that the Akkadians, Assyrians, Babylonians and Medes, to name a few cultures of that time, were constantly exchanging ideas as well as territory. There is enough evidence to say that Solomon Nigosian, a Canadian scholar of the ancient Near East and comparative religion, is mistaken in his opinion that Ezidi is an Islamic sect "incorporating Jewish, Zoroastrian, Christian and Manichaean elements".[90]

Shaykh Adi bin Musafir, writer of the second Ezidi text, was originally an Arab Muslim Sufi, born in 1075 in Syria. He studied with Shaykh Abdul Qadir Jilani (1077–1166), a Kurdish Sufi and the founder of the Qadiriyyah order, under Imam Al-Ghazali in Baghdad.[91] After completing his studies, he resided in the valley of Lalish, an area in southern Kurdistan inhabited by Ezidi Kurds. According to *Mes-haf-e Resh*, God foresaw the arrival of Shaykh Adi in Lalish: "Then I shall send Shaykh Adi bin Musafir from the land of Syria and he shall come and dwell in Lalish."[92] Shaykh Adi spent the rest of his life in Lalish, leaving only for pilgrimage to Makkah (Middle Eastern scholars' preferred spelling of Mecca) with Shaykh Abdul Qadir Jilani in 1116.[93]

Shaykh Adi was a Sufi with high spiritual qualities and power. According to Shaykh Abdul Qadir Jilani, if the gift of prophecy could be attained through striving, Shaykh Adi would certainly succeed. Even Imam Al-Ghazali, the great Muslim Sufi and jurist, was happy to write a letter of encouragement to a Sufi master recommending Shaykh Adi.[94]

The teachings of Shaykh Adi mark a new era in the history and beliefs of the Ezidi religion. He was recognised as a spiritual leader. After his death, in 1162, his grave soon became a shrine for Ezidi pilgrims, and to this day, it is considered their holiest place. A black snake, a symbol of wisdom according to the ancient Akkadian texts of the *Epic of Gilgemesh*, marks the shrine's entrance.

Today, the cardinal principles of the religion are known by scholars, as opposed to Ezidi people, who rely on a capricious oral tradition, through the three recorded documents: the *Hymn, Kitab e-Jelwa and Mes-haf-e Resh.* The *Hymn* contains the mystic utterances of Shaykh Adi, and bears comparison with *Shatahat* of Bayazid Al-Bistani (died 874) and with the writings of Ibn Al-Arabi (1165–1240), all of whom were Sufis. The *Hymn* expresses a deep feeling of ecstasy arising from the mystic experience of *fana* or 'absorption in God':

> All who are in the universe are under me,
> And all the habitable parts and the deserts,
> And everything created is under me,
> And I am the ruling power preceding all that exists.
> And I am he who spake a true saying,
> And I am the just judge and the ruler of the earth.
> And I am he whom men worship in my glory,
> Coming to me and kissing my feet.[95]

Kitab e-Jelwa contains five sections that address the ideas of the eternity and power of God, the transmigration of the human soul and divine retribution. *Mes-haf-e Resh* contains metaphysical speculations on the Ezidi religion. It deals with the concepts of the Creator and creation, original sin, reincarnation and the tasks of the Peacock Angel, Malak Ta'us, in the universe.

The distinctions between the semitic religions, of Judaism, Christianity and Islam, and Ezidism become apparent in this 12th-century foundation text of *Mes-haf-e Resh* in several ways. Firstly, the Ezidis believe that on each day of the week, God created seven angels to govern the universe. On Sunday, He created Azazil, the Peacock Angel, also known as Malak Ta'us and appointed him the chief of angels. On Monday, He created Darda'il, on Tuesday Israfil, on Wednesday Jibra'il (Gabriel), on Thursday Azra'il, on Friday Shemna'il and on Saturday Nura'il. Six of these angels have equal rank, while Azazil (who is known as Iblis or Satan in semitic religions) is the chief of them.[a]

The Ezidis believe that God created the universe with the assistance of these seven angels, in particular Gabriel.[96] This is why the Ezidi religion is called a 'cult of the angels'. It is stated in *Mes-haf-e Resh* that God commanded Gabriel to collect earth from the four corners of the world and make man out of it. He then endowed man with a soul, by His power, and commanded Gabriel to take the man (Adam) to paradise and leave him there, where he might eat of all fruits, except wheat.

It is noteworthy that in the Torah and the Bible, the forbidden tree is the tree of knowledge: "You may eat from every tree in the garden, but not from the tree of knowledge of good and evil; for on the day that you eat from it, you will certainly die."[97] But the name of this tree is not mentioned in the Qur'an: "We said: 'O Adam! Dwell you and your wife in the Garden; and eat of the bountiful things therein, as you will; but approach not this tree, or you run into harm and transgression'."[98]

The Ezidis' understanding of Adam's transgression in eating the forbidden food is essentially distinct from that of Judaism and Christianity, particularly in relation to the culpability of Eve. It is also distinct from the Qur'an, which blames Adam and Eve equally.

According to Ezidi belief, God created Adam first, an idea consistent with the story of creation in the Torah, Bible and Qur'an. The *Mes-haf-e Resh* states that the Peacock Angel asked God: "How shall Adam increase and multiply and where is his offspring?" God said to him: "Into your hand I have surrendered authority and administration." Then the Peacock Angel came to Adam and said, "Have you eaten of the wheat?" He answered: "No, for God has forbidden me so to do and He has said, 'Thou shalt not eat of it'." But the Peacock Angel told Adam: "If you eat of it, all shall go better with you." After Adam had eaten, his belly swelled up, and the Peacock Angel drove him forth from Paradise, left him and ascended into heaven."[99]

This story of the Fall is interesting from the feminist point of view. The Torah and the Bible condemn the woman (Eve) as a sinner, because the snake seduced her to eat from the tree of knowledge. She also pressured Adam into committing the same sin: "When the woman saw that the fruit of the tree was good to eat and that it was pleasing to the eye and tempting to contemplate, she took some and ate it. She also gave her husband some and he ate it."[100] These verses and their interpretation by male clergy have placed women in a disadvantageous position in Judeo-Christian theology. Since woman's sin, through Eve, is greater, God has increased their labour and groaning.[101] But the creation of woman, according to the *Mes-haf-e Resh*, came 100 years after the fall of Adam and his banishment to earth. As a consequence of this, man (Adam) alone is responsible for the sin and woman is innocent theologically. She is set apart from Adam's act of disobedience: "And Gabriel continued to be absent from him for a hundred years and he was sad and wept. Then God commanded Gabriel and he came to create Eve from under Adam's left armpit."[102]

Another major difference is that in Ezidism, Azazil was forgiven by God after Adam's transgression and God kept him as the chief over all the angels. Ezidis therefore believe that his name should not be taken in vain, and this respect for the Peacock Angel causes misunderstanding by their Muslim neighbours. Yet Ezidis believe neither that the Peacock Angel is God nor that he is God's opponent. For them, with the exception of God, the creator of everything, nothing is eternal or uncreated.

For Ezidi, evil is not associated with the Peacock Angel's temptation of Adam or with the concept of 'original sin' but is a human act involving choice. Since evil comes from human error, the human soul can be purified only by undergoing many cycles of rebirth. This doctrine of the transmigration of the soul is vividly expressed in the second section of *Kitab e-Jelwa*. As well, Ezidis advocate the idea of the incarnation of the Peacock Angel in the world as saintly human beings. Shaykh Adi is considered one such incarnation.

Although there are similarities in rituals between Ezidism and Zoroastrianism, the latter dating from the seventh century BC, Ezidism is substantially different from Zoroastrianism in that it is a monotheistic religion. It does not accept the notion of more than one God, whereas Zoroastrianism teaches the reality of two uncreated cosmic powers.

The Ezidis baptise their children with sacred water from the valley of Lalish, where Shaykh Adi is buried. Those who don't live in Lalish use local water sprinkled with dust from Shaykh Adi's shrine. As in both Judaism and Islam, Ezidism recommends male circumcision, and followers who live among Muslims often choose to have the ceremony of circumcision performed on the knees of a male Muslim, as a gesture of peace and friendship.[103]

The Ezidis do not have a public place for prayer or worship. They pray to God three times a day, in private, facing the position of the sun in the sky. At dawn, they face east, at sunset, west and at night, east again.

Every Ezidi religious community is functionally divided into seven ranks. The *mir*[b] is a non-religious leader responsible for appointing the *baba shaykh* the spiritual leader of the community. The *baba shaykh* is the chief *shaykh*, a person of the highest order of priesthood. His function is similar to that of the Pope in Catholicism or the *imam* in Shi'ite Islam. He is the major religious reference, who teaches the *shaykhs* the inner doctrines of the faith.

The *shaykhs* constitute a clan or caste and are chosen by the common followers. The chosen man or woman fills his or her right palm with water from the sacred spring at Lalish and the commoner drinks from the hand of the chosen one. After this, the chosen person becomes the 'other brother' or the 'other sister' and must protect the commoner from bad fortune and wrongdoings, as well as performing duties at marriage, birth and death. The functions and responsibilities of the *shaykhs* are like those of the *ulama* in Islam and the *brahman* in Hinduism. They are allowed to marry only within their own caste.

The third rank is the caste of *pir*[d] or elders. The members of this caste are the custodians of the local shrines. The guardian of Shaykh Adi's shrine, the Ezidis' holiest place, is called Baba Chawash, or 'the doorkeeper', and his position is the highest among members of his caste. The next rank, *qawals*, are those who visit Ezidi communities to recite religious poems and sing during festivals. The *faqirs* are devoted Ezidi and spiritual advisers in the absence of the *shaykh*. The *kochek* are those who leave home and reside in the valley of Lalish to take care of pilgrims, while the *murids* are the common followers.

There are six festivals each year. The feast of Sarisal,[e] a Kurdish term for New Year, is celebrated on the first Wednesday of April. Shaykh Adi is commemorated in Lalish from 18 to 21 July. The *baba shaykh* and the *kocheks* fast during the day to celebrate this summer feast. The feast of the convocation of Shaykh Adi takes place from 23 to 30 September. A special feast is also celebrated after three days of fasting from the first Friday of December, while a winter feast is observed after a 40-day fast in January.

Post-Islamic Religious Sects

Today, the majority of Kurds are Sunni Muslims and follow the Shafi'i school of Islamic law, but there are also Kurds in northern and eastern Kurdistan who are Shi'ite and Alawi.[f]

Arab Muslims established Islam in Kurdistan after a bloody four-year conflict. During the time of Umar bin Al-Khattab, the second successor to Muhammad, ruling between 634 and 644, the Arab Muslims marched towards Iraq and defeated the Persians. After the fall of Al-Mada in 637, an army of 12,000, headed by Hashim bin Utbah, reached Jalula, a Kurdish town in southern Kurdistan, to spread Islam.[104] The Arab Muslims were able to capture Jalula, after heavy fighting:

> The unbelievers started fleeing right and left away from the clearance facing their trench. They perished in [the iron stakes] which they had set up against the Muslims. Their horses were injured, and they had to return on foot, pursued by the Muslims. Only an insignificant number got away. That day God killed one hundred thousand of them. The whole clearing was covered with corpses, in all directions, hence Jalula was called Jalula Al-Waqi'ah on account of the dead bodies covering it.[105]

Some troops went further, capturing Mehran and Khanaqin, Kurdish towns to the east. Many Kurds were taken prisoner, the women among them becoming concubines. The booty was distributed among the Arab Muslim soldiers, each man being given 9000 *dirhams* and nine animals. The surplus booty was sent back to Madinah, the Muslims' capital city.[106]

The Arab Muslims imposed land tax on Kurdish peasants who did not convert to Islam, and these 'unbelievers' were not permitted to sell any land, except to Arabs.[107]

Despite this initial conquest, not everything went smoothly for the Arab Muslims in Kurdistan. Even Al-Tabari, the first scholar to study the Qur'an, mentions that the Kurds of every township were dissatisfied with the damage to their land.[108] They had no alternative, however, as they had been defeated and were subjects of the Arab Islamic empire. From then on, Kurdish culture was Islamicised, and today, apart from having a Sunni Muslim majority, Kurdistan has become fertile ground for Sufism and the rise of extremist Islamic groups such as the Alawi, Qizilbash, Bektash, Shabak, Kakai[g] and Ahl-e-Haqq.

Sufism is a popular practice in the rural areas of Kurdistan. The word Sufi derives from the Arabic *suf*, or 'a rough woollen robe worn as a disregard for material things'. This mystical movement began in the eighth century, and like the early Christian gnostics, the Buddhists and the Hindus, all of whose beliefs the Sufis studied, the Sufis believe that deep intuition is the only way to true wisdom and knowledge of the Divine.

In Kurdistan, Sufism is advocated by either *sayyids* or *shaykhs*. *Sayyids* claim to be descendants of Ali ibn Abi Talib, generally known simply as Ali, the fourth caliph, who ruled between 656 and 666, and his wife Fatimah, daughter of the Prophet Muhammad. *Sayyids* can become *shaykhs* if they lead a Sufi order called a *tariqah*, but *shaykhs* who are not originally *sayyids* achieve this rank by prayer and devotion and are usually called *shekhi bermal*.

In southern and eastern Kurdistan, the Qadiriyyah and Naqshabandiyyah orders are two dominant Sufi *tariqahs*, followed mainly by the peasants. The Qadiriyyah order was named after Shaykh Abdul Qadir Jilani (1078–1166), a Kurdish Sufi who studied in Baghdad.[109] The Naqshabandiyyah order was founded by Baha Al-Din Al-Naqshabandi (1317–1389), from Bukhara.

These two Sufi orders have spread throughout Central Asia, Indo-Pakistan and some parts of the Middle East. The differences between them are not substantial, as both preach purification of the human soul and reunification with the Ultimate Reality, but the Naqshabandiyyah Sufis stress silence as a significant part of living spiritually and invoke God by chanting silently within the heart. In contrast the followers of Qadiriyyah are called 'dervish',[110] and chant *'Allah Hay'* or 'God is alive' as they dance in a circle.

Maulana Khalid Al-Naqshabandi (1779–1827) spread Naqshabandiyyah Sufism in Kurdistan in the 19th century. Maulana Khalid was a Kurd from Sulaimani, in southern Kurdistan, who travelled to India, where he adopted this Sufi order before returning to Sulaimani, preaching and attracting many followers. However, when faced with resistance from a dominant Sufi order in Sulaimani, he was forced to migrate to Damascus.

Another Sufi order or brotherhood is the Kakai. Matti Moosa lists this sect as one of the Shi'ite groups called Al-Ghulat or 'the extremists'.[111] Although Kakais revere Ali ibn Abi Talib, and their founder claimed to be a *sayyid,* many Kakais consider themselves Sunni Muslims. C. J. Edmonds, a British representative in the Kurdish region of Iraq and author of *Kurds, Turks and Arabs* (1957), also believes that the Kakais have remained on the Sunni side and even celebrate marriage according to the Hanafi school of law.[112] According to Matti Moosa, some historical sources relate this sect to the ancient Arab order of Futuwwa and call it by its Arabic name, Akhiyya. However, the origin of this sect, as explained by the Kakais themselves, does not support these views.

The founders of the Kakai, Shaykh Isa and Shaykh Musa, were brothers, who migrated from Hamadan, in eastern Kurdistan, to southern Kurdistan and settled in the village of Barzinja, in the province of Sulaimani. Shaykh Isa had three sons, but late in life married the daughter of Mir Muhammad, chief of the Jaf tribe. In 1272, his second wife bore him a son, Ishaq, who was to become the most celebrated figure of the Kakai. The narration says of him:

> Sayyid Isa's *takiya* needed repair, but when the new beam for the roof was hoisted on to the walls it proved to be too short to span the space between them. When Ishaq saw his father's distress he immediately climbed on to the wall, seized one end of the beam and called to his father "*Kake bikeshe*!" (Brother, pull!). So they pulled the beam that was too short, made it longer and placed it in position.[113]

After this event, the sons of Shaykh Isa and his first wife became jealous of Ishaq. Ishaq, today known as Sultan Ishaq, decided to leave Barzinja, and settled in Pirdiwar, a village in the Hawraman region of southern Kurdistan, where he built his own Sufi brotherhood and *taqiyah* in 1316.[114]

In organising his *taqiyah* and the spiritual affairs of the Kakai brotherhood, Sultan Ishaq formed three groups of disciples. The first group was the 'Seven Companions of Ishaq' or Haft Tan, while the second group was the 'Seven Sons of Ishaq', or Haftawan, two of whom left no male children. The other five sons of Ishaq founded families named after them, these being Mirasuri, Mustafai, Ibrahimi, Khamushi and Bawiseyi. The male offspring of these families are known as *sayyids* by the Kakais.[115] The third group of disciples became known as 'Seven Vicars', or Khalifah. Ishaq chose them from among the 72 elders to be the guides or *dalil*. Daud, a member of the Haft Tan, a companion of Sultan Ishaq, supervised these guides.[116]

Sayyids and *dalil*s have religious duties to perform at religious festivals and ceremonies, and every Kakai must be affiliated to a *sayyid* and a *dalil* as his or her *pir*. Like other religious groups, such as the Ezidis and Alawis, the Kakais are secretive about their beliefs. They do not discuss them with strangers (that is, non-Kakais), but they are cohesive and cooperative with each other, preferring marriage within their Kakai community. However, *sayyids* are not allowed to marry non-*sayyids*, and a commoner cannot marry the daughter of a *sayyid*, because she is his spiritual sister.

Their religious feast is celebrated in winter after three days of fasting called Seshewa. Cooked food is sent to the Kakai religious centre, or *jemkhane*, where it is prayed over by the *sayyid* in the presence of at least seven male members of the sect before being distributed among the people. The Kakais have been accused of having communal sex and a ceremonial meal of love during this festival, but this is untrue: women do not attend the ceremony and Kakais categorically refute the claim.

Kakais consider *Zabur*, the name they give to the Psalms of David, to be sacred, and among other books, they respect *Saranjam*, which contains Sufi utterances. The theological understanding of this sect is not dissimilar from the pantheistic concepts of some other Muslim Sufis, such as Al-Suhrawardi (1154–1191) and ibn Al-Arabi (1165–1240), in that they describe the universe as the manifestation of God. All that is is God. It is also believed that God is inaccessible and incomprehensible to the human mind. For this reason, the Kakais advocate the doctrine of the incarnation of God, or *hulul*, according to which God reveals himself at different times (Adwar Al-Duhur) in human form, to communicate with human society. They also believe that by passing through the cycle of rebirth 1001 times, the human soul can be purified.[117] Today, the Kakais live mainly in Hawar[22], Hawar'e Kon, De'retoo (near Halabja) and some areas in Kirkuk province. In Iranian Kurdistan, the Qalkhanis Kurds are Kakais.

As both Sunni and Shi'ite Muslims are represented in the Kurdish population, the main disagreement between these two main branches of Islam needs to be clarified. The difference stems from the political question of Khalafah—that is, who was to succeed Muhammad on the Prophet's death in 632 AD. The Sunni Muslims believe that the successor could be any Muslim elected by the believers. In contrast, Shi'ites hold the view that a caliph should be from Ahl Al-Bayt, a descendant of the Prophet Muhammad. For this reason, because the Prophet Muhammad had no legitimate sons, they believe that Ali ibn Abi Talib (died 661), the son-in-law and first cousin of the Prophet Muhammad, was his rightful successor, and Ali's male offspring are seen as the *imams*, the leaders of the Islamic *ummah*. The Shi'ites have produced as proof their own traditions of the Prophet Muhammad called the *hadith*, in which the Prophet stated that Ali was to be his successor and that the followers of Ali were true Muslims. To quote from these *hadiths*:

> I swear by God, the Almighty, who is the Master of my life, that Ali and his Shias shall be successful on the Day of Judgment.[118]
>
> When people come into the presence of God, your (Ali's) Shias will be there content with God and He with them and Your (Ali's) enemies shall

be subjected to God's word and their hands shall be tied to their necks.
Oh Ali, only those with faith are your friends and only the hypocrites are your enemies.[119]

Ali is with the truth and the truth is with Ali.[120]

On the event of Tabuk the Prophet appointed Ali as his deputy and he told him, "You bear the same relationship to me as Aaron had to Moses except that there will be no prophet after me."[121]

A significant event is known as Ghadir Khum, when the Prophet openly acknowledged Ali as his successor. The event was named after a place situated near Makkah, on the way to Madinah. After his last pilgrimage to Makkah in the 10th year of *hijrah*, the Prophet was on his way back to Madinah when he stopped at Ghadir to pray. There he told the people: "Whoever recognises me as protector must recognise Ali as protector after me. May God be the ally of those loyal to him and the enemy of those disloyal to him."[122] According to Al-Kashiful Ghita, a spiritual leader from Iraq who died in the 1970s, there are thousands of such authentic reports to support the claim of the Shi'ites.

Other Shi'ite scholars have connected the origin of the Shi'ites with the conflict over the legitimacy of Ali as the true successor and first caliph after the death of the Prophet. Thus Shi'ites do not recognise the legitimacy of the three caliphs before Ali. As well, they advocate the doctrine of the *imamate*, which states that Muslim society should be led by a divinely guided, infallible spiritual leader, or *imam*, who is a descendant of the Prophet Muhammad. They believe in the Redeemer or Al-Mahdi, but whereas the Sunni believe Al-Mahdi to be a messiah, for the Shi'ites Al-Mahdi is the last hidden *imam*, who will come at any time before the Day of Judgement.

Shi'ism is generally understood as loyalty to Ali ibn Abi Talib. The majority of Shi'ites believe in the 12 imams, and are therefore called 'the Twelvers', but there are other groups. The early Isma'ilis, named after Isma'il, eldest son of Ja'afar Al-Sadiq, accepted seven *imams*. They are called 'the Seveners' because the founding members regarded Isma'il, who died in 762, as the legitimate seventh *imam*, rejecting the authority of his brother Musa Al-Kazim (745–799) and all other *imams* after him. The group is also called Batiniyyah, due to its claim that, in addition to its outer form, or *zahir*, the Qur'an has an inner esoteric meaning they call *batin*.

Another Ism'aili group, the Nizaris, believe in the continuity of the *imamate*, while the Zaidis believe in four *imams*. Some Kurds are Shi'ite Twelvers and live in Khanaqin, Mandali, Qasri Shereen and Kirmanshah, but the majority are not.

Many Kurds who live in northern Kurdistan, mainly in the Dersim region, are Alawi. Another Alawi group, called Shabak, live around Mosul, in southern Kurdistan.

Generally speaking, the term 'Alawi' describes all Shi'ite clusters, because Alawi means 'pro-Ali' party, but the modern use of this term refers specifically to a Shi'ite group known as Al-Ghulat, or 'the extremists', who are quite different from the Twelvers, Seveners, Zaidis and Isma'ili Shi'ites. They are called extremists because they deviate from the Qur'an's concept of God, and do not follow the five pillars of Islam, such as praying five times a day facing Makkah and going on *haj* (the pilgrimage to Makkah).

According to Alawi theology, each *imam* has an assistant, called the *bab*, or 'gate', who is responsible for transmitting and interpreting the divine knowledge from the *imam* to the people. For example, Salman Al-Farisi was the *bab* of Ali. The 11th *imam*, Hasan bin 'Ali, also called Al-Askari (846–870), had Abu Shu'aib Muhammad ibn Nusayr as his *bab*.[123] The 12th *imam*, Abdul-Qasim Muhammad bin Hasan, also called Al-Mahdi, who disappeared in 870, did not have a *bab*. This meant that for some followers, ibn Nusayr retained the position of *bab* for the last *imam*.[124] This point is the first technical distinction between Alawis and other Shi'ite Muslims. The Twelvers, unlike the Alawis, do not recognise the authority of ibn Nusayr as the *bab* of the last *imam*.

Alawis, like the Kakais, hold the view that logical categories and human attributes cannot describe God, because God is beyond human understanding. God therefore incarnates in human form in order to make Himself accessible, having done so seven times. Jesus is one of these incarnations, while Ali ibn Abi Talib was the final and most perfect.

This process of incarnation always takes place in three dimensions: *bab* (or gate), *ma'ani* (Arabic for 'meaning', but in Shi'ite interpretation, 'essence') and *ism* (Arabic for 'name, or signifier' but in Shi'ite interpretation, 'veil'). Thus, the theology is close to the doctrine of the Christian Trinity. In the last incarnation, Alawis believe, God's essence was Ali, the gate was Salman Al-Farisi and Muhammad was the veil through whom the Qur'an was revealed. However Ali recorded his wisdom in the highly respected book *Najat Al-Balagha*.

Some Alawis believe that Ali, as God, dwells in the sun. These Alawis venerate light and are called Shamsis. Another group venerates the moon, saying that Ali resides in the moon. This group is called Qamari. For Alawis, all 12 imams are divine beings whom God created thousands of years before Adam. They were celestial or spiritual beings, given physical bodies when they descended to earth.[125]

Other Shi'ite sects, such as Qizilbash, Bektash and Shabak, are Alawis, who are associated with the Isma'ili Shi'ite tradition.

Then there is the Safavi, a Sunni-Sufi brotherhood founded in eastern Kurdistan by a Kurdish Sufi, Shaykh Safi Al-Din (1252–1334). The brotherhood gained popularity in Iran and Turkey, and called for a *jihad* against the Timurid Mongol regime, which had its capital in Samarqand. Although this Sufi brotherhood adopted Shi'ism at the time of Khwaja 'Ali, who died in 1429, Isma'ilism became popular in Kurdistan only under the influence of Isma'il Haydar, known as Shah Isma'il, who captured Tabriz in 1501 and proclaimed himself divine and the king of Iran. Since he came from the Sufi Al-Din line, he most likely had Kurdish ancestry, although some sources claim that his mother was Turkish. Shah Isma'il established the Safavid dynasty, which ruled Iran from 1502 to 1736. Under his influence, the Safavids went through the change from Sunni Sufi brotherhood to Shi'ite Islam, and so spread Shi'ite Islam throughout Iran.

Qizilbash are the followers of the Safavi Sufi order. They are called Qizilbash, or 'redhead', because they were ordered by Shaykh Haydar ibn Junayd, father of Shah Isma'il, to wear a red cap with 12 folds. It is possible that Shaykh Hayder was inspired by Ali ibn Abi Talib, who ordered his troops in the battle of Safin (657) to tie red material around their heads.

The Bektash are not essentially distinct from Qizilbash. Both belong to the same

Shi'ite tradition, but venerate Jesus as well as Ali. The Qizilbash believe that Jesus and Ali ibn Abi Talib are incarnations of God,[126] and similarly Haji Bektash Tekke, founder of the Bektash Sufi group, incorporated many mystic ideas of Christianity into the Alawi faith. The idea of Ali as God is explicitly expressed in Bektash Sufi literature, particularly in this poem, published by Richardson in the *Missionary Herald* of July 1856:

> God, Muhammad, Ali are all God.
> The Divine Reality, Muhammad, Ali is true.
> If you ask what I have in this world,
> My answer is that
> Muhammad and Ali is one God I have.
> God forbid that anyone should see them
> As separate from one another.
> Muhammad is Ali, Ali is Muhammad and
> With God, they are but one God.[127]

The Alawis have several distinct rituals. Unlike the other Islamic groups, they fast on the first 12 days of the month of Muharram by abstaining from drinking water. The end of this fasting is on Ashura (the 10th day of the month of Muharram) and is celebrated to commemorate the massacre of Kerbala and the killing of Ali's son Hussein by Yazid's army on the same day and month in 680 AD (61 AH, after *hijrah,* in the Muslim calender). On this day, a special type of food is cooked and distributed among the people. In other ceremonies, like Abdal Musa, sheep are sacrificed and the cooked meat shared. The Alawi also celebrate Newroz, New Year for all Iranic people.[128]

There are other Alawi groups, with different names. The Yareshanis, for example, live in eastern Kurdistan. These people consider one of their spiritual leaders, Nurali Ilahi, an incarnation of God after Ali. They also revere Nurali Ilahi's book, *Burhan,* as their holy scripture. Ali Illahis ('deifiers of Ali'), Ahl-e-Haqq ('people of the truth') and Sarliyyah also belong to the Alawi tradition.

There are no reliable statistics on how many Kurds are Ezidi, Sunni, Shi'ite, Alawi or any of the other Sufi sects, but all these religious beliefs and creeds have played a significant role in deconstructing and reconstructing Kurdish culture and history. The history of the Kurdish people is not only political, even though the politics and religious stance of a leader were and still are intimately linked. Thus, history has witnessed the rise or fall of a particular religious ideology according to who is in power, and this has translated into intermittent but extensive persecution of Ezidi and Alawi Kurds by Sunni Muslim rulers and their followers, some of these followers being Kurd.

Sadly, in the late 20th century, under the influence of regional, Middle Eastern and international politics, Kurdistan has witnessed a rise in Islamic fanaticism and sectarianism. As in many other parts of the world, this religious fanaticism relies on the politics of terror. It uses religion as a political tool to unite followers and to make war on those who are different, while failing to address the central issues of humanity. Invariably, religious fanaticism distorts the central premise of all religions—that is, to acknowledge a sense of the Divine, and to encourage a love of our fellow human by giving followers some basic rules of behaviour. In a land with so many divergent religious groups and practices, this phenomenon may lead to undesirable outcomes.

ABOUT Dr Abdulkader Maronesy

Born in 1952, Maronesy's first 22 years were spent living among Ezidi in villages, such as Kaboosi, close to the town of Sinjar, which the Kurdish call Shingal and which in ancient times was called Sangarah, in southern Kurdistan, after his father, a Muslim scholar, moved from Dohuk because he opposed the injustices perpetuated by the Iraqi government of the day. At first, the Ezidi wanted to kill Malla Hussein Maronesy, but when the sheep of the chief Muslim of the village strayed onto a field of wheat owned by Ezidi, the Ezidi leaders came to Abdulkader's father for his judgement, to test his sense of justice. When Malla Hussein Maronesy forced the Muslim chief to reimburse the people for the damaged wheat crop, the Ezidi accepted him, and from then on brought their problems to him to solve. They would say of him not "He is a good Muslim" but, rather, "Zelam'e Khodeh", or "He is a person from God".

At the age of 20, Abdulkader Maronesy became a *peshmerga*, or freedom fighter, in charge of 100 men, under his 60-year-old father, who commanded 1000 men. His father's main command was, "Don't go to their land. Don't start a fight. Just defend yourself". From 1972 to 1975, they were in the *ha'ez*, or 'force', under the personal command of Malla Mostefa Barzani,[a] leader of the Kurdish and good friend of Malla Hussein Maronesy. Abdulkader greatly admires Mostefa Barzani: "He was a very brave and honest man. He related to the poor and weak and would call the old men to sit with him and talk. In the latter part of his life, when he knew the ordinary people could not easily approach him, he asked his brother, Shaykh Bab'e and my father to bring the people who needed his help. He always had time for people. He would listen carefully, often quoting verses from the Qur'an and Kurdish sayings in reply."

When the revolution ended in 1975, Malla Hussein Maronesy decided to escape to Kurdistan of Iran with Malla Mostefa Barzani. He had already been in prison three times and knew the next time would mean death.

In eastern Kurdistan, Abdulkader was surprised to observe similarities in the people, even in the way they dressed, to the Ezidi with whom he had grown up. In 1977, he went to Tehran University and studied Iranian history. Although Muslim, his interest in the Ezidi grew, so his teacher encouraged him to do a PhD in Ezidism. The degree was called 'Persian Language and Literature', because the Farsi consider Kurdish history, language and literature to be a branch of Persian.

After years of studying many religions, Abdulkader's faith in God and the religion of Islam grew. He feels Islam is the religion most reflecting the truth about human nature, the universe and God. He says, "Day by day I see the various sciences prove what is in the Holy Qur'an and what Muhammad, Peace Be Upon Him, said about heaven, earth and humanity." He is aware of the historical persecution of Ezidi by some Muslims, but says this is not in accordance with Islamic teachings: "In understanding and following the true teachings, a person cannot be unkind or dishonest to any human or animal, even their enemy."

In 1995, he and his family came to Australia as refugees. When he returned to southern Kurdistan in 2000 to visit relatives, after a 25-year absence, to see firsthand a

Maronesy with five fakirs at Lalish

free Kurdistan, he was amazed by the developments. These proved to him the long and civilised heritage of the Kurdish nation. As for the rise of Islamic politics in Kurdistan, he would like to think this cannot be compared with that in other parts of the Islamic world. "I sincerely hope that Islamic groups in Kurdistan understand their history and what has happened to the Kurdish people, and will not act like extremists in Iran, Afghanistan, Egypt and Algeria. If they take their principles from the Holy Qur'an, Muslims and the Ezidis will continue to live in peace, but if not, they will do as the Ottoman and Safavid Empires did and also what Meere Kurah, from Rowandoz, did to Ezidi villages."

Ezidi: The First Monotheists?

An essay by Dr Abdulkader Maronesy

According to Ezidi oral tradition, Ezidism is one of the oldest religions in the world. One oral tradition states that Ezidism existed at the time of Noah, or Nuha,[129] whom I date as having lived between 8000 and 4000 BC, relying on what we know of the agricultural and building practices, social structures, beliefs and language of the people living in ancient Mesopotamia. The Ezidis also say, "We are not the sons and daughters of Adam and Eve", although there is an oral tradition that Adam was their father.

The Ezidis maintain that theirs is the first monotheistic religion, despite the many idolatrous elements that have been incorporated over time. In this essay, I provide evidence to support this claim, suggesting that Mandaeanism, the other ancient religion that makes the same claim, and Ezidism have a common heritage. I show that the ancient tribes of Mesopotamia practised Ezidism, and that according to many traditions, Noah's boat came to rest on the mountain of Judi in Kurdistan. Thus I propose that Ezidism was the religion of Noah.

The antiquity of Ezidism and its influence on many civilisations' religious beliefs, symbols, festivals, music and art are further explored by tracing back major Ezidi celebrations and elements of belief to a mythological god-king named Jamshid, mentioned in religious writings from Mesopotamia to India. The legendary Jamshid is said to be the founder of civilisation, its religious, social, economic, military, administrative, literary and musical attributes and institutions. I describe how elements of Ezidism featured in the civilisations of Sumer and Akkad, the kingdoms of Babylon, Assyria, the Chaldeans and Urarians, as well as those of the Mitannites, Hittites, Medes, Persians and Aryan Indians, and how they continue to be practised by modern-day Ezidi. Thus I propose that through migration and intermarriage, Ezidism's influences spread far beyond Mesopotamia.[130]

Furthermore, I provide evidence that the ancient peoples of Mesopotamia were originally one people made up of different tribes. Some remained in the area for thousands of years. Some, such as Abraham's family, permanently migrated, while others, such as the Hittites and Medes, migrated, then returned after 2300 BC.

Before embarking on the evidence, I acknowledge the many problems involved in studying Ezidism and its origin and the origin of the Indo-European peoples. The prehistoric nature of such studies means they rely heavily on mythology and oral tradition. Definitive conclusions are difficult, due to the lack of archeological research; the obstacles in accessing what little research there is; the unreliability of dating processes; the lack of texts and confusion regarding existing texts; and the influences of and on Ezidi beliefs. As well, there is the universal difficulty of establishing causal relationships between, as opposed to independent origins of, ideas and practices. All I can say is that the conclusions presented in this essay are based on many years of research; they are not flashing revelations for which I then gathered evidence!

Ezidis claim to be the first monotheists. The name of their religion, which was in use at least as far back as Babylonian times, their name and their view of God are the primary evidence for their monotheism. The term 'Ezidi' comes from Ezdayi, which means 'the creator of me' in Kurdish. Ezidis call this almighty creator Khodeh, and describe Khodeh as "God, the Creator, Sustainer and Keeper of All". Literally, Khodeh can be translated as 'one who gives himself', meaning 'not dependent on any relations or associations, physical or otherwise; only dependent on himself'. The term 'himself' implies not male or female but, rather, a conscious presence.

The Ezidi Creation story also confirms their original monotheism. In the beginning, nothing existed except God, who then made a brilliant star. After 40,000 years, God threw the star so that it exploded, its parts becoming smaller stars, planets and moons, its smoke becoming the sky or atmosphere. Then, on each day of the week, God created seven angels from the star's light and each angel created a planet. For example, the angel Malak Ta'us was created on Wednesday[a] and was responsible for creating the morning star of Mercury. The sun and its warmth, light and fire is also from Ta'us.[131] After this, God ordered Ta'us to stay in Paradise, which Ezidis call 'ain Al-Falak', or 'the eye of the universe', where he was to await further instructions. In the meantime, he read the 'keeping board', another name for the 'Table of Destiny', mentioned in the tablets of Ashur-banipal of Assyria in the seventh century BC as the most ancient sacred knowledge. After some time, God ordered Ta'us to create the first human from clay, God giving

Adam a soul. Following the creation of Eve, the couple entered Paradise, where abundant life knew no death and where God ruled they could eat of the fruits but were to abstain from eating wheat. However, Ta'us advised God that if Adam and Eve were to multiply, they would need to eat wheat, so God gave Ta'us the role of guide and caretaker of humans. According to Ezidi belief, because the sun's warmth and light come from Ta'us, under God's orders, Ta'us encourages goodness, good fortune and the productivity of useful plants and animals.[b]

God ordered the seven angels to kneel only to God, but after 40,000 years, God tested the angels, ordering them to kneel before Adam. All knelt, except Ta'us. When God asked Ta'us, "Why do you not kneel?", Ta'us answered, "You ordered us to kneel to no-one but you. You are the light. Adam is of mud. How can we forget your will?" God rewarded Ta'us by making him chief of all the angels, because he was the only one who believed in the aloneness of God.[132]

The similarities between the Ezidi Creation story and that of Judaism, Christianity and Islam are self-evident—the first known version of the story of Adam being found in the clay tablets of Sumer. In the Sumer legend, Adam was the offspring of the god Enki, also known as the Serpent Lord of the Euphrates, and a local woman. Enki wants to teach Adam knowledge, but Enki's half-brother, Enlil, wants to keep Adam and his offspring ignorant servants to the gods. I will provide evidence that Ezidism was around in the time of the Sumers, and therefore that the story of Adam was part of the Ezidi-Sumer tradition long before it was incorporated into Judaism.

As in many religions, Ezidis claim that after death, a person must account for their life's deeds. When a person dies, their soul is taken to a place known as Perasalatey, or 'bridge of prayer', where angels question the person as to their deeds. If God is dissatisfied with the person, the bridge becomes as narrow as a hair, so that when the person goes to cross, he or she falls into hell. However, if God is satisfied, the bridge becomes wide and the person crosses it into Sukga Marifatey, 'the shopping centre of knowledge'. Here, the individual is again brought to account, by their *shaykh* and *pir* (two ranks of Ezidi holy people), *moorabi* (coach) and their brother and sister of the hereafter. Every Ezidi has one of each. If these are satisfied with the person, they will defend him or her, allowing escape from the *zabani*, the representatives of God in death. The *zabani* have a negative connotation, because if the individual is deemed lacking in virtue, the *zabani* will hit and torture the soul in the gorge called Wahweyl'e, in the valley of Lalish,[133] the centre of Ezidism, located near Mosul, in southern Kurdistan.

However, no state is permanent, and other oral traditions describe a process of transmigration whereby a person's soul enters a succession of physical bodies—animal or human—depending on his or her thoughts and deeds in their previous form. The human form is privileged, because humans have more choice than any other form. Ezidis call this changing of forms Kerass Gunureen, or 'changing clothes'.

As in many ancient religions, Ezidism is inherited from both parents. One cannot convert. However, a person can become a non-Ezidi if they marry a non-Ezidi, if one parent is not Ezidi, or if they stop wearing a special undergarment of handknitted wool with a circular neck called a *geeriban*. If someone says, "Tear your *geeriban*", it is like swearing, "You are not Ezidi".

As in the Indian caste system, brought to India by Indo-Europeans migrating south-east from 1500 BC, Ezidis are ranked according to their closeness with God. This rank is inherited from generation to generation. The *mir* is the political and religious head of the Ezidi and the *bab'e*[c] *shaykh* ('gate' or 'father') is keeper of the Temple at Lalish. Then there are the ranks of holy men called *shaykhs* and *pirs*. All these ranks are considered closer to God than ordinary followers. To be one, you must be born into a family of that rank. However, a very holy *mir, bab'e shaykh, shaykh* or *pir* can gain special power from God, some becoming so close to the Divine that they are ranked between human and God. They are deified and worshipped accordingly, not as God but, rather, as God's assistants. This is what happened to Shaykh Adi bin Musafir, who lived in the 12th century and whose mausoleum is at Lalish. He became known as Shaykh Khodan, or 'the Lord'. Likewise, Ezidis are known to say of Shaykh Shams, who lived in the 13th century, "Shams is the power of religion".

That Ezidis refer to very holy people as *khodeh*, their word for God, does not imply that the person is synonymous with the Creator, like Jesus is in Christianity. Rather, he was or is God's representative on earth, and is prayed to as God's intermediary, similar to some Sufis and Christian saints.

As in other old religions and in Sufi beliefs, different colours signify a person's closeness to God. The lowest order of person is signified by the colour blue, indicating a conscience tempted to make bad choices. The next rank is yellow, representing a conscience able to ask itself why it thought or acted in the way it did. The colour red indicates a conscience inspired to do good and, in so doing, attracting good fortune. White signifies a firmness of position in the realm of good thoughts and actions, while green is a position of satisfaction and black is a level of even greater fulfilment. The highest order of colour is no colour—the colour of air: the pure soul, or one completely absorbed in God.

The Mandaeans, now living in southern Iraq and Iran, also claim to be the first monotheists, but there is much evidence to suggest that the Ezidis and Mandaeans have a common, ancient heritage.[134] Strong foundations of both religions are that God is one, without relatives, and that everything comes from God. There is no independent power of evil, as in the later Zoroastrian religion. While Ezidis practise many superstitious beliefs to guard against bad fortune, this fortune comes from human, animal or object rather than from an independent power and is considered 'bad fortune' only because we do not understand the greater scheme of God. Both religions believe God lets humans choose their way, and that after death, a form of judgement leads to a state of either paradise or fire, although the latter is not eternal, as God is merciful.

The Ezidi and Mandaean Creation story is also similar. Both religions have a hierarchy of angels whom God gave specific roles to create the world. In the Mandaean ceremony of Fa'al, the followers celebrate the day the angel Malkar Hayool created life on earth, after preparing the earth as did the Ezidi angel Malak Ta'us. Many religious celebrations show strong similarities in their use of symbols and plants.[135] As well, the religious leaders of both religions do not shave their moustaches and beards and traditionally do not cut their hair. They wear long white robes, with a rope around the waist tied with a special knot.

The two religions share many sacred symbols. Water is a source of cleansing and purification for both. The Mandaeans baptise themselves whenever they feel the need to purify. Likewise, Ezidis wash in Kania Spee, or the 'White Spring', at the Temple of Lalish, believing it to be water from Noah's flood, pure and sacred.[136]

The circle and snake (serpent) are symbols also held in common. I think the circle signifies the sun, seasons, and orbits of the planets. The Mandaeans make a circular 'crown' from a particular plant, placing it on the head of the person performing a ceremony. The collar of the Ezidi undergarment is circular. In the 12th century, when people in Lalish asked what Shaykh Adi was doing, he told them he was listening to the preachings of the great Shaykh Abdul Qadir Jilani,[d] 450 kilometres away in Baghdad. He then drew a circle and asked the people to step inside so that they could listen too.

For the Mandaeans, the snake is a symbol of water. Snake is *mar* in Kurdish, and 'Mar' is another name for 'Mad' or 'Median'. The snake is guardian of all things valuable and necessary for human survival, including knowledge and wisdom. Consequently, the term *mar* also refers to 'saint' or 'holy person'. Even modern-day Assyrian and Chaldean Christians in the Ezidi areas of southern Kurdistan refer to their saints as *mar*. Thus Saint Marcos is called Mar Marcos. The snake is depicted on the entrance of the Ezidi Temple of Lalish, and likewise, many of the ancient civilisations of Mesopotamia depicted snakes on valuable objects and buildings.

Linguistic and geographic evidence also points to Ezidi and Mandaeans having a common heritage. The term 'Manda', sometimes written 'Amada' or 'Mada', is derived from 'Mad', 'Madi' and, in Arabic, 'Mah', pointing to the land of Mad: the land of the Kurds.[137] Like Ezidi Kurds, the Mandaeans believe that Noah was their ancestor and that they thrived in the area of Noah. In Mandaean texts quoted by the Mandaean Salim Berengi,[138] it is written that the ship of Noah cast anchor on the Mountain of Quardoon, 'Quardoo' and 'Kurdoo' being variations of the same word. Salim Berengi says Quardoon refers to the mountain of Judi in the holy Qur'an, where the Mandaeans established a village and multiplied. 'Mand' or 'Mad' means 'continuance' or 'to stay'.[139] From here, the Mandaeans scattered. Consequently, they believe Babylon was once Mandaean. Some went to Judah, some of these people later returning to Haran, the city of Abraham's brother and nephew in Kurdistan, before moving south.

In fact, the common origin of all the religions and people of Mesopotamia from the time of Noah is dramatically highlighted by the legend. All versions tell of a great leader who saved his family, animals and seed by building a boat in accordance with God's instruction before the coming of a great flood in which all other people perished. According to the holy Qur'an, Noah's boat came to rest on the mountain of Judi. In Arabic, *judi* means 'of genuine benefit'.[140] In old Kurdish, to which the Kurmanji North dialect is closest, the mountain is called Harowrad, *harow* meaning 'mountain' and *rad* meaning 'genuine'.[141] In modern times, Judi Mountain is known to be part of the Ararat Range, 150 miles south-west of Mount Ararat. The still-inhabited ancient Kurdish city of Shairnakh, which means 'city of Noah', near the Hizal River just to the west of the Turkey-Iraq border, and the southern Kurdish town of Zakho are close to the village which Noah built. This village is called Hashtian in old Kurdish. *Hashtian* means '80 people'—the number who accompanied Noah, including his three sons Shem, Ham and Japheth and their wives and families. Unfortunately, due to the difficulty of getting permission to do archeological research and the political unrest in the area, no-one has been able to research the archeological date for Hashtian. However, until 1974, the people of this area practised the very important Ezidi feast of Jemayi,[e] calling it the Feast of Noah.

Similarly, among scholars, there is no generally accepted date for the Great Flood. Some date one around 4000 BC, but new evidence suggests a date of 5500 BC. Consequently, it is difficult to say which people known to have lived in the region came before the flood. The Sumerian king list gives the names of kings before and after a flood. Halafian culture was established in eastern Turkey and northern Syria by 5500 BC. They built the first towns, such as Tel Halaf, whose ruins are within walking distance of the village of Noah. There was also the Ubaidian civilisation. Other equally ancient tribes of the area were the Hurrian, Mosakhian, Qurtie or Kurtie (another name for Kurds), and Elamites. Tribes known to exist in the area after 2300 BC include Guti, Lulubians and the Arun (or Alan) from Azerbaijan, formerly a part of 'Mad' or Medea. To this day, these names are represented in the tribes of Kurdistan, many of whom still practise elements of Ezidism, albeit often under a different name.

Modern scholars note the similarities between the story of Noah as told in the Torah, Bible and holy Qur'an and that of King Uta-napishtaim (also known as Zi-u-sudra) of Shuruppak, a Sumer city on the Euphrates River, as told and retold in Sumer, Akkadian and Assyrian clay tablets. King Uta-napishtaim was told by the god Enki (father and teacher of Adam and god of the kingdom of Sama, east of Haran) to build a boat and leave all his possessions to save his family, animals and seed from a coming flood.[142] In the Sumer version, there are many gods, but the king chooses to follow one, Enki, just as Noah followed the one true God. While the Sumer legend dates back 5000 years, the Torah, as we know it, was not compiled until 600 BC, when the Jewish elite were living in exile in Babylon. However, it is known from the three holy books that God revealed texts to Moses and, possibly, to Adam.[f] God gave Adam the names of things, and in Islam, according to the interpretation of Surah II in the holy Qur'an, Adam knew how to read.[143] We are told that all the ancient texts were destroyed when Nebuchadnezzar II sacked Jerusalem and took the King of Judah and others to Babylon. I conclude that, as with all histories, the Sumer legend was written from the perspective of the rulers of the day, the only difference between the versions being in the names given to Noah and God. All versions have the same theme: that of a leader following the one true God to save his people, an indication that they could have a common origin.

Likewise, changes in names and emphasis distinguish Mandaeans and Ezidi. Whereas Mandaeans place more emphasis on water, Ezidi give more importance to the sun. As a consequence, light and fire are essential components of Ezidi household rituals and religious celebrations (as they were for Sumer and Babylonian ceremonies). Ezidi households light special candles every Wednesday night in remembrance of the day the Peacock Angel, Malak Ta'us, was born.[144] The Sama ritual performed in the Jemayi celebrations in autumn is also centred around fire.

It is the mythological god-king Jamshid who is said to have been the founder of Jemayi, a ceremony practised by both ancient Babylonians and modern-day Ezidis,[145] versions of which are also practised by the followers of Mithras and Zoroastra. Although few modern Ezidi know of Jamshid, he is intimately linked with Ezidism, as he is with other religions from Mesopotamia to India.[g] He is mentioned in the *Vedas*,[146] considered to be the ancient and eternal truths of neither God nor human, their earliest writings dating from 1400 BC.[147] He is also found in the Zoroastrian writings of the *Avesta*,[148] one of the oldest parts, *Gata*, thought to be written by Zoroastra, dating these sections between 600 and 1080 BC.[149]

Jamshid is said to have had a twin sister called Jamay. *Jam* means 'twin', and the twins are sometimes described as two branches of the one plant. Christensen[150] retells the myth of Jamshid, using as his sources scholars of the calibre of Abu Raylan Beerooni, an Islamic scholar of medicine, philosophy and mathematics in the 10th century, who studied in the Kurdish town of Haran. According to the legend, Jamshid lived, like others of ancient times, a long life: 700 years. He ruled for 500. He can be likened to a combination of Adam, Noah and Solomon—the first man of knowledge, a great leader and a wise king. He is said to have been the first to spin, weave and sew clothes from linen, silk, hair, cane and animal fur, before teaching these arts to others. He ordered *deva*, or small gods, to pour water on soil to make the first mud bricks, and from these bricks he made communal baths, palaces and temples. He discovered precious stones like diamonds and precious metals like gold and silver and useful metals like iron, and for each he gave a use. He was the first to make tools of war, the first to discover medicines and cures for the sick and the first to develop writing.

He divided society into four groups. The role of the first group, the Asowrwan, was to worship, and he told them their place was in the mountain.[h] The Arishtaran were those whose role it was to fight and defend. Thus Jamshid created the first army. The third group was Astarooshan, the workers, farmers and merchants, while the fourth category were the rulers or ruling family. Cuneiform tablets describe how the centres of administration in each Sumer city-state were the palace of the dynastic family of Anunnaki god-rulers (male and female) and the temple. According to Assyrian sources, the land of Mad or Medea was also a series of autonomous regions, each of which, according to Herodotus, a Greek historian of the fifth century BC, was ruled by a council.[151]

After Jamshid set up the structures of civilisation, he made a throne of valuable metals and gemstones. Legend has it that the *devas* lifted him as he sat on his throne and, seeing his radiant beauty, likened him to the sun. The people showered him with gemstones and other precious items, the day becoming a celebration known as Newroz or New Day.

On his throne, Jamshid could travel from country to country—vast distances in an instant—returning to the Temple of Jamshid in Shiz, or the holy mountain of Damawand, near modern Tehran, from where he ruled, his kingdom stretching to the highest summit of Ararat.

Jamshid had special God-given powers, energies and protection known as *farr'e*, as did all the kings and leaders of the early civilisations, including those of the Sumerians, Egyptians, Hittites, Assyrians, Babylonians, Medes and Persians. Accordingly, the king or leader was worshipped as the 'chosen one' or 'god-king'. However, like Adam, legend has it, when Jamshid wronged God in some way, God took away his *farr'e* or 'god-like power'. I suggest it was when he introduced idolatrous elements into the religion.

The Temple of Jamshid is the earliest archeological evidence of Ezidism. Its ruins and the red soil that was brought there—red being the Ezidi symbol of holiness and good fortune—can still be found in Shiz, located between Tabriz and Urmia Lake, in eastern Kurdistan. According to myth, the temple had seven halls, each painted one of seven holy colours and each with its own idol and pictorial representations of the sun, moon and five planets closest to earth. These were the seven symbols of seven 'gods'. It is said Jamshid would go to a different hall each day, dressed in the colour of the hall, and those to whom he gave audience also had to dress in that colour.[152]

The metal idols in the Temple of Jamshid combined animal and human forms, as did the idols of the old religion(s) of the Hurrians, Lulubians and Guti (from the land of 'Mad') and the Caspian people (from further north). Similar metal idols and other artefacts depicting half-animal, half-human forms have been found in Ziweh (the ancient site of a Mede citadel), close to Ushnaviyeh, in eastern Kurdistan. Assyrian friezes and pictorial representations on artefacts, and descriptions in Assyrian clay tablets, show or describe the same idols, describing them as part of the Hurrian religion and mythology. This would indicate that the religions of Jamshid, the Hurrians, Guti and Lulubites are related, and if Jamshid is considered the founder of Ezidism, then these tribes were Ezidi or, at least, were influenced by Ezidism.[153]

Thus, according to the Jamshid legend, Jamshid yielded the forms, which enabled the development of early civilisations' economic, political, legal, military, religious and artistic structures. So was Jamshid an historical figure and, if so, when did he live? The dating of the original Temple of Jamshid is difficult, because in the mythical time of Rostrum, a Herculian figure, and that of Kay Kavus,[i] second king of the Kayanyan, the temple was converted to a Zoroastrian fire temple.

Nevertheless, the temple, legend and other artefacts from the area would indicate that within Jamshid's own lifetime, Ezidism took on idolatrous elements. In so doing, the sun, the moon and the five planets visible from earth became the symbols for angel-like messengers or smaller gods, as they were for the Babylonians and Assyrians and still are for Ezidi. The same symbols and beliefs are described in the holy Qur'an's story of the prophet Abraham. All people, including the Babylonians and Abraham's own father, Azar (known as Terah in the Torah), worshipped these symbols, especially the sun, which Ezidis still face to pray. The Qur'an relates how Abraham rejected these symbols. When he sees a star, he says, "This is my Lord", but after it sets, he says, "I love not those who set", and similarly, he rejected the moon and sun as gods, concluding, "I am now free from giving partners to Allah".[154] In so doing, he returned to the original monotheism of Noah.

According to the Jamshid legend, when God took away Jamshid's *farr'e*, he became weak and was overthrown by the tyrant Dahak. It is said that Jamshid voluntarily stepped down from his kingship, unwilling to use his army to maintain his power. After many years of tyranny, Kawa the blacksmith rose up and overthrew Dahak, but he could not become king, being of the wrong caste. Instead, he installed Fraydoon as king, because by law, only someone of the same caste or family as Jamshid could be king. In the *Shahnameh*, Firdawsi does not say Kawa was Kurd, but that the descendants of those saved from Dahak's tyranny became the Kurds. I believe that at the time of Jamshid, all people in the story were from one nation and that it was only after Islam that Dahak became a 'foreigner'.

On the surface, Ezidi belief in the legends of Adam and Noah as well as in the legend of Jamshid appears contradictory. Oral tradition often contains apparent inconsistencies, but also, time and time again, we encounter different names for the same symbols and stories. For instance, Christensen overlaps these two ancient traditions by relating that Abraham was a descendant of Jamshid.[155]

From both traditions, it appears that while a people believed in one God with power over all, over time God's assistants, also known as smaller gods, angels or messengers, proliferated. According to Ezidi oral tradition, these came down to earth to marry and live among the people, and over time numbered at least 24, as named in the Ezidi oral traditions handed down through generations.[156] They included goddesses as well as gods, as in most ancient religions. There was the Ezidi goddess Pira Fat, goddess of water, the equivalent to Naheed, an ancient Indo-European goddess represented as a tall, curvaceous girl and the planet Venus. There were also the goddesses Sitia S and Khatoona Fakhrun (or Fakhra), goddess of birth. Shrines to the goddesses Set Khagigi and Set Geebi are still found in the Sheikhan area, north-east of Mosul. In mythology, with some supporting evidence from prehistory, the mother was the head of the family in this area.

Religions were not given generic names in ancient records, but Ezidi gods, the Temple of Ezida and the Ezidi feast of Jemayi, held in autumn, and Sarsa'al, held in April, were mentioned in the clay tablets of the late Sumer period[157] and in other histories of Sumerian-Babylonian beliefs.[158] For instance, Jemayi's Babylonian equivalent, Zagmoog, is mentioned in the Tablet of Nebuchadnezzar I (reigning in Babylon between 1124 and 1103 BC).

While the names of gods and sacred symbols varied over time and between kingdoms, what they symbolised did not, and although all the early religions had a hierarchy of 'gods', 'messengers' or 'angels', there was always a high god, or God of gods, named variously by the different kingdoms. In Sumer it was Anu, in Assyrian times Ashtar, the equivalent of the Ezidi Khodeh. Nevertheless, every city had its own special god or gods, and people gathered to perform rituals for a god on his or her special day, as do Ezidi followers in each Ezidi village to this day. For example, the village of Khankay, on the Tigris River, has a typical Ezidi shrine—a many-sided pointed cone made of concrete or stone—to Shaykh Mand, an Ezidi leader of the 13th century who came to represent snakes and protection.

A number of Ezidi gods can be related to the gods and goddesses of Sumer, also worshipped by the Akkads, Babylonians and Assyrians. In the Sumer tablets, the 'god of air' and 'the guardian of the table of destiny' was called Otodengar, and in Babylonian and Assyrian times, the 'god of the sun' was called Nabu, both sharing similarities with the Ezidi angel Malak Ta'us. Wednesday was the day of Nabu, the day that Ta'us was born. Ezidi represent Ta'us as a peacock, *ta'us* being Kurmanji for 'peacock', the fanned peacock tail representing the sun. The Babylonians and Assyrians represented Nabu as a young man riding a peacock, holding a snake in his right hand.

Samsuditana, the last king of the first dynasty of Babylon (reigning between 1625 and 1595 BC), introduced a chapel with a statue of Nabu in Esagila, the Temple of

Marduk, Marduk being the avenger, and the god of Babylon. Nabu's chapel was named Ezida. At New Year feasts, Nabu was worshipped alongside Marduk. In the Sumer god-king dynasty, Marduk, the avenger, was the father of Nabu. In Babylonia up until the first millennium BC, Marduk took precedence over Nabu. However, in the holy city of Borsippa, Nabu was supreme.[159] He had his own temple, called the Temple of Ezida, which was on the other side of the Euphrates from the Temple of Marduk. Hammurabi, king of Babylon from 1792 BC, is said to have rebuilt this temple, and thus its ruins are dated between 1792 and 50 BC.[160] Over time, Nabu came to be worshipped more widely. In popular devotions, people prayed to Nabu as the one who knows and sees all, especially in the centuries preceding the last fall of Babylon.

As judge of knowledge and wisdom, Nabu was also worshipped by many kings of Babylonia and Assyria. A number of Babylonian kings had compound names based on Nabu.[161] Nabu-kudur-usar (or Nebuh-kuhd-nez-ur) is commonly known as Nebuchadnezzar I. He reigned from 1125 to 1103 BC. Nabonassar (Nabu-nasir) became king of Babylon in 747 BC and was famous for his interest in astronomy. It was Nabopolassar, a Babylonian general, who founded the Chaldean dynasty of Babylon, and who joined with the Medes to destroy the Assyrian capital of Nineveh in 612 BC. His son Nabu-kudur-usar, more commonly known as Nebuchadnezzar II, reigned from 605 to 562 BC and was responsible for capturing the King of Judah and other notables from Jerusalem, bringing them to Babylon. Another, Nabondus, was king of Babylon between 556 and 539 BC.

Ezidism also had a marked influence on the religion of Assyria. The half animal, half human idols already described have been found in many Assyrian friezes and artefacts. Ezidis call the angel (as in Malak Ta'us) or symbol of the sun Shams, Shamou still being a common name for Ezidi people to this day. (The sun itself is called *roas*, pronouncing the 's' as in pleasure). The Assyrian 'door of the sun' found in Nineveh, an Assyrian capital located east of modern Mosul, was called Bab Shamsh. Shamshi-Addad (Addad being a variant of Khodeh), was a god in the Assyrian pantheon, and became god of many important towns and cities, including Ashur, by the end of the third millennium BC.

Likewise, tablets from the Mitanni city of Borgas dated between 1350 and 1000 BC also mention gods worshipped from Iran to India, including Naheed, the goddess of water and the planet Venus, indicating a common origin of these gods and people.[162]

Similarly, the Babylonian, Hittite, Mitanni, Persian and Greek god Mithras, known as Mitra in Sanskrit texts, god of the sun, light and good,[163] has the same elements and responsibilities as Malak Ta'us.[164] Mithras was also the god of contracts, oaths and mutual obligation, and is mentioned in the 15th-century BC cuneiform treaties between the Hittites and Mitannites. Vedic texts also mention Mitra as god of friends and contracts.

Mithras was worshipped in Hatra, a fortress founded by the Parthians in the first century BC, located in the modern state of Nanowah in southern Kurdistan, the capital being Mosul, and later the Persians were to worship Mithra alongside Ahura Mazda. Thus Mithra was an important god, whose close links with Ezidism will be amply demonstrated. For instance, Mithras's birthday is the same as that of Malak Ta'us's: 25 December. The addition symbol '+' is a Mithraian symbol expressing the control

Mithra has over the four corners of the world, and to this day, Ezidi put this symbol on their properties so that God will bless them with abundance.[165] In a sacred cave near Lalish, there are paintings and drawings of a sun, snake, peacock, bull and scyth (representing Mithra), the same symbols being common in Babylonian and Assyrian friezes. Similar art is found at Galy Zardack, *zardack* meaning 'yellow', in caves of yellow rock on each side of a valley leading to the centre of the mountain of Muqloob, north-east of Mosul. The sacred site overlooks flowing water. It dates back at least to the first millennium BC, and was the place of feasts similar to Jemayi, which is still practised in the Lalish Valley, in worshipping places overlooking flowing water.[166]

Religious celebrations show a deep connection between the Babylonians, Ezidis and Mithraians. In the Babylonians' annual ceremony called Zagmoog, which was held at the Temple of Marduk, and the Ezidis' Jemayi ceremony, held in the House of God at Lalish starting on 6 October, there is a 'gathering of the gods' around seven fires. To this day, the gathering is re-enacted by 14 Ezidi religious leaders performing the Sama ritual for seven nights in front of a circle of followers. Religious music is played by religious men called *qawals* on a sacred seven-notched pipe called a *shabab* or *mezamir* and another instrument called a *duff*, a tambourine-like animal-skin drum with metal discs on its sides. These holy instruments are the same as those used in Babylonian and Assyrian rituals.

The leader of the Sama is the keeper of the Temple of Lalish. In the Sama, he is called Faqiri Sardari, or 'the one who serves God'. He represents the highest of the smaller gods at the gathering, Malak Ta'us, or Shaykh Adi in modern Ezidi oral traditions—the symbol existing long before the life of the *shaykh*. Faqiri Sardari is dressed in black robes and turban, black being the highest order of colour unless one is completely absorbed in God. He is followed in every step and gesture by six pairs of barefoot *shaykhs* and p*irs* dressed in white, representing six of the lesser angels, the six pairs adding up to the 12 months of the year. They in turn are followed by another angel, who is not part of the main seven, called Bab'e Cho'oosh,[j] a eunuch who forms the tail apex of the snake.

Every aspect of the Sama is symbolic. The Faqiri Sardari takes a single step, with right hand resting flat on the left shoulder, then stops, each pair and the Bab'e Cha'oosh taking their turn to do the same. In this manner, seven times they slowly circle a candelabra of seven small sacred fires, which burn continuously with oil. This candelabra, called a *chaqalto*, symbolises the planets and moon orbiting the sun.

As in the Ezidis' Jemayi celebrations, in the Zagmoog ritual there was always one god, God of Heaven and Earth, higher than the seven smaller gods. In the presence of Jamshid, the master of ceremonies, he would hand out roles to the lesser gods for the following year according to what each of the seven could promise in the form of favours (indicating their power and therefore their capacity to represent the people) and duties.[167] He did this by asking, "Who will be God of Earth this year? How much will you give me to become God of Earth?" Likewise, on the fifth day of the annual gathering of Jemayi in Lalish and other places, Ezidis re-enact the auction of the gods, known as Pariswarrkiran. In this re-enactment, people bring dyed materials to be auctioned, the money going to support the House of God.[168]

Another rite of Jemayi is Qabagh, also performed on the fifth day. A group of Ezidis climbs the northern face of the mountain that elevates the House of God at Lalish and lights a fire to start the ceremony, then descends to the place of worship. Men and women begin dancing to the *shabab* and *duff*—holding hands and jumping, moving in a circle, the modern forms of Kurdish dancing derived from the ancient Ezidi rituals. While the people dance, the Mir of Shaikhan province brings a big bull, ordering the people to guard it from bad fortune. The armed guards promise to keep the bull safe for Shaykh Shams, but two people secretly join the people, one of them stealing the bull. All the people cry and mourn until the bull is found. Then the people express their joy as they lead the bull to Shaykh Shams at the House of God, hitting it with sticks and shouting. After this, the bull is sacrificed, for good fortune and fertility in the coming year.

Similarly, in Mithraism, Mithra catches a bull created by Ahura Mazda and takes the bull to his cave. The bull escapes, and by order of the sky god, Shamis, Mithra finds the bull and kills it by beating it, then stabbing it with a knife up to the handle. When Mithra withdraws the knife, a quantity of useful plants, including grasses, come out to make the earth green. Wheat comes from the bull's bone marrow and grapes from the bull's blood. From these grapes, a holy drink is made, used in religious rites.

At the end of Jemayi is the rite of Chel Meran or 'meal of 40 men'. A bull is killed and cooked, and the *mir*, Bab'e Shaykh and the *shaykh*'s *wazir* (adviser) take the cooked bull's meat from the pot, throwing the pieces to the people. Eating the meat is a blessing and a promise of good fortune. When the feast is finished, the *mir* binds a white ribbon on the heads of each Ezidi attending the feast, a sign of blessing for having participated in the holy rite, before they return home.

Likewise, in Mithraism, on the day following the sacrifice of the first bull, another is beheaded and cooked, and religious men and other people who have newly entered Mithraism gather around to eat the holy meat, the occasion being known as the 'Last Supper remembrance', which was celebrated by Mithra and his followers at the end of their struggle, before they returned to the sky.

In Sanskrit texts, Mithra participates in the sacrifice of a god called Soma, who often appears in the shape of a white bull or the moon.

For modern Ezidis, the day after the feast of the bull, huge numbers of people climb the mountain and religious leaders throw bread from above. People take the pieces of holy bread down the mountain to Kania Spee (White Spring) and wet them in the holy water, before taking the blessed bread to distribute to their families and neighbours. In Mithraism and Zoroastrianism, there is also a rite of holy bread whereby a piece of bread is placed in a glass of water mixed with a holy drink called *homa*, in front of the priest. While the priest sings religious songs, he gives a piece of the holy bread to each person to eat.[169]

Jemayi is the most important Ezidi celebration. Others include Roejien Ezi, held in February, when Ezidis fast for three days and pray, believing this will prevent the sun from disappearing. On the fourth day, when they hold a feast to celebrate the sun rising again,[170] everyone gives each other coloured boiled eggs.

April is also a special month. It is the holy month of the gods, when Ta'us and other gods come down to earth and marry. Out of respect, Ezidis do not marry in April. Likewise, the Hittite gods came to earth and married.

There is much evidence that the Medes, a commonly cited ancestor of the Kurds, were Ezidi. The Medes were divided into six clans. One was called Bodeen, whose name changed to Botan, a Kurdish tribe still living in the area between Diyarbakir and northern Syria. Another Mede clan was called Moghan or Mogh, which is another word for *pir*, both the Mede and Ezidi names referring to an inherited line of religious leaders. The archeological findings around Hamadan (the site of Ecbatan, the capital of Medea) and Ushnaviyeh show that the Medes practised the ancient Ezidi festivals of Jemayi and Sarsa'al, using flowers and colours. Like the Ezidis, the Medes believed that our world is a reflection of God's world.[171] They buried their dead in the ground, unlike the Zoroastrians, who left their dead on structures for the birds to eat of the flesh. The Zoraostrians then collect the bones and put them in a *dukhme*, or special box, which is often stored in the cellar.

Half-animal, half-human statues have been found in and around Ushnaviyeh and have been dated to the time of the Medean Empire (727–550 BC). After the Achaemanid Persians conquered the Medes and adopted Zoroastrianism, they called these statues 'bad *devas*'.

Zoroastra was probably born in modern-day Azerbaijan,[172] in the ancient land of Mad (Medea). Two Iranian academics, Jhala Amoozgar and Ahmed Tafazooli, provide evidence that dates him between 1200 and 1000 BC, at least 400 years earlier than believed by many scholars. Their evidence includes a study of the language found in part of the *Avesta* called *Faroardeen Yasht*,[173] all the *Avesta* being written in what is known as 'the alphabet of the *Avesta*', taken from ancient Aramaean.

Zoroastra can be seen as a reformer of Ezidism, borrowing many symbols and rituals while changing much of the theology. For instance, in Zoroastrianism the Jemayi feast is called Mehregan-Al-Mehrajan, in which there is a gathering with the Zoroastrian god of light and goodness, Ahura Mazda. *Mehr* means 'sun' and 'love' and *gan* is equivalent to '-ian' (as in Austral*ian*), the feast relating to both sun and joy. The Iranian scholar Jhala Amoozgar suggests that the celebration of Iranian Newroz comes from Mehregan, but when the Persian Zoroastrians adopted the Egyptian calender in the time of Darius I (522–486 BC), the celebration was moved from autumn to spring. The Zoroastrians took many Mede traditions and artefacts and claimed them as their own.

Ezidis did not accept Zoroastra's religious teachings, so he travelled east. In 550 BC, the half-Mede, half-Persian Cyrus the Great took over Medea and formed the Archaemanid Empire of Persia. In this time, the Zoroastrian religion became widespread, but Ezidism persisted among the Medes, who were still an integral part of the aristocracy. Thus, when an early Zoroastrian king of the Achaemanids, Kambujiya, died on his journey back from Egypt in 522 BC, an Ezidi *mogh* named Giamat claimed he was the son of Cyrus and brother of Kambujiya. He attempted to take over the kingship, but was not accepted, because he was of a different religion.

The Zoroastrian religion became even more entrenched when the king, Kay Kavus, united his people by banning the ancient Ezidi beliefs and practices, forcing people to worship the Zoroastrian god Ahura Mazda. It was in this time that the half-animal, half-human forms came to be seen as devils or bad *devas* and the people who refused to follow the new religion of Zoroastra—the Ezidis—were accused of being 'devil worshippers'. Eventually, after numerous uprisings against this religious tyranny, Ardashir II, reigning from 383 to 379 BC, was forced to place Naheed, goddess of water, and Mithra beside Ahura Mazda.[174] Thus the influences of Ezidism persisted, albeit under different names.

Just as the names of various gods and symbols changed in ancient times, I suggest that it was after Islam came to the area, in the seventh century AD, that the seven Ezidi angels were given the names Israfeel, Izraeel, Mikaeel, Jabraeel, Dardaeel, Shamkhaeel and Azazeel. [k] However, these names represent ideas and roles that go back to prehistory.

The names of God's assistants continued to change in the post-Islamic era. Malak Ta'us came to be known as Azazeel and later as Shaykh Shams, the highly respected Ezidi who lived in the 13th century, and who became known as 'the flying *shaykh*', because of his ability to travel vast distances in an instant. All three names are used to represent the symbol of the sun or the one who is responsible for light, food and good fortune. The other angels were also assigned Ezidi religious leaders of the 13th or 14th century. One became Malak Shaykh Sin, responsible for the pen and the 'unseen board'; another was Malak Faqir Al-Deen, responsible for the moon and infant diseases. Another was Sajadeen, the sender of the taker of souls, and another Nasirdeen, the cutter of throats. Khatoona Fakhrun, a female, was responsible for birth and Shaykh Mand became responsible for snakes.[175] (Although Shaykh Mand was an Ezidi *shaykh*, he was made Emir of Halab by one of Salahaddin's descendants of the Ayyubiad Empire.)

But it is not only about name-changing. For Ezidis, there is no time as we understand it. Ezidis believe in transmigration and incarnation, so people and God's angels from separate times can meet together and great figures like Jamshid can exist over many eras.

Thus aspects of Ezidi religious beliefs, symbols, language, rituals, music and art spread over Mesopotamia and beyond. This spread is not surprising, given the evidence that the kingdoms after Noah, including those of late Sumer, Elam, Akkad and Babylon, Assyria, Mitanni and Hittites, Medes and Persians were not different nations but, rather, different tribes of the one people. I propose that some of these tribes stayed in the area, while others scattered west to Africa, north to Europe and east to India, whether through overpopulation, enforced exile or a search for new frontiers. Of these emigrants, I propose that some were to return, to come to prominence at various times.

There are several points to support this theory. The qualities of the ancient languages of Mesopotamia distinguish them as a group. Scholars suggest an unwritten proto-Indo-European language existed 6000 years ago and this spawned the three main groups of Indo-European languages spoken from Ireland to India, classified as European, Iranic and Aryan Indian.[176] From religious sources, we are likewise told that in the time of Noah, there was one language, and it was only in the time of Nimrod and the Tower of Babel that people began speaking in different tongues.

The first known written language is the Sumer cuneiform script, its earliest tablets and cylinders dating from about 3200 BC. In the past, scholars have said the Sumer script[l] is unrelated to any known language, but more recent scholarship has found similarities between it and proto-Elamite and Akkadian, suggesting it was part of a proto-Indo-European heritage. It was to form the basis of the cuneiform scripts of Babylon, Assyria, the Hittites and Persians. Unlike modern languages, in these ancient languages or dialects a noun changes its form in both its vowels and consonants, depending on its place in a sentence, and if the object of a sentence is plural, then the verb is plural, rather than depending on the subject.

The legend of Noah also supports the theory that these tribes were originally one nation,[m] the division of semitic and non-semitic people being based on who descended from which son of Noah, the descendants of each son remaining in the area, or migrating west, north or east, taking their families and animals with them.

Linguistic and historical evidence supports the legend of Noah and his descendants' movements. In modern Kurdish, spoken in areas around Sulaimani and Kirkuk, 'one who stays near water' is called *kurmanj* or *kurdman, man* meaning 'water' and 'staying in the one place', while a traveller or nomad is called *kurd*.[177] (*Kurd* also means 'strong' and 'brave'.) Many Kurdish tribes have lived for thousands of years in the same place. These ancient sites include Shanidah, Jerwan, Mosul, Arbela (the old name for Arbil, known as Hawler by modern Kurds), Zanjah, Kirman, Shahir, Elam,[178] and the land of Shinar (Shinoe in Kurdish and Ushnaviyeh in Persian). However, tribes like Abraham and his family, who became the Israelites, the Aryan Indians and the Aramaeans, to name a few, migrated never to return, the names of these peoples still being found among modern Kurdish tribes—for example, Sperti or Spartans, Mosaki, Khalti and Alani.

Other tribes like the Guti, the Hittites, Kassites, Mitannites, Medes, Scythians and Persians were known to be nomads before they established their kingdoms or empires in the region. When these tribes began arriving after 2300 BC, there was no major conflict with the indigenous people. Nor did communication appear to be a serious problem. For instance, the scholars Sergei A. Starostin and Igor Diakonov claim the Hittite and Hurrian languages derive from a common parent language,[179] indicating the Hittites were originally from the area to which they returned. The invading tribes worshipped the same family of Aryan gods, quickly formed an aristocracy and integrated with the local cultures. They also readily exchanged ideas with neighbouring kingdoms, indicating they had a lot in common with each other.

There are many stories from both prehistory and recorded history of people moving from the area. The most famous is that of Abraham and his followers. From what we are told, Abraham was a descendant of Noah. I have already described how Ezidis believe in an almighty God but introduced idolatrous elements, against which Abraham rebelled. As well, Ezidis practise circumcision, as did Abraham and his descendants.[n] Also, from what we know of Abraham's geographical origin and an ancient Kurdish tradition known as *warr*, I conclude that Abraham grew up among Ezidis.

Abraham came from the Sumer city-state of Ur, in southern Mesopotamia. However, his family were both important and widespread, as indicated by his brother Haran and nephew Lot, who came from Haran in the north, close to the modern Kurdish town of Raha.[o]

There is an ancient tradition among the Kurds called *warr* or *varr*, meaning 'test of trust'.[p] When a person proposed a new idea or was suspected of a wrongdoing, he or she was put in a fire or forced to eat sulphur. If the person survived unscathed, their rightness or innocence was proved, but if the person was affected in any way, then the person was wrong or guilty. According to the holy Qur'an, the prophet Abraham was tested in this way after he objected to his own father and the people of Babylon worshipping senseless stone idols and praying facing the sun (as Ezidis do). The Qur'an describes how Abraham destroyed the smaller statues claiming, "Your Lord is the Lord of the Heavens and Earth ... And I am a witness to this truth." When the statues lay broken and silent, he asked the people, "Do ye then worship, besides the one true God, Things that can neither be of any good to you, Nor do you harm?" The people said, "Burn him", and Abraham was put into the fire, but the fire 'remained cool' and Abraham was unhurt.[180] Traditions among Ezidi and Islamic scholars say that Abraham's test occurred in Babylon in the time of Nimrod, King of Babel and Akkad.[q] Some Islamic scholars say it was Nimrod, and if not Nimrod, another king of Babylon, with whom Abraham debated. When this king claimed, "I give life and death", Abraham replied, "But it is God that causeth the sun to rise from the east. Do thou then cause it to rise in the west?"[181]

There are at least three traditions describing the lineage of Nimrod. The Torah and the Bible say he was the great-grandson of Noah, through Ham and Cush. Another tradition states he was the great-great-grandson of Arphaxand, the six times great-grandfather of Abraham.[182] Although in the second tradition there still seems to be a discrepancy of time between Nimrod and Abraham, one must remember that while patriarchs like Peleg had their first offspring at the age of 30, others were well over 70, 100 or even, in the case of Noah, 500.[r] Chistensen describes a third tradition, which relates both Nimrod and Abraham to Jamshid. This tradition claims that Abraham's father and Nimrod were cousins.[183]

The great Islamic scholar Tabari (died 923 AD), claimed that the individual who advised Nimrod to put Abraham in the fire by way of a battering ram was a Kurd and from the nation of Abraham. Tabari's sources, indirectly, were Abdullah Bin Abbas and Abdullah Bin Omar, two students of the Prophet Muhammad.

It was after this test that Abraham was exiled from his homeland and began his travels, west to Syria, south-west to Egypt, then north to Canaan. Thus, I propose, Abraham grew up among Ezidi, rebelled against the idolatrous elements and reaffirmed the religion of Noah. In so doing, he became the father of the three major monotheistic religions in the world today.

As for modern Ezidis, while many of their beliefs, practices and names have remained remarkably consistent for thousands of years, others have changed, especially after the arrival of Islam. This causes some confusion as to the original Ezidi beliefs and practices. The source of this confusion is their reliance on oral tradition, because reading and writing were forbidden to ordinary followers.[184] That Mawlik Shaykh Sin is responsible for the pen indicates some Ezidi were allowed to write, but perhaps the idea that writing was bad came from Zoroastrianism, which teaches that bad *devas* taught people to write. Whatever the case, rather than rely on texts, the Ezidi religion has been passed from generation to generation by blood, word of mouth, imitation and ceremonies. Above all, it has been a secret religion, its followers not wishing to broadcast it, or have their beliefs and customs contaminated with foreign, often dominating and antagonistic influences.

Many scholars and followers of Ezidism claim the first Ezidi texts were the books *Kitab e-Jelwa* and *Mes-haf-e Resh*, or *The Black Book*. These are said to have been written in a secret script, by the great Sufi Shaykh Adi bin Musafir and his nephew Shaykh Hasan bin Adi, in the 12th century.[185] However, the style of writing and the subject matter of these books do not reflect the originality and reality of the Ezidi religion, its symbols, myths and rituals that were and still are, practised by Ezidis.[186] The books even contain stories of the prophet Muhammad, these having caused some scholars to say that Ezidism is a branch of Islam. Ezidi scholars like Hudar Sulaiman, head of the Ezidi Institute in Germany, maintain that these books, in their modern form, were written not by these two Sufis but some time after they died. However, these two Sufi *shaykhs* did write books that contain a lot of instructions, especially for Sufis.

Famous Ezidi *shaykhs* and scholars have written less well-known books. These include *Maqualate (Book of) Shamshi Tabrizi*, written by Shaykh Shams, and *Diwan Shams*, written by Shamshi Tabrizi's student Mawolana Jalaludeen, from Balkhi, who moved to Qunauri a short time before the Mongol invasion.

There is no doubt that Islam, particularly through the books thought to be the first Ezidi texts, has influenced uneducated Ezidis. This influence has also caused controversy as to the origin of various religious sects of Turkey, Syria, Iraq, Iran and Lebanon, many of their followers being Kurd. While these sects have incorporated elements of Islam, they do not necessarily follow Islam's five pillars, and they continue to practise many Ezidi beliefs and customs, such as a belief in incarnation and respect for fire, including the Newroz ritual of dancing around or over a fire. For instance, many Kurds from Elam practise Ezidi beliefs and culture, including the way they dress, but have called themselves Muslim ever since the Safavid Persians adopted Shi'ite Islam and began persecuting them, claiming their money, land and animals were contaminated. This was because they were accused of being the followers of Yazid ibn Mu'awiyya, the Islamic leader who was responsible for Ali's son's death. It can thus be concluded that these sects were originally Ezidi, but took on elements of Islam as a form of protection when governed and surrounded by Muslims.

Today, followers of Ezidism are Kurdish people living in Kurdistan of Iraq, Turkey and Syria and also in Armenia, Georgia and Russia, as well as in the diasporas, especially Germany. It is impossible to estimate population numbers, as no census in the Middle East takes into account religion. Although some Arabs and Turks are followers of sects already mentioned as having originally been Ezidi, there is only one non-Kurdish group that acknowledges its practise of Ezidism. They are a small group of Arabs living in Basheekha, close to Mosul and Lalish, who came from Syria with Shaykh Adi Bin Musafir in the 12th century as his *moreed* or followers.

Fortunately, in the last three decades, Ezidis have given greater priority to education and more Ezidis are writing about their religion. It is also hoped that with further archeological research, there will be greater clarification of the legends of Jamshid, Noah and the flood, as well as of Ezidi influences and the origins and migration patterns of the Indo-European people of Mesopotamia.

ABOUT Siamand Minehzadeh Morowatdost

Siamand Minehzadeh Morowatdost (Minehzadeh meaning 'born of Mineh', Morowatdost meaning 'brave man', a name given to his grandfather) was born in Mahabad, in eastern Kurdistan, in 1969. He learned classical music and poetry by ear from musicians and poets he admired. While at school, he acted in a local theatre group and began singing and playing music for public performance. After school, he worked as a taxi driver, before coming to Australia in 1992, where he continues to study music and to play the *ba'aghlama*, the Iranian *tar*, lute, violin and keyboards. In Melbourne, he writes his own music and poems, does some volunteer work at Radio 3ZZZ, runs a steam-cleaning business and drives a taxi.

A Musical and Poetic Tradition

A personal view based on interviews with Siamand Minehzadeh Morowatdost, with additional references from Dana Kadar

Kurdish people love music and poetry. Simko, the leader of Kurdish uprisings in the 1920s, had a piano in his house. There is always music, singing and dancing at every gathering—weddings and picnics, especially at Newroz. Our music and poetry are very, very old, rich traditions, but we do not have the history books to tell us everything. We know only from mouth to mouth.

For thousands of years, the Kurdish people have been shepherds in the mountains, passing the time by playing a flute that we call a *shemshal*. The *shemshal* is a simple pipe made from bamboo or hollowed-out sugarcane. Slowly, the shepherds adjusted the holes when making their next pipe, so the sounds became more natural, a little higher or a little lower. In this way, the *shemshal* developed into what we call the *nay*, in eastern Kurdistan[a] or *may* in Turkey and Russia. It has a wonderful sound. The *nay* can have a metal mouthpiece that goes between the teeth, and by changing the position of the tongue, you create a lower or upper voice for so many different scales and melodies. It is very lyrical music that goes straight to the heart, and some very good musicians play the *nay*, the greatest being Jamshead Andalibi, from the city of Sanandaj in eastern Kurdistan. Andalibi was born in 1957 and plays mostly Kurdish classical music.

Another very important traditional instrument is the *tapel* or *timpo* drum. People love it, especially when they dance. It is much smaller than the big, loud drum called a *dohul*, played in northern Kurdistan.[b] The *dohul* is hung from the neck and beaten with one thin stick and one thick stick, whereas the *tapel* rests on the knee, the larger end played using the 10 fingers. Traditionally, it is made from clay and particular leaves, which are shaped into a curved round hollow vase, then baked in a fire. On each end is glued a thin, hairless sheepskin, which has been heated and stretched. Slowly, the *tapel* evolved, so sometimes the vase shape is handmade from wood or metal.

The *dootar*[c] is the ancestor of all our stringed instruments. It has a tiny bowl made of timber, with a very long neck, and originally had only one string. Over time, another string was added (*dootar* meaning 'two strings') and they shaped the bowl differently, making the flat bottom more round. When they added a third string, the *dootar* became the *sehtar. Sehtar* means 'three strings'. Then came the *ba'aghlama*, with six strings arranged in three pairs, each pair playing the same note. The *ba'aghlama* has a hole in the bottom, unlike the Western guitar. It has seven frets or *parda*, so 21 notes can be played with a plastic plectrum.

More and more strings were added, so now some *ba'aghlamas* have more strings, and the Indian *sitar* can have up to 30 strings (*sitar* means 30), although a modern *sitar* usually has seven, nine or 11 metal strings. All these instruments are related. Traditionally, the frets and strings were made from the intestines of the goat or sheep, which were dried out in the sun and twisted. Now the strings are plastic or metal—either steel or copper—although some are still made from animal intestines. The bowls are usually made from walnut wood.

Gradually, as people travelled from the villages to different regions and cities, they would see and learn to play other instruments and incorporate them into Kurdish music. That is how we got the *zorna* (or *zirna*), a woodwind instrument with a reed mouthpiece and a very distinctive high-pitched sound. It is played all over the Middle East, especially with the *dohul* or *tapel*, for dancing, and also accompanies the Iranian *tar*.

The Iranian *tar* is a handmade stringed instrument with two small heart-shaped bowls, one smaller than the other, the tops of the bowls made from sheepskin, not all-wood like the bowl of the *ba'aghlama*. Like the *ba'aghlama*, the *tar* has six strings arranged in pairs, but it has 28 frets, each with a specific distance between them to produce the right classical sound. The material on the surface of the neck is also different. It is always white—either a hard plastic, ivory or seashells. In the *tar*, the three pairs of strings are plucked with a metal plectrum we call a *berenge*, and in Kurdistan we also use our fingernails, to make it sound like a classical guitar.

In classical music from the Middle East to India, there are seven skills, or seven different ways of tuning and playing each instrument. Each skill has its characteristic notes and chords, rhythms and tempos. We call each skill a *maqa'am*. The same notes can be played in different skills, by making them sharp or flat or by combining them in different ways. In Sorani, we call these seven skills *shoor, mahoor, nawal, homa'ayon, sehgah, chahargah* and *rast panjgah*. Within each skill, there are many 'doors' or different ways of playing. For example, the *shoor* skill has five 'doors', called *abu atar, byatiturk, afshari, dashti* and the Kurdish *byatizand*. Each of these 'doors' has another 13 to 15 offshoots.

A skill has its own mood and purpose, although different skills can be played in one song. Most dancing music and happy songs are played in *mahoor*, whereas *shoor* is for sad songs and love songs. Very sad, slow, quiet songs can be played in *homa'ayon*, with low, drawn-out notes, sliding into gentle trills. To me the love skill is *homa'ayon* and the 'doors' of *dashti* and *afshari* from *shoor*, but also *sehgah* and *nawal*.

Seh means 'three', *chuar* means 'four' and *panj* means 'five', so the skills *sehgah, chahargah* and *rast panjgah* refer to the beats and rhythms, as well as the purpose for which they are played. The *rast panjgah* skill is music for praising God. Muhammad H. Barqui writes in his book Th*e History of Kurdish Music* (1996) that the skill relates back to the *Avesta*, Zoroastra's holy books, in which followers are told to pray five times a day. *Rast* in Sanskrit means 'singing in a beautiful voice for praising God'.

After Islam came to Kurdistan and Persia, the Arabs assimilated a lot of the culture and the skills came to be played throughout the Middle East, but they are distinct. You can tell whether the musician is Arab, Persian or Kurd by the way he plays the skill. For example, an Arabic singer might sing in *shoor*, but we call it *shoor Arabi* in Sorani, or *sarbha* in Farsi, the *'shoor* that belongs to Arabs', and it is distinct from *shoor Kurdi*. It might have the same notes and patterns, but is like another dialect, a different sound. It might have one note that is different or the same note played differently.

As well as the seven main skills, there are five major skills, or *maqa'ami Kurdi*, unique to Kurdistan. One is *khurrshidi*, based on folklore. *La'ook*[d] is the skill of storytelling in song or chant, while *hayran* is a skill slow in tempo and played for love and story telling in Dohuk and northern Kurdistan. Another Kurdish skill is *qataru alawaysi*, based on classical poetry and made popular in the 20th century by the singer Alawaysi, from Saghez, in eastern Kurdistan.

The fifth major Kurdish skill is *horra*, Kurdish for 'praying to God', based on classical poetry for praising God. It is commonly played in Luristan. Muhammad H. Barqui says *horra* relates to Ahura Mazda, the god of Zoroastra. *Ahur* comes from *horra*. *Maz* means 'powerful' and *da* comes from *dana*, meaning 'wise person'. So from his research, Barqui concludes that this Kurdish *maqa'am* could date back as far as 2600 BC or earlier.

No-one knows for sure how old the skills are, but they have been around for thousands of years, definitely at the time of the Persian king Darius II (423–404 BC). There are stories of the musicians and singers performing at the *darbar*, or king's house. In the mountain of Keri Bestoon, in eastern Kurdistan, there are reliefs dating from the time of the Medes and the first Persian Empire, from the seventh century BC, depicting all the instruments. The same instruments are depicted in even older Assyrian and Chaldean reliefs, so the skills could be at least 4000 years old. We know the Sumerians were musically sophisticated. They played the lute, which is like the modern *oud*, the flute and the lyre from 3800 BC. Also, the names of the skills and musical instruments like the *tar* are in use as far afield as China.

One unique feature of the Indo-European music of the Kurds, Persians and Indians is a kind of note we call a quarter, or *sori*, between a flat and a sharp. To my knowledge, it is not played anywhere else in the world. It is not found in Western music, but in our music, some skills cannot be correctly played without the *sori*.

Most Kurdish musicians, myself included, learn to play and sing by ear, teacher to student, heart to heart, and sometimes with the ear, we make mistakes. Still, knowing the skills helps us learn and play together—they provide a blueprint and help in improvisation.

It takes a long time to learn the richness of classical music, but some very good musicians, like Mazhari Khalaqi, have good knowledge of all seven skills. Mazhari

Khalaqi is one of the top Kurdish singers and melody-writers in eastern Kurdistan. He also plays the *tapel*, but is most famous for his singing. He has a deep, mellow voice, like a gentle wind that massages the heart. For nearly 25 years, he ran a Kurdish radio station, but he now lives in London.

One of the greatest Iranian Kurdish singers, Saed Ali Azghari Kurdistani (1882–1937), sang all over Kurdistan. Important Kurdish leaders would invite him to sing for them, and several times he sang for Shaykh Mahmud,[e] leader of the Iraqi Kurdish uprisings in the 1920s. While in Iraqi Kurdistan, he was imprisoned in Kirkuk for not having the proper papers to cross the border. The first recordings of his songs were made when he was 47, but his songs are still played, even by big orchestras. I have heard from many older musicians in Mahabad that his voice was so penetrating that it could be easily heard a kilometre away, and that when he sang, window glass would break within a 500-metre radius. He had a range of six and a half octaves!

One of his most famous songs is about love, but whether it is love for a person, God or something else is left ambiguous. The song says, "All friends come together and know my pain and love. But do not believe anybody who comes to you saying, 'I love'. Do not be tricked, because true love is something you cannot see". This song is sung very, very high in the *shoor* skill, in the 'door' of *byatiturk*.

Many singers wrote their own melodies and songs about romantic love, love of God and country, Newroz, the heroism and sacrifice of our freedom fighters, and the suffering and pain of our political oppression. Other singers became famous for reviving classical poems and folklore. They include the famous *maqa'amaht* singers Rasoul Ghadi, Ali Merdan and Tahir Tofeq, from Iraqi Kurdistan, and from eastern Kurdistan, Khalaqi, Hasan Zirek, Khalil Sadeeqi, Muhammad Mamli and Aziz Shahrokh, who all learned music in the time of the Pahlavi Shahs.

Hasan Zirek was born in 1921 in the village of Hermila, in the Bukan region. He could not read or write, but sang from an early age and, like Khalaqi, sang throughout Kurdistan of Iraq and Iran. Several times, he was imprisoned and tortured. In 1953, he made recordings for the Kurdish radio station in Baghdad, and in 1957, he returned to eastern Kurdistan and recorded songs in Kirmanshah. He brought his own style to hundreds of folk songs. His voice had a good range and was multidimensional, quite deep and slightly gravelly. He died in 1972.

Khalil Sadeeqi died about 50 years ago and Muhammad Mamli died in January 1999. Shahrokh is still alive. Mamli and Shahrokh were from Mahabad. Muhammad Mamli was our neighbour, so my father knew him and I went to him for lessons. He was illiterate, but he created his own poems and melodies and he has over 100 songs on cassette. His voice is soft, of a medium timbre and sharper than Zirek's. Today, people love his music and respect him as a top musician, but in our culture, professional musicians, especially those who play at weddings and parties and make people dance, are not respected, so when he was young, people treated him very badly just because he was a singer.

From long ago, people have called musicians *chawash*, which means 'cheap, doing anything you like without caring what other people think', whereas in the Middle East, you must care what the family and community think about you. This attitude towards musicians is why too few Kurdish people have become top musicians—nobody wants their son or daughter to become *chawash* and nobody wants to be known this way. Then, after the revolution in 1979, the new government banned music, particularly Persian and Western music. Throughout the 1980s, Ayatollah Khomeini was very strict, believing music and dancing distorted people's minds and encouraged sexual attraction, but no law can stop people making music or dancing.

Our way of dancing is communal. We usually dance in a circle or line, with a singer and musicians playing the *tapel* (or the *dohul* in northern Kurdistan) and perhaps the *zorna*. One man leads by waving a small piece of material in the air, and the dancers—men and women mixed—hold hands and follow his steps. There are hundreds of different types of dances. In south and east Kurdistan, one slow, easy dance is called *sechkah* and others are called *sepayi*, *dargha* and *sanari*. With *sechkah* and *sepayi* (meaning 'three steps'), we interlock all the fingers and the arms are held down, but with *dargha*, we interlock only our little finger and swing our arms up and down, then turn our body and swing one arm in front and one arm behind. In *bahshanan*, the feet move slowly but the shoulders vibrate very fast. Each dance has its own music, but most dance music is in the skill of *mahoor* or *shoor*.

As far as I know, in Sorani Kurdistan[f] dances do not vary from village to village, but in northern Kurdistan, they have many different ways of dancing for each area or village. Sometimes, they dance with daggers, or the ladies dance with vases on their shoulders, or they tell a story with their dance. I have seen one such dance that tells of a girl who goes to the river to get some water and a boy who comes and tries to talk to her about love. Her brother sees them, and tells the family he has seen his sister talking to a boy, so the family tells the boy's family. The girl's brother and the boy have a fight, but a woman comes between them, and later they become friends and dance together. The dance is like a piece of theatre, whereas Sorani dancing is more for happiness and movement.

At a celebration, usually the men start to dance while the women look on. When two pairs of eyes meet and linger, a couple knows they are interested in each other. If the woman likes the man, she joins the line of dancers by opening the right hand of the man she likes. The musicians in the middle of the circle approach the couple and, keeping face-to-face with them, make up words in their song about the goodness of the man and how he loves a young woman with beautiful eyes, skin, nose and lips. The musicians make the man feel proud, while they often make themselves appear small or funny. Finally, the man or woman feels so shy that the man must put his hand in his pocket and give the singer money, the more the better. Only then do the musicians leave them and concentrate on another couple. The musicians and singer make their money this way, and it is for this reason that parents never want their children to pursue a musical career.

This is the way many couples meet. It is a good way, because in our culture, a boy cannot walk straight up to a girl and start talking about his true feelings—the girl is very shy and might walk away. So while they are dancing and holding hands, the boy tickles her palm with his middle finger, letting her know that he loves her. She might shyly put her head down, but later they might start talking, or when the celebration is over, he might find her telephone number and call her. The boy's parents discover their son is in love, and if they like the girl, they will go and ask her family about marriage. Perhaps Ayatollah Khomeini does have a point when it comes to the effects of music and dancing!

For weddings and parties and also at Newroz, we usually wear traditional Kurdish dress, whereas at work, by law we must wear Western clothes. However, in the street, I used to wear Kurdish clothes, even to school. There are several types of Kurdish clothes for men, the variations being mainly in the vest. Some styles of vest are left open, as in the *rankoochogheh* or *moradghani* styles, made from stiff material, while the *kawapatol* style is buttoned down the centre. In all the ways of dressing, we have five metres of cloth wrapped around the waist, and big loose pants that narrow at the ankle. Our traditional shoes are called *kaloush*, made with sheepskin soles and bleached white rope on top, and our shirt is usually white to match.

The Kurdish shirt has sleeves with long wings extending past the wrist. These are tied around the wrist, leaving the end to hang down. Many old men, like my grandfather, tie their money in the material, or carry a bag over their shoulder by putting the wing of material through the handle of the bag. They also use the wing to hold up their sleeves to wash before praying, and as the piece of material they wave as the leader of a dance. The men also wear a turban, which is wrapped and placed on the head in different ways, depending on the area of Kurdistan in which you live.

I always loved dancing and music, but for many reasons I could not become a good musician in my country. My parents did not want others to call their son *chawash*. They told me, "You must become a doctor or a professor", but I was not interested. Since I was eight or nine years old, I would only have to listen to the radio once to remember the music, and I would go out to the street and play the music, using my mouth as an instrument. We had five-kilogram tins for oil, and after the oil was finished, they were used as rubbish bins and put in the street to be emptied. People would call me over and give me an empty tin, saying, "Come, play and sing for us". I used to sing to all the girls and women in the street, and they would say, "You have a beautiful voice, a beautiful feeling. Why don't you become a singer or musician?" My dream was always to be a great musician, but when I was 10 years old, music was officially banned.

Because I did not have much money and the people close to me were discouraging, I just had to listen to music, and as a teenager, when the feeling grew stronger, I would go to the mountain every day, summer and winter, to practice singing for up to five hours. If I did not know the skill of a song, I would visit one of the musicians in Mahabad, such as Muhammad Mamli or Aziz Shahrokh, and ask them about the skill. They used to tell me about its history and meaning, and then I would go and learn another 10 or 20 songs in the same skill.

I could not afford to own my own instrument until I was 19 years old. Working as a taxi driver, I slowly saved money and bought an Iranian *tar*. It was the first real instrument I ever played, even though it is more Iranian than Kurdish and I used to play and sing mostly Kurdish music. However, I became interested in Iranian music, because I wanted to be professional. I also believe music is universal—you can borrow and mix from any country's music. All good music is meaningful. It goes from heart to heart.

My other great interest is poetry. Kurdish people really love poetry, which is a very strong tradition in Middle Eastern culture. Singing the great classical poems of poets like Mawlawi[g] (1806–1882) has made many singers famous.

Modern poets, like Sherko Bekas (from Iraqi Kurdistan), as well as poets from Mahabad, like Marif Agha-e (who wrote a collection called *The earth is hard, the sky far away*), Abdulkhaleq Perhezi and the blind Nasser Aghabra, and the modern female poets, such as Jheela Husseini, Zara Nadri, Seemin Gaychi and Kalsoom Osmanpoor, write in free verse, which has no rules, but I wanted to write classical poems so that I could adapt them to music.

The classical styles of Arabic poetry that existed before the Qur'an are called Al-Jar Hahli, or 'poetry before Islam'. Some of these styles died with the introduction of Islam. Other styles were inspired by the Qur'an and its *sajah,* Arabic for the poetic style of the Qur'an. Three hundred years ago, Ahmedi Khani wrote *Mem U Zin*, in the *sajah* way, and many songs have come from this 6000-line narrative. *Sajah* is not true classical poetry, but the end word of each couplet is the same or rhymes. Also in *sajah,* as in the true classical poetry, there is a balance, a continuous rhythm, so that even if the lines are read, they sound like music, like a melody with soft and strong beats.

Classical poetry is called *qasidah* in Arabic, *hornrowa* in Sorani. All classical poems have two basic rules, called *wozen* and *ka'afia*. *Wozen* refers to the weights, beats or metre of each line. *Ka'afia* refers to the rhyming of the last word, or the last three letters of the last word, of each couplet or verse. For poems inspired by the Qur'an, if the Arabic has 15 beats on each line of the couplet, then even if you write in Kurdish, you must have the same number of beats.

These basic line rules are applied in one of five ways. In *masnowi,* the two lines of the couplet have to be equal in the number of beats, but the next couplet can have a different number of beats. Also, the word at the end of each couplet line has to rhyme, but the words ending the next couplet do not have to rhyme with the previous couplet. In *khomasi* (*penjkhoshtaki* in Sorani), the poem or verse has five lines. In *rhubiyyad,* the poem or verse has four lines, and in *doobaiti,*[h] the poet must use only two lines to impart the meaning of a long story. There is also *qasidah,* where every line of the poem must end with the same word.

These five basic line rules apply to at least six kinds of classical poetry, which are classified according to mood and subject, like the skills in music. One kind is *ghazal,* or *ghuzul,* which are love poems and poems describing women. They are usually very long. *Mahdah* are the poems for praising people in power. *Ratha* are poems of sadness and *wosof* are descriptive poems. *I'eeni,* also called *parasti,* are religious poems and *haja* are poems where two people have a contest, retorting to each other by making up alternate lines that have the same beats and rhymes as the previous line of the couplet.

In poetry, my main inspiration is love. I started writing at 13, but it was not until I was 16 that I dared show a poem to another poet. I was at a wedding at which there was a beautiful but selfish girl. A boy was admiring her beauty, but she embarrassed him in front of everyone, saying, "If they inject your blood into a donkey, the donkey will die." The boy was so hurt, he ran away, and this made me write a classical poem about beauty and ugliness. I composed a melody to go with it. I knew it was a bit out of balance, but people loved it.

I went to an old man who called himself a poet and showed him the poem, asking, "Could you please correct my poem?" He was very critical of it. How he phrased his criticism was a poem in itself, but translated, it meant, "This person who calls himself a poet is better to go and eat one finger of faeces than attempt to write poetry." I was shocked, but said respectfully, "Thank you very much". I told a friend what the old poet had said, and my friend advised, "Don't worry. We will go to Urmia and visit the great poet Hemen Shaykh Islami and see what he feels about the poem." Hemen had spent many years in the mountains with *peshmerga*.

I showed Hemen my poem and the old man's, and Hemen gave me a reply in the form of a poem with the same number of beats as the old man's criticism. It, too, was very rude! Translated it meant, "Whoever reads this boy's poem, if his feelings do not wake up, that person has to go and shame himself". I showed the old man Hemen's reply and he knew immediately who had written it!

That was my first meeting with Hemen, and my friend and I visited him another five times, eager to learn the classical traditions. He loved our poems and their youthful feelings. He told us to go to the Community of Poets in Mahabad, where we could listen to some well-known poets and get advice. We went every Friday afternoon. The old men would read their poems, correct each other and talk about which was best, which poems had true feeling. Each time I went with a new poem, they could not believe it came from such a young man. I did not have too much knowledge, I had not read many Kurdish books, but I wrote from the heart.

Very few of my friends wrote poetry. Maybe they thought it too old-fashioned or were too lazy, but I was doing so many things at that time: I was acting in the theatre, doing tae kwon-do, studying at school, learning music, singing and writing poetry.

Later, when I was in the army, I went to another poet in Karaj, near Tehran. His name was Abdul Rahman Sharafkandi, a very famous poet and the author of many books. He compiled the Kurdish-Persian dictionary called *Nomostahajhaj*. Having always dreamed of meeting him, I ended up visiting him three times. He was old and sick, but I showed him my poems. He told me I would have a wonderful future if I continued writing, that I was very sensitive. He was from Mahabad, and when he died, I went to his funeral. Like Hemen Shaykh Islami and others, such as Mamoosta Abbas Haqeqi from Bukan and Mamoosta Hajar, he had been a great poet. They all wrote in Sorani, but in the classical style of Arabic culture.

Throughout those years, my poems were about the love I had for one girl, love I can still taste, so I wrote with joy in my heart. When I was 16, I had moved into a different stage at school, where I made a new friend. One night, he invited me to dinner. Four houses down, I saw this beautiful girl standing in the doorway. A week later, I asked my friend to give me her telephone number, but he said, "I cannot. She is a very good girl. She will not talk to you". I pleaded with him until he did. I waited two weeks before phoning her, and when I finally did, the person who answered refused to call her to the phone. My friend would go and talk about me to her mum, and it turned out that her mum and my mum were friends when they were young, so eventually, I convinced her I was sincere.

I would sit at home day and night, not eating, drinking or sleeping, just writing poems. Sometimes at three or four o'clock in the morning, when I had finished a poem, I could not hold it in, so I would ring her up to read it to her and she would cry.

In Iran, if the *pasdars* (religious police) see you talking to a strange girl in the street, they can take you away or make you marry on the spot. One time, the police caught me talking with her and took me to prison, where I was beaten so badly that I went into a coma. When I woke up in the cell, I found a note: "When tomorrow comes, we will hang you". They could do this. They killed many people for no reason. But my mum came to the prison, screaming, "Why did you take my son?" and they released me after two days. I wrote a poem about it all. Two lines, translated, read: "My tears are blood but my eyes do not close, Sorrow and torment are the food of my mind ..."

After my army service, I told my parents, "I'm going to marry this girl", but they said, "No, first you must go to Australia and establish yourself there. Then we will send her to you." I came to Australia, and after two and a half years became a permanent resident, so I rang my mum and said, "I want to marry Anar now. I can support her." My mum said, "No, we don't like this girl. There are many other girls."

My mum objected because in our culture, girls must be quiet and listen to older women. They must not show their intelligence or have an open mind and they must not be honest about their feelings. Anar was very smart and honest and articulate. She would say that she loved me, and my mum did not approve of that. Never should a girl tell a boy, "I love you."

Love is not sex. If you live with another person and never touch each other, you can love the way you look at each other, the way you communicate, but parents do not understand. I wrote to Anar. Her parents went to see my parents, but because my parents refused their permission, her parents became upset and made her marry someone else. This broke my heart.

To be honest, in our culture there are too many complications about falling in love and marrying, because you cannot marry unless both sets of parents agree. Rarely does true love end in marriage or happiness. But not all love songs are sad. In some, the lovers get together, and the song is about their memories of the happiness they briefly shared. This is not sad for us. It is romantic. In life, there are two worlds: normal life, where you work and mix with other people, and love, where you are with your love, heart to heart, deep inside each other, together inhabiting another world. But mostly in our culture, young people have to deny their love and go with something practical, what their families want, because our parents have more experience and we are too young to make these major life decisions. I made one very big mistake because I did not listen to my friends and family.

After I heard that Anar had married, I married a Filipina in Australia. The marriage lasted 20 days. I lost $23,000 in the two months we were together, because she insisted on a joint bank account and turned out to be a gambling addict. I divorced her. I do not hate her, because it was my mistake and we were from different cultures. Now I will marry someone my parents have chosen. We have a different way of living, and our marriages usually last. I do not care about money, as long as my wife and I are happy, have a roof over our heads, some bread and cheese to eat and respect for each other.

Many Kurdish poems and songs are about a romantic love. They are often sad because, usually, the love is unfulfilled or ends in tragedy. For instance, Aziz Shahrokh sings a love song based on an old poem written in Persian by a Kurdish prince from Bitlis in the late 16th century, about Khadji and Siamand. Khadji was a king's daughter. She and Siamand wanted to marry, but Khadji's father opposed the idea, so one day Siamand secretly took Khadji away. They rode to the mountains, unaware that the king had sent his soldiers after them. On top of a mountain, Siamand slept with his head on Khadji's knee. All of a sudden, Khadji saw a calf and woke Siamand. Thinking the calf was dead, Siamand went over to the animal, but the calf woke and threw him from the mountain to the trees below. The soldiers from the palace approached Khadji, who told them, "Siamand is dead. I do not want to live". Throwing herself off the mountain, she died next to Siamand.

Another Kurdish legend, which has inspired many poems and songs, is at least as old as the Medes. In a big mountain called Keri Bestoon or Bisitun (meaning 'without columns'), between Mahabad and Kirmanshah, there is a huge carving of a man on his horse protruding in high relief from giant cliffs, and another carving in faint lines, visible from eight kilometres away. People say the carvings were done in the time of Cyrus the Great. They show Cyrus and the Medes he put on trial, and there are inscriptions in five languages, including Sumerian, Old Pahlavi, also known as Hawrami, Egyptian hieroglyphics and Greek. As well, there is a cave-like structure, a deep, two-storey tunnel, called Taq Bestoon ('room of Bestoon'), with old cuneiform script and relief carvings along the walls. The legend is that a man called Farhad built the palace of Taq Bestoon to prove his love for Shirin.

Like Khadji, Shirin had a father who was a king and who objected to his daughter's love. He tells Farhad, "If by hand you can cut a tunnel through the mountain and make water run continually, I will give you Shirin." Farhad spent years making the tunnel, digging for a spring and carving the rock. When he finished, he went to the king and asked for Shirin, but the king refused, so Farhad secretly asked Shirin to meet him on Bestoon. He wanted to surprise her with his work of art.

But when Shirin arrived, she found Farhad dead, killed by her father's soldiers with the tools Farhad had used to carve the rock. Like Juliet, Shirin killed herself with one of Farhad's tools, saying, "If there is no Farhad, I do not want to live". The story shows that, with love, you can accomplish the impossible, but it is also a story of betrayal.

Other poems and songs are about our brave fighters, how they and the enemy feel and what they do when they fight. A poem or song might describe how one fighter is equal to 10 of the enemy.

Always there is singing, music and dancing at Newroz. The songs of Newroz celebrate the end of all the cold, rain and snow of winter and the coming of spring's new life, green grass and flowers. It is a time for throwing away all the problems of the passing year, a time to forgive one another, to make a fresh start with a new attitude and a new way of relationship, to be happy. Mostly, Newroz songs are happy songs from the skills of *mahoor* and *shoor*.

Other poems and songs celebrate the beauty of Kurdistan and how much we love our land. For instance, *Agaremo Wajana Bushara Khahom*, sung by Mazhari Khalaqi, is very popular, especially for Kurds now living far from their country. One song says,

"Oh God look after our land and our people, because our land is gold, our water is from heaven and our people's hearts are diamonds."

By far the most famous Kurdish song is *A-Rhaqeeb*, written by the poet Yunis Re'uf (1917–1948), from Koi Sinjak in Iraqi Kurdistan. His poet's name is Dildar. *A-Rhaqeeb* became the Kurdish national anthem when the Kurdish Republic of Mahabad was established in 1946. After 11 months, the Iranian army threatened to attack, and rather than have bloodshed, the president of the republic, Qazi Muhammad, gave himself up. He was put in prison, and hung in March 1947, with other leaders, at an intersection we now call Chwarrah Azadi, 'Intersection of Freedom', only 200 metres from where I lived. So I sing *A-Rhaqeeb* with all my heart.

> Oh observer of life and history, there is a living Kurdish Nation
> No enemy[i] in history[j] can break it.
> *Don't say Kurds are dead, Kurds are alive and will never die.*
> Kurdish youth stand up like heroes
> To draw the crown of life with their blood.
> *Don't say Kurds are dead, Kurds are alive and will never die.*
> We are of Medea and Keyxusrew,[k]
> Our religion and our belief is Kurdistan.
> *Don't say Kurds are dead, Kurds are alive and will never die.*
> We are the sons of red colours and revolutions
> Look how bloody is our past
> *Don't say Kurds are dead, Kurds are alive and will never die.*
> Kurdish youth are always ready,
> Ready to sacrifice their lives.
> *Don't say Kurds are dead, Kurds are alive and will never die.*

To come to Australia, I had to sell my *tar*. I needed the money. In Australia, I began studying the violin and learnt to read music. However, I could not sing while playing the violin, so I began to study the piano. I could not get an Iranian *tar* and I wanted to play classical Iranian-Kurdish music, so I bought a very old *ba'aghlama* with a wonderful sound.

Before I left Kurdistan, the religious police could take people to prison for having a drum, because this drum makes people dance. You must not dance and listen to music. You must fill your ears with the Qur'an. Now, I have heard, this attitude is relaxing. Slowly, even the religious people have come to understand that people cannot live without music. More people are sending their children to music lessons. Although modern Western music is still banned, musicians are being allowed to play traditional Kurdish music, with traditional instruments like the *tar*, *sehtar* and *tapel*. Even so, I have been told that if there is an orchestra playing classical music on television, they do not show the musicians' faces or instruments. They believe that even seeing an instrument can cause bad thoughts!

That is why I am in Australia: I want to become a good musician. Through music and songs, I can be something for my people. We need good Kurdish musicians so that people around the world can appreciate our culture's richness and beauty.

ABOUT Abdulwahab Talabani

Abdulwahab Talabani was born in 1946 in the oil-rich city of Kirkuk. As a child, he would visit Baba Gurrgurr, or 'Place of Fires', where two pools of fire, each about three metres in diameter, have burned for thousands of years. It is where people used to pray to Anita, god of fire, but now the area is closed to the public.

His family had a large library of Kurdish books. When Talabani was 14, his father, a moderate intellectual *malla*,[a] was secretly informed, "Your son must leave Kirkuk". The government had discovered that Talabani was a member of the Kurdistan Democratic Party (KDP) Student Union. He continued his schooling in Sulaimani, having contact with the many writers and poets in that city, until in 1963 the army attacked the city and he and his friends in the student union were arrested at school. While under arrest, Talabani escaped, and joined the KDP *peshmergas* in the mountains at the age of 17. After 18 months, in late 1964, following Mostefa Barzani's negotiations with President Aref's moderate Ba'ath government, Talabani went to Baghdad, where he had access to Kurdish books on history and culture in Baghdad's libraries. After completing his schooling through a technical college, he studied for a degree in applied statistics at the University of Baghdad, also working as a broadcaster for Kurdish Radio in the Ministry of Information.

From 1971 until 1974, Talabani worked as a researcher and demographer in the Ministry of Municipalities' Planning Directorate, and as a journalist for *Al-Ta'akhi*, the KDP newspaper in Baghdad, before returning to the mountains and working as a radio broadcaster for KDP radio. From the early 1970s, the Ba'ath government forced 250,000 Kurdish to leave the Kirkuk area, and in 1974, two of his family's houses in Kirkuk were confiscated. His family moved to the mountains, then to Iran, before returning to Hawler in 1977.

During the amnesty of 1975, following the abrupt end of the Kurdish revolution, Talabani went back to his old job in the Planning Directorate in Baghdad. After a month, he was exiled to the south for four years—working in the Shi'ite towns of Najaf and Amara, then in Saddam Hussein's hometown, Tikrit. In 1979, he returned to Baghdad with the help and protection of a Kurdish friend, Hamid Osman, leader of the Iraqi Communist Party in the 1950s, who remained a respected and influential figure.

From 1980, Talabani worked in Hawler as director of the Arbil branch of the Kurdish Cultural Publishing House. In 1983, he returned to Baghdad to work as an editor for the Kurdish newspaper *Hawkari*, then as the managing editor for the Kurdish magazine *Bayan,* two of the four Kurdish publications published in Baghdad and distributed throughout Iraq. He also worked for *Pa'ashkoi-Iraq*, a Kurdish-Arabic newspaper issued by a Kurdish organisation that had split from the KDP, published through Dar Al-Iraq Press. In 1984 and 1986, he studied journalism in Czechoslovakia and Hungary, after which he became a member of the International Organisation of Journalists. He translated many stories and poems from Kurdish to Arabic and published his own short stories and articles on national and international issues.

Like many Kurdish writers, he felt that by working in the 'Iraqi media machine', he was able to keep alive Kurdish history, culture and language, especially for the 600,000 Kurds who lived in Baghdad. But the work entailed much compromise. The front page of any legal Kurdish magazine or newspaper had to cover the president's activities and statements, the information being received by fax every evening from the Ministry of Information. However, all other pages could be devoted to Kurdish news and issues. There was no censorship at the time of writing and publication, but if a writer directly criticised the regime in an article, they would be questioned by Internal Security. This produced much self-censorship. Most Kurdish writers made compromises so that their writings could be published.

In 1989, he started his own Kurdish newspaper called *Auso*, or The *Horizon*, with 31 staff, until the government closed it down a year later. Between 1990 and 1992, he was editorial manager *of Pa'ashkoi-Iraq* newspaper. After writing some articles critical of Ba'ath policies, including one on the Arabisation of Kirkuk and another on the expense and role of the Kurdish civilian army called the *Forsa'an*, in late 1992 his house was searched twice. He was secretly informed that he was under observation, his life was in danger, and he should leave Baghdad within three days. In November 1992, he and his family escaped to Hawler, where the Kurdish parliament of the no-fly zone was located. Disenchanted with the lack of political cohesion in the Kurdish-controlled territory and aware of the ever-present danger of numerous Iraqi intelligence agents, he and his family escaped to Damascus. Here he worked as a journalist on a Syrian-supported radio program critical of Iraq and for newspapers based in Lebanon and London.

In late 1994, the Iraqi Ba'ath Ministry of Information and Culture issued a decree banning Talabani's writings, recalling all newspapers, magazines and books to which he and other controversial writers had contributed. Realising he was not safe even in Syria, he applied for himself and his family to be accepted as refugees to Australia.

Since arriving in Sydney, on 25 December 1995, he has continued to write, for Australian and overseas Arabic and Kurdish print and electronic media. In March 1998, he launched a weekly Kurdish newspaper, but the venture failed after six months from lack of advertising revenue. He remains concerned that Kurds in Australia do not have access to accurate detailed information about what is happening in Kurdistan. He says, "Having worked for 30 years in the media kitchen, I understand how the news is cooked".

Abdulwahab Talabani is no longer affiliated with a Kurdish political party. He believes all parties have suffered from too much in-fighting and would like to see Kurds in Australia learn to independently express, discuss and accept a diversity of views without feeling they are still under the heels of political leaders back in Kurdistan. He considers the main obstacles to his people's aspirations for autonomy, federalism or an independent homeland are the lack of unity among Kurdish people and the fact that Kurdistan is rich in oil and water. From the

Kurdish mountains, the Euphrates and Tigris rivers supply water to Turkey, Syria and Iraq. Turkey's allies have helped build 12 dams on the Euphrates and a huge dam on the Tigris, all in Kurdistan, both for hydroelectric power and to control water flow. He predicts that water could be a source of conflict in the coming decades. Another prediction is that Kurdish issues can no longer be ignored, especially as Kurds will soon constitute a majority of the population in Turkey.

While in Australia, he has read the poetry of Kath Walker, a leading indigenous poet, and directly relates to her ideas. Abdulwahab Talabani describes Kurdish people as being like the indigenous people of Australia, intimately attached to the land. Every rock, tree and singular feature in or around a Kurdish village, town or mountain is named with meaning and history.

An Introduction to Modern Kurdish Literature

An essay by Abdulwahab Talabani, translated from Kurdish to Arabic by A. Talabani, then into English by Isma'il Qaradghi, with further translations of modern poetry by Sam Zakhary, Myrna Chaar and Udai Joni

In every reading of Kurdish affairs, the Kurd's mouthpiece repeats Faust's famous statement, "In such crowdedness I long to be, to tread on free land in the companionship of a host of liberals". Since 1923, the Kurds have made enormous sacrifices to liberate their land from the occupiers' yokes. These occupiers, fanned by winds of racial hatred and chauvinistic annexation and assimilation, have had the support of international sharks after they smelt the wafting scent of oil, tasted Kurdistan's fresh spring water and sensed the jingling of precious metals underneath its surface. Against this fragmentation of a homeland, along with the shedding of Kurdish blood, Kurdish literature has become a powerful tool of resistance. In defiance of the attempt to extinguish a nation, or perhaps because of this diabolical hell, Kurdish literature has emerged as a humane anthem, reflecting the darkness that overshadows a crucified people.

In this context, it is not surprising to discover that the first known poem written in Kurdish,[a] by an unknown poet over 13,000 years ago, describes invaders who set fire to farms, killed the people and plundered villages. The anonymous poet condemns the invaders and decries their barbaric misconduct. It is also not surprising to know that this poem was found near the town of Halabja, site of a more recent genocide: Saddam Hussein's chemical bombing on 16 March 1988, which killed more than 5000 civilians and injured another 10,000.

Until the 20th century, Kurdish literature was mainly a poetic tradition, echoing a land of fire, snow and honey: the Newroz fires of freedom, lit each spring on the great mountain chains of Taurus, Ararat and Zagros; the hues of timeless rocks, gorges, waterfalls, rivers and distinct seasons; the long, snowbound winters; ancienct forests and meadow carpets woven with the myriad colours of spring's flowers. This dramatically beautiful landscape and its people's passionate life-and-death struggles inspired the universal themes of love and courage, humanity and self-sacrifice, in Kurdish literature.

Historically, the Kurdish dialects in which this literature was written reflected the politics and social developments of each region. The Indo-European language of the Kurds can be divided into two main groups: Northern Kurmanji and Southern Kurmanji. Northern Kurmanji includes a number of dialects and subdialects spoken in Kurdistan of Turkey, Syria and the Dohuk area of northern Iraq. Southern Kurmanji includes a number of dialects spoken in other Kurdish areas of Iraq and Iran. When people talk of the Kurmanji dialect they are referring to Northern Kurmanji, which varies slightly between regions. The main Southern Kurmanji dialects are Sorani-Mukriani, Lur and Hawrami, the Northern Kurmanji dialect of Zaza being closely related to Hawrami.

The different dialects came to prominence in Kurdish literature at different times from the 10th century, according to the rise and fall of Kurdish princedoms such as Botan, Hakkari, Ardalan, Baban and Soran. Thus, when the eastern territories of Luristan and Ardalan enjoyed political stability and power in the 10th century, this was reflected by the great poets Ali Tarmoki and Baba Tahir Hamadani (935–1010), who wrote their immortal poems in the Lur dialect. The realm of poetry then moved to northern Kurdistan during the Botan Princedom of the 11th century. In Botan, the poets Ali Hariri (1010–1077), Sufi mystic Malla Ahmedi Jeziri (also known as Seyida Ehmedi Ceziri, died 1200)[187] and Feqiye Teyra (1307–1375) distinguished themselves. Their poetic tradition culminated in the writings of the great philosophical poet Ahmedi Khani, also spelt Ehmedi Xani (1650–1706), who mastered a mixture of Kurmanji subdialects.

In the 18th and early 19th centuries, the realm of poetic creativity again moved south, where the great classical poets Nali (1797–1855), Wafa'i (1800–1866), Mahwi (1830–1905) and Kurdi (1809–1849) wrote in the Sorani-Mukriani dialect. To the east, the great Sufi poet Mawlawi (1806–1882) composed his masterpieces of love in the Hawrami dialect.

Following the emergence of the Baban and Soran princedoms, in the 19th century, and the Iraqi Kurdish National Movement of the 1920s, and due to the outlawing of the Kurdish language in Turkey and the more liberal attitude in Iraq and Iran, the literature in the 20th century has tilted towards the Sorani-Mukriani dialect. This dialect absorbed a great deal of the atmosphere, environment and vocabulary of the other branches, and became the official Kurdish language in southern Kurdistan's schools. Nevertheless, despite its outlawing, writing in the Northern Kurmanji dialect has continued, with the appearance of many verse collections, stories, newspapers and other literary works in this branch of Kurdish.

What hampers the reading of Kurdish literature is that Southern Kurmanji varieties use an Arabic-based alphabet, while modern Northern Kurmanji uses the Latin script in Turkey and the Cyrillic script in Armenia, Georgia and Russia. Given this diversity of Kurdish scripts, many Kurdish intellectuals are looking for some scientific criteria that

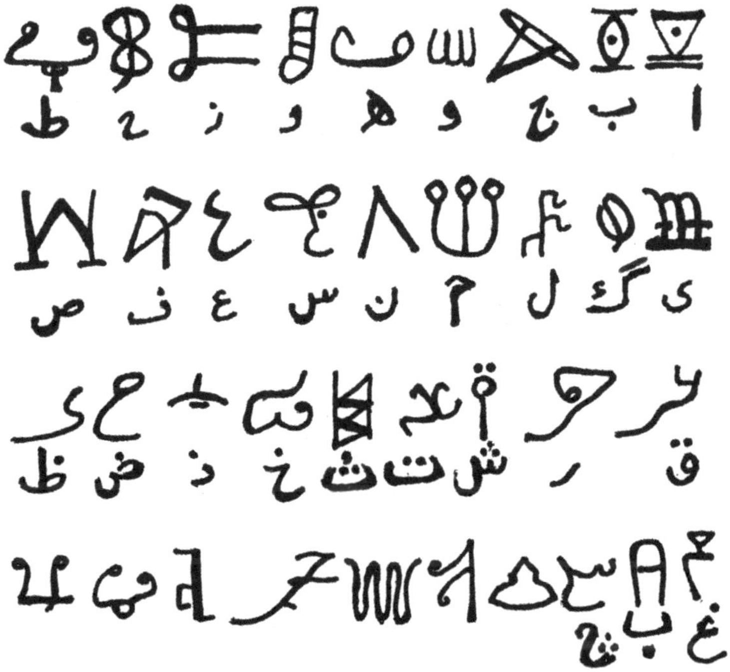

Pre-Islamic Kurdish Alphabet (with Arabic-Farsi equivalents)

will eventually bring together a unified literary standard, modern radio and television often using a mixture of spoken dialects.

Before a Kurdish literature developed, an extensive folklore of proverbs, poems and stories was passed from generation to generation, through a highly evolved oral tradition. Its extent causes a number of Orientalists to agree that Kurds are poets and storytellers by nature.[188] The land and its people's experiences have always ignited a flame of passion in the Kurdish heart and a love of beauty, nature, woman, life, fire and freedom as eternal and deeply rooted as the ancient fires of Baba Gurrgurr.

Within this oral tradition, there are thousands of proverbs, epigrams and witticisms that graphically expose the conditions of Kurdish life, imparting social ethics and standards of behaviour. Through them we are told:

> If you cannot be a flower, do not be a thorn.
> If one wishes to be a horseman, one must be prepared to fall off the horse.
> Truth is bitter.
> Among a thousand words, only two are useful.

Thanks to the scholarship of Shaykh Muhammed i Khal and Ala Din Sejadi in the 1950s, these sayings from southern Kurdistan have been collected, written, explained and published as anthologies.

Likewise, an oral tradition has preserved thousands of morality tales, which often employ anthropomorphised animals to act out the human condition and the relevant aphorism. All this folklore reveals a deep humanity, using allegory to express the human being's limitless capacity for love and suffering.

Based on the earlier oral tradition, Kurdish folk literature has immortalised many tragic love tales with political overtones, the most famous being *Khadji and Siamand, Mem of Alan* (or *Muhammad of the Alan Mountain*), and *Shirin and Farhad*, in the tradition of Romeo and Juliet. These tales and many more are woven into the Kurdish consciousness. They throb with the people's journeys between winter dwellings and summer pastures, the first whispers of love blowing like a breeze over the season's harvest, fanned by the fires and feasts of Newroz. For although Kurdish history is male-dominated, its folklore and literature revering the heroes of many uprisings, such as Isma'il Agha Shikak, Shaykh Mahmud Hafeed and Shaykh Seyid Piran, 'woman' is ever present. All love is hers: she is the beloved, the symbol of land and freedom, the lady who ruled and who fought wars throughout Kurdish history. Among such women are Qadam-Khair, Princess Khanzad of Rowandoz, and the Fayli Queen of the Lur, who ruled in the 16th century and in the early 18th century, respectively, Adela Khanum (also known as Adela Xatun), from the Jaf tribe of Halabja, and the truly great Hapsa Khan Naqib, from Sulaimani. In the 1990s, Leyla Zana joined these ranks of heroines when she was sentenced to 15 years in prison for speaking about Kurds in the Turkish parliament, expressing her voters' will that Kurds and Turks live as brothers.

Despite a rich oral storytelling and poetic tradition, up until the 1950s there were only isolated examples of novels and writings about history, sociology, politics and literature in the Kurdish language. Kurdistan's neighbours—to the east the Persians, to the west the Turks and to the south the Arabs—attempted to dominate the literature of the day. The state of affairs imposed on the Kurdish nation meant that many Kurdish writers were forced to land on the shores of other languages in order to express the spirit of their people. Consequently, the Kurdish Prince of Bitlisi wrote the first great book of Kurdish history and culture in classical Persian, in 1598. Amir Sharaf Khan Bitlisi served as a military officer for the Savafid Empire, but when the Shi'ite Savafids discriminated against his Sunni Kurdish background, he escaped to Istanbul and became a military leader for the Ottomans. He retired to work on his masterpiece, the *Sharafnameh*, which is the most important source of Kurdish history. In it, he describes each tribe and the 20 Kurdish emirates. It has been translated twice into Kurdish, the first time by Muhammad Owni Kurd and the second by Jamil Rojbiani, and also into Arabic, Turkish and French. Some sections have been translated into English.

In the 20th century, many Kurdish writers have made great contributions to the cultural heritage of their adopted language, so much so that Adonis, a contemporary poet from Syria, claims that the key to the Arabic language lies in the pocket of the Kurdish poet and novelist Salim Barakat. Barakat, also a journalist, came from Kurdistan of Syria but now lives in Sweden. He has written many important poems and novels. Two of his greatest novels are *Areesh* (*The Feathers*) and *The Dark Preachers*. His romantic style is unique in its lucidity and his sophisticated command of the Arabic language unsurpassed, yet although he is considered by Arab intellectuals to be one of the greatest writers in Arab literature, the majority of his creative writings reflect the experiences of his people. As he says, "I write the beats of my Kurdish soul in the Arabic language." In so doing, he takes no heed of the criticism levelled against him by some fanatical political writers.

Likewise, the late Abdul-Mecid Lutfi from Khanaqin, in southern Kurdistan, wrote scores of short stories in the Arabic language about Iraqi society during the 1960s and '70s, but never denied his identity. His stories are peopled with Kurdish characters expressing a Kurdish point of view.

Another outstanding writer, Yashar Kamal, wrote his best novels in Turkish, but his symbols of the white horse of freedom and birds flying over fires and lakes atop Kurdish mountains are rooted in his affiliation with his people and their beliefs. In 1996, the Turkish government threatened to take Kamal to court after he wrote of a mountain lake being converted to steam but its fish miraculously surviving. Fortunately, court action was avoided, following protests from international literary organisations.

Like the storywriters, the poets of the early 20th century often wrote in the foreign language of the occupiers. The late Bilind Al-Haydari, from southern Kurdistan, who spent the last years of his life in Britain, was one of five innovators who left behind the constrictions of the classical tradition of Arab poetry. His legacy is considered a momentous contribution to modern Arabic poetry, as is the poetry of another pioneer, the late Abdulwahab Al-Bayati, whose mother was a Kurd and whose father was from the ethnically mixed tribe of Bayat (Kurd, Arab and Turkoman).

It was not until the 1920s that the first novel was published in the Kurdish language. *In My Dream* was written by Jamil Saa'ib and describes the time when Shaykh Mahmud ruled Sulaimani. Like so many literary figures before and after him, Saa'ib had ideals for his people not matched by the reality of his times, and it is thought there is a link between the content of his short novel and his assassination in unknown circumstances.

In 1956, the poet Ibrahim Ahmed, then secretary of the Kurdistan Democratic Party (KDP), experimented with the short-story form, such as in a tale about a Kurdish family called *Ja'ani Gal* or *The People's Suffering*. By the 1960s, there had emerged a whole generation of short-story writers who had been exposed to the European short-story tradition. They include Kaka Mem Botani, Jihan Omar, Ahmed Muhammad Isma'il, Muhammad Rasheed Fattah, Dr Kawis Qaftan, Ra'uf Begerd, Hasan Jaf, Muhammad Mawlood (also known as Mem) and Muharram Muhammad Emin, from southern Kurdistan, Abdullah Sarraj, who now lives in Finland, and Hasan Kezelchi, from eastern Kurdistan, all of whom describe contemporary Kurdish society.

Mostefa Saleh Karim was one prolific writer who set a story in the 1600s, retelling the legend of Khano'i Lapzerin, or *The Prince With the Golden Hand*. Lapzerin's broken hand had been replaced by one of gold. He was appointed prince by Isma'il Safavi, Shah of Iran, and built his kingdom in the Bradost Mountains, constructing high on a hill a huge walled fortress town, which he called Qala'i Dimdim. After his power was established, he announced that he was King of Kurdistan. He printed his own currency and refused to pay taxes to the Shah. The Shah's army surrounded Qala'i Dimdim and demanded he surrender. He refused. Food became short, so he told his people, "You may go out of the city or stay with me. If we do not surrender, all they will take are our corpses." An *imam* decided to tell the Safavid army of Qala'i Dimdim's secret water supply, which was deep inside the hill but outside the town's walls. It could be accessed by another underground tunnel, which surfaced outside these walls, so the Safavids were able to block the water.

Khano'i Lapzerin smuggled his son out of Qala'i Dimdim, then gave his people another choice: "Leave now or we will burn together." On 5 December 1608, his people set fire to the town. When the Safavid army entered, all they found were ashes. They could not even find the *imam* who had told them of Qala'i Dimdim's secret, but the people survived, through Khano'i Lapzerin's son.

A second and third wave of short-story writers includes Shirzad Hasan and Salam Menmi, who rose to prominence in the 1970s, and Salah Omar, Jelil Kaka Weys and Shirin Kamal in the 1980s. They all wrote stories set in Kurdistan but dealing with universal themes. Many have been translated into Arabic and English. Shirzad Hasan is one of the most perceptive of these writers. His stories of Kurdish life are layered with magic realism and his recent novel *Hasar* (*Big House*) has received much acclaim.

The first full-length Kurdish novel was written in 1959, by the outstanding writer Rahimi Qazi, from eastern Kurdistan. It is called *Peshmerga*, meaning 'those who face death without fear'. Qazi follows the *peshmergas'* daily life (walking from village to village, falling in love with village girls), and describes how they established a democratic republic in Mahabad in 1946.

The post-1960s period witnessed dynamic activity both in political developments and in literature. Poetic treasures from the 10th century were authenticated, collected, analysed and published by the scholars of proverbs already mentioned and others, such as Muhammad Ali Qaradaghi, Abdul Karim Al-Mudarris, a Kurd who was Mufti of Iraq in the 1980s and a very wise thinker, and his son Muhammad i Mullah Abdul-Karim, a progressive. While father and son do not agree on some religious matters, they have written and published numerous collections together. Other scholars of literature are Izzuddin Mostefa Rasoul, who wrote *Realism in Kurdish Literature* and *Ahmedi Khani—The Thinker, The Poet, The Philosopher*, and Ma'ruf Khaznadir, who wrote about the great classical poet Nali.

As well, Turkish, Persian, Arabic and English literature was being translated by the distinguished Abdullah Hasan-Zadeh, a man of letters from eastern Kurdistan, and Shukr Mostefa, a member of the Kurdish Scientific Academy in Baghdad who now lives in Hawler, among others.

Until this time, Kurdish literature suffered from a lack of academic analysis. Criticisms were no more than ordinary newspaper articles, but in the 1960s, the scholarship of Refiq Hilmi, who wrote the first history of Kurdish poetry, and of Ala Din Sejadi, the writer of *A History of Kurdish Literature*, laid the path for the critics of the 1970s—people like Kamal Ghambar, Fuad Majid Misri, Fuad Qaradaghi, Azad Abdulwahid and Beroj Akreyi.

As a result of their analyses in newspapers and magazines, writing flourished, and today there are three bright names in Kurdish novel-writing. One is Muhammad Mukri, from Kirkuk, whose most famous novels are *Ejdiha* (*The Dragon*) and *Segwer* (*The Bark of Dogs*), a very brave novel written from personal experience, critically exposing the activities of Kurdish political leaders and others. Mukri was a non-aligned *peshmerga*, a true independent, well known for saying exactly what he thought.

The second novelist is Hussein Aref, who wrote *Sharr* (*The City*). The main character in the novel is his city of birth, Sulaimani, the cultural capital of Kurdistan. Its history is described in terms of a character's development, as influenced by the various forces at play and by its people, such as a *malla*, a communist and a teacher. These subsidiary characters come and go, often illustrating social taboos and reflecting the changing mood and atmosphere of the city.

The third novelist, and perhaps the greatest, is Bakhtiyar Ali Muhammad, who wrote *Marrgi Taqanay Doowam* (*The Second Lonely Death*), a black epic set in Sulaimani. Having found asylum in Germany, he is an avid reader of European literature, using language like a poet, making the reader dance with words, images and deep ideas within an excitingly rich narrative that spares nothing. He is bold in his subject matter, multilayed in his symbolism and modern in his techniques. His magic-realist style brings us closer to the controversial issues about which he writes and has been likened to that of South American writer Gabriel Garcia Marquez. Through strange, almost unbelievable events in his characters' lives, he examines his society and the effects on his people of the Ba'ath regime's political, economic and social corruptions.

As for theatre, its roots in southern and eastern Kurdistan go back to the 1920s. In 1946, the Kurdistan Republic in Mahabad set up a community theatre, and after 1958, local theatre groups were established in southern Kurdistan, culminating in the 1980s, which saw a theatrical renaissance in Sulaimani, Hawler and Dohuk. These theatre groups would perform in different towns, offering a new experience for many Kurds.

The late Rafiq Chalak, writer, actor, journalist and communist, pioneered this new dramatic movement. After returning from Palestine, where he had been working with the great modern Kurdish poet Abdullah Goran in Jaffa Radio, he was imprisoned for his political views. On his release, he worked for Kurdish Radio in Baghdad. Then, in the late 1950s and 1960s, he started writing plays. One was based on Ahmedi Khani's narrative poem *Mem U Zin*.

Most of the prominent 1970s playwright-actor-directors were graduates of the Baghdad Academy of Fine Arts, except for Jalil Zangna, who learnt from experience. They include Ahmed Salar, Tal'at Sama'an and, from the 1980s, Shamal Abdullah. All these writers continue to live in Kurdistan. Ahmed Salar began by directing the European classics of Sophocles and Shakespeare, before creating his own plays, based on the Kurdish classics, to expose the contemporary experience. He used very sophisticated poetic language to recreate the stories of historical figures such as Nali, who was exiled to Istanbul after the Savafids invaded Baban. Others writers of theatre live in exile. These include the actor-director Shamal Omar and his wife, Nigar Hasib Qaradaghi, based in Holland, who have started their own experimental dramatic movement.

Unlike southern Kurdistan, northern Kurdistan has a very long tradition of village dances that are more like theatrical events, reliving historical milestones and legends. In the second half of the 20th century, youth groups in Diyarbakir secretly began performing theatrical scenarios in the suburbs. It was a dangerous pastime in Turkey, where public performances in the Kurdish language remain illegal.

The greatest Kurdish filmmaker, Yilmaz Guney, is from northern Kurdistan. He is famous for writing and directing movies from inside Turkish prisons, his friends smuggling out the script and his directions. Born in 1937 in a village outside Adana, he studied cinema in 1954 and became a projectionist. He began writing short stories and scenarios, but for one of these, called *Three Secret Reasons for an Unequal Society*, he was imprisoned in 1958. In 1963, he was released. He continued to write and make films, for which he found himself in and out of prison. In 1974, he was sentenced to 19 years' imprisonment, during which time he wrote his most famous screenplay, *Yoll* (*The Road*), about five Kurdish criminals who are let out of prison for a week to visit their families. The screenplay relates little of the prison's brutality, concentrating on family life.

In 1981, Guney escaped from prison and went to Paris, where he made *Yoll*, before dying in 1984, aged 50. Despite his troubled life, he made 119 films.

Above all literary forms, it is poetry, considered the highest art form throughout the Middle East, in which Kurdish writers traditionally have excelled. Until modern poets dared break the mould, all Middle Eastern poetry was governed by strict rules of prosody concerning rhyme and rhythm. It was besieged within the walls of the mosques, the *takia* or religious schools that studied *sharia* law, and fed the poor on Fridays, and the princes' palaces and mansions of the tribal chieftains, and invariably imbedded with mystic philosophy and its manifestations. Its themes of sorrow, love, religion and praise of the powerful were explored in an ornamental, euphuistic and rhetorical use of language, achieving the highest musicality and eloquence. When written in Kurdish, it borrowed many words from Arabic, Persian or Turkish.

The first known poet to write in Kurdish was Ali Tarmoki, who lived in the 10th century. He wrote his poems on the leather of the gazelle and on paper brought from China along the Silk Route. After him came Baba Tahir Hamadani (935–1010), who composed poetry using the Persian style and rhythms, although he employed the language of the Lur. He introduced the quatrain to Kurdish poetry and dealt with religious and esoteric themes.

But even classical Kurdish poetry was not devoid of nationalistic undertones. The poems of Malla Ahmedi Jeziri, from the 16th-century Botan Court in northern Kurdistan, clearly express a love of nation, and a sense of nationalism is encountered in the first epic narrative poem of Kurdish literature, a tragic love story called *Mem u Zin*, composed by Ahmedi Khani (1650–1706). In the deep structure of this tragic love story is a description of an era of national subjection and coercion of the Kurdish people, and its instigatory tone encourages a vision of salvation from foreign domination, calling for a national renaissance. These were also the preoccupations of the great nationalist poet Haji Qadir Koyi (1815–1892) from Koya, in southern Kurdistan.

The same tone, though lower in pitch, appears in the elegant poetry of the Kurdish poet Nali (1797–1855) from Sulaimani, one of the princes of classicism, among whom are Wafa'i (1800–1866), Mahwi (1830–1905) and Kurdi (1809–1849). Perhaps the greatest of all was Mawlawi (1806–1882), the *imam* of the *Ghazal*, a poetry of love in all its forms.

Shaykh Reza Talabani (1835–1910) was another poet of this time whose singular voice featured a rebellious ironic tone. He was uninhibitedly courageous in satirising and revealing the malpractices and social abuses of the time, sparing not even his relatives from his acid tongue. In his poem about the Baban princedom of Sulaimani in the 19th century, he says of Baban: "(It) neither surrendered to the Persian's Rule, Nor submitted to the slavery of the Ottoman's." He was fearless in using very rude words and erotic imagery. Thus he writes: "Although my age is eighty, My manhood is as iron..."

While an oral tradition of poetry has always been popular in Kurdistan, until the second half of the 20th century Kurdish poetry in literary form was inaccessible to the common people, the main reason being the very low level of literacy. Teaching was limited to religious schools and mosques, attended by a small minority. Moreover, the language of tuition was either Arabic or Persian. True, a few enlightened clergy played a significant role in preserving Kurdish as a literary language, writing poems and becoming spokesmen for their people, but the majority taught and wrote in Arabic or Persian, for religious reasons. Another obstacle was that publications and other means of communication like radio were virtually non-existent. Poems were often written by hand on scraps of paper and circulated from person to person.

The cause of this backwardness is threefold: the isolation and land-locked nature of the Kurdish mountains, all overland routes requiring journeys into neighbouring territories; the feudal system, made stronger by the powerful Ottoman and Savafid Empires; coupled with the power of the clergy. It suited the purposes of the Ottoman sultans and Persian Shahs to strengthen the affluence of the tribal chiefs, in return for their loyalty in times of war, or as a force against anyone disobeying the 'rightful ruler'. These feudal *aghas* were usually supported directly or indirectly by the clergy, who had great influence over the people. Their powerful message was that whoever disobeyed the Ottoman caliph or Persian Shah was a 'non-believer'.

As a consequence, although a few tribal leaders led isolated rebellions, any secular education or sense of Kurdish identity was actively discouraged. The Kurdish people were kept in isolation by the empires, their intermediaries and *aghas*, leading to widespread ignorance, poverty and disease. Even the aristocrats and princes' sons had little access to anything other than a religious education, if that, and a limited knowledge of their neighbouring princedoms.

The majority of Kurds were farmers, who were openly exploited, yet the limited urban population fared no better. The detrimental policy of imposing the ruler's language on Kurdish society, which could be effectively enforced in the towns and cities, meant that the empires' languages of Turkish or Persian were seen as the languages of the educated. High social status was attached to imitating the appearance, behaviour, conduct and speech of the rulers, and thus the Kurdish city elite often abandoned their language and culture.

Another blow to Kurdish language, literature and education followed the creation of the Republic of Turkey in 1923, after which the Kurdish language was outlawed. In the 1940s, the Turkish gendarmerie would fine Kurdish farmers going to town to sell their livestock five Turkish kurush for every Kurdish word spoken, at a time when one sheep was worth 50 kurush.[189]

Despite this and other forms of coercion, Kurdish villagers continued to speak Kurdish, knowing no other language. Retaining their language and traditions in the unruly topography of Kurdistan enabled the Kurds to survive as a nation.

Realising that the countryside was the fountainhead of Kurdish identity, the 20th-century regimes that control Kurdistan began eliminating Kurdish villages and deporting Kurds into non-Kurdish villages and cities. The first to do so was Turkey. It began its deportation policy during World War One, when militant nationalist unionists led by statesmen Talat Pasha and Enver Pasha decreed a 'holy war' on the Armenians. While the Armenians were being slaughtered, it was decreed that Kurds must be deported from Kurdistan, and distributed among Turkish villages in a number not to exceed five per cent of the total population. This policy was continued by President Mistefa Kemal after 1923 and is still going on. It is estimated that eight million Kurds have been deported from their homeland, and since 1984, 4000 Kurdish villages have been destroyed in Turkey. Thus, modern Kurdish literature for the estimated 19 million Kurdish people who live in Turkey is seeded on very hard rock.

Across the border, the policies of ethnic cleansing in Iraqi Kurdistan up until 1975 were more sporadic. As early as 1920, the British Secretary for War, Winston Churchill, advised that Kurds and Afghanis should be bombed using chemicals, to 'teach them a lesson'.[190] In the 1930s, Prime Minister Yaseen Al-Hashimi ordered Arab clans to settle in Hawijah, near Kirkuk.[191] Between 1975 and 1991, President Saddam Hussein removed all life from the countryside, destroying more than 4000 Kurdish villages, deporting the people and killing about 250,000, and burning and poisoning the farmlands. This genocide climaxed in the chemical bombing of Kurdish villages and the town of Halabja in 1987–88.

In Iran and Syria, the measures have not been so excessive, but in Iran, hundreds of Kurdish villages have been destroyed, scores of thousands of Kurds deported, distinguished Kurdish leaders executed and many people imprisoned. In Syria, for a short period in the early 1960s, the government deported Kurds from border villages and replaced them with Arabs. As well, 200,000 Kurds lost their citizenship.

Tormented by these raging storms, the Kurdish people nevertheless managed to establish a number of progressive cultural and political organisations. On 22 April 1898, Miqdad Bedrxan established the first Kurdish newspaper, in Cairo. Due to Ottoman pressure, it relocated to Europe, but after 21 issues was forced to close. This did not stop other newspapers starting, in the midst of a renaissance of Kurdish consciousness, largely due to the Kurdish uprisings in Iraq, Turkey and Iran from the 1920s until the present day. The growing awareness has been aided by advancements in the means of communication, including radio, the first Kurdish radio station starting in 1936 in Baghdad.

Another advancement was in the area of travel. Roads were built to serve the military but indirectly benefited the Kurds. There was also greater access to publishing, and in southern Kurdistan, when Iraq was a British Protectorate, the Kurdish language became the language of tuition in the 1920s, when Shaykh Mahmud's sister-in-law, Adela Khanum, set up the first Kurdish schools, one for boys and one for girls, in Sulaimani.

In the second half of the 20th century, the number of literate Kurds has increased exponentially. Illiterate parents have given top priority to their children's education, often having to move from their village to do so. The greater access to education and the many Kurdish uprisings have meant that the cobwebs of feudalism and unquestioned autocracy are gradually being torn aside. This has led to considerable progress in the extent, quality and innovation of Kurdish literature, particularly poetry.

New voices began to be heard. They were born from modern circumstances, rather than in the traditional atmospheres of classical poetry, which served only an esoteric-loving elite. The modern poets sought to break the constricting chains of the classical forms in both style and content, to express the essence of the Kurdish reality in a unique personal voice, yet one to which everyone could relate. No longer bound by puns and word plays, their words pulsate with the life of their people, their poetry becoming known as 'realistic poetry' or 'prosaic poetry'.

This revolution in poetry began in the late 1940s. The poets of the 1940s, such as Ahmed Hardi, Muhammad Saleh Dilan, Kakai Falah, Dilzar, Medhoosh and Hesip Qaradaghi, continued writing in the classical style about mystical Sufi subjects, using words woven like silk. However, others, employing the classical rules, began opening the horizons of their subject matter to deal with their people's everyday life and their nation's fight for freedom. In this group of poets are Asiri (died 1950), Ahmed Mukhtar Jaf (1896–1935), Sahab-Qoran (died 1936), Faieq Bekas (1905–1948), Ziwar (died 1948), Bakhtiyar Ziwar (1908–1952), Ka'ani (died 1967), Jasim Jelil, Ali Bapir Agha, Sabri Botani (died 1999 in Sweden), Hemen Mahabadi[b] (1921–1986) and Hejar Mukriani (1921–1991). Also in this group is Yunis Re'uf Dildar (1918–1948), who wrote the poem *A-Rhaqeeb* (*'Observer'*), which became the national anthem for the Kurdish Republic of Mahabad in 1946.

In both form and subject matter, Pire-Merd (1867–1950) and Shaykh Salam (died 1959) were the bridge-builders between the classicists and the innovative realists. Shaykh Nuri Shaykh Saleh (1905–1958) kindled the first flames, relying on the stress and accentuated stress of Kurdish folk poetry rather than on the metre and prosody of the classical forms. But it was the great poet Abdullah Goran (1904–1962) who really dared to challenge the poetic castles of the princes of classicism. He laid the foundations of modern Kurdish poetry, pioneering a personal realism of sweet melodies liberated from conventions.

In his *Caravan of Modern Kurdish Poetry*,[192] the poet Kakai Falah describes how Goran lived in hell from the moment he was born until he died, but argues that his catastrophic life fed his talents and originality. Born in Halabja, Goran was not yet three years of age when his father died. His uncle took care of him briefly, until he also died. This left his mother as sole carer during and after World War One, a time of famine and British occupation. In 1923, when the British used their air force in the Sulaimani region of Iraqi Kurdistan for the first time to put down a people's uprising, he and his mother were forced to flee to the mountains, along with many others. Goran's poem *Ta'awe Negera* (*An Irretrievable Moment*) reflects his sentiments about what was happening:

> The wheel of fortune did not retrieve for me one moment of chance,
> Never is the string of my violin without sadness, not even for a second …

Goran's early poems employed the highly atmospheric, euphuistic language of the classics, until he came under the influence of the Turkish innovative writers Tofik Fikret, Jelal Sahir, Abdul-Haq Hamit and others, as well as his countrymen Shaykh Nuri Shaykh Saleh and Abdul-Rahman Nafoos. Subsequently, he developed a poetry stripped of the classical laudatory panegyrics and amorous clichés that so much depended on borrowed ideas and words. His poems came to rely on an organic unity of form, subject and meaning, and a mastery of powerful personal imagery that reverberates in the reader's mind. Yet, in his lifetime, this new poetry was to bring him merciless derision from those who considered the classical forms inviolable.

In defiance of the relentless disparagement of his poetry, Goran's life experiences made him a true free thinker and, above all, a clinger to ideals. He saw the European West as endorsing and perpetuating the reactionary and racist Middle Eastern regimes' policies of exterminating the ordinary people, particularly his own Kurdish nation. Initially a leftist, he later distanced himself from communist orthodoxy. He came to hate every shackle and restrictive net that cages thought and freedom or denies the right to life and justice. Always affiliated with the poor and downtrodden, those who lack even the freedom to cry out their complaints, he writes:

> Prior to anything else, it is because I am a Kurd
> That, like a sparrow, I am placed in a thousand-threaded net.
> My flying wing is weeping bitterly.
> The knife is so close to my neck,
> That, even if I am a nightingale, as long as I am in the cage
> I am tongue-tied, dumb ...

Goran was self-educated, yet had a good knowledge of the English, Turkish, Persian and Arabic languages and their literature. This scholarship empowered his poetry to ring with the resounding bells of innovation and personal truth, but not without personal cost. He often strained against the incongruities in his life, suffering from confusion and feelings of inadequacy. Thus, to the Kurdish folk musician Darwish (or Dervish) Abdullah, he writes:

> I've listened so often to the spirit of foreign music
> That my Kurdish taste is disturbed, oh Darwish Abdullah.
> Help me by chanting your La'ook, Ay-Ay and Hayran[c]
> That are the people's genuine taste, to cure and overwhelm my sad soul.
> You, Darwish, are much more versed in my soul and closer to it than Beethoven.
> Darwish, go ahead and sing the complaint of the soul.

Many of Goran's poems are about nature, love and feminine beauty, but he expressed these sensual equations in an internal voice, which revealed ever-deeper meaning. One of his poems, *Dwa Serinj* (*The Last Side-Glance*), serves as an example of his inner world:

> Oh, blonde girl, tall girl,
> Why do you stand before me in my weakness?
> Why do you hold your sad chin in your hand
> As you see me driven away?
> I see the butterfly intending to converse.
> Two hearts stand on your rose lips.
> Alas, I wish it would fly. I wish I knew
> What it has in store for the sorrowful soul.
> But Ehrehem, who sees to it that the gardens' leaves fade and wither
> Is upset at hearing the Kurdish birds' singing.
> The forest hunter, who disturbed the quiet, set the net
> Upon the area where the innocent bird will feed on grains ...

This silent dialogue between two strangers was inspired by a moment when a beautiful woman witnessed Goran being transported in chains from Mosul prison to Kirkuk prison after he had been arrested for his progressive ideas. To Goran, she seemed to understand the depth of his tragedy and returned his questioning desire. He yearns to know what she might have said to him, but Ehremen, the symbol of evil in ancient Zoroastrian mythology, stands between them as the source of life's misfortune, the fountainhead of withering gardens and misery. Yet Goran rejects Ehremen's unjust laws, the forest hunter's disfigurement of nature in a place where even a Kurdish woman's beauty can be seen only in terms of sorrow and loss. One cannot fail to see in this kaleidoscope imagery the myriad-levelled parallels with a nation besieged by the hunter and the demonic. Thus, a momentary personal experience is transformed into a statement about a nation.

Goran died on 18 November 1962, leaving a considerable legacy. His use of the Kurdish folk rhythms of five beats to a line and his reliance on the depth and musicality of the Kurdish language were inherited by the generations of poets who came after him. Through his influence, these modern poets launched into new creative spaces that went to the heart of the changes in Kurdish society.

With the intensification of the Kurdish revolution in southern Kurdistan in the 1960s and 1970s, the new generation of poets wrote with a firepower reflecting the armed struggle. They were well versed in progressive nationalist ideology and multiple foreign languages, and aided by translations of Middle Eastern and European literature. Their poetry reflected the impact of the international movements of modernism and postmodernism, leftist ideology, Western surrealism and Dadaism. For example, one of the new forms was called 'poster poetry'. Pioneered by Kameran Mukri, poster poems are only two to six lines, loaded with meaning, power and even shock. One example reads:

> I went to sow in the fields
> To find the children's toys buried under the earth.

A number of manifestoes were published to charge the new creative energies. The most important of these was Th*e Ruwangeh Group Manifesto*, *ruwangeh* meaning 'vision', declared on 14 July 1970. It was signed by the poets Jalal Mirza Karim, Sherko Bekas, Latif Helmet and Jamal Sharbajeri and the novel and short-story writers Hussein Aref, Kaka Mem Botani and Faha'ad Shakeli, among others. Likewise, in 1995, a declaration was published in the *Weran* periodical under the title Th*e First Manifesto of Leftist Poetry*, signed by the poet Ferid Zamdar and other avant-garde poets in Hawler, calling for a 'new' experiment in the writing of leftist poetry. Modern Kurdish poetry is full of such revitalising movements, which act like running rivers taking their course with each generation.

The modern poets were aided by the publication potential in southern Kurdistan, which was far greater than that of eastern or northern Kurdistan. Like Goran, they focused on personal observations, daily events and values to uncover the secrets of the human experiment. They aimed to express their own intuition, an inner vision of the moment, sometimes supported by an ideology, using boldly audacious language and even spelling to dynamically extend the breakthroughs of Goran. No subject was taboo.

No longer relying on borrowed words and rarely veiling reality in esoteric vagueness and hypocrisy, they wrote, sometimes on cardboard, often by hand, their poems being read in the teahouses, in the caves that shelter the Kurdish revolutionaries, in the schools and on the buses.

It must be admitted that not all of the modern poets were, or are, as capable as others in steering the internal content and rhythms into a cohesive organic whole reflecting the 'true self' of modern poetry, but all eloquently express the pain of their people. The best of them rise above party politics and shabby sociopolitical conventions to deal with the greater Kurdish reality. They are truthful, natural and unafraid of censorship. Their use of historical, natural and humanitarian symbols cuts to the core. Defiant in form, tone and subject matter, they dare question their 'masters' in their attempts to understand people and events, to comprehend the heart of the matter. Their wish is to free the mind's siege and embrace the paradoxes of love and hate by making new relationships between words, between ideas and between words and ideas, to create a new harmony.

One of the greatest proponents of the modern form is Dr Rafiq Sabir, born in 1950. Sabir grew up in the town of Qaladiza, which was destroyed and dozens of its inhabitants killed by Saddam Hussein's aerial bombing of 1974. Sabir's poetry rises out of the injustices he experienced in his first 25 years and from the memories of Qaladiza's rubble. After graduating from the College of Literature at the University of Baghdad, where he studied languages, and classical and modern poetry, he wrote poetry and articles in newspapers and magazines. In 1978 he left his homeland for Bulgaria, only to return to Kurdistan and join the *peshmerga* in the mountains in 1979. In 1982, he again left Kurdistan, to continue his studies in philosophy and sociology in Belgrade, where in 1987 he obtained a doctorate on *The Role of Broad Knowledge in the Consciousness of the Kurdish Nation*. His acute feelings of alienation in exile made him return to Kurdistan, before he escaped yet again to live in Sweden, where in 1993 he published his first collection of poetry. He now manages a Kurdish cultural magazine called *Rarboon*.

From his painful memories, Rafiq Sabir explores the cruelty and bitter truth clouding his and his people's lives and souls. He gives voice to the voiceless, writing of the agonies and dreams of spirit, mountain and nation. In *The Beggar*, he observes the strange, lonely labyrinths of the exiled:

> I realise there exists no other time beyond the present.
> Beyond 'here' there is no other place for me.
> I am the lost wanderer.
> My personal death has been my guide so far.
> I am that beggar who spread his prayer rug across your door.
> I am the beggar approaching your hands
> For the things I have lost,
> For the times that suddenly vanished.
> I beg for light.
> I beg for freedom.
> I beg for those unfaithful words
> That never arrived at the rendezvous.

The aloneness and alienation of the exiled, disconnected from their childhood, touches a nerve in *There, at the Alley's Eclipse*:

> Scattered in railway stations,
> In ports,
> In the city taverns.
> Were you pursuing your childhood
> There amid the alleys of murdered Qaladiza?

And, later in the same poem:

> You resembled a void between two voids.
> In your paralysis, you were like a corpse.
> But your childhood was
> A star afraid of its orbit …

Sabir's poem *Vigilant* reflects the Kurdish people's sense of betrayal, when it asks:

> Why do we believe the morning when it shreds its own dawn?
> Why give due to death if it does not give meaning to life?

Rafiq Sabir is witness to the torment of oppression: the unnecessary and heedless violence not only in the midst of battle, but in the aftermath, with rape, murder and kidnappings, the loss of innocence, love, humanity, and pride in oneself and one's nation. War brings shame to everyone. In this context, he does not spare the Kurdish leaders in their fooling of the people. He lances the arteries of their propaganda and opens the myriad doors to their zigzagging political games, by asking a forest of questions. His accessible language and elastic ideas give to his people what they need most: courage, hope and dignity.

As Rafiq Sabir's life and poetry demonstrate, the world of Kurdish literature is now divided not only by the borders of nation-states, but also by those writers who, in ever-increasing numbers, live abroad and those who continue to be captives in their homeland.

Those who remain in Kurdistan are subject to the alien social and political forces imposed on them by a continual state of war and instability. It is far more dangerous for them to take flight in free expression. Consequently, their poetry sometimes resembles a broken-winged bird. To avoid answering to the fascist authorities, these poets are forced to look for loopholes, for pen and paper invisible to the occupiers of their land. They must often use more ambiguous language if their writings are to be published or broadcast, and for their efforts, they mostly remain unrecognised internationally. Nevertheless, the poetry from the homeland resists with hope and dignity the dark domain of the modern sultans and, like the poetry of those in exile, can be a resounding canticle against those warlords who practise an unjustifiable Kurdish fratricide.

Among the most remarkable of the modern poets who have stayed in their homeland are the 1970s poets Jamal Sharbajeri, Ferid Zamdar, Enwer Qadir Muhammad and Salah Muhammad, from Sulaimani; Mu'ayyad Tayyib and Muhsin Qochan, from Dohuk; Mohsin Awareh, Sa'adullah Perosh and Newzad Rafa'at, from Hawler; Ahmed Taqan'e, from Kirkuk, Muhammad Bedri, from Bedra, Abdullah Abbas, now living in Baghdad; and the late Dilshad Mariwani, who was assassinated in 1990 by the Iraqi regime.

Others have spent time overseas, only to return to their homeland. Like all Kurdish writers who have experienced exile, they are more influenced by European and American schools of writing, and their poetry is often composed from a broader perspective. These poets include the late Jalal Mirza Karim and Sherko Bekas.

Jalal Mirza Karim was born in Sulaimani in 1935. He went to the USA in 1975, to return to the no-fly zone of Kurdistan in 1992, where he died a year later. He is known for the depth and simplicity of his language. In *Cherpay Janeki Khinkow* (*Whisper of* the *Painful Drowning*), he writes:

These recurring nightmares
Of my soul
Are a forest killing my dreams.
In the dense fog, I lose my way,
But the heavy rains
Come to revive
My field of dreams,
To grow tearful roses in my eyes.
Yet, I wish to escape these streets of spring
And walk between the tombs.
Standing near autumn's door,
Knocking, knocking,
I am not coming to steal the two-metre marble slabs
That you wear.
I am coming to care for the bodies of the children of Kurdistan.

Likewise, Sherko Bekas, born in 1940 in Sulaimani, left for Sweden in 1987 after spending years in the mountains, only to return to Kurdistan to become Minister of Arts and Culture in Sulaimani. His sophisticated poems masterfully employ lyrical images of nature and womanhood to explore philosophy and transform experience, as in *Love Song*:[193]

It was the first time that a sugarcane
Rebelled against her field.
This slender and pale maiden
Had given her heart to the wind.
But the field did not consent to their marriage.
Consumed with love, she said,
"He is to me beyond compare.
This is where my heart lies".

To punish the maiden,
Whose eyes were already wet with dew,
The indignant field called the woodpecker,
Who drilled a few holes
Into the heart and body of the plant.

From this day on,
She was a flute,

And the hand of the wind
Endowed her wounds with melodies.
She has been singing for the world ever since.

In contrast to the reality of disunity, he writes in *Together*:

The blind man saw with the eyes of the deaf man.
The deaf man listened with the ears of the blind man.
The mute understood both by reading their lips.
Together, all three smelled the scent of the flowers.

He was one who preferred to return to Kurdistan than continue his experience of exile, as his poem *Tunnel* so well describes:

The hours of exile
Are like the wagons of a train.
Connected to each other,
Every day they travel back and forth.

At the station of waiting,
At the station of farewell,
Their restless doors
Continuously
Open and close me ...

Every pain that gets off
Is replaced by a hundred new ones ...

Such a long tunnel of exile!
Where is it leading me? ...

The poets who have stayed in exile have more freedom to explore the issues, as guaranteed by the laws of their adopted countries, while remaining tied to the poetic trends, concerns and symbols of their homeland. They dramatically express a concern for what is happening in Kurdistan and the pain of nostalgia for land, family and friends left behind, often in the context of less traditional personal values. These poets include Salam Muhammad (originally from Kirkuk), Muhammad Amin Penjweni (from Sulaimani), Sami Shorish (now living in Britain), Faha'ad Shakeli and Jewher Kirmanj (who both live in Sweden) and Latif Helmet (now living in Holland). Helmet's poem *The Homeland is my Love, Not my Beloved* likens his commitment to his beloved Kurdistan to "the union of flesh and bone", in contrast to the vagaries of modern love:

But one night,
This girl with lovely lips
Deserted me,
And I became a jar of perfume
For someone else's braids.

The remarkable poet Salah Shwan, born in 1947 in Kirkuk, now lives in Norway. In *The Poet and his Colleagues*, he describes humility and sacrifice, using multiple images:

No candle
Stands through the night
Alone,
Not wanting to burn
Until the morning.

A candle
Cries all night
As it gives light.
And in the morning,
It is thrown into the dark.

A scared rat, trembling
As a bullet is fired,
Hides in his hole.
Has its plague already spread
Among the guerillas?

The dog is
Silent through the night,
Not bothering anyone.
No-one remembers to feed him,
Not even a piece of bread.

Abdullah Peshiw writes from Finland. Born in Hawler, he completed a Master's degree in the Soviet Union. He is now called the children's friend, because his poems often address the loss of childhood, as in *Twelve Lessons for Children*, which begins:

During your trip
To the island of blood,
What did you bring
For children?
Speak! What did you bring?

The poet remembers a time when "Mothers of this homeland fed babies with rivers of milk", but mourns:

It has been a long time
Since we saw a prophet come down
The mountains of this homeland …

So he journeys back to his beloved Kurdistan:

I cut through the mountains' chains
One by one,
I tear the calender. One by one,
To catch a glimpse of her eyes.

He expects a warm kiss:

Instead, I received yellow spit
That defiled my face
From the black-booted person.

Oh, children,
Who are hungry and whose lives are bitter,
I glimpsed a small grave
On the lungs of Baba Gurrgurr,
In the land of petrol,
On which is engraved a few words
At the flaming falls
Of ascending gold,
Which say:
"Here lies the body of a Kurdish girl
With great hazel eyes.
She died from hunger."

In an interview in 1998 on Med TV, a satellite Kurdish station in Europe, Peshiw said, "I would have written more poetry about women had not the Kurdish situation been so catastrophic. The tragedy in Kurdistan has induced an oblivion to a woman's beauty and to love." He honestly and bravely criticised the present Kurdish leaders, and the civil war in southern Kurdistan. When the interviewer commented that Abdullah Peshiw hit these leaders with words, he replied, "I wish I had a better dictionary so I could do more than just hit."

Likewise, the great novelist and poet Bakhtiar Ali Muhammad may not have published *Broken God* if he still lived in Kurdistan. From Germany, he writes:

He used to say, "Because of the pieces of the broken God,
I do not see my faith.
Because of the pieces of broken lovers, I cannot find my heart.
Because of all the false moons, I cannot see the sky."
Oh, how whiteness blinded me!
I was a child inhaling the smoke of the Emperor's burning.
I was dismissed from the white team of sweet children
And went towards the white fog of remote, honourless seas.

The latest generation of poets includes Abdul Rahman Mizuri, Jamal Ghambar, Dilshad Abdullah, Karim Deshti, Barzan Hestiyar, Qubadi Jeli-Zadeh, Faradoon Abdul Berzingi, Hasan Sarraji, Enwer Masifi, Botan Jelal, Jutiyar Khalid, Mukarram Talabani and Isma'il Berzinji, all from southern Kurdistan. From eastern Kurdistan are the new poets Abdulkhalaq Perhezi, Nasser Aghabra, Sulaiman Kawa, Rizgar Khoshnow, Aziz Nasri and Farzar Wali Zadeh, all of whom continue to live in Kurdistan.

Of this generation, the poet Marif Agha-e, from eastern Kurdistan, writes:

You look like a candle flame
And I like the candlestick.
Believe it.
When I am all melted
In your love,
Your flame of pain will be over.

Powerful disillusionment is similarly found in Dilawar Qaradaghi's *Sins*:

Sins wear prayer clothes
And the sinners lay prayer mats for them.
The wrongs are set in the frame of rights
And the lies are justified.
From the day the workshop of our thinking operates,
We want to create
A pure God, a beautiful God,
But so far, every God we have made
Has reneged and turned into an idol.

In Australia, the poems of Abbas Boskany, from Sulaimani, blaze with a language of elegant nobility in their depiction of dreams that are tossed by the winds of frustration. Examples of his poetry can be found in this book, as can the poems of Riza Colpan, from northern Kurdistan, also known for his novels and short stories, and likewise, examples of Shahin Baker's writings. Another well-known satiric essay writer living in Australia is Ghiathaddin Naqhshabandi.

Numerous Kurdish newspapers, magazines, and publications of novels and poetry in the more liberal countries of exile, particularly in Sweden and Germany, have enabled Kurdish writers to evolve and to be exposed to the world, which they could not have done in their homeland. For example, the Australian-Kurdish broadcaster Mustafa Khalil celebrates Kurdish literature every week in his radio program on 2000 FM.

Another exciting development is the number of excellent female poets who have broken through the male bastions of poetry. They include the courageous feminist poet Venos Faiek, from Khanaqin in southern Kurdistan, who now lives in Holland. Kajal Ahmed, from Sulaimani, is another female poet of great conviction. Back in the 1980s, when I edited a newspaper in Baghdad, I advised her that I dared not publish some of her poetry, for it would invite retribution on both of us. This did not hinder her inspiration, and in 1998, still living in Sulaimani, she wrote *Birds*:

According to the most recent classification,
The Kurds belong to the birds.
Look at them. Here they are
On the faded, tomb pages of history,
Migrants recognised in long-distance caravans.
Yes, the Kurds are birds.
Even if no place is left
To embrace their pains,
They will find the illusion of
Journeys between green highlands
And purple lowlands of their country.
That is why it is not surprising to me
That the Kurds fly
From one country to another
And never become a settled, civilised dream.
Nor do they enjoy a nest

Or in their last landing
Go to visit Mawlana.[d]
Nor, as did Nali, do they sacrifice themselves to the dust
Of a fast-fading memory.

Modern female poets from eastern Kurdistan include Zara Nadri, Seemin Gaychi, Kalsoom Osmanpoor and Jheela Husseini. The blind Jheela Husseini died very young, but her poetry remains. Then there is Dya Jwan, a Kurdish woman from Syria, who has a unique sensibility. In her poem *To the World Mother*, she uses the Arabic word *'ishq*, which Kurdish use too, the Kurdish equivalent of *dildari* or *awin* in Sorani, *avin* in northern Kurmanji. Below the word is translated as 'love', but it is a very deep love, one of total loyalty, dedication and commitment to a beloved:

Forgive me
If the mountains of my homeland
Are so high
That I cannot see the mountains behind.

Forgive me
If the illnesses of my people
Are so chronic
That I cannot feel the pain of others.

Forgive me
If I love my country so devotedly,
It leaves no place in my heart
To love another.

Many Kurdish poets have now had their work translated into Arabic, Swedish, German, English, Russian and French, and it is to be hoped that through these translations, the humanity of the Kurdish people will be validated.

An Apology

I apologise for not being able to acquaint the reader with all the creative writers who act as historiographers for the new culture of the Kurdish people, and also for any discrepancies in the dates of birth and death, especially of some classical Kurdish poets. I have taken the dates most nominated by various sources.

A. Talabani

ABOUT **Mosa Dashtani**

Mosa Dashtani was born in a village in the Bahdinan region of southern Kurdistan. He grew up in the city of Dohuk. After finishing school, he went to Baghdad, where he studied for three years at the Tourism Institute, qualifying as an international chef. He worked as a head chef in Sarsing Summer Resort in Kurdistan and at the five-star hotel Al-Rashit in Baghdad. After the Kurdish uprising failed in 1991, his family escaped Dohuk. He followed, walking from Dohuk over the mountains to the border with Turkey, he and his family staying in a village, near Hakkari, where 60,000 Kurds sought refuge. At the end of March, when a no-fly zone was declared over southern Kurdistan, most refugees went home. Mosa decided not to return, living for two years in a Silopi refugee camp, before coming to Australia in 1993. In 1996, he went back to Kurdistan and married. His two children were born in Australia. His mother also lives with the family, continuing to wear traditional Kurdish clothes.

In 1998, Mosa completed a Certificate in Commercial Cookery at the North Melbourne Institute of TAFE, and has worked in various capacities in restaurants and hotels. He is in the process of writing a Kurdish cookbook. Mosa's extensive knowledge of Bahdinan village practices comes from spending his early years and every school holiday in his family's village and also, as an adult, travelling to different villages. For descriptions of preparing goat's-skins, yoghurts and cheeses, he relies extensively on his mother's knowledge.

Foods and Cooking of the Bahdinan

Based on interviews with Mosa Dashtani

Despite a cross-fertilisation in food culture throughout the Middle East, in particular with our Turkish, Arab and Persian neighbours, Kurds continue to have special ways of cooking. These vary from region to region and from village to village.

About the Bahdinan Region

The Bahdinan is a rich agricultural area with large tracts of fertile land and many springs and rivers. Thirty-five tribes have traditionally inhabited the region, each tribe living in 80 to 140 villages. Some villages were one extended family; some villages had 100 people, others 5000. The region maintained its independence as a Kurdish emirate until 1842, when the Ottomans took more central control of their territory. After World War One, the Ottoman Empire disintegrated. When the British and French, in negotiation with Mistefa Kemal, determined the borders between Turkey and Iraq in 1923, my village was cut in half by the border. Most of the Bahdinan area became part of the state of Mosul, within Iraq, Dohuk becoming an independent city in 1969.

Until 1975, excess produce particular to a village or group of villages was bartered for another region's specialties. Otherwise, villages were self-reliant, growing their vegetables, grains, herbs and fruit. Every household made its own bread, fat, yoghurt, cheese, tomato paste and other staples, as well as clothes, soap and other necessities.

Food Storage

The seasonally cool climate means the ability to store fruit and vegetables is vital if people are to get through the long, cold winters. To store all kinds of fruit, a wooden platform is built into a tree and covered with dried grass and tree leaves. The fruit is layed in the grass and covered with more grass. Vegetables such as potatoes, turnip, beetroot and radish are buried under the earth floor of a house, to be dug up when needed. Other vegetables, like tomatoes, eggplants, okra, green and red pepper, zucchini and beans, are sun-dried.

Kurdish Bread

The staple of many cultures is bread and it is the same in Kurdistan. There are two basic families—breads with yeast and breads without yeast.

Bread with Yeast

Bread with yeast is baked in a *taneer* oven, called a *tanoor* in the Sorani dialect. There are three types of *taneer*. The traditional *taneer* is a stone and baked-clay igloo set into the ground in the courtyard outside the house. It has a hole at the top, into which the wood and then the bread is placed, and another hole at the side to let out smoke. The wood is burnt to embers before baking begins.

Another type of *taneer* is similarly made of baked clay but is set above the ground. The modern *taneer* is made of iron, with one casing inside the other and a metal plate at the bottom. It is built on wheels, so it is mobile, and is heated by portable gas from under the plate, the heated gas rising between the two casings.

Plain Bread

The dough is made from warm water, salt, yeast and flour. The mixture is covered with a cloth to prevent drying out and is left in a warm place, but not in the sun, for over 40 minutes. When the dough has risen sufficiently, it is cut, and made into balls by hand. These are then shaped into long, thin loaves or round, flat ones, poppy seeds or sesame seeds often sprinkled on top.

The loaves are baked by having the undecorated side sprinkled with water, so that the bread will stick to the inside walls of the *taneer*. The loaf is placed on the *taneer* wall by hand, or using a padded cloth paddle, which has a handle at the back for the hand to slide into. When cooked, the loaves fall away from the wall, and are removed with a two-pronged wooden or metal flat paddle. In the Bahdinani dialect, we call these paddles *gazik*.

Bread with Fillings

Often, this bread dough is baked with fillings pushed into the dough. This group of

Baking bread in a taneer oven

breads we call *sowik*, each type named according to its filling. Each home may have its own special fillings, and sizes and shapes of loaf.

Again, the dough is shaped into a long loaf or a round flat loaf. For *sowket gejneesh* (*gejneesh* meaning 'coriander'), the sauce is made from tomato, onion and coriander. Sometimes, vegetables and meat are added. For *sowket paneeri* (*paneeri* meaning 'cheese'), we make a mixture of cheese and herbs such as chives, onion, spring onion or garlic, sometimes with vegetables added to the cheese mix.

Once the sauce or mixture has been pressed into the bread, the sides of dough are pulled and pressed together to cover the mixture, then the loaf is reshaped.

We cook *sawik* by placing the loaf on the wall of a *taneer*. If the loaf is not cooked through after it has fallen away from the wall, a metal rod may be put down the hole of the *taneer* and the loaf rested on it.

Another way of cooking the *sowik* is in an oven called a *koochik*, using a *se'el*. An old-fashioned *koochik* is made of stone, the walls shaped like a parabola, open at the front. The modern *koochik* is made with three iron walls, open on the fourth side. A metal rod spans the opening. On the metal rod and the three walls sits an iron *se'el*—like an upturned iron bowl or wok, forming a curved surface about two to three millimetres thick. The firewood is placed on the floor of the *koochik* and burnt to embers or glowing charcoal, heating the iron *se'el*. The bread is then cooked on the top of the *se'el*.

Bread Fried in Oil

Sowket reeni or *sowket na'afreeni* is bread fried in oil. Normal dough is made into round loaves, and fried in animal fat or vegetable oil over an open fire until puffed and brown. To the dough, some people add herbs, different cheeses or chopped vegetables before frying.

Corn Bread

In villages near the Turkish border where corn is grown, there is another kind of bread, made with yeast and cornflour instead of wheat flour. The cornflour is mixed with yeast, water and salt, shaped into balls of dough and flattened. The round, flat loaves are cooked in a *taneer*. The baked bread is like a hard biscuit and very tasty, especially when eaten fresh with yoghurt, but it dries quickly, breaking and crumbling, and after two or three days, its taste becomes bitter.

Breads without Yeast

The main bread made without yeast is called *na'an'e tanik,* or thin bread. The *na'ane tanik* dough of wheat flour, water and salt is rolled out on a low, round, wooden table with a one-metre-long, thin, wooden rod. The bread is flipped into the air and rolled again for several minutes, to make it paper-thin and anywhere from half a metre to a metre in diameter. It is then placed on the *se'el* for cooking, and is turned over with a wooden paddle.

Once cooked, the sheets of *na'an'e tanik* are piled on top of one another. There may be 100 to 200 sheets in a pile. The bread becomes very dry—you can crack it easily—but providing it is stored in a cool, dry place, it is edible one month later.

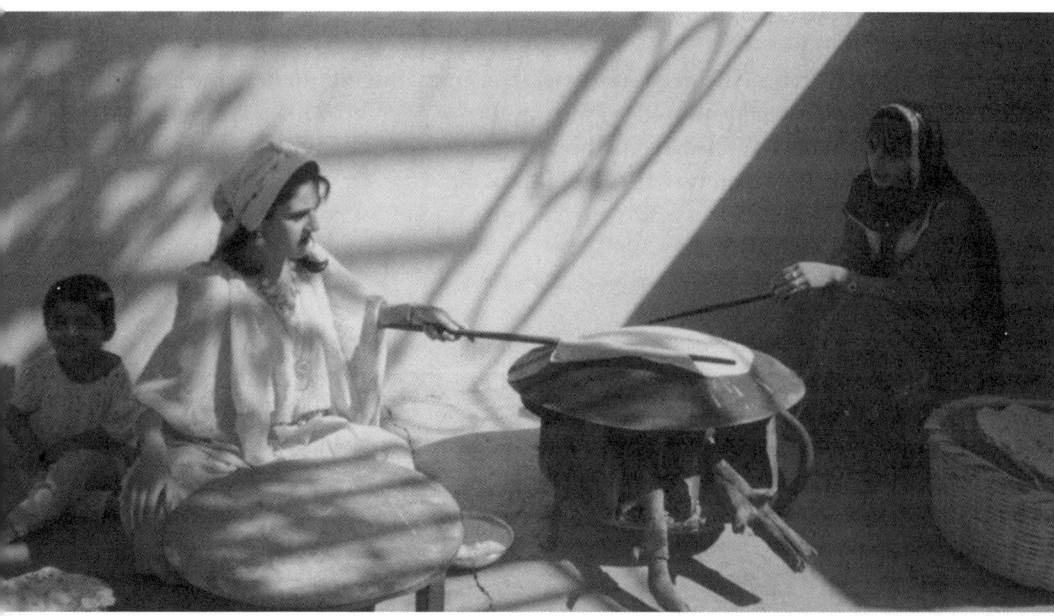

Woman rolling na'an'e tanik on a se'el

Before eating, it you sprinkle cool water over it, then leave it on a tray or in a clean cloth. After two or three minutes, it becomes soft and very good to eat.

Everyone eats *na'an'e tanik,* but it is a staple for shepherds when they are out minding the sheep and for the freedom fighters in the mountains.

Rice

Kurdistan grows at least four types of rice, often in terraces up the side of hills and always where there is plenty of water. One rice is called *reetick,* meaning 'without hairs'. It has a white, medium-sized grain, sometimes coloured green. Another rice, called *semah,* takes three months to grow. A longer-growing rice is called *shashmah,* meaning 'six months'. One very long-grained rice is called *kasnaditi* or 'nobody has seen before'.

These different rices vary in taste, and like most of our fruit and vegetables, are very tasty, because our soils are rich, our air and water are fresh and we do not use chemicals or freezing techniques.

We have many ways of cooking rice. Apart from steaming rice as an accompaniment to other dishes, we make rice soup, rice sauce and also a rice dough. We also cook rice with yoghurt (see 'Yoghurt' section, page 104).

Cooking Rice

There are four main ways for steaming rice. Usually, the water is boiled. Salt and oil are added, then the rice. Sometimes, washed rice is put into boiling salted water without oil. Most of the time, the rice is steamed with herbs, spices or some finely chopped vegetables, for taste. After the rice is cooked, melted fat or butter is poured over it. The dish is then covered for five minutes before serving.

Another cooking method involves first melting the butter or fat, then putting the washed rice into the fat and frying it for two or three minutes, then adding the salt and boiled water for cooking.

A fourth method is to boil the rice for five or 10 minutes, then strain it. A tray is oiled and the flat bread, *na'an'e tanik,* placed on the tray, the rice on top. This is covered with another tray or a lid, to flatten the rice and make the dish airtight. The dish is put in the oven or over embers and cooked very slowly, without fat. A brown, crispy skin is formed at the bottom. Rice cooked this way is dry to eat, not fatty, and very healthy.

Rice Dishes

Kulaf

Kulaf means 'hat', and there are various ways of cooking this dish. In my family, we cook the rice first, grill slices of meat and chopped vegetables, then layer the meat, vegetables and rice in a deep baking dish, with or without *na'an'e tanik* or another flat bread at the bottom of the pot. The layered food is baked for 10 minutes, so the layers stick together, before upending the pot and removing it. If the dish has been cooked with bread, the bread comes out on top. *Kulaf* is also known as *parda palow.*

Brinjab Zazawot

Brinjab Zazawot is made with uncooked meat, sliced vegetables such as eggplant, capsicum, zucchini, beans, potatoes and snow peas—whatever is available—and half-cooked or uncooked rice or uncooked ground wheat. The diced vegetables and chicken or meat are put in the pot on the stove, with butter, garlic and cloves. Tomato paste is mixed with herbs and such spices as pepper, a little chilli and somac (the pulverised red conefruit of the sumac tree, which gives the dish a slightly sour flavour). The tomato-paste mix is then spread over the vegetables and the rice added. The pot is covered with a lid until the rice is cooked. The mix is turned out on a tray before serving.

Briani

This rice dish is cooked with briani pepper, salt and a very little oil, then left. Chicken or other meat is taken off the bone and grilled, then added to a mixture of roasted almonds, sultanas, brown spices and fried butter. Sometimes, fried potato and beans are added to the mix, which can be served either separately or mixed with the rice. Boiled eggs can be used for decoration. Sometimes, people put a thin bread in a pot, the *briani* on top, heat for five to 10 minutes, then turn the dish out to serve as they do *kulaf*.

Dolma

Another way of cooking rice is in *dolma*. The rice is washed and strained, then mixed with onion and herbs like thyme, basil or dill, plus parsley and garlic, perhaps chilli and tomato paste, some vegetables like capsicum, and sometimes uncooked chopped meat (preferably not mince). The mixture is then wrapped in vine leaves and placed in a pot.

The same *dolma* mixture can be used to stuff vegetables like hollowed-out capsicum, eggplant, zucchini, tomato, potato or onion. The different stuffed vegetables can be cooked in the one pot.

Over the *dolma* or stuffed vegetables, we pour tomato sauce and water, or water and lemon juice, or water and sumac—the liquid strained from soaking the redcone sumac fruit in water—or tartaric acid and water, or just plain water.

The *dolma* are covered with liquid, whereas the stuffed-vegetable pot is only half-filled, because the vegetables already contain a lot of water. The food is then cooked slowly on the stove until all liquid is absorbed.

Rahek

Rahek is similar to *dolma* but without the vine-leaf wrapping. Minced meat, garlic and onion, uncooked rice, herbs and spices, salt and pepper are mixed together according to taste. The mixture is made into balls, then put into the palm of the hand and squeezed into short, thin sausages. These sausages are placed in the pot in lines and layers, one on top of each other, with water then added. The cooking is similar to that of *dolma*.

Kotellk with Rice or Wheat Dough

Kotellk are balls made from a mixture of fried mince meat, onion, parsley, salt, black pepper and other herbs to taste, encased in rice or wheat dough.

For rice dough, the rice is boiled without fat until it is sticky. The very thick rice paste is left to cool, then seasoned with salt and pepper. Before making balls of the dough, we put our hands in cold water, to stop the dough sticking. A hole is made in each rice ball and the meat mix pushed in. The rice dough is then pinched together to cover the mixture, rolled or flattened, and cooked in boiling water or a sauce.

In Kurdistan, when making the wheat dough, we use an uncooked ground wheat that sticks together, but in Australia, unless we find the special wheat in an Arabic or Turkish shop or, nowadays, in a supermarket, we have to use a wheat and semolina mix so that it sticks together. The wheat is soaked in warm water for about 10 minutes, strained, and then handmixed with some semolina.

The dough is kneaded to make it elastic, salt and pepper is added, and the mixture left for five minutes. The dough is shaped into round or flat balls, with a hole in each for the prepared mixture. The dough is pinched together, and rolled to become round or flat. The *kotellk* are cooked in boiling water or a sauce.

Fries

Kotellk can be reheated by grilling or frying. We also fry in hot oil round patties made from a thick mixture of onion, parsley, meat, some flour, water, salt and pepper.

Yoghurt, Butter and Cheeses

Yoghurt

We eat a lot of yoghurt on its own, and it is often used in cooking. We call yoghurt *ma'ast*. It is usually made from sheep milk, but also from cow or goat milk.

The milk is heated in a pot, and stirred continuously so it does not stick to the bottom. The cooking time varies for different kinds of milk. The full-cream milk in Australia takes longer than sheep's milk, and the longer the boiling, the thicker the liquid, but it is important not to overboil. It spoils the taste. When the milk starts bubbling, it is taken off the heat and left to become warm.

One spoon of yoghurt and one spoon of milk are combined. This *heven* is to yoghurt what yeast is to bread. The warm milk has a skin on it, and a small opening is made at the side of this skin, so the *heven* can be put underneath and stirred in. The pot is then covered with a lid, put in a warm place, covered with a blanket and left for two or three hours. The yoghurt is then ready to eat.

Making Butter and Cheeses

Preparing a Buck's Skin

To make butter and cheeses, we prepare a skin from a young, black billygoat we call a *mashik*. The procedure may be done only two or three times in a lifetime. The animal's neck is cut, usually by a male member of the household. Through a hole made in the skin of a leg, air is blown by mouth or through a hose, so that the skin begins to separate from the body. This is repeated for each leg, the limbs being cut off at the mid-joint. A hand is put inside the neck, then up each leg, to completely separate the skin from the body. No knife is used in this procedure. The body is removed through the neck.

The skin is rubbed with a mixture of salt, water, and a natural acid such as that made from the somac fruit's skin after it has been soaked in water. The goat's-skin is then left in a warm, covered place for two or three days, making it easy to scrape the hair from the skin. The hairless goat's-skin is then rubbed with a pulverised mixture of dried pomegranate skin and salt, to give it strength. Each leg and the neck are then tied to make the skin airtight except for one opening. The skin is blown up again, the remaining hole tied, and the result left outside to dry.

Butter

When butter and cheese are to be made, the prepared goat's-skin is soaked in water. Two lengths of wood, each with a hole in the middle, are joined by another length of wood being inserted into the two holes of the crosslengths. The forelegs of the goat's-skin are tied to each end of one crosslength; the hind legs tied to each end of the other. With the length of wood between the two crosslengths above the skin, the skin is hung from a tree, or a wooden rafter inside the house, by rope attached to each crosslength.

The yoghurt is put into the skin through the opened neck, along with ice or iced water, which helps the fat stick together. The neck opening is tied, and for a good 20 to 60 minutes, someone sways and shakes the skin.

The mixture is then poured out of the neck and into a pot. The thick layer of fat or butter, called *nevish,* that forms on the top is collected, for eating at breakfast or use in cooking.

Yoghurt and Creamed Cheese

The watery yoghurt underneath the buttery layer, called *dow,* can be drunk as is or reboiled. The boiled liquid is strained through a cloth. The cloth, heavy with the residue of *dow,* is hung where it can be regularly checked for how dry the *dow* is becoming. The result is dry yoghurt that in English is called 'creamed cheese'. We mix herbs like dill and spring onion with it. To make a yoghurt drink, you just add water and shake.

Being boiled again can further dry the *dow*. It is left to cool, strained through a cloth, then rolled into balls and put in the sun for 10 days or more. These balls of dry *dow* we call *kashk*. As hard as rocks, they can be stored for up to two years. When required, the balls of *kashk* are put in water. The *dow* becomes soft and edible, and the leftover water, which is like a watery yoghurt, is used to boil rice.

Goollool

This thick yoghurt-rice mixture is put on a tray or into small dishes, where it sets like gelatine. It is eaten cold, with melted butter, another fat, honey or a syrup poured over it.

Fetta

Dow is also used to make white fetta and other types of cheeses. To make fetta, we put the cleaned duodenum of the sheep in a pot, with watery *dow* on top, adding crushed hot chilli, whole black pepper and a dried root, similar to ginger, that we call *shap*. This mixture is left for 10 or 20 days and is cheese *heven*.

One cup of this *heven* is added to sheep's milk so fresh, it is still warm. It is mixed through, covered with a lid and a blanket, and left for an hour or more, depending on how strong the *heven* is. The result is a block of fetta.

Chopped herbs or green vegetables can be added to the fetta by slightly warming the block on the stove until it begins to break. At this stage, you add the prepared herbs or vegetables, put the mix into a cloth, and hang it to dry for less than a day, to remove excess water. The still-soft cheese mix can be sliced for eating with bread or in salads.

Ricotta and Fetta Mix

Another popular cheese dish is *jhaji*, a mixture of ricotta, fetta and herbs such as dill, thyme, and dried garlic. *Jhaji* is stored in a skin or plastic pot to be eaten over winter.

Sauces and Soups

We have four common sauces, which can also be used as soup bases.

Tomato Sauce

Homemade tomato paste is dried and stored for later use. Tomatoes are crushed in a pot and the mixture strained through a sieve. The seedless liquid is put onto a tray, covered, and left in the sun for seven to 10 days.

Sometimes, the liquid is just boiled, to make it thick, but too much boiling makes the taste a little bitter; drying the sauce in the sun gives it a better taste. To use the dry tomato paste, we add water and herbs.

Dishes with Tomato Sauce

Beans, eggplant, zucchini, potatoes or whatever vegetables are available, even dried vegetables, can be cooked in the tomato sauce on top of the stove.

Tepsi is made in the oven. For *tepsi* dishes, potatoes, eggplants, onions, capsicums and broad beans are sliced and slightly grilled. The potatoes and eggplant require more grilling than other vegetables. The vegetables are layered in a shallow tray, sometimes with layers of grilled mincemeat balls, flat mince patties or grilled fish. One and a half cups of tomato sauce are poured on top. The dish is covered, and baked for 10 to 15 minutes. To make *tepsi* more like a lasagne, we spread a mix of butter, flour and eggs between the layers.

Tershik is a dish made with a watery lemon-soured tomato sauce (*tershik* means 'sour'). If using eggplant, the eggplant is cut in half, then scored with a knife to open the flesh. Celery, onion, eggplant and chickpeas are boiled in the red sauce before the *kotellk* are added and cooked.

Thick White Yoghurt Sauce

Gerara dow is a thick, white sauce made from boiling rice in watery *dow*. *Kotol dow* is a dish of chickpeas, rice, yoghurt and *kotellk*. The chickpeas are boiled for 15 minutes, then the *kotellk* added. The mixture is boiled for another five minutes, before the rice is added and cooked until soft.

Rice Sauce

Ofshring is what we call a sweet, watery soup made from boiling rice in more water than can be absorbed. Lemon juice and onion can be added, as can mint and other herbs. The mixture is then cooked for five minutes. To this, we add chickpeas, salt, pepper and, afterwards, the *kotellk*.

Herb Sauce

Herb sauce is made from finally chopped wild green-vegetable leaves and onion. Called *curry*, this can have a very hot chilli-ginger flavour and, unless further prepared, is too spicy. It must be boiled, drained and squeezed; more water is then added, and the mixture cooked again. You can also cook *kotellk* in this. Many different types of leaves can be used to make the sauce, to which rice, vegetables and meat can be added.

Sweets

For thousands of years, the traditional sweet pastries of Kurdistan have been of two types—*kasma* and *ka'ada*. They are made at special times such as weddings, or when a newly married couple revisit their family homes seven days after the wedding, or at religious festivals, whether Ezidi, Jewish, Christian or Muslim.

For *kasma* and *ka'ada*, a pastry base is made by mixing flour and butter, then yeast, a little salt, cinnamon and milk. The mix is left to rise while fillings are prepared.

Kasma are pastries with a date filling. The date seeds are removed and oil added to the date meat, the mix mashed into a soft paste.

For *ka'ada*, a nut mixture is prepared by grinding almonds and some sugar. Sesame seeds, coconut and sugar, or other types of nuts, can also be used.

Once the pastry has risen, it is rolled out. For *kasma*, the pastry is made into a long rectangle, the date paste is added, then the pastry is wrapped around the mix to form a roll. The roll is cut into sections, so that you can see the filling at either end.

For *ka'ada*, circles or squares are cut out of the rolled pastry. The filling is put on top, and the sides are lifted and pinched together in different ways, a knife or fingernails being used to further decorate the pastries and to indicate the different kinds of fillings.

The pastries are placed on a greased tray, brushed with beaten egg, and oven-baked.

Wild Foods of Kurdistan

The wild foods in the mountains are so plentiful that some people rely on them rather than on agriculture. In spring, there are many wild mushrooms, herbs, green vegetables, wild grasses and fruit that come out only at this time. Groups of villagers, young people or women and children, go to the mountains for a day to gather these foods and the leaves of trees for *dolma*. The day in the mountains becomes a day of celebration. People make a fire for a barbecue, and sing and dance as well as collecting the foods.

On a day in late summer or autumn, people again go collecting wild foods. Each village or group of villages has a special mountain territory that is theirs to pasture sheep and collect wild foods and grasses. For some tribes, the heads of all the villages come together to agree on a day when everyone can go out collecting. According to tribal law, people cannot go before this day—otherwise, some people might miss out, which could cause trouble.

A number of species of wild mushrooms need a very cold climate to grow. One species has a single mushroom weighing up to 500 grams, with a 20-centimetre diameter. Another type of mushroom can grow only in special grass the shepherds collect to feed their sheep in winter.

Once collected, the herbs, vegetables and mushrooms can be used immediately in cooking or dried and stored. Different herbs are used for flavouring tea. Some of the herbs and grasses have medicinal value.

Some plants that we collect for eating also grow in Australia, but here, people do not eat them. One is *tollk*, or mallow plant, with its round, green leaf and white flower. We slice the mallow leaves, put them in boiling water for five minutes, until they soften, then squeeze the water out. The cooked leaves are added to chopped onion, which is fried in a pan. One or two eggs are cracked over this and mixed together. It is a very tasty combination, eaten hot or cold with bread. Sometimes, the *tollk* leaves are used for *dolma*.

Similarly, we eat the leaves of the *pertularea*, a yellow-flowered plant that grows in Australia. Some people even eat stinging nettles, after the nettles have been boiled, squeezed and boiled again. The nettle leaves are also used for treating certain skin conditions.

Other wild foods are found in the broad valleys and plains where wheat is grown. *Dombalan* is one. You hardly ever see it in the market, because nobody grows it. It grows under the ground. You know it is there when there is a patch of broken ground, although it has one small stem, a green-yellow flower and tiny leaves. The *dombalan* is white, about the size of a potato but sweeter-tasting. It can be baked, fried or grilled.

Another food found underground, with a taste similar to, but sweeter than ginger, we call *sefbina'ad* or 'underground apple'. I also find it in the markets in Australia. *Sefbina'ad* is eaten raw or used in pickling.

Fruits and Nuts

In Kurdistan, we grow many types of tomatoes, grapes, stone fruit, berries, apples and nuts.

Tomatoes vary in size. Some are red, some are yellow, some are multicoloured. When cut, their insides can look as creamy as butter. All are very tasty.

Grapes are eaten fresh, or made into sweet syrups used in cakes or to preserve other fruit, fresh or dried. Wine, sherry and arak are also made from grapes.

We have at least eight varieties of grapes, many growing wild in the mountains. Some varieties need watering in summer. Some do not. *Slopi* grapes are long, white and very sweet. The sweet *zarik* grapes are golden, round and small, like sultanas. *Chavga* are like big, black, round cow's eyes (*chavga* means 'cow's eyes'). *Mirmirka* grapes are very small, round and bitter. The *rashmeo* family of grapes is the first to ripen at the end of spring. These varieties are sweet, black or red, large, and oval in shape. *Kerrkerana*, the last to ripen, are crunchy, and so tightly clustered that you must bite into the whole bunch. These grapes are very good to store for winter. *Teifi*, a long, red grape, can also be stored for winter.

Many varieties of stone fruit are farmed near spring water, without the need for irrigation. We grow black, pink, yellow and red peaches—all different sizes and tastes. There are at least three kinds of apricots, which vary in size, and many types of plums, which we call *haleek*. *Halee halhalook*[46] are small yellow plums, *halee rushk* are medium-sized black plums, *halee arroo* are the first to come out in spring, while *halee gorlk*, a very big, green plum, is the last to come out in autumn.

Halhalook are wild fruits called cornel berries, without a stone. They can be red, yellow and orange in colour. Some are bitter, but most varieties are sweet. We have wild black and red berries but no strawberries. Cherries, grown in other parts of Kurdistan, are sold in the market.

We grow gold, red and green apples—bitter, sweet, acidic or sour to taste. The trunks and branches of the trees can also be different colours—some black, some yellow. There are big orchards in the Dohuk region, close to the Turkish border. The Barwari tribe, the biggest in the area, is famous for apple orchards (and sheep).

Many wild trees grow nuts, some not found in Australia. One big tree, called *qazzun*, grows the bitter-tasting *terebinth* nut, which is so hard, it can crack your teeth. It can be ground and mixed with sultanas, to eat as *murrameat*. Ground *qazzun* can also be made into soap, as can the smaller, less round *terebinth* relative called *bemk*.

Other nut trees include the *barnif* (almond), *binduk* (hazelnut), *fistuk* (pistachio) and *gees* (walnut). Walnuts are put in the fire before being eaten. We also have peanuts, oak nuts, and others from the acorn family. One type of acorn, called the *burri marsk*, is stored undergound, then given to sheep in winter. The *burri*, the true acorn or oak nut, is also given to sheep, but if people run out of food, they eat it too. Sweeter than the *burri marsk*, it can be baked to eat or ground into flour. It becomes even sweeter after storage.

The Politics of Food in Kurdistan

The first evidence of agriculture and pastoralism has been found in the mountains of Kurdistan. The huge varieties of wild and cultivated foods have had a significant influence on Arab, Persian and Turkish food culture. Before 1975, orchards and other agriculture covered all of southern Kurdistan except the mountain summits. There were enough insecticide-free apples, stone fruit and grains for all of Iraq, and more for export, but the Iraqi government did not develop the region. The villagers survived on homegrown produce and bartering between villages and were not reliant on outside currencies or governments in any way.

With the gradual introduction of a cash economy, the biggest problem in Kurdistan was that excess produce was impossible to sell in the local markets for a decent price, and the lack of roads and other infrastructure made other markets inaccessible. We could not process the food, because there were no factories to make tomato sauce or to can the fruit. People could not develop such businesses, because under the Ba'aths, everything is government-owned. Even a Kurdish clothes-making factory was closed down and moved south.

In 1975, all hope for autonomy within Kurdistan was destroyed with the signing of the Algiers Agreement between Iraq and Iran. Iraq agreed to give Iran rights to use the Shatt Al-Arab waterway and hand over three nearby areas of land (Tombol Sora, Tombol Cobra and Abu Moosa, where Arabs lived) if Iran promised to stop supporting the Kurdish revolution.

Iraq began a policy of forcibly deporting people from the villages. People unwilling to be herded south fled to Turkey, Syria and Iran. Others, given some choice, went to the cities and towns of Kurdistan. The army then bombed their houses, mosques, churches and synagogues, burnt and cut down the orchards, bombed and concreted up the springs and lit fires in the beehives. The people were left with nothing—no homes and no means of survival. Between 1975 and 1980, two factories were built in Dohuk, one for tomato paste and the other for Kurdish dresses, but otherwise, there was no employment outside the government, except in shops and the trades.

By 1991, 80 per cent of Kurdish villages (4500) had been destroyed. In April 1991, after the Kuwait War and Kurdish uprising, America declared a no-fly zone to stop

Saddam Hussein using his air force over some of Iraqi Kurdistan, but the zone excluded oil-rich towns like Mosul and Kirkuk. Many refugees who had fled to Turkey and Iran returned home. Some found their homes bombed; others returned to a pile of burnt possessions in the centre of the room. People started to rebuild houses, orchards, crops and animal herds, with the help of the UN and other local and international aid organisations. However, many places remain unsafe, and much of Kurdistan has not been rebuilt, because of the unstable political situation and two trade embargoes, one from Saddam Hussein, the other an international trade embargo against Iraq.

In 1992, under UN Security Council Resolution 986, it was agreed that the no-fly zone was to receive food in return for 13 per cent of Iraq's oil revenue reserved for the purchase of food and medicine. This was 50 per cent of the total generated, the other 50 per cent going to pay for war damage. But Iraq's refusal until 1997 of the 'food for oil program' meant many people were lucky to eat once a day. Since 1997, the 'food for oil program' has been established, meaning conditions have improved. Yet this program prohibits the buying of locally grown agricultural products! The UN—not the Kurdish regional governments in Hawler and Sulaimani—decides where to buy food and at what price, and with all the cheap imports, homegrown foods are constantly undercut in price. All this has had an extremely damaging effect on Kurdistan's agricultural base.

More and more people choose to live in the towns, often because this is the only way to educate their children. Unemployment remains at over 50 per cent, but instead of growing food and making their houses, clothes and other necessities, people now rely on shops, markets and aid. In just 25 years, a many-thousand-year-old lifestyle of self-reliance is breaking down and a wealth of knowledge is being lost.

ABOUT Mihriban Astare, Seher Cinar, Ayten Sengul and Helin Diyar

Mihriban Astare was born in 1956 in a village on the Perisu River, which she called *Cem*[a] in Dimili, meaning 'river', close to Elazig.[b] *Mihriban* means 'red fox' in Dimili. As a child, she had red-blonde hair. Her father was an Alevi *de'de* (a *rahper* or *pir* in Kurdish), a holy person responsible for many families.

In 1972, Mihriban left home to live with her married sister in Istanbul, then at 18 she migrated to Australia under the Family Reunion Program. One and a half years later, she went back to Turkey for three months and married her cousin. Her three children were born in Australia.

After working in factories and as a volunteer in the Turkish and Kurdish communities for many years, then part time at a women's refuge for two years, Mihriban began a Bachelor of Social Science at the Royal Melbourne Institute of Technology. In 1996, she divorced her husband.

Seher Cinar was born in 1958 to an Alevi family, in a village two hours' bus ride from Kars, a town near the border of Armenia, an area ruled by Russia until the end of World War One. When she was three, her parents moved to Ankara, so Seher grew up a Turk. She remembers her mother listening to radio broadcasts from southern Kurdistan, but regrets not knowing more of her Kurdish history. In 1987, she migrated to Australia as a single woman. She has a diploma from the Melbourne College of Textile, and would like to open a studio for weaving, tapestry, design and printing.

Ayten Sengul was born in 1960 in the Alevi village of Kacaran,[c] renamed Dayilar by the Turkish government, a three-hour bus ride from Tunceli,[d] the Turkish name for Dersim, where she attended boarding school from age seven. Brought up an Alevi Kurd speaking the Kurmanji dialect, she trained as a nurse and married a Zaza Kurd, who speaks the Dimili dialect. In 1987, she and her husband migrated to Australia with their five-month-old daughter. Her son was born in Australia. After three months' supervised work experience, she was able to work as a nurse, but at present is a full-time mother.

Helin Diyar was born in 1968 in the Alevi village of Zara, 30 minutes from Sivas. In 1975, her family migrated to Australia, where she attended school and learnt English and Turkish. At 16, she returned briefly to Turkey and married her cousin. They have two children, aged 11 and five. For the last 10 years, Helin has worked as a social worker and community development worker for the Kurdish community. She is completing her final year of a Masters degree in Social Work.

A Dialogue Between Women

Four women from Alevi villages in northern Kurdistan speak about history, village life, health, school, religion, marriage, family and PKK.[a]

Helin: Life makes a person who they are. Kurdish women have had to be strong, living a village life—caring for animals, tending crops, collecting wood, carrying water, making bread and yoghurt. As well, because of all the wars and uprisings, not only have they often been left to raise large families, without husbands or fathers, they have had to protect their family and themselves from soldiers and outsiders. Most Kurdish women derive their strength from their children and a belief in family. This keeps them going when facing disaster after disaster, and these women become role models for their daughters.

Seher: When the men left to be soldiers during World War One, my mother told me that the women did everything like men. They worked very hard to keep the farms going, and when Ottoman soldiers came to the village, the women fought them with shovels, sticks, knives, anything they could find, because they were always in danger of being raped and bashed. Close to the village lived Russian and Armenian people, and my mother said they had a good relationship with them, but when the war started, the Ottomans and Armenians also started fighting. My mother said there were massacres on both sides and the Armenians left the area.

Helin: My grandmother told us that in World War One, very few people had anything to eat. She was pregnant, and had to search for leftover food in the *fiske*,[b] where the Ottoman soldiers fed their horses.

Seher: They would pick out the wheat from the horse manure.

Helin: Or from the horse feed. They moved from village to village, and at one time had to hide for three months in a stable. They saw families being massacred and thrown into mass graves. My mother says it was the Armenians who did this, but during the war, many Kurds were killed for not joining the Ottoman army and also by Russian soldiers. I can still hear the fear and anger in my grandmother's voice as she told these stories.

Mihriban: When my mother was very upset, she sometimes swore, "You are *Oorus*", meaning "You are Russians".

Ayten: My grandmother's family had a big farm, with many animals—cows, sheep and goats, and made yoghurt, cheese and butter. They had fruit trees, and grew wheat, chickpeas, lentils and vegetables in summer, drying tomatoes, beans, peppers and eggplants for winter. Many people had nothing to eat during the two World Wars, so my grandmother fed these people.

Helin: My grandfather came from the Magara people, who lived in cave dwellings around Dersim, but after World War One and the collapse of the Ottoman Empire, during all the internal unrest, my grandmother said, they went and lived in a village near Erzincan.[c] She told us Armenians came to their village and to other villages. They took people away in small groups, separating women from men, and many people 'disappeared'. They burnt the fields, destroyed the farm animals and poisoned the beehives, leaving people dying of starvation. A man called Ibrahim Harman escaped to the nearby village of Harman, to tell the elders what was happening. A wise, clever man took a horn to the valley near my grandmother's village and blew it, the sound echoing through the valley. The Armenians, hearing this, thought the Ottoman soldiers were coming, so they ran away. My grandparents fled the village for the safety of Kars, returning some years later. The problem is that all these stories are confusing, vague and undocumented. Why would the Armenians do this?

Mihriban: Either the government used the Armenians to kill Kurds, or they said that the people responsible were Armenian, or it was in retaliation because the Ottomans formed a Kurdish army unit called *hamidiye* to kill Armenians.

I was named after my aunt, a very dominant woman. My father told me she protected other women and their children from Turkish soldiers who came to the village during the Dersim uprising of 1936–37 and the Kurdish genocide of 1938. She would stand up to the soldiers and have her say, even if the soldiers beat her.

Ayten: During the Dersim genocide, when my grandmother was pregnant with the youngest of her nine children, the body of her husband was found. Afterwards, Turkish soldiers came to the village. She hid the children under the house, and when soldiers knocked on the door, she was waiting behind it with her gun. After nine hours, the soldiers left and went to other houses, but for two or three days, she did not leave her post. Whenever the soldiers came back, she was ready. The soldiers finally gave up, because she was a fighting woman. Other people were killed. My grandmother told us how one man was shot, and held his intestines in his hands. A week later, he died.

Mihriban: The Turkish parliament admitted that in Dersim, they killed 10,000 Kurdish people, including women and children, by chemical gas. My mother tells a story of how they put the chemicals in a dry ravine, and one woman survived under all the bodies. One of my dad's cousins from Dersim was the only one in her family to survive. She married, and had one child. This child had a son, who joined the Turkish Socialist Party, but he was killed in 1971.

Ayten: The Turkish government killed 80,000 Kurdish people in the Dersim area in 1936–38. My grandparents and parents would describe how soldiers took a whole village of people into a field and gassed them with chemicals or shot them all, or raped the girls and killed the men and children. To avoid rape, many girls jumped from a cliff or into the river. Sometimes, the soldiers would tell the women that if they handed over their gold, they would not be harmed, but afterwards, they were shot. We were told that soldiers used scimitars to cut babies from the wombs of pregnant women.

Other people were blindfolded and had their hair cut. They were put into trucks, families being split up, and taken to different Turkish cities. Many people went missing.

Helin: My grandmother told me that it was the Armenians who did all this to them in Dersim. That was the story given to them.

Ayten: The stories told to us were so powerful, it did not matter that they were not part of our personal experience. I will never forget when I was seven years old. I was looking after the lambs and kids in our field opposite our house. There was a little tree in the middle of the field, and when I saw soldiers coming, I hugged the tree and wet myself. I cry every time I think about it. Even in Australia, when I see police or soldiers, I am scared.

Seher: It affected us psychologically. I lived in Ankara and did not know where Dersim was, but my father told me how Ataturk's soldiers came and killed 40,000 Alevi Kurds. He would say, "That means they can do it again."

Mihriban: That is why my mum was so protective of her children. She had eight daughters, and she would not let us go anywhere, in case she never saw us again.

Ayten: There were always Turkish soldiers in the villages. My father had seven daughters and his two sons were away, so he was always scared something would happen to the girls. To protect ourselves, we had to be very nice to the soldiers, even though we hated them.

Mihriban: From the 1970s, there were many politically active young people who were partisan socialists in my area. These young students came to the villages to give seminars, and some people spied on them. In the winter of 1972, about 100 soldiers came and searched every house, arresting and torturing anybody suspected of being socialist. At around this time, my 19-year-old cousin was studying at a teaching college in Dersim. He was killed for being a partisan socialist. Soldiers roped his body to the back of a jeep, then dragged it along the road for more than an hour, until it was mangled. If a person was politically active, the soldiers could arrest the whole family, and even if they were in prison only a few days, the women were not spared torture. They would put electric shocks to their nipples, everything.

Helin: When I was young, soldiers came to the village, but I never saw anyone harmed by them and I did not fear them, though I remember my uncles being fearful. It was like, "Get the girls inside. Hide them." The men would stand guard and do anything for the soldiers. What made it more difficult was that many people did not speak Turkish, and we were an Alevi village, so our women were not covered, and the soldiers, thinking Alevi women were 'easy', would take them away and do as they pleased. The truth of this is very difficult to work out, but tension and fear were there all the time. That was life.

In other ways life was hard too. Women had many children, and worked very hard right up until they had their baby. A couple of days later, they went back to work, especially women from poor families. They would keep the baby in a swinging cradle, but also, the children were very quiet and well behaved. They saw the hard life, and took responsibility at a very early age for looking after each other. Women also had a lot of help from grandmothers, aunts, neighbours and even uncles and grandfathers. It was quite normal for children to grow up with their grandparents or other relatives in the next village. Often, it was only the first three or four years of a child's life that the mother was really involved in.

Ayten: At harvest time, the women worked in the field with the men, one woman always staying home to prepare the food. I remember my pregnant mother getting up early to do the housework and make the bread. She would then walk a few hours to the fields, carrying an older child on her back, and a bucket of food in both hands to feed my father, brothers and sisters harvesting the wheat. She would come back, milk the cows, sheep and goats, boil the milk, make yoghurt for the next day, then cook dinner.

Seher: It was always the women who cared for the animals in the barn and did the milking. While a mother was working with the animals or in the fields, she might carry her baby on her back, giving the baby some dried fruit or cheese wrapped in a thin, white cloth to suck, or putting the baby under a tree and covering it with a light cloth.

Mihriban: I heard of children being bitten by snakes and dying. My cousin was one and a half years old, and while my aunt was busy, he tried to get out of his crib and hung himself. Two of my sisters died. One was three years old. My father was so disheartened that not even a doctor in a big city like Konya could save his child, he moved back to the village.

Ayten: Two of my mother's children died.

Helin: Three of my siblings died. One died when I was four. I was looking after her and gave her a drink of milk that was too hot. My parents tried to treat her and she died, I think from internal burns. The child mortality rate was very high, because of the isolation, and travel being so hard, and many girls were very young when they had their babies, and some did not have help or enough experience to take proper care of the baby. Also, many women did not want to go to a male doctor, and for a long time people used natural remedies and therapies. Every family had its own therapies. These were the women's domain, and they would teach their daughters.

When Western medicines became available in the cities, if a child was sick and the family was poor, the father would often go to the city without taking the child to see the doctor. He would bring back medicine and give it to the child, and often the child would die. This is what happened to one of my sisters. She had a common cold, and my father gave her an injection with air in the mixture. There was conflict between the *de'des* and families who wanted to use the new medicine, because of the bad omens the death of a child brought to the village. I remember the teachers having meeting after meeting, trying to educate villagers not to use medicine without a doctor's advice, but I also remember parents carrying their child on their backs for 10 or 15 hours, walking to the nearest doctor.

Seher: Often, they died on the way. There were no roads, and in the winter, there was too much snow, but now they have built roads for all the army vehicles.

Ayten: Once my sister had a small, pimply rash, which spread and became like red wounds all over her face and body. My family thought somebody had put a bad eye on her: *nazar* in Turkish or *cavinkir* in Kurmanji. Twice my father took her to the doctor in Elazig but the creams did not work. One of my father's friends told him to take her to a special place for sick people where there was a *se'el*, like an upturned metal wok, over a fire of charcoal. They rubbed charcoal on her wounds, and after a week, the rash disappeared. We could not believe it, but to take someone to this special place, you had to believe in the remedies. Otherwise, they did not work.

Mihriban: When my cousin had a *yilancik*, an abscess, his parents took him to a holy tree near Erzincan where there is water and a snake. The snake sucked the abscess out. I also saw women putting leeches on their leg veins to make them disappear. In springtime, people would go to special thermal waters that were good for rheumatism and skin diseases.

Helin: Many women died in childbirth. Babies were born at home with help from the village midwife, but sometimes a woman was alone. When I was about five, I was with my brother taking the cows to the field. Around us were green fields full of flowers, and I remember looking for *yemlicks,* like spring onion grass, to eat. We would always eat things we found on the way. I heard a woman scream. Scared, I yelled to my brother, and we ran over. The woman was covered in blood, and was banging a rock on this long cord attached to a baby. After she tied the cord and wiped herself, she told me to go back to the village and let the people know. I ran all the way. When I arrived, I turned around and was shocked. She was right behind, her baby wrapped in her clothes.

It was always a very exciting, important time when a baby was born. The children dressed in colourful clothes and went door-knocking, to give everybody the news of a new baby in the village. Everyone celebrated.

Ayten: My mother would make a special traditional food called *shioriqurt.* She would cook the bread, then cut it and put garlic and yoghurt on top. When the bread had softened, she made a hole in it for melted butter. She would take it to the new mother, whose visitors would eat the bread by taking a piece with a fork and dipping it into the butter. It is gluggy, so it makes a funny sharp sound when you swallow, which is why it is called *shioriqurt.*

Mihriban: When a woman gave birth, all the people cooked different things to take to her house and we stayed up all night singing and dancing. In our culture, we do not leave the woman alone, because a bad angel might come and take the baby or the mother's life. My mother was always telling me that when she was giving birth to me, there was fighting between two villages, and nobody was at home except for my 12-year-old sister. My mother called to her, "Please stay. Maybe a bad angel will come", but my sister left her alone and she was very scared.

Seher: Someone had to stay with the mother and child for 40 days, because if they are left alone, we believed, an ugly woman with wild hair, called Qilkagizkine in Kurmanji, or Alaqalakur,[d] would come to harm the woman and child, to make them sick or die.

Ayten: It is hard to explain, but that belief stays with you—you can't get rid of it. I am a trained nurse, but when I had my son in Australia, I put a clove of garlic under my pillow to keep that thing away. If Qilkagizkine visits a sleeping baby, it is dead in the morning.

Seher: We also believe that if Qilkagizkine comes to the barn to play with the animals or to ride the donkey or horse, and we catch her and put a pin in her collar, she cannot take out the pin. She becomes human. She stays with you, working in your house. When she cooks the food, especially bread, the dough never finishes. She makes bread endlessly. But if you let her free by taking out the pin—they say some people have done this—she disappears, and after two or three minutes, you can hear screaming and see blood. People say she is like a genie, and if humans touch genies, they cannot go back to their world. The other genies kill her.

Mihriban: When a baby comes out bruised and blue and dies, I heard people say "Tarva" in Dimili. I think it means something like 'ghost' or 'bad fortune'. We have many ghost and angel stories. When I was about six, Helika Gizken, the Dimili name for Qilkagizkine, visited me. I felt something very heavy stuck on my chest. I could not breathe. I was very scared, and called, "Mummy, mummy", and she came and put a needle in my pillow so Helika Gizken would go away. Helika Gizken is a bad angel or devil.

Seher: A woman who could not have a child would ask her husband to buy a sheep for sacrifice, a tradition from when Abraham was going to sacrifice Ishmael.[e] Also, she ties material on the branches of a special holy tree and makes a wish to have a child. Sometimes, these things worked.

Mihriban: There are many trees and stones that we believe are holy. We go and tie a ribbon or something around them, kiss them and make a wish or pray, "God please help us." There are holy mountains, like Duzgunbaba, the biggest mountain in the Dersim area. I remember when I was 10 years old, we went to Duzgunbaba and met a very rich Turkish Sunni woman from Istanbul, who was visiting the holy place a second time. She could not have children, but after her first visit, she gave birth to twins, so every year, she told us, she came back and gave money and clothes to the villagers.

In my village, all the Alevi women made candles, and every Thursday night, my mum lit candles all around the house to remember the spirits of our dead people.

Ayten: If we did not have wax, we cut a piece of material, put it in melted butter and lit it.

Mihriban: In summer, the whole village moved with the sheep to one or two *war'e*, Dimili for 'a place of lovely pastures and weather'. Each family had a stone house where they lived for the summer months. Before we moved into the house, my mum would light a special candle made from wax and cotton and leave it burning while she sang a prayer-song which translates, "Snake, snake, beautiful snake, if you are living here, please go. My children and I are coming to this house. Please go ..."

Helin: Ours was a very traditional village. Most of the people had no contact with the outside world, so we had many superstitious beliefs and people believed in all these ghost stories, particularly the women, who would tell their children. I remember when women walked past the cemetery, they would carry special things in their pocket, like a soft cheese that goes harder the longer you store it and a yoghurt called *chokelik*, to protect them from ghosts. Women were told not to go out of the house alone at night, especially when the moon was up, because they would be seen by ghosts. If they had to go out, a man had to accompany them. Thinking back, it was a good way to stop them leaving the house! As babies, my sister and I had a little *muska* pinned to the inside of our clothes to keep away misfortune, but I do not know exactly what a *muska* is.

Mihriban: When babies got sick, there was no doctor, so where did the people go? The Alevi went to a *de'de* and the Sunni went to a *hoja*, like a *mullah*, and the *de'de* or *hoja* wrote, even if they did not know how to write, something on a bit of paper, and the person believed this *muska* would cure them.

Ayten: They fold the paper, sew it in a special cloth, and pin it to the clothes or hang it around the baby's neck, or they put it in water and drink it.

Seher: When I was about 12, we opened a cloth *muska* to see what was inside. We were very excited, but all we found was a scrap of exercise-book paper with a quote on it from the Qur'an, in very primitive handwriting—half in the Latin alphabet and half in Arabic.

Helin: The Qur'an had nothing to do with ours.

Mihriban: There were also good ghosts! In our village at New Year, when there is snow everywhere, a man would dress as a hunchback with a white beard, to make himself look like Kalkek in Dimili. Children were sent from house to house to collect food, and everyone came to the home of the poorest family and cooked and ate together.

Seher: Alevi Kurmanji people call him Galek'e Khizir and Sunni call him Galek'e Sersel.

Helin: Galek'e Khizir was meant to represent a spiritual, non-existent person, like an angel or holy man who comes to do good and reach all those who are suffering in their time of need. He can turn up at your doorstep in any form.

Seher: Galek'e Khizir comes in January for Sunni and in February for Alevi. These things happened in the old days—I never saw it. My mother told me.

Ayten: This tradition has been going on from the time before Islam.

Helin: People lived in such isolated, mountainous places. I have relatives by marriage who literally live under the ground. You have to walk down stairs to their house. The women have access to nothing outside the village.

Seher: Now there is communication like television.

Helin: My village did not get television until 1986.

Ayten: My village did not get electricity until 1991. We had little lamps. At six o'clock, you were in bed, and at six in the morning, you were up to take the animals out.

Mihriban: We lived in a two-storey house, made of white stone that my parents had to cart on their backs, because the place where it is found is inaccessible to donkeys and horses. The animals were kept on the ground floor, and we lived on the top floor, in two big rooms and a large corridor. All the children slept on mattresses in one room, our parents in another room. The visitor's room was whitewashed, and our bathroom had a cement floor, a fire to heat water, and a big metal basin.

Whoever was at home would bring water in a copper bucket from a big cement pool fed by a nearby natural spring. My mother made tomato paste and yoghurt, and would grind wheat in a handturned *degirmen*, or she would take the wheat to a *degirmen* moved by water. She made bread on a *sorj* in Dimili—a round metal plate resting on three stone walls, with a fire burning underneath. When there was not enough wheat, she would ration the bread, and my parents would feed the children before they ate.

In winter, sometimes the bottom storey of our house would be buried in snow, so we had to use the top-floor window to go outside. My mother sometimes boiled the snow to wash clothes. Children from five or six nearby villages came to the village primary school, but when there was too much snow, they had to stay overnight in our houses. The river would ice up, and my father had to cross it by donkey or mule to get things, although in summer, he always stored whatever he could under the house, to be ready for winter. In winter, he sometimes cooked and helped mum in the house, but I don't know how we survived with one jumper, one vest and one pair of socks.

Helin: For families who had no animals, the women would spend summer days going to the fields and wild pastures to collect firewood and animal dung, called *tezek* in Kurmanji, which they used for fuel, as well as wild berries and green vegetables.

Seher: Those with animals put them in the barn at night, and each morning would take all the animals out to pasture. The women would collect the manure, carrying it out in a barrow, and make paddies, adding hay if it was available. They dried the paddies in the sun, on the grass or on earthen bricks, and stored them in piles beside the house or on the flat roof. They always had to prepare for winter.

Ayten: For drinking and cooking water, we had a special pipe coming from a spring between the rocks on a hill. The water, very cold in summer and warm in winter, tasted beautiful. A creek running through the village gave us water for washing clothes, dishes and ourselves and for the animals. In winter, this creek became ice, so my father had to walk half an hour in the snow, on special wooden platforms attached to his feet by string, to get to the main stream. In summer, my mother usually got the water and the women and girls collected wood for winter. If you ran out of wood, it was bad luck!

Mihriban: Your neighbours and relatives would help you. As Alevi, we must always keep the fire burning. For Muslims and Christians, fire is a symbol of Satan, but fire is holy for us—it saves lives in the cold, snowy mountains—and we never put water on a fire. We believe this brings misfortune, the end to our family.

Ayten: The fire burns throughout the day. At night, the woman arranges the ashes so that the fire is there the next morning. If the fire needs to be relit, the woman goes to her neighbour and asks for their fire. Before she brings the fire home, she says a special prayer that the fire will not bring bad luck or misfortune or a curse upon the family.

Helin: The neighbour must agree to her taking the fire, because it is their fire and energy.

Seher: I remember one winter in Ankara when I was about 10. The wood heater was burning and the room was warm, but my mother told me, "Put more wood on the fire. Always keep the fire alive." I said, "Mother, we don't have enough coal and wood. We can let it go out." She said, "No, no. It must burn always", but we later changed this lifestyle, because we did not have enough wood or coal. One night, I went to put water on the fire and she said, "Don't do it! That is a very bad thing. Let the fire die itself." Then we got an enclosed coal heater and lost this fire culture.

Helin: As well as farm work, women generated an income for the family by using their resourcefulness. They worked long hours sewing clothes, mending, and making woollen doonas, *kilims* (woven matts), tapestries and socks, yoghurt and cheese.

Mihriban: My mother generated income for the family by making *kilims* and doonas to sell. She learnt the craft when she lived in Konya and she taught the other women.

Helin: On my visits back to Kurdistan, my grandfather and uncle would comment that it was the women who kept the family together and took all the responsibility for the children and the elderly. In many ways, they did all the planning and controlled the home life and domestic finances. They decided what food was needed and what had to be saved or stored.

Seher: Inside the home, the Kurdish woman is very strong. She is the backbone of the family, because she serves everyone, and it is women who carried on the Kurdish language and religion, not men, but still, they were completely dominated by men. When you talk about finances, most people think of money, whereas in Kurdish villages, the lifestyle did not involve a lot of money and women did not understand financial matters. It was invariably the man who did the buying and selling outside the home, and it was up to him how much money he handed over for the household.

Ayten: My mother made butter, cheese and yoghurt to sell, but my father would sell it, because my mum had never gone to school, so she could not speak Turkish or read and write. She never knew how much money he got for the things she made. Even in 1996, when I went back to Turkey and went to the shops with her, I offered her money to buy clothes and she said, "Darling, I don't know how to spend money."

Seher: Many men did not want their women to go outside and communicate with other men.

Ayten: For my mother, it was because she did not understand Turkish or how to read. When my parents moved from Dersim, people made fun of the way she spoke.

Seher: In Ankara, my family wanted to buy a house. My father did not like the house my mother chose, and later we bought a house he liked but we did not. It was his decision because he controlled the money.

Helin: I am not suggesting women were independent.

Mihriban: Kurdish society was and still is a very patriarchal society. The men make all the important decisions, like, in the past, which children were educated, for how long and where. Sometimes, it was a matter of finances; other times, the father did not want to send the girls away to school. In my case, I went to the village school when I was seven and learnt Turkish for one year, then started preparatory class. In Grade Four, we had a fanatic Sunni teacher. He was Kurdish but very arrogant. He would come to class with a gun in his pocket, and my father was worried he might hurt us. At the time, I was a class monitor responsible for seeing that my fellow students had clean nails and uniform and a suitable haircut. During the Alevi 12-day fast, this teacher made me cut the boys' hair in the shape of a cross, saying, "If you do not do it, I will cut your hair". To shave or cut a male's hair is taboo for Alevi during fasting, but this was the teacher's way of flouting Alevi traditions, to make us angry. After that, the people had a meeting, signing a petition asking the teacher to leave the village. We never saw him again, but we could not go to school until another teacher came.

In my last year of primary school, I did an exam to enter a boarding school for training teachers. Although my father wanted me to have an education, he was worried about letting me go. A woman in the village said, "How can you send this girl far away to school? Anything could happen to her!" The next day, he told me I could not continue my education. I was very angry. One teacher in particular pleaded with him, saying, "Please—she is really good at school." Instead, I was sent with the other village girls to learn from two women how to make *kilims* and do tapestry and embroidery, to prepare ourselves for marriage.

My father had spoilt me from when I was a baby, especially after my three-year-old sister died. If a day went by and I did not see him, I missed him terribly. As a family, we ate together, not like other families, where the men and boys eat first. I was always with him and he was very loving, so when I was 13 and he suddenly decided to marry a second wife, my world turned upside down. I thought, "He doesn't love us. All he wants is a son." I asked if I could go and live with my married sister in Istanbul and my father said no, but I said, "Again, you are stopping me for no good reason. I'm not going to listen to you." In our culture, you always listen to your parents. When my uncle came, I thought, I am going even if my father kills me, and this time, he did not argue. I think he felt guilty about taking me out of school, so I travelled with my uncle to Istanbul, where I had to learn proper Turkish.

I attended a sewing course for two years, then had to leave for want of income. For two years, I stayed at my sister's, looking after my nephew and sewing, then in 1975, decided to come to Australia, where another sister and her family lived. I was 18. My father said, "It is too far. I have heard they eat people in Australia!" I said, "I have to make my own life. I do not want to get married yet." The teacher who had shown special interest in me later saw my father in Elazig and asked, "Where is Mihriban?" He said, "She is in Australia." My teacher said, "You didn't let her go to school—how can you let her go to the other side of the world?"

In Australia, I worked for 12 years in factories, in between having three babies, then completed a child-care course and worked for three years in child care. Now I have nearly completed a Bachelor of Social Science.

Ayten: My older sisters never got a chance to study, because the school was far from our village and did not accept us. In our culture, girls cannot rent a house in a big city to study, like my brothers did. Also, my father could not afford to send us all away. When my turn came, he decided to put me and my younger sister into a boarding school in Dersim, but even this opportunity was stopped later, when the government brought in a policy saying that whoever did not live in the area could not go to this school. One family of cousins did not go to school at all.

The boarding school was for boys and girls, so many fathers would not have sent their daughters. I remember that when my father took me to the school, he told the principal, "She is your daughter now. You can do what you like with her." Afterwards, I would say to him, "Remember what you said? How could you say that? After those words, they had the courage to do whatever they liked with us." From the age of seven, I was under the control of the principal and teachers.

There were 520 students, studying from Years One to Five in primary school and Years Six to Eight in secondary school. The boys would tease the girls, call us names and always put us down. Most girls would get upset and go quiet, but I always stood up to the teasing. Actually, I exchanged punches with a few boys! If a teacher saw us fighting, we were made to stand in a corner of a room, and sometimes the teacher would hit our hands, toes, bottom or back with a piece of wood.

One Sunday, I was in the playground with my eight-year-old friend from the same village and the vice-principal was doing routine work. He called her into his office, and an hour later, she came out crying. I said, "What happened?" She did not want to tell me, but I persisted. She said, "Please don't tell my parents. They're going to kill me", and described how he had touched her everywhere, undressed her, raped her, then walked out of the office and shut the door. She was so young, blood was running down, so I took her to the toilet to clean her and change her clothes.

I knew where the principal lived, and we sneaked out and went to his place. I told him what had happened. He said, "I'll refer you to the court". Her parents were notified, and walked for two days from the village. There were no buses back then. They took her to the doctor and got a report, then took her home. Before the court case, the vice-principal told me, "I am going to kill you if you dare to be a witness in the court." I went to the principal, who was very kind, and told him, "He's been threatening me. He will not let me go to court", and he said, "I will come and pick you up."

The court case took six months. The judge kept wanting more evidence, and during this time, my friend's father said to me, "How could you let my daughter go through all this?" I said, "What can I do? I am a child too. I only wanted to help her." He nearly bashed me in the schoolyard. Finally, the vice-principal was sentenced to some months in prison, before being transferred to another school! I do not know how many girls he had touched, because most would have been too scared to come forward.

My friend never came back to school. She went through months of depression and twice tried to commit suicide. She could not get married, because everybody in the village knew what had happened, and the family had to move. In 1987, my mother told me she was happily married with kids, but that experience will stay with her.

We had only three Turkish teachers at the school. They came from Izmir and the Black Sea and they were very racist, right-wing people. When they told people they were going to teach in Dersim, people said, "How can you go there? Those Dersim people will kill you", but when they came and no-one did anything to them, they started to take advantage of the young Alevi girls, caressing their hair, neck, back or breasts. When the boys saw this, they confronted the teachers, "How can you come from Turkish states and abuse our girls? If you don't leave, we will kill you". The boys bashed those teachers, and over a period of a few months, all three teachers were forced to leave the school.

Many bad incidents happened to me. There was a boy who came from Varto, near the city of Mush.[f] He lost all his family—grandparents, parents, uncles and aunts—in an earthquake. He was crying day and night, saying, "I have no family, no place to go." We were at sport, and he was upset and I was patting his back. The sports teacher shouted, "Are you trying to seduce him?" I said, "No! I am comforting him because all his family have died". The teacher ordered, "Come here." He dragged me to a wall, held me against it and pressed his thumbs into my eyes. It was so painful, I said, "What are you doing?" "It serves you right. You must not go near boys". I was crying and the principal came—a different one to the one who had helped my friend. He said, "What's wrong?" I told him. He said, "You're an *agha's* daughter". He thought my father was a rich *agha*, and this principal was against *agha* landlords, thought to be the richest people on earth in Turkey. He said, "What this teacher did is not enough", and smacked me with a stick on my hands and back.

There were some kind teachers. One morning, we were at assembly and were being made to say, "I am Turkish. I am proud of being Turkish". A friend and I started saying, "I am Kurdish. I am proud of being Kurdish." A Kurdish teacher standing on the stairs heard, and shook his finger at us, saying, "Don't do that", but we kept saying it. After assembly, he said, "I want to see you two". He took us to a classroom and said, "Do you know what you are doing?" I said, "We are not Turkish. We are Kurdish." He said, "You are studying at a Turkish school and you have to follow their rules". That teacher was a bit soft—you could answer him back—and he said, "Because I am sensitive with you, you are taking advantage of me. Hold out your hands." We had to cup our fingers, and he hit them with a ruler, which is very painful, but we started laughing and he became angry, so we ran away!

Seher: At school, we were never taught anything about Kurds, except a few lines in one book about Shaykh Seyid Piran. The book said he was a religious leader who staged a religious uprising that was defeated by the Turks.

Helin: My mother talks about teachers coming to the village in the late 1950s, and how the village leaders had arguments with the teachers over religion and teaching the children in Turkish. They forced the teachers to leave. Over time, the government became strict about villages accepting teachers, so when my mother was 13, a school was established in the village. She attended for one year, before marrying at 14.

The teachers were always men from Turkish towns and cities. They had been thoroughly indoctrinated by the Turkish education system. Consequently, many people felt it was bad for Kurdish girls to be educated. They would be contaminated and corrupted, morally and culturally. Also, many were afraid to send their children to school, because the government would intentionally put extremely violent Sunni or Alevi Kurdish teachers into Alevi villages. I think this was a systematic policy, although it is not documented, so it is hard to prove, but these Kurdish teachers were actually more aggressive, physically abusive and disrespectful than the Turkish teachers. They hated Kurdishness and were very harsh on the students, perhaps because many had come from Dersim, and had been taken away from their parents after the Dersim uprising, to be raised in boarding schools. They had been abused as children, so they were abusive. They also had to prove their loyalty to the Turkish system more than did the Turks, and perhaps thought it was their duty to force education and the Turkish language on people they considered backward.

I started school very young, when I was five, because I had my older sister's identification papers. So many children died that a girl born afterwards would often not be registered. There were 50 to 60 children in the classroom. The older children were on one side of the room, the younger ones on the other. I was never abused personally, because I was a very keen, obedient student, so the teacher took a liking to me, but the abuse I saw was horrific. In the first week of starting school, I saw this Kurdish teacher heat a metal rod on the stove and beat a little boy until he was bleeding, because the child did not have a pencil. When the boy collapsed, the teacher sent a child to bring the mother to take her son home. This teacher would punch students in the face. We had wooden hangers in the classroom, and he would hook a child on a hanger, leaving them dangling for hours. One boy nearly choked on his uniform. The child may have had dirty hands or a torn uniform or been unable to understand Turkish. Every day was the same, and I feared going to school. The teachers had so much power that parents were too afraid to do or say anything. All they could do was not send their children to school.

Seher: If a parent complained, the chief of the village would say, "Shut up. The teacher is educating your child. What more do you want?"

Helin: If the leaders in the village made a petition to remove the teacher, it was often rejected, so sometimes, they took matters into their own hands. But some of these teachers were children of *de'de*, people we were meant to respect. The system made Alevi Kurd hate Sunni Kurd and traditional Alevi hate 'progressive' Alevi.

Seher: They created a division, to stop Kurds coming together in a nationalist movement.

Mihriban: My parents and other people taught us to hate Sunni Kurdish more than Turkish. The way they explained it was that under the Ottomans and in the time of Kemal Ataturk, the Sunni Kurdish hurt and killed the Alevi Kurds more than anybody.

Seher: There is an old saying, "If you are Sunni and you kill 10 Alevi, you go to heaven".

Mihriban: People who go and live in mainly Sunni areas are told, "The Alevi are communists. They are against religion". They are taught to hate and fear Alevi.

Helin: They assume we are against religion because our villages did not have mosques. I never saw a Qur'an. No-one prayed or fasted in our house.

Ayten: Ninety-eight per cent of the people were Alevi in the villages in my area, but in the mid-1970s, the government came and built a mosque in every village. They forced people who had never been inside a mosque to go and pray. Over time, people used these mosques to stable their animals, which is very disrespectful.

Mihriban: There is still no mosque in my village. Two hundred years ago, it was an Armenian Christian village, and now it is an Alevi village. But in the last 10 years, more and more mosques are being built in the Dersim area and people are becoming conservative.

Ayten: In our family, we were never forced to believe or practise anything like fasting. It was our choice. The only thing my parents said was, "We are Alevi and we are different to Sunni", but at boarding school, we had to go to religious lessons and they forced us to pray and learn the Qur'an. We were against it, asking, "Why can't we practise our own religion?" The Qur'an contains some really healthy stuff, but men interpret the Qur'an and take every right, leaving women with nothing.

Seher: Alevi are under a lot of pressure, because Sunni rule Turkey, and they say Alevi are against Islam, they are infidels. In 1995, 35 Alevi were burnt to death at a conference in Madimak Hotel in Sivas. Some fanatic Sunni Muslims began throwing stones, then set the hotel on fire, while the police stood around, taking no action for six hours. They said they did not have the numbers to do anything, and eventually, the army came. People were taken to court, and some political people were implicated but later released. The investigation is still going on. Alevi cannot practise ceremonies such as Jem.

Mihriban: Jem is in autumn. They celebrate with food, music, singing and dancing. At Jem, my father's *de'de*, a dervish, would come. We were his *talip*, the families he was responsible for, and he would play the *saz*[g] and go into a trance. One time, I was laughing while everybody else was crying. My uncle's wife threw me out!

Seher: Today, many singers, artists and Sunni Kurds celebrate Jem, but even when my mother was growing up in the village, Jem was practised secretly; otherwise, the gendarmerie would come. Being Alevi in Ankara, we could practise only inside the home. We fasted for 12 days without water, and at the end of fasting, we ate the sweet soup called *ashura*, with 12 ingredients. Mum always lit candles on a Thursday night, to remember the holy people, but we kept our beliefs and identity secret, because people said, "Alevi have dirty beliefs. They are gypsies, low-class people." If people called us Alevi, we said, "No, we are not Alevi", and if they said, "Oh, dirty Kurd", we said, "Kurds live in our village, but we are different." We denied everything, yet the Alevi philosophy of loving people as equals, being tolerant of different people—is very good.

Helin: For me, Alevism is about respecting life: human and animal. For instance, many Muslims do not allow animals inside their home or near the tap, whereas we love our animals, our cats and dogs. But because of Turkey's assimilatory policies, many Alevi are leaving behind their culture. I still have some of the culture, but I do not clearly understand it.

Seher: Some people say Alevism comes from the older religions of Ezidism and Zoroastrianism and was influenced by Islam. Like Ezidis, you can only be an Alevi if you are born to Alevi parents—no-one can convert.

Ayten: I only heard about those old religions after I came to Australia.

Mihriban: In Turkey, Ezidis are called Satan worshippers.

Seher: Other people say Alevism is a branch of Islam, with Christian and Shamanist beliefs, but if it is, it has broken away to such an extent, it could be called a different religion, like Christianity is to Judaism. Also, there are differences between Arabic, Turkish and Kurdish Alevis. The Arab Alevis are more influenced by Islam, whereas the Kurdish Alevis are more influenced by Ezidi ideas. The Turkish Alevis have been influenced by the Kurdish Alevis and *de'de*, but today, most Turkish Alevis have completely lost their identity.

Mihriban: My father was an Alevi *de'de*. He came from a family of *de'de*, and my brother should have been a *de'de* but is opposite to our father in every way. In summer, my father farmed wheat and vegetables. He had only two cows and no sheep, because he did not have a son until his second marriage. But in winter, when he could not work, he would visit his *talip* in the villages and in the cities of Elazig, Kars, Varto, Dersim, Erzincan and Sivas. A *de'de* and his *talip* have a common background. He would pray for them and help them. If one of his *talip* went into the army and left a young wife and children, my father would take food, such as a sheep. If there was a problem or argument, the people would come to him and he would calm the situation. He loved his *talip*.

He taught us the basic Alevi rules: be true with your tongue, hands and body. Do not gossip, use bad words or insult people; do only honest work; never hurt people; and do not abuse your sexuality. Look with desire only on your husband or wife, look on others as your brothers and sisters. When I asked, "Where is God?" my father would answer, "God is not in the sky or in the earth. God is in your heart", but he would also say, "God is in the shiny face of the moon", and he believed Ali was the incarnation of God. He told us many stories about Ali. Ali could protect people by turning into Aslan, Turkish for 'lion'. In Kurmanji, they say, "Ali yeh Shair" ('Ali the Lion'). Later, the socialists said that Ali was like any other Muslim leader, killing people if they did not convert to Islam, but my father loved Ali and his wife, Fatimah, the Prophet Muhammad's daughter, who was like Mary is to the Christians—a holy woman—and their two sons. We had pictures of Fatimah, Hasan and Hussein in our house. My father believed Muhammad was a prophet, and we called Jesus Peygamber Esa, or 'Prophet Jesus', but he believed Ali was God and would one day return to earth.

Devout Alevis like my father fast for 12 days about a month after Ramadan. In those 12 days, my father ate only bread and a yoghurt drink at night, no meat or onions or water, because Ali's son Hussein and his followers died from not being given water at Kerbala. At the end of the 12 days, he would sacrifice a sheep and eat a special sweet soup. Every 12 years, he sacrificed 12 sheep for everyone to eat.

Helin: All religions teach basically to love and respect one another, but our ideas are based on the information we are fed. We were taught that Ataturk and the Turks protected Kurds from trouble. Soldiers would come to the village and collect the young 'troublemakers'—people they suspected of being politically active—and people were told that this was done to protect them. We were in Australia when my uncle's son joined one of the leftist organisations. I remember my mother being very angry, crying, "How could he do such a horrible thing?" She thought he had joined the enemy. She had become Turkish in Australia! She was 28 years old when she came. She could not speak much Turkish, but in the hostel, we were surrounded by Turks and any translations were done in Turkish. In the mid-1970s, we mixed with Turkish migrants. At that time, Kurds from Turkey denied their Kurdishness. I went to school with Turkish children, and if I said I was Kurd, they would say, "Oh, dirty Kurd", so until I was a teenager, I denied my identity. I got used to saying, "I am a Turkish Muslim." When I started being honest and outspoken about my identity, I got into many arguments.

Mihriban: My experiences in Istanbul changed my views on Sunni Kurds. When I was 16, my brother-in-law arranged to meet his daughter and me at his friend's restaurant. This friend was a Sunni Kurd, and I was really scared, but when I went inside, the restaurant was bright and crowded. The people greeted us warmly and invited us to their house. They insisted we eat with them, and when we went to bed, they gave us lovely pyjamas. The way they acted was exactly like in our culture.

Helin: The division among people has been politically created. Alevi culture has many similarities with Sunni culture. For instance, in our dress code, we may not cover our heads, but traditionally, we were required to wear socks and long skirts.

Ayten: I had a Sunni neighbour in Australia whose father-in-law went to Makkah for *haj*. One day, she was visiting him. She had her head covered, but when he saw a little skin on her chest, he said to his son, "Tell your wife to cover herself. I don't want to see her like that again." Can you imagine? She was his daughter-in-law! To me, that is putting a woman down, and compared to that, Alevi women are free.

Mihriban: Even though my father was a *de'de*, he never pressured his six daughters to practise the religion or cover themselves. He would put me on his lap and kiss me and say, "This is my daughter. She is strong. I am proud of her." That is why I feel Alevi women are more independent. We stand up and have our say.

Ayten: In the Dersim area, 60 per cent of Alevi girls finish high school, whereas the

Sunni Kurds around Diyarbakir and other places often do not let their daughters go to school after a certain age, because they believe a girl should marry, have babies and stay at home.

Seher: Muhammad was not against women's education, but the reality is that men interpret Islam to suit themselves. If you argue, "Muhammad said that", they might say, "Ah, that is true", but they still do what they do.

Helin: Generally, Alevi boys and girls, men and women, socialise more freely.

Ayten: This is why so many Sunni put Alevis down. When I was studying for four years to be a nurse in Canakkale,[h] near Gallipoli, the hospital manager was Sunni Kurdish, and he would say untrue things in front of people, like, "Alevi girls have indiscriminate relations".

Helin: Yet, many politically progressive Sunni people are more open than traditional Kurdish Alevi, and it also varies within Kurdistan of Turkey and between other parts of Kurdistan, between traditional and progressive villages, towns and cities and from family to family.

Ayten: Helin is right. In some areas, people are leaving behind the restrictions of the past, while in other places, where Islam is affecting people's lives more and more; they are becoming more conservative, even Alevi people.

Mihriban: I am spiritual. I am not religious. I am not against religion, because it gives many people strength and solace, but I think Islam has let women and children down. It has conditioned society to think a certain way. In the Qur'an, it says women must cover and be modest, so people make value judgements based on that.

Seher: On Turkish SBS radio in 1996–97, there was a report about a 14-year-old girl from a Kurdish town like Diyarbakir, where Sunnis live. Her mother killed her because someone caught her looking at a young boy and said bad things about her. This is an extreme example of how common law, gossip and people's opinions affect people's lives.

Helin: I think that incident is very uncommon, and the media like to make an example of it for their own reasons, but it is true that in Alevism and Islam, there have always been strong codes of behaviour. People are unforgiving if you make a mistake—if you disobey your family. If you fall in love with the wrong person, you may not be allowed to have contact with your family. You have to live in a form of exile. Kurdish men and women are very much controlled by community opinion, which is formed not only by religion but also by culture.

Ayten: One big problem is that our mothers do not explain anything. They are shy, and also, because I went to boarding school, I saw my mother only once a month, so when I got my period, I was scared. I thought I had lost my virginity. I cried, "Where can I go? What will my parents say?"

Mihriban: It is taboo to talk about puberty and sex. They never explain. If there is women's talk, they say, "Girls, go into another room."

Ayten: I was lucky. When I was crying, a girl two years older than me came up and asked, "What's wrong?" Her stepmother was from Istanbul and had educated her about these matters, so she showed us a pad and said, "Don't be scared. It is normal. We are all going to have this". Later, we asked one of the four female teachers to give some information to the young girls, and so in Years Six, Seven and Eight, they started to educate girls about puberty—only a little information, but it was helpful.

Mihriban: When my older sister got her periods, she cried and went to my mum, saying, "I have cancer". My mum laughed and said, "No, you are becoming a woman."

Helin: We never saw or heard our parents showing each other affection.

All women: We do not have female circumcision, not in Turkey, not in Kurdistan.

Interviewer: Until recently, it was common practise to circumcise young girls in Kurdistan of Iraq and Iran, but the women always did it in secret.

Seher: Really! I have never heard about it. I have only read that it is done in Africa.

Ayten: I heard that they circumcise prostitutes, so they do not have pleasure.

Mihriban: In our village, girls would talk to each other about the boys. When one of us liked a boy, she would write a letter, put it in a matchbox and throw it out the window, and the boy would come and get it.

Seher: If we had a crush on a boy, we kept it secret, because we thought people would gossip and use it against us.

Ayten: At boarding school, I would never let anybody know I had a crush. I was very active and brave, and to tell you the truth, the boys were scared to come near me. After I finished Year Eight, we had a ceremony, and our parents were coming to pick us up the next day. A boy came and said, "I'm in love with you and I'm going to your parents to ask for you. You have to give me an answer: yes or no". I said, "Don't be stupid. We don't want to be like our parents and get married at 15, and I will never marry a Zaza!" We were all Kurdish, but 70 per cent were Zaza people, speaking Dimili, and 30 per cent were Kurmanji-speaking kids. But later, I married a Zaza!

Mihriban: It is not like in Australia, where an Anglo-Australian will marry an Italian or Lebanese or whatever. Because I was Alevi, I would never think of marrying a Sunni Kurd. But for both Alevi and Sunni girls, virginity has always been a big issue. It still is, but 20 years ago, even more so. Before the wedding night, a woman who was like the bride's matron of honour would come to the bride, give her a special cloth and say, "This is for the virgin." That first night is very hard for the girl. She does not know what to expect. She might have a romantic dream of what marriage is going to be like, but she has never been touched by a man, let alone kissed and so on.

The next morning, all the women come to the girl, check the cloth for blood and have a party. Alevi and Sunni do this, and yes, this happened to me! My husband did not want it, but his mother insisted, because I had been living in Australia for one and a half years!

If the girl is not a virgin, the husband tells his mother, who tells the other women, so they do not come for the party. In the past, the husband or his family would return her, or her parents would say, "If you want, kill her".

In the late 1970s, socialist women spoke up against this wedding-night practice, and now, people claim to be open-minded. They forget it still goes on. We are very good at keeping secrets.

Helin: On my visits back to Erzincan and our village, I was surprised by how the girls are still very concerned about their reputation. They would not walk down certain streets or near a group of boys, and did not want to be seen out at night.

Seher: This is the people's mentality, even in Ankara. These days, if they know a girl is not a virgin, they might not say anything to her face, but they say bad things behind her back. Sometimes, the husband will keep it a secret, because it is still a dishonour to marry someone who is not a virgin.

Mihriban: In the past, it was usual for girls to marry as young as 12, and it was always the father who decided who his children married. If the mother was clever, he might listen to her, but often he would say, "She's my daughter. I will decide."

My maternal grandmother died when my mother was six weeks old, so her grandparents raised her. When she was 12, she had a crush on a boy, but her grandparents made her marry my father, who was 10 years older, because they wanted her to be taken care of before they died. She always told us, "Until I had three children, I was always remembering that boy. I loved your father later", and she advised us, "Don't ever marry someone you do not love." But she had no say, and when my father married a second wife, my mother had no say. My dad was 60, my mother was 50 and his second wife was 25. My sister was older. They all lived in the same house, and my mother was very unhappy, but she was very good to my stepmother. They did not fight. My mother said, "It is not her fault. She is like my child. It is your dad's fault that he got married", and later, after they moved to Bursa, my father got sick and died. That was in 1983. His only son to my stepmother was 12 years old. My stepmother remarried, leaving her three children with my mother. My mother really loves children and all us children love each other.

Before he died, my father wanted to arrange all his daughters' marriages. My sister in Istanbul had an arranged marriage when she was 14. She had five children by the time she was 23. When my mother was pregnant with me, my father's brother's wife was also pregnant. They agreed that when the babies grew up, they would marry. We became each other's *beshikkertme*, or 'promised one', before we were even born! We grew up together, and I loved him very much, but as a cousin, so when it came time to marry, I fought with my father and said, "I am not going to marry him." If I had married him, I would have become an *ana*, because we were both from *de'de* families. An *ana* still has to do everything her husband says, but she has respect in the community and solves problems among the women.

I came to Australia when I was 18. One and a half years later, my father asked me to come back to Turkey to marry. I went to my village, and I was going to marry a journalist who worked for a small political newspaper, but his father was always arguing with my father, so my father was against the marriage. I met a cousin on my mother's side, a schoolteacher, and we decided to marry. My mother loved her nephew but did not want any trouble, so we ran away at night, two hours by car, to his family. I had never been to his village, but his family were very happy that their son was marrying me, and one week later, we had a big party for three days and three nights, with drums and *zirnas*[i] playing and everyone dancing in the street. Twelve sheep were sacrificed. I was at the celebration from the beginning, but I was so scared, because I did not know anyone and, as the bride, had to sit inside while all the young girls came and talked to me.

The journalist was tolerant and accepted the situation, but his family was not. His father and uncles had a physical fight with my father and male relatives. My family had to leave the village and move to Bursa, outside Kurdistan. It was terrible. One month after my marriage, I came back to Australia. My husband followed eight months later.

After I divorced, I changed my surname. My brother, who lives in Australia now and is a very close friend, said, "Why don't you change back to your maiden name?" I replied, "Our father got married to have a son. You carry his name. That is enough." But also, I really love my father. Some people swear by God, but I swear by my father. I was very angry with him when he got married a second time. I felt so rejected and, afterwards, would confront him. Once, he told me how his relatives had pushed him to marry his second wife, and that if he had wanted to do it, he would have done so when he was much younger. Once, he cried, saying, "I am old. What if something happens to me? What will happen to my children?" I felt sorry for him. Even so, he made trouble for every daughter!

Ayten: It was very unfair what my father did to my sisters. My older sister was in love with someone, but our father forced her to marry his uncle's grandchild, who came from the city. He thought she would have a more comfortable life, but she lived in misery, until the whole family was killed in a car crash in 1982. He also forced my younger sister to marry someone she did not know. My mother was very upset for her daughters. She cried day and night, cursing my father. A couple of times, he beat her, because a woman is not meant to speak against her husband like that.

My father thought he also had control over me, but I chose my partner. I met him when I was working as a nurse in Konya, and we were friends for 15 months. I told my father, "It is my decision. If you don't agree, I will pack my bag and go". He was very upset, saying, "Even my sons do not speak to me like this", but I said, "Father, I love and respect you, but please, I am going to spend the rest of my life with my husband. I don't want my marriage to end in divorce." My husband and I signed the papers in a marriage office. Neither family came and there was no celebration, but later, we went on a honeymoon. Over time, my father came to accept my choice and now really loves his son-in-law, because my husband is a very good man with a lot of respect for my family.

Helin: Nowadays, in Erzincan and our village, most people decide whom they marry.

Seher: I was very independent and free-thinking. I knew I would not find a suitable Turkish or Kurdish man. I was eight years old when I first learnt about Australia and Aborigines in geography. I thought, "Australia is in Europe but it has African people!" From the beginning, Australia fascinated me. I read more and more, and from when I was 10, I decided, "Australia is my country. I am going there", but my family never expected I would do it. By the time I was 30, I was still single, so when I got my visa, all they could say was, "Look after yourself". Even the Turkish community in Australia was shocked that I came as a single woman.

Ayten: It is not only the men who are dominating. In the past, brides would live with their mother-in-law and suffer a lot. A mother-in-law would treat her daughter-in-law like a slave. My mother ran away with my father when she was 12. He was 22. Her mother-in-law and brothers-in-law made her suffer terribly. I remember my mother crying and telling us how her mother-in-law would hit her with a hammer! My mother had a broken head, a broken leg, a broken arm and a broken shoulder. True! My grandma never let my mother go and see her own mother. My mother's mother would have to visit her in secret. If her mother-in-law found out, my mother would be bashed. Her mother-in-law would say to her son, "Your wife's done this and that", or "She answered me back", so then my father would bash my mother, saying, "How dare you do this! I don't care if she is wrong. You must respect her".

Later, my father gave my older sister the key to the house to hang around her neck. This meant her duty was to look after the house, and prepare the food for when he and the others returned from the field. Twice, my grandma came to my sister and said, "Give me the key. I'll mind it for you." The first time, she hid the key in the stable. When my father returned and asked my sister for the key, she told him, "Grandma has it", but the old woman denied everything, saying, "The girl must have lost it." My father hit my 12-year-old sister over the head with a shovel so hard, he nearly split her head in two. There was blood everywhere. Two months later, my father found the key in the stable but said nothing.

The next time my grandma tried that trick, my sister followed her and saw where she hid the key. When she told our father, all he could say was, "Don't go near your grandma, or if you do, hide the key", so he must have realised what she was like. She was a very nasty woman. Her husband had died when she was pregnant with my uncle, and I think that made her harsh, always wanting to keep control. Even when she was bedridden and dying, she demanded to know what was going on around her. She would not shut her mouth. I was 11 years old at the time. She never liked me, and would curse me. Even today when I talk about her, I hope she is burning in hell.

Seher: There are a lot of Kurdish and Turkish stories about mothers-in-law, but I have never heard of a kind one! They had these rights because they were older and claimed they were educating their daughters-in-law, and how they treated their daughters-in-law reflected on how they were brought up. It is psychological.

Ayten: In a village, up to 60 families lived together, and they all got ideas from each other, so they were all the same.

Mihriban: They were not educated; they did not know any better. It was the only way they knew how to control their family, to make them listen. But there is also a personality factor. My mother-in-law lived with us in Australia for five years. I tried to make her feel comfortable and show her that my home was her home. I respected her, but I also kept a distance, refusing to become involved with any little comment or argument. Also, she knew I could stand up for myself, so we had a working arrangement. However, my sister-in-law is not so outspoken, and my mother-in-law makes any excuse to fight with her. In our culture, the weaker person is often picked on.

Ayten: And that usually is a girl or woman. Even my older brother expected his sisters to wash his clothes and serve him a drink. He would say, "Girls should not go to school." At least he never hit us, and my younger brother was a good friend, but boys were brought up to think that men were number one in the family and that everybody should respect them and what they said. No-one could disagree. Fortunately, this value system is slowly changing. When I look at young couples in our community in Australia, I am very proud of the respect most of the men have for their wives. The wives are making more decisions. My older brother married last year, and the way he treats his wife, I am so happy. He never answers her back or swears at her. My younger brother is the same.

Mihriban: Society is changing. Even in the villages back in Kurdistan, girls and boys go out together and women get divorced. Women are realising, "Why should I be a slave or share someone I love with another wife? I am not stupid. If he can make his choice, I can make mine." Before, women had no education, they did not know the Turkish language, they had nowhere to go, they could not get a job. It is still hard to find a job in Kurdistan, but some do, and more live in the towns and cities, so why should a woman take too much pressure or abuse from her husband, especially if he wants to marry another woman?

Ayten: My uncle's son married a second time. His parents arranged his first marriage to a girl who was only 12 years old. She did not even have her period, and after three years, they still had no children, so her mother-in-law started nagging her son to marry another woman. My cousin was always away working in factories. He met a widow with no children, and she came to the village with him. After that, the first wife had six kids in a row, including four boys, and the second 'wife'—they did not have a marriage certificate—had eight girls! She became jealous of the first wife, even though they lived in separate houses, and made sure the first wife got bashed by the husband nearly every other day. As well, the husband was saying to the second wife, "If you don't have a boy, I will kick you out." The first wife lived with her in-laws and looked after them in their old age, but I don't know what happened to them, because in 1996, when I visited Kurdistan, the village was empty.

When this cousin visited my husband and I, I explained to my husband that he had two wives. My husband said, "Oh, isn't he lucky?" and I said, "Why? Do you think you are going to have another one?" Since coming to Australia, my husband has worked as a taxi driver. Sometimes, I joke, "If you see a beautiful woman, I give you permission to have another wife, but never, never come back to this house."

Seher: Now, women have more opportunities and do not have to accept their husband taking another wife. It is insulting.

Ayten: In the old days, a divorced woman found it difficult to remarry, but now, it is her choice, especially if she has no children.

Seher: Divorce under Turkish law is still very hard. The court always tries to keep the family together, even when a husband has done many bad things, and if a couple divorces, it is very rare for the woman to keep the children. Usually, the husband or his family takes them.

Mihriban: Sometimes, the girls go with the mother and the boys go with the father, but it is a very hard life in Turkey as a divorcee or a widow. When you work as a single woman, everybody teases you or sexually harasses you in the workplace.

Ayten: Still, the woman gets the blame if she separates or divorces, and when a husband leaves his wife, she also gets the blame! People say, "She did not respect her husband".

Helin: Generally, we are very family-oriented, so if a woman behaves inappropriately or gets divorced from her husband, the community does not feel comfortable with her choice. It is too different or threatening. She is not respected, and it affects what she can do, and what she has access to when something happens. For instance, if she is in need of money, she is not helped, even by her own family. She is ostracised by women as well as by men.

Mihriban: Even in Australia, this happens. I worked with my community for a long time and I was a good asset and well respected, but when I divorced, because my husband also works with the community and is well respected—when he talks, people listen—people were scared. If they talked to me or helped me, what would my husband say? What would other people say? They did not want to come between us, and even people close to me did not believe my reasons for leaving—that I felt my husband had no respect for me, that he did what he wanted without caring for my feelings. They said, "Even if this is true, you should put up with it."

I left the family house. I was renting, but no-one would tell my husband that under Australian law, I had every right to stay in the house with the three children and have a settlement. I had a lot of economic and personal problems, but I isolated myself from other people, to be with my children and to avoid criticism and advice. People did not understand. Four years later, I live a life apart from my community. People might say, "Hello" in the street and women might invite me to their houses, but I avoid visiting many families, because if the husband and wife have trouble, the husband might say to his wife, "Are you going to be like Mihriban and divorce me?" It is very, very hurtful. I think they are more conservative here than in Turkey.

Helin: If anything goes wrong, the woman is usually held responsible. We have a curse about the bad fortune a wife can bring! The man says, "What have you done to us?" or "It's your fault that this hasn't worked out!" But if the wife does something good, the man will say, "I taught her". He will take the credit for himself.

Mihriban: Like my ex-husband. When I cooked for visitors and everything was nice, the people might ask, "Who cooked this?" My husband would say, "Me, of course!" If later I said, "Why did you say that when I have cooked all day?" he'd say, "You and me, what's the difference?"

Ayten: My father was the same. If something went wrong with one of the children, my dad would say to mum, "She's your daughter" or "He's your son", but if something good happened, he would say, "Oh, she's my girl".

Seher: It is the men's mentality. Also, I believe Kurdish men escape responsibility in some ways when they say the household is the women's responsibility, because then they can go out and relax, come back and ask the woman, "Where is the food?" From what I see, Australian men are different. They contribute more within the household.

Helin: Kurdish women are generally more self-sacrificing in the family, but in my experience growing up in Australia, Kurdish women make their own decisions as to whether they are going to study or work, and some men are quite comfortable about giving their wife support; others are not. Many first-generation migrants are still struggling with the new culture, and that can create a lot of tension and conflict between husband and wife, especially when the woman wants to take more control of her life. But the second-generation women are more fortunate, because they can pick the good aspects of Kurdish culture and combine it with the opportunities in Australia, so they have more choices and, often, a more equal partnership.

Ayten: Some first-generation migrants and refugees are very strict with their daughters. They do not let them go out at all. Then they take them back to Turkey and arrange their marriage. We cannot give up our culture easily, but more young people are choosing their partners, although when it comes to marriage, generally the Kurdish like their children to marry Kurdish.

Mihriban: The boys can go out, but if the girls go out, they have to do it secretly.

Helin: Of course, it varies between families, and now, there are more Kurdish families and a much better support network, and young people are more able to socialise within the community. But when I came to Australia, at the age of six, there was not such a large Kurdish community. Two years after we arrived, my mother had to take sole responsibility for the family. She worked and cared for the children, and from when I was seven, I contributed to the family's income by helping my brother deliver newspapers. Later, I got jobs at Coles and other places. I had the freedom to work but not to go out and enjoy myself! Then, when I was 16, I went back to Turkey and married my cousin, but he was prevented from coming to Australia for another three years. Now we have two children, and I am completing a Masters degree in Social Work and working full time as a social worker. My mother has been a strong role model. Although she has some very traditional views, she has been very independent, so it is important for me to be independent, while still taking my role as wife and mother very seriously. My husband manages his own business, so we are both busy, but he is very supportive of my studies and work and I am very supportive of his business and other activities. We share the child care and household chores and make all the decisions together. It has been a balancing act for both of us, but we manage.

Mihriban: I think these days, Kurdish men are more supportive of their wives studying and working, especially in the diasporas, because it makes it easier for them. If a Kurdish woman speaks English, she is not calling on her husband to interpret for her. I know some men who are upset when their wives stay at home. They say, "I tell her to go to school, but she won't, and every time something happens, she calls me at work asking, 'What am I to do?'" They like the extra income, but still do not want their wives to argue with them.

I have been here 24 years, longer than I have lived in Turkey, so I call myself Kurdish Australian. I have taken what is good from the Kurds—the respect and love for family and neighbours—and what is not good, I have left behind. I do not want my children to be raised like me: to be shy and not say what they think, to be subservient to a dominant male and a religion. I know that even in Western societies, women do not have equal status and the same opportunities as men, but that does not mean we must turn away from educating ourselves and speaking out.

Seher: To strive for democracy inside as well as outside the home.

Mihriban: But many Kurdish women still prefer to remain silent than argue a point.

Ayten: Everything starts in the family. If the husband does not respect his wife or the wife does not respect her husband, it is hypocritical go out and scream for your rights. But as I have said, it is not just the men who want to control women. Women have a lot to say about other women's behaviour, even in Australia. If a woman is trying to be independent, to do something in the community, other women go to their husband or friends, saying, "Do you know what she did? She is not taking care of her family". Women gossip, and express opinions to be more acceptable to their husband and community, and the woman being gossiped about becomes scared, because she also wants to be accepted.

Seher: When the family and community are more important than the individual, many people cannot accept an individual's independence.

Helin: I must admit, Kurdish women find it difficult to accept different ways. This may be an unconscious thing.

Mihriban: In the four years since my divorce, I have not gone back to the Kurdish Association, although nobody has stopped me. I joined the International Socialists, because I am an active person; I cannot just stay at home and feel sorry for myself. I have to study and work, and if I believe in something and know it is of benefit for the Kurdish, or women in general, I go for it. But it is hard. Ten months after I left my husband, I saw a Kurdish friend from Iraq and he said, "I hear you are divorced." I said, "Yes", and he said, "If you were in Kurdistan, they would have killed you!" I think he was joking, but I said, "Fortunately I am not in Kurdistan; I am in Australia." Three years later, there was a Kurdish function and I went with my brother. I sat near this man from Iraq, and when my brother sat next to me, the man got up and left. Later, I said to him, "This is my brother", but I felt like saying, "Even if he was my boyfriend, it is none of your business". After my divorce, my sister died, and many relatives have been killed back in Turkey, and my family and my husband's family still put pressure on me to go back to my husband, but I am strong. I am educated. I stand up for myself.

Helin: I think this is why Mihriban commands respect. If she walked into the Kurdish Association, the men would not show her disrespect, because she has shown strength. While people may criticise her for divorcing her husband, they are attracted to this strength, even if they resent it on occasions. As far as I am concerned, in her strength she is a typical Kurdish woman. In the last 16 years, there are thousands of Kurdish women who have been left without partners and have had to support themselves back in Turkey as a result of PKK's war with the Turkish government. Some have joined PKK, some have died for PKK.

Mihriban: Although politically active people in my village were getting arrested, tortured and even killed since the early 1970s, when people first heard about PKK in the late 1970s, we were scared, because we were told by the media that they were terrorists, that they were killing people indiscriminately. Nobody told us they were Kurdish people fighting for our rights.

Seher: In the Turkish newspapers, they did not call the 'terrorists' PKK, they called them Armenian or Apocu, Abdullah Ocalan's nickname being Apo, meaning 'uncle'. It was reported that these terrorists were killing children, and burning down government utilities like schools. Under the influence of the Turkish media, we thought they were very bad people, but always I wanted to ask, "Who is Apo?" There was no information.

Helin: I can understand why people were against PKK, because we were very misinformed at school and in the media and, historically, we have been set up against each other.

Ayten: Every time there was a Kurdish uprising, the government recruited Kurdish soldiers, and put the Kurdish soldiers out in front to kill and be killed.

Seher: That is why Ocalan said we had more enemies within the Kurdish people than outside, and I agree with him. It is why we have never achieved anything, because we are too busy fighting each other.

Helin: I don't agree. Our problem is that many Kurdish people in the villages are innocent and easily led, or basically just want to be left alone to live in peace. But the rise of PKK has affected every Kurd's life, in and outside Kurdistan. People are influenced by PKK's political views, especially regarding women.

Seher: From the start, PKK established a policy about women, and always discussed the issues in their literature and seminars, asking women, "Think! What is your status? What do you want to achieve? What do men think about you? What do you think about men and their status? How has this feudal society affected your life?" When they formed the liberation army in 1984, they recruited and trained women just like men.

Helin: In Turkey, it is very difficult to know whether PKK policy has impacted on women for the better, because the Turkish government has taken such a strong stance against PKK. Government forces have completely destroyed thousands of villages and schools, and arrested and killed so many people that many are basically in fear of PKK, but PKK believe this sacrifice was necessary to save the Kurdish identity.

Mihriban: I went back to Kurdistan for a holiday with my three children in 1985. On the aeroplane, my three-year-old son was singing a Kurdish song in Turkish, about a beautiful Kurdish bride, "Gelini de gelini de Kurdi gelini". *Gelini* is Turkish for 'bride' and I said, "You cannot sing this in Turkey or the soldiers will take us to prison." We stayed one night in Istanbul, then went to Dersim. At each checkpoint, there were soldiers with machine guns. We stayed in my husband's village. Every day, helicopters flew over, and every night, army trucks full of soldiers drove through the village, the soldiers shooting at the sky. Or they shot the dogs and looked at the young girls. It was so intimidating that my children were really scared, day and night. They could not sleep. They would cry, "Please, can we go back to Australia? It's all soldiers and guns here."

Some people had children who were politically active, and soldiers would come to their houses and question them. Even so, most still saw PKK as terrorists and were scared. People were being killed and there was a lot of confusion. If somebody did not like a person, he could join PKK and kill the person and people would say, "PKK killed him", but it had nothing to do with PKK. In the 1990s, my uncle was the village *mukhtar*, the elected government representative, and he was killed. People said that PKK had done it because he was spying for the government, but later, we found out that people who knew him, but who were PKK, had killed him for personal reasons.

Many of the village children were without fathers. When we went to the little river to wash, we saw that children were dressed in rags. My children were affected, and we gave our clothes away. We went to Dersim to buy more and gave those away too.

For two months, I could not leave the village. I felt it would be selfish, that it was my duty to help the families. The women had to look after the animals and get wood and water and collect the wheat from the fields, but were scared to go outside the village by themselves. The soldiers could just come and take them away. My 15-year-old relative was taken away to an army base for four days in his underwear. They nearly killed him, but an Alevi soldier saved his life.

When I was very young, I had been too scared to go into the field, because of snakes and other animals. By the time I was 10, my parents would not let me go to the field, but when I went back, I was strong. I helped the women in the field. I lost 17 kilos! When I saw how the people were living, I felt it did not matter if the soldiers killed me.

Tension was everywhere. One day, we walked for three hours with some people to a *war'e* on Duzgunbaba Mountain. Soldiers arrived by helicopter, giving out lollies and pamphlets, saying, "If you don't keep your children at home, they will be killed like this". The pamphlets had photos of dead people lying in pools of blood. I did not realise they were doing this because PKK had declared an armed struggle the year before.

We went to Bursa, where my parents lived, a place where there is beautiful holy water, and there were 300 to 400 soldiers. One asked my six-year-old daughter, "What's your name?" We were pushing her away, trying to keep her silent, but she said, "My name is Dersim." It is taboo, against the law, to use the Kurdish name of Tunceli, so the soldier could not believe his ears. She is a confident girl, and knew about the Dersim uprising, because in our house, we are always talking politics. The soldiers followed us everywhere after that.

From all the stories about PKK terrorists, I feared them, like everyone else, but after a while, wherever I went I came across them, and they were so gentle and nice. One was a bus driver, one a teacher. I thought, "My God, they are normal people." They would talk freely, explaining women's issues, the war, how we are being affected by society, why we were not independent. They were well-educated people.

After three months, we flew to Athens for one night, and still my son did not say anything. Next day, when we flew out, about 100 metres up in the air, he started singing, "Gelini de gelini de Kurdi gelini". For three months, he had not sung that song.

We had not visited my village, because the situation was even worse there. In 1994, the Turkish government burned it and more than 2200 other villages in the Dersim area. Some people were still in their homes when the villages were burned. By 1998, a few old people returned to the village to rebuild, but many of my extended family and neighbours in the village have been killed for their socialist activities. When I walk around the villages of Kurdistan, I feel the bones of my people under the earth.

Ayten: In 1994, my family was told by the government, "Leave or we burn you with your house." They were forced to move to Izmit.

Seher: After PKK's armed struggle began in 1984, my village grew from 10 houses to nearly 100. The government brought people from other villages and backgrounds. This policy of mixing Alevi Turkomen, Sunni and Alevi Kurds, Kurmanji and Dimili speakers, means the people could not unite, so the government has more control and can gather information. The government employed many village guards, or *korucu* in Turkish, to protect the village from attacks by PKK.

Ayten: When more army came to Dersim in the early 1980s, they closed a college and made it into an army base. Many boys in Dersim have been killed, or have left for the cities, so the teenage girls are lonely and vulnerable. Some fall pregnant. After that, the family does not accept them, and they have to run away to the mountains and fight for their nation, or kill themselves.

Seher: They trick the girls. They say, "You're beautiful. I will marry you." I read one story in a Kurdish newspaper about four years ago. A girl disappeared from the village and people thought she had been killed. Two years later, she sent a message to her family: "I am here; help me". She had been taken to a brothel, but the family could do nothing but go to a newspaper journalist to research the case. Also, I have read in the newspaper that soldiers and police were giving the young people in the villages drugs, to make them addicted, so they would do anything for drugs.

Helin: I went back to my village in 1987 and 1993, and the people were still very anti-PKK and against what PKK was doing. Those who had gone to the cities and were assimilated thought PKK were Armenians or Ezidis trying to divide Turkey. The people believed the media. They had no other information. Many have lost knowledge of their background and culture and can no longer speak Kurdish. They are not even allowed to give their children Kurdish names. Eighty years of this systematic policy to eradicate our identity means people cannot distinguish what is happening in terms of right and wrong. I was shocked at how many people in the Erzincan area still felt it an insult to be called Kurdish!

Seher: I heard that some female university students in Ankara and Istanbul joined PKK. Through PKK, the more educated women began to understand more about Kurdish issues, feudal slavery and exploitation, but the civil war has affected Kurdish women in the villages very badly. The Turkish army had already been in Kurdistan for a long time, like sharks waiting to attack people, and when the war started, they found every excuse.

The army put pressure on the women especially. When they come to a village, they beat the woman, or take her clothes off in front of people, to make the men angry. When the men react, the soldiers attack.

Ayten: When people in PKK get killed, they have to educate other people, and if you bring a young person, you can educate them the way you want. If I am a 14- or 15-year old village girl in Kurdistan and you explain Karl Marx or Lenin to me, I cannot understand. But if you tell me I am Kurdish, that my people are being destroyed by the government, that I need my identity, that I am a woman and need my rights, and ask me, "Why are we not free to live and say what we like?" I can respond.

Seher: If women believe in religion or in the politics of a party, they are very strong in their beliefs, so in many ways, if you win the women, you win the people.

Ayten: Many women joined PKK or supported PKK, but many others had husbands and sons who were forced to become village guards. In Kurdish newspapers and on television in Germany, people said, "When we refused to become a village guards, they burned our houses, animals and crops, so we had to leave." If they became a village guard, they were then under pressure from PKK.

Like Mihriban, in 1996, I saw the hard life with my own eyes. I wanted to visit my sister and the village where I was born and my husband wanted to visit his parents' graves. About three or four kilometres from Dersim, we were stopped at an army checkpoint, and the soldiers searched suitcases and looked into my personal bag, shaking my bras and pants. I was disgusted, saying, "How dare you look in a woman's bag! She might have private things", and the soldier answered, "Why not? You are all terrorists, aren't you? We have to make sure you are not carrying guns."

To go to my father-in-law's grave, we had to go to four offices—the government, council, police and army—just to get permission. When we finally got it, we were told we could not take food or drink and had to come back by six o'clock.

Seher: If you have more than one pair of shoes, they take them, saying, "You are going to give them to the terrorists."

Ayten: The grave was in a village 45 minutes by taxi from Dersim, but the roads are very bad, so we had to go slowly. Some 150 families had lived in the village. By 1996, seven remained. The others had moved out, because of the hard life. Basic things like flour, sugar, eggs, tea and rice were strictly rationed so that villagers could not feed the PKK guerillas. For example, a family with four to six children could buy only 15 to 20 kilos of flour and two kilos of sugar a month. Fruit and vegetables were not rationed, but because of the rationing and the way the soldiers demanded to be fed, the villagers were scared they could not feed their children. Many mothers ate very little, just so they could feed their kids.

The husbands were suffering, too, because there are no jobs, and if you have 10 fields, you are allowed to plant only one or two with vegetables, and the rest must be wheat for winter. If you go over the limit, they will burn it, assuming you are growing food for PKK.

Seher: This is an excuse to slowly destroy the people. With all the checkpoints, army bases and police stations, it was impossible for PKK to enter most villages easily.

Ayten: In Dersim, my husband wanted to take a video of a statue of a Kurdish man who had lived through the Dersim uprising. In the 1980 military coup, soldiers came to Dersim, and this man ran down the street, saying, "The Turks are killing us again." He went crazy, and after he died, the people of Dersim made a statue of him. While my husband was filming, an unmarked car came up with two policemen inside. One said, "Excuse me. Do you have permission to tape this?" and I said, "Why should we need permission?" They took my husband and brother-in-law to the police station, and my father, my sister, her mother-in-law, the children and I sat in the park, waiting for them. I was so scared. After two hours, I went to the police station and asked, "Where are they? I don't want my husband and brother-in-law to disappear in broad daylight. I must talk to them." They checked the tape, and said we could tape anything only if we had permission from the police station. We went to Munzur River and ate watermelon. I filmed the army cottages on the hills on each side of the river, their sewerage going straight into the water that people drink. My daughter drank the water and got diarrhoea. She was vomiting all night, so we had to take her to hospital the next day. We waited in a queue of cars, buses and vans at the checkpoint in a 36-degree heat. They were even checking the identification papers of people walking, and when they searched the women, they felt in intimate places. They had no respect at all.

After two hours, my daughter said, "Mum, I'm dying." I felt so helpless. I went to the policeman and said, "Please, my daughter is very sick. Check us and let us go." He said, "You have to wait", and I said, "Look, please, I do not want to be rude, but my daughter needs to go to hospital or she will die", so he said, "Okay, you can go." When we got to the hospital, we were lucky. A doctor who comes from Elazig once a month was there. They told us, "Go to the chemist and buy some medication and a drip", and they kept her overnight.

Another day, we wanted to go to Ovaçik,[j] a town near Dersim. We got to the checkpoint at seven o'clock in the morning and were kept waiting until midday. Finally, they came to the van, collected all the passports and went away. They looked and looked—I don't think they understood anything, because it was all in English. They called my husband and asked, "Where are you going and why do you want to go?" My husband gave them the address, explaining, "We have a friend and need to give him money from his parents", but they said, "Because you have Australian citizenship, we cannot allow you to go, for your own safety". I was so angry. I said, "I do not want your protection. This is my country, my birthplace. How can you be so ridiculous? Protect me from whom?" My husband told me, "Shut up. We are not going." The next day, we left Dersim. That is the life of hell for these people.

Mihriban: In 1995, I went back to Turkey. With my brother, another friend and my daughter, I went to a Newroz celebration in Izmir. There was a crowd of 30,000, and in between the people were policemen and soldiers with gas masks and machine guns. I had not wanted my daughter to come, but she had insisted, "What I do in Australia, I do here." A policeman put a machine gun to my shoulder and said, "What are you doing here?" I could not believe that my daughter was not scared, but she saw all these children folk dancing, like colourful flowers, and said, "Mum, look at those kids. I don't care if they kill us. All these people will be killed if something happens." There were so many friendly people. Maybe 80 per cent of them were Ezidi. The women wore Ezidi rings with black stones and dressed in traditional Kurdish clothes. They held a meeting, and I went and heard them talk about how they had lost their sons in the war, but they were saying, "Even if my other children die, I want an independent Kurdistan. I want identity for my children." It was really amazing. We were introduced to one of the Kurdish leaders of HADEP, a democratic party. He later talked through a megaphone, saying, "The Turkish government say the terrorists are in the mountains, but the real terrorists are the Turkish government." Now he is in prison.

Ayten: If we had our identity and right to practise our culture and speak and write and broadcast in our own language, we would not have all this fighting and all these people would not be killed or imprisoned. We are homesick. You know how you miss one food or fruit you love so much? Well, we are craving for our identity. I just want to be accepted for who I am and not be abused for it. Even in Australia, when I say, "I am Kurdish", many Turkish people hate me. When I was working for two Turkish doctors in a pathology lab, a patient needed my help with the language and asked me, "How come you speak Turkish so well? Are you Turkish?" I said, "No, I am not Turkish, but I come from Turkey." He became very angry and shouted, "If you are from Turkey, you must be Turkish!" He stormed out and did not return. Another Turkish patient asked, "How can you support terrorists?" I said, "Just because we are Kurdish does not mean we are terrorists". She went to the doctors and asked them to sack 'the terrorist'. The Turkish doctors were happy with my work, and we would discuss the issues. They would say,

"You don't have to kill people to get your identity", and I would reply, "We have been forced into a situation where we must fight for our lives. Kurds were killed in the Ottoman army and they were killed in Cyprus fighting in the Turkish army, but Turkey has done nothing for us."

Mihriban: Turkey has 3000 to 4000 radio stations. They say we are brother and sister. If we are, why don't they give us one radio station to speak our own language? If we could teach the children in Kurdish and live in a democracy, no-one would want to go to the mountains to fight.

Helin: Although PKK activities have had mixed consequences for people's lives in Turkey, I think PKK has had a very positive impact on Kurdish women living in Australia. PKK's encouragement of women to participate in politics, and their stance that the freedom of Kurdistan is going to be achieved by Kurdish men and women working together, have given women reason to be more involved in education and politics. They have more information, they read more and, in their activities outside the home, they have more support from their family and friends.

Mihriban: In Australia, I worked for the Turkish Association, but after PKK became active, many Kurds migrated to Australia, and we established the Kurdish Association in Melbourne in 1988. We were so excited to have our own association, because even in the Turkish Association, if we talked about Kurdish issues, they would say, "We are socialist. We do not want to talk about nationalism." After I started working for the Kurdish Association, an amazing thing happened. There was a Turkish night at Latrobe University, and I saw a Turkish man I had worked with for many years giving out socialist pamphlets. When a Kurdish man gave him a pamphlet, he looked at it and said, "This is PKK!" He gave the Kurdish man a scornful look, screwed the pamphlet up and threw it in the rubbish bin. I said, "What have you done?" It was like he was throwing all the Kurdish people into the rubbish. Until then, I had not thought about PKK, but that incident made me realise how fascist Turkish nationalism is. You can work with people and agree with them for years, but as soon as you present a different opinion, they reject you completely, without thought. I began to understand why PKK had taken the actions they had. It also reaffirmed to me that I am Kurdish and that I must work for my community.

But a big problem is that what PKK says in its literature is not always put into practise. Now, it is okay for a woman to be educated and talk about nationalist issues, but it is still not acceptable to talk about women's issues. For instance, when I worked for the Kurdish Association, I asked a couple of feminists to give a seminar. Lots of men were there, and one man said, "When I come home from work, I am tired, so if nothing is ready, I will punch my wife." A lawyer on the panel said, "When you're about to go home from work and your boss says you have to stay another four hours, do you punch him? Does your wife punch you for being late?" After that, the men said, "We do not want feminist issues brought into the association. We have to work for Kurdistan's independence." I argued that we could not become independent if half the population is not respected.

Helin: I think feminism must be one of the goals for the liberation of a people. But also, the Kurdish people have been divided in so many ways that I think PKK is doing as much as possible to patch things up and progress. More education and debate is the way to achieve progress, and obviously, women need to be included. But people make up PKK, and they still put traditional family values above the needs of the individual, so that is why there can be a clash between PKK policies and feminist issues.

Ayten: We need to fight for our identity first, then address feminism.

Mihriban: I strongly disagree. PKK call themselves socialists, and socialism is about equal opportunity, and that includes women. Also, many women and girls are involved in PKK, so their views and status must be considered. But the issue goes beyond feminism. It is about being tolerant of different views. People in PKK or the Kurdish Association can say, "You are a good revolutionary, a strong patriot." But when a person says, "PKK has done lots of good things, but this is a mistake", you are ostracised, even though you are only speaking out because you love the cause so much that you want to fix the mistake. In a true socialist party, which PKK claims to be, the opportunity to express different views must be a goal.

Ayten: That is true. But in PKK, although not many women are in high positions, they get some opportunities, and we must start with little things and work our way up. I am saying it is a start. They could have said, "No, we don't want any women in the army or organisation. They must stay at home."

Seher: When women joined the liberation army, they went to a special training school where they were educated politically. It was the first step to being able to choose what they wanted to do with their lives, not necessarily just to become soldiers.

Mihriban: PKK was in an armed struggle for 16 years. Where are the prominent female leaders?

Ayten: A couple of times, I have mentioned this as well, and there are reasons for it. I will give you a small example. In the Kurdish Association, we had two women who were in positions to make decisions, and now we have a female president, but if there are no other women there to support them, or if they are criticised for what they say or do, how can they be effective? Women need other women's support. I used to be on the women's committee, but often, there was too much arguing.

Mihriban: We have to be able to debate issues.

Ayten: But there was so much waste of time and effort to arrive at a decision, then have it rejected by the management committee, that I decided to withdraw. I preferred to spend more time with my family. I want to go there when I can be helpful.

Seher: And many women will say and do only what their husbands want.

Helin: I agree that there is a lot of inequality, but there is a difference between process and inequality. In any association, all decisions need to go through the management committee, and there is always politics involved as to who is selected on the management committee.

Mihriban: Even a female president cannot work for women's issues.

Helin: The female president of the association is young, passionate and hard-working, and a good role model, but she must follow the rules. Her appointment is a positive step, but it can also be seen as tokenistic, particularly because men surround her. But also, even the management committee cannot break policy and make autonomous decisions.

Along with process, which may need reviewing, there is real inequality. Many Kurdish women lack the confidence and self-esteem to be outspoken around men. They do not like taking the risks that are necessary when making a decision and acting on it, probably because they are more likely to be criticised and ostricised.

Seher: Few Kurdish women have the experience to lead or negotiate effectively, especially when they are breaking new ground. When I came to Australia, I did not know the rules of the management committee. I thought it was going to be an easy, fun thing and I discovered it is very hard. If something went wrong, I wanted to fix it or finish it. I learned many things, but for most Kurdish women, this kind of negotiation and responsibility is a new experience.

Helin: We are generally very good organisers. For any event, like Newroz, the men come up with the ideas and the women do the actual work, but women need to become more involved on an intellectual level. It is changing slowly.

Seher: Also, women have a house to run and children to look after, but that is why women must push themselves, leave the dishes to one side and say, "That can wait."

Ayten: My husband sometimes works 20 hours a day, sometimes seven days a week. I cannot expect him to come home and mind the children while I go off to meetings.

Seher: Australian women are more educated and have more opportunities to work. Society is less judgemental and more tolerant of differences, so the women have more choice in their personal and working lives. In Kurdistan, most people are poor. Unmarried girls must stay at home and be looked after by their father.

Ayten: In Australia, a couple can live together, get to know each other, then choose. With us, once you choose your partner, you have to put up with him, although I hear it was like that in Australia 25 years ago.

Mihriban: During World War Two, when the men went to war, Australian women went out to work. When the men came back, the women had to stay at home, but many were dissatisfied and fought to go back to work. Then, in the 1970s, divorce became easier and more socially acceptable. As Kurdish and as migrants, we are now going through a similar process.

Ayten: I worked with an Australian friend in the clinic, and she preferred our culture, because her husband ran away with another woman when she was pregnant and never came to see their child. She said, "I like the way you stick together." I said, "It is not so simple. A husband can do whatever he wants, but if the woman does something wrong, she is labelled and treated badly. For you—you have a child, but you can still have a boyfriend in the future."

Helin: In some ways, we *are* better off than Australian women. We have very strong community bonds and Kurdish women stick together. We support and help each other on a daily basis, especially if a woman is newly arrived, has just had a baby, is sick or going through some difficulty, or is organising an event like an engagement ceremony, wedding or funeral. Other women will come and help with the cooking and household chores, mind the children and, for the newly arrived women, help with settlement issues like interpreting, moving house, lending money and so on. It is common for Kurdish women to spend a significant time just listening to each other's daily issues, and there is no expression of stress or burden over what they do for each other. There is a strong sense of companionship and a deep, ongoing involvement in each other's lives.

Seher: If a woman has a job, a grandparent or a relative will often look after the children.

Ayten: And Kurdish men are very family-orientated. They love their children and play with them.

Mihriban: Australian culture is not so child-friendly and supportive of mothers and children. Working at the women's refuge, I met Australian women who had been sexually abused as children, or bashed by their husbands, same-sex partners or even their teenage children! The coordinator was lesbian, and I had to adjust to this, but she was a role model for the women. She always encouraged women to be themselves and make decisions. Yet, I learnt that being more educated and having more choices does not mean that Australian women are happy. When a single woman has three children, no income and no outside help, it is hard anywhere.

Seher: For me, feminism means standing up for what you believe, like Leyla Zana did when she was elected to the Turkish parliament and said, "I am Kurdish." She was sentenced to 15 years' imprisonment for that. But throughout history, there have been strong, courageous Kurdish women without famous names, and today, in any Kurdish meeting or demonstration, you see Kurdish women participating. We have achieved many things, but still have a long way to go.

Mihriban: Neither sex should dominate the other. We must be able to debate issues and grow. That is the equal opportunity I want—to no longer hide behind men or blame them. Historically, women have always been ignored and told they are there to make men happy. Domestic violence was behind closed doors. But since the 1980s, there are even women's refuges in some Turkish cities. Over the last two decades, we have definitely seen some progress, as a result of a few women, informal groups and organisations working very hard—writing, researching and becoming political. Now, feminism is in a wide range of cultures.

Seher: If people respected each other, there would be no need for feminism or nationalism. The hope is that as more Kurdish women go overseas and compare their lives with other women's lives, and as women in Kurdistan become more educated, they will start asking questions about themselves and what is happening around them and will have more choices. They are going to have more power and influence, I believe.

ABOUT Dr Azad

Dr Azad comes from a merchant family who lived in Baghdad for five generations. Growing up in the Iraqi capital, he had friendships with people from all backgrounds and political persuasions, including influential Arabs, but his father, secretly a Kurdish nationalist and democrat who rejected socialism, was his greatest influence. Consequently, he came into contact with many Kurdish leaders of all parties. In 1966, Jalal Talabani, the future leader of the Patriotic Union of Kurdistan (PUK), lived in his neighbourhood. In 1971–72, during the autonomy agreement between Kurds and the Iraqi government, he went with other students from the Kurdish Democratic Student Union for a conference in Haji Omaran, where he met the young Masoud Barzani, who was representing his father, Mostefa Barzani, leader of KDP.

Dr Azad kept his Kurdish allegiances secret, and the only discrimination he experienced was not being able to study overseas because he was not a member of the Ba'ath Party. After graduating from medicine, he worked in Sulaimani as an intern before serving in the army. In 1974, his father foiled his plan to join the Kurdish revolution, by asking his son's connections to leave without him. His father was afraid the family would be arrested. But in other ways, Dr Azad was a revolutionist: "In 1979, I fell in love. I personally went to my future wife's family to ask for their daughter, and this is very unusual in our culture. My father refused to come to our wedding. He wanted me to marry a girl from a rich family, but I told him, 'If you have any objection based on her reputation, tell me now. Otherwise, you are not marrying the girl. Money does not make the man. The man makes the money.'"

Dr Azad was a doctor in Baghdad before moving to Hawler, in 1980, to serve his people. In August 1982, on hearing that the Mukhabarat was asking about him, he went straight home and told his wife to pack a few things. On their way out, the gardener asked them, "What is happening?" and his wife, who was crying because of this sudden need to flee, told him, "My mother is sick—we are going to see her". Within 48 hours, the government had sold the contents of their house, the surgery and the pathology laboratory.

Although a KDP supporter, Dr Azad, his wife and two children stayed at a PUK base in Balisan, then, with a letter of safe passage, were taken to Iran, where he worked as a doctor in Kirmanshah, supplying *peshmerga* with medicines, and going to the refugee camps most Fridays to treat common ailments.

In 1987, Australia accepted Dr Azad and his family as refugees. Of life in Australia, he says, "My three children have adapted well. We have everything we need, but I continue to find life very hard and far too busy".

Iraq: The Politics of Oppression

A personal view based on interviews with Dr Azad

Since the Ba'ath coup of 30 July 1968, Iraq is a country ruled by fear and violence.

The founders of Ba'athism advocated violent revolution to create a pan-Arab form of socialism, a socialism based on nations not on class. From the beginning, they dreamed of unifying the Arab world by glorifying Arab history, culture and faith. They painted these as being antagonistic to Western influences, whether capitalist or communist.

Ba'ath rhetoric has never been encumbered by fact or logic. History was simply rewritten. For example, in the early 1970s when I was the only Kurd attending a meeting for army personnel, the lecturer proclaimed, "Iraq has always been an Arab country". He then asked me, "What do you think?" I do not know what came over me, but I answered, "If you can take away the palace of Khusrau I at Ctesiphon,[a] you can claim Iraq is Arabic". Likewise, the Kurdish fortress town of Arbil[b] is thought to be the oldest continuously inhabited town in the world. The Kurdish cities of Sulaimani and Kirkuk are also thousands of years old, but the pan-Arabists prefer to start history with the spread of Islam in the seventh century. They use Islam as a political tool to play on sentimentality and unify the people.

Ba'aths claim to be socialist, but rely on one-party dictatorships, which use a fascist form of control. These dictatorships seek support from anywhere. One of the Iraqi Ba'aths' top ministers was to tell me, "In the late 1970s, we were not directly under the influence of America, so the USSR preferred us to the Shah. President Brezhnev advised us, 'Shut up about petrol prices. Do not show your muscle or put yourself in front of the saw—it will cut you. Let the Shah, their policeman, do this in the name of OPEC. America will then deal with him, because he is wanting more than his limits."

From the beginning, Ba'athism had some surprising friends. Numerous newspaper articles in the Middle East and Eastern bloc claim both Israel and the USA supported its foundation and expansion. Many Ba'aths in Iraq would argue against this, saying they started as a small group believing in Arab nationalism. However, from the 1950s to the late 1980s, when world politics was dominated by the Cold War, the Ba'aths proved a useful line of defence against the growing popularity of Soviet communism in the Middle East, and in the last 40 years, through various means, the Ba'aths have consolidated their power and oppression in both Iraq and Syria.

Consequently, I aim to show that the politics of oppression have many layers, which I will describe in relation to Iraq, but I cannot name my sources, because it could cost them their lives. I can say only that, given my family background and upbringing in Baghdad, having gone to the best secondary school with sons of the Arab elite, including one prime minister's son, I had a wide variety of contacts who rose to high rank in the Ba'ath Party and secret police. Although I also knew communists, socialists and Kurdish leaders, to survive and prosper I kept my Kurdish loyalties to myself and a few close friends. I never discussed Kurdish issues with Arab friends—I knew I could not change what they thought. Even many communists did not accept Kurdish aspirations for sovereignty. Often, I heard them say, "Kurds are stupid for dreaming of an independent country." To those loyal to the Ba'ath Party, I was a childhood friend interested in movies, music, joking, playing ping-pong and having a good time. I kept so silent, some people thought I belonged to the Mukhabarat (Saddam Hussein's personal intelligence service). Also, as a doctor, people spoke to me when otherwise they would not. I mixed with many people in different situations, and over time, incidental comments and events add up. If you are observant, if you keep quiet and listen and follow up what is said, evidence is easily gathered.

To introduce the long-term nature of this international game, I will tell you a story. To get to my primary school in Baghdad, we had to pass a Sunni Islamic centre called Majit Huzrat Shaykh Gaylani, where an old cleaner worked. He never wore shoes; his feet were thick with calluses and dirt. His hair was long, white and straggly. One day, the children I was with started throwing watermelon skin at him, and he chased them away, a terrifying glint in his eyes. We thought he was strange in the head, but he had worked at the centre for some decades. Even my grandfather remembered him.

Suddenly, he disappeared, and nobody thought more about him. Then, one day, not long before Brigadier Abd Al-Karim Qassem's successful 1958 military coup against the monarchy, government and army vehicles blocked the street in front of the Islamic Centre. Soldiers and guards stood everywhere as a cavalcade of official vehicles drove down the road and stopped outside the centre. Out of one vehicle stepped the highest-ranking officer of the cavalcade; his British army uniform covered in stars. People were shocked, gaping open-mouthed, because this officer greeted them by name and knew their business. He was none other than the mad cleaner.

Looking back, I wonder how many clerics this man had influenced or informed on in his many years of service at the centre. From that day, I realised how smart the imperialists had become. Now, they use the country's own people to do their business. The British established the Faisal monarchy in 1921, but did nothing to support the monarchy at its end in 1958, despite the British-inspired Baghdad Pact of 1955 promising to support the governments who were its signatories.

In the late 1890s, the British had discovered the richest oil fields in the world, around the Kurdish city of Kirkuk. In August 1921, following the League of Nations' signing of the Treaty of Sevres, which recognised the right to self-determination of all nations affected by the Ottoman Empire's collapse, modern-day Iraq was made a British protectorate and the British imported an Arab leader from Saudi Arabia to be king. King Faisal was a Hashemite descendant of the Prophet Muhammad and cousin to the Hashemites of Jordan, and as such, a rival to the Saudi royal family. He had been a leader of an Arab revolt against the Ottomans in Syria, fighting alongside Lawrence of Arabia, so the British said, "We owe this man." They prepared the Iraqi elite to accept him, by spreading propaganda that he was a brave, pious man.

For a brief period, the British toyed with the idea of making Iraqi Kurdistan an independent buffer state between the Turks and the Arabs, but the proposal did not include the oil-rich regions of Mosul and Kirkuk. In 1918, they made Shaykh Mahmud, an influential Kurdish religious leader, governor of Sulaimani, expecting him to take orders, but Shaykh Mahmud said, "No—you take orders from me." He covered his hands with cloth before shaking hands with the British. It is my opinion that if he had been more cooperative, the Kurds may have had more authority and influence in Iraq. Instead, Shaykh Mahmud organised a Kurdish uprising against the British and the foreign king. Then, in 1923, all hope for a Kurdish nation-state covering eastern Turkey and northern Iraq was lost when the Treaty of Lausanne recognised a Republic of Turkey and clarified the borders between Turkey, Syria and Iraq.

Under King Faisal I, there were instances of Kurdish oppression. The first atrocity was when thousands of old, handwritten Kurdish books were collected, supposedly for publication. Instead, they were burned. The monarch's army fought Shaykh Mahmud's uprisings until the Shaykh was finally captured, in 1932, the same year Iraq was given its independence and Shaykh Mahmud was put under house arrest until his death, in 1956.

King Faisal died and his son Ghazi took over. Ghazi was more ruthless than his father and held Nazi German sympathies. In 1933, he launched a genocide of the Assyrians. In August 1937, his prime minister, a Kurd named Bakr Soodkhe, was carrying a letter discussing military matters to the German government when he was assassinated at Mosul airport by a British secret agent. Ghazi realised he was next. Sure enough, a few months later, he was killed. His young son became King Faisal II, an uncle acting as regent until the king came of age. Between 1937 and 1941, there were six attempted coups, the government practising a policy of divide and rule. As a result, in the early 1940s, Malla Mostefa Barzani was drawn into fighting the government, but not as a nationalist. It was more a tribal war, and in October 1945, he escaped with his fighters and their families to Mahabad in Iran, where he became a hero of the Kurdish Republic of 1946.

However, at least under the monarchy, Kurds could rise to high positions in both the government and the army. One was Bakr Soodkhe, the prime minister, but a far more noble character was Seyid Qazaz, the long-time Internal Minister, who took a stand for his nation on numerous occasions. When the Revolutionary Court of 1958 decided to hang him, he said, "I will be hung, but my feet will be above those who do not deserve to live." However, all this social elasticity was to change after Iraq became a republic in 1958.

1958 was also the year that the chief founder of Ba'athism, Michel Aflaq, arrived in Baghdad, calling for Arab unity. Aflaq had been a Christian Syrian schoolteacher, who converted to Islam to co-found the Ba'ath movement in Syria in the early 1940s. In Baghdad, he failed to get support from the new Iraqi leader, Abd Al-Karim Qassem,[c] or his followers.

Abd Al-Karim Qassem was so nationalistic that some people say he was patriotic, but I think he was the beginning of the end for Iraq. Although his regime rewrote the constitution, supporting a democratic government to incorporate the Kurdish and Arab nations, in practice he was ruthless and devious. After letting Mostefa Barzani come back to Iraq after 11 years of exile in the Soviet Union, he brought all the Kurdish leaders to Baghdad, claiming he wanted to negotiate. Really, he was trying to control them. When Barzani realised this, he returned to the mountains. Over the next few years, Qassem tried to have Barzani assassinated a number of times. One attempt illustrates the character of Qassem. Abdu Jabar Hashim, one of Qassem's closest friends, had helped Qassem come to power. Qassem sent him to meet with Barzani in a school in the Barzan area between Mosul and Hawler. However, Barzani had received information from Baghdad and told Abdu Jabar, "I have changed the meeting place." They went to a mountain overlooking the school. Barzani supporters then sent a message to Iraqi agents, saying the meeting had commenced. Barzani said to Abdu Jabar, "Take these binoculars and see how your friend Qassem treats you." Aeroplanes came and bombed the school. Barzani said, "Now, go back to your friend."

In 1959, there were two coups against Qassem, in Mosul and Kirkuk, but the government used communists and some Kurds to squash the 'civil unrest'. On 1 May, a communist demonstration of half a million people called for government representation, then in October, a Ba'ath group attempted to assassinate Qassem. One of the group was the 22-year-old Saddam Hussein. When Qassem caught some of them, he freed them, going on television to say, "God forgive them for what happened". It was a puzzling decision from such a man, but according to some top Ba'aths, he was under pressure to appease the growing Arab nationalist movement.

By 1961, Qassem's regime was in trouble. He refused to legalise the popular Communist Party and the Ba'aths had grown sufficient in number to lead a successful demonstration in Baghdad. Between 1961 and 1963, their popularity rose further, with strikes of workers and students, and other activities. In this time, communist papers reported that Michel Aflaq was in collusion with, or was at least supported directly or indirectly by, MOSSAD—Israeli secret intelligence—to get rid of Arab intellectuals, particularly communists, because they had become too strong.

The regime was also playing a treacherous game with the Kurds. Barzani did not want to engage in armed struggle, but in September 1961, the government pushed him into war by attacking a tribe Barzani was obliged to defend. It was a war the government could not win—Barzani had many loyal supporters and the Kurdish mountains were his fortresses. Nevertheless, many Kurdish cities and villages were bombed and destroyed.

Meanwhile, the Iraq government exploited the petrol from Kurdistan, selling 43 per cent of all Iraqi oil to US companies, this percentage rising over the decades. At the same time, it kept Kurdistan weak and undeveloped. In the late 1950s and early 1960s, multinational companies helped the government build two large dams, Darbandi Khan and Dukan,[d] in Kurdistan, to supply Iraq's electricity. But no irrigation systems were built in Kurdistan's rich agricultural areas, and unlike Arab farmers in the south, Kurdish farmers were never helped with money and agricultural machinery.

Behind the scenes, outside forces were giving advice. In 1963, I read some British documents written in 1962, obtained from England through the *Freedom of Information Act*. Translated into Arabic, they contained a map of Kurdistan and a proposal to change the Kurdish demography of areas, villages and cities, particularly Kirkuk, Khanaqin, Sinjar and Shaikhan, by moving Arabs in. These areas would then be considered outside

Kurdistan, if the Kurdish ever got a state. Straight away, I sent a copy to Barzani's headquarters.

On 14 February 1963, the Ba'aths launched a successful coup, Qassem was arrested and killed the same day. On 8 March 1963, Ba'aths came to power in Syria.

America was involved in the Iraqi coup. How do I know this? A family friend, an old man whom I trusted, worked as a driver at the American embassy in Baghdad, and was present when Qassem turned up to speak to the US ambassador. Qassem was unpredictable, a man full of surprises, and on this day, he told the ambassador, "If America does not leave us alone, I will take the American skull and crush it under my feet." After he stormed away, the US ambassador laughed, saying, "What do I tell my country? Qassem does not realise it is his skull that is going to be crushed". Later, the Ba'ath Minister of Defence was to say on the television news, "We came to power on an American train." However, other Ba'aths to whom I have spoken have argued: "America did not organise the coup, but after the coup, they took advantage of the situation and bought cooperation."

A month after they came to power, to avoid fighting on all fronts, the Ba'ath government declared they recognised the rights of the Kurdish people. An agreement fell short of autonomy, but Barzani agreed to stop fighting. *Khabat*, a KDP newspaper written in Arabic, was established in Baghdad, and Barzani sent a delegation to continue negotiations, headed by the honest and sincere Salih Yousifi, later to be killed by a letterbomb sent by the government. Jalal Talabani was one of the delegates. The new government began killing and arresting communists, some of whom escaped to join the Kurdish, and by June 1963, war with the Kurdish resumed. The government was wracked by in-fighting between sympathisers of President Nasser of Egypt and the more right-wing radicals inspired by Michel Aflaq, so in November 1963, there was another coup.

The new president, Abd Al-Salam Aref, lent towards the politics of Nasser. His prime minister was Ahmed Hasan Al-Bakr, although Al-Bakr lasted less than a year in this position. The government negotiated a ceasefire with the Kurds in May 1964, but Iraq resumed the war in April 1965. A Kurdish delegation in Baghdad was arrested, and from October 1965 to January 1966, an unprecedented policy of destruction of Kurdish villages was carried out. Nevertheless, Barzani was to have some outstanding military successes. In May 1966, about 3000 Iraqi soldiers of the fourth brigade were killed by Barzani's *peshmerga* and communists on Handren Mountain, near Rowandoz, resulting in a ceasefire agreement in June 1966.

The prime minister of the time, Abd Al-Rahman Al-Bazzaz, attempted to introduce democratic reforms and negotiate a peace with the Kurds. An educated man, he appeared on television, saying, "If we have six Kurds carrying guns in the mountains, we have trouble." He limited the privileges of the military and began implementing civilian rule, but his prime ministership lasted less than a year, because he was regarded as too pro-British. Afterwards, he became a political adviser to the King of Kuwait, and then, in 1969, the Iraqi government accused him of being a traitor. He was advised by Talib Shabibi—Iraq's ambassador in London and Iraq's representative in the Arab League—to return to Iraq to clear his name. In October 1969, he was arrested on charges of being a Masonic agent. He was tortured and spent the next 15 years in prison.

From the mid-1960s, the Iraqi government began implementing British recommendations to change the demography of Kurdistan. Arabs were encouraged to move in with the promise of free land, a house or farm, a car, a machine gun and about 10,000 Iraqi dinars (US$30–$40), a huge amount at the time. Initially, the government advised Kurds to sell their houses, claiming, "We want to make a park" or "We need to build an army base", as an excuse to bulldoze large areas of Kirkuk and Khanaqin. Kurds were not allowed to repair or renovate their houses, or buy other property in the area, so they had no choice but to leave. After the 1968 coup, the more radical Ba'ath government used more forceful tactics, Kurds receiving no warning or compensation when their houses were bulldozed. If Kurds went south to an Arab area, they were able to take their possessions. If they stayed in Kurdistan, they could take nothing.

A year after the devastating Arab defeat in the 1967 Six-Day War with Israel, on 17 July 1968, a group of right-wing Ba'aths and others with US and British connections staged a successful coup in Baghdad. For 13 days, no-one knew who was in power. After another coup on 30 July, many of the principal players in the first coup were exiled or assassinated, because of their 'imperialist' links. One, Ibrahim Al-Daud,[e] commander in chief of the army, was known to provide the CIA with information in return for money, position and future promises. He had been appointed Minister of Defence between 17 July and 30 July, but after the second coup, he was sent to Jordan before being arrested and imprisoned in Baghdad. He now lives in exile. The other was Abdul Razzaq Al-Nayef, head of the army intelligence service, and known to have connections with the British Intelligence Service. He was appointed prime minister but, after 30 July, was promptly arrested and exiled. He escaped to Britain, and survived an assassination attempt in 1973, to be shot dead by Saddam Hussein's Estikhbarat (Military Intelligence) in 1978, in front of a London hotel. MI5 turned a blind eye and the assassins escaped.

The president before the mid-July coup, Abdul Rahman Aref, and his family were put on an aeroplane to Turkey. Nasir Al-Hani, chief planner of the first coup, who became foreign minister for two weeks, was less fortunate: his bullet-riddled body was found on a Baghdad street in November.

In August 1968, it was publicly announced that the Ba'ath President of Iraq and commander-in-chief of the army was Ahmed Hasan Al-Bakr. He was also the secretary-general of the Ba'ath Party and chair of the Revolutionary Command Council (RCC). At least Al-Bakr had academic, military and political qualifications, whereas the vice-president, head of Internal Security and deputy chair of the RCC had a less inspiring profile. This was Saddam Hussein. He had only a high school education, no military background and no experience in politics, except as an assassin.

How did someone like Saddam Hussein achieve such a meteoric rise to power? In 1956, as a 19-year-old thug, he joined the Ba'aths, the party becoming his life. In 1959, the party elected him as one of the hit team to kill Qassim. Afterwards, it is known, he escaped to Syria, where he lived underground from 1959 until 1963. During this time, Michel Aflaq and Saddam built up a personal relationship. The small, intellectual Alfaq was impressed by Saddam's physical stamina, personal charisma, steely determination, streetwise cunning, ruthless discipline and aptitude for assassinating Ba'ath opponents.

He suited Aflaq's contention that the Ba'aths should control the military. Top Ba'aths have told me that the young Saddam had a simple, charming manner. He was a good communicator, related to people easily and was very committed. Consequently, he was liked by the Ba'ath elite, and in 1966, on Aflaq's recommendation, he was elected assistant secretary-general of the Iraqi Ba'ath Party. No-one knows Saddam Hussein's exact movements between 1964 and 1968, except that for some time, he was imprisoned in Iraq, but 'escaped' and lived in Cairo, where some say he worked as a nightclub bouncer. It is known he studied one year of law at Cairo University. Rumours and some Arabic newspapers also maintain that during this time, the CIA and MOSSAD trained him. Whether or not foreign agents had a direct or indirect influence, in a secret meeting just before the 30 July 1968 coup, in which the Iraqi Ba'ath Party decided on everyone's future position. Saddam was nominated vice-president.

In the new regime, the president was to be elected by the RCC, the RCC having power to overrule parliament. All parliament members had to be members of the Ba'ath Party, unlike in Syria, where under president Assad a number of parties formed a United Arab Front.

The new Ba'ath rulers proved ruthless in every way. In 1969, there were a series of public hangings of Jews and 'pro-Jewish' in Liberation Square, Baghdad. The act was a psychological tactic, to blame Iraq's social problems on innocent scapegoats, a tactic used time and time again ever since. In November 1968, the government went to war with Mostefa Barzani's freedom fighters. The Iraqi air force used napalm, and atrocities were constantly reported on the illegal Kurdish radio and in underground newspapers. One was when 67 women and children escaped artillery shelling by hiding in a cave near the village of Dakan. Soldiers burned them to death.

All Ba'aths were oppressive, but Al-Bakr was an educated man who knew some limits. However, within a couple of years, it was evident that his vice-president was in control. Saddam's portrait came to dominate every public space, and over time, Saddam succeeded in getting rid of all Al-Bakr's men by either assassination or 'accidents'. Both Al-Bakr's son and son-in-law died in 'car accidents'.

Why did Al-Bakr allow Saddam so much latitude? Firstly, Al-Bakr was an old man and not as ambitious as Saddam. They were related by blood and marriage, and Al-Bakr depended on Saddam to get rid of opponents. Also, Saddam had quickly built a strong base within the party by forming a civilian wing of the Ba'ath Party, and by reorganising internal security so that it permeated through every office and level of society. To do this, he was advised and supported in the training of personnel by Cuban and East German secret police and military as well as the KGB. These advisers used to live in well-guarded compounds in Baghdad, and Iraqi people were not allowed to associate with them.

Saddam quickly developed a system where spies spied on spies. From the beginning, he established his own personal intelligence service, the Mukhabarat—civilian secret police who spied on Ba'ath Party members and on those who worked for the government. All other police and intelligence services were accountable to them. Within the Mukhabarat, there was a Special Security Section, controlled until 1982 by Saddam's half-brother, then by his sons. As well, under the umbrella of the Department of Internal Security, there were the normal police, called Short'ha, the emergency police (Shurtat Al-Najdah) and the Amn (State Intelligence Service). *Amn* operated in every office in every town. Then there was the Estikhbarat, a Military Intelligence Service, belonging to the Ministry of Defence, which spied on both army and civilians. All could arrest and kill people at will and were directly or indirectly answerable to Saddam.

Likewise, Saddam increased the numbers and powers of the military. The Forsa'an was a military group established in the early 1960s, named after a famous horseriding regiment in Arab history. The Arab Forsa'an units, called Waleed, and the Kurdish units, called Salahaddin, were sent to the mountains to fight the Kurdish freedom fighters we call *peshmergas*. The Kurds could join the Forsa'an in preference to going into the army, and would be well paid to guard army installations, kill *peshmergas*, and remove Kurdish people from villages before the regular army moved in. Usually, they would be sent to areas where their families did not live, but sometimes, they were forced to inform on their own families or fight a family member who was a *peshmerga*. Others tried to do as little as possible, and some would secretly give information and cooperate with the *peshmergas*. People were often forced to join because their *agha*, or tribal chief, was allied to the government, or they had no other source of income. In the mid-1980s, when so many soldiers were deserting the war with Iran, and when many were suffering unemployment in the new collective villages, Saddam formed two other Kurdish groups. They were the Jahafal Kaffeefa, or 'light battalion', who acted like the Salahaddin, and the Jayeesh Al-Sha'abi, a civilian militia who continued to work normally while serving the interests of the Ba'ath Party. All carried a gun, and mostly, they protected institutions and gathered information. Kurds came to call all these Kurdish groups *jahsh*, or 'donkey's foal', a term of derision.

By 1980, one-fifth of the Iraqi workforce—about 3.5 million people—were employed in either the army, the police or one of the secret intelligence services, and all people were pressured to join the Ba'ath Party. If someone working in, say, a government office was not a member, the Ba'ath representative would encourage him to join, first by giving some advantage, then through harassment, until eventually, the *amn* would be brought in, and the worker forced to join under threat of losing his job. Many were made to sign a letter saying, "If I work against the government or join any other party, the government has the right to kill me". Two Iraqi soccer players were hung in the late 1970s after signing this letter, because they were found to be members of the Communist Party.

As soon as a person joined the party, they were made to commit a crime, such as writing a damning report against one of their friends. After that, a person loses their self-esteem and becomes a tool, as the authorities can expose them at any time.

In 1975, the government issued a policy that all teachers had to be members of the Ba'ath Party. Only a few non-members remained in the system, and they would be sent to remote areas, to be continually harassed to join with interviews and threats. Teachers would ask students, "What did your parents say when Saddam Hussein appeared on television?" If a child said, "My father does not like Saddam", or "My brother spits on Saddam", this member of the family would disappear. All secondary school students were made to join the Ba'ath Party Student Patriotic Union; otherwise, they would fail their subjects. If they failed two consecutive years, they had to leave school.

Yet, many resisted the pressure to join, myself included. As a medical student between 1966 and 1972, I helped re-establish the Kurdish Student Union at Baghdad University, after it had been disbanded in 1963, when some Kurdish students were hung. The new union had two or three people in each cell. We called each other by political names, so if anyone was caught, they could not identify the others. After the 1970 Autonomy Agreement, we pressured Kurdish government ministers to lobby for the allocation of 20 places in the medical school to Kurds without a criterion of marks, and they achieved this goal.

Very few people knew about my activities. After I graduated, I had to go into the army, and in 1973–74, an Arab army officer friend came up to me, saying, "Join us". I laughed, asking, "Which Ba'ath organisation are you talking about?" He said, "I am directly connected with Saddam Hussein's office. Whatever you like, we will give you. If you want to make a Kurdish party, we will donate millions of dollars. I am not asking you to join the Ba'ath Party—that is only a name." I told him, "You want me to work for Arab nationalism! I am not against Arabs, but I am Kurdish. If I betray my identity, I am capable of betraying you to someone who will pay me more. Leave me alone. I am not a politician. I am a doctor." "No, Dr Azad, you are wrong. You are like my brother. Join us." I said, "No—please do not ask me again", and he responded, "I will give you three months to think about it." When he came back, I said, "No", and that was it—they left me alone for years. When I was working in Hawler, a Ba'ath Party leader said, "Why don't you work for us?" and I told him, "I am working for you every time I work in the hospital."

After 1976, while I was a doctor, I joined a group that distributed underground literature, collected money for the KDP party, and relayed information to *peshmergas* inside the city. We also bought secondhand clothes imported in big bales from Europe and the USA, to send to the *peshmergas* in the mountains.

But life was becoming more and more difficult. If you had a set of binoculars in the Kurdish territory and you were not *jahsh* or army, they could hang you. Zoom lenses for cameras were not allowed. To own a typewriter could cost you your life. If you had permission to own one, the *amn* had to have a copy of its typeface on file and you had to keep your typewriter in a locked iron container. If it got stolen, you had to inform the *amn* at once. I needed to type pathology reports, but preferred to handwrite them, giving *amn* no excuse to search my home. There were no computers with printers, or photocopying machines, except in lockable government offices, because people might use them to produce articles against the government. In Iran, I was surprised to see photocopiers on the street and people paying to copy whatever they wanted.

You could be arrested for anything. If someone reported you throwing a newspaper with Saddam's picture on the ground or in the bin, it could cost you your life. There were checkpoints on every road, inside and outside the cities, to search every car. As you walked down the street, secret police, army or ordinary police could check your papers at any time.

I was on a medical committee in Hawler in the early 1980s, and sometimes, we went to the prison. It was a small, crowded place for family of *peshmergas* and others. One day, I was walking through the prison yard when I saw a child of nine months, crying and being comforted by a lady. I asked, "Why is he here?" and she said, "He is not my child. His father and mother are *peshmergas*, so they gave him to another family to mind. To blackmail his parents into surrendering, the *amn* took the child and put him in prison. They were not feeding him, so I take care of him".

Some prison stories are so terrible, you do not know whether to believe them or not. One Kurd who worked with me belonged to the Islamic Movement. He was a very devout Sunni and swore by God that his story was true. He said, "I was arrested on my way to the mosque, for being an Islamic activist. They took all my clothes and put me in a cell. That night, they brought a girl to my cell. She was Al-Da'awah (a Shi'ite political group) and they took all her clothes, telling me, 'You have to have sex with her.' When they left, I told her, 'You are my sister. You are suffering like me. I will never touch you.' In the morning, they saw that nothing had happened between us, so they tortured me, hanging me from my legs and hitting me. Then, they raped the girl in front of me." I have heard similar stories from people I trust. There was a lot of sexual abuse in the prisons—breaking taboos is a good way of breaking people. They must live in shame long after their release.

Everyone was under observation. I was told by an insider, who had firsthand knowledge of their importation, about special long-distance directional microphones the government would place on power poles to pick up conversations inside a house. Most of the people who worked on the telephone switch had to cooperate with the secret police and listen in on calls. I could usually tell who were secret police in the hospital. They were the ones who could come and go without permission. Always, any one of the people who brought the tea or cleaned the rooms could be secret police, listening to conversations and reporting on visitors.

Speaking simple truths was very dangerous. One morning in 1981–82, I was watching television in the hospital and drinking tea with a doctor friend, Malih Habib, a Chaldean Christian, a kind man who helped many people. A news report was showing the Abadan oil refineries in Iran blazing after an Iraqi bombardment. Habib said, "Why are we fighting these people? What grievance do we have with them?" There were three other doctors in the room, and I knew one worked for the Mukhabarat. No-one else knew—I found out only when we were walking down the street and a senior *mukhabarat* stopped his car and warmly greeted him.

I pinched Habib's hand and told him quietly, "Shut your mouth", but he ignored me. "Why do we destroy them and they destroy us?" After we finished our tea, I took his hand and said, "Let us walk, Habib". Outside, I asked him, "Why do you say these things?" "But I have not said anything wrong". I said, "You have made a big mistake. Please take your family and run away. I cannot tell you more than that". Habib said, "Why?" I just repeated, "Take your family and run. Now. The *peshmerga* are not far. They will help you escape." He repeated, "I don't understand." Three days later, he disappeared. His family found his body in a sack in a street close to their house. It had been cut to pieces and the head burnt in an oven. To do their very dirty work, the Ba'aths choose people who are psychologically abnormal: violent people who can commit crimes for no reason or desperate people who will do anything for money.

By developing such a ruthless, pervasive, institutionalised system of control, Saddam became invincible. In this kind of society, you can never be spontaneous—you always have to check yourself. You are never safe, whether alone or in company. Yet, nothing is black or white. Some Ba'aths you could trust, whereas others who were not Ba'aths, you could not. It depended on the individual and how long you knew them. For instance, one of my university friends became a high-ranking officer in the army's secret intelligence. As a student, he had been a member of the Ba'ath Party of Syria, working in opposition to Saddam, so he would meet with us, but later, he was told, "We will kill you if you do not join us." One day, he came to visit me at the army base and joked, "Oh Azad, why have you not run away with Barzani?" I joked back, "Sorry—I have had no luck to run away—I would appreciate your help in doing so." He laughed, then went over to my commander, saying, "Don't give Azad any holidays. He is a good friend of mine. Take care of him."

Many times people wrote reports saying that I was not supportive of the Ba'ath Party, then friends with inside information would warn me to be extra careful. People would write a report either from jealousy or for political advancement, or after being pressured.

But cooperation with the Ba'aths is no guarantee of survival. If you know too much, question some decision, or have greater loyalty to the wrong Ba'ath member, you are killed. This is what happened to Jabar Kurdi. Jabar Mostefa was his real name. A Kurd, he had become a civilian Ba'ath Party member before 1963. He worked as an assassin. It was he who was involved in the plan to kill Iraqi Defence Minister Hardan Al-Tikriti, from the same town as Saddam, in October 1970, after Al-Tikriti ran away to Kuwait. Jabar Kurdi's crime was supporting Ahmed Hasan Al-Bakr more than Saddam. He had no fear of Saddam. He would go around saying, "We made Saddam", so in the late 1970s, he was killed, and all the people who worked for him met a similar fate.

Likewise, death awaited Nadhim Gizar (also known as Nazim Igzar or Kzar), whom Saddam had appointed head of Amn in 1969. Gizar had organised five *imams* to negotiate with Mostefa Barzani in Haji Omaran in 1971. One was given an explosive device to wear, after being told it was a tape recorder. The *imam* exploded, Barzani survived and all but one *imam* were killed by *peshmergas*. Nor were they meant to return to Baghdad: both cars had been rigged with explosives.

Gizar was responsible for thousands of communists being killed and tortured. He ordered terrible things, such as pulling out their eyes, but in July 1973, Gizar was discredited and Saddam Hussein ordered his hanging, after it was claimed he tried to organise a coup while Al-Bakr was overseas. The real reason was that as head of Amn, Gizar had too much power. Following his execution, the television showed pictures of nitric-acid baths Gizar had used for disposing of bodies, the government claiming they had not known of these.

This is the terrible situation for Arab and Kurd alike in Iraq. As for the Kurdish situation, in March 1970, the Ba'aths negotiated an Autonomy Agreement with Mostefa Barzani, which was to take three years to implement. It promised that Kurds would be represented in the parliament in Baghdad, so until late 1973, there was a break in fighting and about 30,000 *peshmergas* were paid to be border guards. All Kurds supported the treaty, although many thought it would take too long to implement. At least there was time to recover from 10 years of war. Too many villages had been destroyed. People had lost their livelihoods. There were no teachers for the schools and a lot of people were unable to go to university.

Generally, life did improve in this brief time of peace, and the government built some much-needed hospitals and schools. But the agreement turned out to be a big mistake, because Saddam also used this time to build up his power base, the armed forces and intelligence, and to improve relations with the USSR. Between 1958 and 1963 and from 1968, Iraq bought arms from the USSR and the Eastern bloc. As well, demographic changes continued, particularly targeting Kurdish intellectuals and leaders. If they did not escape the country, they would be forced to move south or were assassinated. The Ba'aths also bought the loyalty of more and more *aghas*, by supplying money and arms for their *jahsh* forces.

By 1973, it was obvious that the government was not sincere in its negotiations, and in March 1974, full-scale war resumed, the Kurds united behind Mostefa Barzani and Ibrahim Ahmed (father-in-law to Jalal Talabani, who was to become leader of the other major Kurdish party, PUK, formed in 1975). The revolution was supported with money from the USA,[f] which was channelled through the Shah of Iran, with the Shah also supplying hardware. A friend of mine who worked for the Parastan (KDP intelligence), tells a story from this time. In 1974, he was in the Haji Omaran area when he heard sirens. Everyone ran for cover, but when no aeroplanes flew overhead, he went outside to investigate. He ran into a line of mules, looked up, and saw Henry Kissinger dressed in Kurdish clothes. He was quickly pushed aside, and concluded, "We will either get a government soon or be destroyed." I can only conclude that Kissinger was on his way to meet Barzani.

In February 1975, US and Iranian support of the Kurdish revolution suddenly came to an end when the Shah of Iran and Saddam Hussein, still vice-president at this stage, signed the Algiers Agreement in Algeria. In return for the Shah discontinuing his support of the Kurdish revolution in Iraq, he was to be given rights to use the waterway of the Shatt Al-Arab and some pockets of land along the border. An amnesty was declared, and Mostefa Barzani asked his *peshmergas* to cease fighting and hand over their guns. He left for the USA, where he died in 1979, days before his scheduled to return to Kurdistan of Iran following the Iranian revolution.

From 1975, persecution of Kurds escalated dramatically. All Kurdish border villages were evacuated and destroyed. Two hundred thousand people were forced to escape to Iran. In the beginning, government agents were sent to buy the animals and land at very low prices, but later, people received no compensation. To hurry the evacuation, particularly after a newly formed political coalition called the Patriotic Union of Kurdistan (PUK) started activities inside Iraqi Kurdistan in 1976, the army burned the crops and the orchards. They put cement in the springs, destroyed other agriculture with chemicals, and laid landmines in the 'liberated areas'—areas under *peshmerga* control. Soldiers and the pilots had orders to shoot anything on sight—animal or human. People were moved south to camps or to government-built collective villages. These massive treeless complexes on the plains near army bases were more like prisons, with few ways to go in and out, each road having a checkpoint or army base every 200 metres. People would have to get permission to travel, and even when they had permission, they would be interrogated at every point.

Around these complexes, there was no farming land and no work, so the people, who had known only farm work, were unemployed. Those who could get permission would go to the cities, where they could find poorly paid labouring jobs; otherwise, they were forced to join the Forsa'an, having no other source of income.[g]

If a Kurd in Kirkuk had a visitor staying with them from Baghdad or from another Kurdish area, they had to tell the *amn*. At any time, the *amn* could come to a house and check who was there. If they got information that you bought more bread or milk than usual, or a report was written about you, they would come and search your house and take away anyone considered suspicious, many never to return.

Around 1978–79, Saddam issued a ruling that an Arab marrying a Kurdish woman was entitled to more than US$15,000 in dinars. If an Arabic woman divorced a Kurdish man, especially a Fayli Kurd, she also got money.

The Fayli Kurds[h] were a particular target. They had been merchants in the suburbs of Baghdad, like Tappakurd and Aggid Al-Akrad, for 200 years. There were 700,000 Fayli Kurds living in Iraq, and because the Fayli are Shi'ite, the Sunni Iraqi government regards them as Iranian, but because they are Kurds, the Iranian government does not want them. The first deportation of the Fayli occurred in 1942, under the monarchy. Then, between 1968 and 1971, about 70,000 to 100,000 were deported to Iran. The third and biggest wave of deportations occurred in 1980, when 200,000 Fayli were sent to Iran. The Iraqi government invited 500 Fayli merchants in Baghdad to the Ministry of Commerce for a meeting. *Amn* surrounded them, took their money and identification papers, put them on buses and took them to the border. They were accepted into Iran, but the Iranian government refused to give them identification papers, making them non-citizens, even though, when the Shi'ite Arabs of the south were deported from Iraq, the Iranians gave them all necessary documentation.

Back in Iraq, all the Fayli families' property and assets were confiscated. Women and children were allowed to follow, but males between 15 and 50 were kept back and imprisoned, so they would not join the Iranian government or *peshmergas*. In 1980–81, 7000 young Fayli men from Baghdad disappeared without trace.

Under the Ba'ath regime, no family remained unscathed. In 1981, my younger brother disappeared. I had been told he was under observation, although he was not politically active. I had warned him, "You must leave the country; otherwise, they will kill you", but he was a young student and said, "I can manage myself". I became angry, saying, "Leave this place, please. I can arrange for you to join Barzani or Talabani, or with their help go to Iran or Turkey, or I can arrange for you to go to Kuwait or Jordan." "No". A Kurdish person informed on him, and he was arrested on a Baghdad street and taken to a police station. I was told where he was and went to visit him. He said, "Please be careful. They may do it to you." I told him, "Don't worry about me." I made inquiries and was told, "Your brother is under arrest until the war with Iran is finished." He was transferred to Abu Ghreb prison, the most secure prison in Baghdad, where I visited him once. It was after that visit that I fled with my family to Iran. No-one knows what happened to him. Afterwards, my mother died of breast cancer and grief at the age of 42. My father was forced into exile by the government and can never return to Iraq.

My wife's family has also suffered. One brother was imprisoned and tortured for being a member of a Kurdish student union. Another was assassinated in 1987.

His body was found in a mass grave near Hawler after the 1991 uprising.

Living under these conditions for four decades affects the mental and physical state of everyone. There are no statistics—anecdotal evidence is all we have—but suicide has become more common. Sometimes, the suicide is long after an event. For years, many people dream of their experiences. Eighteen years after leaving Iraq, I still dream about secretly going to Baghdad and having the intelligence service observe me, record my conversations or chase me.

Too many people suffer depression, which can manifest in tiredness, a sense of worthlessness or unexplained crying. Many experience an inability to make decisions, or lack motivation, long after becoming refugees in a new land. Some become tolerant or numb to what is happening, then have a delayed reaction or no reaction at all. The first time you experience someone die, you might feel extreme sorrow, but when death becomes an everyday event, you can build up a tolerance. In the Iraqi-Iran War, one could travel between two cities and pass 20 to 40 cars carrying coffins. Down every street, there were plaques on several doors, saying a family member had died or was missing in the war.

After so many years of living in fear and a state of siege, many find it hard to trust others. They may feel unwelcome in other people's homes and are unable to make new friends, being paranoid and suspicious of everyone's intentions. In extreme cases, they might think they are being followed or watched, their conversations overheard or taped. Sometimes, they have good reason to feel this way, because even in Australia, it is dangerous to talk freely. There are agents everywhere, and at any time, they can cause a family member in Iraq to suffer. They know where we are, what we do.

Others suffer from mania, one minute passive, the next extremely aggressive or angry over a trivial matter. Later, they might apologise, realising there was no reason for their behaviour, but some do not have this awareness. Fortunately, a lot of family violence is prevented by mediation from other members of the family. Many Kurds are very critical, especially of their own community. Sometimes, they have good reason to be critical, because of their experiences back in Kurdistan. When people change their allegiances, they change their story.

People can feel guilty. If people supported the Iraqi government, or handed themselves over in an amnesty, or if they become refugees, leaving family and friends still suffering, they say, "I should have stayed to protect and help them." This is illogical, because if you stand against a huge storm, it will destroy you.

Some suffer from an ill-defined anxiety, and a few from obsessive neurosis, perhaps turning the light off, then coming back to check it, or washing their hands again and again. They have lost all confidence in themselves. Finally, when a person has lived through so much pain, it is hard for them to have compassion for others whose life experiences are very different.

Then, there are physical symptoms. Living under so much stress means a high percentage of the population have diabetes, blood pressure and heart attacks as young as 24 years. Depression and anxiety can manifest in insomnia, terrible headaches, backache, stomach problems and joint pain: multiple symptoms, unrelated except by their psychosomatic source.

Some people have a strong tolerance to pain. It is like any disease. If a person is not so tired and rundown at the time of the trauma, they may be better able to deal with it. It can depend on economic and other environmental factors—whether you have support from relatives and friends. People who seek connection with other people are better able to handle trauma than those who are isolated, but when a person has been betrayed by friends, it can be very hard to connect. A strong belief in something like God or the Kurdish cause can keep you strong, or it can leave you feeling betrayed, with many questions, like, "Was it all for nothing? Why have I put my life and other people's lives in danger when the people who cooperated with the enemy have a much better life?"

Then, there are people who may show an acceptance of the past but, over the years, lack a sense of optimism or joy in life. It is a subtle form of depression. Past memories lie dormant, but can surface at any time—when you sit alone or see something. You think about all your friends who have disappeared or are dead. If you are a strong personality, you say, "This is life". You do not surrender yourself easily, but the quality of your life may be questionable.

Most Kurdish people, even as refugees in a new land, do not seek professional help for their mental conditions. Some have already experienced disbelief from UN or immigration officials. They are told by people with little understanding, "These are made-up stories", while people who know how to cheat the system are believed. Sometimes, the less painful story is more believable. Many people try to forget rather than remember. They do not want to talk about their deepest suffering, particularly if their experiences are taboo or shameful.

Otherwise, people can sit with other people, talk and sometimes joke, or listen to sad songs or watch a sad movie and have a cry. Songs and movies can reflect and elevate one's own experiences. Some go to a doctor about physical symptoms and end up talking about their suffering. I tell them, "We suffered, but there were good times and bad times and life is about struggle. We have lost a lot, but it is not the end". It is important for people to mourn, have their experiences validated, and then find a way to rebuild self-esteem, a sense of safety and a feeling of control. This may take a lifetime, a generation or longer.

Despite the long-term trauma, the national and international games of oppression continue, the main players not necessarily in total control of the forces they unleash or their consequences. To make my point, I will go back to the early 1970s, when I was at university. I knew science graduates who were being sent to study bacteriology and virology at European universities. They came back and worked on top-secret projects such as the hybridisations of viruses: making more virulent cultures of typhoid, cholera, anthrax and equine encephalitis. A Kurdish man working at Arbil Hospital told me that he had been employed as a chemical scientist at the Samarra Drug Company, working in an underground chemical factory. They transferred him when they discovered he was a Kurd.

Chemicals were being imported from European countries, and Russian scientists were being housed in well-guarded compounds in Baghdad. In the early 1990s, PUK claimed they could list 20 Russian scientists involved in chemical and biological weapons research in Iraq. From personal experience, I knew that prisoners were being used in experiments from the mid-1970s.

In 1976, when I worked part time in my own surgery in Kifah Street, Baghdad, a friend I trusted—he had been a *peshmerga* back in 1963—came and told me, "My brother was in army personnel and was told by the army hospital that he has encephalitis. I trust you—could you please examine him?" His brother was skin and bone. He had lost his hair and was suffering severe headaches and some paralysis. I told my friend, but not his brother (I did not know if I could trust him), "You must tell no-one what I am about to say. He does not have encephalitis. It looks like they have given him a poison, but I do not know which one. Were there other people with him?" He told me, "Yes. There were 17 people. Some were civilian and others were army personnel. All were put in one prison for a short time, interrogated, then given some yoghurt, kebab, bread and tea before being sent home. Two months later, the symptoms appeared in all 17. Some are completely blind and some have worse paralysis than my brother." All who were arrested used to work for or were associated with Jabar Kurdi. All were to die.

In the 1970s, Saddam Hussein visited a house, after the whole street was cleared and guards posted everywhere. He asked one of the children, "I am your president—do you love me?" and the child said, "No". Saddam said, "Why not?" The child said, "You imprisoned my father." Saddam told the guard next to him, "Release the father." The father came home, and died three months later. A neighbour to the family told me this.

In 1980, I knew of another death by poison. The secretary of the medical college at the University of Baghdad had a son who ran away because he was a member of an Islamic party. When the authorities took the mother in for questioning, they gave her something to eat. She went home, and died two months later.

By 1981, a person with the same symptoms as the *peshmerga's* brother I had seen escaped to England. British doctors discovered he was suffering from a thallium overdose. A BBC Arabic program claimed there was proof that two people had died in Iraq from thallium, and another 15 were profiled. That is how I found out the Iraqi government was using rat poison, and I know or have heard of 200 people who died this way.

Mosul prison was another experimentation centre. I knew a building contractor who was one of 10 men arrested for a small crime, like bribery, or taking more money than they should have, in about 1980. They were put in Mosul prison and exposed to chemicals. All died. Doctors who did the autopsies told me the bodies were a bluish colour, and that there was bleeding from the mouths but no signs of torture. The authorities buried them without letting their families see the bodies.

In the late 1980s, four prominent Kurdish people suffered from poisoning. Dr Mahmud Othman, formerly a KDP central committee member and later head of the Kurdish Socialist Party, Adnan Mufti and the poet and journalist Sami Shorish were present at the dinner. *Amn* or *mukhabarat* planted in the house a Kurdish woman servant, who fed them thallium-laced yoghurt. The four prominent Kurds survived, but two at the dinner did not.

Chemical and biological weapons were being developed in Iraq from the mid-1970s, financed by oil revenue and foreign banks and helped by chemical and biological imports from foreign chemical companies. By 1987, these chemical weapons were being used to bomb Kurdish villages and *peshmerga* bases, culminating in the chemical bombing of Halabja on 16 March 1988, when over 6000 Kurdish civilians were killed. To my knowledge, no Western leader reacted, except Australia's Foreign Minister at the time, Bill Hayden, who strongly condemned the massacre.

Also, from 1976, one year after the Algiers Agreement, there was evidence that Iraq was planning a major war. In that year, a friend who was director of a leather company told me the Iraqi government had sent him abroad to buy leather for two million army boots. At the time, Iraq had a maximum of 240,000 active army personnel. Another friend who was in the army told me, "They have ordered two million army uniforms from Rumania. I am being sent as part of a delegation to finalise the details". My comment to both was, "God help us".

In about 1977, I heard the Voice of America say that Saudi Arabia and Kuwait could live on the interest from their assets in America and Europe for the foreseeable future, without selling another drop of petrol. The wealth of Iran and Iraq was also becoming apparent. Again I thought, "God help us. What is going to happen?"

Apart from the obvious profits in supplying arms for an eight-year war to two of the richest countries in the world, the Iraq-Iran War had political value. The 1973 Arab oil boycott of Europe, which was being used as a bargaining chip for the return of land Israel had claimed in its victory in the 1967 war, was a turning point in US policy in the Middle East. The USA was determined to get more control of the governments and their oil. Also in 1973, a Soviet-backed coup in Afghanistan had overthrown the monarchy; then, in 1978, the USSR supported another coup, and the new communist government signed a treaty of friendship and defence with the USSR. The next country about to fall was Iran. The communist Tudeh Party and Chereek Fadaiee and many socialist parties were very popular in Iran, and throughout 1978, thousands of Iranians in every city and, finally, one million people in Tehran demonstrated against the Shah. What did the USA do? In February 1979, they brought in an Islamic government, to stop communism's spread westward, then 19 months later, encouraged Saddam Hussein to invade Iran, to stop the spread of Shi'ite Islam.

From 1964 to 1978, Ayatollah Khomeini had been allowed to live in Iraq, even though the Ba'ath regime was bombing Shi'ite holy cities in the south, executing Shi'ite religious leaders (five *ulama* in 1974 and eight in 1977) and deporting Arab Shi'ites to Iran. In the Algiers Agreement of 1975, the Shah had asked Saddam Hussein to expel Khomeini, but this was not done until October 1978. Khomeini was flown to Kuwait, but when Kuwait refused to accept him, fearing retribution from the Shah, Khomeini found refuge in Paris, where he stayed until February 1979.

The thousands of Iranians who demonstrated against the Shah were not necessarily Khomeini supporters, although many were inspired by the *ulama* speaking in the mosques. There were a number of potential leaders—both religious and secular—but when Khomeini flew in from Paris on a special aeroplane, after the Shah had fled the country, it was he who claimed victory. Dr Saddeq Kutep Zadeh was with Khomeini on the flight. As foreign minister in the new government and in response to the American hostage ordeal, he asked the Iranian public, "Why say 'Death to America'? America brought us to power. I should know—I was the contact between the CIA and Khomeini."

After that, Khomeini publicly admitted, "Yes, we came to power with America's help, but we misled them. We tricked them." Dr Zadeh was hung for his indiscretion, and all documentary evidence of this early period has disappeared, including cassettes of Khomeini's first speech at Tehran airport.

Following Khomeini's return to Iran, President Al-Bakr came under increasing pressure to go to war with Iran, because of the fear that the Shi'ite revolution and its anti-American feeling would spread to Iraq. Al-Bakr refused, saying he was not going to use his country as an imperialist tool. I have heard that Prince Fahd, now the Saudi king, realising Al-Bakr was too moderate, began supporting Saddam Hussein with money, information and secret deals.

Four months after the Iranian revolution, Al-Bakr was declared 'sick' and supposedly 'retired'. In reality, he was put under house arrest and stripped of all positions. A number of high-ranking Ba'ath members and members of Al-Bakr's family claim that Saddam killed him personally or at least organised his death. Saddam went into the RCC and announced he was president. Some RCC members protested, saying they had a right to vote for the new president, and over the next two months, one-third of the RCC and 500 top Ba'ath officials were executed. Fifteen months after becoming president, Saddam declared war on Iran, saying he was not going to ratify his part of the Algiers Agreement, which he had signed under duress.

Saddam Hussein is easy to understand and predict when you know his early history. Like Kemal Ataturk of Turkey and Hitler of Germany, he came from humble origins. Born in 1937 in a village called Al-Ouja, near the town of Tikrit, he never knew his real father. His mother was not a respected woman. She married four times, so Saddam has only half-brothers. In our culture, people would have treated him very poorly under these circumstances.

When he was 10 years old, his maternal uncle promised him a daughter in marriage if he killed another uncle. Saddam carried out his first assassination. As vice-president, he developed a way of compensating for his inferiority complex with delusions of grandeur. A friend who worked in a Baghdad bookshop told me, "Saddam purchased a copy of Th*e Prince* by Machiavelli. One week later, secret police collected all the copies of the book from the market. The book had been put on the forbidden list." All I could say was, "God bless us." Saddam claims descendancy from Ali, the fourth caliph, and fosters his reputation as a modern-day Nebuchadnezzar II. But unlike Kemal Ataturk, Stalin and Hitler, who at least tried to build up their countries, Saddam has, in my opinion, no commitment to an ideology or his nation. His only hunger is for personal power and glory, and to this end, he does not mind destroying his people. Even Hitler had more dignity. When Hitler realised all was lost, he committed suicide, but Saddam has no limits. For instance, Saddam's personal psychiatrist, an Assyrian, went on Iranian television saying, "One day, Saddam requested my attendance. On walking into his room, I noticed a body lying in a pool of blood on the floor. It was a girl of about 16 with a bullet hole through her head." Afterwards, the psychiatrist decided he had to escape the country—he knew too much.

By understanding his psychological profile, Saddam's international supporters prepare the ground, knowing how Saddam will react. Australian journalist John Pilger, in his book *Distant Voices*, names both Britain's Margaret Thatcher and US President George Bush in this respect.

According to a top Ba'ath Party source, in September 1980, the night before Saddam attacked Iran, he was in Saudi Arabia seeking assurance of full financial and military support from the Gulf states. There are no official documents that the US Carter administration was behind this meeting, but according to the same source, it is well known that Saudi officials do not make such an important commitment without US approval.

Saddam expected a quick war that would gain him territory, power and glory. One BBC Arabic report claimed Saddam made a big mistake attacking the south of Iran rather than the important army bases like Dezful, north of Abadan. This mistake led to a protracted war of eight years, the USA and Europe supplying weapons to both sides, often via the Eastern bloc, Saudi Arabia and Kuwait.

As the war entered its third and fourth year, the number of Iraqi deserters increased dramatically, especially among the Kurds. Captured deserters would be lined up in front of their families, wearing the label 'coward'. The family would have to applaud their son's execution and pay for the bullet. Television showed merchants making large donations to the war effort. Some medical colleagues, who had highly paid positions with the government, told me how they used to bleed to death patients in the prison hospitals, the blood being needed for injured soldiers.

In 1982, my family and I escaped to Iran, and what I saw made me realise that the countries were two faces of the same coin. 'Ba'ath' means 'God's messengers' and 'Hezbollah', led by Khomeini, means 'God's Party'.

Despite the war, Saddam continued fighting the Kurds—the *peshmergas* in the mountains and the civilians in villages and towns. In 1983, after KDP joined forces with Iran for an operation inside Iraq, over 8000 of Barzani's men were rounded up from a collective village near Hawler. Their fate remains unknown. Following the formation of a United Kurdish Front in 1987, in February 1988 Saddam launched the Al-Anfal operations. His relative Ali Hasan Majid, known as 'Ali Chemical' to Kurds, admits to 100,000 'disappearances'. Kurdish leaders have gathered a list of 182,000 Kurds who disappeared over six months. Later, mass graves were found in the south. Between 1300 and 4000 villages were destroyed by chemicals and conventional bombing, and over 6000 civilians killed in Halabja in a matter of hours. It is all documented, yet no-one has ever seriously attempted to take Saddam Hussein to the International War Crimes Tribunal.

The eight-year war ended in July 1988, a month before the end of Anfal. Both countries lost. Iranian media was to claim that two million Iranians and one million Iraqis lost their lives. Instead of oil revenue paying for infrastructure, industry and education, it was used to buy weapons and pay armies. The winners were the powerbrokers, the armament industries and the US and European economies. The bonus was that the Middle East would remain unstable, in preparation for another war. We did not have long to wait.

Saddam had proved a terrible tactician, but not even his closest friends could advise him. Dr Ryard Al-Samarahi, who assisted the young Saddam financially and politically, was minister of health before and during the Iraq-Iran War. In a few meetings, he questioned Saddam, saying, "If you cannot solve the problems of Iran, leave them to their own men to solve. If we can't win this war, end it", and on another occasion, "Why are university professors paid worse than a soldier in the professional army?" After this, the doctor disappeared. The general public was told he had been caught importing toxic medicines that poisoned some wounded soldiers. A knowledgable source told me Saddam killed the doctor personally. Before he died, Al-Samarshi was meant to have said, "Even a prostitute is more loyal to their benefactor."

From statements made by Colin Powell and General Schwarzkopf in 1991, it appears the Pentagon began devising another trap for Saddam and a means for further military intervention in the Gulf from as early as 1989. In January 1990, huge quantities of US weapons, equipment and supplies were sent to Saudi. The USA directed the Kuwait government to undercut OPEC oil prices and increase supplies. Kuwait was also directed to demand that Iraq make an immediate repayment of all outstanding loans from the eight-year war with Iran, and to break off all negotiations with Iraq over these matters. Saddam Hussein was understandably angry, and Kuwait City is only 100 kilometres from the border.

On 25 July 1990, April Glaspie, the US Ambassador to Iraq, met Saddam and later went on television to say, "It is Iraq's business if it has a problem with another Arab country. It is a regional dispute in which America will not involve itself militarily." Three days later, on 2 August 1990, Saddam invaded Kuwait. The invasion was said to be without warning, except that all the Kuwaiti royals and important ministers had already escaped the country.

The Allied intervention was to go beyond numerous conventions of war.[i] On 16 January 1991, the Americans and their 27 British, French, Egyptian and Gulf state allies began a 42-day war that, per day, was by far the most expensive ever fought. The damage to Kuwait's infrastructure is estimated at US$30 billion. For its share of the Allied war expense, it owes US$16.5 billion. Saudi Arabia owes US$51 billion, plus interest. Untried high-tech weapons were tested, and others, such as napalm, heat-intensive devices and uranium-depleted missiles, have caused long-term damage to the environment and human health. It is estimated that between 149 and 231 allies lost their lives, as did more than 100,000 Iraqi soldiers. Some sources say 25,000 Iraqi civilians were killed. The Red Crescent Society of Jordan estimates that 113,000 civilians were killed. Military and civilian targets were hit, but the Allies did not target Iraq's elite Republican Guard, or Saddam's main area of support, around Tikrit. The four-day ground war began on 24 February. When Schwarzkopf, the US commander-in-chief of the Allied forces, was 200 miles from Baghdad, at 8 am on 28 February, President Bush announced a ceasefire. Schwarzkopf appeared on television, saying, "President Bush decided to stop the advance because of humanitarian concerns". They quickly shut his mouth. He was a conqueror, so why did he suddenly resign from an illustrious military career?

But no concern was shown for the Iraqi people. The Shi'ites in the south and the Kurds in the north rose up against Saddam in early March. During the Kurdish uprisings, books were destroyed, buildings burnt and agricultural machinery, tanks and other weapons, as well as the windows and doors from schools and the power lines in the street, were sold to the governments of Iran and Turkey. There are three reasons for all of this, two being a lack of leadership and some unpatriotic people wanting to make money. Also, I have friends who say they worked for both the CIA and the *peshmerga* at the time. No-one knows who was behind the selling of agriculture and military equipment, but I do not think it happened haphazardly. What is known is that in all the chaos, many secret intelligence documents were taken to the USA, and this evidence of Saddam's activities remains unavailable to the people to this day.

On 28 March, one week after the Kurds had succeeded in taking control of oil-rich Kirkuk, the UN announced a no-fly zone for Saddam north of the 36 Parallel. This excluded Kirkuk and allowed Saddam to use all his ground forces and helicopters against the Kurdish people. Saddam took his revenge. Despite over 700,000 US ground troops, not to mention Arab, British and French troops plus navy and air force, present in the region, they did nothing to stop Saddam's slaughter of the people.

The world's decision-makers let Saddam survive and maintain his grip on Iraq, even though no Middle Eastern country had anything good to say about him, except for the PLO and Jordan. The PLO supported him because he supported their cause. Palestinian students had freely studied at Iraqi universities, and many had been used in Iraqi army and intelligence. The King of Jordan also disagreed with the war, despite being an ally of the USA and Britain, because of the Allies' disregard for the Geneva Convention and civilian life, but there were other, hidden reasons. More undercover than if Jordan appeared an ally, the CIA in Jordan was able to bug Iraqi computers with viruses, and Jordan became a one-way information super highway—out of Iraq.

Nine years after the end of the war, there is still an international trade embargo on Iraq. Even medicines and food that are meant to be available in exchange for petrol revenue under a UN agreement are not getting through, because of bureaucratic obstacles devised by the US Security Council. Some of the supplies that do get through are being sold outside the country. While Saddam continues to build his palaces, mosques and other edifices in the tradition of his hero, Nebuchadnezzar II, the Iraqi people suffer. If you make a people hungry, they are easy to control and less likely to start a revolution. Consequently, the USA's insistence on maintaining the trade embargo serves only to maintain Saddam's power base. Saddam also uses continued British and US aerial bombing of targets inside Iraq for propaganda purposes, to achieve the same end, at the same time scapegoating its citizens, with deaths in custody and extrajudicial killings being a common occurrence.

Western frontmen justify Saddam remaining in power by saying there is no-one else strong enough to keep Iraq unified, even though we have thousands of educated people in Europe and the Middle East who are united in their opposition to Saddam. Saddam serves too many purposes. People in the Middle East used to demonstrate against the USA, but when Iraq invaded Kuwait, they begged the USA to come and protect them. Now, the USA directly controls the oil reserves and governments of Kuwait, Saudi Arabia, Bahrain, Oman, the United Arab Emirates and Qatar—the main sources of oil for Europe and Japan. Saddam is just the wolf to threaten and destabilise the area so Arabs buy arms and invite protection.

The Iraqi people do not want him, but they are made powerless, fearful and confused by the system Saddam has created. All assassination attempts and coups against Saddam have failed. Why? Firstly, I think he gets information beforehand—from national and international intelligence sources. Secondly, he is paranoid, taking extreme preventative measures. Saddam lookalikes, some of whom have undergone plastic surgery, act as decoys. Before he goes anywhere, he has hundreds of guards posted in the street and on every roof. Helicopters fly over, and three or four hours after everything has been cleared, Saddam's entourage passes through—20 to 30 cars with tinted windows.

Once in Baghdad, his entourage was passing a traffic policemen standing in the middle of a square. As the policeman adjusted his uniform, he happened to put his hand near his hips. One of Saddam's guards shot him dead. Another time, when Saddam had just made himself president, he attended one of the local Ba'ath Party meetings in Medina Thowra, now called Medina Saddam, in Baghdad. A Ba'ath Party member put his hand in his pocket to take out a poem glorifying Saddam. He was shot dead, and afterwards made a martyr. Another time, Saddam's convoy was passing through a small village called Dujala, near Baghdad, when some people tried to hit his car with an RPG missile. The car blew up, but he was not inside. The village was destroyed and all the people killed, as a warning to others.

There have been several unsuccessful coups, which go unreported in the media. In March 1995, there was a major operation devised by two high-ranking officers from the Delaim family, one of the officers being Muhammad Mathloom Delaimi. They led their units from Rumadi in the west, but the Republican Guard stopped them one hour from Baghdad. A soldier from an influential family told me that special security people, led by Saddam's son Udai, went to these officers' town, faces covered, and raped the men in front of the women. Their families were killed and the town destroyed.

Saddam surrounds himself with *mukhabarat,* and relatives from Tikrit who know that if anything happens to him, they will lose all their privileges or will die with him, so they defend him with their life. In return for this loyalty, Saddam thinks nothing of killing them. In August 1995, Saddam's two daughters and their husbands, Major General Hussein Kamil Hasan Al-Majid and his brother, Saddam, escaped to Jordan, but were convinced to return to Iraq. Why did they go back, knowing Saddam? Their return can mean only that they could not get asylum, because they had too much information. Both sons-in-law were killed.

I conclude that the international game players prefer dealing with the leaders they know, including those in the opposition movements. As such, I believe no Kurdish leader can remain in power for decades unless they are directly or indirectly supported by the governments who rule Kurdistan and the superpowers. For instance, Ocalan and his PKK, who fought the Turkish government from 1984 to1999, were allowed to stay in Syria for 20 years, but it took only two weeks of Turkey threatening war with Syria for Ocalan to suddenly find himself homeless in October 1998.[j] The USA and Israel have made a lot of money supplying arms and training the Turkish armed forces to combat PKK's armed struggle in northern Kurdistan. While the region remains unstable, the USA is assured of maintaining its military bases in Turkey, and then there is the question of access routes to the potential oil wealth of the new republics further east.

Now, I see the main economic power struggle in the Middle East is between Europe and America. The Europeans have lost much of their market in the region and want it back, so the European Union is considering making Turkey a member. However, even if it becomes a member, it will remain America's policeman in the area.

Iraq's future is more unpredictable. All I can presume is that Iraq's next leader is already being groomed. Saddam's infamous son Udai effectively became vice-president in May 1995. He is responsible for countless assassinations of Saddam's opponents, as well as personal vendettas. What I am sure of is that outside forces are planning the future and no event can be seen in isolation. For instance, during the 2000 Israeli-Palestinian peace negotiations, it was suggested that half a million Palestinians be airlifted into Kirkuk, in northern Iraq, to further Arabise the area. The Palestinian government refused and many educated Palestinians were horrified. Unrest between Israel and the West Bank suddenly flared up in October, and Palestinian families, including individuals injured in the unrest, were paid by the Iraqi government to fly to Iraq.

The Kurdish no-fly zone established in April 1991 and run by a Kurdish parliament since May 1992 will not continue forever. Racked by civil war between 1994 and 1998, due to a tribal culture, high unemployment, extreme economic deprivation and an oversupply of weapons from Iraq, Iran and Turkey, it remains subject to the international trade embargo against Iraq and another imposed by Saddam Hussein. Having lived so long under the Ba'aths, the Kurdish leaders tend to act like Ba'aths. Their egos are more important than their nation. Criticism of the parties or their leaders is regarded as an act of betrayal, and those who want to rise above party politics are marginalised. After decades of war, military tactics often dominate political strategies.

In 2000, the Iraqi government was again making overtures regarding reunification to Kurdish leaders, but whatever happens in Iraq, Kurdish issues are international issues, because they cover four countries. As such, I predict that the future of the Middle East is more likely to be determined by the Kurdish question than by the Israeli-Palestinian conflict.

Some people compare the homelessness and genocide of the Kurds to that of the Jews and look for parallels to likewise solve the Kurdish problem, but I see too many differences. The Jews are joined by religion; the Kurds have many religions. The Jewish elite has traditionally been better educated and closer to the seats of power, money and media. All the Kurds have had are their mountains of self-reliance, and these have been turned into deserts.

After seeing what has happened in Kurdistan, I believe people should pick up a gun only when they have no other choice. War brings destruction. A good article can reach more people than a thousand bullets. The Kurds' first priority must be to solve internal divisions and develop political strategies. Communication with the surrounding regimes is important, but for the good of Kurdistan rather than to ensure a personal power base. One must know and understand the enemy. We have a saying: "The intelligent enemy is better than one thousand stupid friends." That enemy will challenge you to do better, as long as you do not let him divide you, or influence you with his negative characteristics.

Thirty years ago, I would have said I would prefer to cut off the hand who shakes the Arab, Persian or Turkish hand, but I have seen how Arab and Persian families have helped the Kurds. Now, I know it is not a question of Arab, Persian, Turk or Kurd. Now,

I say put humanity first, talk through the issues, then consider Kurdistan. The leaders must be accountable; otherwise, we could just as well end up with a ruthless, paranoid Kurdish leader like Saddam—destroying and oppressing the people. I would prefer a humane leader, whatever his nationality.

If armed struggle continues to be necessary, the Kurds must learn from the past and plan for the future. We cannot continue to bring the war to Kurdistan and let it destroy our people, homes and land. It must be fought on our enemies' territory, targeting the head of the snake rather than its tail. Instead of saying, "We have no friend but the mountains", we must establish connections with international and national institutions and use our exiled diasporas as did Archbishop Makarios of Cyprus. After being deported in 1956, he continued negotiations while living in exile in Britain and, four years later, became the first president of a unified independent Cyprus under Greek-Turkish control.

With people like Saddam Hussein in power, Kurds cannot give up the gun entirely, yet I do not blame Saddam alone. The new global economy is like a super colony in which solutions to human oppression are not a priority. The weak nations are far more vulnerable to this new 'invisible colonisation', which uses the nations' own people, education, media and business interests as well as Hollywood wars as means of influence. These means are harder to oppose or rise against. Until there is a marriage between global economics and humanitarianism, there is no foreseeable solution to Kurdish oppression, the oppression of all Iraqi citizens, or any other states of oppression.

ABOUT Eziz Bawermend

Eziz Bawermend was born in Kurdistan, and moved to Australia in 1974. He holds a degree in business administration, and has held supervisory and managerial positions in both privately owned and publicly listed industrial organisations. He currently lives in Sydney, where he has been active within the Kurdish community since the early 1980s. He continues to keenly follow unfolding events in the Middle East.

A Time for Rose and a Time for Primrose

An essay by Eziz Bawermend

"A time for rose and a time for primrose" is a Kurdish way of saying "There is a time for war and a time for peace" or "Things happen not by force but in turn." This is akin to the saying in English that discoveries, inventions, etcetera occur only when their time has come. The question is: has the time come for peace and reconciliation between the Kurds and their neighbours?

Before answering this question, it is perhaps imperative to understand why the Kurds are in perennial conflict with their neighbours—the Turks, the Arabs and the Persians—or, more correctly, why the Kurds are in perennial conflict with the governments ruling these people. More often than not, problems loom too complex, too intractable, when looked at in isolation rather than in a proper framework. It is therefore appropriate to understand the context within which these conflicts occur, and what seems to be the world's utter indifference and duplicity in relation to these conflicts.

The best way of saying who the Kurds are is to say who they are not! The Kurds are not Turks. The Kurds are not Arabs. And, unlike the Turks and Arabs, the Kurds speak an Indo-European language related to Farsi—the official language of Iran—much the same way as French is related to Italian, or Spanish to Portuguese.

Since time immemorial, the Kurds have lived on a piece of land known as Kurdistan. Kurdistan is slightly larger than France. With its high mountains, deep fertile valleys and plains and abundant water, located at a major crossroad of the world, Kurdistan has always been a sought-after prize. Muslim Arabs conquered Kurdistan, along with Iran, in the seventh century AD, and the majority of the inhabitants were converted to Islam by the sword—then basically left to govern themselves as various principalities and tribes. In the 1180s, perhaps the most charismatic Kurdish leader in history, Salahaddin, Prince of Chivalry, led the Ayyubiad Empire to victory over Richard the Lionheart.

The Turks, on the other hand, were marauding nomadic tribes who moved west from Central Asia in successive waves from the ninth century, were militarily defeated along the way, converted to Islam, settled in Anatolia, and opposed the Byzantine Empire in the 11th century. Around 1300, the Turks formed the Ottoman Empire, named after its first ruler, Othman, in western Anatolia. In time, this Sunni Muslim empire expanded from the Iranian frontiers to the gates of Vienna, encompassing all the Arabian peninsula and north Africa, helped by the fact that the majority of Turks, Arabs and Kurds are Sunni Muslims. The empire's expansion in the east was halted only by fierce opposition from the Shi'ite Safavids of Iran.[a]

In 1639, Kurdistan was divided for the first time, when the Sunni Ottoman and Shi'ite Safavid Empires agreed to a border through the Zagros Mountains. On either side of the border, the Kurds enjoyed a good deal of autonomy under various Kurdish *emirs*, or princes, appointed by the relevant empire. As a sign of sovereignty, during the Islamic Friday prayers, the name of the *emir* would be mentioned. Yet each *emir* was obliged to pay tribute as well as supply warriors on demand to the Ottoman sultans or the Safavid shahs.

The situation and border remained pretty much the same until the aftermath of World War One. In 1920, according to the Treaty of Sevres, an Independent Republic of Kurdistan was to be recognised by the international community, if Kurdish leaders could prove that was what their people wanted. However, the Treaty of Lausanne, engineered by the Anglo-French victors and the new Turkish leaders three years later, made no specific mention of the Kurds. The treaty divided and annexed Kurdistan to the newly created states of Turkey, Iraq and Syria. While Turkey got immediate independence, Iraq and Syria remained mandated states under the control of the British and the French for another 25 years. The part of Kurdistan controlled by Iran remained as it was, with only minor changes to the borders.

Whilst the Treaty of Lausanne did not mention the Kurds, it did guarantee basic rights and fundamental liberties to minorities in Turkey, as did the 1926 Anglo-Iraq treaty that created Iraq under a British-imported Hashemite king from Saudi Arabia. The Anglo-Iraq treaty stated that the recommendations of the International Commission of Inquiry (January to March 1925) be respected. These included that, "The desire of the Kurds that the administration, magistrates and teachers of their country be drawn from their own ranks and adopt Kurdish as the official language in all their activities be taken into account". However, in dramatic contrast to the British protectorate of Iraq, within six months of the proclamation of the Republic of Turkey, Kurds in Turkey officially lost their Kurdish identity. The use of the Kurdish language was outlawed, even in private conversation, and all works of Kurdish literature were collected and burned. Over the next 10 years, Kurds became known as 'mountain Turks' and the words 'Kurd' and 'Kurdistan' were removed from dictionaries and reference materials.

The Turkish president, General Mistefa Kemal, who had a rubber-stamp parliament give him the title 'Ataturk' ('father of the Turks') ruled the republic for 15 years until his death. His ways proved far harsher than those of Chile's General Pinochet. Nevertheless, the West—that is to say, the UK, France and the USA—not only supported Kemal and the new republic, but turned a blind eye to his excesses against the Christian Greeks in Asia Minor, as well as the Christian Armenians and largely Muslim Kurds in eastern Turkey. This was because Turkey served both to contain Soviet expansion and to keep the emerging Arab nations in check. The following account from the US Consul in Smyrna (Izmir) in 1922 is worth noting:

> I have often been impressed with the hopelessness of making people who have not been eyewitnesses, comprehend the dreadful character of the massacres which are carried out by the Turks against the Christian population of the Orient... One of the keenest impressions which I brought away with me from Smyrna was a feeling of shame that I belonged to the human race ... the Turks were glutting freely their racial and religious lust for slaughter, rape and plunder within a stone's throw of the Allied and American battleships because they had been systematically led to believe that they would not be interfered with... And this, the presence of those battleships in Smyrna harbour, in the year of our Lord 1922, impotently watching the last great scene in the tragedy of the Christians of Turkey, was the saddest and most significant feature of the whole picture... Christians were abandoned, as no Christian power desired to offend the Turk, from whom great benefits were expected... It is a curious fact that the Turk is still able to deceive Europeans, despite long observation of his tactics... [194]

From 1919 until 1938, a series of heroic uprisings against Mistefa Kemal's brutal rule took place, led by traditional leaders, each event ending in more pain, more suffering and more destruction than the previous one. Through mass executions and deportations of over 1.5 million Kurds,[195] the very fabric of Kurdish society, with its tribal ties and loyalties, was largely destroyed. Turkey's impoverished Kurdish region remained off-limits to foreigners until 1965 and was officially referred to as *mahrumiyet bolgesi* or 'region of deprivation'. Through an ever-accelerated and pervasive process of enforced assimilation, particularly through education and the media, more and more Kurds became utterly ashamed of their ethnicity. The word 'Kurd', if used at all, came to mean 'ignorant, stupid, rude and uncivilised'.

Strict restrictions on the use of the Kurdish language took a heavy toll. Kurdish words were forgotten or were replaced by 'Turkish' words, these being largely adaptations of Arabic or French words. Many educated Kurds—that is, the sons of landowners and religious leaders loyal to the government, who became known as 'feudal collaborators'—placated the Turkish rulers, maintaining, "Kurdish is not a real language, only a dialect" or "Kurdish is not suitable for contemporary life, because it has too few words and expressions." They accepted the official Turkish ideology's 'Sun-Language Theory', which claims that all languages are derived from Turkish and that Turks are the founders of all civilisations!

Despite the Turkish government's systematic policies of genocide, deportation and political imprisonment, Turkey was accepted into NATO, in 1952. Afterwards, during a visit to Turkey, US President Eisenhower formally declared Turkey the 'watchdog' of Western interests in the Middle East.

When the Wolf is Hungry, No-one Knows What it Will Do!

This Kurdish saying means, "Desperate situations call for desperate measures." The late 1960s and early 1970s in Turkey saw the maturing of a generation of passionate, educated young men and women craving freedom to express themselves, to state the obvious, to reject official lies and to pursue social justice. By the mid-1970s, many left-wing publications had become available that struck a chord with these young people. They read about the Turkish lies, as elucidated by Turkish sociologist Dr Isma'il Besikci. These included the state's claim that Mistefa Kemal Ataturk was the 'torchbearer' of the oppressed and downtrodden, conveniently forgetting his brutalisation of Armenians, Kurds and anyone else with a different political view. Other lies were that he was 'anti-imperial and anti-colonial', when in fact, he was the imperialists' local agent and collaborator, and that he believed in a 'multiparty, pluralistic democracy', when in reality, for his 15 years of rule, he was the head of the only legal party. That all languages are derivatives of Turkish, that all civilisations were founded by the Turks, that there are no Kurds in Turkey and that there is no such language as Kurdish were also exposed as fabrications. Dr Isma'il Besikci was quick to point out that because of all these lies on which the Turkish Republic was founded, the state could not afford to allow a democratic environment where any subject could be freely discussed and debated.[196]

Then, in 1975, the young Kurds of Turkey witnessed the betrayal of the Kurds of northern Iraq, under the leadership of Melle Mistefa Barzani,[b] by US Secretary of State Dr Henry Kissinger, following Kissinger's engineering of the infamous embrace between Saddam Hussein and the Shah of Iran in Algiers. This agreement was specifically designed to achieve an end to the Kurdish revolution in southern Kurdistan. It was instrumental in causing much death and destruction for the next 16 years, not only for Kurds. The terrible eight-year war between Iraq and Iran, which killed up to 1.5 million Iraqi and Iranian soldiers, was a direct outcome of the 1975 agreement.

By 1980, because the Turkish regime felt so threatened by the new political awakenings of its citizens, a military takeover was orchestrated in Washington, to save it from collapse. That Washington was involved, I learnt conclusively in 1988 from an advocate of the coup, during a conference in Lisbon organised by the Washington-based Centre for Strategic and International Studies. At that conference, US Professor Samuel Huntington was openly proud of how the US government-engineered coup had saved Turkey.

After the coup, thousands of citizens were arrested and tortured, as a gang of generals issued edicts carrying the full force of the law. All avenues for peaceful change were blocked. A prominent Kurd named Serafettin Elci was sentenced to 27 months in prison simply for saying, "I am a Kurd. There are Kurds in Turkey". Turkish sociologist Dr Isma'il Besikci was imprisoned for 10 years for writing in a private letter that there are Kurds in Turkey and that they are being oppressed. A distinguished Kurdish elder, Mr Musa Anter, affectionately known as Apê Musa ('Uncle Moses'), recounts a personal experience that occurred before the 1980 military coup:

> I was managing a dormitory in Istanbul when I received a call from the police, directing to me to show up at the police station immediately. As soon as I stepped into the station, several policemen started beating me up with their fists and boots, and rained all sorts of verbal abuses on my family, as the sergeant looked on. During a respite, I asked, "What is my crime? What have I done?" The sergeant asked, "Do you not have a radio?" I said, "Yes, I do." He continued, "Do you not have a record player?" I replied, "Yes I do." "So, when you can listen to beautiful Turkish music, why do you—son of a bitch—whistle Kurdish tunes in the dormitory?"

In 1992, Mr Musa Anter was gunned down in broad daylight by so-called 'unknown assailants'—in other words, a Turkish government-sponsored death squad.

In the late 1970s, a group of young Kurds and Turks gathered around a charismatic young man called Abdullah Ocalan, who had found salvation in Marxism. In 1978, this handful of youngsters established a new party, called PKK (Partîya Karkerên Kurdistan), Kurdistan Workers' Party, now mostly known to the world as a terrorist organisation, thanks to the efforts and resources of the US State Department. During the 1980 military coup, most PKK members crossed into Syria, and on 15 August 1984, they mounted simultaneous attacks on two Turkish military outposts deep inside their Kurdish homeland. Many Kurds thought them crazy and suicidal. The Turkish state, backed by the USA, Israel and Germany, had unlimited supplies of fighter jets, helicopters, tanks and artillery. But these young men and women had probably read Mao Tse Tung's *Protracted Guerilla War*, and in any event, they so fervently believed in the justness of their cause that they were unstoppable.

Dramatic or Protracted Guerilla War?

The booklet *Protracted Guerilla War* was ideally suited to a people colonised by a faraway country for the purposes of economic exploitation only, where the coloniser has no intention of obliterating the culture and identity of the colonised, nor any emotional attachment to the colonised lands. Certainly, when Holland colonised what is now Indonesia, it had no intention of turning the Indonesians into Dutch men and women. The colonisation made sense as long as it was an economically viable proposition, and with institutionalised freedom of expression, the citizens of the colonising country could freely debate, and thereby sway public opinion on, the merits of waging a costly war against the colonised. Additionally, the people of the colonised country typically enjoyed the support of neighbouring countries. As well as Indonesia, the same can be said for India, Vietnam, China and numerous African countries occupied by Europeans.

The situation of Kurdistan was quite different. Kurdistan is not just a colony. It is an international colony, divided between and annexed to four neighbouring states as integral parts of those countries, not just for economic exploitation. Moreover, Turkish nationalism has all the hallmarks of a religion, and the forced assimilation of the Kurds is about spreading this religion.

Yet, PKK's armed struggle, like other Kurdish uprisings, was confined to Kurdistan, and appeared very much in line with the principles laid down in *Protracted Guerilla War*. Would the situation and outcome have been different if PKK had taken the war to the Turkish heartland, relentlessly pursued media hirelings around the world, or adopted the Turkish government's ruthless policy of eliminating leaders, writers and journalists? I believe one thing is clear: despite media rhetoric, history will record that Mr Ocalan's greatest weakness in his struggle was his love of ordinary men and women, and that in fighting the monsters, he chose not to become one himself.

Nevertheless, from 1978 and throughout the 1980s, Mr Ocalan was seen as a serious threat not only to the governments ruling Kurdistan but also to other autonomy-seeking Kurdish leaders and organisations, as well as the established Kurdish-Islamic culture that supported feudalism and the oppression of women. This was because the

Marxist-Leninist movement began by challenging all aspects of the existing social order. Unlike many other Kurdish organisations, the aim was for a united and independent Kurdistan, and a new Kurdish society free from the tyranny of religion and the remnants of feudalism.

This threat did not diminish with the organisation's maturation, chiefly because, with its greater emphasis on saving Kurdish identity, PKK became more broadly based during the 1990s, attracting members from all strata of Kurdish society, including the devout of many religions.

Splendour in the Grass and Glory of the Flower!

From the late 1980s, it became fashionable in the tightly controlled Turkish media to blame PKK for all the country's ills. These ranged from hyperinflation to earthquakes. As well, successive Turkish governments, under military tutelage, were at ease in explaining all their failures, corruption, and repressive laws and policies, particularly in regard to freedom of expression, as a necessary response to PKK activity. The propaganda continued through the 1990s, despite PKK feeling they had made sufficient progress in saving Kurdish identity to declare unilateral ceasefires on three separate occasions. All ceasefire announcements were ignored, the Turkish government justifying their stance by saying, "The state does not negotiate with terrorists". This statement is ironical in the extreme, given the prevailing view outside official circles that the generals who really control the Turkish government are above the law, and that 'criminal gangs' have deeply infiltrated state institutions, creating a hotbed of graft, corruption and other unlawful and immoral activity against which the judiciary and politicians are helpless.

The government interpreted PKK's ceasefire announcements as signs that their scorched-earth policy of burning Kurdish villages and farms and forcing the inhabitants into squalid unemployment in the big cities was working. The Turkish generals were even more convinced of the effectiveness of their brutal policies when PKK reduced its demands to "recognition of the Kurdish identity and cultural rights".

In the second half of 1998, in an attempt to entirely eliminate PKK, based for 20 years in Syria, the Turkish government threatened to attack Syria unless the Syrian government got rid of Ocalan and PKK bases on Syrian-controlled soil. Turkey's threat was backed by US naval and airforce manoeuvres close by. In October, Ocalan travelled to Russia, then Italy, but was unable to find asylum, largely due to US pressure. When news of Abdullah Ocalan's abduction from Kenya hit the world media, in February 1999, many Turks danced in the streets, believing him to be the evil behind all their hardships.

Like no other event, the international collusion behind Ocalan's kidnapping and transport back to Turkey outraged and united Kurds all over the world. Nevertheless, some Kurds, from Sydney to Stockholm, rejoiced in the news, due to longstanding political differences, animosities and petty rivalries, though quite wisely, they controlled any urge to dance in the streets. Unfortunately, some Kurdish leaders appear to prefer subservience to an arch-enemy over cooperation with fellow Kurdish leaders. A stark and dramatic example of this reality is currently being played out in southern Kurdistan, which has been divided into two 'principalities', the two ruling parties having close ties to a foreign government known for its oppression of Kurds.

Since his capture, Ocalan has been the sole prisoner on the prison-island of Imrali. From his cell, Ocalan directed his PKK fighters to stop fighting and withdraw from Turkey's internationally recognised borders. It is generally believed that most have withdrawn into southern Kurdistan. He has repeatedly called for a 'democratic republic' in which Turks, Kurds and others can live in peace and harmony. Arguably, these calls are in line with the promises and calls to arms by General Mistefa Kemal, who claimed the need for a common struggle against Western aggressors, promising his Kurdish supporters complete autonomy within a republic, before its proclamation in 1923. Ocalan's order that the names of various organisations be changed to delete the word 'Kurdistan', to which the Turkish rulers are so allergic, also seems in keeping with policies after 1923. However, Ocalan's calls also reflect a prevailing view outside the establishment that democracy in Turkey is nothing but a façade, with elections just a military-designed tendering process in which the PR firms of Turkish state ideology, going under the name of various political parties, compete to implement the generals' will.

The obedient Turkish media have encouraged a cynical interpretation of Ocalan's calls and overtures as attempts to save his own neck from the impending noose. Others have claimed that he has been given mind-altering drugs or that two years' solitary confinement have had an effect. It is more probable, however, that Ocalan, based on his past experience and accomplishments, now has more faith in democratic process than in a continuation of a protracted guerilla war.

The official reaction to Ocalan's calls for a peaceful solution has been the same as before, namely, "The state does not negotiate with terrorists". Yet, echoes of his calls are found in pronouncements of the newly elected Turkish president and the head of the Court of Appeals, who are asking for the supremacy of law and a civilian constitution. Likewise, some emboldened politicians, including current Deputy Prime Minister Mesut Yilmaz, are calling for more genuine democracy. It is worth noting that Turkey has never had a civilian constitution. The present constitution was drafted by those behind the 1980 military coup, and was put to a 'referendum' in a period of heightened nationalism, under emergency measures that banned criticism altogether. The previous constitution had been engineered in a similar manner, following the 1960 military coup.

With Ocalan behind bars, will democracy advance in Turkey? Will corruption vanish, torture cease, freedom of expression be respected and scientific explanations offered for earthquakes, now that PKK can no longer be used as a scapegoat? Let us all hope that the Turkish government will want to achieve more than just the brutal suppression of its citizens. Let us all have faith, while bearing in mind that faith is belief without evidence.

The Jews: The Problem and the Solution

The late Indian Prime Minister J. L. Nehru, in his *Glimpses of World History*, wrote of the Turks and the Kurds:

> And so the Turks, who only recently had been fighting for their own freedom, crushed the Kurds, who sought theirs. It is strange how a defensive nationalism develops into an aggressive one and a fight for freedom turns into one for dominion over others. But how can one crush forever a people who insist on freedom and are prepared to pay the price for it?

Nehru's acute observation of this conundrum is also applicable to the powerful Jewish lobby.

There has been no historical animosity between the Kurds and the Jews, nor any reason for animosity before the 1980s. Some Kurds are Jewish, and have escaped persecution or nationalism by moving to Israel, although their exact number and impact on Israel's foreign policy are hard to ascertain. It is now public knowledge that, for strategic reasons, Israel secretly supported Mistefa Barzani's Kurdish revolution in northern Iraq, giving considerable material assistance, particularly via Iran, until 1975, at which point the Kurds were abandoned by the USA, Israel and Iran, and left to the mercy of Saddam Hussein. However, while supporting the Kurds of Iraq, Israel was oblivious to the persecution of the Kurds in Turkey and Iran.

The majority of Kurds are Muslim, and are therefore required to protect the Jews as a people with a holy book. Yet, although the Turks also are overwhelmingly Muslim, the Ottoman and Turkish governments have not always followed the Islamic teachings in this regard. Even educated Turks have been known to blame the Jews for Ottoman military defeats, saying that during Ottoman rule, Jews controlled key posts in treasury and supply departments, and would withhold supplies until they arranged their cut. These Turks go on to relate that the decline of the Ottoman Empire began a generation or so after the arrival in Istanbul of Jews escaping persecution in Spain during the Spanish Inquisition.

While there is no doubt that Jews suffered less at the hands of the Ottomans than they did from the European Christians of the times, there is little moral justificatoin for Israel's present allegiance to Turkey. In this regard, it is worth noting what New York-based Dr Vera Beaudin-Saeedpour, of the Jewish faith, wrote in a lead article in *Kurdish Life* (No. 6, Spring 1993), describing where Israel stands vis a vis the Kurds and the world at large, opening with the statement:

> Turkey's repressive Kurdish policy represents the antithesis of values Jews espouse. Yet the state of Israel has not only kept silent on Turkey's treatment of the Kurds, it has been at the forefront of promoting Turkey's image and Turkey's interests abroad.

It is strange how a people who have been faced so many times with a choice between forced assimilation and death and have chosen death can so readily conspire, collude and collaborate with the Turkish rulers to annihilate Kurdish identity. They have done so not only by promoting Turkey's image and interests abroad, but by ensuring a steady supply of aid, ranging from hardware and hard cash to strategies for Turkish death squads and scorched-earth policies. By supporting Turkey, Jewish politicians, as well as Jewish intellectuals, columnists, writers, pillars of communities and even Nobel laureates, both in and outside Israel, have chosen to ignore the plight of the Kurds, to actively support, and justify in the world arena, such brutal measures. For instance, it was a Jewish syndicated columnist, William Safire, an ardent supporter of Kurds opposing Saddam Hussein, who coined the expression "good Kurds, bad Kurds". The 'good Kurds' are the ones fighting an enemy of Israel—namely, Saddam Hussein—while the 'bad Kurds' are those fighting an ally of Israel—namely, Turkey. In hindsight, I realise how naive I was 10 to 12 years ago in believing that William Safire was concerned about human rights, justice and other ideals when advocating the rights of Kurds in southern Kurdistan. In view of his condemnation of the Kurds waging war against the Turkish regime—a war fought, essentially, in support of the same rights—I can conclude only that his concern for Kurdish rights was in direct proportion to his perception of Kurds' utility in ensuring Israel's safety and security.

PKK's public defence of Palestinian rights and entitlements and its general left-wing rhetoric against imperialism and Zionism could have made Jewish leaders around the world suspicious, moving them to nip in the bud any real or imagined threat to Israel. Moreover, Israel has long coveted the waters originating in Kurdistan and, since the collapse of the Soviet Union, sees Turkey as the gateway to the perceived riches of Central Asia.

However, there is little doubt that if a Kurdish organisation or splinter group resembling Palestinian Hamas should develop, and was ready to commit, particularly in Turkey proper, acts of violence dwarfing the atrocities allegedly committed by PKK, the West would be more likely to reconsider its position on PKK. Hamas has made the PLO look far more reasonable than the PLO could ever portray itself to be. Let us all hope that the winds of peaceful change are strong enough for the Kurds not to feel the need to resort to such tactics.

From a Vicious Circle to a Virtuous Circle: The Challenge for the Kurdish Diasporas

With globalisation rapidly shrinking the world, social, political and technological paradigm shifts appear by the day. There is but one superpower left, reminiscent of the days of the Roman Empire. Yet, the great Roman Empire was conquered not by wars but by Christians employing peaceful means, which included a shift of consciousness, in the form of changing religious and social values.

Likewise, we are seeing a shift of consciousness in the modern world. For instance, when I was visiting an Australian family of Anglo-Macedonian origin recently, their young, unmarried daughter introduced a young man as her live-in boyfriend—not her fiancé, not even her intended, just a boyfriend who nightly shared her bed, in her parents' home!

This situation is a bewildering and astounding contrast to the ongoing 'honour killings' of women in southern Kurdistan and, indeed, in many Islamic countries. These murderers of women not only go free but often are hailed as heroes, because they have 'cleansed' the family honour, despite it being reported that, more often than not, the victim's 'heinous crime' is merely holding hands or going to a movie with a boy.

The Kurdish diasporas must take the initiative to bring about a paradigm shift in the Kurdish psyche, and impart to the struggle for freedom a real sense of equality and democracy, faith and momentum, in the means they employ. Perhaps the most essential faith and emphasis needed is that the struggle now requires more brain than brawn, more conspicuously outstanding achievements than superior marksmanship.

The Kurds have proven track records in all fields of endeavour, and therefore possess a heritage to build on and to publicise. For example, Turkey's most celebrated author, Yashar Kamal, is a Kurd. Turkey's most popular singer, Ibrahim Tatlises, is a Kurd. The late Yilmaz Guney, Turkey's most acclaimed film producer/director/scriptwriter, is a Kurd. There can be little doubt that in the world of business, trade, commerce and organisation building, the Kurds are also in the forefront in Turkey. How else can one explain the Kurds' achievement in establishing a Kurdish satellite-TV station based in Europe? Assimilated Kurds have also risen to high positions in the Turkish political, judicial and education systems. Many such achievers are no longer ashamed of being Kurdish, thanks largely to the achievements of PKK and the charismatic leadership of Ocalan.

Perhaps the beginning of the paradigm shift that is required to move away from the vicious circle to the virtuous circle is a critical look at some of the truisms on which the vicious circle is based. For Kurdish parties and their leaders to avoid being used, abused and then abandoned time and again by foreign powers, the Kurdish diaspora could spearhead the rejection of such time-honoured truisms as, "My enemy's enemy is my friend" and "My enemy's friend is also my enemy." As well, although the US and Israeli governments are close allies and supporters of the highly undemocratic and repressive regime in Turkey, it does not follow that US and Israeli citizens are enemies of the Kurds. The recognition that there are ways of influencing these governments other than by direct confrontation may be the catalyst for the required paradigm shift. This does not mean there is no place for armed struggle, nor that the Kurds must now embrace Gandhi's non-violent philosophy regardless of what is done to them.

Gandhi versus Genghis Khan

Some Kurds around the world find it hard to see the need for such a paradigm shift. They justifiably point out that the Kurds have had their own Gandhis, such as Mistefa Barzani's elder brother, Shaykh Ahmed Barzani, in southern Kurdistan, and Saeed-i Nursi, in northern Kurdistan.

The philosophies and impact of these two great men appear inadequately documented, consisting mainly of hearsay and whispers. Nevertheless, they provide invaluable insights. From the 1920s, the young Shaykh Ahmed Barzani expressed opposition to armed conflict between 'people of the book'—that is, Jews, Christians and Muslims. Convinced that many such conflicts were deliberately instigated in the interests of the British and French and their local surrogates, he advocated that individuals independently create a non-violent zone around their home, village or region. He and his message were intermittently glorified or condemned by successive Iraqi governments, depending on whether they were in the mood for negotiations or war. He was particularly condemned when he explained that Muslims were obliged to submit to 'legitimate' authority, not to any gang that happens to take power in Baghdad. Forced to flee into Kurdistan of Iran in 1944, with his brother, Melle Mistefa Barzani, he was promptly imprisoned for 11 years on his return to Iraq in late 1946, after which an armed struggle was forced upon his people. In 1972, Shaykh Ahmed Barzani died. Some say Iraqi agents poisoned him, but given his advanced age, believed to be about 80, he most likely died of natural causes.

In a similar vein, Saeed-i Nursi came to the attention of the Turkish authorities in the late 1930s. He was originally known as Saeed-i Kurdi, or 'Kurdish Saeed', but given the Turkish government's strong dislike of the words 'Kurd' and 'Kurdistan', the change of name was effected in all official documents. Nowadays, Turkish authorities refer to his followers as *nurcuylar* when there is a raid, followed by the inevitable arrests, although rumours persist that his followers continue to have strong networks, and that some occupy high positions in the Turkish establishment.

In today's Western vernacular, Saeed-i Nursi's ideas might be described as humane, contemporary interpretations of Islamic teachings. It is said that as a young man, Saeed-i Nursi was puzzled by the observation that thieves were honest with each other, and would invoke God's assistance before embarking on an enterprise of stealing. Moreover, they blamed authorities, rather than themselves, for their circumstances. He considered the prescribed punishment for theft to be barbaric, serving no higher purpose than to protect the interests of the better-off. He also observed the lower status of women, despite their significant role as mothers in shaping their offspring's characters.

To disseminate his teachings, Saeed-i Nursi used a method called *ayin*, where men, women and children learned and prayed together, in so doing, sharing something intangible that may be termed a raising of spirit or social consciousness. He believed that through *ayin*, antisocial behaviour could be prevented, because crimes were committed when a society failed to impart sufficient social consciousness or provide for life's necessities. Therefore, offenders were in fact victims of the authorities, who were failing in their duties to the people. He concluded that violence between individuals and between governments did not and could not solve any problem, that a raising of social consciousness was the answer.

His observations and studies of Islam were secretly published as *Risale-I Nur*, or *Booklets of Enlightenment*, all of which were banned. Merely possessing them can bring lengthy incarceration, with physical and mental torture.

In the aftermath of the bloody suppression of a number of Kurdish uprisings in northern Kurdistan in the 1930s, any Kurd, particularly a religious one who could gather a handful of people around him, was seen as a threat to the secular authorities, and so Saeed-i Nursi was arrested. For a number of years, he was moved from prison to prison, until in a penultimate insult to Kurds, he was declared insane and institutionalised. One traditional way of treating the mentally ill was to beat them into unconsciousness, presumably to drive the devil from their system. Saeed-i Nursi died in captivity, his grave unmarked, to prevent it becoming a shrine to his followers.

There is an argument that Gandhi's philosophy can work only in societies where respect for the rule of law is paramount, that such non-violent philosophies can hardly see the light of day in countries where there is no problem that cannot be solved by Genghis Khan's sword. In a country that still adheres to the sentiments articulated by Mahmut Esat Bozkurt, a Turkish Minister of Justice in the 1920s, "There is no Kurdish problem where there is a Turkish bayonet", it is hard to achieve democratic, peaceful change. However, one must not lose sight of the fact that the Turkish government does not stand still, or that the government and the Turkish people are not impervious to pressure and influences from the rest of the world, particularly the West, on which the government is increasingly dependent.

Where There is Treasure, There is Heart Also

Even with a fundamental shift in Kurdish thinking and strategies, a just cause attracts no more support than a better mousetrap creates a beaten path to the inventor's door—unless the invention is accompanied by a massive advertising campaign. Also, the victims of an abusive situation—in this case, the Kurds—may not be the best people to tell the world about their plight and aspirations. Educational, humanitarian and financial institutions, media and PR firms, as well as external governments, may do a far more effective, credible job. Just as many so-called autobiographies and other non-fiction literary works are the product of professional ghostwriters or collaborative efforts, many just causes would have remained unacknowledged if left entirely to the victims to broadcast them and effect change. Thus, the people of South Africa, East Timor and Kosovar needed international support to effect change, as do the Kurds now.

Even so, the victims must take a measure of responsibility, and nowadays, members of the recently established Kurdish communities around the world have tremendous opportunities and resources available to help them achieve in almost any field of endeavour. With achievement comes recognition and, sometimes, tremendous financial reward, which can lead, in turn, to more achievements that can change attitudes towards and perceptions of the Kurdish cause. For example, financial resources open channels to effective mass media via films, documentaries, novels, non-fiction works and editorials, and can put in place educational programs for Kurdish youth both in and outside Kurdistan. Such resources can also help finance an exchange of skills between the Kurdish diasporas and those in Kurdistan as well as diplomatic efforts to promote change. It is therefore imperative that Kurdish community leaders begin to see themselves as talent scouts, encouraging the development of talent and the accumulation of capital and other resources.

Charity and Democracy Begin at Home

To its credit, PKK underwent a remarkable transformation in only one decade—from a bitter, battle-hardened guerilla organisation to a more reasonable, sensible political force—a transformation few would have believed possible. But, to be a political force with even greater appeal, PKK needs to demonstrate that it can stay true to this transformation, that it is undoubtedly different from the corrupt and despotic Turkish political parties, whose leaders rarely change, decade after decade. The Kurdish diasporas can assist PKK to maintain and advance this transformation, by ensuring that democratic processes within PKK are both visible and convincing. The Kurdish communities, particularly in Europe, appear to be doing a very good job in this regard, and this is having an impact on Kurds in Kurdistan, who are pushing for more internal democratic processes, and not just in terms of voting for a leader.

Yet, it would be wrong to altogether tie to PKK as a political organisation the success of the Kurdish diasporas in advancing the Kurdish cause. Kurdish community members around the world may prefer to see the significance of PKK's achievements in the face of appalling odds more in terms of PKK ideals, including the empowerment of women and children in the family, than in terms of the organisation itself. In any event, PKK may have fulfilled its historic mission, and the time may come when it needs to voluntarily pass the torch to new guardians of the Kurdish quest for freedom, democracy and equality.

Whatever happens to PKK in the future, its conspicuously outstanding achievement is having saved Kurdish identity and culture in northern Kurdistan from the dustbins of history. Its undisputed legacy is having motivated Kurds to proudly embrace their heritage, by reigniting a deep-rooted desire for recognition and future achievement.

We must hope that the cycle of war and destruction is over, and that PKK's efforts have laid the foundation for the inevitable transformation of the Middle East through peaceful, democratic means. Reconciliation is essential—like a discovery whose time has come, Kurdish aspirations are now irrepressible.

— II —

FROM BAHDINAN TO BABAN VIA SORAN

ABOUT **Faiek Jamil Ali**

Faiek Jamal Ali was born in Koi Sinjak, in Arbil Province, in 1932. In 1956 he graduated with a degree in Literature and Social Science from a college in Baghdad and in 1976 attained a Bachelor degree in Law. After his retirement from law, for 15 years he wrote Arabic and Kurdish general and political articles, which were published in newspapers and magazines. For a short time he translated Arabic short stories into Kurdish. He continues to write Kurdish short stories.

A Known Stranger

A short tale by Faiek Jamil Ali

First man, frowning and staring, asked another: "Who are you?"
Second man: "I … I am nobody."
First man, surprised: "How come you are 'nobody'? Don't you see that you are standing in front of me, talking …?"
Second man: "My brother—your eyes are blurred."
First man: "All right. What is your name?"
Second man: "I do not remember. I have forgotten."
First man, coming closer, frankly: "Where do you come from?"
Second man, calmly: "Friend, I do not know. I am here."
First man: "How long have you been here?"
Second man: "Today. Yesterday. Since last year. God knows."
First man: "So you are a vagabond?"
Second man, beginning to laugh, yelled suddenly: "God damn it. You are a crazy man." Placing his hands on the first man's shoulders, he shrugged, "What can be my identity and home?"
First man, removing the other man's hands from his shoulders, shouted: "*Ma'alet bahkur gyr'e*. Your home is buried in mud. *What* are you?"
Second man: "Stupid! Haven't I told you that I am nothing? Am I a free man to have an identity and home?"

Enough

A life story based on interviews with Sami Barwari

There are two types of war: one you believe in and one you don't. I have experienced both.

On 11 March 1970, Mostefa Barzani, leader of the Kurds, and the Iraqi government signed an agreement for Kurdish autonomy in northern Iraq and the 10-year war between the Kurdish *peshmergas* and the Iraqi forces came to an end. I was in my first year at high school. All my life I had been afraid, but after that, there was hope.

It soon became clear that the government was working against the treaty. Over the next few years, there were at least five attempts to assassinate Mostefa Barzani. One famous attempt was on 29 September 1971. The government sent five *imams*, with four others, from Baghdad to Galala, a village near Haji Omaran, near the Iranian border, to negotiate. Government officials had secretly put an explosive device under the clothes of one *imam*, saying it was a tape recorder. When Barzani came into the room and everyone was being served tea, the *imam* exploded. Nothing happened to Barzani because, the *peshmerga* serving tea stood between him and the exploding *imam*. Two *peshmergas* died instantly and others were injured, but *peshmergas* managed to kill three *imams*. One *imam* gave information. Then one of their two cars exploded. The other car was also rigged with dynamite.

The incident was reported in the underground Kurdish Democratic Party newspaper. At school, on the street and at home, people talked about it. The government newspapers from Baghdad wrote: "We don't know about this plot to kill Barzani. Maybe it comes from Iran or America or another country to start a fight between us. We do not want to fight the Kurdish people," but we knew who was responsible.

From late 1972 it was obvious that the Autonomy Agreement was falling apart. The Ba'aths refused to carry out a census in Kirkuk to establish its Kurdish population, claiming the towns of Kirkuk, Khanaqin and Shingar were not Kurdish. In Bagdad some Kurds were killed and others were put in prison, accused of being communist.

In March 1974 Kurdish leaders returned from negotiations in Baghdad, having achieved nothing. After the Iraqi army bombed the towns of Zakho and Qaladiza many went to the mountains to join the *peshmerga*. I was in Year Nine, just 17 years old.

We had two weeks' training to learn how to use the Russian and Chinese Kalashnikov and the Czechoslavakian Burno rifle, which can kill at 300 metres. I was in a unit of 15 to 25 men. The youngest was 15. Most were under 30, and one or two were in their mid-forties. By this time the *peshmerga* were organised more like an army, with about 1000 fighters in each battalion, a number of battalions under one leader instead of under tribal leaders. Mostefa Barzani was being supported from the USA through the Shah of Iran, so he was able to maintain 12, 000 volunteer fighters.

Peshmergas on route in the mountains.

For one year I was in the mountains. We moved from village to village, staying with families for a couple of hours or a couple of days. They would feed us too much. In winter it is very hard, with all the snow, but still we moved. I saw real fighting three times. One fight was in autumn, near Dohuk, on a big mountain we call Mateen, close to my home village of Barwari. KDP got information that the army was coming. Seven to 800 *peshmergas* armed only with their Kalashnikovs and nine rounds of ammunition each, 30 bullets in a round, went to the top of the mountain. We positioned ourselves for maximum view and protection and good escape routes and waited between huge boulders, in caves and holes, between the wild oak and walnut trees.

Three hours later, at dawn, 2000 soldiers started climbing. Among them were the Kurdish 'civilian' military, called Forsa'an. When they were established in 1961–62 we called them *chatar,* meaning 'bandits who ambush to rob or kill', but Mostefa Barzani began calling them *jahshek*[a] or 'donkey's foal', a term of abuse in our culture, and this became their name. Tanks reinforced them from behind, staying on flat ground, and aeroplanes were bombing from overhead.

The fighting lasted on and off for six days and nights. Sometimes the soldiers were one kilometre away, sometimes as close as 200 metres, but we were backed by a second support line and a third supply line, and we had the advantage of position. We were also very focused, determined to keep control of the routes. And we were young and not afraid of dying. Old men know more about dying.

I did not pray, but many did—before and after fighting. This was normal. Sometimes the fighting lasted two or three hours, sometimes a whole night. When the soldiers failed to capture a position, they would stop fighting to make another plan. In this time, we had a chance to sleep, taking turns to watch, and eat bread, cheese and water supplied from the third line in the villages.

In those six days three *peshmergas* died and two were injured. I knew them and their families. The bodies were taken to battalion headquarters and back to their families. Later when I visited, I told them, "He was a good, strong man and he fought very well." What else can you say? We killed about 12 soldiers, and caught eight.

Once I took some very nervous prisoners to the back line. We gave them food, water and cigarettes and they told us, "The government forced us, but Kurds and Arabs are brothers." They were taken to the Kurdistan Democratic Party (KDP) prison.

The army could not win. The mountains were our home and I was with friends. We felt we were doing something good for our people and our homeland. We did not care about dying, because we were fighting a government who was killing our people, so people would say, "He died to make our lives better." This fighting was the opposite of my seven years in the Iraqi army. Army was a prison—you have no say about joining and you just take orders, orders, orders.

In 1975 Saddam Hussein and the Shah of Iran signed the Algiers Treaty, the Shah agreeing to stop supporting the Kurdish revolution in Iraq. Turkey and Syria promised the same. Within 24 hours Iran pulled out its artillery and all borders closed. All supply lines were cut. The Kurds were completely isolated

Many families were still in the mountains, and over 200,000 people escaped to Iran because they feared what the Iraqi government might do. Mostefa Barzani was under a lot of pressure. From Tehran he sent a message, "We must stop fighting—I don't want everybody to die. We should accept the amnesty and see what happens." He went to America to get support, but in 1979 he died of a heart attack.

Some people say he should not have given up so easily, but people can say this when they are somewhere safe, with enough to eat and drink. I think Barzani was right in his decision. Many people were displaced and in danger. Maybe the fight could have continued for one month or one year, but how many would have been killed and to what end?

The Iraqi government ordered all Kurds to hand over their guns, promising to pay 70 dinars for every gun. It was terrible. We came down from the mountains and gave up our guns and it was like dying: nobody talked; everybody's face was yellow and nervous. I saw old men crying, an unusual sight in our culture. It was a very black time.

Soldiers came to the villages, looking for guns and anything else they wanted. Over the next months, all the villages near the borders were destroyed and maybe 500,000 people were moved south to live in tents and new government built-towns. My uncles and many relatives had to move to these towns. The towns were all cement—no trees, no farming land, no jobs, nothing. Electricity and water were supplied for only a few hours a day or a week, the houses leaked in the rain.

The government gave people some money—say 100 dollars for their house, land, farm and animals. No-one could argue. The government could then say Kurdish people sold their land, like what happened to the Palestinians in Israel. People could take only clothes, so when they came to the new towns they had to spend their 100 dollars on food, blankets and furniture from the government supermarket.

Kurdish people have always lived a hard life. I was born in my great-grandfather's village of Safuri, deep in the mountains, near the large village of Dershish, capital of the Barwari tribe, the biggest tribe in the area. He was *agha* of Safuri. He owned the land and the village: a few old-fashioned mud houses with wooden rafters and flat, compacted earth roofs. There was no electricity or road, and Safuri was totally isolated in the long snowy winters.

The natural animals are the wolf, the black bear and the brown bear, and we have many old stories of a bear taking a child from the village, or of a male bear taking a woman, or a female bear taking a man. In winter wolves came in packs of up to 50, looking for sheep and other animals. When I stayed with my uncle in Safuri, I would see him shoot one, and leave its body and wait for other wolves to come and eat it, so he could shoot them. Sometimes people would stuff a skin with straw and put it on the roof of their house.

My father was a farmer until he was conscripted into King Faisal II's army, but he only had to serve three months, because his family paid money. He had married my mother when he was 17 and she was about 13. My mother did not know her age. My dad knew his age because the family must register a son with the government to get a license for citizenship. If this does not happen, a man can do nothing in Iraq. My mother came from the village next to Safuri, and from the same tribe as my father. My two grandfathers were friends, so they gave their son and daughter to each other. This was normal.

At the beginning of World War Two the British army came to the area and contacted each tribe's leader, asking for men to become soldiers. The British approached my grandfather, saying, "If you send your sons to our army, we will make them officers and pay them well," so in 1941 my dad and two or three uncles joined the British army and took many people with them. My dad served in the British army until 1951. During World War Two he was a parachute trooper in Italy, Greece, France, Britain, Russia and throughout the Middle East. He even went to China.

After the war, the British offered to bring all the officers' families to Britain so that the officers could continue to serve in the British army. They promised each family a house, and that the government would pay for the children's education, but my father said, "I want to stay." He was not a *peshmerga*, but he admired Mostefa Barzani because Barzani had spent his life fighting for Kurdish rights. He was from a powerful family belonging to the Naqshabandi sect, and in his area they were always fighting over religion. When he was 18 months old he spent nine months in Mosul prison with his mum. He had gone to a religious school and at age 16 he fought beside Shaykh Mahmud of Sulaimani against the Iraqi monarchy and British army. In the early 1940s he led 2000 *peshmergas* against Iraqi and British forces when they tried to invade Barzan territory. At that time the Iraqi government had only 10,000 in the armed forces, and Barzani's men killed 700, but the *peshmergas* lost, Barzani and his *peshmergas* and all their families escaping to Iran in October 1945. In March 1946 he became one of four generals in the Kurdish Republic of Mahabad, but when the republic collapsed in

December, he and 500 of his followers walked for 52 days through Iraq, Turkey and Iran, being bombed and attacked all the way. Barzani was given asylum in the Soviet Union, where he lived until 1958.

The KDP of Iraq was formed back in 1946, and was active throughout the 1950s. Barzani was its absentee leader, and my father worked secretly for the party—talking to people about our history and situation and about what the KDP would like to do for them. He believed in an independent Kurdistan. When Barzani returned to Kurdistan my father met with him in Baghdad, and again in the village of Galala. Karim Qassem drew up a new constitution for Iraq, which recognised the Kurdish and Arab nations. He said he wanted peace, but he tried to assassinate Barzani many times, so Barzani went from *agha* to *agha* to gather support.

He approached the uncle of my father, who was now *agha*. Before an *agha* dies he, or a group of men in the tribe, chooses the best man to be *agha*. Usually it is the *agha*'s son. My father's uncle was a good man and highly respected. He had a law degree, but when his father died he returned to Dershish to be *agha*. The *agha* is like the government of the area. He has advisers, and together they talk about big decisions, like going to war, with the *agha* makeing the final decision. He gives the orders, and he can catch and put in prison. If the Iraqi government wants to put a road through, officials must talk with the *agha* who decides what will happen. When Barzani got support from an *agha,* all the men in the tribe followed. If the *agha* joined the government, all his men went with him. One *agha* might have 50 followers, another might have 1000 and up until the 1970s he was the one who led them in battle.

Back in 1960 Mostefa gathered a lot of support, including that of the Barwari tribe, and although he did not want to fight the Iraqi government, by 1961 he was forced to go to war, when the government attacked a tribe he was obliged to defend. Because of my father's support of Barzani he was put in prison and over the seven months my family contacted a big man in the government to arrange for his release. They made him promise on paper not to work with anybody outside the government. It said, "If we hear anything suspicious about you, we will kill you straight away." After that he kept his ties with Barzani very secret.

I was born in 1957, after my father had married a second wife because my mother had been childless for so long. My mother was in her early twenties but she had no choice. In our country the man is everything, and until my father's generation, 80 per cent of men had two or three wives. This was normal. They liked many children to help on the farm. Problems only occurred if the man was no good, or could not control things, or loved one more than another. But if the woman was unhappy and went back to her family maybe they would return her.

When I was a baby my father decided to move his family to Barwari, 60 kilometres east of Dohuk. Barwari was a modern village with electricity and a road, and 400 to 500 houses made of stone, with flat roofs of concrete or wood and nylon sheeting and compacted earth on top. The rows of houses looked like giant steps going up the mountain. Below in the wide, flat valley, people grew rice, vegetables, potatoes and tobacco, and grazed their sheep in the summer. There was an airport, built by King Faisal so he could come for summer holidays to Barmuni, a village on the opposite mountain, about eight kilometres away. Later, Saddam was to expand the airport for his army.

There are many waterfalls, springs, caves and tunnels. Some tunnels go right through a mountain, and others twist and turn, becoming very narrow then opening into chambers. It is very dark and cold inside, and the wind or moving water can make the caves echo with strange sounds. The high air pressure can make a lamp go out, and some people are afraid to go inside, telling stories of *jinn* and genies who inhabit the caves. Other caves were made by people thousands of years ago. The one I visited had a small door leading into a chamber with ledges carved into the stone. Caves near Dohuk and Sulaimani have line drawings carved into the stone, of a cow, birds and snakes.

Every day my mother would bring the spring water in a lamb's skin, a clay pot, or a plastic container, and bake bread. In Kurdistan, when a family asks for a girl to marry their son, the first question is, "Can she make bread? Can she cook?" My mother worked too much, washing and cooking and cleaning, but to all of us she was a very good, quite, gentle woman.

There were three rooms in our house. Each wife had a room, where they slept with their children—four girls and me from my mother, three girls and one boy from my second mother. I can remember only one big disagreement, and when my dad came home everything was peaceful. The women worked together. It was like having two mothers—I loved them both, and I do not think about my sisters or brother being from another mother, but I was lucky because I was the first boy and a boy in our country is treated very special. Whatever I did at home nobody told me "No."

My father was also a very kind man. I never saw him angry or nervous. He always talked quietly. He did not drink alcohol or go to a club or café. He prayed five times a day, and talked to me a lot, especially when I grew up a bit—about religion, politics, his life, and the Kurdish people and their problems. For 20 years he worked as a government clerk in the administration office at the Darbandi Khan Dam, one of two very big dams built in Kurdistan to supply electricity to the rest of Iraq. In about 1964, when I was seven, we moved there to be with my father. An American engineering company had made the dam, and we lived in one of 200 very modern, European houses built for the foreign people who had worked on the project.

I started school in 1963—a little late, because of all the fighting. It was a boy's school. We wore Kurdish clothes, and had one class of Arabic a day. The rest of our classes were in Sorani. I grew up speaking the Bahdinan dialect, but only the accent and a few words are different. All my schooling was in Kurdish, and our Kurdish textbooks were printed in Baghdad. But many times I was too afraid to go to school because there were too many helicopters, tanks and soldiers coming to the market, looking for people. Our teachers were also afraid, because they were all Kurdish and the government was suspicious of them belonging to KDP.

At the time KDP was the only political party, even though Jalal Talabani and others began operating independently of Barzani from 1964. In 1966 Talabani negotiated with the government. He wanted Kurdish police instead of Iraqi police, and a university in Sulaimani. He began setting up councils in various places, wanting to take power from Barzani, but most people remained loyal to Barzani. From 1966 to 1970 there was fighting between their *peshmergas* in the area around Sulaimani, north of Darbandi Khan. My father and most of the people thought Barzani and Talabani should talk and solve things without using the gun, especially because it meant the Iraqi army was active too. Army personnel would come to our front door. I was afraid. Everyone was afraid. No-one knew what was going happen from one day to the next, and in the mid-1960s the army burnt many villages, including Barwari and Safuri.

Then in 1968 we heard there was a coup in Baghdad. At first nobody knew who had taken over, but after a couple of months it was announced that they were Ba'aths, with Ahmed Hasan Al-Bakr as president and Saddam Hussein as vice-president. Nobody had heard of Saddam Hussein, but my father told me what people were saying in secret: that after the Ba'aths took control in 1963, there had been a lot of killing, people put in prison, and villages destroyed. In 1969 fighting between Kurds and the army broke out in Mosul, but we never got much information about what was going on.

I went to a boys' secondary school in Sulaimani, renting a house with my mum and two sisters. One time we were in class and an army officer and 10 soldiers carrying machine guns came into the classroom. Somebody had reported that two students were politically active, so they had come to catch them, but the students were not at school. They asked many questions but we were all too scared to answer. Another time, about five soldiers came and took our teacher away. After four or five days, he came back, but we did not ask him anything and he did not tell us. The worst was when two *peshmergas* come inside the school, silently, followed by soldiers. In the shooting, maybe 10 people died, including women and children. The army stayed until four in the afternoon, so nobody could remove the bodies.

We played soccer and volleyball at school and soccer after school. We would go fishing in the river, which was just a series of waterholes because of the dam, using our hands, a fishing line or a bomb. There were many kinds of fish, but most common was the yellow carp.

Newroz was always the best time. Every year the government would announce over the radio and television: "Do not make fire," but nobody took any notice. For two weeks young people would collect wood and old tyres for the fires. On the night of March 20 we would go on the roof to see the fires everywhere—on people's roofs and in the mountains—on every high place. There was dancing and music, and we would visit our neighbours and relatives and join in. The next day everyone went for a picnic. Each group had a fire with food, dancing and Kurdish music. People played the *ba'aghlama, oud,* and *zorna,*[b] and sometimes a *tar* or piano accordion. Two or three men in each group sang about Newroz, the spring and the bringing of new life.

The story behind Newroz is of Kawa, a blacksmith, who rises up against the cruel Zohag. There are a number of versions. Zohag had a wound on each shoulder. Some say a snake grew out of each shoulder, but that these wounds or growths caused him so much pain, to live he had to treat or feed them each day with the brains of two children. Every day two children were killed. Over time the cook took pity on the people and devised a plan, saying to the people, "I will kill a sheep instead of one of the children, but only if the child I spare goes to the mountains and looks after the sheep." It is said that these people are the ancestors of the Kurds.

One day the slaughterer came to Kawa who had already lost seven of his sons, but Kawa thought, "Enough! I will go to Zohag's palace and kill him." He told the people, "If I succeed I will light a fire on the mountain. When you see this fire, everybody must come and kill the soldiers." Some people say he went alone and others say he took men, but he killed Zohag with his big blacksmith's hammer. At midnight the people saw the fire and knew that Kawa had succeeded, so every year at Newroz we light the fire of freedom.

Zohag was real. Some people say he lived more than 6000 years ago. This is why Newroz is celebrated in Kurdistan, Iran, Afghanistan and Pakistan, because long, long ago we were all one people, but the Persians like to say Zohag was the last Mede king and Kawa was Persian. Some Kurds say Zohag was either Assyrian or Persian and that Kawa was Kurd! No-one really knows.

At the Newroz picnics we would visit other groups and join in the dancing. It is not like it is in Australia. In the Middle East you have many friends. When you move into one street, after a week you know all the people, because they come to welcome you and you visit them and they visit you. If the men are not there and just the daughters are at home, you leave. If their mother is there, maybe you sit down and drink tea and talk. Otherwise young boys do not have contact with girls. We went to separate schools, and were not allowed to talk to a girl on the street unless the girl was a relative, or we knew her family, and then only a little, like, "Hello. How are you? Do you need anything?" If you talked more and somebody saw you and told her family, it was a big problem.

I left school when I went to the mountains in 1974. After the amnesty I stayed at home; then in July 1976, I was called into the army. Between 1976 and 1990 I served seven years, five of them fighting in the war with Iran. I did not believe in that war. In eight years more than half a million Iraqi soldiers were killed and maybe more than one million Iranians. I fought in three big battles—the first major one at Somare, then at Saifsa'ad and the last: Basra.

Basra was also my first taste of army life. It is in the south, a modern town of more than one million people in the middle of a flat, very hot desert. Every six months 2000 or 3000 soldiers came for training.

We learnt everything about the Kalashnikov, clothed in uniforms from Romania. I was very fit from the mountains, so the exercise was easy. We spoke Arabic. Some Arabs were good—you can live with them like brothers—but some, no. If you talked politics, you did not see your life again.

After three months, I was sent to a nearby camp to train on Italian-made SPG-9 anti-tank guns. They had a range of nearly two and a half kilometres, and were classified according to the size of the barrel opening: 60, 80, 120, 130, 135, 175, or 230 millimetres. The gun was too heavy—it took four men to move it—so it was mounted on a 4WD vehicle and loaded from the back. But to launch it you just had to press a lever with one finger. The shells came in two sizes—a 30-centimetre long rod and one nearly 70 centimetres, and fire came out the back, like an RPG. If you were within six metres, you could burn.

Every 30 days we were given five days leave to visit our family. After one year, while on leave, I decided not to go back. I escaped to Barwari village and stayed with my sister and uncle's wife. At about five o'clock one morning, when it was still dark, people came to the house saying, "Get out! The army is coming." All the people ran up the mountain and hid in the trees. We watched as the trucks and about six tanks come up the road, several helicopters flying overhead. The tanks and artillery bombed the village, and then about 300 soldiers got out of the trucks and went into every house, taking anything they wanted. I was more scared for my life: if they caught an army deserter, they killed him straight away.

I wanted to go with the *peshmerga*, but in 1977 there was trouble between KDP and the Patriotic Union of Kurdistan (PUK), which had formed in 1975. PUK *peshmergas* were wanting to set up bases in KDP areas, and I heard that about 500 of them were killed around Hakkari by army, KDP and tribes loyal to Barzani. It was a terrible thing. If *peshmergas* fight the Iraqi army for one year, perhaps 100 *peshmergas* die. I did not want to hear of Kurd fighting Kurd, so after three months of living as a deserter, when the government called an amnesty I had no choice—I had to go back to the army.

One year later I was released. I went to Dohuk, stayed with my sister, and studied at a general secondary school in preparation for college. I also worked in a cold store for meat and fish, at the Pepsi Cola factory, and at a cigarette factory built by the Ba'aths in the late 1970s. All jobs in Iraq are the same: government jobs with the same pay — up to 200 Iraqi dinars a month. Then in June 1980, a special agency in every city broadcast that men born within a certain period must report to the agency within 30 days. I had already done two years in the army, but in Iraq you cannot say no. I spent three months near Mosul, before we were given orders to go into Iran.

Anyone should be afraid of war, but when you are in the middle of it, something happens to you. You forget your life and family. You do not think or care. You are crazy. You become like a machine trained to kill. The people beside and behind you think the same—and those you face think the same, so you must kill them before they kill you. You are just a soldier following orders.

After a day or a week you start thinking about what happened: a friend was killed, others injured. Slowly you realise that you have killed too, and that those people have family and friends and probably did not want to fight this stupid war, but then you go and do it again.

We travelled in convoy to Baghdad and then to the border. In front were the tanks; in the rear were up to 200 cars and trucks. I was behind the anti-tank gun in a small Land Rover. It was night. We did not know where we were going, what we were going to face. At this time, you feel nothing. You just look and wait and wonder when the fighting will start. Everything is danger. Everyone is tense and silent.

For four days and four nights, we did not sleep. We ate two or three times. We just kept moving through trees, mountains and hills, villages and farms. All the villages were empty. The people must have seen our headlights and escaped.

From the villages we knew they were very poor. The houses looked big, but inside the courtyards would be land for vegetables, and just one or two small rooms, with no furniture.

The days were very hot, the nights very cold. Thirty kilometres inside the border we come to the village of Naftshahr, where we stayed 10 or 15 days. At night we prepared the ground, making trenches and underground L-shaped holes—two or three metres apart, one and a half metres down, and two or three metres long—covering their openings with branches and stones. It was all work and not enough sleep. People were saying, "Maybe after one or two months, this war will finish," so we did not worry. We just worked and talked and sometimes joked.

From Naftshahr we moved west to a smaller village called Somare,[c] south-east of Khanaqin, still in the mountains. We dug more holes. We were very tired. Two days later a unit was attacked on the other side of the village, and we got orders to go and help. It was night. Everything was still. Two cement bridges over a narrow river were broken. About eight Iraqi tanks and five Iranian tanks were burning. The Iraqi tanks came from Russia, the Iranian tanks from the USA. Every Iraqi tank carries four people inside, so there were burnt black bodies and pieces of body everywhere, some still in their holes.

For the next few nights our job was to pick up the bodies and put them into trucks so they could be taken back to Iraq. Sometimes if you touched one, it crumpled to ash. It was the first time I understood the meaning of war. I began to think, "Today or tomorrow, this will be me."

After Iraqi aeroplanes and tanks bombed another part of Somare territory, we moved in. We stayed for six months, the Iranian front line 500 to 1000 metres away. Ten to 12,000 Iraqi soldiers were trying to hold the area against I don't know how many Iranians. They told us 8000. They moved, we moved. The fighting was with tanks, aeroplanes and anti-tank guns, no close contact. Sometimes the Iranians shot 300 to 400 bombs in one hour and the Iraqis returned fire. I would just keep pressing the lever.

Otherwise we stayed in our holes. Bombs could land half a metre away, but the L-shape protected us from shrapnel. If they came within 30 metres, the noise was shattering: you could hear nothing for the next 30 minutes.

From Somare we moved to Saifsa'ad for 40 days as a supplementary unit for more fighting. After 400 bombs, the whole area smelt of chemicals, and soldiers would come out of their holes stumbling, clutching their hair, with red eyes. Then we were sent back to Somare. I returned to the same hole. One to three people lived in a hole, 30 to 45 soldiers in one area. Some holes you could stand up inside, others you could only crawl into. At night we had to be quiet. If the Iranians heard an engine or someone talking, they would shoot, but night was the time we had to go outside and get ammunition and food, and if there was no bombing we ate together in someone's hole. They fed us well—chicken or red meat, rice and vegetables.

The first hours of the morning were the most dangerous. It is the coldest time, and when you're the most tired. It is the time to pray and it is the time to attack. Otherwise most days all we did was sleep, our gun beside us, while the other person kept watch, gun in hand, or we would talk or play cards or dominoes.

For six months I shared a hole with a Kurd I had known from before. Often we would ask ourselves, "Why are we fighting for our enemy?" Many times, we planned a free Kurdistan. When they moved my friend to another unit, I stayed by myself. Many holes had one person. For three years I lived like this around Somare, then one year around Naftshahr, 40 days in one place, three months in another. Over time, many soldiers, especially Kurds, started deserting. Many had lost their land and home, as well as their relatives to death or prison, and now they lived like mice in the ground for Saddam. They would say, "Our enemy is not Iran. We will go and join the *peshmerga*."

When everything was quiet, they would give us five days' leave. It took one day's travel to go home, so I would be at home for three days. I would see friends and relatives and start to feel a little human, a little less empty. I would not tell them what was really happening. I did not want to worry them.

Finally, in early 1985, I was sent to Basra: 1000 kilometres, taking two and a half days by convoy. We arrived at about 4pm. It was a dark time for the people of Basra, with tanks and aeroplanes coming and going, and the Iranian bombardment. They asked us, "What is happening?", but we knew nothing.

At about 9 pm we were ordered to move inside Iranian territory under Iraqi control—between Abadan and Khorramshahr, on the Shatt Al-Arab. We drove straight into heavy fighting. At any time over the next 15 days, there were more than 60,000 Iraqi soldiers and maybe 100,000 Iranians. There were thousands of tanks and aeroplanes, and every second 1000 bombs exploded from both sides. Night was day, with the sky full of white flares dropped by parachute, and the red and yellow fire of bomb explosions. The air choked with a thick mixture of sulphur and phosphorus, and the stench of dead bodies.

On the ground, tanks moved in packs and soldiers ran. The bombs might land two, three, five metres away, but we could not duck for cover. For two days I fired the anti-tank gun non-stop, my head millimetres away from the gun, each time a crack of lightning going off in my ear. For two days we had no sleep, no food, no water. They could not get supplies through. We felt weak, but I could not leave the gun. If I had to go to the toilet someone else would take my place, but when you neither eat nor drink—there's little need.

When the tanks moved, we moved. Sometimes the tanks were 500 metres away, sometimes 30 metres, coming from every direction. Every minute, I saw five or six people die. Everwhere were pieces of body, looking like they'd been sliced with a knife—just a hand, or a leg, or a head. I watched one man from my unit run from one hole to another. When a bomb blew his head off, he ran another five or six metres, then fell. A bomb explodes—when you open your eyes, three people are dead beside you. After five years of fighting this stupid war, those were the worst two days of my life.

When a bomb hit our Land Rover and killed two, I was injured by shrapnel, and after a few hours they took me to Basra Hospital. It was not a big injury—a bit of shrapnel about the size of a fingernail in my left scapula and smaller pieces in my right. They are still there. If I am cold and move my shoulder, I feel them.

I was in hospital for three days. People had lost eyes and limbs. Some had lost their mind. I was given 15 days leave. For four hours I sat silently at home. My father said, "Don't tell your Mum about your injury. She is sick," but slowly, slowly I told her. Over the next two weeks I socialised, but in my mind were the people I saw die and the thousands in the hospital.

On my return to Basra, I heard that the Iraqi army had been forced to retreat after five days. Of my unit of 300 only 10 or 12 were still alive. In total, Iraq lost maybe 50,000 soldiers at Basra, not counting those injured, and 90,000 were taken prisoners of war. Fifteen years later, many have not come home. Iraq and Iran continue to talk about an exchange of prisoners.

I saw more terrible things and asked a doctor friend to extend my leave. He gave me five days. From the television, my father knew what was happening. He said, "You have been to the army three times. It is enough. Next time, you die. If they put me in prison, I do not care. Go to Dohuk, and we will follow soon." After so many years of war, nearly every Iraqi house had a black mark on the door, with a name and a place and a date. One family had lost seven sons.

It took me a while to settle down. In five years of war I felt I had lost everything: my memory, my feelings, my humanity. I had seen too many people die. But when I saw families, especially the children, I wanted to leave the war. I did not want to stay crazy or nervous or hard like some people.

The hard army life had also strengthened me. Before the army, I liked to sit and eat and do nothing, and because I was the first boy in the family, if I wanted money, clothes, anything, my father never said no. I did not care about school or work. But after the army life, I told my father, "I must work." My father knew the danger but liked the change. He understood without talking. He had seen enough war: World War Two, 25 years fighting the Iraqi army, and now the war with Iran. Maybe other people would go crazy from all this fighting, but we grow up with death. I was seven when I first saw *peshmergas* die on the road.

For a deserter, Dohuk was more dangerous than Barwari, because if the army came, you could not escape to the mountains. I would sit in my sister's home with no job and no money, feeling nervous every time there was a knock at the door. Friends and relatives could visit, but I could only go out in secret, with people who had government connections. All the time, I was scared. There were too many checkpoints, and at any time soldiers could stop you and ask for your identity papers. Once, the army came looking for me, but I was not home. I wanted to join the *peshmerga* in the mountains, but my sister begged me to stay. She was widowed, with four children, and if I went to the mountains, she would have to come with me too. She did not want the life.

In July 1985, my family rang saying, "Come, your mother is dying." She died before I arrived. I was very sorry. For so many years I was not with her. They brought her body to Dohuk for burial and for three days, all the family stayed in Dohuk so that friends and relatives could visit. My father was very upset, but I did not cry. Yet when I saw my sister crying I felt my stomach and heart were being squeezed. I told her, "That is enough. Everybody dies."

Ten months later, news came that my father was sick. Straight away, I went to Sulaimani and took him to hospital. After five hours the doctors disconnected him from the oxygen and intravenous fluid, saying, "We can do nothing." I asked, "He dies?" "Yes." I cried a little—the first time for many years, and the last.

We took our father's coffin on the six-hour journey back to Dohuk. We could not bury him near our mother, because she was buried in a cemetery the government was to convert into a market, and afterwards, the rest of the family moved to Dohuk.

Seven months later I became engaged to my cousin Leila, and after five months we married. I refused to have a big party—I only wanted a honeymoon. My father's death was too recent.

Marriage was something very new—the best thing in my life. It is not like it is in Australia. We cannot have a girlfriend, so from when we are very young, we look forward to this time. After so many hard years, our two-week honeymoon in Sulaimani was peaceful and quiet. I felt relaxed, and close to Leila, but I did not tell her about the bad times. I just wanted to talk about the good future we would have together: having kids, building a big house and owning a car. But if someone had said, "Are you really going to have all this?" I would have had to say, "Sorry—I cannot." Leila knew I had deserted from the army and would have problems finding work.

I had some money in reserve, and five of my sisters and my brother were teachers. Leila and I lived with my other mum, three sisters and my brother. My brother did the shopping. It was my house—a modern house with five rooms—and Leila and I had our own room. I found work for four hours a day, sometimes as a mechanic, and sometimes as a storekeeper for a relative, who would pick me up in his car. At times I would go home by bus. Whenever I was out, they would worry, "Maybe he does not come back."

When Leila was nearly nine months' pregnant, my elder sister took her to a good hospital in Hawler, to avoid any questions. After one month Leila returned with Venwar.

Between 1985 and 1988, while the war with Iran continued, the *peshmerga* were strong and Iran supported their revolution, but in February 1988 Saddam launched Anfal. The word 'Anfal' was used in Muhammad's time. Al-Anfal, meaning 'the spoils', is the title of the eighth surah in the Qur'an. It refers to Muslims fighting non-Muslims. They can take anything from their enemy. It is *halal*—allowed. By using this word, Saddam was saying that Kurds were not Muslims and that he could take humans, animals, crops and villages. Saddam's forces used chemicals and normal bombs, and between February and August, up to 4000 villages were burned or bulldozed. The army and Kurdish militia forced all the Kurdish people to move from their villages. Some were taken south, some came to the towns and others escaped. 182,000 people disappeared. In Halabja, 5000 civilians[d] were killed in a matter of hours, but it was not until I came to Australia that I saw a video cassette of all the death in the homes and on the streets. The government maintained silence. Nobody talked about these things in any Arab country.

Anfal was happening mainly in the villages, but the government also deported Kurds from Mosul and Kirkuk, the two main oil areas, and 5000 to 6000 soldiers were stationed in Dohuk. They were everywhere—in the street and in every shop—and we saw many tanks moving north.

The Iran–Iraq War ended in July 1988, but at about eight o'clock one night in 1989 the army came looking for me. They pulled up in a truck and asked for my ID and told me to come. I could not even go home and say goodbye. I deserted after seven months. Back in Dohuk we would listen to the short-wave radio from countries like France, Britain and the USA broadcasting in Arabic. In late July 1990, we heard that Saddam Hussein was moving thousands of tanks from Baghdad to Basra. Nobody knew why. When the army moved inside Kuwait on 2 August 1990, the radio and TV announced that all men born between 1950 and 1968 must go back to the army. I said, "No." Two years after one war, we were in another. People could not believe it, but nobody could say what they thought. Iraqi radio would say, "Saddam Hussein is winning," and Iraqi television showed pictures of the Kuwaiti people shaking the hands of Iraqi soldiers. After two or three weeks the news stated, "Kuwait is part of Iraq. It was taken away by the British, so we are claiming it back."

Everyone was scared, but when we heard on the foreign news that America was going to enter the war, we were hopeful, and when the Americans and their Allies started bombing Iraqi forces in January 1991, we were very happy. When the bombs reached Baghdad, Saddam Hussein announced, "America bombs Baghdad, but we will cut off their hand so they will never bomb Baghdad again." Within two or three hours of the first bombs, all electricity was cut, and for the next two or three months we had no electricity, no television, no lights—just the battery radio. Everyone was hoping the Americans would go into Baghdad. Everybody loves his country but nobody liked Saddam and we all knew that the Iraqi people could not remove him. The Iraqi Arabs felt the same, because Saddam hurts the Arabs too.

When we heard that America had stopped advancing towards Baghdad, everyone thought it was like a contract between Saddam Hussein and the USA, that America was afraid the Shi'ites would take over Iraq because most of the Iraqi and Iranian people are Shi'ite Muslim. Syria has many Shi'ites, too. It means three countries could become very strong, and America does not want this.

Then we heard that the Americans were encouraging the Iraqi people to rise up against Saddam. The Iraqi soldiers returning from Kuwait threw down their guns and joined the uprisings in the southern Shi'ite towns. Within days Kurdish civilians and *peshmergas* were taking control of all the towns in Kurdistan. Two days after Sulaimani came under Kurdish control, civilians in Dohuk went to the office of the Ba'ath Party and killed an important government official, some Revolutionary Guards and several police. In the morning we woke to learn that Kurds controlled the city, that *jahshek* had joined the uprising and that hundreds of *peshmergas* had come into the city.

Over the next two weeks we saw thousands of soldiers in Dohuk just leave their tanks and guns and start walking. The Kurdish people gave them food, and came with trucks to take them to Mosul and Baghdad, and at night *peshmergas* came and took the guns and tanks.

We could not believe that Dohuk was free: no Saddam Hussein, no soldiers on the street, no security. For the first time in 30 years, men and women could walk the street after four o'clock in the afternoon. There was no-one saying, "Where are your papers? Where are you going?" No-one would shoot you on sight, then plant a gun on you to justify it. Families were walking, talking and laughing in the street at eight o'clock at night.

Over the radio *peshmergas* began calling for anybody with experience in army technology and strategy so I approached the KDP inside Dohuk. Most Kurdish boys from five know about the gun, but the *peshmerga* needed my knowledge of how tanks shoot and how to shoot tanks, so I went with my uncle, who was the head of one group, to the mountains behind Dohuk. We were there to give signals so other *peshmergas* could organise.

After just two weeks of freedom, we heard that US President Bush was telling Saddam, "If you want to control Iraq, we don't mind. We just want you out of Kuwait." The Kurdish people were shocked. A no-fly zone was declared on 28 March so Saddam's air force could not go past the 36 Parallel, but on the same day Saddam's army, tanks and helicopters began advancing north and bombing Kirkuk. The *peshmerga* told the people to leave Dohuk, because they were afraid Saddam would use chemicals. Over five days two million people left Kurdistan.

I returned to the mountains, because the *peshmerga* wanted to protect the people. For three days and nights, Saddam's helicopters and aeroplanes flew over, dropping 100 bombs at a time, killing many people on the road and in the mountains. The *peshmergas* with me managed to shoot down one or two helicopters but the tanks were three kilometres away, on low ground, so the anti-tank gun was useless. We would sleep two hours a night in a cave or hole covered by stones, always under bombardment.

On the afternoon of the third day, I saw three people die from a bomb dropped by a helicopter. By this time, three-quarters of the people had left Dohuk, and we were told to go and save our families. At 6 pm I left the mountain and walked twenty minutes back to town. As night fell, all I could see were the lights of vehicles leaving.

My family had packed blankets and food. My brother and I went and brought a truck for Leila and our three children, my mother, two sisters and one brother, their children,

Refugees leaving for Turkey, photographed by Mansour Razaghi

and other relatives. At two o'clock on the morning of 13 April 1991, we left. My mother said, "Close the door." I asked, "Why? We are not coming back and if the soldiers come they will break it."

The road was choked with cars, and thousands of people were walking. In the morning we arrived in Zakho and by nightfall we had reached a village called Bagoora.[e] One thousand people were camping under the trees. We made a fire, and sat in the rain, protecting the children with blankets.

From there we had to walk to the border. The next morning we started out: 500 metres up and 500 metres down, the line of people stretching as far as the eye could see, sometimes three abreast, sometimes in single file, always at a very slow pace. Leila carried our baby daughter. I carried our three-year-old son and five or six blankets. Five-year-old Venwar walked. Some mountains were still covered in snow and for one and a half hours we walked through snow. Otherwise it rained. There were rocks 200 to 300 metres high and gorges with sheer drops of half a kilometre. We had to cross some rivers, sometimes half a metre deep with melted snow. We saw many old people walking—in danger, you are stronger than normal, but my mother was finding it hard. She was over 60 and too tired and hungry to move. I would carry her on my back, then put her down. She was a heavy load—a big woman. At the top of a mountain, she would say, "I can go on a little bit." Then I would go back to help Leila. I did this for two days. At dusk on the second day, I went back for Leila and could not find her.

There were too many people, and in the growing dark I could not see very well. After an hour I saw my sister, who said, "Oh Leila went the other way." There was a fork in the trail, and Leila had gone by accident to the left, the rest of us to the right. I continued to search and after four hours I found her, but then we lost Venwar, my sister and brother. They had gone a very difficult way, in the snow. The next morning I walked behind a man I knew, who was carrying three children. I watched him put his smallest child under a rock and cover her with a small blanket. I asked, "Did she die?" "No, but what can I do? I cannot carry all of them. I leave her to die so I can save my other two." I picked up his child and carried her in my arms, my son on my back, stopping every 200 to 300 metres. At nightfall, the child's uncle came up to me and I handed him the child, He said, "We won't forget what you have done for us."

We fed the children bread. They were very good, very quiet. Other kids were crying, sick from diarrhoea, lack of food, and the rain and cold. Some died. By the third day every 200 or 300 metres there was a dead body on the roadside, mainly old people and children. Some people dug a small hole and covered the body, placing two stones to mark the grave.

I wanted to help all the people but I could not. When I saw an old man unable to go any further I told him, "Don't worry, uncle. Maybe a relative will come. They will not leave you here." He said, "Yes, I have a son, but he cannot carry me and his kids. I am an old man. Leave me and save your children." "Sorry uncle. If I have time, I'll come back and help you." "No, no. Just go."

For three days, we walked to the top of a mountain, only to see another and another. For two nights we sat under the trees around a fire in the constant rain, and sometimes in the snow. Halfway down the last mountain, the trees stopped and we could see across a large valley to more mountains, and below, the winding, steep, rocky-banked Khabor River, which marks the border with Turkey. The river varied from five to 15 metres across and was running fast and cold with melting snow.

It was five o'clock in the afternoon and raining. There was one small bridge, with no handrail—only three wooden planks, supported by stones on each bank. On the other side, Turkish soldiers with machine guns stood every 10 metres. We approached them, but they shot over our heads saying in Turkish, "Go back. We kill anyone who comes across."

Everybody was exhausted. In seven days, I had slept for two hours. Venwar, my sister and my brother were still lost. We had two blankets between 10 people. We put the five kids under the blankets and the rest of us sat around a fire in the rain and snow. By 7 am half a metre of snow had fallen. During that night, one man near us lost his wife. He had five children aged from one to five. At 8 am, the smallest one died. He went to bury him, then came back to find another child dead. His mother and sister had also died.

The Turkish government was not accepting people into Turkey, so we stayed between Iraq and Turkey for one week in the rain and cold. On the second day our food was gone, so two others and I went back to the truck we'd left on the other side of the mountains. Without the crowd and the children, it took us four hours.

Every two days, three times in all, I went back for food. Then the Kurdish people from Turkey started bringing truckloads of food—bread, rice and vegetables. They would give it to the soldiers, who would call us one by one saying, "How many people are in your group?" After 10 days the United Nations brought food in big army aeroplanes twice a day. The plane would roar low overhead, and drop a one-ton load by parachute—not enough, because in this one place, there were maybe 50,000 people. Some had been walking for 15 days, and every day 50 people were dying.

The planes also brought clothes, blankets, and white nylon or plastic, to make tents. Everything was stamped 'United Nations', or Made in USA, (or Australia, Japan, Britain or France). Everyone would scramble to cut the rope with knives and grab whatever they could. Sometimes the parachute did not open, and the food parcels would strike the ground and break and the food would be scattered in the mud. Later, in the second camp, it was more ordered. We organised into groups and one person collected the food.

It was a city of tents and fires in the mud and rain. People went to the toilet anywhere. Each day I climbed the mountain to collect wood, weak from not enough food or sleep. Leila would cook, and wash the children. We would eat rice and bread, sometimes vegetables, and too much cheese and some sort of cream. At night two or three families would sit around a fire in the rain, talking. People were afraid. There was no singing or dancing. There were no arguments, only a laugh if somebody fell in the mud or into the river. All we could think was about what would happen to us, but I was determined not to go back to Iraq. I was an army deserter.

After 14 days I heard from a local Kurd that there was another camp one hour's walk over the mountain, and he offered to take us. I told Leila, "We should go. Maybe we will find Venwar and your mum and dad." It was a small camp, just 3000 people, and we found Leila's parents and Venwar. When Venwar saw her mum, she cried, saying, "I walked all the way in the snow. I saw many things." Our relatives had food and a tent, so we stayed.

People from the UN started to encourage people to go back to Iraq, but they also said, "There is a refugee camp near the Turkish border and the UN will supply food." After two weeks at the second camp, they took us to a place near a Kurdish village called Ekmala. About 75,000 people were staying here. Within two days the US army and the UN came and organised everything. There were toilet blocks and water from an underground spring. They brought food and tents by helicopter, and organised people into groups of 20 or 50. Relatives put their tents together and the children played in the rain.

My mother, brother, one sister and Leila's parents decided to go back to Iraq. I told them I was not going back. My uncle and brother tried to change my mind, saying, "You are the oldest son and you should care about your sisters, your land and your village." But I told them, "I don't care about those things. If I see only two people left in this camp I will stay." I said to Venwar, "We won't go back to Iraq," and she replied, "Okay, I don't want to see Saddam again."

The US army told everybody to write their name on a list for going back or another list if we wanted to stay. Only 5000 people stayed. Over four days they brought trucks to take the people to Silopi or back to Iraq. We said goodbye to our family, and Leila cried as they waved from the back of the truck. I was afraid for them. The Americans promised protection, and this is the case 11 years later, but when the Americans go Saddam will return Kurdistan.

For eight hours we sat on top of our tents and blankets, travelling on rough roads through the mountains. The 20-odd Kurdish villages we passed through were very, very poor—no electricity, no water except for the river, very few animals, no school, no hospital. In winter, they would be isolated.

Silopi is a camp for people going to Makkah, but it looked more like a prison. It is on a plain, mountains on the horizon. A high concrete wall with barbed wire surrounded it and Turkish soldiers in khaki green guarded the two big wooden gates. Inside there was a hotel where the police and army stayed, and two bungalows, two toilet blocks, and flat land for the tents, which were arranged in 200 to 300-metre rows at different angles around a cement yard about 1000 metres square.

Twelve thousand people had already arrived. The Turkish officials gave us two tents, two blankets for each person, some plastic sheeting to put on the floor, some towels, a gas bottle and a one-burner stove, then showed us where to go. Many people came and helped us. Food was brought in by truck and every fourteen days government officials distributed for each person half a kilo of rice, some oil, sugar and tea and every day, they would bring a bread roll for each person, enough for one meal.

It was a very, very hot summer, and there were no trees or other shelter from the heat. Mice ran over us as we slept or sat. If you killed two, four more would come. What can you do? The water and two toilet blocks were 600 metres away from our tent, seven toilets in each —14 toilets for what became 23,000 people. Water was brought in morning and evening by tank and everybody had to queue. If the pump broke down there was no water. Tall lamps lit the camp at night, but inside the tents we only had kerosene lamps.

The tents were very close to each other. If one tent caught fire from a lamp or when a bottle of gas exploded, the whole line caught fire. Once, 10 tents burnt in the next row. People had to throw everything out very quickly and people were injured.

After two months one married sister and her family, and my unmarried sister, decided to go back to Iraq, as did many people. Only 10,000 stayed, and more left later. After four months they gave us new tents, and started a school in one of the bungalows. There were more than 200 teachers in the camp, so they volunteered to teach four hours a day, six days a week. At first the children sat on the floor, with paper and pens supplied by the UN. Then people from Israel donated chairs and a blackboard for three classes.

With winter coming, it became very, very cold. It would snow 40 centimetres in one night, and there were 50 days of snow. Mud was everywhere. Leila continued to have pains in her legs from sleeping in the wet and cold, but the children were well. All they got was flu.

There were four UN personnel and the rest were Turkish. We kept away from the Turkish. On a number of occasions, warehouse supplies were stolen. One day a man was saying, "Those supplies are meant for us." Soldiers overheard and took him away for several days, beating him badly. They assembled all refugees, and over a loudspeaker a Turkish official told us they would shoot anyone who complained. The UN could do

Iraqi Kurdish refugees at camp on Turkish border, photographed by Mansour Razaghi

nothing. They said, "If we protest, they will dismiss us, so for your sake we say nothing."

The only happy times were when people from an embassy came and accepted people as refugees and there would be a small party. At Newroz, in 1992, the Turkish officials said, "No fire," so we sang and danced without a fire.

We passed the days visiting, sitting and talking, or listening to a small radio. People had different politics, but there were no problems. Everyone had lost everything and we were all living in the same conditions. A hundred people a day were allowed to get a pass to go out of the camp to Silopi town, 10 kilometres away, usually for one or two hours. In one year, I left the camp twice. On the first occasion, I went to the border to see my family. They were well, but they said, "Come back. Care about your kids—they will die there."

The UN started interviewing three months after we arrived. For three hours they asked us about our history: "Why did you escape? Why don't you go back?" They gave us refugee status, made their report and sent it to the different embassies. No-one could choose the country they wanted to go to. It was up to an embassy, and if one rejected you, the UN gave your file to another embassy. I had a friend in Australia, who had sent me a sponsorship letter, so when the Australian Embassy official came, he told me, "Fill out the form and we will send the form to the embassy in Ankara. If you are lucky, they will accept you." After three months we saw our names on the list. I knew nothing about Australia. I had no dreams—I just wanted to leave the camp. After 25 days, we heard that the UN had our temporary residency visas for Australia, but that my sister and her family were rejected because my sister has a small eye problem. She can read and drive a car, but in test after test the Turkish doctors did not pass her.

Because we were being sponsored we needed 16 and a half million Turkish lira for the aeroplane tickets. Leila had some gold rings, and a traditional Kurdish necklace of three chains, hung with gold medallions. It was nearly one kilo of gold, so I went to Silopi, where there were three little jewellery shops owned by Kurdish people. They knew I came from Iraq and needed money, and the first one I visited offered me less than half the gold's worth, not enough to buy five tickets, but the other shops offered less. A good friend in Sydney loaned me the rest of the money.

On 2 April 1992, we gave our tent back to the UN and everything else to my sister and friends. I was very happy and very sad—happy because it was as if I had passed a very big examination, and we hoped for a different life, but sad and worried for my sister. She lived for two years at Silopi before the USA accepted her. Also I knew we were going far from our country and might never see our family again. After 10 years, I still see no way to go back for a visit.

There was no-one to meet us at Melbourne Airport. I rang my sponsor but he had changed address. I had one letter from a person, so I rang him asking what to do. He told me to go to the immigration office at the airport and ask them to take us to the hostel. At Springvale hostel they gave us a flat and we ate at the restaurant for 28 days. Then we moved to a flat. Now we live in a house.

I do not know a country better than Australia. It is very quiet. There is no big problem and everyone can live as they like. The children go to good schools, and learn Kurdish for one hour every Saturday. My only worry for them is that in Kurdistan, our life and culture and religion go together, whereas in Australia, children grow up free. Even when they are 15 years old, they are allowed to go to any place. In my country, this would never happen. It would be a shame on us if our daughter went out with a boy we did not know.

There is no postal service in Kurdistan, so friends bring letters, and sometimes we phone our families. For some years, even though they worked as teachers, they did not have enough food, but now life is better.

I respect Kurdish culture, but I left politics back in Iraq. Enough of politics and fighting! Yet Kurdish people cannot escape politics. When the Iraqi Kurdistan National Assembly was elected in May 1992, we thought, "This is the first stone, and in the future we can build, stone by stone, a state." But in 1994 civil war broke out, and at the end of August 1996, Saddam Hussein's forces attacked Hawler and many people were killed. The region under Kurdish administration became divided, DPS's regional govenment operating from Hawler and PUK's regional government from Sulaimani, which is outside the no-fly zone. Each time we heard the news, it was like being thrown into freezing snow. It was a black thing for Masoud Barzani to invite Saddam back to Kurdistan, but also it was a big mistake that PUK allowed Iranian soldiers into Iraq at the end of July. We do not want a Shi'ite government, where everything must be done inside the mosque.

All sides have made big mistakes, with a hand from outside. Turkey, Syria and Iran want to make problems for Iraq, and for the Iraqi Kurdish parties. They help one Kurdish party against the other but kill their own Kurdish people. None of these governments wants Kurds to do anything for themselves.

Still there is uncertainty. The Turkish army comes into Iraqi Kurdistan whenever it wants, bombing villages and killing people, with weapons supplied by America. American and British planes bomb the area, but if the UN leaves Kurdistan tomorrow, the *peshmerga* will have to take up guns—it is the first and last choice when people like Saddam Hussein are in power.

No-one is willing to give good, solid support for a peaceful solution. In September 1998, America invited Barzani and Talabani to Washington to sign an agreement to stop the civil war. In the same month they helped Turkey put pressure on Syria to get rid of Abdullah Ocalan, leader of PKK. They helped capture Ocalan in Nairobi in February 1999, and he was taken back to Turkey, where he remains in prison. Ocalan is a Kurdish leader, like Barzani and Talabani. They can come and go to Europe and America. Why is Ocalan treated differently? Most Kurds live in Turkey, and they have been denied all rights. It is all about politics and power. To solve the problems might take another 50 or 100 years. We might have to talk with the gun to Iraq or Turkey or Iran, but if we use the gun between ourselves, it is a big problem. Only when we leave the gun and talk face to face can we help each other.

A Question

By Abbas Boskany

Loving you was a lexicon
In colours.
The mind was lacking in
The black-and-white unsaid words.

I used to believe that
Every story had to have you
As a starting point.
Yet, you ask me, "Why?"

You did not know that
Your "whys" were the manacles
Of the heart's violet wish.
You would not know that
Your questions were both
Embers and kisses upon my lips.

I did not know that
While I was singing with
The pastoral birds for you,
You were pulverising
My night-breaths into dust.
You did not know
That I do not know
How to spell a mountain of injuries.
I did not know
What question to ask
So that you would not say, "Why?"

ABOUT Abbas Boskany

Born in 1969, Abbas Boskany grew up in the city of Sulaimani, at the foot of the Azmar and Goijha[a] Mountains. His love of poetry began at high school, his main inspiration being the deep insights of the classicist Mahwi (1830–1905), and the powerful images and questioning of the revolutionary realist Abdullah Goran (1904–1962). He particularly empathises with Goran. Boskany says, "He was a true free thinker, constantly questioning the society around him, communism, poetry, and himself."

While at high school Abbas acted in the Sulaimani Acting Group, and after being cast as the prince in *The Little Prince* adapted from the story by Antoine De Saint-Exupery, he dreamed of becoming a poet–performer. However, the Ba'ath government decreed that all students wanting to attend the Academy of Fine Arts had to be members of the Ba'ath Party. Instead, Abbas went to the Institute of Technology, graduating in civil engineering.

In the army Abbas was employed as a foreman on a military project in charge of three groups of Vietnamese labourers involved in the construction of Badush Dam near Mosul. The project came to a halt when Saddam invaded Kuwait in August 1990. Kurds were being sent to the front line, so Abbas escaped to the mountains. Disillusioned with what he saw of the political activities, he crossed into Turkey, where he started writing poetry.

One and a half years later, in 1992, he came to Australia as a refugee. He is now married to a Kurdish woman, has a son and works as a security officer. In Australia he continues writing articles and poetry. A collection of his poems is about to be published by Rabun Publishers, Sweden, owned by the Kurdish poet Refiq Sabir. He says of his inspiration, "I like the confrontation of words that go deep and explode the status quo. I write about life and the hidden bridges to the other side. I explore new meanings, images and feelings, trying to transform the truths that we see as impossible and reconcile these into a harmonic body—that is, the poem. Yet when I reach the other side, I find no meaning, only questions, and become like a child trying to touch the moon in the river. I am both bright-eyed and black-eyed. That's the only way I can catch my identity and delay the decision of suicide."

Travel Delirium

By Abbas Boskany

The mummies have turned into deities
Taking over the warbles.
Once again
Eve is astray after Adam.
The trees are overtaken by hysteria
The birds start wheezing

Love is the alphabet
Love is the dizzy hollyhocks' hide-and-seek
Love is the meaning.

Together we block the way
We dare not look a butterfly in the eye:

The butterfly was an eyewitness
Of the time when we turned our festival into a funeral,
Its eyes witnessed that ominous evening's eagles.
We peeped at the fading colours,
And rusty bells
That wrinkled the shadows of the churches, mosques and idols;
Those colours and bells
Turned violets into thorns
And banned the melodies.
Side by side, rubbing shoulders
We blocked the way
And together we grew angry.

It was the witness:
Every defeat took us to that oasis' pilgrimage
Which our mothers marched to,
Only there with questions' sobbing
Did we bitterly weep,
And weep.
Love was indeed our identity.

How many seconds
How many epochs
I waited for the rendezvous?
Waiting; has become a photograph-album.
An album of falling leaves.
Still, you did not come.
I transformed the frontiers into a few short lines
And took a decision:
I can approach your drowsy eyes,
I can turn eyesight into words
I can turn parting into reunion.
It did not take long:
The lovers around you revolted
They cut off all the trees to make torches.
It did not take long:
The deities of your pink nights
Broke the necks of all the buds
For a tryst.

Exile has turned into a meaning for night, and
The notebook rests as a few torn pages
Scattered on the streets.
And I, like the
Torn map of my homeland,
Am smashed to pieces.

Only God Knows

A life story based on interviews with Ali Hussein

All my life I have preferred literature and languages to politics. My favourite Kurdish writer is the Sufi mystic, poet, storyteller, linguist, historian and scientist Ahmedi Khani. He wrote the *Nubihara Bicukan*, a Kurdish–Arabic dictionary, in a such a poetical way, it is truly a masterpiece.

In my village of Khabor a storyteller was a very important person. There was no electricity, and even if someone had a radio it was all in Arabic, so on long winter nights, all our relatives would come to our house and listen to my father tell stories.

By day he was a farmer of barley, wheat, lentils and all the grains, as well as tomatoes, cucumbers, eggplant and melons. He and my four uncles owned small plots of land, and in the years they let them lie fallow, they worked other people's land. But by night my *bab* was a storyteller. He would only have to hear a story once and he remembered every detail, and his way of telling had a special charm. He knew more than 100 stories—mainly fables about life.

One was about a boy whose father was a rich, wise man. The old man's advice was to be more close to animals than to people because animals are more loyal. The boy grew up and married, and after his father died he inherited his father's wealth, yet his wife remained childless. One day he went to the mosque where he met a man and woman with a baby boy. They were too poor so the rich man brought the baby home to raise as his own.

Another day he found a sick snake and brought it home and fetched the animal doctor. Another time he found a mangy dog howling with hunger. He took the dog home and cared for it and this is how the boy, the snake and the dog came to live with him.

When the boy was a teenager he fell in love with his adopted mother and developed a plan to get rid of his adopted father. He went to the state's treasury and stole money and the next day informed the sultan that his father had stolen the treasury, showing the gold as proof. His father was taken into custody. When he went before the court he told the judge, "I am innocent. I have a lot of money—I do not need to steal. Everyone knows this and respects me." But the judge put him in prison.

The prison was underground. After a few days the dog and the snake started missing their master and the snake said, "I will look for our master at night," and the dog said, "I will search for him by day." One day the dog went into an underground drain to find water. As he was walking he smelt his master and followed the smell. They greeted each other happily, the dog promising to help. He went home and told the snake, "I have found our master in the prison." The snake said, "It is my turn now."

The sultan's wife had just given birth to a son so during the night the snake went and coiled around the sleeping baby's neck, resting his head on the baby's chin. The baby had been crying all day so he was very tired and slept quietly. In the morning when his mother found the snake coiled around her child's neck, she screamed and all the soldiers and courtiers came running. When everyone was assembled and saw the snake a courtier informed the sultan that it was a sign that the sultan had committed a sin. The sultan replied, "But I have never mistreated anybody in my life." Another courtier said, "There must be someone to whom you have been unjust." The sultan thought for a long time and finally murmured, "There is a man I put in prison but he stole from the treasury." They brought the man to the room and before everyone the snake uncoiled and went to his master. People asked, "Why has this happened?" and the master of the snake replied, "I am an honest man. I think it was my adopted son who betrayed me." The sultan executed the boy and asked the wronged man, "Please come and be my *wazir.* " So that is how the wise old man's son became the sultans's adviser.

In all other respects, I prefer not to remember the past, but people must know what happened. Khabor was one and a half hour's walk from Zakho, close to the Iraqi-Turkey-Syrian border. Far away, but so big they felt close, we could see the mountains of Ararat, where Noah's Ark is said to have come to rest.

There were 30 houses, mostly two rooms, made from mud, with flat roofs of wood rafters and compacted earth. The earth was pressed with a stone roller, and in the rain it became like hard clay. Our family had a water tank, but when this was low, my mother or father would go to the river one kilometre from the village. Water was carried back in tins or goat's-skin bags on the back of a mule or donkey, and stored in clay jars.

In spring the river would flow very fast, and sometimes flooded with melted snow, but in summer all the children would go and swim. Until we were seven, girls and boys would swim and play together. We played in the hills around the village, making swings to hang from the trees, and a seesaw, or we played leapfrog, marbles, hopscotch and soccer, in between minding the animals for our family and collecting firewood. In winter we made snowballs and had snow fights, or we made sledges to slide down the hills.

Some families had 500 animals—mainly sheep and goats, and also herds of cows, mules and horses. The shepherds would take all the animals to the mountain pastures and, before dusk, bring the animals back to each family's house. In the summer hired motors would bring water from the river to irrigate the crops. One or two families with large farms owned the machines or hired the lorries. They would take a lorry of food to sell in Zakho markets and all the farmers would share in the profit.

I was only four when the revolution started but I remember it clearly. Men in the villages went to the mountains to become *peshmerga*. Soon aeroplanes came and bombarded the villages, and we would run and hide in caves. When the bombing got too heavy, my family walked for more than eight hours to a remote village. For me it was a big adventure. We hid under the trees so that the aeroplanes did not see us.

That year is like a dream, but I remember minding the sheep and goats in the mountains. My father and big sister would go back to Khabor, hide in a cave until nightfall, then tend the crops, cut the barley and wheat, and bring the food back to store. But the government burnt some crops. They did not want Kurds to eat. My father did not like killing, but he would always carry a rifle for self-defence—mainly against humans.

When we returned to Khabor, the houses were still standing. We just had to clean up the mess. (Before I was born, in 1970, my parents had had to completely rebuild.) My father and all my relatives continued to feed and help the *peshmerga*. Some were relatives. Everyone loved and respected them, because they were sacrificing their lives for our freedom.

When I was seven I started school in a nearby village, walking from seven o'clock to get to school by eight. School was in Arabic and finished at 12. In the afternoons I played or did homework, or helped my parents with the animals. Twice that I can remember, the soldiers surrounded the village and came into our home carrying machine guns. They warned, "We will kill you if *peshmergas* come and you do not tell us."

My mother could not read or write and my older sisters did not go to school, but my father had learnt some reading and writing in the army. He decided to sell the animals and move to Zakho so that my brother and I could be educated. In Zakho Kurds are allowed to buy houses, not like in Kirkuk, so my father bought one that had electricity and water.

I kept busy studying and playing soccer. I saw how hard my father worked, and how he had left the village for our education. He wanted us to stay away from politics, and we did, except every student had to join the Ba'ath Student Union, but you did not have to be active.

In the 1980s Saddam employed many Kurds as mercenaries to stop them becoming *peshmergas*. We called these people *chatar* in the Dohuk-Zakho area. They were either deserters from the war or people who were about to be conscripted. Instead of going into the normal army they approached their *agha* and asked him to put their name down as a *chatar*. They would get papers, and continue living a normal life, in return for being asked to do various duties—sometimes as agents or spies, or in a joint effort with Saddam's army.

Officially the *chatar* were paid very well, but sometimes the *agha* would not pay them and would keep Saddam's money for himself. But with so many *chatar*, army and secret police, many people were being arrested, tortured and killed for their political activities. This happened to some of my friends in 1985. They had been secretly circulating pamphlets and putting up posters for KDP. They were 17 and 18 years old. Eighteen young people from Zakho were executed, and afterwards the government completely destroyed their families' homes. Many just disappeared, or the body would be delivered back to the family.

The Al-Anfal operations of 1988 were the worst. My family in Zakho was not affected, but the *chatar* and the army went to Khabor and told our relatives, "If you don't leave, we will kill you." They referred to people as animals and destroyed Khabor. Our relatives were forced to move into town. A few went to the new government-built residential complexes near the towns and army bases, away from the mountains.

In 1988 I went to Mosul University and studied Arabic, English and French in the Department of Translation. I aimed to be a translator, but I could not finish my degree because on 2 August 1990, Saddam invaded Kuwait. There was no warning. Friends who heard about it on Iraqi Radio came to the university and told me. My reaction was like everyone else's: "It's crazy." On the radio there was all this shouting, chanting of slogans, and Saddam Hussein making long speeches. He claimed the Kuwaiti leaders were traitors to their people and that Iraq was liberating Kuwait. Later he claimed that Kuwait was part of Basra province before British imperialists partitioned it off because of its oil. After World War One, the British and French had divided the Arab fiefdoms into 20 countries, so Saddam claimed the war was about defying the imperialists and their Arab slaves.

If a government person came and asked, "Do you support our invasion of Kuwait?" I would have answered, "Yes," but what happened in Kuwait was unbelievable, particularly when you know that many Iraqi Arabs from the south are married to Kuwaitis and have relatives there. But I also think the Americans encouraged the war. They want Muslim to fight Muslim.

In January 1991 the US-Allied forces started bombing Iraq. All universities closed down and I went home. There were food shortages and blackouts. We used kerosene lamps and listened to a battery radio—Arabic programs on the BBC and Voice of America saying one thing, Iraq saying something else. I would watch the fighter planes flying low over the town day and night, and could hear the bombs being dropped in the distance. Neighbours and relatives were being killed on the front line. Everybody was hoping the Allies would kill Saddam; but the Allies did not hurt Saddam, they only killed people. Always the dictatorial leaders do not get hurt; it is the poor people who suffer. That is why I do not like politics.

The BBC reported that the Iraqi forces were retreating from Kuwait and being destroyed and that the Shi'ites in the south were rebelling. Then we heard that the Kurds in the north were attacking government offices and bases. I went to the city centre and saw soldiers surrendering. The *peshmerga* were telling them, "Put down your weapons. You are free to go." Some of these soldiers left for Syria or Turkey—they thought the government would kill them as traitors because they did not fight the Kurds. Others walked south. Now they were unarmed and the *peshmerga* were armed, yet I did not see one soldier being treated badly. Many were from poor families and they did not want to fight.

I did not see any violence but I heard that some *chatar* and Ba'aths were killed. Kurds were announcing on megaphones, "We have liberated our area," and the Kurdish flag was raised on buildings. We all felt happy. People were talking freely, and singing Kurdish songs over megaphones. We no longer were scared of the Ba'ath Party, the secret police and all the security checkpoints. There was a sense: Is this truly happening? It was a miracle. No one could believe that Saddam had left our country, and deep inside there was the fear that Saddam was going to come back. Everyone became a *peshmerga*. Everyone carried a weapon—a gun or a grenade. Even I carried a rifle, because although we had hope, we were also scared, and felt we had to defend ourselves at any moment. At night I did not feel safe. I did not know whether I would wake the next morning.

When we heard from the BBC and the Voice of America in Washington that Saddam was attacking the Shi'ites in the south, we knew he would come to Kurdistan and we knew how savage he could be. Then we heard that city after city was falling to the government. They fell as quickly as they had been liberated.

I was with my nephew in the mountains to the south-east of Zakho helping to bring his family's sheep down when we saw planes and helicopters dropping bombs overhead. We returned to Zakho, passing *peshmergas* going to the mountain in an attempt to stop the government helicopters, tanks and soldiers following the people. Families were already leaving. There was no plan.

My father and brother-in-law had waited for us. It was about 11 or 12 at night, 29 or 30 March, when we left the house. I took nothing. We walked along the road with thousands of other people: people crying, people carrying food, blankets and children on their back, people shouting the names of people they had lost, old people sitting beside the road. It was like the end of the world. We were heading for Turkey, knowing Turkey killed Kurdish too.

Everything is a blur. I do not want to remember. It took two days and two nights to cross the mountains through snow and mud. The ground and sky were white, the pines, sycamore and junipers, the bare oak and oleander branches weighed down with snow. I had never been through these mountains—it was a forbidden area.

It was so freezing I could not move my fingers. Sometimes we rested around a fire, but not for long—we were too scared that Saddam's army was going to chase us. On the second day people starting dying and graves were dug beside the road. More on the third day. Some organisations started dropping food from aeroplanes, but it was all a nightmare. All we could do was follow the people: angry, hungry, tired and desperate. We reached the border on the morning of the third day. It was marked by stones and in other places a wooden fence. Turkish soldiers refused to let us cross, so we gathered around fires, waiting in the rain and mud. At the end of the day we were given permission to cross.

My nephew, brother-in-law and I had lost the rest of the family, so we went to one camp for a few days. For the next five days Kurdish people in Turkey, and maybe some good Turkish people, sent trucks of canned food, rice, chickpeas and oil. One time I saw a truck coming and, as the hungry crowd swarmed the truck, soldiers began shooting in the air, then at the people. One man was shot under the chin. Another soldier threw an old woman into the mud. They were whipping us and hitting at us with batons, the butts of their guns and their hands. People were saying, "We run from one dictator to another. What's the difference?"

Big carrier aeroplanes began dropping boxes of food by parachute. I saw one woman crushed to death. If you were not fast and strong, you missed out. For 10 days we relied on these food drops, not one Turkish soldier smiling or treating us as human, but after the UN and American soldiers came, people felt safer and it was more organised. They used helicopters to ship in the food, and they grouped people so that a leader would go and collect for the group.

We moved to another camp on the Iraqi side, trying to find our family. Over the next five days, this camp grew from 10,000 to 100,000. The Americans brought megaphones, and people would call through the megaphones the names of their lost relatives. People sat silently all day, some listening to the radio, some crying.

The land was undulating, with many trees, but by the time we left, all the trees had been cut for firewood. We would gather leaves to sleep on, under blankets we had sewn together for a tent, too tired to care about the mud, cold, rain and the stench from dysentery.

We still could not find our family, so after some days we changed camp. There were 200,000 people, but at last we found them. There were doctors—Turkish Red Crescent and, afterwards, UN doctors, and they brought bottled water and treated the outbreaks of cholera, typhoid and jaundice. The UN starting asking people whether they wanted to go back to Iraq. 850,000 Kurds from Iraq went to the Turkish border and most returned.

My family and I followed the long line of people back, but I was confused. I wanted to discuss things with my father. It was now May; springtime, with flowers and trees budding. At the bottom of the mountain there were cars, trucks and even a few American Chenook twin-blade helicopters to take people back to the cities.

After a few days in Zakho, I told my father, "I want to leave Iraq. I can't go back to university. There is no future for me here. What if Saddam's army comes back? I know English, so maybe I can get a good job and help the family." My brother wanted to come too, but I told him, "One of us has to look after our parents." When I said goodbye, my mother cried and my father was sad and silent.

As I passed people returning to Iraq we would say "*Marhaba,*" (Hello in Kurdish), but more frequently, "*Assala mo alay kom*" (Go in peace), and in reply "*Wa ala kom assala'am*", (Peace be upon you). To me these are the most beautiful words of humanity. There is nothing more precious than peace.

I was allowed over the border, and walked for one and half hours to a camp at the bottom of the mountain, where I stayed for five days. Then the UN brought trucks and took us to Silopi. Silopi was ideal for refugees because we could not get out. Some people managed to escape to the town for a few days, but Turkish commandoes would do night patrols and guard the perimeter, inside and out, and there were always guards at the gate. If people were caught escaping, they were sent back to the Iraqi border. One big problem was that we did not understand the language. Some guards were kind. Others, you could tell by their eyes, really hated Kurds.

I worked as a translator for the UN personnel when they were interviewing people. We worked five to six days a week, sometimes until 10 pm. The work was terrible. Many stories were far worse than my own, so it was very upsetting and stressful, but better than sitting around doing nothing. The food was inadequate and got worse. Time passed slowly and life was monotonous. People were depressed. Basically, we were waiting for life to begin again.

A lot of my friends went to Europe and Canada. I did not choose Australia, but my chance was Australia, and after nearly two years at Silopi, I did not want to stay a day longer. But when the time came to leave I was upset, thinking I would miss my friends. I knew I was going far from my family and country. There was a lot of trepidation. We had no idea what Australia would be like.

It was March, the beginning of spring 1993, when we travelled by bus to Ankara. In Melbourne they took us to the immigration flats in Springvale. I shared a flat with a few single men. The Australians were kind—our fridge was filled with food and we were given food vouchers, but we still felt awkward and strange.

After a few months we started English school. I had to busy myself somehow. I applied to go to university, and was disheartened when they told me they could not recognise my previous studies. I studied for one year, but left when I found a job as a tram conductor. I worked on the trams for three years, sending money back to my family whenever I could, until the tramways started sacking people.

I have a few Australian friends, but generally I stick with my community. We have the same understanding, and in 1995 I returned to Kurdistan to marry. My mother had sent a photo of a girl and we exchanged letters. I stayed with my family in Zakho for 16 days, and found life so hard it made me want to return to Australia. My future wife and I met and talked, and then we signed a contract with the *imam* and another in the court. A week later we had a big celebration—maybe 1000 people came to my family's house for a night of music and dancing. Then my wife arrived.

Our culture is very different to Australia's. Commitment is more important than love—a commitment to agreed values and responsibilities. Back in Australia, the woman might feel lonely and homesick, but gradually she learns English. What all Kurds miss is the strength of community back in Kurdistan—everybody knowing, visiting and helping each other. Here, you stay for two years in one place and do not even visit your neighbour. My neighbours are Chinese, Vietnamese, Indian, Italian, Greek, Arab and Turkish—they might say hello but they might not.

Yet Australia is a good country. There is no war. You can relax. It is more democratic than most places, but no country can fulfil all one's dreams. All over the world, politicians say one thing and do another, so I still stay away from politics. Politics causes tragedy. Yet as a Kurd I know every act and event has political meaning. The media is political. Getting a job is political. What we eat is political. But I never belonged to a Kurdish party and in Australia I try to avoid political discussion. I sympathise with all parties that work to liberate Kurdistan, but politics must serve the community, not destroy it.

Meanwhile I pray and practise the five pillars. Muhammad taught us first to worship God. All things depend on God, and only God knows what will happen.

Falling

By Abbas Boskany

Like the last bead
In a broken rosary
Falling down.

Like the last breath
In the light game of love,
It gets out and
Mingles with all things.

"In that square room
He was squatting and was
Bent on playing a game of draughts with himself.
Every time,
No-one emerged as winner
Other than himself."

Hatred
Had become the logos, the beginning of all beginnings.
With a pair of menacing eyes,
Hatred took over and embraced
All that night's tableaux.

Anger
Was not only the solitary tide.
Anger became the facial features.
Revenge
Became the attention.
Waiting for the arrival of the new ships,
All the guards and dogs became busy.

The love of a bygone history
Like the final raindrop which,
After God's final promise,
Falls on dry land and
Disappears.

He was alone.
He was lost,
And imprisoned
Like the last valiant effort of a bent flame.
He dreams to stand,
Like the flame flaring against the north wind.

He bends his neck,
Unaware that
He too is the last bead
In a broken rosary,
Falling.

Air Waves

A life story based on interviews with Rebwar Bibani

When I was about three or four, my father told his mother, "I am a slave to my wife." He said this because he was holding me. My mother was carrying my sister. From that night I lived with my grandma. She raised me like her son.

My grandma was tall, skinny and bronze-skinned, with black hair and light-blue eyes. She looked and behaved like a man. She would speak to men without hesitation and was more powerful than my grandfather. She controlled the house and made all the decisions, and the whole village respected her because she was so generous and wise. She was a peacemaker, always helping people. For visitors, she would have the best chicken killed—my grandfather would protest, but she always won the argument. To me, she was very kind. I cannot remember her hitting me. The most angry she ever got was when I was eight years old. I had a catapult for birds and when I could not find any leather to make a new sling I cut the strap from my aunty's special shoes. A month later, when my aunty was dressing for a wedding she could not find her shoes. My grandma asked me, "Can I see your catapult?" I handed it to her and she broke the catapult and threw it at me, but I was already running. I went back to my father's home for three days.

In 1961, when I was six, the Barzani leaders were forced into fighting with the government and launched the Kurdish revolution. One morning I woke to hear tanks, trucks, cars and soldiers driving through the village. They went to the furthest village, and we watched as one by one, each village, about eight in all, went up in smoke. All these villages were on a plain about 20 kilometres from Kirkuk, far from the mountains, so it was accessible for ground forces and there was no place to hide, not even among the fig, maple and poplar trees.

We knew they would come to Kaloor, so my grandma and I helped my father climb down the well in the field. We did not have springs, so wells were dug 20 metres deep to reach water. They would also dig a small hole in the side of the wall above the water line, so a person could use a rope to go and hide without being seen from the top.

Our mud house consisted of a visitor's room, where my grandfather always sat and slept, and a big family room, where my grandma, two uncles, one aunt and I slept on cotton mattresses. Inside a big courtyard, about 1500 metres square, there were other rooms. One was for storing seeds and grasses, another housed chickens, a third held six or seven cows, a big room sheltered 120 sheep in winter, and a small one near the *tanoor* oven was for the dried dung fuel.

By mid-morning we heard the sound of five tanks, and many trucks and cars. Five hundred soldiers surrounded the village and began checking homes one by one, taking all the men over 16. I was in the courtyard when the soldiers came into our house, before hearing an announcement over a loudspeaker that everyone had to go and sit on some land about 500 metres away.

Four hundred people sat for eight hours, watching the soldiers take away the animals, pour petrol inside each house and burn the village, building by building. My mother had six-month-old twins, and also my younger brother and sister. One soldier helped her get out of the house by taking one of the babies strapped in his wooden cradle. Other soldiers helped people through the fire and smoke. We saw two soldiers burning as they left one house. They died from their burns. One soldier lost his way in the smoke, and a man of the village would boast afterwards that he had pushed the soldier back into the flames.

I did not understand why all this was happening and I was very upset, always keeping one eye on the well.

It was summer and very hot, and the fires made it hotter, but we were not allowed to move. Yet the soldiers could not stop one old lady bringing water to the people in a big lamb's skin. She was known to talk too much and was always making trouble, but after that day people would say, "You will go to heaven."

In the field, all the men over 16 were collected on one side and the women, children and old men on the other. The soldiers began blindfolding the men, tying their wrists behind their backs. We thought they were going to be shot. But just before dark the soldiers made the 60 or 70 men walk to the military trucks in their baggy Kurdish clothes, with their Muslim caps underneath black and white turbans. They were being taken away so they would not become *peshmerga*.

After all the soldiers left, the old men, women and children tried to save what remained of the houses. We helped my father out of the well and carted water to put out the fires. People cleaned up any rooms still standing, and those who had lost everything stayed with neighbours until they could rebuild. Part of my grandma's house was not burnt, so all the family lived in one room.

About 90 families lived in Kaloor. It was hard for the women to do all the farm work, knowing that the soldiers could return at any time. My father had to rebuild all the houses, and plough the fields with a metal-and-wood plough pulled by two donkeys. He sowed black wheat for livestock and white wheat for bread, then six months later took the wheat by donkey to a grinding machine in a faraway village. The journey took two days.

During this time, one of the twins died from sickness. We had very little food. The government was trying to weaken the revolution by allowing people to take only one kilo of sugar and one kilo of tea past the main checkpoint outside Kirkuk so there would be no spare food for *peshmergas*. We relied on bread, and the cheese and yoghurt from sheep that had been grazing outside the village when the army came, and also what my grandma had stored in the hay under the earth floor when the revolution began.

In Kaloor there was a primary school, with six classes for up to 80 children, who came from four villages, some students old enough to grow moustaches. For the first few years we sat on the mud floor, the blackboard in front of us. If we misbehaved, the teacher might cane our hands 10 or 20 times or the class monitor would hold us upside down so the soles of our feet could be beaten. But when the army burned the village, the teachers from Kirkuk were too afraid to come back, and the school closed.

After nine months the government made a peace agreement with Barzani and released all the men from prison. Athough they were skinny and beaten, on their return the whole village celebrated. Two shepherds, dressed in the heavy, sleeveless, five-centimetre-thick, compressed lambswool coat we call a *farenji*, each played the old music on a home-made *doozala*—two straight pipes of bamboo joined together with holes in both pipes. People sang and danced the *sepayi* and *choppi* holding hands and weaving like a snake behind the leader. Those who could afford to killed a sheep, and the whole village ate together, everyone sitting and talking and laughing.

The ceasefire lasted eight or nine months and life in the village returned to normal. Us boys went back to our games like *khow* or 'get hat', which involved two teams of up to seven. Each member of one team wore the Muslim cap, placing their left hand on the ground. With his right leg a boy had to kick any members of the other team who tried to get his hat. If he kicked first the opposition had to wear the hat, but if the other boy managed to grab the hat, he shouts *khow* and runs with the hat to a wall. Or else he gives it to a fast runner, because the runner has to get to the wall without being caught.

In 1963 the government came and again burnt down Kaloor. Most families escaped to villages under *peshmerga* control. About 10 young men joined the *peshmerga*. Of these, Khosheed and Ramazan were killed. By law we could not go to Kirkuk without permission, so my family went secretly and rented a room, but because we did not have an official address and I did not have a certificate from school, I could not continue my education. To support us my father found work in a factory cleaning the sand and small rocks for concrete and using a hand shovel to load the trucks. In so many ways life in the city was not so free. In the village, if there was a problem it would be solved by the *agha*. After Karim Qassem overthrew the monarchy in 1958, the *agha*s did not have so much power but the men continued to go to the mosque to pray and have meetings, and the *shaykh* would give advice according to Islam. Every family contributed *zakat*, or ten per cent of their income, to the *shaykh* and the poor, but after the Ba'aths came to power in the 1960s, the government paid the *shaykh*. When the *peshmerga* became strong, they set up village councils, so there were all these alternatives, whereas in the city, people had to solve disputes between themselves or go to court.

In the village, men and women worked together on the farms, although men controlled everything and it was normal to hit a woman, but in the city women were not allowed to go out without their husbands, not even for shopping. This did not affect my mother so much, because she was busy with four children and was to have another five.

Living back with my parents was a big change. My father did not have an education and is very old-fashioned. He would never argue with his mother because her decision was final, but towards the other women in his life—my mother and sisters—he was very strict. He believes they should cover their hair and body and should always follow and serve the man. He did not let my first two sisters go to school, but after school became compulsory in 1973, he let my two younger sisters complete high school and one finished university.

In my parents' generation, a husband and wife's relationship was not close. They had no privacy. Also, my mother was not a strong personality like my grandma. She was often crying but around my father she was quiet. If she was unhappy she would not say so, but she was clever. By controlling all the small household events, she could work step by step for bigger outcomes. For instance if she did not like a family, there are 100 tricks for making them feel unwelcome: the way she greeted them, what food she served, and so on. If she was unhappy, she would drag her lips down, and after days of silence my father would become nervous.

It was my mother who chose the husbands for my three sisters and a wife for one brother. She wanted one of my sisters to marry her brother's son, even though everyone else, including my sister, did not agree. I was away when she managed to convince everyone except my father. Then she told him, "I will leave you and go back to my family." That threat was her last resort. My sister told me that she had finally agreed to avoid problems between the families. In our culture 90 per cent of marriages are between cousins. It keeps the families close. We have a saying: if two people from different families marry, 100 people fight!

After a year, Barzani and the government made another peace agreement, and I chose to return to Kaloor with my grandparents so I could go back to school. In our absence Arabs had partly rebuilt and occupied the village, but by the time we went back, the government had moved them out, so Kaloor was empty.

I was in Year Four. School was in Arabic, so it was hard, and many students struggled because of the language difficulties. Only old people, women and children were living in the village, and my grandparents had to rebuild. They hired a tractor at an hourly rate from Daraman, a big village nearby, and sowed the fields. One of my uncles would take the sheep to pasture, and sometimes two or three families would join together and pay a shepherd to look after up to 500 sheep. After school I would take the lambs out.

One day my cousin and I heard shooting while we were playing on some fallow land. We saw Arab civilians with guns, so we followed all the people running to the mosque. Inside everyone was silent, waiting. We heard voices, then a sound of smashing glass. A gun was poked through the window and fired. The women and children cried, and my cousin and I hid under a blanket. The Arabs came inside and took away the blankets, watches and money from people. They even took the old men's coats. The government had told them that Kurdish people were rebels and outlaws, so according to Islam, they were allowed to kill Kurds and take their property.

An Arab came over to my cousin and I and tried to tell us something, but we did not understand his Arabic. He waved us to go outside. We ran, not knowing where to go, and heard many people talking and crying inside a room. Inside an Arab man held a gun to the neck of the only other man in the room, saying, "You knew we were coming so you killed the sheep." Women were crying and pleading, "Please don't kill him. He killed the sheep to eat. You can take the meat." Later they released the people in the mosque, because all the young men had hidden in the field or escaped to the mountains.

At this time there was only one Kurdish party, but in 1964 some progressive leaders like Jalal Talabani, his father-in-law Ibrahim Ahmed, both lawyers, and Noshirwan, broke with Mostefa Barzani because they disagreed with his strategies, claiming the KDP leadership was undemocratic. They escaped to Iran, and after some months of fighting, came back to negotiate, but Barzani killed some of them, so Talabani refused to rejoin him. Barzani gave Talabani permission to stay in Sulaimani as long as he was inactive.

In 1966 Talabani negotiated with the Iraqi government and was given guns, money and control of Bakrajo, a town near Sulaimani. The government allowed Talabani to open offices in most Kurdish cities and to publish magazines, so to this day Talabani is called *jahsh* 66.

In June–July 1968, a coup brought Ahmed Hasan Al-Bakr and Saddam Hussein to power. They entered new negotiations with Mostefa Barzani, based on the 1966 proposals put forward by Prime Minister Abd Al-Rahman Al-Bazzaz. Before he was forced to resign Al-Bazzaz had tried to stop the war by giving Kurds national rights, making Kurdish an official language and holding free elections for local administrative councils.

The Ba'aths were stalling for time. The economy was weak and Iraq was politically unstable, so they made peace with the Kurds while they set about killing all other opposition. But by 1969 the government was back attacking Kurdish towns and villages. By this time Talabani had enough support and strength to stand up to Barzani and fight for control of the Kurdish revolution. Talabani's *peshmergas* succeeded in pushing Barzani back from his established territories, but then something unexpected happened. Saddam Hussein and Barzani negotiated an Autonomy Agreement. After this was announced on 11 March 1970, Barzani wrote a letter to Talabani and the other leaders, asking them to come back to his party. They met with Barzani and consequently advised all their followers to join the revolution. All the Kurdish people were happy about this. They did not understand the causes of disagreement, and when Talabani and Noshirwan escaped to Egypt and Europe because they were frightened that Barzani would kill them, nobody said good things about Talabani. He had been supported by Saddam and fought against Barzani, and he had lost.

During the 1970–1973 peace, Talabani worked for Palestinian groups and contributed to magazines, basing himself in Egypt. When war began again in 1974, Mostefa Barzani led all the Kurdish *peshmergas* against Iraq.

Back in 1968, after the negotiations with the new government, we were officially allowed to live in Kirkuk. Every suburb had a person responsible for registering the names of all the people, so my father registered our family and I was able to start secondary school. We lived in one room, with a kitchen on the balcony and a bathroom shared with two other families, about 20 people in all.

I was a good student, even though school kept changing from Arabic to Kurdish for one year during the peace process, then back to Arabic, then to Kurdish, then to Arabic. I had to sit only half my exams, because in Iraq, if you get 90 per cent for a subject, you do not have to sit the final exam. Some teachers were Arabic; some were Kurdish. One Kurdish teacher taught us Kurdish national songs and always took time to explain our rights. One day tanks and soldiers came to the school. Soldiers entered our class and took this teacher away. He came back eight months later, after the peace negotiations of

1970. We asked him, "What happened?" He said, "They removed my fingernails, and took me south so I could not go back to the revolution." He looked a bit older, his fingers were still red and he was quieter.

In school holidays I went back to my grandma in the village. In the 1991 exodus, she had to walk for three days through the mountains in the snow. There were many children, and she insisted that the little food be given to them. She never thought of herself. When they arrived in Iran, conditions were so bad that after 20 days she died from cold and hunger.

In 1975 I started studying electrical engineering at Sulaimani University. University was free, and students received an allowance, which we would have to pay back. There was pressure to join the Ba'ath Student Union. But by law, it was not compulsory, so I refused. I was told, "You must be working for another party, so we will follow you." My answer was I did not want to be involved in politics. I lived in a student house, four students to a room, and always they planted a Ba'ath supporter to watch and listen.

It was compulsory to study the history of the Ba'aths for one hour a week. We were never taught the truth—that Saddam Hussein rose up in the Ba'ath Party because he was a ruthless assassin. We were taught that he was a natural leader. When Al-Bakr stood down as president in 1979, he announced, "I choose Saddam Hussein because he is the best, most skilful horseman." In Arab culture, a good horseman is given the highest honour.

It was at university that I became political. It was a big shock for the Kurdish people when the revolution collapsed in 1975. At the time, Barzani controlled 90 per cent of Kurdistan. It was said he had 100,000 military, over 300 engineers and 100 doctors, but from Tehran he sent a message to the leaders saying that the revolution could not continue without support from the Shah of Iran and America. Ninety-five per cent of the people were behind his decision, but some leaders and many educated people criticised his dependence on outside support. They wanted to continue the revolution, but Barzani left for America and Talabani escaped to Europe.

The government took control of the cities and mountains, began sending Kurds away from Kirkuk, and destroyed villages near the borders. After three months, in June 1975, Talabani held a meeting in Syria with Kurdish leaders. They established a coalition of three parties: Komala (a Marxist-Leninist party), a General Alliance of independent patriots, and the Socialist Movement, made up of ex-KDP. They called the new collective the Patriotic Union of Kurdistan (PUK), and announced that their objective was to establish democracy in Iraq and autonomy for Kurdistan.

About six months later, Barzani's sons and old friends in Iran renewed KDP. By May 1976, they had established military bases in the mountainous Bahdinan region, in the border triangle with Turkey and Iran. The people in this area have always been loyal to Barzani, and some had guns from 1975.

By 1976 PUK had trained up to 200 *peshmergas*. Talabani had negotiated with Syria to supply weapons and money, and permission to travel across the border, and PUK felt strong enough to become active inside Kurdistan. Talabani sent a letter to Mostefa Barzani in America, asking for safe passage of PUK *peshmergas* and their equipment, emphasising that their fight was with Saddam, not Barzani, and that they needed to negotiate about sharing bases on Bahdinan lands. I have never been told whether Barzani replied to this letter, but a group of 36 armed PUK *peshmergas*, led by Ibrahim Azo from Bahdini, a former Iraqi three-star officer who had trained on Volga rockets in Russia, approached the border after a one-month walk from Syria to Turkey.

It is said that at the border, they met with KDP leaders, with whom they negotiated to form bases inside KDP territory and to proceed with a joint effort, but after entering Bahdinan territory they were followed. They slept in a cave called Bav'e, but by morning only one survived. KDP supporters apparently killed the others. The KDP denied that those responsible were KDP *peshmergas*, but PUK believe that Mostefa Barzani had told the people that these *peshmergas* were from Saddam and were coming to kill them.

This was the first confrontation between the two parties, and Talabani again wrote to Barzani, asking for an investigation, explaining that his *peshmergas* had to go through this area to establish bases around Hawler and Sulaimani. KDP promised they would send an investigation team, but this never happened.

Some PUK managed to get through, and in the villages, towns and universities, they told people that PUK was a progressive organisation opposed to old-fashioned tribal values. Slogans started appearing on walls: "The world is against Saddam". One day there was a protest at the university against the Iraqi government's destruction of Kurdish villages, and some students were taken to prison.

The next incident between KDP and PUK occurred in 1977, when a group of 12 to 18 PUK *peshmergas* led by Hasan Khoshnow entered Bahdinan territory with three Russian-made Doshka machine guns. Although initially given food and safe passage by the villagers, all were later killed.

About 1000 PUK *peshmergas* had established a base in Nowzang, an area between the Iran and Iraq border near Qandil, a high mountain famous for its flat top, where a spring forms a lake. Nowzang is a very isolated, mountainous region with long cold winters, and both Iran and Iraq were attacking the *peshmergas* whenever they crossed the border. As KDP still controlled most of the border areas, Talabani felt trapped. He wanted to establish his main base in the Bahdinan, where he would be close to Syria as well as to the major towns. In 1978, 700 to 800 PUK *peshmergas* travelled in two groups across the border triangle into Turkey, Iranian bombs killing some before they reached the border.

PUK believe Mostefa Barzani announced that these PUK were *jahsh* and ordered the villagers not to give them safe passage or food, instead declaring that if one was killed, the villager responsible could take his gun. The villagers would only exchange food for bullets, and sometimes if PUK entered a village, the people would shoot. After a week, the *peshmerga* had neither strength nor bullets. In the subsequent fight near Hakkari in Kurdistan of Turkey, up to 100 PUK *peshmergas* were killed by KDP *peshmergas* and local villagers. The Turkish army killed 30. Another 180 PUK returned and surrendered to Iraqi soldiers. Some died of hunger and cold. Others escaped into Turkey. Those arrested by KDP were held for two months. Barzani ordered that the leaders be killed. It was a big shock for PUK. Only seven returned to Nowzang safely.

The *peshmergas* and Kurdish people always argue about these events. Always the first question from our people was: "Why are you not united?" Mostefa Barzani had led the

Kurds for a long time and was a very strong man, so they could not understand the reason for the fighting. But after Hakkari, people had more sympathy for Talabani and his *peshmergas*. PUK received help from Kurdish *peshmergas* in Kurdistan of Iran, and started to move inside Iran to bring food, people and guns into Iraqi Kurdistan. Talabani, Noshirwan (Talabani's deputy) and other leaders gathered 300 *peshmergas* and rebuilt their bases in the Nowzang area, which became known as 'The Valley of the Parties'. Seventy parties from the Kurdistan of Iraq, Iran and Turkey lived in the valleys of three big mountains, about four hours' walking between the furthest points.

At university I was kept informed of these events by friends from Mosul University. They would give me PUK literature every month or three. After I graduated in 1979, I was meant to go into the army. I wanted to join the *peshmerga* but was worried that the government would confiscate my family's house. My mother grew suspicious of the strange people visiting me. But if I had told her the truth, she would have made such a fuss it would have been dangerous.

I tried to convince my family to put their house in another person's name. My father refused, so I went into the army for six months, and was sent to Basra for training on Russian rockets. I found the army very hard, always being moved around, always feeling tired. When they stationed me in Kirkuk I could go home each day, and after 10 months of army life, I deserted. My father knew this meant joining the *peshmerga* and warned me, "You are bringing trouble on your family." After I went to the mountains, the secret police or *amn* regularly visited our house asking for me, and my parents were forced to transfer the house into the name of a relative.

So on 26 June 1980, three months before the start of the Iraq–Iran War, I joined the *peshmerga*. The PUK organisation in Kirkuk had given me an address. I chose the code name 'Rebwar', and after one week, representatives told me to go to a bus terminal, where I was taken by special car to a small restaurant on the main road to Sulaimani. I still had my army identification papers, so I could easily pass the checkpoints. After a meal we started walking to the mountains. Two hours later, we were in the forbidden area where helicopters shot anything that moved. That first night, we slept on the ground, covering ourselves with grass. The next morning I met a famous *peshmerga* leader, Ali Bichkol, who'd been fighting since he was 14. In August 1979, when Saddam became president, he gave amnesty to all political prisoners except his personal enemies in the Ba'ath Party. Ali Bichkol had been released and now led a unit of 60 *peshmergas*. He was to be my leader for 21 days.

On the first day they gave me a Kalashnikov. Always you had to keep the loaded gun with you, making sure you had six packets of 30 bullets in your army belt. We would enter a village an hour before dark, to eat and rest and talk to people. Most villages had at least one spy who could contact the Iraqi forces by walkie-talkie, so we would have to leave in the early hours of the morning, taking a little food and sometimes blankets to sleep in the mountains.

When a new *peshmerga* arrives they send him to Talabani's base in Nowzang, so after 21 days we headed for Pira Magroon, a very high mountain. We stayed by a spring and rested and ate for three days, to prepare us for a three day walk, which involved a very hard climb. A *peshmerga*, who was like a postman, led the way, often at night to avoid the Iraqi military bases. When we finally arrived at the main base of Toojhala, on a hill in a valley, I was expecting something more imposing, but at that time the 150 *peshmergas* lived in tents, their only possessions being blankets, rice, some plates and cooking pots. They had just been bombed by Iraqi aeroplanes, which had killed three *peshmergas*. For two months I learned the programs and met the leaders, except for Talabani, who was overseas. We also prepared for winter, building permanent rooms, with rocks and mud and help from villagers. To make the rooms safer under bombardment we used the side of the hill as one wall, but it was always wet. When there was a lot of rain or the snow was melting, it became a waterfall, and you had to sleep between the channels. Otherwise each room had a small window covered in plastic, and a blanket over the door. The communal toilet was a hole in the ground, with rice-bag walls—no obstacle for the icy, howling winter winds. We used kerosene lamps, and later they brought 10-amp generators from Iran, though these would last only six months, because we couldn't get parts.

At the beginning, I lived with Ranja, a good friend. We'd been through secondary and high school, university and the army together. I was assigned to broadcast radio, which operated from a base 14 minutes' walk up the hill. My job was to take the one-hour recorded cassette and transmit it over short-wave radio every night at six. I had headphones and an American TX4 transmitter (later a Kenwood model), an NEC amplifier and a one-kilo radio unit, the three parts imported across the Syrian border. The radio was like a $500 hobby unit, and would overheat after an hour. We transmitted on wire strung in a T-shape between two poplars.

The program consisted of PUK news, information about the government, speeches from Ma'am (Uncle) Jalal or another leader, a segment encouraging people to join the *peshmerga*, as well as music. From 1981, singers (like Hama[a] Jaza) joined the *peshmerga*, and recorded cassettes.

Ma'am Jalal considered the radio very important, and every day he would listen, then send notes or come and talk to the writers. After a year, we began repeating the night program at about six in the morning, but the government started blocking our signal with noise. Somebody would advise us by means of a wireless communication device, so we would move up and down the band or change the broadcast time, sending a new timetable to the city for weekly distribution.

I worked on the radio two or three hours a day, the rest of the time spent working for our life: building rooms, cutting wood, making food. For heating in each room we built a *sopah*, making a mud wall around a 10- to 20-litre metal container, with a flap at the front for the wood, a small hole on which a pot could rest and a pipe going up through the roof.

For general cooking, we had a *kwanoo*. It had two or three parallel walls of rock and mud supporting two metal grilles. The wood was burned on the first grille, fed by the air below, while food cooked on the top grille. Mostly, we relied on stores of dry food such as rice, noodles and beans, but in the summer we grew vegetables like tomatoes, eggplant and beans.

Food preparation was important, because after a year, there were 55 people involved in the radio and publications' centre, where they prepared and roneoed leaflets and books. As well, up to 300 *peshmergas* from different parties could turn up for three or four days at a time so leaders could discuss tactics and people could dance before they went to die. The two designated cooks for that day had to cater for everyone. If *peshmergas* arrived at midnight, they would have to wake up to feed them. If you offered poorly cooked food, you had to cook again the next day—and it was a very hard job in the cold and snow and rain, relying on wood for the fire and washing dishes in freezing water. Most people lived in the valleys, where it's warmer, but we needed to be high up for the radio.

There were only two women at the base, wives of *peshmerga*, but later, two unmarried women came after their *peshmerga* fiancés had been ambushed and killed in Sulaimani. The women had been imprisoned, then released. They worked in the radio, but because of their behaviour were not accepted. Then, a year after I came to Toojhala, two girls arrived: Ashti and Shirin. Having worked secretly for Komala in Hawler, they were forced to escape when betrayed to the government. I was 27 and had never had a girlfriend.

But it was very hard to meet them! They kept to themselves, living and working in one room. Ashti's job was to record the news from the BBC, Voice of America, Baghdad Radio and Tehran, summarising the main points for the radio and newspaper writers. They had been at the base for a week and I had not even seen them so when I was looking for an axe and was told Ashti had borrowed one I made this an excuse to go to their room. I called, "*Howrey*," which means 'one who travels the same way' and Ashti half-opened the blanket over the door. I was shocked. She was 17 and very beautiful. She said, "Bring it back," and all I could say was, "Okay." No one had told her that the axes were for everyone.

The only times I saw Ashti were at our monthly meetings. From the first meeting, I realised she was a woman with strong opinions and feelings. Someone asked her, "Why do you not come and introduce yourself?" and she replied loudly, "In our culture you have to welcome newcomers and give us information." Her outspokenness impressed me, as did all her reading, and the way she wanted to be active for her country. Her friend Shirin was shy and quiet, but Ashti was like fire—an unusual girl in our culture.

Her cooking ability, however, horrified everyone! When it was her turn, the rice was so bad she was asked to cook again the next day. After the second day, she was told, "This is still bad. You'll have to do better tomorrow," but she replied, "This is the only way I cook. Even if you kick me out, I won't cook tomorrow."

When I returned from a one-month visit to my mother to find my old room flooded, I began living with Ashti's brother, Azad, and Ardalan, an artist who designed the pamphlets, book covers, posters and calenders for the publishing centre. Two of Ardalan's brothers were to be killed by the Ba'aths.[b] Over the next three months, I learned about Ashti's family. Her father, a highly respected *peshmerga*, was killed by *jahsh* in 1964. Three cousins had died fighting the government in the 1970s; one had been dragged through the streets of Hawler by rope from an army truck. Two *peshmerga* brothers had survived.

Over time, I made it clear to Azad that I liked Ashti and thought she'd make a good wife. I think Azad also told Ashti about me, and eight months after Ashti's arrival, Azad approached her about the idea of marrying me. I was told that she did not say no.

Greatly encouraged, I approached her directly. She said, "I must ask my mother first." Kak Noshirwan[c] wrote a letter recommending our marriage, and Ashti and Azad walked to Darrgala to contact their family. I followed two weeks later.

I had sent a letter asking my mum to come to the mountains: "I want to marry a girl called Ashti. I am not asking your permission. I just need your help to organise the marriage." My mother thought I was marrying Ranja's sister, also called Ashti. The family had moved to the mountains after their house had been confiscated, so when my mother arrived, she was very surprised. She had brought a ring and some gold, and although she found Ashti beautiful and lively, I could see she wanted the other Ashti. For once, she said nothing.

Instead of a *shaykh* overseeing the signing of a contract, Azad and I went to a shop and wrote out an engagement contract. This meant we were engaged, and my father, brothers and uncles visited us in Darrgala. That was 1982. Back at the radio base, we continued to live separately, and although we could now talk at work, on a walk or when visiting other people, we were always chaperoned by Shirin. Ashti's mother had warned, "Many people ask for marriage. Be careful what sort of man he is, because later the problems fall on you."

Ashti read so much that Shirin would joke, "One day she'll go crazy! Reading so many books is not good for the mind." She also enjoyed discussing politics, but her only opportunity was in meetings, where she was always one woman among many men. It was a lonely life for her. Apart from Shirin, her other friend had been a leader of the Alay Rizgari party of northern Kurdistan, a very intelligent woman in her mid-thirties, but she had been forced to leave their base after many people criticised her for having a relationship with a man from Komala of Iran.

Ashti did not agree with the way the personal lives of single female *peshmerga* were always under scrutiny. She felt that the revolution did not value women or give them useful roles, that it was all fighting and that not enough was being done to educate the people. She also worried for the safety of women in the villages. She was often torn. To make a contribution she had to be respected, and this meant she had to act in acceptable ways, which stopped her contributing as much as she wanted.

Three months after our engagement, on 8 November 1982, Ashti and I moved in together. This was our marriage. We did not have a honeymoon—our whole life was a camping holiday. Toojhala was a beautiful place, except for the bombs.

We call marriage 'the golden cage'. It was a big change. For two years I had taken care of myself, sleeping when I wanted, eating with the other single men, not caring how my room was organised. Now I had to consider two people. I would walk for an hour to the tent shop to buy biscuits and jam, and on coming back be disconcerted to find Ashti had rearranged the room. When bombs came, I felt more responsibility. And communication is very different with a woman. In a group of men, we talked politics, but with Ashti we talked about our families, and she liked me to talk about my feelings, which I was not used to doing. I am not romantic! But although it took some adjustment, marriage was good. We lived in an isolated area, and the winter nights were very cold.

The year 1982 was a busy one on all fronts. Ma'am Jalal had organised weapons and radio equipment to be brought from Syria to Iran, but the Iranian government would not release them unless PUK fought the Kurdistan Democratic Party of Iran (KDPI), which PUK refused to do. Abdul Rahman Qassemlou, the leader of KDPI, met with Talabani and asked for help. PUK, KDPI, and Komala of Iran formed a united force and Talabani sent up to 2000 *peshmergas* to fight Iran. It was a very dangerous decision to fight another government, especially because KDP had formed relations with the Khomeini regime and was helping *pasdars* (the religious police in Iran) to fight KDPI, Komala, and other Kurdish groups.

As well, in 1982 the KDP, led by Masoud Barzani since 1979, formed a National Democratic Front in Iraqi Kurdistan. KDP joined with smaller parties like the Kurdistan Socialist Party, PASOK (a small conservative nationalist group) and the United Socialists (formed when the Socialist Movement split from PUK after 1979), and later the Iraqi Communist Party. From 1982 until 1985, PUK was fighting this front, with KDP making incursions from their bases inside Iran and the Bahdinan region.

As well, soon after my marriage, Iran started bombing Nowzang, partly because of the presence of the KDPI, who had been forced to withdraw there. When we were not working on the radio, we were making *nowzaji*—a bread fried in oil—to send to the front line which was within earshot.

The situation got worse in 1983 when Iraqi forces moved towards Haji Omaran and Halabja, attacking PUK bases. PUK was trapped. PUK leaders sent a letter to KDP to negotiate a ceasefire, saying that if KDP refused, PUK would be forced to negotiate a ceasefire with Saddam Hussein. KDP refused. We were all was very sad. We knew it would be our last winter at Toojhala, and we could not call in the removalists!

Talabani ordered all the women to return to the city, so five months after our marriage, Ashti secretly went back to Hawler. While she was away, in the spring of 1983, we moved the main radio base to Sarshew,[d] a day's walk from both the Iraqi border and Iranian borders. It took two days to cross the mountains and gorges. The horses had to walk between two and five in the morning, when the snow was hard, or they would sink in the snow. It was dangerous and slippery, and in many places a long way to fall.

Sarshew, a very old village on a saddle between two high mountains, was destroyed by Saddam in 1978. We lived in canvas army tents, but made a small room from rocks for the radio, erecting a 70-metre antenna by joining two poplars with nails and rope. There were three engineers, plus those involved in publishing, and the guards: 70 people in all. We relied on people going to the city to bring food and supplies. It was a hard, busy life.

To let Ashti know I was safe, I would regularly play a particular song on the radio. After two months, I played another song to tell her it was time to come back. I sent a person to Sulaimani to bring her to Haladin. My mother and uncle came with her, and then Ashti and I walked the two days back to Sarshew down deep gorges and over high mountains, one overlooking a lush valley full of fruit trees and *gulala surah*—the bright red poppies with black centres.

Two months later, the Sarshew area became a battleground in the Iraq–Iran War. One night a bomb hit our fireplace. The next morning we left Sarshew as the bombardment continued, transporting the radio and two petrol generators on three horses. A river called Harzna, at the point we had to cross, was in flood. It was in a gorge

60 metres below, with banks of quartz sand and stones, some the size of watermelons.

An old pulley system of rope cables spanned the 100 metres across the river. On our side the cables were tied to rock, then descended to the opposite bank. Ashti was too scared to cross alone, so we were roped together, attached to the cable by a metal hook. At least she did not bray like the donkey that had gone before us!

On the other side, we walked, rode and travelled by tractor for two days before arriving at Bargalo, an important base since Barzani's time, in a deep valley between high mountains, with many caves. There were about 20 houses, a one-roomed hospital and a prison, but no room for us. For 10 days we lived under giant oak trees, before being given an army tent. At least the food was better than in Toojhala or Sarshew because Bargalo is close to Sulaimani, so families could bring cooked food and other supplies.

We built a room for the radio and made an antenna higher up the mountain, a 30 minutes' walk away, and started work, broadcasting a morning and an evening program. In winter you could sink into snow up to your chest and lose your way.

Because PUK could not fight the United Front, Iran and Iraq at the same time, Talabani's only choice was to ask the Iraqi government for a ceasefire. He sent Qassemlou to Baghdad with the message, including a demand for some Kurdish rights, then went to Baghdad in November 1983. For the next 11 months, there was a 'cold war', and we were able to produce education, history and music programs because we were no longer reporting *peshmerga* activity. Three times, we were able to visit our families and friends in Kirkuk and Hawler.

After so long in the mountains, we were amazed at the number of *jahsh* in the cities. There was an informer in every street and office. At the beginning of the 1980s, there were only 6000 *jahsh*, who worked in the Kurdish militia called the Forsa'an and the Jayeesh Al-Sha'abi—a compulsory civilian army for anyone working in a government office or educational institution. Because so many soldiers were deserting from the war with Iran, and people had no work in the collective villages, in late 1984 Iraq established Jahafal Kaffeefa, to replace the Forsa'an. Kurdish civilians, individually known as Moosta Shahr, meaning 'consultant' or 'adviser', would be asked to make a list of names to form a foj unit of 300 to 400 volunteers. He would be in charge of the unit, and for every name on the list, he would receive 90 to 100 dinars from the government. As some were in charge of up to three *foj* these Moosta Shahrs became very rich. The members might guard collective villages or army bases, or act as spies; although many did nothing but have their name on the list. In this way, by the end of the 1980s, the number of *jahsh* exceeded 250,000.

The only time I was personally in danger was one time in Kirkuk when *amn* came to my home and took me to prison. Straight away, my family went to the PUK office and they contacted Central Intelligence. After four hours I was taken to Central Intelligence, where a PUK representative was waiting for me to arrange my release.

During the ceasefire there was no bombing and no military attacks but Iraq always tries to kill leaders in these times, and in 1984 they managed to kill Ma'am Reesha, a *peshmerga* leader who became a hero in 1982, when he led 12 *peshmergas* in a stand against Iraqi forces in the village of Hamak, near Kirkuk. Four *peshmergas* were killed, and another four injured, but it was a turning point: after that, *peshmergas* would fight if a village was surrounded, rather than escape.

In August 1984, Talabani made a new agreement with Iran. The negotiations with Baghdad were breaking down, so in October all *peshmergas* were asked to return to base. By this time there were 70 buildings and 200 PUK *peshmergas* at Bargalo. Another 300 could pass through at any time on their way to and from the front line in the nearby Daban Mountains, where *peshmergas* were defending the four main PUK bases: Bargalo, Sargalo, Haladin and Yehksemar. Although they managed to keep the Iraqi forces near Pira Magroon, on the other side of Daban, we were under continual bombardment, usually by aeroplane, but also from missiles launched by Russian-made Kartoosha rockets. A truck would carry a pack of 40, and these could be launched within three minutes. If they were captured, a smaller pack of six could be carried by horse.

Every hour or so, we would hear an aeroplane or the sharp lightning-crack of a bomb exploding, or see the white and grey streaks in the sky, and would run to the main shelter—a cement room two metres by 10 metres, and two metres high, built half into the ground, with a cement roof covered in rock and mud.

There were the loud conventional bombs, which blow a one-metre deep hole into the ground, and destroy a house and your eardrum. Then there were the cluster bombs: *heshoo* in Kurdish, *encoodi* in Arabic. These have a fan on top, which twists open a container about 500 metres above the ground, releasing 250 little bombs, each about twice the size of a grenade, which fall in a 10-metre radius. If you're outside the big bombs kill you, but the *heshoo* cause many injuries. We could not stay in the shelter all the time—we had to continue our work—so all our life was in danger, and many people were killed.

Our custom is that a dead body is washed, then wrapped in a white cotton cloth. All the villagers come to take the dead to be buried in the village *gorrstan*, Kurdish for cemetery. The family stay home for three to seven days so that people can visit, and read the Fa'atiha, the first surah of the Qur'an. This time of visiting is called Sarah Khawshi in Kurdish. *Sarah* means 'head' and *khawshi* means 'save', meaning 'when the heads of people are saved' or 'end of disaster'.

Despite the danger there were a few funny moments! At the beginning of one bombardment, a *peshmerga* taking a shower had to run to the shelter wearing only a towel. Another time, Sherko Bekas, a poet, was asleep when the planes came. He woke and ran to the shelter. When he went back to bed, he found part of a bomb had hit his pillow. He came back saying, "Look what I found in my bed!"

Sherko Bekas had been a *peshmerga* since 1965, and worked in the radio station between 1984 and 1987. He went to Sweden and published seven volumes of verse and two plays, but after the no-fly zone was declared in 1991, he returned and became Minister for Art and Culture in the National Assembly. Since 1996, he has worked for PUK's regional government in Sulaimani.

We had decided not to have a baby, because of the hard life, but one of our friends in radio had just had a lovely little girl, and Ashti started saying, "Let's have a baby." I knew it was not the right time, but Ashti was not working and felt lonely. After she became pregnant, her blood pressure dropped and she had to lie down for up to five hours a day. There was too much dust in the tent and smells would make her vomit. There was not enough food and no vegetables, and she was running to the bomb shelter up to 10 times a night. I feared for the baby, and wanted her to leave Bargalo, but our family was living in Hawler, which was under government control. If Ashti was caught, they would execute her and our family too would be in danger.

In January 1987, a month before Hema was born, Ashti went to Hawler to stay with her sister and mother. I was worried, especially when I got news that the baby was born very small and weak. But it was still very happy news, because in our culture we like boys. Boys can defend and work for the family, while if a girl makes a mistake, she brings shame. This happened to the sister of my schoolfriend, who became pregnant to her cousin. The family asked the cousin to marry her, but he refused, saying she was sleeping with other men. This brought shame on all the men in her family, but her father loved his daughter very much and could not bring himself to kill her. Instead he married her to an old Arab who lived far away, telling her she must never return home. She was lucky. Another way of punishing the girl is to ostracise all the women in her family from village activities. Rarely is the boy killed because this might start a blood feud.

One month later, Ashti and the baby returned. When I first set eyes on Hema, I was shocked: he was so small and ugly and black. I said to Ashti, "The toy battery dog I bought him is better looking!" But he changed our mind and attitudes, and his problems became more important than Saddam's bombs. Ashti could not breastfeed, so we gave him powdered milk. He would sleep for half an hour before another bomb would wake him. He was always crying. After 15 days, my eyes were red from lack of sleep. When our friends escaped his crying, I told them, "You encouraged us to have a baby! Now you have to pay the price too." But after 10 months he started to put on weight and sleep better.

Back in May 1986, all the Kurdish parties had a meeting to form a United Kurdish Front, Iran having worked hard to reconcile PUK and KDP as a weapon against Saddam. By 1987 the *peshmergas* became very strong, making successful hits on many army bases. Iran was also gaining territory in the south, and after Iran joined forces with Iraqi Kurdish *peshmergas* to attack Kirkuk, Saddam responded by using all the weapons he had, including chemicals.

The first chemical attack on Bargalo was in late 1986, while Ashti was pregnant, but the chemicals were weak. Iran began supplying masks and protective clothes to *peshmergas*, but civilians were unprotected.

Very strong chemicals were used in the attack in mid-1987, when Hema was four months old. First, Iraqi aeroplanes dropped normal bombs. Then they changed to chemical bombs. The thick brown smoke was tasteless, but it smelt like fruit or garlic, and collected in the valleys. We wrapped Hema in a wet towel and ran up the mountain, hiding between 10-metre-high rock walls. Hema was so still, we feared for his life. When we looked down on Bargalo, it was like a tornado of brown dust, with 10 or 20 chemical bombs hitting the ground at any one time.

After four hours, the smoke cleared and we went down. It was just before nightfall. Four injured *peshmergas* were affected by chemicals. Their breathing was heavy, their saliva yellow, and their skin developed bubbles. They died in a matter of days. There was chemical dust on every surface. The whole area was poisoned. People made fires near their houses to get rid of the chemicals, but all the food had to be thrown out. We did not eat for two days. People who ate the poisoned food developed stomach ulcers, and some died months later. My throat and mouth were sore for two months, and in those months I made Ashti take Hema back to Hawler.

Around the same time, Iraqi forces chemically bombed the village of Balisan and seven other villages in the Khoshnow Valley, and around the mountain of Qaradagh. Other targets were villages like Shaykh Hosanan village, in a valley near Pira Magroon. Many people died. They had no protective clothes and it seemed the government was making the chemicals stronger and stronger. In the chemical attack on Halabja on the night of 16 March 1988, they used a concoction that killed people within minutes.

The villagers were scared because they could not trust the food they grew or the water. Fortunately, our water came from springs inside the mountain. But in the villages the spring water was collected in various open concrete sinks, one for the women to do their dishes and clothes, another in the mosque for the men to wash before praying, as well as in the public baths. (In Islam you must wash or submerge yourself three times after sex, so men gather in the men's pool and woman in the women's pool. You always knew who had been having sex the night before!) These sinks of water remained poisoned for a long time. Also, the water would flow through open channels or pipes to the public toilets and then out in other open channels to the agricultural lands, so the chemicals affected the whole system.

Because of increasing threat from Saddam's forces, in October 1987 I was sent to Dohlakoga, close to the mountain of Qandil, to set up a spare radio base in case Bargalo was destroyed. Ashti and Hema came with me. Nobody lived in this rugged, isolated area, and we would be completely cut off from the outside world for the four months of winter.

During the first five months, we did not transmit. There were about 50 guards, but I was the only engineer. We lived in tents while we built rooms, bomb shelters, and a public toilet—a three-metre hole in the ground, under a one-metre metal channel so that water could flush the wastes down the hole—as well as a communal shower with cement-block walls. Underneath the shower room, we made a one-metre pit for a wood fire. Over this, we placed a metal plate and 10 centimetres of concrete. A hole from the fire pit to the outside provided circulation. The fire would heat the whole room, as well as a 40-litre container of water on the floor. But the shower was operational only once every week or two, and then we had to be quick. Too many people wanted a wash!

I was also busy cutting wood and stocking up on food for winter. We would walk for seven hours to the Iranian border to buy supplies, bringing everything back on rented horses.

Apart from Ashti, there were two women married to *peshmerga,* and a woman from the village of Sharenair, about eight hours' walk from Dohlakoga. She had come with her husband and five children to make bread, and wash clothes. The family built their own small house for winter, receiving food from the *peshmerga* and earning US$200 a month, a very high wage. A *peshmerga* received 25 dinars (US$12.50) a month, so family and friends always had to help financially. But this lady worked a 12-hour day for her money, even though she was pregnant with her sixth child. One week after the birth, she was back making bread.

At the beginning of winter, Ashti discovered she was pregnant. She was very sick and frightened, because Dohlakoga would soon be completely isolated, so in November we decided that she must go to Iran. I was not allowed to leave the radio. Friends took her to Kirmanshah, while Hema stayed with me.

I was used to preparing Hema's milk, but he was sick. Ardalan, with whom I had lived in Toojhala, helped me. He would wash Hema's clothes and play with him while I worked, and bring me food so that Hema did not have to go out in the cold. Ardalan was one of those special people you met in the mountains—people willing to sacrifice everything and share a hard life for their beliefs. It made the life easier to bear, and sometimes if a person lost a few good friends, the pain was so great that he went back to normal life.

After two months Ashti sent a radio message asking me to pick her up in Nowzang. There was too much snow, but more was coming. I would have to leave the radio without permission. Ardalan offered to mind Hema. I asked, "What if I am unable to come back?" "Don't worry. I will take care of him, and when you come back he will be walking." I was worried—if Ashti became sick she would have to be carried out on a blanket between two poles. I reached Nowzang, but we had to wait a week because of snow. When the snow eased, a group of seven, including the writer Muhammad Mukri, decided to chance the journey to Dohlakoga.

We hired a local guide called Moa'ala. He was a strange man—very strong and stupid. He had never seen a city, and like many village people, he had no understanding of time. Ashti asked him, "How old are you?" He told her, "I am nine years old." "How old is your wife?" "Three years old." "How long is the way?" "About one hour."

We were in danger. We had to walk for two hours through a valley with *jahsh* bases. The *jahsh* would ambush people. If they killed or caught someone, they took him to the Iraqi government in return for money, a house or a car. A *peshmerga* alive was worth more than a dead one. Everybody in the group had their gun ready to fight, except Ashti. She never liked guns. She questioned what good they were in all the snow. I said, "If trouble comes, at least I can kill you and then myself."

From the valley, our way was up the mountains to an area famous for its sheer black cliffs, deep ravines and avalanches. We were walking through snow up to our shoulders, so we took turns to walk in front, because breaking the new snow was very tiring. Moa'ala would tell us, "Oh, this is a dangerous way, but don't worry. It is only 10 minutes to the next cave and there we will drink tea and relax." He would sing and then go quiet and 10 minutes would turn into two hours. On a tea break, he would talk about how he had fought with bears and wolves and lions, although lions have not been seen in the area for a long time. He would talk about strange beasts that come out in the dark, his words like dreaming and lying mixed.

Moa'ala told us of his family, who lived in an isolated village of two houses called Khoolaharrmeh. He was worried about his unmarried sister, because the people in this area of 10 to 15 villages around Nowzang practise a tradition unique in the Middle East.

A girl or woman can run away with a man without permission from her family or husband! The couple go to the *shaykh's* house in the man's village, and the *shaykh* sends a message to the girl's family to come and negotiate with the man about how much money he has to give them. The price for a married woman is two or three times higher than that for a single girl! A widow is cheaper. To stop any arguments, KDPI set a price for each situation. Of course, people from other areas say, "This is a very bad tradition."

As we were crossing an icy ravine about four metres wide, Ashti slipped. It was a 500-metre fall below. Muhammad Mukri grabbed her but also began to slip. I caught Ashti by the back of her coat. Mukri saved himself. I was slipping too, but managed to stop the fall and drag Ashti back. When we reached the other side, I asked Moa'ala, "Why did you bring us this way?" He replied, "So we don't waste time. There is an easier way." I became very angry, and told him, "If Ashti had died, I could marry your sister, because I have a child to care for."

I was very frightened for Ashti. Her blood pressure was so low she was unable to walk for more than a few minutes. Muhammad Mukri and I had to drag and push her. Then it started to sleet. If it developed into snow, we would lose all visibility, and if night came, we would have to stay in one place and would die of exposure, but finally we reached a valley, where the snow was less and it was easier to move.

People at the radio base were expecting us, and as we walked in just on dusk, we were greeted by five *peshmergas* waiting for us on the roofs. One *peshmerga* had already died that winter. We entered our room and Hema was crawling on the floor. I had been away 20 days, but Ashti had been away two months and had not seen him crawling. She approached him, but he crawled away. She started crying, saying, "He doesn't know me."

The weather became worse. After three or four days of continuous snow, the trees in the valleys would be buried under 30 metres of snow. The radio base was 30 metres from our room, and every day we had to cut a new road. We kept warm with a *sopah* and two blankets. No pillows. Sometimes we shivered until morning. That winter in Dohlakoga made me understand the meaning of Newroz, how the spring brings a new, easier life.

One person always manned the walkie-talkie to receive reports from the PUK wireless. All PUK bases have this type of communication, most units having been taken from the Iraqi army bases after a successful attack, or when PUK *peshmerga* were helping KDPI in Iran. It was in this way we first heard of Al-Anfal, the worst operation against the Kurds in the twentieth century. In the operation called Anfal Number One, the government forces surrounded the PUK bases at Bargalo, Sargalo, Haladin and Yehksemar. PUK used 90 per cent of all *peshmergas* to defend the bases, and in one month of fighting 100 *peshmergas* died and 400 were injured.

After Bargalo was bombed, our radio became active. We received the program on a walkie-talkie, recording it on a one-hour tape before broadcasting. Wireless reports came in of a joint attack by PUK, KDP, other Iraqi opposition groups and Iranian forces on Halabja and the surrounding area. A couple of days later, on 17 March, I was manning the walkie-talkie. I picked up a statement from PUK leaders saying that Ali Hasan Al-Majid had attacked Halabja with cyanide, nerve and mustard gas in the early hours of the morning. Over 5000 civilians were dead and another 7000 injured.

At first I could not believe that even Saddam would do this to civilians. On all the wireless lines people were saying, "It can't be true!" But later that day, Asalan, a leader responsible for radio and publications in Bargalo, confirmed the report. Many civilians had died in the underground shelters paid for by Saddam to protect them from Iran. Piles of bodies lay in the streets. On overseas television, people saw Iranian soldiers suffering from chemical burns in Iranian hospitals, but they had been wearing special clothes and masks.

In the next Anfal operation villages were destroyed, and the army was told, "If you catch anybody in the Kurdish areas outside the cities after 19 March, they must be killed or taken south to camps." Half a million Kurds were deported. Tens of thousands of people escaped to Iran, and for a month there was a line of people coming through Dohlakoga. The way was too snowy and mountainous, so they could carry only money and small things. PUK ordered that we give all our food to them. One evening we were making food for the people and one lady was crying. "Why are you crying?" I asked her. "Three hours ago, Iraq bombed us and my 10-year-old son was killed. All we could do was cover him in snow." When people talked of family being killed, they would say, "*Rizgariboo*" in Kurdish, or "*Najatiboo*" in Arabic, meaning, "He has got his freedom. He is no longer suffering."

PUK started withdrawing to the border area, where they were attacked by chemicals. Seventy people died. After this, in June 1988, we were ordered to move the radio base to Saghez, inside Kurdistan of Iran. Reports of Anfal Number Three came through. Saddam's forces attacked Garmian and the Darbandi Khan area near Sulaimani. Most of those who disappeared during Al-Anfal came from this area, more than 100,000 people. They were not protected by *peshmerga* bases. Because the Iraqi government controlled the area, the only way to escape was through Koi Sinjak, a one-month walk. Some who tried died from hunger and exhaustion.

Ashti and I stayed in Saghez. Most *peshmergas* had escaped into Iran, but PUK did not want to leave Kurdistan completely, and Iran gave PUK permission to leave some *peshmergas* in the Halabja area, where Iran still had bases, to start a radio base to replace Dohlakoga. As a result I was ordered to go to the high mountain of Bufrimeri. *Bufri* means 'snow'. *Meri* means '*agha*'. This area, known as Hawraman, is divided between Iraq and Iran. On the Iraqi side, there are about 23,000 Hawramans, who speak their own dialect, but when I went there with Jabar Farman, now Minister of Defence in Sulaimani, there was no-one. Halabja was a ghost town. Sixty per cent of the buildings were damaged, and I saw a mass grave containing 500 bodies. A blind cow blundered around, hitting things and falling over. Other animals lay dead on the ground.

When we arrived at the radio base, the *peshmerga* asked if we wanted to eat wild-pig meat. As a Muslim, I had never eaten pork, so I refused. The men were saying they could shoot one of these big black pigs 10 times with a Kalashnikov but the pig would continue to run for 10 minutes, even if its insides were falling out. They cooked this 50-kilo pig in a big kerosene container with water and all the oil we had, about 20 litres. They brought us the heart and liver, which we ate. We made a big hole in the spring to store the meat, and ate twice a day until it finished. When people came back to collect things, we would share the meat but did not tell them it was pork.

The area was full of landmines. One time we were near an old army base, choosing a spot for the antennae, when we saw what looked like upturned grey metal sugar bowls with wires in between. Others were buried. For half an hour we stood still, afraid to lift our feet. We knew we had to go back, so we began jumping from one big rock to another, using a piece of wood to check the ground ahead of us. It had taken 20 minutes to walk into the area but two hours to leave.

After one month I returned to Ashti in Saghez, to take her to a big hospital in Tabriz. She was having contractions in the waiting room, but a nurse told her, "Your baby will not be born tonight." We think she was an Iranian Mujahadeen, who thought we were supporters of the Shi'ite government she opposed because we had papers to enter Iran. I was not allowed in, and later Ashti told me how she went to the bathroom and washed in cold water to delay the baby. Women had to tell the nurse, "There is a lady about to give birth in the hallway!"

For a month, we stayed with a friend who ran a big house for wounded *peshmergas* and their families. In July we heard that the Iraq–Iran War was over. One to two million people had died and billions of dollars were spent on that eight-year war, all for nothing, but it was a shock to us, because it meant we might not be able to return to Iraq. Also, Saddam was now free to concentrate on slaughtering the Kurds.

We returned to Saghez. PUK were organising groups to go back inside Iraq. Casualties were high. The next Al-Anfal operation was the bombing of Koi Sinjak, followed by bombing of the KDP-controlled areas of Bahdinan. For the last Anfal operation, Saddam's forces gathered around Hawler. PUK sent in more than 1000 *peshmergas*, led by Khorserat, and for 20 days there was heavy fighting. Iraq used chemical and conventional bombs and all available forces. A rocket from a helicopter killed PUK leader Azad Howrami. The other leaders and *peshmergas* withdrew, and on the way to Iran 30 disappeared, probably killed by Iraqi forces.

In the six months of Al-Anfal at least 1300 Kurdish villages were destroyed, no villages remaining in the mountains, and 182,000 people disappeared, although Ali Hasan Al-Majid claims that only 100,000 were killed. In 1991 mass graves were found in the south. Many had been put in a big hole to be shot or simply covered with earth. One boy escaped from a grave when soldiers went to collect shovels. He met some Bedouins, who hid him and treated him like their son. After the uprising in 1991, he returned to Kurdistan to tell his story. In the grave near him, he said, was a little girl still alive, but she refused to escape with him, saying, "I stay with Mum." Her mum was already dead. Governments and international organisations knew what was happening but did nothing.

Ashti did not want me to go back to Iraqi Kurdistan and leave her alone. There was a problem with manning the different bases and I was preoccupied with what I should do: Ashti felt I was not consulting her, and not thinking of her and the children. It was true. All was confusion and heartbreak. I knew the revolution could not continue this way.

Eventually we decided to go to the PUK office and ask for papers to apply for overseas travel visas. If we were unsuccessful, Ashti wanted to stay in Iran until we saw what happened in Iraq, but either way we had very little money. To live in Saghez, Ashti had sold most of the gold we had been given and she had bought after our wedding. In our culture, family and friends give money and gold to newlyweds. Talabani and Komala had each given us 200 dinars, so Ashti had managed to buy 250 grams of gold when she went to Hawler. At the time I said, "You are just like other women who like to collect gold," but that gold saved us in Iran. Now it was almost gone.

We asked PUK to help us, but PUK had distributed about two million Iraqi dinars to people crossing the border. Noshirwan called a big meeting in Qasmarush, on the border, saying, "Because the war is over, Iraq is strong, and we can't afford to give money to all the *peshmerga*. We can help only important people. Now that Saddam has announced an amnesty for people to return to Iraq, everybody is free. You can go back, but we know some people have been killed."

We did not know what to do. It was a big decision. Finally we decided to take the risk after hearing that a friend was safely living in Hawler. We caught a bus to Mariwan, close to the border, and went to a friend's house. It is not our custom to be blunt, but he said, "How can you think you will be safe under the Iraqi regime when you have fought against Saddam for so long? You have not been inside an Iraqi prison. If they kill you, you are lucky. Or maybe you are not afraid because you are going back to join the regime? If not you are mad."

We arrived at the Iranian side of the border early on the morning of 2 February 1989. Soldiers and secret police checked us for everything, taking whatever they could find—gold, money, anything important. We'd hidden some gold in Hema and Heja's clothes and I had put 25 dollars in my pocket so that if they said, "You must have something," I could reply, "Only this." They took all our photos, our memories, and tossed them into a rubbish bin.

At about 3 pm, we were taken by bus to the Iraqi border, a half-hour drive away. Again the Iraqi soldiers and secret intelligence took what they wanted, except one soldier. He found the gold and said nothing.

By this time it was 3 am. It had been one of the hardest days of my life. They put us into military trucks, and on the way Ashti asked the driver, "What will they do to us?" He asked, "Are you civilian or *peshmerga*?" She replied, "I am going home because the war is finished," and the driver said, "God save you." He told her that they were taking political prisoners, and she came back to me, worried.

The bus took us to the Iraqi intelligence base in the Seyid Sa'adiq area. We were interviewed—first together, then separately. I told them the truth: I worked in PUK radio. I knew that many people had gone back already and had probably given information, so I thought that if I lied, they would know and might torture me. After the interviews, women and men were separated and put into military trucks. That is when I became very frightened. I thought of Anfal.

The men were taken to the military intelligence base in Kirkuk, where we were loaded into three locked buses with blankets covering the windows, soldiers with machine guns guarding the 40 men on each bus. We were not allowed to talk. After four hours, the buses stopped and we were told to get out. The soldiers pushed us into groups of three or four, covering our heads with a blanket. Thirty or 40 men were taken to a room. There was not enough space to sit. Some were *peshmergas*; others army deserters. Five of us knew each other.

The room had one small high window, which was blocked up with bricks, and a door of solid metal. We slept in two rows like cigarettes in a packet, with shouting and arguments, and sometimes physical fighting because someone had accidentally put a limb into someone else's mouth. After three days they took some of us by covered utility to the Central Intelligence Prison in Al-Katham, a suburb of Baghdad. This is a modern, multistorey, top-security prison.

They like to investigate straight away, allowing the prisoners no chance to talk to each other, so 10 minutes after I arrived, they blindfolded me, tied my hands behind my back and took me to the interrogation room. A many-starred commander opened the proceedings, armed with two off-siders and a tape recorder. The commander asked, "Have you any qualifications?" When I said, "I am an electrical engineer," he became angry, swearing and saying in Arabic, "You are an electrical engineer and you became a *peshmerga*? You are stupid. The government lets you have an education, so why did you go to the mountains?" I replied, "I have my beliefs, so I joined PUK." I was not thinking. This was a very dangerous answer. He said, "I don't believe you. I think you went to the mountains because you are a donkey." This is the worst insult in our culture. He kept repeating, "You are just a donkey." Becoming nervous, I could not control myself: "I did what I had to do." I thought he was going to hit me, but one of the officers said, "Leave him."

They wanted information, repeatedly asking, "What were you doing in PUK? How many people were with you?" I told them the truth about myself—they knew it anyway—but when they asked me about other people, I would not give them names or details. After the interrogation, I was taken to a cell off a 30-metre-long corridor. Some guards looked as though they hated us; others asked silly questions like, "Did you have relations with an Iranian woman?"

The cell was three metres square. Each of us was given two dirty blankets, and we took turns to sleep in a space 10 centimetres wide. A dim light burned 24 hours a day. There were nine to 13 prisoners in my cell, from all nationalities and regions. Everyone was a political prisoner, but not necessarily a *peshmerga*. Some were witnesses; some had been overheard swearing about Saddam (it was seven years for that one). Others were ordinary civilians who had made the mistake of returning during the amnesty. Some stayed in prison for 25 days, others for five years. The government was unpredictable. They knew many people were against them, so they gave amnesties, but even if they released a prisoner, they could later kill him in his home or in the street, by gun or explosion, with no-one knowing who was responsible.

For 90 minutes a day, they let us out into a concrete yard surrounded by four-metre walls, with barbed wire. The rest of the time, we were locked in the cell. Everyone was nervous, so small problems became big problems. If an argument or fight started over, say, someone making too much noise while others were sleeping, others would try to mediate, because if the guards heard a disturbance they would hit everyone with a length of wood called a 'donkey'. They were not allowed to carry a gun inside the cells.

There was a lot of time, and a lot of talk—sometimes about politics. When someone wanted to pray, we would stand up and give him room. I did not pray. In Year Five, I had started fasting for Ramadan and praying five times a day, but by Year 11, I stopped praying. At university, I stopped fasting. I still believe in God but I'm less serious about religion.

Food was served in the cell. We got tea and bread for breakfast. For lunch and dinner, they would bring half a bread roll each, and a main dish (tomato paste and rice, or rice and onion, or beans) for 40 people. Officially, they had to give us army food, but instead they would bring in a 20-litre pot half full of water, with a little salt, some oil and one cabbage. It smelt terrible, but we ate to live. Sometimes, a guard would not give us the food, instead throwing it in the rubbish bin.

The guards wore civilian clothes or grey military uniforms. All used false names. They were Saddam's students. If one came into the cell, we had to turn our faces to the wall. If they called our name, we had to turn around, keeping our eyes on the ground. When we were being walked somewhere, guards taunted us, sometimes kicking a prisoner's legs to make him fall, or getting another prisoner to kick him. One guard had a habit of hitting a prisoner's ear with a cupped hand to break the eardrum, so that his ear would bleed and become infected.

The worst time was going to the toilet. Eight people were forced into one toilet, the guards would count to 10 and you had to be finished. Sometimes the ground was covered in urine and faeces. As we came out the guard would hit us with a stick. On entering our cell another guard would hit us with his stick. I tried to eat very little, just one piece of bread a day, to avoid going to the toilet, but you have to go.

Every few weeks a guard would shave us. You had to move your face against the blade in his hand. My face would bleed from a hundred cuts, and he would spit into my eyes, saying, "Your beard is like wood!"

At the beginning it was hard, but most people adapted. One or two went crazy, crying or shouting, swearing at the guards, not caring about the consequences. It depends on the personality but I think people are stronger if they have lived a hard life. I handled it.

Surprisingly, after two months they sent some of us back to Kirkuk intelligence base. One man had sold his house to take his family to Iran, but had come back during the amnesty. They had taken all his money, and he was crying, "How do I feed my wife and seven children? I blame God. Why were we born Kurdish?" We were taken to a Jayeesh Al-Sha'abi base in Sulaimani, where a man handed each of us a letter for the army, saying, "*Allah kareem*," "God will help you." It was as if the time in prison was to break us so that later, the military or civilian intelligence services could make people work for them.

I was allowed to go on one week's leave. I visited Ashti and my family and friends in Hawler. Ashti was living with my family. For two months, she had not known whether I was alive or dead. When they took her, she had given them a false name and was released, but had to live in secret in case anyone discovered her background.

I had no idea how long I would be in the army, or whether I would be sent back to prison. I knew they had sent a letter to the army base. I had heard that under the amnesty agreement, a deserter had to serve two days in the army for each day of army service they had missed, but that a *peshmerga* had to serve two days in the army and two days in prison. By my calculations, that meant 17 years in the army and 17 years in prison! However, two months earlier, in April 1990, an English journalist called Bazoft was hung for being an American spy. The government claimed he was in possession of photos of chemical factories near Baghdad. The UN tried to save him, but after Saddam executed him, problems flared between America and Saddam, and Saddam declared a new amnesty: "People coming back to Iraq will not go to prison, but they still have to serve in the army."

In June 1990, I arrived at the rocket base near Basra where I had been in 1979. Ba'ath agents were everywhere, watching and asking questions. Several times they sent me to a panel for investigation at the rocket base's intelligence section in Baghdad. Later, I was moved to Mosul, then back to Basra.

Every month, I had five days' leave and would visit Ashti and my family. Ashti was lonely and disillusioned. She believed people had no appreciation of what the *peshmerga* had tried to do for them. She knew she was a burden on my family, and relied on interest from the last of her gold. I decided to escape, but was told that the Iranian border was officially closed. I would have to live in secret, without Ashti and the children. I had no choice but return to the army.

After Saddam invaded Kuwait on 2 August, they sent our army unit to a military base inside Kuwait. My job was to fix the dynamos in the trucks and cars. We were fed rice, bread and sometimes vegetables and meat. All the soldiers thought Saddam Hussein's invasion of Kuwait was very bad. No-one wanted to fight. Then after a month they sent all *peshmergas* back to the Central Intelligence Prison in Baghdad. My grey military uniform was exchanged for a dirty *galabeya*.[e]

I like tea, but all we would get occasionally was hot water with a couple of tea leaves in it. One day I had been washing the yard for three hours when Ahmed, an Assyrian Christian guard, told me, "If you clean the kitchen, I will give you a cup of tea." While I was cleaning, he asked the guards, "Could you bring tea?" He poured it, but in my hurry to find the sugar, I used salt instead.

One day Ahmed brought in two big trays of rice and beans. It was the only time we had a full meal, and afterwards he made us tea. This was a very kind act. He had a sense of humour too. At two in the morning, he would knock, open the door, and come inside, totally against the rules, and make jokes. Sometimes he forced all of us to sing and dance. Assi, which means 'stuck', lived in my cell. He had been born with a disease that made him very thin and weak, so one night Ahmed forced him to climb a tree and imitate a rooster and a dog—just to make us laugh.

One afternoon Ahmed came to tell us, "Because I have been good to you, they are sending me away." Another guard had caused problems, especially when he learnt that Ahmed had informed one family that their son was in prison. One prisoner suggested that Ahmed must come from an important family or know someone important in the prison. Otherwise they would have hung him for treating the prisoners so kindly.

Everybody was so hungry that some people would fight over a scrap of dirty food. After a while I persuaded the people to divide the food evenly, and take turns to eat five spoonfuls of soup each. This was working well until a big, strong man joined us. He argued that by getting only a little amount each time, we were left hungrier. He convinced a few others, so after a few days of argument I said, "Eat as you like." He took half the rice for himself. Other people became angry and the tray of food was upturned. The guards came in and hit us, then made us lie on the floor with our legs on the wall for three hours. They did not give us food until the next day.

One day I was taken to the military intelligence court. The judge said, "I will read out a list of what you have done against the government and you must object if anything is false." As he read I was silent. When he finished he asked, "So you admit to everything?"
"Yes."

He said, "You have a very bad record." I had no idea of my sentence.

I had been in prison for four months when the American forces started bombing Baghdad. At four that afternoon the guards had given us bread, and a 20-litre tin to use for a toilet. That night we heard loud explosions. The whole prison shook, and dust, metal and building materials were falling everywhere. We climbed on top of each other to see out of the 10 by 60-centimetre window. Outside, the night was as bright as day with all the bombs, and Saddam's anti-aircraft missiles firing from the tops of buildings. We were very happy and one Arab from Basra jumped and shouted, "Yes!" When no guards came to stop the noise we realised they must have gone to the shelter. I got new energy from the thought that the war could change my situation.

At about 1 pm the guards returned. They blindfolded us and tied our hands behind our backs, then loaded us onto buses. After three hours we reached a very old civilian prison, built of stone with doors of wood, in the middle of a date-palm forest in the Bahkooba area, famous for its oranges, apples and stone fruits. Two hundred prisoners lived in one hall 12 metres square. Plaster peeled off the walls and the wet concrete floors were black with dirt. The food was very bad and the water came through an open channel. They gave us water twice a day, but if we drank it we got diarrhoea. All the toilets were blocked, so we had to walk through five centimetres of mud and faeces. We each had a blanket for sleeping, but we also had to use this to clean ourselves. We all became sick.

New prisoners kept arriving and were put with long-term prisoners. It was very disorganised. There were no interrogations and no rules—they could keep us in the hall all day. After 17 days Saddam Hussein sent a message that all prisoners had to be sent back to the army to fight. We were put into groups of four and taken by utility. American forces were bombing all the army vehicles going from Basra to Kuwait. We passed many wrecked vehicles, many bodies, and even dead camels. When the bombs exploded near us, the guards would get out of the car and lie underneath, but we were handcuffed to our seats.

After three days we arrived at a base that was like a prison for soldiers inside Kuwait. A bus had been bombed four minutes before we arrived, and the soldiers were all in the shelter. When an officer heard the sound of our utility, he came out and swore at the driver, "Stupid man! How can you lock them to the seats? Can't you smell the bombs and see the fires? Let them go." The driver said, "You must sign for them," but the officer refused, saying, "How can you expect prisoners to fight against American aeroplanes shooting from 1000 kilometres? You bring these people to die." The driver insisted, so the officer said, "I will sign for them, then let them go."

He meant he was not going to keep us at the prison base. Instead, we were distributed to other bases, and the next morning I was taken to the base I had been at before. I was happy. The first thing I did was go to the toilet. It was so good not to have a time limit! Then I drank tea, but I was very, very weak. I could not walk normally. That night I went to the main officer and asked to go and see my family. He said, "Nobody can leave." I answered, "If you don't give me permission, I will go anyway." He said, "I will give you a paper saying you are going to bring information about salaries." I did not have any money, but a Kurdish man gave me 75 dinars, saying, "If you come back, I will collect the money." He knew I would not come back.

After two days, I escaped with two others. We took a truck, then walked across the desert to avoid the checkpoints. Later we hung onto the back of an army truck going to Basra. We used a boat to cross one river, then took different buses to Hawler via Kirkuk, taking two days and living on onions.

I arrived in Hawler at four in the morning and went straight to my family. I did not expect Ashti to still be there. I had been away for six months without contact and I knew she had been having problems. My family had very little for themselves, and for a long time we had depended on them. They had grown tired. The revolution had taken nine years of my life, and my family's attitude was, "You chose this way, so you must take the consequences."

They told me where Ashti was living, and also that one of my cousins had died in a car accident on his way to Baghdad. It was a big shock. After visiting my uncle's home, I went to Ashti's. I walked through the open door. She was cleaning. When she saw me, she started to cry. I think she was shocked at my physical condition. She was angry too, because I had been in town for seven hours. She asked, "Why did you visit all these places before coming to me? Why has no-one sent me a message that you were free?" I knew she had been alone, with no-one to help her. I had tried to send a message, but people leaving prison had too many messages to hand out. She had gone from place to place, asking people if they had any information about me, and had been living without electricity or water and with too little food. Also her mother had died. We did not hug—it is not acceptable in our culture to show one's wife affection in front of others, even relatives. We sat and talked. Hema recognised me but Hesha did not.

Over the next few days, we heard that PUK and KDP leaders had met in Iran to start an uprising. They had written to all the leaders in Iraqi Kurdistan, and the radio began announcing that all *peshmergas* should find guns. They asked *jahsh* and other people to hide their guns and organise into groups, urging Kurds to unite. They claimed that the government was weak and we were ready to fight. I was very worried, not knowing whether I should go back to PUK or not. I was still very weak, Ashti was depressed, and I worried for my family, who did not have food. If the uprising failed and Saddam came back, I would be punished and killed. Ashti and I made the decision to escape Iraq; it was just a matter of when. But I was excited too. I was always asking people for news.

I visited friends at the radio in Sulaimani who told me *peshmergas* were entering Iraq from Qasmarush. Noshirwan was in the mountains close to Sulaimani with 200 or 300. Another group were approaching Rania, avoiding Qaladiza where 10,000 houses had been destroyed seven months earlier.

Seventeen days after I arrived back, in the first week of March, an uprising led by Ali Nabi started in Rania several days before the plan. Ali Nabi was from a big family, and had been a famous PUK *peshmerga* until 1987, but had returned to Rania and worked as *jahsh*. Iraq had ordered all *jahsh* to hand over their arms to Central Intelligence. *Amn* were searching houses for army deserters and tensions were rising, so without orders, Ali Nabi attacked an Amn office in Rania and took control. When people heard the shooting, they came with guns to help. Tens of people—civilians and *amn*—were killed in the fight. Some *amn* officers escaped, wearing Kurdish clothes. Civilians started attacking army and police bases, and in one morning they took control of Rania.

Three days later, PUK *peshmerga* took control of Sulaimani, then Koi Sinjak. All the people were supporting the uprising. Day by day the radio reported the uprising moving from city to city. No-one expected victory to be so quick and decisive. On 11 March Hawler was liberated, the day before civilians and *jahsh* liberated Dohuk. It took us by surprise. Hawler is a big city, needing a lot of *peshmergas* to attack from different directions, but all the government people were escaping, so PUK reached Hawler quickly. At about 7 am I went out to see a wave of 200 people walking down the street shouting excitedly. Perhaps one person carried a gun, but people just pushed themselves through the gates of the military bases and police stations. Everything was disorganised, and many people were attacking from different points, sometimes accidentally killing each other with grenades or gunfire. Some military and intelligence forces defended themselves, while others threw down their guns and escaped by rushing into the crowd so that no-one knew who they were.

In the centre of town, I saw people collecting food, furniture, government cars, guns, even RPGs from government stores, schools, shops and other buildings. A tank was being driven down the street, its tread ripping up the bitumen. People were breaking into government houses. I had a friend who went home to find people had stolen everything except his clothes. A man was trying on his trousers, so my friend asked, "What are you doing?" The man said, "I want some trousers." It was madness.

A Kurdish writer's son told me, "I went to the city that first morning. When I saw people throwing the books out of the library, I told them, 'These books are for our education.' But the people said, 'This is not your job. We need the paper to wrap up food to sell.'" He concluded, "I came away swearing at the Kurdish people, saying, 'Saddam Hussein was better!' It was not a revolution. It was animal behaviour. Some people were fighting for our country and others were fighting to destroy it."

There were no soldiers in the street, and no traffic or any other rules. People took documents from offices, many of which were deliberately burnt because people knew their names might be on them. Everything was mixed up. A person would name someone as a guard or interrogator and people would be sent to kill him. Some were raped, or cut into pieces, because they were held responsible for imprisoning or killing people.

It was a big shock. I did not expect life to change so rapidly. After two days, my uncle told me PUK radio was calling for me to go to the radio base in Sulaimani. They wanted me to go to Kirkuk and bring back a 10-kilo radio. Ashti was against it, saying, "Maybe the government will come back, and you will be away when I have to escape, so we will lose each other." I said, "Nothing like that will happen," and went to Kirkuk.

Kirkuk had been liberated after a two-day fight led by Noshirwan. Ali Hasan Al-Majid had strongly defended the city with tanks and army in the hills around. In the first wave of fighting, from 4 am until 5 pm, many *peshmergas* died, but during the night, some PUK *peshmergas* managed to bypass the army and enter the Kirkuk suburb of Rhahimarwa, on the road to Hawler. By dawn, they controlled the central intelligence and police bases in that suburb, but they had run out of bullets and had to wait for reinforcements

Ali Hasan Al-Majid continued to bomb and hold the city in a state of siege, until at 3 pm on the second day, *peshmergas* attacked some tanks with RPGs and destroyed a few. The soldiers just ran from their tanks and vehicles. On Newroz, 21 March, *peshmergas* entered the city and civilians pushed towards all the government bases. Al-Majid escaped by helicopter, and after that the army lost point by point. All Saddam's people escaped on foot or in cars.

In Kirkuk I visited another uncle. He had news that Saddam had started bombing the Shi'ites in the south and that Iran was advancing towards Basra. I visited a friend responsible for a *peshmerga* unit protecting Kirkuk, who said, "Masoud Barzani has come back with *peshmergas* via the Hamilton Road, and has got through Rowandoz and Shaqlowa and is now in Salahaddin, but if Saddam comes back it will be hard to defend Kirkuk. The *peshmergas* are too disorganised." When I heard this, I knew I had to get back to Ashti and escape.

Back in Hawler, I arranged to get a government car, but we could not find petrol. The next morning, two days after the government took Kirkuk, we heard that Saddam's Republican Guard had reached the outskirts of Hawler. We found one truck with eight families in it and without asking I threw Hema, Hesha, Ashti's sister's son and the women into the truck, then climbed in myself. A lady started complaining, but there was no time to be polite.

The truck moved slowly through the traffic. We had two blankets and some food, but many people left with nothing. Masoud Barzani and Ma'am Jalal had already escaped to Iran. When we reached the outskirts of the city, Iraqi aeroplanes started dropping bombs on Hawler, while Iraqi helicopters shot rockets and bullets into the crowd of people leaving. I saw American aeroplanes flying above the aircraft, but doing nothing to stop the killing. We passed a car shot to pieces, with a dead child, man and woman inside, and three or four times we had to climb down from the truck to escape the bombs and the shooting. We reached a hill outside Salahaddin at about 5 pm, but then Iraq started bombing Salahaddin. The truck stopped in the middle of a traffic jam. When a bomb exploded near us Ashti and I decided to get out and walk. The road zigzagged up the hill. Suddenly we realised we had left the bag containing our passports back in the truck. I told them to continue along the road while I went back for the bag. I was going against the flow of people and was being pushed and shoved. The bombs kept coming, but I found the truck and retrieved the bag. Then I could not find Ashti. There were cars going back and forth, shuttling people up the mountain, and I went up and down three times looking for them. I shouted. I ran to the top of a rise to look for them. I was still weak from prison, and very tired and nervous. Hundreds of people were crying or shouting for their friends and families, so you just had to look for faces.

At last I found them waiting on a truck. The truck took us through Shaqlowa, Hareer and Rowandoz to Diyana, four or five hours from both the Turkish and Iranian borders. It was night, and people were sleeping everywhere in the cold and rain. We found a destroyed building and rested, two blankets between us. In the morning we had no food.

Saddam had taken Kirkuk, then Hawler, Dohuk and Sulaimani, following the *peshmergas* two ways—along the Hamilton Road to Halabja and along the narrow road to Shaqlowa. But PUK and Islamic Movement *peshmergas* and civilians destroyed seven tanks and blocked the army, stopping them from following the people after Salahaddin. In Sulaimani, they also stopped the army.

Thousands of people started arriving in Diyana. We stayed for a week trying to decide where to go: Iran or Turkey. I decided on Turkey—I had seen what happens in Iran—but Ashti's sister returned home with her children. After a two-day walk across the mountains, with no blankets and only biscuits for the children, on 1 April we reached the Turkish border. It was the same day that Ma'am Jalal and Masoud Barzani were called to Baghdad to negotiate with Saddam Hussein, and both kissed that cheek of poison. Ma'am Jalal was to claim that this was a custom when negotiating, but it was a wrong thing they did. Saddam was weak, and unable to control Kurdistan. Under the protection of America and in full view of the world media, they could have announced our independence.

After three days we were allowed across the border. We walked to a camp at Robarrock. We had not eaten properly for four days, and when a food truck arrived there was a mad crush. Two days later, American aeroplanes started dropping food by parachute. Over the next days, most people decided to return to Iraq. But we were staying, and the UN took us to Shamzina'an and gave us a tent, blankets, pots and pans, and enough food. There were toilets, a water tank, and wood in the mountains for a fire. After two months, they took us by truck to Silopi camp.

On the way we were stopped in a village by Kurdish women saying, "We will not open the road until the government releases our men." Apparently PKK had come to the village and taken some village guards, so soldiers had come and taken all the men. We watched as the army arrived in tanks. They collected the women and children, hitting them, and putting guns to their heads, pushing them into a big hole near the road. We were let through at this point so we did not see what happened to them.

Silopi was a big camp of 10,000 people when we arrived. Many found life in the tents, in the heat of summer and the mud of winter, queuing for water and toilets, too hard. Two or three times we heard bombs and shooting in the distance, probably soldiers and PKK fighting, but I felt free and happy. I was determined never to be under the Iraqi government again. PUK invited me to go back to work, but I did not accept any offers. I was planning to take my family to a safe country, to do something for my children and Ashti, because I had never given them priority in all my life. Always I had thought of the revolution.

It was different for Ashti. She is sensitive. She laughs easily and becomes angry easily, and in the camp she was sad because she thought we might have to stay a long time or even be forced back to Iraq. Sometimes she felt we were deserting the revolution. Then the UN started interviewing and our hopes were raised.

Ashti wanted to go to Europe. It was closer to Kurdistan and we knew people there, but I wanted to go to Australia. I thought there would be less discrimination and a better future for our children. When Australian Embassy officials came to the camp, I told them, "I have 300 dollars: accept us or not," and we were one of the first 10 people accepted as refugees. This meant our aeroplane tickets would be paid for, but Ashti cried for a week. Seventeen days after we left the camp, they posted a list of people who had been accepted into Holland, and our names were there, but by then we were in Australia.

In Sydney we stayed in a hostel, then moved to a flat. We studied, and I got my license for fixing televisions and videos, then found work painting houses. Now I run my own house-painting business. It is hard work, and with the standard of living there is a lot of pressure, but recently we bought a house, and I have been able to help my family back in Kurdistan. We communicate with our families by special express—sending letters with friends who are going back. There was not even a phone service until they established a satellite service in the mid-1990s.

Back in 1992, I had hope for the Kurdish democratic parliament and for Kurdistan. KDP and PUK cooperated, but all the nation-state governments surrounding them wanted to divide and destroy what the Kurds were building, and there were American and Israeli interests not wishing to make Kurdistan stable. With two trade embargoes against Kurdistan, people could feed their children only once a day. Water and electricity supplies were unreliable. People had no work. Also, each of the Kurdish leaders wanted to take the power for themselves, and people were more loyal to their different parties than to Kurdistan. All the men have guns, and since the 1960s the gun had been their friend. When civil war began in 1994, a lot of people died. By 1996 the region under Kurdish administration, which goes beyond the no-fly zone, was divided, but then the UN 'food for oil' program began in 1997 and the civil war ended in 1998. Conditions improved, and now the people are not hungry. But the future can go many ways, depending on how long the no-fly zone goes on for; what happens between KDP, PUK, PKK and the Islamic groups; what happens inside Turkey, Iraq, Iran, Syria and Israel, and between these countries; and other influences from the USA, possibly Europe, and Islam, a new factor in the equation.

After eight years living in Australia, we now have Australian problems and Kurdish problems. Australia has its own issues to face, like how to treat its Aborigines, but I still think Australia is the best country for people from the Middle East, because there are a lot of migrants here and discrimination is less than in Europe.

I have become calmer over the years. Ashti still worries too much about what is happening in Kurdistan. If she sees someone just living for themselves and not caring, she confronts them. But Australia is a different country, and I appreciate this country—it is safe and democratic. I hope that Kurdistan will one day be like Australia.

You are still asleep

By Abbas Boskany

You are still asleep
While I am a rambler on the road:
Hurriedly,
At two iron arms' length
Opposite the way, I slip with time.

Last night,
With an army of flowers and a sea of pain,
I knelt down to you,
Yet it looked like
You enjoyed your silence,
And took pleasure in my brilliant intoxication,
Not letting meaningfulness attend the oasis.

Together,
Night, flowers, pain, wine, tears and myself
Were unable to make you wear a hope-anklet.
Last night,
I launched all my armies
Into the battlefield and was defeated.

You are about to close the doors of my tears.
You are about to turn me into
A beggar at the false mosques;
The red-tulip plain into a desert;
The streets into stripes.
You are still asleep and unaware
Of how I came to ask:
"How shall I disclose the oppressiveness of piety
If not by the illumination of wine?"[a]
You do not seem to know that my groans annoy the angels,
And outrage the Deity.

At two iron lines' length,
Side by side with time,
Opposite the way, I drift far away.
My gasping breaths take flight back to you
Who is still asleep.

Cry of the Partridge

A short fiction by Abdulwahab Talabani, translated by Sam Zakhary and Shorsh Ako

There is a broad, golden valley between the mountains of Peermam and Qarachug,[a] but now the land is naked, completely stripped of its spring beauty. All green has fled, tired from fighting the early summer sun. Already the plain has burnt to desert. Siamand noticed that even the partridge, which had bonded with a young girl called Shirin, was no longer singing for the new morning. The small bird was behaving strangely: circling above Shirin, then suddenly darting high into the atmosphere, seeking the cool breeze from the icy mountains.

It was time the caravan moved to mountain pastures. The *shaykh*, leader of the nomads, sensed something unusual. He had given no orders but he watched his people pack their few belongings and fold their tents, as they sang their mountain songs. These chanted melodies echoed over the plain, like rainbows of silk floating on the north wind.

As the sun stretched its golden elbow over the distant peaks, the sheep and cows began moving eastwards towards their destination, leaving behind clouds of dust and the caravan.

The *shaykh* called Shirin to his side and gave her the reins of the best horse, then kissed her eyes and forehead. The young girl's smile was innocent between pomegranate cheeks. She understood that she had been chosen to lead her people because she was the most beautiful girl among them.[b]

She mounted the beautiful horse, placing the partridge on her shoulder. The *shaykh* checked that his people were ready to go, then gazed after the beautiful Shirin. He wondered what was on her mind, and how she would cope with her new responsibility, asking himself, "Is your heart still that of a child, full of laughter, or has it started to pulse with the dreams of love, like a butterfly about to break from its cocoon? I think so. Yes. I sense how eager you are to see the mountain's deer and to hug the twinkling stars of the dark, summer sky."

Eyeing the land around him, he pondered why the shallow lake had dried up so soon, as if the season had lost its mind, as if the whole atmosphere had ominously forgotten time.

Out in front, Shirin with the smiling face looked around from time to time, ever watchful to secure and regulate the march of the caravan. Her smile was like a diamond that reflected the sun's rays, warming the hearts of those behind her, drawing them to follow ever nearer, although no-one dared to overtake, for she was like their queen, leading her nation to their beloved mountain, their source of safety and freedom.

Siamand made sure he was closest to her shadow. As he rode, he watched her dark strands of hair, loose from her plait, being tossed by the northern breeze. In the hot, rising sun Shirin's caravan looked to him like a series of howdahs filled with gold, roses and honey moving towards a curtain of silver dust on the horizon.

The *shaykh* rode on his handsome horse between his people, his son, not yet 15, riding next to him, listening to his father narrate stories of past travels, stingingly cold winter days, the times of melting snows that caused avalanches and floods, and the warm Newroz fires and happy nights. In so doing his father was teaching him about the life.

Closer to the mountains the people wanted to stop and rest, but in his heart the *shaykh* knew it was neither the time nor the place. He ordered them to continue, wishing they could cross the valley in one jump. It was as if the further they went, the darker the horizon behind them grew, like a nightmare chasing his caravan.

For no apparent reason, the dogs began to bark strangely, sounding like the moans of the sick. The horses were agitated too. They bumped into each other, then panicked into short gallops. The *shaykh* was worried, and confided in his son, as if the boy was older than his years: "I burn with a strange feeling. I feel fire on my face and I see its flames flickering everywhere. It is as if a venomous storm is approaching us."

He called to Shirin, "Don't take your eyes from the peak of Halgurd."[c] Suddenly the partridge took flight. Shirin's eyes followed the small bird as it flew higher and higher, looping and hovering with fluttering wings aloft in the heavens, to abruptly return like an arrow to her shoulder and begin to sing. But the song was more like a cry. It confused Shirin, and she gently stroked the bird's feathers.

The barking of the dogs intensified. The horses jerked their heads left and right, pacing quickly. The *shaykh* took a strong grip of his reins. He looked this way and that, his throat tightening as if he had swallowed bile. He thought, "Is this the coming of a flood, like the one that destroyed my caravan last year? There are too many ways to die, and I feel the death facing us now is the worst of all." He asked himself, "Is it possible for a human to feel what it is like for a tree to be ripped from the earth?" "No way," he answered himself. "That is a fact." Yet his thoughts continued, "But now I think I feel the rip, the tree's crack of pain. It is as if I am being broken piece by piece. My veins are emptying of blood as the plain has been emptied of water. I am losing all sense of colour, sound and life. Alas, how is this happening?"

Helicopters emerged from behind a nearby mountain, landing on flat spaces, blocking the road and byways. Black troops alighted, machine guns ready, mechanically darting here and there as they performed the ceremony of soul-searching. The skeletal, metallic-like forms began shooting randomly, as if they had been blown there by a black wind from the caves of a dark and brutal history.

All colour left the *shaykh*'s face. His skin felt dry. He raised his eyes to the sky, asking silently, "What kind of plague is spreading in this world?"

The mechanical forms began chasing the people: women, old men and children, rounding them up, tying their hands with ropes and their feet with chains, pushing them towards the waiting army trucks. Shirin was in the midst of the nightmare. At first she thought it was a dream, but gradually she came to understand the reality of her fate, and panicked as people began dying around her. Her memory flashed to her family and how they had been kidnapped by similar mechanical forms the previous year, to be taken to a place of no whereabouts, never to return. She gripped the reins of her horse and looked up to Halgurd, unresponsive to Siamand, who was trying to release her hands and save her from the fire. Her mind cried to the mountain, "Oh Halgurd, a small part of heaven, the crown of all mountains, now they steal us from you because they cannot uproot you. Stay, Halgurd. Wait for the return of our caravans. Guard your eagles' nests and embrace the nests of the partridge." From the eye of the sky, two tears of fire fell to a trembling earth, which was quaking under barbarian boots.

Slowly Shirin took the partridge from her shoulder. She softly whistled to the bird, then whispered, "Fly free, my beauty. Do not leave the spaces of the sky. Do not come with me. You cannot survive the bitterness of this journey, the isolation, the cage of exile, or the rusty knife's slaughter. Fly high to heaven." She thrust him into the air, her eyes as pure as the sky as they said goodbye, following the small partridge as it flew away. Below, the earth shook as the air filled with the bullets of rapid machine-gun fire.

As one of the mechanical forms attempted to drag Shirin off her horse, Siamand threw himself around her. A single shot reached its target. Siamand felt a violet curtain drop in front of his eyes. Violet turned to red, the red becoming darker and darker, before turning white, and fading into a thousand colourless spots.

Siamand's bullet-holed veins swam in dunes of salt. An ocean of water was needed to wash away these deadly salts. He tried to scream, but his cry choked in his throat as everything turned to a silent, tranquil grey. Siamand's body fell to the ground like the torn flag of an oppressed nation. The awkward boots of brutality trod over his body, as his open eyes gazed upon the black hurricane now engulfing Shirin.

Burning into Paint

A life story based on interviews with Ahmed Faiek, translated through Dr Muhammad Kamal.

What made me become an artist? I was motivated from within, always wanting to express through artistic creation my concerns about human oppression. From primary school, my teachers encouraged me to develop my art and participate in different school exhibitions, but it was in middle school that I began drawing and painting with a commitment beyond the usual. Although I did not follow a particular political ideology, and as a Kurd I was not able to directly express my political concerns, from the beginning these formed the basis of my art.

I made the issues universal. When I was 15 I did a poster of a white horse rearing up on his hind legs. In another poster, I painted a dove laying its eggs in a khaki-green military helmet. In the background are mountains and cliffs dripping blood onto a plain. Two doves fly up into a blue sky, symbolic of people being deported or having to escape their villages.

My Arab teachers in Kirkuk were as afraid as the students to talk about the political situation, but they liked the quality of my art and saw the symbols as international, relating the themes to Zionism and imperialism. In this way they accepted my ideas, and one teacher encouraged me to continue studying art beyond school.

I always used strong colours, because I see the colours of Kurdish life to be very sharp: Kurdish dress, Kurdish carpet, and the seasons of the year are vibrant. What happens in Kurdistan is dramatic, a raw struggle of life and death, whereas in my mind, Australia is more subtle in tone. Its colours are those of nature: subdued greens, earth browns and pale blues.

People's life experience and concerns back in Kurdistan are very, very different to most people's experience and concerns in Australia, and I find it very difficult to bridge the gulf, to share a point of reference. I identify more with Australian Aboriginal people, because I can understand their suffering, but I have yet to find ways to meet them. As for the people I have met, they have not lived in constant fear of being arrested or kidnapped by the secret police or soldiers. Most Australians do not see the government and army as their enemies. The majority of children have proper care, food, clothes, medicine and toys, whereas in Kurdistan, children grow up without these things.

From my earliest memories, my life has been filled with anxiety and fear. Sometimes the fear was ill-defined, something vague and unknown, but looking back, these feelings have formed the substrate of every experience. Even now, living in a free country, they are my main motivation. I am not at peace. Fear and anxiety are still with me, because I leave behind a whole nation of fear and poverty.

Sometimes these feelings motivate me and advance my art. At other times I cannot lift a pencil or a brush. I cannot describe the exact links, but such feelings push me to explore certain subjects, often subconsciously, although at other times it is after intellectual analysis. Sometimes both processes are at work, as in the painting I did of a potato floating in a fiery red, sky being eaten by a black crow: food being eaten by evil. The colours red and black are in many paintings, and I think they refer to fear.

My family did not object to me pursuing a career in art. Sometimes they encouraged me. My father was a fireman in the fire brigade, and I was one of 11 children—a soccer team—so we did not have time to sit and talk about our private feelings and talents!

In 1981 I went to Sulaimani to study at the Institute of Fine Arts. Those five years were an exciting time. The institute was co-educational, and Sulaimani was a progressive city, full of artists and writers. For the first two years, all the students and teachers, even the dean, were Kurdish, and we were free to meet and talk and study together. After that, Arabic teachers and students and the Ba'ath Party's Student Union were introduced to the school. Many refused to join the union, and some were put in prison because of this, but I stayed as far away from politics as possible.

At the institute, I loved learning how to draw in all mediums—lead and colour pencil, charcoal and oil pastels. We learnt all about colour, juxtaposing colour, and how to mix them in watercolours and oils, as well as using various graphic techniques with different materials. We had still-life and life-drawing classes, but our human models were always clothed! I used my own brain to work out the form, and studied books of anatomy. I did sculpture for a short time, but concentrated on painting.

The Kurds have never had a strong tradition in the visual arts. In a number of caves near Mosul, there are prehistoric lined carvings of cows, snakes and other animals. Near Sulaimani are famous caves with ancient stone drawings and inscriptions from Akkadian times, before the Assyrians and Medes. On one mountain near Qaradagh, 40 minutes from Sulaimani, there is a giant face carved into a sheer cliff. The Medes left a few stone fortresses and castles on top of strategic mountains, and some sculptures, but to my knowledge no Mede paintings have been found, although very little archaeological work has been done in Kurdistan. The Mede capital, Ecbatan (near modern-day Hamadan), as well as Hawler and Sulaimani, are cities built on a succession of cities thousands of years old, and these and many other sites warrant investigation.

Examples of calligraphy have been found to be more than 2500 years old. Some of the earliest texts discovered in Kurdistan were carved into stone or clay in a cuneiform-Aramaic script, and some describe wars with the Assyrians from the Mede point of view. Other writing was done on the leather of gazelle in the Hawraman script.

Various Kurdish princedoms left castles elaborately decorated with plasterwork and animal carvings. One example is at Qaleh-I Yzdigird, at the edge of the Zagros Mountains, dated at the end of the Parthian era of 226 AD. The griffin motif found there was considered the hallmark of the Sassanian Persians four centuries later, but Mehrdad Izady of Harvard University thinks it to be a derivative of the Ezidi 'Peacock Angel'.

In my region, Kurds developed ceramics for daily use, sometimes painting the vessels, but there was not even a strong tradition of carpet-weaving. In other parts of Kurdistan, there is a loom in nearly every house. But even in these areas, such as Hawraman, carpet-weaving did not develop into an industry, as it did in Turkey and Iran, maybe because Kurds have been kept isolated by mountains and have had to be self-reliant. The Hawraman Kurds are also well known for making fine and coarse woollen materials, as well as a special kind of shoe. The soles are made of strong leather, reinforced with nails in the toe and heel, and the upper part of the shoe is made from a bleached rope-like wool.

Poetry and music have always been the more developed traditions, especially since Islam came to the area in the seventh century. Islam put religious taboos on representing God, people and even animals, in case these images were worshipped. Music is also more accessible to larger numbers of people. A painting needs more individual interpretation. As a result of the taboo on images, and our geographic isolation, there are few famous Kurdish artists. One called Malva, originally from Syria, is now known internationally. He lives in Austria and paints as an impressionist, exploring light and colour. Consequently, at the institute we studied mainly European art, from prehistoric cave paintings to modern times, as well as the history of Islamic art and the influence of Islam on art. Our teachers taught us that making images is not a sin, that it did not contradict Islam, because we created for self-expression and a sense of aesthetics.

One teacher at the institute, Abdullah Rasal, inspired me very much—as an artist, a teacher and a person. He had two styles of work—one was academic and the other was expressionist, in which he painted his own face in different expressions and mediums. He had been a freedom fighter, but did not present any particular political ideology, and he revealed himself as a friend, which was very unusual for a teacher in our culture. After I graduated, he was forced to leave the institute. He went to the mountains, then to Pakistan as a refugee, and from Pakistan to London.

In 1986 I finished my studies. The Iraq–Iran War continued, but for a while I was employed at the museum in Sulaimani, in the Department of Old Civilisation, to make scale models for a festival of Nebuchadnezzar II's Hanging Gardens of Babylon, built around 580 BC. On plaster models, three metres high and four metres long, we painted the details of the walls, entrances, windows and trees, our ideas being taken from history books. The models were then put on trucks for public display: a mobile museum. I enjoyed doing the work because the Gardens are a masterpiece of history. At the same time I was aware they were distinct from Kurdish history, as opposed to other displays, which included stamps and vessels from caves near Sulaimani, and homo-sapien remains that show evidence of burial rituals dating from about 35,000 BC.

After I finished at the museum, I set up a studio in Kirkuk, making a living by selling my own paintings, mainly still life and portraits, selling frames and framing. Some artist friends and I did a mural together for a Kurdish Club in Kirkuk, based on the poetry of Omar Khayyam, a Persian astronomer, mathematician and poet born in 1050 AD.

I had a personal exhibition in 1985, and in 1986 I was part of a national exhibition in Baghdad. Every artist in Iraq is a member of the Artists' Union, so when there is an exhibition, they write a letter to all the artists, asking if we want to participate. I did not go myself; I sent my paintings, because I am not a salesman, a speaker or a writer, even in everyday life.

As an artist I did not live a traditional life. We used to drink alcohol and have girlfriends, but in 1987 I was conscripted into the Iraqi army and my artistic life came to an end. Fortunately, I was just an office clerk in Baghdad, then in Mosul, and in 1988 I was sent to Al-Fow, the second-last city before the Kuwaiti border, but all the time I felt that the army was ripping out my soul. I could not paint.

Around the end of 1990 and the beginning of 1991, I was called back to the army for a few months during Saddam's invasion of Kuwait. I served as a clerk in Tikrit, the city where Saddam was born. The whole city was covered in portraits of Saddam. When the government announced they needed primary school teachers, I applied to become a teacher in Kirkuk, and was sent back, but I never started teaching because the Kurdish uprising began in March 1991.

Like everyone else, I was optimistic. Saddam had been defeated in Kuwait and we were told his army was weak. When *peshmergas* took control of Kirkuk on Newroz, 21 March 1991, the Iraqi army withdrew, and everybody celebrated at home and in the street. For the first time in my life, I had great hope for the future. But seven days later, early in the morning, Saddam's helicopters and aeroplanes attacked Kirkuk without discrimination, one of the bombs hitting my family's house. We escaped to the underground shelter of our Christian neighbours where we stayed for two days, listening to the bombs and the radio. I felt a strange mixture of feelings—clinging to a hope that we must succeed, but also feeling very bleak.

On the third day, my family escaped in two cars to Sulaimani, where we stayed for a month with relatives, including my cousin, Layla, whom I had loved since childhood. The radio broadcasts grew grimmer. Kirkuk had been emptied of people. We heard the Americans say, "This is an internal conflict between Saddam and the Kurds. It is not our business," and we feared Saddam would come to Sulaimani.

When news came that the army was ready to attack, everyone started moving towards the Iranian border. Some walked and others were in cars, but it was like one big, slow procession. We walked all day, taking turns in the car. Many children were separated from their parents, but no-one could help them. The night was particularly horrible, absolutely dark and cold and raining. We had to sleep beside the road, hearing constant footsteps.

Sometime during the second day we decided that the women and children should return to Sulaimani while the men continued. We guessed that Saddam wanted only men. That was a very sad parting for Layla and I. We were both crying, not knowing if or when we would see each other again.

After they left, I felt we were walking to nowhere. I could not think. We reached the Iranian border by nightfall, and decided to sleep around a fire, under one blanket. There were four of us. We took turns to stay awake and tend the fire. We were so close to the fire, I was afraid the sparks would ignite the blanket or our clothing. What if the person watching fell asleep? It was after midnight when I felt something touching my knee. I was dreaming that the fire was burning me and I woke up shouting. It was rain. We were all wet and the fire was out. Those experiences on the road are so deep, I cannot paint them, but it is not necessary for an artist to put everything directly into a painting.

The Iranian soldiers could not stop one million people crossing the border. They put a photo of Khomeini on the front windscreen of the car, like a passport, allowing us to continue. We had a relative, a cousin of Layla's father, living in Mariwan, so we went and met these relatives for the first time. We stayed a month, hearing over the radio that

Saddam had recaptured all the cities. When Saddam announced an amnesty, we returned.

Back in Sulaimani, I was very depressed. When I see refugees on television, I remember my own experiences, and it makes me very unhappy that another nation is going through the same trauma. But 1992 was a creative year for me. Hope for the future was rekindled. For the first time I voted in elections for a Kurdish parliament. I opened a studio, and felt part of a Kurdish renaissance of artists, writers and musicians. The quality of my exhibitions was good, but it was hard to earn a living. There were shortages of everything.

It was in this year that I married Layla. We signed two marriage contracts: one for Sulaimani, under Kurdish control, and one for Kirkuk, under Iraqi control, because neither recognised each other's documents. In both cases, it was a civil marriage witnessed by a magistrate, with Layla present, a modern marriage without a *malla*, and we celebrated in a club with food, drums, a *ba'aghlama* and dancing.

We went to live with my brother's family. It was a difficult time. Often there was no electricity or kerosene oil to heat the house. No-one had enough food. The food in the market was too expensive, and no-one had money. Very few people had work. Most people relied on food-distribution centres, but not all food was distributed and rations were small. Sometimes in the morning, we used to eat yoghurt and bread and that was it for the day. We ate meat once a month. Several times, Layla went to the market and sold her own clothes to buy food. Despite this life, in 1993 I participated in an art exhibition organised by the Ministry of Culture of Federal Kurdistan, and our first child was born.

But the situation was getting worse. Kurdistan was not being given help to organise and rebuild a stable society after three decades of war. The main form of employment was in the Kurdish army. By May 1994, internal conflict between the Kurdish parties erupted into civil war. The last thing on people's minds was art. Everyone was disillusioned. We felt that our genuine effort towards democracy was not being given a chance, that yet again we were hurtling towards disaster. This psychological state reduced my ability to paint.

I started to think we must leave Kurdistan, and in 1994 I went to Istanbul with photographs of my work to see if I could sell paintings through Turkish art galleries. The manager of Erguderler Gallery showed an interest, which made me confident I could earn a living in Istanbul. I returned to Iraq. One year later we left for Turkey on 15-day visitor visas, crossing the border from Zakho. Straight away, we went to the United Nations office in Ankara to register as refugees, then on to Istanbul, where we lived with my brother.

The man at the Erguderler Gallery gave me a contract: he would supply all materials in return for a commission on each painting. I would produce the paintings according to his recommendations on subject matter, style and colours. The buyers wanted light, bright, naive paintings of smiling people in traditional dress. I was working as a painter, not an artist, and fortunately the man liked my work.

I saw how Turkish artists have many advantages. They have access to Europe and European schools of art. They can bring European professors to teach at the universities and they have more freedom. They are financially in a better position to travel, and the galleries in Istanbul are lovely, modern, well-lit buildings, the openings often lavish affairs. The people who come to see the exhibitions understand and appreciate art. In Kurdistan, all this contact with the West is not possible. We have few galleries, with few educated people and even fewer able to afford paintings.

Financially, we were all right. My brother-in-law in Australia was trying to sponsor us as refugees on humanitarian grounds, but we were rejected, and had to stay on illegally because we were unable to renew our visas. If we were caught, we would be deported back to Baghdad, so we lived in constant fear. My brother-in-law then contacted members of parliament, telling them I was a Kurdish artist, that I would be a great asset for Australian culture and that my life was in danger. One year later the Australian Embassy in Ankara gave us visas.

In Turkey we were depressed, sustained by our hope of coming to Australia, but when we arrived, I continued to feel lonely and disoriented. I was anxious about being completely cut off from everything I had known or imagined. Everything was new to me—even the air. Layla had the same feelings, and many times we felt like going back. My paintings were dark and abstract, islands of colour in a sea of black.

Over the next few years, life became easier for Layla. Sometimes she is stronger. It is still not easy for me—every moment seems so unreal. Now my inspiration is a combination of Australian colours, loneliness and a sense of nostalgia. The colours are softer, the images and symbols more apparent. I do not transcend realism easily, and I do not explain a painting.

I have had a few exhibitions—solo and with other artists—and I have met several Australian artists. It seems to me their personal relationships are very much disturbed, but I think it is inevitable that the state of the artist is to live in conflict and emotional turmoil in one way or another. Artists should be sensitive to their own and society's problems, so even when I am not worried, I worry because I am not worried!

Always a Sun Behind the Clouds

A life story based on interviews with Mahabad Fatah

I love Sherko Bekas's poem "Counting":

> If you could count every single leaf
> In this garden,
> If you could count all the big and little fish
> Of this ocean,
> If you could count all the birds
> During their migration
> From the north to the south
> And
> From the south to the north,
> Then I would also promise
> To count
> Every single victim
> Of this beloved Kurdistan!

Growing up I was always thinking about Kurds getting their freedom. All my relatives wanted a free Kurdistan. I was named after the Kurdish Republic of Mahabad, established in 1946. My brother Jabar became a *peshmerga* and three cousins in one family were *peshmergas*. One died in 1979–80, fighting the army in the mountains. I remember a driver, knocking on our door, saying, "I have your cousin's corpse in the car." We went over and saw the wooden box: what we call a *ta'aboodt*.[a] I was seven, and straight away ran to my aunt's house, saying, "Come—they have brought his body."

A year later, my dead cousin's *peshmerga* brother came secretly to his home in Hajiowa, a town near Sulaimani, for his wedding, but somehow the *amn* found out. They surrounded the house and started shooting. They shot him, then came into the house. They thought he was dead, but when the body moved, they took him to the prison hospital, where he died. They took everyone else to prison—my cousins, their mother and the bride, all except the father and one son, who were working on their farm. One cousin was a *peshmerga*. They killed him in prison. The bride had been working secretly with the *peshmerga* in the city, but later she was released and managed to escape to the mountains where she worked in *peshmerga* radio. The mother of the family was pregnant, so she told them, "You have killed three of my sons. Don't worry. I will make another *peshmerga*." She gave birth to a girl and called her Kurda.

I was 13 the first time I remember *amn* coming to my home. It was summer, so my sisters and I were sleeping on cotton mattresses on the roof. The soldiers just kicked the front door down. Five *amn* came up to the roof and pointed machine guns at us. I pretended to sleep. One *amn* talked in Arabic on a mobile telephone, "We can't find anyone." Another one said to me, "Wake up! Did you see a boy in a black shirt?" "No, no. I have not seen anyone." They thought anyone who wore a black shirt, or grew a beard, was politically active.

After they left, I was crying and my mother was crying. They had emptied all the cupboards and ripped up the carpet looking for guns, or Kurdish books, especially rare ones about Kurdish history and politics. They had gone through the pockets of my brothers' clothes and stolen 100 dinars after hitting him in the stomach with the butt of a gun, ignoring my mum's protests. We could not go back to sleep, and the next day, people told us that 100 *amn* had searched the area.

We were afraid of the soldiers in the street, especially the Republican Guard. For a period in 1980–81 *amn* came every night to every house. They captured my brother, Jabar, who had started secretly working for PUK in the city. It was the time of Qorban, when we kill a sheep and eat meat to remember Abraham being told by God not to kill his son Ishmael. They kept Jabar for 15 days. *Jahsh* would say our family liked *peshmerga*, and Jabar went to prison several times, but he was lucky. Many did not come back.

When a boy turns 18, he has to serve in the army. One of my brothers served seven years but Jabar served two years. When they asked for people born in a certain period to go back into the army he escaped to the mountains.

Our area of Sulaimani is called Majibeg. It is close to a village, and at night the *peshmerga* would come to talk to people, and also to take *amn* or *jahsh* and advise them that what they were doing was wrong. When I saw the *peshmerga* coming, I would straight away open our door and ask, "Do you need help?" Sometimes they needed water, food, clothes or shoes—their shoes were always worn out from walking. Sometimes they needed to hide in our house. We always helped them.

Saddam Hussein was trying to deport Kurdish people from Kurdistan and settle Arabs in Kirkuk and Khanaqin, but he was too afraid to move Arabs into Sulaimani, because the people of Sulaimani are famous for being brave. Instead, he moved people out. My sister's husband was a guard in a government department, and they moved him to Rhumadi for five years because he refused to join the Ba'ath Party. It was a form of exile.

My mother could not read or write. My father had gone to a religious school and had learnt from the Qur'an. I went to a Kurdish school. Although my teachers were Kurdish, a few times a year all the students would be told to go out into the street to march and clap for Saddam. I would always run away when the teachers were not looking. I never clapped for Saddam, but the Arab people were too scared: they had no choice.

I did not meet Arabic people, and we did not speak Arabic except when the Ba'ath government tried to change the school system, when I was in primary school. In high school, we had one Arabic lesson a day, and we were expected to attend Ba'ath Party meetings once a week. We could not refuse to go, so we would start walking to the meeting, but then, if no officials were in sight, we ran away.

In 1982, when I was 12, all Kurdish students demonstrated in the street with flags. We were against the Ba'ath government and wanted a Kurdish government. We marched and shouted, "We do not want Saddam. We want peace. We want freedom. Leave Kurdistan alone. This is our land." Truckloads of soldiers would arrive, and once I ran to a house. I did not know the people, but I knocked on the door and said, "They are going to kill us. Please, can I come in?" Most people in Sulaimani would open the door straight away, and this family gave me pyjamas to wear so that if the soldiers arrived, I would not be wearing jeans and a T-shirt. At home, girls usually wear pyjamas or a kaftan. Another time I ran to a house and they had Saddam Hussein's photo hanging on the wall. I was scared, but they did not say, "You have to go." Maybe they had the photo to protect them from the soldiers.

This was the life for Kurdish people. We were always under the regime of Iraq, so we talked of freedom. Even in primary school, I wondered, "What is freedom like?"

My brothers had more freedom in some ways. They would go out all the time, whereas I would go visiting only with my family. Yet my family was an open-minded family. My brothers would make tea for themselves, and would help serve visitors, lay out and roll up the mattresses, and wash the courtyard.

Our one-storey house was made of cement, with three rooms, a modern kitchen with an electric fridge and a mobile metal *tanoor*, and a bathroom. Our bathroom had a fire under the cement floor for heating. There was no bath or shower. We had a tap for cold water, and for hot water we had a metal container surrounded by concrete, with a fire underneath. We used a small jug to wash. The toilet was a cement hole in the ground. We had a television and a lounge and bookshelves, although we ate on the concrete floor, the food on a tray, or a nylon mat we call a *sifirah*.

My father did all the shopping and my mother did the housework. They would visit people perhaps twice a month, and as I was the youngest, they always took me. Otherwise, every day we had visitors. Men finished work at two in the afternoon, and people spent the rest of the day visiting. It was always a full house. My father's mum lived with us when I was young and my mother's mum would come and stay for months at a time.

My mother was very quiet, serious and hard-working, with nine children, but she always had time to kiss and cuddle. She was plump and very pretty, with two long, black plaits down to her waist. She wore Kurdish clothes: big loose pants and a long dress, with a leather cap decorated in a stitched pattern of black cotton and a bead and cotton crotcheted border, covered by a scarf. When she went visiting, she wore the traditional gold chains of medallions around her scarf and neck. We call it a *lageera*. She was friendly with everyone, and very religious. My mother prayed at home and my father often went to the mosque, and sometimes the *malla* would come to our home for dinner.

We never asked our parents about their personal history, but I know my mother's family came from Sulaimani and her father died soon after she was born. Her mother remarried. When she was 16, she married my father. His family had come from eastern Kurdistan in 1932, when he was five years old. When he was young, he supported KDP in the city.

They did not know each other before they married. Their friendship and love grew afterwards. They respected each other, and always discussed family decisions, whereas in some families, the husband and wife remain strangers and the man makes all the decisions. My father was a gentle man, who rented a shop and sold clothes for a living. He was always telling us fables and stories about our history. This was the only way we learned about ourselves, because we did not study Kurdish history at school and *amn* would confiscate any books they found. It was my father and brother who told me about Shaykh Mahmud, that he was a good man who loved his people and worked hard for freedom. The British appointed him Governor of Sulaimani in 1918, but were dishonest, so in 1919 Shaykh Mahmud rose up against the Iraq monarchy and the British. They exiled him, then brought him back as governor in 1922. When he announced that he was King of Kurdistan, they attacked him and his people again—the British using their air force for the first time against civilians—in 1923.

Only recently have we read that Sulaimani is 7800 years old. Three times it has been a city. We have a very long history and Kurds have many ancient stories, customs and beliefs. For instance my friends would talk of ghosts who could influence a person or event. If a person was sick or having bad times, they might ask the *shaykh* to write a letter, which they would put in water and drink. After this, they believed, things would get better. When my brother's child was sick, his wife came and asked, "Mahabad, please help me." She heated a metal plate on the stove and put it on her sick child and then asked me to ask her, "What are you doing?" I had to repeat this question three times and each time she would answer, "I am getting rid of the scary things," as she sprinkled a little water on the plate. Maybe these things worked. Maybe not.

Our happiest times were when all the family came together for Newroz and weddings, but these times were rare, because when Jabar and my cousins became *peshmergas* in the mountains, they could not join us.

Newroz is a big celebration of freedom and new life for Kurdish people. It is the first day of spring. The night before, all my brothers, sisters, cousins and I would collect old car tyres and wood, take them to a vacant lot and make a pile up to 10 feet high. Ten or 15 of us would gather to have a picnic, then in the late afternoon light the fire and dance. Other people went to the mountains to make fires, especially the highest, Peri Magroon, and we would watch the fires from our roof. Sometimes, just before Newroz, the soldiers collected all the boys and put them in prison, but this would not stop us. The air would be black from all the burning tyres.

The next day, 21 March, everyone goes for a big picnic in the countryside. We collect firewood and make a fire, and eat delicious food like barbecued shish kebab, dancing and singing until the fire burns out. There are special songs like *Amrojhi Sali Tazaya Newroz Hatowa*: "Today is Newroz, the time for Kurdish people, a day for celebrating freedom." The ancient legend of Newroz tells of the dictator Zohag, who killed many people, until Kawa the blacksmith killed him and lit a fire on the highest mountain. Fire became a symbol of freedom, and now Zohag represents all tyrants. In the ancient Ezidi religion, and for people who follow Zaradash,[b] fire is a symbol of the sun's light, warmth and happiness, the end of the cold, dark winter. The fire burns all death and darkness away and like the sun, brings new life.

My life was to change completely when I was 16. When I was eight years old and still in primary school, I was visiting a neighbour who was one of my best friends at school, and that day her 14-year-old cousin Sarbast was also visiting. I was very shy and quiet with strangers, so I did not take much notice of him.

I was naturally shy. In my culture, a girl is expected to be. There is a saying, "A shy woman is worth a city, a shy man is not worth a comb." A girl must be careful not to bring shame on her family; otherwise they will make her stay at home, or even kill her. My friends and I thought this was terribly wrong but we were careful. When I was in Year Seven, my friend's older sister told me, "Sarbast is now a *peshmerga* and he would like to marry you." I was shocked. I was too young and said, "Please don't tell my parents. I would be too embarrassed." Afterwards, when my friend and her sister came to my house, or I visited them to study, my friend's sister would say, "If you are free one day, Sarbast would like to talk to you." I would say, "No, I want to finish school." Girls were not allowed to marry and continue their schooling, and I was only 13.

One day I was visiting my married sister with my sister Bahar. Bahar means 'spring'. She was always a very kind sister. As we walked, Sarbast's cousins called us over, saying to Bahar, "Sarbast is here. He wants to talk to Mahabad." Bahar asked, "Who is Sarbast?" and they told her, asking, "What do you think about Mahabad marrying Sarbast?" I was 14, so they knew I could not make the decision. She said, "Let him talk to me." Sarbast came to the door and said, "Hello, *hanam* Mahabad." I was shocked. '*Hanam*' means 'madam'. I felt very uncomfortable.

Bahar told him, "Mahabad is too young and she likes school too much." He said, "Yes I know, but I want to talk about marriage." Bahar said, "I will tell my parents if you want, but it is up to her." After that Sarbast's family came to our house while I was at school. Bahar told me that our mum told them, "You are a good family, we have known you a long time, and we always help *peshmerga*, but my daughter is too young, and she can't even get a glass of water because she is so scared of the wild cats around the house."

But they kept coming back. This is not rude in our culture. They would not give up because Sarbast would not give up. One day, when I was in Year Seven, Sarbast's mother told me, "If you just agree, we will wait for you. You can come to our house and finish school there." My parents said, "It is up to you." I did not know Sarbast, but I liked that he was *peshmerga*, so I could not say no.

In 1984, while the *peshmerga* had a ceasefire with Saddam, Jabar came home secretly from the mountains and we had many visitors. Towards the end of the year, Sarbast came to our house. It was a big shock for me, but he had come to tell Jabar that they had to go back to the mountains. The negotiations had been unsuccessful and a terrible time was coming.

Some months later an old man came to our house with the *malla* and Sarbast's parents, and they said, "Sarbast is in the mountains, but he has signed this agreement to be made between Mahabad and this old man." I was so shy I could not go into the room and my father became angry, saying, "Mahabad, if you don't want to marry Sarbast, I will not agree, but if you want to marry, come and sit down." Even the *malla* told me, "The Qur'an says a woman cannot be forced into marriage. It is up to you." I told the *malla*, "Yes, I want to marry," and signed the contract.

I was engaged for one year. When *jahsh* came to know something was happening at our house, *amn* would come every week, thinking maybe we were hiding someone.

They would break the door and my father was always repairing it. The soldiers never spoke to me, but a few of my neighbours had husbands who were *peshmerga* and the soldiers would go to their house and ask, "Where is your husband?" When the wife said, "I don't know," they would bulldoze the house. It would be up to the family to repair it.

During my year of engagement, we visited Jabar in the mountains. He relayed a message from Sarbast: "Tell Mahabad to come to my village." Jabar asked my brothers, "Will Mahabad come?" One brother said, "I do not know." I was so shy I could not say anything so Jabar told them, "How can she stay home and we go?"

My family travelled in three cars to Qoolarush, about 28 kilometres of winding road over Azmar Mountain. Sarbast shook everybody's hand, but when he came to me I was trembling. After lunch he suggested we go for a walk in the orchard, and I insisted, "My family must come too."

Before the wedding, my mum and Sarbast's parents bought all we would need. Sarbast's parents joked, "But please, Mahabad, don't buy a big bedroom suite. *Peshmergas* have to be mobile, and he cannot carry too much on his back!" My mum bought very nice dishes and blankets, and a small gas stove.

As the wedding day neared, I became very scared, because I could not talk to my mother about private matters. She told my sister, "Please tell Mahabad not to be shy. Sarbast is a good boy." The night before I was to leave, my parents, cousins, friends and I stayed up all night talking and joking. In the morning my female relatives, some friends and I went to the hairdresser and beautician and dressed for the wedding. I wore pink pants underneath a long pink kaftan. Over this was another kaftan, of pale pink embroidered netting. It had the traditional long wing sleeves that are tied at the back, and on top of everything I wore a full-length pink sequined coat. We left by car, my mother crying as she sprinkled water on the road to bless us with good fortune.

At each of the four checkpoints there was a wooden roadblock with up to 10 soldiers. They would look at all the passengers—my sister, Sarbast's cousin, the driver, his wife, and me—and ask the driver, "Where are you going?" He would answer, "To visit relations." They must have known I was a bride, but maybe they thought I was going to marry a villager, so they let us through.

We arrived in Gappelon and were greeted by many people, including Jabar and Sarbast's family. Sarbast came up to me, saying, "Come, *hanam*, let's dance." I protested, "No I can't," but he took my hand and pulled. My mind was blank with shock. I was too frightened to enjoy the dancing, I did not speak to Sarbast and I ate very little. It was like I was in a dream. I could not believe it was me. I was only 16.

Sarbast had prepared a little room for us. He had put up curtains to divide the room and had made a table and an inside bathroom with a shower, and a hole in the ground for a toilet. We used a kerosene lamp and candles for light. But even on our 'honeymoon' I was too shy to eat in front of him. I am very different now. After 13 years of marriage, I talk to Sarbast, I go out, we do whatever we like to do, but back then it was slowly, slowly. It is not a good way. I was too young and I did not know anything, but Sarbast was very kind and reassured me, "I like you. I want to make a happy family and for us to have many visitors." Sarbast's friends came and gave us presents and made me feel one of them, and very quickly I began to feel happy, even with bombs exploding in the distance.

In our culture, a bride goes back to her family after three days. I had only been with Sarbast three nights, but back in Sulaimani I would wake up and wonder, "Oh my God, where is Sarbast?" I was thinking, "How can two people come to love each other so much in so short a time?"

After a few days, my family took me back to Gappelon, which was surrounded by very high mountains capped in snow and covered with wild galnut, walnut and oak trees. The village had about 50 houses, with flat land growing grapevines, fruit trees and vegetables. It was summer, and I saw how hard the village women worked with the men in the fields as well as looking after the animals and making yoghurt, cheese and bread. They were more religious than city people, but their life was more open and free. Everyone knew each other and worked and talked and laughed together, whereas in the city, girls would just go to school and come home.

For the first few days, Sarbast had a friend cook for us, or someone would invite us for a meal, so when it was finally my turn to cook, it was very hard. I had never cooked before, and even had to ask Sarbast how to cook the rice! Sarbast explained, "One glass of rice for each person." I asked for more help, but Sarbast said, "You have to learn yourself." He killed a chicken, and I plucked and boiled it, but because a visitor arrived there was not enough rice.

Sarbast worked as a mobile-radio operator, but he was often at home, and it was good to have Jabar there too. The *peshmergas* were spread over a number of villages, and would come together for meetings. I did not go. In our village there were about 20 to 50 *peshmergas*, mainly from the city, and some had wives and children. Their wives did not visit too much, because they did not know me, and also after 15 days Saddam's forces started bombarding us day and night. All the village people had to leave. Some sold their animals, some took them, and others left them behind.

The bombs were falling everywhere—some right next to our room. People had helped us make a concrete and earth shelter, like a small room within a room, half underground. We had to crawl through a little door to get into it. The shelter could fit six people, but sometimes we had to squeeze in 10 or 15 people. We would sit on a mat, and there was a pipe through the earth roof for air. Sometimes I took bread, but in a bombardment you are not hungry.

Qadir was the father of Kak Faridoon, our leader. He had spent a lot of time bringing the rocks and making the shelter strong. The young ones had not helped, because they were too busy working on the newspaper and radio, or working secretly between the village and the city. Most were not married, so they also had to cook and clean.

One time when everybody was crammed into the shelter Qadir became angry, saying, "When there were no bombs none of you came to help me." Some laughed, saying, "Don't worry Qadir, we will help next time." One funny man joked to make Qadir crankier: "Maybe this shelter will fall down on top of us. Maybe it is better to be out with the bombs!" We were lucky—only one bomb hit our house.

Kak Faridoon was on the Central Committee of Komala. I came to know him well. He was very intelligent, university-educated and a writer, who contributed to the PUK

Mahabad and Sarbast Fatah

newspaper, as he still does. Back then he lived a simple life. He liked to talk and joke with people, and visit *peshmergas'* families, especially if somebody was sick or in need of help. When a couple married, he gave them a present. He was Muslim, but I don't think he was serious in his faith. Ma'am Jalal was more religious. He prayed five times a day, and fasted for Ramadan, but he was also a simple man who shared our life.

In that month, my mum came to visit me and was shocked: I was not afraid of anything! She could not imagine me like this and she was proud. My life with the *peshmerga* was to be like a school for me. I could talk to anybody, maybe because I was married and nobody would misunderstand me, but also I saw how strong the *peshmergas* were, how they lived a hard life and cared about people, with no concern for themselves.

After two weeks of bombing, Sarbast said I had to go back to Sulaimani because the army was coming and all the *peshmergas* had to go and fight. I said, "No, Sarbast. If anything happens to you I want it to happen to me too. I can help; I can make bread." Sarbast answered, "This is fighting!" But I said, "I won't leave you."

One morning Qadir told Sarbast, "I can take Mahabad." I was crying, saying, "No, no, I am not going." Sarbast said, "We have no choice." Qadir and I started walking. I was wearing *peshmerga* clothes. It was raining, and we had to walk through a river up to our thighs. After four hours we arrived in Gurrudiah, which was deserted except for a few *peshmergas*. We went to one family—a mother and her three sons, and a wife of another son who was a famous *peshmerga*. I stayed with them, crying all night for Sarbast and Jabar. The bombs were close—we could hear the explosions and saw red streaks in the sky.

For three days we ate white beans. When other *peshmergas* came, we fed them what little we had. We used a spring for water and the village toilet. News came that all the houses in Gappelon had been destroyed. I thought about the things my mother had bought us and wanted to go and get them, so I said to Qadir, "I have to go back to

Gappelon. Sarbast might still be there." He said, "No. He will send us a letter when he has time," but I insisted, "I have to go." I was crying, so the poor man came with me, walking through the rain. When we arrived, we saw that the whole village was empty and silent. If you heard a slight sound, it was scary.

We walked back to Gurrudiah, but when the bombing became worse we walked in the rain to another village, where we found an empty house. We had only some blankets and a little rice. I was very tired, and worried because nobody knew where I was. That night I heard sounds, and the next morning Qadir told me, "The *peshmerga* came and Sarbast's cousin was with them. I told him you are safe." I said, "You should have woken me—I would have gone with him."

There was nothing to eat. We picked some spinach from the village gardens, and with the remaining rice the woman made *dolma*, simple but delicious. A few *peshmergas* came to eat. One of them was my cousin. He was surprised to see me, saying, "Come—we will send you secretly to your family." I said, "Good, but where is Sarbast?" He said, "Don't worry, Sarbast is safe. They are fighting Saddam."

For four hours we walked on a narrow trail through the mountains. By now, I was very strong. I was also pregnant. The next morning, a truck came. I changed out of my *peshmerga* clothes, and my cousin arranged with the driver to take me to Sulaimani.

When I opened the door in the wall of my home and walked into the courtyard where we kept chickens and grew a mulberry tree, Bahar ran to me. Mum came out and she was crying, and we were all hugging and kissing, mum saying, "God is good. He has brought back my daughter." She asked, "What about Sarbast and Jabar?" I said, "Leave it to God."

The doctor in Sulaimani confirmed my pregnancy. I was very unhappy. How could we raise a baby in the mountains? I thought, "I shouldn't have this baby. I should kill myself." I was always crying, but my eldest sister said to me, "Mahabad, this is your first baby and you should be happy and proud." I was fortunate—I did not have morning sickness or any other medical problems.

I could not go anywhere. No-one was allowed to know I was in the house. I passed the time with relatives and friends visiting, or reading. Sometimes I would read the PUK newspaper, printed in Kurdish and Arabic, but most of the time I read poetry. My favourite classical poets are Ahmedi Khani, Nali and Mahwi. Of the modern poets, I like Pire-Merd, Abdullah Goran, Muhammad Salah Dilan, Kakey Falah, Kameran Mukri, Hezip Qaradaghi, Hemen, Abdullah Peshiw and Sherko Bekas. I was always thinking of Sarbast, so Bekas's poem *Hope* was a favourite:

> If my love for you was rain,
> I would already be standing in it.
> If my love for you was fire,
> I would already be crouching in it.
> Oh my beloved Kurdistan!
> My poem says:
> "As long as there is rain and fire
> I will be alive."

Every night I would dream about Sarbast. Sometimes I dreamt he had been killed. After

26 days I went to Sarbast's family, and my mother-in-law cried, "Sarbast is not here, but you are. You are Sarbast for me." We locked the doors, and listened to the *peshmerga* short-wave radio reporting on the fighting and how many *peshmergas* were killed, but I heard no news of Sarbast.

After 40 days someone came in secret to my family with a letter from Sarbast, and my mum brought it. Sarbast wrote, "We are in Shadala if you want to come back." He drew a map, and wrote, "Go with your mum in a car to this place, catch another car to there, then walk. Bring some things, because we have nothing—no clothes, no bread, no blankets." My mum said, "I will take you." It was safer for women to travel—the army did not check them so much.

At about six in the morning my mum picked me up from Sarbast's family's home by car, and we drove through flat wheat country, then hills. After three hours, we got another car, and travelled over a very rough road. Finally we walked for three hours on a narrow trail, carrying blankets, food and a little stove. It was winter, but there was no snow, only grey clouds, and thick mud that stuck to our shoes. Beside the road were big rocks, and hills covered with yellow grass and bare trees.

We got to Shadala at about seven in the evening. Sarbast met us along the path and was hugging us both. He led us through a room where a villager kept sheep and goats, up an internal staircase to our new home. It was empty.

My mum stayed overnight, and the next morning Sarbast walked with her until they met people going to Sulaimani. I told Sarbast I was pregnant and very unhappy, but he was glad, saying, "It is nothing to worry about. We are Muslim, so we must accept it. It will be lovely to have a baby. Another *peshmerga* is coming."

Sarbast worked on the radio inside our room. There was a *peshmerga* group in Shadala, but no other women, although other *peshmergas* lived 20 to 120 minutes' walk away. Sometimes the owner of the house would visit to feed his animals grass and grains, but from the first night the bombs came, and the mud walls of our room would shake. I was not scared. I was determined to remain calm and quick thinking.

All day and night I would stay inside the room. I had brought some rice and lentils, and from a little shop in Shadala, Sarbast would buy the thin bread we sprinkle with water to make it soft. Sometimes, if we had money, we would buy a chicken from the local people. Our families would always help us with money, and PUK also gave us a little. But we did not have vegetables. The village was deserted and it was winter.

After a month, a bomb hit the house opposite us, and other bombs killed three *peshmergas*. They were buried quickly, in the clothes they were wearing or in their sleeping bag. Someone from the city came and told us that the army was coming, that we must escape. After we left, the army destroyed Shadala. I went back to Sulaimani for two weeks to get supplies, and then to Chokhmah. We had one mud room upstairs, and a covered wooden verandah for a kitchen. Villagers would wash in a communal spring, but because the bombs had destroyed everything, Sarbast made a new toilet and a shower: a metal drum with gas underneath to boil water, and another drum of cold water. The walls were of nylon plastic. In other places he used mud or metal sheeting.

In Chockhmah Sarbast was the only *peshmerga* from our group, so he was busy, and

I would see him only for meals. There were about four or five women and 25 *peshmergas* with their leader, Shaykh Ezzeddin Hosseini, a Kurdish nationalist from Iran, and sometimes we visited each other for meals. They were able to go to Sulaimani by car. The army roadblocks did not search their car because Iraq was helping them, and a few times they took me so that I could get supplies. We would pass up to 10 checkpoints, and when I saw the soldiers I was very nervous.

Otherwise we could buy yoghurt from two village families and for the first time I made bread from flour and water, baking it in the traditional earthen *tanoor*, remembering how my mother did it. In the winter we had rice, sometimes meat, white beans, lentils, and tomato paste. In the spring we could sometimes buy green vegetables, but never enough.

Still we were being bombed. In the daytime you could always see the planes circling, so I could not go out except to collect wood or water. I never went to the shop, a tin shed selling basic things like soap, rice and tea, even though it was only 15 metres away. I was often alone, and I would cook, read poetry, or put on the short-wave radio to hear the pilots' plan. Although it was all in number code I wanted to listen in case there was something I could understand, and I would help Sarbast by writing down the messages. We never argued. We respected each other, and kept silent if we knew the other would not like to hear something.

But after four months, Sarbast told me, "Mahabad, Saddam's army is coming. Go back to Sulaimani, because next month is your last month for the baby." I said, "No way!" but Sarbast talked to me until morning. After breakfast he said, "Mahabad, today you have to go back. We have been given orders to leave."

Sarbast and his friend were at the shop buying cigarettes when I heard the loud rumble of planes. We did not have any shelter, so I sat in a corner, covered my ears and prayed, before dashing down the outside stairs to Kherman, who had a baby in a wooden rocker. Two *peshmergas* came inside, one man's hand and forehead injured from the bomb, so I got some material and tore it, bandaging his injuries to stop the blood. Suddenly Sarbast came running into the house, shouting, "Where is Mahabad?" He was frantic, having seen blood in the courtyard. He hugged me, even though it is not considered polite in front of others.

We had to leave immediately, in case the planes returned. There was another village close by where some more Iranian Kurdish *peshmergas* lived, and they would help us. I took nothing, and about one kilometre from Chokhmah, I suddenly remembered we had left a rifle behind. I decided to go back for it. On my way I passed a spring, 50 metres from a house, and a lady lay beside it. Next to her was her baby. She had come from Iran only three days ago to visit her husband after a long separation, and now she was dead. Her husband was going crazy beside her, a few people trying to calm him. When I saw this broken family, I forgot about myself.

I walked back to Sarbast and the other *peshmergas*, a woman and a child. After two hours we arrived in the next village, and Sarbast insisted that I go back to Sulaimani the next day. We had something to eat, and slept without blankets, but a few hours of bombs and seeing people dead and injured makes you tired.

The next morning Sarbast told me, "Mahabad—you must not come back until you have the baby." I was too tired to argue. On the way we were very scared, because Saddam's army was searching all the cars, even the Iranian *peshmerga's*.

It took us four hours, and I went straight to Sarbast's family. They were kind, but I was missing Sarbast. We knew there was heavy fighting, and there was no news. Every day my mum came to see me, but I did not want her at the birth. I was too shy; we had never talked about how a baby comes. Even now, with my own daughter, I do not talk about these matters. So far, she has not asked.

As life goes, my mum was at the birth, along with Sarbast's brother, aunt and a Kurdish nurse. I was so shy with my mum, but Sarbast's brother was like a friend. Sarbast's aunt said, "Please, Mahabad, it is normal. Your mum would like to be here." I was in pain, but I did not know I was in labour. I began crying for Sarbast as soon as the pain passed. My mum took the baby. Three days later, a doctor visited us and circumcised Zirian. We had a quiet dinner, not the usual celebration, because I was a *peshmerga*'s wife. There was never a celebration for a daughter's circumcision. A midwife would do it all in secret. I do not agree with this practice and fortunately, most people in and around Sulaimani do not do it any more.

Sarbast sent a letter through an Iranian Kurdish man, and I was crying for happiness as I read: "I told my friends that I had a dream last night. I was in the water and I grabbed one big fish." To dream of a fish means good news is coming. It was the next day, on 14 May 1987, that Zirian was born. The man went back to Sarbast and said, "I have good news for you, but you have to give me a present first." Sarbast laughed because he already knew.

In the beginning, I was not so close to the baby. My mum knew I was young and missing Sarbast, so she and my sister-in-law looked after him. But over the next month I began to enjoy breastfeeding, carrying and changing him. When he was one month old, my sister took him to hospital to be vaccinated. Ten days later, Sarbast wrote, "Come back. Everything had been destroyed," so my mum and I took money, blankets, clothes, another little stove, and some powdered milk for Zirian. My mother accepted all this as part of the *peshmerga* life.

It took us five hours by car and truck to get to Sarbast's family's village. We stayed overnight and mum and I continued by truck. As we drove into Shadala, I saw Sarbast standing with a group of *peshmergas*. He came over smiling, and straight away asked, "Please give me the baby." He was hugging the baby, and me and my mum all together. He took us to his friend's house. We did not have time on our own, but it was very good to be with him.

The next morning he said, "Mahabad, you have to go back. Where I am going, we don't have a house. I will send for you as soon as I can." I cried, and my mum scolded me, but then we got in the car with Sarbast's brother. A little way from the village, a plane flew over, heading in the direction of Shadala. We hid under rocks and soon heard the bombs. We were worried about Sarbast and Sarbast was worried about us.

About three weeks later, Sarbast sent a message to come to Yehksemar. We lived in a shelter Sarbast had made from four poplar poles and a roof of poplars, leaves and soil. No walls. There were about 30 or 40 *peshmergas*, and only three other wives, although Jabar and my cousin were there. When the planes came, we would all go to the shelter and Zirian would cry and cry. Sometimes the shelter was full of water, and I would have to sit in the water with Zirian held above my chest. It was dark and I would lose his bottle.

I was always tired and worried. My mother sent powdered milk, but sometimes we ran out, and when there was not enough food for ourselves, my breast milk dried up. Also there was nowhere for the baby to sleep except on the ground, and it was summer, so there were many snakes and scorpions. Sarbast found a suitcase, and we took off the lid and put some nice material in the bottom and hung it with thick rope from a wooden pole. It became Zirian's rocker.

At least we had electricity from a petrol-run generator, and a communal bathroom. Two *peshmergas* cooked for the whole group, and mostly we ate together in the *mukharr*, Arabic for *barrigah*, the group house. My days were spent reading poetry, praying and looking after Zirian. Even so, I can say I enjoyed this life. It was hard, but simple and we had chosen it. We believed in it. There were not the worries we have now about having enough money.

But in late September 1987 the chemical bombs came. There was no warning, except that the sound was different—they were not big explosions, more like balloons bursting. Then came a smell like onion or garlic. It affected our eyes, skin and brain. We ran up the mountain. There were no trees or rocks to hide behind, and all we could do was look down at our shelters and up into the wide blue sky. There were about 20 people, including Talabani and his wife. Zirian was the only child. After three hours, we went back down to find a white powder over everything, including the water in the tank. I had to clean and wash everything.

The Iranian government heard about the chemical attacks, and sent protective clothes made of stiff nylon cloth, and a hard helmet with a clear visor, and a mask connected by black plastic tube to an oxygen bag. The oxygen could last for 30 minutes. We received training in how to use the clothing and mask, and in how to give ourselves an injection in the thigh after a bomb.

For winter, we moved down the mountain to the valley, where Sarbast had prepared a room with a concrete floor. Under this we could make a fire to heat the room to wash in. There was also a verandah, where I cooked, using a kerosene lamp for light. Sarbast hung some nylon for a front door and dug a hole and put up some nylon walls for a toilet outside. He also prepared an underground shelter three metres from the house.

It was a very cold winter, with lots of snow. For warmth, we used a traditional *sopah*, but still we were cold. Three families lived in this village, and we often visited each other and sometimes ate together. Jabar and my cousin were living in the next valley, in a village called Kuzlur. I sometimes walked there, two hours over the mountain, and they would also visit us. On 31 December 1987, I invited them for dinner with two families. When it came time for Jabar and my cousin to leave, I hugged them, saying, "Please come back for Newroz." Jabar replied, "*En Sha Allah*."[c]

In February 1988, we sensed danger. One wife of a *peshmerga* went to the city and never returned. She simply disappeared. Her husband waited 11 years before he married again. We knew that the army was heading towards Yehksemar, and Sarbast was always telling me, "Keep Zirian's clothes and powdered milk in a suitcase, and pack some money and gold jewellery, so that if something happens, we are ready." It is a Kurdish tradition to give a baby a gold necklace with a blue charm to protect the child from the evil eye, and we had put this and some money for Zirian in a money box in the suitcase, as well as all our photos and other precious things.

At about three in the afternoon, on 24 February, I went to my neighbour's house and she exclaimed, "Mahabad, did you know Zirian has his first tooth? You have to have a party." This is a tradition. We cook a special soup called *shorba*, made from wheat germ, chick peas, meat, salt and water, which we take around to our neighbours, but these ingredients were difficult to get. Instead of the soup, Sarbast went and bought some chickens from a wooden shed that was taken from village to village on the back of a truck. I cooked the rice and chicken with white beans in a tomato paste followed by custard from powder my mum had sent me. When the party was finished, one family went home and the other settled down to sleep.

At 1.50 am we woke to bomb explosions so loud the room was shaking. Zirian was crying. Sarbast told us to put on our protective clothing, but Zirian did not have special clothes—all I could do was wrap him in one dry blanket and a wet blanket. We were confused about what to do, because the bombs were mixed—normal and chemical. Should we go to a high place to escape the chemicals or go to the underground shelter? There was snow and it was very, very cold, so we all packed into the shelter—five adults and four children—and prayed.

The shelter was shaking and the noise made our ears whirr. Then we heard screams for help. Sarbast went to see who was hurt and when he came back he told us, "Six neighbours have been killed. Others are injured." Sarbast used the radio to call Ma'am Jalal's *barrigah* for help, but he could not get through for some time.

We waited around a fire. All of us had a headache, some were vomiting and some could not see at all. I was very worried for Zirian. A *peshmerga* told me, "Keep the wet towel over him and *en sha Allah*, nothing will happen to us before the car arrives." The land cruiser came at about 3 am. It had not been able to start in the cold. The driver took everyone, seven kids and six adults, up the mountain to the *barrigah*. When people saw our red eyes, they said, "You must go to the hospital in Bargalo."

We piled into the land cruiser, but halfway there the car ran out of petrol, so we walked through the snow in the dark night, unable to see, still hearing bombs.

At sunrise we crossed a river by linking hands, Sarbast holding Zirian. It was numbingly cold. Some *peshmergas* from Bargalo came running down to help us and saw immediately we were not well. Sarbast was very sick. He had water streaming from his eyes and nose. Kak Farhad, a good friend, took Zirian, saying, "I will give the baby to my wife to feed." Zirian was crying with hunger and cold and the noise of the bombs, but Kak Farhad told me, "Go to the *barrigah* and then to the hospital and get an injection." At the *barrigah* they prepared a breakfast of yoghurt, cheese, jam and thin bread, but we could not eat because of the effect of the chemicals. Everyone was vomiting and our headaches were worse. My mind was like a heavy morning fog. It was daytime, but my vision was so dim and blurred, I thought it was night. Some people were panicking because they were blind. The hospital was only 200 metres, but we were so tired it seemed further. There were two clean rooms and no beds. We were taking showers and being given injections when the bombs started again. We went and hid under some rocks. Soon, injured people started arriving. I saw one man who had lost a hand, and another whose face, body, legs and arms were black with chemical burns.

After our treatment we went to Kak Farhad's house. That night there was another bombardment of conventional and chemical bombs. We could see the chemicals, and my eyes and skin were burning. Sarbast was so sick they took him to a shelter, but the rest of us walked up a narrow way between two cliff faces. Sometimes we had to squeeze through sideways, and more than 20 people climbed up to a narrow entrance of a cave, then down into a small chamber.

We had no food or water and there were people pressing on all sides. My back was stuck against a rough wall, and my bangles cut into my skin when I tried to breastfeed Zirian with both knees up to my chest, Zirian lying between them. The cave had a hole in its roof to the open air, which was good for breathing but no good for the rain that fell all night. We were all hungry, wet and cold. The bombardment continued. At least no-one was vomiting because there was no food in our stomachs!

At sunrise a family went down to their house to get some bread and water for everyone. Later we heard a Iranian helicopter land and we came out of the cave. The *peshmergas* who were most affected went on the first flight, but the doctors sent a letter telling the Iranians that we all needed hospitalisation.

All day we stayed in the clearing, eating only a little bread and water. Some of us continued to vomit, but later, in Iran we were told this vomiting expelled the chemicals from our bodies. In the afternoon we went down, but when the bombing resumed we went to the shelter. After a few days, a helicopter had room for us.

The journey to Baneh, in eastern Kurdistan, took about 45 minutes, flying between high mountains covered in snow, green valleys far below. Zirian was crying, but Kak Farhad's wife had given me powdered milk, plus a change of clothes for him and me. I will never forget her kindness. On the flight, I felt hopeless, that there was no safety anywhere: we had lost everything.

When we landed near Baneh hospital, all the nurses and doctors came out wearing special clothes, saying, "We don't want to touch you, because of the chemicals." They gave us fresh orange juice, took us to a room with beds and gave us an injection. We stayed some hours, and then were taken to Saguez. Bombs starting dropping, so they sent us to Khomeini Hospital, a modern multistorey building in Tabriz. We were there for 18 days.

Every day they gave us an injection, and fresh fruit and vegetables, and every few hours they made us take cold showers. The treatment was free. But then Iraqi bombs started dropping near the hospital. A siren would go off ,and everyone would run to the hospital shelter.

I was worried about my family and friends back in Iraqi Kurdistan, particularly Jabar and my cousin, who had gone to the fighting. Sarbast was sad all the time and had grown a beard. In our culture, if someone close dies, men do not shave. After a week, we went for a walk. I wanted to buy a shirt for Jabar and my cousin, as I had always promised to do if we ever went to Iran, but Sarbast advised, "Don't buy anything until they get here."

When the hospital let us leave, we went to Saghez, five hours by public bus. All the *peshmergas* were in Saghez, and they sent us to a hotel where PUK were paying for Iraqi Kurd families to stay. We shared a room with two other families.

I could not relax. People were talking about all the relatives they had lost. The next day Sarbast said, "Mahabad, we are going to have visitors." When they came, they told me Jabar was dead. I screamed and cried uncontrollably. I had lost my dearest brother. He was seven years older than me, but he was my closest friend. Everyone was crying with me, and Sarbast pleaded, "Mahabad, it is not only you. We are all sad. Please calm down." Jabar was killed in fighting on 28 February, while we were in Bargalo, but Sarbast had not wanted to tell me. He had held back his tears until this day.

Jabar was very handsome, very quiet and kind, and very funny. He joked with everyone, and was a very good listener. I could talk with him always, particularly when we lived the *peshmerga* life. If Sarbast and I were having a small disagreement, he would always distract us and make us happy. When I was too sad from missing my family, he would say, "*Peshmerga* must be strong. Look what a stupid enemy we have!" Even when we were young, we would go out together and dance. He was always joking and singing, but he gave up the life for Kurdistan.

After a week, we heard that our house in Yehksemar had been destroyed, along with our suitcase, and we were told it was not safe to return. We went to look for a house in Saghez, a modern city with high-rise buildings and concrete-brick houses, but we did not have enough money, so we shared two rooms with another family. It was very cold and we had no blankets. Zirian became sick. The house belonged to a Kurdish family who lived in another section, but after two nights we all had to leave, because we discovered their brother-in-law was working with Khomeini and for Saddam.

We rented a room in a house with one bedroom and a kitchen. We told the other family to have the bedroom; we stayed in the kitchen. There was no tap water. We had to pump the water, with a very hard pump. The house was far from the shops, so we were always using a taxi. Finally we found another room, with a family in Bilwar, a suburb where rich people live, closer to the city. When we arrived, our neighbours came and welcomed us, and when the lady saw we had only a rug and two blankets, she brought us blankets and pillows. After six months, we had to leave this family because their cousin was coming, and their neighbours told us, "Please stay with us." We said, "Thank you. We will come, but we must pay rent." They agreed, "All right, pay what you can." We stayed for two years.

Sarbast continued to work on the *peshmerga* radio. He would get some money from PUK, and our families sent a little, but there was never enough. Fortunately the Kurdish family with whom we lived was very kind to us. They were teachers, with three sons, and were always giving us food. Sometimes they invited us to eat with them, and at other times I would cook them our dishes. That we spoke the same language and shared a similar culture helped.

In Iran, Kurds and Persians celebrate Newroz with a 14-day holiday. As well as going to the mountains for picnics, it is customary for Iranian Kurds to plant wheat on a plate. When the green sprouts come up, they give away the plate to be used as a table or windowsill decoration. They also boil and paint eggs to give to children. Zirian was 18 months old, and our neighbour gave him a plate of sprouts and two colourful eggs.

But it was a life we had not chosen. We had never been so far away from our family and country, and we did not know if we could ever go back. Zirian was growing up without relatives and spent all his time with me. I was always crying, and Sarbast was constantly worried about *peshmerga* matters, but I think we grew closer because we had to rely on each other. Friends visited, but I mourned all the people's lives and the villages that had been destroyed. Also we could not plan for anything.

Three times in those three years I went back secretly to visit my family. A month after we arrived in Saghez, one brother came to Iran, by car and truck and on foot, to ask if we knew anything about Jabar. People had heard he had died, but my family were not sure. Before he left, he told me mum was sick. I knew she had high blood pressure, because of all the worry about Jabar and us, but that was all. Sarbast warned, "If you want to visit her, you can, but you know it's dangerous."

Sarbast and I travelled in secret, taking turns to ride a horse. I had never ridden a horse before, and had to carry Zirian tiedin front of me by a blanket and belt around my waist. Snow was everywhere. Sometimes it was flat country, at other times a steep climb or descent as we skirted Qandil. Once, when Sarbast was carrying Zirian, his horse lost its footing. Sarbast fell, keeping hold of Zirian. Occasionally, we heard the roar of a river beneath the snow and the horse's leg would go through into the river.

In the first village, Iranian *peshmergas* showed us the way to avoid an Iraqi army base. We slept overnight in another village and rode the horses and walked until we found a car with a trustworthy driver. Sarbast said goodbye, telling me to go to an Iranian *peshmerga*'s house in Rania, a small city on the plain. We had lived with these friends in Chokhmah when I was pregnant. It was strange: they were Iranian Kurds allowed to live in Iraq, and we were Iraqi Kurds allowed to live in Iran!

In Rania, the Iraqi government and army were everywhere, and the next morning Zirian and I got a taxi to Sulaimani. The driver kept asking me, "Why are you travelling alone?" and I became scared that he might be *jahsh*. I had to lie, "I am a teacher and I go to visit my parents."

When I saw my mum, I was shocked. Her right side was totally paralysed. She was bedridden. I was crying, because nobody had told me, and we were all crying for Jabar, even though no-one told mum about Jabar's death for another three years in case she died of grief. But I think she knew. All the time she would cry, and ask, "Where is Jabar? Why have we not heard?" She spent the last 10 years of her life in bed. Bahar refused to marry, saying she had to look after her. Mum died in 1997. My father died of a heart attack in November 1998. Bahar is now in Syria, and I hope to bring her to Australia.

I went back the way I had come. It took two days, but if you go by the Hamilton Road it takes two hours. In July 1988, the Iraq–Iran War ended and Saddam turned all his troops and weaponry to fighting the Kurds. We were very scared. Now only Kurds were fighting Saddam.

Sarbast was working every day on the *peshmerga* radio, so during 1990 I kept busy helping to establish a group for women called the Women's Union of Kurdistan. We produced a monthly magazine, in which we published women short-story writers and poets, and articles advocating that women be more active outside the home. We also wanted to educate people against the killing of women in the name of family honour.

In August 1990, we heard that Saddam Hussein had invaded Kuwait. I was not surprised. The following winter was very cold. We had no kerosene for heating water or the room. It was just before the uprising, and Sarbast was so busy that we might not see each other for a week. Always I was listening to *peshmerga* radio. They were reporting, "Secretly, we are coming to the dance at this time and place, and we will walk together." People knew the meaning—that an uprising was being planned in every city.

When the uprising started in March, my hope returned after three long, dark years. Sarbast went back to Iraqi Kurdistan. After three weeks, my neighbour asked me to come to her house to take a telephone call. It was Sarbast. "I am in Sulaimani now. We are successful." I was so happy. For so long, I had been looking forward to the day Kurdish people would be free. He continued, "I will send you a letter or call you to tell you when to come back."

A few weeks later, I was watching Iranian television at a friend's house when the news showed Iraqi forces bombing Kurdish cities. There were pictures of people escaping across a big river, using ropes. Some fell into the river. Many could not swim, especially the children, and some drowned.

I went with friends looking for people in the camps near Saghez. The camps were like prisons: rows of tents or concrete rooms surrounded by high concrete walls. People were not allowed to leave. At one camp, a Kurdish man told me, "Sarbast's family is in the next camp." I took a taxi. Sarbast's family saw me through the wire, calling, "Don't worry, Mahabad—we are all safe, and so is your family." I was given permission to take them, 30 people in all, to my house. My neighbours gave me clothes and anything they could spare.

Finally, Sarbast arrived home. He had been away for 40 days. All we could think about was how to build the uprising again, but we were also worried about Sarbast's *peshmerga* brother, and I still had not seen my family, except my father, who had turned up on my doorstep one day. Sarbast came with me to the camp where they were living. It was night time, and my mum was very sick. A Kurdish ambulance driver helped us take her back to our house, and when we carried her in, she was crying out with pain.

In June, the Kurdish people and *peshmergas* began another uprising, forcing Saddam's army out of Sulaimani, so we decided to go back with the family. We went around visiting our relatives, staying one night here, a few nights there. We had enough food, and were happy to see our city without soldiers on the street, but it was a hard time: so many *peshmergas* had been killed, and people were scared that Saddam would return.

We spent 10 months in a village called Galala, Sarbast working on the radio. We were free, but still I was scared for Zirian. There was food and no bombs, but in the heat of summer there were too many scorpions. At night, Sarbast would kill up to 15 at a time.

Sarbast started to talk about going to Australia. "If we don't like it, we can come back." He was tired of the life, and the threat of Saddam. We discussed it, and headquarters agreed. Sarbast's family did not. His mum asked, "Why do you go to another country? For a long time you have paid for our dream to come true." Sarbast explained, "Before, we could not leave the Kurdish people to Saddam's army, but now that we are free, we can have a rest in Australia." We knew it was going to be a permanent move, but told our families it was a holiday. We were all crying.

We left by bus in October 1991, with my brother and another family. Two days after we arrived in Ankara, we went to the PUK office. Ma'am Jalal was there. When we told him we were going to Australia, he said, "I will write a letter saying you are *peshmergas*." The letter was helpful. At the Australian Embassy, everything was fixed up in one day.

We told the embassy that people in Australia could sponsor us. We did not realise this meant we had to pay for the flight, so it took five months to arrange the money for the tickets. It was hard, because Turkey was very expensive. To rent a house, you had to pay six months in advance, but Sarbast found an apartment being vacated. We were lucky to eat twice a day. Sarbast sold my gold for about $1500, but it was not enough for the tickets and we did not want to ask our family. We had to borrow from our friend in Australia, who had to borrow from a bank. In Australia, we paid him back every month.

We flew out from Ankara on 21 March 1992. Newroz. By the time we arrived in Sydney, I was panicking. Friends came to meet us, but I was crying all the way to Liverpool because I realised how far away and strange this country was and that I might never see my family again.

We went to our friends, then to a very clean and tidy hostel in Villawood. After four days our friends helped us rent a flat, with help from Social Security. Without this help, we would have had no food, nothing.

The language was the hardest thing, even though I had learnt some English at school and from television. I went to English classes, and although I was five months' pregnant I dreamed of going back to study and finding work.

I continue to pray at home, and fast at Ramadan. It is not hard to be a Muslim in Australia. People can be whatever they want. I have never worn a *hijab*, except for praying. For me, the most important thing for a Muslim is to be kind, honest and reliable. Having said this I would still like my children to marry a Muslim and a Kurd.

Despite the civil war in Kurdistan (1994–98), in August 1996 we went back for a holiday. We were in Europe visiting friends when Saddam's army bombed Hawler on 31 August. We flew to Iran, still hoping to cross the border, but in Mariwan, Sarbast's brother told us that our family and all the PUK *peshmerga* had escaped and were living in Iranian refugee camps.

For 30 days we went from camp to camp outside Baneh and Saghez, visiting family and old friends. At the checkpoints, they could not understand our Australian travel documents. We stayed in Sayranbek camp, and could hear bombs. There was not enough food. Darya, my daughter, became sick. We were only in Sulaimani for 12 days. There were no shops open, all the buildings had been damaged, and although Saddam's forces had left, KDP and PUK were fighting outside the city. The people felt that Masoud Barzani had betrayed their country by inviting Saddam back to Kurdistan, and were very angry.

However there were other changes, which became even more accentuated after 1998. Although Islam is getting stronger and most women are expected to wear a *hijab*, when they did not before, girls in Sulaimani are no longer expected to be quiet and shy! Women are now active in every profession, many becoming writers, singers, actresses and teachers. Yet even now you would never see couples kissing and hugging in public or unmarried couples living together.

In Australia, my relationship with Sarbast has become closer, but really there is no difference. Sarbast continues to work too hard, now as a house painter and also for his community. Before I had my fourth baby, I was trying to find work. Sarbast did not mind as long as it did not affect our family life, but it was very difficult for a refugee without experience, and the jobs expected up to 12-hour days and a minimum of five days a week. I thought how difficult it must be even for Australian women with a family.

In most respects I am glad we are living in Australia, but we miss our friends and family. We love our country too much. If we forget our first mother, then one day we will forget our second mother. We can care for both Australia and Kurdistan, and here we have freedom to speak our language, and practise our culture and choose our way of life. But true freedom is when people have their own country and are free from war.

I try to be a good mum. Zirian speaks Kurdish and English. He does well at school and has many friends, but says he would like to go and live in Kurdistan to be with his cousins, and when asked, "Would you like to be a *peshmerga*?" he says, "I'd give it a go."

My third child, Daroon, is three years old. He wears a traditional necklace, made of cotton, with little gold charms, including a tiny Qu'ran and an Australian koala. Darya is eight years old. Her only experiences of Kurdistan are of sleeping in a refugee camp, not having enough food, becoming sick, falling off a donkey into a cold river and hearing the sounds of fighting. But when her last tooth fell out, she put it in an envelope for the tooth fairy. When, later, she opened the envelope and saw her father's gift of $100, Sarbast commented, "Wow, the tooth fairy was generous. You can put it in your bank account," but Darya gave me the money, saying, "No. Keep this for Kurdistan."

We will never give up our hope for Kurdistan, it is just that we do not want our children to suffer as we did.

The Lost Golden Poplar Trees

By Abbas Boskany

Like a shy hill-partridge,
You come and bring all colours with you.

Like a timid gazelle in a forest,
You run and take away all colours:

"When you are not around,
Everything is black and white."

In the Land of a Thousand Sighs

A life story based on interviews with Sarbast Fatah

Peshmerga means: "You see your death before you die, so you are not afraid." I became a *peshmerga* because I wanted my country to be free and democratic. I had just turned 18. The representative of my cell had wanted me to work inside Sulaimani, or go into the army where I could obtain information, guns and bullets, but I had always dreamed of going to the mountains. My family did not agree with my decision, although my father had been a *peshmerga*. But most families had at least one member who had joined the revolution.

On 25 December 1982, I walked to Fa'el, a village 20 minutes from Sulaimani. It had not snowed as much for 20 years. I stayed with my aunt, waiting for a letter of introduction from my representative in the city. After five days, I set out alone, the temperature 10 degrees below zero, wearing only a shirt. I walked in snow up to my knees, in a long valley with snow-covered mountains on either side, passing through small villages of 10 to 50 houses every half hour or so. After six hours, I arrived at Qazlar, staying the night with a Komala cadre.

I was so tired. The cadre fed me, and gave me two blankets, and I slept on the floor, the next day walking for three hours through even deeper snow until I reached Chokhmah. That night I stayed with Mamoosta Ra'aof. *Mamoosta* means 'teacher'. He was to be killed by chemical bombs in the village of Shanakhsi in 1988.

On the third day, I walked for four and a half hours to the village of Haladin, where I was directed to a house. Two *peshmergas* stood guard at the door. I showed them the letter and they let me in. Ten men aged from 16 to 45 were sitting in a circle, Kalashnikovs nearby. They immediately began laughing at me, saying, "Here's another crazy man who wants to leave the good life in the city!" I gave my letter to Jabar Farman, the PUK political representative for over 100 villages in the area. The others started asking: "How is the city?" "Do you know so-and so?" "What is happening at the university?" All were single men, except Jabar Farman and the two from the village.

So began my 10-month stay with this political branch based at Haladin. Heavy snows continued until April. It was a quiet period, because Saddam was busy with his war with Iran, so my family was able to visit three times. Otherwise, I would get news from people travelling through.

There was no formal training. A small group would sit in a house or under a tree and someone would show us how to clean and use the gun. Whether or not I chose to go to the front line, I had to be familiar with the Russian Kalashnikov, and the heavier Russian BKC machine gun, all our weapons being taken from government stores. Other types of weapons were useless. We would often run out of bullets and have to grab ammunition from a soldier. It was not until 1986 that PUK began buying smuggled weapons on the black market.

There were meetings once a month for new people. The policies, strategies and goals of PUK would be explained: what we were fighting for, how the strategies used in the revolutions of Vietnam, Algeria and Cuba applied to us, how to keep ourselves safe, and how to communicate new ideas, while at the same time respecting the mosque and village customs.

Our aim was for self-determination within a democratic multiparty federal government of Iraq. Once this was achieved, a referendum could be put to the people to find out whether they wanted to separate. The majority of us hoped for independence.

There were only two areas of disagreement. One was how we should work with the other parties. Cooperation requires open communication and tolerance, and some people argued that KDP was too traditionalist and conservative. The other argument was how to deal with *jahsh* after we achieved democracy. Not all *jahsh* were our enemy. PUK had a special branch whose members worked inside the army or administration, although no one worked directly for the Amn or Estikhbarat. From these we would receive information indirectly, via two to three links. Also, many *jahsh* passed on information to their relatives.

Between meetings we travelled from village to village in a unit of about 25 *peshmergas*, educating people about Komala and PUK and our wish to build a democratic government. Sometimes the village people did not accept our modern ideas, saying the old ways had served them well.

In the Sulaimani region, there were more than 15 tribes, with an *agha* for each tribe. Until the 1960s, their power was so great that if an *agha* liked a girl, she had to sleep with him. Her family could do nothing. If there was no marriage, the family would have to leave the area out of shame. By the 1980s, the *agha*s in the liberated areas from Sulaimani to Hawler had less power. They were not *jahsh*, or if they had a link with the government, it was secret. Some supported PUK and some belonged to PUK, unlike most *agha*s outside the liberated areas, who were paid by the government to organise their followers to spy, or capture *peshmergas*. In this way, the government maintained these *agha*s' power base, so they continued to administer the law at their own discretion.

When PUK found out about an *agha*'s link with Saddam, they would send him a warning letter. If we were not sure about the link—maybe an informant had a personal vendetta—PUK would observe the *agha*'s activities, and if the link was proved he would be warned. Some escaped, but if after two or three warnings the *agha* still kept his link, he would be killed.

To replace the *agha* system and teach people about democracy, from 1983 PUK began setting up village councils called *shura* or *anjuman* in the liberated areas. The PUK team leader responsible for social activities would go to a village and announce that in a week's time, there would be a meeting to elect three to seven representatives, who would liaise with the *peshmerga*. Most people in a village knew each other, many were related, and during that week, everyone would discuss who should be their representatives.

The meeting would always be held inside the mosque, as was the tradition, so women could not attend. Village women never went inside the mosque, but PUK could not change the venue, because already we were sometimes accused of being against God in our socialist ideology. Most women did not come to the meeting, and those who did had to sit outside. They could not directly vote—all they could do was talk to their husbands beforehand.

There would be a show of hands to elect the representatives, and sometimes the elected men did not support PUK. The *peshmerga* would still go to the village, because we had to pass through one village to reach another. We knew the families who were sympathetic, and usually we would stay with them two days in every month. They became our friends.

But even if *peshmergas* came to a strange house, the women would put on the *samowah*, prepare a meal, and usually stay and talk, whether their husband was present or not. The people were poor but they fed us whatever they had available. They would give us blankets to sleep in their visitor's room, or in the corner of the mosque, or in some villages a special room for travellers.

Over the next few days we would ask the village representatives what they needed and some would say a new mosque or a room for a school. Most villages did not have a school, and from 1982 the Iraqi government did not allow teachers to go to the liberated areas. A few villages did not want a school, but if they did, PUK would help the people build one and would supply a teacher.

We would then return to base and stay two to 14 days in every month, the longer periods being in winter when there was too much snow and rain. At the base, we made our own meals and washed our clothes, taking turns on guard duty.

In those first 10 months, sometimes I was happy, sometimes I was lonely—thinking about a better life. I would ask myself, "Why are we here?" especially when we were at the base doing nothing but reading books about revolutions and some novels. (One novel I read was *Janegal* or *Nation of Pain* by Ibrahim Ahmed.) We would get very restless, and I would be reminded of a Kurdish proverb, 'At the beginning work is sweet. By the end it can be bitter. Fortunate is he who can swallow both ends.'

The solitude and mountain air would flood my mind with memories. They still play like a tape in my mind. Since Iraq was established, all our problems have stemmed from politics, so 90 per cent of Kurdish people lead a political life. My family was no different. My mother told me that at the time of my birth, she lay under a native tree called a *coa'ot*, with only my aunt to help her, while Iraqi jets and helicopters bombed and shot at our village of Qoolarush,[a] machine-gun bullets showering down five metres from where she lay. I was just a few weeks old when the aeroplanes returned, backed by soldiers on the ground. To protect us my mother covered my brother and me with her body.

The Kurds have a long history of struggle. About five to 10 minutes' walk outside the village there was a special place marked by four enormous, very old trees. Two were galnut trees that we call *mazzoo*, their nuts used to treat skin conditions and injuries. Two were walnut trees that we call *barroo*. These trees mark the graves of Muslim soldiers killed fighting Ezidi and Zoroastrian Kurds. No-one touches them, because the people believe misfortune will befall anyone who does. Every village has graves from that fighting. There are landmarks all over Kurdistan, always with a story behind them.

Between Sulaimani and Kirkuk there is a big rock called *Barda Karraman* or 'Rock of the Hero'. Shaykh Mahmud was injured behind this rock when fighting British and Iraqi forces between 1919 and 1931.

Qoolarush is about 28 kilometres north-east of Sulaimani, in a little valley behind a big mountain called Azmar. Once it was a village of 90 houses, but when I was growing up there were only 10 mud and stone houses, with cement floors, and flat roofs of timber covered with plastic and mud, built on small hills close to the springs. All the people were our relatives.

Next to the village, my father had a big farm, where he grew grapes, apples and vegetables like beans and okra, and raised sheep. Our house had three rooms, plus another for visitors. The Kurdish custom is to have many visitors, and in the early 1970s, I remember KDP *peshmergas* visiting our home at night. The *peshmerga* were my heroes. They would sit, eat, and discuss with my father their dream for an independent country. I would dream of a soccer team playing under the Kurdish flag.

Four army bases or *raba'aya* were located on Azmar. Three *raba'aya* had about 10 soldiers, the main one about 50, and always they watched the village through binoculars. If they saw anything suspicious, they would send in the helicopters. A helicopter would fly over about once a week, the soldiers shooting a few rounds just to scare people. Many times the military came searching for people, and three times they burned the village. The first time was in 1961—before I was born. When the soldiers came, my father went to the mountain and hid in a hole in the side of a well for two days.

My father liked reading—he had about 50 history books written in Kurdish, but they were burned with the house. He could rebuild the house but he could never replace the books. Throughout our history, our books have been taken from us. He always encouraged our education, and I liked studying. Seven children from the village, including four of my brothers and I, would walk for 90 minutes over the mountain to a school in the village of Khumza. I was the youngest. School started at eight, and I remember crying at the thought of walking through the snow and dark of winter. I was always scared that a wolf or a fox might attack us. We were taught in Kurdish, sitting two or three to a desk, mostly one teacher for all classes. In Year Five, we began studying the Arabic language, but our schooling was often interrupted by the revolution.

When the Ba'aths came to power in 1968, I was four years old. Ahmed Hasan Al-Bakr was president and Saddam Hussein was vice-president, but people used to say, "There is no difference between the black dog and the white dog." Like all the governments, they negotiated with the Kurds, then fought, then negotiated and fought again. When the fighting resumed in 1974, the revolution was very strong. People were united behind Mostefa Barzani, and the USA and the Shah of Iran were supporting the revolution, so KDP were able to buy BKCs and RPGs.

At the end of the summer of 1974, when I was about 10, the front line came to Azmar. We could hear gunfire and bombs exploding and could see soldiers. That night, at about 3 am, we escaped. My father and mother took us six children up a small mountain track between the trees. It was a dark night, with no moon and many stars, and there were snakes. I was scared by every noise, even the scampering rabbits. We looked back to see 200 soldiers leading horses loaded with cans of kerosene. There was no road for trucks. We watched as they ran between the houses, setting everything on fire.

For the next nine months, my family and our 1000 sheep lived in pastureland between the two villages of Mararush, which means 'black snake', and Moakeba. Three brothers from Mararush owned the land, and let us live there freely. They even sent people to help us build rooms for winter. I did not go to school. Then in March 1975, the Kurdish revolution collapsed when Iran and Iraq signed the Algiers Agreement. Under instruction from the USA, the Shah of Iran called Barzani to Tehran and gave him two choices: "If you continue your revolution, we won't support you and you will have to leave Iran, or you can end your revolution and you and your *peshmergas* will be safe." Within 24 hours 130,000 *peshmergas*, including my father, stopped fighting. Most handed in their guns. It was very sad for us. After this I vowed I would never join KDP. Fortunately, another party called Komala had been secretly formed by this time. It was politically active, although all *peshmergas* supported Barzani.

Three months after the end of the revolution, on 10 June 1975, Jalal Talabani announced a confederation called the Patriotic Union of Kurdistan. Apart from some non-aligned people, there were three groups, each with its own secretary. Talabani was secretary of Khatigushti, a group of modern-thinking *agha*s, rich people, and some non-aligned people. Noshirwan was secretary of Komala, and Ali Askari, until he was killed in battle at Hakkari in 1977, was secretary of the Socialist Movement. The heads of each branch in the three groups voted for Talabani to be secretary-general, and a year later, PUK became active inside Iraqi Kurdistan.

We returned to Qoolarush in April 1975, but having missed a year of school, I had to sit an examination in Sulaimani. I failed, and repeated the year, so it was not until 1978 that I graduated, going on to a boys' secondary school in Sulaimani. I lived with my uncle's family, working in my uncle's baklava shop after school. Over the next three years, Saddam Hussein tried to change the language of tuition from Kurdish to Arabic three times, but students protested in the street. Each time, soldiers shot a few students, but the people of Sulaimani have a record of protest. Saddam and his forces call Sulaimani the 'head of the snake', because the majority of people there supported the revolution.

At night I would visit my family in Qoolarush, taking care to avoid the army bases on Azmar. When PUK started the revolution in 1976, my father was sympathetic, so PUK *peshmergas* would come secretly to our house, my father giving them information, food and money. They described and joked about the hard life: sleeping in caves or on the mountains under the stars, sometimes without blankets or food, crossing freezing rivers carrying their clothes on their heads.

One early afternoon in 1981, when I was 17, I was walking down a narrow, deserted backstreet on my way to the baklava factory. It was the time when everyone takes a siesta. Two *amn* caught me, then hit and punched me, and pushed me to the ground, jumping on my back and feet. One of them had a small pistol and told me to get up. He pressed my face against a wall, saying, "Stand there! Don't look round! I am going to shoot you." I was scared, but after five minutes, I turned my head. They had disappeared. As I continued walking, a lady came to her door, saying, "Come inside." She had probably heard my screams but was too afraid to come out. I felt nothing but hate and anger. I thought, "One day I hope I have the power to kill those people." Now I feel only sorrow for a world that has such people in it.

Within months of that incident, on 18 October 1981, I secretly went to my first Komala meeting. It was a small cell of students who met to discuss political issues. We made friends in the hospital so they would give us medicines for the *peshmerga*, and we went around painting posters and putting stencils on walls saying, "Join Komala and PUK," "Ba'aths are bad," and "Unite to fight for freedom." I would talk to students and people who came to the baclava shop—people I could trust—and after six months, I joined PUK.

Meanwhile, I completed a three-year electrician's course at a technical college, living with my brother in a house my father had bought. We cooked our own meals, our mother visiting once a month. When I turned 18, I had to choose whether to go to Baghdad University or to the mountains. I was determined to avoid the army, where I might have to fight against my own people.

So that is how I ended up a *peshmerga*. In the slow times, I consoled myself by thinking, "We have chosen the life," and I hoped all our discussions were preparing us for a better future. Then after two quiet weeks, we would go to another village or to a meeting, or there would be news of a fight, and I would feel useful. Friendships helped. Most *peshmerga* were young and single. Many died, and I will never forget them.

In 1983 PUK divided southern Kurdistan into four regions, establishing a malband for each region, not counting Talabani's base at Yehksemar. Malbandi One's headquarters was at Qaradagh in the Kirkuk-Girdamand area. Malbandi Two covered the Sulaimani region and part of Kirkuk, with its headquarters at Sargalo. Malbandi Three operated in the Bahdinan region of Zakho-Dohuk, its headquarters at Warti, and Malbandi Four covered the Hawler area, its headquarters at Balisan.

Each malband had five to eight teams. Each team had three leaders—a military commander, a political commander, and a social leader who liaised with the villagers for meetings, elections and solving problems like land and family disputes if the village council could not solve them. Each team had six branches, each branch with 20 to 60 *peshmerga*, although a few had as many as 100, the team also being led by a military leader, a political leader and a social leader. (KDP was structured similarly, but used different titles.)

From 1984 all PUK positions were elected. Each branch would send a representative to the PUK congress, held in 1984, 1992 and 2000. (Iraq bombardment and civil war prevented a congress being held in 1987 and between 1994 and 1998.) In an election, a central committee of 25 was elected, then the central committee elected a politburo or Maktabsyasi of five. Four of these were the political-military leaders of each malband, the fifth politburo member working from PUK headquarters. The politburo would re-elect Talabani as general-secretary and liaise with him.

There was a fair amount of independence between the branches. Sometimes a branch would not have a radio operator for a week, so for small operations the branch leaders would decide on an activity, carry it out, then inform the team and malband leaders. To plan a major operation, the team and branch leaders would meet, sometimes for days or weeks. Only for very major operations would leaders have to get approval from the malband's headquarters or Talabani's headquarters.

In October 1983 I was transferred to a mobile branch of a team called 47 Pira Magroon, named after the high mountain north-west of Sulaimani, part of Malbandi Two. I began working as an operator in radio communications. Most people had code names for family reasons, and I chose the name Zirian. Zirian means 'angry weather'. I was going to be stormy wind and rain for the Ba'aths!

Qadir Haji Ali was the political and military leader of Malbandi Two and its 1000 *peshmerga*. He worked with a group of six representatives: one for political matters and others for military, financial, community, media, and communication—the person I was immediately answerable to, although all my messages went directly through Qadir Haji Ali.

He was a university-educated man in his mid-thirties, and over the next few years I found him to be a very good leader. Everyone respected him. He had a good brain, and was very careful in his planning, but not for himself. He was very brave, and sometimes those under him would advise him not to go to the front line—he was too important. They wanted him alive.

My branch moved between the villages of Fa'el, Qaslar, Yehksemar, Chokhmah, Sargolo, Balekh, Gappelon, Ma'alooma and many others—depending on the next operation. It was my job to relay number-coded messages about *peshmerga* and Iraqi troop movements. I would receive messages from the city or another branch telling us of a new checkpoint or that a spy had information about *peshmerga* movements. After relaying the message to headquarters, if the orders changed I would relay new orders to the branch. The army would listen to our radio, but most of the time they could not understand our code, especially as it was changed every three to six months.

It was when I joined the mobile branch that I met Tarik. Tarik was to become my closest friend for four and a half years. He was from Sulaimani, the same age as me, a handsome man with light brown hair and honey-coloured eyes, with a passionate, truthful personality. He was always joking and laughing, and when he laughed, his whole body shook. Sometimes on our way, we would say to each other, "We are stupid! Why are we walking around these mountains? The people don't care!"

I made many good friends, but he was the closest. We could share the innermost secrets of our heart. He loved a village girl, and when he went to her village he always wanted to stay at her place. I would tease him, saying, "Oh, let's go to another house this time," and he would go red in the face. He was a fighter on the front line, and before an operation he might half-joke, "Today I do not feel like killing soldiers... But what can I do?" Once we did not see each other for a month. He wrote me many letters, and I kept them, but in Al-Anfal I lost them, along with my photos and diary. At the beginning of 1988, Tarik was going on an operation, and I was hugging and kissing him as we all did before a fight. This time I had a strong feeling that I would not see him again, but I could not say, "Don't go." The plan was to attack a military base, which had many guns and a radio. He was travelling with four others. Just before they reached their target, an RPG blew up their car. All five were killed. The government buried them in one grave, alongside the grave of another 15 *peshmergas*. After the uprising in 1991, we found the grave and opened it. There were still clothes and bones, and we dug a grave for each person and had a ceremony. I buried Tariq properly. But for those intervening years, his face, his laughter and his anger were often on my mind and the memories of him kept me going. Tarik had a good heart and a sound way of thinking. If people like him were alive today, they would do good things for Kurdistan.

On occasions we secretly went into Sulaimani to talk with the people about PUK or to capture *amn, estikhbarat,* and *mukhabarat.* People would tell us, "This person has taken people to the secret police," or "He has killed people," and "This is the best time and place to catch him." We would travel to the town's outskirts at sunset and wait for dark, when the soldiers left their checkpoints in fear of *peshmerga* attacks. Then we would enter—Sulaimani being the size of a suburb of Sydney—avoiding government buildings. People would come onto the street and welcome us, giving us food, chocolate and cigarettes. Up to 400 would gather to listen to our political representative talk through a loudspeaker, while 20 *peshmergas* stood guard around the crowd.

Late in 1983 about 30 of us entered the city. We were describing our goals to the people when we heard that a force, speacially trained for night operations, was approaching. We told the people to go home, and hid behind the one-and-a-half-metre walls around the big roundabout. Five trucks and a tank pulled up with about 50 *qoowatkhaza,* equipped with the latest models of semiautomatic weapons, mostly Kalashnikovs, and wearing uniforms of dark green with black and yellow spots. They did not realise we were 50 metres away and had them surrounded, so we took them by surprise. It was the first time I was involved in actual shooting. We killed nine, and after the others ran away, we escaped.

From late 1983 we were coming under heavy bombardment from either Iraq or Iran. As well, the Iraqi communists were ambushing PUK *peshmerga* after PUK had attacked their headquarters in Pishtashan, close to Qandil, following a number of ambushes on PUK. Life was becoming so hard that in December 1983, PUK announced a ceasefire agreement with the Iraqi government. Until October 1984, there was only occasional fighting with *jahsh* units.

I moved with my branch to Kanibardina, 20 minutes' drive from Sulaimani, and then to Balekh. We had a big Newroz celebration of one million people in Soordash. We held educational seminars, and every week a small group would visit two to three families who had lost a member in the fighting. We had a soccer team to play young people in the villages, and a theatrical group performing little comedies or dramatic scenarios about *peshmerga* and village life, some of them being videoed.

We also visited our families, and once I took the chance to visit a special person. Mahabad was not my relative. I first met her when I was 14, and she was eight. She would come to my uncle's house because she and my cousin were friends. Over the next four years, I spoke to her a couple of times but she was very shy. In 1983, just after I had secretly joined PUK, I told my cousin, "I like Mahabad, and I want to ask her if she would be my girlfriend." My cousin passed on the message, but Mahabad refused. Then I left for the mountains. A year later I sent her a letter, through my cousin, saying I loved her and wanted to marry her, but again she refused. She was only 13. I decided to wait.

I had lots of time to think about her in the mountains, and under the stars I would

Sarbast fourth from left at Newroz

write of my love … Not really poems! During the ceasefire I saw her once, when we entered Sulaimani and Mahabad came out of her house with all the people. She greeted me … and all the *peshmergas*. I tried to see her on another occasion, but she was too shy to talk, saying, "My brother would not like it." I managed to say, "If we have a son, his name will be Zirian." All she said was, "I want to finish school." I knew she liked me underneath, and I saw our future together.

By August, it was apparent Iraq was not willing to make any concessions. The Turkish government had threatened to cut Kirkuk's oil pipeline to Turkey if Iraqi Kurds were given autonomy. PUK ordered us to go back to the mountains and I moved with my branch to Gappelon. I feared I would not see Mahabad for another 10 years.

From 1985, it was a major attack time. To avoid bombardment we were constantly on the move, sometimes going by car or transporting the radio equipment by horse or mule, usually walking, always staying clear of checkpoints and army bases. I could carry the radio on my back, using a special antenna to transmit while I walked, but if I wanted to receive or transmit over any distance, I would have to put up wires in the trees.

In some areas we had to be careful of Iraqi mines. Two specialists would go ahead and clear a one-metre-wide path. Sometimes we did not know the mines were there, and many *peshmergas* lost their legs, arms, eyes or lives this way.

Times were made harder because all the villages in the liberated areas were being targeted by bombardments, with people being forced to leave the villages and to live in caves and under rock ledges in the mountains. They would take their sheep with them but to tend their crops or get their stores of flour, rice and oil, they would have to sneak back to their village at night. Many village children lost their education. Even those who could continue with a PUK teacher could not sit the official examinations.

We slept under the stars, using a Kalishnikov and waistband material for a pillow and had to rely on our own supplies—flour, rice, oil, tea, sugar, powdered milk and dried beans—which we bought at high prices from people coming from the city. Two *peshmergas* would cook for the day, but often we did not have enough.

Despite the danger, I could not stop thinking of Mahabad. A few times I wrote to her on a chocolate wrapper or a cigarette cover, sending the 'letter' with *peshmerga* friends to my cousin. I could not write a proper letter. If it was discovered at a checkpoint, they would kill her. Sometimes I hesitated to give it to my friends, because of the danger, but they insisted on taking it. Mahabad never replied. I was heartbroken.

I decided to send my mum to her family to ask for marriage. Her family responded, "We must ask Mahabad first. Come back in two weeks." Mahabad refused. I asked my mother to go back and again Mahabad refused. I asked my mother to go a third time. My mum said, "She will only refuse again," but I said, "No—she has to accept me." This time Mahabad's family said, "All right," because when they asked Mahabad, she was silent, saying neither yes nor no!

After that, I sent an old man to sign the marriage agreement on my behalf in front of a *shaykh*. Under Islamic law, the agreement must specify how much gold a husband will pay his wife if he divorces her. I told the old man, "I don't care what you write. I don't believe in broken marriages." It was not a government-recognised marriage, because that was too dangerous with me being a *peshmerga*.

We were engaged for a year. Gappelon was close to PUK's headquarters, and we were being bombed all the time. Mahabad worried about me, and always followed the news, but we accepted that our marriage had to be like this. It was not as if we lived in a free country. Once I walked for three and half hours, over mountains and through valleys, back to Qoolarush, so that Mahabad could visit. She came with her family. We were never alone. Another time, I tried to see her but she was too shy to come, even with all her brothers. She never gave me even a small kiss until the night of our marriage!

It was 27 July 1986, summer, when she arrived at our base at Gappelon. We had a party with some of our family and all my *peshmerga* friends—150 people in all, singing and dancing and eating. We were lucky that day—there were no bombs.

It was wonderful to finally hold Mahabad's hand as we danced. I was concerned that I was putting her in danger, but I loved her, and told her, "If we die, it will be together."

Mahabad stayed for three days in the room I had prepared. She was still shy, but we were very happy. Then, according to tradition, she returned to her family in Sulaimani for a few days. When she came back, they gave me a holiday from the radio, but there was no holiday from the bombs.

From the beginning I tried to teach her to rely on herself, in case one day I was killed. I sometimes joked, "Don't worry, in a couple of days we will be killed, so it doesn't matter." I taught her to use a gun and protect herself, to be strong in a difficult situation, and to use the radio. I was surprised at how well she adapted. She loved PUK. Her family was close to PUK, especially Jabar, her brother. But when the bombing became too heavy, we had to leave Gappelon, and I insisted that she go back to Sulaimani.

After she left, I worried for her safety—what if the Iraqi secret police found her? I missed her so much. Sometimes I would cuddle the pillow and dream. My friends would joke, "You are single again!" But when I was working, I had to concentrate, because if one number was wrong, it could mean disaster.

The year 1986 was even worse than 1985. It was the year the army destroyed Qoolarush for the third time and the year I became involved on the front line. Some 150 to 1000 *peshmergas* from several branches or teams would join in one operation. There would be five to seven levels of command, and I would have to liaise directly with each commander.

One typical operation was at the end of August 1986. It was planned by Qadir Haji Ali and the other six leaders of Malbandi Two, and involved entering a collective town called Kareza—1000 houses built in 1979 to house the people from 10 border villages that had been destroyed, on the other side of a hill from the old village.

No-one liked to stay in these collective villages, because for the first year, they were without water and electricity. There was no work, no open spaces and no trees. The two-room houses were made of concrete blocks, with a wall around a small front courtyard, although sometimes people made a small yard on the street for their animals. By 1986 they had electricity and water, but sometimes in the middle of the day, the electricity was cut. In summer, it was like living in a baking oven.

Of the 1000 houses, maybe people in 800 were totally against Saddam. Of the people in the other 200, maybe 50 worked as spies and a few as guards. They had no other income. Otherwise, most of the guards on the streets were Arabs working for the Estikhbarat and Qoowatkhassa.

To plan the attack on two Estikhbarat guard points, and the Amn and Estikhbarat headquarters in the centre of town, Qadir Haji Ali sent someone to contact people secretly working for us. Without their information about the best routes and times to avoid the guards, as well as their help to hide us and give us water and food, we could not succeed in any operation. It was very dangerous, because we had to pass a big army base, and soldiers watched over every entry and exit point. There were guards on every street. The leaders told me, "You shouldn't come. You have been married only 27 days and maybe you will die." I responded, "Everybody is going, so I am coming too." I had chosen the life, and if something happened it was either fate or luck.

One hundred and fifty *peshmergas* were involved, in three lines. The third line, to supply food and medicine, was to be stationed just outside the built-up areas; the second line on the outskirts of the modern village. My cousin Sarkawt, my friend Kawan (who in 1988 was severely burnt and lost his sight in a chemical-bomb attack) and I were on the front line. I carried a gun, the radio on my shoulder. To pass through the military area in the valley, we walked carefully, covering any steel or glass so that no light was reflected. We approached the town from three sides, entering at exactly the right time to avoid the guards, darting from one concrete wall and asphalt street to another. I was scared only for the first five or 10 minutes. When the first bullets started flying I kissed my hand and thought of Mahabad, "Maybe I will not see you again."

Soon there were so many bullets whizzing around, I was not feeling anything. I do not know how we managed to safely pass from street to street. The three-storey Amn and Estikhbarat headquarters, which was also a prison, was on a high point in the centre of town. The walls of the building were made of 40 by 40-centimetre concrete blocks, with only an occasional 10 by 10-centimetre window. On the flat roof, behind a wall, I could see the barrels of RPGs poking through holes.

There were 30 of us around the building. We were under heavy fire both from the building and from soldiers and guards in the streets, so we were always on the move. The soldiers fired everywhere, whereas for us, every bullet counts.

I was constantly reporting and getting information for Qadir Haji Ali beside me. After one hour, *peshmergas* blew open the door with an RPG, and while several BKC machine guns provided cover, six *peshmergas* ran into the building. They were inside for an hour, those outside continuing to shoot. Eight to 10 *amn, estikhbarat* and *jahsh* were killed, but most escaped through an underground tunnel. A few were captured and taken prisoner. Three *peshmergas* were killed and some were injured.

After the *peshmergas* came out of the building, the shooting went on for another half-hour before we managed to escape to a predetermined meeting place within the town. Those who had attacked the two Estikhbarat guardposts were to meet us there, so we would know if somebody had not made it.

In the attack on the Amn headquarters, they had been successful in capturing many secret documents with valuable information, including future plans to attack *peshmerga* bases and the names of people in the area who had links with Saddam Hussein. They also released one prisoner—a Kurd from Iran. He had been captured the night before our attack. Prior to the operation, we had learnt that the Iraqi army was planning an attack. He had gone to talk to the military, to stop them, saying it would endanger too many Iranian Kurds, whom the Iraqi government had agreed to protect, but the *amn* had decided to execute him.

We left the town before sunrise. As we ran through the valley, with no cover, a soldier's bullet killed the Kurdish man from Iran. Now that *was* fate! Three or four *peshmergas* took turns carrying his body over their shoulder. We came under bombardment several times, and lay on the open ground or behind small rocks. Two more *peshmergas* were injured. After 100 minutes we reached the safety of the mountains. We took the body of the Iranian Kurdish man to the village of Kanima'asi, where his family lived, and later we had a ceremony and buried him.

After we moved our base to Shadala, I wrote to Mahabad telling her to come back. She arrived by truck, and when she told me she was pregnant, I was very happy. That Newroz we killed a turkey and prepared to celebrate with music and dancing, but when we gathered in the evening, a bomb killed Gafoor. In our sadness, we could not continue. After six weeks, the bombs started hitting the village and we had to escape. Mahabad had to go back to Sulaimani while we moved our base to Chokhmah.

After I prepared a room, I sent for her. There were only a few villagers remaining, and behind our room, there was one house, where Shaykh Ezzeddin Hosseini and his family lived. He was a representative of the Iranian Kurdish people who had joined with Qassemlou of KDPI to negotiate with the Shi'ite government in Iran. He was a tall, thin man with a grey beard and a whisper of a voice. He would say, "I carry the Qur'an in one hand and my nation's problems in the other." Now he is living in Sweden.

We had been in Chokhmah for four months. One day, while another radio operator and I were in the small village shop, four aeroplanes bombarded the village with cluster bombs and rockets. I started to run home to Mahabad, who was seven months' pregnant, but my friend stopped me. We stayed until the bombardment had finished, then before the aeroplanes came back, I headed home, passing a man crying over the body of his wife and child, who had recently arrived from Iran. As I came through the front courtyard, calling Mahabad, I saw a pool of blood. I thought, "Somebody has been killed." Then I saw a donkey, which had been hit by a rocket. I called Mahabad again and she came, calmly, but she had blood on her hands. "What happened?" I asked. "One of Shaykh Ezzeddin's *peshmerga* is injured, so I bandaged his arm." I found her composure unbelievable. From then on, I knew she could handle the life.

Shaykh Ezzeddin and his wife were injured, and afterwards he complained to the Iraqi government. They had promised not to bombard where he was living. The next day, Iraqi authorities ordered Shaykh Ezzeddin and the other Iranian groups to leave the area because they were going to destroy it. I told Mahabad that she had to go too. We had been given orders and were going into heavy fighting. I did not see her again until after Zirian was born.

The 100-square-kilometre area around Sulaimani was under continual bombardment. Often we were forced to spend up to 10 hours inside a metre-long L-shaped covered shelter. Always the bombs kept coming, and we were losing many people on the front lines.

In October 1986, while we were staying in the deserted village of Qoolajakh, I had another narrow escape. Qoolajakh was in a valley. The military were attacking us with bombs and missiles from aeroplanes and tanks. I was inside a house and very scared, but when soldiers started coming over the nearest hill and shooting at our front line, the 50 of us on the second line had to leave. The front line would cover our escape.

To make a good radio receiver, I had put wires in the trees, but I could not go out and retrieve them, so I had to pull in as much wire as I could, then cut it. I picked up the four-kilo radio, the wires and car battery, as well as my papers, put them in a backpack and ventured out, knowing the soldiers would target the radio. We had to walk in single file in full view and range of the fighting, another *peshmerga* helping me with the battery. After 10 minutes we descended down a steep slope, where there were more rocks and trees for cover, and I put the radio equipment on a donkey. As the bombs kept coming, we hid behind rocks and under ledges. When the danger is so great, you are not scared. It is only when there is a chance to save your life that you are scared.

We were heading to a village called Singr, 30 minutes away, but we could not go directly in case the aeroplanes spotted us. We separated, and after dark went inside the village. Most families had left. Their grape farms were unattended.

We were a big group, relying on our own food—dry bread, a little butter and cheese—and water from the springs. We slept under the trees in our sleeping bags or blankets. It was an ink-blue starry summer night but we were all too tense to appreciate it. Bombs were dropping every 15 minutes or so, showering us with shrapnel and earth.

Sometimes we would only have two or three nights' sleep in a week and our nerves would be strung tighter every day.

Just after 4.30 am, we made tea and I put up the wires in the trees to tell headquarters we had lost Qoolajakh. We had to keep the mountain, because both PUK's and Malbandi Two's headquarters were only two and a half hours' walk away—20 to 30 kilometres—so the front line was expected to fight to the death.

Sometimes we would send letters rather than use the radio because the Iraqi forces and our radio would be speaking. The *peshmerga* would swear at them, saying, "You are fighting for a dictator. You should leave our country." Mostly the soldiers would say, "We don't want to kill you," to remind us they were human too. We would answer, "If you leave our mountains, there will be peace." Some soldiers let us keep a mountain easily. Some even gave us information, such as their plans for the next day—both Arab soldiers and *jahsh*. The Arabs came from the south, and the government had told them that we were thieves and rebels. When they discovered what we were fighting for, a few were sympathetic.

I know of three Arab soldiers who became *peshmergas*. Two of them were killed. One fought in my branch for three years: a good man—my age, very educated. He had made Kurdish friends in the army, and decided to desert because he was against Saddam. We called him Azad, meaning 'freedom', and he learned to speak good Kurdish. We would tell him, "When we have pushed Saddam out of our land, this land will belong to you too." Unfortunately, he did not live to see the uprising. Before one operation in 1987, there was a feeling that made a few *peshmergas* say, "Azad will not come back this time." We tried to tell him not to go, but he insisted. The operation was attacking three *raba'aya*, on the lowest hill of Pira Magroon overlooking Shadala. The operation went well. The only *peshmerga* killed was Azad. His body was brought back and we cried for him. PUK sent his family some money, and a letter saying their son had died honourably.

When a *peshmerga* died, it would be announced on *peshmerga* broadcast radio, along with a summary of his life. One man died two weeks after his wedding and they played this song:

> Say to my first-night bride, if she comes to my grave,
> She mustn't say he was killed for his country, and he does not live for my love.
> I have to do my duty, to give my life for my country,
> Because this country, its valleys and mountains, grew you for me.
> If God gives you a baby boy, tell him,
> "Your dad asked his wife to have a tear for him, and asks you to follow his path."

In a fast retreat, the bodies of dead *peshmergas* could not be brought back. But if possible, injured *peshmergas* would be carried to the second or third line, where each branch had a medic. Once the medic had done all he could, the *peshmerga* would be taken by horse, donkey or tractor to the nearest vehicle, which would take him to Bargalo hospital, sometimes a two or three-day journey. The doctors would operate with a minimum of equipment and medicines.

There was also a prison in Bargalo for captured soldiers and *jahsh*. At times, there were as many as 300 prisoners. At first it was a mud and rock building, but in 1986 they built a cement-block prison with inside toilets and showers, and a big clean room with two rows of beds, each with a blanket and pillow.

Prisoners would be kept a month or two, while we waited for information from the city, then usually released. We did not have enough food or space to keep them longer. Every week, the *peshmerga* had a meeting with them to explain the revolution. We would tell them that we are not enemies of the Arab people, that we just wanted our land, human rights and democracy.

Even *jahsh*, if they had avoided killing people, were released, unless we received information that a *jahsh* had killed in return for money. Then he would be charged and the *peshmerga* would ask the people what they wanted. If they said, "Kill him," he was shot. Some *jahsh* had killed 20 people. Some were rejected by their own families.

For difficult cases, five lawyers at PUK headquarters or the five PUK politburo leaders had a special meeting to decide whether the death penalty was appropriate. They might doublecheck information or get more information to reassess the case. Sometimes, if they found out that although the person had killed people, he had also helped people, the death penalty was reversed.

I have not been to prison but at the beginning of 1987, my 17-year-old brother was put in prison for 11 months after he was caught in a liberated area. *Amn* and *estikhbarat* tried to get information from him by using electric shocks, and tying his hands behind his back and hanging him from his ankles. They did other things I do not want to mention. They put bottles inside some people. When I heard they had taken him to Abu Ghreb in Baghdad, I knew they were going to kill him, but my father bribed a succession of *jahsh* to use their influence. In total, he paid over 10,000 dinars (US$30,000).

After Zirian was born, Mahabad come back by tractor to Shadala with her mum, cousin and the baby. It was so good to see them and hold Zirian, but I insisted that Mahabad return to Sulaimani. She did not want to go, but there was too much danger.

While Mahabad was away, in August 1987, I was transferred to the Control Station at Talabani's headquarters in Yehksemar, near the mountain of Jheelwan, backing the front line. Sometimes I would be sent into an area for a big operation, then return to headquarters, where I would be in contact with PUK's 60 stations, each area having two to three stations, a large area having up to 15. When I was not busy, I would talk to European and Arabic operators on their short-wave hobby radios, dialling the country's code and exchanging information.

Although the cities were still under government control, we were expanding the liberated areas in the countryside to include smaller towns. The bombardments continued. The enemy surrounded us on three sides—the other side being the Iranian border—and sometimes we had to protect little pockets of liberated areas surrounded on all sides. When *peshmerga* captured tanks, they had to destroy them because we did not have enough petrol, spare parts, or trained people to operate them. But in any operation, *peshmergas* would try to capture weapons for the new recruits, because every day, more and more people were joining PUK.

KDP were not operating in our area. They were in Bahdinan, and they also had a base close to Tehran until 1979, when the new Khomeini government allowed them to move closer to the border. From 1981, maybe five times a year, during the summer, they would send a small unit inside Iraqi Kurdistan, to attack an army depot, protect a village, or make trouble for PUK. Then in 1986, talks began between all the parties in the Bahdinan region to form a united front. In 1987, the United Kurdish Front, or Baray Kurdistani, was announced, and in the winter they conducted some joint operations. I think the first was capturing the town of Kanima'asi, in Bahdinan province. The operation had its problems. Some locals had relations with the KDP, others with PUK, and there were arguments as to who should or should not be killed. But after the Front was formed, the Iraqi government became even more desperate.

In August 1987, three weeks after moving to Yehksemar, I sent for Mahabad. We were living in tents and there were many bombs, but I was too worried for her safety in the city. If Mahabad and Zirian were with me, at least we would be killed together. Every day, friends were dying, so my thinking was, "Tomorrow, death may come to us too."

It was in Yehksemar, in late September 1987, that chemical bombs first hit us. The chemicals were nerve gas, or *guz asa'ab* in Arabic, cyanide and phosphorus. The phosphorus burns the body, and all of the gases make you vomit and breathless. Your eyes go red, making it hard to open them or to see anything but intense light. That day, we put a wet towel around Zirian, and ran up the mountain to escape the gas.

For winter, we moved into a room at the foot of the mountain. One night I received a radio report saying 11 army trucks were approaching the area, each truck carrying a Rajimah Kartoosha, each station consisting of 40 gun rockets. We knew they could be chemical. I did not tell Mahabad. The next night, 24 February 1988, was beautiful, cold and clear. We had been celebrating with two *peshmerga* families Zirian's first tooth. After dinner, everyone went to sleep on blankets. At 1.55 am we woke to conventional bombs cracking like grenades and chemical ones making a low whistle, exploding with thunder-like rumble. They were close.

We had special clothing and two masks, but nothing for Zirian and the others. All we could do was wrap Zirian in a dry towel, then a wet towel and another dry towel, and go to the shelter under the verandah. People were shouting, "Chemical, chemical!" and we saw the starbursts in the sky.

It was dark inside the shelter—one metre deep, one metre wide and five metres long—crowded with five adults and eight children. Our eyes were sore. When I heard people outside shouting, "Please help us," I went out. Bombs were still exploding, their gas filling the air. I could not see, so I went back to the shelter. We waited for one hour, until the bombardment ceased, then went outside. All but one member of a family of seven had been killed instantly when a chemical bomb hit their house. The man who survived had lost his mind. As we stood around the fire he would talk about the chemicals, then laugh, then suddenly get angry and swear at Saddam. He was taken to hospital but unluckily for him he did not die. He was still crazy four months later.

After another half-hour a 4WD arrived to take people to safety. We were driven up to headquarters, and when they saw us, they said we had to go to Bargalo hospital, a 90-minute drive. There were 17 people in the vehicle, and in the mud the car nearly rolled and then got stuck, so we had to walk. We could still hear bombs. It was dawn, about 6.30 am, but many of us could not see, so we just followed in a line. Close to Bargalo, we had to cross a four-metre-wide river. I held Mahabad's hand, carrying Zirian in the other, then crossed and recrossed helping the other children. When everybody was on the other side, I held Zirian, but I had no strength left. I called out to people nearby, shouting like a crazy man, "Bakhtiar! Rozgar! Farhad! Come and help." *Peshmerga* came, and I gave Zirian to one, saying, "Save Zirian. Maybe I will die." I was blind and had to lean on someone to walk.

At the hospital, three doctors and five assistants checked us. I was with the men, and they took our clothes and made us go outside to the showers, but instead of showering us, they hosed us like cows—with very cold water. Meanwhile, the bombs started again—normal and chemical.

They quickly put a blanket around each of us and gave us an injection, but it had no effect. Our clothes were contaminated, so people gave us new ones. Then we ran to one of the shelters. Still, I thought I was going to die.

More bombs came later that day. Mahabad took Zirian to a cave, but I was too sick. The next morning, still leaning on a *peshmerga*'s shoulder, I went up to see them. The smell of chemicals was everywhere. Inside the cave, 25 people were huddled, mostly in silence. I said hello to Mahabad, but I was so sick they took me back to the shelter.

That night, we were bombed again with chemicals. I was in the shelter and bombs were dropping every 15 minutes, some landing one metre away. We just sat in silence, waiting. This was Al-Anfal.

Mahabad and Zirian came to the shelter the following day. We stayed as a family for three days. Nobody had slept much and people were too tired. Everyone knew we had to leave Bargalo, so people killed all the chickens and invited us to eat, but even the smell of food made me vomit. For five days I could only drink water and juice. I felt faint and dizzy. I could not walk more than 20 metres without falling over. My mind felt strange and I was numb all over.

I had a strong feeling that I had lost somebody very close. Jabar had been sent to the front line, and I insisted on staying by the two-way radio because I wanted to talk to him. But the people on the radio refused to call him. I went crazy, shouting and swearing in anger. I had no control of my emotions. The radio operators were my friends, but I hit and kicked one operator because all he would say was, "Jabar is all right but he can't come to the radio." They understood that I had lost my normal routine.

Iranian army helicopters were taking people to Baneh, inside Kurdistan of Iran. When we were in the helicopter, I kept asking people, "What has happened to Jabar?" One of his injured friends whispered, "*Shaheed.*" This is a special word used to refer to someone who has gone straight to heaven, having given their life for their beliefs. The Bargalo radio operators had not wanted to tell me that Jabar had been killed on the first day of Anfal, 28 February, and I could not tell Mahabad. She loved her brother so much.

When we landed, they took us briefly to Baneh hospital, but when Iraqi planes started bombing Baneh, they sent us 50 kilometres by bus to the hospital in Saguez. While we were waiting in Casualty, Iraqi aeroplanes started bombing the military area close to that hospital, so the hospital staff said, "It seems the aeroplanes are coming where you go," so we were taken 11 hours by bus to Khomeini Hospital in Tabriz, where up to 200 *peshmergas* were being treated.

We stayed in one room for 18 days with two other families. During this time, Iraqi long-range missiles bombed Tabriz three or four times. In the first few days, I could recognise Mahabad but not others. I had no control of my memory, vision, hearing or language. People would talk to me but I did not understand them.

They did x-rays, and gave us some medicine and injections three times a day. Every three hours, we had to take a shower to wash away the sweat from the chemicals. Slowly, slowly, I started getting better. After 18 days I was able to walk, eat and talk normally, but Jabar's death had affected me very badly. I did not shave. Mahabad asked, "Why aren't you shaving?" and I told her, "Iranians like people to have a beard."

When we left the hospital, we went to Saguez and stayed in a hotel, sleeping on blankets. After a few days we heard from the radio and saw on television the chemical bombing of Halabja. Iran took teams of doctors and media in, but Western countries ignored the genocide because they supported Saddam. When I heard and saw what had happened, I feared for the future. After Halabja, I told Mahabad of Jabar's death. She cried and cried, but by that time, everyone was grieving.

We stayed in the hotel for a month, then rented a room. Every month, PUK paid each family 3000 to 5000 tomans. It was enough for bread and rent. Because of Anfal, all *peshmergas* were pulling out of Iraqi Kurdistan, but after Anfal, Saddam Hussein called an amnesty. I never believed in the amnesty and did not want to go back to Iraq while Saddam Hussein was in power. For three years we lived in Saguez, situated on a high plain with a population of about 500,000, and only one factory: a cigarette factory. Some of our friends married Kurdish girls from Iran, but inside, the reality was sad.

Many people think the uprising of 1991 was spontaneous, but it was not. It was a new way of thinking. During Anfal we had lost the villages, so rather than keep fighting in the mountains, PUK planned a people's uprising in the cities, with the aim of forming a Kurdish parliament. Anything like that takes good planning and organisation. A training camp was set up near the border, and groups were reformed to go back to the Sulaimani and Bahdinan areas—six to 30 volunteers in each group: a total of 250 young, strong and mostly single men. They were going back to extreme danger and hardship, initially far from the cities, to areas that had been cleared of all life, where soldiers had orders to kill anything that moved. They were often without food for days, yet by the end of 1989, 20 radio stations had been established inside Iraqi Kurdistan to support them. We manned the two-way radio 20 hours a day but could open it only at certain times, sending coded messages like, "If you hear us, please open your radio on this frequency." To get supplies, they would travel at night to the outskirts of a city, then hide. When they radioed through their location, I would radio PUK in the city to drop food at a certain place. Then slowly, throughout 1989–90, PUK began establishing cells in different cities to obtain information and to build up relations with the people.

Back in Saguez we worked from a two-storey building, on a floor more than half underground, with three home-made antennas on the roof—basically, three lengths of cable with positive and negative wires inside, all supported in the middle by a five-metre pole. Depending on the weather conditions, the frequency we wanted to use, and the distances involved, we plugged the appropriate cable into one of three sockets in the

100-watt Iraq military radio. With this set-up, we could reach all over Iraq and Europe. With my little bit of English, under the code Y16SUL, I talked to Swedish, Russian and German people and once to an Australian. Arabs would talk to us from Jordan and Kuwait. Kuwaitis would say, "You lie about Saddam," and we would tell them, "Be careful. One day Saddam might come to you too." When Saddam killed an English journalist some months before he invaded Kuwait, PUK knew he was heading for trouble and began consolidating their plans. We had to calculate which army bases to attack first, the weakest points, and the best time and season. I was not involved in the planning but I relayed the messages.

Then Saddam invaded Kuwait on 2 August. Reports started coming in from Iranian and Montecarlo radio describing the atrocities committed by Iraqi soldiers in Kuwait City—the stealing and vandalism, the raping of women, people in the street being killed because they had a mobile phone. We were not surprised. It is Saddam's way. For the Kuwaitis and those sent to the front line, the invasion was a catastrophe, but for Kurds it was a blessing. We heard America had deployed tens of thousands of troops to Saudi Arabia, and our dream for a people's uprising grew steadily.

In September 1990, we sent a representative, Khalid, inside Sulaimani to make contact with the Moosta Shahrs and other *jahsh* who had previous links with PUK. He informed them of our plan and asked them to start collecting weapons and ammunition. From that time, PUK began sending letters to every *jahsh* organiser, *agha* and important representative in each town, asking them to join the uprising.

In December, PUK made contact with Barzani's people on the border and in Karaj, close to Tehran, to discuss the uprising and a future plan for the United Kurdish Front. At first KDP did not accept the idea, saying, "We will not be able to hold the cities and too many people will die." PUK argued, "We have to do something, and it is better if all parties join together."

In mid-January, a joint US, British and Kuwaiti air force began bombing military and civilian targets inside Iraq. In February, PUK headquarters set the date of the uprising: 7 March 1991. They planned that by 21 March, all Iraqi Kurdistan would be liberated. They sent a plan to KDP, who agreed to have 50 KDP *peshmergas* operating with every PUK group. In the plan, 2000 PUK with 50 KDP would liberate Kirkuk and 2000 KDP with 50 PUK would liberate Mosul.

In early February, PUK announced over broadcast radio that a people's uprising was soon going to bring a Kurdish victory and all *jahsh* who changed sides would be forgiven for their mistakes. By mid-February, 7500 *jahsh* and other people had pledged their support.

Around this time Iranian officials asked PUK about the plan. PUK promised, "We are not going to make trouble for Iran. Our revolution is in northern Iraq." In that month, the United Front and Shi'ite opposition groups from the south of Iraq had a meeting in Iran. The Kurdish Front suggested that it was best to coordinate and start the uprisings on the same day. Initially the Shi'ite groups agreed, but I think the Iranian government must have stepped in, telling the Shi'ites that they would support them to defeat Saddam, so the Shi'ites did not remain in regular contact. Also there were a number of differences between us, apart from religion. The Shi'ites were not happy with how the Americans had violated the international conventions of war. The Allied Forces were bombing Basra, not caring about the civilians they killed, and the Shi'ites were not as organised.

At 4 am on 24 February, Allied Forces began Operation Desert Storm. The Allies put a blackout on news reports for the first 12 hours of the ground war, but later we heard that in the first 24 hours they had bombed 200 of Iraq's 1000 oil wells. Iraqi conscripts began surrendering in their thousands. Some became refugees. We were very happy with the news, but more concerned about special forces like the Republican Guard.

By 27 February, the Allied Forces had liberated Kuwait City, and as the Iraqi troops withdrew, they set fire to 500 Kuwaiti oil wells. On the same day, there was a big tank battle, and various news services reported that 800 Allied tanks had destroyed 200 of the 250 to 300 Republican Guard tanks. Yet if they had destroyed that number, the Republican Guards would not have recovered so quickly; within a week, they were attacking the Shi'ites cities, and within a month, Kirkuk and Dohuk.

Through BBC, CNN and Arab broadcasts, we heard that the Americans were heading towards Baghdad, but when they were six hours away, at 8 am on 28 February—after only 100 hours of ground war—President Bush announced a ceasefire and Schwarzkopf was ordered to retreat. We were shocked and angry. I said to friends, "Bastard America, they want Saddam Hussein to stay in power."

I am sure American spies knew of plans to overthrow Saddam. The day after the ceasefire announcement, on 1 March, President Bush said it was not America's business to destroy Saddam—it was the task of the Iraqi people. At the same time, I heard American soldiers on the news say they were ordered to give the Republican Guards fuel for their tanks so that they could return to Baghdad! It was very different to what they did to the withdrawing Iraqi forces and civilians on the highway of death from Kuwait to Basra where, after the ceasefire announcement, the Allies continued bombing, massacring with heat intensive devices that burnt everything to a cinder, napalm, cluster bombs, and uranium depleted missiles that left the area radioactive.

Also on 1 March, Shi'ite radio reported that columns of tanks had rolled into Sa'ad Square in Basra, and that an Iraqi commander had shot at a picture of Saddam, telling a crowd that their humiliating defeat was a result of their leader's irresponsible miscalculations. The people cheered him, and while soldiers left their tanks and weapons, the people stormed Ba'ath headquarters, police stations and security offices. Guns were handed out from the government stockpiles, stored even in schools in case the Allies started parachuting into the cities. In this way Basra was liberated on 2 March, and the Intifada quickly spread to other Shi'ite towns. Committees were set up to distribute food and reopen essential service, and the *imams* issued *fatwas* to encourage people to keep calm and not loot or kill.

On 3 March Iraq accepted the Allied conditions for a permanent ceasefire. Suddenly, on 4 March, we got news that our plan for an uprising in every city on 7 March was pre-empted by *jahsh* linked to PUK in Rania, a town 60 kilometres from Sulaimani, becoming involved in a clash when the government tried to take their weapons. The United Front had yet to get *peshmergas* into back-up positions in the mountains, but on the 5 March Khalid, the PUK representative in Sulaimani, suggested that it was best to bring the date forward: the people were ready. However, there was a two-day delay in getting permission papers for *peshmergas* to leave Iran, and heavy rains made it difficult to travel. PUK answered Khalid over broadcast radio, "We will make *zamarwund* (dancing) together in two days." By early morning on 7 March, hundreds of *peshmergas* entered Sulaimani. By evening the city was liberated.

Before the uprising, PUK had announced over the radio, "Please do not cause damage to the hospitals, schools, universities and councils. Please bring any documents you find in the army or Amn bases to the centre. Do not kill soldiers and other Ba'aths—take them to the centre." But there was a lot of killing in Sulaimani, especially of *amn*, *estikhbarat*, *qoowatkhaza* and *mufrazakhaza* (Kurdish army units who were paid 1000 dinars for every *peshmerga* they killed). Everyone had lost someone, and civilians of Sulaimani took their revenge. One woman cut off the head of a secret policeman who had killed her two sons. After 70 years of oppression, many people had something boiling inside. If you remove the lid, all the steam comes out.

In just two days, one town after another came under Kurdish control. Then news came through that Republican Guard units were dropping napalm, cluster bombs and scud missiles on Basra and other towns in the south. We knew we might have a big fight on our hands but we thought we were safer than the Shi'ites. In the south, there were more army, and also fear of Iranian Shi'ite influences. By 16 March, the Iraqi army had succeeded in squashing the Shi'ites. In 10 days, 4000 people were killed in Najaf, a Shi'ite holy city, and many more were raped or arrested.

The 50,000 Iraqi soldiers who were stationed in Kurdistan heard over the radio that city after city had fallen to the Kurds. By 13 March, the Bahdinan area had been liberated. The normal conscripts' morale was low—without shooting a bullet, they dropped their guns, left their tanks and equipment, and surrendered. Over the radio we called for anyone with specialist knowledge in tanks or rockets to come to certain places, but not enough came, and some who did we could not trust. The army had stopped feeding the soldiers, so Kurdish people set up big pots of free food in the mosques, for the soldiers.

I was working 18 hours a day but I did not feel tired. Every five or 10 minutes, we received messages about another base being attacked, another area being liberated, how many people were involved, how many *amn* were killed. I would write down the details and telephone them through to broadcast radio, so the news could immediately be relayed to the general population. On 11 March we were ordered to disconnect our radio equipment and take it back to Iraqi Kurdistan, but we were forced to spend one night on the border because so many vehicles were getting stuck in the mud. What I saw still makes me angry. Many bulldozers and trucks were waiting to cross, having been sold to Iran! It was a big betrayal of the nation, because this equipment was needed to rebuild our roads and other infrastructure. The Kurdish leaders must have known and I do not know why they did not stop it. All I was to see was a few individuals become rich very quickly.

As soon as I set foot on home soil, I cried. It was spring and everyone was smiling. But on the way to Sulaimani, I saw too many destroyed villages, and thousands of landmines beside the road. I cried again, thinking, "We may have a free Kurdistan, but how will people rebuild their villages and farms?"

In Sulaimani I thought, "I hope to die this day because I will never see such happiness again." All the people were kissing and hugging us, and giving us food and clothes. As soon as we set up the radio, I talked with Mahabad back in Saguez.

Hundreds queued at the PUK centre to donate blood and food for the front line, or to volunteer in whatever way they could. Others were stealing from government buildings. Thousands of *jahsh* and Moosta Shahrs began asking PUK if they could join the party. They were told, "You cannot join," or "You can join but we are not going to give you positions of responsibility." Many then approached KDP, who gave power to some very big *jahsh*, such as Tahsin Shawayes.

For a week, I worked very hard on the radio, relaying messages as to where *peshmergas*, food and blood were needed, sleeping at the office. Then on 20 March, we heard that over 2000 PUK and 50 KDP *peshmergas* were attacking Kirkuk, with Saddam Hussein's army fiercely defending the city. After a two-day battle, on the evening of 21 March, PUK announced that 75 per cent of Kirkuk was liberated. The only place left was a big military camp. The people welcomed the *peshmergas*. Kirkuk is a very important city, as rich in our history as it is in petrol. The 8000-year-old site of Jarmo, near Kirkuk, is as old as Jericho.

Over the next seven days, PUK called on the UN, the USA, Europe and the world: "Please recognise us and help us keep Saddam Hussein out." But of the 30 countries that had fought for Kuwait, not one responded. There was talk of a no-fly zone being established north of the 36 Parallel, where Iraq would be banned from using aeroplanes. PUK told UN officials, "If you make a safe haven for the Kurdish people, Kirkuk, Khanaqin and Sulaimani are Kurdish cities too, so the no-fly zone must start from the 34 or 34.5 Parallel." But seven days after Kirkuk's liberation, on 28 March, President Bush announced that Saddam would not be allowed to fly his aeroplanes north of the 36 Parallel. In this way, the USA gave Saddam Hussein the green light to attack Kurdistan with all the ground forces, tanks and helicopters at his disposal. It seemed no-one wanted the Kurds to have the strength or economic base to demand a state of their own.

On the same day as the announcement, Iraqi forces, including Republican Guard and Mujahadeen from Iran, moved to attack Kirkuk. KDP had failed to move on the oil-rich town of Mosul, and it was the beginning of the end of the Kurdish uprising.

After Kirkuk, Saddam's army went to Dohuk and quickly captured the Bahdinan province, then Hawler. People began escaping to Turkey or Iran. PUK wanted the people to stay and protect the towns. The price was high, but we were willing to pay it. If we remained united, we could dictate our own terms, but when the people started escaping the *peshmerga* were stranded.

The Kurdish leaders again appealed to the world for support, reporting that Saddam was bombing civilians with helicopters and tanks, but no-one responded, despite all the Allied Forces still in the area. We knew Sulaimani was next. On 1 April, PUK announced to the people, "Do not leave Sulaimani—we will protect you." On the night of 1 April, we were ordered to disconnect the equipment and take it to Azmar, where Jabar Farman, Mamoosta Jamal and 50 *peshmerga* had destroyed three tanks and stopped the army's advance.

They fought on during the day of 2 April, but by this time, Iraqi forces, secret agents and units like the Mufrazakhaza were back in Kurdistan. After PUK received information from inside the army that Saddam had plans to bomb Sulaimani heavily, the order came through on the night of 3 April, "We can't stop the regime. Take the radio by truck to Tawela [on the Iranian border]." PUK announced to the people, "We advise you to leave Sulaimani." I asked myself, "Why did the Allies fight such an expensive war for less than one million Kuwaitis but are unwilling to help six million people who have been suffering for decades, let alone the millions in Turkey, Iran and Syria?"

We put the equipment on the truck, and at 4.30 am on 3 April, I started walking with other *peshmergas* the 50 kilometres to the Iranian border. More than a million people walked over Azmar, the hills and the plain. In some places there were landmines. Bombs were exploding and helicopters were shooting into the crowd. One helicopter killed 11 people in a truck, including a close friend, Dr Ali, a medical assistant.

On that 36-hour walk people trudged through heavy rain and mud. It was very cold. It seemed that whatever Saddam was doing, God was doing also. From the highest peak, we had come down too rapidly, and everybody was angry.

For a long time I walked behind a lady carrying a baby, three children by her side. When I looked hard, I could see her baby was not moving. As I got closer, I saw it was dead. She thought he was sleeping, and I wondered what she would do when she put everything down. I saw another woman give birth on the road while three women held a blanket around her. Children walked without shoes or food. But still I had hope. The Kurdish have been destroyed time and time again, and still we survive to fight another day.

At the border, thousands of people milled about. Bad people were trying to rob others of guns and bags. From their eyes, you could see they did not care. The Iranian soldiers were body-searching every man, rummaging through the suitcases and looking at the women. I was told that some tried to find people to work for them secretly, to find out such information in the camps as who had guns or alcohol. But a few Iranian soldiers showed great kindness. Some brought their own food from their base for the people. PUK had set up a temporary office at the border, and were giving people with responsibility papers so that they could cross easily. I was given papers, and travelled by public bus to Saguez. Other people were taken to camps.

I went straight to Mahabad. As I walked in the door, it was a strange mixture of feelings. For a brief moment, we were very happy to see each other, that we were still alive. We hugged and kissed—but then the whole situation took over. After all the sacrifice, we had lost everything, and we were very upset and angry. Yet even in all the blackness, there was a sense of humanity. People in every street had collected bread, potatoes, biscuits and clothes for the refugees. It was not easy for them. It was heartening —like a rebirth of the Kurdish nation. Help was also coming from Persian people in other cities.

Our family was in a camp at the border, so the same day I arrived we went and brought them back to our place. I continued my job as a radio operator. After 10 days we heard that Saddam had invited the Kurdish leaders to come to Baghdad and negotiate. All the Kurdish parties had a meeting, at which it was decided that they had no alternative. America was not going to help and too many people were outside the

Iraqi Soldiers killed in the second uprising in Sulaimani, June 1991, photographed by Mansour Razaghi

country. They feared Saddam's army would kill people, both in Iraq and Iran, and they needed to stabilise the situation.

People were horrified when they saw Talabani and Barzani kiss Saddam in Baghdad. Three months later, Saddam announced that he would not accept any of the points Kurdish leaders had presented. He did not accept a federation and claimed Kirkuk would never be a part of Kurdistan. He tried to divide PUK and KDP over Kirkuk: PUK insisted Kirkuk must be included. KDP was more willing to compromise. He was offering less than what was offered in the 1970 Autonomy Agreement, so by May–June, the negotiations broke down.

PUK leaders began planning a second uprising. They advised people not to cooperate with any government authorities, so that the Iraqi government would be encouraged to leave Kurdistan. The people could harass but there was to be no fighting.

The second uprising was not so organised. Saddam was back in Kurdistan. His army bases had never left and Iraqi soldiers were on the streets of Sulaimani, which was outside the non-fly zone. It was not safe to go out, even though the UN was putting pressure on the Ba'aths not to hurt anyone. During this time, the United Kurdish Front announced they would hold elections to set up a Kurdish parliament, with or without international support. The atmosphere was very tense, and over some weeks in June, there were several incidents in Sulaimani. Civilians were shot or bombed by soldiers and homemade molotov cocktails burned five to six tanks. The last straw was when one *raba'aya* of 20 to 30 soldiers bombed a girls' school, killing two girls. People from several streets in the Arbat area, including some PUK *peshmergas*, collected 60 soldiers in one room and shot them. Although PUK denounced this action, Western media reported it as a human-rights abuse, blaming PUK. The UN announced they would police the no-fly zone.

During the months of June, July and August, people all over the Kurdish region began harassing one base or checkpoint after another—telling the soldiers and *amn* they had to go. Slowly the government started withdrawing soldiers, government workers and equipment. In Hawler, Dohuk and other cities, the people would clap as they left. Some did not leave peacefully, but finally the government was pushed back to Kirkuk.

In July, Mahabad and I returned to Sulaimani. After we had visited our families, PUK sent us to the communications base in Galala, a destroyed village near Haji Omaran, 20 kilometres from the Iranian border, surrounded by mountains. These were dotted with wild gallnut and walnut trees, springs and small waterfalls, and on the lower slopes were small orchards of stone fruit and apples, vineyards and pastures. We made a platform for a bed, and the 25 *peshmergas* at the base would cook and eat together.

But in late September, Saddam began dropping bombs from helicopters near Kirkuk and in and around Sulaimani. There was fighting for two or three days and many people were killed. It was during this time that we found the mass grave, and reburied Tarik's body in the cemetery, bombs falling one kilometre away. Otherwise, those 10 months at Galala were peaceful. But still I felt uneasy. I had been a *peshmerga* for nine years and was very tired. I had lost too many friends and I feared for Zirian's future. I told headquarters, "I want to go for a rest." I had heard Australia was a good country, and a friend had offered to sponsor us.

We left for Turkey on 18 October 1991 and arrived in Australia on 23 March 1992. I was unsure about everything. All my thoughts were for Kurdistan. In the Kurdish election in May 1992, 150,000 people in Sulaimani did not have access to polling booths. I blame the UN observers. They did not want one party to win. Also different electorates had varying population numbers, although this happens in many countries, including Australia. But what was different was that on the ballot sheet, there were no candidates' names, just a colour representing each party—yellow for KDP, green for PUK, and five other colours for the other parties in the United Front: Sami Sinjari's People's KDP, the Socialists, the Communists, the Islamic Movement of Kurdistan, Zahmet Keshan or the Toilers' Party, and the Assyrians. People voted for a party.

KDP got 44.51 per cent and PUK got 44.02 per cent of the vote. This translated into 51 seats and 49 seats, with five seats reserved for the Assyrians and Turkomans. The Islamic Movement, a confederation of Islamic parties, came third, with 5.1 per cent. It failed to reach the 7.0 per cent that would entitle it to a seat. There was talk of PUK forming a coalition with some of the Assyrian independents, but then KDP and PUK negotiated a 50:50 split. It meant there was no opposition or shadow ministry.

Despite the difficulties, until 1994 I was full of hope for the democratic parliament in Hawler. People tried to rebuild the country though customs revenue, although the trade embargoes continued and all other supplies came through the UN, Care Australia and other humanitarian groups. Factories for processing wheat, sugar, cement and cigarettes were rebuilt, but always there was a problem with spare parts and electricity—the generators at Dukan and Darbandi Khan dams were very old. Sometimes Saddam would cut the supply from Mosul, to put pressure on KDP. Doctors and teachers were working for no pay. In school, ten kids would share one book.

To add to the problems, the Islamic parties were gaining power. The Islamic Brotherhood from Egypt had established itself in Kurdistan by the late 1960s, but was not important until it spawned what were to become the most dynamic Islamic organisations: Bizootnowa, Yegerrtoo'i Islami and, to a lesser extent, Rabitai Islami, which together make up the Islamic Movement of Kurdistan.

Bizootnowa was militant, whereas those who did not believe in armed struggle joined Yegerrtoo'i Islami, the political party, or its welfare wing, Rabitai Islami. These last two groups believed in staying in the towns and cities, working from the mosques, holding meetings to educate people about Islam and Islamic politics, distributing food, money and other essentials. They also supported poor families to send their children to Islamic schools. As a result, they grew in popularity, and Yegerrtoo'i Islami is now the strongest group. But my two brothers were *peshmergas* with the more militant Bizootnowa.

Islamic political ideas were being spread back in 1979–80, both in Iraqi Kurdistan and among the mainly KDP supporters in the refugee camps in Iran. In late 1982 Bizootnowa announced a political organisation and army, so in 1983 my older brother went to one of these camps in Iran to secretly join. In 1987 he came and visited me in the mountains. He was armed, but he looked at our conditions and commented, "You are living like kings." After the uprising, he and others in Bizootnowa came back and established themselves in Rania. PUK said, "Welcome," even though there were a few arguments. By then, my older brother was a commander of a group. In 1991 my 20-year-old brother also joined became a member of Bizootnowa, working secretly in the city before joining our older brother's *peshmerga* unit.

On 6 May 1991, my older brother went to a deserted army building, looking for guns. Sometimes the soldiers would boobytrap the weapons they left behind, and as my brother was examining an RPG, it exploded. He left behind a wife and five children.

Our country is Muslim and my brothers were religious; they prayed five times a day. But after they joined, they became dedicated to Islam in a political way. I believe in God and the Qur'an too, but I was more attracted to PUK for its democratic and socialist principles. Before I came to Australia, I advised my younger brother, "I won't push you to leave your party or what you believe, but think about where they go, what will be the result. We all love our country, but some leaders in your party say, 'We must have Islamic law, an Islamic government and an Islamic leader.' They say democracy is an idea borrowed from the West. Remember—before we become Muslim, Christian or Ezidi, we are born Kurdish. That does not mean I am a fanatic nationalist, but your leaders say,

Sarbast's brother, killed 6 May, 1991

'We must do everything in the name of Islam.' Yet our Islamic leaders like Salahaddin did nothing for their people. All the Islamic empires have squashed and oppressed us. It is because of Islam that we do not have a land called Kurdistan. Always the Kurdish lose when they think they are Muslim before they are Kurdish."

An Islamic state does not have to be a dictatorship, but in reality Islam does not encourage democracy. A non-Muslim cannot represent a region in an Islamic state. Muslims believe that the Qur'an is God's law. In Muslim societies, the man decides everything, although some exceptional women have become powerful. For instance, Hapsa Khan Naqib, the sister-in-law of Shaykh Mahmud, had no official position, but because of her personal charisma, strength, vision and family position, she wielded great influence. She was an excellent mediator and was the first to open Kurdish schools.

As well as the Islamic Movement of Kurdistan, there are also unofficial groups like the Nahazah and Hamas, as well as the Hezbollah, led by Shaykh Muhammad Khalid Barzani (cousin of Mousad Barzani), and Lashkiri Islami Kurdi, which have been active in the Bahdinan area since the early 1980s. To me, it is not about religion. It is about dividing the people. Because these groups are well financed by Iran and Saudi, they are able to distribute welfare and gain support. Consequently more and more Bizootnowa *peshmergas* began establishing themselves in PUK territory, telling the people that PUK was against God. They began putting acid on girls' legs if they considered the girls were not dressed properly. Hairdressing shops were burned. They wanted to take away the few rights Kurdish women have, and PUK wanted to stop these actions. It was useless talking; sometimes you have to use force.

In 1994 the Bizootnowa ambushed and killed two or three PUK *peshmergas* in Garmian. PUK called on the other parties to tell them to stop, but the other parties did not intervene, so PUK decided to take over Bizootnowa's headquarters.

At around this time, I had a dream that a flood came and destroyed my family's house and orchards. I said to Mahabad, "Something has happened to my family." In the front line of fighting to take over Bizootnowa's headquarters, on 5 June 1994, my younger brother was killed by my own party. He was 24 years old. Also killed in the fighting, on the PUK side, was one of my closest friends, Jelal Hama Muha. He had been a PUK *peshmerga* since 1977, always visiting our family, hundreds of times kissing and playing with my younger brother. My mother treated him like a son. She would feed him and wash his clothes, standing guard outside the house so that he could sleep. This is how utterly stupid all this killing is.

I was angry that my brother had not listened to me, that brother is still killing brother in Kurdistan. I thought, "We lose everything by our own hands. We have to stop this unhappiness." That my party was responsible for my brother's death was too, too painful.

But I also think the Iraqi and US governments and the CIA support this fighting. It is like in Afghanistan, where the USA supported Islamic groups to push the USSR out, and now the Islamic groups fight—some supported by America and others by Russia. Similarly, in Kurdistan, I believe the Muslim groups are being supported indirectly by America, because they get money from America's allies.

The year my youngest brother was killed, civil war broke out between PUK and KDP—over power, territory and money. It was a terrible time. Many agreements were signed, but the war continued until 1998, helped by outside forces. PUK bought weapons from Iran, as well as on the black market. Today approximately 30 per cent of PUK's budget is spent on weapons, 60 per cent on rebuilding villages and farms, running parliament and developing businesses, and 10 per cent goes into the hands of people.

In Australia it took me three years to get a job, because of my poor English. Then in 1995, I started my own house-painting business. Yet even now—eight years after we arrived—my heart and mind are still in Kurdistan. Most of my friends and family are there, as are all my memories and roots. I continue to be a PUK member. I support them with radio broadcasts, and we talk with MPs and the local council about the needs of the Australian-Kurdish community and forming links with Kurdistan. I am a Labor Party member too, and have asked them, "Why does the Australian government not involve itself with the Kurdish problem?" Care Australia has done a lot of good in Kurdistan and there are still many Australians working there for UNICEF, but the Kurdish people need political support to establish a stable country.

Of my five surviving brothers, one is a member of Bizootnowa, another is a member of Rabitai Islami. Of the three who do not work for any political party, two work on our father's farm and the other is a geologist. I send money to my parents, five brothers, sister, my sister-in-law and some friends whenever I can, because there are still no jobs and it is a difficult life. Sometimes I support them before I support my immediate family.

If Kurdistan becomes a free country, I will go back to live, but it is hard because I have three children born in Australia and Zirian is going to high school. I want them to be well educated, but also I miss my friends and I love my country too much.

The Kurds have had three chances for a nation-state. The first was when the 1920 Treaty of Sevres recognised the Kurds' right to self-determination. The second was in 1946, when the Republic of Mahabad was formed in eastern Kurdistan under Qazi Muhammad, a great Kurdish leader. Our third chance is now. We are a nation of 30 million people. Our hope is the new generation, with its greater education and understanding of the world. Through them, we may achieve self-determination for a free country in four parts: a federation of states—Northern, Southern, Eastern and Western Kurdistan—that can preserve Kurdish culture and language, and aspire to human rights and democracy. It is a real possibility, if the Kurdish people unite. If a family is united, no-one from outside can destroy them, regardless of their problems. I saw 10 *peshmergas* fight and win against thousands of soldiers, because they were fighting for their beliefs, they trusted each other, they knew the land and they had the stamina. This was in direct contrast to the Iraqi conscripts, many of whom questioned why they were fighting the Kurds on Kurdish land. Few believed in Saddam. If Saddam could kill his two sons-in-law, he is capable of killing anyone, but even if Saddam sent thousands of tanks into Kurdistan, he could not defeat a united people.

But Kurds have many traditions, thousands of years old, that stop us coming together. Foremost is our tribal mentality: if I start a fight with another person, my family or party will support me, whether I am right or wrong. This happens with Kurds even in Australia. Instead of sorting out the problem in a just, objective way, people make decisions based on loyalty to their tribe or political party. Then there is a long history of Kurds betraying each other to our enemies, who have always been strong and oppressive. In the past, these outside forces have been Islamic empires. Today, they are the governments of Iraq, Turkey, Iran and Syria, which also use Islam as a political tool, and because the majority of Kurdish are Muslim, they are influenced by these Muslim countries.

Despite these obstacles, many of us maintain the hope of one day coming together. Most of all, we need education, objectivity, and relations with the outside world. But if all else fails, we have lost so many people in the last 80 years, we must be prepared to lose more in a final war. I would go back and fight if I thought it was a final solution. Zirian is also prepared to go. If he was killed, it would be for Kurdistan.

Parting

By Abbas Boskany

Contemporaries we were:
Close and intimate.
Like two children in the alleys,
We fostered hopes and
Were busy with soil playing.

As close to each other as night and dew,
As the morning breeze and the first cock-crow,
As mornings and soarings.
The sight-range was all bright.
Yet it cracked with a hair's line of light.
As the night's tar turned into definitions,
Into poetry,
And into parting.

Contemporaries we were:
Close and intimate.
Together we used to call,
"Cup-bearer, pour wine into the cup"
Fill it, cupbearer.
Tonight is a unique night.
We started with a word, and were
Like two rivers mingling.
Likewise, with one word, we are through.
Contemporaries we were:
Close and intimate we were.
Close and intimate we are.
"Cheers!"

A Fortress of No Tomorrows

A life story based on interviews with Maryam Rowandozi, translated through Aso Walid

Rowandoz is an old, old town[a] built on a half-kilometre wide ridge. To the west is the wide Gali Valley, bordered by the Korak Mountains, but my family's house was on the eastern side, just two metres from the 500-metre cliffs dropping to the Kharand Valley. We looked across to Handren Mountain, one kilometre distant as the bird flies, its steep, grey cliff faces so high that the sun does not shine on Rowandoz until nine or 10 am.

Handren, about two and half kilometres by road from Rowandoz, has always been a strategic mountain. It is where Fakhir Mergasori led a few thousand *peshmergas* against an Iraqi force of 10,000 in 1965. As a result of this battle, the Iraqi government was obliged to negotiate with Mostefa Barzani. On Handren's lower slopes, near the village of Kowlokan, was an army base of 5000 soldiers, with binoculars, tanks and helicopters.

We could not see the army base, but we overlooked Kowlokan, and the river Kowlokan, which is a section of the Big Zab. The river flows through steep gorges from Haji Omaran in the east. Along the river winds the British-built Hamilton Road, and near the river and Kowlokan village, we could see Muhammad Pasha Kora's castle on top of a hill. *Kora* means 'blind'. Muhammad Pasha had one blind eye. The castle was built in 1784 of mud bricks and stone. After his father died in 1810, Muhammad Pasha became a ruler of the Sorani kingdom, which extended south to Sulaimani, but in 1837 the Ottoman sultan paid the *malla* in Khat'e village, behind Korak, to say that whoever fought the Ottomans was fighting against God. In this way, the Ottomans were able to capture and kill Muhammad Pasha. Ba'athss destroyed the castle in 1969. Now, only part of the four-metre high wall remains.

But Rowandoz was famous long before Muhammad Pasha Kora. In 1540 Khanzadi Soran became Queen of Bani Hareer, the low pink hills behind Korak on the southern bank of the Big Zab. Princess Khanzad wanted to unite the Kurdish tribes to defend the area against the Ottoman and Safavid empires, and she would ride a horse into battle. Her brother was Sulamein Beg, and when he died in 1590, his son, Ali Beg, became ruler. The wide Gelieli Beg River, a continuation of the Kowlokan River to the west, and the waterfall are named after him.

Balakian River and Khalani Bieow River also run into the Big Zab. Upstream, in the 1970s, Saddam Hussein built Bekhma Dam, with help from European and Japanese construction companies. The dam serves to divide the Bahdinan and Sorani lands.

In winter, up to a metre of snow surrounded our house. In spring, the valley's green pastures were cut by creeks running with melted snow, but in summer, the creeks dried up. But Bekhal Waterfall, at the bottom of Korak, never dries up. Nor does the spring of

Megr, even when the rest of Kurdistan is in drought. The spring comes from a hill at the southern end of Rowandoz, and all the people of Rowandoz depend on its water. In 1950 the government made a big concrete tank near the *garda gard*—the sports field at Megr. Big pipes gravity-feed the water to each house, where it is stored in a *kani*, a small concrete tank with a tap, dug about one and a half metres into the ground. At about the same time, the government built a gas generator, which supplied Rowandoz with electricity until 1996, when KDP sold it to Iran. Now Rowandoz is without electricity.

During World War One, the government made a rough road from the Hamilton Road up to Rowandoz by cutting into the Kharand cliffs. The road zig-zags up the cliffs so dangerously that every year, at least one car falls off. The road enters Rowandoz at Garachi Khwar'e, or Lower Rowandoz, and continues to Garachi Sar'e or Upper Rowandoz, where my family lived.

In the centre of town, opposite my father's shoe repair shop, is a cannon built by Wastah Rajab for his king, Muhammad Pasha. But Wastah Rajab's cannon could not save his king from the Ottomans. Nor did it save the Rowandoz area from being bombed in the early 1920s as the British air force and newly imposed monarchy attempted to curb the activity of Kurdish rebels, led by Shaykh Mahmud.

When I was growing up, Rowandoz had one small hospital, one council building, four primary schools (two for girls, two for boys), and two high schools. There were five cafes, where the men drank tea and played backgammon and dominoes. The houses were made of mud mixed with straw, with poplar rafters supporting flat mud roofs. Our house was one room, five metres by six metres, with two very small windows, a wooden door, and a small kitchen. We had no furniture. For heating we burned wood in a *sopah*, a metal box with a chimney. We slept on thin cotton mattresses we call *doshak*, with a *lef* to keep us warm: two lengths of material sewn together and stuffed with cotton or wool. In summer, we slept on the roof, cooled by the wind blowing from Handren.

We washed in one of two big public baths: circular buildings, about 30 metres in diameter, with cement basins along the wall. Each basin had a cold-water tap, and one for hot water, which was heated by gasoline. In the centre of the room was a round heated stone—one metre high, and one and a half metres in diameter—heated from underneath by a gas fire. Before gas, they used wood. It heated the whole room, and we would relax by resting our backs on it. Women would go to wash in the morning, the men in the afternoon. We washed in our underwear, saying hello to our relatives and friends.

My family was rich, and owned land on the plain between Rowandoz and Diyana, where relatives grew wheat, grapes, watermelons and vegetables, and raised sheep and goats. The produce was shared between our relatives who worked the land and my grandfather and father, who passed on the shoe repair shop from one generation to the next. We would get milk, yoghurt and cheese from our relatives, or sometimes my father bought supplies from street sellers, my mother storing the dairy products in a small tin bucket in the cool water of the *kani*. If people did not have a *kani*, they stored food in the icy water of a spring.

We were Sunni, and my parents prayed five times a day, my father at the mosque and my mother at home, but they did not make us children pray. They were not fanatical.

My father's mother was a Christian from Diyana. When she married my grandfather, she became a Muslim. We called her Nana, and she was a very good and gentle woman.

My mother's life was more disrupted than Nana's, because my father was involved in politics. Her family came from Haji Omaran, and when they settled in Rowandoz, the two families were neighbours. My eighteen-year-old father liked the look of this young girl he would see from afar, and his family sent mediators to negotiate a marriage. My mother's family refused five or six times over a three-month period. This is the custom to preserve the family honour. But eventually my mother's family agreed, and my father's family bought for my mother the traditional necklace we call a *gardanay rowandozi*: two 24-carat gold chains from which Constantinian lire coins and other gold medallions were hung.

My father, uncles, and cousins were all involved in politics. In the late 1950s and early 1960s, my father collected and supplied food, clothes and money to KDP *peshmergas* led by Mostefa BarzaniIn 1961, when Abdul Karim Qassim pushed Mostefa Barzani into war, my father was arrested and taken to Nograsalman Prison, south of Baghdad. Relatives hid my mother, because KDP worried that soldiers would take her.

When my father was released, he continued working for the *peshmerga*. My mother was worried for his safety, but believed in the struggle. When Jalal Talabani went to Baghdad and negotiated with Saddam Hussein in 1966, my father supported him, because he felt that Barzani was dishonouring the Kurdish cause, that he was interested only in his own power and in making all the decisions. In 1975, when PUK was formed, my father became a member, and would often visit Talabani in Balisan, a village behind Korak. Until his death in 1999, my father supported Talabani.

I am the eldest of six girls and two boys—about one year between each child, so there was always a baby in the wooden cradle. My first memory is when people warned my father that Republican Guards were looking for him. He and my mother escaped with my two little sisters, but accidentally left me behind. Half an hour later, about 20 Republican Guards arrived in army vehicles. I stood outside the house, watching as they went in to search for guns and secret documents. One asked me, "Do you know where the guns are?" I told him, "There are no guns," and he called me a liar. I was not lying. My father had taken them. They brought the cotton mattresses and *lef*, and the tins of sugar, wheat, rice, salt and flour outside, and ripped the bedding with their knives. They poured the food onto the ground, then set everything on fire. Although I was shocked I did not cry or run away. When the soldiers asked me several times where my parents were, I replied truthfully, "I don't know," and they became very angry, and left.

My father was hiding in a relative's cupboard, and at sunset he went to a *peshmerga* base on Korak. Every day my mother took food to him, walking six hours there and back, sometimes leaving my two sisters and I locked in the house.

My parents had a strong relationship based on clearly defined roles. Babum, my father, made all the decisions, and these were never discussed. But if he had spare money, he would give it to our mother to save. Dykum, my mother, was very kind and patient, calm and quiet. The only time I saw them argue was when my father would hit one of the children for being too noisy or fighting, especially in winter. Dykum would ask, "Why do you hit my daughter?" It was the only time she questioned him, and my uncle or cousin would come and calm them down and solve the problem. Always Kurdish people do this. No-one is allowed to argue by themselves!

When a child became frightened from a bad dream or a bomb, Dykum would put seven hot coals in a dish of water, and splash the water over the child, saying, "Go away fright."

The women always helped each other. They made bread together, cooking it on a big iron plate resting on three stone walls, wood burning underneath. Often neighbours cooked their meals together, or a person would cook a special dish and share it with everyone. If two or three families were visiting, or when there was a celebration like a wedding, all the women helped cook, and all the children played together. Every week there was a celebration and everyone danced the *sepayi, sooskay* or *shaikani* together. Everyone got on well. I never saw a man hitting a woman. Very few people divorced. If they did, when the children turned six or seven, they would go to the father's family. The woman returned to her family, but even her family did not respect her.

The only domestic disturbance I remember was when I was a teenager: a neighbour was shot dead by her husband because she was cheating on him. Her lover escaped. It is against Kurdish custom for a wife to cheat on her husband, so I thought her husband had a right to kill her. The husband went to prison for a couple of months, but within a year, he married again. Every five or six years, we would hear of this type of killing in Rowandoz. In 2000, the PUK administration in Sulaimani legislated stricter laws about 'honour killing', but laws often apply only to poor people.

Otherwise Rowandoz was a beautiful, peaceful place—until I was seven. In 1968 Rowandoz became divided. Because Rowandoz is a strategic area, the Ba'aths brought in soldiers, police and *amn*, and employed *jahsh* in the Kurdish civilian army. Upper Rowandoz was under the control of Kurdo Noori Bawil Agha and his 1000 *jahsh* followers, while Seyid Agha, son of Asad Agha, and his 1500 *jahsh* controlled Lower Rowandoz. When these two *agha*s families had been allied with the monarchy, they had taken the peoples' land by force. After the coup in 1958, Karim Qassim gave the land back to the people, but in 1968, these two *agha*s and their followers formed a link with the Ba'aths and, again, took control of the land. A big *jahsh* headquarters employed 5000 to 10,000 *jahsh* and people in Rowandoz were united in their hate for them. That is why the majority of Rowandoz's boys joined the *peshmerga* and other families went to Hawler. Because of these *agha*s, my family had financial difficulties. We had to buy our food instead of getting it from the farms.

Life changed. There was always a curfew at night. The day after a *peshmerga* attack inside the town, it would be announced over the mosque's megaphone that people were not to leave their houses from morning until evening, and schools would close for the day.

My mother could not read and write, but my father dreamed that one day I would go to university. I started school in 1968. I had never spoken Arabic. At school we listened to the Qur'an once a week, and in Year Five they started teaching us Arabic. All the teachers were Kurdish, and kind to their students. There was one class for each year, and each class had up to 25 students, so although there were four primary schools in Rowandoz, many children did not go to school. Some families were too poor, and needed their children to work on the farm or in the shop. Also the majority of 14-year-old boys joined the *peshmerga*.

I was a gentle child, always smiling. I never liked fighting or arguing, but I was strong and looked like a boy. My father would cut my hair very short, which is unusual for a girl. He treated me like a boy. He was a tall, intense man—very intelligent and often angry in a quiet way. He never shouted, but he smoked too many cigarettes. Injustices made him angry: when the government captured or killed people, he would secretly visit the affected family, and talk about it with his friends. He was never angry with me. When I was little, he would play with me and tell me the old fables, featuring sheep, goats and wolves, often with a political message.

One story was about the legendary Rostami Zal, who was like a Kurdish Hercules who fought injustices in a time before Genghis Khan. He lived alone on top of a mountain near Quzvienca,[b] in a forest near the Caspian Sea. The Persian poet, Firdawsi, wrote about him.

My father did all the shopping, often taking me. The shopkeeper would always give a fair price. Bartering is an embarrassment in the villages, because of the strong relations between people. My father also took me to help him clean his shop, and he was always giving me advice, "Be good to your neighbours. Don't fight with your siblings. Stay away from the soldiers. Study hard at school so that one day, you will be something."

Until I was 13, he would take me to the *peshmerga* base near the village of Fahqian, on Korak, in spring. We would see the goats and sheep in the pastures of the Alkoiyan Valley being tended by shepherds wearing long, woollen waterproof coats, playing the *shemshal*. We would climb up the steep cliffs of Korak, where after 1975, the Iraqi and US governments built a big satellite dish to spy on the Soviet Union. Iran destroyed the dish in 1986.

We always took with us some boiled eggs, and *na'ani teeri*, the thin dry bread we sprinkle with water. We would stop by one spring to watch the partridges come to drink. We consider partridges very special birds. We eat them and use them to catch other partridges. In summer, a male is put in a cage surrounded by camouflaged traps—loops of string each connected to a length of wood. When the caged male sings, other male partridges come to fight him. The intruder's leg or neck is caught in the loop, and as he struggles, the loop tightens.

Before sunrise and around sunset, we would see gazelle high up on Korak. I never saw wolves, I only heard them howling, especially under a full winter moon. Some people hunted the wolves for their skins, selling a skin for 150 dinars. My father told me that 40 years before, tigers used to live on Korak. One woman, whose job was to circumcise young girls, was known as Fatima Pling, *pling* meaning 'tiger', because a tiger on Korak killed her husband. (Most Rowandoz families secretly circumcised their five-year-old girls. It was optional, but people believed what they were told—that it was part of the Muslim religion—so the practice was passed down from mother to daughter.)

At the base, the *peshmerga* would give me boiled eggs, and sometimes biscuits, cake, and lollies, and play with me. I would often learn that one had been killed in fighting. Most casualties were buried at the site of the battle, because if the body was returned to the family, it could be dangerous for them. As I grew older my father never worried about taking me to a man's place because they were all relatives and close friends and he trusted them. Two of his daughters were to marry *peshmerga*. My sister's husband, Bahzad, was Talabani's bodyguard, but he was martyred at Balisan in 1985.

After the 1970 Autonomy Agreement, there were some peaceful years, but in 1974, war broke out again. In May, the army attacked Rowandoz with weapons like napalm. I was shopping with my father. We hid, then during a break, walked home, passing five families who were buried under the rubble of their houses. Our house was destroyed, and that night we walked down to Kharand Valley while the bombing continued. For three days we hid in a cave, surviving on boiled eggs and bread. Then we caught a jeep to Haji Omaran, where an Iranian army truck took us to a refugee camp in Ushnaviyeh.

The family lived in one tent. There were public toilets and taps, but sometimes people argued, because they were unhappy—they had lost everything. The teachers from Rowandoz set up a school and I would go there. For money, my father went and worked in the border area, and when the snows came, we were transferred to Sardasht, where we lived in a house with my grandparents and an uncle's family.

After the 1975 Algiers Agreement, Mostefa Barzani ended the revolution and Saddam announced an amnesty for all Kurdish people, so in the spring of 1976, we returned to Rowandoz by lorry and bus. We took food and blankets, and at the border Iraqi doctors gave us a triple injection against TB and other diseases.

Most houses in Rowandoz were flattened. Some had walls or just their windows and doors broken. There were no shops, just an open-air market. All the primary schools had been destroyed, although parts of the high schools remained. There was no electricity. We camped on our land, putting sticks into the ground to make walls with blankets, sleeping on blankets under the stars. Thank God there was not too much rain that year. Over the next two months my father rebuilt our house with wood and cement. The government supplied cement to each family, as well as 500 dinars and food for one month. We were happy to be back, but were also afraid—there were even more police and army, and new Ba'ath Party offices called Munazama (Rekhrow in Kurdish).

After one month I went back to school—three classes in one room. I had to make up for the year I had lost. I studied and looked after my sisters and brother. My other brother had died. From when I was 12, I had to cook, make bread and wash the clothes in a big tin.

In the late 1970s, fighting between PUK *peshmergas* and the government broke out behind Rowandoz, near Fahqian village. We were happy that PUK was fighting, and would send medicine, food and money, even though we had little to give. Ours was always the first house to which the *peshmergas* came for a meeting. I would serve them tea and food, and listen to their political discussions. Sometimes I would say, "One day we will get our freedom and you will be able to come back to the city." They were brave, honest people, paid just five dinars a month, and I would dream that one day I might become a *peshmerga* too. None of my girlfriends wanted to be a *peshmerga*, but we all talked about the day we would be independent, when there would be no more *jahsh* and soldiers in Rowandoz. Because of his political activities, several times my father was captured, beaten, and taken away for one to three days to the offices of the *amn* or *jahsh* for questioning. As a result he decided to sell up and leave Rowandoz.

The journey to Hawler took three hours by taxi. We cried all the way. We rented a house until my father built a new one, and I went to school and made new friends. Many relatives from Rowandoz lived in Hawler, but life was not so good. When I was in Year Twelve, the teachers, who were Kurdish but 100 per cent Ba'ath Party members, put pressure on us to become members of the Ba'ath Student Union. They frightened us, saying that if we did not join, we would fail and would be expelled, but we told them it was not important for us. We had a clear history. Many students, includinng myself, failed and had to repeat.

Most of all, I missed Rowandoz's mountains, valleys, rivers and expanse of sky. Hawler is a noisy, crowded city, its only interesting feature the fortress castle on the hill in the centre, visible from every house. The hill had grown higher and higher over thousands of years as buildings were built on top of others. But the old mud-brick shops in the arches around the fortress were demolished in 1968. During their demolition, people discovered two underground tunnels. One, 20 kilometres long, went east to Kaznizan, on the way to Koi Sinjak. It led to an underground spring higher than the fortress, so its water came by gravity. On the western side, they discovered a five-kilometre underground tunnel to a guard's tower, so if the guard saw invaders, he could secretly return to the fortress. Over time, people kept taking the bricks of this tower, and now it is destroyed.

Hawler is on the plain, and we lived on the eastern side, on the way to Shaqlowa, next door to my mother's sister's family. My aunt had a son, Aso, who was the same age as me, studying at the University of Baghdad. We had known each other all our lives, but when he finished university, he came back to Hawler and we came to like each other. He worked secretly for the Kurdistan Socialist Party's newspaper, also sending information and medicine to *peshmergas* in the liberated areas. After a while, I told my father that I wanted to marry Aso. My father said, "It is your choice." I passed my final year of school in 1984, and after two months of teaching primary school, Aso and I signed an engagement contract in front of Malla Hussein. Five days later, Aso received a letter from the Kurdistan Socialist Party saying many members were being arrested. They advised him to go to a liberated area, in case his name was given to government agents.

Aso had secretly become a member when he was a school student, after the Kurdistan Socialist Party leader, Rasoul Mamand, split with PUK on 8 August 1979. Rasoul Mamand and Talabani had argued about Talabani refusing to give Kak Rasoul more power. Talabani did not want the split, and from December 1979 onwards, PUK ambushed and attacked many Kurdistan Socialist Party *peshmergas*. In 1982, the Kurdistan Socialist Party, which only had 2000 *peshmergas*, was forced to join with KDP, PASOK (Party of Socialist Kurdistan) and the Iraqi Communist Party in a united front against PUK. The front's leaders thought that Jalal Talabani wanted all the power. People like my father hated all the in-fighting, saying it was no good for the Kurdish people. He knew Aso was on the 'other side', but did not stop our marriage. Many families were split along party lines.

After Aso received the letter we discussed our choices. I was not a member of any party, but I told him, "I go with you."

My parents knew we were in danger. We went by car to Choowarta, a small village close to Qalachorlan, a PUK base in the Sulaimani area. That night we crossed a big mountain on horseback, arriving at the Kurdistan Socialist Party's base at Kanarway the next day. Then we went by car into Iran and turned back, riding horses over mountainous country to the headquarters near Kowlan village. I had never ridden a horse before, so sometimes I was afraid, but it was great to be back in the mountains. The mountains are a different world. I felt strong and free.

At the base, we rested for a few days, then discussed with Kak Rasoul and other leaders what we should do. Aso was an electrical engineer, so Kak Rasoul told him, "Tomorrow, you must go to radio broadcasting and work with the other technicians, Hardi and Noza'ad Rosh Biani." (Hardi surrendered in 1987 and was executed.) He then turned to me: "Would you like to be a program reader on the radio?" Kak Rasoul smoked too much, but he was a progressive-thinking man who made no distinction between men and women in his party. I was surprised but pleased. I was happy to serve the Kurdish people in this way.

Over the next two years, Kak Rasoul would often invite me to go with him and the eight members of the central committee, including Mamoosta Sa'ad, a writer for the radio, Kalahaji, and Hama Haji Mahmud to meetings at the various *peshmerga* bases, so Aso came too. When they discussed the content of the daily one-hour broadcast, they asked my opinion. At least twice a week the program devoted time to describing the lives and activities of martyrs—*Shaheed* (those who go straight to heaven)—and how they died. Other news described *peshmerga* and government activities in the mountains and cities. I suggested that we play music as an introduction so from then on, we began each broadcast with *The Internationale*, the song of the proletariat in all communist countries. Another suggestion I made was to read letters written by people working inside the cities, describing their situation, detailing who had been captured by *amn* and advising of any student demonstrations. The central committee accepted the idea and the segment was successful, although for safety reasons, we could not mention names. There were no radio programs about women.

There were other women active in the party, all married to *peshmerga*, because it was not customary for single women to become *peshmergas* in Iraqi Kurdistan, unlike PKK in Turkey or Komala in Iran. Miriam Khan worked with her husband, Dr Ali. Although not a trained doctor, he had experience in treating injured *peshmerga*. She was a brave, gentle woman. In 1982, she was captured by PUK in a big battle on Qandil, while she was helping injured *peshmergas*, but was later released. Tameem, wife of Hama Haji Mahmud, fought on the front line, shoulder to shoulder with other *peshmergas*. Her husband is now the leader of the Kurdistan Socialist Party.

At the radio, I worked alongside Aso and the other technicians, writers and readers. The men respected me: I was the first woman reader and I was confident in my job, whereas most women would refuse this sort of work. Many could not read or were too shy, and in Kurdistan, the man is very aggressive. However, the men around me appreciated that I worked very hard in other ways too. As well as taking care of my home, I cooked for special occasions, like Newroz, when we make *dolma* or cook lamb stuffed with rice. I also developed a strong relationship with the women in Kowlan.

Kowlan is a very old village, its 20 houses built like steps going up a hill, north-east of Qandil. *Kowlan* means 'rubble'. At least twice, an avalanche completely covered the village. The winter is six months long. Often, more than two metres of snow buries the houses, so people walk on the roofs. In autumn, everyone planted wheat, and in spring they planted tomatoes, potatoes and other vegetables. In July, they harvested the wheat, all in a line, singing to the rhythm of their scythes. The food was stored for the long, harsh winter in a small room, under straw.

The Kowlan women were very angry about the *agha* of the village, who'd grown rich from controlling the people and taking their produce, goats and sheep. This put them under pressure, and with so little flat land to farm, they had to bring food from Iran by car, mule and horse. They did not have the power to stand up to him, and our party could not get involved, because we needed the base and relied on the people to help us.

My two neighbours were Fatim and Khaleh. They were always tired from working and from taking care of their children. Another woman made bread in the *tandoor* each day for the 200 *peshmergas*—the *peshmergas* buying the flour, paying her to be the *khaja khol* ('bread maker'). As well, she had to look after her own children, clean her house, milk the cow, and make yoghurt and cheese. Yet despite their hard, busy lives people would turn on their radios after lunch to listen to me read the program. The women were especially encouraging. Otherwise, they were uninterested in political or social issues. None could read or write.

I know nothing of the theory of Marxism. I did not read books. At a monthly meeting, a central committee member would explain socialism, and Marx and Lenin's theories, but usually I was too busy to go. All I know is that socialism teaches that people should be treated equally, that men and women should work shoulder to shoulder, and that all our work should help people.

Aso was also busy. He worked between eight and 24 hours a day on the radio and typing the newsletter, and sometimes he went away with other *peshmergas*. Both of us carried a weapon—either a Kalashnikov or a small pistol. I knew how to use guns but never had to fire one. At night we slept with a Kalashnikov under our pillow.

Although I was happy in my marriage and liked being a radio reader, I was always tired, and sad about what I had to read. Everybody in the United Kurdish Front hated PUK, especially after November 1983, when PUK signed an agreement with Saddam Hussein. From 1982 to 1985, 12,000 *peshmergas* were involved in fighting, Kurd against Kurd, perhaps 2000 to 3000 losing their lives. This meant that while we were in Kowlan (1984–85), I broadcast too many stories about martyrs being killed by their own Kurdish brothers. It was my husband's party fighting my father's party. Aso's two brothers and nephews also belonged to PUK, and they sent Aso a letter asking him to change sides so that the whole family could be PUK. Aso did not reply. The women of Kowlan would often ask, "How can brother fight brother?" but at that time, I did not like PUK. I joined my mind with my husband's mind. I had no contact with my family. I did not see my father for eight years—until after the 1991 uprising.

Our hopes for peace were raised in 1985 when PUK sent Kak Faridoon, Azad Howrami and other representatives to the Kowlan base and asked the Kurdistan Socialist Party to discuss a ceasefire with KDP, PASOK and the Iraqi Communists, saying that we must unite against Saddam for the good of the Kurdish nation. Back in 1983, they had approached KDP to negotiate but KDP had refused. By 1985, KDP was weaker. Many refugees were in Iran and in return for support, Iran was using Barzani men in its war with Iraq, so KDP's Idris Barzani was ready to negotiate, and on 27 and 28 May 1986, central committee members from all the different parties had a meeting at our base in Kowlan to sign a peace agreement. At the time, I was about to give birth to our first child.

When all the leaders arrived they greeted each other with hugs and kisses. From PUK, also called Yekiti, there were Kak Faridoon, Shaykh Dara and Azad Howrami. From KDP (PDK) were Fazil Mutni and Malazim Yunis. Representing the Kurdistan Socialist Party were Qadir Jabari, Mamoosta Sa'ad and Amin Qadir, and from PASOK were Azad Pasok and Jamal Pasok. I attended the two-day meeting in between preparing the lambs and *dolma*, reading the radio program and having contractions on the second day. With me was Kalsoum, Qadir Jabari's wife. Qadir Jabari had been based in Damascus, and this meeting was the first time husband and wife had seen each other in 11 years.

The most important point discussed was a ceasefire, and the forming of a united *peshmerga*, with fighters from the various parties permitted to travel through PUK-controlled areas to cities like Hawler and Sulaimani, and talk to the people. All the parties except PUK had been restricted to Iran and the border area. PUK agreed to this. The second point was to pool money into one treasury. The third point was to operate a single radio broadcast.

When the second day of negotiations had finished I went into labour. The baby was coming. I had already prepared food for that night and the next day. I had severe pains and thought there was some problem with the baby. Until then, I'd had a healthy pregnancy. Aso went and told the village midwife. Goola, a very gentle, experienced woman of about 70, had delivered every baby in Kowlan for the past 50 years. She felt my stomach and told me, "The boy is naughty. He has twisted around." She rubbed sheep's-fat oil on my stomach and reassured me. We had kerosene lamps for light, three blankets and two pillows. Fortunately there was a spring three minutes' walk away. It was *kani jnan*—a special spring bordered by a one-metre-high, circular stone wall, in which women wash their face and hands before praying. Goola heated water on the primus and *sopah*.

When Aso came back for a meal, we laid the mat, and were sitting down to eat when a snake fell from the roof onto the dinner table! It was a large and very poisonous copperhead, and in the middle of a contraction, I ran out the door! Aso killed it with his Kalashnikov. Goola said, "It's a lucky day for you." It was a good sign to kill a snake—an enemy.

Aso went back to work. All night I paced the room until the pain became so bad, I had to lie down. I shouted and cried. When Aso returned at 7 am, I was still like this. Two hours later, I gave birth. Goola immediately cut the cord, washed the baby and wrapped him in material, then put him next to me. At last I could rest!

Six days later I went back to reading the radio program. I had to take my son, his crying going on air! After a month Aso discussed the difficulties with Kak Rasoul, who said, "We will find a lady in the village to look after your son while Maryam is broadcasting," so that was arranged. Seven months after my son was born, we left Kowlan base. After the peace agreement, Aso had visited his relatives in the PUK bases of

Bargalo and Yekhsemar. They again asked him to join PUK, and he was promised a position on PUK radio.

When Aso changed his mind about PUK, I changed my mind too, but when he told Kak Rasoul of his decision, Kak Rasoul became very upset and they argued. He suspended Aso for two days, so we left Kowlan to join the Twelfth Team of Soran, based at Garawan. All the women of Kowlan cried for us.

Three thousand people lived in Garawan, in a valley bordered by Handren and Korak, about 12 kilometres south of Rowandoz. The area was where Malbandi Three operated, and Aso's brother was there. Aso's family came to visit. Mine could not, because my father was under constant surveillance and my mother was unwell. There was no radio—it was a commando base—and Aso's job was to introduce new *peshmergas* to the PUK program.

On 1 April 1987, when I was expecting my second child, we were in Fahqian village visiting Aso's brother. When Iraqi aeroplanes started bombing, the *peshmerga* announced over the minaret's megaphone that everyone must leave the village, but we could not escape. I was having contractions. The bombs kept coming, some exploding a kilometre away. Then Saddam Hussein's tanks and ground troops started to attack from two kilometres away. All the people had escaped, and the *peshmerga* had gone to the mountain to fight, so we were the only ones remaining. At 4 pm, I gave birth. Aso cut the umbilical cord and washed the baby.

After five days and many, many deaths, the *peshmerga* regained control of the area. We returned to Garawan. In the evening, I heard a strange noise, a bit like a tractor, then as the sun set behind the mountain, we heard four or five low booms. After five minutes, the *peshmerga* announced: "This is a chemical bombardment. Please go to the top of the mountain." Two hundred people obeyed. Everyone was frightened.

I was still weak, and it was a very cold, windy, black night with heavy rain. We knew the road, but it was very steep and narrow, wide enough for only one person, a cliff to our right. I carried the baby in my arms, Aso holding our 11-month-old son. We found a cave, its arched entrance leading to a flat area about three metres square. The rain continued throughout the night, so until sunrise, 200 people stood in the cold, damp darkness of the cave, surrounded by mosquitoes, bats and yellow scorpions. In the morning we went back to the village. There was no chemical dust residue, because the bombs had been dropped some distance away, so many people went straight back to work harvesting their grapes. But the scratches people got while cutting the branches began to burn, and people's eyes ran. They were transferred to Khat'e hospital, and Dr Zirian said, "Your symptoms are from chemicals. Nobody must touch the branches or eat the grapes." The people were transferred to Iran. After six months, they came back to the village, but over the next six months, two died.

The village people and *peshmergas* decided to rebuild the village further up the mountain. In between breastfeeding my two sons, I carried the mud to Aso in a big flat dish, while Aso's sister looked after the babies. After the one-roomed houses were finished, we covered them with trees and leaves to camouflage them. Aso found a new spring with fresh, cool water, made a channel, and laid a hose to siphon water from the spring to a point just metres from our house.

The village had two or three shops. These sold powdered milk, canned food and frozen chicken, which they got from smugglers coming from Rowandoz. Everything had to be brought in illegally, because the government had put a checkpoint on the outskirts of Rowandoz, so things were extremely expensive.

Over the radio we heard about the start of Anfal, and the chemical bombing of Halabja on 16 March 1988. Aso says 12,000 were killed of a population of 71,000, but no-one dares speak the true figure. Then at 7 am on 23 May 1988, there was a call over the mosque's loudspeaker for all *peshmerga* to go to Garawan base for a meeting. Aso went and did not return. I heard no news for a couple of days, but assumed he had gone with the others to Chelchel.

Three to 400 *peshmergas* of the Twelfth Team of Soran, led by Sa'aid Muhammad Ziyad and Qadir Katchal, the First Branch of Korak, as well as Abdullah Boor's 19th Team, were stationed on Chelchel mountain. Chelchel is the highest point east of Rowandoz, close to Korak. Nearby on Korak was the Iraqi base, but if Saddam controlled Chelchel, he could control the area. He sent the Minister of Defence, Adnan Khrola, to plan the attack, along with the elite Republican Guard, backed by air force, ground troops and every modern weapon.

On the first day, we heard over the radio that Iraqi aeroplanes and tanks bombarded Chelchel. Then at 2 am the next morning, news came that Iraq had sent in six battalions of ground troops, about 2000 to 3000 soldiers, including *jahsh*, from many sides. In 34 hours of continuous battle against 200 *peshmergas*, many soldiers lost their lives, the *peshmergas* prepared to fight to the last bullet. After 34 hours the Iraqi forces pulled back to Korak, and over the next week they would attack and retreat.

In that week, Sa'aid Muhammad Ziyad telegramed Kusrat Rasul in Balisan, requesting that he send more *peshmergas*, but Balisan was also under heavy attack. When the *peshmergas* on Chelchel ran out of bullets, we heard they were risking their lives to retrieve bullets and guns from dead Iraqi soldiers. The first martyr by knife was Shaheed Ali, killed when trying to take ammunition. Many friends died in that battle.

I was on the third line, in Garawan village. For a week, more than 20 women made *na'ani teeri* and packed sheep's cheese and yoghurt in material, to send to the front line. We were nervous and fearful for all the people and did not sleep, only resting for a few hours a day. During that week, I heard news that Aso was three hours' walk away at the back of Chelchel, manning the *rakal* (the transceiver equipment used to relay messages to Garawan base), with two others, Azad Qasarb and Mamoosta Rashad, who now live in Canada. After that, I heard nothing. For three months, I did not know whether he was alive or dead. Fighting continued for a month on Chelchel and, as the *peshmerga* withdrew, for another two months in the Alkoiyan Valley and on Handren. Saddam continued to use chemicals and destroy every village.

After that first week the *peshmergas* announced that all women, children and old men must escape to Iran. I was sad. I wanted to keep fighting Saddam so the Kurdish people could have a homeland. I travelled by horse with my older son tied with fabric onto my back, and my baby tied to my front. Others had babies too. Some people carried chickens and blankets. Others carried injured *peshmergas* by horse to the KDPI hospital at Pishtashan[c] on Iraqi soil, close to Qandil. It was step by step for two

Displaced family at Penjwan, photographed by Mansour Razaghi

days over five mountains, sometimes through snow. Some children died on the way.

I did not eat until we arrived in Bahdinowa, on the other side of the border. It was very hard. I saw 5000 dusty, tired people lying and sitting in Bahdinowa cemetery, without food, drink or blankets. The Iranians began distributing tents. It is said PUK paid for this, but Aso thinks the Iranians gave PUK this money.

Every day *peshmergas* would arrive from the front, but no-one knew the whereabouts of Aso. One day in August, I saw this dusty bearded man carrying a Kalashnikov walking up the road. I did not recognise him until he was two metres away. When I saw who it was, I cried. He said, "Don't cry. Just thank God I am safe." A few days later, the Qandil battle was fought, and then all *peshmergas* pulled out of Iraqi Kurdistan.

On Aso's return, my cousin, a rich man who was very close to Barzani's family and who lived in Ushnaviyeh, came to the camp and took us to live with his family. After a month, in autumn 1989, PUK called all *peshmergas* to go to PUK headquarters at Qasmarush, near the border, close to Sardasht. Aso went and Jalal Talabani said, "We must fight against Saddam Hussein to the last life. All available *peshmergas* must go to Mamandan Mountain and Dohlakoga, because it is still under PUK control." The *peshmergas* became divided on that basis. Many did not have duties at that time, and they could not be active inside Iran, so they either had to go back to extreme danger or give up when Saddam announced an amnesty. When many engineers gave up under the

Iraqi Kurdish Women making bread at Penjwan, photographed by Mansour Razaghi

amnesty, Talabani asked Aso to man the broadcasting unit in Saguez, along with two engineers, Peshko Abdul Khlik Marouf and Redarr. Every 21 days Aso came and visited us for seven. This continued until the uprising.

In early January 1991, Aso told me there were big plans for an uprising. Talabani had sent a letter to Masoud Barzani, who was in Rajhan, near Urmia, saying, "We must unite, and go inside Iraq to talk to the people, because nothing remains of Saddam Hussein's soldiers in Kurdistan. Now is the time for an uprising." Between 15 and 17 February 1991, there was another big meeting in Qasmarush, and after a week, Aso went inside Iraq to work on the radio. I stayed in Ushnaviyeh.

The first town to be liberated was Rania. Many Ba'aths were killed. I was very happy when I heard the news on radio and television. Then we heard of Sulaimani's liberation on 8 March, Hawler's on 11 March, and Dohuk's a day later, but there was no news of

Aso. I started to wonder whether he was alive. Along with 20 other women, on 20 March I caught a mini-bus back to Iraqi Kurdistan, crossing the border at Haji Omaran. When we arrived on Iraqi soil, we thanked God. We were back in our land. In Hawler, I went straight to Aso's mother's house. She told me that Aso was in Kirkuk writing a report about the battle for Kirkuk's liberation. After eight years of not seeing my family, I visited. We cried and hugged, and I stayed some hours before returning to Aso's mother.

Kirkuk was liberated on 21 March, but when Saddam's forces approached and began bombing seven days later, Aso returned to Hawler, going first to PUK headquarters, where he was told, "Tonight, Saddam Hussein will attack Hawler." He came home to find us all asleep on the roof, and became very upset: "Why did you come back to Iraq? All of you must leave." We did not believe him and went back to sleep. Half an hour later he came back saying, "Wake up! Saddam is going to attack." At midnight the bombardment began.

The *peshmerga* were not allowing civilians to leave Hawler until the *peshmergas'* families had escaped, so at 12.30 am, Aso gave me his *peshmerga* card to show to the checkpoint. We walked to the checkpoint, then caught a lorry to Ushnaviyeh. Aso stayed behind. At 9 am the next day, after fighting Iraqi ground troops and tanks near the Koi Sinjak Road, the PUK *peshmerga* pulled back to Salahaddin. They managed to stop Saddam's advance on Shaqlowa at Darbandi Koray, between Shaqlowa and Salahaddin. Masoud Barzani was at the KDP base in Sarirush, close to Shaqlowa, so *peshmergas* controlled Salahaddin and Sarirush.

Aso stayed two nights at Shaqlowa, then a week at the radio base at Galala, before coming to Ushnaviyeh. He was shocked by what he saw in Kurdistan and on the border. In Haji Omaran, many bulldozers, tractors and cars, and much military and hospital equipment waited to be transported across the border. He saw tank tread, copper and aluminium pipes, while on the other side were Iranian intelligence carrying Kalashnikovs from Iraq. In PiranShahr, Sardasht and Ushnaviyeh, we both saw these vehicles and this equipment in council yards. They had been sold to the Iranian government! Someone from PUK told Aso that tanks, RPGs and BKCs were also being sold to the Iranian and Turkish governments.

Later I saw Iraqi soldiers' uniforms and boots being sold at temporary roadside stalls. Perhaps the leaders lost control over what people were doing. It was a time of chaos, and everyone had become a *peshmerga*, including *jahsh*, but Aso blames the Kurdish leaders, saying that they must have allowed the people to do this. He argues, "The ordinary people could have taken the boots and clothes, but the people in top positions must have been responsible for disposing of the large equipment. Aso says, "If the Iraqi Kurdish leaders had kept the tanks and heavy weapons, we could have defended Kurdistan or attacked the biggest city in Iraq. Without the bulldozers, how could we rebuild Kurdistan?" Kurds were coming to Iran and paying up to 20,000 Iraqi dinars for a donkey or horse because they had no way of ploughing their land. An Iranian official told a man buying a donkey, 'Why did the Kurds sell all the equipment in the first place? You must be dumber than donkeys!'" Aso says, "To my mind, this is all proof that Kurdish leaders don't want Kurdistan to be independent. The only modern Kurdish leader to ask for independence is Abdullah Ocalan, and that's why he is now in prison."

Later, when we visited my family, my mother asked, "Why were people put in prison or killed because their family had *peshmergas* while Jalal Talabani's father, Shaykh Hossamadin, was able to walk free through the middle of Kirkuk?" Aso said it showed that Kurdish leaders had been working with other governments for some time.

After what he saw, Aso no longer wanted to work for PUK. He decided we must escape to another country, so he went to Tehran to apply to go to Australia as refugees. When the Australian Embassy refused our application twice, he decided we must return to Hawler, but I did not accept that. Our third son had been born in Ushnaviyeh in 1989 and I was concerned for the children's future.

In April 1991 I became extremely angry as I watched on television Jalal Talabani and Mousad Barzani in Baghdad for negotiations hug and kiss Saddam Hussein. I asked, "How can they do this? Have they forgotten Anfal and Halabja and the decades of fighting?" To negotiate with Saddam was betraying the blood of their people. After that, I saw no hope for Kurdistan. Kurdistan was not my country any more. But Aso insisted we had no choice but to return to Hawler, so in February 1992 we did.

The streets were filthy, because there were no garbage bins or garbage trucks. Every wall was sprayed with bullet holes. Electricity was available for only two hours a day, water for one. Some people were buying water. There were no medicines or equipment in the hospital. People were hungry. The only food came through the UNHCR and other aid organisations, but it was not getting to ordinary people in the cities and towns. It was going to refugee camps, some villages, people in power, and those working as volunteer doctors and teachers. People killed for food, or stole a pot of *dolma* while it cooked on someone's stove. There was thieving of food from aid organisations, with people becoming rich overnight: leeches sucking the blood of the people.

My sister worked as a volunteer teacher, paid in food by the UNHCR, but in the classrooms there were no books or pens, no chairs, no doors, no glass in the windows. My sister continues to teach. Since 1996, she has been paid 500 dinars every few months.

People were preparing for the election of a Kurdish National Assembly in May, and everybody was divided along party lines. This time they were fighting not with guns but with colours! PUK wore green and KDP wore yellow. *Peshmergas* tied yellow or green material on their Kalashnikovs and every office displayed a colour. If someone with the wrong colour was in the wrong place, they were in danger. It was so stupid. Some people would argue in the street about politics, but in other places people were too afraid to talk. Now there was no Saddam. Instead, they were afraid that KDP or PUK or some other party, such as the Islamic Movement of Kurdistan, would kill them if they dared criticise the party controlling that area.

It was obvious the election was going to be won by either PUK or KDP, so many in the Kurdistan Socialist Party (including Rasoul Mamand, Adal Morad and Adnan Mufti) and members of other small parties left to join one of the major parties.

There was a Kurdish radio station, newspaper and television channel for each party—seven television channels—but Aso soon discovered that the people in power employed *jahsh* and informers in high positions in preference to *peshmergas*. Aso says, "The leaders knew that if I and other *peshmergas* saw something unjust, we would not shut our mouths, but the *jahsh* were used to shutting or opening their mouths in return for money and position." At least Aso could buy food on the black market, because we had savings, and Aso's mother had given us money after selling their house.

As the May election loomed people came under increasing pressure to vote for KDP or PUK. Voting took place from 8 am until midnight, but many people did not have identification papers or money to catch a car or bus to the booths. There were long queues, and I heard people were arguing, even fighting, while they waited to vote. We were told that some people cheated by voting a number of times by using different identification papers, especially in the Dohuk area. People were being given money, rice and flour if they voted KDP. Everyone over the age of 18 could vote, but Aso advised me not to. He said, "While those leaders are in Kurdistan, never vote for them." We did not vote.

After the election, it was announced by all the parties' media that KDP had won 51 seats and PUK 49, but many people believe that PUK would have got the majority of votes if people had not cheated. On the day they announced these results just for a joke I told my neighbour who supported KDP that PUK had won. She became very upset saying, "I will have to move from this street." She went to tell the news to her neighbours. When she found out the truth she said nothing.

The parties agreed to form a United Peshmerga Force and to share power in all government departments. It looked like a good chance for the Kurdish people, but nobody trusted the leaders—it had been the same in 1986. The ink of any agreement they sign always seems to fade within months.

At least there was no curfew, and people could read Kurdish books and broadcast in Kurdish, and there were fewer police and soldiers on the streets. But over the next 18 months, people still fought a war of colours, and day by day, the situation worsened. The united *peshmerga* never acted like a united *peshmerga*. Every party set up checkpoints. Between Haji Omaran and Hawler, Aso counted 22; in Saddam Hussein's time, there were 10. There was no overriding law and order. The court calendars and prisons were bursting, and many prisoners were tortured and executed without being charged. Officials were not complying, even with the Iraqi code of conduct, under which there is no cross-examination.

There were explosions, people were being ambushed and taken hostage, and some were assassinated. Aso's nephew had been in the Islamic Movement, but decided to join PUK during the uprising. He disappeared in 1992. We discovered what happened to him only through a 1996 Amnesty International report. The Islamic Movement had captured him in Hawler and taken him to Diyana. After burning 'PUK' into his chest with hydrochloric acid, they executed him.

In the second half of 1993, fighting broke out between PUK and the Islamic Movement in the Sulaimani, Hawler and Shaqlowa areas. Many people were sacrificed. It was a clash over social values as well as over power. The Islamic Movement was closing bars that sold alcohol, and women's hairdressers. All women were made to wear the *hijab*.

Throughout 1993 KDP and PUK leaders visited each other and signed many agreements, but it all came to nothing. I lost all hope. All Kurdish people felt the same devastation and sense of betrayal. Aso said we must build a new life for the sake of our children, and I agreed. He went to the Australian Embassy in Tehran, and this time they accepted us. On 24 March 1994, we flew out of Tehran. Five weeks later, civil war broke out between KDP and PUK.

In 1996 I was attending an English course at Liverpool Migrant Resource Centre in Sydney. At the centre were banners made by Cook Islanders and South Americans, and a group of us asked if we could make a Kurdish banner. In July, 10 to 15 women started meeting every two weeks, most from Iraqi Kurdistan. We came up with a design, which included a man and woman in traditional Kurdish wedding dress, a woman holding a baby in the mountains, sunflowers, a white dove of peace, and the Kurdish flag's colours (green, white and red, with a yellow star in the middle). As well, there was a map of Australia surrounded in gold, with a lonely, sad-faced refugee woman behind a window. A red wave represented our suffering, a blue wave love, harmony and hope.

Most of the banner was sewn in fabric, and we were at the stage of sewing our individual pieces onto the banner when we heard that on 31 August 1996, Saddam had bombed Hawler, at the invitation of Masoud Barzani. When we came into the migrant resource centre the following week, PUK supporters were saying, "Barzani has sold Kurdistan to Saddam," and KDP supporters were saying, "Barzani had no choice. PUK had taken over Hawler and allowed Iran into Kurdistan. We are proud of what Barzani did. He saved Kurdistan from Iran." No-one felt like working on the banner.

At the next meeting, we discovered a yellow border had been sewn onto the banner. PUK supporters said, "This yellow border represents KDP. If it stays, we won't be part of this banner." I explained to the project officer why it was unacceptable. The PUK women decided to buy a dark-blue ribbon for the border. Despite these problems the banner was completed in September.

Now there are two regional governments in the Kurdish region of Iraq, and two satellite television stations: K-TV in Dohuk and Kurd-Sat in Sulaimani. All this makes me happy to be in my second country. It is a democratic country, unlike my first country. I sometimes feel lonely because I am far from my land and people, and day and night I have fond memories of Rowandoz, but otherwise all my memories are of war, from generation to generation.

I was a happy child, but as I grew up I saw too many things. When I was in Year Five, I watched as *jahsh* hit my father with their Kalashnikovs, making him fall down. They tied his hands, and I swore at them and went onto the roof and swore at them as they took him away to *jahsh* headquarters, where they hung him upside down. I knew too many people who died, and saw too many villages destroyed, so I became a *peshmerga* with my husband to take revenge on the government who did this. In the mountains, I did not smile. I was quiet, serious and sad, because I thought the revolution would mean freedom, not brother killing brother.

So I came to Australia. Australia has been good to us. Life in Australia is freer for a Kurdish woman. Back in Kurdistan, women are always under pressure. The man fights and negotiates and the woman stays at home. If a father wants to marry his 14-year-old daughter off to an old man, she must do it. In Australia, I make more decisions, like sometimes choosing the food, clothes and furniture when shopping, whereas back in

Kurdistan, Aso would decide everything. In Australia, I am free to talk about anything. Very occasionally, I might disagree with Aso about a political point, but not enough to be a problem.

In Australia, my daughter will marry whom she chooses, but we will have to know his family, because marriage is only once in a lifetime. I will not let her have boyfriends. I will not let my sons have girlfriends. I would like them to study, serve the Australian government and protect the Australian land.

I am not greedy. I pray to God that if I become rich, so will all poor people. If Kurdistan became independent, I would like to go back, but I do not think our children would want to live there. They are used to Australian culture and are not interested in politics, although they like to watch videos about Kurdistan, hear about our hard life and listen to the old stories, particularly our eldest son. None dreams of becoming a *peshmerga*.

I am happy here, but I am still angry with Saddam Hussein, especially when I see documentaries showing how the Iraqi people contiune to suffer because of that man. I often say, "I would like to throw Saddam to the Great White Shark. They are both savages."

Colour War

By Abbas Boskany

I stole a butterfly wing's colours
And cast them upon your colourless days,
Illuminating my native land's dark night.
Yet the sight to your eyes became a black tent.

It was a full-coloured night.
You and I,
Nothing lay in store that we had not done to each other,
Yet I did not know whether I was able to offer you everything.

You, like a butterfly,
Followed the thundering of my madness,
You wanting only to give moral support
To the butterfly's colours and my native land's dark night.

Price of Freedom

A life story based on interviews with Dr Bewar

The first day I arrived in Australia was the day I was born. My over-riding feeling was that I was truly free. I had never felt like this. All my life, my thinking has been brewed by politics. In south Kurdistan, there are about six million Kurds, but until 1992, we had no official Kurdish media that was not controlled by the Ba'ath Party. It was against the law to listen to *peshmerga* radio or to buy Kurdish political magazines or books. If the army or police caught people with one, they were often executed straight away. Many people just disappeared. Yet in Australia, with a Kurdish population of just 12,000, we have three hours of Kurdish radio a week, broadcast in Kurdish, and are free to talk about Kurdish news, culture, history, social issues and health. We have a Kurdish magazine and newspaper, and access to books written in Kurdish. The Special Broadcasting Service (SBS) shows Kurdish movies. Had I such rights and opportunities in my country, I would never have become involved in politics.

In 1982, when I was in my first year at university, there were big demonstrations in all the towns of Kurdistan—Kirkuk, Dohuk, Sulaimani and Hawler—in memory of the bombing and destruction of Qaladiza on 24 April 1974, when 1000 people were killed. My friends and I distributed leaflets among shopkeepers and business people, asking them to join the student demonstrations. On successive days, people from all parts of society joined us, chanting, "Long live *peshmerga*! Long live the Kurdistan revolution! Death to Saddam and his regime!" We were also shouting, "No racism in Iraq! No nationalism! Long live all Iraqi people!" but no Arabs joined us.

It was very, very dangerous. At first the army faced us with shields and batons, just hitting people, but as tens of thousands of people joined the demonstrations over three weeks, they started shooting. Hundreds were injured and many students killed in each city. Thousands were arrested, but each day more and more people marched. These were the first big public demonstrations against Saddam's regime in Iraq.

On 25 April 1982, I was marching down Sala'am Street, the main street of Hawler, when the army started firing into the crowd. Everyone scattered. Ten people were running in the same direction, and we broke into a house to hide. We were on the roof when 12 heavily armed intelligence officers caught and blindfolded us, then took us in vehicles to prison. They beat us with rubber cables and put us in a small, dark room. For the first two days, they fed us nothing—no food, no water.

We slept on the floor, without blankets. The food was poor and portions small. When they took us to and from the toilet, they beat us, and they also beat us every day during questioning. I denied having been in the demonstration. I said I had been going home from the university, but the interrogator asked, "Then why are you wearing jeans and sports shoes?" Every day the interrogator asked the same questions: "How did you organise the demonstration? Who is supporting you? What is your organisation? Give us the names of your friends." When I did not give information, they beat me, but if you do admit to anything, they give you 10 years in prison or they hang you, so the best strategy is total denial. None of us gave information. It was a matter of life and death.

Our families did not know where we were or even whether we were alive or dead. We had no legal rights, and none of us expected to come out alive. We did not know that all the Kurdish university students were boycotting lectures and demonstrating, demanding our release, and one day at about 1 am, two months after our arrest, officers blindfolded us and put us in jeeps. They released us a day before one of my final exams. I had to resit it four months later.

I had always wanted to be a civil engineer, but decided to study medicine to help my people. I attended Salahaddin University in Hawler. This university had been started in Sulaimani in 1966 at the time of Jalal Talabani's negotiations with the Iraqi government, but because of student unrest, it had been moved to Hawler in 1980–81.

University is free in Iraq, except for the books, but Kurdish students always had problems. If students did not belong to the Ba'ath Party Student Union, they were not allowed to attend some tertiary institutions, and they could not become teachers, participate in international sporting teams, or travel outside Iraq. Kurds who lived at the university had to stay in a college isolated from the others, and Kurds not belonging to the Ba'ath Party were not allowed to visit friends in other colleges. Outside college, Kurds were not allowed to gather in a group.

For four months after my release, I had an intelligence officer following me everywhere. I knew that he was not a student, because his uniform of grey pants and white shirt was new. He would attend my classes and exams and follow me to the library and university gates. On the last day of the exams, I jumped over a half-wall on the other side of the room. I thought they might be intending to catch me on my way home. Other people were also targeted. It was so obvious that it seemed as if making us aware of them was a tactic in itself.

In 1984 there was another big protest, because all students were being forced to join the civilian army, called the Jayeesh Al-Sha'abi, one day a week and during summer holidays. All Kurdish students at Salahaddin University refused to attend the final exams, so we failed and had to repeat the year.

In 1988, the year of Saddam's Anfal operations, I graduated, and started working as an intern in Hawler Teaching Hospital. All interns and registrars lived in, and were on call 24 hours a day, six days a week. Saddam had ordered that no doctor was to treat people suffering from chemicals, so when people came in with breathing problems, burning eyes and blisters, my colleagues and I treated them by writing up false diagnoses for respiratory-tract infections and conjunctivitis.

In mid-1988, there were chemical attacks on the Bahdinan people of the Zakho-Dohuk area, as well as on the Garmian people between Kirkuk and Sulaimani, and thousands had escaped their villages and come into one of three camps—at Bahirka, Hushtralu, and Ankawa, a suburb of Hawler. They had been at the camps for a week, sleeping on the ground in the open without food or drink. Many had become dehydrated, so people brought them to the hospital.

We gave these people intravenous fluid. After introducing them to solids, we discharged them and admitted others. The hospital was chaotic. A three-storey building built by the British, it had roughly 800 beds. Four big halls had 40 beds each, but there were sixty patients in each hall. Small rooms had two, four or six beds, and another two or three patients on the floor. Outpatients was crowded too. We worked around the clock for two weeks, grabbing a few hours' sleep here and there.

People in Hawler collected food, clothes and blankets to help the Bahdini and Garmian victims. On a number of occasions, the government set up checkpoints and confiscated supplies, so people became resourceful in finding other ways to reach the people. Still, hundreds died. In our hospital dozens died.

I finished my internship in 1990, and was meant to go into the army, but I refused to join an army that was killing my people. I had always dreamed of joining the *peshmerga* in the mountains, but at that time the *peshmerga* were weak and scattered after Anfal.

I decided to escape Iraq. I travelled with a friend by car to Haji Omaran. After that we walked. Our idea was to get to Ankara, then decide where to go. We were very worried, always keeping our hired guide in front of us, talking to him as little as possible. My only thoughts were, "Is this man going to betray us? Are we going to live or die?"

It was the beginning of winter, very cold. After two days' walking, we reached the Khabor River, on the border. It was midnight, and there was a searchlight on the Turkish side that turned 360 degrees. We had to cross before the light did its sweep. The river was about 50 metres wide and fast-flowing. I cannot swim, and the water was up to my chin, at one stage going over my head. I lost my bag in the current.

The water was freezing, but we were colder when we got out. We were dressed in Kurdish clothes. We call it *ranku joghal*—grey balloon pants and a tunic tucked into a thick waistband of black material—and the *jamadani*—the turban around a cap. We took these off. Underneath we were wearing jeans and jumper.

A Kurdish guide took us to the nearest village, where we knocked at a house shown to us. The people were Kurdish, and let us sleep the night. At six the next morning, they gave us bread and water and told us the trail through the mountains, and in this way, we went from village to village. It was a hard, mountainous, isolated way, but we wanted to avoid soldiers.

The villages were very poor. The houses were made of mud and straw, with flat roofs atop which were stored hay and piles of cow-dung patties. Very few people had paid work but everyone was friendly. They would give us whatever they were eating: yoghurt and bread mainly, sometimes nuts, honey, rice and different soups. They would warn us to avoid certain areas, and at a distance we passed huge army installations, with long rows of tanks.

It took us three days to reach the village of Shemdinli.[a] It was a village of several thousand people, with traditional mud homes and others of brick and cement. We walked into town thirsty, hungry, and very, very tired, so when we saw three soldiers coming toward us, we were in a daze. They stopped and questioned us. When we could not answer in Turkish they accused us of being PKK and took us by military truck to an underground police prison in the centre of town.

We stayed one night in a cell with two filthy mattresses on the floor and no blankets. They took us out separately and fired questions like, "Where are you from? What

A typical Kurdish village

religion are you? Why did you come here?" I kept to my story, that my father was Turkoman, but I was raised by my Kurdish mother. They kept asking, "What do you know about PKK?" We were scared, hungry, thirsty and tired—they had not given us food or water.

The next day they transferred us by jeep to the military prison. Here they treated us as if we were a cross between enemy soldiers and criminals. We were put in a small cell with a double bunk, and interrogated. The next day I kept to my story. They were sure we belonged to PKK. We told them we knew nothing about PKK. They told us, "Then we will send you back to Iraq." I asked, "If you send us to Iraq, they will kill us. Please take us to the Iranian border."

After two days of interrogations, our luck changed. They had found out I was a doctor, and their prison doctor was on leave. A Kurdish prisoner had suffered an epileptic fit and gone into a coma. They asked me to help him before they deported us. He was on Tegretol and intravenous fluid, and he had an in-dwelling urinary catheter. At first I refused, because they did not have the proper equipment. I was in doubt about the patient's condition. All I could do was adjust the medication. After four days, I took the catheter out, and on the sixth day I removed the IV. The patient told me his fit had been an act so that they would not deport him.

I don't know why they trusted me, but over the next three weeks, I was asked to treat two soldiers with gastroenteritis. I asked for Buscopan, a pain-killer for abdominal cramping and pain, and gave them an injection, a soldier always standing guard.

They continued to question us, but less aggressively, until finally they accepted us as refugees and we were transferred to Hakkari, a civilian refugee camp. Hakkari is on a mountain, and when we were there it was all snow and very beautiful. We were housed in a big school-like building, with 80 other people, for a month, until they transferred us to Tatvan, where we lived in a hotel. It was luxury—good beds and good food, with television, pinball, chess and dominoes, except it was heavily guarded, and we were not allowed to leave the building without an escort. I kept busy working as a volunteer doctor for the refugees. Then, when the Kurdish uprising started in Iraq, they decided to transfer us to a military prison in Siirt, 10 hours by bus. It was to be my worst time in Turkey.

It was the beginning of March 1991. We arrived at about 8 pm in four buses, each carrying 40 men. We saw rows of tanks and so many soldiers and dogs I thought they were preparing to fight a whole country, not 200 refugees. We refused to get off the bus saying, "This is a military prison not a refugee camp." Soldiers with guns, sticks and dogs boarded the bus then beat and dragged us—three soldiers to every person. They grabbed people randomly from the crowd, including my friend. A couple of days later, he came back and told me, "They let the dogs attack us, then they beat us."

The rest of us were taken to a soldiers' hall in an old building with paint peeling off the walls, and double bunks. The mattresses were filthy. We had one blanket each. We were made to get up at 6 am and had to line up in a canteen for insufficient food. We had to bring cold water in tins to wash and drink.

For the first two months, the soldiers beat us, barked orders and verbally abused people. There were about ten Turkomans from Kirkuk and the Turkish military worked them like secret police. If they heard any conversation that went against the Turkish regime or the soldiers, they made a report and the offenders were interrogated, as was anyone else they thought was suspicious.

Most of us were very tired, stressed and depressed. Some isolated themselves completely, just sleeping or writing. At Newroz, when the men began singing in Kurdish, soldiers came and beat them. There was no more singing.

The place, in the middle of a brown plain, had a high security fence heavily guarded. We felt vulnerable and isolated. We were not allowed newspapers or magazines or any way to reach the outside world. But when I began working as a doctor, I had the chance to mix with the nurses. Through one Kurdish nurse, I was able to send letters on behalf of the prisoners to the UN, the International Red Cross, the US President and the European Community. I do not know whether these letters got through, but three months after we arrived, the International Red Cross came and interviewed us, always in the presence of a Turkish soldier.

I remember little about those seven months. My mind was always preoccupied with work and leaving the place. I was lucky because of my profession. When I was sitting with the medical staff, I would not bring up the subject of Kurds, but when they did, I listened. All the staff were Turkish, except for a nurse, but they were all critical of the Turkish regime and how it was treating Kurds.

One day at the beginning of our second winter at Siirt, they gathered us to say they were transferring us to Silopi, a civilian camp. As we got on the buses, some swore at the soldiers. For the nine-hour ride, we were singing and joking.

Silopi was covered in snow. On first impression it looked like Siirt, but there were families, the treatment of refugees was better, and there were options to play soccer or volleyball and other facilities. I started working voluntarily as a doctor, with six other refugee doctors and a UN team, in one of the permanent buildings. I was responsible for the pharmacy and the emergency unit, with its five beds, IV fluid, oxygen, ambu bags for ventilation, and thermometers. Otherwise each doctor was given a stethoscope, an opthalmoscope, and a sphigonamometer for measuring blood pressure. Two mobile intensive-care units were donated, but were stolen within a few days. There were a couple of ambulances, but these also disappeared, as did medications. I would accompany patients to the hospital in Cizre[b], about one hour's drive away, and one day the manager asked me to check some medicines in the hospital's pharmacy. About 50 per cent of their medications came from Silopi.

As a doctor I had my own tent, and a bunk in the pharmacy. The Turkish doctor in charge gave us permission to open the pharmacy from morning until evening, so I took on the responsibility. We had only a few confrontations with the Turkish authorities. One was over me playing a tape of Kurdish songs. A soldier came into the pharmacy, saying, "You are not allowed to play that song." I said, "Why not? I have a right to play whatever I like." He wanted to destroy the tape, but another soldier told him to leave it alone and they went out.

People were suffering from depression, gastroenteritis, respiratory-tract infections, sports injuries, often caused by playing on cement, and burns from gas stoves and kerosene lamps. At one stage, two or three tents burnt down and people were treated for first and second degree burns. We gave them intravenous fluid, tetanus shots and antibiotics. Very bad cases were transferred to Diyarbakir hospital, three or four hours' away. The worst case was when we treated a family for carbon monoxide poisoning from kerosene fumes. All of them had diabetes, and with the poisoning, one of them went into diabetes ketoacidosis, caused by a rise in blood sugar. It was night, and we could not transfer the comatose patient to a hospital, so I stayed with him until morning. I was very worried because we did not have a glucometer. We had no pathological or biochemical checks. All I could do was treat him with saline insulin. In the morning they transferred him to Diyarbakir, and he eventually improved.

At one stage there was an outbreak of hepatitis A, transferred by contaminated food, water, utensils and faeces. We did not have a vaccination program, so all we could do was advise people to drink lots of fluid and eat sweet things. We observed the worst cases in a temporary tent hospital of 20 beds.

I also worked for the Australian and Canadian delegations when they came to the camp to do medical checks. They asked me to accompany them to other camps in the area. At one camp near Mardin, the people were all refugees from Anfal and the chemical bombing of 1987–88, many from Bahdininan villages. I worked as an interpreter, taking blood and doing medical checks. Families of nine or 10 had been living in a tent, sleeping on blankets, for three years. Some were still suffering from the effects of chemicals. Eventually some were accepted as refugees. Others went back to

Kurdistan either by choice or because they did not pass their medicals. Sometimes their x-rays showed they had previously had TB, or that they needed glasses. At times the decision to reject people on medical grounds appeared arbitrary, particularly when you consider that these were refugees.

I would estimate that 90 per cent of people in the various camps suffered from depression and extreme isolation. They were emotionally broken. Some would talk to me, but I did not have time to counsel. I was too busy treating physical conditions, and I was also very depressed and under a lot of pressure—especially because I was unable to treat people properly. Many children died, as did some adults.

I did not know what had happened to my family until friends came to Silopi and told me they had escaped to Iran. Later someone brought a letter. They had left Hawler by car, but a bomb had exploded and shrapnel had punctured the car tyres, so they had to walk.

As a humanitarian refugee, I was given three choices—the embassies of Australia and Canada accepted me, while Norway offered asylum through the UN. I chose Australia because English is spoken, the Australian delegation was very friendly, the medical system is the British system, as in Iraq, and the climate is good. So five months after coming to Silopi, in February 1992, I was on a bus to Ankara.

When I arrived in Australia, I had very little money in my pocket but more happiness than I had ever experienced. For a few months I lived at a migrant hostel. In the first week, I applied to do the Australian Medical Council (AMC) examinations to get my medical degree recognised in Australia. In August I applied to the University of New South Wales to do the three-year transition course. I passed all the exams and was accepted for 1993. I continued with the AMC exams so that I could become a doctor either way.

I found the Australian medical course more practical than the course in Iraq, but otherwise the same. As a single man it was hard changing from being part of a big family to living on my own, but in other ways it was better, because I was very busy with study and new friends. I did not finish university, passing all my AMC exams in September 1994. I chose to work in the western suburbs, as it is where many Kurds live. The most common ailments I see relate to post-traumatic stress—depression, weakness, tiredness, insomnia, difficulty in concentrating, and psychosomatic complaints like stomach-ache, backache and headache, as well as chronic arthritis.

In early 1994 I went back to Kurdistan. At that time, the situation had changed for the better—we could speak freely about Kurdish politics, and at last we had a free Kurdish media. But there were many internal problems, and most people relied on food and medicine supplied by the UN. When I visited the teaching hospital, people were dying as a result of shortages of medicine and equipment—especially children with gastroenteritis and respiratory problems. The situation became worse during the four years of civil war, and when Saddam Hussein's forces entered Hawler and bombed the city in August 1996, my family feared a repeat of 1988 and 1991.

I am not confident about the future of Kurdistan. The international community is turning a blind eye to Turkey's invasion of Iraqi Kurdistan. There is a Kurdish saying, 'Kurds have no friends but the mountains,' and it was confirmed yet again when no country offered political asylum to Abdullah Ocalan, leader of PKK in northern Kurdistan, after he was forced to leave Syria in September 1998. When he was illegally abducted in Nairobi on 16 February 1999, Kurds felt they had been betrayed by the whole world. The Greeks, who are meant to be our allies, CIA and MOSSAD were involved. Turkish commandoes took him to Turkey, where there was no hope of fair treatment or a fair trial.

I felt the despair, anger and frustration of all Kurds. Once again, we did not feel safe anywhere. Protests at Greek embassies around the world were the only way we could turn media attention on the fact that Ocalan had been captured by an illegal collusion of forces. It is easy to criticise some of the demonstrators who vandalised property, and the often violent struggle in Kurdistan when you live in a country that has never faced major problems of attack and bombardment, political imprisonment, execution and deportation. If the protests had been legal, as in getting permission from the police, they could not have occurred as an immediate response to the kidnapping. If they had been peaceful the media would not have reported them, as we have discovered since then. Time and time again the world media does not report what is happening in Kurdistan or our peaceful attempts to provide information. Even people in the Middle East are ill-informed, because Arabs also oppress Kurds. Even Kurds can get news only via friends and the Internet.

The hypocrisy of world attitudes was highlighted a month after Ocalan's abduction, when NATO went to war for half a million Albanian Kosovars while the plight of 40 million Kurds remains ignored.

The future of southern Kurdistan will depend on America's vision for the area and what happens after Saddam. But international institutions, governments and people must realise that the Kurdish problem will not be solved by more humiliation, imprisonment and killing. By denying the problem, it does not go away.

I have a good life in Australia but I am torn for my family and people. The tragedy of a nation, means I cannot feel settled or at peace. Freedom is the issue. We need practical, political solutions. For this, Kurds must unite and stop the different parties seeking neighbouring governments' military support, no matter what the risks. We have to build up a strong base. All Kurds must support a declaration of independence for southern Kurdistan, by trying to educate people, governments and international institutions wherever we live about the Kurdish situation. Whatever we have to sacrifice to do this, more has already been sacrificed.

Together

By Abbas Boskany

Together
Before lightning,
With arms round our necks,
We narrate myths.
Heading towards
The fountainhead of illumination,
We performed our ablution with light
And said our prayers to love.
Together,
We pause to meditate about the caravan's emptiness,
Without confounding the false slogans' lexicon,
Without reciting the Old and New Qur'an.
With gold-sand, rosewater, and wheat-stems,
We build a hospice for the homeless questions,
With interrupted sobbing,
A briefcase of love-stories,
A gripful of the new cities' soils,
We will throw a different correlative
At your adamant looks and
We will wait.
Could it be that you pardon us our eternal journey?
Can the exile nights,
Our motherless lamentations,
And our statelessness
Grant us heavenly forgiveness?
We come and are ignorant
Of that faceless dawn.

We come, and in the ambiguity
Are ignorant of the prayer-call
And the prayer itself.
Together in this thick darkness,
Like juxtaposed enemies,
Like reciprocal patricides,
We have turned into statues in front of each other.
The sullen frown in the face,
And the sparks of wrath
Have become the bridges between us,
Have become the exegeses of revenge.
Opposing each other, we squeeze the palms of our hands.

Shade will not come out of
Ideology, love, or the deities.
We started together and pondered,
Like a lantern of rancour, we shone together;
Together, we have turned into the exile's walnut-game players.
When the score was 2:2,
We lost.

A Way Through the Mountains

Experiences and views based on interviews with Dr Ali Zibari

In May–June 1987 Abu Saddam, Chief of the Ba'ath Party in Akre, a Kurdish town 100 kilometres north-west of Hawler and 60 kilometres east of Dohuk, came to a funeral and made a speech. I listened in shock: "We are pleased that Ali Hasan Al-Majid, esteemed uncle of Saddam Hussein, has become secretary-chief of the Ba'ath Party for Northern Iraq." (Iraq is divided into three regions, each with a secretary-chief directly answerable to President Saddam Hussein.) Abu Saddam continued, "Al-Majid has very important duties, the main one being to clear the north of outlaws." Abu Saddam was referring to *peshmergas* and all Kurdish people living in mountain villages. "I want you to tell your relatives that we have set a date, and until that date we offer amnesty. If the outlaws surrender, we may forgive them. After that date—let me state this clearly—we will kill every human and animal and destroy all green in the forbidden area. We will use all weapons—forbidden and unforbidden."

I went home shaken. I told my family that I had to leave the country but I was concerned for them. The family decided to leave too. The question was, where to go?

All the Kurdish parties were active in the area, but our family was traditionally sympathetic with KDP, although at the time I was not a member. However the Ba'aths considered it a crime to believe in freedom and democracy. We sent a letter to a KDP *peshmerga* called Babakir, who had been an officer in the army before becoming a *peshmerga* in the 1960s. We asked for permission to come to the mountains, and requested help to escape. On 8 August 1987, at 3 am, I walked out of Akre, along with my parents and three brothers, one brother's wife and their four children, aged between three months and five years.

By the following afternoon we had arrived in Esumara, a small mountain village, where we hired mules. From here two *peshmergas*, Yusef and my cousin, Khalil, were to be our guides. Khalil was based in Iran. He would work for a month or two, then return to Iraqi Kurdistan for two or three months of military activities. His family survived by working on a cotton farm near Saveh, 200 kilometres south of Tehran.

On the second day of our journey, we were travelling through the Barzan area, on the eastern side of the Big Zab River, Zab being Arabic for the Kurdish 'Ze'. The Ze is one of four tributaries of the Tigris, and winds its way through deep gorges. Our tribe, the Zibar, has always lived on its western side. My father grew up in the village of Birakapra, where I was born, five to 10 kilometres from the village of Barzan. In 1975, half the area's population escaped to Iran; the other half, some tens of thousands of people, were taken by army trucks to desert camps in the Aldiwaniyeh province south-west of Baghdad. After some years, they were allowed to return to camps in the north, like Qooshtapa near Hawler, but never to their homeland. It had become a forbidden area.

On dusk we neared Barzan and four Iraqi aircraft flew over. We feared they would see us, but they flew on to bomb Barzan, the village and surrounding area close to every KDP's heart, because it is where the Barzani family originates.

That night the army arrived from two or three directions and the area became a battlefield so my father took us to hide in a cave. The army was intent on destroying the villages and lands with dynamite, including old religious schools and other sites very precious to the Barzan tribe. They met with some opposition from Hezbollah forces, supported by *pasdars*[a] from Iran. Many of the Hezbollah were Kurds who had been living in Iranian refugee camps. KDP was against either of these forces being in the Bahdinan, and in the battle no KDP from Division One came to help.

The next day helicopters flew over and we stayed in hiding. The *pasdars* were escaping, and as one *pasdar* passed by, Khalil asked him, "Why are you leaving?" His answer was, "The gun cannot fight the tank." I kept silent, but the question in my mind was, "Well, why are you here?" My conclusion was that it was only to make trouble for the local people and KDP *peshmergas*.

It took two weeks to cross the mountains. At one stage we stayed at a KDP base. The *peshmergas* fed us from their own meagre supplies. As mobile units they had to carry whatever they needed, because most of the villages had been destroyed. Like us, they travelled mainly at night.

It was a very isolated route—many mountains, gorges and rivers, and deserted villages. To avoid an army base, we had to illegally cross into Turkey for five hours. When we saw Turkish soldiers, Khalil said, "Don't worry." He was experienced in these matters, offering them cigarettes to enable us to pass safely.

The last area on the Iraqi side is Khagurg—a forbidden area like Barzan. We crossed the border illegally, along with hundreds of other families escaping the battlefield, and went straight to Ushnaviyeh, the first town on the Iranian side. After a few days, we reported to the authorities and applied to be accepted as refugees. That process took two to three months, no-one bothering to ask our background or how we crossed the border. In fact the Iranian authorities were only to inquire about how we came to be in Iran when we were applying for visas to leave the country! I had been working as a general practitioner in the country for six years—having sat an exam in Tehran.

What surprised me most was that although the people of Ushnaviyeh were Kurds like us, they were not sympathetic. I decided there were two reasons for this. Firstly there had been heavy fighting between KDP and KDPI from 1983 to 1986. Secondly, they hated the Shi'ite government and wanted Saddam to win the war, and saw us as fighting Saddam and helping Iran. To understand the fighting between KDP and KDPI and why Iraqi Kurds helped Iran on several occasions, one must trace events from 1975. After the collapse of the revolution following the Algiers Agreement, tens of thousands of KDP *peshmergas* and their families, and other people from the villages fled the onslaught of the Iraqi army and air force. In Iran they were distributed to camps and towns throughout the country, under SAVAK's[b] strict supervision. They had a reasonably settled life, and were able to work in factories and other low-paid jobs, but they could not travel without permission. Many educated young men left for Europe and the USA.

In 1975 many Kurds were questioning the collapse of the revolution and wanted to establish strategies to prevent a repeat. Some believed that the leader of the revolution, Mostefa Barzani, had relied too much on the support of imperialists like the USA. After being betrayed by both the Shah and the USA, a growing number of KDP supporters were leaning towards Marxism, although the Barzani family did not. Barzani had seen the Soviet system for himself in his 11 years in exile.

From 1975 Barzani lived in America, and while he was alive no-one could replace him as leader, so KDP reformed under a 'Temporary Leadership', which included Barzani's sons, Masoud and Idris, as well as Sami Sinjari,[c] who was the KDP *peshmergas'* military leader in Iraqi Kurdistan. It was Sami Sinjari who led the battle of Hakkari in 1977. Hakkari is in Kurdistan of Turkey, but the local people have traditionally supported Barzani, so 250 KDP *peshmergas* were based there.

PUK had formed their coalition in Syria back in 1975, becoming active inside Iraqi Kurdistan in 1976. To KDP understanding, PUK was a young party, keen to take over the revolution. In 1977 PUK sent two well-equipped units to attack KDP at Hakkari. One came from Syria, led by Dr Khalid, and the other from the mountains north of Sulaimani, led by Ali Askari. In total they numbered about 1000. I have been told that before the battle, KDP leaders met with Askari, saying, "We know you have come to fight us, but it is better if we unite." Ali Askari refused. With KDP totally outnumbered, Sami Sinjari went to the local people, saying, "We follow Barzani. The others follow Jalal Talabani." At the time, Talabani had a bad reputation as a *jahsh*, because of his negotiations with the Iraqi government in 1966. Sami continued, "They have come to attack us, so we need your help." It was a terrible fight for existence, and hundreds of PUK lost their lives, including Ali Askari. It is a very painful memory for all Kurds.

At the KDP congress of 1979, Masoud Barzani was elected leader of KDP, following the death of his father in March. During the congress Sami Sinjari and his followers split from the KDP, Sami Sinjari forming his own party, called the Sha'ab Party or Kurdistan Popular Democratic Party (KPDP). The split was primarily over leadership, which also involved ideological and strategic issues, particularly between Idris Barzani and Sami Sinjari. Idris Barzani was a man of tough decisions and military solutions, whereas Masoud Barzani always looked for political solutions and was more willing to compromise. He knew that for every army base the *peshmergas* attacked, the army would destroy several villages. Yet unlike the old stories of sibling rivalry, Idris and Masoud were like two halves of an apple.

From the late 1970s, KDP was organised into eight divisions. Division One was led by Dr Rowsch Shaways, who became prime minister of the Iraqi Kurdish National Assembly in Hawler in 1996 and president in 1998. The division maintained a permanent presence in the Bahdinan area and was basically self-reliant. Then there were Divisions Two, Three and Four, operating in the Hawler, Sulaimani and Kirkuk provinces. These divisions maintained an office in Ushnaviyeh, from where they would negotiate permission with the Iranian government to cross the border. Zikri, one of my cousins, worked in this office, making trips to Khagurg to supply *peshmergas* with medicine, shoes, clothes, blankets and food. Division Five was based in Baghdad until 1976, when it was disbanded. Division Six is in London, Division Seven is in the USA and Division Eight was in Tehran until 1996, when the central committee of that division were arrested and tortured after the Iranian government accused them of being Israeli agents because of KDP's good relationship with Turkey. The leader of each division was a member of the KDP's central committee, this numbering between 18 and 24.

Divisions One to Four served to maintain a presence in Iraqi Kurdistan, resist the Iraqi army taking over completely, and educate the people. There was no front line. Small groups moved from area to area to trap the army or to raid a base for weapons, aiming to minimise loss of life. If there were heavy *peshmerga* losses, they would leave.

As for education—KDP broadcast daily radio programs, although the Iraqi government was always putting so much noise over the signals that often, the program was inaudible. KDP also printed a newspaper called *Khabat*, but in government-controlled cities like Mosul and Akre, it was hard to get. The death penalty was automatic for anyone caught with the paper. As well, *peshmergas* would go to the villages to hold meetings with the people and the *mukhtar*, or government representative, appointed by the government. The *mukhtar* was expected to supply the government with information and people, so *peshmergas* would warn him—verbally or physically. On two or three occasions, KDP *peshmerga* placed a dinar coin in a *mukhtar's* mouth and sewed his lips up. The *mukhtar* was rarely killed, each one having various degrees of allegiance, many also giving information to KDP.

At village meetings, *peshmergas* would tell the people why the struggle was necessary, but I fear some of this education had negative consequences. The educator did not necessarily have a broad education, and in the mountains the villagers had little or no contact with the outside world. Many did not go to school or understand Arabic. Their lives were hard but simple, and their mentality naïve. To speak to these people about revolution can be dangerous, especially when trigger-happy young men become inspired by rhetoric.

Also, to speak to people about one party's ideology serves to divide them. This was proved in the 1980s when the Kurdish revolution degenerated into fighting between Kurdish parties. From the KDP point of view, it was PUK attacking KDP, the communists, the socialists and any other group, so they could control the revolution. In 1982 these groups formed a United Kurdish Front to resist PUK attacks. There was a joke of the times: A PUK leader is ordered to fight the Iraqi army, then KDP, then the communists, then the socialists. At last he comes back to his base exhausted. He points his Kalashnikov to the sky and says, "God is the only one Jalal Talabani has not ordered me to fight." All most people wanted was for the parties to unite against their common enemy, but each party seemed more intent on weakening or eradicating the others.

I have never been a *peshmerga*. My experience is of the consequences of armed struggle, and after seeing the devastation and suffering, I know there must be a better way. As such, I believe Masoud Barzani is a great leader, because he has always been a realist and a pacifist, often walking a tightrope trying to balance different interests. However circumstances often spiralled out of his control.

After Mostefa Barzani died, his body was brought back from America to be buried on some land he owned on the outskirts of Ushnaviyeh. This land became known as Barzanabad. As more and more *peshmergas* were killed in Iraqi Kurdistan, and others fled, half the land was used for the dying and half for the living. I knew one *peshmerga* who lived in one of Barzanabad's very basic mud houses. Ahmed Beharki had six children and lived next door to four orphans. He took in these orphans and cared for them as his own.

One evening in late 1979, a woman in Barzanabad saw three figures near Barzani's grave, an Iraqi helicopter waiting nearby. She went and told *peshmergas*, who attacked the men and reclaimed their leader's body. The three men were identified as KDPI. No-one knows why they were taking the body, but I have heard they wanted to give it to Saddam. Whoever was really responsible must have wanted KDP and KDPI to fight. KDP had lost some *peshmergas* in ambushes staged by KDPI, but Masoud was refusing to take military action.[d]

When Abdul Rahman Qassemlou and other KDPI leaders declined to hand over the KDPI suspected of the crime, KDP *peshmergas* protested, telling Masoud, "Give us permission to fight if we cannot punish those responsible." Within a few weeks, there were clashes between KDP and KDPI, and over the next three years, intermittent fighting, until finally from the spring of 1983 until 1986, the clashes escalated into full-scale conflict. This was aggravated by KDPI having been pushed out of the cities and towns by Iranian forces into areas where KDP were active. KDP were far more experienced at fighting in the mountains, and were easily able to push KDPI into Iraqi Kurdistan. As the fighting continued, the *pasdars* looked on delighted, taking advantage of the situation by also attacking KDPI. The Kurds of Iran saw this as KDP helping the *pasdars*.

Meanwhile the Iran–Iraq War raged on. In return for being allowed to stay on Iranian soil and other support, the Iranian government asked KDP for help, and on a few occasions, for which they were to pay dearly, KDP joined with Iranian forces inside Iraqi Kurdistan. In the summer of 1983, KDP helped Iran take control of the strategic mountain of Girdamand, near Haji Omaran. One week later, Saddam Hussein's forces surrounded Qooshtapa camp, 20 kilometres south of Hawler, with tanks and forces, taking away all Barzan males over the age of 12. Eight thousand disappeared without a trace. The women and children were rounded up and put in a heavily guarded camp and allowed no contact with the outside world.

PUK had its own foray with the Iranian forces in 1987. A joint force bombed Kirkuk, intent on sabotaging oil wells. Iran claimed the operation a success. Iraq claimed otherwise. Saddam's revenge was to deport the Kurdish of Garmian, an area in the Kirkuk province, and bulldoze the houses. In 1987 the United Kurdish Front of seven parties, including KDP and PUK, was announced. A year later, it helped Iranian forces capture Halabja. Within days, Saddam retaliated with chemical weapons that killed thousands of civilians. Saddam's revenge is based on a tribal mentality: take three eyes for every eye.

By the time I arrived in Kurdistan of Iran in 1987, there was a ceasefire between the KDP and KDPI, but the climate of suspicion and hostility remained. In Ushnaviyeh, we rented a house in the town and I worked as a general practitioner in a government medical centre between Ushnaviyeh and Urmia, also visiting villages in the border triangle. My patients were both Kurds and Turkomans. In my work, I became aware that of all Kurds, Iraqi Kurds are the most fortunate, despite our suffering at the hands of Saddam. Both the Kurds of Iran and Turkey are much poorer than Iraqi Kurds. They have no rights to publish, broadcast or be educated in Kurdish. In most Kurdish towns of Iran, the Shi'ite Turkomans, called Azeri, hold all positions of authority. The reason is that Iranian Kurds are Sunni, while the majority of Iranians and the government are Shi'ite.

After 10 months I began practising in a medical centre inside the refugee camp in Ziveh, Ziweh in Kurdish, which had been receiving a constant flow of refugees since the late 1970s. The other major refugee destination was Naghada. By the end of 1988, these two places had become overcrowded chicken pens for the hundreds of thousands of people escaping Al-Anfal, especially during the operations known as Great Anfal, which were carried out in July–September 1988, after the Iran–Iraqi War finished. All the north was being cleared of life, and at the beginning of winter, an unprecedented number of refugees began arriving. People were dying of cold, malnutrition and lack of medicine. One day a person working for the Iranian health authorities told me, "Last night 20 infants died from cold in Ziveh."

In October, after the forbidden areas had been completely cleared and the refugees had stopped coming, Mostefa Barzani personally led a *peshmerga* force of a couple of thousand for a month of fighting in the Khagurg area. They fought battalion after battalion, their basic message to Saddam being, "We will never die."

In Ziveh the people were housed in a giant one-storey store built by the Shah. The space was divided into tiny cubicles by temporary two-metre-high brick walls. If a family had five to six square metres, they were lucky. The people had no employment, or help from the Iranian government, but the human is very resilient. People shared what little they had, cooking on a small kerosene burner, which was also their only heating. There was one toilet for 40 families, and no washing facilities. The stench of humanity was overpowering.

Tents were erected when there were no more cubicles. People were suffering from typhoid, dysentery and malnutrition, as well as burns from stoves. They could not afford medicines and tests, even when these were available. I served my patients as best I could.

There had been peace between KDP and KDPI since 1986, but in 1990 a terrible incident occurred in Ushnaviyeh. A Kurdish man from Iraq and another from Iran were in love with the same girl. One day in the market, the Iranian Kurd told the other, "You must not talk to this girl. I am going to marry her." The next morning, the Iranian Kurd was found dead. We think it was Iranian intelligence forces who killed him, to cause trouble between Kurds. If so they succeeded.

The Iranian police came and took the Iraqi Kurd to prison, spreading the rumour that Iraqi Kurds had started killing Iranian Kurds. When my family heard this, we stayed at home, afraid to venture out. Later we were told that many Kurdish men, women and children stormed the prison and took the Iraqi Kurd. They gouged out his eyes, killed him, then tied his body to a truck, towing it through the streets. People threw rocks at the body as it passed, while the *pasdars* looked on.

The truck towed the body towards Barzanabad—even though the Iraqi Kurd was PUK. When the people of Barzanabad heard what was happening, they rang Masoud, asking, "What do we do?" Masoud told them, "Don't interfere with them unless they come inside Barzanabad. If they do, fight them, even if they are led by the president himself." The people knew that Barzani's *peshmergas* were battle-hardened, and did not venture inside Barzanabad. The KDPI leadership criticised the people for their actions, but that night *pasdars* captured 70 KDPI in Ushnaviyeh. These people were tortured on the pretext of investigating the crime. It was this incident that made my family and I move to Urmia, a big multicultural city, where we felt safer.

In my work and social life I was in constant contact with KDP *peshmergas* living in Ushnaviyeh, Urmia and Naghada. A very old man, Aris Bedar Rooni, who lived in Naghada, had fought alongside Mostefa Barzani in the early 1940s, escaping with Barzani to join forces with the Mahabad Republic of 1946. When Qazi Muhammad, president of the Republic, surrendered to the Iranian authorities, Aris Bedar Rooni returned to Iraq with Mostefa Barzani. Barzani decided not to surrender to the Iraqi authorities, and gave his followers a choice—surrender or follow him to an unknown destination. Mostefa Barzani's brother, Shaykh Ahmed, was one who surrendered to stay with his people. He was imprisoned in Basra, his hands and feet in manacles, until 1958. Four others who surrendered were ex-army officers. They were executed. However, Aris Bedar Rooni and 500 men chose to follow Mostefa Barzani into the unknown. Rooni was a widower. He had four sons, but he told Barzani, "I will leave my sons, or kill them so that they are not left to the mercy of our enemy." Their mother's brother took care of the children for 14 years while Aris Bedar Rooni, Mostefa Barzani and others lived in exile in the Soviet Union until 1958.

Living in Ushnaviyeh was Abdullah Kadu, who had been a *peshmerga* since the early 1960s. He was killed fighting PKK in 1996. Babakir, whom we had contacted to help us escape, also lived in Ushnaviyeh. In the late 1970s, his two teenage brothers were accepted as refugees by the USA. The elder one worked to pay for his younger brother's education, and now the younger brother is a highly respected vascular surgeon specialising in liver transplants. Babakir returned to Iraqi Kurdistan during the uprising of 1991, and is now the *peshmerga* leader of the Dohuk province. So many of these veteran *peshmergas* had lived a very hard life, seeing many family and friends killed, but they never gave up. Even as refugees in Iran, they were optimistic for the future.

From April 1991, a new wave of refugees began arriving, after Saddam came back into Kurdistan following the Kurdish uprising. Until September I worked in one refugee camp of 50,000 people. Initially they slept in the open, until Austria supplied high-quality tents. The camp was far better organised than the camp in Ziveh. Even so, an average of eight people died each day. When this camp closed, I worked with the refugees in Naghada until September 1994.

Since 1991 Masoud Barzani has never been photographed with a gun. In 1992 Kurdish people held their first democratic multi-party elections. Women and men were allowed to vote, and Barzani won. He proved what he was willing to do for peace when he shared the Kurdish parliament and administration 50:50 with PUK. But this power-sharing indicated that the Kurdish decision-makers, although well-meaning, did not have enough understanding of how democracy works, and it was soon to collapse, because in Kurdistan, a loser never gives up. They will not allow the winner to control what they perceive as their territory. It is a mentality based on the gun, the gun enabling an immediate response.

I was fortunate to have an education, but I had no exposure to democracy and little idea of how it works until I came to Australia with my wife and children in September 1994. Only when a person is exposed to different views in a peaceful environment can he or she step back and take a universal view. But even in Australia, Kurds find it hard to sit around a table and discuss matters. They often keep the mentality of the 1980s, with all its ideological and military conflicts. As Kurdish SBS radio broadcaster, Shahin Baker, said, "When the Australian parliament sits, they argue and accuse each other, but after the session finishes, they go and socialise together. The Kurds go and kill each other." The 1980s was the worst decade for Iraqi Kurds, but we must forgive each other so that we can move forward. This takes time, peace, exposure to democratic processes, and an understanding of what 'freedom' is.

My hope is that much can change in a generation, in just one or two decades. My earliest childhood memory is of running away and hiding in caves while the army destroyed our village. My illiterate father moved to Akre so his four children could be educated. Now one is a teacher, another is an architect in Akre, I am a doctor in Australia, and my youngest brother is working with computers in Sweden. Faris, the man married to my wife's sister, was orphaned in Iran. From the age of 12, his oldest sister raised her siblings. To live, they worked on apple orchards in the school holidays. Now Faris is a dentist and his brother is an engineer, their sister remaining head of the family.

Conditions in Iraqi Kurdistan were shocking until 1997, when the UN 'food for oil ' program began to be implemented. Since 1997, 13 per cent of all money received by Iraq for rebuilding infrastructure goes directly to Kurdistan. There has never been so much money available for the development of Kurdistan. Our civil administrations are putting this money to good use in both KDP and PUK zones within the limitations of two trade embargoes. Our children are being educated in Kurdish. They are not being subjected to the brainwashing of the Ba'aths, and there is more freedom in publishing and broadcasting than ever before. The people's economic circumstances are far better than in the rest of Iraq. People are not so caught up in politics, and I see this as a good sign. In January 2001, Masoud Barzani and Jalal Talabani met several times to discuss a reunification of the region under Kurdish administration. In just three years, the Kurdish administrations have proved what they are capable of, given the chance. If peace and connection with the outside world are maintained, and if we continue to have protection from the aggression of our neighbours, I am optimistic for the future.

A Fox is not a Camel But He Must Think Like a Camel

A life story based on interviews with Wria Rekar

Sa'adi Shirazi was a Persian poet who studied under the great Sufi masters Gilani[a] and Suhrawardi. In the 13th century he wrote a story about a fox that was running away in terror. A passer-by asked the fox, "What is your trouble?" The fox answered, "They are taking camels for forced labour." The passer-by was puzzled, "But the fate of camels has nothing to do with you. You don't even look like a camel." "Silence," said the fox, "for if an intriguer were to say I was a camel, who would work for my release?"

I was constantly reminded of this story in prison after someone informed on two friends and me. To this day I do not know for sure who it was, although when I was in a refugee camp in Iran in 1986, a person from my student union cell gave me a name.

Back in 1982, at eight o'clock one morning, I was walking with a friend from the student hostel to Baghdad University, where I was studying Science. A taxi and a Fiat pulled up and two plainclothes *amn* got out, one asking, "Are you Wria?" "Yes." "You must come with us." They made me get into the car between them, and wear dark sunglasses so I could not see, then placed an open book on my lap! Later, my friend told me that they had taken him a short distance, then released him.

I asked, "Why are you doing this?" No answer. After an hour we stopped and they took me inside a building, into a small room, where I had to sit on a chair. A tall, dark-skinned, overweight *amn* stood in front of me and asked, "Are you Shapol?" I answered, "My name is Wria." He slapped my face, saying, "Son of a bitch—I know your name is Wria, but in the Kurdistan Student Union, your name is Shapol." I denied it.

Four or five *amn* took me to a special room, stripped me of my shoes, wallet, belt and watch, blindfolded me and handcuffed my hands behind my back. I was to remain this way, in the same clothes, night and day, without a wash, for the next 14 days.

They tortured me with a tube that delivered an electric shock when pressed against my ears, jaw, neck and arm muscles. They hit my back and legs with a rubber cable, and made me lie down and put my legs in wooden shackles, raised from the ground, so they could hit the soles of my feet. My handcuffed hands pressed into my back, and I cried and shouted, thrashing around like an animal being slaughtered. One *amn* put his foot on my mouth to keep me still. This torture went on for half an hour, and when they asked me to get up and walk, I could not. They pushed me from one to another, saying, "Your name is Shapol," but I kept saying, "No."

For two days of torture, I told them nothing. The worst was when they swore at me and insulted my parents, saying, "Fuck your mother," and "You bastard Kurdish dog."

At first the insults ate into me, but over time, strange things became normal.

They repeated the same questions: "Why don't you belong to the Ba'ath Party?" I would say, "I don't want to join any party. I just want to study and enjoy life." An *amn* asked, "Do you like Sir President Saddam Hussein?" To my shame, I answered, "Of course." They would stop the torture when I lost consciousness or when they wanted to ask questions. Then they would begin again. This went on each day for up to an hour before lunch, and again in the afternoon, always with the same interrogators.

It was nothing to what I was told other people went through. The electric shock could throw prisoners across the room, so they must have been using a low voltage on me. How you were treated depended on when and where you were arrested, as well as on who was your interrogator. I was lucky. There was a light-skinned *amn* of high rank who seemed more pleasant. He never insulted me, or let the other *amn* insult me in front of him. He would ask, "Do you need water?" because after the electric shocks, I was always very thirsty from shouting. He would speak quietly, saying, "You can talk to me." It was a good technique. It made me feel like telling him everything, but I did not.

They asked if I wanted to talk in Kurdish. I refused, even though my Arabic was poor. On the third day, they took me to the interrogation room and removed my blindfold and handcuffs. There were about seven *amn* . The 'nice' one was sitting at the desk. They sat me on a chair in front of him, one standing on each side of me. I sensed that this time was different. I was very scared. Suddenly, all of them except the 'nice' one shouted, "Fuck him!" The *amn* on each side of me grabbed my pants at the front, the 'nice' one looking on. I knew he had the power to stop them.

I have never been so scared. I felt I was going to vomit. My vision blurred. They became faceless. The 'nice' one said, "Stop. Give him water." Without thinking, I drank the lot. I wanted to evaporate. The 'nice' *amn* said, "We know everything—how you distributed leaflets. You do not need to deny it. If you don't tell the truth, I'll go out and these people will fuck you. But if you confess that you belong to the Kurdistan Student Union, I promise no-one will touch you. Think about it."

All eyes were on me. I tried to avoid their gaze, wanting to think, knowing my decision was critical. If I confessed, maybe they would want to know more and I would not be out of danger, but I decided to confess. I said, "Yes." The 'nice' boss continued, "You have worked for the KSU for one year." "Yes." "You distributed leaflets." "Yes." "Your code name is Shapol." "Yes." I never imagined I would confess. I never imagined how scared I would be when threatened with sexual abuse. I felt weak and ashamed—I had failed a big test.

People react differently to prison and torture. Some people who appear strong outside become weak inside. Others who are weak outside become strong. Sometimes, the more you believe in a cause, the stronger you are, whereas the person who thinks only of himself may crack under the pressure.

After my confession, they continued the torture, but not so intensely. They asked me about the person who had got me to join the KSU. I told them, "He joined the *peshmergas* in the mountains." They asked, "Who are your friends?" "Who are your relatives?" "Is so-and-so working against the government?" "What do you know about this person?" "Do you know anyone who secretly owns a typewriter or photocopying machine?" and I would say, "I know nothing," which was the truth. I remember they took the blindfold off to show me a photo, asking me to identify the man. In the light, I could see nothing, and I said so, but they thought I was lying, and they started torturing me again.

One day the 'nice' *amn* asked me, "What is the aim of this Kurdistan Student Union?" I was silent. He said, "We won't torture you. Just tell us." They listened as I said, "The Union wants our schools and universities to teach in Kurdish." They replied, "But they teach in Kurdish." I told them, "Day by day, you are reducing the Kurdish language. Under the Autonomy Agreement in the early 1970s, Science and Literature were taught in Kurdish, but after 1979 only the science subjects are taught in Kurdish and we do not study any Kurdish history. University is in Arabic." They asked, "What else does your union want?" "The union wants an Independent Union of Students, and it also wants to stop the Arabisation of Kurdistan." "What do you mean?" "I am told Arabs are being moved into Kirkuk and other towns and Kurds are being forced out." "Do you believe this?" I was silent. "What else does the student union want?" "In general, the union wants to solve Kurdish issues in a peaceful way." An *amn* pushed my head forward, saying, "You donkey! You believe whatever you are told."

Sometimes during interrogation, I would hear women crying under torture. Torture is physical pain, but hearing other people's pain is more disturbing. Also, you cannot trust your senses. It is very disorientating, because I did not know whether the women's screams were real. I now suspect they were on tape.

Once I was in the room with seven or eight *amn* , who were taking turns to slap my face and kick me. In the process, my blindfold moved a little, and I saw they were laughing. I still wonder how people can enjoy inflicting pain, even if they do the job to avoid going into the army, or to earn good money and have status, or even if they are proud to be Arab and hate the Kurdish. I think back to one night in 1980 or 1981 in Shaqlowa, when *peshmergas* threw a grenade into the *amn* office. Over the next few days, *amn* randomly arrested about 30 people and brought interrogators to torture them. These interrogators were teenagers from Saddam's tribe. My point is that from the beginning, some people are taught to torture, scare and insult others. They are brainwashed by a group mentality into believing Arabs are the best people in the world. They become desensitised and brutal. In prison, I heard that one *amn* would be angry all day with the other *amn* if there was no-one to torture. To sleep at night, he would drink too much alcohol. What I fear most is that even if Saddam Hussein loses power, most of the Iraqi secret police would stay in their positions, using the same skills in the service of the next regime.

On the seventh day of torture, I couldn't handle it any more. I was in the toilet, which had a water jug for washing afterwards. I put one foot on the tap, the other on the jug, and stretched for the electric light. It was too high, but I hoped that somehow I would reach it. I couldn't. When I came outside, the *amn* guard somehow knew I had tried to kill myself, and kicked me badly.

After torture, they would return me to the cell, always blindfolded and handcuffed, so I never saw the room properly or knew who was in the cell. We even had to sleep this way. It was very cold. We had no blankets. I would sleep sitting up, back against the wall, so that guards could not kick me from behind. Many times, as I sat blindfolded and handcuffed, a guard would prod my face with his boot. It was done to humiliate. One night an *amn* told me, "Tomorrow, we remove your nails," but it did not happen.

They brought tea and food to the room three times a day, putting it on the floor—eggs or bean soup in the morning, rice and soup for lunch, meat and bread for dinner. They took off our blindfolds and bent our heads. When we were eating, we were not allowed to move our heads from this position or they would hit us. Our blindfolds were put back on straight after the meal. Otherwise, the only time our eyes and hands were free was when we were in the toilet. Whenever they took us out of the cell, *amn* would hit us for no reason. Once I was kicked in the testicles and fell unconscious.

In the cell, we were hit if we talked. We sat in silence, so there was plenty of time to think. Most of the time, I thought, "Worse is yet to come," and I wanted to die. I reflected on how crazy my society had become. I remembered when Saddam became president in 1979, and all the bus stops in Hawler were labelled 'Gift from the President', as if the money had come from his own pocket. Even when Saddam was vice-president and Hasan Al-Bakr was president, it was Saddam who was always active, visiting other countries and signing agreements.

I remembered back to the time of peace between 1970 and 1974, when there was a treaty between the Kurds and the government. Saddam used this time to start a relationship with the Soviets and some Western countries, and to build up his army and internal security. Meanwhile, whole families in Baghdad were being killed as they slept in their beds. People would say Abu Tabar was responsible. *Abu* is Arabic for 'father', and *Tabar* is Arabic for 'big knife', and just mentioning the name would put fear inside people. One person was eventually arrested, and confessed on television, but to my mind, Abu Tabar had to be Saddam's internal security forces, who killed Saddam's opponents, and also ordinary people, to cover up the politically motivated murders.

To distract the people from what was happening in Iraq, a wrestler called Adnan Qaysi was promoted as an Iraqi who had lived in the USA but loved his country so much that he'd come back. The government brought wrestlers from Britain and other Western countries to fight him, and these fights were televised. Adnan Qaysi always won, even against wrestlers twice as big. At school, we wrestled, sticking our elbow into each other and shouting, "Adnan Qaysi." His name was everywhere, and everyone talked about him. To my understanding this was a ploy borrowed from the West to distract people from what was happening.

In my home town of Shaqlowa, half the population are Kurdish Muslims, and half is Chaldean Christian. At Newroz between 1970 and 1974, young people would take car tyres to the tops of the mountains of Safin or Soork to light a big fire and sing Newroz songs. In one area of Safin, halfway up is a cave that is holy for Christians and Muslims. For spring picnics, both communities would walk up the narrow path, on one side a sheer cliff, on the other the mountain full of natural tunnels. But after fighting resumed in 1974, the army put landmines all over Safin and people were forbidden to go there. Some people joined KDP in the liberated areas. My family stayed behind. When Iraqi forces and *jahsh* entered the town, the army randomly collected men, saying they were going to shoot them, but later set them free. Sometimes the *peshmergas* came into the town at night. Iraqi bombs and rockets would fly over us every night, targeting surrounding villages. It was very frightening, and at the beginning we could not sleep, but we grew used to it.

The police station was located on a high position. Day and night, they would shoot randomly into the houses or streets, the purpose not to kill but to terrorise. Still, one woman died. Twice, five or six soldiers inspected our house. On the first occasion, the officer in charge was nasty, throwing everything around. The second time, the officer just routinely inspected, without destroying anything or insulting us. One neighbour said we were not harmed because I had recited the Ayat Kursi verse from the Qur'an.

The Iraqi government put sanctions against many cities and towns, so we had a ration-card to buy essentials. It was forbidden to bring anything from other cities to Kurdistan. During 1974, we had rice only a few times. Twice a week, my parents would send me to buy kerosene. Our neighbour's children and I would wait in a queue, each with a tin. At this time, the Kurdish communists were accusing Mostefa Barzani and KDP of being a puppet of USA, Israel and Iran, so the Iraqi government tolerated them. One or two communists with their Kalashnikovs always accompanied the donkey cart with the kerosene. Everyone was entitled to two gallons a time, but the communists got more, and often the kerosene would be sent straight to their homes. So much for equality.

The rationing continued until March 1975, when the revolution stopped, but resumed during the Iraq–Iran War. I remember that in the summer of 1983, my brother Hiwa and I would wake up at 5 am and queue for kerosene. For seven days, we waited until 11 am, but the kerosene always ran out before our turn. My mother complained, "Why do other people get kerosene and not you?" I told her, "Ask your husband. If he is not a member of the Ba'ath Party or an *amn* or *jahsh* or Jayeesh Al-Sha'abi (the popular civilian army), we cannot get kerosene." One day there would be no eggs in the shop, another day no chickens... I think the Iraqi regime did this deliberately—everyone was too concerned about what would be available in the market to think about politics.

My father had been an ordinary member of KDP, but at a meeting in 1972, he had told the other members that KDP should be cautious about totally depending on the Shah of Iran. He asked, "You must wonder—when the Shah denies Kurds their rights in Iran, why is he befriending us?" My father was never asked to another meeting. Yet, one evening in 1975, he was listening to an Arabic radio program on either Voice of America, BBC or Israeli Radio. After a while, I saw tears falling from his eyes. I was shocked. I had never seen him cry, but I did not dare ask him why. Later, I discovered it was because the Kurdish revolution had collapsed. He criticised the Kurdish leaders, saying they had left the country and abandoned the people. Many thousands of people were killed. Jonathan Randal, in his book *Kurdistan: After Such Knowledge What Forgiveness?*, says that CIA director Calby was personally warned of the possibility of these massacres, and was advised that to avert them, the USA must intercede through Iran. Nothing was done. When a US official asked Henry Kissenger why the USA had stopped supporting the Kurdish and was not helping the tens of thousands of refugees fleeing into Iran, he said, "Covert action should not be confused with missionary work."

The Iraqi government opened a Munazama, a Ba'ath Party political headquarters, in every town and city in Kurdistan. All books written in Kurdish or in Arabic about Kurdish history disappeared from the library. Later I heard that members of Munazama collected these books and burnt them. All activities like learning music or sport were under Munazama control, and many institutes and colleges began rejecting students who did not become members of the Iraqi Student Union. In this way, a few students from Shaqlowa became loyal to the Ba'ath Party and were forced to write reports about others. The report-writers would gain an extra 10 marks in the final exams, enabling them to attend the best faculties at any Iraqi university, and some, although none from Shaqlowa, got scholarships to study overseas in the communist-bloc or Western countries.

Arabs replaced Kurds in most government offices and in the schools. Until this time, our education had been in Kurdish. Our new teachers asked us to join the Iraqi Student Union. Most students in my class eventually joined, except the communists, who were exempt until the Communist Party was outlawed in 1977–78. I did not join, because my father told me not to. My father would say, "One day, our fate will be the same as that of the Kurdish in Turkey."

When my teacher unfairly failed me in the Arabic exam, I approached him. He told me, "While you are not a union member, I will never let you pass." There was only one high school for boys and another for girls, and I had no chance to go to another city. If someone twice failed in one subject or more, they had to leave school. I could not cope with that idea, so I joined the union, against my father's wishes. After that, I got a better mark than I deserved.

Three times, I went to Iraqi Student Union meetings. There would be a three-hour lecture in Arabic by some Arab Ba'ath cadre, about the great Arab nation and the mighty Ba'ath Party. Ethnic and religious minorities were never mentioned. This total negation of our identity was degrading and humiliating. At one meeting, a cadre said, "The autonomy we have given the Kurds is much better than the system in the Soviet Republic or that of the Switzerland Federation. In Iraq, Kurds have more rights than Arabs." What kind of rights, I did not know, and no-one dared ask. All I could think of was the right to see and hear Saddam on the news four times a day instead of twice because all Arab news was repeated on Kurdish television.

Going to these meetings made me feel guilty—especially when I found out that being a member of the student union automatically made me a member of the Ba'ath Party, so I stopped going. Twice I was warned, "If you don't go, you will be sorry." My excuse was, "I forgot."

In my first year at Baghdad University, members of the Iraqi Student Union three times asked me to join them, but I rejected their pressure. In 1979–80, they would ask students to go and demonstrate against President Anwar Sadat of Egypt, after he signed the Camp David Agreement which offered Sinai's return to Egypt in exchange for peace with Israel. Saddam was against this agreement, so all students and office workers had to demonstrate against Sadat. All the campus doors would be closed, except the main gate, so that no students could escape going, but one female student showed some of us how to jump a fence, and in my four years of study, I escaped more than thirty rallies. Office workers would also be made to go, with the warning, "If you don't go, you will not be paid this month."

I also avoided elections. Only Ba'ath Party members and sons of *aghas* and *shaykhs* were allowed to stand, but whoever the government liked most always won. Iraq's elections are a sham and the parliament is a sham. That is why I never voted. As a student in Baghdad, I could avoid it. Office workers could not.

Throughout university, we had to study a subject called Al-thaqafa Al-qawmiya or 'National Education', which was devoted to praising the Arab nation, the Ba'aths and Saddam Hussein. Once, the lecturer, Dr Ali Attia, who had a doctorate in nuclear physics, asked, "Why was the last prophet chosen among Arabs?" He answered his own question, saying, "Because God knows Arabs are clever, smart, honest, generous and brave, so he chose Arabs to spread the last message of God to all nations." Another lecturer claimed, "Imperialism and Zionism created the war between us and Iran in order to destroy our economy." He went on to assert that our economy was better than it had been before the war. Now, we had juice cans in the shops! It was true that Iraq imported a lot of food during the war, but no-one dared question the obvious contradictions, and in the exams I hated every word I wrote.

It was in my second year that a Kurdish friend asked me to join a PUK branch of the Kurdistan Student Union. Unfortunately, there was no union for all Kurds, only for particular parties. All of them were illegal, but my friend assured me, "The structure of our organisation is so strong that Iraqi secret police will never find out about our membership." A year later, I was arrested.

In prison, we were referred to as dogs or donkeys. But it was always being blindfolded that particularly made me feel very depressed, pessimistic and helpless. I was so desperate, I began thinking about God. I look back now and think how selfish I was. Only when I really needed help did I turn back to God. Yet until I was 15 I had been a very devout Muslim. On Fridays I went to the mosque, and I would not pray just five times—I would pray 25 times. I would be dizzy with prayer. My aunt had written the words on a piece of paper for me to memorise. For some time I did not understand them, but Malla Majid used to say, "If every day you say more than 500 times, 'There is no God but God, and Muhammad is his Messenger,' your sins will be reduced and you will go to heaven." My parents did not like my obsession, but they did not stop me.

I told my Chaldean Christian friends, "You are going to hell unless you convert to Islam." One told me, "Wria, you are really stupid if you believe all that." When I was 16 I began reading some books and decided I *was* stupid to believe only Muslims go to heaven. I questioned why praying and reading the Qur'an is always in Arabic. Maybe *mallas* think Allah listens only to Arabic. I decided the main reason Islam is such a chauvinistic religion is that from the beginning, the Arab Muslims forced or obliged other nations to become Arabised. Religious leaders would encourage parents to give Arabic names to their children, convincing them that this was their children's ticket to heaven.

Also, most of our *shaykhs*, *mallas* and *sayyids* supported the central government of the Islamic empires. Then, from the time of the British, the authorities maintained good relations with the religious leaders, feudal *agha*s and *begs*, because of their influence in our society. These leaders never wanted the people to be educated, because uneducated people ask fewer questions. They accept things, and follow humbly. In Shaqlowa, one feudal lord, Sadiq Beg, was a parliamentary representative under the monarchy when people in Shaqlowa signed a petition to have a high school. He argued against it, and all the signatories were deported from Shaqlowa. My father was one of them. Of course, the government listened to their representative rather than to the people's wish. It was only after Iraq became a republic in 1958 that they opened a high school in Shaqlowa.

After 1975 an Arabic school and an Islamic school opened in Shaqlowa. At the time, I heard 11 Islamic schools were opened in Kurdistan. Students were paid money to attend an Islamic school. These Islamic students would graduate as Arabic or religious teachers or *mallas*, or they could work in an office, in turn recruiting and teaching religion to the next generation. It was a good way of assimilating Kurds into Iraqi Arab culture.

Most religious and tribal leaders support Islamic laws. Even the Iraqi government complies with Islamic laws to some extent, particularly regarding marriage and divorce. I decided that the inferior position of women in Kurdistan was the direct result of Islam and the feudal system, and by the time I went to university, I was an atheist. Yet in prison, I was constantly asking God for help. I would pray, "*Khwa'a ya* please kill me." (*Khwa'a* is 'God' in Sorani. The Bahdini say *Khodeh*.) When I was released, I continued to pray each morning, and now I believe in God, but I do not need any religion to come between God and me.

After 14 days, they stopped torturing me. A doctor examined me and gave me some tablets. I was transferred to a room with up to 40 prisoners, surrounded by iron bars, and was finally released from my blindfolds and handcuffs. All the other prisoners stared at the new arrivals with a strange intensity. I sat down quickly, and a man came up and asked in Kurdish, "Are you Kurd?" "Yes," then straight away, I asked him, "Will they torture me any more?" "No." I believed him and did not stop laughing for 10 minutes. It was the happiest moment of my life, and as it turned out he spoke the truth.

Each cell had a head prisoner, who assigned someone to clean or do whatever other duties needed to be done. We were allowed to shower once or twice a week, and one prisoner gave me his pyjamas before being released, so I had a change of clothes, except I wore the same underwear the whole time.

Sometimes the room was so crowded, there was no room to lie and sleep. We slept crushed together, but still I was happy: the torture was over. Time went slowly, and the guards never let us settle—they always made a big noise as they brought new prisoners in or took others out—so after a month, I was no longer happy!

We were allowed to talk in the new cell, and I overheard one Kurd telling his story to another prisoner: "When I went to court, there was a judge, a state prosecutor, and the state defence lawyer." Political prisoners could not hire their own defence lawyer—if they could, lawyers in Iraq would be millionaires. He continued, "No-one else was in the room. When I said I was innocent, the defence lawyer became very upset and started attacking me. He seemed more worried than the prosecutor! After 10 minutes, the judge announced I was to be sentenced to death." His crime was that he was thought to be a member of the Communist Party. He had already spent a year in prison when they told him, "You will be executed next week." After a week, they said, "Your execution has been postponed by three days," but he was brought to our cell, then released two days later. At the time, many communists were given amnesty.

Generally I talked freely with most Kurdish prisoners, but with others it took time to know whom to trust. They would place secret police inside each cell, to act like prisoners for 15 days or so, and one of these people came to me and said, "I am going to be released in two days. Give me the names and addresses of your relatives so I can tell them where you are." I said, "No thank you." Afterwards a prisoner told me, "It is good you said nothing. I have seen him in here before."

I had started to hate Arabs in the other section of the prison, but in the cell there were Arabs and Kurds, and at one time an Assyrian, and sometimes the authorities were harder on Arabs who opposed the regime, because they wanted to bring down the whole government, whereas the Kurds wanted only their rights and to rule Kurdistan. One Arab told me, "My brother went missing in the war between Iraq and Iran, so I used to listen to Iranian Radio, hoping to hear his name when they read out the names of the prisoners of war. One of my friends told the secret police and I was arrested. They hung me from my hands, and burned my testicles with a lighted newspaper. The other prisoners in our cell had to feed him and help him go to the toilet. After one day, the guards took him. I don't know where.

They were particularly hard on Shi'ite Arabs, who form a majority of the population but have no voice. One Kurd who had been with Shi'ite prisoners told me, "They took me to the torture room, brought in an Arab Shi'ite and burnt him with a hot iron. Another time, they brought in an Arab Shi'ite brother and sister and pressured them to have sex in front of us." I think his stories were true. He had been badly tortured, and was sentenced to death for trying to help some Arab Shi'ites escape through Kurdistan into Iran. However, his father talked to a *jahsh* leader, who used his connections, so he was later released.

Three truckdrivers had been arrested for pretending they were Saddam's guards so they could demand free meals at a restaurant. Another very thin prisoner arrived so weak he could neither speak nor stand for more than a few minutes. After 20 days his health improved and he told another prisoner that he was *amn*. He said there are four floors of our building, which was in the Amn headquarters. We were on the top floor. The further down you went, the worse it became in terms of food and fate. He had been on the second floor.

Another prisoner told me he was arrested because a 'friend' tape-recorded him telling a joke. The joke was that one day, a shoe-seller was serving Mrs Saddam Hussein and he farted. Mrs Saddam said, "How dare you fart in front of me. Do you know who I am?" The shoe-seller replied, "Yes, I know—your husband shuts our mouths. Now you want us to shut our arses!" He was expecting a seven-year sentence for this.

I soon learnt that the innocent fox was right when he feared he would be treated like a camel. Eleven Kurdish students were brought in. One had been arrested, and under torture had confessed he was KDP, giving others' names. Later I learnt he was not a member of any party. The others also confessed under torture to being KDP, when really they were Communist, Socialist, KDP, PUK or did not belong to any party. Likewise, one Arab prisoner told me how he was arrested. "I went to A'athamya Cinema in Baghdad to watch an Indian movie. It had a bit about democracy, and I commented to my friend, 'There is no such thing in this world.' Suddenly, there was a hand on my shoulder and a man saying, 'Come outside.' I asked, 'Why?' and he growled, 'Son of a dog, come out.' Three people forced me into a car, one saying, 'How come you are insulting the government?' I said, 'I was talking about India!' For eight days they tortured me. They chained my legs to a gas cylinder and hung me upside down. They told me, 'You are a member of Al-Da'awah (a Shi'ite political group)' and I replied, 'I am a taxi driver,' which was the truth. They said to me, 'You are communist,' and the next day they accused me of being something else. After eight days, I decided to say, 'I am whatever you say I am,' but I never got the chance. They brought me here." To stop the torture, people confess to anything.

Every day, they would give each cell a newspaper called *Al Thawra*. Always on the front page was a half-page picture of Saddam. At lunch time we put newspaper on the floor to eat on, but we had problems with Saddam's head! We would hide the page or hand it back to the guard. Most mornings we would get eggs for breakfast, and a tiny pinch of salt. I asked a Kurd, "Why do they give us so little salt?" He told me, "In the 1970s, they arrested members of PUK in Baghdad. This group saved their salt until one day, when a guard opened the door, one called Jwamair threw the salt into the guard's eyes. Somehow they managed to escape. They were recaptured and tortured and Jwamair had his eyes gouged out. Apparently he did not show any reaction, so when a prisoner does not cry under torture, they ask, "Are you Jwamair?"

At the end of Ramadan, the head of Amn, Fazil Barak, came to visit us, in full uniform. He had a very arrogant, scary manner. It is a time of doing good deeds, called Jajhini Ramadan in Kurdish, Eed Ramadan in Arabic, and he asked each prisoner why they were there. Sometimes a guard wrote down a name, and these people, all Arabs, were later released. Saddam Hussein was to execute Barak in the late 1980s.

After three months of prison I had a dream. I was in a very nice, clean bathroom with a mirror and a window. I took a shower and shaved, and looked at myself in this beautiful mirror. Since then I have had similar dreams, and always, good news follows.

The next morning officers read out a list of names. Mine was among them. They collected about 100 Kurdish students in a big hall. The 'nice' *amn* interrogator addressed us: "Most of you have done bad things against the government, but all of you come from good families who serve the president." He then announced, "The president has decided to give amnesty to 3000 Kurdish prisoners. You will be released today. How generous is your leader." I was very lucky. In 1982, the government was losing the war against Iran, and in Kurdistan there were big student demonstrations. Some Kurdish *mallas* had met with Saddam, demanding the release of political prisoners. Saddam wanted to ease the tension. Before and after this time, people were killed for my crime. When I saw people in the street, I thought, "How can you act normally with what is happening behind those walls?" But after a while, I started to forget that others were still being tortured. This is life.

I took a bus to Hawler. An old man beside me asked, "Why are you wearing pyjamas?" I told him the truth and he was silent. I stayed with my sister, and the next day journeyed to Shaqlowa. My family were very happy to see me.

For a while, I did not like touching anything electric. I would be scared to open the fridge in case I would get an electric shock. I did not talk to people, except close friends, because I feared they might be secret police. I was allowed to go back to the university after the summer holidays, and between Baghdad and Shaqlowa are many checkpoints, and sometimes guards check your ID against a list of names. After prison, you cannot guess how scared I was that my name was on that list.

I had to repeat Year Three, and I felt very isolated and lonely. Twice, I went to the doctor about a pain in my heart, and after intensive checks, he said, "There is no physical problem. Maybe you are depressed." I still have back pain from where they kicked me.

Two months after I returned to university, I had a dream. I found some coins on the ground and was very happy. When I woke, from past experience I knew something bad was going to happen. My mum had taught me that if you have a bad dream, you should sit beside the river and tell the river your dream, then ask God to take it away with the water. If there is no river, you should turn on the tap. The next morning, I turned on the tap, but sometimes this does not work.

A short while later, I was walking to an exam when I heard someone call, "Wria!" I looked around and saw two *amn*. I recognised one from my interrogation sessions. I could not speak; my heart was thumping wildly in my chest. "We want you to talk to Kurdish students and see what they say about the government and Kurdish politics." I told them, "I just want to concentrate on my studies." The one I knew said, "You were released on condition you work with us." I said, "I do not remember any conditions. All that was said was that the Revolutionary Command Council had given amnesty to 3000 prisoners." He gave me a friendly punch in the shoulder, saying, "Stupid! We are the RCC! Don't worry about your exams. You will pass everything and we will give you money and a pistol." "I have never touched a gun, and I am doing all right in my studies without your help." He threatened, "We will take you back to prison and torture you if you refuse to cooperate." I asked for a week to think about it.

I was too nervous to sit the exam. At the appointed time and place a week later, I saw the *amn* I had recognised from prison. He asked, "So what have you decided?" "I just want to continue my study." He asked, "So what do you want to do with your life?" The *amn* promised me many things, but I refused, and from that day they never approached me.

In Year Four I was assigned a room with two students at the student hostel. One, a quiet Shi'ite from the south, was very scared of the regime. The other was Jordanian. There were many students from other Arab countries studying in Iraqi universities. The Iraqi government spent a lot of money on them so that they would be loyal to the Ba'ath Party. This Jordanian wore Saddam's medal on his jacket and praised Saddam and the Ba'ath Party. One Christian friend who belonged to the Ba'ath Party told me, "They keep on asking what you are saying about the government." I took it as a warning that I was under surveillance.

During university holidays and when I finished university, I stayed at home in Shaqlowa, too scared to go out more than three or four times a month. At this time, 1984, PUK had a partial ceasefire with the Iraqi government in effect, but there was still fighting between the Kurdish parties. I was sick of Kurdistan being a war zone. I wished they would all make peace, but our Kurdish leaders spend a lot of time and money smearing rival parties and their leaders. The fruit of this is more hate and bloodshed. I do not understand how their conscience allows them to do this. Only when our leaders retire or become refugees abroad do they say that Kurds should stop killing each other, yet most of them have blood on their hands. If they directed all their effort against the enemy, instead of their fellow Kurds, we might have a free Kurdistan by now.

In general I was safe, because I was not meant to go into the army until the winter of 1984–85, but when the time came, I decided not to go. Nor did I want to join the *peshmerga*. Finally I joined two friends who were going to a KDP-controlled area in the mountains. We had to walk through deep snow across hard country for 11 days with *peshmergas* as guides, and my feet became bloody and blistered. In one village, a lady treated them with henna. When we got near the border, my friends told the leaders that we wanted to cross into Iran. It was night, snowing and very cold. We would have to cross in the early morning, when there was less water in the river. My feet were so sore I could not walk easily, and the leader said, "On this walk, no-one is your brother. If you cannot keep up with us, do not come." My friends and I decided to go back to a *peshmerga*-controlled village. We walked at night to avoid the army bases. This time I went to a village under PUK's control, where I met my brother. Three months later, he helped me go to Iran. I paid money to a smuggler to cross the border, but we met Iranian soldiers and had to surrender. After two weeks, they took us to a refugee camp. One year later, I flew to East Berlin on a visa to Syria. The Syrian government had sent invitations to Iraqi opposition groups. I was not a member of the Kurdistan Socialist Party but they gave me an invitation so I could escape.

Straight away, I went to West Berlin by train and on to Hamburg, where the police discovered I had no official travel documents. They sent me to Stuttgart refugee camp. From there, I was sent to a refugee house. Just before New Year 1988, I was visiting a Kurdish friend in Heilbroun. Another Kurd, who was also visiting, told me, "Wria, have you heard news from your family?" "No—I do not ring them in case the call is monitored." He said, "It is better you call them." I asked, "Why?" and he told me, "In November, December Iraqi secret police surrounded Shaqlowa and captured 100 people. All but 22 were executed. The name Hiwa was mentioned." I telephoned my relatives in Hawler, but they told me all my family was well. On New Year's Day I rang a friend in Berlin: "I heard people were executed in Shaqlowa and one was my brother Hiwa. Is it true?" He said, "Yes, and also your cousin and uncle." I sat crying in the gutter in the snow. Two girls who were passing thought I was drunk. Two weeks later, a friend told me that my father had died a year before of diabetes, having developed the problem while I was in prison. I felt responsible.

I came to Australia as a humanitarian refugee in 1988, the year of Anfal. Some years later, my family told me that when *amn* came and took Hiwa in 1987, a masked Kurdish man from Shaqlowa was also in the car, pointing out houses to target. After Hiwa disappeared, *amn* came to the house saying, "Do not make inquiries about your son; he has been executed." Then a soldier came to the teahouse where men play dominoes and said, "I saw people from Shaqlowa in Mosul prison." The government likes to play such games with the minds of families. Over the next four years, my mother and sister searched everywhere for Hiwa. They paid a lot of money to a *shaykh* in Kirkuk, who claimed he could find where Hiwa was because he had influence with the government. He was a relative of the vice-president, Izat Durri. Like many people, my family also paid a fortune to fortune-tellers, to be told different stories each time.

It was not until the uprising of 1991, when people found mass graves outside Hawler, identifying the bodies from the shoes and clothes, that my family knew that Hiwa had definitely been killed. A friend was to tell me he read documentation of what had happened. My brother and two others had died after three days of torture. My uncle and cousin were shot. Unfortunately, a lot of government documentation went missing during the uprising. Kurdish informers burnt some, and crateloads were sent to America. According to Middle East Watch, the USA has enough evidence to charge Saddam Hussein and others in the Iraqi government with genocide and war crimes, particularly during Anfal. But although the Clinton administration has tabled a proposal to the UN Security Council to view the documentation, there has been no further progress. Neither has any evidence been taken to the International Court of Justice in the Hague.

After the uprising failed, there were many suicides. I knew of five people in Shaqlowa who committed suicide by shooting or burning themselves. People were depressed and angry, feeling no hope. My 16-year-old brother, Daria, committed suicide in 1993. He was a very bright student, but perhaps the family were mourning the dead rather than supporting the living.

On hearing the news of my brother's suicide, I immediately returned to Kurdistan via Turkey. People were living in terrible conditions. I saw many beggars on the streets of Hawler. What really surprised me was the strong Islamic feeling among ordinary Kurds, many of whom had joined Islamic organisations. Mistakes being made by PUK, KDP and the other parties were driving people to look for alternatives. After so many years of war and hunger, it was a comfort to look beyond this world. But also Saudi Arabi, other Gulf States and Iran were financing the Islamic organisations and these were distributing food and other necessities. There were rumours that Iraq and Turkey were also funding them. To my mind, this was being done to weaken nationalist feelings. By increasing the number of fanatical Muslims in Kurdistan, it makes it harder for democratic parties to achieve democracy and self-rule.

Yet the move towards Islam was not unified. Some old *mallas* are very good, humble people—patriotic, too—but they did not approve of Islam's young political recruits, Kalashnikovs slung over their shoulders. The *mallas* would say, " This is politics. It has nothing to do with religion." The young recruits saw the *mallas* as old-fashioned and illiterate about the true meaning of Islam. Meanwhile PUK and KDP were trying to appease the new Islamic groups, and I feared for the future, especially that of women.

I journeyed back to Istanbul by bus, feeling very pessimistic for Kurdistan. Seeing that my friend and I were Kurdish, the driver invited us to sit with him at the front of the bus. He played a cassette of Kurdish music, but before the commandoes boarded at each checkpoint, he took the cassette out and put Turkish music in the player. It served to remind me that all the time, Turks, Arabs and Persians try to persuade us that we do not have a genuine history and culture, that we are a backward, violent people. When they give us a basic right, like speaking or publishing books in Kurdish, they think they are being magnanimous. Yet we are not a minority group who has migrated to a new country. These things are our legitimate right, as is our right to live peacefully in our homeland. They talk, read, sing, laugh, cry and study in their own language. Why is it right for them but not for us? We did not occupy their countries. They occupied ours.

It takes time, even in Australia, to feel safe, and for years I dreamed of returning to Kurdistan, but now Sydney is my home. Yet until the day I die, there will be a sadness in my heart for my dead brothers, Hiwa and Daria, and also for my sister Baran, who died in Australia of accumulated pain and loneliness.

At least now, I am free to say whatever I feel and think. I can go to the library and read books. There are far more books about Kurdistan in Australian libraries than there are in Iraq, so I am learning more and more about my country. For instance, it was not until I read Rosita Forbes' eyewitness report, quoted in David McDowall's *A Modern History of the Kurds*, that I discovered Kurdish women went to war with babies strapped to their backs during the Mount Ararat uprising of 1928–30 led by Ihsan Nuri Pasha against the Turkish government.

There are two ways for the future: give rights to Kurds or go on fighting and killing. I fear the latter is more likely: there is a greater concentration of power and profit in selling weapons than in building a life for people. My only hope is that day by day, Kurds will make more friends around the world, and also among Turks, Arabs and Persians. We must start with a dream, if it is ever to come true.

The Man and His Donkey

A Kurdish fable retold by Rebwar Tahir

On the way to the market with his son and donkey, a farmer says to his son, "You ride the donkey and I will lead." As they pass people sitting by the road the farmer hears one say, "Look at that foolish man. He lets his young son ride while he walks." So the farmer changes position with his son. A little further on he hears the men say, "Look at that careless man. He lets his son walk while he rides." The farmer scratches his head and decides they should both ride the donkey. Some passers by say, "Look how that man does not care for his donkey," so the farmer says to his son, "Let us both walk." Seeing this, people in a cafe say, "Look at that man—he has a donkey but he does not use it." The farmer becomes so frustrated he sells his donkey. When he returns home, his wife says, "You are the donkey to listen to others and sell our most valuable asset!"

A Nightingale in a Golden Cage Sang, "Oh My Country"

A life story based on interviews with Waleed Bamirny

Growing up in Baghdad was hard, particularly when there was fighting in the north. The Iraqi media portrayed Kurdish *peshmergas* as traitors trying to divide and destroy Iraq. The news showed Iraqi soldiers surrounding unarmed villagers and *peshmergas* handing over their guns. Successive rumours described *peshmergas* as blood-sucking draculas who live in caves, kill Iraqi soldiers, and eat their flesh because they have nothing else to eat. When fathers, brothers and sons in the army were killed in the north, people tried to get some sort of relief by discriminating against the Kurds among them. Many hated and feared the Kurds, blaming Kurds for all their suffering. Shopkeepers and taxi drivers would say, "Why are you living among us, using our services? Go back to your land." If the police were called to a confrontation between a Kurd and an Arab, the Kurd knew there would not be a fair resolution.

At school, most students were Arab, and many would taunt, "You are our enemy. Why are you killing our brothers? Why are you disobeying the government?" They would tell bad jokes about Kurds just to make me angry. When someone picked a fight or bashed me, everyone would stand around and watch. Even my Kurdish friends were too scared to help. I was always desperate for an older brother or cousin, but I was the eldest in my family and had no cousins in Baghdad.

It is difficult to socialise with people who have something in their heart against your nationality, especially when everyone has relatives working in the army, police, secret police, or a government office. I had some Arab friends, those who were more educated and realised that the conflict was political rather than being based on nationality, but usually I felt safer playing with Kurdish children. With Arab children, you never knew what was going to happen next. The teachers also believed what they heard about the Kurds, so they treated Kurdish students unfairly, hitting us at the slightest excuse. I did not enjoy school.

My father had only finished primary school, so he chose to make a career in the army, where he had a few days' leave each month. He was an administrator in an engineering unit involved in building temporary bridges and laying mines in the 1967 and 1973 wars against Israel. A few of my father's Kurdish colleagues were accused of being communist or KDP, but my father did not have trouble. He worked mainly on the Jordanian or Saudi borders and he was dark-skinned, so no-one could tell he was Kurdish. Also he was dutiful in his work, and always careful in conversation.

My mother could hardly speak Arabic and her only friends were Kurdish. She came from the same village as my father—Barmuni—but in the mid-1960s, her parents had sent her to Mosul to keep her safe from the fighting. In Mosul, my father saw this young, pretty girl from a distance, and sent members of his family to ask her family for permission to marry her. When he was transferred to Baghdad, she came too. In Baghdad she wore Western clothes, but we always spoke Kurdish at home, whereas some Kurdish families spoke Arabic.

We rented apartments but as Kurds it was easy for a landlord to evict you. My earliest memory was our family of four children living in one room in an apartment shared between three Kurdish families. After a year, my father rented a whole apartment, but then our landlord said that there was an Arab family in need of a room. But it turned out to be a good experience. Us seven children and their children played like brothers and sisters. We shared the bathroom and kitchen, so my mother showed good hospitality, making the Arab family popular Kurdish dishes like *briani*, and if there was an argument she was the first to calm the situation.

In Baghdad I did not have a clue about Kurdish history or Newroz. On television, occasionally there would be a Kurdish singer singing Kurdish songs, always loyal to the government. There were Kurdish radio programs with music, poetry and the Iraqi news, and one Kurdish newspaper, *Hawkari*, but I was too busy playing soccer and my mum was too busy doing housework and looking after the children. But from 1975—when I was eight years old—my mother began sending me to Barmuni to stay with my grandparents for the three-month summer holidays.

Barmuni is close to the mountain of Mateen and the Turkish border. It is where King Faisal built his summer palace. The army destroyed the village in the 1960s and again in the 1970s, so it was rebuilt as a modern village of 1000 cement-block houses with electricity and water. There was a big tourist hotel nearby in Sarsing, but everything was so different to the skyscrapers and life in Baghdad. I loved it there.

The government ruled by day, the *peshmergas* by night. My uncle was a *peshmerga*. After the revolution collapsed, he told his family he was going to hand over his Burno. On my 1975 visit I would follow him everywhere on the farm, carrying our lunch of fruit and dry bread in a goat's-skin bag. I was proud of him. Then he secretly escaped to Iran, and did not return to Barmuni until 1986. He gave up being a *peshmerga* when Kurds began killing Kurds. He was loyal to Kurdistan.

In 1979, when I was 12, my family was asked to move again. The Arab family we lived with had found out that my father and uncles had bought land in Dohuk (cheaply, because my father was in the army). Before my father had finished building our house the landlord said, "I cannot extend your lease." While on two days' leave, dad hired a truck and we moved our bits of furniture—a fridge, one bed and the cotton mattresses—to our house with no windows or doors. Fortunately it was autumn.

That is when I began to really enjoy life. Among my cousins and uncles, going to weddings and parties every week, and celebrating Newroz, I felt proud and safe. We did not feel our father's absence so much. When I was told the story of Kawa, who killed a tyrant and freed his people, I felt proud to be Kurdish.

My secondary schooling was in Dohuk. There was an Arab teacher whose job was to recruit students into the Ba'ath Student Union. One day in Year Seven, it was my turn to be interviewed. The teacher told me: "If you don't join the Ba'ath Party, you are going to find life very hard. You will always be questioned. You have a choice, but you have to join." It was confusing! I went to my dad, who told me he was in the Ba'ath Party—otherwise, he would not have his job. He advised, "Join, but don't get involved. We are not a family who knows people in power to support us. You will not be followed and you will be able to continue your education and have more opportunities." So I joined the Ba'ath regime. We had to pay a monthly fee and attend monthly meetings in the school holidays, and do army training in the Jayeesh Al-Sha'abi in the school holidays.

When the war between Iraq and Iran started in 1980, my father served behind the anti-tank gun, living in bunkers for eight years. During Al-Anfal in 1988, my grandparents had to escape from Barmuni when Iraq used chemical weapons in the area. Their cows, sheep and chooks were affected by poison, and their house and farm were damaged. When they arrived at the refugee camp in Kurdistan of Iran, they needed treatment because they were sick from chemicals. My mother was always depressed and crying because her family had vanished. One year later, we had a phone call from my uncle. My mother cried again when she found out they were alive.

I wanted to go to university and study engineering, but because my father was in the war, I had to look after my family. I went to Mosul University, 45 minutes by minibus, and studied maths and science. I lived in the college for five days, returning to my family on weekends.

I did not tell the university I was a Ba'ath member. I did not realise that the Ba'ath network is so extensive you cannot escape. Everyone is graded according to his or her degree of affiliation. The *moyayid* believe in the Ba'aths, the *nuseerr* are supporters, the *ozo* are members and the *rafiq*, Arabic for 'comrade' or 'political friend', are at the top of the hierarchy.[a] It is the *rafiq* who recruit supporters, lead meetings and catch army deserters, in return for bonuses, prizes and promotion. When my file was sent to Mosul, the senior students of the Ba'ath branch, called Hezob Al-Ba'athi, became angry, saying, "You have been here two years and did not tell us you were a member. We must recruit you or you will be thrown out of university." The lecturers and professors all belonged to the Ba'ath regime, and I had nearly finished my degree, so I said, "Okay, I will join."

The war with Iran continued, and I knew I would be conscripted, so I purposefully failed my last year. I finished just in time for the Kuwait War! The Iraqi government was recruiting all males between 18 and 45, and if you avoided army duty, the penalty was death. In September 1990, I was sent for training at an anti-aircraft base in Babylon, 120 kilometres south of Baghdad, learning about the Soviet-made Strella anti-aircraft rocket. In the following months, more and more soldiers came south, until the hotels were packed with soldiers and others were sleeping on the streets. They had to buy their own food.

In January, US and British aircraft bombed Babylon. Buildings fell, people died, women screamed and blood was everywhere. The worst sight was a mother wailing over the body of her dead child amid people running for shelter. I was only 21. I did not believe in the war, and was afraid. I prayed for my life and to see my family again. After two days of bombing, some friends and I decided to desert. We wore casual clothes, and hid among civilians leaving their shops and houses, heading for remote areas.

We paid a driver of a Landcruiser 10 times the usual rate to take us north along roads without checkpoints. If we were caught, we would be shot as deserters by the Republican Guard or units called 'prosecutors'. In Baghdad we saw the destruction from Allied bombing. There was only one train and about 4000 people trying to board. The packed, unlit train travelled slowly through the night. If someone lit a cigarette, everyone would shout at him to put it out. Occasionally there would be a flash of light in the sky as Allied aircraft bombed military installations. Eleven hours later, we arrived in Mosul.

A taxi driver from Dohuk drove us across the mountain, avoiding checkpoints, again for good money. When I reached my house, I was in tears. I was housebound, and after a few weeks *rafiq* came and knocked on our door, saying, "If you have a deserter, he has to surrender. There is an amnesty." I hid in the chooks' pen!

Allied forces began bombing Dohuk. Our house was shattered, but such things can be replaced. We lived in hope that Saddam would be killed or deposed from power. On 28 February, Montecarlo and BBC radio announced that the Allies had won the war. The next day, President George Bush encouraged the Iraqi people to rise up against Saddam. We felt relief that at last, a superpower was supporting the Iraqi people. Our hopes were further raised one week later when we heard that army deserters and civilians were taking over the police stations and army barracks in the south.

I did not know of any plan for an uprising in Kurdistan, but when it happened, everyone supported it, including *jahsh*. Some said that the *jahsh* were pointing their guns at their Kurdish brothers one day and at the Ba'aths the next, but this does not entirely reflect the situation. In KDP areas, many tribal leaders had become *jahsh* so they could save their people. Only two *jahsh* tribes, who were enemies of Barzani, shot to kill. The others, when ordered to take over an area, always warned the *peshmerga* beforehand. They would take over a deserted hill or mountain, then, after they left, the *peshmergas* would return. I knew many *jahsh* who believed in the Kurdish cause and were in constant communication with the freedom fighters. Then there were people like my father, who served the Iraqi army for 30 years, and on retirement in 1990 had been ordered to join the Jayeesh Al-Sha'abi as an armed guard for the Ba'ath administrative offices. It was a dangerous job, because weapons stored in the offices were targets for *peshmergas*, but unless people appeared loyal to the Ba'aths, they could be imprisoned and their families thrown into hardship.

On the day of the uprising, all Dohuk's shops closed. People rushed home saying something was going to happen, that soldiers had abandoned checkpoints and were travelling to Mosul. At sunset we heard bullets and shells exploding in attacks on army bases and police stations. As the night progressed, we heard more explosions and many people shouting. People drove vehicles, including Landcruisers taken from Ba'ath bases, beeping horns and playing Kurdish songs. Over loudspeakers, they asked people to unite, telling them the regime had gone and they were free. For some hours, I stayed at home. Outside, it was impossible to distinguish friend from foe. Around 11 pm, my cousin and I ventured out. People were breaking into government buildings, releasing prisoners, wrecking furniture, looting portables, throwing police and *amn* documents out into the street and burning them in piles. Next morning, rubbish, broken glass and chaos were everywhere.

Many soldiers simply left their tanks, artillery, and machine guns and walked away. They were sick of war, but 50 kilometres from Dohuk, Iraqi authorities were recruiting them. But I met Iraqi colonels and majors who said, "This is our opportunity to leave the country." At last I felt safe on the street with all the people shouting and singing. My father was very happy too.

Over the next few days, KDP *peshmergas* began arriving, holding meetings with important *jahsh* and tribal leaders to join the United Kurdish Front or Baray Kurdistani. They began using government buildings as their bases, and convinced hundreds of people to attack and capture a large Iraqi army base in the small town of Fydiyah, 15 kilometres to the south. In the first attack, the people kicked out the soldiers, but when they went back for the weapons and ammunitions the Iraqi regime killed about seven and captured 10 to 15 others, taking these south by helicopter. (The army base continues to operate because it is just outside the no-fly zone.)

The hospital was collecting blood to treat the injured. People had enough to eat because it was customary to store food for hard times. As well, government food stores were raided and the food was given to the shops to sell.

But on 28 March, we heard news that Saddam had retaken Kirkuk. Next, Iraqi helicopters and ground artillery began launching rockets and missiles on Dohuk. We realised that the USA was letting Saddam take control. After one day of bombing, *peshmergas* went around in Landcruisers, announcing, "Evacuate Dohuk. Take the women, children and old people. We will fight on." They feared Saddam would use chemical weapons, and we heard that in Kirkuk they had been separating men from women, shooting the men and using women as human shields. We heard that the United Kurdish Front, including Barzani and his men, had stopped the Iraqi army at Salahaddin, and people were joining the *peshmergas* to defend Dohuk, but it was not a fair fight.

Events were confusing. For instance, on the last day I was in Dohuk, I saw Jalal Talabani and his wife, Hero, Ibrahim Ahmed's daughter, come to our street in a motorcade of cars marked PUK. *Peshmergas* stood guard on the roof of a house owned by the head of the *jahsh*, Adel Barwari, and while Dohuk's people fled, Talabani had a meeting with him.

We left Dohuk, 10 families in a truck. Rumours spread that Ali Hasan Al-Majid was bringing his forces and throwing people out of the helicopters. I think it was a government tactic—to encourage the Kurds to flee. People became paranoid and scared, and we joined the human wave walking to the border.

It was Ramadan, so my family was fasting, but we broke our fast before sunset. I was carrying all our food, and people were saying, "There are planes dropping food." I left everything except bread, not knowing it would take us four days and nights to cross the mountains. We were walking through black snow and freezing black rain under black clouds. People were pushing, and yelling. Some of the way was so narrow, people fell over the edge, only managing to save themselves by grabbing onto a tree or rock. Animals were dying from exploding landmines, and dead people were being buried between two big rocks, small rocks piled on top. Women left their dead babies behind. Others left their old people too weak to walk. When my five-year-old sister lost her shoes in the mud, she complained, "I won't walk in bare feet. We're not hippies. I must have shoes to continue." My mother told her, "This is not a situation in which you can decide to walk or not. We have to save our lives." My sister started crying, and we had to grab her hand and force her to continue.

At dusk on the fifth day, we arrived at the border. We heard gunfire but we were more scared of Iraq's army and helicopters. The Turkish soldiers demanded we drop all we carried, and we were allowed through to a Kurdish village of 50 houses called Dashtan, where we stayed for two weeks. The people were friendly, but they could not help—they were too poor and we were too many.

Turkish trucks bringing up food would get stuck in the mud, and as 400 or 500 people converged on one truck, soldiers on top of the trucks fired their guns. I saw two people killed by this form of crowd control.

Turkish officials began saying, "If you go back to the refugee camp in Iraq near Chakoorja (Cheli in Kurdish), you will be safe and have food and medicines. The sooner you get there, the better accommodation you can arrange." My father, brother and sister were sick, so I decided to go ahead of the family, walking for two days. There was a big crowd going the same way, but when we arrived, we discovered it had all been lies. There was nothing but bare land. People were setting up tents behind a well-guarded wire fence, which separated the camp from the village. The village had shops, but people were not allowed to go there.

I was shocked, and worried for my family because I had taken all the blankets, but the border had more or less closed, so I decided to wait for them. They arrived after a couple of days, having suffered a lot.

American aircraft started dropping food parcels, but not enough. Kurds from Europe came searching for family members. Some took videos, which were used in world news releases. When the US Foreign Minister, James Baker, visited the camp, people complained about bad treatment by Turkish soldiers, so the Americans promised to run the camp with Allied troops. US and British soldiers came within days, immunising people and erecting toilets, but too few. The camp stank.

The weather became very hot, and many people were sick with diarrhoea, cholera, and a disease that made people's hair fall out. I acted as an interpreter, telling people to put a powder in the water to prevent diarrhoea and how to take other medicine. After five weeks, Allied Forces suggested we return home, saying the no-fly zone would protect us. Because we were so sick, I decided not to risk living in a Turkish refugee camp. They brought tractors and big trucks to take the people, and in this way, on 19 May, we returned to Dohuk.

It was strange to be back. After a two-month long nightmare, it was good to be living in a building with electricity, water and proper meals. Nearby in Zakho there was an Allied Forces camp, where I got medicine for my father and sister, but the Iraqi government was still in Dohuk, and as an army deserter I was worried.

Two weeks later, the Iraqi regime pulled out and all government services left Dohuk. That meant there was no health, education or administration. Twelve or 13 Kurdish factions led by KDP organised the Baray Kurdistani to manage government affairs, but they had no money to pay anyone. Because of my English, I was able to work as an interpreter with the US army in Dohuk. They had teams helping with water sanitation, electricity, immunisation, food and kerosene distribution and resettlement. Civil engineers were being employed to fix machines.

I was stationed at the information gate. People were reporting any explosive devices, bullets or RPG shells they found, so the area could be made safe. Others would complain of a shortage of water, food or medicine, or another problem, and expect the Americans to wave a magic wand and fix everything. I remember one man coming to the office demanding compensation for the Allies' bombing of Dohuk. One of his sons had been killed and another blinded. When told it was up to the Iraqi government to compensate him, he became angry and threatened to kill an American in compensation. Everyone was put on alert. I was sympathetic. Our lives had been shattered for nothing. Seeing *jahsh* leaders being rewarded with good positions, we had lost faith not only in America but also in the Kurdish parties.

I had been working for seven weeks when the US army and its humanitarian program left Dohuk and went to Zakho. I was unable to go with them because of family responsibilities. Baray Kurdistani was advertising that they needed teachers, so I went and taught high school science and maths in a middle school for Years Seven to Nine in the mornings and in a senior school for Years 10 to 12 in the afternoons. I was paid, but only enough to feed the family for two weeks in every month. We relied on savings.

Despite all the shortages and disruptions, both students and parents valued education as the only way to a good job and survival. There was no social security system.

The style of teaching involved a lot of explaining. Students were not allowed to interrupt or ask questions until the teacher had finished. But the students respected their teachers. In Iraq, looking directly into a teacher's eyes is seen as a challenge to authority, and teachers are allowed to use the cane.

In science, we could do only simple experiments that did not require equipment. We taught in Arabic because we were still using the Iraqi curriculum and textbooks, but we left out the brainwashing and the extracurricular activities, such as the Ba'ath Student Union meetings, army training and students being forced to march in government demonstrations.

Young people were the majority of the population, and far more politically active than Australian students. In the lead-up to the first free election involving Kurdish parties, KDP and PUK representatives were going around trying to convince the people to vote for them. People were wearing yellow and putting up yellow material in their shop, yellow being the colour of KDP. Very few wore green in Dohuk. Everyone carried a gun, but there was no trouble—we were determined to build a democratic government. There were many rumours and media reports about what was happening in the different parties, and in class I would allow an exchange of ideas for five or 10 minutes. Sometimes there was an argument, but it was always friendly. The Sha'ab Party or Kurdistan Popular Democratic Party (KPDP), led by Sami Sinjari, an engineer by training, was concentrating on youth issues, education and sport, so it had the support of many students.

Just before the election, I accepted a job as a field officer for Care Australia. The only way people were getting basic necessities was through these humanitarian programs. Care Australia was the biggest humanitarian organisation operating in the no-fly zone, having taken over from Care USA when the US army and Care USA pulled out in July

1991. The UN World Food Program, UNICEF and the UNHCR worked through Care Australia and other non-government organisations. These liaised with Baray Kurdistani and employed teams of locals. As manager of the kerosene distribution program, I collected data from the towns and villages so 100 litres of kerosene could be distributed each month to each family.

I remember only one incident of violence before the elections. A Kurdish delegation from Turkey was staying at the Babylon Hotel when a car bomb blew up the hotel. There were a few injuries, and those responsible were not identified.

In May 1992, all men and women over the age of 18 were allowed to vote, and everyone did—even the disabled and the blind—coming by bus and by any other means to queue at the polling booths. Even so, outside forces tried to sabotage the election. For instance, people could use their fingerprint if they had no identification papers, but Turkey sent ink that could be removed with water, allowing some people to vote several times.

It was a very close vote between KDP and PUK, and because Masoud Barzani is a wise person, he tried to keep the peace by sharing power with PUK rather than having PUK go into opposition. There were also five seats reserved for minorities like the Assyrian Christians. The Kurdish National Assembly oversaw four governates: those of Dohuk, Hawler, Kirkuk and Sulaimani—even though Kirkuk and Sulaimani were outside the no-fly zone. If a majority within a governate voted for one party, then the governor was appointed from that party, the deputy governor from the other. Dohuk and Hawler had KDP governors, Sulaimani and Kirkuk PUK governors.

One of the first priorities was to set up a judicial system based on Iraqi law and encourage everyone to put down their guns. A police force and a United Peshmerga Force, made up of *peshmerga* and *jahsh*, was formed, but the lack of resources made it hard to catch and process criminals. People still had guns, and Iraqi agents were acting undercover: bombing, kidnapping and executing, then spreading rumours about who was responsible. An independent member of parliament was executed, and between 1992 and 1994, we would hear of women and men being killed monthly in Dohuk by political groups, or unidentified persons. The victims were said to be working as informers for Ba'ath agents.

Life continued to be hard. All UN organisations had to get permission to enter Kurdistan from Baghdad, and from June to October 1992, this was withheld from UN groups. Care Australia and the smaller NGOs continued to operate, sometimes bringing in supplies and personnel through Turkey. The Kurdish National Assembly relied on customs revenue, but with the two trade embargoes against Kurdistan, they could not import machinery or infrastructure, although TVs and videos were smuggled in. The lack of currency meant many teachers and doctors continued to work for little or no pay. However, NGOs like Karitas and Shelter For Now were helping people rebuild villages, and a German organisation was supplying goats and chickens to people who had lost everything. Also, local and internationally funded Islamic humanitarian organisations began building a mosque, school and medical centre, and connecting electricity in the rebuilt villages. But from 1993, Iraq cut off electricity supplies from Mosul, and the Dohuk area has since relied on diesel generators, costing families 200 dinars a month.

In early 1993 fighting broke out between KDP and PKK. From 1992 PKK were being forced into the no-fly zone by the Turkish army. KDP had been accepting them, giving them the red scarves of KDP, on condition they would not make military incursions into Turkey, but PKK claimed they had every right to attack the enemies of the Kurds. When PKK attacked Turkish army bases, then retreated to the no-fly zone, Turkish forces would follow them, attacking villages and killing local civilians and KDP. PKK had no villages or family in the area, so had nothing to lose. Some people accused KDP of letting the Turkish forces come, but after Saddam Hussein became president in 1979, the Iraqi and Turkish governments had an agreement that they could go 10 kilometres into each other's territory to chase Kurdish rebels.

PKK guerillas were occupying more and more villages and land, including my village of Barmuni, forcing people to go to their meetings and spreading rumours about rival parties. They virtually took control of certain areas, and this was not appreciated. They were guests acting like intruders, so KDP started defending the villages.

In 1994, disputes between KDP and PUK escalated, especially over the amount of income coming from Customs on the Turkish border. A portion of the income was meant to go to the parties and the rest to the treasury. These disputes were inflamed when Turkish representatives gave Talabani paperwork indicating that KDP was getting more than its fair share. PUK asked KDP to give a correct report. KDP told the truth, but PUK did not believe them and confiscated 20 million dinars from the Treasury in Hawler, claiming it was to pay workers. By mid-1994 it was full-scale civil war, but not in Dohuk. In December PUK took over Hawler, where the Kurdish parliament sat.

KDP was getting weapons from Turkey, so PUK asked the Iranian government for support. The Iranians put conditions on their support: PUK must put pressure on the KDPI, based in Koi Sinjak near Sulaimani, and recruit Iraqi opposition from the Shi'ites in Iraqi Kurdistan to make an Iranian army unit. PUK recruited Shi'ites, with Iranian soldiers coming in to train them. In late July 1996, 3000 Iranian soldiers entered Iraqi Kurdistan and attacked the KDPI base at Koi Sinjak. Afterwards, PUK used Iranian artillery to attack KDP on the Hamilton Road. Barzani asked the USA to solve the situation, but the Americans were more concerned with supporting the Iraqi opposition than with helping the Kurds. Barzani was desperate. Iraqi regime representatives approached KDP, offering help, saying it was an opportunity to kick the Iranians out of Iraq and PUK out of Hawler. KDP knew how treacherous Iran could be, and therefore Iraqi and KDP intelligence made a deal, with the Ba'ath regime agreeing to attack Hawler, causing a minimum of damage, and then withdraw.

I am sure the USA supported this plan. They disliked the Iranian government more than the Ba'aths. On 31 August 1996, all US personnel pulled out of Hawler by helicopter. That night, KDP entered from the north and Iraqi forces attacked from the south. After two days of bombing Hawler and PUK bases, kidnapping and killing PUK supporters and Iraqi opposition, and destroying the US communications network set up for the Iraqi opposition, the Iraqi forces retreated to Kirkuk, bombing Sulaimani on the way. That was the end of Iraq's invasion. Afterwards, PUK refused to send their parliamentary members back to Hawler, preferring to operate their administration from Sulaimani.

But all that was yet to come. Throughout 1993, I continued working for Care Australia. We did a lot of travelling in UN vehicles to the villages and were ambushed three times on mountain roads. You could buy Kalashnikovs and hand grenades in any local market, and the Iraqi government was paying people thousands of dinars to hide behind rocks on mountain roads and fire 50 bullets or a couple of shells, then run away, or to ambush and take hostages. They were targeting people who worked with the UN and the NGOs in particular, to make these organisations leave the no-fly zone or request Iraqi government protection. We had our own guards, and once we got to the village we were safe, but a number of friends were ambushed and killed by Iraqi agents, including one Australian. (Care Australia was to finish its contract with the Iraqi government on 31 March 1995.)

I had become scared for my life but I was also facing another obstacle. I liked my second cousin, Nareen, whom I had known since childhood. I felt she was my other half, so I asked my mother to ask her mother—they were cousins—if we could marry. But Nareen had older unmarried sisters, and in our culture, it is considered unfair for a younger sister to marry first. Her mother told my mother I had to choose one of her older sisters, but I said, "No, my heart is with Nareen," but her parents refused our marriage.

Twice I had wanted to leave the country, but stayed because I felt responsible for my family. This time, my brothers were old enough to look after the family, so I told them there was nothing to keep me in this part of the world. They were surprised but understood.

I could not bring myself to say goodbye to Nareen. I had to leave secretly, so I said goodbye to few people. Care Australia held a party to raise money for me to live in Turkey. They had not done that for anyone else. Every day for a week, I went to the border only to be knocked back by the Turkish guards. That was a very emotional week—saying goodbye to family every morning, my mother crying, only to return in the evening. Eventually I got through, on 17 November 1993. I spent five months in Turkey, arriving in Australia on 21 April 1994. I lived for two months in the Victorian countryside with the family of Regan Netherton, my Care Australia manager, who was my sponsor to Australia. The nearest neighbour was half a kilometre away and I was used to a crowded environment, even in a Kurdish village. I moved to Melbourne when some Kurdish friends offered to share their inner-suburban flat, to be in contact with the Kurdish community, to do an English course and to establish a career. I discovered that my Bachelor's degree was recognised by the Overseas Qualification Unit, so that all I had to do was a Diploma of Education, and maths teachers were in demand.

But I was still in love with Nareen. I met many girls of different nationalities, but they were just friends. Back in Kurdistan, Nareen and her sisters remained unmarried, and my mother was always trying to find somebody suitable for me. Eventually I announced I was going to marry a girl in Australia and my family was very unhappy. I explained, "I can't have the girl I want, so it doesn't matter who I marry!" They approached Nareen's parents, saying, "Waleed may not be back for another four years. At least let Nareen be his fiancée." When her family agreed, I was delighted.

Our families made a verbal agreement in September 1995, and together they arranged a dowry of two rings and some gold. I had to decide whether to study for a teaching diploma or take a job as a production worker with Toyota. I asked Nareen, "Should I make money and return as soon as possible, or study and then find work." She advised the second option, and from then on, my phone bills were enormous!

University was a good experience—very different from university in Iraq. In Australia, you have to look for resources and attend lectures with up to 500 students, whereas in Iraq, it is a class of 15 students, all wearing a uniform. If you are absent too often, you cannot continue.

When it came time to go into the schools to teach under observation, I worried how students would to handle my accent. I had been warned that Australian students often give teachers a hard time. I have hot blood, and can lose my temper quickly, but in Australia you have to be patient with students.

The first time I went teaching, I explained my background to my supervisor, who was very supportive. I told the students that if they found my accent too difficult, they should stop me and I would explain the work in another way. None of them had any idea about Kurdish people. I was asked, "Is it a type of food?" Everybody was aware of Saddam Hussein, but otherwise the students had no knowledge of political issues, even Australian politics. Their lack of information surprised me. In some ways, I like the Australian way, because schools concentrate on education, and I think high school students are too young and gullible to become involved in politics. A teenager can quickly become very fixed on one idea, then refuse to listen to others. Politics is not like maths or science. You have to draw on a wide range of information and be aware of the subtleties of political argument, and there is not the perspective of hindsight. But by telling the truth and showing that I was human, I gained the students' trust. Fortunately, maths does not involve a lot of talking, and when they were cheeky I did not take it personally.

Meanwhile I was missing Nareen. She and her family were living without regular water and power supplies or enough food. I felt it was unjust, that I was being selfish unless I brought her here, and in 1995 I asked my lecturers if I could take leave to bring my wife to Australia. They agreed I could go after my teaching rounds. I did not have an Australian passport, so I could not rely on the Australian government for help if I was arrested in Syria. Instead, I told my travel plans to a friend in the Department of Immigration, so that he could trace me if I disappeared. Friends lent me money for my airfares and expenses, all the time saying, "Why take the risk?" Regan from Care Australia said, "We worked hard to bring you here," but I had to take the chance. Only when I had arranged everything did I tell Nareen I was coming. She said, "Don't come if you're going to be in danger, or if it will harm your studies," and I said, "I don't care, because I am really suffering without you."

When I arrived at Damascus airport, the authorities claimed that I was entering the country illegally, even though I had a visa from the Syrian Consul in Sydney. After 10 hours of detention, I was regretting having come. Then a Kurdish policemen advised me to pay the police. I handed over US$40 and they let me go.

In Qamishli, I went to the police station for permission to enter Iraqi Kurdistan. Every day they told me, "Come back tomorrow. We are still investigating you." I also had to give Nareen's name and details to Syrian intelligence officers. I showed them our marriage certificate, because we had married by proxy, but after nine days of this treatment, having travelled 27,000 kilometres and with only 80 kilometres to go, I was fast losing hope. Only when I asked to see someone in authority and explained that I had never been political did they let me go.

The border is marked by the Euphrates River, which you have to cross by small boat. On the other side were Nareen and my family. Travelling by car to Dohuk, I could not believe I was back in my country. It was like a dream. I was legally in the no-fly zone, but the Iraq border is near, and there are many checkpoints along the road, so there was always a chance of being arrested by an Iraqi agent.

I saw big changes in Dohuk. A university had opened some months before, and at both Dohuk and Hawler universities they were conducting research projects into Kurdish history and culture. Archaeological diggings in Hawler and Zakho had uncovered coins, vases and other artefacts up to 3000 years old. The schools were well run. Sports, especially soccer, were being played everywhere. All television broadcasts were in Kurdish and some were about Kurdish history. There were Kurdish books for sale and several Kurdish theatre groups performing. New houses, shops, shopping centres and hotels had been built, providing more jobs, although unemployment was still over 70 per cent. But the people were happier. Under the Ba'aths, all big businesses and factories were government-owned. People could own small businesses and shops. People still could not build factories or businesses, because of the trade embargoes, but some generators had been imported, a shoe factory had started, and there was more trading generally. As well, people could discuss politics at school, in the mosques, at the markets and on the buses.

Islamic organisations were continuing to build schools, medical centres and water supplies and run distribution programs, and a few people in Dohuk had begun supporting Islamic political parties. People were looking for some fresh air in the middle of all the political pollution. Islam teaches a practical justice, but the problem is that political figures use Islam to recruit the uneducated and undereducated for their *peshmerga* groups. Clashes were occurring between Islamic *peshmerga* and KDP in Hawler and Halabja, a concerning development. Political leaders can use culture rather than Islam to take society backwards, and our tribal culture is much stronger and older than Islam, especially in regard to women. There is nothing in the Qur'an and Hadiths to stop women from being educated and taking a role in society. Honour killing is tribal, not religious. According to Islamic law, if a person has a relationship outside marriage, there must be four witnesses and a judge must decide the punishment. But in both Islam and in our culture, mothers are highly respected, and our custom of having big families has meant that most women have been too housebound to play an active role in politics and the arts.

I was very busy organising the celebration of our marriage, when one night, PKK attacked a police post on Speirez, a mountain 500 metres from Dohuk. PKK began entering Dohuk at night, clashing in the street with KDP, then returning to the mountains. On the roof, you could hear the whizzing of bullets and shells exploding. People were killed, and my father wanted me to leave Dohuk immediately, but I insisted we go ahead with our celebration. I borrowed a car and collected Nareen. At last she was sitting next to me. We drove around town in a procession, everyone beeping their horns, before arriving at the reception, where 300 people welcomed us with music, dancing and food. As we sat watching everybody dance, Nareen was smiling, but she was also sad: she was leaving her family *and* her country.

For some girls, it is even more frightening. Many have never met the man. Very few Kurdish men remain single, and most want to marry a Kurdish girl, so a man living overseas may see a girl on a videotape or in a photo and, if her family approves the marriage, exchange a few letters with her. That is all. The girl takes the risk in the hope of getting a good husband, a good home and a safer, better life for her children. In Kurdistan, with so much unemployment, many people cannot afford to marry, so the girl's family sees an overseas marriage as a good opportunity for their daughter and themselves. She and her husband can send money back. People do not have the luxury of feelings: the circumstances control the decision.

To be honest, love does not come to many of these marriages, but they work on a practical basis. In Australia, it is even harder for love to grow, because of the social pressures. People live as a nuclear family, the husband works from morning till night, coming home tired. The woman is not used to this isolated life. In Kurdistan she often lives with relatives and her husband finishes work at one o'clock, comes home for lunch, spends time with the family, and then goes out with friends, while she visits family and neighbours. The family have dinner together, then watch television or socialise with visitors. It is a more relaxed life.

In Australia people's lifestyle and expectations change. There is tension if the woman wants to study, work, wear clothes her husband dislikes, or buy things her husband cannot afford. Many send money back to their families, raising the question of which family has priority.

Parenting is also different. In Kurdistan, children play freely with neighbours and cousins. We are not as demanding of our parents' time and attention. If my father was angry and hit me, I would go to our neighbour's and sleep over, or my uncle's in the village and stay for all the summer holidays. It is normal for grandparents, aunts, uncles and married siblings to raise children not their own. In Australia, parents must take full responsibility, and a breakdown between parent and child causes huge problems, making parents from other cultures particularly protective of their children. In many ways, the community does not support parents teaching children moral values. People might think me old-fashioned, but I think it's much harder to raise children in a Western country.

My 17 days in Dohuk passed quickly. I took Nareen straight from the border to the Australian Embassy in Damascus, where she had an interview, and after five days she was given an Australian spouse visa. Then it was a matter of getting permission to leave Syria. We had to go to the Department of Intelligence, where they asked her about her political opinions and views on the fighting between PKK and KDP. After three days, they gave us the necessary documents, which we then had to take to the passport office. This time, we asked a knowledgable person to come with us, so we could pay a suitable bribe to the right person. I did not show Nareen how worried I was, but six days later, we finalised all the official documents. As we boarded the plane, I thought, "At last, the nightmare is over. We are flying to heaven."

Nareen had advantages over many Kurdish women. She had taught English in primary school for two years, and she had friends here. Her teaching qualifications were recognised, so she did voluntary work, then taught primary school for eight months. Now she is a full-time mother of our son and I am a full-time teacher.

At first some students did not believe I was qualified to teach maths, because I came from Iraq. They would ask, "Sir, if your whole life has been bombs, guns and wars, where did you learn maths? In the caves?" I knew they were ignorant of the rest of the world, and would explain. Sometimes other teachers asked me to speak about my experiences as a Kurd. Students asked a lot of questions, though not about politics. My size and physical appearance helped. The students nicknamed me 'Arnie' after Arnie Schwartzenegger, asking, "How come Arnie does not go and destroy Iraq?" I explain the reality of war, but they stick to the movie answers.

What a society considers important or heroic affects children in every way. Sometimes I tear out the pictures of celebrities that students have pasted in their books, saying, "That is no ideal to follow." In my day, maybe a Kurdish political leader or a *peshmerga* was considered a hero, but for me it was a highly educated person or one who had suffered for being true to their beliefs. Today, young people in Kurdistan are probably closer to the West—a sportsperson or singer might be their hero.

I teach full time, tutor private students and help the Kurdish community, especially new arrivals, because I have a better knowledge of English than most. I often feel I am under too much pressure, and sometimes Nareen feels lonely and homesick. The Kurdish diasporas are all coping with culture shock and a sense of exile, but the phenomenon is also giving us knowledge of democracy. In Kurdistan we were brainwashed by a dictatorial government that allowed no participation or consultation. Until 1975 the armed struggle was full of idealism, but when the Kurdish parties started fighting each other, and after the uprising, when so many *jahsh* got positions of power, and Kurdish authorities began acting like Ba'aths, people became disillusioned. It is a new and wonderful experience to be in a country where you can speak freely, approach a member of parliament or a local council and vote in free elections.

Unfortunately, many Kurdish leaders, although they have spent time in Europe and the USA, have also been military commanders. But it is hoped they will use more diplomacy, and that people with non-military backgrounds, who have strong democratic ideals, may have a chance to become leaders. The problem is that superpowers like dealing with dictators. One person is easier to convince than a whole population. As a result, our leaders are supported by outside forces, politically and financially—Barzani by the Americans and Talabani by the British—and neither is being allowed to win against the other. (The French are in between, having a strong relationship with the Iraqi government: there are oil contracts to consider. Only President Mitterrand tried to help the Kurds, influenced by his wife.)

Since 1997 the United Nations 'food for oil' program has been operating, so water and electricity supplies are being developed, schools and villages are being rebuilt. There are many Australian engineers and communication technicians, and others involved in dismantling landmines. The media is using an ever more extensive vocabulary and all schools teach in Kurdish. Students are not having their education disrupted by sudden changes into Arabic, war, having no teachers, or having to escape to the mountains.

The justice system is improved. My brother-in-law is a lawyer. He is paid by the regional government in Hawler, but also has private cases. There is less crime. There are local elections every three years in the two KDP governates, and the student unions hold elections.

Yet, though the war between KDP and PUK stopped in 1998, there is still fighting between PKK and the Turkish army, or between PKK and KDP, or between PKK and PUK. During fighting, people cannot farm their land, but no more is it about ideals and courage. With neighbouring governments bribing the different parties, Kurdish politics has become big business.

Meanwhile, unemployment remains extremely high, even among KDP members, although if you are a party member, you can get a better position in a government department. In the Dohuk–Hawler governates a principal of a school must be KDP. The rich are getting richer, while the majority struggle. These days, there are no shortages in the shops, but people cannot afford to buy.

There is still no postal service. There is a local telephone network, but to ring nationally or internationally, people rely on telephone centres. Calls are expensive. Organisations working in the no-fly zone, like UNICEF, UNHCR, WEFP and the NGOs, have access to the Internet because they have their own satellite telephone systems, and many administrative departments are getting computers and Internet access. Computer courses are being taught, and more shops are selling computers and software, but with the electricity always being cut and few private telephones, even people with computers rarely have email or Internet access.

The Kurdish diasporas cannot finance businesses back in Kurdistan, because of the international trade embargo, but they can help by explaining the political and humanitarian abuses of Kurds in Turkey, Iran, Iraq and Syria to the people and government of the country in which they live. We have no representative at the UN, and even if we did, human-rights issues become important only when the world's economy is being threatened or it is politically strategic. All Amnesty International or Middle East Watch can do is write another report.

The Kurds in Europe may have more chance to help the Kurds in Turkey by lobbying the European Union, the IMF and the World Bank to pressure the Turkish government to address their human-rights abuses, but because Iraq and Iran are oil-rich, they rely less on outside funding, so pressuring them is more difficult. Oil companies do not want to boycott these countries.

World economic and social trends are making it even harder for people like the Kurds to develop economically and politically. The new global economy does not respect borders, local communities or the environment. All I can hope for is that international bodies decide democracy is more important than profits and put pressure on governments to develop democratic processes. If this can be done, perhaps Kurds can hold a referendum, like the East Timorese, or create some form of confederation within present borders. Kurds could rule themselves in cooperation with each government, because no nation of people can survive when fighting enemies on all fronts. Our only hope is peace. Only then are there opportunities to build a life for the people.

The Moon Rises after Sunset

A life story based on a struggle for women's rights, from articles and an autobiography by Surma Hamid, translated from Kurdish by Dr Toma Hamid and Dr Muhummad Kamal

In Iraqi Kurdistan, between 1991 and 1997, one woman was killed every 24 hours in the name of family honour, tradition or morality. Her crime varied. She may have disobeyed a male relative or husband, or had a disagreement with one of them. She may have left her home without permission, even to visit her daughter or mother, or to attend a funeral. She may have talked to a man in the street, or taken a job outside the home. She may have refused to join the political organisation her husband belongs to. She may be in love and want to choose her life partner. She may want to remarry after being widowed or divorced. She may have refused to marry, or be refusing her daughter's marriage. She may want a divorce, or be refusing a divorce. She may object to her husband taking another wife. She may have been raped. She may have committed adultery, sometimes in return for a little food to feed her children. She may be ill, or be accused of being possessed by *jinn*. A war against women was being raged. Between 1991 and 1997 it involved the murder of more than 5,000 women by their husband or a male relative, with thousands more being forced to live under terrifying conditions.

The women so murdered are often buried without funerals, while their killers are allowed to walk free. The perpetrators are rarely arrested and imprisoned for any length of time, nor do they receive any other punishment. Indeed, many are congratulated.

While many Kurdish men and women are very much against 'honour killing', it is supported by an entrenched, tribal patriarchal culture that has caused Iraqi penal law to be amended on a number of accounts, particularly in 1979, after Saddam Hussein became president.[a] Iraqi law is still applied in Iraqi Kurdistan. As well, a person in Iraq has always been able to buy a court's decision.

The dominant culture also accepts other punishments of women because of 'sexual misconduct' or 'disobedience'. Common punishments include mutilation, such as the chopping off of a woman's nose, or punishment by stoning, burning, having acid thrown over her, or being forcibly imprisoned inside the home. According to the dominant culture, a raped woman can be killed although in some cases the man who rapes her is also killed.

Then there is Islamic or Shariah law, which covers civil, family and criminal matters, and which form the basis of some Iraqi laws, particularly in regards to marriage, divorce and custody of children. Accordingly, men are allowed to marry up to four wives, and a woman is unable to ask for divorce unless there is evidence of extreme violence or neglect. After divorce, usually initiated by the husband, a mother is denied custody of her children when they reach a certain age, and in a court of law, there must be two concurring female witnesses to counteract a male witness.

This type of gender discrimination is not new in the Middle East. That the culture and these laws continue to be practised in the 21st century is worrying enough. What is more disturbing is that in the chaos after the Kurdish uprising of 1991, and during the civil war between 1994 and 1998—although accurate statistics are hard to gather as many cases go unreported—the frequency and brutality of 'honour killings', mutilation and house-imprisonment of women, increased dramatically in Iraqi Kurdistan, to a rate far higher than other areas in the Middle East. Women became scapegoats for a traumatised society.

After the region came under Kurdish administration in 1992, some members of the ruling parties upheld the culture of 'honour killing'. Consequently, in 1999, when relatives of 13-year-old Kalthum Ahmed discovered a neighbour had raped her, they ordered her 12-year-old brother to kill her, because the rape had brought 'shame' on the family. Her brother shot her in public, the governor of Rania witnessing her murder. In another incident in Dukan, a woman was murdered under the supervision of a top official of PUK, a party that claims to be progressive.

What was more frightening was the establishment of death squads, which approached families and accused a daughter or a wife of being a prostitute, of going against religious and moral values in some other way, or of being an Iraqi agent. The family would be told: "You must kill this woman," and if the family agreed with 'honour killing', they would kill her. If they refused, the squad would kill her. Many women were suspected of having a relationship outside marriage, because they were alone for months while their husbands were away fighting.

A progressive doctor told me about one of these vicious campaigns, which was orchestrated by the KDP, with help from the Islamic Movement. KDP had organised six special squads led by well-known murderers such as Ashti Kuchar, Tahsin Kemaki, Waheed and others. In July 1994, they murdered 71 women in the city of Dohuk alone, including women from all sections of society. One victim, Fawzia Muhammad, a supporter of PUK, was kidnapped at 3 am from Azadi Hospital.

Women were not the only ones being killed in Dohuk. The authorities in Dohuk refused progressive organisations such as the Workers' Communist Party of Iraq, Displaced Peoples' Association and Unemployed Union permission to open offices in the town or to distribute their publications. Consequently Aram Ali, a member of the Workers' Communist Party of Iraq, was kidnapped and brutally murdered in the district of Sumeel in 1993, mainly because he insisted on taking his party's publications to the bookshops after being warned and interrogated four times. He had not believed KDP would carry out its threats to kill him. At around the same time, death squads assassinated other progressive people, such as Faranso from the Assyrian Democratic Movement, Abu-Nasir from the Iraqi Communist Party, and Renas from the Kurdish Toilers' Party. The Christian minority in the area was also persecuted.

What has exacerbated the situation is the rise in popularity of Islamic fundamentalist groups, which promote the attack and killing of women who do not dress or behave in accordance with their ideology. They are responsible for attacks on hairdresser shops, cinemas, and other venues that, in their view, have a negative influence.

With the growing despair, progressive doctors reported that thousands more women were burning themselves, many succeeding in their intention to commit suicide. Although there is a UN presence in the no-fly zone, the UN has refused to intervene in these crimes, or fund organisations wishing to intervene.

My own family experienced an 'honour killing' in 1989. My mother's brother killed my mother's cousin Garha, a mother of nine children, because her daughter was exchanging letters and having a platonic relationship with a boy. My uncle thought it was bringing shame on the family.

Although my father was a kind man who treated his wife and daughters with respect, my family were subject to the strict patriarchal culture through my uncles. We lived in Arbil, the old name for Hawler. My parents were poor, struggling to raise their seven girls and two boys, but in 1987, when I was 11 and my mother was 27, my father died in a car accident. In accordance with Islamic tradition, my uncles took control of our family because my brothers were too young to take the responsibility. These uncles told my mother to go back to her family and give up her nine children, but my mother refused. She continued to live in our father's house, so we had a house, but no money. Every two days, we would eat once: just bread and tea. Every night we went to bed without food and my mother would cry in fear that her children would starve.

My uncles were angry because my mother had refused to obey them, and always they made trouble. When they told us, "Your mother is no good," and we defended her, they beat us. When my older sister tried to get a job to support us, they said, "No," and beat my sister, because they did not agree with women working outside the home.

Our circumstances were not unusual. Every day, our neighbour beat his wife and we heard her screams for help, until she died. Then he married a woman 43 years younger than himself, and he beat her too – for any little thing. Growing up, it seemed to me that most women's situations were horrific, and I began to challenge my uncles. When they wanted me to wear the *hijab* and read the Qur'an, I was resilient, even when they beat me. I still remember my mother's advice: "Keep silent and wait for your brothers to grow up," but I waited for the day I could emancipate myself.

I was the only child in my family to go to school. My brothers and sisters and 15 cousins did not. Many children could not be educated, because families could not afford pencils, books and clothes. Instead, children were sent onto the street to shine shoes, clean cars or sell small things, but my father had told my uncles, "Surma is very intelligent. She must go to school." He loved his daughters the same as his sons, and even from his grave my father's wishes were binding. However, my uncles tried to stop me, ripping my books and beating me. My education was a threat to one uncle in particular, because he and my father had arranged for his son and I to marry while we were still in our mothers' wombs.

My fiance, Yunis Mahmud, had a gun and worked as a *jahsh* until 1991, when he became a PUK *peshmerga*. His father knew that an educated woman would not consider his illiterate son for marriage, so in 1993, when I was in Year 10, I was forced to leave school. My mother's brother threatened my mother that if she refused my marriage to Yunis, he would kill her as he had killed Garha. She was afraid, so I was forcibly married to an illiterate, reactionary boy. We were both 17.

Yunis was also caught unawares. He lived with his aunt. One day his parents asked him to come home. He did not know it was for our wedding. He had no understanding of marriage. There was no movies or sex education, and on our wedding night, he was more afraid than I. We sat in a room for five hours without touching.

Sexual relations can be a big problem for Kurdish women. Ninety-nine percent of women in Iraqi Kurdistan have their clitoris cut when they are four or five years old. I still remember being taken for a bath and two women coming in and twice cutting me with a razor. I cried, and my sister put her hand over my mouth. For a week, I was in pain and bleeding. My family said they would give me a toy if I stopped crying. Because of this cut women have desire, but it is very hard to have an orgasm, and it can cause psychological problems. Some women come to hate having sex.

Yunis's family was too poor to take care of us, so we rented a room. We had no furniture, nothing, because Yunis gave up being a *peshmerga* and had no work. I would not eat for two or three days. He would go to his aunt's or uncle's, returning after some days. I would be hungry and angry, saying, "This is not a life." He would answer, "You are my wife and cousin. My life is your life. If I do not eat, you do not eat." I would say, "Find some work," and he would beat me. Sometimes he worked at an electrical-goods repair shop, but would spend the money on himself. He would not allow me to find work, because a woman's economic dependence is a powerful weapon in a patriarchal culture. I would say, "Give me a divorce so I can go back to my mother," and he would say, "I will shoot you first." Even his father would tell him, "Go home to your wife. She has not eaten for three days and she will die. You must find work," and he would come home very angry saying, "All my problems come from you. I should kill you." I would go and stay with my mother for one week or a month and Yunis would tell his father, "Surma does not want the marriage," and my father-in-law would come to collect me. I would tell him, "Your son does not feed me. My mother has to give me clothes," but he would take me back by force. After this happened a few times, when my mother defended me, he beat her so badly she was afraid to protect me. Sick and crying she told me, "Go back to your husband and count yourself dead."

When the economic condition of my family worsened my uncles allowed my sister Farida, to work on a poultry farm. It is there that she met Suaad, a female worker who was an active member of the Independent Women's Organisation (IWO). When I met Suaad, I told her about my problems, and she promised to help me.

In response to the increase in the oppression of women, in May 1993, some progressive Kurdish women led by Dr Nasik Ahmed set up the IWO in Sulaimani as an independent, non-profit, non-government organisation funded by its members and individual donations outside Iraq, mainly from Europe. It had no affiliation with existing parties, although it had an informal relationship with the Workers' Communist Party of Iraq, and IWO members studied and believed the Marxist-Leninist view that the oppression of both women and men is due to the patriarchal, capitalist system. As a consequence, men as well as women became members of the IWO. My dear brother was one. Throughout our lives, he demanded the right for his seven sisters to live normally, and the right for our mother to remarry. My mother had never wanted so many children, but because her first five were girls and the family wanted a boy, she had one after another. This tradition of big families puts pressure on both parents, the man having to support them all. For all these reasons, the IWO saw men not as enemies, but as victims of the same system.

The most immediate task of the IWO was to prevent 'honour killings', by documenting and exposing such crimes in Kurdistan and abroad, and by insisting that the perpetrators be brought to justice. The other primary task was to raise people's awareness and to campaign for the repeal or amendment of laws that discriminate against women. Other campaigns included the release of women from home imprisonment and the prevention of female genital mutilation. In the future IWO, which from 1997 assumed the name 'Committee in Defence of Iraqi Women's Rights' outside Kurdistan, hopes to address contraception, health and education by visiting women in schools, camps, factories and other work places, as well as open more shelters to protect women. To do all this the organisation needs support from the international community.

To protect women facing domestic violence or death, to mediate in social, family and legal disputes, and to help women suffering psychiatric illness, by the end of 1994 the IWO had opened offices in all cities, except Dohuk. These offices became secure sanctuaries guarded by a women's army, after the women had received six months' training, mainly in how to use a Kalashnikov. In Dohuk, there is an underground IWO group of men and women. They educate people by putting posters on walls, and report incidences of 'honour killing', suicide and violence against women, and have saved several women from death by taking them to Arbil or Sulaimani, or by helping them escape to Turkey.

From 1995, I secretly became a member of IWO, working under the name of Frishta. After a short time I was promoted to the committee of Public Office, which networked with other organisations. Every time I went to work, I told Yunis that I was visiting my mother. In 1997, Yunis realised I was working. He kept quiet, but used this favour to exploit me. He would say cruel things and beat me, then rape me, and I could tell no-one. I had to obey him in every way. If he beat me in the street, no-one would help. If he beat me in front of his grandmother, she would say, "You have to be a good wife." But through my work I gradually became more conscious of my rights and more frequently challenged my situation. When my uncles continued to order me to wear the *hijab* I refused. When they accused Farida of working with prostitutes at the poultry farm I defended her. If they threatened to beat me I would not cry, I would say, "I will take action against you." However, I stayed married and at home, working in the Arbil office.

Many women were too afraid to come to our office. Hezmat was 28 when she asked for help. Her husband was a drinker, and she had separated, but she needed a divorce and wanted custody of her daughter. We employed a lawyer, took her case to court and won. She supported herself and her daughter by washing and cleaning in other peoples' homes. Another girl, Negas, aged 18, came to my home asking for assistance. Her poor father had sold her to a rich man twenty years her senior for 20,000 dinars. I made a report and the IWO took her case to court. The court decreed she could divorce as long as her father repaid the rich man his money. However, her father had spent some of the money, and we had to raise it. I gave 1000 dinars of my own money to help her.

While the IWO was not fundamentally opposed to any specific culture or religion, it opposed all violations of basic human rights, and thus it was in conflict with reactionary organisations, which supported such actions. As the IWO became more popular, and more effective in defending women's rights by taking issues of domestic violence and divorce to court, the more we were threatened by other organisations. In 1996, Islamic groups attacked a women's meeting in Arbil. Fortunately, the police came and the Islamic supporters ran away. Frequently, male relatives of a woman we were trying to help came to the office and threatened violence unless we handed over the woman. The women's army would throw them out.

Some clergy, in particular, became angry and issued orders known as *fatwas*, against almost every member of our organisation. On 16 April 1998, Malla Bashir, a leader of Bizootnowa in Arbil, sanctioned the killing of all six members of our executive committee. I was one of them. Dr Nasik Ahmed, the secretary of the IWO, decided we should go to court. The television channel, controlled by KDP, broadcast an interview with us in the courtroom. We lost the case: the court called us anti-Islamic in our faith and values, and issued warrants for our arrest.

The next day, a group from the Workers' Communist Party of Iraq came to express their support and solidarity. Islamists including members of the Hezbollah and Bizootnowa, attacked the centre with machine guns. Two members of the Workers' Communist Party of Iraq—Shahpur Abdul Qadir and Qabil Adil—were killed. The KDP closed down our centre, and the Islamists put our photos on city walls, labelling us immoral and corrupt, demanding information on our whereabouts. I escaped that morning to a friend's house where I stayed in the basement for four months. I was pregnant, and from all the fear and stress I had severe stomach pains.

Both the Islamists and my uncles were trying to find me. The IWO suggested I go to the IWO Centre for the Protection of Women in Sulaimani, founded in August 1998, to help women escape abuse. I did not go, afraid my uncle, who had an important position in PUK, would kill my mother. Instead, with help from my mother and sisters, I changed my name to Shukriyah Zahir Maoulud and obtained a false passport. Covering my face with a veil, I left Arbil for the Turkish border. Before we reached Turkey, my son was born prematurely in the back of the car. I named him Tuana, meaning 'strong'.

In Ankara, I sought refugee status through the UN. A feminist called Fakhr Al-Nisa conducted my interview, and after 20 days I was accepted. Over the next nine months, while I was waiting to get my visa to Australia, I worked with the Committee in Defence of Iraqi Women's Rights. We were trying to influence the UN to accept widowed and divorced women, with or without children, as refugees.

On 8 July 1999, I arrived in Melbourne with my one-year-old son and immediately began working for the Committee in Defence of Iraqi Women's Rights. I learned English, and now hold seminars at educational institutions, with help from Dr Muhammad Kamal and different women's organisations, to inform people of the killing of 5000 women in Iraqi Kurdistan in the name of protecting family honour and patriarchal culture, and how necessary it is to change Iraqi family and penal laws.

With help from sympathisers, I hold fundraising events and distribute reports put out by the Committee and by the Centre for the Protection of Women in Sulaimani. This shelter accommodated women and their children in either an open section or a secret section, for women who need to go into hiding. In 1998 there were 400 women in the two sections.

The cases that the shelter dealt with are horrific. In December 1997, a 13-year-old girl, Sorma Rasool, was found not to be a virgin on her wedding day, because a neighbour had raped her. Her husband prosecuted her, and her relatives threatened her with death. The shelter was able to take her away from the police and provide accommodation and protection. One shelter resident, Samera Said Zorab, had been stabbed 11 times and shot twice following allegations of adultery. Twenty-six-year-old Kazal Khider, was accused of adultery by her male relatives, who humiliated and beat her, then cut off her nose. Her execution was postponed because she was pregnant. The IWO rescued her and her two-year-old child.

Many women sought the shelter's protection to escape from being forced into an arranged marriage or to escape abusive marriages. Kalthoom Hussein was forced to marry according to *jhin-be-jhin*, a marriage arrangement where two families exchange sisters, daughters or cousins. As a consequence, Kalthoom set herself on fire, resulting in severe burns to 50 percent of her body. After receiving hospital treatment, she came to the shelter. The shelter tried to assist these women get a divorce by taking their cases to court. Others who were divorced, came to the shelter in need of protection or because they had nowhere else to go.

The shelter also endeavoured to find women who had gone into hiding, or who were being held in house imprisonment. Nahida Rostam Ahmed, aged 45, was beaten by male relatives for refusing to remarry after separating from her first husband. Having attempted self immolition, she escaped, but was found and imprisoned in her family's bathroom for eight years. A note she managed to throw out the window was picked up and brought to an IWO representative. Five armed women from the women's army went to the house in a small town near Sulaimani, in November 1998. When they asked to see Nahida her father told them that there was no woman of that name inside. They forced their way in, and discovered Nahida in the corner of the bathroom, her mouth taped and her legs and hands in chains. She was allowed to wash her hair once a month, and perhaps this was when she wrote the note.

Many victims of mistreatment develop psychological problems and the shelter cared for these women in the IWO's Solidarity Centre, a special centre for psychiatric cases. Amira Noori Muhammad, born in 1974, developed postnatal psychosis four months after childbirth. Her husband wanted to be rid of her, because of her illness. Nineteen-year-old Banaz Mostefa, was forced to marry three times. The first marriage lasted 15 days, the second and third, two days each. Her father chained her up, and as a result she developed a psychological illness.

One of the most taboo subjects in our society is incest. In a well-known case occurring in 1992 in Kirkuk, a son raped his mother. Police beheaded him. I have heard of three cases where a brother raped his sister. However, many incidences would not involve sexual intercourse because of the importance placed on virginity. Yet few dare talk about incest, let alone make a report or seek treatment. It is still a deep secret in our culture.

Wherever possible, the IWO entered into negotiations for women. Kazhal Omer Muhammad, aged 27, was in love with a man of whom her family did not approve. She asked the shelter to negotiate with her family. Meriam Abdul Wahid Aziz, 52 years old, suffered two broken ribs and broken teeth when her husband's cousin, Sardar Rashid

Ahmed, tried to rape and strangle her. She needed assistance in bringing about his arrest. Neighbours of Aghtar Taofiq Amin, a 45-year-old widow and mother of three children, were attempting to evict her from her house on the grounds that she was engaged in a suspicious relationship. People from the shelter helped her stay.

Other women sought assistance with problems unrelated to marriage and 'sexual misconduct'. Thirty-one-year-old Najea Rahim Khadir was threatened with death by her brother because she had a job. In June 1998, Shadan Mustafa's brother threw boiling water over her because she was late returning home. Nasima Kaka-Hamallah Faraj did not give her brother money, so he shot her, rendering her paralysed. Rizan Raoof, aged 34, was beaten repeatedly by her brother and threatened with death in July 1998, because she wore Western clothes. Twenty-three-year-old Bahar Ali, was beaten up by her brother because she spoke to a stranger. In October 1998, she attempted self-immolation and was hospitalised. Forty-year-old Naayma Karim sought help because she is hermaphrodite.

Some women sought help for political reasons. An editor of *The Tribune* newspaper, Nithal Al-Haj, was shot in November 1998, by Muhammad Hamid, a supporter of the Ba'ath regime. Galawish Ali Hamasaid was kidnapped by PKK. After she escaped, she was in danger of being killed by her brother, so she contacted the shelter.

The shelter worked under very difficult circumstances. It had a contact number but no fixed address, having to move one to three times a year; the number of staff was insufficient with just one lawyer, two doctors and one social worker to handle the workload; the facilities were highly inadequate and overcrowded. Often it was hard to feeding everyone adequately, and there was no schooling for the children. The shelter had only eight security guards and was in desperate need of more. Due to the non-availability of transport and the lack of finances, there were many instances in which staff arrived on a scene too late to save the woman.

Despite these obstacles, the IWO also set up a Centre for Homeless Children, for children orphaned or thrown onto the street by their parents, or by their father after their mother died. At any one time, the centre had between 20 and 30 children, awaiting adoption, or reunion with their families.

While the KDP and PUK regional governments in Arbil and Sulaimani did not support IWO, they tolerated its existence, and it was largely through the work of the IWO and other organisations, as well as the implementation of the 'food for oil' program in 1997, and the end of the civil war in 1998, that both 'honour killings' and suicide decreased after 1997. However, in 2000, the shelter in Sulaimani was forced to close down. A number of developments led up to its closure.

The IWO, the Iraqi Workers' Communist Party of Iraq and other organisations in Kurdistan were lobbying the Sulaimani administration on several family, civil and penal law matters—to some effect. For instance, in April 2000, the PUK administration amended articles within the penal code 111, that sanctioned 'honour killing', although whether this amendments will be enforceable remains unclear.

The Iraqi Workers' Communist Party was calling for a referendum to be put to the people that Iraqi Kurdistan become independent of Iraq, as opposed to both Talabani and Barzani's view that Iraqi Kurdistan should by part of a democratic federation of Iraq. Perhaps because of the stand by the Iraqi Workers' Communist Party, and our informal relationship, or perhaps because several organisations were having an impact that did not suit some PUK leaders, one of whom had a female relative in our shelter, on 8 July 2000, the authorities cut the shelter's telephone line, water and electricity, claiming it was part of an overall action to disarm all militant political forces and close down their offices in Sulaimani.

Six days later, armed men attacked the IWO office of Dr Nasik Ahmed. That afternoon, a shelter vehicle came under fire and two security guards were killed. A week later, on 21 July 2000, PUK armed forces came to the shelter and ordered the IWO office, the shelter, and the Centre for Homeless Children be shut down within half an hour. No reason was given and all IWO documents were confiscated. PUK forces arrested 12 women and their five children, as well as the female security guards and IWO members who were present at the time. The PUK leader's female relative was taken from prison and killed for refusing to return to her violent husband.

After seven days, the other women and children were released, but the IWO documents were never returned. When the women and children protested to the PUK administration that their lives were endangered by the shelter's closure, they were again arrested. Seven months later, these women and children were still in prison in Sulaimani, living in fear of humiliation, torture and death.

Fortunately, IWO offices in other cities and the secret section in Sulaimani are still operating. As well, IWO members continue to hold seminars and meetings and to publish a newspaper in Sulaimani. The voice of IWO is now being heard through the offices of the Committee in Defence of Iraqi Women's Rights, operating in cities throughout Europe, North America and Australia. The Committee is responsible for letting it be known that in October 2000, Saddam Hussein went on national TV stating that all of Iraq's problems could be traced to women, because they take men's jobs, wear short dresses and lipstick. He ordered that women be kept at home to raise families.

Following this announcement, the Iraqi regime began beheading women accused of sexual misconduct. Ali Hasan Al-Majid, a military commander during Al-Anfal, began the campaign by killing 10 women in Mosul. Subsequently, special military forces led by Udai, Saddam's elder son, killed 50 women in Baghdad. The government women's organisation, known as the General Union of Iraqi Women, played a major role in this sadistic operation, informing authorities of various women's 'sex crimes'. In a two-month period, 200 women were decapitated in front of their families. For several days, their heads would be publicly displayed on the front door of their family's home as a warning to others.

Between 1991 and 2001, as a result of UN economic sanctions against Iraq, at least 6000 Iraqi children die every month. Meanwhile the Hussein regime continues to build mosques and palaces. The inhumane economic sanctions have only stabilised Hussein's power, by creating extreme poverty for the Iraqi people. Many are unable to eat even once a day, and some women have chosen to sell their bodies to feed their families. The wave of terror against women was just another round of the regime deliberately scapegoating its most vulnerable citizens, to try and deflect blame for the peoples' hardships. At the same time, these murders serve to intimidate others. Many of the women had been falsely accused of sex-crimes. One was progressive doctor. By nailing her head over the doorway, a warning was sent to other democracy activists. During the same period, 100 political prisoners were murdered, all these actions serving as a political purge of the progressive anti-Hussein movement in Iraq.

In response to the beheadings of women in Iraq, on 25 November 2000, 200 people marched in Melbourne, demanding that the UN and the Australian government condemn the Iraqi regime's killings. Moreover we demanded that the UN lift the devastating economic sanctions on Iraq, and that the Australian government open its borders to refugees and free asylum seekers from the detention camps. In Iraq we would like to see sex workers organise a union for their own protection, then assist them individually or via their union to find alternative means of livelihood.

We are concerned about what happens in Iraq because it directly impacts on Kurdistan. Saddam Hussein is putting increasing pressure on Kurdish leaders to negotiate for the region under Kurdish administration to come back into the fold of Iraq. The no-fly zone cannot continue forever, but the present day Kurdish leaders do not have the courage to carry out a referendum for independence while they have the opportunity to do so. Whether Iraqi Kurdistan comes under Ba'ath control or becomes independent, many people are in danger of being killed and persecuted either by the Ba'aths or neighbouring governments, so in my view, it is better to establish an independent democracy.

Similarly, a long-term strategy must be taken in our struggle for women's rights. Kurdish women do not necessarily escape persecution by leaving Kurdistan. In December 2000, the Committee in Defence of Iraqi Women's Rights reported that Kazal, a Kurdish woman living in Holland, was invited to her aunt's house to reconcile with her estranged husband. Her husband and his two brothers cut her to pieces, but while they were putting her remains in the boot of a car, a neighbour reported them to the police.

Other women have been lured back to Kurdistan to be killed. Yunis wants me to go back, or help him come to Australia. Day and night, he and my father-in-law and other uncles put my mother and sisters through extreme pressure, with all kinds of threats, to force me to reunite with Yunis. But my very sick mother advises, "Never come back or they will kill you." My aunts and cousins and uncles ring me and say, "You bring shame on all the family." My 19-year-old sister begs me to come back, fearing my father-in-law will make her marry another of his sons. She cannot marry without her uncles' permission and the law does not allow a girl to travel outside the country without the signature of her male guardian. Yet if she did find a way to leave the country, one of my uncles most likely would kill our mother. If I divorced Yunis, most of my family would never talk to me again.

In Australia, many women from Muslim backgrounds must totally obey their husbands and tolerate all kinds of abuse. Often, they tell no one. On a number of occasions I have received threats for speaking about the discrimination against women in the Middle East. Coming home on the train one day I was accosted by a bearded man who spoke in Arabic. I told him I did not understand. He said, "I know you speak Arabic. I heard you speaking at a seminar against Islam. If you do that again I will cut out your tongue." Another day, when I was wheeling my son home in a pram, a group of men pushed me towards a car and threatened to cut out my tongue if I spoke publicly about women's rights. I reported them to the police, asking my friends what else I should do. They advised, "Continue your work." I continue for the sake of all people, particularly the women who are powerless in the face of terror.

Leyla Zana[a]

By Abbas Boskany

You did not know what to say
When all the exhausted non-deities
Brought you to the shore of bewilderment.

I am a have and a have-not.
Between my haves and have-nots
Dangles the hangman's rope: the borderline.

Neither the morbid swashbuckler's rusty sword's swashing
Nor the unfortunate cravens' crowing
Durst have anything to do with
The hangmen's false mosque anthems.
How had you the courage
To search for love
Amidst the lurid canine fangs?

How was it possible that
Between life and extinction,
Love and departure,
No bridge lasted?
How?
Leyla,
Leyla,
My nights and days, my days and nights,
Are all stray and homeless:
Between your not-being-around and
The sense of having-you-around,
A temple of certitude and vindictiveness rises.
For a moment, I fear
The poetry you are making.

Between
Your lofty chin and
The hangman's yellow smile,
I witnessed two things:
Your immortality and
My wrathfulness.

Hey, Fighters! Don't Forget Peace

How civil war started in the no-fly zone, based on interviews with Haval Dasko Aziz, giving the KDP point of view, and Sarbast Fatah, giving the PUK point of view, with an introduction by Hussein Tahiri

After the no-fly zone was established in northern Iraq in April 1991, US President George Bush ordered 7000 American soldiers to join British, French and Dutch troops to construct refugee camps for the return of over two million refugees who had fled to Iran and Turkey. However, there was no offer to help establish a provisional Kurdish government, or to rebuild infrastructure destroyed by 30 years of war.

Consequently, a United Kurdish Front began negotiations with the Iraqi government for an autonomous state within Iraqi borders. Without international guarantees, these negotiations collapsed, particularly over whether the oil-rich city of Kirkuk was to be part of the autonomous region. Nevertheless, the Front was determined to establish autonomy and democracy, and on 19 May 1992 it held an election for a Legislative Council and a Leader of the Kurdish Movement. Thirteen parties competed for 105 seats, five of which were reserved for ethnic minorities. Four candidates stood for Leader of the Kurdish Movement: Masoud Barzani, Jalal Talabani, Mahmud Osman, and Shaykh Osman Aziz, leaders of the KDP, PUK, Socialist Party and Islamic Movement, respectively.

There was no electoral roll. Many people had been displaced, or carried different identification papers. Polling booths were unevenly distributed, and the PUK and KDP accused each other of loading their supporters into trucks and carrying them to different booths, yet miraculously, peace prevailed. KDP won 51 seats, while PUK, with 14,000 fewer votes, won 49. However, PUK claimed the voting had been unfairly rigged, so in a climate of hope and cooperation, KDP agreed to share power 50:50, Masoud Barzani claiming he did this to avoid war. In the election for Leader of the Kurdish Movement, Barzani received 44.6 per cent and Talabani 44.3 per cent of the vote. They agreed to conduct another election for this position at a later date.

In June 1992, most of the Allied troops withdrew from the no-fly zone and the Kurdish Legislative Council began its work. KDP's Jawhar Namiq was nominated president, and Foad Ma'sum, from PUK, prime minister. A unified *peshmerga* force called the Lashkiri Kurdistan was formed under the Minister of Defence, Jabar Farman, a PUK leader. A judicial system was set up, based on Iraqi law. The Kurdish leaders wanted the Legislative Council, also called the National Assembly, to be a democratic model for the Middle East. On 4 October 1992, it voted for Iraqi Kurdistan to be part of a federation within a united and democratic Iraq.

But the alliance was fragile. The 50:50 policy was applied to all government departments and offices, from heads of departments and their deputies down to the cleaners. In every department, the manager was from one party and the deputy from another. Both were deemed to have equal power, yet each was more loyal to his party than to the government. The other major destabilising factor was that the National Assembly was not recognised by neighbouring countries and their allies. For this reason, Barzani and Talabani decided not to directly participate, remaining free to negotiate with outside governments. This lack of direct involvement served to weaken the administration. Also, they could not agree on strategy—for instance, in making a deal with the Iraqi government, Barzani was willing to forgo Kurdish claims to Kirkuk, but Talabani was not.

The Kurdish leaders did not trust each other. PUK regards Jalal Talabani as an educated Kurdish politician who supports democracy over tribal affiliations. They see Masoud Barzani as the conservative heir to a tribal structure. On the other hand, KDP accuse Jalal Talabani of being as changeable as the weather, of using alliances with different governments like a sunflower who always wants to face the sun.

On 7 September 1992, three smaller Kurdish parties—the Kurdistan Socialist Party (KSP), the Kurdistan Popular Democratic Party (KPDP) and the Kurdish Independent Party (KIP)—united to form the Kurdistan Unity Party (KUP). In the summer of 1993, KUP united with KDP, changing the balance of power in KDP's favour. PUK was alarmed. However, the first military clashes occurred not between KDP and PUK but, rather, between them and minor parties who thought KDP and PUK were monopolising power. In December 1993, KDP clashed in Sulaimani with a group led by Hama Haji Mahmud. The attack resulted in several deaths, causing friction between KDP and PUK as to how to respond. In the same month, clashes occurred between PUK and the Islamic Movement of Kurdistan. In the 1992 election, the Islamic Movement had not achieved the seven per cent threshold required for parliamentary representation, and so, allegedly with support from Iran, established its own jurisdiction, educational facilities, and welfare services, distributing food and financial assistance. All this assistance was welcomed as Kurds were living in great economic hardship. The Islamic Movement rapidly gained support, and these gains threatened the existing power base of PUK. The Islamic Movement and PUK accused each other of terrorising their supporters. After the Islamic Movement forces killed two PUK *peshmergas*, in Rania and Halabja, PUK attacked Islamic forces in the Kifri area, near Darbandi Khan. Barzani asked Jabar Farman, Minister of the United Peshmerga Force, to calm the situation amidst claims that PUK were misusing the *peshmerga*, but the fighting continued, and hundreds of *peshmergas* from both sides were killed.

Meanwhile, those in the National Assembly who chose to serve the general community were replaced by party faithfuls. By early 1994, each side was accusing the other of misusing parliament, blocking decisions and diverting money. In such a climate, it needed only a spark to start a fire. This spark occurred on 1 May 1994, in a clash between KDP and PUK supporters over a civilian matter in Qaladiza, 50 kilometres east of KDP headquarters at Salahaddin. The clash developed into a civil war that lasted until 1998.

What follows is not about perpetuating the conflict but to show how tribal traditions, years of war and intrigue, a gun mentality, a lack of trust and information, and frequent misunderstanding can cause often well-intentioned people to be distracted from their goals, irrespective of whether outside forces are involved. If dates and descriptions of events contradict, it is symptomatic of the problems—Haval Dasko Aziz and Sarbast Fatah relying on the documents available to them. Finally, these interviews are also about a sincere attempt to reconcile, with indications that significant psychological changes have taken place since the late 1970s.

Haval (KDP): To understand what happened in 1994, one has to go back to 1966, when Kurdish individuals who had left KDP were supported by the Iraqi government to fight against the Kurdish revolution. At the time, KDP was the only Kurdish party. In 1975, after the Algiers Agreement, the rebels of 1966 and others formed PUK, becoming active in southern Kurdistan in 1976. On 26 May 1976, KDP leaders, including Masoud and Idris Barzani, and Sami Sinjari, formed a 'Temporary Leadership' and began a new revolution. PUK entered the Bahdinan area, a KDP stronghold, and attacked KDP several times, culminating in a big battle at Hakkari in 1977, which PUK lost.

From 1982, PUK was attacking KDP and other Kurdish parties coming into 'their' territory. In late 1983, PUK negotiated with the Iraqi government, and were supported by the government for 11 months. Fighting between the Kurdish parties continued until 1986, when KDP and PUK reconciled, and from mid-1987, they and five other Kurdish parties formed a United Kurdish Front.

After the uprising of 1991, everyone agreed that a democratic multi-party election was the only way forward. In the May 1992 elections, KDP won the majority of votes. However, PUK did not accept the result, and Masoud Barzani decided to put the needs of the Kurdish people above the needs of the parties, and split government 50:50. If KDP had not made this decision, civil war would have started in 1992.

PUK demanded that for the first two years, they should hold the posts of Prime Minister, Minister of Treasury, Minister of the United Peshmerga Force and Minister of Industry. To avoid conflict, KDP agreed to this, but said that another election in 1994 should determine future positions. The manager of the Bank of Kurdistan was also PUK. The parliament was funded by customs revenue from Ibrahim Khalil Bridge, on the Turkish border, and from the customs point on the Iranian border. KDP and PUK representatives controlled these points, working from the same offices. This meant that both parties were aware of the revenue going to the parliament's treasury, and to the eight officially recognised parties.

In January 1994, after PUK's military operations against the Islamic Movement in the Sulaimani area in 1993, KDP called for an election to solve the growing tensions. Before anything could be arranged, trouble began. When Talabani was asked on MBC-TV in Washington in 1998, "What was the cause of the civil war?" he replied, "We had to solve the balance of power problem. We had to decide once and for all who should govern the region under Kurdish control."

Sarbast (PUK): PUK never intended to start a civil war. Talabani was more concerned with convincing European governments to press for the no-fly zone to be pushed back to the 34.5 Parallel, to have the trade embargo against Iraq not apply to Kurdistan, and other matters. After civil war broke out, many Europeans lost sympathy. Civil war was to no Kurd's advantage. Before Talabani went to Paris for a meeting with President Mitterrand on 22 April 1994, he ordered that all *peshmergas* follow Barzani's orders.

Haval: Talabani left before the trouble began. Some people say he had a plan to begin the fighting while he was out of the country, to distance himself, so that once PUK had taken over the no-fly zone, he could come back and negotiate with KDP and make himself a hero. Whatever his reason, following his departure, he was not in communication with Barzani. This made it very difficult to solve disputes.

Sarbast: They were in telephone contact.

Haval: There was no contact between Talabani and Barzani.

Sarbast: The trouble began over a civilian matter. Back in 1973, the Iraqi government had given some land to a very aggressive *agha*, the father of a young KDP security guard, Ali Haso Mirkhan. In the 1980s the government had cancelled this land distribution and built government buildings, which were destroyed in the 1991 uprising. After the uprising, the owners from prior to 1973 built shops without permission from any authority, so in 1994, Mirkhan attempted to reclaim the land for development.

Haval: After Mirkhan produced documents to prove the land was his, parliament gave him permission to redevelop the site.

Sarbast: It was the KDP party that gave him permission, and PUK requested that the matter be decided by parliament because Mirkhan had not paid money for the land. But before parliament could settle the matter, on 1 May 1994, Mirkhan and his supporters set fire to the shops. The people were angry, and Ali Nabi, a PUK supporter, came to mediate, suggesting the matter be settled by the parliament.

Haval: Ali Nabi brought 20 armed men to negotiate with Mirkhan and his 11 armed men. In the confrontation Ali Nabi was killed.

Sarbast: KDP supporters ambushed and killed Ali Nabi and Isma'il Warti a few kilometres outside Qaladiza, on their way to Rania. Angry PUK supporters attacked Mirkhan and his supporters, killing most of them. I believe both incidents happened within a day.

Haval: It was a few days after Ali Nabi's death that Mirkhan was ambushed and killed, along with 12 of his supporters, by PUK military. In the intervening days, the parliament had sent a team to investigate. The team decided it was a civilian matter and asked for it to go before the court, but PUK supporters took their revenge before this could happen.

Sarbast: The PUK leadership say these PUK supporters acted without orders from the party.

Haval: Is there any system in the world where 100 military can act without permission from their leadership?

Sarbast: Both the KDP and PUK leadership saw the trouble as a civil matter and advised restraint. An investigation team decided both cases should be taken to court.

Haval: Before the court dealt with the deaths, PUK *peshmergas* entered Rania and took control of the town, except for two KDP buildings. They demanded that KDP withdraw from the buildings.

Sarbast: They did not take control of Rania. The people were angry over the death of Ali Nabi, and PUK went to KDP and advised them to leave the town for their own safety.

Haval: KDP withdrew from one building peacefully. The Iraqi National Congress (INC), meant to represent all parties, and the Communist Party tried to mediate over the withdrawal from the other building, saying that PUK was doing this to protect KDP from angry PUK supporters loyal to Ali Nabi. Barzani sent orders for KDP to withdraw on two conditions: that no-one was killed, and that the building and documents be put under the control of INC and the Communists. But one hour after the KDP people were taken away by car, PUK took over the building and took KDP documents.

Sarbast: This did not happen. The Communists and INC remained in charge of the building and the documents.

Haval: After taking control of Qaladiza and Rania, PUK *peshmergas* occupied Sulaimani and Koi Sinjak. They arrested all KDP leaders and members and took them to Halabja.

Sarbast: KDP were not arrested. They were taken by bus to Halabja with an armed escort for their own protection. UNHCR personnel and other parties witnessed this.

Haval: In response to these aggressive actions, KDP announced all PUK *peshmergas* must withdraw from the Dohuk and Zakho area.

Sarbast: PUK agreed to withdraw from Dohuk and Zakho, but as PUK were withdrawing from Dohuk, a PUK group led by Rebaz was ambushed by KDP on 5 May. Rebaz was killed, along with about 20 *peshmergas*.

Haval: Two PUK leaders, Hasan Kuwestani and Rebaz, were based in Dohuk. They had been asked to leave peacefully and go to Shaqlowa. Kuwsetani did, but Rebaz stopped in Akre and gathered PUK military. Fighting occurred between them and KDP, and Rebaz escaped to a farm close to Akre. He killed the owner of the farm, so the owner's son killed him. If KDP had wanted to kill Rebaz, they could have done so in Dohuk. Two weeks later, Kuwestani was killed in fighting when PUK tried to take control of Choman and Haji Omaran on the Iranian border.

Sarbast: On 17 May, Hasan Kuwestani was on his way to Qaladiza for negotiations when he was killed in an ambush. PUK was angry over the deaths and KDP having stopped distributing revenue from Ibrahim Khalil Bridge, so PUK maintained control of Qaladiza.

Haval: The revenue distribution ceased as a result of the fighting. It was not the cause. You do not give money to your enemy.

Sarbast: In Talabani's absence, without a definitive chain of command, and because the parliament and its judicial system were powerless to mediate, intermittent clashes continued.

Haval: Talabani was not in regular contact with his own supporters, if you can believe them. Because of the clashes, two or three weeks after the death of Mirkhan 8000 KDP *peshmergas* surrounded Shaqlowa, north of KDP headquarters in Salahaddin.

Sarbast: Too many PUK *peshmergas* were being killed in small ambushes, and Barzani did not appear to be taking any action to prevent recurrences, so angry PUK leaders decided not to follow Barzani's orders and to try and solve the situation once and for all. Jabar Farman moved 2000 PUK *peshmergas* to the mountains around Salahaddin. He intended to take control of KDP headquarters if KDP did not come to the negotiation table, but Iran sent PUK party headquarters a message, "If you achieve your aim, it is like capturing Qom." Qom is the holiest city in Iran. Talabani ordered PUK to refrain from attacking KDP headquarters.

Haval: Jabal Farman was meant to be the Minister of the United Peshmerga Force, but his PUK *peshmergas* never reached the Salahaddin area. If you know Kurdistan's geography, you would know it is not possible. They would have to go through the Shaqlowa area, where 8000 KDP *peshmergas* were based, or fly in.

Sarbast: There is the road from Hawler, another from Koi Sinjak, and other ways.

Haval: At this point, Barzani sent messages to the PUK leadership to stop fighting and negotiate. He offered to withdraw his forces from the Shaqlowa area if PUK withdrew. The PUK prime minister, Kusrat Rasul, and another PUK leader, Malla Bakhtiar, went to Salahaddin to meet Barzani. They told Barzani that they did not know the exact whereabouts of Talabani and that PUK activities were being organised by Jabar Farman who, although second in command of military activities after Talabani, was not acting under direct orders, but he had other support. In effect, Rasul was saying Farman was out of their control. As a result of the meeting, Barzani ordered the 8000 KDP to withdraw from the Shaqlowa area, which they began to do, but then Jabal Farman moved his forces in.

Sarbast: KDP did not withdraw from Shaqlowa as they had promised.

Haval: We have INC eyewitnesses to say they were withdrawing. Talabani returned to Hawler from Turkey by Turkish helicopter after his aim to occupy the whole of the no-fly zone had failed. A leader of another Kurdish party made a joke with him, "The first time you left Kurdistan, your military occupied the headquarters of the Islamic Movement. The second time you left Kurdistan, your military occupied KDP headquarters in Sulaimani. The next time you leave, I will transfer my headquarters to PUK headquarters!" When PUK took over the Islamic Movement's headquarters in June 1993, Talabani came back to negotiate with them and make himself a hero. The same tactic did not work with KDP. He had to meet with Barzani and other leaders in Hawler on equal terms.

Sarbast: On 16 July 1994 representatives of Talabani and Barzani went to Paris to sign an agreement. It outlined the return of PUK and KDP forces to their original positions, a constitution to be drafted by December, and a census to be carried out for another election in May 1995. Other points were that appointments to all positions were to be made on the basis of merit, and new institutions were to be set up, such as a General Auditing Office. When returning through Turkey the KDP representative gave the details of the agreement to the Turkish government. Nevertheless, two or three months of peace followed.

Haval: Revenue from Ibrahim Khalil Bridge began to be distributed as before.

Sarbast: Revenue was withheld from when the fighting began in May. It was never to go back to normal. Under pressure, KDP made one payment between July and December, but this was hardly enough to pay government workers. As well, Barzani kept his *peshmergas* in Shaqlowa, and up to 3000 *peshmergas* in Salahaddin, only 30 kilometres from Hawler, the seat of government. The Ba'ath government was supplying KDP with weapons and business opportunities. It appeared to PUK that Barzani's plan was to push PUK out of the Bahdinan region, traditionally a KDP stronghold, because PUK was gaining support, particularly among young people. They preferred PUK's democratic style to the tribal leadership of KDP.

Haval: Where was this support? The 1992 election result in Dohuk speaks for itself. An overwhelming majority voted for KDP.

Sarbast: There were other points of disagreement. Like KDP, we want a federation within a democratic Iraq, but to negotiate a federation, there has to be a change of government in Baghdad, because we do not believe the Ba'aths will ever introduce democracy. Otherwise, we wanted to implement the Paris Agreement, but KDP was avoiding all points. KDP continued to withhold revenue from Ibrahim Khalil and was illegally taking other revenue. In December 1994, when Talabani and Barzani were meeting in the parliament to solve the problems, 3000 KDP *peshmergas* attacked Shaqlowa and by 23 December, after two days of fighting, took control. All houses belonging to PUK, including Talabani's, were destroyed. Barzani claimed he had not given orders for this to happen. Talabani asked Barzani to order his *peshmergas* to leave Shaqlowa, and Barzani promised to calm the situation, but in the following week, there were clashes between PUK and KDP outside Hawler and mounting evidence that KDP were moving *peshmergas* from the Bahdinan region closer to Hawler. On 24 December two KDP battalions (2000 *peshmergas*) under Barzani's control attacked PUK around Hawler. Fifty-three parliamentarians went on a hunger strike in protest against the escalating violence. After more confrontations, PUK entered Hawler on 27 December and by 29 December had KDP in the Sheraton Hotel surrounded. On the same day, KDP captured PUK *peshmergas* in the Bahdinan.

Haval: Two hundred PUK *peshmergas* from Sulaimani entered Hawler on 15 December 1994. Talabani was wanting to take control of the no-fly zone. Once inside Hawler, PUK burnt all KDP newspapers and journals, took equipment from the hospital, and confiscated houses from some KDP members of parliament. Some KDP supporters, including university staff, were kidnapped or killed.

Sarbast: PUK did not touch the hospital or, to my knowledge, any university staff.

Haval: PUK immediately held 800 KDP hostage in their party offices at the Sheraton Hotel. PUK cut the electricity to the building and allowed nothing in or out. Fortunately, the people inside had enough food for a month.

The smaller parties convinced KDP to withdraw from the Sheraton, and over some days they did so, taking their documents with them. When there were only 30 KDP *peshmergas* left inside, they refused to leave. PUK attacked the building and took control of it on 15 January 1995.

Sarbast: The Sheraton Hotel was the only big fight that occurred when PUK took control of Hawler. But according to my information, following a ceasefire on 1 January the Sheraton was handed over to INC. But on 2 January, KDP resumed attacks in Haji Omaran, then on 5 January attacked PUK on Speelik Mountain, close to Hawler. On 15 January, KDP unsuccessfully attacked Hawler, and over the next two months bombed the PUK party offices in Hawler several times, killing about 10 citizens and destroying many houses. They did this with Iranian supplied rockets, their other target being the parliament itself.

Haval: KDP bombed the PUK party offices because PUK was bombing Salahaddin. The parliament was never a target and the KDP bombs were not Iranian. They were taken from Iraqi army stores after the 1991 uprising. But the most important point is that by entering Hawler PUK was threatening the Kurdish parliament.

Sarbast: The parliament continued to operate, although there were many heated arguments over the occupations of Hawler and Shaqlowa. If PUK had not taken over Hawler, KDP would have. Their plan was to destroy PUK.

Haval: KDP's headquarters at Salahaddin were only 30 kilometres from Hawler. If KDP had wanted to take over Hawler they could easily have done so.

Sarbast: During 1994–95, they were bombing Hawler, and attacking PUK around Hawler, but PUK was too strong.

Haval: In March 1995, 95 parliamentarians stayed inside the parliament building and went on a 25-day hunger strike, insisting that all *peshmergas* leave Hawler. On 28 March, the PUK Minister of Agriculture, Sa'adi Ahmed Pir, and PUK *peshmergas* entered parliament and escorted the KDP parliamentarians out of the building, taking them to Salahaddin. From this time, the parliament ceased to operate.

Sarbast: The KDP parliamentarians walked out of their own accord. PUK *peshmergas* did not enter parliament on any occasion. From February to August 1995, Iraq launched more than 10 attacks on PUK areas. One attack was on 7 April 1995, when Iraqi forces from the Iraqi army base outside Hawler bombed the city to make trouble for PUK. This proves Iraq supported Barzani.

Haval: This attack did not happen. In August–September 1995, talks in Dublin did not achieve a resolution to the fighting, and the civil war intensified throughout 1996. PUK was attacking on many fronts and KDP were forced to defend their positions.

Sarbast: PUK was willing to leave Hawler peacefully if revenue from Ibrahim Khalil Bridge was distributed fairly and KDP stopped relations with the Ba'ath government. But to add to the problems, on 28 July Iran attacked the KDPI base at Koi Sinjak, staying 48 hours in the no-fly zone. PUK had allowed KDPI to have a base at Koi Sinjak since 1992. After KDPI *peshmergas* attacked an Iranian army base, PUK put pressure on them. But Iranian forces took matters into their own hands and entered PUK territory. Iran gave PUK no choice in the matter, but PUK was able to warn KDPI that the Iranian army was coming.

Haval: PUK allowed Iranian forces to enter Iraqi territory. Because KDP did not cooperate with these forces, the Iranians supported PUK's offensive against KDP with artillery and helicopters on 17 August 1996, along the Hamilton Road.

Sarbast: Iran did not give PUK support in any offensive.

Haval: PUK had completely taken over Hawler and many other towns and areas. The parliament was not operating, and after Iran's ease of entry into Iraqi Kurdistan, Masoud Barzani called for assistance from the USA or from any other government. The Iraqi government was the only one who responded to Barzani's request for help. Barzani did not approach Saddam Hussein directly.

Sarbast: Barzani personally wrote to Saddam Hussein asking for help, saying Iraq's territorial integrity must be defended. His real fear was losing power. On 31 August

1996, 40,000 Iraqi troops, including four elite Republican Guard units, and 350 tanks entered Hawler accompanied by KDP *peshmergas*.

Haval: KDP did not accompany Saddam's forces, but KDP forces took advantage of the time to attack Hawler from the other side of the city.

Sarbast: Over the next few days, about 1000 people were killed, kidnapped or arrested by Republican Guards and KDP. Afterwards, Barzani went on television saying that he was forced to ask for Saddam's help as the survival of the region under Kurdish administration was at stake.

Haval: I would like to see a list of names of the people who PUK say were killed or kidnapped by KDP. As far as we know, about 20 to 25 PUK leaders were arrested by KDP and sent safely back to Talabani's area.

Sarbast: America's response to Saddam coming into the no-fly zone was to call it an internal matter and bomb army installations around Baghdad, 400 hundred kilometres away. There was no thought of protecting the Kurdish people in Hawler. Representatives of INC say the CIA was given prior warning of the attack, and fled to Turkey before Saddam's forces arrived. The only other people who knew of Saddam's invasion were KDP. Other UN and NGO relief workers left the country quickly afterwards. My personal opinion is that the CIA and, possibly, other outside forces must have given the green light for Saddam to invade the no-fly zone, as they must have done for Iran's incursion in late July. Iran's invasion achieved nothing but trouble for PUK and for PUK's relationship with both KDP and the Iranian government. Similarly, Turkey must have had permission to maintain a permanent presence in the no-fly zone since 1992.

Haval: The US did not support PUK, because PUK was making an aggressive grab for power.

Sarbast: The US and other governments do not support PUK, because PUK wants to establish a modern democracy and these governments prefer to deal with dictatorships. Barzani suits them, because he is an old-fashioned dictator. His family rules KDP like royalty.

After Saddam's attack on Hawler, KDP and Iraqi forces arrived on the outskirts of Sulaimani. PUK *peshmergas* had already evacuated the city. Many citizens also escaped to Iran, fearing a repeat of 1991. I was in the border area at the time. There were no proper facilities to handle all the people.

Haval: Iraqi forces did not go to Sulaimani. They returned to Kirkuk.

Sarbast: After seven days, Saddam's army left the no-fly zone, but Iraqi secret police did not, and there are still more than five Iraqi army bases near cities under Kurdish control.

In 1996, Barzani's *peshmergas* and Iraqi secret agents stayed in Sulaimani throughout September. Barzani did not think PUK had the power to come back. But PUK were still in contact with cells inside the city, and after about 40 days of KDP's occupation, thousands of PUK *peshmergas*, and civilians who volunteered to support PUK, returned to Sulaimani in three days of fighting. They forced Barzani and his *peshmergas* to withdraw to Azmar and the hills. KDP took up defence positions for four hours, then left the area. Because the mood of the people was so antagonistic after Saddam's return to Kurdistan, when Barzani and his *peshmergas* headed for Salahaddin, they went via

Kirkuk rather than taking the shorter route along the Dukan Road. Kirkuk is under Iraq's control, but hundreds of people came out and threw tomatoes and eggs at Barzani's convoy, shouting, "You are *jahsh.*"

Haval: I think there is some confusion here. In September, when Talabani and PUK *peshmergas* escaped Sulaimani, Talabani visited Mahabad, in Kurdistan of Iran, and hundreds of people came out and threw tomatoes and eggs at his convoy because the people of Mahabad support KDPI. Since 1994, Talabani had put intermittent pressure on KDPI at their base in Koi Sinjak. Also, many KDPI in the area were being killed, arrested or handed over to the Iranian government.

Sarbast: Talabani was not in Mahabad in 1996, but when PUK *peshmergas* were travelling through Baneh and another border town, people were shouting, "Shame on you! Why did you let Iran go into Koi Sinjak?"

Haval: A non-partisan eyewitness saw Talabani in Mahabad. When PUK returned to Sulaimani, they were supported by Iranian forces, which entered Iraqi Kurdistan and stayed for a couple of weeks, until PUK had established control over Sulaimani, Rania and Qaladiza.

Sarbast: Iran did not help PUK. I was at the border. *Peshmergas* had to buy weapons on the black market to arm themselves. When people began returning home, Iranian soldiers at the checkpoints thoroughly screened them and the UN were interviewing them. I saw one UN helicopter land, and other UN teams were sent overland to interview people returning to the front line. No Iranians were among the *peshmergas.*

Haval: When PUK fled Sulaimani, they went empty-handed. When they returned, they had Kartoosha rockets and other heavy weapons. There is no black market on the border that sells those kinds of weapons. CNN showed footage of heavily armed *peshmergas*, but when Barham Salah, now prime minister of the Kurdish Regional Government (KRG) in Sulaimani, was asked if Iran had supplied these weapons, he denied that PUK had Iranian support.

Sarbast: The mood of PUK and its supporters was very strong. After they had seen how KDP and outside forces tried to destroy them, there were no half-measures—when we fight, we fight, an eye for an eye. After taking control of Sulaimani, PUK *peshmergas* advanced to Qaladiza, Dukan, Rania and Koi Sinjak and were on their way to Salahaddin. As they closed in on Shaqlowa, a US official telephoned the PUK leadership and warned that there would be more trouble if they did not stop the advance. He advised them to attend the Ankara Agreement on 17 October. Iraq also sent a message warning that if PUK did not stop advancing, there would be a repeat of 31 August. Once again, PUK was forced to back down, not wanting to take on the US and Iraq.

Haval: After the ceasefire KDP asked PUK to reform the joint parliament in Hawler.

Sarbast: PUK refused because the parliament had broken down on points that were still unresolved. PUK preferred to operate from its own administration in Sulaimani. From this time, the Kurdish region was split, Iraq warning PUK that De'gala, on the Koi Sinjak Road, was like the red line, and that if PUK crossed it, then Iraq would return. The civil war continued, and in October 1997, KDP invited Turkish forces to fight PUK. PUK lost 60 people from one jet fighter.

Haval: KDP did not invite Turkish forces inside the no-fly zone. PKK had joined with PUK to fight KDP, and were in the PUK area, so Turkey decided to bomb. Through 1995–97, PUK was the aggressor.

Sarbast: We were fighting for survival. Then on 17 September 1998, Talabani and Barzani signed a ceasefire agreement in the White House in Washington. The Washington Agreement called for a general election within a year, but KDP has not complied.

Haval: The Washington Agreement was a package of four main points, the election being the third, and KDP wants to clear up the other points first, such as the return of civilians to the KDP area. Also, after so many promises had been broken the leadership of the two parties had to start building trust. However, in 1999 there were a number of meetings, and as a result the public service, health and education are coordinated between the two regions.

Sarbast: Now, all secondary schools and the universities in Hawler, Dohuk and Sulaimani are under the control of an independent committee, which decides the syllabus, books and examinations. Also in the 1999 meetings, Talabani and Barzani discussed a future election, and later Talabani announced he would accept Nechirvan Barzani, son of Idris Barzani, now prime minister of the KRG in Hawler, as the head of a temporary joint government, so that a general election could be planned over a six month period.

Haval: I have heard this said by PUK supporters, and read it in an Australian–Arabic newspaper, but I am not aware of any official document or formal approach, although a major problem is that a lot of documents held by both parties are never published. If they were released, I do not know whether it would solve the problems or create more, but certainly, it would give people a chance to look at events in a fresh way.

Sarbast: I would like all documents to be available to the leadership of all parties, but not to our neighbouring governments. Some independent-minded people have collected documents and written an analysis, but their work has yet to be published. I do not know why. I would like to see international media interview Talabani and Barzani side by side so that people could judge for themselves.

Haval: Despite the internal conflict, the two trade embargoes and pressure from our neighbours, since the 1997 'food for oil' program was implemented under UN resolution 986, the people's situation is improving. In Kurdistan, there is not the same corruption as in southern Iraq. However, a big problem with this program is that the UN buys the food from outside Kurdistan rather than from local producers, which is undermining our agricultural base.

The KRG is very concerned about this, and in 1996 a German organisation helped set up a dairy-cow breeding project in Ankawa. More than 83 cows are milked daily, half the milk going to hospitals, kindergartens and humanitarian organisations, the other half being sold. An irrigation project in Ajga village, 10 kilometres east of Salahaddin, was constructed with the cooperation of the British SCF Organisation and the Ministry of Agriculture and Irrigation. Several springs provide water for the project and two 350-metre-long canals control flooding. A college of agriculture is being built to concentrate on animal breeding and horticulture, and the Ministry of Humanitarian Aid and Cooperation is helping to build a Visiting Lecturers' Program.

In 1997, the Hareer Tinning Factory was overhauled and provided with water for the manufacturing of tomato paste, preserved fruits, jams, grape juice and vinegar. South of Hawler, a textile factory employs 750 workers. Other public and private factories have been established since 1998 in Hawler, Dohuk, Akre, Zakho, Soran and other areas. In 1998, a UNESCO project provided computers and schoolbook printing facilities, and other projects began restoring postal services and expanding telephone lines. Salahaddin University Press, still using equipment from the 1970s, with the exception of some computers, publishes scientific and cultural books, newspapers, magazines and posters.

In these and other ways the KRG in Hawler, in cooperation with the UN, is trying to build and rebuild after years of neglect and destruction. The cabinet formed from 1996 gave priority to building roads—vital for economic development—as well as villages, health centres, schools and government buildings. The next cabinet concentrated on establishing and maintaining the rule of law and the independence of the courts, to provide citizens with a sense of security they have not felt for decades.

But there are still many obstacles to overcome. Since 1994, a non-government international organisation called Emergency has been working to help those affected by the huge number of anti-personnel mines planted in Kurdistan by the Iraqi regime. In 1998 an emergency hospital was opened in Hawler to treat burns and paralysis and to counsel patients with morale and self-confidence problems.

Yet our biggest problem is that the people of Hawler still have only one hour of electricity a day, and water is also cut, because these services are supplied from Dukan Dam, which is under PUK control.

Sarbast: The electricity is not cut for political reasons. The generator is too old and cannot handle the demand.

Haval: In the October edition of *New Kurdistan*, a PUK newspaper, it was reported that Sulaimani has power for more than 18 hours a day.

Sarbast: This is because the administration has set up diesel generators in the suburbs to supplement Dukan.

Haval: The KRG in Hawler held elections in 1998 and again in 2000 for 50 representatives. Because a party must gain a minimum of seven per cent of the vote, all KRG representatives are KDP.

Sarbast: In the KDP zone, the PUK newspaper is banned, whereas the KDP newspaper is sold in the PUK zone. PUK is trying to establish a modern democracy. In February 2000 a multi-party election for 56 councils was held in the PUK region. It was the first time that candidates' names were listed at each polling booth. Also at each booth was a representative from each party and an independent observer with a solicitor's background. As a result of this election, two councils are now run by an Islamic Movement majority, two are run by the Rabitai Islami, and 52 councils by PUK, with other parties also represented on these councils.

Human rights and maintaining law and order are top priorities. Back in 1990, PUK set up the Women's Union of Kurdistan among the refugees in Iran. In 1995, they, along with other women's organisations and individuals, marched from Sulaimani to Hawler in protest against the civil war. But between 1991 and 1997, many women were being killed and many incidents went unreported. Some involved women who before 1991 were selling their bodies and information to *estikhbarat* and *amn*. These women were often widowed or separated from their husbands due to fighting, but they were killed for the information they were selling rather than for their sexual misconduct. One well-known case is a *peshmerga*'s wife who began working secretly for the Amn. She put thallium into the yoghurt at a dinner gathering in Owag'e. Those present included Dr Mahmud Osman, Dr Shivan and Sami Shorish, all of whom recovered from the poison.

Fortunately, since 1997, the murder of women is decreasing. The Women's Union of Kurdistan now has offices and more than one refuge, as well as a Centre for Homeless Children in the Sulaimani area. They organise computer, English-language and radio courses, sports and weaving activities, and run a coffee shop.

In 2000, the KRG in Sulaimani amended legislation to ensure 'honour killing' was treated as a crime of murder, to be tried before a court. This was a very brave move, because in Iraq, the culture condones a woman being killed if she has shamed her family. Likewise, the KRG in Sulaimani passed another law saying that a man cannot marry more than one wife unless the first wife agrees. Other conditions apply. For instance, the first wife must be unable to have children. But I must admit that the new laws are very hard to implement. The culture supports 'honour killing' and having more than one wife, so some men feel that this is their right. Attitudes must change before there is real change.

Still, there is the dilemma of when to use force. In June 2000, PUK closed the Sulaimani offices of the Iraqi Communist Workers' Party, which was established in 1993. Its members are young, keen and very critical of PUK, but PUK tolerated their presence until their announcement that they were going to start military action.

As well, there is the continuing problem of PKK and the Turkish government's presence in Iraqi Kurdistan. The Turkish government constantly puts pressure on KDP and PUK to destroy PKK. When PKK came to southern Kurdistan in 1984, PUK had good working relations with them. PKK is Kurdish, too, trying to make a stand for the rights of 19 million Kurds in Turkey. After the 1992 election, more PKK came to Iraqi Kurdistan. The United Kurdish Front tolerated their presence, providing they did not carry out military activities or make military incursions into Turkey. However, PKK continued their attacks in Turkey. Because most PKK were in KDP's area, there were many clashes between PKK and KDP. In autumn 1992, the United Peshmerga Force fought PKK, then negotiated. But clashes between PKK and KDP continued, so many PKK moved to the Sulaimani region.

Problems intensified after mid-1999, when Ocalan ordered that all PKK leave Syria and Turkey. They had nowhere else to go but Iraqi Kurdistan. Ocalan announced that the liberation army was to be disbanded, but they still had weapons. Until his imprisonment, Ocalan was a great Kurdish leader, but now he has become a tool of the Turkish government. In 2000, in a letter to his brother sent via his solicitor, he is quoted to have written, "Do whatever you can do—but do not fight the Turkish army." It is reported that he told the Turkish government, "I can solve the problems of Iraqi Kurdistan if you let me. PUK is the real problem because it is supporting PKK." After Talabani returned from Ankara in October 2000 and asked PKK to leave PUK territory,

PKK attacked PUK, and fighting continued until December, with Turkish forces coming close to Rania. In December 2000, Iran negotiated a ceasefire and offered PKK asylum in Iranian refugee camps. If PKK go to Iran, their presence will be used as a weapon in negotiations with Turkey, but also PUK must keep peace with Iran to have a door to go in and out. We pay a big price for this door.

Haval: In January 2001, Barzani and Talabani met several times to discuss unification.

Sarbast: They are talking about holding one election for one government—to make the Washington Agreement a reality.

Haval: The region under Kurdish administration continues to be protected by US and British air forces based at Injerlic. In December 2000, Turkey gave the US permission to use the base for another six months. How long this protection lasts depends on other Middle East problems, because the no-fly zone is not just about protecting Kurds. Meanwhile, the Iraqi government is making overtures to Kurdish leaders to resume a dialogue. The KRG in Hawler is willing to negotiate a federation within Iraq, as long as Iraq becomes a democracy. I cannot say we agree with PUK on this point, because they change their mind so often.

Sarbast: While Saddam is in power, no-one is safe, but Saddam Hussein's sons are even worse. Udai kills for any reason, or for no reason at all. His brother Koosai is responsible for Internal Security, so unlike Udai, he uses other people to do his dirty work. The only chance for Iraq is to get rid of this family as leaders. But even if they are overthrown, I think Iraq will only become a democracy when present world thinking changes.

Intermittent rumours say that the US is proposing an independent state of Kurdistan in northern Iraq, with pressure from Europe because of the growing refugee problem. It is my personal view, as opposed to PUK's view, that all Kurdish parties should come together and work for an independent Kurdistan in northern Iraq. To do this, we would need US, European and Arab support.

Haval: To be a free country is the hope of all Kurdish people, but our aspirations must correspond with our power base. Our neighbouring countries strongly object to a federation in Iraq, let alone an independent Kurdistan, and KDP does not want fruitless bloodshed. Yet if there is no democracy in Iraq when the no-fly zone ends, for sure we have a plan. Until then, all we can do is work towards establishing stability and democracy in the Kurdish region. As Abdullah Goran wrote in *Kurdistan Hymn*:

> Home of abundance,
> Instigator of revelation and inspiration,
> Kurdistan...Kurdistan...

— III —

FROM PAZIKAN TO BOTAN, JUMI TO HAKKARI

Why Kurdish?

An extract from *Mem U Zin* by Ehmedê Xanî (Ahmedi Khani), Shakespeare of Kurdistan, in which he explains the significance of writing in Kurdish circa 1690 AD, before the French Revolution and the concept of 'nationalism' – translated by Eziz Bawermend

When ignorance reigned supreme,
Empty found Khanî the chair of wisdom.

So, not because of his qualifications or competence,
But just for the loyalty to his people and passion to preserve,

In short, due to determination, or helplessness and desperation
He did commit this act, against the prevailing custom and tradition.[a]

He threw caution to the wind and took the plunge.
Seemingly made of pearls and precious stones,

The language of the Kurds he reorganised,
And thus for the people he suffered,

So that no-one can say, "The Kurds are unjust, baseless, without origin;
Various people have Books,[b] only the Kurds do not."

So that men of thought cannot say, "The Kurds
Did not choose love as one of their aims.

Altogether they neither want nor are wanted,
Altogether they neither love nor are loved.

The taste of love did not fall to their lot,
Devoid are they of metaphoric as well as true love."

Definitely not! The Kurds are not so green,
But they are waifs and powerless.

Unwise and ignorant they are not,
Just deprived and dispossessed.

If we had a leader to look after us,
A compassionate one who knew the subtleties;

If science, intellect, maturity,
Poetry, prose, reason and wisdom

Were the things he valued in his court,
Honoured as valid currency and legal tender,

Then I would raise the flag of poetry
To the top of a mast that towered the earth.

I would recall from the heavens the spirit of Melayê Cizîrî,
And along with him I would resurrect Elî Herîrî,

I would give such joy to Feqîyê Teyra,[c]
So they would remain content for all eternity.

But what am I to do? The market is rather still.
There are no customers for vintage wine.

Especially in this day and age, the purse
Has become the friend and darling to us all.

That is, greed for money and gold,
Each, has become our sweetheart.

If you sell all of science for one cent,
If you give all philosophy in exchange for a pair of shoes,

No-one will take them to blaze the trail.
No-one will come to the party.

When we realised that such is our day and age,
When we realised fighting is all for money,

We took to becoming alchemists,
And when we saw that this was not possible,

We acted with fairness for a while
And we cleaned counterfeit jewels[d]

Deception wasn't the heart's desire,
As a go-between, it never acted.

Faith we lost in religion, and gold we never came by,
Out of desperation, at the end, we became coppersmiths.

For exhibition we brought out our hidden copper,
All blank were they, with no seals, so we prayed.

Our prayers were answered in the positive,
Vehicles they became for our task.

Although these coins are not legal tender,
They are simple, clean and precious.

Without deceit and pretence, they are complete,
And handy are they for people to do their business.

It is pure Kurdish, no doubt about it.
Gold it is not, so they cannot say, "It is low in carat."

Silver it is not, so they cannot say, "It has faded."
Our own red copper it is, this is quite clear.

Of our currency do not say, "Worthless it is."
It lacks only the stamp of those preceding the Shahs.

Had it been decorated with seals and stamps
But with no demand, it would not have remained.

It is a darling unattached to anyone.
Therefore, deamed guilty, without intention.

Currencies of people with no powerful backers,
Unless stamped with the seals of sovereigns,

Are spoiled and useless, according to many scholars,
But are highly regarded by many philosophers.

Yet the sovereign of our time, knowledgeable man,
Did not listen to us with an ear to understand,

Mîrza[e] is this gentleman's name,
Whose looks are pure alchemy.

Deceitful hearts he transforms to crystal,
Counterfeit coins he transmutes to pure gold.

Were there a hundred loads of red counterfeit coins,
To yellow he would instantly convert with one look.

He brings down the exalted to the lowest with his wrath,
And elevates the lowest to the pinnacle with his favour.

He detains generals like captives,
Then releases them like derelicts.

Without obligation or expectation of anything in return,
He makes rich with his benevolent hand

Thousands of poor and desperate every day,
Hundreds of beggars every moment.

Had he looked at us once,
Had he turned his blessed face towards us,

All these coins would be transmuted into gold,
All these words would be turned to poetry.

But very dear is his look.
Therefore, he did not look at us specifically.

However, a blessing for the populace is he,
So, oh God, grant him continuity.

He Who Does Not Fight Has a Sharp Sword

In memory of Sayideh Ibo, based on interviews with his wife, Nas'e Ouso'eva, and son, Dr Aziz Iboyan, with translations from Russian by Loretta Jew

Nas'e: A human like Sayideh Ibo is born once every thousand years. He was a shepherd boy who became Armenia's top paediatrician. He became known as 'the god of the children'. As a man, as a doctor and as a writer of stories and poems, Sayideh was so wise; his observations so acute, his knowledge of Kurdish culture and command of the language so rich, yet he could talk with ease to people of any age, background and level of education. With the children he joked; they could tell him anything. People were important to him, especially his Kurdish people. Everyone revered him.

Aziz: My father worked for the good of society. He had a peaceful character—polite, well organised, knowledgable, strong—the list goes on and on. He advocated a democratic view on all points. For nearly 30 years he practised and taught at Erevan Medical Institute, a major teaching hospital, and in 1974 was one of three doctors selected from the USSR to go to the International Congress of Paediatric Nephrology in Washington.

Lenin's point of view was, "The family is the smallest political unit, so to create the right society, we have to create the right family." Every family, movement and country relies on its leaders. Our family relied on my father, as did the Kurdish community in Armenia. He was a household name, and 20,000 people attended his funeral—people from every ethnic background and profession: Armenians, Georgians, Azeri, Russians, Ukrainians, doctors from as far away as Moscow, writers, patients, relatives of patients, family and friends. People came from every town and village in Armenia. It was very traumatic for everyone, particularly because his death was so sudden and violent.

Nas'e: For two days while he was lying in state in our apartment, men on top of the building were taking photos of everyone who entered and left the building. I do not know who these men were, but neighbours thought they were KGB, police and other agents.

Then on 21 January 1991, Sayideh's body was taken by hearse in front of a long procession through the streets. Traffic stopped. It was a very cold, snowy winter's day, and when the people standing at bus stops and in the street were told it was Sayideh Ibo's funeral procession, they took off their hats and bowed. We travelled 60 kilometres to Sayideh's village of Upper Karhoon, six kilometres from the town of Ichmadin, in the province of Ichmadin.

The open coffin remained at Sayideh's elder brother's house for a day and was then transferred to the club. Busloads of people arrived. The people formed a long queue out

Sayideh Ibo's funeral

in the snow, waiting to file into a big hall to view his body. As Sayideh's wife, I sat next to the coffin, shaking everyone's hand as they passed, while Sayideh's relatives sat in rows of chairs on one side of the hall. It was a long day.

A bag of telegrams included a letter of condolence from PKK. On 24 January a hearse took the coffin to the village cemetery, where Aziz, Sayideh's brothers, and close relatives carried it to the grave site, each taking their turn. The procession was calm and orderly until they got to the grave. A scuffle broke out—I do not know why—but it was quickly stopped. By 10 am the cemetery was crowded, although I do not remember a single politician. Later the investigators showed me a video, and pointed to some strange men and asked if I knew them. I did not.

It was a big cemetery, and I had sold a lot of gold to pay for a large red marble headstone engraved with Sayideh's name, date of birth and death, and a crack to symbolise how his life had been so tragically cut short. For more than four hours people made speeches, which were broadcast through loudspeakers, the only formal part of the ceremony being the Kurmanji prayers of the fat Ezidi *shaykhi* of the village, Shaykhi Ahmed. I did not like the man, but probably Sayideh's brothers had asked him to attend, and he made a lot of money from donations.

It was customary to have a long table of food for the guests at the cemetery, but for Sayideh, each of his five brothers provided food in their home. For the elder brother's house, I had paid for the slaughter of four cows, which were cooked in four big cauldrons, the beef being served with bread, fruit and alcohol.

I stayed three days. I had already cried too much, but whenever I was alone or surrounded by women, the tears flowed. My life had been so happy before this time. I had my problems, but my marriage was made in heaven.

I remember the first time Sayideh took me to his village. His little nieces were so shy of this new lady; they pulled their dresses over their faces, not realising that I could see everything underneath. The family was very close, Sayideh's mother at the centre, and I was immediately swept up into this all-encompassing love. Yet for a long time, the village's ways were very strange for me. As a 19-year-old city girl from Tbilisi, Georgia, I had grown up in a modern apartment, although for bathing we used the public baths, whereas Sayideh's mother, a number of his brothers and their families still lived in the stone house with three rooms and a small kitchen, featuring an old-fashioned wood fuel stove. Water was from a communal tap outside, though waterpipes were later laid to each house. They had electricity but no bathroom, and the toilet was down the back of a big garden. There was no sewerage—they just dug a deep hole, and covered it when it was full.

Whenever we visited, the family would kill a sheep and prepare a feast of delicious dishes. The first time I met the village *shaykhi* was at one such feast. Women did not sit with the men to eat so on this occasion Sayideh and his brother sat on either side of me. When Shaykhi Ahmed arrived and took his place he turned and looked me up and down disdainfully, saying loudly, "Where did this one come from?" A man nudged him and whispered, "She is Sayideh's new wife." Shaykhi Ahmed was unimpressed, "Well, she shouldn't be sitting here." The man murmured, "If you don't like it, you better get up and leave."

Each visit was like a holiday for the whole village. All the families would come and sit, reminisce, philosophise, tease and joke, and as a young woman I was very naïve and often shocked. For instance one time, after a man had died, a villager confided, "We have already paid our respects and we will bury him tomorrow, so we picked up the body and threw it in the shed." Horrified, I looked over to Sayideh, who later said, "You will believe anything!"

All the Kurds in this area were Ezidi, as was I, but my family did not practise or believe so much. I know very little about the religion except that it is a very, very old religion. My father had told me that it is a composite of Buddhism, Christianity and Islam, and what I do know is vague and confusing: although Ezidis believe in one God called Hodey[a], they pray facing the first light of the sun, called Shamsh. Although Hodey is all-knowing and just, Ezidis have many rituals to ward off the evil eye. Accordingly, mothers often pin an amulet of blue stone, with an eye drawn on it, to a child's clothes or hat.

There is an Ezidi *shaykhi* in each village, and the people believe that it is he who sends the sun's light to earth. People bow or otherwise pay respect as he passes, but in my opinion these *shaykhi* were dirty, uneducated people, who kept their followers backward so they could keep power and control. In their teachings they would say, "School is not good for your children," and girls would often be married at a very young age. The *shaykhi* goes from home to home to collect donations in return for a prayer. At a funeral they wail and cry in return for a donation. To me it was not right. I always felt there was a black element underlying this religion, ever since I was nine years old and my maternal grandmother took me to a *shaykhi*'s house because she was sick. Ezidis believe that if you stay overnight in the *shaykhi*'s house, your illness will be gone by morning. We went by horse and cart, and were met by this very old, dirty, smelly *shaykhi* who trembled. He had a cloud of flies around him, and the thought of kissing his hand was repulsive, but my grandmother insisted I do as she did, and afterwards I went away and spat and spat to get rid of the taste. We stayed the night, sleeping on thick mats around a pit with a large fire in the centre, where the bread is baked, and the next morning my grandmother was no better.

When we came for a visit to Sayideh's family, with mixed feelings I would see Sayideh's mother pray at sunrise and sunset. Sayideh did not pray, yet when he left our apartment of a morning, he would say, "Shamsh," not necessarily looking at the sun. It was like saying, "God help me through the day," and even though I did not believe in this ritual, I would do the same. But at other times during our marriage, I was horrified. Whenever Sayideh and I attended a funeral, he would line up with the other people to kiss the back of the *shaykhi's* dirty hand before giving a donation. I once asked Sayideh, "You are an educated man—why do you do this?" He answered quietly, "In honour of my parents."

The Ezidi have no religious buildings for worship, and some would go to an Orthodox church in the town to light candles and pray but not to attend the service. I often went to a church to pray. Sayideh did not. However one day, as Professor of Paediatrics, he was asked to take a delegation of professors from Moscow to the head priest of the Armenian Orthodox Church. In front of the atheist delegation Sayideh kissed the head priest's hand, then turned to the delegation, saying, "You see, I am a believer. Now you can take me off the committee!" To his surprise everyone clapped.

We would respect some Ezidi celebrations. For three days, on the Tuesday, Wednesday and Thursday after 10 February, Ezidis fast between sunrise and sunset, but Sayideh and I would fast for only one day. On the fourth day, called *I'ed*, everyone visits each other. Another Ezidi celebration is Khudernavi, which is like the Christian Easter. Everyone colours boiled eggs and gives them to children, and I have heard that some people practise a ritual of jumping over a fire.

I do not know if this was practised in Sayideh's village, but at first everything was a challenge, especially Sayideh's mother. As an educated city girl, I did not understand her at all. Hodjai, or *anay*, Kurmanji for 'mother', had been left a widow with nine children at the age of 30. She could not read or write, but she was very clever and very strong of spirit and body. Even her sons were afraid of her. When I was about five months pregnant, we came for a visit. As soon as we got out of the car, *anay* rushed out of the house to welcome us. She was about 45 by this time, dressed in traditional Kurdish clothes and speaking Kurmanji. On seeing my swollen belly, she dropped to her knees, tears in her eyes, saying, "Thank God you are giving me a grandchild from my son!" I felt very awkward, and Sayideh went over and picked her up, and they cried in each other's arms. Over time I came to see *anay* as an example of everything a mother should be: strong and very warm, and loving to one and all. When we both visited, she would say, "Today the sun shines brighter."

Sayideh's family was not originally from Armenia. They had migrated north from the village of Igdir, near Kars in Turkey, close to the Armenian border, where his grandfather had been chief of the village police and highly respected, and where his father had received some education. They had been forced to escape when the Ottomans began persecuting the Ezidi, probably in the 1915 genocide of the Christian Armenians, and had moved to one village, then to Upper Karhoon on the plain, where they bought land and settled along with other refugees—both Ezidi Kurd and Christian Armenian. For those times, the family was rich and Sayideh's father prospered as a farmer, but in 1920, during all the fighting that followed the October 1917 revolution, the authorities took the family's property and wealth.

Sayideh was born in 1924, the fifth son of six boys and three girls. Some time after his birth the authorities arrested his father and one brother. They were in prison for some time, because informers were reporting people considered 'privileged'. I know nothing of the Soviet Union persecuting Kurds because of their ethnicity.[b]

The Soviet Union persecuted the Kurds of Nakhichevan, now calledKarabakh, an area between Armenia and Azerbaijan. The Kurds living there had a good economy but in 1929 the leader of the communists of Azerbaijan told Stalin that the Kurds wanted autonomy, so the Kurds wre forcibly dispersed between the various republics. In 1937–44 Stalin began another wave of mass deportations of Kurds from Azerbaijan, Armenia and Georgia to Central Asia.

When Sayideh's father was released from prison, he had a problem with his lungs, and this was the cause of his death when Sayideh was nine years old. Sayideh's three sisters were married when they were 14 or 15, and Sayideh's brothers helped by working on the collective farm, where they grew grapes and vegetables and tended livestock.

People were also allowed to own some land and livestock, so Sayideh's brothers planted vineyards, using the grapes for eating, drying and making their own wine and vodka, and kept sheep and cows. From a young age Sayideh worked as a shepherd, but always he would take his books, climbing onto a haystack and covering himself with hay so he could read without being disturbed.

The skin of every sheep they slaughtered would be salted and dried in the sun for making and storing a delicious herb cheese. To earn extra money, they would sell wool that *anay* did not need for stuffing pillows and doonas, or for weaving *kilims* on a small loom, in traditional designs of red, green, black and white, but never blue. (In the Ezidi religion, blue is never used in clothing or other materials. I do not know why.) As well as being the village midwife, *anay* would milk the animals, and make butter and yoghurt for the family's needs and to sell. It was Sayideh's older brothers' and cousins' job to take the yoghurt in clay jars or metal containers by bus into the town of Ichmadin, where they would walk the streets hawking the yoghurt. Sayideh's short autobiographical story, *The Benefits of the Yoghurt Jar*, describes the first time he was made to go with them. In the story a 10-year-old shepherd boy called Savek comes back from shepherding very tired and hungry. His mother serves him food saying, "Now is a good time for you to learn how to earn a living for your family. Tomorrow you will go at first light with your brothers and cousins to sell yoghurt in the town." The young boy shakes with terror—the thought of going to town and selling yoghurt being so foreign to him. He asks, "Who will mind the sheep?" but his mother says, "Don't be anxious, my son. It is time for you to learn the ways of the town." When an older cousin calls by and Savek's mother tells him to call for Savek at dawn, the cousin asks incredulously, "Why? You cannot make anything out of that boy! He will amount to nothing!" All Savek's brothers think the same. But Savek's mother is unbending. The next morning his mother wakes him, "Quick—get up. The others have already started walking to the bus. You must go and keep the family honour." He runs after them, carrying a heavy container of yoghurt.

On arriving in Ichmadin, the others walk the streets, calling, "Fresh, cold yoghurt, high quality yoghurt for sale." Savek is too shy and embarrassed and reasons that there is no need to shout. People will see his container and come and ask him, "What are you selling?" but by the end of the day, nobody has bought his yoghurt, and at the prearranged meeting place the others laugh and laugh at him. Worse still, Savek's yoghurt has curdled with all the heat and movement. At home his mother shields him, saying, "Never mind. Give him time." That evening his big, rich uncle visits, and asks Savek's mother to call Savek. Savek comes into the room, his knees trembling, and sits quietly in a corner. His uncle tears into him, "You have wasted the day!" then, turning to Savek's mother, he asks, "Why do this to him? He is not a good shepherd. He cannot sell yoghurt. He is no good for anything except reading books. Why don't you send him to school?" Savek's mother answers, "All right. In the autumn he can go." Many years pass and when Savek thinks back to that day he is very, very happy that he did not sell any yoghurt!

All Sayideh's siblings attended the village school, but Sayideh was the only one who went on with his education. God blessed him with an exceptional ability to learn. He spoke Kurmanji at home. School was in Armenian, with its own alphabet and script, but at the village school the teacher and all the students were Kurdish, so they often spoke Kurmanji. Students would sit on mats writing with nib pens, warming themselves with a cow patty fire. Sayideh's aptitude was obvious, and his teacher would reprimand other students by saying, "After you die, your bones will lie at Sayideh's feet."

At the age of 15 Sayideh went to Ichmadin to study Armenian Orthodox theology in a religious seminary. Sayideh did not want to become a priest. He went because of his love of learning. He lived at the school, but after one and a half years his studies were cut short. World War Two had broken out in 1939. Two of his brothers went to war, but Sayideh fell upon different circumstances.

One summer, when he was about 16, he was accompanying his mother and the sheep to summer pastures, where they would live in a tent and cook on a fire. On their way, a middle-aged man accosted them, started an argument and went as if to attack *anay*. She kicked him hard in his private parts, and a year later, when the man died, people thought it was a result of this incident. Rather than let *anay* go to court, Sayideh said it was he who had caused the injury. The judge sentenced him to four years in a prison camp.

Sayideh never talked of his life in prison. During the war it was hard for everyone. My own father returned a semi-invalid, suffering from shrapnel in his legs, and headaches. Sayideh told me only two stories from this time. In the middle of one very cold winter, the prisoners were surviving on hot broth once a day. The guards used to allow them to walk around the camp, and one day, in a deserted corner of the camp, Sayideh found a battered old cloth hat with sideflaps. He picked it up and put it on, but it felt unusually tight. He took a closer look and saw stitching, which he unpicked. Inside was money. That night, when everyone was asleep in their double bunks, Sayideh told the old man in the bunk underneath him of his find. The old man advised, "Don't tell anyone about this gift from God. Occasionally buy a little bread for yourself." Sayideh said, "I can't do that. We are all starving." The next day Sayideh called the men together and they decided to divide the money into portions, and over time with each portion they bought a loaf of bread, which they would slice with a length of string.

The other story was of how he dreamt that the village *shaykhi* came to him and gave him a long black coat. The next day he told the old man, who advised, "It is a good dream. You are going to live a long life." A few months before Sayideh's death, he dreamed the same dream, but this time the *shaykhi* brought him a short black coat. He told me quietly, "It means my time is coming soon."

When Sayideh was a young boy, a malaria epidemic had swept through the region, causing many people to become sick and die. He had caught malaria too, but had recovered, and ever since, his dream was to become a doctor. So, after he was released from prison, he moved to Erevan to study at the medical technicom for nurses, hospital and laboratory staff. He lived on a scholarship or government allowance, and it was here that he was taught the Russian language.

Sayideh was in his early twenties, still studying at the medical technicom, when a cousin's family insisted that their daughter become his wife. For Ezidi, there is no formal marriage ceremony or government registration. People have a party. Sayideh did not want this marriage, but his cousin's parents brought her to his home. After the party he told his mother, "Until such time as she no longer lives here, I am not coming home." He went back to town to continue his studies, and eventually the girl returned to her parents.

After some years Sayideh finished at the medical technicom so brilliantly—he attained the top mark in every subject—that he was accepted into the Erevan Medical Institute to study Medicine. It was when he was in his last year of Medicine that I met him. I was studying my fourth year of a five-year course in Russian Language and Literature at nearby Erevan University.

Like Sayideh, I have a sixth sense. From dreams and coffee cups, I can tell something of the future. One Christian religious holiday, all the little girls were playing together. We have a belief that if you stand a mirror vertically behind a glass of water and drop a wedding ring into the glass, then look at the mirror through the glass, you will see the man you will marry. When my turn came, I saw a man in a white coat, with thick black hair and a moustache, looking through prison bars. The first time I met Sayideh, I felt that his face was familiar, and later I remembered the face in the mirror.

All the Kurdish students from the different universities either knew each other or knew of each other, and people would talk of this extremely clever medical student called Sayideh Ibo. Every student received a government allowance, but he was the only one on a Stalin scholarship. He also wrote Kurdish poetry in the Russian Cyrillic script, and this had been published since 1948 in the Kurdish newspaper *The New Way*, or *Ria Taza* in Kurmanji, and in magazines. I had never met him, but his poetry grabbed my soul.

I too had just had a narrow escape from entering an arranged marriage. My mother was married by 14. My mother's older sister had a son and they dreamed we would marry. I was against it, and my father, a railway station workman, supported me, but my mother was prepared to force the issue. When I showed my opposition, she refused to talk to me. On one visit she pushed a betrothal ring on my finger, and a wedding party was arranged while I was away at university. I was 18 when, on my next visit home, during the summer holiday, it was announced I was to marry. I knew I could not openly refuse, so I had to make it look like my cousin did not want me. I begged him, "Help me. I love you as a brother, but please, can you refuse to marry me?" He said, "No, I could never do that." I went to my aunt and said, "I can't do this," but my aunt said, "I know you don't love him, but for love of me, marry my son." One day while I was visiting my grandmother, my cousin arrived. It was a critical moment. I ran up, hugged and kissed him, and said in front of everyone, "Oh, my dear brother, it is good to see you." From that moment everyone, except my aunt, understood I could not live with him as a wife. The wedding was called off, but to the end of my aunt's days, she refused to talk to me, and from then on there was a problem between the sisters. It seemed both Sayideh and I had narrowly avoided being sacrificed to our old-fashioned customs.

At university I had many suitors, and apparently Sayideh had seen me from a distance. He began putting about a rumour, which spread like wildfire among the Kurdish students, that we were meeting in secret and were to be married! I was the last to know, but when I heard I was puzzled and upset. One day the editor of the Kurdish newspaper *The New Way* invited people to attend a reading to discuss the articles about to be published. Sayideh sat next to me, although I actually thought his friend, who was sitting across from me, was Sayideh and the man beside me was Sayideh's friend. We talked, but there was no exchange of names, and when it came time to leave, Sayideh offered to drive me home. He was friends with my cousin, and assured my cousin, "I will look after her," so my cousin let me go with him. On the front door step of my university accommodation, I thanked him for bringing me home, calling him by the name of his friend. Sayideh laughed and laughed, saying, "No, no. I am Sayideh." I pulled back abruptly and he asked, "Is everything all right?" Stiffly I said, "It is difficult to talk on this matter. Goodbye." and briskly shut the door.

On my next holiday to Tbilisi, my mother, father, uncle and other relatives tackled me about this rumour, saying, "This is not the way a young woman should behave. You are bringing shame on your family." Later I was to ask Sayideh, "Why did you set up this rumour instead of acting in a gentlemanly fashion?" His justification was, "I might have lost you to someone else!" He was a man who knew his mind in all areas.

Sayideh was such a strong character and I was just a foolish, young girl. At first I was not interested in him at all. As a young man he was thin, and not tall. He had a thick mop of curly, dark hair, intense eyes, a mountain of a nose, full lips and a strong jaw—the features of a peasant. I knew he was well educated and very talented and highly thought of, but he simply did not attract me.

After he finished his studies, he left to be a general practitioner in Spitark, and from Spitark he wrote to a close Armenian friend who was studying Medicine. (She had a humped back and came from an orphanage, but she was a brilliant student.) She visited me, saying, "Sayideh wants your address to ask you to send him some technical books." I agreed, fully understanding the implications, but feeling I would appear uncultured if I refused.

I received a very long letter from him, which I still have, in which he apologises for troubling me, but could I send him a particular newspaper? He goes on to say, "Would you mind if I wrote to you occasionally or would this be meddling? Maybe you have someone in your life, and by me writing I would be causing you trouble." I wrote a simple letter back, agreeing to send the newspaper but saying, "The rest is my own business." I was a determined young lady and morally very strong. He wrote a few times asking for the newspaper, and I sent them. After a few months I received a letter saying that he was coming to Erevan and would I mind him calling and thanking me for all my help? At about 11 am one Sunday, he turned up with flowers and a huge box of sweets.

On Sayideh's subsequent visits I came to realise what an exceptional man he was. He had a kind heart and a deep mind—completely different in his thinking to anyone I had met. He would read me his poems in a voice ringing with emotion and music, then ask my opinion, appreciating my background in literature. It was always a pleasure to listen to him, but at first I was intimidated, and his use of the Kurdish language was so rich in unfamiliar words, idioms and imagery that sometimes I had to ask him to explain. We would have deep discussions on literature and Kurdish culture, and I became completely absorbed by him—although I must admit, it took me a while to get used to his humour! He loved to tease, and every time he would pull me in—until I knew better. The was the case the first winter, when we were visiting his village. I wore a coat with a fox fur collar. He said, "I hope you are not planning to come to the village in that! The moment you step out of the car all the dogs will attack the fox!"

He made everything a joke. He was like a child in his humour and honesty with me, although he was mainly serious with others.

When he finally asked me to marry him, in my last year of university, I was ready to say yes. I did not even know his age: that he was 12 years older than me. During our engagement, when we visited my family in Tbilisi, my family took the subject of marriage very seriously and asked many questions, but over time they came to adore him. My mother would cook special dishes and every second sentence was, "Sayideh this, Sayideh that..."

The first time both our families met was at our wedding party in 1958, a year after our first meeting. We had a simple celebration at my parents' house. There were no Ezidi traditions and no music or dancing. No special dress. I did not want fuss, but we ate well. After the party, the custom is to tie a white ribbon across the street. The newly married couple is given a gift of money before they cut the ribbon and drive away, but the only vehicle we could find to take us to the train was a truck. I felt it was crude, not at all what I had imagined—and when this little old Kurdish lady came up saying, "Our little beauty has been swallowed by a bear," my tears flowed.

It was easy for Sayideh to adapt to married life. We went to Spitark for one year—Sayideh working as a doctor, and I as a schoolteacher of literature and language for the senior years of high school. When our daughter was born we employed nannies to look after her, but when she was six months old, we had to go to Moscow for Sayideh's dissertation and I gave her to my mother in Tbilisi. It was a common role for grandparents. I visited her every two months.

The Erevan Medical Institute had recommended that Sayideh go to Moscow and sit an exam at the Institute of Paediatrics, part of the Academy of Medical Sciences. Of the 15 sitting the exam, only one would be selected, and Sayideh was the one. His first dissertation was on new treatments for whooping cough, for which he was to receive his Candidate or Bachelor of Medicine. While he did his research and worked in the institute's hospital, I studied the development of children, also at the institute.

We both loved Moscow: its physical beauty as well as it being the educational and cultural centre of the Soviet Union. We enjoyed going to the Bolshoi Theatre and seeing Chekhov's production of *The Seagull*, and to the Bolshoi Ballet to see Galina Ulanava dance *Swan Lake*. Sayideh completed his dissertation before the three-year time period, and it was published in a Russian medical journal as were many of his subsequent papers. We returned to Erevan, on the way collecting our three-year-old daughter—neither she nor we having any problem adapting to the new life.

Sayideh became Assistant Professor of Paediatrics at the hospital attached to Erevan Medical Institute, treating children with every condition. He also started his second dissertation on lung problems, for which he would get a doctorate eight years later. It was then, in 1970–71, that he became a professor.

All patients were treated for free, and the Armenian government paid doctors.

Sayideh received the highest reward, but nothing like the remuneration in Western countries. However, we lived well and were able to buy a nice apartment in the suburb of Komitass, named after an Armenian composer. As Ezidi Kurds we felt no discrimination. It was the antithesis to the Kurdish situation in Turkey. Under the Soviet system the Kurdish people could speak, publish and perform in Kurdish. We had our own newspaper, radio programs, language schools and theatrical groups. These theatrical groups came from the villages and were partially funded by the government but mainly supported by the people. They would visit Erevan and put on stories of Kurdish life, doing all the scenery and costumes to a very high standard. Then in about 1980 Erevan started its own Kurdish theatre. We were free to play Kurdish music, and Sayideh loved music. He would wander around the house singing Kurdish songs. Kurdish people could work in the government, but there were no Kurdish politicians, only a Kurdish community representative.

Despite these freedoms, always we were aware that Armenia was not our land, and because the Kurdish were a small community—there were only 600 to 700 in Armenia—we helped and supported each other. Sayideh was constantly asked to help, whether it was to treat children, help them go to university, or give advice on any scandal or problem, even to negotiate a modern marriage between families, after a man and woman had fallen in love!

The Armenian people were friendly, but deep down they felt a difference. I remember one day I picked up the phone to ring Sayideh and found myself in the middle of a telephone conversation. One woman was asking the other about her very ill child and the mother answered, "I do not know what to do. I need help." The other woman suggested, "Why don't you take your child to that professor." The mother said, "You mean the Ezidi professor? I have heard that he is very good but he has a very long waiting list." I broke into the conversation saying, "Excuse me. Could you ring tonight after seven o'clock and I will arrange for your child to see my husband." The mother asked, "You can help? Oh I am terribly sorry I called him Ezidi. Please forgive me."

Sayideh was like a doctor from God. Even when he was assistant professor the professor would send him all the hard cases, and even the *shaykhi* would bring their sick children. He could diagnose a problem when others could not. I remember one child who was suffering from severe allergies. Many doctors had tried various remedies until finally the parents brought him to Sayideh. Sayideh asked them to stop all treatment for one week, then bring the child back. He prescribed a medication and the child got better, and afterwards the parents wrote and sent greeting cards, even after they moved to America.

Working with children came easily to him. His office was full of toys, and the children would come in at any time, unlike the doctors. One day a boy came in for a chat, and after Sayideh gave him some sweets the boy offered, "I know where my father keeps his pistol." "Oh, where?" asks Sayideh, and the boy told him. When the boy's father came, Sayideh advised, "I think you had better hide your pistol somewhere else!"

Sayideh's powers of observation helped in making accurate diagnoses. For instance, one day in early spring, while travelling by car, we saw some Kurdish children selling snowdrops beside the road. Sayideh stopped and bought some, saying, "You must be the son of so-and-so, and you must be the daughter of ..." Later I asked, "How did you know those children?" and he said, "By their faces." Rarely did Sayideh feel under too much pressure.

Few cases weighed heavily on his mind. One was when parents of an 18-month-old child suffering a neurological problem came to him. Sayideh had no remedy and knew the problem would be ongoing. The child's parents begged him to give them a medicine to end the child's life, but Sayideh refused and could only advise them to try and do the best for their child.

Usually he worked from nine to five, treating patients and also giving lectures to doctors, but at any time of the night he might be called out on urgent cases, and if the patient was in a different town he would be taken by helicopter. Over time he would treat several generations in the one family and relatives of patients would always visit us on New Year, which in Armenia is a big event, like Christmas is in Australia. Everyone sets their table with food and leaves their door open for visitors. One Christian family would bring their child every year. When the child was two to three months old, he was pronounced clinically dead, but Sayideh saved him. The parents renamed their child Sayideh, which was very unusual—Christians did not give their children non-Christian names.

As well as working at the hospital, for 30 years Sayideh did a radio program in Kurmanji, called *Advice from a Doctor*, on an Armenian radio station, for one hour twice a week. It covered pregnancy, birth, motherhood and how to treat infectious diseases, and was to become the basis of three paediatric books. He was always busy, and so was I. I continued to teach the senior years Russian language and literature, and also taught university students language-teaching methods. This was my choice. We did not need the money, but I love teaching, especially literature. Sayideh did not want me to work so hard, so I compromised. I could have done a dissertation, but Sayideh said, "One professor in the family is enough!" Yet he often helped me in the house. When Aziz was born and starting to eat solids, Sayideh would prepare all his food, and weigh him once a week. When the children were young, Sayideh would crawl around on the floor playing with them. As they grew older, he would sit them on the lounge and read to them or tell Kurdish folk tales or stories about his life, speaking mainly in Russian but sometimes in Kurmanji. He ensured his daughter and son had a good upbringing, morally and materially.

Aziz went to a preschool, and when both children were going to school, I would drop them off, then go on to my school. I finished at one, so I was home when they came home at three. On arriving home, Sayideh would put on an apron and wash the dishes. I would say, "Rest—you have worked hard enough," but he would say, "I don't want you to be tired," or he would ring up from the hospital and say, "Don't cook tonight. We will go out to a restaurant." I was understanding of Sayideh's work, and how it often took him away or kept his mind preoccupied. Of course I felt lonely at times, but I knew he did not belong to just me—he belonged to everyone.

Oh, we had our arguments! That is life. Quite often, I had a contrary point of view—usually stemming from my different background—but rather than have a lot of arguments, Sayideh would whittle me down until I saw his point, or I would change his mind. Or he would do something really bizarre and funny to relieve the tension and make me laugh. In a gathering of friends, he might joke, "Why argue with a woman? Listen carefully to what she has to say, agree with her, then do whatever it is you have to do." Sayideh could express himself so thoughtfully and articulately that some people, even his own cousins, were too shy to speak freely and openly in his presence. All his family turned to him for advice, including his older brothers. If a child misbehaved, they would be told, "Don't do that or we will tell Sayideh." However, both his mother and I always felt free to be ourselves, and to each other Sayideh and I were open books. We shared our minds, our hearts and experiences, which is unusual in Kurdish culture.

I was always the first to hear or read a new poem or story he had written. In 1963, after we came back from Moscow, the Armenian government published his first book. *My Era* or *Khornar Men* was a collection of lyrical poems, with political themes describing Kurdish life before and after the 1917 revolution. Other poems satirised Kurdish characters, or described a love of place, whether it was Moscow, Leningrad, or his motherland, Kurdistan. His use of Kurdish idioms, metaphors and symbolism make his work hard to translate, but his love of his homeland and his knowledge of the people goes to the heart of any Kurd. In one of the satirical poems, called *Mother-in-law, Father-in-law and Son-in-law,* he describes a Kurdish family gathering. The whole conversation is taken up with self-praise: they are the best family, with the best homes, the best food, and the best lives, and they go on and on until "their tongues are stuck to the roofs of their open mouths". This is a Kurdish idiom: they have paralysed their tongues by speaking so much rubbish.

Though Sayideh was invited to join the Soviet Communist Party, he never became a member, unlike others who wanted to advance. However, until the late 1970s, he was a big believer in socialism. He had great faith in the Party and respected its program. This is shown in the poem *The Party Program,* written in 1961, when we had just moved to Moscow. Sayideh compares the life of 100 years ago to that after the revolution, and concludes that the program had greatly improved the Kurdish people's lives in terms of education, health, work, food and shelter. In another poem, entitled *My Era—My Soul* or *Rhohay Mun—Khorna Muna, rhohay* meaning 'soul' and *khorna* meaning 'era', also written in 1961, he describes how the soul responds to the good and bad of an era.

Sayideh wrote epic poems and short poems, and epigrams of four to six lines, and also short stories. We would discuss his ideas in depth and with my soul and spirit, I understood him, but when it came to his knowledge of the Kurdish language, I continued to have to ask him to explain. However his books were very popular with the Kurdish in Armenia. The Armenian government would pay for a run of 500 copies that would sell out within a day, to be followed by more editions. The biggest problem in accessing his work is that although it is written in Kurmanji, the language of northern Kurdistan and parts of southern Kurdistan, Sayideh wrote in the Russian Cyrillic alphabet, which the Kurds from other parts cannot read.

In 1966 his second book was published. *Crossroads* or *Deriyan,* for which I suggested the Russian title *Pair'e'khry'o'stok,* was a collection of short stories about Kurdish village life, full of Kurdish idioms. For example in the story *The Sacrifice of Tayjo* the shepherd character, Tayjo, is so strong and healthy that people say, "He could use his teeth to mill a stone." Then one day, his eyes fill with pain, and as he rolls on the ground in agony everyone stands around offering remedies. One bystander suggests grinding sugar for his eyes, but the big, moustached *shaykhi,* fingering his string of beads, says imperiously, "No, no—you must sacrifice a sheep. That is the only cure." The village is poor so the people continue to try all the other remedies. In desperation one villager uses a Kurdish idiom to say, "If you had a broken leg, 'on my eyes, and on my face and on the heads of my fathers for seven generations' I would know how to help you." Finally the people decide to sacrifice a small goat. They put the wet goat's-skin on Tayjo, and in their rush only half-cook the meat. After Tayjo dies from cold and diarrhoea, the *shaykhi* saves his pride by saying, "You took too long to follow my advice."

In *Twenty Years Later,* or *Bist Sol'e Dun,* a collection of poems published in 1970, Sayideh describes the long hard road travelled by Kurdish people from traditional life to Soviet socialism. He shows how traditional Kurdish life had some elements of socialism, in that everybody shared and helped each other, but also it was controlled and kept backward by a feudal *agha* system. However with exile and communism the *agha* system had broken down and when Sayideh was growing up, the government controlled everything. Kurds had far more freedom than they had in Turkey, so Sayideh concludes that communism delivered all their dreams.

In 1975 his third collection of poems was published, under the title *Seenum,* the name of a girl. In the poem *My Dream,* he describes three dreams, three loves: that of his birthplace, the world and a free Kurdistan.

A red line of love for his people and culture run through all his writings, and one poem, *My Childhood,* written in 1964, the year our son Aziz was born, was set to music and sung by Arame Tigran, an Armenian who dedicated his life to Kurdish music.

Aziz: I regard Arame Tigran as second only to Sivan Perwer. Every new year, he would visit my father and play the *ba'aghlama* and sing. The song became very popular, and to this day it is played over the radio.

Nas'e: It was sung at Sayideh's funeral. Paraphrased, it goes:

Where is my childhood?
I am looking for my childhood that passed like lightning.
It ran away and left me alone.
Come back, return to me, my sacrifice (*mun hiyran*)
I turn to my son and see you tall and handsome.
To me, you are a deep sweet kiss.
You are spring and I am winter.
I am not mistaken *that you are my head*[c]
The rule of life is that one grows old so another can grow.
Through you, my son, life continues.

Sayideh's language was also rich in metaphor. In the poem *Dirty Hands,* Sayideh describes a young man whose hands are so impregnated with dirt from hard work that the skin is as hard as a cow pat. His face is as black as the dirt at the bottom of a well, but he is not ashamed of this hard-earned dirt.

Sayideh's first novel was published in 1979. It is called *A Kurdish Traveller* or *Kurdo Waiwee.* Set at the time of the October Revolution, it describes the events in Armenia and their effect on the lives of the people, dramatically relating how most Kurds did not understand what was happening or why, unable to throw from their mind's eye the weight of the *aghas* and *shaykhi* and their ingrained traditions to see the reality of their harsh lives. However young Armenian revolutionaries attract some Kurdish youths to their ideas and cause upheaval in the village.

Re-reading the novel, I am struck by its humour: the way Sayideh described the characters, their conversations and situations. I was also crying. Everything he writes has the ring of truth, and he saw so much hypocrisy that it made me wonder about all the people who had been so kind to me before he died. Reading his description of a *shaykhi* woman, I could see her in front of my eyes: her unwashed, dishevelled hair, and her constantly hitching up her dirty baggy pants, her appearance and that of her *Shaykhi* father matching their characters and actions. To heal sick babies, she would unwrap the swaddling material and pronounce a diagnosis, then wrap the baby up and pass it under the belly of an animal saying, "Okay, now the baby is cured." If the baby died she would gaze to heaven saying, "What can I do? It is the will of God." *Shaykhis* held the people in their hands, and belief in their power was in the blood of generations.

Another character was the *agha*. He owned 1800 villages (Sayideh was prone to exaggeration), and was given to speak expansively of his lands and power. Then there was a holy man called Pir Meerzo, a two-faced person who kissed the hand of authority while spreading nasty gossip behind their backs, and a rich man who acted like a judge. These three held the village in darkness, while Hamza, a young educated man and a serf to the *agha*, tried to open the eyes of the people. The novel begins with the police coming to the village and arresting him because of these activities, his older illiterate brother, Shabeli, also a serf to the *agha*, unable to understand why Hamza is being arrested.

Two shepherds feature in the story. One, Karam, is involved in the inevitable love story. He is the upright son of a shepherd who was out minding sheep one day when a pack of wolves attacked and killed 50 sheep. The *agha* ordered Karam's father to work for the rest of his life for food only, to pay back the loss of the sheep. Upon his death, Karam inherits his father's debt, his mother working at odd jobs around the village to help, sometimes receiving only a crust of bread for her cleaning or repairs. Karam and the *agha*'s beautiful daughter, Zaytoon, fall in love from a distance, but as in the tragic tales of Khadji and Siamand and Shirin and Farhad, theirs is an impossible love.

Sardar, the son of Pir Meerzo, is married to Shabeli's daughter, but Sardar decides he wants the *agha*'s daughter for himself. He divorces Shabeli's daughter, sending her home to her father, but keeps their son. Zaytoon does not want the marriage, but her father beats her, her mother beats her, and she is betrothed against her will, even though everyone knows of her love for Karam.

Ahmed, the *agha*'s son, and Sardar go to Karam while he is out minding the sheep. They start a quarrel, and Sardar kills Karam with a sabre. Shabeli's son, who is aware of his mother's mistreatment, finds Karam's body and, thinking that the *agha*'s son is responsible, goes and kills him. He leaves home and becomes involved in the revolution. One has to wait to find out the fate of the *agha*'s daughter. It is in the unpublished second half of the novel, which lies in storage in Moscow!

Throughout the novel, Sayideh's descriptions are magnificent. Of the arrival of spring he relates how the winter snow melts, separating into glistening medallions like those on a bride's traditional necklace, melting further into silvery-white snakes that slither down the hill to reunite in the river. In another section, Sayideh describes a heavy brown fog around the mountain of Senak, likening the fog to the washed and combed wool of the sheep. Hovering above the fog, the tip of the mountain appears as if tied to the sky. In another passage, a sombre grey day is compared to an old woman's face, the rain falling like her tears.

The novel is dense with Kurdish proverbs, such as, 'The goat knows her time has come when she goes and eats the bread of her shepherd,' and 'Let us agree and arrive at the same conclusion so neither the metal skewer nor the meat will burn.' In a conversation a character says, "Of course your son will listen to you. If he does not, I myself, 'at your feet', will cut his throat." Karam's mother tells Pir Meerzo, "I am your servant. 'I am the earth under your feet'."

During the 1980s, when it became apparent that the Soviet system had no more to give to the people, Sayideh gradually moved away from his belief in communism. He criticised a lack of fairness, despite the rhetoric.

Aziz: In my view the USSR was not truly socialist, because the government owned everything. True socialism promotes equity in opportunity and decisions, and ownership by the people. I see 10 times more possibilities in Australia than in the former Soviet Union.

Nas'e: This loss of faith was reflected in his writing. He no longer praised communism. Instead, in his last collection of poetry, *Freedom* or *Azadi*, published in 1988, the two epic poems and many shorter ones have patriotic themes about Kurdish people, their history and situation, constantly calling for the need to unite. One of the epics, *The Origin of the Kurds*, is based on a Kurdish legend. Paraphrased, it starts:

> Four thousand years ago,
> Among the beautiful roses,
> In one of the big black tents
> Lived a good and clever man called Kurdo.
> He came from generations of good families.
> One day music rang and drums beat outside his tent
> As people brought him a beautiful bride
> called Walday.
> This couple had seven handsome boys,
> Who supported their father.
> When all seven married and raised families
> Step by step the Kurdish nation was built …

However Sayideh goes on to describe how over time, they go their separate ways and become each other's enemies.

The second epic, *On the Other Side of the Araz* (the river bordering Turkey and the Soviet Union), describes how the river divides a homeless people. The poem compares the lives of the Kurds in the Soviet Union with those in Turkey, and Sayideh's pain on seeing that on their own land, they have become serfs to the Turks, or have been pushed off, just as the Turks were pushed off their land by the Mongols. In this collection, Sayideh laments how each fragmented Kurdish community always maintains it is the best, and urges that now is the time to unite against their mutual enemies. One poem in this collection, *A River*, is a good example of his use of symbolism:

Discarded white wool floats down the river
The river spits onto its banks and asks for sweet songs
From the lips of the plants.
The river gives breath and life,
To the pregnant roses.
The flowers are soft in comparison to the stones on the bank.
This small river is poor in comparison to the vast ocean.
The ocean is like a huge man who eats too much,
When compared to this lamb of a river.
The ocean is hungry. It swallows everything and remains insatiable.

For as long as I knew him, Sayideh dreamed of an independent Kurdish state, with all the lands taken from the Kurds returned to them, but he wanted a bloodless revolution, one that used diplomacy rather than armed struggle. He thought all the Kurdish parties must come together to discuss the issues and decide on one course of action. As a united front, they could then have dialogue with existing governments and international institutions. Only then would the world recognise and help them.

Aziz: My father did not get involved in party politics. He took a more universal, philosophical overview. He saw this absence of cooperation between the parties as the biggest obstacle to the promotion of a Kurdish consciousness and identity, and to the recognition of the Kurdish nation. It still is. There is a lot of talk about unity, but no action.

Nas'e: He always followed events in other countries, and he admired Mistefa Barzani very much. Although Barzani used armed struggle, he was always ready to negotiate, and back in 1970 Sayideh had great hopes for Barzani's Autonomy Agreement with the Iraq government. Later he realised it was not worth the paper it was written on, and in the following 20 years, he felt, the Barzani leaders and Talabani made many mistakes. But Sayideh always did what he could. After Saddam Hussein's genocide of the citizens of Halabja in 1988, he had a meeting with other Kurdish intellectuals. His ideas formed the basis of a letter asking for acknowledgment of the genocide, and his was the first signature on the petition sent to the governments of Armenia and Russia, and to the UN.

He also admired Abdul Rahman Qassemlou from Kurdistan of Iran as a true democrat. As for the PKK in Turkey, he respected their aims, as did all educated Kurdish in Armenia, but he rejected some of their strategies. He recognised that the Turkish government had been far harsher on its Kurdish population than had any other government, but it pained him that so many young people were being killed, and that the armed struggle was perpetuating the genocide. Yet in many poems, he called for people to stand up against tyrants, like in *Advice of my Brother*, written in 1961 and published in *My Era*. Paraphrased, this poem goes:

"It was early in the morning when the enemy fell upon us."
He turns to his mother, saying, "Oh mother, my wound is heavy,
I am dying and you are remaining.
Fight the fascists.

Oh mother, my wound is heavy.
I am dying for my homeland.
Fight the enemy so Alagaz[d]
Will always be great.
Oh mother, my wound is heavy
Let your daughter-in-law paint her eyes and comb her hair
Let her be like she was before.
Don't let her grief break her.
Oh mother, my wound is heavy ..."

I would describe Sayideh as a pacifist, but in one incident another side showed through. We were on holiday at a sanatorium, and we were taking a walk at sunset. We sat on a bench, and people gathered around to talk. To everyone's silent astonishment, a man walked up to the group and verbally abused one of the women in a very masculine way. Sayideh calmly stood up and suddenly, with a wide sweep of his arm, slapped the man's face. The man was so shocked, he shut up and walked away. Later I asked, "Why did you do that? You did not know the woman." Sayideh replied, "I had to re-educate him." So I think he may have thought that at the point when your family are being slaughtered, you cannot sit by and talk.

Before *glasnost*, the borders were closed. KGB even checked private letters, but after *glasnost*, PKK were the first to come to Armenia. They opened an office in Erevan, visiting every Kurdish family in the town and in all the villages, holding meetings and discussions. They visited us too, in 1991, to pay their respects after Sayideh's death.

Aziz: I knew them only by pseudonym and they struck me as highly educated and articulate.

Nas'e: In the late 1980s, the developments in the Soviet Union concerned Sayideh greatly. He did not like the era under Mikhail Gorbachev, wary that Gorbachev could not deliver all that he promised. Nor did he have faith in Yeltsin.

Aziz: Gorbachev introduced *perestroika* and *glasnost*, but he did not have the backing of a strong group. He always made the decisions, often too late to save the situation. He was unable to control the forces he unleashed, and many of us hold him responsible for all the tragedy that followed.

Nas'e: Sayideh thought change was necessary but the spilling of blood could have been avoided. While Armenia did not have the bloodbaths of some Soviet states, in 1988 Armenia began negotiations with Karabakh, after its local council voted to be under Armenia's administrative control. (Karabakh was a territory annexed by Azerbaijan under Lenin's auspices in 1923, against the wishes of its population, which is 76 per cent Armenian.) In response to these negotiations, from 1989 the Azerbaijan authorities began expelling Armenians from Karabakh, and some Armenians became casualties in the escalating violence, many escaping to Erevan, Russia and the USA. In Erevan, these people were lining up each day with their sick children to see Sayideh. He gave the patients from Karabakh first priority, distributing the necessary medicine without prescription, from that chests of medicine in his room, donated by aid organisations. The children were mainly suffering from diarrhoea, malnutrition, scarlet fever, diphtheria, measles, rubella and lung problems—all caused by extreme hardship.

For my part, I would collect clothing for the beggars who had come to Erevan.

Aziz: My father spoke out strongly against civil war. He tried to help and calm everyone.

Nas'e: In November 1989, the Armenian Nationalist Movement formed. Azerbaijan had blocked roads and railways to Armenia, and Azerbaijan soldiers attacked Armenian villages in the Azeri enclave of Nakhichevan (the Armenian side of Karabakh), so the Armenian authorities isolated Nakhichevan and began expelling Muslim Azeris. There were no casualties, but many Muslim Kurds became frightened, migrating to Russia, Kazakhstan and other places, although some may have been coerced to move.

Traditionally, Ezidi Kurds did not like Islam and never married Muslim Kurds, and with all the trouble, the Ezidi wanted to distance themselves even further. They started going on Armenian television and radio saying they were not Kurdish, that their nationality was Ezidi.[e] There were very few wealthy Ezidis. The majority were poor and uneducated, and we wondered how they were able to finance their media presence, and who had the most to gain by aggravating divisions within the Kurdish populations of Armenia, Georgia and other parts of the former USSR.

To discuss the growing tensions, in late 1989, early 1990, the First Secretary of the Armenian government called Kurdish Muslim and Ezidi leaders to a meeting. One of the Ezidi leaders was Sayideh's third cousin. On this occasion, Sayideh voiced his opinion: "We are all Kurds, but some have stayed with the old religion while others have followed the new." After the meeting, when everyone was leaving, Ezidi people beat up some intellectuals who had attended the meeting. A group of Ezidi youths recognised Sayideh and, for his own protection, bundled him into a car and took him home.

While Sayideh always voiced the truth when asked in private conversation, he made no public statements after that meeting, but many people began using his name for their own purposes. One newspaper article quoted Sayideh as having said the Ezidi need to be given a portion of Armenia to form a state of their own. This was the wish of a particular Ezidi leader, not Sayideh.

Throughout 1990 rumours spread about that Professor Iboyan gave lethal injections to Armenian children or that he had been arrested and sent to Moscow. People were gossiping about him everywhere. He was invited to go on television to refute the rumours, and afterwards people phoned, saying how relieved they were to hear it was all wicked gossip. Now I believe those rumours were in preparation for what was to come. On 23 August 1990, the central government in Moscow ignored an Armenian declaration of independence. These were uncertain times, and many robberies were taking place.

Aziz: From that time until now, there were many killings, not only of Kurds but of Russians and Armenians too. No-one knew why it was happening, but it became increasingly evident that the killers were targeting clever people.

Nas'e: On the winter evening of 17 January 1991, it was dark by 5 pm. Aziz, who worked with his father at the hospital, had gone to bed, but Sayideh was reading the newspaper in his armchair, near the heater in our hallway. When the doorbell rang, he asked me to look through the peephole. I saw a short, dark, thick-set Caucasian man, with another in the shadows. The man announced, "I have come to see Professor Iboyan. I have a sick child."

"Well, I am sorry—he is not here." The man thought for a while, then left. I went to the balcony, and saw the two men under a streetlight. When they saw me they quickly got into a small white car and drove away. After Sayideh's death, Prokooratora, the people above the police who were investigating the case, suggested that if I had let the men in, they could have killed us.

An hour later, Sayideh suggested we go to our *dacha*, some 30 minutes' drive, to check the gas heating pipes, because the weather was so freezing he was worried the pipes might burst. Aziz drove us. Along the way, we became aware that an imported car was following us, and Sayideh suggested that Aziz slow down. The other car accelerated, overtook, then cut in at an angle in front of us. Aziz put his foot on the accelerator and managed to pass. The car continued to follow us through hills of wild shrubbery and into the village, stopping outside the orchard around our *dacha*. They waited as we went in, then sped away.

On the morning of 18 January 1991, before Sadiyeh left for the hospital, he advised me, "Don't open the door to anyone." I told him crossly, "Why say this? I am not a child." There was a metre of snow on the road, and to get to the hospital, Sayideh had to drive up a steep hill. After he passed, some big trucks came and blocked the road, so doctors who came later could not get through. The doctors always had a five-minute meeting before starting work, but Sayideh never made it.

At about nine am, the telephone rang. A woman speaking in Kurmanji said, "Nas'e, how are you?"

"I am okay. Who is speaking?"

"You must remember meeting me in a shop in Moscow." I could not remember. She continued, "Do you know what has happened to Sayideh?" "No. What has happened?"

"Don't you know?"

"Stop talking in riddles. Who are you and what do you want to say?"

"Look—ring the clinic and ask Sayideh what has happened."

I rang Sayideh's office. Nobody answered. I tried 20 times, pacing the room in between. I was anxious and worried, but at that stage I did not believe anything was wrong. Many people had been saying strange things about Sayideh.

I could not ring Aziz. The evening before, Aziz's friend had rung him, saying, "My turn has come for the car I want to buy. Can you come with me to the co-op?" Aziz had turned to his father, asking, "What do I do?" Sayideh said, "It is rounds tomorrow." Aziz asked, "I will only be away from the hospital for an hour." Looking back, I feel this was all part of a plan.

At 10.30 am, a jeep pulled up outside our apartment block. It was Aziz's friend's brother. I let him in, and he said, "Please, Aunty Nas'e, don't be worried, but Sayideh is not feeling well." I immediately thought Sayideh's heart was causing him trouble. The man said, "Get dressed and we will go to the hospital." He took me to the office of the director. All the doctors were sitting quietly, red-eyed and distraught. I said, "Where is Sayideh? Take me to him. It must be his heart." The director spoke. "I am sorry, Nas'e. It was not his heart. He was shot." I murmured, "Who?" then immediately passed out, biting the end of my tongue.

When I came back to consciousness, I was still in the office. Aziz had joined the other doctors, and there were also some investigators. Aziz quietly told me the details: "A lady doctor saw three or four men, and a woman with long hair, come into the hospital grounds (a restricted area) in a small white car. She talked to the passengers, and noticed that the woman hid her face, but she thinks the woman looked like Sayideh's new secretary (the daughter of one of his cousins). Other staff saw strange men on the ground floor of the hospital and on the first floor near Sayideh's office. The men must have entered his office. There was no sign of a struggle. He was shot in his right temple by a silenced Mukaroff pistol." Aziz was very distraught himself. When he arrived at the hospital and was told the news, he had started shouting uncontrollably, "Where is my father?" Some hospital attendants had to restrain him. Afterwards, they took the body away for an autopsy.

I was taken home. My blood pressure was very high; I was in a state of shock. I felt no pain from my tongue. All I wanted to do was lie on my bed and be left alone, but people kept coming and going and talking. I could not understand what they were saying.

The next day, relatives ordered a coffin, and I sat trembling as I waited for Sayideh's body to be brought home. When his body arrived, he looked like he was sleeping. At 67, he did not have one grey hair, but when I saw the bullet wound, I fainted again. After I regained consciousness, I wanted everyone to go so I could be alone with him, but family and friends kept coming and going. I would lie down, then 10 minutes later get up and walk, then sit, then lie, then walk. People began discussing where he should be buried. The President of Armenia, Levon Ter-Petrossian, had been out of Armenia for two days, but on his return he sent members of the Party to offer Sayideh a burial place in Panteon, a special cemetery where famous artists, writers, scientists and politicians are buried. However, Sayideh's relatives wanted him buried in the village, and I was in no state to speak out.

I was in shock for a long time. On my return from the funeral, I would pace the apartment, unable to think or to do anything. I still have a swollen ball of blood at the end of my tongue. I have had an operation, but to this day, if I talk too much, it hurts.

Before Sayideh's assassination, everyone was our friend, but afterwards, Aziz and I felt we were on our own. It would have been a blessing if someone had taken my life too, but I was worried for Aziz. He was the son of a leader, and whoever was responsible for Sayideh's death might fear that while Aziz remained alive, the case would not be closed. My daughter had come from Moscow for Sayideh's funeral, and told us she had been accepted as a migrant to Australia. Sayideh and I had come to Australia for a holiday a year before his death. We liked Australia very much, and Aziz and I decided to apply.

My only strength came from God. I felt his presence, that he would open the road for me, and frequently I went to the Armenian Orthodox Church to pray that the authorities would discover the people responsible and bring them to justice according to the law. (After *perestroika*, capital punishment was abolished.) In the first eight months, I was interviewed a number of times by investigators, but over the next three years the investigation went nowhere. It was a well organised operation, with many people involved, but it felt like the investigators were dragging out their investigation on purpose, and in 1994 I took the case to the KGB.

The KGB let it be known that it was a political assassination, but again, every time I approached them, they would say, "Go home and wait. When we find out something, we will let you know." Over the next two years, they also failed to come to any conclusion. When it became obvious they had closed the case, I demanded that they give me an affidavit to say they were unable to find the people responsible. I said, "If your hand is not involved in his death, then you must give me this paper." They may not have been able to gather enough evidence, or there could have been political reasons.

When Aziz left for Moscow to do his dissertation in paediatrics, I was alone. In September 1991, following a referendum, Armenia declared its independence from the Soviet Union, and the government signed a ceasefire agreement with Azerbaijan. Two months later, the agreement collapsed, and in December, when the Nagorno-Karabakh parliament declared its independence, there was more conflict. In the same month, Armenia joined the Commonwealth of Independent States, which replaced the Soviet Union. But all the politics were a background haze for me, and in January 1992, a year after Sayideh's death, I moved to Moscow to live with Aziz.

We were both still in a state of terrible grief and shock. We did not have many visitors. I withdrew from people, preferring to spend my time reading, praying, visiting the Russian Orthodox church, and visiting Erevan to wind up our affairs: packing and storing all Sayideh's unpublished manuscripts and our personal effects, then selling the apartment. Occasionally I would visit the House of Kurds in Moscow, an institution that had been established by PKK. One night they put on a memorial evening for Sayideh and people read his poems. Another time, some injured PKK came, and I used my influence to get them medical attention.

Aziz: By the 1990s, about 10,000 Kurds lived in Russia, and thousands of these were in Moscow, including many intellectuals from Armenia and a few from Iraq and Iran. PKK organised concerts, theatrical performances and conferences for political and educational purposes at the House of Kurds. I saw a number of theatrical scenarios. Some were brilliantly prepared, such as the 1994 presentation of *Mem U Zin*, a love story in the vein of *Romeo and Juliet*, written by Ahmedi Khani, which Sharaf, a professor of history, and a member of the Kurdish parliament-in-exile in Brussels, had adapted for stage. At the House of Kurds I met PKK representatives, including one central committee member known as Mahiar, now living and working in Russia, and from 1995 we were able to watch the European-based, Kurdish satellite television broadcasts.

Back in Armenia, by 1994 Kurdish newspapers and other institutions were closing down. It was the same for many non-Kurdish institutions, although some people failed to see the wider economic and political problems and claimed that ethnic minorities were being targeted. Some people's struggles are based on lies, some on truths.

Nas'e: In December 1995, we came to Australia. I had to leave all Sayideh's unpublished manuscripts, our carpets, antiques and other paintings, because these cannot be taken out of the country. The authorities were not even going to let me take Sayideh's portrait, but I insisted, saying, "It is all I have of my husband."

Aziz: Arriving in Australia was a cultural shock. Here, everything is clean, organised and quiet. People smile. In Armenia and Russia, life is grey and difficult.

Nas'e: Here, I converted to Christianity. I find some comfort in prayer, but life is lonely. Aziz is working and studying very hard to be accepted as a doctor and I do not have many friends. I go to English classes and I have taught two students Russian. In 2001 I am going back to Moscow, Armenia and Georgia. I will visit Sayideh's grave and my parents' graves and see friends and relatives. I want to ask the police about the investigation, and get Sayideh's papers that are being stored with a friend in Moscow. If the authorities let me, I hope to bring them to Australia.

I feel betrayed by the Armenian authorities. For more than 40 years, Sayideh served the people and the communist system, but they could not find who killed him. Both Aziz and I have taken out Australian citizenship. This country has been good to us. It is my country now, although I am still haunted, day and night, by memories. Sayideh was my best friend, a true humanist. Now, health permitting, my life's tasks are to be here for Aziz, work towards getting Sayideh's stories and poems translated and published in the Latin alphabet and, if possible, unravel the mystery behind his assassination.

The Power of Observation

A fable retold by Eziz Bawermend

After they had successfully completed their religious and administrative studies, a Kurdish prince commanded his three sons to go out into the world dressed as peasants and observe the world's nature and manners. After a long day's journey, they met a worried camel driver. He asked them if they had seen his stray camel. The eldest brother said, "Tell me, is your camel blind in the left eye?" The relieved camel driver replied, "Yes, indeed it is. Where did you see it?" The middle brother fired his question, "Tell me, is something wrong with the right hind leg of your camel? Does it limp?" The camel driver was even more relieved, "Yes, yes, that is definitely my camel. Where can I find it?" The youngest brother finally asked, "Are two teeth from the right-hand side of your camel's mouth missing?" "Yes, yes, there can be no question about it. That is my camel! Please tell me where you saw it?"

The three brothers looked at each other approvingly and together said, "Sorry, we have not seen your camel." In utter disbelief, the camel driver accused them of having stolen his camel, and quickly lodged a complaint with the nearest town's judge, who promptly ordered the three brothers to be arrested. To the judge, the brothers admitted the conversation but repeated their claim that they had not seen the camel. In their defence, they offered the following explanation:

The eldest brother said that he had observed the grass, which had been eaten from only the right-hand side of the path, so he concluded that the camel was blind in the left eye. The middle brother had noticed fresh hoofmarks on the path, as if a camel had been dragging its right hind hoof in a way that only a limping camel would do. The youngest brother said he had noted the grass cuttings along the path. The cuttings could only have fallen from the mouth of a camel with two missing teeth on the right side. Finding their explanation thoroughly convincing, the judge set them free.

Sacred Fire

A life story based on interviews with Temur Childargushi

I am an Ezidi Kurd from Tbilisi, the capital of Georgia. There are about half a million Kurds who live in the former Soviet Union, and about 150,000 are Ezidi. Kurds are concentrated in Armenia, Georgia, Azerbaijan, Kazakhstan and Uzbekhistan, but after the collapse of the Soviet Union, many Kurds became refugees and settled in Russia, mainly in the Caucasus, and many Jewish Kurds migrated to Israel.

My family was originally from an Ezidi village in northern Mesopotamia. Some centuries ago they had to flee Muslim persecution, so they settled in Sarhad, a village near Agri in northern Kurdistan, near the mountain known as Chia Agri, or 'Mountain of Fires', because it was once a volcano. It is known today as Mount Ararat, and some people think it is where Noah's Ark came to rest.

My direct ancestor from seven generations ago had 40 grandchildren and was known as Chalo Molla Childargushi or 'home of the 40 children', so my family name, Childargushi, is a very old name. As Ezidi, we have to know our father's name and our father's father's name, and so on, for seven generations, and it is custom to swear "I know this is true according to my father and my father's father, for seven generations."

My family lived in northern Kurdistan until 1915, when the Ottoman army collected a Kurdish army unit known as Hamidiye and used this unit to kill Armenians. The Armenians asked us for help, and we hid them in our houses, so then the Ottomans started killing Ezidi Kurds. To escape the genocide, the Ezidi and Armenian people fled north to Armenia.

My grandfather was 25. His wife had died after the birth of her second son, so with his 18-year-old sister and two children—my father aged eight, and my uncle aged four—my grandfather walked north, taking only a few clothes and some sheep. Before they got to the border, my grandfather was shot dead. My great-aunt took my grandfather's gun, and hid my father and uncle in caves by day. There was so much shooting of people trying to escape that they had to make their way at night, moving like snakes along the ground. For food, they would kill a sheep. Eventually they arrived at Araz River, marking the border with Armenia. In Kurdish we call it A'awa Rush or 'Black Water' because so many people were shot trying to cross. My aunt made a raft to cross, then they walked another 30 kilometres to the village of Bar Roj, Kurmanji for 'facing the sun', where they lived with relatives.

As children we heard this story of our aunt's heroism many times. Our maternal grandfather, and the old men who were neighbours, would tell us other legends about our fighting history and our love history, but the story that stands out in my mind is that of my eighteen-year-old aunt saving my father and uncle.

It was in Bar Roj that my father married. My mother was 10 years younger. Her family had escaped to Armenia before she was born, but both families came from the village of

Sarhad and knew each other. The people of Sarhad were from the Banduri tribe.

In 1935, after my great-aunt died, my parents went to Georgia to begin a new life in Tbilisi, so I have never visited Kurdistan. I tried in 1997, but Turkish officials would not let me leave the airport. I had Australian travel documents, but they told me I needed a visa.

In Tbilisi my father worked hard as a labourer in a big shop. My mother managed the house and raised seven children—five girls and two boys. Like many Ezidi women, she wore the necklace of black beads known as 'night stones' or *show'w* in Kurmanji.

We had a very different life to Kurds in other countries, particularly the Kurds of Turkey. The socialist system claimed to be international, so all ethnic groups were allowed to keep their language and culture. We were free to talk Kurdish, the government funded Kurdish-language schools, and a Kurdish theatre in Tbilisi, in which I was an actor for 10 years. We were allowed to celebrate Newroz with street marches, and as Ezidi we would make a small fire, and the children and young people would jump over it.

We were able to keep our culture alive but there was a ceiling on what we could do. The communist system officially discouraged religion, so any religious practices had to be done secretly, inside the home. There were other discriminations, more than in Armenia. In Georgia, a Kurd could become a doctor but not a specialist, and we could not become members of government. We could not buy or own land. Our family rented a small two-bedroom flat in a district for Armenians, Kurds and other ethnic minorities. The Georgians lived in another part of town.

All Kurds have a similar culture, but there are differences depending on where we live and on our religion. As Ezidi Kurds in Georgia, we had a mixture of very old beliefs and traditions with a relatively modern lifestyle.

I cannot say exactly how old our Ezidi religion is, but there is evidence that the religion came out of ancient Mesopotamia. Our holy men teach us to say, "We are not the children of Adam and Eve; we are from another world," and we have the symbol of the snake on our most sacred temple at Lalish. One of our smaller gods is a very, very old Sumer god called Un or Anu, which is why we add *-un* after the name of any object that is holy. Our holy blanket for visitors is called *khodun*,[a] and at night we kiss and pray over the *khoduni marli* or holy bedding—special blankets and pillows—which the family cannot use. They are reserved for guests, and our prayers are to bring guests to our home, for guests are holy and bring good fortune. We always leave a light on so that the *khodun* are never in dark.

The Kurdish calender begins in 700 BC (on 21 March), when the Assyrians record that our ancestors, the Medes, established a dynasty with its capital at Ecbatan. Newroz goes back to at least this time, but the importance of fire, and the Ezidi calendar, is even older, dating back to a time when, we believe, all Kurds were Ezidi, before they became Jews, Christians and Muslims.

The Medes were in Mesopotamia from before 2000 BC. Assyrian clay tablets from around this time recorded their presence, and this is also the date when 12 clay tablets from Nineveh were written narrating the *Epic of Gilgamesh*, about a King of Uruk called Gilgamesh (*gilgamesh* is Kurmanji for 'big water buffalo'). Gilgamesh travels back in time to meet the King of Shuruppak, who reigned at the time of a great flood. King Utanapishrim of Shuruppak is told by a god to build a boat to save his family, animals and all the seeds of life, because another god is angry with mankind and wants to destroy them.

Some people describe Ezidism as an offshoot of Islam, but certainly it is older than the time of Zaradash (also called Zoroastra or Zarathrustra). Many books say he was a Persian who lived in the seventh century BC, but he was a Mede, who had a vision of the good God, Ahura Mazda, in the mountains. He taught that this God of Good always wins against the God of Evil, Ahriman, and he and his followers wrote 13 books called the *Zendavesta*, describing his revelations and the Zoroastrian rituals for priests.[b]

We are told the Ezidi did not listen to Zaradash, so he travelled to Persia, Afghanistan and India, where the Parsees still practise his teachings. But there are a lot of similarities between Ezidi and Zoroastrian beliefs. You cannot be Ezidi or Zoroastrian unless both your parents are of that religion. Like Ezidi, Zoroastrians believe in fire and celebrate Newroz with fire. The Zoroastrians have as their symbol the phoenix—the bird that rises out of the ashes, while our symbol is the peacock, a bird of beauty whose tail symbolises the sun's rays.

Both Ezidis and Zoroastrians acknowledge the struggle of good and evil in each person and in the heavens. But Ezidis believe in one supreme God we call Shams, God of the Sun, because out of the fire of the sun comes all light and life. *Shamps* in Arabic means 'sun', so the Arabs probably took the word from the Ezidi. We believe Shams is a good force, and does good things for people, and our most important prayers are to Shams. In the morning, every practising Ezidi wakes up to witness the first arrow of the sun and prays, "God, give this world freedom and peace. Help all people—of all nationalities. Help people who are travelling, help the poor and heal the sick." We must ask for God's love and grace for everyone else in the world before we ask for help for our family and ourselves. Only then can we pray for our own protection against all bad thoughts and actions, and to be guided to do, say and think what is right. I do not know any other religion like this. Ours is a very humanitarian religion, and Ezidi people are free to worship as they wish. In Georgia and Armenia, the Ezidi swear by Shams or Khodeh. In southern Kurdistan, they swear by Shaykh Adi,[c] and each village or household has their own special angel to swear by for protection.

We believe in seven angels or messengers, who help the Supreme God create and maintain the universe, and we pray to them so that the universe can be protected from bad choices, words and actions. The 'dark' angel we call Apik, but we do not believe it is like the Christian's Satan, the Muslim's Shaitan, or the Zoroastrian's Ahriman, which became the embodiment of all evil. For us, Apik is one angel who was a little bit of a troublemaker, but Shams is forgiving, and this is why we must not say a bad word about Apik or even say his true name. As a consequence, some Muslims accuse Ezidis of being devil worshippers, and when Islam came to Kurdistan in the seventh century, a few Ezidi converted but many resisted. Between the 10th and 15th centuries, Ezidis were one of the most executed people, many having their tongues cut out. Others were buried alive. In the Shingal area, there is a cave filled with the bones of Ezidis killed because of their beliefs.

Ezidis were forced to keep many of their beliefs and practices secret. To know these secrets is proof you are Ezidi. If a person says, "I am Ezidi," you may reply, "Prove it," and the person must say secret words, and name his or her *pir* or *shaykh*, and say who is the god of their home.

Every Ezidi family has a *pir* or *shaykh* who visits their home to pray and to help in any way, and in return, each family gives a gift, which is passed on to someone in need. Some are teachers; others are healers. You cannot study to become a *pir*—you must be a son or daughter of a *pir*—and a *pir* must marry a *pir*. There are about 40 or 50 families of *pirs*. The father *pir* teaches the son to help men, and the mother *pir* teaches the daughter to help women. But it is not just outward teaching. Because various healing powers are passed on from generation to generation, the *pir* has something inside that is magic.

In the 12th century, many were converting to Islam, so Shaykh Adi came to the Ezidi people. Some people say he was a Sufi who knew the religion of Ezidi to be good, so he made the people strong in their faith. He became a holy man, and wrote a book called *Mes-haf-e Resh*, or *The Black Book*. It is written in a secret script,[d] because the Ezidi did not want the Muslims to read it. I have not read it. Ezidi do not really have a holy book: our beliefs and practices are passed from generation to generation by word of mouth, but it was probably after Shaykh Adi that Ezidis stopped eating pork and incorporated some Islamic beliefs.

Shaykh Adi's mausoleum is in the village of Lalish, near Dohuk in the Shingal area, where 80 per cent of Ezidi live. Lalish has become the holy village for all Ezidi people, and many go there to pray to Shaykh Adi, and to wash their face in the holy water called 'White Spring' to clear their soul of impurities. There is also a holy fire in the mausoleum.

Shaykh Adi was the first Ezidi *shaykh*, and afterwards some people were called *shaykhs*. Like the *pir*, they can become a *shaykh* only if their family are *shaykhs*. The *shaykhs* took from the *pir* their knowledge and traditions and, over time, became stronger and more numerous. In Georgia, a *shaykh* would visit our home for prayers, donations and special ceremonies, like when a boy is one year old, the *shaykh* says words and cuts some of the boy's hair, making the boy officially Ezidi.

We have many rituals and symbols to bring good fortune and to ward off evil. We believe a horseshoe brings good luck. To keep away bad luck, we wear an eye with a blue stone in it. At Newroz, we eat a special cake called *kloch*. It is hard and square and has a blue bead inside. The first cut goes to the father of the house, and if his piece has the bead, it means good fortune for the following year. Traditionally, the second cut goes to the shepherd of the cows, the third to the shepherd of the sheep, and the fourth to Khatoona Fakhrun, the angel who helps women in marriage, childbirth and sickness.

Ezidi weddings also have their own distinct rituals. We always marry under a tree, which we decorate with sweets, chocolates and other little presents. When the bride comes to the tree, the groom drops pieces of apple on her head. For a joke, my cousin caught the apple at my wedding! Then the groom's best man shakes the tree so that little sweets and presents fall on the bride and groom, to give their marriage a sweet future. All the children run to pick up the presents, and the adults are kept busy watching the children. While this is happening the evil eye is distracted from the newlyweds, so they have time to slip away into their house. In Georgia, before they go inside, they step on a plate and break it. Ezidis believe that if people watch the newlyweds going inside, it might bring bad luck to jinx them.

In the villages, the bride wears a traditional Kurdish dress, with a fine, red netting draped over her head and face. Red is the colour of freedom, good fortune and luck. In the city, the brides usually wear a white dress. My wife wore white.

Ezidi dancing is similar to other Kurdish dancing in that everyone holds hands, but the steps are different. Each village has its own dances, which have been handed down over the centuries, some celebrating victory in battle or another major event. Similarly, each village has its own music and songs. Ezidi songs tell about our history, much of which has never been written down—about a kind *agha* or one who is victorious in battle. Sometimes two *aghas* have a competition to see who can sing best by singing different sections of the same song. Traditional instruments are the *tambour* (a stringed instrument like the Greek *bouzouki*), the *zirna* (like a high-pitched trumpet), and a large drum called a *duhol*. The drum is made of skins, and is beaten on one side with a thin stick and on the other side with a thick stick. We also have the *may*—a pipe, partly made from bamboo, with a reed in the mouthpiece that vibrates to make a high sound, and which often accompanies a singer.

Alongside our old beliefs and traditions was our modern life in Georgia, where girls and boys went to school together, unlike in Kurdistan. Classes were in Russian. I speak Georgian, too, but at home we always spoke in the Kurdish dialect of Kurmanji. As we grew older, some of us had girlfriends and boyfriends, whereas in Kurdistan, young people do not mix outside the family. In Georgia, we had arranged marriages and love marriages. My marriage was both. My wife is the sister of my cousin's wife. Our grandparents knew each other and our parents knew each other, so we knew each other.

Although in Georgia the Kurdish man is still a little more advantaged than the woman, I think the average Kurdish woman has more education and more say in family matters in Georgia than in Kurdistan. I am always asking my wife's opinion and advice, but as for the final decision—maybe it is my decision, maybe it is not. I am a very soft man.

Then there was our nationality and politics. My brothers, sisters and I spoke perfect Kurdish, so we did not need to go to the Kurdish-language school. Our father was very interested in Kurdish politics but he was not politically active, he was too busy working. Our mother read Kurmanji in the Latin alphabet, but in the Soviet Union, the government changed the Kurmanji script to the Russian–Slavonic alphabet called Cyrillic, so us children mostly read Kurmanji books and magazines written in Cyrillic, printed in Armenia. It was not until I was 18 or 20, when my older brother and sister and I became involved in politics, that I learnt to read and write Kurmanji in Latin.

My older brother and sister encouraged my interest in Kurdish politics from when I was about 14. We had contact with Kurds in Europe, from Sweden and Germany in particular, every month receiving Kurdish–European newspapers. We also attended lectures and meetings, and as artists, my brother and I designed posters and placards, and printed T-shirts with slogans like 'Long live Kurdistan'.

After I finished high school, I studied for four years at an art college in Tbilisi before doing my two years of army service. When I came back, I became a member of a Kurdish *komsomol* group that helped Kurdish students in their studies. In the socialist system, all children belong to a *pioneer* group and teenagers join a *komsomol* group. The government, in our case the Georgian government, ran these groups. After this, people could decide if they wanted to join the Communist Party.

I worked with my brother, who was an interior designer. My brother would design the stained-glass window, picture or metal relief and I would fill in the colour or press the metal. We did mosaics and other ornamentation for a couple of restaurants, and a few fountains.

It was my interest in Kurdish culture that made me become an actor in the Kurdish theatre. We would rehearse three times a week after work and put on drama and comedy. The writers were Kurdish people from Armenia, like Askari Boik. One of his comedies was about a young couple in Armenia who wanted to marry. They were students at university and had lived together, so when they went back to Georgia to visit their families, their parents were very unhappy and objected to the marriage. Eventually the couple convinced their parents they were sincere, but then they came up against other traditions. Custom dictates that the parents of the groom give money or a gift to the parents of the bride. We call it *kalen*. The girl argued she did not want to be sold, and they decide to elope.

Before the USSR broke up, everyone was friendly—Russians, Georgians, Kurds and other minorities. If someone gave me the smallest reason, I would tell them about our history, culture and my dream for a free united Kurdistan, one Kurdistan, like it was under the Medes. People would ask me, "Why have Kurds not been able to create a country since the Medes?" My answer to this was, "Kurds have always lived at the crossroads of Europe, the Middle East and Asia. Every army going east or west—Persian, Greek, Roman, successive waves of Mongol and Turkic tribes, then all the Islamic empires—would go through Kurdistan to expand their territory. This stopped Kurds forming a country of their own, but no-one could take away our independence in the mountains, and the Kurds became notorious for taxing passing travellers and caravans. In this way and because they were self-sufficient, they were able to maintain their fiefdoms, princedoms and kingdoms right up until the late 19th century. But in 1923, the Treaty of Lausanne, signed by Britain, France, Greece and Turkey, divided Kurdistan, and for the first time the Kurds lost their independence. I would describe the Kurdish uprisings, the first being in northern Kurdistan in 1878–81, led by Shaykh Ubaidallah Al-Ineheri, who wrote to the British setting out claims for a land called Kurdistan. Then in 1925, around Diyarbakir, there was a big Kurdish revolt led by a Sufi, Shaykh Seyid Piran, but Turkish forces and the air-force of the Soviet Union squashed it, and hung Shaykh Seyid and many others.

The people I spoke to were very interested. Big changes began all over the USSR in 1985, when Gorbachev became president. I was 30 years old. In the first couple of years, I liked him, because he was trying to introduce economic reforms under *perestroika*, and something close to freedom of expression under *glasnost*, to move towards a socialist democracy.

It was because of *glasnost* that we were able to protest when we heard of Saddam Hussein's Al-Anfal operations between February and September 1988, particularly after the chemical bombing of Halabja in March. Many people wrote to the Soviet and Georgian governments to protest against the genocides. In April 1988 a Kurdish friend and I went to the post office to send a telegram to Gorbachev, but they would not accept our telegrams. Many other people had a problem sending protest telegrams and letters, because to send anything to a government minister, you had to get permission from the people in the post office. Most refused. Some letters got through. Eduard Shevardnadze, the Foreign Minister of the Soviet Union at the time, replied through the newspaper, "There is no proof chemicals were used." There was plenty of video evidence, but the Soviets considered that Saddam's Ba'ath Party was socialist, so they supported it.

We felt powerless. All we could do was march in demonstrations in Tbilisi in 1988 and in Moscow in 1989, more and more people joining us in sympathy. We wanted to inform people how Saddam Hussein's army was destroying Kurdish villages, and of the disappearance of 182,000 people and deportation of up to half a million, because none of it was being reported in the media. We heard only through Kurds in Europe.

Gorbachev eventually changed his mind about Halabja, but it was too late. The socialist government continued to support Saddam, as did the Western powers and the Arabs. No-one did anything to stop the genocide, or hold the Ba'aths accountable.

In 1990, Kurds from all over Europe and the former Soviet Union gathered for a big conference in Moscow. There was another international conference in Sweden, and I was invited. We discussed Kurdish problems and how we must unite. People made submissions to the United Nations about the use of chemical weapons and other social injustices, but the biggest obstacle is that if, say, Australian Aborigines go to the UN, they are protesting against one nation, whereas the Kurds are protesting against four. Even when these countries fight against each other, like Syria and Turkey, or Iran and Iraq, when it comes to the Kurdish people, they are united.

At the time, Gorbachev was opening up society, with good intentions, but no structures were being put in place to make the changes work. From a society totally controlled by the communist government and the KGB, suddenly it became a society virtually without rules. It was very dangerous, and by the end of the 1980s, there was a big blow-up. In the anarchy, leaders did whatever they wanted, inciting their own particular ethnic group to demand a separate land, from Yugoslavia and the Eastern bloc to the various republics; inciting normal people to start killing each other, using weapons stolen from the army. It was nationalism at its worst, and I blame Gorbachev for creating the conditions for it to happen.

Being active in the Kurdish movement, I also followed Georgian politics, so I could see that fighting was going to start. From 1988, people were demanding "Georgia for the Georgians," the sentiment growing stronger and stronger.

The three main ethnic groups in Georgia have lived together peacefully for centuries: the Georgians, the Ossetians from Ossetia in the south, and the Abkhazians in the north-west, around the Black Sea. All speak their own languages, but are basically Middle Eastern cultures, with varying degrees of European influence. The Georgians are mostly Christian, the Ossetians follow a number of religions, and the Abkhazians are half-Christian, half-Muslim. Under the Soviet system, everyone had cultural autonomy but no political autonomy, and for a long while, the Abkhazians had been pushing to leave Georgia and join Russia, believing they would have more freedom. However, in the push to become an independent republic, the Georgians did not want to lose access to the Black Sea, so they were determined that Abkhazia should stay part of Georgia.

The first signs of war were in April 1989. Soviet soldiers killed at least 20 Georgians who were peacefully demonstrating for an independent republic. The protesters belonged to the National Democratic Party, led by Gamsakhurdia. They were against the Soviet system, and when Gamsakhurdia won the elections in 1990, he began pushing for independence. In May 1991, he was elected the first President of the Independent Republic of Georgia. His government was based on Georgian nationalist sentiment, so when the Ossetians and Abkhazians began demanding their rights, a full-scale war broke out on a number of fronts. The anti-socialist Georgian army fought against the communists, led by Eduard Shevardnadze, the Soviet's former Foreign Minister, and against the partisan armies of the pro-Russian Abkhazians and the Ossetians, each of whom was demanding territorial autonomy. Civilians started killing civilians, and many Abkhazians and Ossetians were forced to flee to Russia.

Gamsakhurdia's government cracked down on all opposition, declaring a state of emergency in October 1991. In January 1992 Gamsakhurdia fled to Armenia, and in October the communists took power under Eduard Shevardnadze, who instituted measures to stop the fighting. The new republic faced severe food shortages and an inflation rate of 1500 per cent. Kurdish-language schools and theatre, and other ethnic institutions, were shut down.

We had no future in Georgia, and after I came back from the conference in Sweden, I decided to leave with my family. We arrived in Australia as sponsored tourists on 26 December 1990, but had packed up everything, hoping for permission to stay.

We immediately applied for refugee status, but were rejected. We had no help, no access to anything. Fortunately, after 20 days, I got work as a bricklayer. Early one morning in late 1991, the Federal Police knocked on the door, saying, "You have 28 days to leave." I went straight to the Kurdish Association for help. We went to a solicitor, who wrote a letter outlining our appeal. After a long wait, we were rejected again, but in 1994, visa requirements were changed to allow Chinese students affected by the Tiananmen Square massacre to stay, and the government introduced a course and some tests for improving English. I did a certificate and passed, and after five and a half years of living in Australia, we got permission to stay.

While I was bricklaying, I had seen tilers at work, so 18 months later, I started working as a tiler. I did the first job for no money—just to show I could do it—and after that, I studied for a certificate in tiling. Now I earn good money.

In those early years in Melbourne, I spent a lot of time trying to help Kurds from Georgia come here as political refugees, but the Australian government refused to give the rest of my family visas. Their life was becoming more and more difficult. High unemployment is everywhere in Georgia, but it is worst for Kurds and other minorities. To this day, my family in Georgia barely survive. My brother is unable to get work as an interior designer. My elder sister, who used to teach Kurmanji and produce Kurdish radio programs, is also out of work. Each unemployed person gets a pension of $8 a month. With that, they can buy two kilos of meat and bread. That is it. People sell everything just to eat. They live without gas or electricity. They use kerosene for lighting. In winter they have no heating, in summer no fridge. I send money, but I cannot do all that I would like, and I feel guilty because I have a good life while they are suffering.

In Melbourne, we have tried to start a Kurdish theatre group, and I continue to do art as a hobby—painting posters, doing mosaics, sculpting in plaster and bronze, and taking part in a couple of Kurdish art exhibitions. I have made medallions in plaster and bronze of famous Kurds like Yilmaz Guney, the Kurdish film producer, who made most of his films while inside a Turkish prison, secretly passing the scripts out and giving directions to friends. In 1982 he received the Palme d'Or at the Cannes Film Festival for his film *The Way*. Another medallion is of Qanate Kurdo, a Kurdish professor at the academy in Leningrad who wrote many books and compiled two dictionaries: Sorani–Kurmanji and Kurmanji–Russian. A third medallion is of Abdul Rahman Qassemlou, the General Secretary of the Democratic Kurdish Party of Iran, who was assassinated in Vienna in 1989 by Iranian agents.

The hardest thing about coming to Australia is making a new beginning when you are in the middle of life: learning a new language, finding new friends, a job, housing—everything. The other difficulty is not having our extended family around us, particularly knowing their life is so hard and may not be safe. The best thing about Australia is that here, my children have a future.

At home we speak Kurdish, so my children speak, read and write in Kurdish, unlike many children from northern Kurdistan whose families have been forced to speak Turkish since the 1920s. I would like them to marry Ezidi, purely to keep their religion and culture. If one parent is not Ezidi, then their children cannot be Ezidi. There is no way back. In politics, it is a different matter. The Kurdish people belong to five different religions, but this should not stop us forming a democracy.

The border between Georgia and Turkey is now closed, because Georgia is trying to be friendly with Turkey and is clamping down on PKK, which started operating (in a political sense, not as a liberation army) on the Georgian side of the border after *perestroika*. The Georgians do not want to encourage any Kurdish movement on their territory.

But we are all Kurds—we are without a country and our people are suffering—so we must be political. My conscience would not let me simply live a comfortable life—it is my duty to work for my people. We meet at the Kurdish Association, organise cultural events and help new arrivals. We write protests about what is happening in Turkey. We try to do what we can for Kurds in Australia and back in Kurdistan, but I would like Kurds in Australia to be more united. There are too many disagreements among Australian Kurdish associations over what is happening in Kurdistan.

In 1992, there was big hope when the Kurdish parliament was formed in Iraqi Kurdistan. It recognised the minorities in Kurdistan: the Assyrians, Chaldeans and Armenians. But many things destroyed the parliament.

We have no support from the UN, Europe, America or the Arabs, so parties have had to rely on regimes close to home, which always want something in return. Our enemies are strong and they use the different Kurdish factions against each other. Turkey supports and allows border access, then uses Barzani against PKK; Syria supports PKK to use them against Turkey, and Iran uses Talabani and Barzani against KDPI. It all ends up in Kurds killing Kurds. So, the biggest question is whether we can unite. However until some outside powers are willing to support Kurdistan for the sake of the people and not their own self-interest, there will be no Kurdistan and no end to the fighting. Many agreements have been made, but agreements do not feed children. They do not make a nation if there is no economic infrastructure and protection from far stronger enemies, yet I am sure one day we will see a state called Kurdistan.

Goat Girl

A Kurdish fairytale retold by Seher Cinar

I will tell you what I can remember of a story about love and beauty regardless of a person's skin covering. Underneath we are all human. We all want to be loved.

Once upon a time, there was a girl who lived with her family in the countryside. She was called 'goat girl' because her family was so poor that they had to kill a goat and use the skin to make the girl's dress. Her goat's-skin and her poverty hid her beauty.

One day her family sent her to the brook for water. When she arrived, she removed her goat's-skin to bathe, and placed her only personal belonging—a shiny ring—carefully on a stone by the water's edge.

While she was in the water, a handsome prince passing by, stopped and dismounted to allow his horse to drink. As the animal neared the edge, the sun's reflecting off the ring frightened the horse, which bolted. The prince went to investigate, and caught sight of the ring, then the naked girl in the river. Awestruck by her beauty, he fell in love with her.

The goat girl did not know who this strong young man was, and became nervous, but he called her and placed the shiny ring on her finger. They spoke for a long time then, together, the goat girl and the prince rode away to his country.

Sabir Bagdas, photographed by Hasan Bagdas

They Speak First of the Lioness, Then of the Lion

A life story based on interviews with Sabir Bagdas, translated from Kurdish through her son Hasan Bagdas

"I was born one to three years before 1900, in the Kurdish village of Bozhuyuk, near Sivas. Bozhuyuk is on the southern bank of the great Jaihoon River, whose source is in the mountains some 20 kilometres away. The river was six to 10 metres wide at Bozhuyuk and never ran dry. On the contrary, in March it sometimes flooded with melted snow, and in the summer the farmers built little dams and water channels to irrigate their fields. On the other side of the river is the mountain of Binboga, 1000 metres high and partially covered in wild juniper forests with trees up to 70 metres tall. Binboga was where we took the sheep in summer. To the west, east and south are rolling green hills.

About 100 families from the tribe of Melan, or Sennamili, meaning 'branch of Melan', lived in Bozhuyuk. In those days Bozhuyuk was the biggest village in the region. There were no shops, but people from other villages would come with their donkeys or horses to stay at the *agha*'s house for a few days and sell sugar, sultanas, fabric, tools—whatever they had.

My father was the richest person in the village. Our heavy, white-stone house had many rooms, and a large storeroom for butter and yoghurt, and there was water from a spring only 100 metres away. It was the best house in the village, better than the *agha*'s house. Its flat roof was made of junipers and earth, and the floor was of earth."

Sabir never knew her father. He joined the Ottoman army in about 1902 to fight the war in Yemen. Normal army duty at that time was about six years, in war or peace. He once wrote asking for money. Sabir's mother, Ele, sent five gold coins, but many months later the coins came back. They did not know where he was or what he was doing, and Ele took over the running of the farms. She organised the farm workers and the shepherds to take care of the crops and the livestock. She was a very strong, clever lady, very powerful and attractive.

In the days of the Ottoman Empire, government officials came in the autumn and collected animals and crops for taxes. Bozhuyuk was near the border of Turkey and Kurdistan, so Turkish villages surrounded it. Turkish people would also come and take sheep, cows and fruit by force. Sometimes, they would attack the village, and there would be a gun fight. This went on until the 1960s. In 1963, when Sabir's son-in-law and cousin were behind a stone wall defending the village from Turkish people, they were killed.

Ele was highly respected, and people called Sabir's family by her mother's name. Sabir was called Ele's Sabir. Sabir learnt much from her, but it was her father's mother who raised her. At night her grandmother told her all the old Kurdish stories, and it was her grandmother who taught her from the age of six how to use the loom to weave the rugs we call *kilims* in Turkish, *ber* in Kurmanji. When Sabir was about nine, she was given space to make her own *ber*. Her grandmother taught her all the patterns of her family—strong geometric designs, each pattern with a name. They used wool from their sheep, spinning and dying it themselves, making the dyes from earth and plants.

One day when Sabir was about 10 years old, the village *agha* received official government notification of Sabir's father's death. Her father's sister demanded that Ele marry another brother's son, because there were no men in the family. He agreed to the arrangement—Ele being much older was no problem for him—but Ele was angry and refused. Instead she went and talked to the village *agha*, Mullah Ali, from the next richest family in the village. He had become more powerful when Sabir's father failed to return. He was a religious man, and in those days was the Ottoman government's representative, so it was his job to solve disputes.

One night Ele and Mullah Ali talked, and the next night Ele went to his house as his second wife. There was no contract. Sabir was very upset about her mother leaving. She cried and cried, but Ele had made up her mind. Sabir stayed with her grandmother.

Sabir says, "I cannot read or write. When I was about 10, I went to Arabic school to learn the Arabic alphabet, but after three months my mother married the *mullah* and I had to leave school to look after the farm." She started going on *zozan*—when the sheep are taken to the mountain pastures in the spring, living with her grandmother and uncle in the Kurdish black-felt tent we call a *kon*, and making yoghurt, butter and cheese, before returning to the village in autumn.

The *agha* effectively took control of their land, making use of it, even though the titles remained with the family of Sabir's father. A few months after Ele's marriage, another letter came to Mullah Ali, this time from the army, saying Sabir's father was alive. Still he did not return. They heard he went to fight in World War One and later, by word of mouth, they heard he had died. Then six years after marrying the *agha*, Ele became sick and died.

Sabir's family were Alevi, and Sabir grew up practising the Alevi traditions. Some Kurdish Alevi say, "We are not Muslim," because they take many beliefs and traditions from other religions, such as the Ezidi and Zoroastrian religions, but under the Ottomans they called themselves Muslim to escape persecution. Like Ezidi, Alevi jump over a small fire at Newroz, and each year a holy man or *de'de* visits the homes of devout Alevi. In Bozhuyuk, a *de'de* would stay in the village for two to four weeks, and the people would gather in a house, usually the *agha*'s, to listen to him talk about Alevi beliefs and how to be a good Alevi. The families cooked special food for him. After the religious ceremony, Alevi play the *ba'aghlama* and dance a special Alevi dance called the *sema*, people joining hands and dancing in a circle around pairs of men and women.

Nearly every winter night, when no-one could work because of the snow, people collected in a house—one night in one house, another night in another house—to drink tea, play the *ba'aghlama* and sing special Alevi songs. Men usually sang, but in Sabir's village Sabir and one or two other women also sang. The songs were about how Alevi must respect humans, more than the prophet Muhammad, more than Makkah, and about the pressures put on Alevi because they are different. Alevi are more relaxed and flexible in their ways. There was no mosque in the village, because Alevi do not pray in a mosque since Ali, the nephew and son-in-law of Muhammad, the fourth caliph, was killed in a mosque. Alevi do not pray facing Makkah or believe in *haj*, when people go to Makkah and pray. Alevi say our *haj*, our Makkah, is the human face, that God is in every human. It is the good you do in this world that is important. There is no reward or punishment after death.

After the Turkish Republic was established in 1923, Alevi did everything in secret because it was against the law to do anything not considered Turkish. If police knew about a ceremony, they would come and take the people away. But although the Turkish government outlawed the Kurdish language and the wearing of Kurdish clothes, they could not stop the people, and Sabir always spoke Kurmanji. She did not know a word of Turkish and, until the 1950s, always wore traditional Kurdish clothes. In Australia, she still does.

Every tribe had a different way of dressing, but the woman's dress from Sabir's area is called a *zubin*. It is in three parts, with a split down each side, over loose pants caught at the ankle. These pants are white or pale in colour, unless the girl or woman is working in the fields or with the animals. Then she wears dark-coloured pants, with a black cotton apron, called a *xillik,* tied around the waist. On her head, Sabir wore a hat about a hand's width in height, called a *koffi,* under a *sar*[a] (scarf) of brown or black cotton. Being from a rich family, she also wore chains of gold medallions wrapped around and around the *sar* and *koffi* and over her chest. This jewellery we call *kize*. A girl from a poor family might be given the *kize* when she marries, but nothing too expensive. Above the *kize*, Sabir tied a second *sar* of material around her head like a turban.

Everyone attended all the village weddings, and Sabir loved to dance to the *zorna* and the *dohul*. If the family was rich, the music and dancing would continue for a week before the bride came. Usually the party lasted two or three days. On the last day the husband's relations and friends form a procession and go to the bride's house, singing, playing music and holding the old Kurdish emirate flag: red, white and green stripes with a yellow circle in the centre.

The bride's trousseau—the rugs, dresses, socks, and so on she had made or collected—was packed into boxes and placed outside her family's house. The bride's brother or cousin would sit on these boxes, waiting for the groom's family, and when they arrived, he would ask them for a gift—money, a pistol, an ox or a horse. If the groom's family did not have what was asked, bargaining would begin!

The bride remained in her home, often crying, because she was usually being married without her permission and did not want to leave her family, not knowing her husband or what her new life would be like.

Once the deal was done, the bride's boxes were loaded on a donkey or a horse, and two girls from the groom's family escorted the bride outside. She rode to her new home in front of the procession, the *zorna* and *dohul* being played along the way. If the distance was short, she might walk.

The groom would wait for his bride up on the roof of his family's home. On her arrival, he dropped a very special apple. If she caught it, she was clever and understood what she wanted, and it promised to be a good marriage, but if she dropped it, her standing with her new family was lowered. If someone else caught the apple, he asked the couple for a gift, and they had to give something important to save the bride's dignity.

Sabir remembers 1915 clearly. It was the year that the Christian Armenians came to the village to escape the Ottoman army. Everyone was very much afraid, but families hid the Armenians in their houses until it was safe for them to leave. Still, many Armenians were killed either in the villages or trying to escape the country. It was also around this time, when Sabir was about 15 or 18, that it was decided she should marry the cousin Ele had refused to marry. Sabir had known this man since she was small and in all ways disliked him. She thought him far too old. "I don't care about his physical look. He was a bad character, very dishonest; basically an opportunist."

She refused to marry, and cried for many, many days, but she had no say. The senior men in the village and the women in her family forced her, because she was the only child of a rich family. "They wanted a wedding party, but I refused. This upset the man, but I wanted nothing to do with him."

Sabir's grandmother lived with them until she died. Sabir ran the farm. "My husband did not join the business. He was very lazy—just sitting at home. Always we had problems. I did not let him into my bed. Always we fought and argued." She would be the one to decide what had to be done on the land not being used by the *agha*. She would organise the workers so that everyone knew their tasks. If a worker was taken to the army or had a problem, they would send someone else to do the work. She was a young woman, but the workers respected her mother and her family, so they respected her orders.

In the winter Sabir made *kilims*. "Always I was busy." She also made saddlebags, pillows, aprons and socks. Most saddlebag patterns are similar to those on the rugs, but some are specific to the pillow and saddlebag. They are sewn as a wool tapestry, with a thick wool backing woven on a loom, then decorated with colourful wool tassels and beads. The intricately patterned socks are knitted using five needles.

World War One was still going on, and after a year of marriage, Sabir's husband joined the army. He was away for four years, but she did not miss him. All the men had gone and most did not come back. Government officials would come to the village and take things to feed the army, and Sabir says, "There was enough food for everyone."

It was around this time that the first truck came to Bozhuyuk. Sabir remembers watching the children run after the noisy beast. When it stopped, people gathered and tried to feed it grass as if it was a cow. She also remembers the first radio. All her neighbours came and asked, "When you go out, if this man says he is hungry, what do I do?" Someone told them, "If you don't touch him, he will not ask for food."

In 1918 people brought news that the war was over, but the men still did not come home. Some were serving in the Ottoman army, some were stuck in Russia, Yemen and other Arab countries. Others joined Mistefa Kemal in Anatolia.

Mistefa Kemal did not affect Sabir's life in the beginning. There was no political activity in Bozhuyuk, and she did not hear until much later about the Kurdish uprising in Qocgiri[b] in 1919, only 200 kilometres away. In those times, news did not travel. The village was the world. Nor did she hear about the Treaty in Sevres in 1920, which promised Kurds their right to a homeland, but in 1923 news reached the village that Mistefa Kemal had established a republic. People talked about how he wanted to give rights to women, but soon everyone was unhappy because Kemal was creating a Turkish state, and going back on all the promises he had made to the Kurdish leaders in return for their support to get rid of the sultanate, caliphate and the foreigners. Kurdish villages had their names changed to Turkish names, and laws were passed to make even the words 'Kurd' and 'Kurdistan' illegal.

Back in about 1920, Sabir's husband arrived home. "I did not care whether he came back or stayed away. Our life continued as before." Six years after their marriage, Sabir was still childless, so an aunt decided Sabir's husband needed a second wife. She brought a lady to a neighbour's house for Sabir's husband and this lady to have relations. The next day, everyone knew what had happened, so then everyone accepted that they were married, as was the custom, and the lady was brought to Sabir's home. Sabir says, "I was not upset. I did not take seriously what they did. I had no relations with him, and I was always looking for somebody else so that I could leave him. Anyway, this woman and I got along well, though she always had arguments with our mother-in-law. The mother-in-law did not dare cause trouble for me."

For three years, the three of them lived in the same house. Her husband's new wife did the cooking, because she did not weave *kilims* or know about the farm, but Sabir smiles: "She was also childless until I ran away."

Eight years after her mother's death, Sabir would often go to the village cemetery and cry over her mother's grave. A man staying with his relations next door to Sabir observed her, and one day he approached, saying, "Why do you cry for your mother? She is dead. You should be crying for yourself because you have no future in this family." He could see how carefully she listened to his words and how she respected his assessment. There was also a chemistry between them—he was a very handsome man.

The man sent a message through the woman he was staying with, saying that he liked Sabir. Sabir says, "She made a bridge between us." Through this neighbour, Sabir learnt that his name was Mistefa, that he belonged to the same tribe as Sabir, and that he was highly educated for those times. He worked as a schoolteacher, and also played the *ba'aghlama*. At the end of his visit, he told his female relative, "If she wants me, I will marry her."

A month later, he returned to Bozhuyuk and sent a message: "Tonight, we go." Sabir was about 25. All she took were her clothes and jewellery on the 20-kilometre walk to Mistefa's village of Dallikavak, near the town of Sariz, near the larger town of Aizezia, in the region belonging to the city of Kayseri.

In Kurdish culture, some families would see Sabir's actions as bringing shame on her family, but other families do not care—especially if the woman is powerful and they understand her circumstances. No-one was angry with Sabir, except her first husband. One week after she left, he went to the gendarmerie, asking them to bring back his wife and to charge Mistefa for taking her.

The gendarmerie came to Dallikavak, and Sabir and Mistefa agreed to go to court in Aizezia to sort out the matter. To the judge's question, "Why did you marry a second time?" Sabir's ex-husband replied, "Because we did not have children." Unlike in the

Ottoman days, when Sabir would not have been able to present her case in court, Sabir was able to tell the judge, "He wants me back only as a guarantee that he has control of the farms." The judge became angry, saying to Sabir's ex-husband, "You married into a wealthy family, then you have abused your wife's goodwill." The judge kicked him out of the court, saying, "Shut up and go," then wished Sabir and Mistefa good luck.

For two years, Sabir lived on a farm in the house of Mistefa's father, along with Mistefa's two brothers and their families, as well as Mistefa's first wife.

Sabir had known that Mistefa had a wife—the two villages were close enough for people to know these things. She says, "It was very difficult for me, but I knew he did not like her, so I went with him. I could not stay with my first husband any longer." But Sabir came to like Mistefa's first wife very much. They were about the same age, and Fat'e, Kurdish for 'Fatimah', had a quiet, polite, obedient and very kind nature. She always loved a joke, and as time went on, Sabir became upset with Mistefa for neglecting Fat'e. Sabir says, "He did not respect her. He did not share his feelings or sleep with her. He kept saying, 'I do not like her,' so I protected her."

Sabir's new life was very different to her old one. The house was very crowded and she had to fit in, but when Mistefa's father died, the land was split between the sons so Mistefa and his family moved to their own place. Still, it was a poor life in comparison to her youth, and not so free. Her husband would become jealous, especially if she sang or danced at a gathering, even though he often had relationships with women in villages where he taught, giving Sabir some very bad experiences. She was jealous but had no say, and Mistefa ignored her feelings.

After they had moved into their own house, Sabir and Mistefa went back to Bozhuyuk—again by walking. This was normal. It took four hours. They asked the *agha* to give them money in return for some animals and land. Over the years, to keep the peace, he allowed Sabir to sell some things to him and the people, one by one, for a low price.

Each year, Sabir and sometimes Fat'e, would accompany Mistefa to different villages so he could teach Kurdish children in the Turkish language. The people respected Mistefa as a teacher. They would organise a good house and provide some food as payment. Sometimes the school would be in a room of the house. Other times, the house would be next to the school. The government would also pay him once a month, and give him 70 kilos of sugar each year, which was a good income for the family. The government was pushing education, building a Turkish school in each village, then making it compulsory for children to go to school. If people did not send their children in the first 40 days, the father would be fined or go to prison. Sometimes the *mukhtar* (mayor) came and collected the children. Mistefa knew he was a tool of assimilation, but he had no option—it was his job.

Mistefa had learnt Kurdish songs when he was in the army in Erzincan, a Kurdish city, but at school and at most celebrations, he played Turkish music. Only at weddings did they sing and play Kurdish music, and everybody spoke Kurdish, unless a Turkish neighbour came. Between 1945 and 1950, the Turkish flag replaced the Kurdish one in the front of the house at weddings. Otherwise, the people would be prosecuted. Slowly, everyone was being assimilated.

Sabir had to teach herself the Turkish language, and step by step she left the Alevi life. Mistefa was born Alevi too, but in his beliefs he was atheist. He would tell his children, "Don't follow any religion, because no religion benefits the human." Both Kurds and Turks lived in Dallikavak, so any Alevi celebration was done in secret. They no longer gathered on winter nights. At Newroz a fire would be lit and they would dance, but it was called a spring celebration; otherwise, Turkish forces could destroy the village.

Sabir had to watch her children grow up Turkish. At home she would listen to Mistefa helping the children with homework in Turkish. If the children spoke Kurdish, and another child told the teacher, next day they would be made to line up in front of the class to be beaten. Students quickly learned.

Every morning the teacher would make us sing the Turkish national anthem. We had to say: "I am a good Turk. Turks are the most valiant and noble people on earth. One Turk is worth the whole universe." We would be taught about the great Mistefa Kemal Ataturk, how he had built a new country and a new people, and that throughout history the Turks had never lost a single war. We were told it was the Turks who created all the great civilisations—the Sumerian, Egyptian, Babylonian, Ionian and Hittite—and that Turkish was the mother of all languages. One by one, Kurdish children came to think, "We are Turk." By the time I was a teenager, I called myself a Turk and a socialist. I had forgotten my identity. Of course, Sabir was very unhappy that her children were being turned into Turks, but she says, "I had no option. I had to keep silent."

Sabir did not hear about the uprising in the Diyarbakir-Agri region back in 1925, led by Shaykh Seyid, when 100,000 Kurds were killed and 20,000 were buried alive. But she heard about the Dersim uprising, and how the Kurdish put up a strong fight against the Turkish army in the 1930s, particularly between 1936 and 1937. It was well organised, and many people joined the uprising, led by Seyid Ali Riza and Ali San Bey. The Turkish army came to Dallikavak and collected all the young boys and men to fight against the Dersim Kurds. The Turks promised Seyid Riza they could negotiate a settlement, but instead they hung him in November 1937 and proceeded to massacre the people. Some of the boys and men of Dallikavak died. Others came back to tell stories of killing woman and children, destroying villages and burning crops. Some cried as they described the genocide. Poems and songs were written about the uprising and about Seyid Ali Riza and Ali San Bey. Sabir points out, "Seyid Riza's wife, Bese, also fought, but no songs were written about her."

Mistefa was against the power of the village *aghas* and other rich people. He wanted to destroy the landlord and tribal system, which enabled the *agha* to force people to work for no pay. In 1939 or 1940, he decided to take a stand. He collected six or seven people to go with him and ambush the *agha* on his way back from the Dersim Mountains. They bashed him, and a few months later the *agha* died. The gendarmerie came to Dallikavak and arrested Mistefa and the others, and Mistefa was put in prison for six months. Step by step, the *aghas* in the west of Kurdistan lost their power. Village disputes were solved by the elected *mukhtar*, and by the 1950s all *agha*s in this part of Kurdistan were finished.

Sabir continued making *kilims*. She became famous for her speed and her patterns. A rug measuring one metre by four metres took her two weeks to make. "The people copied my patterns, calling them 'Sabir's Patterns'." Some rugs were made for the family, but she would get orders from the businessmen in Adana, where she would go to sell them. From the sheep to the market, she did everything.

Like her mother, Sabir was always busy organising the farm and the animals, as well as spinning, dying, weaving and selling her rugs. Fat'e would cook, make the bread and look after the children. Sabir says, "We helped each other." They had children at about the same time, giving birth at home, the village midwife supervising. Fat'e had six or seven children and Sabir had 10, but Fat'e raised them all. I called Sabir *elle*, or 'mother' (different tribes have different names for 'mother'), and I called Fat'e by her name, but she was more like our mother. She disciplined us. Sabir would not interfere, unless she thought somebody had made a mistake. Occasionally Fat'e would beat us but Sabir would use strong words like, "I explain and explain but if you give him big torture he still does not listen."

In World War Two, Turkey sided with Germany. Hitler admired Mistefa Kemal and his nationalist ideology and methods. For three years, no-one had enough food in the village. There was a drought, but also the government would collect all the food to feed the army. Sabir would gather the weeds around the house and Fat'e would cook them. Mistefa took all of Sabir's jewellery, *kilims* and saddlebags to town to sell, so he could buy wheat and other necessities to feed everyone. By this time, all but two of Fat'e's children had died of sickness. Only one of Fat'e's children survived her.

Of Sabir's 10 children, seven were to die through accident or illness. One son drowned when he fell into a water channel. My sister died after she married the son of Sabir's first husband and second wife. By this time, the children of Sabir's first husband had claimed back the title of their land from the *agha*, so Sabir was pleased for her daughter to marry into the family and gain some benefit from the land. One day, this sister was travelling in a cart driven by oxen. An ox broke loose, and a piece of wood pushed into her stomach. She was pregnant but told no-one of her injury, and after she gave birth, she died.

Another sister married a rich man. She thought her husband was having relations with another woman, and confided to a neighbour, "If my husband is doing this, I will hang myself." The neighbour joked, "Why don't you hang yourself now?" So she did.

After World War Two, life became less difficult. Mistefa continued teaching primary school until 1953, when he retired to look after the farm. The family would go on *zozan* for the summer months, taking the sheep to the pastures in Binboga. But in 1955, hard times returned. Mistefa had borrowed money to buy 120 sheep, and the whole family, except Fat'e, who stayed at home to look after the animals, was taking these sheep to pastures near Adana, a distance of 300 kilometres. They took turns to ride in a truck, walk or ride the donkeys and horses, shepherding the sheep along the road. Sabir went ahead to put up their tents near a Kurdish village where they had permission to stay. Mistefa and their 16-year-old son continued travelling along the road with the sheep. A big truck came along and lost control, killing all the sheep, Mistefa and their son.

A man from Dallikavak came by truck to tell Sabir. She cried every day for many days. "For years I cried so much I could not see properly. It was my son I cried for. Children are more important than a husband. But I am strong. I cried myself into a new life." Sabir continues, "I stopped believing in God when I was very young. My strength comes from having no support from anywhere—from doing everything myself. If God exists, he gave me many bad things, so why should I believe in him?"

Mistefa had left the family with a large debt. One man helped us. His name was Halil, my sister-in-law's father. He was highly respected in all the villages near Dallikavak, so he went from village to village collecting money to pay off the debt. Meanwhile, Sabir and Fat'e continued to live together, Sabir supporting the family by taking *kilims* to the businessmen in Adana.

Sabir had never officially married Mistefa, and all her children had been registered as Fat'e's children, so when Mistefa died, there were some legal matters to settle, and it was then that Sabir took on the name of Bagdas and registered her children as her own. By 1960 she had solved the debt problem, and with 50 other Kurdish families from Dallikavak and the next village, she decided to sell up and join with them to buy a large farm on fertile land in the Caucasian village of Yassipinar, near the town of Pinarbasi, 35 kilometres from Dallikavak. It was an area given to 40,000 Muslims from the Caucasus after Russia invaded Kurdistan in 1877–78 and the Ottomans were forced to negotiate a withdrawal with help from Europe. A rich Caucasian *agha* had decided to sell his land to Alevi Kurds as a lesson to people who were causing him problems. These people were Muslim and they hated Alevi, so after two years, all the Caucasians left Yassipinar.

Life was good, because we had a big farm and many sheep. In the spring the whole family would go to the high mountains near Yassipinar to find water and pasture for the sheep. We lived in black felt tents. Rich people had very big tents with enough room for 20 people, a kitchen and a living room. Sabir liked life in the mountains. She and Fat'e made yoghurt, milk and butter, and this fed us in winter and was also a good income.

In 1969, when I had to go into the army for two years, the family moved to the town of Pinarbasi. After army duty, I opened up a studio for signwriting, decorating and painting. Sabir did not mind life in town either: "I lived with my two sons and their families. Our income was from Hasan's studio and my *kilims*."

After the military coup of 12 March 1971, the gendarmeries from Ankara were very active collecting people who had relations with the Left. Sabir says, "One night, they came looking for Hasan. They took everyone outside and searched all the houses, leaving a big mess, but they did not find him." They were looking for me because all the high school students, teachers, doctors, solicitors and political people would visit my studio to have meetings. For six or seven years, I belonged to the Turkish Workers' Party. They were the first party to mention Kurdish issues in their program.

Sabir knew about my political activities—it was 30 years ago, but still she gets upset. Many times, she would tell me, "Don't mix with politics. I know what will happen to you." Sabir says grimly, "But he did not listen to me."

The gendarmerie called again, and this time they caught me, promising, "If you give information, you will come straight back." They took me to the police station in Kayseri, and two days later to prison in Ankara. Sabir did not know where I was, and cried every day. I was 22 and they gave me hard torture for 45 days.

That was 1972. That year, Fat'e died. It is still like a bad dream. When she was lying sick in her bed, I asked her, "Do you have any pain?" At first she was silent. Then she pointed to her most private part and said, "Here is *very* sore!" In front of everyone! She laughed, and 20 minutes later she died. She was always making people laugh, even on very serious occasions. Sabir had the power. She could do whatever she wanted. Fat'e had no power, but she was extraordinarily gentle and kind.

Fat'e's sister washed her body, and I watched as they put her into a special white cotton bag tied above the head. We call it a *koffin*. They make a special carriage, a stretcher from wood with rope crossbars, and the *koffin* is tied to this, and carried by four people. Every half-minute or minute the carriers change, so many people carry the *koffin* to the cemetery. A man spoke about Fat'e's life and kindness and asked the people, "Do you have anything to say?" and people said, "We are happy with her life. She was a good lady." The *koffin* was then put into the grave.

It was also in 1972 that my uncle sponsored my wife and I to come to Australia. In Melbourne I worked very hard—for the Board of Works and in different factories, until I decided to study art. Since 1991 I have been a full-time artist, something I could never have done back in Turkey. But after I left Kayseri, Sabir's life became very difficult. She had many health problems: pains in her heart and knees. Sabir says, "I did not want to come to Australia, but I had no option. Hasan was here, and my other son in Turkey lost all his money after he bought a farm and a tractor and cows. When I applied to the Australian Embassy, my x-rays were very bad and they rejected me, but we paid money for someone to take x-rays of another person, and we gave these to the embassy, so I passed."

Sabir came to live with us in 1977. Of Australia, Sabir says, "I liked it straight away and I fitted in straight away. I have been to many villages and cities in Turkey, but here is better than anywhere. Life is easy. The health service is very good." She would not be alive today if she had stayed in Turkey.

In 1983 my brother, his wife and their nine children came out on tourist visas and applied to be accepted as refugees. In 1980 the Turkish government had sent me a letter saying I must return to Turkey. When I did not go, they took away my citizenship. For this reason, my brother and his family got refugee status. Sabir's only other surviving child is our 76-year-old sister, who lives in Bozhuyuk.

In 1984 we began hearing about the armed struggle of PKK in northern Kurdistan, and many Kurds in Melbourne realised we had to solve our problems in our own way. Two years later, we formed a Kurdish Association. One activity was to teach children the Kurdish language, because they speak only Turkish. How can you have self-determination with no knowledge of your own language or culture? Of PKK and the Kurdish situation in Turkey, Sabir says, "I always listen to the men talking, and from the beginning I like PKK because they fight against the Turkish government. I don't want blood, but PKK had no option. They must fight for freedom. In Turkey, there is no peaceful way."

The PKK was doing a lot for Kurds in Turkey and around the world, and in 1991 Sabir's 18-year-old grand-daughter, who had grown up in Australia, decided she must go back to Kurdistan and join PKK. She had always criticised our democratic activity in Australia in support of Kurdistan, saying, "It is not enough—we must do more." Sabir says, "I was surprised. She had always been a timid girl, very warm and soft and gentle.

But she was a clever girl, too—always naughty and making problems. I did not want her to go, but she went." It was a big shock for everyone. At first we were very upset, but now we respect her decision and understand she wants to do something good for her people. We have had no direct contact with her. We think she is still alive.

Until 1997 Sabir continued to make saddlebags, socks and rugs, but by February 1999, she had lost interest in living. We thought we were losing her. She would not eat, she would sleep 12 hours a day, and she would not come to meet visitors. Then Abdullah Ocalan was kidnapped in Nairobi by Turkish commandoes with help from CIA and MOSSAD intelligence, and was taken back to Turkey to be put in isolation on the prison-island of Imrali. Immediately Sabir became strong. She began eating well, taking her tablets, and every time we have a visitor or I return home, she comes and asks, "What has happened to Apo?" Her second question is, "Did they give him freedom?" She has a fresh life. She says, "Before I do whatever I do, but now my hope is that Apo will be free. Kurds need an independent homeland."

When the NATO war in Kosovo began soon after Ocalan's arrest, we thought, "This must help the Kurdish situation." Several politicians in different countries noted the similarities between what was happening in Kosovo and the situation in Kurdistan, but the world chooses to ignore what is happening to our people.

The Power of Reason

A fable retold by Eziz Bawermend

There were two brothers. The older one was gregarious, and very competent at explaining and rationalising gross exaggerations. He lived by his wits, and wherever he went, people welcomed him and treated him like royalty. In awesome admiration, his younger brother decided to imitate him by offering exaggerated claims to the public in pursuit of the same royal treatment.

One day the younger brother said to some people, "You know, I was walking alone the other day and I heard the cries of puppy dogs coming from the sky!" In utter disbelief, his listeners accused him of being a liar, one asking scornfully, "Who has ever seen puppies with wings?"

Fortunately, his older brother showed up just in time to defend him: "My brother must be telling the truth. Sure, puppies have no wings, but eagles and other birds of prey could have snatched some puppies and soared into the sky, as they snatch rabbits and lambs." Everyone was convinced, and apologetically agreed that it was indeed possible.

On another occasion, at a gathering of hunters, the younger brother made the extraordinary claim: "The other day I was hunting a deer. I aimed my gun and, bang, with one bullet I hit its hind leg hoof, and its head!" The listeners roared in protest, one saying, "That is ridiculous! A bullet ricocheting from hoof to head?"

The young man could not give a satisfactory explanation, and as the situation grew tense, his older brother came to his rescue once again, saying, "What my brother hasn't told you, and what you haven't considered, is that the deer was scratching its head with its hoof, so my brother easily hit both with a single bullet. Why do you question the veracity of his statement?" Again, everyone was convinced, agreeing that it was not only possible but highly probable, and expressed adulation for the older brother's insight and explanation.

In a bout of jealousy, the younger brother thought he would put his brother's ability for explanation to even greater test. He called out saying, "You know another strange thing happened the other day. When I was hunting, I saw a rabbit looking at me with no apprehension. I came within 20 metres, aimed my gun and pulled the trigger. By the time I reached the rabbit, lo and behold, it had turned into a bowl of stew!" People shouted, "Liar, liar! How can a rabbit turn into a bowl of stew?" His older brother sighed, saying, "Dear brother, where on earth am I going to gather all the ingredients that go into a stew to justify your lie?"

Grass Does Not Stay Under a Rock

A life story by Riza Çolpan, translated from Kurdish by Eziz Bawermend

The year is 1936. The season is autumn, the month September. By this time, most of northern Kurdistan has fallen under the control of the Turkish government—all but a small liberated area in and around Dersim. Dark clouds hover over the land of the Kurds. Every day the Turkish government launches a fresh attack on Dersim. Under such circumstances, my mother, Inci, is picking cotton and my father is collecting the branches of young oak trees for the animals' winter fodder.

There are sounds of cannons and explosions. Terrified, my mother stands to look around and feels a sharp pain. She heads home. Neighbouring women gather around her as she goes into labour, and in a short time I open my eyes to the world. The village midwife cuts my umbilical chord, sprinkles my body with salt, covers me with a specially warmed sandy soil, and wraps me in a length of material, before placing me on a flour and wheat sieve next to my mother. The midwife then turns to my mother, saying, "Congratulations! May God grant a long life to your son. You must name him Riza." Thus I assumed the name of the Kurdish leader Seyid Ali Riza, who is fighting the government. It was also the name of the midwife's dead son.

In that part of Kurdistan there is a tradition practised by Alevis and Ezidis. Whenever a woman gives birth, all boys and girls of the village visit her home and for three days and nights keep the mother entertained with singing, dancing, clowning and recitations of poetry, as well as assisting with the mundane work of the household. The boys and girls of our village live up to expectation, appropriately discharging their traditional obligations.

The year is 1937. Blood pours in Dersim. The springs and rivers of Mizur, Xarcik[a] and Euphrates run red with the blood from the floating corpses of thousands of Kurdish boys and girls, men and women.

When I am six months old, my father takes my mother, my two older sisters, one brother and me deep into the mountains to hide, and thus he saves our lives. But the world remains indifferent to the plight of the Kurds as if deaf, mute and blind. The Kurdish people have once again fallen into the hands of the barbaric and bloodthirsty Turkish soldiers.

It is July 1938, midsummer. The Kurdish liberation movement in Dersim is defeated. Seyid Ali Riza's nephew, who had been in dispute with his uncle over some land, has been bribed with government gold to betray his people. As a result of his treason, Seyid Ali Riza along with 16 of his lieutenants are captured and hung, their corpses burned, and their ashes thrown to the winds so that the tombs of these Kurdish heroes cannot become shrines.

During this cruel time, according to some sources, at least 70,000 Kurds died. According to those who were fighters and eyewitnesses, Turkish soldiers split open the bellies of hundreds of pregnant women in a mad guessing competition: is it a boy or a girl? They pierced the unborn babies with bayonets, lifting them from the wombs to terrorise the population. They chopped off the heads of hundreds of boys and collected them in bags, then threw them into the rivers. They locked up hundreds of children and old people, sealing the doors and windows, then set them on fire. Poisonous gases slaughtered thousands who hid in the caves, or the cave entrances were cemented, ensuring a slow but certain death. They raped, pillaged and slaughtered in village after village, but my family and I managed to survive.

It is 1942. I am a shepherd looking after lambs and kids, goats and cows. My mother has instilled in us a fear of the barbarous Turks, whom she calls 'cannibal Turkish murderers'. When telling stories of their cruelty whilst suppressing the uprisings in Qocgiri, Palu, Agri and Zilan,[b] my mother and others would break into tears, but we were too young to fully comprehend. I had no idea of who or what Turks were, but we were all terrified by the possibility of our heads being chopped off and our flesh eaten.

In those days, my whole world was my village of Kupik,[c] in the county called Mezgir, in the shire of Moxindi.[d] I believed that there was only one place and one country in the world: my village and Kurdistan. There was only one language: Kurdish.

Days, weeks, months and years pass fast into oblivion. Day by day, I start to comprehend the world around me. By this time, the Turkish government has built military barracks and various government offices in Dersim. Turkish soldiers frequently come to our village. Whenever we children spot them, we hide, overwhelmed with fear. In this environment, I grow accustomed to the word 'Turk' but am still very frightened of the soldiers. We call them 'brutes'—that is, 'those with brute force'. They always go to the village headman's home. I hear their voices from outside but cannot understand a single word they say. The village headman does not know much Turkish either, and mixes Turkish and Kurdish words, which annoys the soldiers. He resorts to hand gestures.

I remember very clearly that every summer, during harvest, Turkish government officials, whom we dubbed 'harvest bugs', showed up with the 'brutes' and took much of our harvest by force, leaving us hungry. Hunger and disease took their toll. There was no medicine, no doctor and no hospital. Tuberculosis, which we called *jana zirav,* and measles were grim reapers. Miraculously my family and I survived.

It is 1945. For the first time, a schoolteacher comes to our village and is a guest in our neighbour's house. He rides a horse, and wears a white shirt, a tie and no hat. I have never seen anyone like him. Deep in my heart, I yearn to go to school to become a teacher like him, to ride a horse and wear a white shirt and a tie, without a hat or traditional headgear. That desire grows stronger with the passing of each day and night.

It is the beginning of September 1946. A friend and I are taking care of the animals in the mountain pastures. One afternoon, I ask my friend to look after my animals so I can go to Shilk'e village, some four kilometres away, to enrol at the government school, which had been built in 1942. I go to the office of the teacher, a Kurd called Sukri Can. I speak Kurdish and enrol, then return to the animals.

I tell only my mother of this. She wants me to go to school, and become a public servant with a regular salary, to improve our household finances and to protect the family from the excesses committed by government officials. I do not inform the rest of the family, because my older brother already looked down on me as his enemy. Still, I do not go to school, for fear of my older brother and my father.

After three weeks, two soldiers come to our house with the village headman and tell my father, "You have enrolled your son in school and have failed to send him. You must send him or pay 150 pounds to the state." Neither my father nor my older brother know any Turkish, so cannot say, "We know nothing of this enrolment." They ask the village headman to tell the soldiers, "We cannot afford this kind of money, so as from tomorrow, we will send him to school." The village headman conveys the message as best he can to the soldiers, and afterwards, my father and brother give me a good thrashing, but do not prevent me going to school. The monetary and physical penalties are too heavy. So that is how I start school, on 15 October 1946, without a pen, a notebook or a textbook, without knowing a single word of Turkish. All first-year pupils are in the same boat.

The school building is more like animal quarters. Two hundred and fifty children from six villages sit in a small hall, with one teacher, a Kurdish man who knows a little Turkish. There are 18 to 20-year-old students among us. They are being taught a few Turkish expressions in preparation for being conscripted into military service.

For five years, I attend school in the midst of poverty, deprivation and brutal treatment. I swear I did not have shoes until I was 15. In winter, I wear something like moccasins, and in spring and summer I walk the four kilometres to school barefoot, without breakfast. My mother throws in some dried bread for lunch, if she has any. Our bread is made from millet and barley, since we cannot afford wheat. In winter we have no vegetables, only dried bread and onions. I taste my first orange when I am 15. My clothes consist of the same loose, white-cotton pants and a long shirt. When it rains in the cold of winter, the material becomes as stiff as rock.

At school, we are forbidden to speak our mother tongue. The teacher would select one student from each village to spy on the others. Whoever spoke Kurdish had to be reported to the teacher for a severe thrashing, verbal abuse, and a mark of zero. In our village, I was selected to spy on my fellow students, but thank God, I never reported anyone. There were reasons. Firstly, our house was far from the centre of the village, so I was not in a position to catch other students. Secondly, all the other villagers belonged to the Bamasun tribe. They were *sayyids*, called Sayyidon, descendants of the prophet Muhammad. But my family of Guran (so named when a wolf killed my great-uncle when he was seven) belong to the Izol tribe, and we feared their bad feelings.

The schoolteacher and others would say, "There is no nation of people called Kurds. The so-called Kurds are 'mountain Turks', a branch of Turks known as *oguz*, or 'blood-letting Turks'. There is no such thing as a Kurdish language. The so-called Kurdish language is an irregular collection of words taken from Turkish, Arabic and Persian. The language lacks grammar and rules that all real languages possess." I do not doubt the veracity of these claims. I do not see our treatment as brutal, because I have forgotten my parents' words about the Turks. Our teachers repeatedly tell us, "The Turks are brave, gallant, valiant and hard-working. The Turks are the fathers of all nations and the Turkish language is the mother of all languages." We accepted these teachings uncritically. I too wanted to be brave, gallant and valiant, a descendant of those who fathered the world's nations. I no longer feared the Turks, for I had become a Turk, and not just an ordinary Turk, but a racist, radical, fanatical Turk!

One day, I tell my father, "We are not Kurds. We are Turks." He jumps to his feet and slaps my face, saying, "If we are Turks, why do the Turks slaughter us? What is the crime of the young and the old, the men and the women they slaughter?" My mother quickly embraces me, turning to my father to say, "Why are you hurting the child? He reads books, and that is what the books say. You haven't read a book in your life!" So many times that poor woman defended me from my father and brother, having no idea of the lies contained in those books, and how their pages served to deceive the 47 or more nationalities who live in Turkey.

So this is how I completed five years of primary school. I did not receive a diploma. My father did not have a Turkish identity card and my older brother, who controlled the family finances, refused to give me the 50 krush, or half-pound, to have my photo taken for the diploma. Instead, my brother throws all my books into the fire, then picks me up to put me into the fire too. My hair is beginning to burn when my mother and sister-in-law stop him. After this, I run away to Adana. The day is 14 April 1951.

Half my life was spent in such circumstances, and now I am writing this as an open-minded democrat because, today, the plight of the Kurds is the same as it was then. The Turkish state perpetrates its brutal policies against the Kurds. Since 1984, the Turkish state has burned over 4000 villages and uprooted six million Kurds. Still the world turns a blind eye to the oppression of the Kurds and the suffering of their children.

I am 15. I stay two years in Adana without returning home. I go home when my father dies. At 17 I become responsible for the welfare of my five brothers and mother. My older brother continues to live at home, working on other people's farms, a man full of anger and jealousy, always hitting his siblings. But I love him. He is my brother. I work in foreign towns to support them, often sleeping on the ground without a mattress or a blanket so that I can send more money to my family. God be thanked a thousand times that I was able to proudly discharge my duty.

It is 1955. On 6 or 7 September, a Greek places a bomb in Mistefa Kemal's birthplace in Thessoloniki. This becomes an excuse for the Turkish military to go on a rampage against the Greeks in Turkey. I am a young man. I go out into the street to see what is happening, along with 100,000 other people. Turkish police are urging the crowd to smash, destroy, and terrorise Greeks, saying, "Don't your veins run with Turkish blood? Attack their homes, shops and churches." Calling someone 'Greek' was as bad as calling someone 'Kurd' or 'Armenian'. We burn a church and, armed with the legs of chairs and whatever else we can pick up, we vandalise anything Greek. With a mob, I go into a Greek shop and start smashing electrical appliances. An old Greek lady says, "Please leave one for me." A man hits her with a piece of wood. She falls. The man fetches cold water and pours it over her. I leave, not knowing whether she is alive or dead.

After that terrible night, they arrest 24,000 and take us to the army barracks. Some stay one month. Some stay two years. I run away after five months.

It is 1959. I am conscripted into the Turkish military, serving in the navy for three years in Istanbul. I am a soldier in 1960 when the military junta comes to power.

I am lonely so I send my address to a Turkish newspaper in Cyprus asking people to write. I receive 114 letters! One girl keeps writing. After two or three letters, we become sweethearts. We exchange photographs. Two and a half years later, I write to her family and ask if I can marry their daughter. My mother wants me to marry a Kurdish girl, but I do not have the money to pay the family. I want to marry a city girl. Her family agrees, and we exchange rings. After I finish my military service, the family sends me money to come to Cyprus. I arrive on 22 December 1962. It is the day that the hammer of social awareness hits my head and my political conscience begins to awaken.

Life in that small island is very advanced compared to Turkey. There is a sense of democracy, tolerance and understanding that I have never encountered before. I am always comparing the life, and trying to assess the situation, as far as my knowledge permits. I witness many things, and experience enough hardship to fill several novels, but before all this, just six days after arriving, on 28 December, I marry my sweetheart. We settle in a village, at the time called Balikitro, 12 kilometres east of Nicosia. On 1 October 1963, I become a father. It is strange.

It is 21 December 1963. War breaks out between the Turkish army and Greek Cypriot communities—a very unjust conflict. In that dirty war, I lose everything, because the leaders of the Turkish community frighten us by saying, "You must leave the village. If you don't, supporters of EOKA (a racist, fascist Greek-Cypriot organisation) will come and kill you." For their part, the Turks organise the Grey Wolves, who are even more racist and fascist than EOKA.

It is 1 December 1964. My family and I have found shelter in my brother-in-law's house in Nicosia. In the same month, the Cypriot Turkish authorities come and tell me, "You must do military service, because you have served in the Turkish army. We need experienced people like you. If you don't serve, we will not let you find a job and your family will die of hunger." The Turkish government is paying each civilian soldier or *mujihad* 10 pounds, but the Cyprus government is taking eight and a half pounds of that. Out of necessity, I comply: I become a soldier in the civilian army, living in the army barracks, so that my family does not starve.

Many harsh days follow. I witness ugly events. Everybody is armed, and becoming a soldier, either for the Turks or the Greeks, with both sides committing atrocities beyond imagination. On one side of the street live Turks, but on the other side, Greeks. Children playing in the streets are shot and killed in the crossfire. The Turkish side of Nicosia becomes like the Texan Wild West. Turkish fanatics, with pistols on their hips, move up and down the streets like cowboys. They take the men to the mountains, and abduct the girls, assaulting and molesting them before offering them to the soldiers in the Turkish contingency. Witnessing such crimes, I become angry. I start quarrelling with the other soldiers, opposing what they are doing, but I am alone and cannot change the way events are going.

Thirteen months after our first daughter is born, my wife gives birth to another girl and I beg to be allowed to visit my family. When I return from the visit, I witness a particularly heinous act. Several Turkish police have captured four Greek Cypriot youths and are holding them prisoner. One of the four is a tall, fine young man of 19. They bring him to the regiment where I am serving, immediately taking him to the basement. The commander orders that a policeman named Fuat be called. Fuat's brother, Ali, had disappeared at the beginning of the conflict.

When Fuat enters the basement, the commander and a few other soldiers, including myself, are standing around the prisoner, who sits on the floor, hands tied, shaking. The commander turns to Fuat: "Fuat, now you can take your brother's revenge. It is up to you whichever way you want to kill him." Fuat asks, "What is his crime?" and when none is offered, he says, "I cannot kill this man." The commander repeatedly orders that the young man be killed. He shouts at Fuat, "Don't you have Turkish blood in your veins to avenge your brother and your people?"

Fuat pulls a small knife out of his pocket, walks over to the prisoner, grabs his ear and cuts off a small piece. The youth screams in pain and I feel terrible. My heart burns. Fuat says quietly, "That is enough for me. I am not going to kill this youth," and walks out. The commander orders the soldiers to defecate, telling the youth he will have to eat their excrement before he is buried alive. At first, I do not believe it can happen, but then I see a soldier bring excrement and force it into the youth's mouth. After that, a hole is dug with a bulldozer. The young man is put in the hole and covered with soil. And so he perishes.

Immediately after this incident, I become like a lunatic, not knowing what to do. To this day, I have not forgotten that barbarism and I continue to curse this kind of inhumanity. At the time, I raise my voice and tell others whatever comes to mind. Soldiers surround me, with pointed guns. I am handcuffed and locked in a dark room. They go to my home, throw my sick wife, 13-month-old daughter and four-day-old baby, along with our belongings, out into the street, in the rain. Twenty-four hours later, they take me to a civilian soldier base on Penctili Mountain. *Penctili* means 'five fingers'. I demand to see the commander-in-charge, a Turkish general going under the name of Firtena, which means 'cyclone'. Thank God, he allows me to explain my situation. He becomes very angry with the people who have brought me, saying, "This man has served three years in Turkey and is a visitor to Cyprus. Here he has served two years. Why do you bring him here?" He orders them to return me to my family and to leave us alone. Three weeks later, my family and I leave the island. Although I had served the Turkish state in Cyprus for two years, thank God, I had not killed anyone.

It is 1965. I take my family to Istanbul and find a job. I join unions, befriend left-wing Turks, and become a socialist and a communist, but an ignorant one. In those days, my Kurdish identity and that of the Kurdish nation never cross my mind. I see myself as an internationalist and a Turk. My newfound communist friends teach me, "Our struggle is international. Being a Kurd or a Turk makes no difference. The workers of the world are one, and all should have the same rights." When the subject of the Kurds and other nationalities in Turkey is raised, they instantly cease to be internationalists and become hard-line Turks, expressing racist slogans, "One Turk is worth the whole world," and "How blessed is he who says 'I am a Turk'." They never permit criticism of the Turkish leader Mistefa Kemal and his bloodthirsty ideology. Rather, they venerate him as the first leader to oppose the seven most powerful imperialists. These imperialists are never named.

Following a lot of hard work with the unions, I become a member of TIP, Turkey's Labor Party, and spend long hours working for them. I am seen at many political events, meetings and protests marches, and thus I attract the wrath of the Turkish state. Friends counsel me, "Before you are killed, leave the country." I send a letter to my wife's relations who came to Australia in 1949. They send me an invitation, and leaving my wife and three children behind, I run away to Sydney on 21 January 1970. Seven months later, the Australian government allows my wife and children to join me. Later, I sponsor three of my brothers and their families, although two still suffer under the Turkish yoke.

In my new country, I do not remain politically idle for long. I find myself in a free, democratic, affluent and, by and large, happy society. My horizons widen as I witness firsthand its multicultural nature. Everyone is free to speak their own language, listen to their own music, broadcast over radio and television, and print newspapers and magazines in various languages. At last I come to my senses. I begin searching for my roots, scouring the libraries and bookstores of Sydney for a book on the history of my people. Unable to get any information, I return home hurt and disappointed.

Three months later, a bookshop keeper sends me a 120-page book from Oxford University, but I cannot read it because my English is so limited. I ask friends to read it for me. I become a little better informed, but continue to work with two Turkish left-wing organisations on social and political matters. After reading dozens of books, I am familiar with the theory espoused by Karl Marx, Engels, Lenin and other writers.

I work in a dry-cleaning and pressing business until 1975, then a dressmaking and pressing factory until 1984. Back in 1973, I join the ranks of the Communist Party of Australia, and attend its various functions until 1989, when I leave this party. In 1974 I form the Turkish Labourers' Association in my house, with Kurdish and Turkish members, and between 1975 and 1997 I am a member of the Australian Labor Party. Until 1978 I work with the Turkish Left, but I come to realise that the Turkish Left in Australia is no different from the Turkish Left in Turkey. They are just as racist and in denial of the Kurdish people's existence, saying, "We are brothers. We don't want Turkey's borders to change. Those who want to divide us are traitors to socialism."

In 1978, I decide to avoid such racist people. I approach the Kurdish community to organise members for an association. On 29 January 1979, along with fellow patriotic Kurds, I form the Australian Kurdish Association. Today it continues to serve Kurds and promote the Kurdish cause.

From 1974 the Turkish consulate begins to see me not only as a communist but also as an advocate of Kurdish rights. In 1978 some Leftist friends and I become targets for some racist Turks in the Turkish Right. The man who is handed a gun to kill me is himself a brainwashed Kurd I knew from Istanbul—a friend, or so I thought. When he comes to me and tells me of a plan to kill Kurdish activists, I inform him that I am one of his targets. I was told he made two attempts on my life, but the hand holding the gun was shaking so much that he could not do it.

My Leftist colleagues and I decide to inform the Australian police. We write a letter to the Australian prime minister, Malcolm Fraser. Fortunately, Australian authorities afford us Federal Police protection, and the police inform me they have the suspicious persons under surveillance, that I am safe. To make sure, I decide to visit my Kurdish friend, with my wife, and confront him.

I knock on his door, and he answers nervously, not wanting to invite us in. I say, "What is the matter? Are my wife and I unwelcome?" Inside his home, there are pictures of grey wolves everywhere. The grey wolf has become a symbol of Turkish purity, particularly for young Turkish assassins. The myth is that when the Turks were travelling westward from Central Asia, they lost their way in the mountains. Another version is that they could not cross a great river. A wild grey wolf appears and leads them to safety, and thus the grey wolf came to be seen as the Mother of Turks.

I say to my would-be assassin, "You can kill me now and not spend a day in prison. You can say I invaded your house and threatened you, but you must know your bullet will hurt me more than another's bullet, because we are Kurds and friends. Why do you want to kill me?" He is silent. Before leaving, I say, "If you kill me, you must know that someone else will kill you." He later escapes the country after he is found to be defrauding the social security system.

In 1980 a fascist junta takes power in Turkey. It extends its reach to Sydney. In April 1983, the Turkish consulate send letters to 13 persons demanding their return to Turkey within a month, warning that if they do not, their citizenship will be revoked and any possessions in Turkey confiscated. Of the 13, nine are Kurds and four are left-wing Turks. My brother Ali and I are among them. I do not have any material possessions in Turkey, but the Turkish government cancels my citizenship.

Today, I am not a member of any political party.

I must be honest and say that until 1977, even though my mother tongue is Kurdish, I had not spoken a single word of Kurdish since 1951, when I left my village. I had lost my mother tongue. Moreover, I had forbidden the Kurdish language to my younger brothers, for I had been taught that Kurdish was useless and not a real language. I had made extra effort to learn Turkish well enough so that no-one would know I was Kurdish. I had never seen written Kurdish, but in 1977, for the first time, I become aware of the Kurdish alphabet when some Kurdish patriots living in Europe sent me a copy of the Kurdish alphabet in Latin and some periodicals in Kurdish, and that is how I taught myself to read and write Kurdish in both Latin and Cyrillic.

At age 14, I had begun writing poetry about bravery and love, but it was in Turkish. I wrote a memoir, but left it at home when I ran away. In the meantime, the midwife who had helped my mother in childbirth read it. When I returned on a visit, she was an old woman, and came to me, saying, "Why do you write these things? You know nothing. Let me tell you what it was really like." She described how in 1910, when the Russian army was in Kurdistan, and the Kurdish people had nothing to eat, she saw a newly married woman secretively lift her skirt, pull something out and eat it, covering her mouth as she did so. The midwife pleaded with the young woman, "Please give me a little of what you are eating." Another person whispered to her, "You would not ask if you knew what it is. She is eating animal dung."

Now all my books are written in Kurdish. Today, the Turkish dictionary contains 27,000 words, the majority borrowed from Kurdish, Arabic, Persian and other languages. In dramatic contrast, the dictionary prepared by the Kurdish writer Hejar contains 70,000 words and still does not include all Kurdish words, or any of the contemporary techno words. The Kurdish language is very rich, and it has been a pleasure, a real sense of accomplishment, to use it to write eight published books, and another two that are ready for printing. Of the eight books, five are poetry, one is a memoir and two are novels, one being about the Dersim genocide, the other about Rostam, a mythical Kurdish hero.

But I do not consider myself a poet and a writer. I see myself first as a Kurdish patriot, and I write to be an example for Kurds, so that they may learn how to read and write in Kurdish and abandon wrong beliefs implanted in their minds. My writing is based on my experiences, and the travels that have expanded my horizons. In the mountains, my friends were shepherds. In Turkish cities, my friends were intellectuals, the educated and those with political beliefs. I moved around in many different communities, their people becoming my teachers.

My life has seen three phases: brutal oppression, communist dreams, and now a desire to visit the land where I was born, to see relations and to visit the graves of my parents and grandparents. Today, I am 63. I am free and content. I have four children and three grandchildren. My remaining hope is to see my ashes spread over a free, united Kurdistan. As I write in one poem[e]:

Oh mother, my mother,
My Kurdistan,
I long to show
My heart to you,
Expose my body.
See what I have received from you!
Those abundant flowers,
The trunks and branches of the forests,
The nectar and honey of all your plants
Are my very legs.
Your soil is my flesh.
Your stones are my bones and marrow.
Your mountains and valleys
Are my hands and fingers.
Your plains and hills
Are my back and chest.
Your rivers and springs
Are the tears in my eyes.
You have given me my mind and soul.
You are my thoughts and beliefs,
My religion,
My prophet.
My God.

Mourning In Black

A poem written by Riza Çolpan in memory of Halabja and Anfal, translated by Bênav

It was the year nineteen eighty-eight
When Kurdish patriots
And friends of the Kurds
Mourned Halabja.

It was spring, the sixteenth of March
When the sky: cloudy, dark, and cold,
Filled with a poisonous fog
And the earth and sky mourned in black.

Planes dropped chemical bombs
That melted moaning bodies
While others screamed for help,
The mountains and valleys mourned in black.

The *peshmergas* went out,
But against the wind they could not fight,
As Halabja turned into Hiroshima
The stones and trees mourned in black.

Oh, dear mother, your husband hugged his son
But, weak from gas, failed to lift him.
As they lost their lives together,
Their Kurdish garments mourned in black.

As piles of sightless, soundless bodies
With frozen limbs accumulated,
For days remaining unburied,
The moon and stars mourned in black.

Valleys and ditches filled with bodies
People were buried without farewell.
Kurmanjs, Sorans and Lurs died, and
The Zazas and Gurans mourned in black.[a]

As the poisoned wind ended all life,
The world remained blind and deaf
Even God appeared not to witness the death.
The believers mourned in black.

Oh, pity me, pity me!
Five thousand Kurds were martyred.
After that smog submerged the town,
Wounded hearts could not find a cure.

Elsewhere, the wild, aggressive enemy
Hunted the Kurdish people.
Burning their homes, trees and crops.
The forests and fields mourned in black.

As shepherds attended sheep.
A fog appeared before them.
The animals died; the shepherds died,
Their cloaks and flutes mourned in black.

Children in front of doors
Were playing or walking around,
When the bombs came,
The rain mourned in black.

Old men and women sat at home.
Bawer and Delal[b] were outside.
With all the spring water poisoned,
The rivers and lakes mourned in black.

Fathers, mothers, along with their children,
Young and old
Were wrapped.
Their shrouds and *koffins* mourned in black.

While little babies were breastfed,
Their mothers unaware of the wind,
Alike, honourable heroes and babies were buried,
The picks and shovels mourned in black.

Children screamed,
Mothers mourned and sisters sobbed,
Even the men shed tears.
The dove mourned in black.

Four thousand villages
Wiped out by the enemy.
And from their graves,
Feqî, Xanî and Cigerxwin[c] mourned in black.

Tens of thousands fled their homeland
The world looked on, playing dumb.
As the Kurds tried to escape the hate,
The paths and roads mourned in black.

Tens of thousands were dying,
Their animals and farms falling still.
The Kurds were losing so much,
All of Kurdistan mourned in black.

As the dreadful news spread fast
On television screens everywhere,
Showing pictures of a lifeless land,
A helpless audience mourned in black.

As the Imperialists chose to be silent.
Saddam, Assad and Ozal delighted. [d]
As even the Soviets remained shameless,
Salahaddin mourned in black.

The Holy Peacock and Ahura Mazda
Remained as wordless as the others.
No power did anything,
The Ezidis and Mazdaks mourned in black. [e]

Old Zoroastra did not show up,
Nor did Rostam Zal.[f]
No Kurd remained smiling;
All lovers of peace mourned in black.

Oh, Kurdish brother: learn the lesson.
Find yourself the path.
The world did not ask, "Who are they?"
When even the sun mourned in black.

Forever we dig our own grave,
For a thousand years being killed
By Arab, Mongol, Turk and Persian ruler,
As the centuries mourn in black.

Oh, brothers, open the history books
To learn and never forget.
Revive the soul of Kawa.[g]
Forgotten memories mourn in black.

The tragedies of Halabja, Shaykh Seyid and Zîlan
And those of Dêrsim and Agrî
Broke many hearts like mine.
Riza Guran's[h] family mourns in black.

So look at events with an eye
To distinguish right from wrong.
Unite against the enemy
Or continue to mourn in black.

You and I

A poem by Riza Çolpan, translated by Omar Sheikhmous

You and I exist, my labouring friend,
My brotherly countryman and farmer,
In all corners of the world,
Under the blue sky,
The red and yellow sun
And the round moon.
Mountains have settled between us:
Huge mountains.
Plains, slopes and valleys
Become obstacles in all ways.
Rivers and great seas,
Oceans of infinite depth and stretch,
Have kept us from meeting
Have hindered all contact.

Still,
We are the owners
Of nature and world.
We fly like birds,
As the lightning in the clouds
Cuts through mountains
And dries the rivers and seas.
Our voice thunders on.
As loud as any cannon or tank.
Resounding echoes
Around the world,
And in Kurdistan, too,
Among her *peshmergas*.

Companions!
Our hearts carry a wish,
Our stomachs a fire,
Burning like a volcano
For the poor and those who toil:
Villagers, farmers,
And workers all,
For the deliverance of all people.

Yes, my farming friend,
My working friend,
We have the same rights,
We are the same class.
We must learn to be faithful, and
Commit to each other
With our hearts and souls,
And in our speech,
To struggle without end,
To reach a victory,
A life of equality,
In a hasty race.

Oh! Companions!
Among us,
We have betrayers to our cause:
Unenlightened and unwise people,
Scorpions and snakes with fatal poisons,
Who have become disciples of the
Shaykhs, *mullahs* and priests;
Rapid dogs to the imperialists,
Attacking
The lovers of humanity and democracy
Like wolves of prey.

Come, my companions!
Join hands.
With strength, wisdom and speech
Eliminate all borders and passports.
No more killing of humans,
No more cruelty and oppression,
Abolish
Death, torture and beating,
Conflict and war.
No more spilling of blood.

Come, my companions,
My sisters and brothers,
For a good future,
A square meal,
Clean clothes,
A just and egalitarian life.
For little children,
Barefoot, in rags and hungry,
With swollen stomachs,
Let doctors and medicines come,
Learning and schools, too.
Work hard to change this world
Into blooming gardens.

Come, my companions!
Remember your forefathers,
The tears in their eyes,
That fell, abundant, like
Rivers and springs,
Down their cheeks.
And the lives of women
Youthful brides and the elderly,
Among the herds,
In dirt and dung.
Put an end to these conditions,
My friends:
This great shame of the world.

Come, my companions!
Let us proclaim a just organisation,
Eliminate inequities.
No more servants and slaves of thousands
To a few overlords.
Let us bring forth
A world of equality,
A world of fraternity,
Where no-one eats fine meats, caviar and lobsters
While thousands go hungry to the bone.

As the Hungry Dream of Food, the Musician Dreams of Music

A life story based on interviews with Dursun Acar

In Mistolar, the Kurdish name for the village where I was born, people sang when they cut grass for the animals. They sang while harvesting wheat. They sang at social gatherings. They sang when a person died. We rarely stopped singing and playing music. Shepherds would play hand-made wooden flutes made from rosewood, blackberry wood or hazelnut—woods whose deep sounds and feelings of nature echoed through the hills.

As I child, I watched my father's fingers as he played the *ba'aghlama*. At family gatherings, people sang and played *ba'aghlama* and flute, but it was Turkish music. For dancing, they played the big drum called a *dohul* and the *zorna*, which is like a high-pitched clarinet that is played from Egypt to India. The other commonly played instrument was the Greek *kemence*, Greeks having lived in Turkey since the days of Alexander the Great. The *kemence* is like a violin with a long triangular, wedge-shaped bowl, from the Trabzon region. We did not play the Greek *oud* or *cumbus*, as they do in Diyarbakir and Urfa.

At winter parties and at weddings, everyone danced in a circle—man, woman, man, woman—sometimes the fast, slow dance of the Greeks, to music we call Karadeniz, or Black Sea music, while other dances were Kurdish. Sometimes, an old man or woman would show off by doing a traditional Kurdish dance in the centre of the circle. I never saw a woman playing a musical instrument, but sometimes a woman would sing.

My mother had a lovely voice. When somebody died, a woman or man would sing a dramatic song. It was the only time people sang in Kurdish. There was a small lake 30 minutes' walk from the village. It was pale green, with a centre of deep blue, and in 1969 my 17-year-old brother drowned there. When my mum heard the news, she started singing, "Lo, lo, lo, Lo. Le, le, le, Le. Loa la lor..." "my baby, my son...", without an instrument, just a song from the heart, and people could feel her madness and sadness.

My father would sometimes ask me to sing with him, but as a boy, I was always too shy in front of people. I would tremble with nerves. When my family moved to Ankara, I would go back to Mistolar in the summer holidays. For three months, I would take the cows, sheep and lambs to the mountains. Sometimes it is dangerous to be alone in case a storm comes, or a wolf attacks, and I would walk with other shepherds, but many times I was alone with the animals. I felt free, and I would sing all day, listening to the echo. I sang Turkish songs, because Kurdish music was banned. I heard Kurdish music only on the short-wave radio from Iraqi Kurdistan. After I heard a Turkish song over the radio I would repeat the words and music until I got it right. The songs were usually about love or some other drama—somebody losing a son, or going blind, or dying. Other songs celebrated nature.

I had no money for an instrument and my father was too poor to buy one. He earned 300 lire a month, and the cheapest *ba'aghlama* was 400 lire. Instead, I would beat a stick on my leg or with my hand, making my voice low, then high, making music when nobody could hear.

Mistolar is in the hilly Qocgiri region, about 120 kilometres from Sivas, near Kizil Dag, Turkish for 'red mountain'. The bare, rocky hills are either red from copper or shiny grey from chrome, none of the metals having been mined, because this is Kurdistan. The village did not get electricity until 1986. We used kerosene in a bottle, put a string down and lit it, then covered the light with a glass.

It was an Alevi village, so we did not have a mosque. We did not have an *agha* or a *bey*. Someone might be called *agha*, but they lived like everyone else. It was not like the *aghas* in the east, who are still powerful. All we had was the village *mukhtar*, or government representative. If people had a problem and wanted to approach the government, they went through him, or if the gendarmerie wanted to catch someone, or the judge wanted someone to go to court, they came to the *mukhtar*. He was elected every few years from two or three candidates, each from a different political party.

My grandfather and his sons were farmers, and our family lived in my grandfather's red and black stone house with four uncles and their families. There was a room for cows, ox and horse, another for sheep, another for lambs and another for storing animal feed. Separate, but under the same flat, earthen roof, with one large entrance serving all the rooms, were three family rooms and a separate room for cooking and storing food. My mother cooked in a stone wood-fuelled furnace. She milked the animals, and made yoghurt and cheese, storing them in the cold spring water, or in snow brought from the mountain. She worked inside the house, her daughter-in-laws working outside. The men would plant and the women would weed and pick up, everyone joining in the harvest, cutting the grass and wheat with scythes, singing as they worked. We were poor, yet in the village we slept on wool like kings, or on the roof in summer. When my parents moved temporarily to the town of Merzifon, we slept on dried grass.

I began learning the Turkish language when I started cleaning shoes in Merzifon for money at the age of five. I was 10 when I began school in Mistolar. The Turkish teacher sent spies around to each family's home to discover which families spoke Kurmanji. The next morning, at school, a list of names would be read out. Those on the list had to stand and have their hands or fingers beaten. One day, my grandfather asked me, "What has happened to your hands? Were you naughty at school?" I told him, "No—I was hit because we speak Kurmanji at home."

My grandfather invited the schoolteacher to breakfast, and when the teacher had eaten, my grandfather said, "I respect you. You are educated and you are teaching our children, but why do you hit Dursun for speaking the language of his family and his village? Why do you punish him for being Kurdish?"

The teacher was shocked. He replied, "The government tells me I cannot let the children speak Kurdish because it will hold them back from speaking Turkish." My grandfather told him, "Do your job, teach our children Turkish, but do not try and take our language and culture away from us. You are one person; we are many. There are many ways we can kill you."

My grandfather taught me what I knew of Kurdish history. He told me stories of the uprising of Kurds in the Qocgiri region against the army of Mistefa Kemal in 1919. The uprising was led by Aliser Bey and Nuri Dersimi, a veterinary surgeon, who had gone around and got the support of the *aghas*. Seyid Risa from Dersim, about 200 kilometres away, told the Qocgiri leaders to delay the uprising until after the winter snows so he could join them, but Mistefa Kemal's army attacked before this and defeated the Kurds. Aliser Bey was killed and Nuri Dersimi escaped to Syria, where he wrote books until he died.

Seyid Riza led his own armed struggle in the mountains of Dersim in the 1930s. It reached a height in 1937. In the summer of 1937, he was betrayed to the Turkish government by a local Kurdish *agha*, Diyab, and was captured and taken to Elazig. His two sons were hung in front of him before he was executed.

Other than my grandfather's stories, I had nothing to do with Kurdish culture, especially after we moved to Ankara. There was no paid work in Mistolar, so from 1965 to 1972 we lived in the capital, where my father serviced a block of apartments. In one apartment lived an Italian family, and they gave me my first instrument: a mandolin. I played it like a *ba'aghlama,* and whatever I heard, I copied. I learned quickly.

In 1972, when my family moved back to Mistolar, I stayed with an aunt in Adana to finish school. I would leave for school one or two hours early, to go to a *ba'aghlama* shop on the way, to sweep the workshop for the man who hand-made the *ba'aghlamas.* In return, he would say, "I know you want to learn, and that's why I like you, so I will give you one *ba'aghlama* and you can play for 15 minutes. Then go to school." He did not teach me how to play, but I learnt how to tune the instrument, which is like learning the alphabet before you can read, and I would watch him making the *ba'aghlamas.*

The wooden bowl is all one piece, carved with a chisel. Now, they use a machine. A piece at the top of the bowl is left long and shaped into a V, to extend up the neck so that the bowl and neck can be joined. The neck is made from a white wood that in Turkish we call *googan*. I think it is hazelnut. The neck is covered in a sheet of pine, cedar or spruce, about three or four millimetres thick, and sometimes inlaid with a pattern. Most *ba'aghlamas* have six strings. For more power, some have eight strings, but each pair of strings makes the same note.

I bought my first *ba'aghlama* in 1970, when my uncle, who lived in Sydney, sent me some money. It cost 400 lire, and I took it with me when I went into the army in 1974. I played in the army disco, and I would sing too, which was good experience, because on stage I gradually lost my nervousness.

In 1976, I returned to Mistolar to find its name had been changed to Dagyurdu, a Turkish name. That shocked me. It made me start thinking about politics and what Turks were doing to Kurds. I stayed for four months, but there was no work, so I went to Ankara, where I became a security guard at the University of Hacettepe.

There was a Turkish choral and dance group for students, and I asked to join. They asked, "Have you a *ba'aghlama*?" and I said, "No," because I had sold my *ba'aghlama,* but they allowed me to sing. There was only one other worker in the group—he also lives in Australia now. There were about 20 people playing instruments, 30 or 40 in the choir, and 20 to 40 in the folk dance group.

Three months after I joined, I saved enough money to buy a cheap *ba'aghlama*, and later, a friend of mine offered me a *ba'aghlama*, made in 1967 and very nice to the ear. He allowed me to pay the 1500 lire over time, so then I could play and sing with the Turkish group and the group taught me many skills. I was still learning by ear, but they let me make mistakes and catch up.

In Turkey, every city has different music and folk dances, from Ismir in western Turkey to Diyarbakir, Urfa, Siirt, Bingol, Van, Mardin, and Bitlis in Kurdistan. Basically, the steps and music are different, and also the musical instruments. Sometimes, Kurdish music uses the accordion, even the bagpipes in Artvin, close to Georgia. In the university group, they danced in groups of 10 to 36, with a leader, in a circle, a halfcircle or a straight line—man, woman, man, woman—everyone moving in perfect time. They entered competitions against other university folk-dancing groups, performing dances from all over Turkey—including Kurdistan, though they always called them Turkish.

Until I worked at the university, I knew nothing about Newroz. In our village, nobody talked about it, except to say it was from Persia. One day a Turkish university student told me its meaning. He knew about Kurdish culture from knowing two Kurdish students, Deniz Gezmis and Huseyin Inan, and one Turkish student, Yusuf Arslan, who were executed in 1971 because they were socialist. He and his friends also brought me some books, saying, "You have to learn about your history." For 20 years, I had not understood why different things happened, but after two years at university, I knew.

By teaching me about Kurdish culture and history, these Turkish students were doing something illegal. But they belonged to a socialist group, and from that time on, every 21 March, they would bring me a red rose and say, "Happy Newroz." Now these people are doctors, solicitors and engineers, but I really appreciate what they did for me.

The university choral group knew I was Kurdish. When they heard I was learning about Kurdish culture and history, members would warn me, "Be careful—it will cause you trouble." A teacher in the group asked if I was Alevi, and I answered, "I was born Alevi. Now I don't believe in any religion." In Turkey, maybe 20 per cent of Kurds are Alevi and 70 per cent are Sunni. The Ottoman rulers and the Turkish government always tried to make trouble between us. The Sunni are told, "The Qur'an says non-Muslims must die, and Alevi are not Muslims." People say, "God says this," but I don't think God says anything like this. People kill each other. When I was 15, I decided religion was just old-fashioned politics. The old people were framed by religion, but the young professionals were socialist, pursuing a more just society, and they influenced me. But this teacher was a good man, and not racist. He worked as a conductor on radio, and said he liked Alevi music. He taught the group some Alevi songs, as well as songs from many different towns, but all in Turkish.

I lived in Ankara and worked at the university for 11 years. I married in 1978, to a third-generation cousin. Our parents arranged the marriage. We did not love each other, but we could not defy our parents, and we thought that, over time, we might come to love each other. We did not. We are still together, but with many problems. It is very hard.

During the late 1970s and early 1980s, I would hear the Turkish media say that the Turkish army had gone to an eastern village, to kill people who wanted to divide Turkey. We never heard that they were Kurdish, or that they wanted to live in a free country where they could speak Kurdish, practise their own culture and have some say in politics. Even so, I understood that killing people and destroying villages was wrong—it does not matter who the people are. I believe in a democratic system where you cannot pressure others, whatever their nation, colour, or religion.

The first time I heard of PKK was in 1982, when prisoners went on a hunger strike and some PKK prisoners set themselves alight in Diyarbakir prison. But at the time, I was not thinking about a free Kurdistan. My only question was: "Why are Turks and Kurds killing each other? Why are the Turks changing the names of our towns?" I thought the answer to the problems was a socialist democracy where everyone was free to talk, work, get an education and obtain food and medicine. I thought this way until 1988, when I came to Australia.

Back in Turkey, the first real Kurdish songs I heard were written by a man called Cigerxwin,[a] from Syria, who died in 1984. His songs were very popular, because they were about family, nature, and being free. He would sing about love and his dream for a free country, and why the Kurdish freedom fighters live in the mountains and survive on very little food, to fight for the people's right to live in peace on their own land, to speak their own language and practise their own culture. More people started writing and singing in Kurdish, sometimes taking old poems, such as those of Ahmedi Khani, who lived in the 17th century, or writing their own. One famous songwriter and singer is Sivan Perwer, who ran away to Germany in the 1970s. He brings alive songs from long ago about love, beauty, nature, human rights, freedom, the *peshmerga* and Kurdistan, and also writes his own. His songs ring in the heart of every Kurd.

Now I have many Kurdish cassettes, because Kurdish music is not banned in Australia. Many songs ask questions like why are we not like other nations? Why do people kill each other over religion, politics, or nothing at all? Is it fun? Is it greed? Why always kill poor people and why always destroy poor nations? All our songs explain something; they are not like disco, repeating the same thing over and over.

In Turkey, we were poor and would always be poor. I worked, but my wage was very low. Also, the more I knew about my culture, the more I wanted to speak and sing in Kurdish, live like a human being, instead of always being under the feet of someone else, feeling pressure all the time, especially when I began writing and singing Kurdish songs. I was also concerned for my family's future. My uncle was still in Sydney, and his son, my cousin, was in Melbourne, working with computers. In 1988, he called me, saying, "You can't stay there. You do not belong. If you want to be a Kurdish musician, you must come here. I will send you a letter to help you get a visa at the Australian Embassy in Ankara." At the embassy, they said, "Bring your passport." I went to the passport office, and after two weeks I got it and took it to the embassy. Then they said, "Bring your holiday certificate." I did this, and then they said, "Now get it translated into English," but when I got home my visitor's visa was already there!

When I arrived in Melbourne, I could say just "yes" and "no" in English. I had imagined Australia to be full of big buildings, like Ankara, so when I saw all these single houses with gardens, I liked it. But after two weeks, I thought: "I have to go back. I have no job and I can't get a work permit, and if immigration refuses my application and sends me back, I will be in big trouble—I will lose my job at the university, be put in prison and tortured." I was very nervous and confused, especially because my family was still in Turkey.

My cousin told me to stop this thinking and helped me apply to stay. Immigration said, "But you came as a visitor." I said, "I know. Otherwise, I could not leave Turkey. I do not have a criminal record—you can check—but the government knows me, knows I sing in Kurdish, and knows I sing political songs." They let me apply for refugee status and gave me a work permit.

After 510 hours of English-language classes I got work in a chocolate factory as a machine operator and forklift driver. I completed a quality-control course and a hygiene course, and got a forklift license, then did a computer course. I played table tennis and soccer, and started playing music with a Kurdish group and other community groups. Twice my application was refused and I was ordered to leave Australia. The third and final time I went before immigration officials, I showed them a video of me playing and singing Kurdish songs, telling them, "If anybody says a Kurdish musician can make Kurdish music in Turkey, then you can kick me out straight away." This was in 1992, and they gave me a long interview, conducted by a very experienced old man. He asked, "Are you a PKK member?" I said, "I'm not a PKK member, but I am Kurd." "But why do you always sing under the PKK flag?" "When I sing with an Australian group, I sing under the Australian flag. When I sing with a Macedonian group, I sing under the Macedonian flag, or a Greek flag, or even the Turkish flag. I play for all sorts of benefits to help different groups raise money." Then he asked, "Have you been in Germany?" "No. Why do you ask me this question?"

"Maybe you went there illegally, without a passport." "No." He persisted, "How do you know Sivan Perwer, and the Kurdish musical group Hunerkom?" "I know them because we communicate with each other—they send us music and we send them music." Finally he asked me, "One last question: did you ever kill anyone in the mountains?" I answered, "My weapon is my musical instrument. I have killed no-one."

Two weeks later, I received a letter granting me a temporary visa for four years. I immediately brought my family here. Then in 1994, with a new rule for 20,000 Chinese, they gave us the chance to apply for a permanent visa. We were successful, and in 1996, we applied to become Australian citizens.

Now, we are Australian. If Kurdistan becomes a free country, I will stay here, though I may visit Kurdistan. I spent 30 years in Turkey—for nothing. Now I am 40, and very happy with the 10 years spent in Australia. I know Australia is not really independent, because it is still under pressure from the British and the Americans, but I can speak my language, write songs and sing and play Kurdish music without fear. We live a healthy, comfortable life. In Turkey, there was never enough money. I see my children speaking English and Kurdish, and being well educated.

I still cannot read music. I learn by listening, then writing down the words. Sometimes the accent is difficult, but I listen until I understand the words, and slowly, I learn. Over time I began writing my own songs—composing music on the *ba'aghlama*, then writing words. Sometimes, my daughter sings with me, but she is between three cultures—Kurdish, Turkish and Australian—and she has her own mind.

I enjoy writing songs. One is about living in a sweet country, a free country, like

Australia, but others are for Kurdistan, where people must fight for life and freedom. Like all Kurdish songwriters, I write about human rights. I am not blind any more, and we must tell the world what is happening in Kurdistan, so I sing about Turkey's double standards. They demand human rights for Turks in Germany but do not give those rights to Kurds in their own country. They claim to be democratic, but put people like Leyla Zana in prison for 15 years because she used the word 'Kurd' in parliament when asking that Turks and Kurds live as brothers. If a Kurd speaks up for human rights, the government calls him a terrorist. If a Turk does so, he is sacked, arrested or killed. This is not democracy. My songs ask, "Why is the government refusing to look for peaceful solutions?"

In Australia I have read many books about Kurdistan. Now that I know more about my identity, I realise Kurds have been an unlucky nation. Those in power divided our people before we even knew what a country was, when Kurds still lived in tribes and followed their *agha*, but even the *agha*s could neither read nor write. The mountains were our friends, but they also divided us and kept us isolated. In Turkey, the Ottomans and Kemal Ataturk tried to divide us on the basis of religion, and ever since Ataturk, our language, dress and music have been illegal. In Turkey, being a Kurd is illegal! Now, many Kurds cannot speak Kurdish, and so it becomes harder to unite with Kurds from other parts of Kurdistan.

I used to think cultural freedom in a democratic system was enough, but if it was, then the Soviet Union would not have split up when it started to become more democratic. I began to realise that for self-determination, you need a political system that ensures justice for all, as well as cultural freedom. The Turkish government is very clever. There are no jobs in Kurdistan. Everyone must serve in the army for at least two years, and the government pays big money to the *aghas* in the east to employ Kurdish village guards, who become powerful and sometimes misuse their power.

Every day, people lose their life, or live in fear of being put in prison and tortured, but if you join PKK, it is a really hard life. Yet if I had learnt more about my culture and history and what was happening to my people before I married, maybe I would have joined PKK. Then I could not have come to Australia.

Back in the 17th century, Ahmedi Khani wrote: "We die but the sun always rises and gives new life." Abdullah Ocalan is like the sun—he gave new life to his people. Even so, for a long time many Kurds did not support him or PKK. PKK guerillas were accused of killing Turkish soldiers and even other Kurds, but they killed only those who were collaborators with the Turkish government. When people talk about Kurds killing Kurds, they do not understand how the PKK guerillas or the *peshmergas* of Barzani and Talabani grew up. They live a very hard life, both before and after they become freedom fighters. They live in constant danger. Maybe they make mistakes, but war is different to peace—you cannot judge mistakes in the same way.

In February 1999 Ocalan was kidnapped in Nairobi and taken back to Turkey. All Kurds were united in condemning what happened to him. His abduction, solitary imprisonment, trial and death sentence touched something deep inside. Now we understand. Against all international law, the system today catches Abdullah Ocalan, tomorrow Talabani, the next day Barzani. Today, they kill us; tomorrow, they kill you.

Why the Rich get Richer and the Poor stay Poor

A fable retold by Eziz Bawermend

The 15th of the lunar month of Shaban is known as the night when the fortune of all creatures for the following year is determined. One year, at the time of Shaban, one villager asked another, "With so many people in the world, not to mention other creatures, who can possibly determine in one night everybody's fortune for the following year?" The second villager responded, "The angels get together and from dusk to dawn decide what the rich should get the following year. Only a few seconds are left for them to decide what the vast majority who are poor should get—so they just say, 'Let them have what they had last year!'"

A Rose that Cannot be Plucked, A Song that Cannot be Banned

A life story based on interviews with Veli Toprak

I believe humans do not forget two things in their life: one is particular smells and the other is melodies. Music has surrounded me all my life. Music is universal. It can build bridges and unite. Politics divides.

My grandfather, uncle and father all sang, and played the *cura*, *ba'aghlama* and *tambora*, a group of instruments called *zaz* in Turkish. Each of them has a single bowl, and three pairs of strings, each pair tuned to the same note, with up to 24 frets. The *cura* is a very small *tambora*, tuned an octave higher than normal, while the *tambora* is like a long-necked *ba'aghlama*. It can be tuned to different scales and tones, although I often tune my *tambora* to the *ba'aghlama* sound, to suit my voice—usually G minor or F minor.

My father also played the *ximza*,[a] a very small *ba'aghlama*, which has only three strings and eight frets. His *ximza* was 250 years old—a present from a friend who appreciated my father's music and strong humanitarian beliefs. It had been passed down from this man's grandfather's grandfather. My father taught me on this instrument, which I would practise when I was alone.

In Kuçuk,[b] the Turkish name for our village, people visited each other every second night, especially in winter, and they would play *tambora* and *cura* and sing Alevi songs, about loving people and being tolerant and fair. One line I particularly remember is, "Do not think I am far from God, because if I know myself, if I love people, if I love life, God is inside me." This is Alevi philosophy.

Our family originally came from the Dersim area, but after the Dersim uprising, the government deported my grandfathers, or they escaped, to Kucuk, which belongs to the city of Kayseri. I did not know my grandfather, but I believe he was involved in the uprising. Kuçuk was a farming village, without shops, surrounded by flat land and distant mountains. My parents could not read or write. My father grew fruit and vegetables and kept animals. My mother milked the animals, making bread, butter, yoghurt and cheese.

My parents grew up in Kucuk. My mother was 14 when she married. My father was 30, a widower, with four children under the age of eight. My mother had 10 more children, so she was very hard-working and self-sacrificing, but also very stubborn and impatient, all the time shouting. I was a quiet, serious child and missed cuddles and individual attention. She cared for us as a package.

Our father was different. He was a friend to all his children, always joking and playing with us and telling us stories. He was an easy going man with a great sense of humour, and was always helping people. He would take sick people to hospital and lend money to anyone who needed it. He lived the Alevi philosophy of always respecting and loving the human, though he was not a practising Alevi in a religious sense. He would say, "If there is a God then it lives in the human. Each human is a small god." Although uneducated, he was rich in ideas and experience from all his contact with musicians and educated people. Many Alevis became socialist—having been persecuted by Sunni Muslims for so long, they were used to fighting injustice—but my father did not. He was a humanist, and his progressive ideas and personal dignity influenced me greatly.

At home we spoke the Dersim dialect of Dimili, also known as Zaza. It has a different accent to Kurmanji, but they are similar. It was only when we moved to Adana in 1962, when I was six, that my parents started speaking Turkish. My mother found it difficult. Four years later, we moved to Ankara. My father took on casual work, like cleaning, although in the last 10 years of his life, he could not find work. My mother worked as a housekeeper and cleaner, so both parents had to speak Turkish. At home they started speaking Turkish, and only to Kurdish friends would they speak Dimili or Kurmanji. They especially spoke Dimili when they were upset or arguing, and my mother would storm off to her parents' and my father would have to go and bring her back. Their arguments were mostly over money.

I would try to remember my Kurdish language, but it was very difficult, because all my friends and teachers spoke Turkish. At home we no longer practised Alevi traditions. Many famous Kurdish and Turkish musicians came to our house—people like Aref Sag, Neset Ertas, and Mahsumi Serif. They would sing and play with my father, mainly Turkish songs. Music made Kurds and Turks come together.

I would listen to them, but stopped singing when I went to high school. Instead, I took private lessons on the mandolin, learning to read music, exploring the different rhythms and melodies, what scales harmonise, and how to bring the different melodies together to make a second or third voice. At school we practised as a group, and I was interested in the rhythm section to improve my timing, always thinking of how to transfer these skills to the *ba'aghlama*. Later, I started playing the *ba'aghlama*.

The group I played with was mostly Turkish, so we played Turkish songs. A few times, we performed on radio. I did not feel like an outsider, because music is a universal language, like science, and I was interested in learning the skills. In those days, I never mixed music with my political ideas.

Because I always admitted to my Kurdish identity in Ankara, I began to experience discrimination. Turkish people are under the influence of Kemalism, a very nationalist ideology that can be very humiliating. As a 10 or 11-year-old boy, I remember neighbours, school students, and people in the street shouting after me, "Kurdish people are hairy and ugly. They have a tail, and live in the mountains like animals." In high school, one teacher was a Turkish nationalist from Kayseri. When he was interviewing me, he studied me and said, "Your face looks like you come from east of Kayseri. Are you a Turk or a Kurd?" "I am Kurd." "Are you Alevi?" "Yes." After that, he failed me for two years. If a student had a strong Kurdish accent, other students would laugh.

My uncle worked in the hospital. One day his sister visited him, and they spoke Kurdish in the corridor. The principal of the hospital terminated his job immediately.

I came to believe that we had to defend our dignity. At school, when we were made to say, "I am proud to be Turk," I would mumble, "I am proud to be human." I was not against the Turkish people, but I was against Turkish nationalism and the way it kept people ignorant and racist.

From 1938 until 1960, the Turkish government was so oppressive that people did not dare speak about Kurdish issues in the city, but from 1960, more Kurdish people started going to university and joining socialist organisations. In 1971, three socialist students in Ankara, two of them Kurdish, were hung because they talked to other students about the Kurdish uprisings of the 1920s and 1930s and how socialists must help the Kurdish people.

During the 1960s, it became apparent that most socialists were not ready to fight for Kurdish issues, that they were still under the influence of Turkish nationalism, and Kurds realised they had to form their own underground associations. In 1969 Kurdish intellectuals from a number of groups formed an association called DDKO or Revolutionary Cultural Society of the East. They published and distributed illegal magazines. My older brother, caught carrying such magazines, was put in prison for two months and subjected to electric-shock 'therapy'. His cell was so cold that 20 years later, he still suffers kidney pains.

People were becoming increasingly interested in politics, especially in the suburb of

Tuzlu Cayir, where I lived, a very poor area. Many political associations formed, each publishing its own newspapers, such as *Kawa*, *Rizgari* and *Riya Azadi*.

When I was 15 or 16, one good friend, Riza, was in contact with these political people. Together we read the newspapers and went to seminars on socialism, meeting Kurdish intellectuals like Orhan Kotan, Kemal Burkay and Abraham Richly, very intelligent, articulate men. I also met a short, bald Turkish professor, Isma'il Besikci, when he was in Orhan Kotan's *Rizgari* magazine office. He was in between prison sentences for writing and publishing books about Kurdish history and society. He asked me where I was from, and which tribe, and I told him from the Çarekan tribe.[c] Both Orhan Kotan and Besikci talked about 20th-century Kurdistan as an interstate colony.

In these ways, I was exposed to Marxism. My friends and I were critical of some of the Soviet Union's policies, but thought socialism the best system for Kurdish liberation. As the voice of Kurds became stronger, socialists became increasingly critical of the Kurdish movement, saying it was being used by imperialist countries to undermine and divide Turkey.

Riza was trying to make his own group, and we decided it was safe to meet at my house. At the time, a young political science student called Abdullah Ocalan was hanging around Tuzlu Cayir, attempting to interest people in a new party, and he came to this meeting. Except that he always wore a long leather coat, he did not make a particular impression on me. I more admired the intellectuals, particularly Orhan Kotan, a poet and writer. His poetry was analytical as well as passionate and meaningful, his writings advocating that the Kurds of Turkey form an alliance with Kurds from other parts of Kurdistan to create a democracy. I think Abdullah Ocalan was influenced by Kotan's theories, because initially, PKK formed an alliance with the Kurdish parties in southern Kurdistan.

After the meeting at my house, Abdullah Ocalan disappeared. After a while, there was news that he had formed a group of students and workers, called the UKO or National Liberation Army, and was advocating armed struggle to create a united socialist Kurdistan. I was more interested in researching the theory of our struggle, although I remember being surprised when the UKO announced they were against publishing Kurdish newspapers or magazines in Kurdish and Turkish, claiming these papers were helping the enemy. The magazines and newspapers were published in both languages to educate and include the Turkish people in our struggle, because if the Turkish people do not help the Kurdish in Turkey, the Kurdish people cannot achieve their aims. But Ocalan rejected this idea, choosing to address Kurdish people in one-page declarations. The one I saw was written in Turkish.

UKO supporters began ripping down the posters of other associations and putting up their own. To other organisations, this was hostile and reactionary, but to me the UKO was behaving like any other young Kurdish party that wants to lead the Kurdish movement. I always tried to minimise differences between the groups, and I argued that there should be open communication between Kurdish and socialist groups.

On every corner of every street in Ankara, there were police or army officers. When you went for a walk, they might search you 10 times. At a public bus stop, they would be there with their machine guns to greet you. Despite the danger, a defiant Kurdish consciousness was growing, and in 1975–76 a big concert was organised by a number of progressive Kurdish people in Ankara's sports stadium. Singing Kurdish songs in public was playing with fire, but organisers used the usual tactic of asking permission for a cultural night, then going ahead with the concert before permission was denied. Up to 20,000 people came. When Sivan Perwer started to sing, it was like a magical wave of feeling and people began to scream and cry. Suddenly, thousands of police stormed the stadium and everyone starting leaving. Some police arrested the organising committee, but people helped Sivan Perwer escape. That was the end of the concert. And it was also the end of Sivan Perwer living in Turkey. In 1976, he escaped to Germany.

Around this time, another socialist group formed, KUK. Like Ocalan's UKO, they believed in armed struggle, but unlike UKO they operated more as an organisation without a central charismatic leader like Abdullah Ocalan. Ocalan's UKO went through a number of name changes, and by 1978 started calling itself the Kurdistan Workers' Party (PKK). From that time they gained strength, most obviously because Ocalan promoted himself, his party and his radical ideas simply and aggressively. And, whereas others stayed in Turkish cities, he went to Kurdistan to gain support. Being from a very poor Kurdish village himself, he knew how to reach uneducated people. Otherwise, it is like the rest of life: success being the result of a combination of determination, skills, tactics, and being in the right place at the right time.

From 1978, PKK and a few people in other parties started using the gun, and I heard of instances of fighting between groups and people were killed. I was against such violence, because it contradicts democracy. People should be free to criticise each other ideologically, but at the same time keep the peace and support common goals.

I was not interested in going to university, but after I received a letter from the army, I applied to study science. I studied at the Gazi Institute in Ankara, continuing to live with my family, working from nine am to midday as a foreman in the Road Development Service. I had no time to study music.

The years 1978 and 1979 were very explosive ones for Turkey. Social Democrat, Turkish Nationalist and Islamic coalition was in power. A Social Democrat, Bulent Eçevit, was prime minister, but when it came to Kurdish issues, he was extremely nationalistic, despite the many Kurdish, socialist and progressive members in his party. Even the Turkish Nationalist Party had Kurdish members who had been completely assimilated. Since 1925, it had been illegal to say the word 'Kurd' or speak the Kurdish language. Many did not even know they were Kurdish or would deny it.

In my workplace, there was a struggle between the Social Democrats and the Turkish Nationalists. Both were trying to occupy every workplace. Fortunately my immediate boss, a highly skilled engineer, was a Kurd, and he treated me reasonably well. Then in 1979, the Turkish Nationalists gained more power in the Millet Meclisi (parliament), and when this happens in Turkey, every workplace changes accordingly. More Turkish Nationalists were employed in my workplace. The new engineers were always trying to humiliate Kurdish people, giving Kurdish workers the more difficult work.

The level of violence was escalating in the streets, in the schools, everywhere. Thirty to 40 people were dying every day from fighting and bombs. It was like a civil war between different socialist and nationalist parties, and this gave the government an excuse to get tough on everyone.

The university often had to close, students having to make up time whenever they could. I was going in on a Saturday and Sunday until 11 pm, although I was still active politically. Any time I had, I went to meetings. My parents wanted me to concentrate on study, knowing that what I was doing was dangerous. The police were always harassing me at all the checkpoints between home and work, and university. From my identity papers, they suspected I was a socialist, because of the suburb I came from. If they did not like your appearance, they could bash you. After one particularly long day at university, I was so tired that I went to my sister's to sleep. I woke up to find about 20 policemen around my bed, pointing their machine guns at me. One said, "You are a terrorist," accusing me of planting a bomb. I said, "I didn't do anything," but they took me to a police station for a couple of days, where they bashed and humiliated me. At one stage they asked, "Are you Muslim?" "Yes," so they said, "Then pray." I answered, "I forget how," so they said, "You are an enemy of Turkey. We should kill you."

When the Turkish Nationalists gained a majority in parliament, they terminated all the non-Nationalist workers in my workplace. I lost my job. In December 1979, my father died of a heart attack. Having finished university, I knew the army would send for me, and there was pressure to support my family. Two of my sisters had migrated to Australia in 1970, and were encouraging me to come here. In June 1980, I arrived on a tourist visa. Three months later, on 12 September 1980, there was a military coup in Turkey. Suleyman Demirel, a right-wing Turkish Nationalist, came to power, but looking back, he was more liberal than Eçevit is now.

I was sad to leave my friends, my family, and my familiar environment, especially going so far away. Australia is not like Europe. It was a big step. I lived with my sister, and three weeks after my arrival, I became engaged to a Kurdish girl. We were married six months later, and after five years I was given permanent residency. My qualifications were not recognised, so I worked as a supervisor for ACI, making bottles. Now I work on and off in my brother's restaurant.

I began meeting Kurdish families from all parts of Kurdistan, and became involved in the activities of the Australian Kurdish Association. At the time, Shahin Baker was president, organising cultural events. There were not many Kurdish musicians in Australia, so he encouraged me to play music and to learn Kurdish songs. I wrote to my family and asked them to send my father's 250-year-old *ximza*. I started to perform, and because people liked it, I became more motivated to become a singer and musician. For some years now, nearly every weekend, I perform for Kurdish people, or other people from Kurdistan—Assyrian, Chaldean and Sryani people (Orthodox Christians from Turkey and Syria), and also the Turkish community. If there is a big party, I prepare a band, while for small parties, I perform solo. When singers like Sivan Perwer come from overseas, I play for them, because they cannot afford to bring their usual musicians.

In Australia, I have learned more Kurdish dialects, like Kurmanji and Sorani, and now I can read and write some Kurdish in the Latin script. I love learning all the Kurdish songs, mostly old folk songs which I give new life. One songwriter who has particularly influenced me is Cigerxwin, a famous Kurdish poet, born in 1903 in Dersim. After the uprising he fled to Syria, where he joined Syria's first Kurdish political party, established in 1957. From 1979, he lived in Sweden, until his death in 1984. One of his most popular songs is a Kurdish lullaby:

> Hush little baby, hush hush don't cry,
> They killed your father but freedom won't die...
> Tomorrow you will grow, and become a man,
> And you will have a flag, a free Kurdistan.

Cigerxwin's poetry is always about the beauty and tragedy of Kurdistan and the struggle of its people, always encouraging people to be hopeful. The melodies for many of Cigerxwin's songs were composed by Sivan Perwer, who has become perhaps the most famous Kurdish songwriter, singer and *tambora* player in the world. He is also a political figure, although he has never belonged to a political party, preferring to sing for a united democratic Kurdistan.

Five years ago I began composing my own melodies. Mostly, other songwriters compose the words, people from different ethnic backgrounds with whom I have performed, like Nuri, a Sryanian songwriter, Albert Isaac, an Assyrian songwriter, and Rizgar Khoshnow, an Iraqi Kurdish composer and *oud* player. For the Kurmanji songs I have used the poetry of Shahin Baker and Riza Çolpan, and recently, I brought together some musician friends, and we hired a studio and laid down the tracks, producing a cassette and CD.

Sivan Perwer

For a few years, I kept in contact with my political connections in Ankara, but then I decided I did not want to go on working in the name of a particular ideology. Kurdish politics has brought divisions, whereas Kurds all over the world need to establish a broad, unified base that emphasises all aspects of our culture. I decided to be politically independent so my music could influence all kinds of people. Even so, I keep up with the news. I always listen to SBS Kurdish radio, read Kurdish magazines and the Internet, and talk with Kurdish friends, particularly about what is happening with PKK. I do not agree with all that went on in PKK's armed struggle between 1984 and 1999. Half the Turkish army was moved into Kurdistan, over 4000 Kurdish villages were destroyed, and over two million Kurds were moved to the cities. These people will be quickly assimilated. On this level, the armed struggle could be seen to have failed, but on another level, it has brought world attention to Kurdish issues and has raised the consciousness of Kurdish people in Turkey.

Despite my misgivings about armed struggle, when Abdullah Ocalan was kidnapped in Nairobi and taken back to Turkey in February 1999, it was awful. Mr Ocalan had spent his life defending his people against the Turkish, and when I saw him looking so dishevelled under the Turkish flag, it was humiliating for the Kurdish nation. It made me more motivated to help my people as a musician.

Ocalan's arrest galvanised Kurds and mobilised support as never before. In March 1999 over 150,000 people went to a big concert in Athens to show solidarity between the Greek and Kurdish people. Greek and Kurdish singers sang, including Sivan Perwer.

It is now August 2001. Ocalan has been the only prisoner on the island of Imrali for 32 months. He is kept in a room with a glass ceiling, not knowing whether it is night or day, with little or no access to newspapers or radio, surrounded by masked guards. He has been twice sentenced to death. The Turkish government release his statements, and what saddens me most is the way PKK still see him as a prophet. When he gives orders from his prison cell for PKK to put down their arms and leave Turkey, to make peace with the 'democratic' Republic of Turkey, and not fight the Turkish army under any circumstances, most obey, even though it seems Ocalan has become a tool of the Turkish government.

I am in favour of ending the armed struggle and of PKK changing its strategies, but if PKK is a modern, progressive organisation whose aim is to establish a socialist democracy, then it should have elected another leader or group to decide on future policy and strategy. We do not know what they are doing to Ocalan or who is really giving the orders, and the party has lost focus and direction. The Turkish government is strengthening its position. Under such circumstances I cannot imagine the Turkish government negotiating even limited cultural freedom for Kurds. So I prefer to talk about music.

I have been in Australia for 21 years, and I thank this country for giving me opportunities to improve myself—to learn Kurdish dialects, sing Kurdish songs and become a serious musician. In the future, I would like to record more songs, form a Kurdish music group to travel around Australia and the world, and to continue to learn, to pass on my skills to others. I always encourage Kurdish families to observe and encourage talent in their children. I have taught Kurdish children to play the *tambora*, and have formed children's dancing and chorus groups.

We have to encourage more Kurdish youth to take up music and other art forms, because we are in danger of losing our culture, and also because our culture unites us, whereas politics divides. Music, films and literature are effective ways to spread understanding of Kurdish issues, to awaken the world to what Kurdish people are seeking: recognition of a people, a culture, and a land called Kurdistan. That is why I say Sivan Perwer is more important than Abdullah Ocalan in spreading feeling and understanding for the Kurdish. Through our music, people will come to know that Kurds are like tigers and will never give up until they win their freedom.

A Foot in Australia, Three Souls in Kurdistan

A history of the PKK based on interviews with Ayce Akturk, Hakki Hayri and Ahmed Tigran

Ayce: In 1918, the American President, Woodrow Wilson, voiced his belief that all peoples, including the Kurds, have a right to self-determination. On 10 August 1920, the Ottoman government and members of the League of Nations—namely Britain, France, Italy and Japan—signed the Sevres Treaty, which agreed to a scheme of local autonomy for all people affected by the collapse of the Ottoman Empire. It specifically outlined an Armenian state, and the possibility of a Kurdish state if Kurdish leaders could show that a majority of their people supported the idea and were 'capable' of independence. The Kurdish state was defined as an area east of the Euphrates, south of Armenia, and north of the Syrian and Mespotamian borders, and was to include the Mosul province of future Iraq. That the Kurds did not get a nation-state was largely due to their leaders not matching the ambitions of one man: Mistefa Kemal.

Like Hitler, Mistefa Kemal has some mystery in his background. He was born in 1881 into a lower middle-class family in Thessaloniki, in Greek Macedonia, and may have had Slav or Albanian blood. But he grew up an Ottoman and attended a religious school. When marauding Greek gangs destroyed his father's timber and salt businesses, his father took to drink, dying soon after. Aged 14, young Mistefa began boarding at a military school, where he witnessed numerous incidents reflecting the ethnic violence of the times. After he graduated, in 1899, he joined the Ottoman army, and in 1915 fought at Gallipoli as a lieutenant. From this time the history of Mistefa Kemal was written up as befits a hero.

It was during Britain and France's occupation of the Ottoman Empire following World War One that Kemal rose to prominence. In May 1919, General Kemal was sent to Anatolia to demobilise the Ottoman soldiers in accordance with the Armistice, and to squash unrest, including a small Kurdish uprising in Qocgiri, and scattered conflicts arising between Christians and Muslims. In Anatolia, he attended two congresses of tribal leaders, the majority of whom were Kurds: one in Sivas and the other in Erzurum. It was at these congresses that he realised there was a strong feeling for liberation, and a wish to preserve a degree of autonomy for non-Arab Muslims, although few Kurds had thought of an independent nation-state of Kurdistan.

Moving quickly, Kemal set up a provisional government in Ankara, opposed to the Ottomans in Constantinople, with backing from soldiers and politicians from the 'Young Turks', and tribal leaders. But it was the Constantinople government that went to Sevres in 1920. After Sevres, Kemal lost no time in negotiations with the British and French to form a secular, pro-Western republic to replace the Ottomans. The USA was also keen. To gain the support of Kurds, Kemal promised their leaders autonomy within the republic. In this way, he became the leader of Turkish nationalism, but the theoretician, the ideologue behind him, was a Kurd from Diyarbakir, Ziya Gokalp. In 1924, when it became clear that Kemal had betrayed the Kurdish people, Gokalp committed suicide. Another Kurd who supported Mistefa Kemal was Hasan Hayri of Dersim. After writing in support of the coexistence of Turks and Kurds in a Turkish state for the Lausanne Treaty, Hayri was condemned to death as a Kurdish nationalist. His last words were, "I want my grave to be in a place where Kurds can walk by and spit on me because of my betrayal."

Back in May 1919, the Greek army advanced east, and in August 1922, Kemal led a final, victorious assault. In driving the Greeks out of Turkey, Kemal ensured his hero status. In the same year, he launched a massacre of Armenians. It was not a matter of religion, because Ataturk was to ban Islamic institutions. Rather, the Armenians were killed because they wanted a separate state. Thousands of Kurds were also killed. Despite being responsible for this bloodbath, it was Kemal, not the Ottomans, who attended the Lausanne Treaty on 24 July 1923 and negotiated the borders of modern Turkey.

The Lausanne Treaty made no mention of Kurds or Armenians, the Western powers only too willing to accommodate Kemal in their need for an ally. However, in signing the agreement, Turkey undertook to "protect life and liberty of all its inhabitants, without distinction of birth, nationality, language, race or religion."

From the moment the republic was formed, Kemal went back on all his promises, claiming we were all one Islamic nation. Yet in 1924, he banished the caliphate, and banned Islamic courts and Islamic schools. He became a dictator, killing anyone who questioned him, including some of his most loyal supporters. From then on, the government justified any means.

As a consequence, in 1925 the Kurds launched their first major uprising. Shaykh Seyid Piran, a charismatic Sufi of the Naqshabandi-Dervish order, led the rebellious Zaza tribes between Diyarbakir and Erzurum. The government responded savagely. Shaykh Seyid and 300 leaders were hung, 100,000 people were killed and another 20,000 were buried alive. Whole villages and their crops were destroyed, the livestock taken. Politicians in Ankara immediately introduced anti-Kurdish legislation.

The powerful Sufi orders, and the words 'Kurdish' and 'Kurd', were outlawed. Kurds became known as 'mountain Turks'. The speaking of Kurdish was banned, even in private conversation, as an aggressive, separatist act, although for a few decades, villagers continued to use Kurdish, knowing no other language. Step by step, the introduction of schools replaced the old language, and when a person was overheard speaking Kurdish, they could 'disappear', the authorities denying any involvement.

Also in 1925, the wearing of any non-Western clothes was banned, including traditional Kurdish clothes, but again, Kurdish villagers continued to dress as they had done for thousands of years.

From 1927, millions of Kurds began being deported from Kurdistan, with Turks being moved in. No-one knows the exact figures, because both the perpetrators and the victims suppressed information, many Kurdish parents preferring not to tell their children, to protect them from further persecution.

The next large, well-organised Kurdish uprising was in 1928, around Agri and Mount Ararat. It was led by an ex-military commander, Ihsan Nuri, but by 1930, it was also squashed, the Minister of Justice, Mahmut Esat Bozhurt, saying, "In this country… those who are not Turks only have one right—the right to be servants of the Turks, the right to be slaves."

In 1934, parliament decreed that everyone must assume Turkish names from a list of acceptable names. The parliament gave Mistefa Kemal the title 'Ataturk', meaning 'father of the Turks'. Until then Kurdish people had no surnames. Traditionally, a person was known by their tribal name and their father's name. If my father's name was Ahmed, I would be called 'Ahmed's Ayce'. Sometimes, if one's mother was a strong, well-respected woman, her children would be called after her.

Over time, all village names were changed to Turkish names. My family's town, Dersim, meaning 'silver door', was renamed Tunceli after the uprising of 1936–37 and the 1938 genocide. *Tunceli* means 'bronze hand', signifying that rebels had been conquered and would never rise again.

Hakki: Turkey even used chemicals to squash the Dersim uprising.

Ayce: There were 27 Kurdish uprisings against the Kemalists between 1919 and 1940. Dersim was the last, and afterwards, my grandparents migrated to Istanbul.

Modern Turkey was celebrated as a democracy, but it was not until 1950 that an election was held. In reality, Turkey was founded on an extreme fascist kind of nationalism, like that of the Nazis in Germany.

Hakki: When we draw parallels between Turkey and Nazi Germany, some people say we are exaggerating, but on his 50th birthday, in 1939, Hitler told some Turkish generals, "Ataturk has two great students in this world—Mussolini and me."

Ayce: The Kurdish people were deliberately kept poor and backward. The government limited services to Kurdish villages so that people could not become strong in demanding their rights. There were no jobs or proper roads, electricity, schools or hospitals. People had to travel to school or to a hospital. Often, a sick person died on the way, so people used traditional medicines.

Hakki: The traditional life was for families to travel long distances in the summer to pasture their sheep, paying rent to an *agha* in each place, usually the same ones each year. They might travel 10 kilometres in a day, put up a tent and, depending on conditions, stay one to six days, then move on. Or they might settle for some months, if there were good pastures, returning to their village in autumn.

Ayce: Villages were subsistent, and as there were no factories or businesses in Kurdistan, many sought work in the cities, and were quickly assimilated into the Turkish system.

Ahmed: At school in Dersim, we were made to feel stupid if we did not understand Turkish. As we grew older, everyone spoke Turkish. Armed guards at the high school would check every student's ID. Soldiers and police were on every street. If you travelled 60 kilometres, you would pass five checkpoints, and at each you were interrogated and, possibly, searched. In every way, we were humiliated and made to feel sub-human.

Ayce: With all the persecution, poverty, insults and other inhuman treatment, Kurdish people became subservient. Kurds were called *kuyruklu kurt*, meaning 'Kurd with a tail', or *kiro*, meaning 'uncivilised, uneducated, rude, worthless, one who knows nothing'. Meanwhile, the education system and media indoctrinated people that Turks were the heroes of the world.

Hakki: If you said you were Kurdish, a Turkish person might respond by saying, "We are all Turkish." It was like they were saying, "We're all Australian," but Australia is not based on one ethnic group, and Australians are not forced to deny their origins, or to speak, write and broadcast in only one language.

Ayce: It was illegal to play Kurdish music or celebrate Newroz. Kurdish dances were called Turkish dances. There was no Kurdish radio, no legal Kurdish newspapers or books.

Ahmed: Not hearing your language spoken publicly, never seeing your language written down, and always being told you are crude and uncivilised affects a person's sense of culture and pride in their people, and their self-confidence.

Ayce: Many Kurds began to live in denial of their origins, and would do many things to prove they were good Turks.

Hakki: It was only in the late 1960s and 1970s that illegal Kurdish publications began to be distributed—put out by the socialist parties, or by DDKO, the Revolutionary Cultural Society of the East, a federation of eastern cultural associations formed in 1969. Writers of these underground publications were regularly imprisoned. One was Isma'il Besikci, who had been a soldier in Hakkari in Kurdistan between 1962 and 1964. Besikci decided to do his postgraduate research on Kurdish culture, but because he was a Turk, when he went to Anatolia the people told him lies. He went back to his Kurdish colleagues, who gave him letters of introduction, and he started to be told the truth. After publishing a number of papers, the university sacked him from his research position, and although he was reinstated following an appeal, after the 1971 military coup he was imprisoned. He has been in and out of prison ever since, so far serving between 12 and 20 years.[a] In 1993, of his 29 published books about Kurds and Turkish government policies, 22 were banned. One reason why Kurds do not hate Turks is because of people like Besikci.

Ayce: The government oppresses both Kurds and Turks. We despise the government system and the way it brainwashes everybody.

Hakki: Many people have tried democratic means to change the system. Many were influenced by socialist ideology and have paid with their lives. One famous case is the three Ankara University students who were hung in 1971. Their crime was to belong to a left-wing organisation advocating a socialist revolution. But even among socialists, there were arguments about whether there was a Kurdish identity and language—whether we existed! Any organisation recognising that Kurdish people live in Turkey was shut down.

The only person with any power in the Turkish parliament who arguably tried to do something for the Kurds was Turgut Ozal, although many criticise him for not doing enough. Ozul had a Kurdish grandmother, and while he was president, between 1989 and 1993, he advocated the economic development of eastern Turkey and electricity and telephones were connected to some villages. In 1991, he convinced parliament to let Iraqi Kurds come to Turkey as refugees. Legislation was passed making it legal to speak Kurdish in private conversation, although it remains illegal to broadcast in Kurdish and speak Kurdish, or even mention the word 'Kurd', in court, parliament or government departments. Many Kurdish journalists and MPs continue to be imprisoned for this.

Ayce: Leyla Zana belonged to the Democracy Party (DEP), and when elected to parliament, in 1991, she dressed in the Kurdish colours (red, green and yellow) and took her oath, saying, "I am taking this oath for the friendship of the Kurdish and Turkish people." She and the few MPs who supported her were verbally attacked. Of the 450 MPs in the Turkish parliament, 150 were Kurdish, but most considered themselves Turkish. By 1991, human-rights violations in Turkey had reached unprecedented levels in terms of disappearances, extrajudicial killings, deaths in custody and torture. Leyla Zana went around the country and to the USA and Europe advocating the introduction of universal civil rights in Turkey and an end to the civil war in Kurdistan. In her speeches she would quote the Turkish Human Rights Foundation's figure that 3,134 Kurdish villages had been destroyed since 1984.

Finally on 5 March 1994, after a vote denied parliamentary immunity to her and three colleagues, police came to the parliament and arrested them. They were charged with separatism and were each sentenced to 14.5 years in prison.

Afterwards, DEP was outlawed, to be replaced by HADEP. In 1993, one of Leyla Zana's colleagues, Mehmet Sinjar, was assassinated by the government secret services, as was another HADEP representative, Muhsin Melik, in 1994. Between 1995 and 1996, Amnesty International reported 76 'disappearances', 115 extrajudicial killings and 35 deaths in custody, some victims having been arrested for a minor traffic offence or not having an ID. But these figures are only the tip of the iceberg. In 1996, 200 writers were arrested and imprisoned, many suffering torture. In November 1998, while PKK leader, Abdullah Ocalan, was in Italy, two HADEP members were arrested by police and lynched by a mob. Before the April 1999 general election, many HADEP candidates and members were imprisoned, and government paramilitary organisations continue to attack HADEP members and human-rights activists. Some have fled the country.

Hakki: Between 1991 and 1999, 160 DEP or HADEP members were killed or disappeared. In 1991, Vedat Aydin, president of the Peoples' Labor Party in Diyarbakir, was kidnapped and killed by counterguerillas or secret police disguised as local police. At his funeral, Turkish troops opened fire on 100,000 people, killing more than 10. In 1999, Amnesty International records show that two 19-year-old female prisoners were sexually abused after admitting under torture to being PKK supporters. Anyone who wants democratic changes in Turkey is in danger. Amnesty has documented the arrest, torture and killing of human-rights activists Tacettin Asci and Ahmet Aydin in 1998, and the dismissal of numerous parliamentarians who have spoken up about human rights. In this situation, more and more people came to believe you cannot rely only on democratic change.

Going back to the 1970s, one of Besikci's stories describes a commando unit entering a village, stripping the men, tying a rope to their sexual organs and forcing the women to lead the men around the village. It was an act of total humiliation designed to kill the spirit of the people. People were not retaliating because there was a slave mentality of,

"I can't do anything about this." It was in this climate that the Kurdistan Workers' Party, PKK, was formed.

Ayce: One of the reasons PKK is so different to other Kurdish parties is Ocalan himself. He was born in 1948 of a Kurdish father and a Turkomen mother. They were a poor family living in the village of Omerli, in Urfa province, near the Syrian border. This background is unlike other Kurdish leaders, who come from powerful tribes or *shaykh*'s families. Ocalan is self-made. He grew up a Muslim, but became a Marxist while studying political science at Ankara University. However, from the beginning, he claimed to be more a nationalist. In the 1970s, he set out to organise his own Maoist-based political party, and in 1973–74 formed Apocular, or 'those who follow Apo'. Apo, meaning 'uncle', is Ocalan's nickname.

In 1977, Abdullah Ocalan, Cemil Bavik, Ali Haydar Kaytan and two Turks, Hakki Karer and Kemal Pir, wrote up a program for PKK, then travelled to Kurdish towns like Dersim, Batman, Urfa and Mus to meet representatives and to talk with school students. On 18 May 1977, a secret policeman posing as a revolutionary killed Hakki Karer in an Antep cafe. It brought home to the others Mandela's words, "Your means of struggle is determined by the enemy." After this, Ocalan wrote PKK's manifesto and on 27 November 1978, Ocalan and 24 others held the first PKK meeting, in the village of Fis, near Diyarbakir, capital of northern Kurdistan. All socialists, their intention was to educate students and the poor, to break the traditions that kept Kurds backward, and to create a more open, progressive society. They clearly stated their aim of forming an independent, democratic, socialist Kurdistan, including all parts of Kurdistan. PKK was the first modern Kurdish party to do this.

Hakki: For the first six years, PKK did not have a Liberation Army. The guerillas went to the people to talk about a Kurdish society based on human rights, using Cuba as an example, because they knew that the USSR's socialist system had suffered when 20 million of its best men were killed in World War Two, and from the post-war arms and space races. PKK promised land redistribution, and freedom from the oppressive tribal *aghas* who had collaborated with the Turkish government. Right from the beginning, PKK defended the people against these *aghas*. When an *agha* took people's land or kidnapped a village girl for marriage, PKK would try to negotiate, but when the *agha* did not listen, they were often forced to fight in self-defence.

PKK's first target was Mehmet Bucak, an *agha* of the Bucak tribe, and a conservative 'Justice Party' parliamentary representative for the Siverek district. He had his own small army, which was going around attacking and killing Kurds who were sympathetic to the Kurdish struggle. In 1979 a PKK group paid him a visit in a house in the Hivan district. When they entered the house someone turned off the lights, Bucak put a child in front of him and successfully escaped. His men opened fire and one PKK militant was killed. The Bucak tribe increased its attacks on PKK sympathisers, and PKK were forced to defend themselves. Fighting escalated, and other tribes became involved.

Ayce: In return for PKK's good deeds, village people would feed the guerillas, even if it was only bread, onion and *daw*, a watery yoghurt drink. More and more people in the areas where PKK were active began to listen, but outside these areas, we knew little about them.

Ahmed: Even the villagers who helped PKK did not necessarily think they would win their struggle, but they helped anyway. Other villagers were too scared to help. They knew the government had killed many people in previous uprisings.

Ayce: Concerned about these pockets of activity in 1978 and again in 1979, the government instituted a state of emergency in active PKK areas. In 1979, Ocalan left for Syria, then Lebanon, where he met with Palestinians and began planning how he would educate cadres. On his return to Syria, President Assad allowed him to set up political and miltary training camps just outside Damascus and in the Syrian-controlled Bekka Valley of Lebanon.

With PKK and other pro-democratic activity increasing in Turkey and the people's revolution in Iran taking on a fundamentalist character, USA supported another military coup in Turkey in September 1980, and martial law was declared throughout the country. In Istanbul my family lived where there was a concentration of Kurds. Tanks were in the streets and the gendarmerie were raiding coffee-houses and homes in search of people. If your ID showed you were born in a Kurdish region, you could be arrested, and many of my relatives, friends and neighbours were detained and tortured during this period. The government imprisoned thousands of students, workers and villagers, and about 250 PKK escaped to Syria.

Hakki: In the prisons, 40 to 50 prisoners were housed together in halls called *kogus* in Turkish. People were forced to sing the Turkish national anthem, to pray, and say, "I am a Turk." Prisoners could not even walk into court because they were so skinny.

On 14 July 1982, prisoners in Diyarbakir prison started a hunger strike, protesting against military rule and the conditions in Turkish prisons. After 63 days, four PKK central committee members died of hunger. The hunger strike ended when authorities agreed to some demands, but conditions soon reverted to normal for Turkish prisons.

The PKK tradition of self-immolition also began that year. Mazlum Dogan, a PKK founder and central committee member, was found dead in his isolation cell on Newroz, 21 March. One rumour claims he had burned to death, another that he hung himself. No-one knows what really happened, but he was probably murdered. On 17 May 1982, four PKK militants set themselves on fire to commemorate Dogan's death. When other prisoners moved to put out the flames, the militants cried, "Keep the flame alight. Anyone who stops the fire is a traitor. This is the fire of freedom."

In September 1982, Kemal Pir, one of the Turks who had helped Ocalan start PKK, and M. Hayri Durmus, were found dead in their isolation cells after being on a hunger strike. They were probably murdered.

The four who died in the hunger strike and the four who burnt to death became symbols. It is a sad situation when the only form of protest open to you is to take your own life, but this willingness to self-sacrifice makes a movement strong.

Some militants became legends for the way that they resisted torture. One was PKK leader Mistefa Karasu. He reflected PKK's policy of resistance to the end. PKK were determined to smash the slave mentality. They showed people you could struggle against oppression.

Ayce: Between 1978 and 1982, there were a lot of bombings and much violence in Turkish cities. The incidents were usually blamed on leftist groups and on the ASALA, an Armenian group seeking recognition of the genocides of Armenians in 1895, 1909, 1915 and 1922. In the 1915 genocide, over one million Armenians were killed.

Hakki: With PKK leaders like Dogun, Pir and Durmus dead, PKK realised there was no way they could achieve anything in Turkey without an armed wing. Those present at PKK's third conference, in 1983, voted to declare war on Turkey. The Kurdistan Liberation Army (ARGK) was formed, the armed struggle beginning on 15 August 1984, with attacks on government, police and army headquarters in the towns of Eruh and Shemdinli, Ocalan leading the struggle, politically and strategically, from Syria.

Ayce: From the start PKK established formal military and ideological training for men and women, and female guerilla units commanded by women—never before done by a Kurdish organisation. By 1993, there were 2000 female guerillas out of a force of 10,000 to 12,000. By the late 1990s, the Liberation Army numbered 30,000.

Hakki: In 1985, PKK's military wing, the Kurdistan Liberation Army, separated from the political wing, the Kurdistan National Liberation Front (ERNK). Not everyone who wants Kurdish rights wants the hard life of a guerilla. In the liberation army, guerillas must dedicate their whole life. Unlike *peshmergas* in other parts of Kurdistan, PKK guerrillas are encouraged to have no more contact with their family, and they are not allowed to marry. The rule of no marriage ensures that female guerillas are not in the shadow of men, but also it was a war situation, which requires total dedication. PKK militants had to go wherever the military council sent them. Each cell was constantly on the move, living in hideouts or in the open, not knowing what the next cell was doing. They did not get paid. PKK looked after them, but sometimes they did not eat for three days, and it was never safe for them to return home. Their families would become government targets. Generally, for those who were married before they joined, their wives joined as well. If they had children, some joined PKK, or went to live with other members of their family, or the party looked after them. Some went to be educated in the Bekka Valley base. Others went to Europe. So if a married person did not want to make the sacrifice, they could work for the liberation front, or behind the scenes.

The rules were strict because PKK guerillas were fighting a regime far more brutal than Saddam Hussein's. They could not fight for a few years, then give up in an amnesty, like *peshmergas* in Iraq. The Ba'aths of Iraq at least acknowledge Kurdish identity, and allow the Kurdish language and publications. Saddam Hussein has killed hundreds of thousands, but he has also regularly negotiated with Kurdish leaders.

In response to the increased organisation of PKK, from 1985 the Turkish government approached more and more *aghas*, paying them huge amounts of money to form a village guard, or *korucu* in Turkish, to fight PKK. Most people were forced to join—otherwise, they had to leave their village or their houses were destroyed. PKK guerillas targeted these colloborators, warning them, "Don't take up arms against us."

Hakki: Sometimes, when guerillas entered a village and came under attack by village guards, soldiers or gendarmerie, they had to defend themselves, and civilians were caught in the crossfire.

Abdullah Ocalan always maintained that there should be a code of fighting for a national liberation movement, like the Geneva Convention for international war. But not everything goes to plan. In the early days, people suddenly had the opportunity to carry out personal vendettas, saying they were acting on behalf of PKK. Also, there was a problem of counterguerilla activity within the organisation. One famous case was a PKK commander named Terzi Cemar, who worked for the government from the start. On 15 August 1984 he was meant to have led an attack on a third town, but it never happened. He made excuses. In 1992–93 he committed many crimes during a 15-month period of activity, and in the winter of 1993, when the guerillas went to the mountains and lose all connection with the outside world, he accused guerillas of being spies so they would not trust each other. He killed 20 to 27 of them. One guerilla shouted, "Long live Leader Ocalan," and smashed his own head with a rock to kill himself because he hated being accused of disloyalty. At the time, no-one in his unit questioned Terzi Cemar, because people in Kurdistan think the leader knows best, but at his trial in Syria, he confessed everything, and was executed.

There was always the problem of counterguerilla activity. During the Cold War, secret organisations were formed in different countries with the aim of starting a counterattack in the event of a communist revolution. When communism ceased to be a threat, the organisations dissolved, except in places like Turkey, where the government used them against people in opposition or working for democratic rights.

As well as gathering information, Turkish counterguerillas would commit crimes and blame them on opposition groups. Often, they disguised themselves as PKK guerillas and went to villages to torment and kill people, burning houses, crops and animals, then blaming it on PKK.

The government sometimes used PKK militants who had turned against their people and sought sanctuary from the government. For instance, a PKK militant called Horgir, an aggressive gangster before joining PKK, began working secretly for the government after he joined. He began treating people without respect, causing unnecessary death, then later escaped to Germany, where he was killed as a traitor.

Ayce: In the late 1980s, certain members of PKK began working as spies for the Turkish government. They tried to alienate Ocalan and the guerilla army, intending to form a new PKK. They were unsuccessful, and when it was established that these people had links with the Turkish government, they escaped the country. Ocalan's Turkish wife was among them.

Hakki: There were also PKK militants who acted without orders. In March 1993, PKK declared a unilateral ceasefire while Turgut Ozal tried to convince the parliament to consider a peace process involving different Kurdish groups. Talabani was mediating between Ozal and Ocalan. Ocalan announced that the only conditions for a permanent ceasefire were cultural freedom, the abolition of the village guard, an end to the state of emergency in Kurdistan, and recognition of Kurdish organisations. But Ozal died suddenly, supposedly of a heart attack, on 17 April 1993. A month later, on 24 May, PKK announced the ceasefire would soon end. Without orders, Shemdin Sakik ambushed and killed 33 unarmed soldiers. This caused huge anger in the Turkish community. PKK also saw this as a war crime, and refused to give Sakik any duties for two or three years. In 1998, Sakik deserted, to be caught by Turkish forces in southern Kurdistan.

Another problem was different groups writing articles or collecting money from Kurdish businessmen in the name of PKK.

Ayce: Between 1986 and 1990 the number of guerilla attacks on Turkish military in rural areas, on police stations and on army posts in Kurdish towns and cities increased. In Istanbul we watched television news reports showing close-ups of dead women, children and old people in the eastern villages. Some had been strangled with barbed wire. Some were in mass graves. From these reports we took a negative view about this group the media called Apocular.

Ahmed: Even in Dersim, we were scared of these 'terrorists'.

Many *shaykhs* were also collaborators, making speeches saying that PKK guerillas were terrorists and traitors.

Ayce: The commentary would say, "Those responsible are 'external groups' trying to divide the country," or "They are Armenian Christian." So many Armenians had been killed that they had to develop propaganda against them, and the reports capitalised on anti-Armenian feeling.

Hakki: As time went on, reports named Abdullah Ocalan, claiming he was Armenian. Many Kurds began thinking, "The Turkish government does these things, then accuses others." Later, it became clear, because when PKK completed an operation, they would admit responsibility.

Ayce: In January 1996, 11 village guards were killed in a mini-bus. PKK were blamed, but a human-rights delegation discovered local gendarmeries were responsible.

Hakki: The situation was really mixed up. Some incidencts for which PKK were responsible were blamed on others. One incident involved the deaths of 10 to 12 managers from an iron and steel-making factory employing Kurdish people in Ferokrom. These people had learnt that 180 of them were going to be sacked, to be replaced by Turkish workers who would be paid double the normal salary. In Australia, you might go on strike, but in Turkey, this would be dangerous.

One morning when the workers and managers were travelling to work in two buses PKK guerillas ambushed the buses. The managers were killed, PKK admitted to the action, but newspapers claimed it was the workers who were responsible, because PKK terrorists would have killed indiscriminately.

Ayce: Anyone who befriended the Kurds was silenced one way or another, inside or outside the country. Olive Palmer, a Swedish Social Democrat, invited Ocalan to Sweden, but before Ocalan could visit, Palmer was shot dead in front of a Stockholm cinema on 28 February 1986. Eventually a Swedish man was charged, but released for lack of evidence. No-one has been convicted of the assassination.

Hakki: In the 1990s, PKK's strategies changed. People realised that achieving an independent Kurdistan was going to be a long marathon.

Ayce: The turning point was in 1991. After the fourth congress in December 1990, PKK announced a people's uprising, or Intifada, Serhildan in Kurdish. In all the Kurdish towns, there were demonstrations, strikes, boycotts and shop closures. Even the army could not buy bread! Women played a big role—going and talking to people in towns and villages.

Hakki: This would be unthinkable 20 years ago. In Cizer'e,[b] back in the 1980s, some people were beaten to death because they were caught eating in public during Ramadan. That is how strong Islam is in the area, but at Newroz 1992, an Ezidi Kurdish woman came from Europe to organise a rally in Cizer'e. During the rally, a US-made armoured personnel carrier drove into the crowd, killing up to 150[c] peaceful demonstrators, including this woman. She has become a legend. They still sing songs about her.

Ahmed: In retaliation for these demonstrations the Turkish air-force bombed Kulp and Sirnak, and destroyed 17 villages in the Dersim area.

Hakki: From 1992, Turkey began threatening to cut off Syria's water and electricity supply or go to war if Syrian President Assad did not stop protecting PKK. Under more and more pressure, many PKK went into the no-fly zone of northern Iraq. Turkish forces followed, and since autumn 1993 have been a permanent presence, launching attacks on PKK, KDP and civilians. The world turns a blind eye to this invasion.

Throughout the 1990s Turkish squads under many different names continued to kill Kurdish intellectuals. Where religion was strong, the government used the group called Hezbollah. The Turkish Hezbollah is very different to the left-wing Hezbollah of Lebanon, which has a base in the Bekka Valley near PKK's. The Turkish Hezbollah is a shadowy organisation supported and manipulated by the government. Between 1991 and 1995, it killed over 1000 Kurdish intellectuals. After so many killings, Ocalan decreed that those responsible be killed on sight. From then on, whenever a militant Hezbollah killed a Kurdish intellectual, the people would try to lynch him. The gendarmeries would often save such murderers from the mob, taking them to another city and letting them go. Many began defecting from Hezbollah, to join PKK.

In contrast, PKK's principle is not to harm innocent civilians, but in the early 1990s, a number of operations were carried out in Turkish areas, including a shopping centre and a tourist area in Istanbul, with the intention of making the general population aware that there was a war going on in the east, and to discourage tourists, because the government uses 50 cents of every tourist dollar to build the army and buy weapons.

People were to be given notice before a bomb went off, but once, two tourists were accidentally killed, and on another occasion, people were injured. In one bombing incident, two PKK militants planted a bomb before realising civilian cars were entering the area. As they were trying to stop the cars, they both blew up with the bomb. Nothing goes perfectly, and after these incidents PKK used sound bombs to spread their message.

Ahmed: In Anatalya, guerillas stopped a car, asked the tourists to get out, and burned the car. An Australian tourist was held by PKK in the mountains, but was later released.

Ayce: One incident in Istanbul was blamed on PKK, but Turkish authorities later admitted that a gas main had exploded. I believe most of the incidents were the work of government agents, counterguerillas or other political groups, then were blamed on PKK.

Hakki: In PKK's unilateral ceasefires of 1993, 1995, 1998 and 1999, PKK guerillas no longer initiated attacks but reserved the right to defend themselves. PKK and other Kurdish representatives offered to sit down and engage in peaceful dialogue with the Turkish government, to establish democracy in Turkey, but to this day, the government has refused, saying it will never negotiate with 'terrorists'.

Ayce: Before the 1990s, I knew that we were Kurdish and had a distinct culture and language but I did not have knowledge of Kurdish history. There were no books or magazines. It was only through PKK's struggle that I came to realise what had really happened to our identity. For example, Newroz has always been outlawed in Turkey, but during the 1990s, more and more Kurdish people began publically celebrating it. Then, in about 1995, the Turkish government declared an official Newroz, calling it 'Turkish New Year', saying the celebration came from the days when Turks came from Asia.

In 1994, to be more inclusive, PKK changed its flag from the hammer and sickle to a red five-pointed star in a green circle on a yellow background, and in 1995 went through major restructuring. A presidential council of seven was set up to support Ocalan. A central committee of 29 oversaw different bureaux, with more groups, including religious organisations and others who were not socialist, becoming affiliated with PKK.

Another major innovation was the setting up of a Kurdish Parliament in Exile in Europe in 1995, with intellectual and business support from around the world. It met in The Hague, before moving to Brussels. Its main objective was to diplomatically represent Kurdish issues and human rights to the UN and to governments outside Turkey. It also wanted to attract the support of people from other parties and non-partisans from all over Kurdistan. In the same year, PKK supporters established Med TV, a satellite television station broadcasting across Europe.

Hakki: The more these innovations proved Ocalan was not just a militant, that he had brilliant ideas and was backed by intelligent people, the more desperate the Turkish government became, but the more the Turkish government cracked down, the more popular PKK became. Some people were normal civilians by day and PKK militia by night.

Ahmed: They would raise money, get food and information for the guerillas, and educate the people. I remember one student at my high school debating Kurdish issues with some Turkish socialists. He was the only PKK supporter at our school, but he made us stop and think.

Hakki: People as young as 15 wanted to join. PKK did not want them so young, but there are a lot of emotions and people wanted to do something, especially after friends and relatives were killed. Also, if they did not join PKK, they had two choices: be conscripted into the Turkish army or escape to Europe.

Ayce: Some people have accused PKK of kidnapping young people, but PKK has gone to great lengths to find these youngsters and hand them over to the Red Cross or take them back to their families.

In the 1990s, people in the cities became more sympathetic to PKK. Between 1996 and 1999, the 'Saturday Mothers'—mothers who had lost children in the civil war—would stage a sit-in every Saturday in different places in Istanbul. Often they were harassed, sometimes arrested, but the sit-ins continued.

Hakki: In 1996, they built a new prison in Eskisehi, with single cells, to break the bonds between prisoners of war. Thousands of political prisoners from various left-wing organisations, including PKK, went on hunger strike in protest over the new, harsher conditions. Twelve non-PKK prisoners died from hunger. Another 10 died in Diyarbakir prison on 24 September 1996, when special squads attacked them with nail-studded wooden planks.

Ayce: Despite thousands of journalists, writers, human-rights advocates, teachers and civilians being arrested or killed, PKK stopped retaliating, in defiance of Turkey trying to portray PKK as a terrorist organisation.

Hakki: Alparslan Turkes (a leader of the National Movement Party), who died in the late 1990s, expressed the government's attitude, when he said, "Give me the authority and I will finish the problem within six months," like Hitler's Final Solution. He was not satisfied that between 1984 and 1996, 4000 villages had been destroyed and two to three million people deported or forced to flee Kurdistan. The Turkish government carries out this genocide with the second largest army in NATO, the tanks, helicopters, other armaments and ammunition supplied by the USA, Israel, Russia, Germany, Great Britain, France and Belgium.

Ayse: The Turkish government has accused PKK of getting money to buy arms and to finance the liberation army through drug smuggling and extortion. The truth is that Kurdish people all over the world donate many millions each year for the cause. The Turkish government accuses Greece of selling PKK rockets and missiles, but only PKK know where they came from. One source is from attacking police, army and gendarmarie bases.

Hakki: The Turkish government puts out so much false propaganda about PKK. Back in the 1980s many critics claimed that Ocalan was an ignorant, ruthless dictator who knew only violence. Many Kurdish intellectuals doubted his intentions, but when they met Ocalan, and read about his visions for society, many came to admire him: his charisma, knowledge and the way he was open to new ideas, and by the end of the 1990s, a good many of the 19 million Kurds in Turkey and the 1.6 million in Syria saw Ocalan a prophet, so much so that, in 1996, Franz Schurmann, an American journalist writing for Pacific News Services, called him the new Salahaddin

The more popular and inclusive PKK became at all levels of society and in all parts of Kurdistan, the more it proved itself above feudalism and primitive nationalism, and the more obvious its professionalism, dedication, and ability to adapt became, the more Ocalan and PKK were feared. By the late 1990s, Turkish and Western media were portraying Ocalan as a greater threat to the Middle East than Saddam Hussein.

Not only Turkey and its allies were being forced to reconsider their plans for the area. The new republics of the former Soviet Union to the north-east of Kurdistan have huge oil reserves. Turkey and the USA wanted to build an oil pipeline from Baku (in Azerbaijan) to Ceyhan, a city on the eastern Mediterranean coast, but the Kurdish representatives refused, demanding recognition first. The pipeline has not been built.

In late 1998 some Turkish parliamentarians secretly sent messages to Ocalan, asking for a ceasefire. In response, on 1 September 1998, PKK announced a ceasefire, but Ocalan later decided it was all a conspiracy.

On 9 September, a bomb exploded in an apartment believed to be used by Ocalan. From mid-September, Turkey began threatening war if Syria did not expel Ocalan and PKK. America began naval exercises close to Syria. US air-force planes were already stationed at bases near Iskenderun, Adana and Incirlik. Thousands of Turkish soldiers were moved to the border for military exercises, the Turkish press claiming that 80 per cent of Syria's military and economic base could be destroyed within hours. A regional war would not only destroy PKK but would also change the regime in Syria, to create a more cooperative environment for Israeli and US interests.

At exactly the same time Turkey and the USA were threatening Syria, the USA and other NATO members started threatening Milosovic in Serbi, supposedly because of his persecution of Kosovo Albanians. Also in September, the Taliban in Afghanistan killed several Iranian diplomats, so Iran was preoccupied with its problems, and Barzani and Talabani were in Washington signing an agreement, which involved outlawing PKK activity in Iraqi Kurdistan. The trap was set. At this point, Egypt's President Mubarak stepped in to mediate.

On 9 October, Ocalan escaped to Moscow. Suddenly, Turkish newspapers changed their tune and began talking about peace between Turkey and Syria, and on 20 October Turkish and Syrian officials signed an agreement in which Syria promised to close all PKK bases on its territory.

At first Russia denied Ocalan was in the country but other reports say the Russian parliament voted for Ocalan to stay in Russia. Under pressure from Washington, President Boris Yeltsin ordered Ocalan to leave. With sympathy for him among socialist members of the Italian government, on 12 November he flew to Rome, where he was immediately arrested at the airport.

Ayse: People began saying that Ocalan would be extradited to Germany, where he was wanted for murder, extortion and terrorist acts committed against Turkish-owned businesses and PKK deserters, although these claims are propaganda. He never ordered killings. He has always believed in winning people over.

Hakki: Ocalan was released after 11 days and Turkey and the USA immediately started putting pressure on Italy to extradite him to Turkey. Ocalan announced he was ready to cease the armed struggle and go before an International Tribunal, as long as PKK's actions were considered in the context of Turkish government policies and actions. Turkey refused this offer, demanding that Ocalan be tried in Turkey as the individual responsible for over 30,000 deaths, including those of 4472 civilians. But because Turkey still has capital punishment, the Italian government refused to extradite him.

Ayce: On 16 December a Rome court decided Ocalan was free to leave Italy after Germany withdrew an international arrest warrant charging Ocalan with terrorism. But Kurds were dismayed when no European country was willing to offer Ocalan asylum. Kurdish leaders like Talabani and Barzani can visit different countries whenever they like, and leaders like Kemal Burkay, from the Kurdistan Socialist Party in northern Kurdistan, and Ibrahim Ahmed, from KDP, have been granted asylum in Sweden and Britain, but Ocalan had nowhere to go. In November, to show solidarity and loyalty for Ocalan, people from all over Europe gathered in Rome and Bonn to protest.

Hakki: It was winter and many people camped on the streets. Young Kurds who had grown up in Europe were basically saying, "I want to go to Kurdistan, I want to go to fight." They had such a passion for Kurdistan.

Ayce: Ocalan begged people not to set themselves on fire, but during the following week, more than 55 people burned themselves around the world to show their loyalty and support.

Hakki: Western people cannot understand such absolute faith in one person. They are individualistic but do not trust the individual.

People claimed Italy would split NATO if it refused to expel Ocalan. When the Turkish government started jamming Med TV signals, an Italian member of the European parliament said, "Now I understand why the Kurds have resorted to armed struggle. The aggression they face is incomprehensible."

Ayce: On 16 January Ocalan left Italy for an unknown destination, then on 8 February some Greek officials approached their government requesting Ocalan be given asylum. On 15 February 1999, a car taking Ocalan from the Greek Embassy in Nairobi to the airport was hijacked by Turkish commandoes. Ocalan was flown back to Turkey and shown on television: drugged, tired and confused. The next day Kurds all over the world demonstrated outside Greek embassies. We all felt a terrible sense of betrayal and desperation.

Hakki: Ocalan was completely isolated on the prison-island of Imrali. He was not allowed to see a lawyer for 10 days, and all subsequent interviews were conducted in the presence of masked guards. His lawyers were abused in the streets, their families threatened. They did not get access to all the government files until two weeks before the hearing. On 3 May Ocalan was put on trial for separatism, treason and the murder of 30,000 people. During the trial he was put in a glass box, unable to hear or communicate with his lawyers. On 29 June he was sentenced to death.

Living in isolation for so long is psychological torture. His health is worsening. Despite this treatment, back in mid-1999 Ocalan called for a unilateral ceasefire and for all PKK to leave Turkey. To my knowledge, no ARGK guerilla is accepted as a refugee in a Western country, for 'security reasons'.

Ahmed: Neither is a Liberation Front member or any other member of PKK accepted as a refugee by a Western country. The mantra is they are all terrorists. Yet the same governments are happy to accept Kurdish freedom fighters and political activists from Iraq and Iran.

Hakki: PKK's only place to go was Iraqi Kurdistan, even though since 1993, KDP and sometimes PUK have been attacking PKK. The Iraqi Kurds are angry that the Turkish forces, claiming they are chasing PKK, have committed atrocities and destroyed villages inside the border, but these actions are the Turkish government's responsibility, not PKK's. Both Barzani and Talabani accuse PKK of jeopardising the safety of Iraqi Kurdistan, but they have become slaves to the enemy. They make agreements with Turkey and other governments to fight PKK or to limit PKK activity. Of course, under these circumstances, PKK fights for survival.

Ayce: Since 1992, PKK has carried out education programs and has been very successful in recruiting supporters in Iraqi Kurdistan. Young educated people are attracted to PKK's goal of an independent Kurdistan[d], and its strong progressive ideology that does not depend on individuals. But the stronger PKK becomes, the more the other Kurdish leaders see PKK's organisation and efficiency as a threat to their own power and profit base.

Hakki: In 1999 the parliament in exile was disbanded in favour of a Kurdish National Congress, which aims to act as a representative council, including all the

Kurdish parties, non-partisans and minorities in Kurdistan. Only three parties are not represented, the main one being Barzani's KDP, because of its ties with the Turkish government.

Ahmed: Now Ocalan's stated aim is for a peaceful and democratic republic of Turkey, which is in the interests of both the Turkish and the Kurdish people. Similarly, more and more Turkish people are expressing their wish for peace, negotiations and an improvement in human rights generally. They realise the problems cannot be solved militarily, and also they want to join the European Union. But there are still too many in the military and government who insist that PKK are terrorists and see negotiation as out of the question. These are the ones who claim that the Amnesty International's reports 'lack impartiality'. They pass window dressing legislation to prove they are doing something about human rights, meanwhile stopping any discussion of human rights in Turkey at international forums.

Ayce: Personally, I believe that 40 million Kurds deserve an opportunity for dialogue after all the genocide, war, oppression and pain. One way or another, the Turkish government has to accept the reality—that Kurds form one-third of the Turkish population and will no longer accept living as slaves.

Ahmed: PKK's unilateral ceasefire continues. The problem for the Turkish government is, if there is a peaceful solution, how will it employ all its army and police, who have grown accustomed to power?

Hakki: I always support dialogue, but political processes take time, and it seems war is a necessary part of establishing a power base, as it was in South Africa, Palestine and Northern Ireland. Even when Ghandi passively resisted the British in India, there were decades of bloodshed between Hindus and Muslims, and there has been a lot of death in the pacifist struggles of Tibet and Burma. Everybody loses somebody in a liberation struggle, whatever form it takes.

Whatever happens to Ocalan, he has united us for a period, which was critical in our history. The Turkish government cannot stop the Kurdish struggle now, because PKK has changed the whole dynamic in Turkey and there are many talented people willing to stand up for their principles. Our ultimate aim is for an independent state of Kurdistan but the steps along the way can be debated. Forming a Greater Kurdistan is all about time, what pressure is brought to bear, and if Kurdish people want it. Many people say it is an impossible dream but in World War Two who could have imagined a European Union? If enough people believe in themselves and what they are struggling for, and are willing to work for their beliefs, the rest happens.

ABOUT **Shahin Baker**

Shahin Baker (BA, Dip Ed) was born in 1946 in Mazra, in north-eastern Syria. He studied in Austria and Germany for three years, before arriving in Australia in October 1968. He works in the field of education and as a journalist, broadcaster and writer. His Kurdish works are published under the name of Shahin Bekir Sorekli.

Aunty Zeho

A short story by Shahin Baker

In Kurdistan, it is customary to call all women older than you 'aunty'. I always remember Aunty Zeho. She was the most beautiful woman in our village. Although from a wealthy and well-known family, her husband was rather poor. He owned only a small piece of land, two cows, several sheep and a donkey. When we visited their home, however, I had the impression this was a well-off family, as Aunty Zeho was a woman of quality and taste, always well spoken, well dressed and very generous to her visitors. At the same time she was not as serious as the other women, and in her presence I felt happy and optimistic.

After many years' absence I visited the old village, and Aunty Zeho was one of the first people who came to see me. I felt like a child as soon as I saw her, stood up and walked towards her:

– Aunty Zeho, how glad I am to see you.

– Please sit down, my son. Don't stand up for me.

– If I don't stand up for you, who deserves standing up for?

She blushed, her blue eyes shining, her beauty still apparent.

– How are you, Aunty, how is everyone in the family?

– First tell me how you are. We all missed you so much.

– I missed you too Aunty Zeho. I heard Uncle Oso has left us. May God bless his soul.

– Oso always used to say what a pity you did not return. He had so much admiration for you.

I felt like crying, too ashamed of such attention and respect. In the West, those of us who were born in 'developing countries' often feel reduced to a number, whereas in the villages of Kurdistan, even a stranger is interested in who your father or uncles are and which tribe you belong to.

– And your sons? Where are they?

– They have all gone, disappeared into the cities. Damn the cities. Our villages are half-empty. Do you remember how lively our village used to be? Damn the governments! They only look after their cities. We have seen nothing but hardship from them.

For a moment, I felt I was among the ones she was cursing, for I too had deserted the village, a long time ago, as a young student.

– Oh yes! I remember, and when you were a girl, the village would have been even livelier. I wonder how many young men you turned crazy!

In Kurdish society, only after marriage does the title 'girl' change to 'woman', and Aunty Zeho again turned red in the face, smiling, and at the same time, almost crying. I was tempted to tell her that as a young boy, although she was almost as old as my mother, I too had admired her beauty, but I stopped myself, not sure how the others would take it.

– You are just kidding me. Your mother was prettier than I, God bless her soul. She died so young. She couldn't stand you going away.

– Yes. I always beg her forgiveness but nothing will return her. What can we do? It is fate. But no, Aunty Zeho, my mother admitted you were prettier!

– Did she really? You are just being nice to me, aren't you?

– No, no, I am serious. Everyone knows you were the prettiest. Tell me, why don't you join one of your sons in the city? It would be more comfortable.

– To hell with the city's comfort. The last time I was there, I couldn't stand it more than three days. City life is not for me. They live imprisoned in flats, like birds in cages. One of my daughters-in-law even covers her face when going out in the street. A Kurdish woman covering her face! What is the world coming to? No, no, I would rather spend my last days with my goats and chickens, under a clear Kurdish sky. And besides, they speak another language in the city.

– Yes, but if you were younger, maybe things would be different.

She sighed and said:

– Well, unfortunately, you live your youth only once. Nevertheless, I do not regret anything. I think, despite everything, ours was a better life than that of today's youth. They have deserted our traditions. They just imitate the others. Look at the way they dress. Listen to the way they talk…

– You have a point, aunty, but some would not agree.

The day I left, Aunty Zeho cried.

– I probably won't see you again. May God always be with you.

I could not control my tears. I kissed her on both cheeks, unable to say a word.

An Apple Does Not Fall Far from the Tree

A life story based on interviews with Ruken Heval[a]

I was born in Izmit, south-east of Istanbul, on the Mamara Sea, and grew up in Istanbul. I have never been to Kurdistan. My parents and grandparents used to talk about their life there, mainly choosing to remember the good times, but whenever my grandmother talked about Kemal Ataturk and the Dersim uprising or *katliyam*, Turkish for 'the killings', I could feel the anger inside her.

My father told us about his grandfather, who was a very tall, strong man. He knew Arabic letters, and had such a serious authoritarian manner that people feared him. Before the Dersim uprising, he talked to the Turkish soldiers when they entered the Kurdish village of Kigi[b], trying to make peace with them. When they realised he was trying to help his people, they decided to execute him, but people built a wall in a house and hid him between the walls. He died in 1948.

My father's family were farmers from Kigi, which belongs to the town of Bingol. My grandparents and uncles owned land, grew wheat and vegetables and raised sheep, chickens and cows. They made their own flour, bread, yoghurt, butter and cheese, but in the early 1960s, my father's father emigrated from Bingol to Izmit, looking for work. He found a job in the shipping yards, checking ships' cargoes.

Back in Kigi, my father's family continued to farm. They spoke Kurmanji so when my father went to primary school he could not speak Turkish. He was also expected to work on the farm, and he did not like school. He told us many stories of his childhood years, and I loved hearing them. I would say, "Oh, let's go there," and he would say wistfully, "Not now. Next year, next year."

When he was 10, he went to join his father in Izmit. He started school there, but asked his teacher, "Please certify that I have finished school. I have to work." The teacher gave him the certificate, so he worked from when he was 10 years old, to help support his mother, three brothers and two sisters back in the village. For a year he worked in restaurants, then he went to live with his sister in Istanbul, working with his brother-in-law in a plastics-moulding business. After three years, he and his father had enough money to bring the family to Izmit. He was 14 by then, and began working in the shipyard with his father. Over time, he taught himself to read and write.

Eventually, they bought a house near Izmit with a large garden. Their house had a big living room with a wood heater, three bedrooms and a small hall. It also had a toilet, not a toilet for sitting on, but a hole, with a place to put your feet on either side. There was a bathroom, but no bath or shower, just a wood heater for the water. We would sit on a wooden stool, pour hot water into a big metal dish and wash with a jug. My grandmother handwashed the clothes.

My mother's family also came from a village near Bingol. Hubek was near the town of Harsek. (These are the Kurdish names for the villages. I do not know their Turkish names.) During World War One, when my mother's grandma was about eight or 10 years old, she was separated from her family and a Turkish soldier found her and took her back to Istanbul. She grew up with him, and he looked after her like a father. When she was 15, she met my grandfather, her future husband, in Istanbul and he took her back to his village, Tari, where they were married. Afterwards they moved to Elazig. She could speak really good Turkish, having grown up in Istanbul. My grandma eventually made contact with her two sisters and although their family owned land, when all the daughters got married and went to different cities, there was nobody to look after the land. No-one knows what happened to it.

When I was growing up, my mother's grandma still lived in Kurdistan, but she would come and stay for three months at my grandparent's house in Izmit, so I knew her. Her character was stronger than a man's! Everybody loved and respected her and came to her with their problems, because she was old and had so much life experience. In the old culture, we respect all old people and love the young, but she was special: she was as soft as she was strong. She died in 1993, when she was nearly 90. My family prayed for three days, and every year, on the anniversary of her death, we pray in her memory.

It seems that those Kurds who do not die through illness, accident or war live a long life, probably because they have a natural lifestyle and eat healthy food. My cousin's grandfather, who is more than 110, is tall and strong, and still works on the farm.

My mother's father also came to Izmit in the 1960s, looking for work, and got a job with the railway. When my mother was five, the family joined him, but she would visit her home in Hubek. She has clear memories of how they used to dry slices of salted uncooked lamb's meat in the sun and make *pestil* from grape juice. They would press the grapes, then heat the juice until it became very thick. They would spread out some thin white material on the flat earth roof of the house, sprinkle it with flour, then pour on the grape syrup in a thin layer, sprinkle it with more flour, and let it dry in the sun. The *pestil* is sweet, hard and chewy. Our relatives in Kurdistan would send it in a food parcel with dried pears and apples. I have never tasted fruit so fresh and beautiful. Even the smell was delicious. They would also send *curtan*, a white, hard rock made from dried yoghurt used in cooking. I loved to gnaw at it.

My mother's family lived a big, one-storey brick house, with a tiled sloping roof, on 1000 square metres of land, which grew every kind of fruit. It was in the street next to my father's family's house, so my parents' families were neighbours and became best friends. All their children grew up together.

When my mother finished Year Five, the last year of primary school, she wanted to go to Istanbul and study nursing, but my grandpa refused. Her older sister had married at the age of 16 and went to Erzincan, in Kurdistan, then to a village near Dersim with her husband, a school teacher. Instead of becoming a nurse, my mother went and lived with them for two years, to help her sister look after the baby. After that, they all moved back to Izmit.

My grandpa was very strict with his daughters. My mother could never go out visiting, unless she was in the company of her sisters, and never at night. She could never have a boyfriend. She told me, "I was in love with somebody who was studying to be a doctor, but he moved to Bursa." She could never disobey her father, but her younger sister was like a boy, very strong, and would defy her father. She told her parents that if they did not let her marry the boy she loved she would leave home.

My father was six years older than my mother. He liked one girl and my 14-year-old mum used to deliver their letters to each other, but the girl's parents arranged for her to marry someone else. After two or three years, my father, who was working in Istanbul, and coming to Izmit on weekends, walked up to my mother one day, while she was washing dishes in the garden, and, without warning, gave her a ring. Their parents agreed to the marriage. Although my father's family were Alevi, and did not go to a mosque and pray, and my mother's family were Hanafi—Sunni Muslims—her family were not strict Muslims. In my parents' day, religious differences were not as significant as they are now.

It was a modern wedding. My mother wore a white dress and the two families came together for a party. Afterwards they lived with my father's parents, for economic reasons. I was born in the first year of their marriage, in 1971. A year later we moved to Istanbul, to my aunt's three-storey house. She lived upstairs, her brother-in-law lived downstairs, and we had the ground floor.

Two years later, my parents moved to another suburb in Istanbul, on the European side, and my father continued working with his brother-in-law's plastic-moulding business. We still had little furniture and no fridge, and when my brother was born in 1973, my father went to his brother-in-law to borrow money to buy a fridge, so the baby's milk would no longer go sour.

After my other brother was born, in 1976, my father opened his own plastic-moulding and injection business with a friend, and when I was seven years old, we moved to Uskudar, a suburb on the Asian side of Istanbul. Our apartment was much more spacious and new, taking up one floor of a five-storey building. We had two living rooms, three bedrooms, a modern bathroom and a kitchen, and we ate around a big, high table, unlike the low tables at my grandparents' houses.

In our family, my brothers were treated no differently to me. As the oldest, I was called *abla*, while my youngest brother called his older brother *abi*, terms of respect.

I started school in a building that had been converted from a hospital built by the Ottomans. It was coeducational, and every Wednesday we paid money to see a movie screened in the assembly hall: films like *Tarkan and Bizan's Imperatur* showing how the great Turkish heroes killed many people and won every war throughout history. They made us say, "The Turkish are brave and always victorious." From age six or seven, children were exposed to this. It was the same in the classroom, where they taught us songs about the Ottoman Empire and the great Ataturk.

Neither of my grandmothers could read or write. When I was in Year Three, the Turkish government opened literacy courses for older people, and my grandmothers attended. They would say to me, "Oh, I'm going to beat you!" but they found it difficult.

My father's mother is still illiterate. She came to Australia in her old age. Her family was *de'de*, and when I came to Australia, in 1995, I shared a room with her for six months. I would be woken in the middle of the night by her praying to the 12 imams, counting them and saying their names, especially Ali's. Over time I got used to it, and have come to admire her greatly. She never gives up. She is over 80, but you can never tell her, "You can't do that." She lives with my uncle and his two sons, his wife and another uncle. My uncle's wife works, so my grandma gets up at seven in the morning, makes everybody's bed, washes everybody's clothes and cleans the house. She tends her vegetable garden, prepares the evening meal, brings in the washing, does the ironing, puts the clothes away, sets the table and serves dinner for six people. When she goes to the doctor, he says, "You are in perfect health," except she is a little deaf and wears a hearing aid. It means she hears what she wants to hear! She is like a friend. We can joke together. She has had many difficult times in her life, but she is still standing. After someone dies, she cries and cries, then says, "Okay. This is life. What can we do?" She rebuilds herself.

Growing up in Istanbul, none of my friends knew I was Kurdish, and when I was young, I did not understand the difference. I always spoke Turkish. When we visited my grandparents, they and my parents spoke Kurdish and I would understand very little. My mother often used the odd Kurdish word, and I remember when I was five or six, sitting on my father's knee, with him saying, 'This is *boz,*" pointing to his nose, and "This is *jow,*" pointing to his eye. He would add, "But don't say these words outside the house." When I grew up a bit, I asked, "Why can't we talk Kurdish outside?" My father explained, "Because it will cause a problem for you. They don't like Kurdish people."As I grew older, when my parents spoke Kurdish, especially about us, I would get upset and say, "I know you are speaking Kurdish because you don't want me to understand, but I know you are saying this and that." I learnt by listening, and could guess the rest.

My grandmothers did not wear traditional Kurdish clothes. They knitted big jumpers and sewed long floral dresses and embroidered and crocheted their scarves with beads. They would tie the ends of their white scarf so their neck and hair showed—not like strict Muslims. My mother and I wore Western clothes. The only time I saw Kurdish clothes was when they showed folkloric dance groups on television. They were always called Turkish dance groups, but as each city had its own characteristic dances, they would say, "This is a group from Diyarbakir or Urfa," and then we would know they were Kurdish.

Nor did we practise any religion. I knew we were Alevi, but not what it meant. All my father told us was, "You have to respect people. You must never tell a lie. You must always be honest. Never steal. Be good to everyone." After we grew up, he said, "Your religion is on the inside. It is in your mind, and it is between you and God—it is not between you and other people."

One day in September 1980, my father came home from work early. Someone had painted a red 'X'—the fascists' mark—on the door of his factory, marking him as a Kurd or a democrat. This scared him. It was the day of the military coup, and after that, no-one was allowed on the street after midnight.

Around the same time I remember my mother and her friends becoming very upset after watching a current-affairs program about a girl who was killed because she had shamed her family. I asked my mum, "How could it happen?" and she said, "In that part of Kurdistan, it is tradition. They think the girl has to marry who they want, not who she wants." I was shocked.

I knew nothing of what was happening in Kurdistan until about 1982 and 1983, when I became aware of media reports of terrorists killing 'people in the east'. We did not know who the terrorists were, but my father would become upset.

About this time, a photo of my mother's sister's fiancé, a leftist school teacher, was pasted up by police around Istanbul and Izmit, with the question, "Do you know the whereabouts of this man?" The police knew where he lived, but wanted to shame him. Eventually he was imprisoned for five years. While my aunt waited for him to be released, she would visit and teach us leftist songs containing dangerous words like 'democracy' and 'freedom'. We could not say these words openly or people would think we were political and against the Turkish government!

At high school, I started learning German, but the teacher taught us German by asking questions and giving answers about Ataturk. When was he born? What battles did he fight in? What did he do for modern Turkey? We were taught that modern Turkey owed everything to Ataturk—he reformed the Turkish language, our clothes, and the status of women. It was he who gave women the right to vote. In fact, Ataturk reformed the whole society. I was so sick of hearing about Ataturk in history and Turkish language classes that I discontinued German.

Some teachers were very hard. They hit students on their face or pulled their hair for talking in class, wearing jewellery or nail polish, if their uniform was too short, or if someone was not wearing a tie, so later, when I came to Australia, I could not believe the freedom in the classroom. In Turkey, the school principal and many teachers belonged to the Nationalist Party, which was very fascist. I was 17 when I was in my final year, but some members of the school's fascist group were 24-year-old men. The principal allowed them to remain at school to recruit others into their group, which they called Ulku Ocagi. These recruits had to follow orders, which included harassing students they did not like, and I have heard that later they became something like the mafia.

In the late 1980s I first heard the word 'PKK', on a political program on television. I was surprised. There was an interview with Abdullah Ocalan. He was very sick and the interview did not show him in a favourable light. Newspapers started mentioning that PKK was responsible for the terrorist acts in the east, and for the killing of soldiers and civilians. A relative began buying an underground Kurdish newspaper from Europe called *Ozgur Politika*. Some newsagents would sell it secretly to people they could trust. My parents were sympathetic to PKK, and could not believe PKK was killing innocent people. My father would say, "Ocalan is protecting his people, not killing them." Their views came from what they were told by relatives still living in the villages. PKK female guerillas would come to my aunt's mother-in-law's home to cook bread. They would give her some and take the rest for the guerillas. She would kill chickens for them, and when she became sick, these female guerillas looked after her.

I remember my father saying, "It does not matter whether we are Alevi, Hanafi or Sharfi—we are all Kurdish. Your nation is yourself, your nature, and if you deny that, then you forget who you are. You deny yourself." He did not hate the Turkish, but he hated the people who divided Kurdish and Turkish. I never denied my Kurdishness—I just never talked about it.

The media and many people in Istanbul, including my friends, started complaining about how the influx of ignorant people from eastern villages was overcrowding the cities. All my friends were Turkish, so I never talked about why the people were fleeing from the army. I never openly gave my opinion. Even talking is suppressed in Turkey. I felt like I was living in a cage.

My father gave me freedom. I was allowed to go out with a group of girls and boys, as long as my parents knew them. We would visit each other's homes, and go to the movies, or to cafes to hear Turkish singers and musicians. Only a few places, like discos and big clubs, played Western music.

My father was also protective. He wanted me to go to a university in Istanbul so he paid for me to do a two-year private course in travel at Istanbul University. I felt I did not belong. Most of the students were living in a dream world. All their conversation was about clothes, what they would do on the weekend, and how much money they had spent on what. I was living a double life. There was me out in society, acting as a Turkish girl should act, and there was the other me—a Kurdish Alevi girl.

I was 20 when I had my first boyfriend. We met when we were on holidays at the Black Sea, where his family owned a big house and land, but like us, they lived in Istanbul. We started going out to cafes together, only in the daytime. I was not allowed out at night. My mother knew of this but my father did not. When the boy asked, "Where are you from?" I told him directly, "I'm from Bingol, I am Kurdish." He asked me my religion and I told him, "Our religion is Alevi." He was Sunni, and said, "Do you know what is Alevi?" I said, "I don't care about religion!" He said, "You don't care!" I thought everything was fine, until one day he told me, "We have to separate. I am going to be married." I asked, "What are you talking about?" He was the only boy in the family and his parents had arranged his marriage to a girl he had never met. After that, we saw each other once at a friend's place, then no more. Friends told me that his parents had wanted to separate us because I am Kurdish. It really, really hurt me.

It was towards the end my second year at university that I began wanting to know more about my Kurdish identity. I saw a television program showing the first day of the new parliament. It was 1991, and I watched Leyla Zana swear her oath in parliament, saying Turks and Kurds are brothers. I was shocked. She was so strong and brave, beautiful and proud, and I thought, "After this, maybe they will kill her." It was terrible when she was sent to prison, three years later.

After seeing Leyla Zana on television, I started attending a Kurdish cultural group with some Kurdish friends. We would sing Kurdish songs and have exhibitions of Kurdish handicrafts and paintings. There was no political discussion, but still we had to be careful. After 1991, speaking Kurdish in private conversation was no longer illegal, and Kurdish music was meant to be legal too, but it remained dangerous to talk and sing in Kurdish, even in a private group, and Kurdish singers could not perform in public.

The law had changed on paper only. The police could make up anything. I was made aware of this by a boy I met while I was working in the bar of a hotel, after I graduated. He said he came from Tunceli. I asked, "Why don't you say Dersim?" He did not answer. I said, "You must be Kurdish." He hesitated before agreeing, "Yes." I said, "You must be Alevi." He was silent. I reassured him, "Don't worry. I am Alevi Kurdish too." He then told me how the police had pulled him up and asked for his ID. When they saw he came from Dersim, they took him into the police station and held him for three days, beating him badly. I knew this could happen to me at any time. Although I had never been to Kurdistan, my ID said I came from Bingol.

My father was having business troubles. The Turkish want to do business only with other Turks, and it was becoming increasingly obvious that Turkey was being ruled by the mafia, the military and the USA, so my family decided we should leave in any way possible. In 1995, I came alone to Australia to study an English course. I stayed with relatives, and applied for refugee status on the basis that I was a Kurd from Turkey. I was accepted, and my family came out a few months later on visitors' visas, also applying to stay as refugees.

In Australia, for the first time in my life I was free to simply say without fear, "I am Kurdish." For the first time, I felt human. It was wonderful to see Kurds come together, to be able to form associations, and to speak, write and sing in Kurdish. My two brothers began dancing in a Kurdish dance group. They wore costumes with the PKK flag—a yellow five-pointed star in a green circle on a red background—on their chest. We sent photos of them back to our aunt in Istanbul. In 1995, a Kurdish satellite TV station had started in Europe, and my aunt's husband had bought a satellite dish so he could watch Kurdish programs. From the angle of his dish, the police knew that he must have been picking up Med TV, so they came to his apartment and told him to turn his dish around. When they saw my brother's photos, they arrested him.

In Australia, my brothers study at a technical college and run their own business. I studied childcare, then accounting, working weekends at a take-away food shop. My father does not work, because of his health and the language problem. He allows me to go out with my brothers and a group of friends, and my parents will let me choose whom I marry, though they would like me to marry a Kurd. My mother has adjusted well to the new life. She is a strong woman, and is always caring for people, even if she does not know them. For instance, I had a Turkish friend with three little daughters. They could not decide where to live so they would spend three years in Australia, then go back to Turkey for a year. My friend wrote to me from Turkey saying her daughter's hair had fallen out. The doctor told her it was because her daughter was psychologically disturbed. I advised her that she must settle and she asked if I could find her a flat in seven days. I asked my parents if she could stay with us and they said, "Of course, why are you asking?"

My mother looked after the children while my friend went looking for a house, and when they found a flat my mum said, "You can stay here, you don't have to move."

We are building our lives in Australia, but always we follow what is happening in Turkey. When Ocalan escaped to Italy at the end of 1998, my father went to Italy. Sometimes he dreams about Ocalan. He loves Ocalan for the same reasons I do. Ocalan has let the world know who my people are, and how they are struggling for their rights in an unfair world based on power and money. Other Kurdish leaders think locally, but Ocalan speaks of freedom for all Kurds.

When they captured him in Nairobi and took him back to Turkey, in February 1999, we were shocked. I could not believe it. My dream that Ocalan was going to build a free, independent Kurdistan turned into a nightmare. In July 1999, Ocalan announced a unilateral ceasefire, but the Turkish government continues to arrest people just for speaking about human rights. Ocalan has twice been sentenced to death, and has spent over two years in isolation on Imrali, but I will continue to support him as PKK leader, as long as he lives. After 16 years of armed struggle, his message is, "Peace is better for Turks and Kurds." Now, PKK is waiting. All Kurds from Turkey are waiting for the day the government will release Ocalan, as the South African government released Mandela. One day, I will visit Kurdistan. I will touch the earth of Kurdistan and breathe the fresh air and walk under Kurdistan's bright sun.

Justice in the Kurdish Principality of Botan

A fable retold by Eziz Bawermend

The prince of Botan was known not only for his courage and administrative skills but also for his keen sense of justice. It is said that one day, three Persian traders entered his principality. Just outside the city, they were ambushed and robbed, losing their mules and the loads they were carrying. They explained their dilemma to an innkeeper, asking his advice. The innkeeper reassured them, "No-one is wronged in Botan. The prince of Botan holds court every Friday. Go and tell him what has happened and he will solve your dilemma."

The following day, the three traders went to the court and explained their plight. Unfortunately, the interpreter wrongly informed the prince that they were questioning his authority and telling lies about him. The prince responded, "Perhaps they are hungry and thirsty. Give them some money, and they will be more reasonable after they eat and drink."

The traders returned to the inn and explained that they had been given a small amount of money and told to go away. The innkeeper was astonished, and pleaded with them to remain as his guests and return to the court. After some hesitation, they agreed. The prince was surprised to see them again and, after hearing their account, via the same interpreter, ordered that they be given some more money.

The traders returned to the inn and recounted their experience. More astonished than before, the innkeeper begged them to go back a third time, and so they did. The prince became suspicious, ordered that the interpreter be held in isolation, and requested two other interpreters to tell him what the traders had to say. Thus the truth was revealed.

The prince ordered that the traders' possessions be immediately located and returned to them. When all was done to the traders' satisfaction, the prince asked when they were planning to leave, and they indicated the following day. He requested that one leave via the eastern gate, one via the western gate and one via the northern gate, suggesting they could easily meet at the first spring outside the city and share with each other what they had seen.

The trader who left via the eastern gate saw that the prince's son had been hanged during the night for his crime of stealing from the traders. The one who left through the western gate saw that the accomplice to the Prince's son had been hanged. The trader who left via the northern gate saw that the first interpreter who had also been an accomplice had also been hung.

In the Shadow of Aslan

A life story based on interviews with Saad Barazi

By far the greatest Kurd in world history is Sultan Yusef Salahaddin Al-Ayyubi, born in Tikrit, in Iraq, in 1138. His family was of the Rowundi tribe, from the mountainous Balakian region. They moved south to Tikrit, then west to Damascus, where his uncle was a military leader to the sultan in Syria. Coming from a family famous for being good fighters, Salahaddin grew up to join the military aristocracy of the Umayyad Empire.

On the death of his uncle, history tells us, Salahaddin reorganised the Arab armies, employing Mamluk mercenaries from Turkey, as well as many Kurds. Arab commentators talk about the strange language he used to converse in with his commanders. Due to his military prowess, the Sultan of the Shi'ite Fatimids in Egypt asked him to come to Cairo, and in 1175 he established the Ayyubiad Empire over Egypt in the name of Islam, through diplomacy, the sword and some good fortune. He then took over Syria, before fighting the Crusaders with a cavalry of 12,000, defeating Richard the Lionheart in 1187, thus liberating Jerusalem from the Christians.

History also tells us that the way the Crusaders treated the Arabs, Jews and local Christians when they invaded Palestine could in no way be compared with the way Salahaddin treated his foes. The Crusade armies slaughtered everyone, including women and children, whereas Salahaddin was known not to have killed anyone not fighting on the battlefield. He was very pious, fair and honourable to both his people and his enemies, in peace and in war. According to Islam, conquered non-Muslims must pay taxes, but Salahaddin did not do this. It was done by the Umayyad dynasty based in Damascus, whose empire spread from Spain to Central Asia, and it was done in the Abbasid dynasty, but it was not done in Salahaddin's days.

During the years they fought each other, I am not sure that Salahaddin ever met Richard the Lionheart. Salahaddin was a *tabeeb*, or doctor, and there is a story that when Richard suffered a high fever in Jerusalem, Salahaddin sent him fresh fruits and clean iced waters from the Mount of Harmoun, as well as a *tabeeb* to treat him. Whether this doctor was Salahaddin in disguise, no-one knows, but after Richard was cured he said of Salahaddin, "A man of this spirit will never be defeated."

There were many other famous Kurds in history. The Medes, considered the ancestors of the Kurds, ruled an extensive empire between 723 and 550 BC, at which time Cyrus the Great of Persia overthrew his grandfather, the last Mede king, Astyages. However, the Medes were around much earlier than this. Some claim the beautiful Nefertiti, mother-in-law of Tutankamen and favoured wife of Akhenaten, the Egyptian pharoah who introduced monotheism into Egypt in the 1300s BC, was a Mede. It is recorded that Mede princesses also married into the royal families of the Phoenicians, Hittites and

Persians. When Alexander the Great took over the Persian Empire from Darius II, whose mother was Mede, he married Darius's daughter and they produced a son. Unfortunately, when Alexander died, both his wife and son were killed.

Three hundred years ago, a Kurd by the name of Karim Khan-e-Zand became Shah of Persia. However, his Kurdish successor was toppled by a northern alliance that included a Kurdish prince, after which the Qajars took over Persia until 1925.

Many Kurds speak Arabic, a few having become renowned poets and intellectuals in the Arab world. One Kurdish poet Ahmed Shawqi, who lived in Egypt and died about 60 or 70 years ago, has been called the prince of Arab poets.

Since 1923, a number of Kurds have achieved prominent positions in the army and parliaments of the day. Some have become prime ministers and presidents. In Turkey, there were at least two prime ministers and one president of Kurdish ancestry, and likewise in Iraq, and under the Pahlavi Dynasty in Iran. In Syria, two of the Barazi family—my first cousins—became prime ministers: Dr Mohsen Al-Barazi and Husni Al-Barazi. Another first cousin, Adeeb Shishakly, son of my father's sister, was a president.

Dr Mohsen Al-Barazi was educated in Syria and France. Following France granting Syria independence, in 1945, he was appointed Minister of Education and Minister of the Interior, but after the coup of 1948, led by Husni Al-Za'eem, also a Kurd, but with a military background, Mohsen was imprisoned. Later, Al-Za'eem pardoned him and made him prime minister. Having secured his power, Al-Za'eem probably needed Mohsen's experience.

Al-Za'eem was a strange man, prone to unpredictable behaviour and wild emotional outbursts. He was a dictator, but he tried to do some good for Syria. He forced rich people to pay certain amounts of money according to what he believed they could afford—nothing as regular as a tax. Everybody thought he was taking the money for himself, but in fact he was buying arms for the Syrian army—tanks, ammunition, and so on—to make Syria strong in the event of threats from Turkey or Iraq. Also, Israel had just been established, in 1948, and he probably could see into the future. Unfortunately, he made the army so strong that it thereafter became politically involved and democracy could not take a foothold.

The people did not understand Al-Za'eem's strategies, so after only eight or nine months, there was another military coup led by Sami Hennawi. Al-Za'eem was killed in his presidential palace, and my cousin Mohsen was taken from his home, imprisoned for a few days, then executed. I was only eight years old at the time, but had Mohsen had enough time, he might have restored democracy.

Mohsen was a right-wing democrat, as was my other cousin, Husni Al-Barazi, who was prime minister between 1944 and 1946–before and after Syria was granted independence. Neither cousin had a military background. They were both highly educated, Husni in Syria as well as in Istanbul, and both were staunchly antisocialist, but they were not particularly close—more like family rivals competing for the top job.

Before he became prime minister, as an elected parliamentarian Husni Al-Barazi had worked for Syrian independence, so the French exiled him in the early 1940s, during which time he stayed in Turkey and Lebanon. However, when independence was being negotiated, President Hashem Atassi invited him to return and become prime minister. In Syria, the people vote for a regional representative in parliament, the parliament votes for the president, and the president nominates his prime minister. In 1946, there was a democratic change of government, and Husni lost his position, because he was considered too pro-Western.

It was during the 1940s that a small group of people calling themselves the Arab Ba'ath Movement, one of their chief spokesmen being Michel Alfaq, a school teacher from Syria, started talking about pan-Arabism and violent revolution, opposing all Western influences.

In 1948, after the coup led by Al-Za'eem, my cousin Husni Al-Barazi was made Governor of the Aleppo region. Very much against Al-Za'eem's military government, he was imprisoned and, after a few months, sentenced to death, but was saved when Sami Hennawi toppled Al-Za'eem the same year. Sami Hennawi's government lasted eight months. It was thrown out by yet another military coup, with another coup following in 1952.

His political career finished, Husni Al-Barazi established a newspaper in Damascus called *Annass,* Arabic for *The People*. In every article, he wrote against the military regime of the day, always quoting a line from the famous Abbasid poet, Al-Mutanabbi, meaning 'the one who claims prophecy'. Husni Al-Barazi was also against the Ba'aths and the communists. In the 1950s, the Ba'aths joined with the Socialist Arab Party, led by Akram Horan, to form the Socialist Arab Ba'ath Party, and Husni did not fit into any of these new trends. Instead, he supported the pro-English Baghdad Pact of 1955, between Britain, Turkey, Iraq, Iran and Pakistan. He was given information that he was going to be arrested, so he escaped to Turkey and then to Lebanon, where he lived in exile for the rest of his life.

In the late 1960s, when I was in my late twenties, I would often visit him. I was stranded in Lebanon without a passport, unable to return to Syria in case they would not let me leave again, and Husni was instrumental in my successful application to migrate to Australia. He was in his late seventies, he and his wife living a quiet life on income from his properties in Syria. I found him a very witty, well-read and well-spoken man, interested in Middle Eastern and world affairs, and from time to time, he would talk of how Kurds have a just cause in their struggle for an independent Kurdistan, but I do not know whether he actively supported this cause in his younger days.

His wife, a very strong, dignified lady, for whom he would stand up every time she entered or left the room, was from another old family—the Kailani family, which has deep roots in Syria, Saudi, Iraq, Palestine, Jordan and Egypt.

The 1952 coup in Syria was led by another cousin, Adeeb Shishakly, Chief Commander of the Syrian army. When he came to power, he appointed Fowzi Sello, a fellow Kurd, as president, and stayed on as army commander, but after a short time, he removed Sello and became president himself.

In those days, many political parties were trying to manipulate events to gain power, so Shishakly passed laws to impose law and order. A few political leaders were put in prison, but were then released, and no-one was executed during Shishakly's rule. This was quite remarkable for the times. All males were armed so he made a law that no-one was to bear arms in public places, even a pocketknife, and this law was enforced with spot searches in the street, or anywhere.

He continued to build up the army, because he wanted good security. He supported Arab ties, but not to the extent of Nasser and other pan-Arabists. He was essentially pro-Syrian and tried to develop a strong economy, based on trade in agricultural products like grain and cotton. He established the Damascus International Fair which is still an annual event, but in 1954, his army chief told him, "We must bomb the areas that are against us." Shishakly refused, saying, "I will not allow one drop of Syrian blood to be shed just so that I can stay in power." He was advised, "Go to Lebanon until we fix things up, then come back." But that never happened. From Lebanon, he went to Brazil, where he established a little farm and led a quiet life. In 1965, a Syrian man, whose faction is debatable, went to Brazil and asked to see him. Shishakly, excited at having such a visitor after so many years, came to greet the Syrian, and was hugging the man when he was shot at point-blank range.

After Shishakly, the socialists moved in and turmoil started all over again, with many active political parties fighting in the streets. By 1958, there was strong support for Jamal Abdul Nasser and his pan-Arab socialist ideology, and the Syrian President Shukri Qu'watly went to Cairo and agreed to unite with Egypt in a United Arab Republic.

But Jamal Abdul Nasser of Egypt did not understand the Syrian people. Syrian officials who were allied with Nasser were well treated, but others were not, so in 1961, after two and a half years, the Syrians split from Egypt. But it was during the time of the United Arab Republic that the first of a series of land reforms was to greatly change my family's fortunes.

Originally, my family came from the Syrian part of Kurdistan, near the Turkish border. We were one of the biggest tribes in the region, well established in towns and villages like Arab Bounar and Ain Al-Arab, owning many properties and herds of animals. Under Ottoman rule, the Al-Barazis fought as officers and soldiers in the Ottoman armies in Egypt and the Sudan. In return for his services in Syria, the Ottoman sultan rewarded one of my great-grandfathers the title of *agha* and a choice of property. He chose land in the region around Hama, in the south, 220 kilometres north of Damascus, so in the first years of this century, my family split, one part moving south to take care of the newly acquired properties and also to have political influence in Damascus.

The heads of the Barazi tribe in the north had three titles, *agha*, *beg* and prince, and two of them—Bozan Beg and Shaheen Shaheen Al-Barazi—represented the Kurdish region in the Syrian parliament of the 1950s. The few in the family who achieved an education were backed by wealth, property and numbers, so it was they who became prominent in politics, working for Syria's independence, representing the regions around Ain Al-Arab (in the north) and Hama (in the south).

My father was not one of those to benefit from an education. His father had died when he was two, so he was raised by his brother, Husni's father, some 40 years his senior. However, whereas Husni received a good education, my father could barely read or write. Nor did he receive his rightful inheritance. At the age of 16, he was sent to sell a crop from land he knew was his, so he kept the gold. On his return to Hama, Husni's father asked for the money, but my father replied, "It is rightfully mine. You are not having it." Husni's father kicked him out, so my father returned to the property and took control. Husni's father sent a man to chase him away. My father shot the man dead, so from the age of 16 until he was 51 years old, my father was on the run from the Ottoman government. He changed his name from Aslan Al-Barazi, *aslan* being Turkish for 'lion', to Abdul Karim, and was constantly moving between Hama, the Turkish border and the north of Lebanon to avoid capture or death. His wives had to visit him in secret.

There are many stories from that time, although my father was usually unwilling to tell them. The authorities were to capture him three times. Once, before the soldiers took him on a train heading for Istanbul, his aunt gave him some *kebbah*. She had marked some in which she had cooked hashish, and he gave these to the soldiers guarding him. He was handcuffed to a Bedouin but he managed to unlock his handcuff with the key to his shaving box, and jump out of the train while the guards slept. He travelled by night, carrying a leather waterbag. One time he ran out of water so he decided to urinate into the bag and wait for it to cool, but the leather absorbed the urine. He was in the mountains and he looked up and watched a bird, flying overhead, come to land. He went over and found water.

Another time he was being dragged by rope on foot behind soldiers riding horses. He always travelled with companions, some of whom were wanted dead or alive, and at the time of this capture he instructed one, Abdul, to ride behind the soldiers some distance. Abdul Rajab had come to live on one of my father's properties and it was he who told me this story. My father told the soldiers, "I am tired from walking. Why don't you rent the horse from that man behind us?" The soldiers agreed but Abdul Rajab refused saying, "No-one rides my horse." Following extensive negotiations Abdul Rajab said, "As long as I stay on my horse the prisoner can ride behind me." The soldiers did not realise the horse was a first class thoroughbred who could easily outrun their horses.

When Aslan and Abdul arrived back to one of Aslan's properties they found all the livestock had been killed, the *falaheen* or peasant farmers had been kicked out and the buildings destroyed. They were told the son of the next door neighbour, Refa'at Beg, had been responsible. Aslan and Abdul went to pay this son of Refa'at Beg a visit. They found the army of Refa'at Beg and his son celebrating. When the sentenial on the roof announced their arrival the men got their rifles and started shooting. Abdul Rajab described it this way, "We got off our horses and started walking up the steps under a shower of bullets. Aslan put his arm to his brow and turned to me saying, 'There's too many bullets, don't you think?' and just kept walking. Men with big moustaches were wetting themselves. Aslan came to the son of Refa'at Beg and said, 'I am not going to kill you but I will leave you crippled for the rest of your life as a lesson to anyone who wishes to touch Aslan's property.' He shot him in both knees."

Eventually, the French agreed to pardon Aslan if he handed over his guns and sword and promised not to break the law again. He gave his promise, handed over his guns, but told them he did not have a sword. So after 35 years of avoiding the authorities, my father was able to settle into the life of *agha* and landowner, after which, if asked of those days on the run he would reply, "What's done is done. It is finished."

Hama is a lovely, old city built on the banks of the Al-Asi River, known for its Roman waterwheels. To this day, you can see the irrigation canals built by the Romans. The land around Hama is fertile and green when it rains, but arid in the long, dry summer. Around the river, the farmers irrigate the land, maintaining crops of vegetables and cotton, whereas on the open plains, they grow mainly grain, relying on rain and bore water. My father had 11 properties in the Hama region at the time of the first land reform in 1960, some along the river and some on the plains.

But settled life found my father once again in trouble with the law, when a man was shot dead at a gathering of family and friends. Because of his record, the police accused Aslan Al-Barazi of the shooting. The case was assigned to a public prosecutor from the Arab family of Khateeb. My father knew the prosecutor, and approached him, saying, "Take the side of justice." The prosecutor decided my father was innocent. After two or three years, it was found another Barazi had done the shooting. The prosecutor died, leaving a daughter whom my father decided he would like to marry. He already had two wives, but they were uneducated. He sent some representatives to the daughter's brother, the Governor of Damascus, asking for the woman's hand in marriage, and the governor agreed.

My mother was my father's seventh wife. He was father to nearly 50 children, of whom 15 lived. In Islam, a man can marry four wives. If one dies, he can marry another, or if he divorces, he can marry another, and that is the way it happened. When I was growing up, he had three wives.

My mother was the odd one out in her family. The Khateebs were a family of lawyers and doctors. Her two sisters were highly educated, my mother was the only one who was not. She could read but not write. In her late twenties, she had married Prince Khalid of Algeria, after France exiled the Algerian royal family and they had come to live in Syria. They loved each other very much, and she had a son by him, Prince Nizar. However, Prince Khaled's family put pressure on him to divorce her and marry his wealthy cousin, Princess Zahra. They divorced, but afterwards Prince Khaled decided he loved my mother too much, so they remarried. With more pressure, this time from Princess Zahra, he divorced my mother a second time, but his marriage to Princess Zahra was unhappy and they had no children.

After her second divorce, my mother lived with her family, having been forced to leave her five-year-old son with her husband's family. This broke her heart—she never really recovered from it—but when Prince Nizar turned 16 and was more independent, he started visiting her and they became very close. He was a good son to her, as kind as his father. My mother always loved Prince Khaled, saying, "I hope to meet him in the next world."

If a woman came from a well-established family, she had no trouble finding a second husband after she divorced. If anything, she was more desired, because she had more life experience. My father knew her family and respected them. So while in her forties, my mother had two more children—my older brother and myself.

Each of my father's wives had their own home. One lived on one of the properties, and she would visit my mother from time to time. The other one lived in Hama, next door to us, with an internal door between the two houses. This door would be locked by my father's second wife when she was jealous or angry. My father would have to go around the outside! Otherwise, all the children would freely come and go between the houses, and when my mother ran out of milk for me, my father took me to his second wife, a Jarkas whose family came from the Chechnya-Daghistan area, to nurse me. Later, if I had an argument with my mother, she would say, "Of course I know where you get your nastiness from! You sucked her milk." The other wife's jealousy and the hardness of my father often upset her, but I was close to both women.

To his wives, my father was fair, as he understood the word. It was up to him where he spent the night, and he was the absolute and undisputed boss in all three households. No-one could do anything without his permission. Only one wife dared stand up to him, and he might swear and throw his wooden shoe at her as he left the room, but my mother was totally obedient. She would greet him by kissing his hand, and she never addressed him by name—she used his inherited title, *agha*. Yet they would sit and talk. My mother was a good conversationalist, and very humorous. She had travelled to Saudi, Lebanon and Turkey, so although she was uneducated, she was intelligent and had some worldly experience. When she was young, she had played the *oud* and sung on family occasions and sometimes she would sing or hum to him.

But there was a lot of sadness and jealousy when one wife felt less favoured with his time, attention or gifts, and there were many disagreements, especially over perceived difference in opportunities given to the children. My father usually ignored the problems, as long as they did not affect the children. In the Middle East, ties are through the father, so as far as he was concerned, everything belonged to the children, not the women. It was his way of drawing the line.

Having said that, even though our father gave all his sons equal opportunity, only three of his 10 sons graduated from university, two of them being my full brother and me. To be fair, my father gave his uneducated sons twice as much property as his educated sons, but still there was rivalry, mainly over property, even between children of the same mother.

In regard to his children, I know Alsan loved us more than we loved him. Not in my case—because I loved him dearly—but some of my brothers were unkind to him. It was a matter of greed, and as adults, there were a few confrontations over land and crop distribution. Once we were all shouting and the troublemaker pulled his gun so I pulled my gun and my other brother pulled his. My father slowly and deliberately put his hand on his gun and said quietly, "If you don't stop this, you all know, I will."

I called him *yabo* or *yubo*, always greeting him by kissing his right hand and placing it on my forehead, although as a sign of affection sometimes he would gently slap my hand so I would not kiss his. *Yabo* had lived a very hard life and was a hard man—hard on himself and his family. He was never cruel, but he brought us up to be tough. He expected us to get up early, and learn to shoot, swim, and ride a horse, saying, "You cannot be a Barazi without being a horseman." On the 110 properties in our family, we had 750 Arab thoroughbreds. From when I was six, I remember riding all day with him, going from one property to the next. If one of us lagged behind, he would come back and break a green twig to whip both rider and horse. If we had to go without food all day, so be it.

He taught us, "If it's your life or another's, make sure you take his, but never start trouble." Once he saw a friend and me killing a line of ants. He became angry, saying, "Don't kill unless you have to." No-one questioned his love. He was patient, and would let us jump all over him even when he was trying to sleep. If a child was sick, he would not sleep. He would put money in our pillow case and when we got better this money would be given to the poor. It was his way of praying to God to make us well.

Being born in Hama, of an Arab mother and growing up among Arabs, we always spoke Arabic. My father could not speak Kurdish, and neither can I. We did not practise any Kurdish customs. My father never talked about being Kurdish, but he was sympathetic to the few Kurds who lived around Hama, and they would always come to him to sort out any disputes.

I attended a local Arab school, but at the age of eight, I, along with my four older brothers, left Hama to attend a Christian American boarding school in Tripoli, returning to Hama for the three-month summer holidays. To this day, despite the war, Lebanon has the highest standard of education in the Middle East, and Tripoli is a lovely city on the sea. I remember those days fondly. The students were mainly Arabs from Jordan, Syria, Lebanon and Palestine, with a few American students, and the teachers were mainly Arab, speaking Arabic and English. Some had studied only in the Middle East, while others had postgraduate degrees from the USA.

After completing school in 1959, I returned to Syria and applied to study hotel management in the USA—there was no such course in the Middle East at that time. But the Syrian government refused my application to leave the country, because it was the time of the United Arab Republic, and Nasser had a rule that to go to the USA, a student must have a Syrian Baccalaureate, so I went to Aleppo College for a year, then transferred to the American University in Cairo. I studied political science and economics, with dreams of a career in politics.

I had a great time. Six of us became very close friends—some Muslim, some Coptic Christian, two from Syria. We studied together, went on picnics to the Red Sea, and partied, going to nightclubs and restaurants. Many an evening was spent at the Hilton, and upstairs at the Belvedere Nightclub, at Joha and Ali Baba, and at nice restaurants like Khamis (in Fouad Street, now known as 23 July Street). Some of us were better off. I was supported by my father, and employed a maid full time, although in the last years, I was the poorest of them, after the Syrian government took our lands.

I had only one encounter with the Egyptian authorities. During the exams, we used to leave our apartments and live in a boarding house, where bedding and meals were provided so that we could concentrate on studying. One time, my friend shared a room with an Egyptian diplomat, who had been brought back from Ethiopia and put under house arrest at the boarding house. The diplomat stole my flatmate's passport and ran away to Jordan to seek political asylum. In the subsequent investigation of whether the passport was stolen or had been sold, my name came up. When they asked my flatmate, "If you are so poor, where do you get your money?" he replied, "I live with Saad Barazi, who pays my expenses and gives me food." I was asked to go to the Ministry of the Interior three or four times, where I was interviewed for a few hours, mainly in regard to my friend. It was worrying, because we had heard many stories of how badly people were treated by the authorities, but I was quickly cleared.

It was in Cairo that being a Kurd started to matter to me. By 1961, there was a lot of news about Mulla Mustafah Barzani fighting the Iraqi regime in the mountains and in subsequent years I was to read about his life. The Barzanis had been a leading tribe in the area, next to the Barazis, for 1200 years, but when Mustafah was only 18 months old, he was put in prison with his mother for nine months. Between 1905 and 1908, the Ottomans hung his grandfather and his eldest brother, while his father, a Sufi of the Naqshabandi sect, was killed by religious fanatics. His older brother Ahmed was appointed the Barzani tribe's religious leader, Mustafah becoming their military leader. He had no formal military training, but became famous for his tactics: speed, endurance, deception and dispersion.

After fighting with the tribes of the Qadri sect in 1934, he was exiled by the Iraqi government to Sulaimani, but in 1943 Barzani returned to the mountains and gathered a *peshmerga* force of about 4000 to 5000 men. Armed with British Lee Enfields (from police desertions), Soviet Kalashnikovs, Stens, Mausers and Bazookas, they managed to outwit an Iraqi army of 30,000 soldiers and 12,000 police backed by the Royal Air Force. They became famous for 12-hour marches at night, climbing sheer cliffs and expert marksmanship. But defections of tribal allies brought sudden defeat, so Mustafah Barzani led 35,000 men, women and children to Mahabad, in Iran, where in 1946 he became one of four generals in the Kurdish Republic.

When the leaders of Mahabad surrendered, after 11 months, Barzani asked the USA to give his people asylum. When this was refused, the women and children were allowed to return to their villages in Iraqi Kurdistan. His brother Ahmed returned too, to be imprisoned for 11 years. Meanwhile, Mustafah took 500 followers on a 52-day march into Turkey and back through Iraq and Iran, being attacked all the way. For 11 years, he lived in exile in Azerbaijan.

Of Abdul Karim Qassem, Barzani is quoted as saying, "If that man farted every time he lied, he would sound like a machine gun." The Kurdish Democratic Party had formed in 1946, electing Barzani as chairman, but it was an uneasy alliance, of intellectuals and uneducated tribal leaders. Whereas Barzani spoke in riddles, folktales and legends, intellectuals like Ibrahim Ahmed and young leftist Jalal Talabani were more intent on introducing democracy.

Once Qassem showed he was all talk and no action, the younger *peshmerga* were eager to go to war, but Mustafah Barzani was reluctant, saying their enemy was too powerful, that political strategies were necessary. However, in September 1961, Barzani was pulled into fighting over an incident involving KDP, tribal leaders and the army near Darbandi Khan. Iraqi MIGs and other planes began bombing villages, including Barzan. Barzani was forced to declare war on Qassem's government, and his *peshmerga* did well.

After the 1963 ceasefire, and a verbal promise of Kurdish autonomy, on several occasions Jalal Talabani was sent to Baghdad as Barzani's representative to negotiate, and twice Talabani came to Cairo and had talks with Nasser, who verbally recognised the Kurds' right to self-determination. But over the months, the new Ba'ath rulers, who were also in negotiations with President Nasser and Syria, became increasingly evasive.

Government forces amassed in Kurdish areas, blockaded roads, implemented curfews and deported 150,000 Kurds from Kirkuk. Massive arrests took place in Kurdish cities.

War between the Kurds and the Iraqi forces resumed, and this pattern of 'double-talk' negotiations and war was to repeat itself with the governments of Aref, Al-Bakr and Saddam Hussein.

Barzani's aim was not to separate from Iraq. He fought for peace, security and autonomy. He ate, slept and marched with his men. He never put himself above what he was—a tough, intuitive fighter who believed in goodwill among men—but he also knew that strength and self-interest controlled the relationships between tribes and nations. In his view, Arabs were the brothers of Kurds; their governments were the enemy.

To me, he was a true hero. He was the first to truly awaken a Kurdish consciousness. From him, the Kurdish struggle gained such momentum that it no longer relies on one person. This was proved when he died of a broken heart in America in 1979. The struggle continued.

It was during my time in Cairo that I also heard a little of what was happening to the Kurds back in Syria. The Ba'aths in Syria were moving Kurds from their villages near the Turkish border to establish an Arab Protection Belt, as a security measure against Turkey.

Otherwise, I was having such a good time in Cairo that I was not keen to finish university. When I was given the choice of either graduating or being kicked out, I graduated, and returned to Syria in 1965, to discover that the political situation had not improved. Ba'aths had taken over in 1963, and I quickly realised I had no hope of entering politics.

Personally, I do not like any form of socialism where the government ends up owning and controlling everything. I certainly did not like the way the Ba'aths and other socialists organised power for themselves, all the time leading the country into financial chaos. After two more land reforms, there was still no more equity or income benefit for Syria. Land reform was meant to confiscate the properties of the rich landlords and divide them among the *falaheen*. Instead, the government took from the 'haves' and gave nothing to the 'have-nots', an elite group running the government becoming the 'haves'.

In my case, I ended up owning less than 10 per cent of the property left in my name, yet 40 years later, only 10 per cent of the confiscated land has been redistributed to farmers. Seyid Mor'ee, the Egyptian Minister of Land Reform in Nasser's days, wrote an article many years after the collapse of the United Arab Republic. In it, he described how he had been sent to Syria to investigate applying land reform in Syria as it had been done in Egypt. He came back to President Nasser, saying, "It will not work." This was because the situation in Syria was very different to that in Egypt. In Syria, there were two types of farming—one that relied on irrigation, like cotton, and one that did not. The law was that if the landlord had no irrigation systems in place, the *falaheen* would get three-quarters of the crop and the landlord would get one-quarter. If the landlord was irrigating the land, with all the expense of earthworks, pumps and diesel, then the landlord would get half and the *falaheen* would get half. But President Nasser's answer was, "We cannot have land reform in Egypt and not in Syria. It is one country." In his article, Seyid Mor'ee wrote, "The Land Reform Law in Syria was an act of revenge." It was not in the interests of the country. When the government took over the land, they did not maintain the irrigation systems, so farming became less productive. The farmers were forced into the cities to look for work. Agriculture in Syria deteriorated to such an extent that whereas Syria used to be the grain basket of the entire Roman Empire, it ended up having to import wheat.

With subsequent land reforms, my family's property kept dwindling. It was a great upheaval. You go to bed secure, wealthy and well established and wake up the next morning owning nothing. It affected people differently. Some people had heart attacks and died, but my father was a strong man, and probably the blessing of it all was that he was uneducated and did not understand the political and legal ramifications. When the government took more and more of his property, he wanted to acquire new properties. We had to explain to him that it could not be done. In the last 18 months of his life, he was bedridden. They had to sell his collection of rifles and pistols and other possessions just to buy him medicine. And so he died in 1965, at the age of 79, a poor man, still not understanding or accepting what was happening around him.

My mother lived another 21 years. She was 93 when she died. My family's declining fortune did not affect her so much, because she had always maintained a simple life, and when we became our own bread-winners, we looked after her. And as life would have it, after my father's death, my mother and my father's second wife became best friends, my 'aunt' begging my mother's forgiveness for the way she had treated her in the past, my mother replying, "I forgave you a long time ago."

In the year of my father's death, I reapplied to study hotel management in the USA. My application to leave Syria was repeatedly rejected, because my brother was having a dispute with the Ministry of Land Reform and I was involved as co-owner of the land in dispute, but I finally got my travel documents.

That same year I met my first cousin from Turkey and was asked if I would marry her. I agreed, and when I was in the USA, I assigned someone to sign the marriage contract on my behalf. I thought I was doing the right thing, and we had a son, but the marriage lasted only two and a half years. There was no understanding.

In 1965–66 I finally attained my first dream, that of studying hotel management in Washington DC. To finance myself I worked in big hotel chains like the Mariott, Hilton and Holiday Inn. I was 25 years old and it was the first time I had had to support myself, so it was quite a different life from the carefree days in Cairo, but I adapted well.

When I came back to the Middle East, I took jobs with catering companies in Abu Dhabi, in the United Arab Emirates, then returned to Lebanon. I did not want to go back to Syria. My family was having difficulties, and I feared the Syrian Government would not let me leave, so I applied to migrate to Australia. After 13 months of interviews, medical check-ups and filling in forms, the Australian Embassy rejected my application. I was in trouble: my passport had expired and all doors seemed to be closing. This was when I went to Husni Al-Barazi for help. During his time as prime minister, he had formed a good relationship with an Australian, Lord Casey, who was Minister of State in Middle Eastern Affairs for the Churchill Government in Britain. He was later to become Governor General of Australia, but in 1968, he was chairman of the CSIRO, and he managed to get the decision reversed.

I arrived in Melbourne in October 1969 and found Australian people to be quite welcoming if I made the first move. I took different jobs—lecturing at the William Angliss Hotel Management School, then opening a restaurant for a new franchise in Australia. When the partnership broke up, I worked as a catering consultant for Golden Fleece Petroleum until 1975. I returned to Lebanon to establish a restaurant business, but when war started, I came back and rejoined Golden Fleece until 1978, when I moved to Perth. There I married Ruth, an Australian I had met in Melbourne some years before.

When I decided to go and work in Saudi Arabia, I prepared Ruth for the worst: we would live in a compound and she would not be allowed to drive; there would be no movies, nightclubs or restaurants. Initially the adjustment was difficult for both of us. The housing facilities were terrible. There was no telephone, and no driver, so Ruth was stuck at home all day with no way of contacting me. Sometimes the generator would fail and there would be no air-conditioning in the 55-degree heat. I wanted to return to Australia, but Ruth insisted we stick it out. After a year, my job improved: we were given more luxurious accommodation, Ruth became more mobile, with a driver and houseboy at her disposal, and we were able to travel on holidays to Europe, the USA and Egypt.

Ruth became friendly with an Arab neighbour who had been to the USA with her husband and could speak English. The lady took Ruth to local tea parties, where she would listen to the Arab women criticising their husbands! But when her friend's husband found out that Ruth was Christian, he forbade his wife to associate with her. Otherwise, we made friends with foreigners living in the compound.

Although Ruth is naturally a conservatively dressed woman, in Saudi society all women are required to cover their hair in public. Ruth refused to comply, so on one occasion was confronted by religious police. If they had wanted to follow the letter of the law, she would have been taken to the police station. I would have been called and made to sign an undertaking that it would never happen again. If it did, I would be imprisoned, because as her husband, I was letting it happen. I should have more control over my wife! Fortunately, they let Ruth go. Later she would cover her hair occasionally, but not as a rule.

After eight years in Saudi, Ruth was feeling homesick. Our daughter was growing up and Saudi schools were not what we wanted for her, so Ruth and our daughter came back and lived in Tasmania for seven years, then moved to Sydney. For 10 of those years, I worked in Saudi. Initially, they used to come and visit me, but Saudi is not the ideal place to spend a holiday. I decided they should stay in Australia, and I would visit two or three times a year.

To have such a long-distance marriage was not hard for me, because in Saudi, I had a housemaid and all the facilities I needed. It was more difficult for them. If something happened, I was far away. If one of them was sick, I could not sleep the night, and although Ruth is an independent woman, who kept busy with our daughter and a small business, I know she felt alone at times. We were not building up a lot of shared experiences and our phone bills were huge, but we coped.

In Saudi, I worked for a multinational company that manufactured Kleenex, Kotex and Colgate-Palmolive products, and imported food from the USA, Switzerland, Great Britain and France. We supplied wholesalers and supermarkets, and I ran the Jedda region—up to the Jordanian border and south as far as Yemen. I had a budget of about $80 million a year with 220 employees. I was very happy until I started having disagreements with top management.

I had a lot of contact with local Saudis, because I speak the language and because some of them were well acquainted with my family's lengthy association with the House of Saud. I would be invited on fishing trips and weddings attended only by the men. Coming from a Muslim background, I understood the rules of segregation and the reasons for it. By no means does it degrade the woman. Women have their own life, their own parties and activities. The Qur'an protects women's rights and regards women highly, saying, "Heaven is under the feet of mothers."

Back in 1970, Syrian President Hafez Al-Assad, a moderate Ba'ath, had succeeded in a bloodless coup. When he died in 2000, he was the longest-reigning president in the Middle East. He did a lot for Syria: built roads, schools, hospitals and the army, and developed the economy, but democracy remained an issue, and in February 1982, while I was in Saudi, I heard news of the massacre in Hama. My mother was 85 years old. The army surrounded the city, so no detailed information could get out, but we heard that many thousands were killed over a few weeks. I could not contact my mother to find out if she was safe. Later, I heard how soldiers came into her home and went through all the stores, spilling the flour and sugar, saying they were looking for guns. She asked, "Do I look like a person who stores guns?"

I was also in Saudi when Iraq invaded Kuwait in August 1990. The mood was very tense. Everyone was concerned, especially regarding the rumours that Saddam Hussein intended to take over Saudi as well, so when the US and Allied forces came in January 1991, they were most welcome, despite the most unusual scenes, like American women driving trucks! Inspired by such sights, 20 educated Saudi women from well-established families decided to drive down a main street in Riyadh. They were promptly put under house arrest. Their passports were confiscated, they were never allowed to work again, and no doubt their fathers or husbands were given stern warnings.

Back in 1980, when Saddam Hussein attacked Iran, I was sympathetic with him. He had been forced to relinquish to the Shah of Iran sovereignty over the Shatt Al-Arab in 1975, when the Shah was so powerful he could demand anything. To my mind, Saddam was reclaiming what was rightfully Iraq's. However, the 1988 Al-Anfal operations against the Kurds showed his true colours and the invasion of Kuwait proved him a mere puppet for Western interests.

At the time, the price of petrol had just taken a dive, and Saddam owed Kuwait huge amounts of money for Kuwait's support of Iraq in the Iraq–Iran War. For this and other reasons, I do not believe the invasion of Kuwait came as a surprise to Western powers.

The cost of Operation Desert Storm to Saudi, Kuwait and other Gulf States is estimated to be US$180 to $280 billion and growing (with interest). This will take years to pay off, robbing these countries of any chance to build the necessary infrastructure to make them stable. The war was also a good arena to test new weapons and to establish US military bases all over the Gulf. The ones who are left to pay are the ordinary people of the Gulf States, Saudi Arabia and Iraq, most of all the Iraqi people.

I was based in Jedda, so I was far away from the war, but cousins from Riyadh came to stay with us, to escape the Scud missiles. The missiles were also reaching Al-Khobar and Dhahran. In these cities, the television screen would suddenly go completely red, the sirens would start, and then there would be an announcement on television and over street loudspeakers that there was an air attack. People would be frantic.

We would watch the television pictures of the US Patriot missiles hunting out the Scuds in the skies. The Patriots were still being tested, and the Scuds were hopelessly inaccurate, so sometimes the Patriots would career off in another direction, or the missiles would fall welded together. Only sometimes did the Patriot succeed in exploding the Scud in mid-air. The Scuds usually missed their target, but two of the worst incidencts occurred when one exploded in front of the officers' club in Riyadh and another hit the marines' mess in Dhahran. About 300 marines were killed.

As a Kurd, I wondered why Saddam's chemical bombing of Halabja back in 1988 was made such a feature during Operation Desert Storm when so little attention was paid to it at the time. Why didn't the Americans and Arabs punish Saddam, or stop him from producing weapons of mass destruction, back then? Everybody knew about Halabja—you could see it in *Time* magazine, in *Newsweek*: pictures of dead babies under their mother's body, an estimated 8000 people dying in the street and in their homes.

It took only six weeks for the scales of war to turn against Iraq. The Allies quickly moved into Kuwait. On television, we saw pictures of Kuwaiti oil fields burning. Everybody was predicting it would take up to 10 years to put out the flames, but it took less than a year. At the time, Kuwait City was in permanent night from the burning oil, and the natural habitats of birds and other animals, and human resources from the sea, were badly damaged. Otherwise there was a lot of censorship of the news. In the last CNN interview with General Schwarzkopf, the Commander of the Allied forces, and Prince Khalid, Commander in Chief of the Arab army, Prince Khalid would go to answer a question and General Schwarzkopf would interrupt saying, "No comment." I only heard later that 30,000 retreating Iraqi soldiers were buried alive by Allied troops. When the news broke out, the Pentagon's comment was, "It was unavoidable. Who said war is sweet?" The Saudis did not like seeing Iraqi people being killed on the highway to Basra, but Allied forces maintained that they had to bomb the Iraqi military machine, although they did little damage to the elite Republican Guard. Many from the Iraqi regular army are now living in Saudi Arabia, Kuwait and Jordan.

When I heard about the Kurdish uprising in the north, I felt apprehensive, especially when it became apparent the Americans were not coming to their support, that they wanted Saddam to remain as a buffer against Iran. I knew what was going to happen, and it did.

The Kurds have been struggling for a very long time against all the empires and nations that have ruled Kurdistan, but Kurds have never let go of their heritage and have always produced good soldiers, outstanding intellectuals and strong political leaders.

Kurdistan is rich in natural resources—some of the world's best oil fields are in Kurdistan and the big rivers of the Middle East come from the Kurdish mountains—so governments in the area fear an independent Kurdistan would become a threat to the whole region. The issues cannot be underestimated. About one-third of Turkey's territory is considered by Kurds to be part of Kurdistan. Turkey is a very close ally of the USA.

Syria has its own dealings with Russia and the USA. There are many fingers in the pie.

But Kurdistan is geographically identified; as are its 30 million people, with their own history, language, traditions and culture, and the world must recognise this.

Yet repeatedly, Kurds have put their trust in negotiations only to be betrayed. This is why Kurds find it hard to trust anybody, and feel they must resort to armed struggle.

Each nation-state in the area has its own history in relation to the Kurds. Syria's is different from Turkey's. The Syrian population is about 17 million, made up of a number of minorities, including Turkomans, Assyrians, Chaldeans, Armenians and Kurds. There are also numerous religious groups: Christian, Druze, Sunni, Shi'ite, Ezidi and Alevi. Kurds in Syria account for only 1.6 million, nine per cent of the population. Yet many well-established Kurdish families are recognised by their Kurdish name—names like Barazi, Sorekli, Ayyoubi and Bagdas. Kurds are Syrian citizens and, like all ethnic and religious minorities in Syria, are subject to Syrian civil law.[a] Likewise, in Iran and Iraq, Kurds are recognised as an entity. This is very different to Turkey, where in a total population of 66 million, there are 19 million Kurds, whose existence has been totally denied. But nowhere are Kurds allowed to form political parties. Consequently, their struggle for autonomy is the stuff of legends.

I am an outside supporter of Kurdish aspirations, but I believe KDP is the oldest party and the more reasonable one, having worked more towards unifying Kurds. In comparison, PKK of Turkey is a relatively recent and far more radical phenomenon. For many years, PKK claimed their goal was to create a United Socialist Kurdistan, their main enemy being the Turkish regime, but it is an impossible fight. The Turkish government retaliates by destroying villages and killing civilians, but most of all, you cannot fight both a military power and a whole nation of people who have been brainwashed into believing there are no such people as the Kurds or have been taught to hate Kurds.

KDP and PUK of Iraq have been fighting in a totally different environment, particularly since the Ba'aths came to power in 1968. Nearly all Iraqi people want to get rid of Saddam Hussein, so many Iraqi Arabs are sympathetic to the Kurds. Also, from the beginning, the Iraqi Kurds limited their fight to being against the Iraqi government. They are not trying to create a Greater Kurdistan. As the saying goes, "Let us learn to walk before we start running."

Having said all this, I do not agree with the way Abdullah Ocalan, the leader of PKK, was denied political asylum outside Turkey.

As for the future, I would like to see PKK become more cooperative with other Kurdish parties. Certainly, they should not be jeopardising the semblance of autonomy in Iraqi Kurdistan by carrying out military activities in the no-fly zone. They are giving the Turkish army any excuse to invade, bomb villages and kill innocent civilians, and it does not further any Kurdish cause to have Kurd fight Kurd. This applies to Masoud Barzani and Jalal Talabani as well. Kurds must unite and put all their resources into establishing a strong and stable autonomous state in northern Iraq, then encourage Turkey to do likewise, because their numbers in these regions justify this. Yet this is what Turkey fears most, as do Iraq, Iran and Syria.

Since the 1960s, I have sympathised with the Kurdish struggle, but I have no involvement in Kurdish politics and have had little exposure to Kurdish culture. My family were thoroughly assimilated into Arab culture. Nevertheless I am proud to be Kurdish, because of our history and because of our reputation for being honourable and brave, yet humanitarian and kind. Kurds are tough, stubborn fighters but also very romantic, hospitable people.

In 1996, I returned to Australia to live and established a business, and am now working 11-hour days, six days a week. I am becoming more devout in my religion, though not in a strict fashion. I do not fast in Ramadan. I pray, but not five times a day. The Qur'ran says, "Allah forgives everything except the worshipping of another god beside him." I do not dispute the Islamic teachings. I believe that the Qur'an is the word of God given directly to the Prophet Muhammad. However, the biggest problem in Islam today is that we do not have enough educated teachers to pass on the correct messages. Many things are done in the name of Islam, such as female circumcision, and the killing of women to safeguard family honour, but these are the result of pre-Islamic traditions and social pressure, which are very strong in the Middle East.

But times have changed and will continue to change. Modern marriage is very different from marriage in my father's day. I still think I am the head of my family, though my wife and I share most decisions. She is a good adviser, especially if I am thinking emotionally. Our daughter is 19, and very much involved in drama, music and singing. She has lived in Australia since she was five, so she is thoroughly Australian. Although Muslim by birth, she is not practising. One day, she wants to be a Buddhist, the next a Hare Krishna. She studied Islam at school, but it was an academic rather than a spiritual exercise. She has yet to come to a strong personal realisation. She is proud of her mixed heritage and would like to speak fluent Arabic. I tell her about Aslan, because he is often in my mind, but she finds the tales somewhat barbaric. Her grandfather came from a different world.

Worldly Knowledge

A fable retold by Eziz Bawermend

A dedicated theology student read every book he could find. Within a few years, he finished his studies in Islam and informed his esteemed teacher that he was ready to go out into the world. But his teacher advised that although he had successfully completed all required subjects, it was a cruel world, where ill-informed and ill-tempered people could do him much harm. The teacher suggested that he acquire some 'worldly knowledge' before venturing out. However, the eager student reasoned that he was in God's hands, and that as long as he maintained his faith in God and concentrated on his books, all would be well.

His teacher and fellow students bade him farewell, and he began his search for a village that would accept him as its *mullah*. One day he reached a village just before Friday prayers, so he joined the men of the village in prayer. Within a few moments, the village *mullah* had made numerous mistakes in his interpretations of the holy Qur'an. These made the young graduate increasingly upset. After prayers, he told the *mullah* in no uncertain terms of all his mistakes, asking if he feared God. Unabashed, the *mullah* asked the villagers, "This fellow tells me I make many mistakes. What do you think?" The villagers replied, "You are the greatest *mullah* we have ever seen."

This annoyed the young student even more and he turned to the *mullah*, saying, "Why do you ask these illiterate villagers? What do they know about reading the glorious Qur'an? We need to consult a knowledgeable person." Still unperturbed, the *mullah* said, "Perhaps you and I should have a competition." He suggested they both write the word 'bull', to see who was the better writer.

Each withdrew to a corner of the mosque and started writing. The young man quickly wrote the word, then waited for the *mullah* to finish. Some hours passed, and the villagers began suspecting their *mullah* was not as good as they thought. After considerable time and effort, the *mullah* announced, "I am ready." When the young man showed his writing to the villagers, they could make no sense of the squiggles. The *mullah*, however, showed them a detailed picture of a bull, which they all recognised. One villager told the young man, "Your writing doesn't make sense. It doesn't even look like a cat or a dog, much less a bull. How dare you criticise our *mullah*!"

Forlorn, he returned to his teacher, who asked what had happened. After the student conveyed his story, his teacher suggested, "Next Friday, let us all go to this village and see how this *mullah* interprets the holy Qur'an." He advised his students to observe carefully.

They arrived in the village for Friday prayers and the village *mullah* started making gross mistakes that made the teacher shed tears of pity. At the end of prayers, the teacher approached the *mullah* and gently said, "I can honestly say I have never seen a *mullah* read the Qur'an the way you do!" Failing to appreciate the ambiguity of the statement, the *mullah* felt very proud, and replied, "I am glad you came to hear me. This young fellow was saying I made a lot of mistakes." The teacher replied, "Well, you know what the young and inexperienced are capable of saying and doing. Is it not true that those preceding us have said, 'The young err and the mature forgive'?" The *mullah* felt even more flattered, and said, "For your sake I will forgive the novice." "Thank you," said the teacher, "and as he who possesses a hair from your beard will automatically go to heaven, may I have a hair from your beard?"

Almost intoxicated, the *mullah* repeated to the villagers the teacher's words, ceremoniously pulling a hair from his beard for the teacher. A villager then asked for one hair from his beard, and so did another villager and another, until within a short time, the villagers were pushing and shoving to get a hair. In minutes, the *mullah*'s face was bleeding. He was pushed to the ground and his clothes torn. The teacher turned to his student and said, "This is what I mean by worldly knowledge. You have been avenged, but you should return to the school to learn more."

Black Hens Still Lay White Eggs

A life story based on interviews with Bavi Alan

Where I come from, if there is a drought and no grain to bake one's bread, just to buy the family's bread each day is a special job. The bread buyer cannot do any other work, because he must get up at two or three in the morning to queue outside the bakery. The bakery opens at five, and by 11 all the bread is sold. One day we have electricity and the next day we do not. Tap water came in 1975. Before this, we relied on the well, or *beer*, in the garden. I can still taste that water: natural and clean.

Kobani is in Kurdistan of Syria. The Syrian government calls it Ain Al-Arab. Since 1946, most Kurdish towns and villages have had their names changed to Arabic names. The region's population is about 220,000 and the town's population is about 30,000, and growing rapidly. We used to have many playgrounds for soccer and basketball, but apartment blocks are being built everywhere, because people are moving in from the villages, although there are no factories, only government offices and small businesses.

The region is very flat, except for two hills—Girri Kani, half a kilometre to the east and a kilometre from the border with Turkey, and a bigger one, Mishtanor, over two kilometres to the south. As children, we would swim in Lake Goll, to the west, fed by an underground spring, but the spring filled with dirt, or maybe the source of the underground water was diverted, and now there is no lake.

From our roof, we could see the train line marking the Turkish border, and Turkish soldiers standing with their machine guns every 100 metres. Some of my family lived on Turkey's side. My father's tribe is Eladin, one of the main tribes in the Kobani area, but when he was a child, his family moved to Bingol, in Kurdistan of Turkey, to farm wheat, cotton and sheep on Kurdish-owned farms. Afterwards, they moved to Biracik, just north of the Syrian border. He would go back and forth from Kobani to Biracek to work on his family's farm for a year at a time, before he settling permanently in Kobani in the 1950s, about the time a Turkish soldier shot his wife's uncle at the border. My mother's mother ran to her dying brother, even though the soldier threatened to shoot her, and held him bleeding in her lap until he died. From that day she hated Turks.

Every year on special occasions, such as the end of Ramadan, our relatives from the village of Otmanec would come to their side of the border and we would go to our side. Under the watchful eyes of the Turkish soldiers, and one or two Syrian soldiers, we would shout greetings to each other and swap news. Until the late 1970s we were allowed to shake hands and hug, but when it was time to leave, the Turkish soldiers would separate us with sticks. Then in 1978, when PKK became active in Turkey, all physical contact was forbidden. After PKK began its armed struggle, in August 1984, we were not even allowed to approach the border. They planted landmines and if you tried to cross, Turkish soldiers shot you. Sometimes I would go secretly, to visit my family on their pistachio farm. We would wait until night, then follow a guide, putting one foot directly in front of the other to avoid the mines.

There was no border in the time of the Ottoman Empire. People moved north and south freely. The 1920 Treaty of Sevres promised self-determination for Kurds but excluded Syrian Kurds, while the 1923 Treaty of Lausanne squashed any hope for Kurds to have their own nation-state. Since then, many Kurds from Turkey and Syria moved south to Damascus, Hama, Latakia and Aleppo to avoid trouble, especially in the aftermath of each uprising in Kurdistan of Turkey.

Yet between 1920 and 1946, when Syria was a French protectorate, Syrian Kurds had more freedom than they do today. The French considered Kurds a nation of people, and allowed associations like the Kurdish League, which published Kurdish books and magazines, including *Hiwa,* written in Kurmanji. Kurdish children could attend Kurdish schools, and we had our own representatives in parliament. But after independence, the situation in Syria grew worse for minorities.

In Syria, the Alevi are the largest religious minority—about 14 per cent of the population. There are Kurdish and Arab Alevis. The Kurds are the largest ethnic minority, about 10 per cent of the population. They are Ezidi, Alevi, Sunni Muslim and Christian. The Druze are another sizeable minority, often considered Muslim but also following the Christian gospels, the Torah and Sufi beliefs. People say the Druze are closely related to the Kurds, and Druze leaders like Kamal Jumblatt, who was the leader of the Druze in Lebanon, and his son Walid Jumblatt, have helped Kurds who have fled to Lebanon, and the Druze radio station often plays Kurdish music.

In 1958, when Mustafah Barzani returned to Iraqi to negotiate with the new Iraqi government, Syria joined with Egypt to form the United Arabic Republic. All Syrian political parties were outlawed, including the Kurdish Democratic Party of Syria (KDPS), otherwise called Al-Parti. This was started in 1957 by Cigerxwin, a teacher, poet and songwriter originally from Kurdistan of Turkey, and Osman Sabri, a teacher, as well as others who were inspired and supported by Barzani's KDP. KDPS's slogan was "freedom for a united Kurdistan." The government responded by accusing Kurds of wanting to create a second Israel, especially from 1961, when Syria separated from Egypt, and a full-scale war began between Barzani's *peshmerga* and Iraqi forces, and many Kurds in Syria crossed the border to become *peshmergas* for Barzani. The Syrian military government implimented a series of measures against the Kurds. In 1962, the government announced that for security reasons, they had to create a Haezam Arabi, or Arab Green Belt, about 350 kilometres long and 15 to 30 kilometres wide, along the border with Iraq and Turkey, in the Syrian Kurdish province of Al-Cezira.[a] *Cezira* means 'around water'. Tens of thousands of Kurdish people from 40 to 50 villages were collected into trucks, with whatever they could carry. If they refused to leave, soldiers shot them. They were taken to a town of their choice—the Kurdish town of Qamishli, or towns in Al-Hasaka province, or Arab towns to the south.

The emptied villages were rebuilt, and the Syrian government paid and armed Arabs from Al-Raqqah to migrate and settle in them. Many Kurds tried to go back and reclaim their land, armed from the black market and motivated by KDPS. About 50 people were killed in clashes, but the deportations continued, and Kurdistan of Syria is now reduced to three fingers of land, separated by resettled Arabs.

In March 1963, the Ba'aths came to power in Syria, three weeks after the Ba'aths in Iraq came to power. Both governments believed in socialism, with an emphasis on pan-Arabism and nationalism. They opposed the existing communist parties, which were supported by many Kurds, claiming these parties were agents of imperialism and unable to solve nationalist issues. As a token of their shared views, the Syrian Ba'aths sent 5000 soldiers called Firqa Yermook to help fight against the Kurdish *peshmerga* in Iraq. But the Syrian Ba'aths were overthrown in 1966, so in 1968, when more radical Ba'aths took power in Iraq, the Syrian government changed allegances, and assisted Barzani and his *peshmergas* in their fight against the Iraqi government, to destabilise Iraq and create a tool for negotiation. This secret support for Iraqi Kurds continued until the 1980s, but Syria was far less supportive of its own Kurdish population, and there was isolated incidents of violence. In 1968, 150 people lost their lives in a cinema in Amoda, 50 kilometres from Qamishli. They were watching a movie, but most of them were political, I believe. The army received information and sent people to light a fire. No-one was caught.

Also in 1968, a census arbitrarily declared 100,000 Kurdish people *ajanabi*, or foreigners. In one family some would remain citizens, and others became non-citizens. According to the Syrian Kurdish party Yekiti, these 'non-citizens' today number 200,000. Others were declared Arab, not Kurd, to reduce the official Kurdish population of Syria to half a million. In reality, I believe, there are two million Kurds in Syria.

According to the Yekiti Party's publications, the people classified as *ajanabi* cannot go to government schools or universities, or to public hospitals, unless they pay a fee or bribe. They are not allowed to own land, a house or a car, and they are not eligible, under any circumstances, for a government job, or for government rations of sugar, rice and oil. They must buy these necessities on the black market, where one kilo of rice might be 20 to 25 Syrian pounds, and one kilo of sugar might be 30 Syrian pounds, compared to one, or one and a half pounds through the government. If a woman marries a non-citizen, even if he is her cousin, then their children are non-citizens, and if a non-citizen complains, they are told, "Go back to Turkey or Iraq, where you belong," but they cannot, even if they want to, because they have no official identification papers or travel documents. To travel within Syria, they must get permission from the Syrian Intelligence Service. This is not easy. It takes a couple of days, proof of the reason for travelling, and many questions. When the *ajanabi* arrives at their destination they cannot stay in a hotel unless the Syrian Intelligence approves. Even a farm animal has more rights than these people, yet Kurds have lived in the area for thousands of years.

My family's religion was originally Ezidi, the oldest religion of the Kurdish nation. It goes back many thousands of years, some say 10,000. There are about 20,000 Ezidis in Syria, but my great-grandfather stopped practising for fear of persecution. Some Muslims think Ezidis worship Shaitan and do not believe in Allah. Like Alevis, Ezidis do not pray in a mosque. They pray to Shams, facing the Sun, because the sun is basic to life. Our symbol is Malak Ta'us. *Malak* means 'king' and *ta'us* means 'peacock', so Malak Ta'us is the Peacock King. We believe that he was the king of the angels, and that when God asked all the angels to pray to Adam, Malak Ta'us was the only one who refused, saying, "Why? Before, you asked us not to pray to anyone but you." For his disobedience, Islam calls him Shaitan, but we believe Malak Ta'us apologised to God for his pride and was forgiven.

Ezidis do not believe in Shaitan or in hell, but that our soul is progressively purified over many transmigrations. It was the Zoroastrian religion that introduced the concept of hell, where people who make wrong choices fall into molten rivers of metal, and those who make good choices experience these rivers as sweet, warm milk.

Although my great-grandfather, grandfather and father never practised Ezidism, we grew up with many Ezidi symbols. On the wall, we had a picture of a peacock, and we never put water on a fire, because we respect fire. The way we wrapped babies was a special Ezidi way, and when we made bread the last loaf was always marked with a cross.

My father did not officially convert to Islam, but felt compelled to pray the Muslim way, to save his name and live in peace, even though he did not understand the language. If he needed to call on God in another way he used Kurdish words. As a teenager, I would ask him, "If you don't understand the Arabic words, why do you pray like this?" He would say, "We have to. Islam is getting stronger, so we must be Muslim too." He would add, "People say Ezidi is evil." I did not practise any religion, but I would argue, "If Muslims call it evil, that is their problem. We are Kurd. We have a land and a language, and our own religion, Ezidi." Still this religion is being practised in Afrin, the Arabic name for Jiya-kurd, and in the Qamishli area. He would quietly say, "You were born a Kurd and you will die a Kurd, but you must always respect people and love peace, so do not be so critical."

My father was very kind and gentle, and I respected him in all ways, but as a teenager, I argued with him, because at school I was being exposed to communism, Kurdish books and magazines, and articles written by Cigerxwin, Osman Sabri and others analysing the history and religion of the Kurds. They were highly critical of Salahaddin Ayubbi, because although he spoke Kurdish and employed many Kurdish soldiers, he fought for Islam, and used Islam for political purposes, doing nothing for his Kurdish nation. These writers drew parallels between that black time in Kurdish history and today, when again the pan-Arabs are using Islam as a political force to unite people, saying, "Look at our great history and culture," denying the ethnic, cultural and religious diversity of the Middle East.

These Kurdish writers were not against Islam. Rather, they were against empires and national governments using any ideology as a power base to deny nations of people. They believed that if Turks, Iraqis, Persians and Syrians could have their own government, so should the Kurds, because we are the oldest and largest nation in the area. But to this day, the Kurds are told, "You are Muslim, so why you do ask for a nation-state when already we have one?" The Kurdish writers would counteract such arguments by pointing out that religious people led many Kurdish uprisings. They would describe the uprising of 1925 in the area of Diyarbakir, Midiat and Mardin, in Kurdistan of Turkey, led by Shaykh Seyid Piran, a Dervish Sufi, and tell of how Shaykh Seyid told his people, "Do not let the enemy use us because we are of the same religion. Islam does not deny people justice, their rights as humans, or their nationality." The Turkish government destroyed the revolution, by killing, some say, 100,000 Kurds. Shaykh Seyid Piran and many others were publicly hung.

We never had a Kurdish uprising in Syria. Our population is small, and we do not have mountains to protect us, except around Afrin, yet my father would say, "Son, we must be very careful because we are under a lot of pressure. Remember how harshly the Turks crushed the rebellion of Shaykh Seyid?" He had been a young man at the time.

Apart from our differences in religion and politics, I was very close to my father. He was not a fanatic in any way. My mother's parents were Christians from Kurdistan of Turkey, but in 1915, when the Armenian Christians were being massacred by the Ottomans, many came to their Kurdish neighbours for help, so the Ottomans began killing Kurds, by the hundreds of thousands, and her family escaped to Armenia, before moving south to Kobani, where her father and brothers converted to Islam.

I never knew my mother. She died aged 23, when I was 18 months old. She simply got the flu.There was only one doctor for the whole area, and treatment was expensive. My father would say, "My son—we do not know the doctor so why go to the doctor? We can treat ourselves naturally." When her sickness grew worse, he called the doctor, but it was too late, so he and my half-sister, Avin, raised me.

Avin was kind, but my father did all the cooking; he made the bread and looked after us in every way, in between running his own mixed business buying and selling rice and sugar from Aleppo, and vegetables from farms around Kobani. He was very active. There were no chemicals in our food, he never tasted alcohol, and he was rarely sick.

I would ask him, "Why not marry again?" but he would say, "No, my son, I love your mother and I could not find another woman like her."

Families arranged most marriages, so love was accidental. My father was married before my mother, and had a daughter and a son. His son and his first wife died when Avin was 12. Within a year, he saw my mother in the street and liked her. He watched which door she entered and asked about her, then approached her family directly, saying, "I will do anything you ask to marry this girl, and I will do my best for her." They married in 1955 and had a daughter in 1957 and me in 1959. I have never seen a photo of my mother. For 24 years, I asked my grandmother about a photo and she told me, "I believe your aunty has one." My aunt had moved to Kurdistan of Turkey, then to Ankara, so it was not until 1983 that I could visit. I asked to see my mother's photo, but she said, "Oh Bavi, that was a long time ago. I do not know what has happened to it. It doesn't matter—you can look in the mirror and see her."

During this time, I spoke Kurdish to a friend close to a government building. He said, "Please do not speak Kurdish. They will arrest us and we will go to prison for ten years."

In Syria, we could speak Kurdish at home and in the street, but only around Afrin did the men wear Kurdish clothes. I always wore Western clothes because the Arab *galabeya*, cap and turban, which my father wore, were considered old-fashioned. But my sisters wore the colourful Kurdish dresses in the Barazi—Barzani style, like kaftans in two long pieces, with sleeves that have one-metre extensions, tied at the back, worn over balloon pants, with a little jacket on top, tied at the front. My sisters would plait their hair with material, and wear a little hat called a *koffi* of plaited material that spirals to the centre, about a hand's width in height. Over the *koffi*, they wore a scarf called a *shar*, open at the neck, and around the *shar* they twisted a yellow or red *kunjik* band. Then over the *kunjik* and chest they wore the traditional gold medallion necklaces. In the Afrin or Qamishli areas, the women dressed differently. My wife comes from Qamishli, where traditionally they wore a high striped hat, but now, in Syria, all young people wear Western clothes.

Our single-storey, three-roomed house was made of white limestone and black volcanic stones, cut into square blocks and scratched for decoration. The cement floors were covered in carpets made by my mother. On a sunny day, you would see women weaving carpets in their courtyard or out on the street. We also had a room called a *kalpeech*, its thick walls made from mud and straw. It was cool in summer and warm in winter, so in winter, this was where we slept. The roof was flat, and before the winter, we would have to seal it with fresh soil. Even so, when the rain was heavy, the water would come through, and we would move our mattresses and blankets onto the wide windowsill to keep dry. The next day, we would have to seal the roof again.

A gasoline heater heated water and we used a bucket to wash. In the kitchen was a mud *tanoor* for baking bread, and two gas jets for cooking. Everyone had a garden enclosed by a two-metre-high wall, and we grew vegetables and kept chickens, a sheep and sometimes a lamb, which we would kill for eating.

My father had been to school for two years so could read and write a little. He dreamed of giving his son a higher education and before he died I graduated from university, but his daughters did not continue after Year Four. Avin and her husband arranged for my 14-year-old sister to marry, against my father's wishes. He thought she was too young, and it was a big mistake, but up until the 1970s, 90 per cent of girls and boys would marry very young. Now, it is different—the age of marriage is more like 25.

Although we could speak Kurdish freely, there were no Kurdish radio or television or newspapers, and there were no Kurdish schools as there are in Iraqi Kurdistan. The 100,000 Armenians in Syria are allowed to have a school to learn Armenian, but the

Kurds, a much larger population, are not, so I grew up speaking Kurmanji, but school was in Arabic. It was difficult at first, because up until Year Five or Six, the only person who knew Arabic was the teacher. There were always people going around to check what was happening in the classrooms and once a Kurdish teacher tried to explain something in Kurdish and was taken to the principal. He never used a Kurdish word again.

On 16 October 1970, Lieutenant General Hafez Al-Assad, an Alevi Arab, took over from Noradin Atassi in a bloodless coup that reinstated the Ba'aths. A year later, he became president, and in a land-distribution Act gave a little land to Kurds in Al-Cezira. In 1976, he officially stopped the deportation of Kurds. I believe he was less harsh on the Kurds because he was part of a minority and in the Ottoman days, Assad's own people, from Al-Qardaha village, near Latakia, in the north-west of Syria, were persecuted. He did not want to alienate another minority, but he also had to appease the Sunni majority. The 1946 constitution declares Islam the official religion of Syria and requires the president to be Muslim, so Assad said, "I am Alevi Muslim," and he went to the mosque to pray.

Although Hafez Al-Assad was in competition with Saddam Hussein to be the hero of the Arab world, he was not a madman like Saddam Hussein. He was cleverer. Syria has never negotiated with its Kurds, but nor has it killed and imprisoned Kurds like the Ba'aths in Iraq. Also in 1972, Assad formed a coalition called the National Progressive Front, which included Ba'aths and Al-Qawmi (the Syrian Nationalist Party), as well as the Communist Party, led by Khalid Bagdas (a Kurd), and two other small parties. Any other party was declared illegal, so communists who split from Khalid Bagdas were imprisoned indefinitely. While democracy remains an issue, in many ways Assad did many good things for Syria, and when Iraq invaded Kuwait in 1990, Assad supported the Americans and the Allies, but now Syria and Iraq are getting closer, for political and economic reasons.

I entered high school in 1971, the year Assad became president. As in Iraq, the principal of the school and 90 per cent of the teachers belonged to the Ba'ath Party and every male student was under pressure to join. Teachers who were not members were disregarded in any decisions. Each grade had a Ba'ath management committee, made up of teachers and students, and a representative would give lectures on the Ba'ath Party and the great Arabic language and history. I refused to join, as did most other students, except for one or two Arabs, because membership meant you had to do anything they asked, even spy on a friend, so at our school, everyone avoided anybody who was a member. When the representative asked, "Why do you refuse?" we could not say, "Because this party represents the Arab people, and we are Kurdish." We would say, "Because we don't like politics, we just want to learn." As a result, the teachers would treat us badly and give us low marks.

The girl students were not pressured to join, but there were few of them—maybe five in a class of 25. Syria is freer than Iraq and Iran in relations between the sexes. School was co-educational and we were allowed to speak to each other, and in the villages around Kobani, they were even more open than in the city, where mosques and *shaykhs* dominate.

After being exposed to underground literature my 15 and 16-year-old friends and I began dreaming of a society based on humanitarian principles, where everyone had a right to an education, a job and health services and the freedom to express ideas. Then gradually we came to realise that communist ideology can be used as chauvinistically as religion so we concentrated on Kurdish issues. We would listen to the KDP news on the short-wave radio and follow Barzani's revolution in Iraqi Kurdistan, and we also listened to BBC and Washington Voice broadcasting in Arabic, as well as Kurdish news from Armenia.

By this time, there were three big illegal Kurdish parties and a couple of minor ones in Syria. The three main ones were KDPS, KDPS Peshvaru and Yekiti, a democratic socialist party formed by left-wing, open-minded people. Yekiti was popular because it allowed its members to have a voice at all levels, to criticise the leaders and their policies, and it believes in a political struggle for human rights and cultural autonomy: for Syrian Kurds to have a Kurdish media and the right to be educated in Kurdish.

My political activities consisted of talking about what was happening in Kurdistan and reading Kurdish magazines and pamphlets. But even this was dangerous. We would have to hide any political literature, and some friends were put in prison for three years or more just for it being in their possession. My father would say, "Be careful. Once you finish school, you can help your people in better ways."

The government had forbidden any public celebration of Newroz, and on the night of the 20 March, there would always be a curfew, for 'security reasons'. Everyone would go to their roofs to watch the fires on Girri Kani and Mishtanor. As teenagers, friends and I began going to the mountain, avoiding the Syrian checkpoints, to light a fire, and read poems and sing songs like *A-Rhaqeeb*, disregarding Turkish soldiers shooting few rounds from the border just to kill our feelings.

The Syrian government was too scared to go to the mountains at night, because they knew people might have weapons, but the next day the police would come around and ask who lit the fires. Nobody would say anything, but they would take people they suspected away for questioning and after a day or so, release them. If the person was known to be guilty of making a fire, he might stay in prison for a couple of years for 'endangering a public place'. Many friends were captured.

On Newroz day many Kurdish people do not go to work and most shops close. My father would take us for a picnic. The government could not prevent the increasing number of people celebrating, even in Damascus, so in 1980, they made Newroz 'Mother's Day', unofficially allowing Kurdish people to celebrate their own Newroz. However it was still forbidden to make a fire or sing *Long Live Kurdistan*. In the early 1980s, I attended a couple of big Newroz rallies, always with a large undercover force mingling in the crowd: hundreds of thousands of people dressed in the colours of our flag: red, yellow and green. A stage would be set up for folkloric groups to dance and sing, and perform little theatrical scenarios about the poor, democracy and human rights. People played the *duhol* and *zirna*, and there were food and drink stalls, but if someone wore a political sign or the Kurdish flag on their chest, the security forces took it away, and incidents, arrests and the occasional death continued. At Newroz 1988, people were marching on the streets of Damascus, and during a dispute with police, a man was shot dead. At Newroz in 1993 ten Kurdish political prisoners in Heseke

Central Prison were burnt to death. No–one knows how or why. Over thirty people were arrested on Newroz day 1999, because they made a fire.

Syria likes to say it is democratic. Every seven years, there is a presidential election, but from 1971 until his death in 2000, Hafez Al-Assad was elected unopposed.

Every four years, there is an election for parliament, and in 1975, the Syrian government allowed Kurds to participate as independents, but the election was a formality. In some places, they hid the ballot papers and police took away the ballot boxes. It was not until the 1990 election that representatives known to be leaders of other political parties outside the National Progressive Front were genuinely allowed to stand as independents. Syria could have been influenced by the first free election in Jordan, a year before, although King Hussein and President Assad were not close, and from the three Kurdish provinces eleven Kurds were elected to parliament. Six were PKK.

It was an historic moment for Kurds in Syria. Over the next four years, all Kurdish paliamentarians, except the PKK supported representatives, as well as non-Kurdish political parties, such as the Communist party, and some democratic Arab organisations, approached the parliament to solve the Kurdish *ajanabi* problem, but Fuad Eliko from Yekiti said that whenever they did so, the leader of the parliament would tell them, "The decision must be ratified by the president. Unfortunately, the problem cannot be solved by the parliament. Just wait, keep calm, until the time is right." The Kurdish members of parliament felt useless. They could do nothing for Kurdish areas in terms of economic development, education or health. However, they were able to open the minds of some parliamentarians to Kurdish issues.

In the 1994 and 1998 elections, the government announced that only independents approved by the government could stand, and Kurdish representatives, banned from travelling or advertising, decided to withdraw. All they can do is continue their struggle for human rights—for the *ajanabi* and for people who have committed no crime but who are indefinitely imprisoned without charges or a trial, such as 16 people, mostly teachers from Qameshli, who were found to be in possession of a Kurdish party magazine, or were caught distributing a pamphlet about the *ajanabi*.

Although recently, libraries and bookshops have begun stocking some Kurdish publications, such as Kurdish dictionaries and books about culture, anything political remains illegal. Yet while the Syrian government refuses to consider Kurdish political issues in Syria, it has supported PKK in its struggle against the Turkish government. From 1979 until 1998, Assad allowed Abdullah Ocalan to live in Syria, and PKK to have training camps outside Damascus and in the Syrian–controlled Bekka Valley of Lebanon. Ocalan and other PKK members were free to travel to Syrian Kurdish areas and hold meetings, and many young men and women from our area joined. They were attracted to PKK's original aim of an undivided, independent Kurdistan, and to its progressive ideology, and PKK was very efficient in recruiting new members. Yekiti's articles claim the Syrian government even gave Syrian Kurds amnesty from military service if they joined PKK, on condition they leave Syria. PKK became a very strong political force because of Syria's help, and also from donations from the wealthy Kurds of Turkey and Europe, but because Assad protected PKK, PKK did nothing to help the Syrian Kurds.

Ocalan even announced that when there was a free Kurdistan all the *ajanabi* could go home!

The Syrian Ba'aths had three reasons to support PKK. One was channelling Syrian Kurdish nationalism towards Turkey. The second was to create pressure so they could negotiate with Turkey over Alexandretta, which it called Iskenderun, or Hatay in Turkey, a northern province that France gave to Turkey in 1936 in return for Turkey's cooperation in the looming war. The third reason is that they needed a negotiating tool for water when Turkey began its huge dam project, known as GAP, or the south-east Anatolia Project, on the Al-Fra'at (Euphrates) River in Kurdistan. The Euphrates crosses into Syria near Kobani and travels 750 kilometres south-east to Al-Hasaka province, where it enters Iraq at Abu Kamal. Syria relies on this water for irrigation and electricity. Without it, Syria would be in darkness.

In retaliation for Syria's support of PKK, Turkey began using some fanatic Islamic organisations against the Syrian government, but in 1992, Turkey agreed that an amount of water could come into Syria, providing Syria curtailed PKK activity. As a result, PKK began moving into Iraqi Kurdistan, part of which was being protected by the no–fly zone.

By this time I was living in Australia. Back in the 1970s, I repeated the final year of high school, to get better marks. If you are a Ba'ath member, you are given an extra 20 points, letting you enter a faculty of your choice, but I did not have this advantage. I went to work in various factories in Lebanon, to earn some money for university, but the pay was very poor, and when the first bullets of the civil war began to fly, I left, and was accepted into a Syrian university.

My time at the university was not happy or free. Ba'ath Party members were favoured with cheap accommodation on the university grounds, while friends and I had to rent a flat. Every time we came and went from the university, we had to show our ID to armed soldiers at the front gate. Otherwise, as Kurds, we did not suffer discrimination. Some lecturers, educated in France and Russia, would criticise the government for their handling of Kurdish issues. Some of us, including women, were politically active, reading and distributing illegal magazines, going to meetings, social nights, and attending conferences. It was all done in secret, except for the conferences. If we were caught, we would go straight to prison.

After finishing my degree, I helped in my father's new furniture business in Kobani. Unfortunately, because the incomes of the people were so low, we had to shut down, and the only work I could get, not being a member of the Ba'ath Party, was private tutoring. At least I was free to tutor in the Kurdish language. It was when I was with a student one day that my cousin came to say my father was sick. I went home immediately, but he had died.

I wanted to leave Syria. All the time I felt I was being watched, and I knew I did not have a future, so I applied to migrate to Australia. I had been told it was a free country. In my interview at the Australian Embassy in Damascus, I was asked, "Why do you want to leave your country?" I could not say, "Because I am Kurdish and I am interested in politics," so I said, "I want a better life." The interviewer asked what I thought about terrorist activity and drug–trafficking, and I told him, "I am personally against all terrorism and drugs. I love peace and I believe in equality."

As a single man, I found Australia to be a free, democratic country, although many people appeared more interested in sports and alcohol than in world issues. Sometimes, you need to starve to know how good it is to eat.

I did some voluntary community work, and studied various courses at college and university. In 1987, I was a founding member of the Kurdish Democratic Association. For three years, I was president, before and after it unified with another association and became the Kurdish Association of NSW. We sponsored thousands of people, helped new arrivals, organised cultural days, concerts and conferences, and demonstrated against Iraq's use of chemicals on Halabja in March 1988. Twice we organised concerts featuring Sivan Perwer, who I consider the greatest Kurdish singer in our history.

Perwer's father was an accomplished flute player, his older brother a singer, and his childhood was full of musical gatherings, the whole neighbourhood often demanding that he sing. By the time he was in high school, people were asking him to make records, but he was not interested in recording in Turkish. In the early 1970s, influenced by Barzani's revolution in Iraqi Kurdistan, he became a protest singer, spreading the message about his people's reality. Twice he was imprisoned in Turkey for singing in Kurdish. So many people have been imprisoned, even killed, just for listening to his songs, because he and his music are banned in his country of birth. Instead, since 1976 he has travelled the world as a Kurdish symbol, loved by all Kurds because he stands above party politics. He sings for the whole nation.

He composes melodies for traditional poems, and also for his own words, as in *Delale*:

I met a Kurdish girl
In a street of Europe.
She looked so helpless.
I asked her,
What are you looking for?
She said,
I escaped from the furious wind,
Like thousands of Kurdish girls.

I said, yes, friend,
Sweet and beautiful girl,
What are you going to do here?
She said,
My homeland
Is always on my mind.
I prefer my country
To this rich one,
But I have never met freedom
In my life.
I just want to live a little free.

I took out my Australian citizenship, then returned to Syria for a year. I met a young Kurdish woman studying in Aleppo, and three months later we married in an Ezidi wedding, on the street of my father-in-law's house in Qamishli. Two months later, we came to Australia. We live a comfortable life, my wife's only complaint being the distances one has to travel to go anywhere.

For Kurds back in Kurdistan, the situation is still unpredictable. In September 1998, Turkey threatened to go to war with Syria if Syria did not force Abdullah Ocalan and PKK to leave. If Syria stopped supporting Ocalan, Turkey promised to sign an agreement over water and trade. They thought that once Ocalan left, the PKK struggle would be over.

Ocalan sought political asylum in Russia, then in Italy and Greece, before travelling in secret to Kenya. In Nairobi, he was captured, with the assistance of CIA and MOSSAD agents working in collaboration with the Greek and Turkish governments, and taken to the prison-island of Imrali, in Turkey. After meetings between Syria and Turkey, all PKK were asked to leave Syria. The only safe place they could go was Iraqi Kurdistan.

In mid-1999, PKK announced a unilateral ceasefire, but the Turkish government refused to negotiate with 'terrorists'. PKK now play a waiting game in their mountain camps near the Iranian border. Because they are no longer engaging with the Turkish army, I have been told, some guerillas want to return home to Turkey and Syria. In late 2000, Talabani went to Ankara to ease tension with the Turkish government, and because of this, fighting broke out between PKK and PUK. Three thousand Turkish soldiers entered the Sulaimani area, both Turkey and Talabani denying that they were invited.

The problem for PKK is that they will need their fighters if they resume an armed struggle. Personally, I do not believe they should stop the armed struggle until they achieve their goals, but the leaders have decided to wait to see what is going to happen to Ocalan.

After two and half years of isolation, Ocalan seems mentally dead. Even his own Kurdish lawyer, Ahmed Zaki Ogiklo, reported that the first time he was allowed to meet Ocalan back in early 1999, Ocalan had lost 17 kilos, his brain was not functioning, he spoke very slowly and was confused, yet Apo is famous for being articulate. He is reportedly physically and mentally very sick but non-Turkish doctors have not been allowed to visit him. I believe, when he no longer suits the Turkish government's purposes, they will announce that he became ill and died. I do not believe Apo will ever be freed.

But whatever the Turks do to Ocalan, it will not finish the Kurdish struggle in Turkey. With 19 million Kurds in Turkey, there are many potential leaders. They cannot kill the people's will. European countries, the USA, Amnesty International, the UN and other organisations must put pressure on Turkey to talk with the Kurds.

There is progress—but only outside Turkey. Kurds now have been governing themselves for ten years in Iraqi Kurdistan. Even in eastern Kurdistan, in February 2000, the Iranian government allowed a Kurdish Institute to be established, to publish and hold cultural events. Kurdish can now be taught in schools, and radio and television programs are broadcast in Kurdish. Similarly, it is hoped that Kurdish rights in Syria will be addressed. President Assad died from a heart attack in June 2000, and his 34-year-old son, Bashar, a British-educated doctor of eye medicine, was appointed president and commander in chief of the army. It remains to be seen what he will do about Kurdish rights. However Syria's top priority is negotiations with Israel over the Golan Heights.

My four children were born in Australia. They all speak Kurdish very well and know about their nation. They would be the first to defend Australia, but they will never forget their homeland. They are Australian–Kurds. My eldest, Ciwan, is 20 years old. She was a member of a Kurdish youth organisation, and Abdullah Ocalan's arrest had a big impact on her. She was particularly affected by the young girl who set herself on fire outside the Greek embassy in London. Like many Kurdish people, her response to Ocalan's abduction and imprisonment was, "I have to be more active."

The Flags and The Flame

A poem by Shahin Baker

Full of pride, I watched you, my Sydney
Opening your heart to the world
Of lively youth and colourful flags.
As the ocean kissed your shore
And your rivers flowed with joy,
Millions witnessed you being crowned
The queen of all cities.
You are the city of water and life,
Proud of your Aboriginal heritage,
Cosmopolitan, yet Australian.
Your harbour offers hope to millions,
Like the family watching TV the other night:
As the Olympic parade passed,
With flags raised, one by one,
A child whispered to her mother:
"There is a flag for Andorra,
There is flag for Aruba,
Why isn't there one for Kurdistan?"
Her mother, hiding warm tears,
Kissed the child, and proudly said:
"But Australia has a flag,
And you are an Australian Kurd.
Maybe, one day, like Cathy Freeman,
You too will light a flame,
And those who govern Kurdistan
Will wake and feel the shame."
The child was overjoyed
To know she also had a flag,
And in her heart, a dream was born:
To one day light the flame.

Necessity: The First Teacher

A short fiction by Lorin Miri

I hate soldiers, police and informers. I hate the governments that occupy Kurdistan. I love my homeland and my mother. As we travelled north, I remembered her dream of a dove on the roof that flew away. When I told her, "Maybe that dove is me," she became worried. That was nearly two years ago, and I have not seen her in that time, nor do I expect to. Death is more likely. Too many people have already died—20 relatives from my village. We do not know what happened to them.

My mother has lost two children to sickness and two to politics. Even before I left, I saw her shed rivers of tears when she thought no-one was looking. My brother spent two years in prison. He had been stopped at a police checkpoint when taking a Kurdish woman from Turkey and three German tourists in his taxi to the archeological sites around Afrin. After four days all the others were released, even the Kurdish woman from Turkey, who turned out to be a PKK cadre. In Syria, PKK from Turkey are safe; it is PKK from Syria who are not.

My brother was held in Afrin, Aleppo and Damascus prisons, the interrogators constantly asking him, "How do you know these people?" When he explained, "They asked to be shown the sites," they did not believe him. My father paid people in the government to get my brother released. He came home—his body thin and bruised—and straight away joined PKK. I did not see him for seven years.

Our whole life was a prison. That is why I joined PKK. Now I must forget family, forget marriage— forget everything except the revolution. I accept this. I was always interested in politics. I would hide political books under the floor in the storeroom— in amongst the hay. My mother was proud that I could read and that I knew so much, but she would worry when I argued politics with the men, because in her day, a girl had to respect a man's opinion. When I started going to meetings, she told me there would be no happiness in the life I was choosing, but she did not stop me— half of her believed in what I was doing.

As we travelled in two 4WD vehicles over the rough road, often no road at all, I remembered back to 1985, when I first heard about PKK. Some people were saying it was a terrorist organisation that killed innocent people. Others were saying that PKK was fighting for our nation. I went to a PKK meeting to find out more. A very serious female cadre talked to about 30 young women. She spoke very powerfully about how our land had been taken, our villages destroyed, our people killed and imprisoned. It was the first time I heard about PKK members dying in a hunger strike and from self immolition in Diyarbakir prison in 1982. She told us, "We do this because we want a free, united Kurdistan. But for now we must concentrate our fight in Turkey, because the majority of Kurds live there, and the Turkish government is the most oppressive of all."

She described how PKK encourages women to work for their people. "We believe that if 50 per cent of the population are left out of the revolution, it will not succeed." Her speech inspired me. I felt, "I must do something for my people." Slowly the Kurds of Syria were becoming Arabised, forgetting their language and culture. She finished the meeting with, "If you want to join PKK, you can, but I must warn you— it is a hard life. As a guerilla fighter, you might not eat for days. You are constantly on the move. Unlike the *peshmerga* in southern Kurdistan, PKK guerillas cannot marry and do not get paid. If they capture you, you will go to prison and be tortured." A few women joined immediately but I was not ready.

I began reading PKK literature and came to realise Abdullah Ocalan had a great vision for his people. At other meetings I would hear how PKK guerillas attacked military bases, police stations and *jahsh* in the villages. Twelve months after that first meeting, I heard that the PKK cadre who had spoken had been killed in fighting.

In the 1990 elections for parliament, six representatives supported by PKK were elected, but they discovered they had no power or voice, and in the 1994 elections, the government chose the representatives for the three Kurdish regions. However, from 1990, PKK began organising their own Newroz festivals. The word would spread for people to gather at a certain time and place, and at four in the morning, we would join hands and walk in a great line to the park. The police could not stop thousands. They did not shoot into the crowds as they do in Turkey.

I joined a theatrical group, which wrote scenarios and secretly performed in different places. We did our own scenery. Everything was simple but effective. Many people in the towns and villages had never seen theatre so they loved our performances, and after a year, we were invited to perform at Bekka Valley training camp. I was very excited. It was while I was there that I decided to stay and commit my whole life— especially after meeting Ocalan.

I was so nervous about meeting him. I had heard so much. He was a tall, solid man who stood erect, hands clasped in front or behind. His presence was imposing, and his voice strong and assertive, yet he lived as one with the cadres. People all over the world donated money to PKK. Apo could have become a very rich man, but he chose a simple life. His one personal belonging was a photograph album of martyrs and friends. Otherwise, he owned two changes of clothes— a military uniform and a civilian suit.

Over the next six months, I was able to observe his routine. Up at 6 am, he did one hour of exercises, before eating a simple breakfast of bread, tea and soup— like an ordinary villager. He would spend much of the morning planning activities and preparing speeches. His shortest speech was two to three hours, most of his lectures being recorded on video, transcribed and published. He would not have lunch until two pm and would eat the same food as the other cadres, though he had a special cook, for security reasons. After lunch he would spend an hour playing soccer or volley ball, just one of the team, his underlying aim being to get to know the inner personalities of each player. He made it his business to know every cadre— if not personally, then from political reports.

At the camp or when he visited towns and villages, Ocalan would meet with PKK groups and diplomatic representatives from different areas, and other countries.

Sometimes, the meetings went until the early hours of the morning, but always there were telephone and CB calls. He was in continuous contact with the bases and semi-stationary units in all parts of Kurdistan, and it is said that every operation he controlled was successful. He was not directly involved in the fighting, and I think that helped him make wise decisions. He abhored unnecessary bloodshed and meaningless war, as opposed to our struggle to live as any other free nation. His love and knowledge of Kurdistan was inspirational, and so was his attention to women's rights, education and participation. Women even had their own party within the party, but at the camp everyone mixed together and shared the duties, the men always treating the women with respect.

No words can describe the extent of Ocalan's personal sacrifice. He did not smoke or drink alcohol and was not dependent on tea or coffee. He avoided anything that would detract from his mental or physical health. He always operated from his mind, not his heart. His high intelligence and powers of observation impressed cadres and visitors alike. Above all, he could see the big picture, and by 1996, most Kurds in Syria supported PKK. People no longer believed the Turkish propaganda that PKK were terrorists.

At the camp I lived in a room with a girl called Shirin. Like the other cadres, she was not afraid of anything. We both loved reading, and sometimes after a day of training, lectures, and duties we would stay up all night, studying books. This was not uncommon among the cadres. Many were university-educated.

After I had been at the camp for three months, my brother arrived from the academy near Damascus. He was very surprised to see me, but after our initial greetings we only talked as other people talked. Then after six months of intensive education, I was sent into towns and villages to go from home to home to organise women's meetings and speak about PKK and to collect money, food, clothes and new recruits. I would tell people, "Meet at 4 pm at such and such a place," and from 4 pm people would trickle in one by one so as not to attract attention. I always spoke passionately about freedom for all Kurdistan: freedom to live in peace, to publish and express ourselves, to use the resources of Kurdistan and to make a government, like any other country. I was 19 and speaking to women up to four times my age, yet they would listen well, although many of village women were shy, uneducated, and restricted by their culture, and you cannot change people in a day.

Some months went by before I received orders that I was to join a unit heading into northern Kurdistan. We were told no more. 15 kilometres from the border, we stayed in a village, waiting for orders. Only a week before, Turkish soldiers had shot three guerillas just north of the border, and there were landmines.

The night came to cross. There was no moon and it was raining, but long-distance lights turned night into day. I focused on Shirin's muddy boots in front of me, comforted by knowing I was travelling with people I could trust. So much of my life had been otherwise. I remember when I was 16 and 300,000 people had gathered in an open area 10 minutes' drive outside the city for a Newroz picnic. The next day, we went to school. It was a girls' school— 90 per cent Kurdish, but we would be hit if caught speaking Kurdish. Every morning we had to say, "There is one Arabic nation. It will live forever.

Our purpose is freedom and socialism." By age 14 I knew that this was a lie. It was all Arab history and geography so I chose to study science and mathematics in my senior years.

The day after the picnic, the principal made us gather in an assembly. She asked, "Who went to that party yesterday?" Nearly all the girls put up their hand. The principal called me up in front of the whole school and made me get down on my hands and knees. She took my long plait, pretending it was the reigns of a horse and made me crawl around, sometimes pulling my plait so hard that my head jerked backwards. All the time, she was snarling through her teeth, "All Kurdish are donkeys like this. What is this language you speak? You are *jahsh.*"

She went along a line of girls asking, "Why did you not come to school yesterday?" She slapped the faces of two girls, but when she slapped the third girl's face the girl slapped her back. The principal announced, "Whoever went to the party yesterday can leave the school immediately. Do not come back." Straight away, 30 per cent of the girls walked out. About 40 seniors stayed behind, myself included. We went to the classrooms telling the students, "Do not come to school until the principal allows us all to come back."

That night, detectives visited some girls' homes, taking them to the police station. Fortunately, they did not know my address. The next day, we went to school, staying in the playground. My friend turned up with a red and swollen face. She told us the police had hit her, then proceeded to ask her who had told her about the Newroz party, who attended, and who made speeches. She answered them directly. Over the next two or three days, people made reports to government officials about what had happened at school, and after three days, all girls were allowed back to school, and some months later, the principal was dismissed. Ever since, I had a germ of hatred in my heart, and when so many other things happened to my family and friends, that germ grew. It gave me energy.

On that first night's walk across the border, I needed that energy. There were 12 of us, each carrying a Kalashnikov, and a small shoulder bag and belt for provisions. Two cadres carried a BKC. We also had an RPG. One cadre, responsible for all the literature, was the unit's teacher. Another was a medic, then there was a person in charge of stores and a CB operator. Our commander was a man in his forties, very tall and thin, with a big bushy moustache, and eyebrows overhanging small eyes separated by a large, flat nose with huge nostrils. He had studied in Europe, then returned to join the revolution, and was completely fearless and dedicated.

Silently, carefully we walked in single file until dawn. As the sun rose, I saw a bare, rocky landscape. Our commander took us to a rock ledge, under which we rested for a few hours, waiting to meet up with another group. Then the 30 cadres continued walking for two days. By the time we arrived in a Kurdish village my feet were sore and blistered.

The 500 flat-roofed mud houses spread out over a hill and into a valley, where the farmers grew apples and grapes, and grazed sheep and goats. There was a mosque but no school or shop. The one or two-roomed houses were without furniture, except for, perhaps, one *kilim* and a few cotton mattresses. At night, they used candles or kerosene lamps, and for heating a metal wood-fuelled heater. Water came from two underground springs, but it was not clean. There was two public toilets for women. Inside the women could see each other sitting on two stones with running water in between. They were not embarrassed to look at you and at first I felt awkward.

Shirin and I were sent to a little room set into rock on the side of the hill, some distance from the other dwellings. The roof was so low I could not stand up, and inside it was very dark. There was only one tiny window about 12 square centimetres. When my eyes adjusted, I saw a very beautiful girl in a bright red Kurdish dress sitting on the earth floor breastfeeding a newborn baby. Her marsh-green eyes were like windows in a smooth, pale moon face. She was perhaps 14. I asked her "When was your baby born?"

"Yesterday."

"Who was with you?" "I was alone." After giving birth she had baked bread.

Her husband was a farmer and often went to town to trade, but I could not believe their living conditions. There was nothing but a worn-out blanket to sleep on, and the room was filled with smoke from an open fire. I asked, "Why don't you make the window bigger?" She replied, "It would be too cold in winter for the baby. It is comfortable the way it is." I felt sorry for her. This was Azeema's real life, her whole life. She did not choose it. When she went outside Shirin whispered, "Why give yourself a headache wanting to discover everything about this girl? She is married with a baby - that's it."

Azeema's husband came home for dinner. All they had was bread and tea. He was a stern, silent man, at least 15 years her senior. She said he was kind. She said she loved him, and that she was very happy.

She also had many questions, like where were we going, and was I married? When I told her, "No," she was incredulous, asking why should an educated woman like me make trouble for herself choosing the life of a guerilla fighter. I asked her, "Why do you say it is trouble? I will live like you. Is your life trouble?"

She laughed, "For me, no. But for you it is hard. Can you make bread?" I answered, "No." "Can you make a fire?" "No." "Can you to cook?" "No." She said, "Oh my God," and we both laughed.

The next morning, her husband returned and said he would be gone for a few days, so Shirin and I could stay. Azeema and I continued our conversations. She asked me about my home, and I told her, "It is true that I know city life, but I was born in a village. My great-grandfather was *agha*. He built the village more than 100 years ago. He was an Effendi, and solved all the people's problems, accompanying anyone who had to go to a government office. He had many children." "So how do the people live?" "Everyone grows olives. There are olive trees on every hill. Come October, everyone goes and picks olives, shedding the branches onto blankets, and then pouring them into big bags, each holding 100 kilos. These are taken by horse or tractor to the olive pressing factory in the village. The village trades in olive oil. But come winter everyone relaxes, and at night men came to listen to my father tell stories. He had no education, but he could work out any mathematical problem in his head, and he was a master storyteller.

I felt warm talking about these childhood memories. Azeema listened as if I was telling her a fairytale but then a sudden wave of guilt swept over me. No guerilla is meant to reveal where they come from, but more importantly, we are taught to leave our past behind. We were creating a new society, one not based on tradition and superstition. I immediately noticed her little baby wearing a bracelet of blue amulets, with an eye on each amulet, to protect him from the evil eye. The women in my village would do the same but I had always been skeptical of such practises. Azeema's face and gaze were open. She was so fresh, her heart so pure. We were of different minds, but somehow there was a link, and I felt relaxed in her company.

I discovered she had gone to school for two years and gave her a pamphlet written in Kurdish. She studied it for a long time, then looked up, smiling, "I have never seen writing in Kurdish before." I offered to help her read it.

Over the next few days, I helped Azeema bake bread, collect water and tend her vegetable garden, in between teaching her to read Kurdish. I was surprised how quickly she learnt. When it came time for us to leave, she cried.

If I had thought I knew hardship, nothing prepared me for where we were going. Moving, moving, sleeping three hours and moving on, always wary of danger over the next hill or behind the next rock, never able to let one's mind wander, one's body relax. Several times, we hid as long army convoys of young soldiers, some grim, some as innocent-looking as my baby brother, passed by. Several times we saw rows of tanks in the distance.

We picked up food in different villages, or would be brought supplies by an old man or woman on a donkey. Whatever the villagers could spare, they gave us. In between, we made our own bread over a metal plate on a fire, and some days, we had only bread and tea. Sometimes, I could not sleep because my stomach growled with hunger.

At no time did I know where I was. We had to avoid towns: too many soldiers and gendarmeries. After 10 days of travelling, one of our group became sick. At the beginning, others carried his provision bag, then him. After several days, he died, and we carried his body for three days before arriving at a special cemetry for PKK, where we buried him.

One day on dusk, we came to the outskirts of a village. Our commander told us we were going to hold a meeting because villagers had reported that the village guards were abusing their power. That night, we stayed under trees on a nearby hill, the sounds of people singing and playing the *duff* and *zirna* wafting on the breeze. It felt so human after 20 days on the move. The next morning, a small, very serious boy came to our camp. My mind flashed to my free-wheeling childhood, riding horses, making cubby houses, and playing with sticks and stones. This boy acted as if he had known no fun, as if the future of the village was in his hands.

Six of us went to the village school— the rest posted at various points outside. As our commander told the men they should join the revolution, there was a sudden burst of machine-gun fire close by, followed by return fire, then an explosion. The villagers panicked, escaping out the door. We took up positions behind the window and door, weapons at the ready, the calm, steely determination of our commander's face giving me confidence. Machine-gun fire broke the window. We returned fire, then an explosion blasted a gaping hole in the wall. The earth roof began collapsing. Under covering fire, we escaped through the hole. Between flying bullets, I saw a tank, and soldiers running between the houses. I ran, following my comrades, mind blank, body numb. Three of us did not return. We would have to pick up their bodies after the soldiers left. The commander led us up rocky crevices and over a hill, then down into a deep cave. For two days, we waited inside the cave, not knowing whether soldiers were still in the area. I was not hungry for the first day.

After collecting our comrades' bodies we headed for a base in the mountains to join our *surre'ye*— 60 to 100 people. Three or four *surre'ye* made up a *cateeb'e*, which controlled an area. We would be in the base through winter, and had to stock up on food supplies, living in caves and nylon tents. Before the snows came, we collected wild greens from the mountains. There were two cows, but after some months, we resorted to hunting wild pigs and goats, even snakes and tortoises, for meat.

Most days it rained or snowed. My body felt like a block of ice. Twice, village people brought us cheese, honey, butter and olives, as well as the staples, on the back of a mule. We would grind our own flour, taking turns to cook. Still, we followed a routine: waking at 6 am, singing *A-Rhaqeeb*, followed by one hour of sport, then seminars of a serious ideological nature and military training, the nights filled with long discussions about strategy. Occasionally we danced, Kurdish style. Shirin and I became close. We filled any spare time by reading about PKK and different revolutions.

After March, we carried out a few operations, once crossing a deep river by using inner tube tyres and attacking an army barracks to get ammunition. In the attack, Shirin was killed. My grief did not hit me until a week later, when we buried her in the cemetery on Judi Mountain, in Botan. Another time, we clashed with village guards, and once had to avoid a flock of helicopters firing rockets, but after 13 months, I found myself back in Azeema's village.

I had been through so much and there was Azeema, smiling, six months' pregnant, thin and tired. She greeted me quietly, "It has been a hard time, yes?" For the first night in a long while, I slept deeply. I slept right through the next day. I woke on dusk to overhear Azeema and her husband talking in hushed voices, his tinged with anger. The next morning, I asked her, "Does your husband mind me staying with you?" Azeema answered, "You are welcome. His mind is full of worries." Over the next few days, as I helped Azeema I wanted to tell her, "You see this life as normal, but it is too hard, because the government is too busy buying weapons and paying soldiers instead of building up our country."

Finally one morning I spoke my mind. Azeema replied simply, "Yes. But what can I do?" I wanted to give her all the answers I had been taught. I wanted to talk to her about human rights, women's rights, socialism and democracy, so that she could tell the other women. They could form a group. But my tongue would not move. What could she do that she was not already doing? I looked at her child and her swollen stomach. I thought, "It would be good for my party, it would be good for my standing in the party, but would it be good for these women?" Azeema trusted me, and I thought, "I am here for only a short time. If the army comes, I can escape, whereas these women will be in danger." Then I worried that I was giving up, or turning away from power, not taking risks for the revolution. Half of me argued silently that the revolution was about a nation, that individuals had to be sacrificed, but the other half saw Azeema, and her love for her little boy.

Azeema must have sensed the war in my mind, because later, when we were washing clothes, she asked, "Sister, do you believe in God?" I was silent. In PKK, we are taught not to enter into religious discussions, to respect the village people's beliefs. After a long pause, Azeema whispered, "I do." I said quietly, "We believe what we are taught," then bit my lip. I had not given time to this subject. My people's struggle was more important. Azeema was saying: "That is so. My family was religious." After a pause, she continued, "But there is a feeling…that gives life and death meaning. And more. I do not understand the mysteries but I know out of bad, good can come." Azeema's soft voice continued as if from a dream. "In my family's village, four hours' walk from here, there were some young people who were politically active. One day, soldiers arrived by helicopter and started shooting everything that moved. They came into every house, killing, killing, killing. I was eight years old and hid in a cupboard. I heard my family dying, then silence. I was too scared to move. After a while, there were footsteps. Suddenly, a soldier opened the cupboard door, his Kalashnikov pointing at my face. He looked down at me for some time, then slammed the door and left. I stayed in that cupboard for a long time. I slept and woke, and when I finally crept out, the village was deserted, except for an old man with a bleeding arm. We walked to this village, where a family took me in. My husband's family. You see, God creates heartaches but offers cures too." She began to sing…

I am an old and helpless man.
I see, but can you see too?
I feel. Can you feel too?
This trouble, this sorrow; this unforgettable event.

Imagine, and remember:
Nagasaki and Hiroshima.
They still try to bandage their wounds.
Think now, I have the same wound. Who can bandage it?

My green Halabja, my homeland
My beauty, my children, my future…

I call the Kurdish leaders
To unite, and come together.
The trouble of Kurdistan
Is official. Our people are in pain.

Write to the world.
Announce and inform,
Shout and cry.
Say: Our future is in danger.

Cry and cry for Halabja,
The heart is breaking,
The eyes are weeping.
My people are suffering.

My green Halabja, yesterday alive,

Today burning.
My beautiful children,
Playing yesterday, dying today.

People! Remember Halabja,
Remember my children,
Remember my beautiful homeland,
Remember the beauty of the world.

It was a famous song by Sivan Perwer. I asked, "Where did you hear that?" "My husband has a cassette." For this simple possession, they could be imprisoned. Or worse.

That afternoon, Azeema's husband came back early, warning, "The gendarmeries are coming. Go to your commander." We were to move out immediately. Azeema and I hugged and kissed and cried as we said goodbye, and as my unit headed out between the trees up a steep hill, on the other side of the river, I looked back to see six army trucks pull up inside the village.

We descended into a valley and after three days, were in the mountains. It was summer, the air was fresh and we passed many shepherds with their sheep. For days, we kept moving. All we had to eat was bread, apart from a bag of food Azeema had given me. I shared the food, but it did not go far. We got water from springs, but you should not drink too much when travelling.

Finally we made it to the base where we would stay for winter. There were 10 other women. One day I overhead the vice-commander criticising a woman for her past history. He finished by saying, "Women are dangerous." Feeling sick inside, I asked, "Can I say something?" "Yes," he says. "Your opinions about women are just like a Ba'ath principal at my school. This woman is working very hard for the struggle." I left the dinner early, and my companion told me, "I agree with you, but you must not get so upset. He is just one man." I replied, "If that man talks about her like that, next he will talk about us in the same way." After that, this man made it difficult for me. I kept more and more to myself, determined to be above reproach. I was lonely. Time can kill in a world of rock, and I was fighting off a pervasive sense of sadness that went far beyond my immediate experience.

When the bombs came, we escaped. Two cadres were killed in the bombardment, and we had to carry their bodies. Three others were suffering from frostbite, so our progress was slow. After 6 long, hard months, we returned to Azeema's village. As we approached, I felt a shiver through my body. The village was empty. I ran up to Azeema's room. Nothing. A scream rose inside me, but I locked it inside. I felt as if my lungs had collapsed, and I gasped for air. The tears fell.

Coming down the hill, I showed none of this emotion to the others. We stayed a few hours, before continuing south. We had orders to return to Syria for training and reassignment. This was very unusual, as most guerillas do not return from Turkey. The only cadre I knew who had returned had escaped from PKK and lived in hiding.

By foot, donkey and car, we eventually arrived at the academy— a big farm outside Damascus. I remember little of the journey. My head was filled with questions, and anguish.

At the academy, I slept and ate little. I was overtired— emotionally and physically. A cadre showed me more attention than usual, and this confused me. I told him to stay away— if people saw us, we would be punished— but I was in desperate need of a kind word, a kind touch, something that went beyond the rhetoric, a communion such as Azeema and I had shared.

One day, some police came to the academy gates and demanded entry. They were confronted by other government forces, who told them, "Go and get a letter from the president and then we will let you enter." This made me wonder why Turkey and the superpowers had not put more pressure on President Assad to stop supporting PKK 'terrorists'. Then I wondered, "If we are terrorists, why do the Europeans allow Med TV to be broadcast all over Europe?" But I kept silent. Then, at one meeting, the leaders were saying, "We put everyone in their right place." I said, "That is not possible, because we are not building schools, hospitals, farms and factories. All we have is fighting! If we took all the money we collect and used it to help our people rather than to attack our enemy..." The commander interrupted, speaking harshly, "In Turkey just saying the word 'Kurd' can get you a prison sentence. Speaking Kurdish on radio or in a government office is illegal. Our problem is political." I protested, "But if the people can't eat?" Again I was cut short. "PKK is changing a feudal, backward society into a progressive one. As a woman, you should be grateful." "But if people are being killed?" The commander ordered, "Go. Tomorrow we will discuss this matter further."

I lost all confidence. I no longer felt clear in my path. I felt cut off from my comrades, all of whom were so sure that what we were doing was right. Questions and memories haunted me. We have to be able to live with what we do, with how we work towards our goal, or we lose everything. And what if Azeema was right, that life does not end in death? How should this affect what we do? She had love, so where did this take her? The awful thing was that I did not know. I had hate and anger, but where were they taking me? At that moment, a tiny quail came to rest on a sycamore and began to sing a heavenly song. And I knew what I had to do.

Our Trouble

Another extract from *Mem U Zin* by Ehmedê Xanî (Ahmedi Khani), Translated by Eziz Bawermend

Bartender, for the love of God, please
Pour some wine into the crystal glass.[a]

Let the glass of wine reveal to the world.
Let there appear here whatever we wish.

Let events ahead of us come to light.
Let us know if the future holds promise for us.

Look, our misfortune has reached its peak.
Will conditions improve, do you think?

Or will they so remain,
Until upon us comes the end of time?

Is it possible, I wonder, that for us, too,
A star will emerge out of the firmament?

Let lady luck be on our side for once.
Let there emerge from within us, too

One to shoulder the earth.
Let there be a king of our own.

Let his sword attest to our might.
Let the might of his pen be known.

Let there be an answer to our trouble.
Let there be a demand for our knowledge.

If we had an exalted leader,
Of good deeds wanting a poem,

Our bullion, too, would be stamped.
It would not be so unwanted and suspect.

However pure and clean they may be,
Value is added to gold and silver with a stamp.

If we had a king,
If God saw him deserving of a crown,

If a throne was appointed to him,
Our luck would turn around.

If he was provided with a crown
Of course, for us, too, there would be respect.

He would feel sorry for us orphans.
He would set us free from bondage to the craven.

They would not be victorious over us, these Turks.
Ours would not turn into ghost towns.

We would not become fugitives: dispossessed, wretched.
We would not bow our head in defeat to the Turks, the Tadjiks.

. . .

Although it is disgraceful to be their subjects,
This disgrace belongs to the persons of repute.

This is a matter of honour for the chiefs, the leaders!
What can the troubadours and the dispossessed do?

Whoever took the mighty sword in his hand,
Established in manly manner a state.

Because the world is like a prize bride,
Its fate, too, determined by the mighty sword.

But its dowry, trousseau, jewels and wedding presents
Are goodness, generosity, kindness and forgiveness.

I asked the world, "What is your dowry?"
"Benevolence", it said to me.

In short, "With the sword and goodness,
The world submits and bows its head to man."

I am puzzled by God's wisdom:
In this world of states,

Why have the Kurds remained stateless, dispossessed?
For what crime have they become fugitives, condemned?

. . .

Like a great wall, the Kurds stand between the Turks and the Persians.
Here and there are the Kurds, occupying all four corners.[b]

Both sides make the Kurdish clans
Targets of their poison–tipped arrows.

As if the Kurds hold the key to crossing the borders,
Each clan is as strong as a great wall.

Yet however rough and stormy they get,
This Turkish ocean and Persian sea,

It is the Kurds who are spattered with blood
And, like a rampart, separate the two.

Generosity, benevolence, bravery,
Chivalry, guardianship and valour,

All are credited to the Kurdish clans.
The fame of their sword and their benevolence is far–flung.

To the same extent, they cherish freedom and independence.
It is submission and obligation they detest.

Yet this spirit of independence and exalted benevolence
Has become the obstacle to shouldering the burden of
obligation.

Because of this, they are always without unity,
Divided and pitched against one another, they stand.

If we had unity amongst ourselves,
If we all, together, obeyed one another,

The Turks, the Arabs and the Persians
Would one and all be in our servitude.

Then would we perfect the art of government and religion.
Then would we acquire all wisdom and command all nature.

Wheat would be separated from the chaff
And the real achievers would come forth.

– IV –

FROM ELAM TO KHOY, VIA MUKRIAN AND ARDALAN

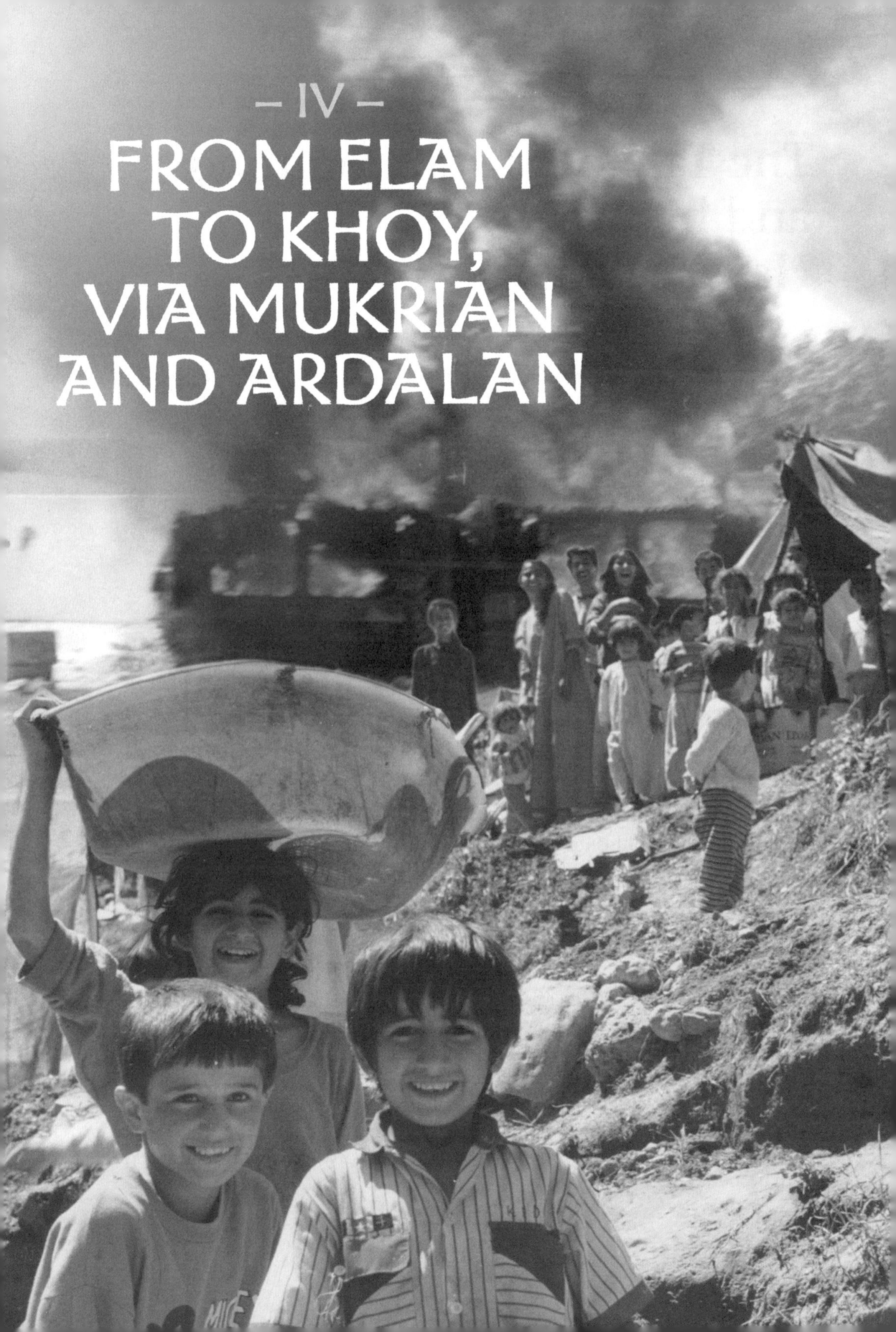

The Tale of Sultan Mahood and his Wazir, Hayaseekhas

As told by Siamand Minehzadeh Morowatdost

My grandfather was a great storyteller. He was eight years old when Russia invaded Iran in World War One. The Russians burnt his town and killed his family. A twelve-year old girl took him through the snow to a village in Russia, where people saved his feet by putting them in fresh horse manure. He stayed, finding work on the construction of railways, before going to southern Kurdistan, and becoming a farm worker. Very religious, he was famous for his bravery and good deeds, but often did not have food to eat. He told me how he sat under a tree, which bore sweet juicy fruits like cherries, but they are not cherries; like plums, but smaller than plums. The black ones make your lips black, and there are red and white ones too. He waited for the birds to come and eat the fruit and drop some and he ate the fruit that the birds had dropped.

Eventually he came back to Mahabad and married my grandmother, and after she died he married another woman, but he knew so many stories about the sultans and their chief advisers. One that stands out in my mind goes like this:

There was a sultan called Sultan Mahood, whose wazir had an exquisitely beautiful wife. Sultan Mahood lusted after Hayaseekhas's wife, and the wazir knew this. The sultan often sent the wazir on missions elsewhere, but Hayaseekhas would always return before the sultan could fulfil his desire. Once, the sultan sent Hayaseekhas away for a whole month. Before the wazir departed, he surrounded his house with oily asphalt, a little here, a little there, so that anybody who came would leave footprints, from which he could identify the visitor.

After the wazir departed, the sultan visited Hayaseekhas's wife, telling her directly, "I want to have sex with you." She replied, "Okay, no problem, but let us eat first." The sultan agreed. The wazir's wife was as smart as she was beautiful, and boiled seven eggs, painting each a different colour. At the table, she offered the sultan an egg, but no matter which egg he went to take she grabbed his hand, saying, "No, the red one—or the blue one—is more beautiful. Look how lovely it is." Finally, Sultan Mahood said in exasperation, "The eggs may be different colours, but on the inside, they all taste the same." Hayaseekhas's wife exclaimed, "Exactly! And it is the same for women. Now, go back to your wife." Sultan Mahood understood and, sorry for what he had tried to do, went home.

When Hayaseekhas returned he saw the sultan's footmarks on his asphalt and, assuming the sultan had been successful with his wife, went away to a faraway village, where he became a shepherd for an old man, in return for food and shelter.

A year passed. The Ottomans were preparing to fight Iran, but first they presented Sultan Mahood with a riddle, promising that if he could solve it within two months they would agree to keep the peace. If not, they would take over Iran. The riddle was this: "We give you seven camels. You must tell us which camel is the great-great-grandmother, which is her daughter, which is her grand-daughter, and so on, for seven generations."

Sultan Mahood knew that only Hayaseekhas had the wisdom to solve such a riddle. He tried to find him but, when unable to do so he devised a plan, ordering his soldiers to give one sheep to each household and to tell the villagers that, in one month, they would return to weigh the sheep. Each sheep had to weigh the same then as it did now. The sultan knew that only the wazir was clever enough to solve this problem.

The people saw the task as impossible. If the sheep ate it would grow bigger. If the sheep did not eat it would die. When the soldiers left the village where the wazir lived, the old man cried all night. The wazir asked him, "What has happened?" and the old man replied, "It is not your worry. You are only a shepherd," but the wazir insisted the old man explain, so he did. The wazir told him, "Leave it to me."

One month later, the soldiers returned to each household to find each sheep either too big, too skinny or dead, but when they arrived at the old man's home, they were shocked to find that the sheep was the same weight. When the old man told them his shepherd was responsible, they asked to see him.

The soldiers sent a message to Sultan Mahood saying they had found a sheep that weighed the same. Sultan Mahood ordered that the man who had looked after the sheep be brought before him. But when they ordered the wazir to come with them, he said, "Tell the sultan he must walk here in his bare feet." Sultan Mahood had no choice, and, without shoes, he began walking to the village. Hayaseekhas met him halfway and they hugged and greeted each other, the sultan saying, "I know why you ran away, but I swear to God I did not sleep with your wife. Your wife is smart, and she taught me a lesson. I am very sorry for my intention but before I tell you my problem please, tell me how you kept the sheep the same weight for a month." The wazir replied, "It was easy. I fed the sheep very well, and when he was full, I showed him a wolf. The sheep became so scared, the food would pass straight through him."

Then Sultan Mahood asked his wazir to return to the city to help him solve the Ottomans' riddle. There were just two days until the deadline. On being told the riddle, Hayaseekhas said, "Tell the Ottomans to come. I need one large, empty space," so this was arranged. Hayaseek has instructed, "Now, put all the camels inside this space and bring me a big stick." In front of the Ottomans and Sultan Mahood, the wazir started beating the camels, one after another. In pain and fear, each one immediately went under her mother's breast. Soon, the seven camels were in a line, one generation after the other, so that is how the wise wazir saved Iran from a war with the Ottomans, and every household in Iran knows this story.

Freedom

A poem by Marif Agha-e, translated by Kamran Avin and Gafoor Muhamad

Which one of us is freer:
I
Or
A caged bird?

One handspan between
The bird and freedom,
The rope and my neck.

Words are Your Own Until they Leave Your Mouth

A story based on interviews and an essay by Ghader Abdi

I was a teacher in Kurdistan of Iran, as well as in Tehran. Later, I taught a series of courses, held in tents, for the Kurdistan Democratic Party of Iran (KDPI). The Iranian government viewed these classes as illegal, and at one stage, we had to escape bombardment. The secretary of KDPI, Dr Abdul Rahman Qassemlou, was one of the teachers, as was Abdullah Hasan Zadeh, the present KDPI secretary, and Hasan Rastgar, a member of the politburo. We all thought educating was the most important activity of our organisation, and Dr Qassemlou was a very good teacher. I once commented, "You enjoy teaching more than being a political leader!" to which he replied, "That's right. In my opinion, being a teacher is more useful."

Between 1794 and 1925, the period when the Qajars ruled Iran, there was no education, except from the Qur'an in religious schools. From 1925, government schools started to be established in the big cities but there were only a few primary schools in Kurdistan. In 1947, the Iranian government built four primary schools in the Piranshahr region, an area covering one town and 100 villages, but there were no high schools until the late 1950s.

I started at Piranshahr's only primary school in 1951, a school with up to 60 students, serving a town of 3000. I was the first in my family to go to school. My mother was illiterate and my father had taught himself to read the newspaper. Famous Persian classics like *Golastan* and *Bostan* by Sa'adi (1184–1291), Shakespeare of the Farsi language, read all over Azerbaijan, Uzbekhistan, Afghanistan, Iran and Iraq, were out of his reach.

Like most Kurdish students, I learnt in a 'foreign' tongue, and was taught mathematics, science, and an Iranian history of empires, shahs and sultans, from a few textbooks, our education being an exercise in memory.

In those days, most girls remained uneducated. My elder sister went to school for two years, then continued her studies at home. Most of my friends left at the end of primary school, but my father, who owned a few general stores, was determined to support my education, as well as my younger sister's, so that we could contribute to our nation's future. He saw education as the key to freeing the Kurdish people from poverty and backwardness. He would say, "The first roads were built after World War One, but only for the army. The first machines to travel along them were army trucks and tanks, not an ambulance, or a truck to transport our agriculture." Three big army bases were built in the Piranshahr area in the 1950s, but no factories, businesses or health services, and there was no electricity in the villages.

We were free to speak Kurdkish outside the classroom, but until 1979, publishing in Kurdish, even writing a private letter in Kurdish, was illegal. There was some underground literature, but growing up, I relied mainly on my father's knowledge and, later, that of his friend Kak Hamadi Khanemi (born Muhammad Hasan Zadeh), a member of KDPI.

My father would frequently talk about our family history and that of the Kurdish movements. During World War One, Russian soldiers killed many Kurdish people in Iran while fighting with the Ottomans. He and his mother were forced to escape from the village, and people were starving because they could not continue farming the land. He was the first to tell me about Simko, or Isma'il Agha of the Shikak tribe, who asked the US, British and French forces to recognise his people, saying, "My people are eating grass." When Simko's demand for self-government was ignored, he gathered some Kurdish tribes and, from 1919 until 1930, fought the Iranian forces, as well as the British and Russians. In 1923, he visited Shaykh Mahmud in Sulaimani and was welcomed as a Kurdish hero, but failed to form an alliance with Shaykh Mahmud or with any of the Kurdish leaders in northern Kurdistan. One reason was that Shaykh Mahmud and the leaders in Turkey favoured the Turkish Kemalists. They thought it best if all Muslims united against the British, but the Turkish army had killed Simko's wife when they had fleed to Turkey, after the Iranian army burnt down his village of Chahrik, so he had fought the Turkish army and made another enemy. Simko looked to Britain as an ally, but the British preferred to side with Colonel Reza Khan, who became Shah of Iran in 1925, thinking he was a better front against the new communist system in the north.

Under Reza Khan, the Iranians formed a very strong army, and some Kurdish tribes deserted Simko. By 1930, Simko had no choice but to negotiate with the Iranian government, even though they had tried to kill him several times. On 21 June 1930, when he went to Ushnaviyeh for a meeting with government representatives, he was shot dead in the street. It was a long history repeating itself. Simko's eldest brother, Ja'afar, had been killed by the Qajars after they sent him a Qur'an in which was written, "Come to a meeting in Tabriz. We promise you will be safe."

In autumn 1931, Johar Sultan led a new Kurdish movement near Hamadan but it was aggressively put down by Reza Khan. In that time, Reza Khan asked some Kurdish parliamentarians to say, "As Kurds, we have no problems in Iran. The Kurdish people think like other Iranians," and Kurdish academics such as Rashid Yasami wrote books with the same message.

It was not until the 1940s that another movement gathered momentum in eastern Kurdistan. During World War Two, the Allied army, including the Soviets, came to Iran, worried by Reza Khan's relationship with German industrialists. Also, they wanted to use the Iranian rail system and Persian Gulf ports to supply the Soviet army. The British exiled Reza Khan, and in his absence, intellectuals and ex-political prisoners organised various political parties, initiating a brief period of democracy.

In 1944, the only representatives of the Iranian government in Mahabad were the police. Kurdish intellectuals demanded that they leave Mahabad and the people took over the police station. An underground association called Komalay Jiyanewey Kurd, meaning 'The Kurds Live Again', was formed. On 16 August 1945, a well-known religious judge called Qazi Muhammad became its secretary-general and its name was changed to the Kurdistan Democratic Party. It was the first Kurdish political party, and it quickly gained popularity. With support from the Soviet Union, in January 1946 Qazi Muhammad declared the Republic of Mahabad, but unlike the Azerbaijan republic formed in the north, the Mahabad republic was not communist. The emphasis was on creating a democracy. A council elected the Mahabad ministers, Qazi Muhammad becoming president, people demonstrating their loyalty in the streets.

The republic made valuable contributions to education and culture. Kurdish became the language of tuition, and new schools were established. The administration gave students uniforms and books, and started printing books in Kurdish. A theatre group formed, their first play being *Dayk Nishtiman* or *Mother of the Patriot,* and in the 11-month life of the republic, there was no killing.

I was born two years before the republic, in Piranshahr, 50 kilometres west of Mahabad and 14 kilometres east of the Iraqi border. Piranshahr is the first city on the main road through a valley of the Zagros Range. It is a continuation of the Hamilton Road in Iraq, the last village in Iraq being Haji Omaran and the first village in Iran, Tamrchin.

The Zagros Mountains are visible to the west of Piranshahr, but the city itself is on the plain 90 kilometres north of Sardasht. It was in Sardasht in December 1946 that the Mahabad forces stopped the Iranian army and maintained a siege. Afterwards, when they agreed to let through food supplies, the Iranian government smuggled in guns with the food. To avoid the bloodbath experienced in Azerbaijan, Qazi Muhammad and other leaders surrendered to the government. When the government took control, the first thing they did was collect all the books and publicly burn them. They destroyed the publishing houses, changed the Kurdish schools into Farsi government schools and, in March 1947, hung Qazi Muhammad and other leaders who chose not to escape.

My father was a peace-loving man, who loved Qazi Muhammad for his intelligence and his devotion to his people. Qazi Muhammad was from a very big, famous family. He could have escaped, become old and written his memoirs, but instead died for his principles.

To attend high school, I had to live in the city of Naghada, 40 kilometres north of Piranshahr, staying with a friend of my father's and visiting my family every few weeks. At school we wore Western-style uniforms, it being illegal to wear Kurdish clothes. Some teachers were kind. Others used the stick, although the Department of Education had banned physical punishment. Even in high school we were allowed no research, discussion or essay-writing. A dictatorial government does not encourage its people to think.

My father's friend, Kak Hamad, became my mentor and my teacher of Kurdish history and politics. In 1958, when Malla Mostefa Barzani went back to Iraq after 11 years in exile, Kak Hamad talked about what was happening in Iraqi Kurdistan. Kurdish people are political, because although we have the usual economic, cultural and family problems, our main problem is government oppression. At the time, KDPI was publishing material and organising support, and the government was very active in arresting its members.

It was in high school that I first read the *Shahnameh,* a collection of stories about the Iranian people before Islam, written about 1000 years ago by a great Iranian poet,

Firdawsi. In Firdawsi's time, there was no separation of nations. He called people and their heroes either Iranian or Turanian. The Iranians included the Kurds, Farsi, Baluch and Afghanis, and the Turanians included the Turks of the region around the Saihoon and Jaihoon rivers, now Turkmenistan, Uzbekhistan and Kazakhstan.

It is in the *Shahnameh* that Firdawsi retells the ancient Kurdish legend of Kawa, the iron-maker, and his rebellion against the tyrant king Azhdehak, from the Persian point of view. In Firdawsi's account Kawa took off his apron of animal skin and used it as a flag, which Firdawsi called the Kuvyani flag. After Kawa killed Azhdehak he asked a member of the Kayani[2] family, an ancient Iranian dynasty, to become king. I have always wondered why Kawa did not become king himself. All I know is that the Kurds continue to be oppressed by modern-day Azhdehaks.

The story goes that Firdawsi sent his book to Sultan Mahmud Khasnavi, the ruler of the time. The Sultan reacted by asking, "Why talk about old heroes? I have many heroes in my army," but later, he reconsidered and sent Firdawsi a gift. By that time, Firdawsi had died, and his daughter returned the gift, saying that the Sultan's recognition was too late.

After three years at high school, I went to a boarding school in Urmia for two years, studying to become a teacher. Urmia is a very multicultural city, with Sunni Kurdish speaking the Sorani and Bahdini dialects, Christian Assyrians and Armenians, Shi'ite and Sunni Turks from Azerbaijan, and a few Farsi. Sunni and Shi'ite mosques and Christian churches exist side by side, yet of the 460 villages around Urmia 400 are Kurdish.

It was in 1961, during my time in Urmia, that Mostefa Barzani started a revolution against the Iraqi government, and this inspired many Iranian Kurds. Barzani was a remarkable leader for his time. He did not trade off his people's rights. He did not go to Baghdad during the fighting. He made the Iraqi government come to him. He would talk to the Shah of Iran, not his underlings, and likewise to Henry Kissinger, the US Secretary of State in the 1970s, and to representatives of the Israeli government: as one leader to another. He became a hero to all Kurds. The problem for Iranian Kurds was that in the 1970s, although Barzani did not believe in the Shah, he relied on support from the USA, which came through the Shah, and this made it difficult for Iraqi and Iranian Kurds to unite in a struggle for one Kurdistan.

After completing my teacher's training, I was sent to the mountain village school of Soliman Kandi, near the city of Saghez. The mud-walled houses had flat, earth roofs with a room for each son's family centred round a central courtyard. There was no electricity, and for water, there was a spring. A big public toilet and wash area was located near the mosque, but some people had their own facilities.

The old mosque had very strong, thick walls and a wooden minaret, and the school was next to it: two small rooms with mud floors, and one very small window which gave too little light. The government supplied us with desks, benches, textbooks, pens and paper, and a blackboard, but no books for a library, so I collected books from friends.

The village was very poor. The people farmed wheat, barley and corn and raised livestock. They grew all their own fruit and vegetables but, sometimes, they did not have enough to eat. It was a difficult life, but people respected the teacher and were friendly and helpful because they knew the value of education. Nowadays, buses go to and from the villages, so the teacher can live in a nearby town.

The government paid me 500 tomans a month (about US$70), average for that time. It was enough to buy food. I lived alone in two rooms, with my own toilet and washroom but no furniture. Students would fetch my water, and families often invited me to eat with them, or the head family would send me cooked food. Otherwise, I cooked on a small oil stove. Life was strange at the beginning, but I have good memories of those five years in the village. I was always invited to weddings and family occasions.

School ran from nine to 12, with a two-hour lunch break followed by another two hours of study. One person in the village had spent five years at high school, and after six months I asked the Department of Education to employ him. I would teach Grades Four to Six, and he would teach Grades One to Three. There were about 40 students, aged from seven to 15—or older. We set no age limit. Not all the children could attend full time, many having to help their parents, so we would help them catch up.

We prepared several students for the exam to go to high school in the city. I tutored one girl in science and mathematics, and when she went to the city, she achieved a first-class pass and her family allowed her to continue her education when her brother joined her. Now she is a teacher in Saghez. Other students from the village have become teachers, hospital staff, university graduates and government employees.

I had no discipline problems. I would encourage my students by giving a pencil or small notebook as a reward for good work. I taught in Farsi, from the official textbooks. If a student talked to me in Kurdish, I would use the Kurdish word, then teach them the Farsi equivalent, and step by step, they would learn the new language. Sometimes students commented, "You are Kurdish," and I might tell them about the Kurdish people, but I kept it simple. Although there was no army or police in the village, unless a problem arose, SAVAK agents were everywhere.

I had a battery radio, and every day after school, students that I trusted would come to my home to listen to the KDP broadcast from Iraq. We would write down points and discuss Kurdish issues, and talk with sympathetic families, as well as teachers from other villages. The broadcasts were illegal and the subjects we discussed such as the government, justice and democracy were dangerous to talk about, especially as a teacher with his students. At the very least, I could have lost my job, but I learned to know who I could trust.

Of the 60 families, two to three were known to be in contact with SAVAK agents. In return for their reports, the government or an agent gave them money. One untrustworthy person caused a problem for me. There was a man with an amputated arm who sometimes went to the border of Iraq to buy grapes or other items to sell in the village. He had two sons in the school, and I liked them, because they were very smart, though their family was poor. The untrustworthy person went to the government and told them that I had sent this man to the border to get information. SAVAK arranged an interview. I was very worried, having secretly joined KDPI after coming to the village (although nobody in the village knew this). I answered their questions truthfully, and was believed, because this untrustworthy person had no proof.

The main family in the village were the former landlords of Soliman Kandi and several other villages—part of a big tribe covering 100 villages. Until the time of the Qajars, the king owned all land, favouring individuals or tribes most loyal to him by giving them land. As land meant power, these recipients became rulers in their own right. There were strict rules within a tribe and between tribes, so that even the wild pastures were demarcated for each tribe's use. But a series of government-enforced 20th century land reforms had broken this old order. Some landlords resisted, but Ali Nahid, the grandfather of this family, knew change was inevitable, so to avoid conflicts, he accepted the 1960s redistribution of some of his family's land. This meant that in my time people farmed their own land.

Ali Nahid had a big library, and although he was in his fifties and I in my twenties, we became friendly, because of our love of books, particularly those about history and politics. His paternal aunt was Qazi Muhammad's mother. One of his sisters was the wife of Qazi Muhammad's brother, Abul Gharsem Sadr Qazi, who was hung with Qazi Muhammad, and one brother had been an officer in Qazi Muhammad's army.

As a child, Ali Nahid had gone to the city and completed primary school, but he was largely self-educated. He had become head of his family after the death of his older brother, who was a member of Reza Shah's parliament, as well as a landscape artist and author of books. They were very precious books, beautifully handwritten both in Farsi and Kurdish, one being a novel set in the time after the 1219 Mongol invasion of Kurdistan, but when the religious police came to the village after the Iranian revolution, they took them all. Now they are lost.

Ali Nahid, his two sons and their families, and three brothers and their sons' families lived in a huge complex. In the middle of all the rooms was an enormous courtyard, with a large spring-fed pool. Outside this area were rooms to welcome visitors. Visitors could not go to the rooms of the women and children, but from a distance I occasionally saw Ali Nahid's grand-daughter Gohertuj, who was also the grand-daughter of Ali Nahid's eldest brother, the writer and painter. She led a life of complete seclusion.

Ali Nahid was the undisputed head of this large extended family, and still commanded much respect in the village. In the old days, there were different leadership systems in each village depending on the personalities. If the main family was not so respected, then the *malla* of the mosque, which was the centre for all prayer, discussions, celebrations, funerals, education and the market, had more power. But in Soliman Kandi, if there was an argument between families, people used to go to Ali Nahid although by my time, such matters were taken to the police. Still, there was no justice, because people could bribe the court.

After two years, I wanted to build a new school to accommodate more children. With help from Ali Nahid and the village people, we built four well-lit mud-walled rooms, the government supplying windows and doors. After I left the village, the government built a second school, to cope with the growing population. This was in spite of a huge exodus to the cities because there was not enough land to feed the people, and no electricity, ways to process the food or roads and transport to take seasonal produce to the markets.

I had been active in KDPI for three years, discussing issues and recruiting new members, when in 1963, at the second congress, Ahmed Tawfiq became the KDPI's secretary-general. I was told that a particular member from Piranshahr had gone to this congress. A few of us knew he had secret relations with the government, and I worried for the safety of the people I had recruited. I did not want them to face a four-year prison sentence.

I was also concerned about the direction of the organisation. Tawfiq was from Mahabad and had been living in Iraqi Kurdistan, working closely with Mostefa Barzani, but under him the KDPI was splitting, some people wanting to be more independent and active in eastern Kurdistan. These concerns made me gradually distance myself from the organisation, until I left altogether. Subsequent events, particularly in the late 1960s, made me glad I had.

After five years, I was transferred to Saghez primary school, after I married Gohertuj, the grand-daughter of Ali Nahid. Gohertuj and I began a new life together, one with electricity, running water, a proper kitchen and a bathroom. Saghez is on the plain close to Baneh, and only 40 kilometres from Soliman Kandi, so her family would often pick us up in their jeep and take us back to the village.

Although the students in Saghez were from poor families, they spoke very good Farsi and had more education and more time for studies than the students in the village. Also, I had to teach only one class, and all this made my job easier. The teachers were very enthusiastic and worked very hard, not because of any government pressure but because we felt a duty to educate Kurdish children. Occasionally my Kurdish background was raised in class. Although we were not allowed to teach in Kurdish, we could speak Kurdish in casual conversation, despite signs on school walls saying "Talk Farsi."

For those three years in Saghez, I was not politically active, instead concentrating on teaching and reading books about the ancient civilisations in Sumer, Egypt and China. My reading made me decide to study social science at Tehran University, majoring in demography, an important subject since Iran's rapidly urbanising population is predicted to be 100 million by 2020.

It was during my studies that I read *Nahzat Al-Qloob*, a book written by the 14th century Iranian geographer Hamdulla Mustofi. He described a people called the Kurds living in an area called Kurdistan, which consisted of 16 states extending from north-west Iran to Diyarbakir in central Turkey. However at Tehran University, there were no subjects in Kurdish history, sociology or geography. There were only two units of Kurdish language, taught by Dr Sadeek Mufti Zadeh.

As well as being a full-time student, it was compulsory to teach in a school each morning. I taught Year Four in a primary school in Ghalaimorhia, a very poor suburb near an army base on the main road south to Saveh, where many farming families from Azeri villages had settled. The Shah's government was destroying Iran's agricultural base, purchasing cheap grains and other crops from overseas.

The streets of Ghalaimorhi were narrow and dirty. There was electricity but no government-supplied water, sewerage or public transport. The people and their livestock lived in crowded rooms made of cement brick, with homemade toilets. They survived by raising animals, or by selling dirty underground water, cigarettes and tissues on the street. It was very much a third-world pocket in a rich, modern city, in a country able to afford the best army and military hardware in the Middle East.

I taught in one of a dozen small rooms, each overcrowded with more than forty students. The students had enough to eat but they were unhealthy because of the dirt and overcrowding. However they were good students and most went on to high school.

There was a rule allowing a teacher to transfer to another school after one year, but I chose to teach in Ghalaimorhi for four years, travelling an hour by bus each day. My salary was lower than my salary in the village, because the government encouraged teachers to go to more distant places. It was hard to support my family on the wage, especially after our daughter was born. We called her Bayan, 'the hour before dawn'.

I made a very good friend at the university, and we also taught together. He agreed with my assessment of the situation in KDPI after Ahmed Tawfiq took over, but told me everything had changed following the third congress, in 1973, when Abdul Rahman Qassemlou replaced Ahmed Tawfiq as secretary-general. Qassemlou was policy-orientated rather than personality-based. He had introduced democratic procedures and a social democratic program, aiming for democracy in Iran, and autonomy in Kurdistan. It seemed that at last, we had an intelligent leader who understood what we could do realistically, and this made me very excited.

I was considering becoming more politically active, my biggest worry being the effect of this on my family, but one Newroz holiday, while my friend was visiting his family in Baneh, he met with some KDPI cadres and *peshmergas*. The secret service found out about the meeting, the army surrounded the house, and in the fight, one KDPI cadre was killed. My friend escaped to Iraqi Kurdistan. This meant I lost my only political connection, and it was hard to meet others, because SAVAK was very active.

During this time I was given an illegal copy of Qassemlou's book and read it many times. Barzani's revolution in Iraqi Kurdistan was going very well, until the Algiers Agreement in 1975, when Iran agreed to close its border and cut its support for the Kurds in return for use of the deep channel in the Shatt Al-Arab, in accordance with an international agreement regarding the use of a waterway on the border of two countries.

The end of the Kurdish revolution was a sad turn of events. In the early 1970s, Kurds were united as never before and Iraq and Iran had a tenuous relationship. In hindsight, if the revolution had been brought to Iran, it may have been supported by the Arabs, who hated the Shah. When the revolution resumed in the late 1970s, it was fragmented by the formation of other Kurdish parties, the number of Kurds who were being forced to work for the Ba'aths, and the eight-year war between Iran and Iraq, which started when Saddam Hussein attempted to take back the Shatt Al-Arab. Thus that expensive, bloody war was a direct result of the governments and their allies wanting to halt the Kurdish struggle.

When I finished my degree, we returned to Piranshahr, where I taught social science at the only high school. My subject covered Iran's constitution, written in 1907, when for a brief period the Qajar shah allowed a democratically elected *majlis* (parliament) to assume power. In the preamble, the shah is described as a symbolic figurehead with less power than the prime minister. The prime minister is elected by the *majlis*, consisting of two to five representatives from each region, depending on the population. However, the next Qajar shah curtailed the parliament's powers, and when Colonel Reza Khan led a successful coup in 1921 and made himself shah in 1925, he became dictator, as did his son, Muhammad Reza.

In class, I trod a very fine line, going to the very edge of what could be said. I could not elaborate on the fact that Muhammad Reza Shah broke his own constitution by assuming absolute power and unlimited access to the nation's treasury. I could not discuss the spending of so much oil money on weapons and the army when a strong society needs schools, hospitals, roads and manufacturing infrastructure. Nor could I mention politicians like Muhammad Mossadeq, who became prime minister between 1951 and 1953. He told the Shah, "We respect you, but like England's king, you should do your job and we will do ours." When he nationalised the British-owned Iranian oil industry, from which Iran was only receiving a very small per centage of the revenue, Britain imposed an international boycott on Iran. Mossadeq tried to negotiate with US oil companies, but the USA decided to support the Shah and organised a successful coup. A year later, US oil companies negotiated exactly what they wanted with Muhammad Reza Shah.

I had no discipline problems. Iranian classrooms are not like Australian classrooms. There are many kinds of democracy and in Western societies an individual's freedom is given priority, whereas in the Middle East the 'common good' is emphasised, at least by the people. Also my students were very keen to learn, and I was very friendly and close to them. It was not like, 'I am the teacher, you are the student'. Even now my students telephone me from Iran, saying, "We learnt from you what we must do in our life."

It was good to be back home living with my parents and my young unmarried sister. She had become a teacher. I saw old friends and made new friends in the teaching profession: people who thought like me —that it was our duty to motivate the students to work hard. Then two years after our daughter was born we had a son. I wanted to call him Siamand, a good Kurdish name, but my father said, "No," because in the Kurdish legend, Siamand dies. Instead, my first son was called Samrand, after a beautiful mountain near Piranshahr, and after my father died, I called my second son Siamand.

In 1976, because of my demographic studies and my contacts in both the city and the villages, I was asked to be responsible for the census. In a 20-day course, I trained people to collect from villages statistical information on population numbers, age, sex and occupation. We established that 70,000 people lived in and around Piranshahr, most being under the age of 20. We did not collect information on ethnicity or religion, but were able to research the percentage of children reaching different levels of education. Only primary school was compulsory, and I discovered that less than 30 per cent were going on to high school, mainly because of economic difficulties and isolation. What surprised me most was that some ex-primary students claimed they had forgotten how to read or write with no newspapers or books to reinforce their brief time at school. I encouraged families and teachers to help children go on to high school, advising the Department of Education to set up schools at which students could live and eat for free. After 1979, the new government introduced such schools.

Discussions about Kurdish issues and democracy outside the classroom became more frequent during 1978, when demonstrations began against the Shah in Tehran and other cities. From the early 1970s, more and more intellectuals and students wanted change. Many were joining the leftist Chereek Fadaiee and Tudeh parties. A few with Shi'ite religious thinking joined the Mujahadeen. Popular outside Kurdistan was a more progressive integration of Shi'ite Islam and socialism outlined by Dr Ali Shariati, a highly respected university lecturer who was assassinated in 1977 by SAVAK, three weeks after escaping to Britain. The Shah feared religious thinking more than communism. He would say, "Our first enemy is religion and backward black thinking. Our other enemy is red thinking." Dr Shariati had written many illegal books opposing traditional Marxism, describing a liberal, democratic form of Islamic socialism, one where neither Marxism nor religion ruled politics, but in which the rights of the poor were assured.

Despite differences in thinking, nearly everyone wanted a fairer, more democratic country. The first to demonstrate were the university students in the cities, then high school teachers in every town began encouraging their students to join the rallies, and after that, the general public walked with us. We marched two or three times in Piranshahr. The rallies would end at the mosques, where the *mallas* spoke about the need for democracy in Iran and a recognition of our Kurdish identity. As more and more joined the demonstrations all over the country, the SAVAK, police and army gradually lost their power. They could not arrest everyone.

The big problem was that while the vast majority of people hoped for democracy, they could not openly discuss how to achieve it. Throughout the country, the *mallas* did the talking, the mosques being the only safe places. Intellectuals like Mehdi Barzagan,[b] Shupour Bakhtiar[c] and Dr Ghulam Hussein Sadgheeqi,[d] and Kurdish leaders could talk only in secret to special groups—not to the general public. Consequently, there were no meetings in Kurdistan between the political parties, nor were there books about Marxism, Islamic Socialism and other models in any library or bookshop. A person caught with such a book could be imprisoned, or even sentenced to death.

The only certainty on which we were all united was that the Shah had to go. We knew that the Iraqi revolutions of 1958, 1963 and 1968 had not brought good changes. However these were not revolutions of the people, but coups organised by elites, and also, because the Middle East has huge oil reserves, outside influences invariably shape events. All we could do was hope change would be for the better.

Schools closed a couple of weeks before the Shah left the country. With news of his departure, people from all nationalities, religions and political parties celebrated in the street. Well-known political leaders such as Mehdi Barzagan led massive demonstrations through Tehran's streets. People feared that the army would stage a coup, but after a couple of weeks, in February 1979, Khomeini flew from Paris to Tehran, immediately promising that the constitution would be rewritten, and the new government would develop rural areas. We hoped he would include Kurdistan but feared our mainly Sunni background would disadvantage us.

The country continued to celebrate, the army saying, "It is up to the people. We go back to our army bases." In some cities, Shah supporters were killed or imprisoned, and there were fires and looting, but the *peshmergas* controlled Piranshahr, so there was no trouble.

I was afraid for my country, that Islamic leaders would not let other political parties be represented in the government. However when Mehdi Barzagan was appointed prime minister in the Islamic Revolutionary Council, a provisional government of 15 members, I thought, "He is an intelligent leader and a balance to the Islamic leaders. He will push for democracy." None of us knew how strong the *mallas* would become, and how they would rid the country of intellectuals such as Shupour Bakhtiar, killed in Paris by an Iranian terrorist in 1991.

The schools reopened one week after Khomeini's return, but there was new divisions among the teachers. One teacher might belong to the Mujahadeen, another to Chereek Fadaiee, one to Tudeh, another to KDPI. It was a time of uncertainty. Parties were openly active, the writing and reading of Kurdish was no longer banned, books, newspapers and two monthly magazines in Kurdish were published and distributed, and there was a new freedom to discuss politics and social issues. However, you cannot go to bed a dictator and wake up a democrat, and some individuals were killed for thinking a different way. Even within a family, father and son might disagree.

Two or three weeks after the Islamic Revolutionary Council was appointed, government representatives led by Darius Faroohar, a minister in Mossadeq's government and now Minister of Work Affairs, were sent to Mahabad to talk with Kurdish leaders. I was asked to attend the meeting by a representative of both Qassemlou and Shaykh Ezzeddin Hosseini, a highly respected religious leader in Mahabad. When Faroohar flew to Piranshahr, I met with him before going to Mahabad. At the meeting Faroohar addressed Qassemlou, Shaykh Ezzeddin Hosseini, students and intellectuals, advising, "First, let us establish our power base for democracy. We must not miss this chance. Then we can talk about autonomy."

Afterwards, Faroohar came back to Piranshahr and held a meeting at the mosque, which he asked me to attend. The people were chanting, "Democracy for Iran and autonomy for Kurdistan," and he repeated, "Democracy for Iran." I asked him, "Why not continue?" He replied, "Because I want what is most important first." I told him, "Until we have autonomy for all nations in Iran, we have no democracy. You must tell us what you think about autonomy." He refused, but I believe he was sincere in his wish to consult the Kurdish people. Throughout the next two decades, he advocated democracy and was to be imprisoned. Then in 1998, he and his wife were assassinated at home in Tehran.

It was at the Mahabad meeting that I met Qassemlou for the first time. His message was that we needed to practice democracy within KDPI, and hold discussions with other parties and people around the country, to build up a common understanding.

A month later, there was a referendum asking whether people wanted an Islamic republic. Only the Kurdish people in Mahabad, Sardasht, Piranshahr, Saghez, and Sanandaj voted 'no', because the Shi'ite leaders were not describing a plan for democratic structures and human rights within the Islamic republic. This 'no' vote meant the provisional government thought we were standing against them, that we wanted to divide the country, or that we supported the Shah. Government representatives came and talked with our leaders, and during this time, I met with Qassemlou a number of times, not as a KDPI member but as a teacher and a resident of Piranshahr. We discussed how to establish a free media, Kurdish schools, a fair justice system, and a local council to govern a Kurdish state.

But step by step, the situation turned for the worse. Three to four months after the Mahabad meeting, people like Faroohar lost power in the provisional government. In Kurdistan, Iranian army and police numbers increased dramatically and people could feel war looming. Many escaped from the cities and villages. It was during this time that I rejoined KDPI. Then five months after the referendum, on 19 August 1979, the anniversary of the 1953 coup against Mossadeq, Khomeini declared that KDPI was illegal and announced a holy war or *jihad* against the Kurds. The first area to be attacked was Sanandaj. After that, the army came to Saghez, then Piranshahr, Mahabad and Sardasht.

The army would approach a city, bombing with tanks and missiles, and the *peshmerga* would defend, but the *peshmergas* were outnumbered and poorly equipped. It must be said the Iranian forces were not as indiscriminate as Saddam Hussein's army. The Iranians are more selective and devious. They have long memories and prefer selective assassination, or to kill with sugar, as in the English saying, 'an iron hand in a velvet glove.' However it was not all sugar. In 1980, *pasdars* came to Gharna, a village near Piranshahr, and shot dead 68 people, including women and children, and the *imam*, as he pleaded for the lives of his people, a Qur'an in his hand. Similarly, *pasdars* killed people in Kalata'an, Soofiyan and Sarookani, because they were suspected of harbouring *peshmergas*.

Some months after rejoining KDPI, and one day before the army came to Piranshahr, I escaped with my family to a village under the control of KDPI. For those three months of war, with our children aged six and four, we moved between villages, staying with relatives and friends.

The government controlled everywhere by day, but the KDPI *peshmergas* came into the cities at night to fight the *pasdars*, who had more power than the army. They even had a minister in the cabinet. The *pasdars* were students, workers and intellectuals who were motivated by Islamic beliefs to police 'unIslamic' activities such as music, and women not wearing Islamic dress.

After three months the government announced that it wanted to negotiate a ceasefire, having come under some outside pressure from other Muslim countries and parties like the Palestinian Liberation Organisation. It was a case of smiling for the enemy while planning for tomorrow. A meeting in Mahabad was organised between representatives of KDPI, Chereek Fadaiee, Komala, Shaykh Ezzeddin Hosseini, and Sabghiyan, a government representative. Before the meeting, Qassemlou asked Shaykh Ezzeddin Hosseini not to tell Sabghiyan that the Kurdish leaders belonged to different parties, but for some unknown reason, Shaykh Ezzeddin Hosseini introduced people by their name and party. Sabaghiyan said, "We are not talking with the Chereek Fadaiee and Komala because they do not represent enough Kurds," and immediately walked out.

During the ceasefire, we returned to Piranshahr by car. *Peshmergas* had replaced the army or police on the streets. Friends had already told us that the army had ordered the burning of our house. The walls had bullet holes, and the doors and windows were broken. Inside, everything was burnt, but a few neighbours had taken some of our carpets and antiques to their houses and they brought them back.

In the spring of 1979, there was an election for representatives of each region to go to the Khobregan to discuss a draft of the new constitution. In its draft form, the constitution recognised ethnic rights and languages, and outlined a system of government where a president would be elected by the people but would have less power than the prime minister, who would be elected by the 270-member *majlis* (Islamic Consultative Assembly). This would include a representative for the Christian Assyrians, Chaldeans and Armenians as well as the Jews, although no non-Muslim could represent a geographical region. Ultimate authority would be in the hands of the religious leader, and an unelected Council of Experts comprising six religious leaders and six lawyers, with power to veto any legislation passed by the *majlis*.

All men and women over the age of 20 were allowed to vote. In our region, called Western Azerbaijan, three members were elected to the Khobregan, one of them Qassemlou. On the day he was meant to go to Tehran, Khomeini called him "the most corrupt of the earth", because Qassemlou advocated democracy and Kurdish rights as opposed to a theocracy. Qassemlou thought it was too dangerous to go, so no-one represented the Kurds in the Khobregan. The ruling *mallas* had free rein in preparing the new constitution, which made no mention of ethnic groups and their rights. From the beginning, the government dictated from the top.

In early 1980, KDPI held a congress in Mahabad, where the government had no power. Nearly 300 people attended, electing 25 members to the central committee, myself included. The central committee re-elected Qassemlou as secretary-general. Knowing Iran was preparing for a general election, we discussed KDPI policies, and what compromises we were prepared to make to avoid another war. We did not want to have villages destroyed and people killed as had happened in Iraqi Kurdistan, so we agreed that if the government accepted just one of a number of points, it was a good sign for future negotiations.

The election for the *majlis* was to be held in the spring of 1980, and I was asked to nominate for the towns of Sardasht and Piranshahr. I was still teaching but the government had stopped paying salaries to teachers of whom they disapproved, which included me. I talked to people in the city and villages, saying, "It is not important that you elect me. Think about the issues and exercise your democratic right." I was elected, but while preparing to go to Tehran some Kurdish city governors and councillors were arrested in Tehran. They had been attempting to negotiate with various ministers about public matters like electricity, health, transport, and oil, but they were imprisoned for one to three weeks, just for being Kurds. There were protest demonstrations in Piranshahr and other cities, and in this atmosphere of terror and anti-democracy, the elected Kurdish representatives sent a telegram to the central government, saying, "We are willing to represent our people in the assembly on condition our security and safety are guaranteed." We waited four months. A reply never came, and the parliament started without anyone to represent our region. In the election for president, a vast majority elected Banisadr, but he was unable to put his democratic thinking into practice. Step by step, war began again.

First, the government came to the cities, then to the villages, forcing KDPI *peshmergas* to take up defensive positions in the mountains. When Iraq attacked Iran in September, we tried to negotiate a ceasefire in Kurdistan, at least until the war was over, but the government refused, continuing to pour soldiers and *pasdars* into Kurdistan.

Iranian media repeatedly reported, "Kurds are atheists, enemies of Islam and the new government. They are backward and uneducated, they know only the language of the gun, and are supported by nations who want to destroy us." We would answer this propaganda in our radio programs and newspapers—saying that we are Muslim and Iranian, that we want freedom and democracy—but had limited ability to reach the people. As a result of the propaganda, the military and religious police who came to Kurdistan, indoctrinated with hatred, were determined to bring the Kurdish atheists back to the one true path.

One story told by a *peshmerga* reflects the extent of this indoctrination. In the winter of 1981, on the road between Piranshahr and Sardasht, a wounded *basiji*, (a section of the *pasdar*) was taken captive. He was put to bed beside a traditional wood-fuelled heater, the government having stopped all fuel coming into Kurdistan. When the *peshmerga* minding him gave his only blanket and shared with him the little food he had, the *basiji* could not believe the kindness saying, "Why you do this? We are told you are wild people." When he heard the early morning call to prayer he was shocked, exclaiming, "Oh Godless, are you ridiculing me?" Where are your atheist leaders? Where are your pleasure rooms?" The *peshmerga* patiently treated him until the *basiji* was able to walk around the village. He saw the extreme poverty, the lack of electricity, sewerage and tap water, and compared it with his own village around Kirman, in the east of Iran. Before returning to his family after two months, he apologised to those who cared for him, saying that if he lived in such bad conditions he too would fight for his people.

It was during 1980-81 that KDPI ran a series of courses in mobile tent schools. I had been sacked from teaching, and at the congress in Mahabad the 25 members elected to the central committee were each put in charge of a duty. I was chosen to organise a series of courses to teach KDPI cadres about the party, history, economics and language so they could understand our place in the world.

We sent letters to all the local KDPI organisations, asking them to send people for the free three-week course. I was not paid. My father had died one year before the Iranian revolution and I had sold some shops, so we lived on reserves. My mother lived wherever Gohertuj lived. Now she lives with my sister in Iran, and still my past activities may cause them problems. At any time, they could be imprisoned, or be refused a job or a university position. For these sorts of reasons, Gohertuj did not like my involvement with politics. She has bad memories of this time, such as hiding the children under a bridge for hours while an aeroplane bombed the village. We had many arguments, because a man's political activity destroys everything—the family, the lifestyle, the children's education—and most of all, the family lives in constant danger.

The first course was held five minutes' walk from the village of Kherajo, where the government was weak. Students came from various places, including Mariwan and Kirmanshah. Some were members of the KDPI student union still going to high school. Others were cadres working for their local organisation. None had seen fighting. All were men aged between 20 and 30. For girls, it is very difficult in our culture to live among men in isolated places, and although more and more women were joining the KDPI, they rarely did so as cadres and *peshmergas*.

We held classes in a tent and lived in tents, about six tents in all, erected under the trees so that aeroplanes could not see them. I gave lectures to about 30 students, all very committed. After the lecture, I encouraged them to ask questions and discuss issues, which was unfamiliar to them.

My subject was political sociology. I taught in Kurdish from Qassemlou's book—about the history and politics of Kurdistan. Briefly I would cover the empire of the Medes and the later empires that ruled Kurdistan, including the Persians between 550 and 331BC, the Greeks until 226AD, the Sassanians until 637AD, then successive Islamic empires including the Khaznavids in Firdawsi's time. I would teach them about the four very destructive invasions of people from the east: the Ghoz Turks at the end of the ninth century, the Seljuk Turks in 1037, the Mongols from 1231, and the Taimooryan (Tamerlanes) in the 1380s. These invasions changed central and western Asia forever.

I would go on to describe the clash between the two powerful empires at the beginning of the 16th century, that of the Ottomans (1300-1920) and the Safavid Persians (1499-1736). I explained how the Safavid Shah, Isma'il Safavi, reigning from 1502 to 1518, replaced Sunni Islam with Shi'ite Islam throughout Iran, but because the Kurds remained Sunni, they became second-class citizens, and when the Kurdish tribal leaders offered to help the young Safavid Shah against Sultan Selim and his Ottoman army in the Chaldean War of 1514 near Khoy, the Shah refused their help. Instead, he ordered their imprisonment. In contrast, Sultan Selim used religious sentiment to ensure the loyalty of his Sunni Kurds. The Shah lost the war, and for the first time Kurdistan was divided—the Zagros Mountains becoming the border between the Ottomans and Safavids.

We studied the 19th and 20th centuries in more depth. Up until 1800, the territory under Iranian control included Georgia and Armenia, extending west to Anatolia and east to Afghanistan, and the term 'Iranian people' referred to all nations in that empire. Then Russia took over Georgia in 1801, and Armenia in 1928, while the British took Kabul, in Afghanistan, in 1878–80.

We discussed the relative independence of the Kurdish emirates, each dominated by a tribe that rose to power at different times. Among others there were the tribes of Elam, Hamadan, Kirmanjun, Lur, Ardalan, Mukrian, Rhurmiah and Khoy in modern-day Iran, and Bahdinan, Baban and Soran in modern-day Iraq. Then there were the emirates of Jumi, Dersim, Zilan, Hakkari and Bitlis, and the powerful dynasty of Botan, which had its own currency and covered an area in present-day Syria and Turkey. In 1842, Amir Badrkhan of Botan led the first uprising in modern history, that was squashed by the Ottomans with help from French and British troups. In the 19th century, the Ottomans tried to centralise control of their eastern region, because the Austro-Hungarian Empire was preventing further expansion in the west, and the Kurdish emirs who cooperated with the government grew in power.

In greater detail we studied the second division of Kurdistan, after World War One, and the subsequent uprisings in each of the four nation-states, analysing why each of them failed. I proposed that there were three main obstacles to the establishment of an independent Kurdistan: our land had no sea access; we were surrounded by enemies; and we were crippled by the divisions between Kurdish tribes. Before World War One, tribes governed the whole of the Middle East. One tribe would come to power and dominate others, like the Ottomans, Safavids and Qajars, but there was no Kurdish tribe able to dominate other Kurdish tribes, perhaps because they were divided by other empires, geography and religions. They were also isolated and underdeveloped, the uneducated tribal leaders having not thought of forming a nation-state. With Kurdistan divided, the Kurdish nation found it even harder to unite, especially with no fair legal or political system in any of the nation-states occupying Kurdistan. In the past, when trouble came, we could escape to the mountains and into other parts of Kurdistan, buy land and settle, but modern borders prevent this.

The liberation struggles of Palestine and Eritrea were studied, as was the program of KDPI, the different types of socialism and democracy. In our thinking, democracy must come first, KDPI's goal being a multi-party system within an Iranian confederation. We were against dictatorial communism, where the government owns everything. We wanted both collective and private ownership, as well as a strong social insurance system and the opportunity to plan our education and other matters, as do the states of Australia and the USA, leaving defence and foreign policy to a central government.

We discussed the necessary elements of democracy, that it must ensure freedom of religion, political parties, languages and other forms of cultural expression. The media has to be decentralised, and the constitution of the country must support these freedoms, with an independent court system, that ensures the people in power are responsible to parliament and the parliament is responsible to the people.

Qassemlou taught economics, covering the economic development of Kurdistan, Iran and the Middle East. Another teacher taught the Kurdish language, its history and its relationship to other languages, because some of the cadres could not read and write Kurdish. We taught Kurdish in the Sorani script. Kurdish has 25 letters of Arabic, plus seven letters not found in Arabic, and no equivalent for some Farsi sounds.

We would teach five hours a day, often talking into the night—there was no other entertainment. The local KDPI organisation was poor, relying on voluntary donations, but they supplied our food, and the local people donated what food they could. Their lives were extremely hard, because the government was not letting basic necessities like wheat, barley, sugar, rice, tea, oil and kerosene into Kurdistan. Sometimes we only ate bread and cheese.

We were in no danger in Kherajo, and after that first course, I stayed with my family for several months in between collecting cadres and organising the next course. People never came to my home. I would visit and talk to cadres and *peshmergas* in different villages, and attend the central committee meetings held over seven to 10 days every two months.

Kherajo had become unsafe, so the next three-week course was held near some villages in the Qaderabad Valley, between Piranshahr and Sardasht, in the middle of very high, snow-capped mountains covered in the deciduous stone-fruit trees we call *go'eejh*. The air was so clear that KDPI had built a hospital there for pulmonary patients. We were more organised and had very good students. Again, we lived in tents, but we had a generator for light, although we had to be careful not to be seen from the air. Before and after the course, aeroplanes bombed the area, killing two or three *peshmergas*.

Our third course was held near the village of Alut, near the town of Baneh, below high mountains in a deep valley at the mouth of the Little Zab River, where people grew apples and pears. Although our circumstances were more dangerous, because we were closer to government places, the course ran smoothly. Not so the fourth course, held in the village of Hamamyan, near the town of Bukan,[e] which was under KDPI control. Some of the students were worried about their families, because Iraq and sometimes Iran were bombing their cities. Two and a half weeks into the course, Bukan was attacked by Iranian forces from the Miandoab front, and *peshmergas* came to our area because it was the best place from which to defend the city. I was teaching in the tent when we heard aeroplanes and helicopters, then bombs exploding, followed by heavy artillery fire. We had to escape by jeep and tractor, with soldiers in helicopters firing machine guns at us. The students were young, and seemed to thrive on the adrenalin, but the reality was that they were now in danger of being arrested by government agents. We stayed with *peshmergas* in a mountain village north of Bukan, next to the Tatahoo River, and after three days we told the students to return to their organisation.

The fifth and last training term of KDPI cadres in which I was involved was held in 1981, in the village of Singan,[f] a rich agricultral area growing wheat and fruit, close to the town of Ushnaviyeh. It was the school holidays, so the teachers allowed us to use the local school. Nearly a century ago, the chief of Singan had built a castle on a hill in the middle of the village, but Iran had bombed this castle the year before. The owner showed us some spots in the soil, saying, "I can make fire from these spots." When he put a match to the spot, it ignited like a gas fire. The bombs had not been conventional.

The students attending these courses were not interested in becoming *peshmergas*. They would go back and work for their local organisations, or teach politics to other *peshmergas* who were undergoing their one to two months' military training. Some have since become members of the central committee, or were financed by KDPI to study medicine, sociology, history and politics at European universities. After 1992, those who studied medicine were asked to work in the KDPI hospital in Koi Sinjak in Iraqi Kurdistan for up to 12 months. They could not return to Iran.

After the last course, my family and I continued to move around for another year, our children having to constantly change schools, to avoid the government finding us. We lived on our reserves, and from trade, paying no rent, electricity or water bills. Our only expense was food.

I wanted to end my political activities—mainly because of the hard conditions under which my family had been forced to live and the way my political activity would affect them in the future, but also because some new political thinking within the party made me feel uncomfortable. I was scared about where we were heading. What was our goal? We were losing more cities to the government, and problems between KDPI and Komala were escalating. KDPI *peshmergas* were being forced to move into Iraqi Kurdistan, although Qassemlou was still in Iran, pleading with people, "Don't leave. If we have only one village, it is better that we stay." I went to the politburo meeting (the politburo being higher than the central committee) held after the fifth congress in Shivajo in

1982, and told them, "I must say goodbye to politics." Qassemlou asked my friends to convince me to stay, but I refused. I always felt responsible for the safety of those who supported us. I do not believe in putting people in unnecessary danger, and the government was not willing to give us any concessions. Fighting was the only alternative. Later, the government softened, giving tokens like allowing Kurdish music, but authorities continued to use the media to fan hatred towards Kurds.

In 1984, there was another election and the government selected our region's representatives. KDPI and other Kurdish political parties continued to be active, so the government laid a trap, announcing that political activists could resume a normal life, although their files would remain open. I sent my family back to Saghez.

Soon after, when visiting a friend's home in Mahabad, two government representatives came to see me, saying, "We know you have been politically active for an illegal party. If we did not have problems with both Iraq and the Kurds, we would kill you. Be careful or we will arrest you and you will never see Kurdistan again." Two weeks later, they arrested me in Mahabad. After six months, I was taken to court. I had no lawyer. I was told what I had done and was allowed to talk for five minutes. I said, "Iran has a political problem. We need democracy and to live together peacefully." The judge said, "No. You are against Islam and the Qur'an." I said, "Thirty million people voted for Banisadr to be president but now he lives in Paris. What has happened to this country?" He replied, "You are advising us how to run this country?" "I am concerned by the political situation." "We do not need your advice." I was not told the details of my sentence.

I was in prison in Urmia and Tehran. Conditions are bad in every Iranian prison, and my experiences would take up a book, which one day I will write. Suffice it to say that Iran's methods are more complex and psychological than the harsh methods used in Iraqi and Turkish prisons. Most of the political prisoners were well educated and in the prime of their life. Some were teachers, and in one cell I was with two doctors. These people could have contributed to their country, but instead, they were in prison.

After six months, the prisons were becoming so full, I was taken back to court. I was told, "We will send you to live in Kirman or Yazd." I said, "In those places, you have taught people to hate the Kurds. To be in prison is better than that. Allow me to stay in Tehran, or take me back to prison." I was allowed to stay in Tehran, provided I report to the prison every month.

I supported my family by buying car parts and sending them to Urmia. Back in Kurdistan, the period 1985–1987 saw heavy fighting between KDPI and government forces, and between Kurdish political parties, the fighting supported by outside elements not wanting any Kurdish party to become strong and stable. In 1988, when the Iraqi-Iran War ended, political activity became even more dangerous. I was afraid the government would catch people I knew, and many escaped to Iraqi Kurdistan. Then in 1989, news came that Qassemlou had been assassinated in Vienna while meeting Iranian government officials. The Iranian government denied involvement.

After seven years in exile, I went back to court and was told, "You can go back to Urmia, but you cannot live anywhere else in Kurdistan," so in 1990, I bought a home in Urmia.

That August, Iraq invaded Kuwait. In many ways, this war and its aftermath were good news for Kurdish people. With Saddam Hussein and his forces preoccupied with the southern front, Kurdish from Iran found a safe haven in Iraqi Kurdistan. Following the Allies' declaration of a no-fly zone and the establishment of a Kurdish parliament in 1992, the KDPI headquarters moved to Koi Sinjak. I had contact with some friends there, and agreed with their policy that they support the Kurdish parliament and autonomy in Iraqi Kurdistan before working for autonomy in Iran. If the Kurdish parliament became strong, it could represent all of us, telling the world about our situation, as the Azeri can do from the independent republic of Azerbaijan. Their parliament represents seven million people, but can also speak at the UN for the 20 million Azeri in Iranian Azerbaijan.

From 1990 until 1994, I lived a normal life, although I had underground contact with KDPI. My file was not finished in the court, and if Iranian secret agents heard of my activities, I could be arrested. I was scared for my life and for my family's future, so in 1995, I decided we should escape.

We had no official visas, but were welcomed by friends in Koi Sinjak. That year, KDPI had become the first Kurdish party to have a democratic change of leadership. Abdullah Hasan Zadeh replaced Mostefa Hejri as secretary-general, Hejri continuing to work as Zadeh's assistant. But the mood at the base was tense—we were not out of danger. In the previous 12 months, at least 130 KDPI and other politically active Kurds from Iran had been killed by Iranian secret agents, and other people paid to kill them. Iran had too many tentacles in Iraq, so I decided to go to Turkey.

When we arrived in Ankara, the UNHCR told us to return to the border. I said, "That is impossible. We could be caught and deported," and we were given permission to stay in Kayseri. After 40 days, our application for refugee status was approved. We were given about US$100 a month, half of what we needed, the rest coming from our savings and our friends.

Australia was my first preference, because I knew some English. After an interview at the Australian Embassy, we were accepted, and 18 months later, we came. We have been here four years, and every day I study English. My daughter is married with one child. My eldest son is studying information technology at a technical college, and my other son is in Year Eight. Both sons have adapted well.

On 28 July 1996, the Iranian army invaded Iraqi Kurdistan and attacked the KDPI base at Koi Sinjak. Fortunately, no-one was killed. After that, Jalal Talabani announced that all Iranian Kurds must leave Koi Sinjak, but KDPI said, "We have nowhere else to go." Since September 1996, Koi Sinjak is under PUK administration, KDPI continuing to be active in education and producing radio programs, the PUK intermittently putting them under pressure, or using their presence as a negotiation tool with the Iranian government.

In Iran, after President Banisadr, Muhammad Ali Rajayeh became president, then Rajayeh Ali Khameni, followed by Hamshami Rafsanjani, Khameni becoming Iran's spiritual leader when Khomeini died. Each president was more conservative than the previous one, and Hamshami Rafsanjani had the constitution changed by the Khobrighan to give more power to the position. When the new constitution was put to the vote, most people voted 'yes', because their education level is low, and they are afraid to oppose the government. However, in 1997, an overwhelming majority elected Khatami as president. He is a liberal intellectual who has visited Kurdistan, but Kurdish issues are a very low priority, and the more moderate *majlis* still has to answer to the theocracy.

While no Iranian census takes into account ethnicity, it is estimated that Kurds are only 10 per cent of the population, and are therefore the third largest nation in Iran, occupying seven per cent of the land. The Kurdish region is rich in petrol, water and agriculture. However, Kurds continue to be seen as backward, third-class citizens, and their Sunni representatives are not able to climb up the Shi'ite-dominated government or military hierarchy as easily as do the assimilated Sunni Kurdish in Turkey. Their voice is small in the *majlis*, and also, if Kurds are given more rights, the central government must then give similar rights to all six nations in Iran, especially the Azeri, who may outnumber Farsi, as well as the Arabs, who occupy a rich region in the south. With six nations represented in the parliament, a constant struggle between conservative and progressive thinkers, and Arab and Western politics playing a role, it is hard to get support for change.

The biggest problem above all others is Iran's excessive population growth. This growth and modernisation are changing every dynamic. There are now better roads, but these can also be used for fighting *peshmerga*. In Kurdish villages, they now have television, an effective tool of assimilation. The government is supporting farmers and making considerable effort to provide schools, medical facilities, electricity, and help for old people, but tends to favour Shi'ite villages. Also, when government officials become more established, they become more corrupt and less concerned with helping the poor.

Under present circumstances, I think it is more practical to work for democracy within present borders rather than for an independent nation-state called Kurdistan, especially because the Kurdish population is growing more rapidly compared to other nations. For example, in multicultural Urmia, the Kurdish population was estimated to be 50 per cent in the 1990s. A Turkish intelligence service report to cabinet in the 1990s predicted the Kurdish population of Turkey would reach 40 per cent by the year 2000 and sixty per cent by 2020. Also our reliance on guns has determined our history. It has made us even more dependent on a hierarchy of enemies, who are more than willing to supply us with small arms.

What is certain is that the whole of the Middle East will go through dramatic changes in coming decades. In the 20th century, the Persian Gulf was the petrol heart of the world. In the 21st century, this mantle falls on newly established republics around the Caspian Sea, to the north and east of Kurdistan. Azerbaijan, with its population of Shi'ite Turks and its close relationship with Turkey, is becoming the new Kuwait.

But the most important dynamic for the region is the scarcity of water—for drinking, let alone for irrigation. The main sources of water for the Middle East are in Kurdistan. A war over water is not out of the question. A war could change borders, and if this happens, the largest nation without a homeland—the Kurds—must be given consideration.

Whatever course the future takes, it is vital for Kurdish people to prepare for democracy. Democracy does not automatically follow a people's revolution. It needs time, method, and practice in catering for different ways of thinking. For this to occur, people have to be well educated and informed, so they have a better understanding of issues and are more flexible and rational when discussing them.

For more informed strategies and leadership, careful, objective and well-documented research and analysis is needed on our history, our present circumstances and, above all, our future role in the Middle East. Whether or not we remain an international colony or progress to nation-statehood, we need to be able to negotiate our place in the region on the basis of our potential political and economic power.

Wish

A poem by Marif Agha-e translated by Kamran Avin

I am angry with these borders
That surround me.
I wish I could live
In the borderless world of your eyes.

Prison

A poem by Marif Agha-e translated by Kamran Avin

Since the day
My eyes were scared of
Prison and cell,
The door of that prison of fear
Was locked inside me.

Mahabad

The Eye Can See But the Hand is Short

A life story based on interviews with Fariba Qazi

Qazi means 'judge'. Qazi Muhammad was my paternal grandfather's brother and my paternal grandmother's cousin. My mother's mother was sister to Qazi's mother and her father was brother to Qazi's father. I was not born when Qazi Muhammad was hung in March 1947, in Maydan Qazi Muhammad,[a] but his image was always with me—in the city of Mahabad, where I grew up, and within my family. He was a spirit in all of us. He wanted peace and dignity for his people and, for this, he was willing to sacrifice his life.

Like his father and his father's father, and in every generation of my family for 500 years, Qazi Muhammad was a judge. My family always sent the boys to another city for their education, where they would be less distracted and learn independence. The Qazi judges learnt the law in the mosques and were respected as being fair-minded. Reza Shah appointed Qazi Muhammad as High Court Judge for the Western Region, so all the most difficult cases came to him.

During World War Two, when the Iranian government was weak and withdrew from Kurdistan, there was fear that the Kurdish tribes might fight each other, so the Kurdish Democratic Party was formed in 1945, under the leadership of Qazi Muhammad. The feeling was that it was time to establish a country called Kurdistan. The aim was independence, not autonomy or a federation, so that the Kurdish nation could be like any other nation—believe in themselves, govern themselves, and not rely on charity.

When the Republic of Mahabad was declared, in January 1946, Qazi Muhammad was the natural leader. His cousin, Muhammad Hossein Seif Qazi, *agha* of the Qazi tribe, became a minister. My mother often told us stories about Qazi Muhammad—how he was a very down-to-earth person and strong in mind and body, swimming every day, even in winter. He would go around the city to talk to the people. He did not put himself on a pedestal. He never took power for granted and always emphasised education and looking after the poor. All his daughters finished 12 years of school and he was the first Kurdish leader to encourage fathers to educate their daughters as well as their sons. When he visited the new Kurdish schools he saw the ragged clothes of many of the children so he ordered uniforms to be given to every student.

When Iranian forces came to Tabriz, the capital of the Republic of Azerbaijan, which had been set up at the same time as the Mahabad republic, they killed many soldiers, and after the republic's president, Pishawairi, escaped to Russia, the Iranian forces massacred more than 30,000 people. The Mahabad republic had a well-trained army, which could have fought the Iranians. My uncle had gone to Russia to train as an officer, but 11 months after the republic was declared, Qazi Muhammad decided to surrender to save the people from slaughter. He gave the other leaders a choice: surrender or escape, and the night before Mostefa Barzani and his followers were to leave for Iraqi Kurdistan, Mostefa Barzani begged Qazi Muhammad to come. "With you, we will get world recognition, but without you, the world will see us as rebels."

Our mother told us that while Qazi Muhammad was in prison, the authorities offered to let him go to England or Russia and save his own life, but he refused, saying, "The people gave me their trust and I swore I would never betray them." He believed that without him his people had within them the belief and courage to gain their freedom.

Qazi Muhammad was hung with his brother and cousin. My mother described how on the day of his hanging, Qazi Muhammad told those present, "Every drop of my blood will become a *peshmerga* who will fight for an independent Kurdish nation." Beside him, his cousin, Muhammad Hossein Seif Qazi Khan,[b] sang *A-Rhaqeeb* as they put the rope around his neck. He was so big that he broke the rope three times, which under Iranian law should have qualified him to live, but they shot him in the head, then hung up his body.

My paternal grandfather, Qazi Karim, Qazi Muhammad's brother, was also a judge. After the hangings he was so overcome with grief he became temporarily paralyzed. His seven sons and their families lived in a complex attached to the old stone courthouse, a huge stone-slab courtyard and a covered pool with living quarters above, in the centre of all the rooms. I lived there until I was six.

Because no-one in the next generation became a judge (my father, Qazi Muhammad's nephew, worked as a government statistician) so one by one each family moved away and built separate houses. We moved to a large house on two acres of land in a new suburb on the outskirts of Mahabad, looking out over high mountains, which encircle the town. There was a room for women visitors, a room for men visitors, a large saloon for living, and five or six other rooms for sleeping, until my father added two more storeys.

Servants and their families came from the villages to live in the separate rooms around the courtyard, many servants staying for years until they had saved enough money to build their own house on land my father would give them. A man made tea for all the visitors and three or four others looked after the yard and vegetable garden. A young girl helped care for the children and an older woman helped my mother cook, but my mother was always in charge of the cooking and never let anyone else milk the cows.

There were nine children in our family. My mother had six years' of schooling, which was a lot for that generation, and she could help us with homework. Most of our teachers were Persian but they respected our family. I did not like school. I hated history especially. It was all about the shahs and how many people they had killed. We spoke Kurdish in the playground and sometimes even in the classroom, but although at home we had books in Kurdish, all printed in Iraq, our parents never taught us to read Kurdish. Also, Kurdish books were illegal until Khomeini came to power, in 1979, so we had to read Kurdish poets like Hafez and Mawlawi in Persian.

Seven of the nine children, including three out of four girls, have tertiary educations. One sister is a lecturer in accountancy at the university in Kirmanshah, Iran's biggest Kurdish city. My two other sisters are writers. Mariam is a year younger than me. Three of her Kurdish short stories have been published in Iraqi Kurdistan. Maybe she inherited her storytelling ability from our mother and mother's mother. When we visited our grandmother in the village of Sarakarmish, she would tell us stories at night beside a kerosene lamp. There was no electricity, no bathroom or kitchen, my grandmother baking bread in a *tandoor*. She told us that her grandmother or great-grandmother was the inspiration for a play called *Mother of a Nation*, performed at the time of the Mahabad republic. In one scene when the woman's three sons lie dead after fighting the soldiers she does not cry but scratches her face and smears her blood over her sons' faces. A soldier watching laughs at her, saying "If you did not want them to die, why did you teach them no better?" and she replies, "I am not putting my blood on them because they die, but rather so you do not mistake their palour for fear."

My mother would tell us all the old fables at night, but I think these stories are boring to kids these days. One of my favourites is about a shepherd who cried, "Wolf, wolf," for no reason, a story also told in Europe. Another tells of three brothers. Just before their father died, he told each in turn, "There is a treasure buried, but I do not know exactly where. You will have to search for it." The three brothers dug up the land but when they did not find the treasure, they thought, "Now the land is disturbed, we had better sow wheat." As they kept on searching, they planted much wheat, and this became a treasure in itself. I think this is the main message, but the story continues. One son found the treasure and hid it from his brothers. Sensing that one of them was not telling the truth, the three brothers went to their wise uncle and asked him to discover who was lying. Their uncle said, "First, let me tell you a story. Once, there was a beautiful princess who loved to walk in her garden. One day the gardener saw her and sighed. She asked him, 'Why do you sigh?' and after some hesitation, the gardener replied, 'For your wedding night. How lucky that man will be.' The princess promised him that who ever she married, she would save her first night for the gardener.

She became engaged to a prince, and after seven days of celebration, on their wedding night, she asked her husband to let her go to her garden. Her husband asked, 'Why?' and she told him of her promise to the gardener. He said, 'Because you are so honest and honourable, I will let you go.'

Dressed in her beautiful wedding dress, she walked alone to the garden. The gardener, surprised and impressed that she had remembered her promise, told her, 'You are too pure and precious to be touched.'" The uncle stopped the story at this point and asked the first son, "What would you have done if you were the gardener?" and the young man said, "I would do as the gardener did." The uncle continued, "On her way home the princess passed a group of men. They asked, 'What are you doing here alone at night in a wedding dress?' When she told them her story, they said, 'We will not touch you—you are so pure and honest.'" At this point the uncle asked the second brother, "What would you have done if you were one of those men?" and the second brother replied, "I would do the same—send her home." The uncle continued, "As she neared home, she was caught by a thief. At this point the uncle asked the third brother, "What would you do if you were that thief?" and the third brother answered, "I would do anything I liked to such a beautiful girl. How can you let such an opportunity pass you by?" The uncle continued, "The thief thought like you, and raped her." Pointing to the third brother, the uncle said, "This is the one with the treasure."

It was in 1977, when I was 15 and studying health in Year 10, that I did two weeks' work experience as a voluntary first-aid assistant at Mahabad hospital. There was so much to do, I stayed for the three-month summer holidays, working in the bandage room.

The hospital was free, so there was always 100 people waiting, when only 35 could be seen in a day. The poor people, especially, were expected to wait for days just to get an injection or to have an infected wound bandaged. Yet a rich person, or someone well dressed or from a respected family, would be seen quickly. I would argue with the nurse, saying, "This person is first in the queue," and the nurse would say, "Who is in charge here?" but I would be adamant. It shocked me to see the nurses treating poor people like dirt. They wore sterile gloves but would touch everything, and shout, "Lie down. What are you crying for?" I would say, "Now your gloves are not sterile, and why are you so rude, just because the patient is poor?" I made myself very unpopular but they had no choice about me staying. The doctor in charge of the hospital was my father's friend, and I would tell him what was happening.

I think my sense of fairness came from my family. My father was very fair-minded, and always treated my mother with respect. If he became angry, he would leave the house for an hour or so, then come back laughing. He was a good friend and treated his daughters no differently to his sons, and this caused me problems later in life. He listened to us and asked our opinion. He even advised me how to clean myself and not eat yoghurt when I had my period and when I told my girl friends they were shocked. He would invite us to sit and talk with male visitors, and never stopped us playing chess, backgammon or table tennis with our male cousins. Most girls were trained to be shy of males and were constantly afraid that their brothers might see them doing something socially unacceptable. Even our mother disapproved of what our father allowed us to do.

I really loved working at the hospital. I felt so mature, and decided I would like to become a health professional. If I had liked books more, I would have become a doctor, but I had seen I could do valuable work as a nurse, and the next summer holidays, with my family's support and encouragement, I returned to the hospital. The same nurses were there, and still hated me, but again they had no choice, and the work was very rewarding.

The same year, I nursed my paternal grandmother. She was much quieter than my other grandmother, but very kind. When I was four or five, I would think, "If you die I want to die with you."

That year, 1978, was when the demonstrations started against the Shah. My whole family went to the rallies, but like any teenager, I preferred to go with my school friends. People were selling books on the pavements—about communism and other ideas, in Kurdish and Persian—and I began to buy the Persian books to read. People would be arrested for selling them, but always others came in their place. Or they would run away when they saw police and come back the next day. I was fascinated—at last, I was reading real history instead of fantasy. I learnt about Mossadeq, democracy, Marxism and evolution, and its application to society. It made sense.

It was in my last year of school that I became politically active. After the revolution in February 1979, political parties were actively distributing their literature and I became interested in the Chereek Fadaiee because they wanted communism for everybody and autonomy for all nations. Our father was sympathetic to KDPI, but we wanted to be different. We also wanted to fight for all people, not just the Kurds. My eldest sister was studying at university in Tehran, and had left some literature, and Mariam and I began reading. I became a member of their youth organisation called Sa'azman Chowarnnan, or Community of Young People, and started selling Chereek's newspapers and books at school and to relatives. I was impressed by communism's goals of fairness and giving people equal opportunities, but as you grow older you realise it is not possible for people to be equal because people are born with different talents and they make choices.

Initially, the new government tried to negotiate with Kurdish leaders, and my father would invite Qassemlou and the Iranian representatives to our house for meetings. My father and Qassemlou were good friends, and I would have political arguments with Qassemlou, saying, "Communism is better." He would say, "You are such a good girl. I wish you were a social democrat." Our father never tried to convince us of his opinion. He respected Chereek Fadaiee because its members were educated and liked books.

Studying health at senior school meant I could go on to nursing or psychology, but during my final year, in June 1979, civil war broke out between the Kurdish *peshmergas* and the Iranian army. The universities closed down. Mariam too missed out on going to university. Only later, as the mother of two children, did she attend, and few women do that in Iran.

The Iranian army went first to Sanandaj. I was doing my final exams. Everyone knew they would come soon to Mahabad, and were buying food to store for the hard times ahead. I went to the hospital and collected some first-aid supplies.

Troops started bombarding Mahabad at 7.30 am one day in September. All the shops closed, and people collected in basements. My family went to our neighbour's, but Mariam and I put on Kurdish trousers and, with my first-aid bag containing antiseptics, sterile gloves, gauze, bandages and sutures (although I had never stitched a person before), we went to the mosque where people were taking the injured. The hospital did not have the capacity, and all the doctors, except one—Doctor Habibi—had left with their families before the bombardment. Also, the hospital was under government control.

That first day was shocking. Injured men and women lay on the floor. People were crying. An 18-month old boy had his stomach hanging out, although he was alert, drinking milk from a bottle. Beside him, his pregnant mother was dying. I could feel the nine-month-old baby was still alive inside her. The woman's husband was talking through a bloody opening in his throat, but was more worried for his wife and children than for himself. I felt helpless. When the mother died, I wanted to cut her open and save the baby, but I lacked the confidence and knowledge. Some of the most severely injured people were sent to the hospital. Others died. During the day, someone told us that our aunt's house had been bombed, killing my cousin and four others.

Mariam and I arrived back at the basement at about 10 pm. I went straight to sleep. The bombing continued for 20 days and nights. Each morning, Mariam and I would arrive at the mosque by six or seven. When people ran to tell us where there was an injured person or a body, Mariam and I would go with them to the site, even as the bombing continued.

After a week, Chereek Fadaiee came to the mosque and organised about 25 first-aid suppliers into teams of three or four. The girls were aged 16 to 18 and the boys 17 to 20. Few had any training, so like Mariam, they learnt as they went. As a team leader, I would show the others what to do and delegate the tasks. I know the boy in our team sometimes felt awkward taking orders from a younger girl, but it was a subtle reaction, and we were all too busy and the situation too drastic for me to care. I am reminded of a Kurdish proverb: 'It is not the beard but the deed.'

We would work until nine or 10 at night. Our family supported our work, although it was dangerous. Even the people who remained in the basements were becoming sick from the overcrowded, unhygienic conditions.

The worst injury I treated was a *peshmerga* who had a deep twenty centimetre long wound from being shot in the leg. I cleaned the wound with antiseptic and stitched him without anaesthetic. The needles broke in his skin and he screamed. I was scared, but I had to do it. Others I did not have the confidence to treat. I remember two *peshmergas* who were dragged out of the battle and brought to the mosque. One had his flesh torn away so I could see his stomach, intestines, liver and kidneys. He asked, "Please kill me.

I know I am going to die," but we took off his clothes and I put sterile gauze over his wounds and sent him to the hospital. The other *peshmerga* had a bullet in his chest and could not breath so I gave him mouth-to-mouth resuscitation. He started breathing and we sent him to hospital, not knowing what would happen to him or the others we sent.

Bodies were also brought to the mosque, or were left lying by the roadside. We would be called to the site and have to drag them to an open place and bury them. We buried people anywhere we could, sometimes burying several together, singing national songs to keep our spirits up. One was "Our land, our land, our beautiful land, Live in happiness, freedom and independence."

We had to bury the bodies as quickly as possible, to prevent diseases spreading, and often I did not know who I was burying. Mariam and I even buried our 13-year-old cousin in my uncle's front garden without recognising him. When we were putting him into the grave, I noticed his black leather coat, and commented, "He must come from a rich family." Some weeks later, when we were visiting his family, his mother, who was permanently in a wheelchair, was crying and calling, "Where are you my son?" and I whispered to Mariam, "Maybe that boy we buried was Omid." His sister was very mentally disabled—possibly a legacy from too many cousin marriages—so this boy was so precious.

Many bodies were lost because we forgot where we buried them, and there were some we could not bury. People told us there was a body in the river a little way out of the city. When we got there we saw that it had been mutilated by dogs and was half-rotten. I did not want to touch it, because of disease, so we threw acid on the body and left.

In those first 20 days of fighting, my father joined KDPI. I was so against war after what I had seen that when Qassemlou visited our house I said, "You should not fight under any circumstances." I did not understand that Qassemlou did not want war either, but was being forced to defend the people.

When Iranian soldiers took control of Mahabad, my father went with KDPI to the mountains, where he was put in charge of the KDPI hospital in the village of Garada, in the Ja'afati Valley in Iraqi Kurdistan. We saw him only when he could secretly return to the city for a night or two.

Over the next six months, the bombing was intermittent. KDPI and Chereek Fadaiee would bring first-aid supplies to the mosque. We did not expect a religious government to bomb a mosque, but they did a few times. During that time no first-aid supplier was injured—despite all the danger of going to the sites. People would say, "Allah is protecting you."

When the war started, I was only 17. Initially I felt strong, but over time, seeing so much death and suffering began to affect me. One day, at a bombsite, I went to lift a woman whose body was lying on the ground. As I put my hand behind her head, the back of her skull was missing and my hand went right into her brain. It was too much. I went into shock, and started to fear the next experience. Over time my nerves broke down and I would get angry easily, and argue with my brothers and mum over any little thing. Fortunately, they were tolerant, knowing why I was upset.

I think those experiences still affect me. They made me less tolerant. I have less capacity to cope with ordinary life and its problems, to process new information and find a way to live again. I am more prone to depression. I don't think such experiences make you stronger.

From 1980 until early 1982, I went to Chereek Fadaiee meetings and worked as a first-aid supplier whenever there was a bombardment. Fighting was mainly outside the city, and mostly someone came to the house to collect me, and we would walk or ride a donkey to a village, to administer first aid. Many *peshmergas* had big wounds and, after my initial treatment, would be sent by vehicle, then donkey and stretcher, to the KDPI hospital across the border. Otherwise, I would stay at home. There were no Iranian soldiers in the street but there was intermittent fighting between *peshmergas* and various government forces in Mahabad until 1987.

Back in 1982, when I was 20, a man who belonged to Chereek asked some girlfriends from Chereek if I would marry him. It was not the traditional way, which made me interested. Many young men, including some cousins, sent family members to my family to discuss marriage, but I never liked the idea. I was against cousin marriages, even though my mother would say, "If the girl is good, it is a shame for the family to give her to another family, and if the girl is bad, it is a shame on the family to give her to another family." My father never encouraged me to marry a cousin, so I agreed to meet this man.

Kamal was a *peshmerga* who had seen some fighting, although not as much as KDPI. He had been to prison and had a reputation for being strong in his beliefs. That was all I knew of him. On our meeting at a friend's house, I liked his appearance, and what he had to say about educating the village people and organising them into groups. Because he was Chereek, I stereotyped him as an open-minded, liberated man. After we met several times over a few weeks, I informed my family that I wanted to marry him, so they said, "We should meet him." I did not see it as risky—it is the way it is done in Kurdistan.

Kamal's father went to my father in the mountains and my father gave his consent. We became engaged and had a party, but two or three weeks later, the day before we were meant to sign our marriage certificates, my 17-year old brother, a KDPI *peshmerga*, was killed in fighting. The wedding was postponed and all the guests came, but instead of a wedding, we had a funeral. We were all crying. I prayed for a miracle to bring him back, even though I did not believe in God. I just could not accept that I would never see him again.

Six months later, the court sent a letter to my mother. Because my father was with KDPI in the mountains, the government was going to take our house and land, and she was ordered to pack her things and go and live in exile in a faraway city called Damghun, in the middle of the south-eastern desert. My mother advised, "You had better marry now, because there is no point coming with me. It will be one less problem." I married, and went to live with Kamal and his family in the centre of Mahabad. Afterwards, two of my uncles were also exiled, but my mother pleaded with the court that as a woman she had to stay with her daughters, so they let her stay.

Marriage was a very different life. I had been used to a lot of freedom. I stopped going to political meetings or being a first-aid supplier. I fell pregnant immediately, and although for the first six months I was happy in my marriage, the family had a very different dynamic. My father-in-law had absolute control over every detail. His wife had to ask him for even the smallest amount of money. In my family, my mother always had money, and if she needed more oil or whatever all she had to do was ask and my father would have it delivered. When my mother-in-law needed something, her husband would interrogate her, "How much is left? What has happened to it all?" He became angry when I dropped a few tea leaves. Once, I heard knocking at the front door and pulled back the curtain of my room to see who it was. My father-in-law entered the room and demanded, "What were you doing at the window?" then closed the curtains. I never dared ask for money so I had none, unless I won backgammon when playing my mother!

When I was six months' pregnant, Kamal got a job at a power plant in Kirmanshah. I remained with his family, feeling like an outsider. One of Kamal's sisters was two years older than me and another was six years younger, but my mother-in-law never asked them to do housework and they were always served the best food, so when I joined Kamal in Kirmanshah, in my last month of pregnancy, it was the happiest month of my life.

But my happiness was short-lived. A week before Arash was born, Iranian troops in Mahabad collected young boys—mainly 16 and 17 years old—and took them to prison. Fifty-nine boys were shot dead. Feeling unsafe, Kamal left for the mountains, and, in retaliation for the young boys' deaths, KDPI *peshmerga* made 59 attacks, killing soldiers and *pasdars* rather than capturing them.

A few days after Kamal's departure, I gave birth to Arash in hospital, then returned to live with my in-laws. Although they allowed me to visit my family, I was very unhappy, but kept my feelings inside. I tried to be a good daughter-in-law—and fortunately, Kamal's two brothers treated me kindly, especially Kawa.

Outside, the situation was very tense. When Arash was three months old, *pasdars* captured a good friend still working as a first-aid supplier. She was 16, and was tortured and killed with eight other girls.

As time passed, I became increasingly sad and lonely. When Arash was 18 months old, I sent a message to Kamal, asking him to come back. I told him, "You could not put up with your father. How do you expect me to?" We went and lived in Tabriz for 18 months, Kamal earning money by driving his own car as a taxi. We struggled financially, but life was peaceful. Kamal and I got along better in Iran, perhaps because he respected my family and knew they supported me.

Then in 1985, a few weeks after our first son's third birthday, *pasdars* arrested my husband, Arash, myself and two visitors: Kawa and Mariam. On the way to Tabriz prison, I told the *pasdars*, "My sister is a visitor. You do not have orders to take her. If anything happens to her, you are responsible." One answered, "We write our own orders."

The next morning they took us by car to Mahabad prison, and for three months nobody knew what had happened to us. It is only after we went to court that they told our family.

I was alone with my three-year old son in a cell one and half metres by one metre. To lie down, I had to put my feet on the wall. There was a small window, but so high up I could not see out. A light globe burned 24 hours a day. We had a bucket for a toilet and a blanket for a bed. If a guard knocked, I had to quickly don a *chador*. We were allowed out three times a day, for up to 30 minutes, to go to the toilet and wash. Otherwise, I would tell Arash stories or play with him with my hands and feet, or pretend I was a horse.

One day, the judge visited me in the cell, saying, "You are Mostefa Qazi's daughter. Your father is a *peshmerga*!" I replied, "Yes, but I am not my father." He asked, "Are you being treated well?" I said, "Look, I have a baby in this cell. Even if I was a murderer and deserved to be here, what has my baby done?" After that, they sometimes took Arash to watch television and play games, but I wonder how my prison term affected him. I was very depressed, but having Arash made it less boring.

Every day, two or three men interrogated me for hours. They would threaten but never hit. I was cooperative, having heard stories of children being tortured in front of their mothers. I admitted to my political activities, and when asked for names, I gave them those of people not in Iran.

Otherwise, I read Islamic books, which were all the male guards would distribute when I asked for reading material. But these books really shocked me. They described the way Islam was spread in Iran. It was *halal*—the Muslim soldiers' God-given right—to take property, rape women, behead thousands, and cut out the tongues of those who did not speak Arabic, because they were making war against *ka'aferr*, people of other religions.

My father had his own beliefs and would laugh when he heard our mother saying, "If you don't pray you will go to hell." I used to argue with her, especially when I began reading about communism. I asked why, if God is all-powerful, all-merciful, does He allow so many people to suffer at the hands of so few? If all things are determined by God's Will, then we have no choice and are not responsible for our actions. But if we have choice, then everything cannot be determined by God's Will. I could not believe in God, because I could see no signs. The books in prison reinforced my scepticism, yet underneath, I sensed there was something that gives life meaning. Over time, when I realised I could not change the world, I came to believe in God, but it is a pure, loving spirit, not an Islamic god or a Christian god.

Other women in single cells also had children, and we would meet in the washroom. One young, beautiful Kurdish woman from Iraq was named Helal or 'new moon'. Her father had brought her to eastern Kurdistan and forced her to marry his nephew, who was in love with another woman. When her husband took this other woman as his second wife Helal found a needle in her food several times. She escaped and lived with another man in another unofficial marriage and had a child to him. He also treated her badly until she was arrested because she was without official papers.

One day, I saw Helal's baby daughter covered in a skin rash, due to infected mosquito bites. I returned to my cell and immediately called a guard, saying, "You are keeping children here but there are mosquitoes and dirt everywhere. As a Muslim, you believe in cleanliness, but in the washroom I saw a baby covered in a rash. You must spray to get rid of the mosquitoes." So they did.

I saw Mariam once, six weeks after our arrest. She was skin and bone, refusing to eat the food because she was pregnant and feeling nauseous. The guards wanted me to encourage her to eat, so I gave them money to buy her the foods she craved. So they did.

After three months, I went to court. I told the judge, "If I had seen a wounded *pasdar*, I would have helped him too, but I never saw one." I was truthful, and I think that is why I got such a light sentence: six months for helping *peshmergas* as a first-aid supplier. After this, they took Arash away and he lived with my in-laws. My mother or brothers would also mind him.

I was put in a bedless room with up to 10 women aged between 20 and 65. Some women were Komala, some KDPI, some Chereek Fadaiee. One, an opium addict, stayed only a few days. Others stayed four or five months. Long-term prisoners were sent to Urmia. Most of the women were from the villages and had little or no education. They could not speak Persian, so I would translate, and straight away I became like their team leader. When I saw the filth I asked the guards for cleaning materials, and was given them.

One day the guards brought some rotten eggs. I told the women not to eat them and called the guards. They said, "You have no right to reject the food," but I told them, "If we eat those eggs you will have to take us to hospital. This is a time of war and the hospital is needed for the injured." The guards would bring burnt bread and the women would cut it into little pieces so they could get rid of it without the guards realising, as bread is holy in Islam. One time I put the burnt bread on top of the rubbish. The guards asked, "Who did this sin?" I said, "It is not bread. Bring a dog. If the dog eats it, we will eat it. The farmer has worked very hard for a year to make the wheat for this bread—why do you waste it?" We never got burnt bread again.

One day the judge and *baba*, the male prisoner-in-charge of bringing food, came to our cell. I said to the judge, "It has been two weeks since my court case and I have had no visitors." The judge said, "No-one has asked to visit you." In front of everyone I said, "How can you say such a lie? When people lose a chicken they go after it. Do you expect me to believe that people who have lost two daughters, two sons and a grandchild do not search for them?" *Baba* had already told me he had seen my mother and father-in-law waiting in the courtyard several times. The judge was so shocked he walked out.

After four months in prison, I finally received a visit from my family. On the first visit, we were allowed to hug and kiss, but after that, we were in two separate rooms, with windows opening to a corridor in between. From then on, they visited once a week and were allowed to bring me food.

One 65 year old woman was very lively and would tell us stories—sometimes about her love life. One I remember was when she was a young girl travelling with the sheep. She was sleeping in a tent and the boy she loved was outside so she put the end of her waist band material under the tent for him to feel all night. It was so exciting for him—just the idea that the material belonged to her. That was their only contact but they were happy! Two of her sons had been in Komala and another was shaheed—gone to heaven—having died fighting in the *peshmergas'* war against the government. She made it obvious to the guards she disliked them, and a few times they became angry and hit her around the head.

After three months in the group cell I was released. I lived with Kamal's family. Kamal was in prison for another 18 months, and after his release, in late 1987, we had to stay with his family for another two years because he was on probation. Had we left, the government would have taken the family's house. His father continued to control everything. Kamal was used to it—I was not. For money, he and his father would go secretly to Turkey and bring back goods like jeans and sequins and sometimes Kamal drove a hired car. Our marriage was going well, our second son, Azad, being born in 1988.

My mother still lived with my sister and various uncles, but then the government took all the family's land—including the land of my father's six brothers—so my uncles asked my father to give himself up, which he did in 1989. He went to prison in Urmia for a month, and the government released all the land and houses.

After Kamal finished his probation, he suggested we leave Iran. We did not have passports, so we paid a smuggler. It was late autumn 1989, but a day before we were to go, my father forbade our departure, saying, "It is too cold and dangerous at this time of year. I am taking Arash home so that you cannot go." I did not mind staying, but Kamal really wanted to escape, so the following spring, we arranged everything, telling our families we were going to Tabriz for a holiday. We travelled to Urmia, taking a 4WD to the border. In the last village, we dressed in village clothes, paying smugglers to take us by donkey through a mountain pass. After 90 minutes, we arrived in a village in Turkey, then were taken on by car to Ankara. We had paid good money.

In Ankara, we went straight to the UNHCR and applied for refugee status. I telephoned my family. My father said, "It is your life. I did not want you to go, but good luck." We rented a flat, then were moved to Konya. Our Turkish neighbours were very friendly. When I was talking to my son in Kurdish one woman asked, "What's that blah, blah, blah?" I said, "Don't call my language blah, blah, blah. Your language is blah, blah, blah to me!" We became good friends.

After 11 months in Turkey we arrived in Sydney on 13 March 1991, at the time of the Kurdish uprising in Iraqi Kurdistan. We were taken to a very nice, fully furnished flat in Auburn. There were even sandwiches in the refrigerator! I was sad to leave my family but more excited about our new life.

Kamal and I went to English classes at the Australian Migrant Service, and while studying, I began working as a volunteer for a child-care centre, then in Westmead hospital. After three English courses, my teachers encouraged me to go to technical college to learn more English. I worked voluntarily in a nursing home kitchen, until they employed me casually a few days a week. Then I did a six-month welfare course, but when I started doing my practical work at the courts, I realised I could not relate to the people needing my help. I decided to study nursing. After another English course and a year studying for my Higher School Certificate, I was ready for the three year nursing course at the University of Western Sydney. Life was hectic—studying, working, and looking after the family.

Meanwhile, Kamal was working as a volunteer for the Kurdish community and in Kurdish radio. When I started getting paid work in 1993, I put pressure on him to seek work too. He found a few months' work in a factory, then got his taxi licence.

I began work for a nursing agency, but never felt that I belonged. The other nurses could talk for hours about trivial things like making a salad, whereas my interests were history and politics—subjects that men are often more interested in. Consequently I preferred to talk with men. Kamal understood I was not interested in gossip. However after his family migrated to Australia, he became more conservative, saying, "Why do you always talk with men? Go and sit with the women," and we would argue.

Life in Australia is very different for Kurdish men and women, especially when it comes to raising children. In Kurdistan, a mother usually lives with her extended family, and everyone helps care for the children. In Australia, a mother has to do everything. There is also a lot more pressure to earn money here.

There are so many adjustments. Life in Australia is freer for women, but a Kurdish man is not used to his wife expressing her own needs, especially sexual feelings. Traditionally, women are not meant to like sex or answer back. Also, Kurdish men are very jealous, possessive and suspicious. A Kurdish woman who works outside the home would not dare let a male colleague drive her home. Kurdish men often bully to get their way, and I have seen some husbands hit their wives, but Kurdish women are too shy, humiliated and afraid to seek professional help.

Kamal was spending more and more time away from the family, and we were having many arguments, because I loved him and I am a woman who expresses herself. In early 2000, he insisted we go to the *shaykh*, to ask for a divorce. I told the *shaykh* I did not want a divorce, so the *shaykh* refused Kamal's request. Kamal disappeared for a week, then came back and said, "We must go back to the *shaykh*." I felt humiliated and angry. On the second visit, the *shaykh* talked with us for seven hours. He was very patient and supportive of the family, doing this mediation for no payment. It was his Islamic duty. Again, he refused to divorce us. Kamal told me, "You are wasting my time. I want a divorce." When we went a third time to the *shaykh* I said, "I do not want a divorce but I cannot do anything to change his mind," and the *shaykh* granted our divorce. We are now divorced under Islamic law but not Australian law.

Kamal asked me to find another place for me and the children to live, but I told him I could not manage the children on my own, so for the last six months, I have lived alone. The children visit after school or I go and pick them up at least three times a week. Fortunately I have a few close friends, but I did not realise how hard and lonely life is on one's own. I would consider marrying again, but would spend more time getting to know the person. The Kurdish way is wrong.

I continue to work long hours. I dream of one day having enough money to set up a fruit-canning factory or some other business in Mahabad. We have good agriculture but no factories, and in season, fruit is sold very cheaply. People dry tomatoes and peaches for their own use but not for sale. I would much prefer to do this than send money. Of course, I long to see an independent Kurdistan, but will it ever happen?

Buried Alive

A short fiction by Mariam Qazi, translated from Kurdish by Fariba Qazi

He could not move. He lay there, opening his eyes a few times, in defiance of the darkness around him. His whole body ached. He attempted to move his legs, and failed. He breathed uneasily, thinking, "Where am I?" Again trying to move, he sighed with pain.

He could hear a young woman crying. He tried to call to her, but his mouth was shut. He became fearful of the relentless dark. "Is it night?" he asked himself, "Or has a ghost taken me? Why can't I move?" As he managed to move his head slightly, his forehead hit Al-had, the stone placed at the head of a grave. He began to believe his fears, shaking with the realisation that he was wrapped in a white *koffin* and covered with earth. He was buried alive.

Soon snakes and scorpions would come, he thought, and he tried to scream, "I am not dead!" but he could not hear himself. The thought of all these creatures crawling towards him drove him crazy. He tried to fling the earth away, but as one clod moved, another replaced it. The descriptions he had heard of death marched in his mind,[a] knitting the form of death.

Shivering, crying, he tried to scratch himself free from his tight, dark grave, calling for God, his hands bleeding. He started to breathe more easily, as he at last tore apart his *koffin*, and was free of the earth and the young woman's cries, at the same time asking, "If this truly is my grave why is it opening its mouth again?"

His wife looked upon his exhausted body, with its torn *koffin* now protruding from the earth, his eyes shocked and staring. She began to laugh hysterically, saying, "What are you doing? How many times do you want to die?" her voice like a shadow moving through the death-odoured cemetery.

The man was scared, remembering that his wife had died long ago. Her laughter was as frightening as the thunder of a storm. Even the sky's dark expanse felt tight around him.

The man sat beside his grave and took a deep breath, not knowing whether he was dreaming or dead, but as thirst and hunger attack him he thought, "I am thirsty! I am hungry! Therefore I am alive."

As the night ruled and the owl sang,[b] the man managed to stand and take a step, but instead of moving forward, he slipped backwards and fell, face pressed into the ground. He became aware that the earth was even thirstier than he, as cracked as his own dry lips. He wanted to sleep but his eyes refused to close. He wanted to cry out for help but his tongue refused to obey. Unable to analyse what was happening, he covered his eyes and tried to think of nothing.

Finally, he fell asleep, only to be woken by a nightmare. Standing, he saw something even more alien than all he had experienced in this short time. The sun was rising from the west,[c] its rays tearing apart the screen of night. The atmosphere filled with noise as all around him, the dead rose from open-mouthed graves. Some were just bones. Some had snakes laced around their necks. Some had worms crawling out of skulls not yet emptied, returning through eyes and nostrils to emerge again. The man covered his eyes in revulsion at the scene of death, with its fetid stench, its howling and wailing, its pain and suffering.

Again, he tried to run but slipped back, hearing the risen dead laugh and jeer. In the next moment, he recognised the beat of his friend's drum. His friend had died two months before, but it was as if he were leading the crowd of the dead. The man looked up and saw his *zorna* falling from the sky. Catching it, he felt impelled to play, as if the demented crowd were demanding, "Play! Play!" He put his *zorna* to his lips, closed his eyes, and played with all his energy. He had been the best *zorna* player in the region, and he played without rest, without pause for breath.

On opening his eyes he saw that from the sky came ashes, which hit the earth and transformed into dancing flames. The fires took the form of boys and girls, and again, he closed his eyes, and played to the beat of his friend's drum, his body bending and weaving with the music.

The next time he opened his eyes, it was winter, snow and cold having no pity. People trailed like ants across the mountains of Kurdistan. Now, he was playing for the three million homeless as they marched backwards. Thousands of women, children and old men, dead from hunger and cold, lay beneath the snow, but these thousands now rose to rejoin the crowd. Among them, shoeless orphans searched for a parent's warm embrace.

Again, he closed his eyes and continued playing, as did his friend. When his eyes opened next, they were standing before 7000 burnt, blistered bodies, which also rose, their cries of pain transformed into shouts of laughter and joy. The small city of Halabja was alive once more.[d] The musicians closed their eyes, tears of happiness falling, as their music of *zorna* and drum reached the sky.

In this way, they saw all the massacres, and each destroyed village and city, going further and further back in time, their music healing the mutilated bodies, until they arrived at Chwar Chira, the Square of Freedom.[e] As they played *A-Rhaqeeb*, the flag of the Kurdish republic rose high in Qazi Muhammad's hand.

Weaving between thousands of Barzani's *peshmerga*, the musicians found themselves on the desert of Arak, where they saw the thousands buried alive rise again. Continuing their journey north to the peaks of Ararat, they found hundreds of decapitated bodies, but then witnessed the heads mending with the bodies, the guilty resheathing their knives, as being a Kurd was no longer a sin. The three mighty powers controlling Kurdistan had stopped massacring the people, and a cry of peace filled the air.

Still, the musicians did not heed exhaustion. Still, they journeyed further back, and those who prayed heard their music and lifted their heads, returning to the fire, and the cries of Zoroastra and Ahura Mazda.[f] In fear, the musicians prayed, "There is only one God and Muhammad is his messenger," before resuming their melodies. Next time their eyes opened, they found themselves in the hall of a great castle,[g] in front of which was a field full of boys and girls dressed in traditional Kurdish clothes, dancing around fountain-fed pools edged by floral borders and elegant statues.

Spotted around the field were tables laden with food. Hundreds of well-dressed people were enjoying the party. In the middle was a throne covered in gold-embroidered red silk, on a platform with 10 stairs. On the throne sat the king and his beautiful Khahtoon, adorned in gold necklaces, her eyes black, her lips small and red, her cheeks a lively pink. Oonmunda, the city of the Kurds 8000 years ago, had risen again. In amazement the musicians relentlessly played on.

Suddenly, the drum tore apart and the *zorna* fell mute. The rumble of an earthquake shook ground and sky. The two musicians gazed at each other with fear as all around them, people ran, this time forwards. Cries mingled with the sounds of crashing buildings heralding the breakdown of a civilisation as the earth opened its mouth like a dragon swallowing life and death.

Suddenly the musicians witnessed two men[h] running in circles, screaming. Every time they completed a circle, the value of nation, country and life decreased. Kurd fought Kurd until not one remained. The two musicians were observing the most harrowing scene of all. They tried to run backwards, but would not. They dashed their heads against stones and trees, trying to kill themselves, but could not. They cried, screamed and fell. Around them, springs gushed blood. Even trees scratched and smote themselves,[i] and the mountains spat fire on human conscience. All the dead who had risen were now searching for their resting places. Finding their graves, they lay down, covering themselves with soil.

An owl hooted from time to time, then there was a long silence, before an agonised sigh of extreme pain shattered the night. The *zorna* player trembled on his grave. He wished the earth would consume him, then recognised his wife's voice calling, "No! No! You cannot die. Now, even your grave rejects you. How many times do you want to die? Get up! Get up!"

Flag

A poem by Jheela Husseini translated by Kamran Avin and Gafoor Muhamad

Your love became a light,
Became steel shoes
And a steel stick.
Your love became sunlight,
Became the root of my heart and insight.
I broke the ice
And came to you.
On the summit of that love,
I grew taller and became a flag.

From Drops of Rain the River will Rise

A life story based on interviews with Mary Razaghi

I was a teenager during the 1970s, when many young people were fired up about the Kurdish cause and Mostefa Barzani's movement across the border. We wanted our freedom and independence too. A local hero inspired me also: a Kurdish doctor who came to Saghez, the first of his kind. Dr Shakeri was not the stereotypical doctor with wealth, a big house, and a flashy lifestyle. He rented a very small house and had a minimum of furniture, reasoning that if most of his patients could not afford such luxuries, why should he? He wore traditional Kurdish clothes, which was unusual for educated people, but most of all, he practised in the poorest neighbourhood and would drive a jeep to remote villages to treat people. He was the first doctor in Saghez to practise in this simple and popular way.

News got around that he had been an activist in his university years and had spent time in prison. There were many stories about his kindness to poor people—how he did not charge them for his time or medicines. The young generation, in particular, admired him, although many from my father's generation were convinced that he was unbalanced. In Middle Eastern culture, it is very difficult to be an individual.

I never saw Dr Shakeri. I did not permit myself to take up five minutes of his precious time, but he became my idol. I yearned to be like him—a doctor helping the poor. From Year Nine, I studied hard and prayed to this end, telling neither friends nor family of my desire.

Although Iran has a public hospital system, the quality of the services was low, and in Saghez, people still relied on advice and medicine from market-stall herbalists, and the midwives who deliver babies at home. My mother and neighbours told many stories of women dying in labour because their husbands did not allow them to see a male doctor at the hospital. Women themselves would claim they would rather die than be examined by a male doctor!

A midwife delivered all eight children in my family: four boys and four girls. Big families were the rule. I remember my mother saying, "Poor me! Poor my generation! If contraception was available I would have had only four children!"

We lived in the centre of town, in a double-storey mud-brick house with a flat soil roof. In heavy snowfalls, we paid someone to clear off the snow. There was no bathroom, so we used the public baths, of which there was one in each suburb. The women's section had a main room with a big heated pool, as well as private rooms, each covered in mosaic tiles, and taps for hot and cold water.

My mother cooked on a kerosene primus stove, and in our large courtyard, she grew vegetables, fruit, and many roses. She kept chickens for eggs and meat, but slaughtering was always my father's chore.

My mother had never gone to school and was illiterate. It was one of her greatest regrets, because she was a very intelligent, resourceful lady. She invented her own baby's bottle at a time when none were available, and earned her own income making pickles and sewing women's clothes. My father did the general shopping, but she would go and buy jewellery and Kurdish clothes: the long floral dresses and big heavy pants, with the little cap under a scarf, until the cap went out of fashion. Even in the mountains, we have fashion! Then there were five metres of material wrapped around the waist, and a small jacket and a thick shawl for winter. Around her head and under her chin, she wore the traditional gold chains hung with coins—but when this fashion also changed, she lengthened the chains and wore them as a necklace. Later, she was forced to sell some of the coins and other jewellery, gold having always been an alternative currency in the Middle East.

My father is a very quiet, pleasant, democratic man. He goes to the mosque daily, and still reminds me to say my prayers. Born in 1903, he remembers both World Wars, and famine so severe people were reduced to eating cats and dogs. He studied for six years at a religious school, where he learnt to read and write in Farsi, a remarkable achievement in Kurdistan 90 years ago, and he encouraged all his children to study and achieve. He worked as a clerk for the sugar department, then the grain department. He could type, too, which was a great asset, but he was not ambitious, much to my mother's chagrin. Once, he made a bookkeeping error, and was conned by a colleague, becoming liable for a lot of money, causing the family financial hardship for some years.

His attitude to life has always been, "I do what I can and leave the rest to God." He did not impose his way of thinking on anybody, and gave his wife a lot of freedom. She would travel to different cities by herself, and on one occasion, she stayed at my elder sister's house in Abadan for three months. In our mother's absence, my second eldest sister cooked for us. When my mother made an investment in carpets in another city and lost the entire investment, he was very annoyed, but I do not recall an argument, then or at any other time. If they did argue, it was not in front of the children.

My mother was our father's second wife, his first wife having died of tuberculosis, along with their nine-month-old son. Some years later, he and my mother had an arranged marriage, when she was 16 and he was 31. They were relatives—I am not sure how close—and like most brides, she had to live with her mother-in-law.

Traditionally, a mother-in-law had absolute power and authority over her daughter-in-law. If the father-in-law was alive, he did not interfere. My father was an only child, an uncommon occurrence, so his mother was presumably very protective of him, and my mother would tell us how he would go out and do as he pleased, leaving her to the mercy of her mother-in-law. However, when she had three sons in a row, she gained some power of her own! For example, she successfully demanded a big circumcision party for each son, despite her mother-in-law objecting after the first two.

Some mothers-in-law taught the young brides good lessons, but even when I was growing up, it was common for mothers-in-law to be tyrants. Each mother-in-law acted as she had been treated. Food would be locked in a wooden chest, to which the mother-in-law always held the keys. If guests arrived and the wife wanted to offer them food, she would have to ask the mother-in-law for the key, but with new technology, like refrigerators, and other social changes, mothers-in-law no longer have the same power. My mother respected her daughters-in-law. She did not intervene in their affairs or breach their privacy.

After her mother-in-law died, I think my mother's life improved, but an undercurrent between my parents continued that is best described as a subtle clash of personalities. Although my mother was also religious, kind, generous and always helping people, she was probably more astute in her dealings with people, and she had a streak of stubbornness. Perhaps she felt she had lost her personality in the marriage, but like most Kurdish women, she was quiet, her dissatisfaction being expressed in subtle ways.

I believe my father was happier in the marriage. My mother died 16 years ago, and the only time I ever saw him cry was at her funeral. For years, he would tell us quietly, "Do not take your loved ones for granted. Otherwise, you will know their value when it is too late." He told me, "In the entire 50 years of our marriage, I slapped her twice." It was a great achievement for his generation. Many a wife was beaten on a daily or weekly basis. Two slaps! The first occasion was when their firstborn was about six months old. My mother was working in the courtyard when the baby started crying inside the house. My father went out and asked her to attend to the baby, but she did not, so he slapped her. I think they had been arguing, because my mother was caring—this was not her usual behaviour. Nor do I condemn my father. It was just the way of life 60 years ago.

To me, he was gentle. I can remember him slapping me only once, when he was very angry because I had hidden when everyone else was preparing for a family photograph. But he might have been less gentle and tolerant when he was younger—my eldest brother remembers harsh physical punishment.

Certainly, other households were less benign. My mother-in-law was married at 16, and during those early years, her husband beat her badly. She told me, "One day, he gave me a black eye. My father came and told my husband, 'It is okay if you beat her, but please don't beat her head or face. People can see the face and a head injury can be dangerous." For this she praised her father as being kind and caring! She has 10 surviving children, four or five others having died from miscarriages or early childhood diseases, but her husband did not give her even one toman.

Similarly my life was very different from other girls'. I had freedom to go to the library, parks and shops with girlfriends, although my brothers had more freedom: they could come home after dark. But within the home, we were treated equally, except that the boys never had to wash their clothes. I can remember washing my brothers' clothes and thinking nothing of it. However, ours was not like other households, where a brother could hit his sisters and order them around.

We spoke Sorani everywhere except in the classroom. Boys and girls were segregated in school, but we had male and female teachers, Persian and Kurdish. Some Persian teachers were married to Kurds, but they never discussed Kurdish issues, whereas a few of the Kurdish teachers wore Kurdish clothes outside school and held study groups. The groups would discuss ideological books written by Marx and Lenin, Russian novels, and Kurdish politics—the Mahabad Republic and the movement in Iraqi Kurdistan.

Apart from my dream to be a doctor serving poor people, I had a teenage passion for my nationality and a dream of freedom for my people—to have our own identity in the international arena. I was not thinking about how to get it, just to have it. Sometimes, I bought Kurdish books on the black market, sold by trusted people, who also had to trust you, because most were illegal. The books were not expensive, but as a girl, it was hard to get hold of them, because it was difficult to get to know the people who sold them, especially when my only older brother living at home was uninterested in the Kurdish cause, being more enamoured with his guitar and Elvis Presley!

I had to hide the books in our house, and my mother was terrified they might be found, but did not discourage us from reading them. (My sisters were more curious than politically motivated.) My father strongly disapproved, but we never studied the books in his presence, and he did not search the house for them. We had a mutual respect and silence on the matter.

Qazi Muhammad and Mostefa Barzani were our heroes. We worshipped Qazi Muhammad as the leader of the Mahabad republic, but most of all because he did not desert his people, whereas my father thought Qazi Muhammad was a good man, but naïve. He sacrificed his life for nothing.

Every Newroz, our father would buy us presents, and we would have a big fire on the roof of our house. On everyone's roof or in their backyard or in the laneways, there would be a fire and fireworks. We believed the Kurdish were the first to celebrate Newroz, and were proud that the Persians had borrowed it from us. At school, I read about the Zoroastrian religion, which considers fire sacred, so perhaps the Newroz fire came from them. The followers of Zoroastra believe in three golden rules: good thinking, good words and good deeds, but I know very little about Kurdish culture before Islam, except for some small rituals based on superstitious beliefs. For instance, there is a belief that cutting your fingernails at night leads to your father's death, and although we no longer believe this, my husband always cuts his nails during the day. He says the light is better!

I used to wear Kurdish clothing during the summer holidays, even after a Kurdish teacher beat my 12-year old relative for wearing Kurdish clothes outside school, the teacher having interpreted this as sympathy for the Kurdish cause. And I love Kurdish music. My favourite singers are Aziz Shahrokh, from Mahabad, and Tahir Tofeq, from Iraqi Kurdistan, who sing revolutionary songs. I used to memorise all the songs. I also read a lot of Kurdish poetry, whenever I could find the books. I had two books of poems by the great Sorani poet Abdullah Goran, and my other favourite was the female Persian poet Farough Farokhzad, who died in a car accident in the 1970s. I would read the poems over and over, and commit them to memory.

My father did not mind my interest in music and poetry, but he disliked my political ideas. His uncles had been killed in a tribal fight, brother against brother, and regularly he would sit us down and lecture, "Believe me, I have seen much, much more than you. I know all this is nonsense and hot air. In the end, the leaders will negotiate and desert the people, and it is always the simple, naive youngsters who are killed. The result is nothing but more oppression and hardship for the Kurdish people. Please don't waste your life on politics." My mother was different. I think deep in her heart, she was sympathetic, although as a mother, she was concerned for our safety. But I had that teenage surge of energy. It was unstoppable, and I did not listen to advice.

In my last year of school, I filled out the university application forms. We had seven or eight choices and my first five choices were medicine, medicine, medicine. Still, I told no-one, thinking if I failed to get a place, I would not have failed in the eyes of my parents and friends.

After a few months, the results were published in the national paper. I was alone at home when the paper was delivered. My teacher rang to congratulate me. After a few hours, my mother and sister came home. I waited for an hour while they unwound and began cooking, then casually said, "The university results are out. I have been accepted into medicine at Tabriz University." My sister laughed with excitement and my mother calmly congratulated me. I was the first girl from our town to be accepted into medical school. I was not the brightest one, but I dared to dream. It was 1975, and in 1976, three other girls from Saghez were accepted into medicine, and another five a year later.

Within half an hour, everybody in Saghez knew, and for a few weeks, I was the topic of conversation. People were very encouraging. My parents did not worry that I had to study in Tabriz, the capital of Azerbaijan, because my older sister, who is much brighter than me, had already led the way. She was the first girl in Saghez to complete her high school diploma. She went on to study chemistry at Tehran University, living with our older brother. Her teachers had wanted her to do medicine, but she did not like the sight of blood.

In Tabriz, I lived in a university hostel for girls. Two of my three roommates were from my high school. The doors were locked at midnight, but we were always back well before then. There was no supervision. The Shah encouraged social freedom, probably to channel our energies away from politics. Some boys and girls went out together. I never had a boyfriend—generally, it was unacceptable—although if I had wanted to badly enough, I could have. A few of my high school friends had one. They would exchange letters and photos, and wait for each other in a quiet laneway to talk and exchange a quick kiss. Even so, most of my school friends and some of my university friends had arranged marriages, as did two of my brothers and myself, if that is the term for when family members introduce you to another family. But as far as I know, no-one was forced into marriage. Some school friends left school to get married, but it was their choice.

There were 120 students from all backgrounds in my year in medicine, including 30 to 40 Azeri girls from Azerbaijan. They were surprised to hear I was the first girl from Saghez to study medicine. Many had aunts and sisters who were doctors.

Medicine involves the study of anatomy, and at certain points, the boys would whisper and laugh which was a bit embarrassing. There was no open discrimination, but boys could become friendly with the professors, go to their offices, talk and look up their books, which we could not do. In summer, they could lie on the grass in front of the medical faculty, and we would envy them for that. Our only resting place was the library!

In my first year, the Shah was still powerful, but one professor taught the philosophy of materialism. I was fascinated. It was a new way of seeing the world. Many students from different groups were leaving leaflets, small books and revolutionary slogans underneath the seats in the lecture rooms. The most popular student organisation belonged to Chereek Fadaiee, a party representing communists from all nationalities. Many of my friends were joining, so I decided to explore new horizons too, and quickly evolved from a nationalist to an internationalist.

We held meetings and study groups, ploughing through all those large, heavy philosophical books by Marx and Lenin, pretending to understand them. I remember being puzzled by Marx's book, *Capital*. I absorbed 10 to 20 per cent of the meaning and followed our group leaders without question. I did not think independently about Trosky's opposition to Lenin, or any other opposition. Our leaders said the opposition was against the revolution and they knew best. Because we were pro-Russian, we did not question Stalin's purges, but being anti-Maoist, we were very critical of the excesses of Mao's Cultural Revolution in China and Pol Pot's in Kampuchea.

The Kurdish nationalists argued that communism betrays the Kurdish cause because Marx analysed society in terms of class, whereas oppression in the Middle East is of nations as well as classes. But we followed our leaders' line that if someone is against the poor and disadvantaged, his nationality does not matter. We wanted to help everyone by changing the whole structure of society, and this did not clash with my sense of nationalism, because Chereek Fadaiee supported autonomy for all nations.

Being at the bottom of the pyramid, I would vote at meetings for a student representative but could not vote for party leaders. The hierarchy was underground and unknown to us. Our other activities consisted of distributing pamphlets, and spray painting slogans on the walls of the university and in the poor areas of Tabriz.

It was in my second year, in 1978, that open demonstrations against the Shah began. I was in three frightening demonstrations when soldiers arrived by the truckload and started shooting. Everyone ran for their life. People were killed, but that did not stop us.

The university closed for several months and I went back to Saghez, and marched in more demonstrations. My mother and sisters joined us. By that time, most people were involved and even elderly women used to march. Everyone wanted freedom. For Kurds, the official word was 'autonomy', but deep inside, we wanted independence. We could not say so directly, because it was unacceptable, nationally and internationally, yet even our local leaders would say over the megaphone, "We want autonomy!" then, turning the megaphone off, "And our independence too!" There would be loud cheers and clapping. In my mind, I was communist, but in my heart, I still dreamed of the Kurdish flag flying high at the UN.

Revolution was in the air but my father never marched. He regarded it all as pure stupidity that would not change anything. Yet as thousands joined the rallies the Shah lost his grip on power and the army and police backed down.

We hated the Shah, but had no clear idea of what would replace him. We imagined a coalition of Mujahadeen and leftist organisations, and although most activity around the country was happening in the mosques, I thought this was more to do with tradition, convenience and safety. None of us in Kurdistan visualised religious leaders monopolising a new government.

When the Shah left the country, I was back in Tabriz, joining the celebrations. We heard that Khomeini's return to the country was imminent, but were not worried. We were young and thought the world was in our hands.

The universities reopened. For a few months, political parties were free to be active, and all the student unions voted for a home meeting room. As Chereek Fadaiee received the most votes, we were allocated the biggest room. Khomeini's supporters got the smallest.

Chereek Fadaiee opened a small library in Saghez. We handed out pamphlets to students and civilians in the streets explaining that Chereek Fadaiee thought it was time for all nations to have a say, that Kurds should have greater access to Kurdish-language education and publications, and be free to wear Kurdish clothes to school, to have our own mayors—basically, the right to be Kurdish without fear of persecution. KDPI was advocating the same, and was very popular, but more moderately socialist, representing a broader cross-section of Kurds, including many religious people.

After every revolution, there is a time of chaos and uncertainty, and I heard there was some fighting and looting. The *peshmergas* controlled all the Kurdish cities and towns, and it was their job to keep order. For most people it was a dream come true to see our beloved *peshmergas* walking freely in the street! Even my younger brother, enthused by me, had become a *peshmerga* for Chereek Fadaiee, so the *peshmergas* were our brothers, sons, neighbours, friends, and husbands. However, power invariably corrupts. I did not witness human-rights abuses, but I saw pictures of tortured bodies, and heard that all over Iran people who had worked for the Shah were being tortured and killed. Blind revenge has disastrous consequences, and even now some friends argue, "When you are fighting a revolution you do not have time for a judge and a court," whereas I strongly condemn capital punishment under any circumstances.

Within a few months, it became apparent that the new government would not allow the political and social freedom to continue. Hezbollah religious police called *pasdars* were introduced to cities and universities: rude, arrogant youths who thought they knew everything, with power to enforce their ideas without written authority. At the university gates, in homes and at checkpoints, they randomly checked people's identification, searching peoples' clothes and bags, if they suspected the faintest possibility of finding something incriminating. My encounters were very unpleasant. At every checkpoint between Tabriz and Saghez, my baggage would be searched, 'sisters' dressed in black *chador* body searching the women.

Some three months after the revolution, war started between government forces and *peshmergas*, the *peshmerga* units from different parties initially united. My brother was involved in Saghez before escaping to Bukan, then to Shiraz. There was no fighting in Tabriz but I participated in Chereek Fadaiee meetings and rallies in support of the Kurdish movement.

Then when the university closed for six months, I went back to my family. As the government took control of towns and cities, the *peshmergas* retreated to the villages, returning at night to attack army bases. In Saghez, we would hear gunfire and shouting in the lanes near our house. Most people left their courtyard door open, in case the *peshmergas* needed shelter. People used to joke that Khomeini ruled by day, the *peshmergas* by night. My father's opinion never changed. He never agreed with the fighting, nor with giving the *peshmergas* or their supporters food, blankets and clothing.

It was during this time that I accompanied him to Tabriz so he could see a doctor. As we entered a hotel, I noticed a jeep full of *pasdars*. I was wearing an oversized top, worn jeans and flat-heeled shoes, and as we waited to be served, five *pasdars* approached and proceeded to search our baggage. They found nothing, but decided to take me into custody. My fragile, pale 77-year-old father begged, "If you want to take her, take me too." He even kissed the hands and face of one of them. How I hated him having to do that.

They took us both. I was put into a single cell, and body-searched by a cold, officious female in a black *chador*. My father was taken somewhere else. After we were released the next day, my father said, "When I entered the cell, the boys were surprised asking, 'Why are you here, *haji*?'" *Haji* refers to someone who has been to Makkah, but is commonly used to show respect for the elderly. No-one expected him to be an activist! It was winter, and he told me, "Those poor boys gave me all the blankets, but I just sat in a corner, waiting for morning." This was my dear father's one and only experience of prison. He thanked God for our release, and begged me, "Please, stop making trouble for yourself."

When the university reopened, I returned to Tabriz. My friends were shocked to see me without a *chador*, or a *makhnah*, a sewn material that fits over the head, neck and shoulders, or even a *roosari*, a simple scarf. Being covered had become compulsory all over Iran, and was enforced everywhere except in Kurdistan, where the government was too preoccupied fighting *peshmergas*.

One morning, as I entered the faculty building, a *pasdar* at the front desk asked for my identification. Checking it against a list of names, he told me to step aside. Six female students were taken to the female detention centre in Tabriz prison, where we were put into a room for 50 to 60 political prisoners. Other students joined us later in the day. There were double bunks, and we were given a blanket but no bedsheets.

After a week, I was taken to a room, and a man questioned me for two hours. He asked about my background, my political activities and people I knew to be active. I answered the obvious questions and named well-known activists. He became angry, saying, "Do you think I am gullible? Everyone knows these people." That night, when I was taken back to the room, I had to walk through a well-lit, asphalt yard. The guard pointed to three pools of blood on the ground, asking "Do you want to be next?" Back in the room, fellow inmates told me that three girls, including one of my classmates, had just been executed. As was customary, the women had been taken out to witness the execution. The girls had been shot from behind before reaching the wall.

As a simple follower, I was questioned only a few times. Otherwise, some of the female guards and male officers were rude but my section was not for prisoners with important information or those directly connected to the *peshmergas*. New people came and others were released. The women, aged between 15 and 45, handled the unhygienic conditions well—joking and talking—except the mothers, who worried about their children. My friend, separated from her three-week-old baby, was always crying, and would express milk daily so she could breastfeed on her release. It was to be some months later.

After a couple of weeks, a friend told my sister of my arrest, and my father and brother were allowed to visit me for 10 minutes. My father did not waste time lecturing me. He was too concerned, and after a month I was released and allowed to return to university. A few months later, they started expelling pro-communist and Mujahadeen students, me among them. This saddened my family, but it was expected—there was a wave of cleansing.

For the next year, I stayed at home. The war with Iraq had been going on for four or five years. There were international sanctions against Iran since 1979, because of the Americans taken hostage, but also government sanctions against Kurdistan. Basic necessities like kerosene (for heating and cooking), petrol, rice and sugar were not allowed in, and those who could afford to had to buy them on the black market stalls set up on the back of trucks.

In the villages, the *peshmerga* from different parties began clashing over their different philosophies and strategies. It was history repeating itself and many people were asking, "Why are we killing each other when we have not won the main battle?" In the mid-1980s Chereek Fadaiee split over strategy. The majority were against armed struggle, wanting to continue the revolution by educating people. I went with this group, but gradually disconnected even from them, bored by long, unproductive discussions over every detail. I decided I wanted to be helpful as a doctor, and had begun to fear for my life. As time passes, people become wiser, or more conservative, and after a year, I was allowed to return to university. The six-year course took me nine years—1976 to 1985.

By 1984, I was doing practical work at Tabriz University hospital, seeing the landmine and bomb injuries from the Iran-Iraq War—amputations, foreign bodies, burns and trauma—including many injured women and children. I was also seeing people with polio, tetanus, rabies and leprosy.

After graduation, doctors were contracted to work for one year in an area of need, so in 1985, I was sent to the small town of Qurwah, part-Kurdish, part-Azeri, two hours from Sanandaj. Its newly built hospital had up to 100 beds, well equipped by Kurdish standards, staffed by Indian and Pakistani doctors because of a shortage of Iranian specialists. Six months later, when one of these doctors left, I was put in charge of the delivery room and obstetrics ward.

At last, I was working as a doctor, helping poor people, but my memories still hurt. I discovered a bitter truth: I was unable to be the doctor I wanted to be. The economy was getting worse each year, with the war and the sanctions and the peoples' lives were harsh. Most women in Qurwah came to the hospital to give birth, but we saw only those village women experiencing difficult labours. If a delivery was normal, we discharged the mother and baby the next day, because of a shortage of beds and equipment. After a caesarean delivery, we kept the mother for up to six days, until her stitches were removed, but discharged the baby on the first day. We could not afford the space. Fathers would drive the newborn back to the village by tractor, travelling hours through cold and snow. The baby would then be at the mercy of a grandmother or aunt. I was the person who signed the discharge forms. It was inhuman, but I had to follow the rules. Even now, thinking about those poor babies gives me a chilling sensation.

I remember patients needing an urgent caesarean but the women refusing, saying, "If you do the operation who will look after my other kids and the house? If I lose this baby, never mind, I have another six at home." For weeks I would wonder about the mother and baby's fate.

For a few months, we had no qualified obstetrician. As a general practitioner, I was not trained for caesareans. I had to refer patients to a bigger town, or beg a general surgeon to do the operation, but we lost patients for lack of qualified personnel and medicines.

When a baby died, the parents would take the body home for burial. If a baby suffered a minor abnormality, like an extra finger, it was taken home, but if the baby was grossly malformed, say from hydrocephalus, it was usually left at the hospital. In one instance, the father said, "I will not take this monster home."

The mothers were as young as 15 and as old as 50. They would tell me how embarrassed they had been by the thought of being examined by a male doctor. I worked six days a week, but for the six months I was in charge of the delivery room, I was on call fulltime, sometimes staying up all night with patients, then doing my rounds the next day.

It was a lonely, unsettling time. I lived in a two-storey building with about 70 single rooms for medical and nursing staff. I had lunch at the hospital restaurant and would buy and prepare my own breakfast and dinner. I was paid little, but enough for food, clothes, and travel to Saghez and Sanandaj.

Sanandaj is where I worked after finishing my contract. It is the capital of the province, surrounded by hills and mountains. Abidar, the tallest and most famous mountain, has waterfalls, rock formations, trees and, from its snowcapped summit, a breathtaking view.

As I was setting up my surgery, Iraqi planes bombed the town, shattering every window in the building. In the morning, I worked at a *dermanga*, or public community health centre, for outpatients, in the afternoon working in my surgery. At the *dermanga*, there was a nurse, a doctor, a small chemist and an immunisation clinic. This was in 1987–88, so some outpatients were Kurdish refugees from Iraq. Some were chemical-bomb victims, as were a few Iranian soldiers. We would dress their burns and blisters after their discharge from the hospital, but the worst cases were transferred to big cities, or sent to Europe for treatment and propaganda purposes, to show the world the cruelty of Saddam Hussein's regime.

Initially, I was the only female doctor in Sanandaj. Men soon learned by word of mouth that I wanted to treat female patients. There were plenty of male doctors for them, and I was never without a patient. I treated an average of 20 patients each afternoon but continued to feel helpless and inadequate. I was desperate for a simple pregnancy test. Either I had to send the patient to Hamadan or ask if they knew someone at the hospital. Even a cleaner could help!

At least contraceptive pills and IUDs were available. During the first few years after the revolution, large families were encouraged, Khomeini making a famous statement: "We want Muslims to take over the world." But after an explosion in the birthrate, the government began advocating contraception.

In both the surgery and the clinic, I saw impetigo, hepatitis, tuberculosis, chicken pox, measles, back pain, gastritis and diarrhoea, but worst were pregnancy complications, because two lives were at risk. In examining many women, I saw no malformation or scars attributable to female circumcision. Until arriving in Australia, I had never heard about this practice in Kurdistan. However, my mother-in-law tells me a midwife advised her that circumcision is a good tradition for girls, asking her permission to perform the small cut. My mother-in-law refused. I believe the Kurdish practice is not as cruel as that in Africa.

Malnutrition was the other major concern. It was most common among village children. The normal scenario was for a mother to be pregnant every other year. During the next pregnancy, the older baby would be put on a diet of biscuits and sugar dissolved in boiled water. This gives babies energy and bulk, but leaves them severely malnourished. I tried to educate the women, knowing they could not afford the diet of dairy products, vegetables and meat I was suggesting. When I suggested follow-up treatment or prescribed a course of medicine, I knew all along they would not be able to manage, or afford it. The problems were overwhelming, and as one person I had my limitations on the number of patients I could help financially. All I could do was listen and show that I cared, but everything I did felt like a drop in the ocean.

I felt useless, hopeless. I often remembered Dr Shakeri, and, at intervals, followed up on what happened to him. He had become a leader of Komala, a Kurdish communist party, that came to prominence after the revolution. He now lives in Iraqi Kurdistan and has a position with the Kurdish administration in Sulaimani. I will always be grateful to him and his impact on my life although I could not sacrifice as much as he did. I had a refrigerator and liked nice clothes!

Despite everything those two years in Sanandaj were easier than my year in Qurwah. The hospital had flats allocated to health professionals, and I shared one with a friend. Then at the end of the second year, 1989, I married a doctor, closed my surgery and came to Australia. I have not worked as a doctor since.

As a mother of three children aged 10, seven and five, I sometimes feel my life has become very narrow. Over time, many dreams fade. As a young person, I was so full of energy, so trusting of what people told me. With maturity and being exposed to a different culture and ideas, I have learnt there is no definitive reality, only perception. Now I try to explore and think for myself and encourage my children to do likewise. Now I try not to lump people into categories, especially with life being in such a state of flux all over the world. Two of my sisters and many friends back in Kurdistan are married but continue with their careers. They negotiate with their husbands, and their daughters will be even better off, despite the obstacles.

Islam is still a powerful influence on Kurdish people's lives. 1400 years ago it was a very progressive influence, giving women the right to inherit property and be witnesses in court. Many Islamic laws and their derivative values, however, are open to interpretation, and the way they are being practised can be criticised.

There are some laws I continue to accept. I consider it fair that a daughter is entitled to only half the inheritance her brother receives, because in the Middle East, the economic burden and obligation to look after the family remains with the father, husband or brother. However, I do not accept that in our culture two women's testimonies are needed to contradict one man's in an Iranian court. I do not accept that there is one standard of honour for men and another for women, and that a man's honour is based on whether the females of his household comply with community values.

In the late 1990s, in Saghez, a brother killed his sister with their father's consent, because she had brought shame on the family. My sister in Iran, a schoolteacher, defended the brother's action. She was shocked and disgusted when I argued, "I think a relationship between two single, consenting adults is their own business, providing they are causing no harm." Like many women, she shared the men's mentality of how women should be treated.

It made me realise that the greatest obstacle for women changing their status is not Islam but their own mentality; that every revolution must start from within. However most Kurdish women do not believe they need more respect, better treatment or equal status. The product of a way of life, they accept it, and feel comfortable within it, trained as they are not to express their feelings or opinions, and being protected from life outside the home. As a result, most grow up shy, lacking confidence and self-esteem. In marriage, a wife is expected to be polite and respect her husband. She wraps herself in a cocoon of silence to avoid argument. In some families, a wife who does not, is physically punished. Few women have the economic means to take an independent stance, and many fear the consequences if they did. It is a fear of the unknown and also a fear of criticism and ostracism from the Kurdish community, even in Australia. It is human nature to want acceptance.

While Islam allows a woman to divorce on grounds of violence or neglect, the divorce rate in Kurdish families is very low, both in Kurdistan and in Australia. Growing up, I knew of a few cases, 98 per cent initiated by men. Men being men, they get tired of their wife's looks or behaviour and seek adventure. Not many could afford more than one wife, (even less so these days), so they divorce to remarry.

I used to think polygamy might suit some women. They could share the responsibilities of children and chores, but a friend whose father had a few wives disagrees. She told me it was chaos. "The wives were always jealous of each other, always fighting. They even tried to jeopardise each other's cooking by adding too much salt!" No-one was happy—neither the husband nor the wives.

Divorce is always a sad story for a Kurdish woman. She does not have government support and, in most cases, she loses respect. She has to rely on her father, or another male relative. She becomes a misfit, but even worse, her children are regarded as their father's property. The usual practice is that children stay with their father or his family, even though Islamic law allows mothers to keep their children until a certain age. However a family friend in her early twenties was divorced recently because her husband beat her. A few times, she was hospitalised. After the divorce, she gave birth to a son and, without even seeing or touching him, sent him to his father. My heart goes out to her. Because of her husband's mistreatment, she was supported by her entire family, and could have cared for her baby, but it is considered shameful for a woman to take her husband's children to her parental home. As a result, most women stay in a marriage without complaint, even if life is miserable. Love has never been essential for a Kurdish marriage.

Our culture expects us to be polite. Also, many aspects of our lives are considered too private for open discussion. There is a lot of self-censorship, in many ways more powerfully limiting than government censorship. With so much suppressed emotion, it is no wonder it can explode in various ways.

But there is hope! With more education and new technology, like the media, exposing people to other ideas, I think the men's mentality and the laws are becoming more reasonable. Now, under Iranian law, the first wife must give her consent for a second or third marriage, although that consent is sometimes obtained by force. Putting up with a second wife is just another sacrifice a mother makes to be with her children.

But the lack of confidence goes beyond marriage issues or distinctions between male and female. Even as an educated woman, I am very embarrassed by the little I know about our history and culture, especially before Islam. There are so few books that even our knowledge of the Kurdish language is limited to daily conversation. The classical poets use words beyond our reach. There is no opportunity to research Kurdish issues at an Iranian university and no government funding for literary and scientific endeavours. The lack of opportunity and resources means there are relatively few Kurdish scientists, philosophers, writers and artists, male or female. There are other reasons for this: our geographic isolation means that until recently, there has been little exposure to different ideas. The main concern for most people has been daily survival. They have not had the luxury of sitting around thinking of new ideas or inventions. Reading has not been a popular pastime. Also, Kurdish people are used to operating in a group, rather than individually, and an individual who takes a stance against accepted values is a target.

But even this is changing. With Kurds now spread around the world, there are Kurdish writers, musicians and artists who now have the freedom to explore their ideas outside Kurdistan, and this is gradually changing the situation in Kurdistan. I have even heard of a Kurdish rocket scientist who works for NASA. Kurdistan may be 50 years behind but with the global high tech 'village' reaching everywhere it will not take us 50 years to catch up.

Much of our culture is worth preserving. I would like my children to keep our culture of being friendly, kind and generous, and respecting their elders. I would like them to remember the language, clothing and music, although I cannot expect them to know our history when I know so little. However, I do not encourage my daughters to be quiet and shy like me. I would like my children to marry someone they love. It would be a bonus if their spouse were Kurdish. I would like them to have the freedom to remain single, if they choose! In Australia, marriage is an option, whereas in Kurdistan, everyone is expected to marry. Otherwise, there is a stigma that something must be wrong with them. Most of all I would like them to leave behind the narrowmindedness. We can have a broader view of the world, even when concerning ourselves with Kurdish issues.

As for the future, I think the struggle for autonomy will continue, at least for a few generations. If we were to gain human, cultural and political rights, we may not be so desperate to have flag in the UN, especially as I see a future where borders will not be so important, as in Europe. All cultures will assimilate into a global, multicultural society. Each culture will lose something, as well as acquire new values. Personally, I am more concerned about the depletion of the ozone layer and the forests, the greenhouse effect, and the pollution of waterways and atmosphere. The time has come to treat our earth with respect and reverence, to put all our energies into creating a world where violence and oppression against people and nature are eradicated.

Good News

A poem by Jheela Husseini, translated by Kamran Avin and Gafoor Muhamad

You would come and share
The glory of this good news, with a warm hand.
In this autumn of life,
Put a butterfly of gladness on the hairs of poetry.
Squeeze frozen fingers and hands of sadness
When I hid my world of gladness in my mind.
The song of gladness and vision
Melted on my lips
The flower of my love silently growing, instead.

See the Mother, Know the Girl

A life story based on interviews with Mariam Sultani

She is always in my heart and mind. Every day I remember her goodness, courage and strength, how she sacrificed her life for us. She was so forgiving, even of the most terrible person in her life: her husband. At Ramadan, she would say, "Go and visit your father. He was horrible to me, not you." She would never let us talk badly about him. When I am dealing with my own children, or my husband, when I speak, when I feel sad for all I have lost, I remember her. When I feel helpless for being unable to assist my children in their homework I remember her. She could not read or write, but when I was doing exams, she would bring me cups of tea and rub my shoulders.

I remember her long, colourful Kurdish dress, a wide band of cloth around her waist, a shawl tied at her throat. She always wore a scarf over the traditional four-centimetre-high, flat-topped sequinned hat made of strong cardboard, her hair peeping out at the front over dark eyes, two plaits down her back.

Religious! She prayed more than five times a day, although in those days the mosque was forbidden to women. Even though she was very poor, she was always generous, helping an orphaned family by giving clothes, food and money, if she had any.

I was born in a city of about one million people, surrounded by beautiful mountains, in eastern Kurdistan. When I was six years old, my mother left my father, taking with her my older brother and sister, Halil and Halima, and me. In those times especially, it was a very brave act to leave a husband, but my father was abusive in every way. To be honest, I hated him. He would swear and shout and hit all of us but was most cruel to my older brother. He took Halil out of primary school, making him work in very low paid jobs like take-aways and barber shops, forcing him to hand over all his pay. Often he would kick him out of the house. Halil loved animals, and kept singing quails in wooden cages, as well as doves and rabbits. Once our father took Halil's rabbit and killed it in front of Halil, making my mother cook it for his meal. None of us could eat the leftovers. Our father always ate first. We could eat only after he had finished, even during Ramadan. I cannot remember him ever having kissed me.

When my mother left him, we stayed a week with our father's brother until my mother's nephew rented us a room, and gave us blankets, pillows, and plates. Our father never gave us money, and my mother's two brothers had died, so it was her two nephews who helped us, Yusef particularly. He was a teacher in another city but whenever he came to our city he was always there for us—materially and emotionally. He is as close to perfection as a man can get. He and other members of our mother's family would give us rice, oil, and money for food and rent, but not on a regular basis, so there were times when we ate very little. My mum was too poor to buy us new clothes, so I would be too shy to go anywhere.

Our father initially wanted us back and sent many people to talk to our mother. She could not divorce him by law, so asked him to divorce her, and after two years, he did so, religiously and legally, and married again. He fathered another four children. We had as little to do with him as possible. He worked as a gardener for the city council and I would pass him on my way to school. Sometimes he would stop me and say, "Would you teach me to read and write. I will pay you a few tomans." After a few lessons he would give up, then ask me again the following year. His second wife resented my visits. She did not like us at all. His only say over our lives was when he had to give us permission to marry.

My mum was happy that all the violent times were over, although she had many economic difficulties. None of the girls in her large, wealthy family had gone to school. She could not get a job, and her health was too poor to do housework for other people, so she had to rely on her relatives and Halil.

Yusef rented a shop for Halil and bought all the equipment to set up a barber's shop. It was opposite a police station, Yusef thinking that this would protect Halil from our father, but because Halil refused to talk to our father, our father sent his three brothers to threaten Halil. The eldest produced a knife saying, "Why don't you respect your father?" then they hit and kicked him. Also, because people were scared of the police, Halil had few customers. Then, when he turned 18 and had to do two years' military service in another city, it was very hard for us. He was the only man in the family, and we missed him, although Yusef would take us to visit him whenever he could.

We moved a lot. Some of the houses had electricity, others oil lamps. To wash, we always went to a *hamam* or public bath. Our mother baked bread once a month with neighbours in a traditional *tandoor*, grew vegetables and kept ducks and chickens.

We spoke Sorani. School lessons were conducted in Farsi, of course, because that is the law. The only other difference was religion. Some teachers were Shi'ite and would describe Shi'ite practices.

In secondary school, I studied religion, Persian, science, maths and a bit of English. They did not teach Kurdish history or speak about Kurdish people, so I learnt very little about my background. We wore Western-style uniforms, but outside school, I wore Kurdish dresses, because they are so pretty. I never covered my hair.

When Halil was in his second year of army service, my mother's sister asked if her son could marry Halima. Halima was only 15 but secretly loved this cousin, and afterwards she moved to Tehran. Then Halil came home. He looked for one job after another but was constantly refused. He felt responsible for the family and his pride was shaken. It was at a friend's suggestion that he become a policeman.

He was transferred to a faraway city with many Shi'ite Arabs, who did not accept him. We wrote every week, but after a while, our letters were returned. Suddenly, Halil appeared on our doorstep, acting very strangely. He was hallucinating, crying, not sleeping, praying a lot, and talking strangely. He would think people were his enemies, and wander off and we would not know where he was. He refused to see doctors saying that the only person he trusted was the friend who got him his job as a policeman. This friend convinced him to let the doctors treat him, and they gave him an injection that put him to sleep. My mum's relatives then arranged for an ambulance to take him to a hospital in Tehran.

While my mum stayed with him at the hospital, I stayed with my mum's wealthy relatives. I could not sleep—I was always thinking of Halil. I felt I came from another world—one that was much lower on the social scale: poor and full of problems.

Halima's friends in Tehran arranged for Halil to go to a good private hospital, where he stayed for a month. They gave him electric shocks and medicines, and when he came home, he was much better. He went back to work, but a doctor's certificate recommended that he never carry a gun. He applied to be transferred to Tehran, and wanted us to go and live with him, but before we did so, he asked my mum and his friends to find him a wife. Finally, one family accepted him and he became engaged. The wedding took place a few months later, in Halil's absence, and we had another celebration in Tehran, after his wife arrived.

I was in Year Nine when we moved. It was the middle of the school year and there was no place for me in the Tehran school. We would visit Halima, who lived in a modern house with a lovely garden courtyard, though her marriage was not so beautiful. For a year we stayed in that big city. It was the time leading up to the revolution, but there was even more unrest and chaos after Ayatollah Khomeini came to power in 1979. Sometimes we could not sleep at night, because of the fights and all the shouting, shooting and fires in the street. Gangs of young men would go around arresting people, and people were burning shops, banks and government buildings.

As a policeman, Halil had to witness all the violence and death. He was too sensitive, and began having nightmares, unable to sleep at night. As he became more scared and nervous, he did not want to go to work, reluctant to see more bloodshed. He just could not cope. Two months after the revolution, our mum convinced him we should return to Kurdistan, where it would be quiet. And it was for a while.

Before his marriage, Halil had a wonderful relationship with our mother, but afterwards, they had many arguments. Our mum was sick with a kidney problem and she would ask her daughter-in-law to wake Halil to go and queue for oil. Halil's wife would say, "No, he is too tired from work." At such times it appeared to Halil that his wife cared for him more than his mother did. After an argument, Halil's wife would sometimes return to her family for a week and we would have to bring her back. The next spring the doctors found my mother's kidneys had stopped functioning. She needed a transplant. Yusef offered to donate his kidney, but she died on the morning before the operation. She was 47. I was 15.

We took the body, wrapped in blankets, home from the hospital in Yusef's car. He did everything for us, and insisted that we take the body to his family's home. His mother and brothers and sisters helped wash it and put it in a white *koffin* tied above the head. Halil was very distraught, feeling guilty about the arguments they had been having, and insisted on burning off some of her hair, using a cigarette. He kept this lock of hair in a special place, sometimes carrying it with him.

We prayed in the house before the men took the body for burial. Women and girls did not go to the cemetery. We stayed at home, crying, sitting, talking and preparing food for the next three days.

The house became crowded with mum's extended family and their friends. Every time a new visitor arrived, we read the Fa'atiha, the first surah in the Qur'an: "In the name of Allah, Most Gracious, Most Merciful, Praise be to Allah, the Cherisher and Sustainer of the Worlds, Most Gracious, Most Merciful, Master of the Day of Judgement. Thee do we worship, and Thine aid we seek. Show us the straight way, The way of those on whom Thou has bestowed Thy Grace, Thou whose portion is not wrath, and who go not astray."

After three days, we returned home, and for the next month had many visitors. Close friends stayed a few days, then visited twice a day. Halil was demented with grief. My father had neither come to the funeral nor offered his sympathies, so Halil vented all his guilt and anger in that direction. He went searching for our father in all the teahouses, and when he at last found him, he screamed, "You killed my mother, so I will kill you." He was brought back home but was always wandering, visiting mum's grave, and bringing back earth. At public baths, he bathed in his clothes. He was a big man and would not listen to anyone, and we were very worried for him—especially because *pasdars* were everywhere. Sometimes, he was so angry, he would beat his wife.

After six weeks, we convinced him to go to the doctor, and he was taken to hospital, but two months later, he came back, worse, so mum's relatives arranged for him to go to the same Tehran private hospital he had been in before. His wife returned to her family, and I had to live for two months with my sister Halima, who had returned from Tehran. Even she was unkind to me. Music remained my friend, but Halima would tell her husband, "Mariam is very bad. She is listening to music!" and her husband would order me to stop because Islam says women must not listen to strange men's voices. I particularly loved the songs of Muhammad Jaza, an Iraqi Kurdish singer. It seemed he was singing for me—about unhappiness and loneliness, about not having anyone, about hoping for a better life in the future.

After two months, Halil came home, much better. I wanted to go back to school, but he and his wife wanted me to stay and help in the house. My sister-in-law became a very unkind, demanding boss. I did everything but cook—caring for their child, cleaning the house and washing clothes. I was not allowed out of the house alone.

This is often the way for a girl without parents, and I was very lonely and unhappy.

The *pasdars*, police and army were everywhere. There was a checkpoint on every road entering or leaving each city, and the *pasdars* in particular had the power to interfere. They were Persian civilians, who wore camouflage uniforms and carried machine guns, and they would tell women and girls to cover themselves so that not one hair showed, or if they heard Persian or Western music in a car, they would stop the car and break the cassette. Most music was banned but folk music was allowed, so we could still buy Kurdish cassettes, but no political songs.

I was never interested in politics, nor was my immediate family, except Yusef. He was a communist in the Shah's time, and had been in and out of prison, and tortured. In total, he had spent six years in prison. After the revolution, there were so many political groups, mostly left-wing, in which I had friends who were active. These friends talked about Kurdish politics, but I did not get involved.

For a number of years in the early 1980s, *peshmergas* would come down from the mountains and enter the city at night, and shooting would start between them and the *pasdars*, army or police. People would hide in homes, shops or offices, and everyone would leave their courtyard door open, so the *peshmergas* or *pasdars* could hide behind the walls. I hated all the fighting. After a night of it, the *pasdars* visited every house in the suburb. They would kick down doors, searching everywhere. If they saw any cassettes or strange books, they destroyed them. Once I was at a neighbour's when they found Kurdish cassettes. I asked, "Why are you taking those cassettes?" and one said, "Because a group shot at us last night." I said, "Well those cassettes did not shoot at you!"

Although I was shy of strangers, I was always outspoken, even to my father. When I stayed with Halima, I would see how she tried to obey her husband in every way, but her husband would shout and hit her over silly things, like the dinner not being ready or the child crying, or a broken plate. Halima would quietly accept his behaviour, but I would demand, "Why are you hitting her? Why are you swearing at her?" and I would advise her to stand up for herself.

In Kurdistan, when a girl turns 16, people start coming to ask for the girl to marry their son, and a few families approached my father and brother to ask for me. I loved one of them, but Halil, my father and Halima's husband did not approve of him, because he was a *peshmerga*. We were neighbours. I never talked to him, but just by looking, we shared our love.

About another man, Halil and Halima's husband disagreed, so when Halima and her husband were on holiday and the aunt of my future husband came to visit, saying, "My son Mostefa has seen Mariam and wants to marry her," Halil said, "We will give you an answer in two days." My father gave his permission, and before the others came back from their holiday, the arrangements were made.

I had never seen my future husband. He had apparently seen me in the street from afar. I felt I had no say, that I was an object to be sold or given away, or a problem they wanted to be rid of. No-one asked me how I felt about the marriage.

I saw Mostefa once. A week before the engagement ceremony he came with his aunt, his friend and his friend's wife to talk about the marriage, but I could not even look at him. I thought he was ugly and far too old. There were 13 years between us. I was very,

very unhappy. I could have refused the marriage, but then my family would have been angry with me. I thought, "What the heck? Who cares?"

My sister-in-law put in an order for what Mostefa had to provide in terms of money, gold and clothes. His family lived in Iraqi Kurdistan, so he had to pay for everything out of his pay from a government office. He told her, "I will try my best."

During the following week Mostefa, my sister-in-law, his aunt and his friend's wife went shopping for fabric to make my engagement dress. I had no say. They took a dress to give my size to the dressmaker.

Both my engagement and wedding dresses had the traditional close-fitting bodice over a long-sleeved dress of sheer material, gathered at the waist, with a full-length skirt. Around the waist was wrapped a wide, folded, colourful, floral band about four metres in length. For the engagement ceremony my dress was pink, with darker pink and white embroidered roses and a silver-white satin bodice. I wore two veils, white netting underneath pink netting decorated with gold discs.

The ceremony went ahead in Halima's absence. About 20 of my family and friends gathered at our house for tea and sweets before Mostefa, the *malla*, and 20 of his friends and relatives arrived in the afternoon. The men all wore Western suits, except the *malla*, a well-known, highly respected figure. Mostefa and I had to repeat after the *malla*, "Allah has no partner and I witness that. Muhammad is his servant and messenger." Halil acted for me, saying, "I give my sister to you, Mostefa." Mostefa had only to say, "I, Mostefa, accept your sister as my wife." There were no promises! We signed the two marriage certificates—one for each of us—and even when we were doing this I could not look at him. The marriage was recorded in the *malla*'s book, and then we exchanged rings. Sweets, fruits and chocolate were served, followed by music and dancing, though it is tradition that the bride does not dance. Nor did I want to. I did not exchange one word with Mostefa. The wedding ceremony was to be in 20 days' time.

When Halima returned from holidays, she was shocked and upset that everything had happened without her. When she and her husband met Mostefa, they did not like him. Between the engagement and the marriage ceremony, couples usually come together briefly, to get to know each other, but I would run away whenever Mostefa visited. I was still in love with the other man. Fifteen days after our engagement, our neighbours told us that Mostefa already had a wife in Iraqi Kurdistan. This news only made my hatred for him grow.

Like my engagement dress, my wedding dress was arranged without me. No-one talked to me about what to expect after marriage. I had never studied biology at school and knew nothing about sexuality. I was very frightened.

For the marriage ceremony, the groom entertains his family and friends at his house, while the bride's family entertains her relatives and friends at her house. We ate lunch and I was washing up and doing the housework. An hour before Mostefa and his party were to collect me, I was told to get ready. I was crying as I dressed in pale-pink with a veil of white stiff netting, chains of embroidered white daisies falling down each shoulder, and the pink veil from my engagement—anxious about what was going to happen, worried about how he would treat me, and very sad about the love I still felt for another.

I heard the beeping horns of the procession of cars, and was told to sit in the car next to Mostefa. An old woman, whose job it was to cook for the wedding feast and to check a girl's virginity on the wedding night, sat on my other side. I felt numb, as if I was attending my own funeral.

A few of my family and friends came to Mostefa's place for half an hour or so, just to drink tea. After they left, there was music and dancing. Mostefa and I joined in. I had no choice: it is tradition. Otherwise, the old woman stood beside me with a special bag. In it, she had a change of clothes, a nightie for the bride, a sheet of plastic, a square of white cloth and a box of sweets. It is tradition that in the early evening, while everyone is eating and dancing, she goes to prepare the bed. She puts plastic over the mattress and the white cloth over the plastic. She calls the bride, advising her, "Don't say anything. Don't bring shame on your family." The groom comes in and, without any talking or preparation, quickly takes the bride's virginity. It is more like rape. The bride dresses, the groom leaves, and all the women come to inspect the white material. If there is blood on it, they put money on the material and kiss the mortified bride.

I know one girl, a daughter of a *malla*, whose material showed no blood, although she was a virgin. Her husband dragged her by her hair all the way back to her family's home. In front of her family, he bashed her, telling them, "You have shamed me." She remained with her family. In such cases, it is very hard to marry another man, especially one from the same city.

On the third day, the families of the bride and groom come together for an afternoon of sweets, fruits and tea. The bride usually wears a red dress and her family brings bedding, furniture and whatever else they can afford, some of it bought with the money given by the groom's family. In my case there had been many arguments over what to buy because of the lack of money.

At the beginning, I hated my husband, but he was very kind to me and my family. He did anything he could to make me happy, gave me freedom in every way, and provided well, so that over several months, I began to feel more comfortable.

Sometimes he would tell me stories about the hardships of life as a *peshmerga* with Barzani in Iraqi Kurdistan. In the first month, he mentioned having been married before. Three or four months later, he told me he had one child. I was very sad. Then I read a letter from his family. It said, "Your boys are fine," and he said, "So my other son is still alive." He told me that he had divorced his wife, but after 17 years of marriage, I found out they were not divorced, that he just left his family, and that he had three children. I was very angry.

After marriage, I refused to be dependent. I would think of my mother's life and my sister's. I understood my mother's dependency, but I would get angry with my sister, because she chose to rely on her husband for everything. I would go and take the snow off the roof, or do the garden or move the furniture, although Mostefa always did the shopping.

After three years my son was born and it was so good to have a baby. I love children and Mostefa was a very kind father. Even now, he is never strict, he is always laughing with them, and he never gets angry with them.

Mostefa worked hard, and after six years we bought our own house. We had everything—a modern bathroom and kitchen, all the furniture we needed, a comfortable life in every way. I was happy. But in 1987, something shocking happened.

For six months, Halil had been working as a security guard in an adult religious school in our home city, while his family lived in Urmia. The war with Iraq continued, and when Iraqi planes started bombing Urmia, he went to bring his family to safety. When he got out of the bus, he saw blood everywhere. More than 2000 people had been killed, and mutilated bodies still lay on the ground. He could not get these images out of his mind, and became very depressed. Four nights after their return, he told his wife that he wanted to kill himself. She did not believe he would do it. All night, he prayed. He kissed and hugged his daughters, then prayed again. The next day, he went to work. Alone in the security guard's room, he shot himself.

The whole family was devastated. His wife was in denial, claiming he was killed by *peshmerga*. We would say, "No—he did not hurt people. *Peshmerga* would not kill him. We have proof from the doctor." I fell into a black depression for a long, long time.

Otherwise, we did not experience the hardships suffered by so many Kurds. The Iraq-Iran War ended in 1988, but during Anfal many Kurdish people from northern Iraq escaped to Iran, and we helped some and two families stayed at our home until we found them a place to rent.

One day, some government agents went into Mostefa's office and checked through his desk. He came home and said, "I have to leave. Maybe I will go to Iraq, maybe Turkey. Are you coming with me?" I was eight and a half months' pregnant. I said, "Please wait until after the baby is born," but he said, "I can't wait. They are after me." I was very angry and upset. My family tried to convince him to stay, but he left early the next morning, taking only a few clothes. I was very worried for him, and cried for a month.

Our seven-year-old son would sit in the corner of the room and not talk. He did not want to go to school. When four secret police officers came to my house, they wanted to know where my husband was. I had no idea. They searched for evidence to use against him, but found nothing.

I went to Tabriz to visit my cousins and Mostefa telephoned, saying, he was in Ankara, and was safe. Soon after, I gave birth to a daughter. I was very happy to have a girl. Mostefa called again, and I pleaded with him to come back, but over a number of phone calls, he always said, "It is better that you come here." I was confused. I missed him very much but did not want to leave Halima.

Government officials came to the house, asking questions, then sent someone to take me to a centre, where investigators questioned me. They took me to the centre six times for questioning, and three times to court. Always they asked me, "Where is your husband? Why did he leave the country? Why does his family live in Iraq?" I would cry during the investigations, but stayed strong. I fought them with words.

When my baby girl was three months old, I decided that if Mostefa was not going to come back, we had to go to him. My son was already on my passport, but when I tried to add my daughter's name, the passport officials said, "You need to have your husband's signature." I tried bribing the official. I tried buying a false passport, a birth certificate or ID. I tried finding someone who had taken a child to Turkey and had come back alone, so that they could take my baby, but after trying everything, my only option was to smuggle my daughter into Turkey.

I wanted the three of us to go together. The people around me, especially my sister's husband, warned me not to trust a stranger, saying, "It is best you go legally and have the baby smuggled in another way." One person knew a smuggler. I arranged to meet him in Naghada. For A$1,000, he agreed to take my five-month-old daughter across the border. She was to stay with his family a week, then be taken over the mountains. It was a very dangerous route, the border area between three countries, patrolled by soldiers, *jahsh* and *peshmergas* from all the parties. Also there was snow. Anything could happen, but I gave the smuggler my daughter, food and clothes, then my son and I went by bus to Tehran and from there took a plane to Istanbul.

Mostefa met us at the airport. I was very angry with him. To my mind, he had been willing to sacrifice us to save himself. He could have returned to Iran. Maybe he would have gone to prison, maybe even been tortured, but he chose to run away and leave me with all the problems and responsibilities, and now I did not know whether my baby was dead or alive. On the bus trip to Yuksekova, a town in the mountains close to the border, I was upset and very worried.

I had arranged to go to the village of Shemdinli, five hours' drive from Yuksekova, to pick up my daughter. Mostefa preferred to stay in Yuksekova, saying, "It is too dangerous. They might arrest me." I borrowed clothes from a Kurdish woman with whom we were staying, dressing in her style: two or three long dresses, one over the other, without a waistband, a hand-made scarf wrapped around my forehead and neck.

We drove through the mountains and on arriving in Shemdinli some men took me to their cousin's house and told me to wait for the man to come with my baby. The family was very kind, making me dinner. We ate on the carpet around a circular metal tray. In Iran, we use a plastic tablecloth.

Night came. I could not sleep. The man was meant to have come, and I was worried something had gone wrong in the four-hour drive to the border and the eight-hour walk across the mountains. It was a very long night. All I could think of was, "I have lost my baby girl."

At 9.30 next morning, somebody came saying, "Is there an Iranian woman in your house? We have her baby." Fifteen minutes passed. I was crazy with the knowledge that my baby was alive. I could not stop crying. Finally, a strange man brought my daughter, but I could not take her. I was not myself. I was on my knees, kissing his shoes, and crying, "Thank you, God. Once again, you have given me a daughter." The man was saying, "Please don't. You are my sister. Get up and hold your baby."

When I held Avin, I was shocked. She was so different from the baby I had left. She looked at me in a different way. She was wrapped in a small, dirty blanket and wore a dirty T-shirt and very wet, soiled pants. She was so quiet, very hungry, and sweating. I do not think the man had fed or changed her in all that time. I had left clothes, food, medicine, every thing he could need, but he had brought nothing but the baby.

I borrowed some clothes from the lady and we gave Avin a wash and fed her. Back in Yuksekova, Mostefa wanted to hug and kiss his daughter—this was the first time he had seen her—but she was crying and would not go to him, or to anyone. Before the separation, she used to laugh and play happily with everybody, but afterwards, she clung to me, and for four months she would not sleep.

The next morning, we left for Ankara. We lived there for two years, in flats in big apartment blocks, with other people in situations similar to ours. We were getting some money from the UN High Commission for Refugees, but after our savings ran out, things became more difficult. I found work in a hairdressing salon, but Mostefa could not work in his profession because he did not know the Turkish language, and was too proud to get other work. Then we moved to Konya for a year.

Konya is a small city, with many old mosques, on the Anatolian plateau. We arrived in winter and rented a small flat. In our culture it is tradition for neighbours to welcome newcomers and bring cake or sweets. When our Turkish neighbour saw we had only a few blankets and nothing else, she could not believe it. "Your children will get sick. How can you live this way? The next day, her family bought us a double mattress and blankets and sheets, and food and firewood. They knew we were Kurdish, but it did not matter. I will never forget their kindness.

In Konya, Mostefa got work as a kitchenhand in a restaurant and I worked in a women's clothes shop, but we did not have enough money and did not know what would happen from one day to the next. It was 1991, and we heard about the Kurdish uprising in northern Iraq and how all the refugees were coming to Turkey escaping Saddam Hussein's forces. I was worried for all the people. We received a letter from Mostefa's first family, saying they had escaped to Iran and were applying to the government to gain ownership of our house. I had sympathy for them, knowing what it is like to be without a father, but I did not want them to have the house, as I was hoping to return. Also, since our marriage, I had put every effort into building the house for my family. In the end, they did not get the house. It is now being used as a government office.

We were being sponsored to come to Australia. We had to borrow 100 dollars here, 300 dollars there, for the airfares, but when we arrived in Melbourne, our friend made us welcome. Australia was so quiet, peaceful and beautiful, I commented, "This is like paradise." At last we were safe and for days all I could do was sleep.

After a month our friends helped us rent a flat, the Smith Family and St Vincent de Paul giving us beds, furniture, plates, spoons, and a few pots and pans. The mattresses stank, but we used them for four years.

I had headaches, and pains in my stomach and back. Doctors and medicines were too expensive in Turkey, but in Australia, after several operations, my health improved. Mostefa and I studied 510 hours of English at the Adult Migrant English Service, and I was quick to pick up the new language. But learning a whole new way of life is like being born again, so we have been born three times. Each time, there were many pressures, and having lost everything, psychologically a refugee finds every little detail difficult. Nevertheless I did two more English courses, then courses to develop my job skills, and found work quickly.

Mostefa did not find work until 1996. He did not speak good English and he was not looking for a job, so when friends found him a position as a general hand in a factory, I told him, "It is either work or divorce." After 10 months, he was again out of work, then after a year got a job as a process worker. That lasted one year. For a long time, he was unemployed, and relied on his son to translate, but now he is speaking English and working.

Still, there are periods when I am so depressed and anxious, I do not want to leave the house. It reminds me of the black time after Halil's suicide. For three years, I had counselling through a government health service, which helped me cope with the new life, to heal some wounds and to build confidence. Sometimes, I take medicines and see a psychologist. I read and force myself to go for walks, do the shopping and see friends, but sometimes, I cannot motivate myself. My love of Allah is getting stronger. I have waves of feeling to wear the *hijab*, but I do not know when I will start. Generally, I am happier when I have a job, because then I have less time to think about personal matters.

Young ones adapt more quickly. My son is doing well at school. Last year, he came first in many subjects and was first in his year. He wants to study computers. Avin has asthma and a kidney problem, and emotionally is very, very quiet—she prefers to keep to herself. She often has nightmares, and is very afraid about being separated from me. She is seeing a psychologist and, thank God, is slowly getting better. She sings beautifully, and would love to be a singer, but in Iran, this profession is frowned upon. I do not encourage her, yet when I listen to her, it is so lovely and I wonder what to do.

If you ask whether I regret leaving my country, I cannot say. In Australia, we get on well as a family, but there are problems, and sometimes, I miss my family and the life terribly. You are not so alone over there. Still, after all that has happened, I would not like to go back.

I Love You Besides Being Angry With You

A poem by Marif Agha-e
translated by Kamran Avin
and Gafoor Muhamad

Again, dark smoke and your sighing.
Again, strange avenues and your shadow.
Again, an exiled traveller's bag and your shoulders.
Again and again,
The open mouth of handcuffs and your hand.
How heavy a load you are
On the shoulder of sadness.

ABOUT Hamid Rashidi Zarza

Hamid Rashidi Zarza was born in 1941 in Goorgawa village in the Shnoo region of eastern Kurdistan. He spent about fourteen years in prison for his political views during both the time of the Shah and the Islamic Republic, being sentenced to death three times. During his time in prison he studied law and received a legal degree in 1970. Of himself he says, "I was fourteen when the angel poet whispered in my ear. To speak and write in Kurdish had its penalties and in the year 2001 nothing has changed. If I was born in a democratic country my poems would have come

from the tongue of a bird. Instead my heart is a volcano and I do not know when it will erupt.

Gaddar[a]

By Hamid Rashidi Zarza
translated by Kamran Avin

I was ebullient with passion in my land
In a place where I was known as Gaddar

My roar in the hieghts and lows
Caused the wide, broad fields to quake.

The snow, water and brook, aqueduct and spring
All knew me as the springhead.

The way I wove field and desert
Watered farm and dry both rejoiced in me.

Shivering dew on cheeks of jasmine would
Twinkle like diamond fragments.

I bestowed green to tree and arbor
Adorning the earth with my capable hands.

When the moonshine was showing off at night
In me she was seeing her beautiful face.

Wherever I passed and blitzed
A thousand plants bloomed.

Fragrant flowers grew by my banks
My breeze combing their tresses.

Their beauty, style and sensuality
In toto were dependent on the outpouring of my grace.

When I wriggled and wound my way
Sands and grit all, were scattered.

Fresh air and the pattering of Spring after Spring
The swashing river and whispering twigs

Were clear in every event and place.
No one was anxious about needing a companion.

But since the day the rain stopped
The clouds became sullen.

I lost my roar and rave over banks and fords
I worried for the dikes and watered farms.

Since I was left with no dike and place, alas
Within mounds and rockeries I was blocked.

I wandered into algae, swamp and lagoon
Becoming a refugee in my own country, my homeland.

Because I have no true leader I have been divided
Otherwise I would have my power still.

Yet by cloud, furrow and hail stone
I will become that great river again.

By my whimper, by the thunder of April's cloud
The valley and field will be embellished once more.

Freezoo[a]

By Hamid Rashidi Zarza
translated by Kamran Avin

I am not Freezoo, but they call me Freezoo
I have strong roots, but am oozing blood.

The sky has created me this way
Has shown my height to be that of vain grass.

They say I have sucked the blood of terra
That it is already too late, the damage is done.

Let them to turn me upside down and inside out.
Let them force me off the farm.

Let them decapitate me,
Let them rend apart my vein and root with ploughshare.

Let them weed me from the tilled field and farm
For even after I am beheaded I grow again.

I am not clod or loam, I will not be sodden.
For I have embraced the land itself, Oh Respected One.

I have taken root in the ground
How can plowing and turning me upside down abate my power?

Just drizzle is enough to wet me
To wash the dust of sadness from my face.

I take root, and take root on taken root
My gnawn root is invisible.

Now stabled at the four corners of the earth
No grown thing can stand against me.

For a shrub taking root is enough, for me just a little loam
Give me chance and time, like a good man.

Give me a barren desert, I will not fill up any space
I will not occupy any flower's place.

A Tale of Three Brothers

By Aza Shirwani

The Fayli Kurds are also known as the Original Lur or Small Lur, one of four groups that make up the people known as Lur. The three other groups are the Mamasani, Korhglawi and Bakhtiari who consider themselves a separate Lur nation. The Lurs have lived for thousands of year in a large territory centred in the Zagros Mountains, extending into eastern Iraq and western Iran. This territory they call Luristan, the Lur's dialects and culture being transitional between Farsi and Kurdish.

Unlike the three other groups the Faylis have always considered themselves part of the Kurdish nation. Up to thirty Fayli tribes come from the biggest mountain of the Zagros Range called Gowra Kuya, its slopes and plains extending into present day Iran and Iraq. The Iranians call this area Pisht-qur or 'the land behind the mountain'. In Iran the Faylis live in the towns of Elam, Kirmanshah, Shoosh, Khorramabad and Mydasht. In Iraq they live in Khanaqin, Bedra, Jassan, Mandali and Shahraban, as well as Baghdad.

The Fayli presence in Baghdad has a long history, Baghdad being the nearest and largest trading city to Fayli lands. One of the Fayli princes of the sixteenth century, Thoul-Fakar Ahmed Sultan Mosloo, made Baghdad his capital for six years until 1529 AD, when Shah Tahmasib Safavi killed him and took Baghdad for the Safavids.

Few studies have been made of the Faylis but some historians believe 'Fayli' comes from the old Sumerian word 'Peali' which means 'fighter' or 'brave man' and later the Arabs changed the letter 'p' to 'f'. Another theory is that an ancient Fayli king was named Peali. A third theory is that they were named after a river that divides them from the Arab population in the south.

The Fayli are not feudal. A person is elected to be a village or tribal representative with the title of *tushmal*. The *tushmal* does not dictate to his people, he is more a mediator between equals.

When making bread the Fayli custom is to make a cross with salt and when making buns they also mark the bun with a cross. One explanation is that they were Christian before converting to Islam.

That the Fayli are firstly Kurd and secondly Shi'ite Muslims has caused them to be oppressed by the Sunni government of Iraq. Deportations started in the forties and resumed in the seventies. However because they are Kurds they are also not welcome in Iran. Yet the Fayli and other Lurs have lived in the area since pre-history when the kingdom of Elam was at the forefront of civilisation, and today they number in the millions.

There are many legends and stories familiar to Fayli families. The legend of one large Fayli tribe goes like this:

Many hundreds of years ago there were three brothers: Ali, Shirwan and Soyla. Soyla had polio and could not walk. As farmers in the Zagros Mountains near Elam, they were forced to pay taxes to a bigger tribe known as the Kaytool. In protest one day one of the brothers cut open and gutted a watermelon, and filled it with manure before dispatching it to the prince of Kaytool.

Soon after, the brothers heard that the angered prince was sending fighters to attack them. Crippled Soyla told his brothers, "Go to the mountains. I can take care of myself." For years Ali and Shirwan fought the Kaytool, killing many, including the prince's son. Finally the prince sent them a letter saying, "You have never believed in me. Now I have lost a son, but I have two daughters. Marry them and give me grandsons. Then we can live in peace." From these marriages Ali had a son called Chirakh, and Shirwan had three sons called Hayer, Safar and Dara. These are the names of four groups in the large Fayli tribe called Ali Shirwan.

Life's Legacy: Blood Cannot Be Washed with Blood

A life story based on interviews and the PhD of Dr Hussein Tahiri

Human beings have the ability to evolve in a conscious manner, and that is what drives me. Gaining an education was an important part of this evolution, particularly since I was born a Kurd, a third-class citizen, from a poor family, of illiterate parents.

The village of Enbe lies between Urmia and the Turkish border, on the skirt of a 12,000-foot mountain. We call its peak Sere Chalawe. *Ser* means 'head' and *chalaw* means 'hole in the ground'. The grazing area is called Chiman. Mountains surround Enbe, but to the east are a few kilometres of flat land where crops and vegetables for the village are grown and where the animals graze.

In my childhood, there was no bitumen road and water came from a public tap. There was no electricity until the late 1990s. A primary school was built in 1973. The 200 houses, on either side of a river, were made mainly of big stones held together with mud or cement. The village was multi-tribal, my tribe being Pacheki.

We spoke the Kurdish dialect of Bahdini and wore Kurdish clothes. We played Kurdish music and celebrated Newroz, but Newroz is not like a Kurdish national day in Iran as it is for Iraqi Kurds, because all Iranians have celebrated it for more than 6000 years. There are still old fireplaces such as one I visited in Yazd, in the south-west, where the guardian claimed the fire has been kept alight continually all this time. In the Zoroastrian scriptures called *Zandavesta*, the fire festival is described as a 'spring festival'. On the Wednesday before Newroz, Persians and Kurds celebrate Kula Charshanbi, or 'Red Wednesday'. We make a bundle of clothes, pour petrol over it and set it alight before throwing it into the air. The Persian tradition is to have a Newroz feast on 21 March, cooking seven foods whose name begins with 's'. My family would just provide the best food they could for our visitors.

When my father wanted to enrol my brother in school, he sent my brother to get his birth certificate. I asked my father to get my birth certificate too. I was accepted into school, my brother was not, because his birth certificate showed his age as 13, although he was a few years younger. Neither of us knows our exact age.

We did not have toys to play with, except those we made ourselves from clay and nature. The first time I touched a pen or paper was when I started at the village school. Classes were in Farsi, a new language. When I was handed my first school books, it was the first time I had ever held a book.

School is free in Iran, but there is the expense of books and stationery, and for middle and secondary school, I had to go to Urmia, over the mountains to the east, where I shared a room with other students. Our families paid for our rent, food and school expenses, and this was difficult for them. Of the 50 students from our village who studied in Urmia, only a few managed to finish high school. Life became even tougher after the Iranian revolution. Queues for food and other necessities were long. In one instance, my housemates and I queued for two days in winter to buy kerosene for our heater. Even after waiting, you were lucky to get what you needed.

Urmia is on the eastern bank of a very salty lake, so salty that no animals survive in it. It also has mountains to the east, north and south. There were small factories for cement, sugar and salt, but otherwise, no industry. People live in three or four-storey houses, for the extended family. It was the first time I had lived among non-Kurds, and the first act of discrimination I experienced was when my future wife's cousin and I went to enrol in Year Seven. The principal pushed him out of the school grounds, because he was wearing Kurdish trousers. At school, there was no mention of Kurdish history or culture, and no discussion or researching of a topic. Politically, we were blank pages.

Our teachers began writing on these pages from the beginning of 1978, when I was in Year Eight. They told us how the Iranian people lived in poverty, without political freedom, while the Shah sold six million barrels of petrol a day, using the money to buy military hardware, build up the army and secret services, and develop luxurious resorts. We were told that if the Shah were toppled, a new government would create a new society, with roads, electricity, hospitals and schools. When the street demonstrations began, teachers and students joined them, and over the next year, I saw many clashes between police and demonstrators.

It was during this time that I began hearing about the Kurdish Democratic Party of Iran (KDPI) and its leader, Abdul Rahman Qassemlou. Qassemlou wanted democracy for Iran and autonomy for Kurdistan, and these ideas were exciting. The son of a tribal leader, he was an intellectual and a very sophisticated politician. He had finished his education in Eastern Europe, becoming a lecturer in economics at the Sorbonne in Paris, and had established good contacts with social-democratic parties in Europe. Under Qassemlou, KDPI emphasised democracy, within the constraints of the party's illegality, and having to work in a state of secrecy and, later, a state of war. The goal was to establish a local government elected by the people, to educate Kurdish children in Kurdish, and develop the region economically. This was all good news in Kurdistan, where the majority relied on subsistence agriculture and pastoralism and where, in 1966, only 21.8 per cent of males and 5.7 per cent of females were literate.

My family was not political. It was too dangerous. The SAVAK secret police and local gendarmeries would arrest anyone on the slightest suspicion. As children, we sometimes got angry and swore against the Shah, to be told, "Don't swear. The walls have mice and mice have ears," so I was clandestine about my political interests and they would say, "Hussein is so quiet. All he is interested in is his studies."

When the violence and pilfering in Urmia increased, schools closed and I went back to Enbe. The Shah fled the country, and two weeks later, in February 1979, Ayotollah Khomeini flew from Paris to Tehran and many supporters of the Shah were arrested. There was talk of distributing oil revenue to people as they do in Kuwait, and in an atmosphere of hope and freedom, every political party became active, KDPI and other *peshmergas* taking control of Kurdish towns and villages. Kurdish books and newspapers were published and Kurdish music was distributed and played.

Article Five in the draft constitution promised equal rights for Persians, Azeri, Kurds, Arabs, Baluchi, Bakhtiyari, Turks and Turkomans. Article 21 emphasised Persian as the official language, but permitted the use of different vernaculars in local schools and media. However, within three months, it became apparent that Ayotollah Khomeini could not reconcile ethnicity with Islam. For him, we were all brothers, the term 'ethnic group' applying only to non-Muslim religious groups. War began when Khomeini labelled KDPI a party of Satan, declaring a holy war against KDPI and Komala (a Kurdish Marxist organisation). On 16 December 1979, after some months of fighting and following weeks of negotiations, the government announced a limited autonomy plan. But Qassemlou refused the plan, because it offered a decentralised administration, not autonomy. Khomeini responded by saying he would ask authorities to guarantee specific constitutional rights for Sunni minorities, but the Kurds also rejected this proposal, arguing that the issues were ethnic and regional, not religious.

Finally, in the draft of the constitution approved by the Assembly of Experts, the *Majlis*-e-Khobregan, there was no mention of equality between ethnic groups, and when people elected Qassemlou to the *majlis* (the Islamic Consultative Assembly), he was prevented from going to Tehran by an outbreak of fighting. Later, Khomeini commented, "It is a pity Qassemlou did not come to Tehran, because we could have arrested him."

The government began using the Peoples' Mujahadeen to gather information about opposition parties, including KDPI and Komala. When the government outlawed the Mujahadeen, the communist Tudeh Party was used to gather information, until it was also outlawed.

The Iraq-Iran War started in September 1980. Iraqi planes flew over Urmia, but initially did not bomb civilian targets. Despite the war, the Iranian government deployed some 200,000 armed forces and established 3000 military bases in Kurdistan. Killing became routine. One day on my way to school, I saw a crowd of people and decided to follow. KDPI *peshmergas* had attacked a military barrack the night before, and at the barracks I saw 13 dead KDPI *peshmergas*.

For the first two years, the Islamic regime alternated between fighting and negotiations, but KDPI's 12,000 *peshmergas* and 30,000 militia were no match for the Iranian forces. By 1982, the government had pushed KDPI out of the towns, and by 1984, KDPI had left the villages. Qassemlou and other KDPI members fought in the mountains for another two years, after which they were forced to withdraw to Iraqi Kurdistan.

The Iranian government victory was made easier by bloody conflict between KDPI and Komala from 1984. Komala was forming village councils and redistributing land, but KDPI did not do this, wanting to represent all levels of society. These sorts of ideological and strategic differences split the two parties. From Iraqi Kurdistan, Qassemlou travelled to Europe to seek support for a political solution. As a leftist who rejected Soviet socialism, he was able to attract support from European social-democratic parties.

Back in 1983, having finished school, I applied for university, but failed the compulsory government investigation into my personal life. Two years' military service was mandatory, so I decided to make a career in the army, hoping to become an officer.

After a year of training, I was selected to become a signals officer and, because of my high marks could choose where I was to be sent. I chose Urmia, and was based at a village between Piranshahr and Sardasht, but after 43 days, I was ordered to go back to the Urmia base. A friend showed me the letter, which said, "This person must be kept under surveillance." Why? Because I was a Kurd. After that, I found myself in a frontline army unit from 1985 until 1988, moving between Khorramshahr, Dehloran, Elam and Naftshahr, in the south and west of Iran.

Iraq's initial surprise attacks on Iran were successful. They had captured 12 towns and a lot of land in the south and west. Saddam Hussein thought the war would be over in a few days, that Iran's armies were too disorganised, but he underestimated Iran's will to fight. If your country is attacked, especially after a successful revolution 19 months before, and you hear news of rapes and other atrocities, no man, especially a Middle Eastern man, can stand by.

Iranian forces took time to organise, but once they did, their morale was much higher than that of the Iraqis. Iran had two armies—the official army, where you had to be over 18, and the Revolutionary Guard, made up of volunteers as young as 13. This was not strange in our culture. At this age, boys are not considered children and many were prepared to die.

After a few years, Iraq was thrown out of Iranian territory. At this point, Iraq wanted to finish the war and was ready to pay compensation, but Iran would not compromise. The war served to create an emergency situation in which the government could crack down on any opposition, and the government had decided Saddam Hussein must be toppled. But after a few years, Iraq became stronger and no longer wanted to pay compensation. The war went on and on. Iraq had superior weaponry, Iran more human resources.

I was luckier than many. As a signal's officer, I was usually based at least six kilometres behind the front, although Iraqi planes flew overhead and long-distance guns could reach us. We lived in underground dugouts about the size of a little room, covered with a metal plate and soil. The soil insulated us from the 50-degree heat of summer, and from cold, but mostly it was very hot. Day and night we sat and sweated in our dugouts in the middle of a treeless desert.

I was a platoon commander, in charge of communication between the ranks and higher command, establishing and maintaining telephone connections, shortwave radios, teletype equipment and radio relay units. Usually, I was mobile.

I did not see many deaths, but in 1986 near Dehloran, Iraqi planes bombarded us with nerve gas. For a few weeks, everything looked red and I could not look at light. At the mobile hospital, I saw several soldiers trembling and jerking so badly that two men could not hold them down. Afterwards, by the river, I watched dead fish float downstream.

Ordinary soldiers would live with three to six others, but as a low-ranking commander, I had my own place, with a soldier to help. A few officers became very good friends. We liked to read books, mainly about psychology and sociology, and discuss their contents. The other officers were Persian, but I could speak freely about the war, saying, "This war will end in a stalemate. No side will be allowed to defeat the other."

One morning, a soldier woke me to say one of these officers had been killed. From then on, everything was different. This was in late 1987, and I made up my mind to leave Iran. I escaped in 1988—one month before the end of the war.

After 30 days at the front, we were allowed home for 10. I went back to Urmia, packed, and crossed into Turkey with my wife and two-year-old daughter. I had been engaged at 19, married at 20. Cheshmi was 16. I had not wanted to marry so young, I had my own plans, but there was some family pressure and enough of me must have wanted to. We had known each other since childhood, and when her family moved to Urmia, I sometimes visited their home to help her father. I would not see her, though, because in our culture, when there is a visitor, unmarried girls usually go into another room. It was not until Year 12 that we met at her cousin's wedding, and felt some romance, so although ours was an arranged marriage, we also loved each other.

Cheshmi's relative guided us over the border to a Kurdish village in Turkey. Around midday on the third day, gendarmeries came to the village. Two Persians had come to the village the day before. One of them and I decided to escape, climbing up a hill behind the village. Cheshmi and our daughter stayed, because it is easier for Kurdish women to say they are from Turkey but cannot speak Turkish.

The Persian with me asked, "Will they come here?" I told him, "Yes." He ran but I was too breathless to go any further, and hid down a creek embankment, under a tree. Bitterly cold, I pulled the hood of my overcoat over my head and dared not move. I heard two gunshots. Then another two. I thought, "They will just shoot from the knees down." It was freezing and I was restless. I started counting to 1000, but after 1000, I was still too scared to come out.

Three hours later, I climbed the embankment and decided to walk up the mountain. The village below was deserted. A shepherd told me, "They have arrested one and shot the other in the back", pointing to a soldier on either side of the valley.

That night, I stayed up the mountain with the guide, and the next day, a local Kurd was sent by the smugglers to find us and take us to another village. I was told Cheshmi had been given an identification card and had already been taken to Gawar, ('Yuksekova' in Turkish), half an hour from the Iranian border.

We were in the hands of people-smugglers. In the evening 12 of us—two Kurds, the rest Persian—were put in a minibus going to Van.[a] To avoid police stations and checkpoints, we would have to get out and walk. On the last leg of our journey after we had walked five cold, dark hours through the mountains, our driver was an hour late. By seven in the morning, we were afraid the checkpoint outside Van would be open, but when we got there, the police were asleep in their cars, so we passed safely, and were quickly distributed among some households.

Cheshmi was staying at another house, so that night I visited her, accompanied by the smuggler. We discussed our trip to Ankara and the smuggler gave us our bus tickets. I asked, "What chance do we have?" He said, "You will have to pay more if you want somebody to take you." I did not have the money, so Cheshmi and I decided to go to the police station in Van the next day.

I told the police, "I escaped Iran for political reasons and am seeking asylum." I did not tell them I had been an army officer, I was unsure how they would react. The police asked why Cheshmi was wearing a Kurdish dress. I told them it was more comfortable for travelling. A Kurdish translator spoke to me in Kurdish, but I said, "I don't understand. I am Azeri." Azeri from Azerbaijan speak Turkish, so they asked, "Why can't you speak Turkish?" "Because my parents talk to me in Persian." Had I admitted being Kurdish, they would have deported me straight away. Later, when they discovered I had deserted the army, they reacted positively. The interpreter told me that in the previous 24 hours, over 50 people had sought asylum in Van. All had been returned to the border. He said, "We didn't deport you, because you were an army officer and you have family."

We stayed in Van while the police sent our file to the UN. Every day, we had to report to the police station. After six weeks they sent us to Nevsehir, in Cappodocia, Central Anatolia, where we had to report once a week.

Nevsehir is a small town made famous by the old churches, mosques, remnants of ancient fire temples and many stunning stone formations. People used to live in the stone cones, and in the caves and underground cities, most of which have never been excavated. I visited one underground city. There were about eight well-ventilated levels, with rooms of all sizes, some very large. Archeologists think the Hittites settled in the volcanic formations and expanded them under the ground in the third and second millennium BC. The Greek historian, philosopher and soldier Xenophon mentions the underground cities in 401BC and between the fourth and 10th centuries, Christians most likely expanded them, possibly building the tunnels that connect some cities to hide from the Romans and iconoclasts and, later, the Sassanids and Turks. But generally, I could not appreciate the history and beauty around us. With no idea what the future would bring, life was very insecure.

I had money for three months, after which the UN helped us a little. We ate meat once a month and stayed in very cheap rooms. Some Turks were friendly, others were not. We let everyone think we were Persian, but this did not stop them interrogating us for hours with very personal questions when we wanted to rent a place. In the end, most would say, "We can't give you the house, because you are foreigners." All their questions were simply to satisfy their curiosity! After two months, the UN came to interview us and we were accepted as refugees. Two months later, we were interviewed by the Netherlands Embassy and were rejected. As we waited, time stood still. Finally, the Australian Embassy accepted us, and after 13 months in Turkey we arrived in Australia on 15 June 1989.

We had been told that we would be given a house and a loan to establish ourselves, and that there would be an interpreter to help us. We were travelling in a group of 12. At Athens airport, we waited 12 hours with no money, hungry and exhausted. On arriving in Melbourne at about 6 am, we were taken to Springvale Migrant Hostel. When we opened the door to two empty rooms, two beds, and a few plastic cups and plates, it was a problem of different expectations.

I knew only a few words of English, but was driven by energy and excitement to overcome the obstacles. For a month, I attended English classes at the hostel, then rented a flat, with help from friends. Before we moved, I found a job as a radio mechanic, but lost it after a month, because of my lack of English. In 1990, I started English classes at Preston College, determined to go to university.

In 1991, I started an Arts degree. Taking half an hour per page, I had to read a few hundred pages each week for each subject. It was hard, but I was determined, and all but one of my lecturers was understanding. The one who was not refused to mark my essays, because of my English, and as a result, I had to defer a year. I began again in 1992, and finished my degree in 1994, going on with Honours in 1995.

Enrolling to do a Masters of Political Science degree at the University of Melbourne in 1996, I upgraded to a PhD the same year. From the beginning of university, I knew my PhD topic: how the tribal structure of Kurdish society has prevented the formation of a Kurdish state, whether as a united nation or as a series of politically autonomous states within present borders. My thesis describes how the tribes have been political, economic and territorial entities since time immemorial. Tribalism requires complete loyalty to the tribe, the tribe's leader having the undisputed right to make all decisions. Coupled with this tribalism was a warrior-based patriarchal culture. All Kurdish boys carried weapons, or were at least familiar with them, and tribes have always risen up against empires, other tribes or a weak tribal leader, solving disputes over land, water and women by fighting.

This tribalism has probably enabled Kurds to survive in large numbers for over 4000 years, but has also meant they have been unable to unite over a large territory, one tribal leader rarely willing to follow another. Alliances were made but also broken, these power struggles invariably exploited by outside forces.

In my thesis, I argue that the Kurdish political parties of the 20th century are an extension of this tribalism. These new tribes are based on politics, and may have central committees, politburos, printing facilities, and radio and television stations, but the party leaders still demand total obedience to the party above any sense of common purpose, and continue to use violence to maintain power.

Fundamental to tribalism are blood feuds, which no system of law has been able to replace. In such a feud a wronged tribe or political party is obliged to exact revenge, even if the person killed is innocent. I argue that in justifying and perpetuating these power struggles, the parties enable outside forces to exploit them, and for as long as this continues, the Kurds will remain oppressed.

Much of Kurdish culture and history is unwritten, or has been appropriated by neighbouring cultures, so initially, I had many problems finding resources, but over the years, I managed to collect articles from Kurdish newspapers and academic journals, books from libraries and friends, and information through the Internet, culminating in a research trip back to Kurdistan in 1997. It was unsafe for me to go Iran, so I travelled to Turkey, Iraq, Syria and back to Turkey.

On arriving in northern Kurdistan, I spent seven days with my mother and one brother. We had not seen each other for nine years, and in that time their life had been tough. My father had died in 1995, although I was not told for six months. My mother and two brothers continued to live in Enbe. They were better off than when I was growing up, because two brothers are welders and two are bus drivers, but generally speaking, the economic situation is grim and many people do not have enough to eat. Before the revolution, one US dollar was equal to seven Iranian tomans. Now, one dollar is equal to 700 tomans.

After the family reunion, I stayed for a week with my wife's relatives in Gawar. The father of the wife of the family was a village guard from the Peniya-Jori tribe, whose *agha* was an MP. This *agha* had chosen to accept a huge amount of money from the government to form a village guard, rather than have his villages evacuated and destroyed. I have read that one tribal leader was given US$15,000 a month to employ village guards, but it is up to him how much he pays them. Usually, each guard is paid US$230 a month, a tremendous amount of money in northern Kurdistan, where the average annual gross income per head is less than US$400 and unemployment is well over 50 per cent. Consequently, by 1996, village guards numbered 70,000.

The village guards were employed to stop PKK guerillas entering villages to collect donations of money, food and new recruits. If a man in the tribe refuses to be a guard, he can be arrested, imprisoned, tortured, killed or have his house destroyed. His only alternative is to go a Turkish city or become a guerilla, which in Turkey means cutting all ties with his family, so this man I stayed with had become a village guard, while others in his family, were very sympathetic to PKK. One week before I arrived, PKK had taken all his sheep and set fire to his hay. From PKK's point of view, a village guard was being paid to kill his own people. It was shameful blood money, so as defenders of the people, PKK felt entitled to do whatever they wished with the village guards' assets.

In Iraqi Kurdistan, the *peshmergas* would kill army, police and Kurdish militia, but not civilians. From the beginning, PKK was more hardline. In 1979, PKK guerillas attacked Mehmet Celal Bucak, a Kurdish tribal leader who was an MP for the Justice Party of the Siverek district, as a warning to others not to betray the Kurdish cause. The attack failed, but there were other attacks, on *aghas*, their followers and members of Kurdish political parties not advocating complete independence. Throughout the 1980s PKK's leader, Abdullah Ocalan, maintained, "We must first start by cleansing from within," and "It is our policy to kill the enemy. If you work for the enemy, you are the enemy."

These tactics were criticised by other Kurdish parties, and also by many Kurds in Turkey, but PKK's more radical goals and strategies can be directly related to the institutionalised brutality of the Turkish government and its complete denial of the existence of ethnic minorities in Turkey. Since the 1970s, government forces have destroyed over 4000 villages, and deported more than 3.5 million Kurds. In a country claiming to be a democracy, there were 340,000 political arrests and imprisonments between 1984 and 1994. The speaking of the Kurdish language, the wearing of Kurdish dress and the playing of Kurdish music were outlawed from 1924 until 1991. Many Kurds in Turkey were completely assimilated, but even they were treated badly. Through indoctrination, a rigid Turkish nationalism had taught the population to hate and fear 'mountain Turks', 'terrorist separatists' or anyone 'opposing' the Turkish nation, and the Turkish forces' behaviour reflects this.

The situation is very different for Kurds in Syria, Iraq, Iran, Armenia and Georgia, where Kurds can say they are Kurdish and speak their language, although Kurdish political parties are illegal everywhere. Ironically, Iraq was the most liberal, until the time of Saddam Hussein, the 1958 constitution recognising that Iraq is made up of the Arab and Kurdish nations. The genocide of Iraqi Kurds began in the 1960s, yet even under Saddam Hussein, there were periods of amnesty. Then in 1991 the UN declared a no-fly zone north of the 36 Parallel to protect the Kurds of Iraq.

However, the superpowers continue to support Turkey and its military solutions. This support has enabled Turkey to buy sophisticated military hardware and permanently deploy 300,000 security forces in Kurdistan since 1990. Since 1991, the war with PKK has cost Turkey an average of seven billion US dollars a year, resulting in rampant inflation. The Turkish government claims that since 1984, over 30,000 people have been killed in the war with PKK. Of these 23,640 are described as guerillas, 5555 as soldiers and 5300 as civilians. Other sources give far higher figures. Even government records admit there have been another 4500 extrajudicial killings of Kurds by 'unknown' assassins.

The use of chemical weapons on the Kurds in Turkey is also shrouded in secrecy. There is evidence that the Turkish government used chemicals to defeat the Dersim revolt in 1938, and, on 11 May 1999, PKK accused Turkish forces of using chemical weapons in an attack that killed 20 guerrillas.

After 1991, PKK's policy changed, largely due to the armed struggle's effect on people's lives. They stopped attacking civilians, other than village guards. Even some of these attacks were said to be 'an organisational mistake', or the work of Turkish forces who had either infiltrated PKK or had independently carried out acts of atrocity, and blamed them on PKK. In 1993 and 1995, PKK called a unilateral ceasefire and asked to negotiate, but the government refused to talk with any party over Kurdish issues and continued to destroy villages, and to kill, imprison and evacuate people suspected of political activity or sympathies. The only concession ever made was when President Turgut Ozal, himself part Kurdish, passed legislation in April 1991 allowing the Kurdish language to be spoken in private conversation. In 1993, he died, officially of a heart attack, though many believe he was poisoned.

The crippled lives of the people as a consequence of this conflict was described in an article by Robert Olson in *Kurdistan Report*, dated March-May 1996. In Hakkari people evacuated from their villages were reduced to searching the garbage for something to eat. The mayor had released a media statement, "Hunger rules this city." The government's response was to put the rubbish in pits and guard these pits with soldiers.

Education was also affected. PKK targeted schools and teachers, believing they were agents of assimilation. The government blame PKK for killing 102 teachers and burning 192 schools, but admits to closing 5000 village schools for 'security reasons'.

For my research, I wanted to make contact with PKK, but knew I could not do so in Turkey. I would have to travel to Syria. My plan was to go first to Iraqi Kurdistan, which was in the middle of civil war. To cross the border, I sought the help of the KDP office in Diyarbakir. A driver took me to Ibrahim Khalil Bridge, from where I went to Dohuk, and then on to Hawler, the Kurdish name for Arbil, the seat of the KDP regional government.

Since May 1992, an elected Kurdish administration had ruled the no-fly zone more or less successfully until a civilian matter in April 1994 ignited civil war. In the dispute, KDP and PUK supporters took matters into their own hands and people were killed, proving the Kurdish parliament and its judicial system powerless. The neotribalism spread like wildfire, and by 1 May 1994, whole areas were plunged into factional fighting, each party taking over different towns and areas. From May 1994, PUK accused KDP of misappropriating funds from Ibrahim Khalil customs point, but by January 1995, PUK was holding 70 per cent of the territory under Kurdish administration, including Hawler. France, Britain and the USA tried to reconcile the two warring factions and negotiate a withdrawal to their previous positions, but both sides believed that if they withdrew, the other side would take over. In March 1995, 95 parliamentarians went on a 25-day hunger strike, asking that all *peshmergas* leave the city. The hunger strike ended when KDP parliamentarians left the parliament building, and from that date, the parliament ceased to operate.

Iraqi Kurdistan was divided: KDP controlled the north-west, PUK much of the centre and south-east, including Hawler. Each side persecuted the other's supporters, in what was to become known as a war of colours. Yellow was the colour of KDP and green the colour of PUK. A Kurdish citizen could be physically intimidated, tortured, killed, deported or have their assets confiscated if found wearing a colour in the wrong place. Despite the Kurdish administration being in danger of annihilation, Kurdish leaders continued to fight, even though neither major party could destroy the other. In the soup of rivalry and betrayal, Barzani and Talabani were using their various neighbours as protectors, but these same neighbours were maintaining the balance of power between them. On many occasions, government representatives from Iran, Iraq, and Turkey agreed they did not want a Kurdish administration in northern Iraq.

The unwilling participants and main losers were the Kurdish people. An Italian aid worker, who lived in Hawler, commented, "When elephants fight, it is the grass that suffers, and when elephants make love, the grass also suffers." After the Ankara Agreement of September 1996, KDP controlled two governates from Hawler, while PUK controlled two governates from Sulaimani, a city officially outside the no-fly zone. Predictably, by the time of my visit in 1997, all negotiations to reform a united parliament had reached a stalemate, and intermittent fighting continued, each side blaming the other.

My research had prepared me, or so I thought, for my journey into the best window of opportunity for Kurdish autonomy since 1920. I approached Hawler, and saw the town rising from a vast, treeless plain, its modern suburbs sprawling around a huge 2000 to 3000-year old fortress, built on even older fortresses. Most of the buildings were noticeably war affected, bullet holes puncturing the walls, and houses were in urgent need of repair. The political uncertainty and the double trade embargo meant no-one was rebuilding.

Everywhere, I observed that life for the ordinary people was very difficult. Unemployment exceeded 75 per cent. Wages were low. Teachers were being paid 300 to 400 Iraqi dinars (about US$15-$20 a month). To survive, families relied on the UN 'food for oil' program, which had become operational in 1997. The program distributed monthly rations of flour, rice, kerosene and other necessities, paid for by oil revenue, for which families had to register and present identification papers to be eligible.

Despite these circumstances, it was a good feeling to see Kurds ruling themselves for the first time in my life. Shopkeepers, police and government officials were all Kurd and Kurdish was spoken everywhere. Everyone was friendly. When I entered a shop I would be offered tea or a cold drink. The shopkeeper sometimes spent the equivalent of what I spent in the shop! People were particularly happy that a Kurd, rather than a foreigner, had at last come to study them! I interviewed officials in KDP, and some Kurdish intellectuals from the Kurdish universities in Dohuk and Hawler, but although I tried for several days I was unable to meet Masoud Barzani. It was the same in Sulaimani, where I was unable to interview Talabani. I do not think either Talabani or Barzani received my messages.

After 20 days in Hawler, I travelled to Koi Sinjak, where I stayed for two days at the KDPI politiburo. I found KDPI the only party offering easy access to ranked officials. It was not so hierarchical. Members of the central committee queued for food, and ate and talked freely with ordinary *peshmergas*. Also, it was a welcome relief to find more moderate and accommodating views being expressed.

Although I come from eastern Kurdistan, it was not until starting my Arts degree that I was able to research the historical details behind the Kurdish struggle in Iran. After World War One and the withdrawal of Russian and Ottoman forces, there was a power vacuum, which enabled Isma'il Agha Shikak, known as Simko, an uneducated tribal leader, to establish authority. His people were starving, and Iranian authorities had killed his grandfather, father, two brothers and other relatives, so from the beginning, he believed the best solution was to form a Kurdish state, asking the Americans, British and French for help. When this help was not forthcoming, he launched an armed struggle, in 1919, successfully capturing Urmia and Salmas. In 1921, he began publishing a newspaper in Kurdish and Persian, and even though he faced major opposition from Iranian and Russian forces, he was able to expand his territory to include Mahabad.

In February 1921, a soldier, Muhammad Reza Khan, overthrew the Qajars. Reza Khan was determined to centralise government and received British help to organise the Iranian army. In July 1922, he sent a force of 8000 to attack Simko's forces near Salmas. Simko's tribal allies deserted. Of 10,000 men, Simko was left with 1000 from his own Shikak tribe, and these were pushed into Turkey. From 1922 Simko tried negotiations and armed struggle, until in 1930, the government invited him back to Iran to negotiate in Ushnu, where he was ambushed and assassinated.

For my thesis, I analysed why his struggle failed. Like so many other Kurdish uprisings in Turkey and Iraq in the 1920s and 1930s, Simko's was a tribal war fought over a limited area, without a clear war strategy, command system, or administrative base to coordinate and advise. Simko even had to apologise to the civilians of Mahabad for the customary looting by his unpaid *peshmergas*. Although Shaykh Mahmud was also uprising nearby, in Iraqi Kurdistan, there was no cooperation between the two, each concerned with forming an independent Kurdish state in his own area. The Iranian government was expert at manipulating tribal enmities, and Simko was betrayed by rival tribes and even his own uncle. In the end, all the bloodshed came to nothing.

When Muhammad Reza Shah made himself shah in 1925, he began a process of detribalisation, forcing tribes into permanent settlements. From 1926, Kurdish lands, which had traditionally been held in common by the tribe, had to be registered in the names of individuals. Tribal leaders became feudal landlords, their tribes people reduced to tenants.

By 1932, Shaykh Mahmud's revolt in Iraqi Kurdistan was defeated, and the last

Kurdish uprising in Turkey ended in 1938, but during World War Two, when Iran was occupied by Russian, British and US forces, another power vacuum formed in parts of eastern Kurdistan. Some Kurdish intellectuals formed the Kurdish Revival Association, which in August 1945 evolved into the Kurdistan Democratic Party (of Iran). It immediately began working towards an autonomous Kurdish state within Iranian borders. Members did not want to rely on armed struggle, or the leadership of *aghas*, *shaykhs* and *mallas*. They put great emphasis on education. In 1946, there were only three Kurds in Mahabad who had completed high school.

The Iranian government was weak. The Kurds asked the English and Americans for support. When this was refused, they relied on the Soviets, who had remained in Iran after World War Two. The Soviets gave financial and military assistance, as leverage for oil concessions from the Iranian government. On 22 January 1946, the Kurdish Republic of Mahabad was declared, Qazi Muhammad, a respected religious judge, becoming president. On 11 February 1946, he formed a cabinet of 14 ministers and a prime minister, the administration making contact with Kurds from Syria, Turkey and Iraq. Back on 11 October 1945, Mostefa Barzani, his brother Shaykh Ahmed, and 3000 *peshmergas* and their families had escaped to eastern Kurdistan after being attacked by Iraqi forces and the British airforce. However, the Kurds of Mahabad were suspicious of Barzani's intentions and did not immediately offer help. Barzani was so desperate, he was ready to return to Iraq, if the Iraqi government promised a safe return for his people and commuted the death sentence to life imprisonment for 35 leaders and himself. It took some Iraqi Kurdish notables to assure the Mahabad leaders that Barzani was not part of a British plan to undermine them, before a reconciliation process began, after which, in March 1946, Mostefa Barzani was appointed one of four generals. He was to become the military backbone of the republic and, thereafter, a hero for all Kurds.

For the first time, the Kurdish language was taught in Mahabad schools. Kurdish books, newspapers and magazines were printed and a Kurdish theatre started. Women were encouraged to participate in political, cultural and social events. An official Kurdish army was formed, based not on tribes but on 70 officers, 40 non-commissioned officers and 1200 soldiers trained by a captain of the Soviet forces. But the Soviet Union was under increasing international pressure to leave Iran. The Iranian government promised the Soviets some oil concessions, to be ratified only after they left. When the Soviets complied, in May 1946, many Kurdish leaders who had supported the republic entered into secret negotiations with the Iranian government, once again proving it was self-interest rather than Kurdish self-determination that motivated them. The Iranian forces were quick to launch a major attack, but Kurdish forces at Saghez forced a retreat.

In hindsight, the Kurdish leadership was politically and militarily naive. When the Iranian forces tried to infiltrate the republic's territory from Saghez, the Kurds inflicted heavy casualties, and blocked the roads to the towns of Sardasht and Baneh, isolating 3000 Iranian forces. The forces were in danger of starvation. The government commenced negotiations to open the road and allow food through. Amazingly, the Kurdish leaders agreed, Baba Shaykh, the republic's prime minister, delivering a speech to Kurdish forces saying, "We cannot let our Persian brothers starve." The Iranians used the opportunity to smuggle in arms.

An Iranian force of 20,000 attacked the Azerbaijan republic, to the north. The Azerbaijan leaders did not resist, and on 13 December 1946, Iranian troops entered Tabriz, the capital. Some Kurds wanted to fight on, but there was no real plan in place. Barzani and other Kurdish leaders escaped to Iraq, but Qazi Muhammad and others decided to surrender, Qazi Muhammad saying he had sworn to protect his people. On 16 December 1946, he went to Miandoab to facilitate the surrender, the next day handing himself over to Iranian forces. On 30 March 1947, Qazi Muhammad, his cousin Muhammad Hossein Seif Qazi, and his young brother Abu Al-Qassem Sadr Qazi were hung in Chwar Chira Square in Mahabad, where the republic had been proclaimed. The Iranian government promptly closed the Kurdish publishing press, banned all Kurdish publications, burned the books, and prohibited teaching in the Kurdish language.

In 1951, Iran enjoyed some political freedom when the Iranian nationalist, Muhammad Mossadeq, became prime minister. Even so, in the 1952 election, the KDPI candidate of Mahabad, after receiving more than 80 per cent of the vote, was replaced by a religious figure from Tehran. In August 1953, a coup organised by the CIA overthrew the Mossadeq government and reinstated Muhammad Reza Shah as absolute ruler. KDPI activists were arrested, some went underground, and many escaped to Iraqi Kurdistan.

Members were divided. The conservative faction, supported by Mostefa Barzani, wanted a temporary halt to armed struggle in eastern Kurdistan, while young leftists opted to continue. In 1967, 200 of these KDPI leftists entered eastern Kurdistan to gather support, armed with four Kalashnikovs, two larger machine guns and 85 old rifles. In clashes with a well-armed Iranian military, most were killed. The remainder escaped to Iraqi Kurdistan, where between 1967 and 1968 at least 40 were either killed, or arrested and handed back to Iran by Mostefa Barzani. By doing this, Barzani achieved two goals. First, to eradicate the leftist KDPI group who had allied themselves with his leftist opponents within KDP, and who opposed his ally, KDPI leader Ahmed Tawfiq, and second, to ensure continued military aid from the Shah.

In 1973, KDPI elected Abdul Rahman Qassemlou as secretary-general. After years of fighting during the 1980s, negotiations resumed when the Iraq-Iran War ended, in 1988. On 13 July 1989, Qassemlou was asked to attend a 'final meeting' in Vienna. It was very final. Members of the negotiating team assassinated Qassemlou and two of his colleagues. The Austrian government arrested the assassins, but the Iranian government, although denying involvement, successfully pressured the Austrians to release the assassins.

Sharaf Kandi was elected to replace Qassemlou. In 1992, he was assassinated in Berlin. The assassins were arrested and brought to trial, this time with the support of the USA, who were trying to prove that the Iranian government was involved in terrorism. At their trial, the assassins revealed that Iran's spiritual leader, the president, and the minister of information, had all been complicit in ordering the assassination. Mostefa Hejri was elected secretary-general, followed by Abdullah Hasan Zadeh, a moderate intellectual. This democratic change of leadership was a first for a Kurdish political party.

Nevertheless, in 1997, the outlook for Kurds from Iran was grim. An open border to

Iran is essential for PUK's survival, so PUK complied with Iranian government pressure to stop KDPI broadcasting its radio program from 18 March 1995. In late July 1996, an Iranian force of 2000, led by Muhammad Ja'afari Sahraroudi, the mastermind and head assassin of Qassemlou, attacked the KDPI politburo base at Koi Sinjak. A member of the PUK politburo stated they had no choice in the matter, but had warned KDPI an attack was eminent. No-one was killed.

Since the early 1990s, both KDP and PUK have not allowed KDPI and Komala to infiltrate into Iran, and the Iranian government continues to be in complete control. In eastern Kurdistan, unemployment and disenchantment are high, and there are claims that the government has played an active role in encouraging the use of illegal drugs among youth.

At the Koi Sinjak base, I was told that KDPI had no choice but to wait for two possible outcomes: long-term stability in Iraqi Kurdistan or fundamental political change in Iran. Meanwhile they felt like prisoners without walls. Iranian government agents had killed hundreds. Consequently, two armed *peshmergas* accompanied us when I was taken at top speed to Sulaimani in a KDPI two-cabin utility. There were many PUK checkpoints and no-one knew who was friend or foe.

In Sulaimani, I sensed the people were in fighting mode. PUK and KDP radio stations, TV channels and newspapers were playing with people's emotions. PUK TV repeatedly showed pictures of Masoud Barzani being kissed by Saddam Hussein, censoring the part where Talabani kissed Saddam. The media was calling for revenge for the treason committed by Barzani on 31 August 1996, when he had supposedly invited Saddam Hussein's forces to attack Hawler. Sure enough, on the morning of 13 October 1997, PUK attacked KDP a few kilometres outside Digala on the KDP-PUK border, in an operation called Cyclone Revenge, or Gardaluli Tula. I spoke to Foad Ma'sum, a PUK leader, who claimed the attack was to impose peace, that KDP had control of all the borders, as well as relations with Iraq, and was using its stronger economy against PUK. They would listen only to force. When asked why PUK did not make concessions in the interests of the people, Foad Ma'sum's answer was, "The pride of KDP should be broken before we sit down for negotiations." The same mentality prevailed in KDP.

About 200 *peshmergas* were killed in two days of fighting. After another five days of fighting, when it became apparent neither side could defeat the other, both sides declared a ceasefire. Like many Kurds, I asked, "Even if the leaders disagree why should they and their *peshmergas* continue fighting each other?" Talking to followers from both parties and seeing the desperate life of the people, let alone experiencing it, helped me understand. Firstly, those in one party thought they were absolutely right and the other party was in complete error. Everyone used half the available information to justify their actions, and party members were not privy to the other side's information. Conversations were quoted as evidence of betrayal, and for many accusations, there was no documentary evidence. Otherwise, there is the possibility of forgery. No-one was willing to make concessions, saying, "If we do, the other side will destroy us," or they would argue about whether a concession was made.

Secondly, people had few options apart from working for a party's *peshmerga* force. After the Iraqi government destroyed thousands of Kurdish villages in the 1970s and

1980s, people had been gathered into collective villages under the control of government forces. They could no longer cultivate their land or care for animals. Often, the only form of employment was in the Kurdish militia, set up in the 1960s to fight Kurdish insurgency. From the 1970s the Iraqi government offered each militia arms and 80 dinars for 15 days' work a month. Two men in each family could join, enabling a family to receive 160 dinars a month when 50 dinars was enough for a middle-class family. Consequently, by the late 1980s, there were 250,000 *jahsh*, compared to 10,000 volunteer *peshmergas* in each of the main parties.

When Saddam left Kurdistan in April 1991, employment in the various *jahsh* militia ended over night. Many men had only one option: to join the United Peshmerga Force in order to survive. They knew no other profession. After the Kurdish parliament was formed, a person in the United Peshmerga Force was paid 400 dinars a month, and any booty was theirs to sell on the black market. Even when it became apparent that the Kurdish leaders were no longer working in the interests of the people, and many Kurds, including *peshmergas*, had lost faith, their only option was to continue serving in a particular party's armed forces. To engage in trade required money, and to leave the country was not possible for everyone. To remain passive meant their family could starve.

All government jobs required the worker to join a party. A European commentator stated, "It is impossible to be neutral or your name is deleted from food distribution lists, you lose your job, you are ruined."

Electricity was being supplied for only a few hours each night, except in Zakho and Dohuk, where electricity came from Turkey. Water was available for an hour or two every few days. When fighting broke out, the water and electricity supply to KDP areas would be cut indefinitely by PUK. KDP would retaliate by stopping the supply of goods from Turkey into PUK areas. Hospitals and schools were operating without resources.

No-one talked about how these conditions were affecting their mental health or family life. Domestic violence is considered a private matter. All families have had some members killed in the four decades of fighting, and men on both sides of the family are expected to support widows and children.

For all these reasons, by 1997 each major party employed about 100,000 *peshmergas*, who were not being paid 400 dinars a month to do nothing, especially when so many weapons were being supplied by the Turkish, Iranian and Iraqi governments.

In the light of these circumstances, it is remarkable that a year after my visit, in September 1998, Barzani and Talabani were brought together by Turkey and the USA in Washington, where they signed an agreement pledging to refrain from fighting and to solve their problems. This agreement was more focused on solving the problems of neighbouring countries. The statement read:

> The Higher Coordination Committee (formed to solve problems between the two parties) will ensure that both parties cooperate to prevent violations of the Turkish and Iranian borders. It will establish reasonable screening procedures to control the flow of people across these borders and prohibit the movement of terrorists [sic]. Both parties, working with the HCC, will deny sanctuary to the Kurdistan Workers Party (PKK) throughout the Iraqi Kurdistan region. They will ensure that there are no PKK bases within this

area. They will prevent the PKK from undermining the peace, or from violating the Turkish borders.

The agreement brought peace between PUK and KDP but it did not unite Kurdistan. The election promised for July 1999 has yet to be called, each side blaming the other for the delay, the situation remaining unstable with the presence of PKK.

Throughout the 1990s Syria came under increasing pressure to stop supporting PKK. PKK moved its bases into Iraqi Kurdistan, particularly into KDP areas, immediately starting an active recruitment program. What made them particularly popular among Kurdish youth in both Iraq and Iran, and a big threat to the status quo, was their original goal of a united independent Kurdistan rather than a series of autonomous states.

As a result of PKK activity the Turkish military have been active in Iraqi territory intermittently since the 1980s, and permanently since 1995. On my visit, I saw Turkish tanks in Qasro and Sarsank villages. Turkish forces have bombed numerous villages in the KDP area, killing many civilians. There are no statistics, no international condemnation, and Iraqi Kurds know they cannot fight and win against the Turkish government. They prefer to negotiate.

Turkey was supplying KDP with arms to fight PKK. KDP deny this supply route, but admit to fighting PKK, because PKK were interfering in KDP matters and the Turkish military were destroying their villages. Consequently, during the civil war, PKK moved into the PUK zone and formed a tactical alliance with PUK. This meant that in the fighting around Digala, both PUK and PKK attacked KDP simultaneously, KDP saying it was a joint operation, the PUK denying this. Then in the same month of the Washington Agreement, Turkey succeeded in coercing Syria to force Abdullah Ocalan and all PKK to leave Syrian-controlled territory, and despite the agreement, PUK and KDP were unable to stop PKK moving across the border.

After Abdullah Ocalan's abduction to Turkey in February 1999, and his August announcement that all PKK must leave Turkey, the last of the PKK guerillas had nowhere else to go but Iraqi Kurdistan. It is a dangerous situation. The PKK remain armed yet Ocalan has ordered them not to engage in fighting with Turkish forces. Iraqi Kurd political parties believe their presence poses a threat to any chance of a federal Kurdish state of Iraq. PKK maintain they have no choice but to stay.

Back in 1997, after 45 days in Iraqi Kurdistan, I came away very disheartened. I entered Syria via Turkey, staying at Al-Qamishli, where I made contact with a PKK supporter. While I waited for instructions, I interviewed a few leaders of various Syrian Kurdish parties. These parties are illegal but tolerated. They want cultural, social and political rights for Kurds in Syria and to have the 150,000 Kurds arbitrarily denied citizenship in 1962 reinstated as citizens.

Yet while Hafez Al-Assad's Ba'ath government was both accommodating and tough on its own Kurdish population, it meanwhile actively supported PKK from 1979 until 1998. Abdullah Ocalan was allowed to establish a PKK base outside Damascus and in the Syrian controlled Bekka Valley in Lebanon, Syria using PKK's presence as leverage for its unresolved territorial and water disputes with Turkey. Turkey's membership of NATO and its alliance with the USA and Israel were also concerns. For all these reasons,

President Hafez Al-Assad allowed PKK to train in Syria and launch attacks into Turkey.

The PKK supporter gave me a contact in Halab, the Arabic name for Aleppo, and from there I travelled to Damascus. I waited in a house for four days, to then be taken to one of two PKK training camps in Damascus. I found the people open and friendly, and for two days was free to observe camp life.

The training camp had four teachers and about 60 students. Many students had been sick or injured, so a number had seen fighting, some as low-ranking commanders. In class, a teacher would raise a topic based on a statement by Abdullah Ocalan, such as, "You rely more on the enemy than on Kurdistan." Then each student would be asked to stand and say what the statement meant to him or her, confessing their deficiencies in relation to the topic. A common reply was, "I still belong to the enemy because I was brought up in the enemy's culture and was taught in the enemy's schools and I must put these influences aside and purify myself." Other students then questioned the student, before the teacher explained PKK's view.

Some students told me that the emphasis on self-criticism pushed them to work harder. The whole idea was to build a new way of thinking, tied to the Marxist-Leninist ideology of PKK. To paraphrase them, "Socialism means humanity. PKK is socialism." Through this sort of education, PKK aimed to create a 'new human being', a 'new generation of Kurds with a new Kurdish culture', independent of tribal, religious, Turkish, Arabic, and Persian affiliations.

To do this, PKK guerillas had to abandon all attachments to the past, including money, possessions and family. Official policy was that guerillas could keep contact with their family, but in practice, this was actively discouraged. Some students thought making contact was a sign of weakness, showing you were still emotionally bound to your past and were not purified.

All personal desires were viewed as a sign of weakness. PKK guerillas are not allowed to marry, even within the organisation, because this would create divided allegiances. Personally, I saw this as a necessary development. In the past, PUK and KDP were vulnerable to government attacks because their *peshmergas* married and often had their families living with them in the mountains. If the families stayed in the cities, the government would harass them. If a *peshmerga* died, then there was the problem of supporting their family. Ocalan had been married to a middle-class Turkish woman who became involved in the struggle, but in the late 1980s, she escaped to Europe, some say because she did not like the violence. To PKK, she is a traitor.

The students claimed, "If people want to marry they must leave PKK. Everyone is free to leave." This was official policy, but from my research, if a guerilla wanted to leave, they had to escape, the penalty for which was death.

All these official and unofficial policies were in place because PKK was worried about security. A deserter or family member would be arrested and tortured until they gave information, or were offered money, safety or a government job in return for information. One way or another, they were intimidated. There was no place to go except a Western country, unless they joined another Kurdish party. KDP accepted them, if only for propaganda purposes, but PKK saw these defectors as traitors, as KDP was their enemy, so they were killed.

What was most surprising to a Middle Eastern man was the PKK's revolutionary policy in respect to women. In the classroom, there were two rows—one for men and one for women. All were encouraged to participate in discussion, and daily chores were shared equally, including food preparation. In their breaks, they would walk, talk and eat together. In the Middle East, this is unimaginable, yet I observed that in the camp, no man dared look at a woman other than as a comrade. He would be punished severely if he did.

There were women's units and men's units, which sometimes fought jointly. In 1993, it was estimated that out of 10,000 PKK guerrillas, 2000 were women. I heard some people criticise PKK for this, saying, "They are corrupting Kurdish society."

As for its political organisation, PKK had a central committee, but Abdullah Ocalan wielded absolute power, always relying on his own judgement and charisma, allowing no-one to establish a personality or gain the neccessary leadership experience. He is quoted as saying he did not like secretaries and advisers, and openly maintained that he led by himself, single-handedly creating and developing PKK, believing there was no-one capable of replacing him, that if there were, he would resign. His followers regarded him as a prophet.

By being in absolute control, Ocalan prevented a split, again unusual for a Kurdish party, although there have been some high-ranking defections, including two top-level commanders and Ocalan's wife.

PKK strategies appeared extreme but were working. The more the Turkish government repressed PKK, the more PKK fought back. The guerillas knew that if they killed a few Turkish soldiers, a whole village could be destroyed, but more and more people became willing to make the sacrifice, for the survival of the Kurdish identity in Turkey. It was largely due to PKK that unofficially Kurdish, legal democratic parties, like HADEP, were allowed. The fact that the Turkish government bans them as soon as Kurdish issues are raised, imprisoning or killing the offending parliamentarians, indicates there was no effective alternative to PKK in Turkey.

Nevertheless, it was not until the 1990s, when Ocalan began manoeuvring away from violence as the main method of struggle, that PKK became more widely popular. This was in spite of, rather than because of his announcement that he would settle for federalism within Turkey's borders, or political and cultural autonomy as opposed to his original goal of a united independent Kurdistan. Even after his 1999 announcement that he would settle for cultural rights, many PKK sympathisers still quote PKK's original aim.

In the early 1990s, the PKK began a Serhildan, or popular uprising, based on the Palestinian Intifada. PKK chose Newroz 1992 for the closing of shops, and protest marches of thousands of people, in the Cizer'e, Sirnak, Nusaybin, Van and Hakkari. The Turkish military opened fire, killing more than 70 people. Many others were arrested, imprisoned and tortured, but these uprisings served to bring many thousands of Kurds face to face with the Turkish military.

In 1993, PKK began targeting tourism in Turkey, which it saw as financing the Turkish war against the Kurds, but this served to reinforce the image of PKK as a terrorist organisation. There are about two million people from Turkey living in Germany, about

500,000 being Kurdish. Of this number, about 50,000 are believed to be PKK supporters, but after several violent incidents in Germany, Turkey persuaded Germany to ban PKK.

In the 1990s, the PKK established various women's groups, religious groups (Sunni, Alevi and Ezidi), as well as European-based groups. Instead of splitting, PKK became an umbrella organisation for a wide variety of organisations. In 1995, PKK supporters in Europe established Med TV, a satellite station broadcasting in Kurdish all over Europe and the Middle East. In the same year, the PKK created a Kurdish parliament-in-exile, based in Brussels, to be a bridge between world public opinion and the national liberation struggle, to establish diplomatic relations with governments and international organisations, and to inform the Kurdish diasporas. It aimed to represent all Kurds. However, in its 1998 elections, of a Kurdish community of over 10,000 in Australia only 640 voted. In 1999 it was replaced by the Kurdish National Congress.

In these ways, PKK grew in strength, raising the consciousness in Turkey as no other party had been able to do. The words 'Kurd' and 'Kurdistan' began being used in conversations although still outlawed. Kurdish was being spoken more than ever before and Kurdish books and magazines were unofficially distributed.

I came away from the PKK camp feeling that if PKK could maintain their dedication, they would eventually win their struggle. My reservations were that the party relied too much on Ocalan's iron grip, and underestimated cultural and psychological resistance to creating a new pattern, even within the party.

Returning to Turkey, I went to Diyarbakir, where there is a HADEP office. This legal democratic party advocates a political solution for Kurds in Turkey. In 1990, HEP (the People's Labor Party) formed as a moderate alternative to PKK, for people who did not believe in armed struggle or an independent Kurdish state. Some people claimed that HEP was established by the Turkish government on the suggestion of the USA, but HEP rivals and the government accused HEP of being a political wing of PKK. When HEP was banned, DEP replaced it. When DEP was banned, HADEP replaced it. While there is controversy over how HADEP is related to PKK, HADEP officials acknowledge that without PKK's support, they are powerless. In the 1991 elections, HEP managed to get 22 members into parliament, but when these parliamentarians mentioned Kurdish issues, they were imprisoned. The most famous case is that of Leyla Zana, wife of the mayor, Mehdi Zana, who had been given an eight-year sentence for speaking Kurdish in court. In 1994, Leyla Zana was given a 15-year sentence for being 'separatist', because she swore her parliamentary oath in the name of Turkish and Kurdish brotherhood.

Despite HADEP's success, HADEP officials described the government doing everything possible to hinder them. Elections were called at times of heavy snowfall, so Kurds in isolated areas found it difficult to travel. The polling booths were located in gendarmerie and military camps, to intimidate voters. Many displaced Kurds were not registered, so they could not vote, and many illiterate Kurds had to rely on government electoral officers. Some Kurds were threatened with violence if they voted for HADEP.

I also met with Serafattin Elci, leader of the Democratic Mass Party (DKP), which had formed in 1997. DKP was most unusual for a Kurdish party, because it took a liberal democratic view, emphasising freedom from government control, and Kurdish cultural and administrative rights within a liberal, democratic Turkey. Elci criticised other Kurdish parties as being too leftist, thus contradicting their present oppression by governments. But in 1999, DKP was banned, again highlighting the difficulty of working within a democratic framework in Turkey.

Despite all that I had witnessed on this research trip, I had mixed feelings about returning to Australia. I had liked being in Kurdistan. It is so dynamic. I missed the quiet safety of Australia less than I had expected. Kurdistan is weighed down by problems but is full of possibilities.

Perhaps most of all, I liked the sense of community. Every country has a particular way of living, and even though Kurdistan has poverty and fighting, the bonds between neighbours and relatives are strong. Walking down the street, you are greeted by nearly every person. With so much unemployment, people are always visiting, talking for hours, and helping each other on a daily basis. A group of women bake bread or cook together. If someone dies, neighbours and family visit for days. People are ready to lend money if they have it, because tomorrow, it might be their turn.

Although many migrants and refugees find life in Australia more secure and financially comfortable, it is often boring and isolating. To some extent, these feelings are the result of exile and culture shock, but it is also related to the nature of the Australian community. Even in Turkey, many neighbours were quick to welcome us and establish good relations. In Kurdistan, you do not feel that sense of emptiness when you are not busy. When a way to legally participate in a democratic government in Kurdistan is found, I will probably go back, but in the near future, this seems unlikely, so I am determined to adapt and contribute to Australian society.

Accordingly, in the 1998 federal elections, I ran for the Australian Democrats in a safe Labor seat in Melbourne. There was little chance of winning, and I think my name and accent went against me, but it was a good experience. I need to improve my spoken English and my knowledge of Australian culture. I could change my name, but I would rather be accepted for who I am. Otherwise, I would like to become an academic of Middle Eastern and Kurdish issues, if that is possible, though the Australian government seems to be reducing, even eradicating courses not directly linked with economic disciplines.

Many dreams cannot be realised. The reality of the Kurdish situation was brought home to every Kurd on 15 February 1999, with the abduction of Abdullah Ocalan in Nairobi, Kenya. Against all international law, he was taken, drugged and blindfolded, back to Turkey, through international collusion. The CIA, the Greek government and Turkish forces have admitted their involvement. MOSSAD, Israel's secret service, has not, yet William Safire, from the *New York Times*, reported in January 1999 that MOSSAD was the first to inform Ankara of Ocalan's arrival in Moscow.

For all Kurds, the kidnapping of Ocalan was history repeating itself. Ocalan had placed his trust in the Greek government, a traditional enemy of the Turks, to take him to a safe haven, but he was betrayed, like Simko in 1930, Qazi Muhammad in 1946, Mostefa Barzani in 1975 and Qassemlou in 1989.

I concluded that Ocalan's predicament was the result of him having nowhere to go, and this was partly his own doing. The Syrian Kurds could not hide him. Kurdistan of Syria is a small region, without mountains. He could not go to Iraqi Kurdistan, because he had made KDP an irreconcilable enemy during the 1990s. KDP say that Syria and Iraq supported Ocalan to destroy any chance of a Kurdish state in Iraq. Iraq or Iran could not accept him, having enough problems and not wanting to strain relations with Turkey. The Russian *duma* agreed to give him refuge, but after a few weeks, President Yeltsin refused him political asylum and Ocalan was asked to leave. Ocalan looked towards Europe, thinking this a good opportunity to gather European support to pressure the Turkish government to the negotiating table. Having already denounced armed struggle, he claimed to be seeking peaceful alternatives.

Italy had been more accepting of Kurds and other refugees than other European countries, and had a socialist government. Some media sources say a few members of the Italian parliament invited Ocalan to Rome, although as soon as he arrived, on 12 November 1998, he was arrested at the airport for travelling on a false passport, and he was detained on an outstanding arrest warrant by Germany. Turkey immediately asked for his extradition. The Italian government refused, on the grounds that Turkey still had the death penalty. When Germany withdrew the arrest warrant, no doubt to ease tensions between Kurds and Turks in Germany, the Italian court set Ocalan free.

All over Europe, there were demonstrations in support of Ocalan and his request for political asylum in Europe. On 11 December 1998, Ocalan announced he would step down as PKK leader if this would enable a peaceful solution for Kurds in Turkey. On 19 December, the Italian prime minister addressed the parliament, saying Ocalan should be tried in an international court. Ocalan was willing, as long as the trial revealed Turkey's part in the war. Turkey continued lobbying, saying that keeping Ocalan from trial in Turkey was a gross interference in Turkey's domestic affairs, a European conspiracy to revive the Treaty of Sevres. Pressure from all quarters intensified.

With hindsight, some people say Ocalan should have stayed in Italy and gone through the process of seeking political asylum. There were rumours he could go to North Korea or Libya, but then he would have been isolated, unable to lobby Europe to exert pressure on the Turkish government. Finally, he agreed to be smuggled to Greece, the Greek foreign minister promising he would be flown to safety. While negotiations for Ocalan's asylum ostensibly continued, it was later related to Med TV by one of Abdullah Ocalan's companions that on two occasions in Greece, the Greek government attempted unsuccessfully to hand Ocalan over to Turkish authorities. Reuters and AP News reported that the Netherlands did not allow Ocalan's plane to land.

It is understandable that no European country was willing to take Ocalan. Turkey wants to join the European Union and 60 per cent of Turkey's foreign trade is done with the EU. Germany is pushing for Turkey to gain 'member-in-waiting' status, and continues to supply Turkey with armaments, on condition that they are not used against Kurdish civilians, while the British and US governments label Ocalan a terrorist.

On numerous occasions, Nelson Mandela has spoken out in support of Kurds. In the 1990s, the Turkish government wanted to give Mandela a prize. He refused. A representative explained, "If you want to know why, just be a Kurd for one day." So the plan was to fly him to South Africa. No-one knows whether the South African government had offered him asylum, but Abdullah Ocalan found himself in Nairobi, hiding at the Greek Embassy, the Kenyan government apparently unaware of his presence for three weeks. There were reports that some Kenyan government officials were paid five million US dollars to arrange Ocalan's return to Turkey. Ocalan sensed something afoot, but was in the hands of the Greeks, and Nairobi had been teaming with CIA and MOSSAD agents ever since the bombing of the American embassy in August 1998, in which 212 people were killed. Escorted by the Greek ambassador and Kenyan security, Ocalan and his companions left for the airport. Turkish commandoes were waiting in a plane to take him to Ankara.

I was sleeping when a friend phoned on 16 February, to tell me Ocalan had been abducted to Turkey. A number of other people rang, but no-one had the details. I phoned the Kurdish Association, who confirmed the news. That night, we met, and talked about holding a demonstration, but no details were decided. The next morning, on my way to the Association, the news came over the car radio that a Kurdish demonstration was being held in front of the Greek consulate in Melbourne. Police had attacked demonstrators, who carried petrol cans. There were also demonstrations outside Greek embassies in Sydney and all over Europe.

I drove straight to the Greek consulate. I saw no violence, though people were very emotional. There was a sense of total betrayal, anger, despair and disbelief. Once again, Kurds felt, "We have no friends but the mountains." A Kurdish delegation went inside to talk to the Greek consul, before everyone dispersed.

I knew that the US had pressured every country to hand Ocalan over to Turkey, but I could not believe it of the Greeks. Later, it was confirmed that individuals in the Greek government were involved, much to the dismay of many Greeks. Yet Greece and Turkey are members of NATO, and therefore bound to cooperate on matters of internal security. Also, they are constantly on the verge of war over Cyprus. An unofficial statement claimed that the USA would organise negotiations over Cyprus, in return for the handing over of Ocalan. The first of many such meetings was held on 1 July 1999.

Ocalan was transported to the evacuated prison-island of Imrali, and Med TV in Europe was closed down by the British Independent Television Commission (ITC), on the pretext that it was inciting violence and showing a lack of impartiality. The same commission had given Med TV a 10-year licence to operate from 1994, but Sir Robin Biggam, a board member of the ITC, was also a director of British Aerospace. At the time of Med TV's closure, British Aerospace was commencing production of assault rifles and grenade launchers for Turkey's security forces.

The USA had many reasons for putting pressure on different governments to cooperate in the arrest of Ocalan, having always maintained that PKK is a terrorist organisation working against a democratic country. Turkey, a strategic ally, is increasingly vital to US interests in the region. A buffer zone between Europe and the volatile Middle East, it is officially a secular state, despite its Muslim population, and the land bridge between Europe and the newly formed oil-rich Central Asian republics across which major gas and oil pipelines are proposed. Turkey provides America with military bases, and since 1980, the USA has supplied Turkey with US$15 billion in arms, an estimated 75 per cent of Turkey's arsenal. This includes Cobra helicopters, Black Hawke transport helicopters, armoured personal carriers, and F-16 bombers used to bomb Kurdish villages. In 1998, the USA trained a special Turkish commando unit to fight Kurdish guerillas in the mountains.

As well, Israel and Turkey have established closer ties. Israel has supplied arms and intelligence to Turkey, and in October 1998 commenced training Turkish special forces to fight PKK guerillas. In return, Turkey has agreed to sell water to Israel. The water's source is in Kurdistan, and it will have to be piped either by sea or across Syria.

While the USA and Israel actively help in Turkey's suppression of the Kurds, the Kurds watched NATO go to war in Kosovo within weeks of Ocalan's abduction. The official line was that Slobodan Milosevic and his Serb forces must be prevented from committing human-rights abuses, arbitrary killings and evacuations of Kosovo Albanians. Also listed among the abuses were the Muslim Kosovo Albanians being stripped of their constitutional autonomy, and being denied the right to speak their own language, run their own schools and shape their daily lives. It was all too familiar to Kurds.

On the prison-island of Imrali, Ocalan has been kept in complete isolation. For the first 10 days he was not allowed to see lawyers. When German lawyers were forbidden to enter the country, 80 Kurdish and Turkish lawyers volunteered to take on his case. In desperation, PKK declared the whole of Turkey a war zone, warning tourists that they came to Turkey at their own risk. For the next 45 days, Ocalan saw two lawyers for one hour each week, the first meeting in the presence of a judge and all meetings in the presence of masked prison guards. His lawyers reported their concern for his mental and physical condition. He was allowed no other contact with the outside world, including newspapers or radio. On 24 March, the day NATO began bombing Kosovo and Serbia, he was meant to attend his first court appearance, but was not taken to Ankara, because of the security risk. His lawyers and the prosecutors met in the presence of three judges, one a military officer, who decided he should be tried on Imrali.

While Turkish prime minister Bulent Ecevit continued to deny the existence of Kurdish people in Turkey, in April he said of the Kosovo Albanians, "I can't imagine the Kosovars living under Serbian rule any more. Independence or a federation would be the most effective solution." In the same month, 37 hazardous words such as 'Kurd' and 'citizen of Kurdish origin' were banned. 'Evacuated villages' was to be reported as 'abandoned villages'.

Turkey held national elections on 18 April. The extreme right-wing National Action Party gained votes on the slogan, "Ocalan must hang." The usual violence associated with voting in Kurdistan went unreported by international media, although Stephen Kinzer wrote in the *New York Times* that government rations such as flour and sugar were to be cut and people told their houses would be burned if they voted for HADEP. Villagers were forced to cast open ballots and there were incidents of violence.

Also in April, a chief judge in Turkey's constitutional court, Ahmed Necdet Sezar, called for legal and constitutional changes in Turkey, saying the current constitution was a remnant of the 1980 military coup. There were calls to end the death penalty, but Ocalan's trial would continue under the present system, which the Turkish prime minister assured the world was just.

The trial was set for 31 May. Ocalan was put in a glass box, communicating with the chief judge through a microphone. He could hear neither the prosecution nor defence, but was allowed two statements. In one, he asked forgiveness from the mothers of Turkish soldiers killed in the war. Edited from most reports was that his statement continued, "but the Turkish government of the 1980s gave Kurds no choice but to carry out an armed struggle. Turkish families could at least bury their dead; PKK could not." He denied allegations that PKK was partly financed through drug-trafficking, claiming that financial support came from donations and that arms were purchased through normal commercial channels. In his second statement, he emphasised his aim for a democratic settlement of Kurdish issues to the benefit of all Turkish citizens. Some sections of his statements have confused Kurdish people, but he assured them that his position had not changed, and they should be patient. Of course, he was sentenced to death. On appeal, he was again sentenced to death, but in November 1999, his lawyers applied to take his case to the European Court of Human Rights.

In July 1999, a PKK council of seven announced a unilateral ceasefire to show they were united behind Ocalan. They promised to refrain from any acts of violence but reserved the right to defend themselves. The Turkish government refused to negotiate, Turkish forces continuing to attack PKK. In August, Ocalan announced that PKK must withdraw from Turkey. The rationale was that the war must end so that Turkey could progress to a democratic republic. Some PKK wanted to continue the armed struggle, but most have complied with Ocalan's requests, although arrests of PKK supporters, Ocalan's lawyers, journalists, and human-rights advocates continue.

Although PKK guerillas no longer attack the Turkish army, clashes between them and Iraqi Kurdish parties have continued. In late 2000, PKK and PUK fought for several months in the Sulaimani region after Talabani requested that PKK leave the area. Both sides accused the other of initiating and continuing the fighting, Talabani accusing PKK of acting on behalf of Iraq, PKK accusing PUK of acting on behalf of Turkey.

Again, history is repeating itself. Despite PKK opposition to tribalism, in practice the PKK leadership carries on tribal behaviour similar to that of other Kurdish leaders and parties. Despite rhetoric about democracy, while many grassroots PKK supporters express progressive views and work hard for Kurdish issues, PKK is more centralised in its organisation and secretive about its hierarchical structure than any other Kurdish party. Ordinary members have no clear idea about its structure or the personalities involved, and are not allowed to express a non-party view or act without orders from the top. Criticism is actively discouraged.

PKK is still based on one person: Abdullah Ocalan. Since going to Europe, I think, he has realised the extent of feeling against himself and PKK. He knows that an independent Kurdish state is an unrealistic dream at the present time, given world opinion and the inherent contradictions in Kurdish society. Although pressure from Iraq and Syria continues to be exerted for PKK to continue armed struggle, Ocalan has so far refused. His own life is at stake. As well, his long term strategy may be for PKK to become a legal political party, so he can be released and assume a parliamentary position.

To find out what is happening in Kurdistan, the Kurdish diasporas rely on the Internet, word of mouth and a few Kurdish journals. In Australia, we have a national weekly one-hour radio program, with other programs broadcast state-wide, and one community magazine. The general media, so effective in moulding peoples' opinions, reports little and seems directed to take a certain line. I was most concerned with the attitude of the Australian media regarding the demonstration outside the Greek consulates in Melbourne and Sydney. There are about 5000 Kurds living in Melbourne, up to 60 of whom went to the Greek consulate. Of these, four or five engaged in scuffles with the police, and two were arrested and charged with 'resisting arrest' and 'assaulting police'. There was no property damage, and most of the demonstrators were peaceful, despite the intense emotions, yet the whole Kurdish community was portrayed in a negative light, some being named as terrorists. A few journalists used very emotive language, writing, "Kurds go home", it being a commonly held view that refugees should leave their problems in their country of birth. Yet if a Western country was invaded and its people subject to genocide and forced to speak a foreign language, many escaping as refugees, could these refugees forget the plight of their family and friends back home?

Since those initial demonstrations, we have had many signature campaigns and petitions to governments, lawyers, and international bodies, with several peaceful demonstrations going unreported by the media. In April 1999, I was part of a delegation that met with Australian Foreign Minister Alexander Downer, who unexpectedly claimed to be sympathetic with the Kurdish cause as a whole, though he did not like Ocalan and PKK, because of their use of violence. We also met with the Senate Human Rights Committee and several senators, proving that we had a just cause and could argue intelligently.

The Kurds' biggest problem continues to be a lack of recognition. Unlike the Palestinians, we do not even have observer status in the UN. Our other problem is lack of unity. While all Kurdish political parties agree that Kurdish identity should be recognised and Kurdish culture and political rights respected, no party leader is willing to trust another to represent all Kurds, putting the nation before his own power base. For these reasons, a party allies itself to one or more neighbouring regimes, to gain more power. The others accuse it of selling out. There is a sense of betrayal on all sides. If party leaders remain divided, so do the party members and sympathisers, even those in the diasporas. People who do not remain loyal are considered traitors or are marginalised. It is the same old tribalism being re-enacted in the 21st century.

A major contributing factor is that Kurds have had no experience of democracy within their own culture, or within the nation-states in which they live. To replace tribalism with democratic processes, there needs to be a psychological and social development so that people learn to accept different points of view. People must be educated, yet only a few Kurds are well educated. In Western countries like Australia, where there is greater access to information, leaders generally must convince the people or listen to them. A politician who disagrees with the party's line can resign, start their own party, become an independent, or try and change the party from within. With legitimate means to encourage change, it is not a life-and-death struggle.

Recent developments offer hope—at least in Iraqi Kurdistan, where despite a four year civil war and two trade embargoes, Kurds have been governing themselves for nearly ten years. What they have achieved in terms of developing democratic processes and infrastructure, and providing for their people, compares most favourably to what is happening under Saddam Hussein's regime in the south. The regional governments of

Hawler and Sulaimani are making concerted efforts of reconciliation, yet both remain officially unrecognised by governments around the world and under constant threat from the nation-state governments surrounding them.

While many Kurds' ultimate dream is for an independent Kurdish nation-state, in present circumstances, most Kurdish political leaders realise that autonomy or federalism is more realistic. Meanwhile, what is most needed in Kurdistan and throughout the Middle East is community development—economic, social, cultural and political. However, for this kind of evolution, all sides must be respectful of democratic processes.

Miracle

A poem by Marif Agha-e, translated by Kamran Avin

Fortune-teller:
A day will come and the world will have changed.
Fire will be freezing:
Freezing fire!

Ice will blaze like fire:
Burning ice!

Destiny will not be so bitter.

Textnotes

I – LIFTING THE VEIL

The Kurds and Their Origins – *Dr Hussein Tahiri*

a *Writer:* In this chapter, the term 'Iranians' refers to 'Iranic' people, the Aryans who migrated to the Midde East. It does not refer to Persians.

b *Editor:* For a description of Enki's role in the evolution of mankind, see Dr A. Maronesy's essay, p. 49

c *Editor:* The Assyrians, Babyonians, Akkadians, Kassites, Hittites and Medes derived their cuneiform script and laws from the Sumers.

d *Editor:* The Medes built citadel fortresses, the mud-brick ruins of two having been found at Nush-e Jan near Hamadan and at Ziweh, also spelt Ziwiyeh or in Farsi Ziveh, near Ushnaviyeh, in eastern Kurdistan. At Ziweh, archeologists have found exquisite ornaments and furniture in bronze, silver, gold and electrum, with forms linking the artefacts to Hurrian and Sumerian mythology.

e Known as Hawler by Kurds and pronounced 'Howwlairr'

f *Writer:* Such differences are common in our era as well. For example, 'Japan' in English is 'Zhapon' in Persian and 'Yaban' in Arabic.

g *Writer:* Kirzioglu M. Fahrettin, in *Kurterin Koku (The Origin of the Kurds)*, Ankara, Ayyidliz Matba'as, 1963, compares Kurdish words to ancient Turkish words. He states that Bano, Dae/daya, Apo, Buge/bike, Kund, Kani and Beran/baran are the ancient Turkish words Baba, Ana, Amuca, Gelin, Kend, Kaynak and koc, respectively, although Baba and Amuca are derived from Arabic. He also uses wrong spellings and meanings to prove his point, misleading those who do not know Kurdish.

h *Writer:* In Turkey, the speaking of any Kurdish dialect was banned. Kreyenbroek states, "For a long time, Kurds who bargained in the only language they knew could be fined a certain sum per word". In other parts of Kurdistan, there was pressure to speak the dominant language as a sign of being cultured or progressive. (Kreyenbroek and Sper, 1992, p. 73)

i Also pronounced 'Alawi'

j *Writer:* I use 'Ezidi' to distinguish it from the fifth Arab caliph, Yazid Ibn Mo'awiyya. His son became the sixth caliph after defeating Ali's son Hussein in the famous battle at Kerbala.

k Pronouced Ta'oos

l *Editor:* Ezidi oral tradition and other evidence date it back to Ubaid-Sumerian times. (See essay by Dr A. Maronesy)

m Also spelt 'Yarseshan' in Dr M. Kamal's essay

n *Writer:* Qizibash is Turkish for 'redheads'. They supported Shah Isma'il, the founder of the Safavid dynasty in Iran. His army used to wear red headgear.

Religion and faith in Kurdistan – *Dr Muhammad Kamal*

a *Editor:* These are the text names of the Ezidi angels.

b Pronounced 'meer'

c 'Baba' is the Arabic for 'Bab'e' in Kurdish.

d Pronounced 'peer'

e In Dr A. Maronesy's essay, the festival is spelt 'Sarsa'al', which is the way Ezidi pronounce it.

f Also spelt and pronounced 'Alevi'

g Pronounced 'Ka'akai'

h Pronounced 'Howarr'

About Dr Abdulkader Maronesy

a *Editor:* Malla in the Sorani dialect, melle in the Kurmanji North dialect and mullah in Arabic means 'man of knowledge' but has come to be interpreted as 'man of religious knowledge'. Some Kurds prefer to leave out the 'malla' when talking of Mostefa Barzani. Others argue that Mostefa Barzani knew the Qur'an very well and deserves the title. Similarly, 'Mostafa' can be pronounced 'Mistefa' in Kurmanji and Bahdinani, or 'Mustafah' in Arabic.

Ezidi: The first Monotheists? – *Dr Abdulkader Maronesy*

a *Writer:* Others use the *Mes-haf-e Resh* as their reference when saying Ta'us was born on Sunday. Some say it is an oral tradition that Wednesday was the day Ta'us revealed himself. However, the *Mes-haf-e Resh* was written after the advent of Judaism, Christianity and Islam and therefore, I believe, served to discredit Ta'us by linking him with the angel Azazeel, who became known as Satan.

b *Editor:* This version of the Creation story comes from oral tradition, rather than from *Mes-haf-e-Resh* as quoted by Dr M. Kamal.

c Kurdish pronunciation of the Arabic 'baba'

d Also spelt Gilani

e *Editor:* The Ezidi feast of Jemayi is not mentioned in the *Mes-haf-e Resh,* according to Dr M. Kamal.

f *Writer:* Across many cultures, a god or a messenger is said to have given humans the ability to write. For Ezidi it was an angel, for the Zoroastrians it was the devas who taught Jamshid's relative Tahmorus, and for the Greeks it was Cadmoos, god of writing.

g *Editor:* In the *Sharafnameh,* written by Amir Sharaf Khan Bitlisi in 1596, Jamshid is mentioned as the fourth king of the Pishdadian dynasty, but Dr A. Maronesy suggests this is written according to the biases of Islamic scholars from the 10th century and after.

h *Editor:* In Exodus 6:3, Abraham refers to God as El Shaddai or 'Lord of the Mountain', also a name for the Sumer god-king Enlil, who tries to stop his half-brother Enki from giving Adam knowledge and, later, sends a great flood.

i Kavus is pronounced 'Kowoos'. The name can also be spelt Kei Kaus. Xosayarsa is another name of the same king.

j *Editor:* Bab'e Cho'oosh is called Baba Chawash in Dr M. Kamal's essay

k *Editor:* As in the seven archangels of Christianity. Note that these spellings of the angels are how modern Ezidis pronounce the angels' names. They are spelt differently in the *Mes-haf-e Resh,* and therefore in Dr. M. Kamal's essay.

l *Editor:* Proto-Elamite and Sumer cuneiform evolved from a vertically written, picture-based writing to a left-right phonetic and picture-based writing.

m *Editor:* Genesis Chapter 10 details the progeny of Noah's sons. Biblical scholars such as Edersheim relate how they migrated: Shem's to Asia, Ham's to Africa and Japheth's to Europe. Thus Shem's sons Elam (the name of a people and area in Kurdistan), Asshur (the Assyrians), Arphaxad (the ancestor of Abraham), Lud and Aram either remained in the area or travelled west as far as Judah. The sons of Ham went to Africa: Cush to Ethiopia, Misraim to Egypt, Phut to Lybia and Canaan to the land of Canaan. Japheth's sons travelled north to Europe: Gomer's descendants, thought to be the people of Brittany and Wales, Madia going north to return as the Medes, Javan becoming father of the Greeks, Tiras of the Thracians, Tubal and Meshech of the German Celts and Armenians. Lastly, Dr A. Maronesy believes Magog to be the father of the Mede priest cast of Mogh, while Eldersheim believes him to be ancestor of the Scythians.

n *Editor:* The Mandaeans do not circumcise boys.

o *Editor:* Other relatives of Abraham shared the names of governors and the cities they governed—including Terah (Abraham's father), Nahor (Terah's father), Serug (Nahor's father) and Peleg (Serug's grandfather).

p *Writer:* The word *varr* still exists in the Kurdish language. Today, if a Kurd wants to say "trust me", he says, "Bavarka je".

q *Editor:* Other sources say Abraham's test occurred in south-eastern Turkey (Kurdistan).

r *Editor:* According to biblical lineage, if Nimrod lived at the time of Abraham, it would date Abraham at about 3000 BC. However, it is known that the Elamites invaded Ur around 2000 BC, forcing the aristocracy to escape north, and this would date Abraham about 2000 BC, the more generally accepted date. It was Nimrod who was meant to have built the second Assyrian capital of Nimrud, also known as Kalhu, or Calah and the Tower of Babel, and according to Aramaean texts of 1300 BC, he was father of an Egyptian pharoah of the first dynasty.

A Musical and Poetic Tradition – *Siamand Minehzadeh Morowatdost*

a north-west Iran
b eastern Turkey
c Pronounced 'durrtar'
d Pronouncing the 'oo' as in 'book'
e Pronounced 'Mahmood' with 'oo' as in book
f north-east Iraq and north-west Iran: part of southern and eastern Kurdistan
g Pronounced 'Moelawi'
h Pronouncing 'oo' as in 'spoon'
i 'Enemy' can be translated as 'army' or 'bomb'
j 'History' can be translated as 'time'
k Pronounced 'Kaycruso'

About Abdulwahab Talabani

a A Kurdish way of pronouncing the Arabic mullah

An Introduction to Modern Kurdish Literature – *Abdulwahab Talabani*

a *Writer:* In a dialect closely related to the Hawrami dialect, considered to be the oldest of he modern dialects.
b Also known as Hemen Shaykh Islami
c *Writer:* The 'oo' in La'ook is pronounced as in 'book'. La'ook, Ay-Ay and Hayran refer to the traditional genres of Kurdish music and singing—mostly epic songs about historical, semi-historical and mythical figures.
d *Writer:* Mawlana is a Sufi word for 'our Lord', or 'a highly respected person, one with deep knowledge'.

About Mihriban Astare, Seher Cinar, Ayten Sengul and Helin Diyar

a Pronounced 'zem'
b Pronounced 'Elaza'
c Pronounced 'Kajaran'
d Pronounced 'Tunjeli'

A Dialogue Between Women – *Mihriban Astare, Seher Cinar, Ayten Sengul and Helin Diyar*

a Partîya Karkerên Kurdistan or Kurdistan Workers' Party, the Kurdish political organisation which engaged in armed struggle with the Turkish government between 1984 and 1999.
b Pronounced 'fishk'e'
c Pronounced 'Erzinjan'
d *Ala* is Kurdish for 'mixed colour' and *qala* is Turkish for 'woman'.
e Muslims believe Ishmael, Abraham's first born, not Isaac, was the son he was going to sacrifice.
f Pronounced 'Moosh' and often spelt Mus
g Also called a 'zaz', referring to several types of stringed instruments, including the ba'aghlama.
h Pronounced 'Janakkal'e'
i In the Sorani dialect, it is pronounced 'zorna'
j Pronounced 'Ovachik'

Iraq: The Politics of Oppression – *Dr Azad*

a Built by the Sassanian Persians in the fourth century, 30 kilometres from modern-day Baghdad
b Otherwise known as Hawler
c *Editor:* Abd Al-Karim Qassem was an army commander involved in the slaughter of the Assyrian community in 1933
d Pronounced 'Dookan' with 'oo' as is spoon

e Pronounced 'Dowood'

f *Editor:* It is reported that the USA donated $300 million to the Kurdish cause in 1974 alone.

g *Editor:* Another source reports that when trying to get work, they would be ordered to go to a centre where they were asked to pay one dinar. Afterwards they were told, "Okay—now you are a member of the Ba'ath Party." They might say, "We thought we were paying to get work", but it was too late. If they caused trouble, they would lose their new house or be forced to join the conventional army or the Jayeesh Al Sha'abi, the civilian army.

h One of the four main groups of Lur people living in the east of Iraq and west of Iran.

i *Editor:* Immediately following the Iraq invasion of Kuwait, President Bush ordered a naval blockade of Iraq without approval from Congress or the UN Security Council. Then the USA bullied and bribed people voting in the UN Security Council so an unprecedented series of resolutions was passed that meant any nation could take all military means necessary to enforce these resolutions against Iraq.

j *Editor:* In 1980 the Turkish army attacked Qamishli in Syria, killing 17 Kurds who had fled the military coup in Turkey. The question is why weren't similar attacks carried out after 1984, when PKK began its armed struggle, operating from bases in Syria?

A Time for Rose and a Time for Primrose – *Eziz Bawermend*

a *Writer:* Briefly, 'Sunni' means 'regular' and 'Shia' means 'irregular', and the division can, to some degree, be likened to that between Catholics and Protestants in Christendom.

b Kurmanji pronunciation of the Sorani 'Malla Mostefa' and the Arabic 'Mullah Mustafah'

II – FROM BAHDINAN TO BABAN VIA SORAN

Enough – *Sami Bawari*

a Bahdinani/Kurmanji for the Sorani *'jahsh'.*

b Pronounced *Zirna* in Sorani

c The 'o' pronounced as in 'coat'

d *Editor:* The figure varies from 5000 to 12000, not counting Iranian soldiers. The variances could be due to the fact that initially only bodies in the streets and houses were counted – not the bodies of people who were in underground shelters or who were buried in rubble.

e Pronouncing the 'oo' as in spoon.

About Abbas Boskany

a 'jh' is pronounced as 's' in vision

Air Waves – *Rebwar Bibani*

a Short for 'Muhammad'

b *Editor:* Ardalan is the *peshmerga* name for Rebwar Tahir, whose painting is on the jacket of this book.

c Kak is a term of respect, like 'Mr'. Karka is the term of respect for an older brother.

d Pronounced 'Sarsheoo'

e Arabic for 'kaftan'

You Are Still Asleep – *Abbas Boskany*

a From the classical poet Mahwi

Cry of the Partridge – *Abdulawahab Talabani*

a To the west and north of Hawler

b This was their custom.

c The name they gave to the peak of Peermam, the highest mountain in the region.

Always a Sun Behind the Clouds – *Mahabad Fatah*

a Pronouncing the 'oo' as in 'book'

b Another name for Zoroastra

c If God Wills

In the Land of a Thousand Sighs – *Sarbast Fatah*

a Pronouncing the 'oo' as in spoon, Qoolarush meaning 'deep, black'.

A Fortress of No Tomorrows – *Maryam Rowandozi*

a *Editor:* Farming communities existed to the north-west of Rowandoz from 7000 BC. Mills, cemeteries and copper beads have been found there.

b Pronounced 'Kazvienci'

c *Editor:* The KDPI hospital moved from the village of Garada, in the Ja'afati Valley or 'Valley of the Parties', to Pshtashun after Anfal in 1988.

Price of Freedom – *Dr Bewar*

a Pronounced Shamdinli in southern Kurdistan

b Pronounced 'Jizir'

A Way Through the Mountains – *Dr Ali Zibari*

a Iranian Religious Police

b The Shah's secret police

c Also known as Sami Abdurahman, from Sinjar (Shingal)

d *Editor:* A Kurdish source who does not wish to be named claims that this desecration of Barzani's grave was carried out by Iraqi Mukhabarat, and was indirectly organised by a KDP leader. Masoud Barzani and others did not want to fight KDPI, but the KDP leader feared the intelligence and popularity of Dr Qassemlou, the KDPI leader, and his alignment with Jalal Talabani. Dr Ali Zibari comments that this is unlikely to be correct because it was of no benefit to the Mukhabarat, who relied on KDPI being inside Iran for them to get intelligence on Iranian targets, etc.

A Fox is Not a Camel – *Wria Rekar*

a Also known as Shaykh Abdul Qadir Jilani

A Nightingale in A Golden Cage – *Waleed Bamirny*

a *Lyanga* is Kurdish for *nuseerr, andam* is Kurdish for *ozo* and *haval* is Kurdish for *rafiq*.

The Moon Rises After Sunset – *Surma Hamid*

a Penal Law no. 3818/1972, states that the murdering of woman for a scandal is not regarded as a crime. Penal Law no. 671/1976, states that if a daughter goes out at night without her father's knowledge and consent, then the father is not guilty for killing her, provided that he has informed the police of what she has done. Resolution numbers 150, 240, 304/General Board/dated 13.10.79, states that a man who kills his sister for having sex before marriage is considered innocent, even if she marries her lover afterwards, because her act resulted in a scandal for the family. Resolution no. 342/18.9.79, states that a man who kills his female cousin for running away from her family's house is innocent because her escape is a scandal. Resolution no. 660/22.4.1979, states that if a witness can prove the murdered woman had misbehaved, and that this was the reason behind her murder, then the offence is to be regarded as having been committed for the sake of honour. Resolution no. 1488/1979, states that if a woman is murdered for misbehaviour, then the murderer is innocent, even if the murder is committed after a period of time, since there was hope that the woman would correct her behaviour during that period. Source: Penal Code no. 111/1969 and its amendments, published 1982.

Leyla Zana – *Abbas Boskany*

a Leyla Zana, a Kurdish parliamentarian in Turkey, was imprisoned in 1994 for 14 and a half years for suggesting Turks and Kurds can live as brothers, and for speaking out against the human rights abuses occurring in northern Kurdistan (Turkey).

III – FROM PAZIKAN TO BOTAN, JUMI TO HAKKARI

Why Kurdish? – *by Ahmedi Khani, translated by Eziz Bawermend*

a *Translator:* Khanî refers to the tradition of writing in Arabic and Persian.

b *Translator:* 'Books' refers to the holy books of the Torah, the Bible and the Qur'an.

c *Translator:* Ciziri, Heriri and Teyra are three masters of Kurdish literature preceding Khanî.

d *Translator:* 'Counterfeit jewels' presumably refers to Arabic and Persian words.

e *Translator: Mirza* is Kurdish for 'prince' and is also used as a name for a male.

He Who Does Not Fight – *Nase Ouso'eva*

a A version of *Khodeh*

b The Soviet Union persecuted the Kurds of Nakhichevan, now called Karabakh, an area between Armenia and Azerbaijan. The Kurds living there had a good ecomony but in 1929 the leader of the communists of Azerbaijan told Stalin that the Kurds wanted autonomy, so the Kurds were forcibly dispersed between the various republics. In 1939-44 Stalin began anther wave of mass deportations of Kurds from Azerbaijjan, Armenia and Georgia to Central Asia.

c An idiom

d A mountain on the Armenian–Turkish border

e *Editor:* In Iraq, Ba'aths have claimed that Ezidi are Arab, and likewise the Turks have claimed Ezidi are Turkish.

Sacred Fire – *Temur Childargushi*

a *Editor:* In old Sumer legend, Anu is the father of half-brothers Enki and Enlil, as well as the grandson of Apsu and Tiamut, the Dragon Queen.

b *Editor's Footnote*: The *Zendavesta* was written in the Hawramani language of Kurdistan. In most books, it is referred to as Old Pahlavi, the language of ancient Persia.

c Pronounced 'Ardi'

d *Editor:* Some say the language is Northern Kurmanji. Other researchers say the script is an old form of Aramaic, and others that it might be Mandaean.

They Speak First of the Lioness – *Sabir Bagdas*

a Pronounced 'sharr'

b Pronounced 'Kojgiri'. The letter 'c' of all Kurdish words in Part III is pronounced as a 'j'.

Grass Does Not Stay Under a Rock – *Riza Çolpan*

a Pronounced 'Carchik'

b *Editor:* These uprisings occurred in 1920, 1925, 1927–29 and 1930.

c Pronounced 'Koopik' as in 'book'

d Pronounced 'Mokhindi'

e Extract from *My Kurdistan*, translated by Omar Sheikhmous.

Mourning in Black – *Riza Çolpan*

a *Translator:* Kurmanj, Soran, Lur, Zaza and Guran are various groups within the Kurdish nation.

b *Translator:* Bawer is a boy's name and Delal is a girl's name.

c *Translator:* Famous Kurdish poets

d *Translator:* Presidents of Iraq, Syria and Turkey

e *Translator:* The Holy Peacock is the angel of Ezidi Kurds, while Ahura Mazda is the ancient god of Zoroastra. The Ezidis and Mazdaks are Kurdish people.

f *Translator:* Rostam Zal is Kurdish hero.

g *Translator:* The blacksmith who rose up against a tyrant

h *Translator:* Guran is the poet's tribal name, Çolpan being Turkish. In the Republic of Turkey, everyone has been forced to assume a Turkish name.

As the Hungry Dream of Food – *Dursan Acar*

a Pronounced 'Jigerhun'

A Rose That Cannot be Plucked – *Veli Toprak*

a Pronounced 'hamza'

b Pronounced 'Koochik', the 'oo' as in book

c Pronounced 'Charikun'

A Foot in Australia – *Ayce Akturk, Hakki Hayri, Ahmed Tigran*

a Depending on which source one reads

b Turkish say Cizre, pronounced Jizer

c *Editor:* Other sources say 45, the figure of 150, or thereabouts, applying to the total number of deaths in several towns. There are no accurate statistics.

d *Editor:* Although PKK's stated goals in this regard changed in the 1990s, it continues to be quoted as PKK's long-term intention.

An Apple Does Not Fall Far from the Tree – *Ruken Heval*

a *Ruken* means 'smiling face' and *heval* means 'friend' in Kurmanji

b Pronounced 'Kier'

In the Shadow of Aslan – *Saad Barazi*

a *Editor:* Saad had not heard that in the 1960s, Syria arbitrarily decreed between 100,000 to 200,000 Kurds to be foreigners, without any rights of citizenship.

Black Hens Still Lay White Eggs – *Bavi Alan*

a Cezira is spelt Cezer'e in Kurmanji and Cizre in Turkish, and is pronounced Jiziri or Jizir

Our Trouble – *by Ahmedi Khani, translated by Eziz Bawermend*

a *Translator:* Khani refers to the legendary crystal ball of the ancient King Jamshid who could see into the future.

b *Translator:* 'four corners' relates to the saying 'four corners of the world'

IV – FROM ELAM TO KHOY VIA MUKRIAN AND ARDALAN

Words are Your Own until they Leave Your Mouth – *by Ghader Abdi*

a Also spelt Kayanyan

b An Islamic democratic thinker

c A member of the Jebhai Mili, an organisation which emphasised a western style democracy

d A minister in Mossodeq's time, and an academic in the social sciences

e Pronounced 'Bookan' as in 'moon'

f Pronounced 'Seengun'

The Eye can See But the Hand is Short – *by Fariba Qazi*

a *Maydan* means 'field'. The square was known as Chwar Chira (four ways, light) before the Islamic republic and became known as Chwar Azadi or Maydan Azadi after 1979.

b 'Khan' is a term of respect

Buried Alive – *by Mariam Qazi, translated by Fariba Qazi*

a *Translator:* 'March' refers to the 1000 to 2000 women who marched from Sulaimani to Dohuk in protest against the civil war raging in Kurdistan between 1994 and 1998.

b *Translator:* There is a Kurdish belief that an owl's song brings death.

c *Translator:* Referring to the Allies refusing to help the Kurds against Saddam after the 1991 uprising

d *Translator:* Referring to when the Kurds won their freedom in Iraqi Kurdistan in 1991

e *Translator:* The square in Mahabad where Qazi Muhammad was hung in 1947

f *Translator:* Zoroastarianism is the religion before Islam.
In Iran, we are taught that Ezidism came after Islam.

g *Translator:* Referring to the time of the Medes, and before

h *Translator:* Referring to Masoud Barzani and Jalal Talabani

i *Translator:* Referring to the way Kurdish women show extreme grief

Gaddar – *by Hamid Rashidi Zarza*

a Gaddar is the name of a river close to Mahabad

Freezoo – *by Hamid Rashidi Zarza*

a Freezoo means 'weed' or 'couch grass'

Life's Legacy – *by Dr Hussein Tahiri*

a Pronounced 'Wan'

Photo Credits for Half-title Pages

PART I: Peshmerga in Nawzang area
photographed by Mansour Razaghi

PART II: Boy at Penjuan
photographed by Mansour Razaghi

Children from Halabja
(anonymous photographer)

PART III: Aslan, Saad Barazi's Father

PART IV: Burning tank and refugees
photographed by Mansour Razaghi

Sources

The Kurds and Their Origins – *Dr Hussein Tahiri*

1 One such text is by Kirzioglu M. Fahrettin, titled *Kurterin Koku* (The Origin of the Kurds), Ankara, Ayyidliz Matbaas, 1963, p. 5. In this book, the author, a history teacher, tries to prove Kurds are of Turkish origin.
2 Kendal, *Kurdistan in Turkey*, Gerard Chaliliand (ed.) *People without a Country*, London, Zed Press, 1980, p. 68
3 Muhammad Abbasi, "Introduction", in Amir Sharaf Khan e Bitlisi, *Sharafnameh*, Tehran, Elmi, 1994, p. 98 (in Persian)
4 Wilhem Gernot, "The Hurrians", Translated by Diana Stein, U.K., Aris and Phillip Ltd, 1989, in *The International Journal of Kurdish Studies* (book review), Brooklyn, The Kurdish Library, Vol. 7, Nos 1 and 2, 1994, p. 112–13.
5 Muhammad Abbasi, *op. cit.*, p. 100
6 Thomas Bois, *The Kurds*, Beirut, Khayats, 1966, p. 8
7 Abdul Rahman Qassemlou, *Kurdistan and the Kurds*, Balinge, JN Wesanin Jina Nu, 1991, pp. 41–42
8 Muhammad Abbasi, *op. cit.*, p. 19
9 Mehrdrad Izady, *The Kurds: A Concise Handbook*, Washington, Taylor and Francis International Publishers, 1992, p. 34
10 Thomas Bois, *The Kurds*, Beirut, Khayats, 1966, p. 14
11 Mehrdrad Izady, Wilhem Gernot, while others like Derk Kinnane talk about 'Iranicised tribes'
12 Peter Bogucki, *The Origin of Human Society*, Blackwell Publishers, 1999, p. 232–36, 338, and *Encyclopaedia Britannica*, University of Chicago, 1991, Vol. 5, p. 625; Vol. 26, p. 54; Vol. 12, p. 98
13 Kurdish Library, "Kurds and Kurdistan: Facts and Figures", *The International Journal of Kurdish Studies*, Brooklyn, The Kurdish Library, Vol. 8, No. 2, 1995, p. 163.
14 *Encyclopaedia Britannica*, University of Chicago, 1991, Vol. 21, p. 922–23
15 *Ibid.*
16 Wilhelm Gernot, *op. cit.*, p. 112
17 Shrikant G. Talageri, *The Aryan Invasion Theory: A Reappraisal*, New Delhi, Aditya Prakashau, 1993, pp. 25, 139
18 *Encyclopaedia Britannica*, University of Chicago, 1991, Vol. 5, p. 583; Vol. 21, pp. 922–23
19 Frank Hole (ed.) *The Archeology of Western Iran*, Washington, Smithsonian Institute Press, 1987, p. 176
20 Thomas Bois, *op. cit.*, p. 10
21 Sheikh A. Waheed, *The Kurds and their Country*, Lahore, University Book Agency, 1958, p. 45
22 Kurdish Library, "Kurds and Kurdistan: Facts and Figures", *The International Journal of Kurdish Studies*, Brooklyn, The Kurdish Library, Vol. 8, No.2, 1995, p. 163
23 *Encyclopaedia Britannica*, University of Chicago, 1991, Vol. 21, pp. 922–23
24 Frank Hole (ed.), *op. cit.*, p. 289
25 Thomas Bois, *op. cit.*, pp. 10–11
26 *Ibid.*
27 Sheikh A. Waheed *op. cit.*, p. 49
28 *Encyclopaedia Britannica*, University of Chicago, 1991, Vol. 21, pp. 922–23
29 *Encyclopaedia Britannica*, University of Chicago, 1991, Vol. 5, p. 951
30 Mehrdrad Izady, *op. cit.* p. 32, 34
31 John Bulloch and Harvey Morris, *No Friends But the Mountains*, New York and Oxford, Oxford University Press, 1992, pp. 56–57
32 Muhammad Abbasi, *op. cit.*, pp. 72–78
33 Sharikant G. Talageri, *op. cit.*, pp. 317–18
34 Mehrdrad Izady, *op. cit.*, p. 32
35 C.J. Edmonds, *Kurds, Turks and Arabs*, London, Oxford University Press, 1957, p. 5
36 Thomas Bois, *op. cit.*, p. 13
37 Mehrdrad Izady, *op. cit.*, p. 32

38 *Ibid.*, p. 32
39 *Ibid.*, p. 35
40 Col. T. Wahby, *op. cit.*, pp. 3–4
41 *Ibid.*. p. 6
42 Basile Nikitine, *The Kurds and Kurdistan: A Sociological and Historical View*, 2nd Edition, Tehran, Niloofar Publishing, 1987, p. 47 (Persian translation by M. Ghazi); Bois 1966, 16; Edmonds 1957, 7; Minorsky in Wahby 1982,16; and others
43 Mehrdrad Izady, *op. cit.*, p. 28–31
44 *Ibid.*. pp. 31–32
45 Sheikh A. Waheed, *op. cit.*, p. 43
46 C.E. Bosworth et al (eds.), *The Encyclopaedia of Islam*, Vol. V, Leiden, E.J. Brill, 1986, p. 447
47 Mehrdrad Izady, *op. cit.*, p. 35
48 Thomas Bois, *op. cit.*, p. 15
49 *Ibid.*
50 *Ibid.*
51 Frederick Millingen, *Wild Life Among the Koords*, London, Hurdt and Balckett Publishers, 1970, p. 207
52 Col. T. Wahby, *The Origin of the Kurds and Their Language*, Lecture delivered to KSSE, U.K. branch, 22 December 1964 and published in *Kurdistan*, of KSSE Nos IX and X, reprinted in Sweden 1982, p. 2
53 Basile Nikitine, *op. cit.*, pp. 56–60 (Persian translation by M. Ghazi)
54 *Ibid.*, p. 35
55 Austin H. Layard, *Discoveries Among the Ruins of Nineveh and Babylon*, New York, Harper and Brothers Publishers, 1853, p. 323
56 Col. T. Wahby, *op. cit.*, p. 2
57 Mehrdrad Izady, *op. cit.*, p. 40
58 Basile Nikitine, *op. cit.*, pp. 46–47
59 Col. T. Wahby, *op. cit.*, p. 5
60 Mehrdrad Izady, *op. cit.*, pp. 172–75
61 *Ibid.*
62 C. J. Edmonds, *op. cit*, pp. 10–11
63 Mehrdrad Izady, *op. cit.*, pp. 43–45
64 Sheikh A. Waheed *op. cit.*, p. 12
65 Kurdish Library, "Kurds and Kurdistan: Facts and Figures", *The International Journal of Kurdish Studies*, Brooklyn, The Kurdish Library, *ibid.*, pp. 63–64
66 Amir Sharaf Khan e Bitlisi, *Sharafnameh*, Tehran, Elmi, 1994, pp. 399,423
67 C. E. Bosworth, et al, *op. cit.*, p. 451
68 Abdul Rahman Qassemlou, *op. cit.* p. 35
69 *Ibid.*
70 Stephen C. Pelletiere, *The Kurds: An Unstable Element in the Gulf*, Westview, Boulder and London, Westview, 1984, p. 22
71 Amir Sharaf Khan e Bitlisi, *op. cit.*, pp. 43, 57
72 C.E. Bosworth, et al, *op. cit.*, p. 461
73 Amir Sharaf Khan e Bitlisi, *op. cit.*, p. 738
74 John S. Guest, *The Ezidis: A Study in Survival*, London and New York, KPI Limited, 1987, pp. 15–16
75 Mehrdrad Izady, *op. cit.*, p. 46
76 Abdul Rahman Qassemlou, *op. cit.* pp. 36–39
77 Muhammad Abbasi, *op. cit.*, p. 56
78 Muhammad Muain, *Persian Dictionary*, Tehran, Ameer Kabeer Vol. 5, 8th edition, 1992, p. 648
79 John S. Guest, *op. cit.*, p. 28
80 Muhammad Abbasi, *op. cit.*, p. 59
81 John S. Guest, *op. cit.*, p. 28
82 Muhammad Abbasi, *op. cit.*, p. 58
83 Sheikh A. Waheed, *op. cit.*, pp. 6–7
84 Mehrdrad Izady, 1992, p. 151

85 *Ibid.*, p. 150

86 Muhammad Abbasi, *op. cit.*, p. 25

Footnote references

Encyclopaedia Britannica, University of Chicago, 1991, Vol. 10, p. 773;

Laurence Gardener *Genesis of the Holy Grail*, London Bantom Press, division of Transworld, London, 1999

Religion and Faith in Kurdistan – *Dr Muhammad Kamal*

87 Qur'an 3:154, 5:50, 33:33, 48:26

88 Some Arab tribes practised female infanticide before the rise of Islam, for moral and economic purposes. This practice was banned by Islam: "Kill not your children for fear of want. We shall provide, sustenance for them as well as for you. Verily the killing of them is a great sin". (See: Qur'an 17:31)

89 B. Adi Hasan, *Mes-haf-e Resh*. Appendix I, from *Survival Among the Kurds: A History of the Ezidis*. John S. Guest. London: Kegan Paul. 1993, pp. 211–12

90 Solomon Nigosian, *Islam: The Way of Submission*. London, 1987, p. 96

91 Ghazali Al-Abu Hamid Muhammad al-Ghazili (450/1058–505/1111) Also named *Hujjatu Al-Islam* (The Proof of Islam). Self proclaimed renewer of Islam (*mujaddid*). Probably the single most important figure in the dogmatic theology and ethics of Sufi Islam. He taught at the Nizamiyyah College in Baghdad during which time he established the fame of the institution as the major educational centre for Islam. Among his most famous works are *Revival of the Religious Science* (*Ihya 'Ulum Al-Din*) and *The Deliverer from Error* (*Al-Munqidh min Al-Dalal*).

92 B. Adi Hasan, *op. cit.*, p. 211

93 John S. Guest. *op. cit.*, Survival Among the Kurds: A History of the Ezidis, London, Kegan Paul, 1993, p. 17

94 *Ibid.*

95 *The Hymn of Shaykh Adi*. In John S. Guest, *op. cit.*, p. 213

96 For Muslims Gabriel is an angel through whom the Qur'an was revealed to Muhammad: "Say: Whoever is an enemy to Gibriel, for he brings down the revelation to your heart by God's will, a confirmation of what went before and guidance and glad tidings for those who believe". (See: Qur'an 2:97)

97 Genesis 2:15–17

98 Qur'an 2:35

99 B. Adi Hasan, *op. cit.*, p. 211

100 Genesis 3:6–8

101 Genesis 3: 16

102 B. Adi Hasan,, *op. cit.*, p. 211

103 John S. Guest, *op. cit.*, p. 36

104 Al-Tabari. *Ta'rikh Al-rusul wa'l-muluk*. Vol XIII. State University of New York, 1989. p. 38

105 *Ibid.*, p. 39

106 *Ibid.*, p. 44

107 *Ibid.*, pp. 47–48

108 *Ibid.*, p. 51

109 J. Trimingham Spencer, *The Sufi Orders in Islam*, Oxford University Press, 1998, p. 41

110 *Ibid.*, p. 14

111 Moosa Matti, *Extremist Shiite: The Ghulat Sects*. New York, Syracuse University Press. 1988, p. 168

112 Edmonds, C.J., *Kurds, Turks and Arabs*. London, Oxford University Press, 1957, p. 190

113 *Ibid.*, p. 185

114 *Ibid.*

115 *Ibid.*, p. 186

116 *Ibid.*

117 Moosa Matti,. *op. cit.*, pp. 172–175

118 Al-Kashiful Ghita, Shaykh M. Hussain, *The origin of Shi'ite Islam and its principles*, Qum, Ansariyan Publications, 1982, p. 25

119 *Ibid.*, p. 26

120 *Ibid.*, p. 28

121 *Ibid.*

122 Al-Muzaffar M. Riza, *The Faith of Shia Islam*, Qum, Ansariyan Publications, 1982, p. 39
123 Muhammad Baqir, Al-Sadr *Shi'ism: the Natural Product of Islam*, Tehran, 1982, p. 25
124 M. Amin Ghalib, Al-Tawil *Ta'rikh Al-Alawiun*, Dar Al-Andalus. 1981, p. 255
125 The Alawis in Syria are called Nusayriyyah, after ibn Nusayr
126 Moosa Matti *op. cit.*, pp. 352–353
127 *Ibid.*, p. 353
128 George E. White, "The Alevi Turks of Asia Minor", *The Contemporary Review Advertiser*, No.104, November 1913, pp. 690–98

Ezidi – The First Monotheists? – *Dr Abdulkader Maronesy*

129 Khalil Gundi, *A Research About the Ezidi Minority in Iraq*, southern Kurdistan, unpublished, p. 3
130 Britannica CD: Ancient Middle Eastern Religions
131 Khalil Gundi, *op. cit.*, pp. 4–5
132 Khalil Gundi, *op. cit.*, p. 5
133 Haso Hormy, *Lalish*, Lalish Centre, Dohuk, 2000, pp. 21–22
134 Arthur Christensen *The First Human Being and the First Prince*, Translated by Tafazuli and Amoozgar, New Distribution, Tehran, 1934, p. 472
135 Salim Berengi, *Forgotten Nation*, Tehran, The World of Books, 1988 pp. 217–27
136 Tawfik Wahbi, *A Short Research about the History of the Kurds' Religion*, Translated by Hussein Said Jamaludin, Tehran, Ahmadi Publishers, 1982, p. 6
137 Salim Berengi, *op. cit.*, p. 16
138 *Ibid.*, pp. 63–64
139 Nikitin Vassili, *Kurdistan and Kurds*, Translated by Muhammed Kazi, Tehran, Drayat, 1998, p. 45
140 Qur'an: Surah 11:44
141 Ibrahim Yunesi, trans., *The Movement of National Kurd*, Paris, Flammarion, 1979, p. 10
142 Britannica CD: Shupurruk
143 Ishmael Ebin Kasir, *The Prophet's Stories*, Beirut, House of the Pen, 1991, p. 31
144 Khalil Gundi, *op. cit.*, p. 4
145 Arthur Christensen, *op. cit.*, p. 472
146 *Ibid.*, p. 285
147 Britannica CD: Veda
148 Arthur Christensen, *op. cit.*, p. 297
149 Dr Shah Nasorideen Al-Husseini, *The Civilisation and Culture of Iran*, Tehran, University of Revolutionary Guards of Iran, 1977, p. 18
150 Arthur Christensen, *op. cit.*, p. 410
151 Dr Shah Nasorideen Al-Husseini, *op. cit.*, pp. 21–22
152 Kayhosrow Isfandiyar, *Dabistani Muza Heb*, Tehran, 'Premier School of Religion' 1983, pp. 15–1
153 Dr Shah Nasorideen Al-Husseini, *op. cit.*, pp. 42–43
154 Qur'an: Surah 6: 76–79
155 Arthur Christensen, *op. cit.*, p. 397
156 Khalil Gundi, *op. cit.*, pp. 12–13
157 Arthur Christensen, *op. cit.*, p. 272
158 Salim Berengi, *op. cit.*, p. 16
159 Britannica CD: Nabu
160 Britannica CD: Hammurabi
161 Khalil Gundi, *op. cit.*, p. 27
162 Abbas and Pirnia Eckbal, *Iranian History*, Khayam Publishers, Tehran, 1991, p. 124
163 Khalil Gundi, *op. cit.*, p. 8
164 Khalil Gundi, *op. cit.*, p. 9
165 Khalil Gundi, *op. cit.*, p. 17
166 Khalil Gundi, *op. cit.*, p. 16
167 Arthur Christensen, *op. cit.*, p. 472
168 Haso Hormy, op. cit., p. 72

169 Khalil Gundi, *op. cit.*, pp. 19–22
170 Haso Hormy, op. cit., p. 9
171 Dr Shah Nasorideen Al-Husseini, *op. cit.*, pp. 42–44
172 Muhammad Muain, *Persian Dictionary*, Tehran, Ameer Kabeer, 1992, Vol. 5, 8th edition, p. 648
173 Jhala Amoozagar and Ahmed Tafazooli, *The Mythology of Zoroastra's Life*, Babylon Book Centre, 1991, p. 20
174 Dr Shah Nasorideen Al-Husseini, *op. cit.*, pp. 59–61
175 Khalil Gundi, *op. cit*,. p. 12
176 Jared Diamond, *Guns, Germs and Steel*, London, Jonathon Cape 1997, p. 343
177 Nikitin Vassili, *The Kurd and Kurdistan*, Translated by Muhammed Kazi, , Tehran, Drayat, 1998, p. 45
178 Britannica CD: Ancient Mesopotamia
179 Britannica CD: Hittites
180 Qur'an: Surah 21: 51–71
181 Qur'an, Surah 2: 258
182 Ishmael Ebin Kasir, *The Prophet's Stories*, Beirut, House of the Pen, 1991, p. 144
183 Arthur Christensen, *op. cit.*, p. 397
184 Khalil Gundi, *op. cit*, p. 3
185 This is according to their Arabic translator, Father Anstans Maari Al-Kameli, who published *Meshaf-e-Reshe* with a French translation in the journal *Inthropos*, in 1916, Vol. 6, pp. 1–39, as referred to by Dr Shah Nasorideen Al-Husseini, *op. cit.*, p. 48
186 Khalil Gundi, *op. cit.*, p. 3

An Introduction to Modern Kurdish Literature – *Abdulwahab Talabani*

General References

- Abdulkareem Mala Mudarris and Fatih Abdulkareem, *Nali: A Collection of Nali's Poetry*, Baghdad, The Kurdish Academy, 1976
- Abdulkhalegh Parhizy, *The Miserable Angle*, Tehran, Unnamed publisher, 1995
- Mir Basri, *Kurdish Personalities*, Riad El-Rayyes Books Ltd, 1992
- Muhammed Ali Qaradaghi, (ed.), *Wafayyi: The Collection of Wafayyis Poetry*, Baghdad, The Kurdish Academy, 2nd edition, 1984
- Naser Agabra, *Hodach of the Heart*, Mahabad, Rahraw Publishers, Iran, 1999

Numerous newspapers and magazines published in Kurdistan, Britain and Sweden.

- Omed Ashina, (ed.), *Diwani Bekas*, Sulaimani, Kurdistan, 1999
- Qira'at Siyasiyyah, political review, *Arabic Quarterly*, Vol. 3, No.1, Florida, World and Islam Studies Enterprises, U.S.A., 1993
- Rafiq Sabir, *Diwan*, Sweden, Self published, Sweden, 1st edition, 1993

Particular Sources

187 Shaykh Muhammad Madhooki, *History of Kurds and Kurdistan*, Assad Press, 1991, p. 270
188 This is the opinion of Abuvion, the Armenian Orientalist.
189 *Kurdistan*, researched and written by the Bureau of Research, published by the Palestinian National Emancipation Organisation, 1982
190 Noam Chomsky, *The Ongoing Invasion*, Arabic translation of May Nabhan, Al-Meda Studies, 1993, p. 43
191 Hasan Al-Alawi, *The Turkish Influences on the Arab Nationalist Project in Iraq*, London, Az-Zawra House, 1988
192 Kakey Falah, *Karwani Shiiri Nwe*, Baghdad, Hasan Press, 1980
193 Sherko Bekas, *The Secret Diary of a Rose*, Australia, Ashti Bibani, 1997

A Time for Rose and a Time for Primrose – *Eziz Bawermend*

194 Report on Turkey, USA Consular Documents, as quoted by Dr Vera Baudin-Saeedpour in Kurdish Life, No. 6, Spring 1993
195 G Ghailand (ed.) *People without a Country: Kurds and Kurdistan*, Zed Books, 1980 edition, p. 68
196 *Ten Questions and Ten Answers* by Dr Isma'il Besikci, printed in Sydney by Committee for Solidarity with the Kurds, 1987

INFORMATION ON TITLE PAGE PHOTOGRAPHS

Part I: Peshmerga in Nawzang area, photographed by Mansour Razaghi

Part II: Boy at Penjuan, photographed by Mansour Razaghi
Children from Halabja, (anonymous photographer)

Part III: Aslan, Saad Barazi's father

Part IV: Burning tank and Refugees, photographed by Mansour Razaghi

Index

B

C

D

E

F

G

H

I

J

K

L

M

N

O

P

Q

R

S

T

Z

BLACK SEA
Artvi
Ankara
Sivas
Erzincan
Erzurum
Kizil R.
Bingol
Mush
Tatvan
Elazig
Malatya
Bitlis
Siirt
TURKEY
Diyarbakir
Batman
Mardin
Jezire
Incirlik
Urfa
Qamishli
Iskenderun
Hatay
Aleppo
Ar Raqqah
Mos
Khabor R.
Euphrates R.
MEDITERRANEAN SEA
SYRIA

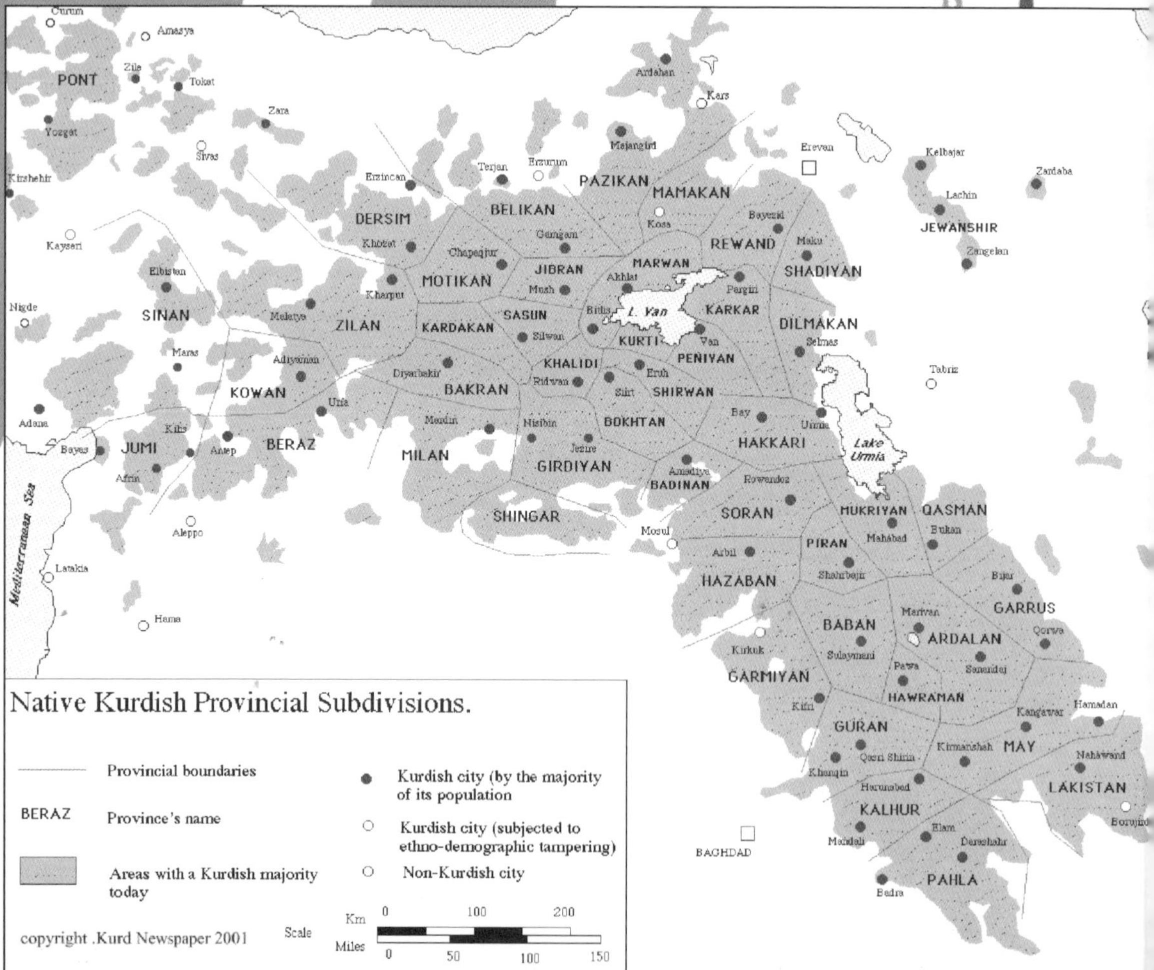
Native Kurdish Provincial Subdivisions.
Provincial boundaries
BERAZ
Province's name
Areas with a Kurdish majority today
Kurdish city (by the majority of its population)
Kurdish city (subjected to ethno-demographic tampering)
Non-Kurdish city
Scale
Km
0
100
200
Miles
0
50
100
150
copyright .Kurd Newspaper 2001
PONT
DERSIM
BELIKAN
PAZIKAN
MAMAKAN
REWAND
SHADIYAN
JEWANSHIR
MOTIKAN
JIBRAN
MARWAN
SINAN
ZILAN
KARDAKAN
SASUN
KARKAR
DILMAKAN
L. Van
KURTI
PENIYAN
KHALIDI
KOWAN
BAKRAN
SHIRWAN
BOKHTAN
HAKKARI
JUMI
BERAZ
MILAN
GIRDIYAN
BADINAN
Lake Urmia
SHINGAR
SORAN
MUKRIYAN
QASMAN
PIRAN
HAZABAN
GARRUS
BABAN
ARDALAN
GARMIYAN
HAWRAMAN
GURAN
MAY
LAKISTAN
KALHUR
PAHLA
Mediterranean Sea
BAGHDAD
Mosul
Aleppo
Kirkuk